THE GREAT REPUBLIC

THE

GREAT REPUBLIC
A History of the American People
Third Edition

BERNARD BAILYN
Harvard University

ROBERT DALLEK
University of California, Los Angeles

DAVID BRION DAVIS
Yale University

DAVID HERBERT DONALD
Harvard University

JOHN L. THOMAS
Brown University

GORDON S. WOOD
Brown University

D. C. HEATH AND COMPANY
Lexington, Massachusetts   Toronto

Acknowledgments

Page 20. "John White Returns to Roanoke Island." Reprinted from David Freeman Hawke, ed., Richard Hakluyt's *Voyages to the New World: A Selection* (Indianapolis: Bobbs-Merrill, 1972), pp. 129–31.

Page 41. "Francis Higginson Describes the 'Aire of New-England.'" Reprinted from Perry Miller and Thomas H. Johnson, eds., *The Puritans: A Sourcebook of Their Writings* (New York: Harper & Row, 1963), Vol. I, p. 124.

Page 64. "An Act for Preventing Insurrections Among Slaves." Reprinted from *The Old Dominion in the Seventeenth Century*, edited by Warren M. Billings. Copyright 1975 The University of North Carolina Press. Used with permission of the publisher.

Page 74. "John Winthrop Defines a Woman's Place." Reprinted from Perry Miller and Thomas H. Johnson, eds., *The Puritans: A Sourcebook of Their Writings* (New York: Harper & Row, 1963), Vol. I, p. 124.

Page 102. "Sarah Kemble Knight Describes New York City." Reprinted from Perry Miller and Thomas H. Johnson, eds., *The Puritans: A Sourcebook of Their Writings* (New York: Harper & Row, 1963), Vol. 2, pp. 441–42.

Page 128. "George Whitefield Comes to Middletown, Connecticut." Reprinted from the diary of Nathan Cole by permission of the Connecticut Historical Society.

Page 173. "Josiah Quincy, Jr., Deplores the Stamp Act Riot." Reprinted from *Proceedings of the Massachusetts Historical Society*, 1st ser. 1791–1883 (20 vols., 1879–1884), Vol. 4 (1858–1860), pp. 47–51.

Page 188. "Jonathan Sewall Condemns the Drive Toward Independence." Reprinted from the Dartmouth Papers with permission of the Earl of Dartmouth and the Staffordshire Record Office.

Page 218. "A Pennsylvania Citizen Describes Frontier Settlement." Reprinted from *Looking for America*, ed. Stanley I. Kutler, 2nd ed. (1979), Vol. 1, pp. 148–52.

Page 223. "American Women Are Urged to Practice Republican Virtue." Reprinted from *Women of the Republic* by Linda K. Kerber. Copyright 1980 University of North Carolina Press. Used with permission of the publisher.

Page 238. "A Farmer Favors the Constitution." New York *Journal and Weekly Register*, Nov. 8, 1787.

Page 264. "Lewis and Clark Encounter the Plains Indians." Reprinted from *History of the Expedition of Lewis and Clark*, Vol. 1, ed. Elliot Coues (New York: Dover Publications Inc., 1965), pp. 160–65.

Page 296. "Harriet Martineau Describes Enterprise in Chicago." Harriet Martineau, *Society in America* (London, 1837), pp. 350–52.

Page 320. "Frances Trollope Attends an Indiana Camp Meeting." Frances Trollope, *Domestic Manners of the Americans* (London: Whittaker Treacher and Co., 1832), pp. 139–43.

Page 338. "Sarah Grimké Writes on the Condition of Women in the United States." Reprinted from *Roots of Bitterness: Documents of the Social History of American Women*, ed. Nancy Cott (New York: E. P. Dutton, 1972). Originally found in Sarah M. Grimké, *Letters on the Equality of the Sexes and the Condition of Women* (Boston: Isaac Knapp, 1838), pp. 46–54.

Page 350. "An Overseer Laments His Slaves' Flight." Reprinted from John S. Bassett's *The Southern Plantation Overseer As Revealed in His Letters* (Negro Universities Press, 1968), pp. 146–47.

Page 415. "Theodore Parker on Slavery as a Barrier to Progress." Reprinted from Theodore Parker, "The Nebraska Question," *Additional Speeches, Addresses, and Occasional Sermons*, Vol. 1 (Boston: Little, Brown and Co., 1855), pp. 379–80.

Page 425. "William Henry Holcombe Argues for Secession." Reprinted from W. H. Holcombe, *The Alternative: A Separate Nationality, or the Africanization of the South* (New Orleans: Delta Mamoth Job Office, 1860).

Page 437. "A Confederate Girl Writes on Secession and the War." Reprinted from James I. Robertson, Jr., ed., Sarah Morgan Dawson's *A Confederate Girl's Diary* (Bloomington: Indiana University Press, 1960), pp. 31–33.

Page 444. "A Union Private Describes Army Rations." Reprinted from David H. Donald, ed., Alfred Bellard's *Gone for a Soldier*, pp. 118–23. Copyright © 1975 by Alec Thomas Archives. Reprinted by permission of Little, Brown & Company and Julian Bach Literary Agency, Inc.

Page 481.   "A Georgia Girl Deplores the Ruin of the South." Reprinted from Eliza F. Andrew's *The War-Time Journal of a Georgia Girl* (Appleton-Century-Crofts, 1908), pp. 32–33.

Page 494.   "A Northerner Educates Virginia Freedmen." Reprinted from Gilbert Osofsky, ed., *The Burden of Race: A Documentary History of Negro-White Relations in America* (New York: Harper & Row, 1967), pp. 160–61.

Page 521.   "A Minnesota Indian Chief's Views on Whites' Treatment of His People." Reprinted from Kenneth Carley, ed., "As Red Men Viewed It: Three Indian Accounts of the Uprising," in *Minnesota History*, 38, September 1962.

Page 564.   "A Tailor Testifies on Working Conditions." Reprinted from John A. Garraty, ed., *Labor and Capital in the Gilded Age* (Boston: Little, Brown & Company, 1968), pp. 20–22.

Page 586.   "A Journalist Describes Going Broke in Kansas." Reprinted from Emporia (Kansas) *Gazette*, June 15, 1895.

Page 600.   "Jane Addams Urges Factory Legislation in Illinois." Reprinted with permission of Macmillan Publishing Company from *Twenty Years at Hull-House* by Jane Addams. Copyright 1910 by Macmillan Publishing Co., renewed 1938 by James W. Linn.

Page 628.   "Polish Peasants Look to the Promise of America." Reprinted from W. I. Thomas and Florian Znaniecki, *The Polish Peasant in Europe and America*, 2nd ed., Vol. 2 (New York: Dover, 1958), pp. 1505–8.

Page 678.   "A Vigilante Group Assaults the IWW." Reprinted from *Looking for America*, ed. Stanley I. Kutler, 2nd ed. (1979), Vol. 2, pp. 309–11.

Page 714.   "Middletown Takes to the Road." Excerpts from *Middletown* by Robert S. and Helen M. Lynd, copyright 1929 by Harcourt Brace Jovanovich, Inc.: renewed 1957 by Robert S. and Helen M. Lynd. Reprinted by permission of the publisher.

Page 740.   "A Teacher Reminisces on the Depression." From *Hard Times: An Oral History of the Great Depression*, by Studs Terkel. Reprinted by permission of Pantheon Books, a division of Random House, Inc.

Page 764.   "A War Correspondent Lands in Salerno." Reprinted from Jack Belden, "Hey, Soldier, I'm Wounded!" *Life* Magazine, September 27, 1943, p. 27.

Page 820.   "A Black Student Fights for Equal Rights." Letter by Patricia Stevens reprinted from CORE, *Sit-Ins: The Students' Report* (New York, 1960). Reprinted by permission of CORE.

Page 835.   "The NOW Bill of Rights." From "Women's Liberation Has a Different Meaning for Blacks" by Renee Ferguson, reprinted from and © The Washington Post, October 3, 1970. Reprinted by permission.

Publisher's Foreword

In the fall of 1982, as our thoughts turned to planning for the third edition of *The Great Republic*, we discussed at some length how to make an excellent text and supplement package even better. Recalling how enthusiastically the first two editions were received, we resolved fully to maintain their great strengths—authoritative scholarship, interpretive approach, and comprehensive integration of the many strands of American history—in this third edition.

At the same time, we, along with the authors, felt a need for making *The Great Republic* more accessible to present-day undergraduates, many of whom have had little high-school preparation in history. For this reason the entire text has been redrafted and carefully edited, on a line-by-line basis. Throughout, the third edition employs a less complex vocabulary and sentence structure. At numerous points definitions and background information have been added. This edition follows a more straightforward chronological structure than did its predecessors, and three of the sections have been thoroughly reorganized. And we are proud to announce a new contributor to this edition, Professor Robert Dallek of the University of California, Los Angeles, who has recast and greatly expanded the chapters in Part 6, on the period from 1920 to the present.

In order to personalize the story told in these pages and to emphasize the strong coverage of social history, stimulating primary source documents have been added throughout the book.

Further, we have greatly expanded the supplement package. We have thoroughly revised the Student Guide and the Instructor's Guide and have increased the number of questions in the latter to more than a thousand. We have added new components to the supplement package, including thirty-five two-color map and chart transparencies and the Archive testing program, a computerized test bank for the Apple© IIe microcomputer that offers instructors a flexible means of test production with 1000+ questions.

We hope that you will agree that the new *Great Republic* is not only a rich and authoritative account of American history, but also a highly effective teaching tool.

Acknowledgments

We are most grateful, as are the authors of *The Great Republic*, to the many historians who offered their reactions to the second edition, whether through letters or through discussions with our representatives and editors on campus and at professional meetings. We especially wish to thank the following for their sensitive and perceptive comments and suggestions regarding the revision:

Michael Batinski, Southern Illinois University
Thomas Buckley, University of Tulsa
Paul Bushnell, Illinois Wesleyan University
Leonard Dinnerstein, University of Arizona
Harry Fritz, University of Montana
Gerald Gill, Tufts University
Daniel Hockman, Eastern Illinois University
David Lundberg, Tufts University
Daniel Richter, Millersville State University
Martin Saltzman, Long Island University
Robert Sterling, Eastern Illinois University
Harry Watson, University of North Carolina, Chapel Hill
Roy Wortman, Kenyon College

A very special word of thanks goes to historian James Miller, whose care and dedication contributed immeasurably to the progress of this revision.

Apple© is a registered trademark of Apple Computer, Inc.

Introduction

This book is a history of the American people, from the earliest European settlements in the New World to the present. We call our book "The Great Republic," adopting a phrase that Winston Churchill used to describe the United States. No one can doubt the greatness of the American Republic if it is measured by the size of our national domain, the vastness of our economic productivity, or the stability of our governmental institutions. Less certain has been its greatness in the realm of culture, in the uses of power, and in the distribution of social justice. Our purpose has been to present a balanced story of American development—a story of great achievement, of enormous material success, and of soaring idealism, but also one of conflict, of turbulent factionalism, and of injustice, rootlessness, and grinding disorder.

Three general themes unify the six sections of this book. The first is the development of free political institutions in America. Understanding the United States today requires a knowledge of conditions in the colonial period that made popular self-government at first possible, then likely, and in the end necessary. In the American Revolution the longings of provincial Britons for a total reformation of political culture were implemented in American political institutions. During the first half of the nineteenth century, democratic institutions and practices expanded to the limits of the continent, and they received their crucial testing in the American Civil War. By the twentieth century, urbanization and industrialization profoundly changed American society, but our democracy survived all of these changes, as well as depressions, international crises, and world wars. To understand why today, in the ninth decade of the twentieth century, no significant groups of Americans question our free institutions requires an understanding of how these institutions evolved from eighteenth-century republicanism to modern mass democracy.

Our second theme is the tension that has always existed in America between the interests of groups with special goals and needs and those of the society as a whole. From the beginning the New World, with its abundant resources, stimulated ambitions among the shrewd, the enterprising, and the energetic that often conflicted with the shared needs of the entire populace. The enormous expanse of the country and the admixture of peoples from every quarter of the world encouraged social fragmentation and fostered cultural diversity. But from colonial times to the present, there have been countervailing forces working for social stability and cultural homogeneity.

The Founding Fathers of the Republic were aware that there would be no automatic harmonizing of regional, economic, and social interests, and they worried that minorities might become subject to the tyranny of majorities. At the same time, they feared a centralized government powerful enough to impose order on these conflicting and local interests and active enough to defend the weak against the powerful. In the national and state constitutions they devised a mechanism for the mediation of struggles and for the protection of human rights. In the years since, the balance between the general welfare and the welfare of regions, states, and economic and social groups has often been precarious, and our book shows how, from time to time, that balance has tipped, sometimes in the direction of social order and stability, sometimes in favor of minority interests and individual rights. Much of our story deals with successive attempts, never fully satisfactory, to reconcile the needs of the whole country with the interests of the parts.

Our third theme reflects our recognition that the history of the United States has always been part of a larger history. Except for the native Americans, who had developed a complex and diverse indigenous civilization, the early settlers in America were all immigrants who brought with them the beliefs, values, and cultural legacy of the European and African societies in which they had been born. Naturally, then, developments in America have been closely and inextricably related to those abroad. We believe that the American Revolution, for all of its distinctiveness, needs to be viewed as one in a series of great democratic revolutions that swept the Western world. We think the leveling of social distinctions and the democratization of political life in Jacksonian America are closely related to similar contemporary movements in Europe. And we have stressed that the urbanization, mechanization, and bureaucratization of the United States by the end of the nineteenth century paralleled, copied, and influenced like transformations in the other modernizing nations.

By the twentieth century the connections between developments in the United States and those in the world at large became even closer, and the final sections of our book trace the emergence of the United States as a world power. We have told the story of our involvement in two devastating world wars, in addition to other, smaller conflicts all over the globe, from Korea to Vietnam to Lebanon. We have shown how, in recent decades, the president of the United States has become the most influential political leader in the world, how variations in the American economy have affected the well-being of all other nations, and how, for better or worse, American popular culture has reached a global audience. At the same time, we have emphasized that changes in other parts of the world have profoundly affected American political life, eco-

nomic growth, and social organization. In short, we have written an American history that is part of world history.

In presenting these three themes, the authors have started from a shared view of the nature of history. We all believe that history is a mode of understanding, not merely a collection of information about the past. Our obligation is not simply to describe what happened, but to explain it, to make clear why things developed as they did. We share, too, an aversion to any deterministic interpretation of history. At certain times economic and demographic forces are dominant, but they are themselves shaped by cultural forces. Great political events are sometimes triggered by economic drives, but at other times they are responses to ideologies.

We do not believe, then, that the course of American history was predetermined. The present condition of our national life has to be explained historically, stage by stage. In the pages that follow, we present both a narrative and an analysis of how the United States has come to be what it is today—a great power, but still a Great Republic, where freedom and equality are dreams that can become realities.

B. B	D. H. D.
R. D.	J. L. T.
D. B. D.	G. S. W.

Contents

PART FIVE
Nationalizing the Republic, 1877–1920

John L. Thomas

CHAPTER 22
Stabilizing the American Economy _____ 544

CHAPTER 23
The Politics of Reform _____ 572

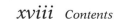

Maps and Charts

PART ONE

SHAPING THE REPUBLIC, TO 1760

Bernard Bailyn

*T*he American Republic was created only in a legal sense in 1776. In a deeper and more general sense it was the product of a century and a half of development that preceded the establishment of American independence. The ultimate origins of this "Great Republic," as Winston Churchill called the American nation, lie far back in time. America's historical roots lie in the desperate gambles of hard-pressed sixteenth- and seventeenth-century merchants involved in overseas trade, and in Elizabethan dreamers' visions of a western passage to the vast wealth of the Far East. They lie in the courage and single-mindedness of religious refugees determined to carve out a new life in the wilderness rather than compromise their beliefs. They lie in the life-long labors of a quarter of a million Africans transported in bondage to the New World. And they lie in the everyday struggles of five generations of transplanted Europeans and their descendants—primarily farmers and artisans—who vaguely sensed that theirs was a new and freer world, more supportive of human dignity and richer, for those whose risks succeeded, than any land known before.

The many peoples in colonial North America did not seek to transform the world. Although they were adventurous, they were basically conservative by instinct, or they became conservative as they sought to establish familiar forms of life in an unfamiliar environment. But traditions could not be maintained in wilderness communities whose basic conditions were so different from those of the Old World. A new pattern of life evolved in the course of the five generations that spanned the first permanent English settlement in North America and the American Rev-

Overleaf: View of New York from the north, 1679. *The Long Island Historical Society.*

olution. Gradually the character of community life was transformed—
its demographic foundations, economy, social organization, religion,
and politics. No theory or grand design guided this transformation;
change did not come about because of anyone's desire or will, or in an
effort to attain an ideal. Change simply took place as a matter of fact.

In the years before the American Revolution, some looked upon
change with suspicion. It was resisted in part, and its effects were limited as the colonists sought to copy the pattern of life in the more traditional societies of Europe. Many saw their provincial world not as a
model for society, but as a regression to a more primitive way of life.
Behavior had changed—had *had* to change—with the circumstances of
everyday life. But habits of mind and the sense of the rightness of things
changed more slowly. Many felt that the changes that had taken place
in the years before the Revolution meant a movement *away from*, not
toward, something; that these changes meant deviance; that they lacked,
in a word, legitimacy.

For most Americans this divergence between ideals, habits of mind,
and beliefs on the one hand, and experience and patterns of behavior on
the other, ended at the Revolution. The American Revolution was an
upheaval that destroyed the traditional sources of public authority and
called forth the full range of advanced and enlightened ideas. Long-
settled attitudes were jolted and loosened. People began to see that the
erosion in patterns of social life that had taken place in the colonial period had been good and proper. In the context of Revolutionary beliefs,
these changes were viewed as steps toward a new ideal—the ideal of a

simpler existence in which the individual would count for more, and the state for less. In this new way of life, the weight of burdensome social institutions would be permanently lifted. The blight of privilege and the misuse of power, it was expected, would be destroyed, and corruption would be exposed before it could sap the nation's strength. As a result of all these changes, the ordinary person's desire for personal fulfillment could at long last be satisfied.

These were the ideals of the Revolution, shaped by a generation of brilliant political thinkers who were convinced that it was their great historic role to set the world on a new course. And in the context of these ideals—which, however modified, remain the highest aspirations of the American people—the changes of the colonial years took on a new meaning. The settlement and development of the colonies, John Adams wrote, could now be seen as "the opening of a grand scene and design in providence for the illumination of the ignorant and the emancipation of the slavish part of mankind all over the earth." The glass was half-full, not half-empty; and to complete the work of fate and nature, further thought must be taken, and changes accelerated rather than restrained.

Social change and social conflict took place during the Revolutionary years, but the beliefs and aspirations of America's founders, unlike those of the leaders of the later French and Russian revolutions, did not require the destruction and remaking of society. The American Revolution did not create new social and political forces; it released forces and intensified changes that had been developing from the day Englishmen first permanently settled in America. Modern America—a massively developed, affluent, and tumultuous technological society of more than 200 million people—is worlds away from the seventeenth century's tiny farming communities and obscure port towns, huddled along the coast of an almost undeveloped continent. Yet there is a clear line of continuity in American history that links those primitive settlements to the sophisticated, dynamic world power of the late twentieth century. Modern America is not simply the product of modern forces—industrialism, political democracy, universal education, a consumer culture. It is the product too of the idealism of the eighteenth-century Enlightenment, reinforced and intensified by the openness and affluence of American life.

This powerful strain of idealism flowing from the very different world of the eighteenth century into all the complexities of modern America is the most distinctive feature of the American Republic as it enters its third century of existence. The central theme of the colonial period of American history is the story of how that irrepressible strain first entered American life, of how it was nourished in the soil of a strangely altered society that grew from confused seventeenth-century origins, and of how the characteristic American mixture of idealism and materialism was first created—reaching so soon an apparently absolute and perfect form in the subtle figure of Benjamin Franklin.

Far from being a quaint introduction to the main story, therefore, the settlement of the American colonies, and the early development of American society, constitute a critically important phase of our history. Without an understanding of the pre-Revolutionary era, none of the rest of our history can be properly understood.

1 The Background of English Colonization

The United States evolved from British settlements on the North American mainland, first permanently established in 1607. But a century earlier, a more powerful European state, Spain, had founded an empire in the Western Hemisphere that was highly developed when the British first entered the colonial world. The growth of the Spanish Empire in the Western Hemisphere and of Spanish-American society forms a remarkable—and revealing—contrast to the evolution of the British Empire and of Anglo-American society. In some ways, to be sure, Anglo-American society in British North America and Indo-Hispanic society in Central America and South America are so different that they can hardly be compared. But we can learn much by contrasting government and politics in the two empires.

By the early eighteenth century, political life in British North America had become quite distinctive. Anglo-American society was marked by free, open political competition, which was made possible by certain underlying institutional and cultural conditions. Nothing quite like this society's unconfined brawling struggles—faction against faction, groups against the state—existed in any other colonial region of the world, and certainly not in Spanish America. Yet there had been a time when this kind of political life might have evolved in the Spanish colonies as well. It is therefore worthwhile at the outset to explore the basic reasons why Spanish America did not have a free competitive political system at the height of the colonial period. By studying this contrast, we can better understand the forces and circumstances that made for so dynamic a political society in the British-American colonies on the eve of the American Revolution.

Points of Contrast: Spain in America

There are important contrasts between Spanish and British America at every stage of development. The very origins of settlement were different. Whereas it took England half a century after its first contact with the Western Hemisphere to establish even a temporary colony there, Spain proceeded swiftly to exploit the lands that had been claimed for it by Christopher Columbus in 1492. Led by its courageous, greedy, and often brutal *conquistadores*—adventurers for whom there are no British equivalents—Spain's exploration of the Western Hemisphere, its conquest of the native peoples, and its establishment of a new civilization swept forward in three main waves.

The Spanish Conquests.
Columbus himself explored much of the Caribbean on his four voyages between 1492 and 1504. Within a generation of his death in 1506, Spanish adventurers had seized possession of most of the coastal lands of Central America and South America. The conquest of the Caribbean basin climaxed in 1513 with Vasco Núñez de Balboa's exploration of the Isthmus of Panama and his discovery of the Pacific Ocean, and with Juan Ponce de León's discovery of the Florida mainland.

The second wave of Spanish expansion in America was stimulated by rumors of vast treasures hidden in a highly civilized state deep in the interior. In the course of this second wave, the empire of the Aztec ruler Montezuma in Mexico was conquered between 1519 and 1521. This most dramatic and bloody conquest was led by the resourceful, ruthless, and incredibly energetic *conquistador* Hernando Cortés. There are no heroes in this tale of slaughter and conquest. On one side were the passionately determined Spanish adventurers, half-mad with greed, who overcame fearful hardships to plunder and ultimately to destroy an ancient civilization. On the other side were the equally courageous and brutal but bewildered and unsophisticated natives. Other *conquistadores* extended Cortés's conquest of the Mexican world to the north. Between 1528 and 1536 Álvar Núñez Cabeza de Vaca circled the northern edge of the Gulf of Mexico and reached the Gulf of California. Between 1539 and 1541 Hernando de Soto cut through the forests of northern Florida and of what would later be the southeastern United States and discovered the Mississippi River. And in 1542 Francisco Coronado, seeking El

1602

...er Ralegh Knight Lord Warden of
...rries ... of the
...f the Isle of Iarsey & her M. Lieute
...al of the Counties of Devonshyre & Cornwall

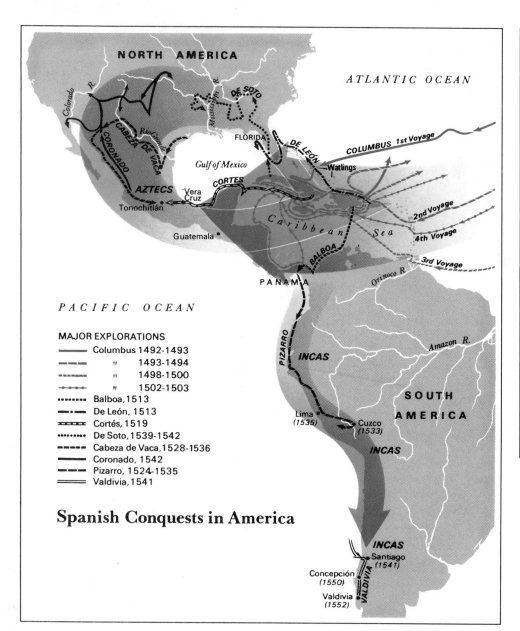

Spanish Conquests in America

MAJOR EXPLORATIONS

- Columbus 1492-1493
- " 1493-1494
- " 1498-1500
- " 1502-1503
- Balboa, 1513
- De León, 1513
- Cortés, 1519
- De Soto, 1539-1542
- Cabeza de Vaca, 1528-1536
- Coronado, 1542
- Pizarro, 1524-1535
- Valdivia, 1541

Dorado, a mythical city of gold and jewels, explored the mud villages of what is now Arizona, New Mexico, Colorado, Oklahoma, and Kansas. While these conquerors were exploring and subduing what would become the northern borderlands of Spain's empire, other followers of Cortés swept through Central America and established Spanish rule in Honduras and Guatemala.

The third great wave of Spanish conquest was led by an illiterate adventurer, Francisco Pizarro, who launched a series of expeditions from Panama through the jungles of Ecuador and northern Peru into the heartland of the elaborate Incan empire, which was

then weakened by civil war. By a trick Pizarro managed to capture the Incan emperor, whom he murdered after extracting a ransom of more than twenty tons of pure gold and silver, and then destroyed much of the Incan army and nobility. Next he proceeded to strip city after city of their treasures, to embroil both natives and conquerors in devastating warfare, and to establish in 1535 the new central city of Lima. From the plundered Incan lands further expeditions were begun—first into Ecuador, then into Chile and northern Argentina (1535–37), and finally into Bolivia (1539). The full conquest of Chile was the work of another almost unbelievably determined and ruthless

BATTLE FOR THE INCAN CITY OF CUZCO
An imaginative depiction by Flemish engraver Theodore De Bry (1528–98). Never having seen either America or an Indian, De Bry portrayed the natives as ancient Greeks, innocent but savage, and dwelt almost sadistically on cannibalism and the brutalities of the conquest. Cuzco appears as a Spanish-American walled city.

PORTRAIT MEDAL OF HERNANDO CORTÉS
The medal, made during Cortés's visit to Spain in 1529, is one of the very few portraits of an early *conquistador*. The image was probably drawn from life.

conquistador, Pedro de Valdivia. His small troop of Spanish adventurers and Indian followers survived journeys through the desert, near starvation, and attacks by native peoples to found Santiago, Concepción, and Valdivia before succumbing to a native rebellion in 1553.

Radiating out from these three main lines of conquest (first, the subjugation of the Caribbean islands and coastal areas; then the reduction of Mexico and the exploration of southern North America; and finally the invasion of Peru, Chile, and northern Argentina), Spain's empire in America expanded in all directions. By 1607, when England established Jamestown, its first permanent settlement in America, Spain's American empire extended nearly 8,000 miles, from southern California to the Strait of Magellan at the southern tip of South America. The empire was the largest the Western world had known since the fall of Rome. Its only competitor in the Western Hemisphere had been Portugal, which had controlled the coastal areas of Brazil until the union of the Spanish and Portuguese thrones (1580–1640) gave Spain legal jurisdiction even there.

Spain's fabulous western empire was acquired through greed, lust for adventure, and a passion to convert the heathen people to Christianity. But it was also the product of remarkable administrative skill.

The Spanish Empire. Despite the difficulties of effectively managing so vast a territory, Spain's American empire was well organized. The structure of government that had evolved during the sixteenth century was elaborate, skillfully designed, and—except for periods when royal authority collapsed in Spain itself—successful. And it was utterly different from the imperial system that Britain would set up during the seventeenth and early eighteenth centuries. Spain's rule of its empire was highly *bureaucratic*: full-time salaried officials enforced decrees and laws governing the behavior of both the rulers and the ruled. These regulations reached down into the daily life of the poorest peasants in the most remote corners of the empire, half a world away from the central administrative agencies in Spain. And the system was *patriarchal*. That is, it was hierarchical in structure, all authority ultimately centering in the patriarchal figure of the

THE WORLD THE SPANIARDS FOUND
The Gold Mixtec chest plate, above, represented the god of death. Macchu Picchu, Peru, right, was the last refuge of the Incan emperors in their flight from the Spaniards.

monarch of Castile,* whose rule in his American lands was conceived of as personal, an extension of his domestic authority.

The establishment of royal power in overseas territories by means of a complex bureaucracy began almost as soon as Spain learned of Columbus's discoveries. This quick response contrasts sharply with the plodding actions of the British government a century later. By 1503 the first major Spanish imperial institution had been created, the *Casa de Contratación* (board of trade). With its headquarters in Spain's leading port, Seville, the *Casa* licensed all trade with America, enforced commercial laws and regulations, collected customs duties and colonial crown revenues, and kept the commercial accounts of the entire empire. Because of its power over colonial commerce and over the flow of money that poured into Spain from America, the

---

*Castile was the largest and most important of the kingdoms that had been united in the fifteenth century to form the Spanish monarchy. Isabella was queen of Castile; Ferdinand ruled the smaller kingdom of Aragon. Strictly speaking, America belonged to—and was governed by—Castile alone.

Casa became in effect a major branch of the royal treasury. From this original agency Spain's imperial government, reaching lands in all parts of the globe and bound together by hundreds of rules enforced by thousands of officials, took shape within a single generation.

In all of its work, the *Casa de Contratación* was controlled by the Council of the Indies, which had been created in 1524. The Council was composed of some of the Spanish king's highest advisers, and it acted in the king's name. It dominated both the making and the enforcing of laws—civil and religious alike—in the Spanish colonies, and it constituted a branch of the royal court of justice. The Council appointed all the clerical and secular officials who enforced its laws. It had a special responsibility for the spiritual and physical welfare of the Indians; it was the court of highest appeal for the entire colonial judicial system; it censored all publications in America; and it audited the accounts of the colonial treasurers.

All government agencies and officials in America reported in some way to the Council of the Indies. The chief governmental unit in America was the vice-

Spanish and Portuguese Empires in the New World

Map labels:
NORTH AMERICA
Santa Fe (1609)
St. Augustine (1565)
Havana (1515)
Mexico (1521)
Panama (1519)
Lima (1535)
SOUTH AMERICA
Santiago (1541)
Buenos Aires (1535-1580)
Rio de Janeiro (1555)
Demarcation Line, 1494 (Treaty of Tordesillas)
Disputed by Spain & Portugal
Spanish / Portuguese

OCCUPIED BY SPANISH
1492-1519
1519-1543
1543-1600
1600-1743

OCCUPIED BY PORTUGUESE
1532-1543
1543-1600
1600-1743

Spain's Imperial Government in the New World, 1550

Map labels:
(Northern Boundary indefinite)
AUDIENCIA OF NUEVA GALICIA (1548)
AUDIENCIA OF MEXICO (1527)
VICEROYALTY OF NEW SPAIN 1535
AUDIENCIA OF GUATEMALA (1543)
AUDIENCIA OF SANTO DOMINGO (1526)
AUDIENCIA OF PANAMA (1535)
AUDIENCIA OF NUEVA GRANADA (1549)
AUDIENCIA OF LIMA (1542)
VICEROYALTY OF PERU 1542
SOUTH AMERICA

royalty. Two viceroyalties were created in the sixteenth century: New Spain (1535), which included all Spanish territory north of the Isthmus of Panama; and Peru (1542), which covered all to the south of the Isthmus except the coast of what is today Venezuela. The viceroys ruled these two huge jurisdictions with broad but somewhat ambiguous authority to act in the king's name, and their capitals were centers of glittering splendor.

The level of government below the viceroyalties was that of the *audiencias*. There were seven *audiencias* by 1550; five more were added by 1661. Originally they were royal courts with direct access to the Council of the Indies and were subject to the Council's veto. Soon, however, the *audiencias* acquired administrative and political authority—power that they shared or contested with the viceroys. More clearly below the viceroyalties were lesser jurisdictions—*presidencias* and captaincies general—that were deliberately created as administrative subdivisions of the larger territorial governments.

These were the main jurisdictions. Below them lay many lower units, whose chief officers were usu-ally appointed by the viceroys or *audiencias*. Normally the Council of the Indies had to approve these appointments; occasionally the king himself did. Below them was the lowest level of civil government, the municipal corporation (*cabildo*). Finally, there were various investigating and superintending officials who were appointed in Spain to strengthen the crown's authority throughout its American territories.

The Spanish imperial government was neither completely rational in its construction, nor altogether efficient in its operation, nor comprehensive in its reach. There were clumsy gaps and overlaps in authority. Lower jurisdictions, especially those in remote areas, found many ways of ignoring the higher authorities; and corruption was widespread, especially in the lower offices. Yet despite these weaknesses, the Spanish Empire functioned as a reasonably coherent state system for more than three hundred years, however inefficient it might appear to a modern analyst. And the system was largely unchallenged. Of course there was resistance to certain regulations and to some of the officials sent from Spain. But there was no openly organized political opposition to the state, only the passive refusal to comply with unacceptable or un-enforceable crown orders (a foot dragging that was reflected in the well-known phrase, "I obey but I do not execute"). Nor was there a body of ideas that would justify sustained opposition to the crown, nor political leaders who were experienced in challenging state authority and motivated to do so. When, more than three hundred years after its founding, Spain's empire in America finally succumbed to corruption, misgovernment, and rising democratic aspirations, there was no corps of native politicians capable of managing free governments and of creating responsible, stable self-government. And the doctrines that shaped the Latin American independence movements of the early nineteenth century were largely alien ideas that only awkwardly expressed the needs of the Spanish-American people.

Contrast with the British Empire.
The contrast with British America could hardly be sharper or more significant. There was never an effective structure of imperial government in the Anglo-American empire. The authority of the British crown and of Parliament was scattered through half a dozen uncoordinated agencies of government, and it was always superficial. It seldom penetrated much beyond the docks or the customs houses, and British control of the American political system was weak. Yet, surprisingly, there was organized resistance to this weak and scattered authority from the start. By the middle of the eighteenth century, resistance had grown into a sophisticated process of competitive politics and had bred politicians who were long experienced in local self-government. Consequently the transition to independence and to responsible self-government was smooth and, once the War of Independence was concluded, entirely bloodless.

This stark contrast between the Spanish-American and the British-American patterns becomes even more vivid and surprising if one considers the fact that, in the early years of the Spanish-American empire, institutions had existed that could have developed into bases for just the kind of competitive politics that evolved in North America. But instead of maturing into centers of open competition with the state, these institutions withered and disappeared.

At the start, for example, the most powerful figures in Latin America were the *adelantados*—feudal lords whom the crown had granted extraordinary powers to subjugate the American frontiers. These men exercised executive and judicial authority that from the beginning was understood to be competitive with the crown's own authority. Yet few of the *adelantados* managed to transmit their authority to a second generation. Another potential threat to the state's overall authority in the sixteenth century was the *encomienda*, a Spanish institution that was transferred to America in 1502. The *encomienda* was a grant of the labor of a specific number of native Americans for agriculture or mining—along with the land they occupied. This was, in effect, a gift of slaves or serfs. The crown had intended to protect the Indians' spiritual and physical well-being, but the *encomiendas* quickly became agencies of vicious oppression. Determined to eliminate the institution, the crown gradually succeeded in reducing the powers of the roughly 4,000 *encomienda* holders by draining away their incomes and eliminating their right to pass the original grants on to their heirs. The dramatic decline of the Indian population also undermined the *encomiendas*. By the early eighteenth century the *encomienda* was no longer a political danger to the crown. In similar ways the threat of other, lesser competing political authorities—provincial assemblies and municipal corporations—was eliminated or reduced.

Why had all these semi-independent agencies and institutions been weakened or absorbed into the state apparatus? Why had organized competitive politics died almost at birth in Spanish America, whereas in British America it grew so quickly and so strongly? There is no simple explanation, but there were certain circumstances in Spanish America that provide part of an explanation, and these contrast sharply with the conditions that shaped the development of the British-American communities.

From the very start the Spanish crown had actively and directly asserted its authority. Even before Columbus's discovery, the monarchy had proclaimed its rule over the lands that had been conquered in its name, and it intended to use this power not merely to regulate commerce, but also to impose far-reaching governmental authority in newly acquired territories. The Spanish monarchs of Columbus's time, Ferdinand and Isabella, declared America to be a separate kingdom that was linked to the kingdom of Castile. The native American peoples thus became direct subjects of the Spanish crown, and the governmental jurisdictions in America were regarded as subordinate agencies of the crown. The papacy—the highest moral authority in the Western world—supported Ferdinand and Isabella's declaration. The popes assigned to the monarch of Castile the responsibility for the welfare of the native Americans, which meant primarily the task of converting them to Christianity. Building upon that central Christian responsibility, legal and religious scholars in Spain developed an imposing body of writings that strongly reinforced and justified the Spanish monarch's claims to personal rule in America. Further, there were no competing intellectual centers from which contrary ideas could develop. The Catholic church, conservative in doctrine and royalist in politics, dominated the intellectual life of Spanish America. Whereas British America became a refuge for religious dissenters, Spanish America became a fortress of Catholic orthodoxy, even more tightly controlled than Spain itself. Dissenters and heretics of all kinds were generally barred by law from emigrating to Spanish America.

Yet declarations and political theory do not in themselves create political realities. There was something in the conditions of Spanish American life that guaranteed a welcome for the crown's supremacy and that helped stifle competitive institutions at their birth. The situation becomes clearer if one turns from institutions to population characteristics and considers what groups would have had the capacity to oppose the crown and also an interest in active, organized resistance.

The Spanish-American Population.

There were five principal categories in the Spanish-American population, of which the most numerous by far was that of the Indians. The Aztecs, the Incas, and the other native Americans whom the Spanish encountered were advanced people in certain ways. But to Europeans of the time they seemed primitive, particularly in technology and weaponry, and they were helpless before the fierce Spanish conquerors. The native Americans were quickly transformed by conquest into a mass laboring population. And beyond the deprivation of their political rights and their severe exploitation under the *encomienda* system, the Indians were being decimated by diseases brought by the Spanish. Reliable studies estimate that the population of the Viceroyalty of New Spain declined from about 25 million at the time of the Spanish conquest to slightly over 1 million at the beginning of the seventeenth century. Losses in the Viceroyalty of Peru may have been equally severe. As the Indian population plummeted, the Indians' abandoned land passed to Spanish landlords, and the surviving native Americans found themselves bound by debt servitude, called peonage. It is scarcely surprising that the Indians, struggling for basic survival, were incapable of organizing their own political institutions to resist the Spanish state.

At the other extreme from the Indians were the major imperial officeholders—the viceroys, *audiencia* judges, high church officials, and governors—who might most readily have achieved some independent authority. But the crown's policies in recruiting and controlling these officers prevented them from moving in that direction. Most of the high church and state officials who served in Spanish America in the three-hundred-year colonial period had been born in Spain. They had no vested interests in America, and they expected to return home to Spain after completing their tour of duty abroad. Furthermore, the crown had devised controls to limit any independence that these officials might have developed. Their time in office was strictly limited, and they were frequently transferred to prevent them from acquiring too strong an identification with any particular locality. Moreover, they depended on the royal treasury for their salaries, and their conduct of office was carefully examined.

A third group was the Creoles, the American-born leaders of Spanish descent. Under favorable conditions they might well have organized and become an active political force. Unlike the Indians they were politically sophisticated, and unlike most high church and state officials they were Americans, with American interests. And indeed, there were conflicts between the Creoles and the Spanish officials, particularly over officeholding and the enforcement of trade regulations. Further, by the eighteenth century the sale of public offices by the bankrupt Spanish state gave the Creoles increasing access to public authority. But in general the Creoles' small numbers and their social position forced them into a dependent political role. Of the total population of more than 9 million in Spanish America in the 1570s, only 118,000—or 1.25 percent—were Creoles. In the entire first century of Spain's colonial period, approximately 240,000 Spaniards emigrated to America. The contrast with British America is startling. In the equivalent period (that is from 1600 to 1700), approximately 400,000 emigrants left the British Isles for America alone, a yearly average two-thirds greater than that of the Spanish. The Creoles' small numbers account for the kinds of occupations they pursued. As a thin overlay on a comparatively large population of Indians, the Creoles never became the mass base of the social structure. Instead they filled the upper strata of the American communities: they were landowners, clergymen, army officers, and merchants. Their identity as a ruling class, and consequently their well-being, derived not from their American birth, but from their European descent, which distinguished them racially from the mass of the population. Thus, despite their local interests, the Creoles continued to identify themselves with Spain, the source of their status, wealth, and power.

Finally, there were two other groups in the Spanish-American population. Blacks were imported as slaves and never acquired an active political role. Politically more important was the increasingly large number of racially mixed persons. By the 1570s the racially mixed elements constituted approximately 2.5 percent of the entire populace. By the end of the colonial period in the early nineteenth century, that figure had risen to more than 30 percent. (This presents another striking contrast with British America, where the racially mixed population was quite small.) Many racial combinations existed, but the most important element by far was the *mestizos*, peo-

TWO VIEWS OF THE FABULOUS SILVER MINE AT POTOSÍ

The external view, far right, appears in an atlas by Hermann Moll, c. 1709–20. The interior view is an imaginative depiction by De Bry that captures something of the degradation suffered by the Indian miners. Thousands of these forced laborers perished in that "mouth of hell" 16,000 feet above sea level. The wealth produced at Potosí for over two centuries after the mine's discovery in 1545 was stupendous, but the cost in human suffering by whole populations of helpless natives, slaving underground by dim candlelight for days on end, was immeasurably greater. The city of Potosí itself (in modern Bolivia) had a population of 120,000 by 1572 but remained a tumultuous mining camp throughout the colonial period, swarming with gamblers, prostitutes, and adventurers of all kinds.

ple of mixed European and Indian ancestry. Yet, although numerous, the *mestizos* were generally considered socially inferior to the dominant Spanish elements, and they constituted a lower-middle class of small farmers and shopkeepers. In a society where status, wealth, and power were controlled by those of pure Spanish heritage, *mestizos* avoided asserting their identity through politics and chose rather to fit themselves as inconspicuously as possible into existing situations. Only a profound cultural change would release their suppressed aspirations and free them to assume effective political roles. When that cultural change took place—and only then—the colonial era of Spanish-American history was over.

These population characteristics, so different from those of the British-American world, go far toward explaining the failure of a free competitive political system to develop in colonial Spanish America. Institutions that originally could have supported these politics were available. But the small elite of high state officials was bound to Spain in every way. The Creoles were a small, self-conscious ruling class in a great sea of Indians, blacks, and racially mixed persons. Their well-being depended on their continuing identification with the sources of authority in Europe. Only the racially mixed were disposed to move toward self-government, but through most of the colonial period they lacked the numbers, the self-esteem, and the experience to create effective political weapons against the overwhelming Spanish establishment.

England's Overseas Expansion

England's entry into the Western Hemisphere was the very opposite of Spain's. Where Spain had been swift, England was slow; where Spain had been deliberate and decisive, England was muddled in purpose. For Spain, America almost immediately yielded immense wealth. For England, America created more losses than profits, at least at the start. The differences were most extreme and of most consequence at the very beginning of exploration and settlement.

For no less than fifty years, while Spain was conquering and exploiting vast areas of Central America and South America, England did nothing to develop its claims to North America. These claims had been established in 1497–98, when John Cabot, who had been commissioned by Henry VII, had discovered and begun the exploration of Newfoundland, Labrador, and Nova Scotia. Cabot's son Sebastian had continued the exploration into the Hudson Bay region of Canada in 1508–09; but throughout the reign of Henry VIII (1509–47), neither the crown nor private enterprise showed any interest in developing these distant territories. The only English contact with America that remained throughout these years was the work of fishermen from England's West Country—the counties of Cornwall, Devonshire, and Dorsetshire—who, together with fishermen from France, Spain, and Portugal, had begun to exploit the excellent fishing waters of the Grand Banks (off Newfoundland) and the mouth

of the St. Lawrence River. These fishermen had become familiar with the southern Canadian and northern New England coasts. They had built crude shacks for use during the fishing seasons, but they had made no attempt to establish permanent settlements or otherwise assert England's claims to the land.

Then suddenly, in the early 1550s, the situation changed. This abrupt reversal marked the beginnings of British colonization. The development was complex, and it is as important to understand what did *not* happen as it is to know what did happen. For there was no sudden emphasis on overseas settlement as such, and there was no immediate English determination to assert claims to America. Instead there were two basic shifts in orientation, both of which would eventually involve colonization, but neither of which was originally directed toward that goal. The first shift was in England's economy, the second in its international relations.

Economic and Diplomatic Changes.
England's prosperity in the first half of the sixteenth century had been based on the growing European demand for its raw wool and woolen cloth, which were marketed largely in Antwerp, in what is now Belgium. Throughout the reign of Henry VIII, more and more capital and labor had become involved in this dominant commercial enterprise, more and more farmland had been converted to pastureland for sheep, and England's financial stability had become increasingly dependent on Ant-

werp. Then in the late 1540s this elaborate commercial structure began to weaken. By 1550 the Antwerp wool market was saturated, and in 1551 it collapsed. English cloth exports fell off 35 percent within a year, and the financial world was thrown into turmoil. The merchants were forced to reconsider the whole of their activities. New markets and new trade routes would have to be found, and capital would have to be risked in ways that a previous generation would have thought wildly speculative.

Changes in England's international position helped channel the merchants' suddenly mobilized energies. Antagonism with France had dominated England's policies throughout Henry VIII's reign, and in this rivalry Spain had been England's natural ally. As a result England had been willing to support Spain's claim to the entire Western Hemisphere except Portuguese Brazil.* This support was confirmed by the marriage of England's Queen Mary (1553–58) to King Philip II of Spain.

But when Mary's half-sister Elizabeth became queen in 1558, a reversal in England's international

---

*This claim had been recognized by the pope in 1493 and was confirmed by the Spanish-Portuguese Treaty of Tordesillas of 1494, which assured Spain of its title to all newly discovered lands 370 leagues west of the Cape Verde Islands. That line, it was later discovered, struck the American continent at approximately the mouth of the Amazon River, thus leaving much of the eastern coast of South America to Portugal.

ELIZABETH I
In the so-called Armada Portrait, painted in 1588, Elizabeth's hand, holding a globe of the world, covers most of North America.

relations began. In contrast to her predecessor, Elizabeth was inclined toward Protestantism, and Protestant political considerations gradually came to shape England's foreign policy. By the mid-1560s it was becoming clear that Catholic Spain threatened England's independence as a Protestant nation, and that England's long-range interests in Europe lay in the support of the rebellious Protestants in France and of their counterparts in the Netherlands who were struggling against Spanish rule. From an ally of Spain, England gradually became an enemy. Although England felt too weak until the 1580s to engage in open warfare with the great imperial power, the country had every reason to want to harass the Spanish people and to plunder Spanish territories in any way possible.

Thus, impelled by a sudden economic need to break out of the safe, conservative commerce of earlier years, and no longer hesitant to attack Spain's overseas territories, England entered a new phase in its history. It did not, however, plunge directly and immediately into colonization; it attempted overseas settlement only eventually, and almost incidentally. In response to the new economic pressures, England expelled foreign merchants and favored English merchants in the conduct of trade. Land that had been converted to sheep grazing in order to supply wool for export was now forced back into crop raising. Textile production was deliberately limited, and new merchants were restrained from entering into trade. Above all, the commercial community poured capital into a search for new kinds of overseas trade and for new, distant markets that would be free of the influence of European middlemen. In 1555 enterprising merchants formed the Guinea Company for trade to Africa, and the Muscovy Company for trade with Russia. In 1579 the Eastland Company organized English trade to the Baltic region. In 1581 the Levant Company was created to control England's commerce with the Middle East. Finally, a series of contacts with India and Southeast Asia led to the formation of the East India Company in 1600.

These were legitimate and official enterprises, but during the same years less legitimate activities were also unfolding. Risk capital, some of it secretly supplied from royal sources, was being channeled into semipiratical raids on Spanish commerce and shipping. These enterprises began in 1562 when John Hawkins of the southwestern town of Plymouth broke into the Spanish trade monopoly in the West Indies

ESKIMO MAN, WOMAN, AND CHILD, BROUGHT BACK TO ENGLAND BY FROBISHER IN 1577

John White (see p. 18) accompanied Frobisher on his second voyage (1577) to Frobisher Bay, an inlet on the coast of Baffin Island, northeast of Hudson Bay, and probably sketched these three captured Eskimos on shipboard. The woman, whose child peeks out from within her hood, is tattooed in blue around the eyes. The Eskimos were sensations in Bristol, where they demonstrated the use of their kayak, but they died within a month of their arrival. Frobisher was convinced that the bay he found was the northwest passage leading to China and that ore picked up at the mouth of the bay contained gold. But his efforts to establish a mining settlement along the bay failed miserably even before it became clear that the ore contained no gold.

and the South American mainland (the "Spanish Main") with the first in a series of illegal but highly lucrative peddling voyages. Hawkins's third voyage, in 1567, led to open conflict with the Spanish. Francis Drake took up the challenge at that point and began what proved to be twenty years of wildly adventurous raids on the Spanish colonial properties. The climax of Drake's career was his famous voyage around the world between 1577 and 1580, a joint-stock enterprise (see pp. 23–24) that yielded a 4,600 percent profit for the shareholders.

By then there was rising English interest in the Western Hemisphere—not primarily as a location for English colonies, but as a route to Asian markets. The Cabots' explorations at the turn of the sixteenth century were recalled, and new commercial and geographical information flowed in to help justify the enthusiasm of a group of adventurers from England's West Country. Led by Sir Humphrey Gilbert, this group was determined to find a northwestern passage through the Western Hemisphere to the Far East. In 1565 Queen Elizabeth's most important official advisers, the Privy Council, heard a formal debate on possible new routes. The merchants of the Muscovy Company urged endorsement of efforts to find an *eastern* passage, north of Siberia, and to exploit the trade of the Baltic region and Russia. The merchants and landowning gentry of the West Country, long fa-

miliar with the North American coastal waters, argued for expeditions to the *west*, through what is now Canada. Gilbert and the westerners were defeated in that debate, but with their support an enterprising mariner, Martin Frobisher, in 1576–78 led three expeditions into the region northeast of Hudson Bay. Frobisher and his London backers, under the direction of a merchant, Michael Lok, organized the short-lived Company of Cathay in response to the reports of gold—which later proved to be false—that were carried back. There were continuous frustrations in all these western ventures, but the search for the northwest passage went on. In the end, after vain and desperate efforts to get through the ice and snow of the Canadian wilderness, Englishmen at least gained a reasonably clear picture of that forbidding region of the globe.

First Attempts at Colonization.

As these overseas enterprises progressed, the idea of colonization gradually developed. In his appearance before the Privy Council in 1565, Gilbert had suggested the value of establishing colonies as way stations along the proposed routes to the Far East. In 1578 he sought and received a crown charter for establishing a colony in America.

Gilbert's attempt in 1578 to establish a colony in New England or Nova Scotia—the first English attempt to colonize the Western Hemisphere—failed almost before it began. His small exploratory fleet was scattered by storms and diverted by the lure of privateering. Yet in the process of launching this expedition, Gilbert acquired valuable experience in the financial aspects of colonization. He also won the enthusiasm of his gifted half-brother, Sir Walter Raleigh, and captured the interest of two cousins, both named Richard Hakluyt and both experts on overseas geography, who became important propagandists for colonization.

The younger Hakluyt's *Discourse Concerning Western Planting* (1584) shows the mixed motives of this advanced circle of enthusiasts. Hakluyt argued that it was England's duty to Christianize the American pagans, especially since an American colony would serve as a base for attacks on Spanish lands and Spanish treasure ships. More important, he continued, American colonies would provide long-term economic gains. They could supply England with exotic goods that otherwise would have to be bought from Spain, and they would create new markets for English consumer goods. The colonies would also absorb England's unemployed workers and turn their labor to advantage. New routes to Asia, new weapons against Spain, a new source of exotic supplies, a new market for English goods, and a new use for England's "surplus" population—all this would justify England's support of colonization.

But Raleigh's and Hakluyt's ideas were not widely shared, and they did not become state policy. In 1584, after Gilbert had died on a voyage from Newfoundland, Queen Elizabeth transferred his charter to Raleigh; but she kept her government from directly supporting his plans for colonization. When Raleigh was planning the expedition that would lead to the establishment of his famous "lost" colony in America in 1585, the queen made a minor financial contribution to the venture and gave it her personal blessing. But her government did nothing to help launch or sustain the enterprise. This one English settlement in America in the sixteenth century was thus of necessity almost entirely the *private* undertaking of a group of merchants and gentlemen from the west of England.

The story of this first English colony in the Western Hemisphere, in the region that the English named Virginia in honor of Elizabeth, the "Virgin Queen," is quickly told. In three successive years separate groups of settlers were landed on Roanoke Island, a heavily wooded spot off the coast of present-day North Carolina. The first group, 108 men, arrived in 1585. The settlers quickly clashed with the Indians and used up their food supply as they explored the North Carolina coast, and they returned hurriedly to England the next year with Francis Drake, who had unexpectedly appeared on his way home from a successful raid on the West Indies. Late in 1586 a party was sent from Eng-

land to relieve the first group; of this party, 18 men were left behind on Roanoke Island, but this forlorn and helpless crew was soon slaughtered by the Indians. The island was therefore deserted when in the summer of 1587 the third and largest contingent of settlers—117 men, women, and children—arrived under Governor John White. The precise fate of these people, the best-equipped of Raleigh's settlers, has never been discovered. White had to return quickly to England to speed on more supplies, but the threat of open war with Spain* and the attractions of privateering kept relief vessels from reaching the colony. When White finally managed to return in 1590, he found all the settlers gone. Apparently they had moved south to Croatoan Island, and there they had vanished. Their disappearance marks the end of Raleigh's efforts at colonization.

In comparison with the bold and hugely successful first thrusts of the Spanish in America, this was a fumbling, failing, almost pathetic affair. Raleigh's Roanoke venture dramatically underscored the limitations that defeated English colonization in the reign of Elizabeth I. Yet it also revealed the basic conditions that would shape the successful English settlements in the early seventeenth century.

Personnel and the Role of the State

Several things of permanent importance had become clear during these earliest and least successful years of English colonization in America. First, there existed in England, available for colonization, a leadership group whose members were quite different from the Spanish conquerors, "drunk with a heroic and brutal dream," as a Spanish poet later described the *conquistadores*. The Spanish conquerors had been the sons of poor farmers and townsmen, many of them illiterate. But the leaders of English overseas enterprise—Gilbert, Raleigh, Hawkins, Drake—were the well-educated younger sons of the West Country gentry, bred in secure landed establishments and familiar with the sea from childhood. English law barred younger sons from inheriting family properties, and these men were eager to find a way of reestablishing themselves on the land in the same genteel condition they had known before.

Second, it was clear that there was in England a mass of laborers available for emigration to overseas colonies. London, whose population rose from 60,000 in 1500 to 200,000 in 1600, was swollen with unemployed workers. The countryside was swarming with migrant farmhands; and in the centers of the wool industry, the West Country and East Anglia (the

---

*This war climaxed, but did not end, with the famous defeat of the Spanish Armada in 1588.

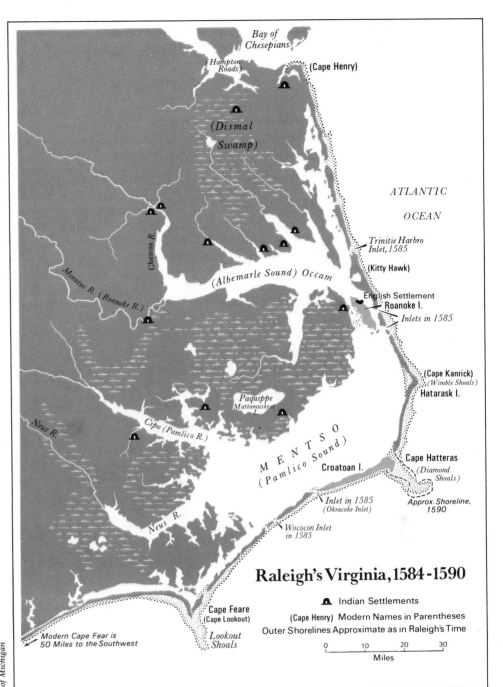

Raleigh's Virginia, 1584-1590

🔺 Indian Settlements

(Cape Henry) Modern Names in Parentheses

Outer Shorelines Approximate as in Raleigh's Time

```
0    10    20    30
         Miles
```

Map labels: Bay of Chesepians; (Hampton Roads); (Cape Henry); (Dismal Swamp); ATLANTIC OCEAN; Trinitie Harbro Inlet, 1585; Chawan R.; Moratuc R. (Roanoke R.); (Albemarle Sound) Occam; (Kitty Hawk); English Settlement Roanoke I.; Inlets in 1585; (Cape Kanrick) (Wimble Shoals); Hatarask I.; Neus R.; Paquippe Mattamuskeet L.; Cipo (Pamlico R.); M E N T S O (Pamlico Sound); Croatoan I.; Cape Hatteras (Diamond Shoals); Inlet in 1585 (Okracoke Inlet); Approx. Shoreline, 1590; Wococon Inlet in 1585; Neus R.; Cape Feare (Cape Lookout); Lookout Shoals; Modern Cape Fear is 50 Miles to the Southwest

NORTH CAROLINA INDIAN MAKING A DUGOUT CANOE, 1585

Detail of an engraving by De Bry of one of the accurate and superbly colored scenes of Indian life and the natural environment made by John White on his voyages to Raleigh's "Virginia" in 1585 and 1587.

In 1590 John White, the first governor of Roanoke Colony, returned to Roanoke Island from England. His account was later published by Richard Hakluyt the younger.

OUR boats and all things fitted . . . , we put off from Hatteras, being the number of nineteen persons in both boats. . . .

We . . . landed at daybreak, and coming to the fire we found the grass and sundry rotten trees burning about the place. From hence we went through the woods to that part of the island directly over against Dasamonquepeio and from thence we returned by the waterside, round about the north point of the island, until we came to the place where I left our colony in the year 1587. In all this way we saw in the sand the print of the savages' feet of two or three sorts trodden the night. And as we entered up the sandy bank, upon a tree, in the very brow thereof, were curiously carved these fair Roman letters CRO. Which letters presently we knew to signify the place, where I should find the planters seated, according to a secret token agreed upon between them and me at my last departure from them, which was, that in any ways they should not fail to write or carve on the trees or posts of the doors the name of the place where they should be seated; for at my coming away they were prepared to remove from Roanoke fifty miles into the main. Therefore, at my departure from them in Anno [Domini] 1587 I willed them that if they should happen to be distressed in any of those places, that then they should carve over the letters or name, a cross ✠ in this form. But we found no such sign of distress.

And having well considered of this, we passed toward the place where they were left in sundry houses, but we found the houses taken down, and the place very strongly enclosed with a high palisado of great trees, with cortines and flankers [entrenchments] very fortlike, and one of the chief trees or posts at the right side of the entrance had the bark taken off, and five foot from the ground in fair capital letters was graven CROATOAN, without any cross or sign of distress. This done, we entered into the palisado, where we found many bars of iron, two pigs of lead, four iron fowlers, iron sakershot, and such like heavy things, thrown here and there, almost overgrown with grass and weeds. From thence we went along by the waterside, towards the point of the creek to see if we could find any of their boats or pinnace, but we could perceive no sign of them, nor any of the last falcons and small ordnance which were left with them, at my departure from them.

At our return from the creek, some of our sailors meeting us, told us that they had found where divers chests had been hidden, and long since digged up again and broken up, and much of the goods in them spoiled and scattered about, but nothing left, of such things as the savages knew any use of, undefaced. Presently Captain Cocke and I went to the place, which was in the end of an old trench, made two years past by Captain Amadas, where we found five chests that had been carefully hidden of the planters, and of the same chests three were my own, and about the place many of my things spoiled and broken, and my books torn from the covers, the frames of some of my pictures and maps rotten and spoiled with rain, and my armor almost eaten through with rust. This could be no other but the deed of the savages, our enemies at Dasamonquepeio, who had watched the departure of our men to Croatoan; and as soon as they were departed, digged up every place where they suspected anything to be buried. But although it much grieved me to see such spoil of my goods, yet on the other side I greatly joyed that I had safely found a certain token of their safe being at Croatoan, which is the place where Manteo was born, and the savages of the island our friends.

When we had seen in this place so much as we could, we returned to our boats, and departed from the shore towards our ships with as much speed as we could.

eastern counties of Essex, Suffolk, and Norfolk), underemployment was generating the discontent that would express itself forcefully in the religious protest of Puritanism. Elizabethans spoke of the "multitude of increase in our people." Responsible officials were convinced that England was overpopulated and that its well-being was threatened by an idle labor force that consumed more than it contributed to the national wealth. For many, the most attractive remedy was colonization and emigration. We know now that there was no absolute "surplus" of people in seventeenth-century England, even though the population of the kingdom rose from just over 3 million in 1550 to just over 4 million in 1600, to 5.2 million in 1695, and to 6 million in 1720. The sense of overpopulation arose from the widespread displacement of a mass population and from the high geographical mobility that had resulted from rapid economic growth, inflation, and the commercialization of agriculture. But however these developments were viewed, they proved crucial to the early settlement of British North America by making a mass of ordinary farm and town workers available for recruitment.

Third, it became evident that there was plentiful capital available for investment in overseas ventures, as well as abundant business interest in mobilizing that capital and directing it to profitable uses in colonization. The costs of financing the Roanoke voyages and the first efforts at colonization had been borne almost entirely by landowning West Country gentlemen, but their resources were clearly inadequate to support further, larger-scale efforts. In 1589 Raleigh transferred control of the Virginia enterprise to a London business syndicate that was headed by Sir Thomas Smith, one of the most powerful merchants of the age. The capital available to these merchants was far greater than that of the West Country gentry, and it would be these businessmen who would launch the first new wave of colonization in the early seventeenth century.

It had become clear, too, in the later years of Elizabeth's reign, that when colonization efforts would be resumed the crown would continue to play only a minor role. It would legalize exploration and settlement and would have some say in the plans that were made. But the crown would initiate nothing and organize nothing, nor would it sustain or reinforce any enterprise that was begun. More important, the English crown had no desire to extend its direct rule over distant territories conquered or settled by Englishmen. Some form of government would be provided, but it would not be direct crown government in depth. The burden of governing the colonies, like the burden of financing them, would have to be borne by the organizers of the settlement or by the settlers them-

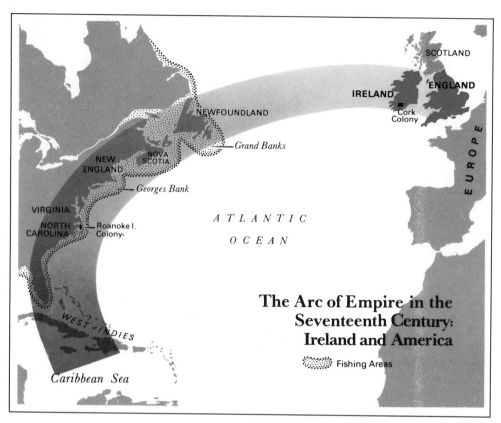

The Arc of Empire in the
Seventeenth Century:
Ireland and America

······· Fishing Areas

selves. At the start at least, colonial government would have to be self-government of some sort, and the imperial government would be a superstructure, an overlay imposed on semi-independent units of local government.

Financial Limitations and the "Starving Times"

England's war with Spain, which had begun in the 1580s, finally ended in 1604. The conclusion of peace released the powerful expansionist impulses that had been building up in England for half a century. The resulting lunge into overseas enterprise in the reigns of James I (1603–25) and his son Charles I (1625–49) was spectacular. The famous settlements at Jamestown, at Plymouth, and around the Massachusetts Bay were only fragments of a huge overall effort that reached into many areas of the globe, that involved hundreds of thousands of Englishmen of all descriptions, and that cost millions of pounds.

The chief target of this great expansion was not North America but Ireland, which in the sixteenth century had been the scene of England's first extensive and sustained efforts at overseas colonization. Henry VIII had tried to bind the native Irish chiefs to him by feudal ties and gradually to introduce the Church of England and elements of English law. But he had

failed to win over the rebellious Irishmen, and in 1566 English armies moved in to conquer what they could by force. British settlements were then established in certain parts of southern Ireland, which formed a "pale of settlement" beyond which lived what Englishmen considered savage, ungovernable natives.

By 1604 the English saw Ireland and America as equivalent centers of overseas expansion and in their minds linked the two lands geographically. As they looked out at the world beyond England, they saw a single arc of overseas territories suitable for colonization sweeping out from their own island. This arc enclosed Ireland, Newfoundland, and the mainland coast of North America south to the Caribbean. It was natural for the English to consider nearby Ireland, which was described in a travel book of 1617 as "this famous island in the Virginia Sea," as the first and primary object of their colonization efforts in the early seventeenth century. When in 1607 two of the most powerful Irish earls resisted English authority and ultimately fled the British Isles, the English confiscated their vast properties. They largely cleared this immense territory—which covered six of the nine counties of the northern province of Ulster—of its native population and sold parcels of the land to prospective "planters" (settlers). London's city government and its major guild corporations took up large grants. After an

TROOPS ON THE MARCH
A woodcut of 1581 showing English soldiers returning to camp after a retaliatory fight with "wild Irish" cattle raiders.

Irish rebellion in 1641, 7 million more acres were cleared of their native inhabitants. Thousands of native Irish were severely punished for their part—proved or suspected—in the rebellion, and most were driven beyond the English pale. Into these Irish "plantations" came a steady stream of English and Scottish emigrants in the same years that the North American settlements were being established. By 1642 an estimated 120,000 English and Scottish men, women, and children had settled in Ireland. This migration was six times larger than the famous "Great Migration" that settled New England in the same period.

Yet Ulster was the scene of only one—if the most extensive—of the colonization efforts of the time. Besides Ireland, Virginia, and Massachusetts, English settlements were established in Bermuda, on several Caribbean islands (Providence, Barbados, St. Christopher, Nevis, Montserrat, and Antigua), in Newfoundland, in Nova Scotia, and on the mainland coast of South America. In addition the English developed fragile contacts with India, first into flourishing trading settlements (called factories) and then into the beginning of a network of political control that would eventually cover much of the Indian subcontinent.

In this global context the first English settlements on the North American mainland were relatively small undertakings, and their early histories become understandable only in terms of the greater whole. For while these American communities would in time have a unique historical importance, originally they shared characteristics common to the rest of the earliest seventeenth-century enterprises. And of these common characteristics, none was more important than the way in which they were financed.

The Financing of the Colonies. Whatever their founders' ultimate dreams, these earliest English colonies—whether in Newfoundland, Barbados, Ulster, Plymouth, or Virginia—had to be financed at the start by profit-seeking joint-stock companies. Eleven commercial companies bore the main financial burden of the settlements that were launched before 1640. They raised their capital (an estimated £13 million) by selling stock to a remarkably broad range of the English population. Thousands invested—landowners as well as merchants, people of ordinary means as well as those of wealth. The funds that were raised by these investments were, for the most part, managed by men who worked not only within the usual constraints of business operations, but also under two very special pressures. These pressures explain much of the hardship and tragedy of life in the earliest American settlements.

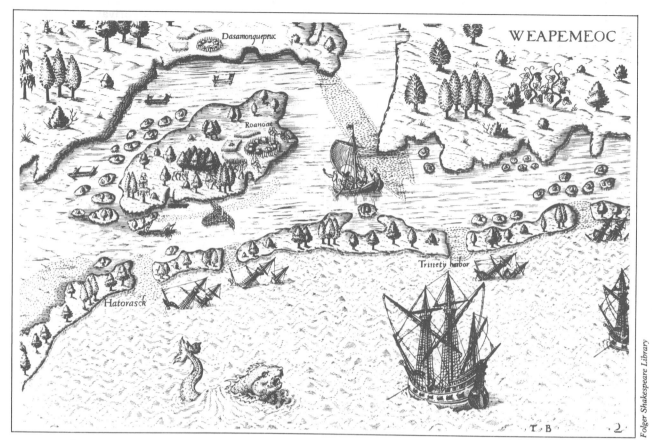

"VIRGINIA," c. 1590

This interesting detail of a map-picture dating from 1590 shows the coast of "Virginia" (present-day North Carolina) and the perilous shoals off Cape Hatteras where many early sailing vessels foundered. The rendering shows Indian settlements on Roanoke Island.

First, the joint stocks—the initial capital funds—of these ventures were not expected to endure. That is, shareholders did not expect to leave their funds in these companies over a long period and to draw a steady dividend income from them. Instead, investors hoped to benefit from the quick liquidation of the whole enterprise at the end of a single voyage or after a set number of years. It was expected that at such a time the original capital plus accumulated profits would be distributed to investors. Whether there would be any further investments beyond the initial one would depend on the business prospects at the time of this complete division of the company's assets. Many of the settlers were in effect employees of the company that had organized the venture, for a stated term of years; thus they were under great pressure to produce an immediate profit. If they failed to ship back tangible proof of the financial value of the settlement, they would be cut off and would be forced to fend for themselves. As a consequence, instead of carefully exploring their surroundings and acclimating themselves to the strange American environment, the first settlers spent much of their time scrabbling for gold in every shallow stream, searching for routes to the Pacific Ocean around the bend of every broad river, and plunging almost suicidally into the backcountry to investigate confused Indian reports of great cities or of vast sources of furs or precious metals.

The pressures on the settlers were further intensified by the technical fact that the shareholders in these early joint-stock companies had unlimited legal liability. The backers of the settlements were personally liable, without limit, for all debts the settlement companies might incur. Investors were therefore extremely sensitive to any possibility of failure. They had no choice but to abandon doubtful enterprises as quickly as possible.

The "Starving Times."

The result of these conditions was desperation, starvation, and at times complete chaos in England's first North American colonies, as well as bankruptcy in the companies that first colonized mainland North America. For there were only three possible sources of quick profits for colonists. First, they might have found valuable resources on the surface of the land, loaded them onto boats, and rushed them back to investors. Second, they might have encountered a docile native population and organized it quickly into labor gangs to dig out the less accessible resources. Third, settlers might have discovered new routes to rich, exotic markets. None of these possibilities, however, proved realistic on the coasts of North America. Consequently, after the first shipments, investors withheld life-sustaining supplies from the settlements, and one company after another failed. Sheer accident provided most of the profits that were made at the start. In Bermuda, for example, ambergris (a substance, produced by whales, that is used in making perfume and medicine) was found in large quantities; a shipment of £10,000 worth of this substance saved the Bermuda Company. (Subsequently the company profited steadily from tobacco production.) Similarly the Providence Island Company had the good fortune to capture a Spanish treasure ship worth £50,000.

Lucky accidents of this kind were rare, however. Sooner or later, almost every one of the companies that had financed settlements in British North America failed, and as they did so the original investors sought desperately to find secondary sources of profit. Some of the stockholders, seeking to recover their losses, funded "magazines"—stores of goods to be sold at high prices to the needy settlers. Some stockholders set up separately financed enterprises: glass manufacturing and silk making were favored in Virginia.

Others attempted to develop "private plantations," that is, personal estates and jurisdictions, in the new land given to them in place of the missing company profits. The Virginia Company alone created fifty of these private domains, but few of these secondary enterprises succeeded. Perhaps the most successful of the lesser ventures within the Virginia Company was the fund that was established to send over a hundred "maids" to Jamestown "to be made wives of." The investors in this venture realized a 47 percent profit on their shares when they sold the women's work contracts to the colonists.

As their financial prospects dimmed, many investors withdrew altogether from the ventures. In these cases colonists found themselves abruptly cut off from their backers, and for most of them the transition to self-sustained community life was desperately difficult. Even in the best of circumstances, the first inhabitants of Jamestown or Bermuda or Plymouth would have had a shock in adjusting to the wilderness environment. Forced to search for sources of immediate profit while neglecting the basics of survival, many found the struggle unendurable and succumbed—to despair, to disease, and to the harassment of hostile natives.

The narratives of the first settlements make painful reading. There was heroism, but there was also murderous selfishness; there was industry, but also laziness and at times suicidal inertia. Death and misery were everywhere. It is perhaps not surprising that the best-organized and most successful of the earliest communities were those in which strong religious beliefs prevailed. For only the otherworldly goals, the fierce determination, and the inner certainty of the Pilgrim and Puritan leaders could withstand the disintegrating effects of the "starving times."

1492–1504	Columbus's four voyages to New World.		**1539–41**	De Soto explores southeastern United States and discovers the Mississippi.
1494	Treaty of Tordesillas divides non-Christian world between Spain and Portugal.		**1540–42**	Coronado seeks legendary cities of wealth in North American Southwest.
1497–98	John Cabot explores Newfoundland, Labrador, and Nova Scotia, and establishes English claim to North America.		**1540–53**	Valdivia extends Spanish conquest of Chile.
1503	Spain establishes board of trade, *Casa de Contratación*.		**1542**	Viceroyalty of Peru established.
1508–09	Sebastian Cabot explores Hudson Bay region.		**1551**	Antwerp market for English woolen goods fails.
1509–47	Reign of Henry VIII.		**1553–58**	Queen Mary reigns in England.
1513	Balboa discovers Pacific Ocean after crossing Isthmus of Panama.		**1558–1603**	Elizabeth's reign in England.
1513	Ponce de León discovers mainland of Florida.		**1562–67**	Hawkins trades and plunders in Spanish America.
1519–21	Cortés conquers Mexico.		**1566**	England begins conquest of Ireland.
1523	Verrazano explores coast of North America, establishing French claim.		**1574**	Gilbert leads expedition to Hudson Bay.
1523–1530	Spaniards conquer Honduras and Guatemala.		**1577–80**	Drake circumnavigates globe.
1524	Spain creates Council of the Indies.		**1578**	Gilbert fails to establish colony in North America.
1528–36	Cabeza de Vaca explores northern periphery of Gulf of Mexico, west to Gulf of California.		**1584**	Richard Hakluyt (the younger) publishes *A Discourse Concerning Western Planting*.
1532–35	Pizarro conquers Peru.		**1585–87**	Raleigh fails to establish Roanoke Colony.
1535	Viceroyalty of New Spain created.		**1585–98**	England colonizes Ireland.
1535–39	Initial Spanish conquest of Ecuador, Chile, northern Argentina, and Bolivia.		**1603–25**	Reign of James I.
			1606	Virginia Company chartered; includes two subcompanies.
			1607	English colony established at Jamestown.

SUGGESTED READINGS

The discovery and conquest of Central and South America by Spain had been the subject of some of the greatest narrative histories written in the nineteenth century, notably William H. Prescott's *History of the Conquest of Mexico* (1843) and his *Conquest of Peru* (1847). This tradition of dramatic narratives continues in our own time in the writings of Samuel E. Morison, particularly in his biography of Columbus, *Admiral of the Ocean Sea* (2 vol. and 1 vol. eds., 1942, condensed as *Christopher Columbus, Mariner*, 1956), and his *The European Discovery of America: The Southern Voyages, AD 1492–1616* (1974), a volume crowded with maps and photographs that was written after the author retraced the routes of the Spanish discoverers by ship and plane. John H. Parry has sketched the general development of European expansion, geographical discovery, and initial overseas settlements in two very readable books, *Europe and a Wider World, 1415–1715* (1949) and *The Age of Reconnaissance*

(1963). And David B. Quinn has summarized the first efforts of the Spanish, English, and French to explore and settle North America in his *North America from Earliest Discovery to First Settlements* (1977).

There are several good introductory histories of Spanish America in the colonial period: Charles Gibson, *Spain in America* (1966); Hubert Herring, *A History of Latin America from the Beginnings to the Present* (3d ed., 1968), parts I, II; Bailey W. Diffie, *Latin American Civilization: The Colonial Period* (1945); John H. Parry, *The Spanish Seaborne Empire* (1966); and Salvador de Madariaga, *Rise of the Spanish American Empire* (1947). An equivalent history of the Portuguese-American empire is C. R. Boxer, *The Portuguese Seaborne Empire, 1415–1825* (1969); on the French empire in America, see George M. Wrong, *The Rise and Fall of New France* (2 vols., 1928), and William J. Eccles, *Canada Under Louis XIV* (1964) and *Canadian Frontier, 1534–1760* (1969).

The best general account of the administrative and constitutional history of Spanish America is Clarence H. Haring, *The Spanish Empire in America* (1947). For a theoretical analysis of the same subject in sociological terms, see Margali Sarfatti, *Spanish Bureaucratic-Patrimonialism in America* (1966). The underlying ideas of empire are described in John H. Parry, *The Spanish Theory of Empire in the Sixteenth Century* (1940).

On economic history, there are two classic works: Clarence H. Haring, *Trade and Navigation Between Spain and the Indies* . . . (1918), and Earl J. Hamilton, *American Treasure and the Price Revolution in Spain, 1501–1650* (1934). In addition, see Peter J. Bakewell, *Silver Mining and Society in Colonial Mexico* . . . (1971); Woodrow W. Borah, *New Spain's Century of Depression* (Ibero-Americana, 35, 1951); and relevant chapters in John Lynch, *Spain Under the Hapsburgs* (2 vols., 1964–69).

There are several studies that concentrate on the particular topics emphasized in this chapter. On race relations and population characteristics: essays by Magnus Mörner, Woodrow Borah, and Peter Boyd-Bowman, in Fredi Chiapelli, ed., *First Images of America* (1976), Vol. II; Charles Gibson, *The Aztecs Under Spanish Rule* (1964); John H. Rowe, "The Incas Under Spanish Colonial Institutions," *Hispanic American Historical Review*, 37 (1957), 156–91; Lesley B. Simpson, *The Encomienda in New Spain* (1929); C. E. Marshall, "The Birth of the Mestizo in New Spain," *Hispanic American Historical Review*, 19 (1939), 161–84; James Lockhart, *Spanish Peru, 1532–1560, A Colonial Society* (1968), and his *Men of Cajamarca* (1972); Charles Gibson, "The Transformation of the Indian Community in New Spain, 1500–1800," *Journal of World History*, 2 (1955), 581–607; Lyle N. McAlister, "Social Structure and Social Change in New Spain," *Hispanic American Historical Review*, 43 (1963), 349–70; Lewis Hanke, *The Spanish Struggle for Justice in the Conquest of America* (1949); and Silvio Zavala, *New Viewpoints on the Spanish Colonialization of America* (1943). Nathan Wachtel, *The Vision of the Vanquished* (1977), is an attempt to portray the trauma of the Spanish conquest from the Indians' point of view. On the dominance of native Spaniards in high office and the slow rise of Creoles through purchase of public office, see M. H. Burkholder and D. S. Chandler, *From Impotence to Authority* (1977), and J. H. Parry, *The Sale of Public Office* . . . (1953). For an extended comparison of the Spanish American and the British North American colonial empires, see James Lang, *Conquest and Commerce: Spain and England in the Americas* (1975). Comparisons of slavery in North and South America have been worked out in books by Frank Tannenbaum (*Slave and Citizen*), Carl N. Degler (*Neither Black nor White*), Herbert S. Klein (*Slavery in the Americas*), and most comprehensively by David B. Davis (*The Problem of Slavery in Western Culture*).

The essential writings on England's involvement in geographic discovery and overseas settlement in the sixteenth century are by David B. Quinn. His *Roanoke Voyages, 1584–1590* (2 vols., 1955) contains every document related to that enterprise, a subject he has summarized in an excellent brief account, *Raleigh and the British Empire* (1947). In addition, Quinn has edited the documents of the colonizing efforts of Sir Humphrey Gilbert (2 vols., 1940), written a biography of Gilbert, edited Hakluyt's writings, and discovered the Pilgrims' original plans to settle on the islands in the gulf of the St. Lawrence. His essays are brought together in *England and the Discovery of America, 1481–1620* (1974) and summarized in his *North America*, cited above. Samuel E. Morison's *The European Discovery of America: The Northern Voyages, A.D. 500–1600* (1971) covers in the same vivid fashion as *The Southern Voyages* the Cabots' voyages and all of the Elizabethan explorations, and it contains in addition an excellent account of the Roanoke expeditions. A more traditional summary is John B. Brebner, *The Explorers of North America, 1492–1806* (1933).

The important role of Ireland in the origins of Elizabethan colonization and the connections between Irish and American settlement are best described in David B. Quinn, *The Elizabethans and the Irish* (1966). See also James Muldoon, "The Indian as Irishman," *Essex Institute Historical Collections*, 111 (1975), 267–89; and Nicholas P. Canny, "The Ideology of English Colonization: from Ireland to America,"* *William and Mary Quarterly*, 3d ser.,** 30 (1973), 575–98.

The masterwork on the financial history of sixteenth- and seventeenth-century English exploration and colonization is W. R. Scott, *The Constitution and Finance of English, Scottish and Irish Joint Stock Companies to 1720* (3 vols., 1912). Theodore K. Rabb, *Enterprise and Empire* . . . *1575–1630* (1967), demonstrates statistically the broad social basis of investment in colonization.

---

*This essay and several mentioned in the references that follow have been reprinted in an excellent collection, *Colonial America: Essays in Politics and Social Development* (Stanley N. Katz and John M. Murrin, eds., 3rd ed., Boston, 1983). Essays and selections from books that appear in this volume are indicated by a dagger(†).

**This journal will be referred to hereafter as *Wm. and Mary Q.*

2 Transplantation

In 1600 the eastern coastal region of mainland North America, some 362,000 square miles from Maine to Georgia and west to the Appalachian Mountains, was largely uncultivated. Much of it was covered with forests, but it was by no means an unbroken wilderness. A native Indian population, grouped in well-organized tribes and sharing approximately the same culture, lived fairly settled lives there. Many dwelled in semipermanent villages of up to 1,000 persons. Concentrated in the fertile coastal plain and the broad river valleys, these native Americans communicated readily along an intricate network of riverways and forest trails. They lived on a generally nutritious diet of fish and farm crops, principally maize (corn), as well as on game and wild foods, and they rarely suffered famine.

But the Indians' hold upon the land was light. Large areas of the Atlantic woodland region were completely uninhabited; the New England coastal population had been decimated by smallpox just before the first English settlers arrived. Anthropologists have estimated the average population density for the entire region east of the Appalachians in the early days of European settlement at thirty-four persons per hundred square miles. In the most populous region, New England and coastal New York, whose population in 1610 has been estimated at 72,000, the average density was between four and five persons per square mile. Nowhere was more than 1 percent of all the land available for cultivation actually being farmed, and nowhere did the Indians think of landownership in terms familiar to Europeans. The Indians did not view land as pieces of property owned by individuals. Rather, land was a common resource that was inherited from ancestors, held in trust by tribal chiefs for future generations, and used by all members of the tribe for their daily needs. Nor did the Indians think of warfare in European terms. Deadly struggles between individuals and tribes were common, and enemies were treated brutally; but the Indians did not go to war to

destroy their enemies completely, to create utter devastation, or to engage in wholesale massacre. Finally, in only one area of the entire Atlantic coastal region were the native inhabitants organized into a political structure that was effective beyond the tribal level. And even in that famous and militarily important organization, the Iroquois Confederacy, control over the separate tribes was never secure.

By 1700 this vast coastal region had been transformed, and the foundations of British North American civilization had been established. The Indians had been eliminated from the seaboard lands—killed in epidemics, destroyed by the invading English and Dutch in savage local wars, and driven back beyond the western fringes of European settlement. The area now contained a quarter of a million transplanted Europeans and their children and grandchildren, all attempting to re-create the familiar pattern of European life in this undeveloped land. The settlers had come principally from England and the Netherlands, two of the most dynamic and economically advanced nations of Europe. They lived in communities that were parts of a commercial network spread across the entire Atlantic basin and that directly or indirectly involved all the nations of western Europe. Within this transplanted European population, and mainly in Virginia and Maryland, there were also more than 20,000 African slaves, who were bound in lifelong, hereditary, and debased servitude.

The transplanted population of 1700 was organized into eleven provinces loosely controlled by the English government, which was only beginning to understand the full importance of the colonial world it had acquired. A small proportion of the settlers, perhaps 8 percent, lived in the five main port towns (Boston, Newport, New York, Philadelphia, and Charleston) through which flowed most of the commerce and communications that linked this world to Europe. The rest lived in village communities numbering a few hundred persons or on isolated family farms or

Enoch Pratt Free Library; photograph from the Maryland Historical Society

"plantations" that were modeled on European agricultural establishments but different from them in fundamental ways.

These tens of thousands of transplanted Europeans and Africans had arrived in no concentrated stream, under no centralized direction, and in no limited span of years. Rather, they had arrived—and in 1700 were continuing to arrive—irregularly and under various circumstances. Migration and settlement were organized by individuals or by private organizations, and the history of this process forms not one story, but many. Yet for all their variety these stories of colonization have a common pattern. They begin with high hopes and great plans—often visions of utopian, or ideal, societies—designed by people who dreamed of starting the world anew, of creating new communities, and, usually, of profiting immensely by doing so. But contact with reality in an undeveloped land brought frustration and the failure of original high hopes. Those who survived, however, learned to adapt creatively to their new environment. This was the persistent pattern of colonization in the seventeenth century: soaring expectations, disappointment, frustration, disaster or near disaster, and then a slow adjustment to the realities of life on the wilderness edge of the North American continent. New forms of society gradually emerged from this process, forms made far more complex by their superficial similarities to the familiar patterns of European life.

Virginia: Squalor, Struggle, and a New Way of Life

The settlement of Virginia is a classic case of high hopes shattered and a new world rescued from the ruins. It began in 1606 when the English crown chartered two Virginia companies, one based in Plymouth, England, and the other in London. These two companies incorporated the interests of the two main groups that had already been involved in western exploration and the planning of American settlements—the gentry and merchants of the West Country, and the London merchants to whom Sir Walter Raleigh had transferred his rights. The companies were given separate although overlapping portions of the North American coast for settlement and were instructed to appoint their own resident governments. In 1607 the Plymouth group, which had been assigned the northern area between the Potomac River and present-day Bangor, Maine, attempted a settlement (called Sagadahoc) on the Maine coast near the mouth of the Kennebec River. But everything went wrong. No signs of quick profits appeared, disease and Indian attacks decimated the small band of settlers huddled in the tiny fort, and within a year the effort was permanently abandoned.

AN INDIAN CHIEF, 1585
A watercolor by John White (see p. 18).

Jamestown. The Virginia Company of London, which had been assigned the southern sector, was more ambitious and better financed. Its leaders, under Sir Thomas Smith, England's most powerful merchant, were vigorous, hard-driving men. In December 1606 they sent out three ships, the *Susan Constant*, the *Godspeed*, and the *Discovery*. These tiny vessels were scarcely able to hold the 144 people they carried, let alone survive a midwinter crossing of the Atlantic. Not until April 1607 did they reach Chesapeake Bay. In May the 104 survivors of the voyage disembarked on a low-lying island thirty miles upstream on the James River. The spot, close to the riverbank, was so soaked with stagnant water that no home site could be chosen farther than 800 feet from malarial swamps, but the location was safe from attack and was believed to be close to passages through the continent to the Pacific. This unlikely place, which came to be called Jamestown, was to be the first permanent English settlement in North America.

The colony survived, but only barely. During the

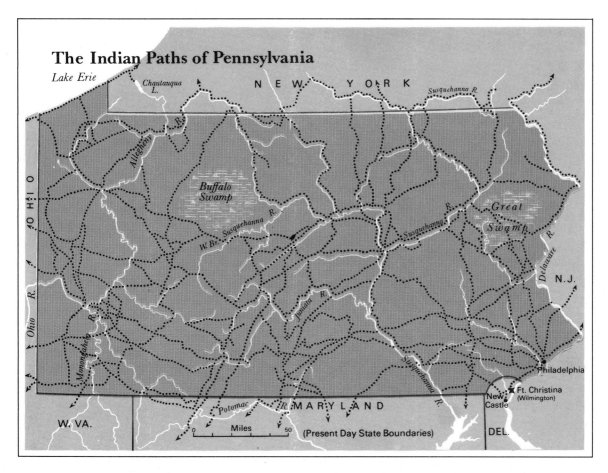

The Indian Paths of Pennsylvania

Lake Erie

Chautauqua L.

NEW YORK

Susquehanna R.

OHIO

Allegheny R.

Buffalo Swamp

W. Br. Susquehanna R.

Great Swamp

Susquehanna R.

Delaware R.

N.J.

Ohio R.

Monongahela R.

Juniata R.

Susquehanna R.

Philadelphia

Ft. Christina (Wilmington)

New Castle

W. VA.

Potomac R. MARYLAND

0   Miles   50   (Present Day State Boundaries)

DEL.

The map above is a composite reconstruction of all the Pennsylvania trails known to have been used by the native Americans. It appears in Paul A. W. Wallace, *Indian Paths of Pennsylvania* (1965), which contains detailed descriptions of every path on the map.

eighteen years of the Virginia Company's existence (1606–24), Jamestown, the main settlement, was a disaster for everyone in any way connected with it. Death was everywhere in the colony. Four out of five of the "planters" died of disease or in Indian attacks. The Virginia Company itself survived beyond its first two years only because of its leaders' persistence in pursuing empty dreams of profits and because of the financial support they were able to mobilize. Seldom has good money been thrown so extravagantly after bad; seldom have hard-headed businessmen been so mistaken in their expectations of success.

It quickly became clear that in Virginia the settlers would discover neither easily mined minerals nor a passage through the continent. Nor would they find a useful native labor force. Hope came to rest on the new idea of giving the colony enough settlers and secure financing to produce more ordinary goods—grapes, sugar, tobacco, cotton, and dye woods. These products could be sold with substantial, although not sensational, profits in England. Once the colonists cre-

ated this kind of firm economic foundation, they could look into more dramatic and profitable ventures.

To establish Jamestown on this permanent basis, the company in London obtained a revised charter and launched a new effort that gave the endangered colony hope for the future. Without this renewed effort of 1609, Jamestown would have disappeared like Roanoke—and it almost did in any case.

By the terms of the new charter, the company was transformed into a public joint-stock company for a period of seven years. (Previously it had been financed by the contributions only of its incorporators and their friends.) In February 1609 the company staged an elaborate publicity campaign and began to sell public shares. One popular way to purchase shares was to pledge personal service in the colony as a settler. Such an "adventurer of person" received one or more shares of stock depending on his "quality" (that is, social standing) or special skills. Each share was to be worth at least a hundred acres of land in 1616, when the company's total assets would be divided among the

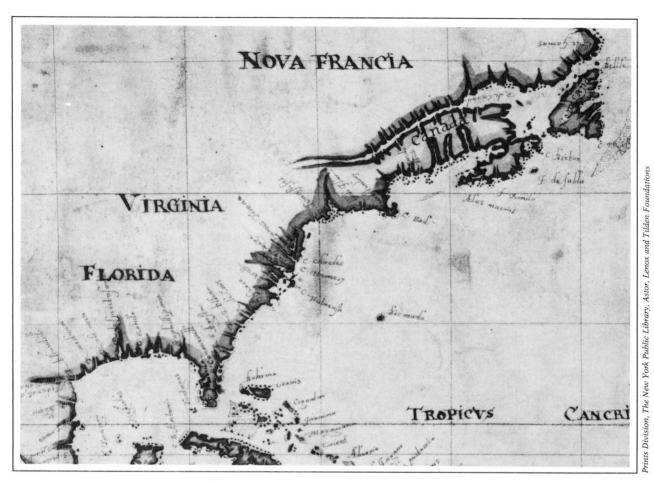

MAP DRAWN FOR THE VIRGINIA COMPANY
OF LONDON ABOUT 1607

Note the detail and relative accuracy of the Caribbean islands
and the fishing areas of maritime Canada, and the vagueness of
the rest, especially the southern areas labeled Florida.

stockholders. At the same time, the stockholders were given more authority, and a new form of government was drawn up for the colony.

Under the first charter the resident government of the colony had consisted of an appointed council that elected its own president. The result had been wrangling among the leaders until Captain John Smith seized power. Smith was a shrewd, stubborn, commanding war veteran, a romantic but intelligent adventurer. By forceful leadership he had prevented the forlorn band of colonists from starving to death. Combining cleverness and brutality, he had kept the neighboring Indian tribes cordial or at least intimidated. Smith had also made important explorations of the Chesapeake region and had surveyed its economic possibilities. The lesson of his leadership was not forgotten. Under the new regulations of 1609, all colonial authority was to be exercised by an appointed governor who was to be advised, not controlled, by a coun-

cil. The governor's power was to be limited only by the "liberties, franchises, and immunities" accorded all Englishmen and by instructions issued to him by the company.

The publicity campaign of 1609 was sensational. Colonization was preached in the churches of London, and the price of the company's stock rose. For the moment, support of the Virginia Company became a national cause. As a result, in June 1609 the company was able to send to Virginia a fleet carrying five hundred men, one hundred women, and large quantities of equipment and supplies. But the whole expedition seemed doomed. The vessel that carried the newly appointed officers of the colony was blown off course and was wrecked in Bermuda. (News of the shipwreck helped inspire Shakespeare's play *The Tempest*.) The four hundred leaderless settlers who arrived at Jamestown were exhausted by the long voyage and weakened by the putrid shipboard food. Disease was

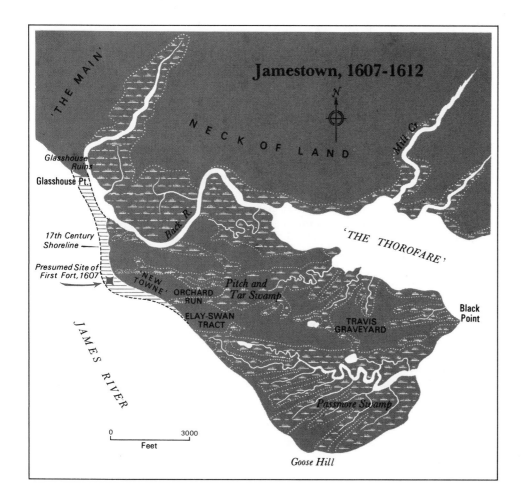

Jamestown, 1607-1612

already spreading among them when they landed. They were too feeble at first to work and then became deeply discouraged by the miserable prospects they found. They had been shaken out of their normal sense of social discipline and were confused by the disordered life around them. They fell into fierce factional struggles, lethargy, and despair, and they failed to plant the crops they would need for the coming year. In the midst of a rich land they starved, and, unable to withstand disease, they died in droves, miserably. When the fearful winter of 1609–10 was over, only about sixty of the settlers were still alive. In May 1610 the new leaders of the colony finally arrived from Bermuda. They found a scene of utter desolation: Jamestown's palisade was in ruins, its houses had been burned for firewood, the last scraps of food (including cattle and domestic animals) had been eaten, and people spoke secretly of cannibalism.

The ravaged settlement, still lacking the supplies that had been paid for by the stock sale of 1609, seemed hopeless. On June 7, 1610, it was abandoned. The settlers sailed down the James River in four small vessels, intending to go home to England by way of Newfoundland.

The Settlement Restored.   The colony was saved by a coincidence, which people of the time saw as an act of God. By chance the departing settlers were met near the mouth of the James River by a longboat from a fleet just arriving that carried three hundred men and the new governor, Lord De la Warr. The despairing and fearful settlers were ordered back, and De la Warr began the slow process of restoring discipline and confidence, creating a sound agriculture, and establishing profitable relations with the Indians. In England the company, with somewhat despairing vigor, continued its fund raising and sent further reinforcements of more than six hundred men with hundreds of domestic animals and shiploads of equipment. By now the emphasis was entirely on developing Virginia's agricultural, industrial, and commercial possibilities. A satellite settlement was founded at Henrico on the upper James (the site of present-day Richmond), and two others were located at the mouth of the James.

Harsh social discipline was imposed by a new code of laws that was published in 1612. Called *Lawes Divine, Morall, and Martiall*, this code organized the community into a kind of military corps. The settlers were required to perform service on common projects, and they were subjected to severe penalties for failure to work or to share military obligations.

Thus reinforced and disciplined, the colony made slow, painful progress toward self-sufficiency. Humble products—furs, timber, sassafras, some experimentally produced iron, and (beginning in 1614) small quantities of tobacco—began to fill the holds of vessels returning to England. But although the settlers had made an encouraging start, these early cargoes were not profitable enough to stimulate sizable new investments in the company, whose expenses were rising dangerously with each lifesaving supply ship that had to be sent to Virginia. More funds had to be raised. Subscribers were dunned for further contributions, unfulfilled pledges were pursued in the law courts, a public lottery was launched, more pamphlets were written describing Virginia's glowing promise, and more sermons were preached on the people's moral obligation to support this "New Britain." But even these intensified efforts did not generate the necessary aid. To popularize the organization further and to broaden its base, the company obtained a third charter in 1612 that again increased the ordinary shareholders' voice in the company's management. Still, the company's finances remained weak. The company was so short of money that in 1616, when the seven-year period of its existence as a joint-stock enterprise ended, it was too poor to provide the surveys necessary to make the promised distribution of 100 acres per share. Despite all the recent reinforcements, the colony's population was still a mere 350.

One last, great effort had to be made if the company was to be saved and any profit realized from the tens of thousands of pounds that had been invested. In 1618 a new group headed by Sir Edwin Sandys took over control of the company from Sir Thomas Smith and initiated the final phase of its history.

Under Sandys's influence the company drew up a uniform and generous policy of land inducements for the established colonists ("ancient planters") and for prospective investors and settlers. It devised the "headright" system, under which anyone who transported a settler to Virginia (either another person or himself) won the right to fifty acres of land. More important, the system allowed shareholders to pool their landholdings into jointly owned tracts, and it granted minor governmental powers to the holders of these tracts and of certain other large personal estates.

The creation of these "private plantations," or "hundreds," began the uncontrolled expansion of settled territory. By 1663 seventy such units were authorized. The lower James valley became dotted with self-contained subcolonies. At the same time, the rigid military discipline of the *Lawes* of 1612 was replaced by a more normal system of civil courts operating under English common law. A representative assembly—the first in American history—was provided for. This assembly consisted of the governor and his council, together with representatives of the private jurisdictions and of four projected urban communities, or "boroughs." At its first meeting in 1619, the assembly made clear that it would not only express popular grievances, as Parliament had been doing for centuries in England, but also protect the fundamental rights of Englishmen as these rights were known "at home."

In addition, the company launched a new economic program. It sent another 4,500 settlers to Virginia, through whom the company made intensive efforts to establish profitable agricultural products. Expert craftsmen began to manufacture pitch, tar, ships, and other timber products, as well as iron, salt, and glass. And the settlers experimented with growing tropical and semitropical crops and with producing salable wine and marketable silk.

It was all a colossal gamble by the energetic entrepreneurs who had taken over the company—and it was hopeless. Simply launching these enterprises drained all the company's cash, most of which had been raised by a lottery. By 1621 the lottery had become such a public nuisance that Parliament stopped it. Only a miraculous parlaying of small successes into basic security could rescue the company; but a single disaster would mean its collapse.

Collapse and Legacy of the Virginia Company.

In March 1622 the final catastrophe struck. The Indians, deprived of their lands, thoroughly terrorized and brutalized, and fearful of the sudden growth of the English population, fell on the whole string of defenseless farms along the James River and killed at least 347 inhabitants. The colony was physically devastated and utterly demoralized. The colonists, fearing that the slaughter would be renewed, and at the same time thirsting for vengeance, abandoned their fields at the start of the planting season and took up arms. The result was both a bloody reprisal against the Indians and a crop failure in the fall that created a near famine. Hundreds who had escaped death at the hands of the Indians died of sickness in the winter of 1622–23. When in 1624 the bankrupt Virginia Company's charter was annulled and the crown took over direct control of the colony, only 1,275 settlers remained alive out of the more than 8,500 who had gone to Virginia. In terms of its original purpose, the company was a complete failure.

Yet in a larger sense the Virginia Company had been successful. It had opened the North American mainland to British settlement. It had peopled a small portion of the mainland, although at a fearful cost in English and Indian lives. It had experimented with the economic possibilities of the Chesapeake, and it had left behind a heritage of the rule of law (at least within the English settlement) and of the practice of self-government, however rudimentary. Above all, the company had set the pattern for Virginia's development.

The general assembly, which the company had created to rally support among the settlers, continued to exist when Virginia became a royal colony. Governor, council, and representatives of the boroughs, or "burghs" (hence the name *burgesses* for the representatives), met together as a single group until the 1660s. By then the burgesses' interests had become distinct enough from those of the council to justify their meeting as a separate body. This central government, along with the county courts that were created in 1643, was the basic public authority in this frontier community, whose everyday life was an unregulated response to the raw Chesapeake environment. By 1642, when Sir William Berkeley first arrived as governor (a position he would occupy for most of the next thirty-four years), the essential character of life in the first permanent English colony in America was clear.

Seventeenth-century Virginia did not offer elegant, easy living on gracious "plantations," and there were no "Cavalier" aristocrats. True, in the first years, when all sorts of exotic rewards were expected, the leadership of the colony had included intellectuals and the sons of noblemen and other prominent people. But this early leadership had disappeared by 1624, casualties of the environment, the Indians, disease, and discouragement. The new leaders established themselves by their sheer capacity to survive on rough, half-cleared tobacco farms and to produce material gains from the raw wilderness. These men were former servants, yeoman farmers, and adventurers of little social status or wealth. They lacked the outward signs of social authority, but they managed to prosper by brute labor and shrewd manipulation.

The leaders of Virginia in the generation after the company was dissolved were tough, unsentimental, quick-tempered, crudely ambitious men who were concerned with making money from the land and with increasing their landholdings. They cared little for the grace of life. They roared curses, drank heavily, and gambled extravagantly, sometimes betting their servants when they had little else to wager. They asserted their interests fiercely. They wanted an aggressive expansion of settlement and of trading enterprise, and unrestricted access to land, no matter what the Indians' objections. From the simple governmental

agencies that existed, they sought legal endorsement of their hard-won gains. They claimed large amounts of land, but it was *cleared* land that counted—and there was little of that to be had. Because labor was in critically short supply, every effort was made to entice over from England workers whose labor could be counted on for a set period. This period was specified in "indentures"—contracts that bound immigrants to service for a number of years in return for payment of their passage to Virginia. Although an average of 1,500 indentured servants arrived in the Chesapeake annually through most of the seventeenth century, their terms of bonded service were short—normally four years for adults, and five to seven years for minors. After completing their service, most of them joined the general population of free tobacco farmers seeking to expand production and competing for hired labor.

Black "slave" labor (the meaning of the term *slave* was at first ambiguous) was known in Virginia as early as 1619. But black slaves were more expensive, at least in the short run, than white indentured servants. The absolute foreignness of the blacks—their appearance, behavior, language, and skills—offended the English, who were suspicious of all foreigners. A black labor force came into being only gradually. In 1640 a mere 150 blacks were reported in Virginia, and not all of them were slaves. In 1650 there were 300; in 1680, 3,000; in 1704, when the white population may have reached 75,600, there were roughly 10,000 blacks. As the number of black laborers rose and as their importance to the developing economy became clear, a new status of bondage took shape—that of "chattel slavery." This kind of slavery was previously unknown under English law. As servitude for whites became progressively more limited in duration and less rigorous in demands, the laws began to specify that blacks would serve for life. Moreover, their offspring would automatically become the property of their masters. Conversion to Christianity would not lead to slaves' freedom; nothing but their masters' discretion could limit the severity of punishment that could be inflicted on them; and racially mixed marriages were forbidden. Finally, the laws specified that a "slave" was no longer simply the lowest-ranking kind of servant, but rather something absolutely different in the eyes of the law. He was a form of property to be bought and sold. This was "chattel slavery," a status applicable only—and necessarily—to blacks and to all their descendants.

These were the main provisions of the "slave codes," so devastating in their consequences for the whole of American history. The codes originated in the latter half of the seventeenth century in response to an acute need for labor, an elemental fear of foreignness, and an insensitivity to cruelty remarkable even for

DETAIL FROM "THE RHETORICIANS' GUILD," HARLEM, THE NETHERLANDS, BY FRANS HALS
The Netherlands, the Pilgrims' first refuge, was an oasis of religious toleration. The scene shows a Calvinist, a Moslem, a Jew, and a libertine debating points of theology.

that callous age. But however unique the conditions that gave rise to these codes, once devised they became a fundamental part of the legal fabric of community life, and they intensified and perpetuated the racial fears and hostilities that had helped shape them. By 1700 it was becoming clear, to some at least, that chattel slavery, rising like some terrible germ-laden cloud, was poisoning the very soil and roots of human relations.

The Pilgrims' "Sweet Communion"

It is difficult for twentieth-century Americans to recapture fully the state of mind of those who led the settlement of New England. The Puritans and the Pilgrims are easily caricatured: the Puritans as God-intoxicated demons of self-righteousness, endlessly contemplating the fine points of their religion, and the Pilgrims as simple Christians, spotless in their devotion to the Bible. Both groups were products of the attempted reformation of the church in England that had followed Martin Luther's break with the Catholic church in 1517. In the 1530s England's Henry VIII had severed all ties with the Roman Catholic church and had established the Church of England, making himself its supreme head. Although under Henry and his daughter, Elizabeth I, the church had undergone considerable change in both theology and organization, the Puritans and the Pilgrims were among those who felt that the church was still too "Catholic," too immoral, and too closely involved in politics. They

sought a more direct experience of God than the existing church provided.

Although the Puritans and the Pilgrims shared this common disillusionment with the state church, otherwise they were very different. Their aims, their styles, and their accomplishments were different, and their ultimate contributions to American life lay in altogether different spheres. The Pilgrims were one of many radical "separatist" groups that first appeared in England in the 1570s. While remaining loyal to the English state, they felt its church too corrupt, the church services too ritualized. Accordingly, they set up their own "purified" churches—often primitive cells where their conventicles (secret religious assemblies) could conduct services that were stripped bare of all ritual. Unaffiliated with each other except for the people's shared aspirations, the conventicles attracted only true believers, who gathered together voluntarily in covenanted brotherhoods. Defiant of the persecution they were suffering at the hands of the government and the state church, and without hope of forcing their views on the world at large, these religious radicals were naturally drawn to America, where in isolation on the far margins of the English world they hoped to find freedom of worship while retaining the protection of the English state.

The Separatists. One such band of pious, humble, and stubborn believers had gathered in the village of Scrooby in east central England. This group, whose members eventually came to be known as the Pilgrim

THE PLYMOUTH PLANTATION
Leyden Street, Plymouth, as it appears in the modern restoration. "The houses," a visitor wrote in 1628, "are constructed of clapboards, with gardens also enclosed behind and at the sides with clapboards, so that the houses and courtyards are arranged in very good order."

Fathers, at first had no desire to settle in America. To escape the corrupting English way of life, in 1609 they fled to the Netherlands—first to Amsterdam and then to the nearby city of Leyden. Although the Separatists were free to practice their religious beliefs openly among the tolerant Dutch, they became increasingly concerned that their children were being attracted to the evils and "dangerous courses" that the liberal environment of Leyden seemed to foster. Fearful that their children would lose their faith, the Separatists eventually decided to move again, hoping to find a place better suited to the establishment of a pure church of Christ. After considering sites elsewhere in the Netherlands, on the northern coast of South America, and on islands at the mouth of the St. Lawrence River in present-day Canada, they decided on Virginia. They had several contacts with the leaders of the Virginia Company, which at the time was offering partially self-governing plantations to groups such as theirs.

By 1619 the Virginia Company had granted the Separatists the right to settle within its jurisdiction, and the English government promised not to molest them there. Financial help came from an investment group headed by the English adventurer Thomas Weston. After many hesitations those Separatists willing to go to America sold their property to purchase shares in the joint undertaking with Weston, with each settler's labor being counted as a single share of stock. In July 1620, 35 of the 238 members of the Leyden congregation took leave of their brethren in a scene so poignant, so prayerful and tearful, that even casual Dutch onlookers wept. They sailed to South-ampton, England, on their own small vessel, the *Speedwell*, to join an English contingent of Separatists and the 180-ton *Mayflower*, which the merchant-investors had rented for them. After two false starts and the ultimate abandonment of the unseaworthy *Speedwell*, many were discouraged from going on with the voyage. But the remaining Pilgrims, along with laborers who had been hired by the merchants, crowded into the *Mayflower*, which had been packed high with furniture, equipment, food, and animals. On September 16, 1620, they set sail for Virginia.

Of the 101 passengers on board the crowded vessel, perhaps 87 were Separatists or members of Separatist families. During more than nine weeks at sea, two children were born; remarkably, only one person died. But by the time the voyagers sighted Cape Cod, on November 9, and disembarked at what is now Provincetown on the tip of the cape, on November 11, they were ridden with disease, primarily scurvy,* and weakened by malnutrition. They had lost the strength and the will to continue on to the land in Virginia to which they had title. At Provincetown they "fell upon their knees and blessed the God of Heaven who had brought them over the vast and furious ocean and delivered them from all the perils and miseries thereof."

An exploring party found Plymouth Harbor on December 11. There, on a slope rising westward from the

---

*Scurvy is a disease caused by vitamin C deficiency. Its symptoms include weakness, anemia, and bleeding gums.

shore, probably the site of an abandoned Indian cornfield, the Pilgrims built the simple village of their desires. Although the weather during this first winter, 1620–21, was quite mild for New England, the early months of the settlement proved to be one of the worst "starving times" recorded anywhere in British America. When spring arrived, half of those who had crossed on the *Mayflower* were dead.

Plymouth Plantation.

Plymouth's history up to 1691, when it was absorbed into the more powerful Massachusetts Bay Colony, a Puritan stronghold, is a tale of both modest triumphs and shattered dreams. The trials, the victories, and the defeats are all recorded in Governor William Bradford's magnificent history, *Of Plymouth Plantation*, which he began writing in 1630. Bradford's work opens with a review of the settlement's early years and continues as a documentary journal and commentary covering the next sixteen years. It is one of the most moving and eloquent documents in the entire literature of American history. Its vivid imagery and biblical rhythms blend perfectly to express Bradford's hopes and struggles, and finally his sense of tragedy and failure.

The Pilgrims' foremost blessing, wrote Bradford, was "to see, and with much comfort to enjoy, the blessed fruits of their sweet communion." Their triumph was that they had finally succeeded in establishing the purified church they had so long sought. But there were troubles from the start, and the first and most pressing problem was financial. For several years the colonists failed in business ventures. The merchants back in England, bickering among themselves and fearful of mounting costs if they continued to resupply the settlers, sold out their shares or simply abandoned their investments. By 1626 the company was bankrupt, but the Pilgrims, more honest than shrewd, continued to honor their original obligations. For years they struggled to squeeze enough profit from fur trading, fishing, and the sale of lumber, Indian corn, and wampum to pay off their debts. But progress came slowly. By the time the colony settled its debts, in 1648, many of Plymouth's founders were dead.

More threatening than debt were the spreading-out of the settlement and the weakening of purpose that grew with the passage of years. After the *Mayflower* a series of vessels had made the long journey to Plymouth, and the population had risen steadily. By 1657, the year of Bradford's death, there were more than 1,360 inhabitants, and Plymouth had changed from a single covenanted community* into a colony of eleven towns. As a result of the growth and

---

*A *covenanted* community is one that has been established by a covenant, or formal binding agreement, especially one with strong religious overtones.

Courtesy of Plimoth Plantation

EDWARD WINSLOW, 1651
Winslow, the only Pilgrim of whom a portrait is known, was one of the better educated and more worldly wise of the group. His career illustrates the cosmopolitanism of the first generation of settlers in British America (see p. 103). His long years of service as Plymouth's chief business agent, Indian negotiator, and propagandist brought him often to England where in 1654 Cromwell engaged him on a diplomatic mission and then appointed him to head the expedition that seized Jamaica from the Spanish. Governor of Plymouth for three years, governor's assistant for over twenty years, he was largely responsible for setting up Plymouth's successful Indian trade and for exploring the adjacent territories.

scattering of the population, the feeling of singleness of purpose had faded. Even if the gentle Pilgrim leaders had sought to impose discipline and control, they would have lacked the legal means to do so. Their original settlement contract with the Virginia Company was worthless in New England, and a document they had received in 1621 from the Council for New England (the official English body that had taken over the legal rights of the defunct Virginia Company of Plymouth) was only a vague land grant and an equally vague license to establish a local government. The colony's government developed slowly and uncertainly, authorized neither by charter nor by the English crown.

The starting point was the Mayflower Compact, a document devised to control the restless non-Pilgrims while the *Mayflower* was still at sea. It was simply an agreement—signed on November 21, 1620, by forty-one Pilgrims, hired laborers, and sailors—to obey whatever laws and officers the community would create. The signing of the Mayflower Compact in the cabin of the Pilgrims' rocking vessel was a dramatic event. But the document was not a constitution. The unauthorized government that in fact developed in Plymouth was primitive in organization. The freemen simply came together annually to choose a governor (Bradford was elected thirty times) and a few assistants to support him. Otherwise the electors convened only on extraordinary occasions, as directed by the governor. The feeble political structure, combined with the second- and third-generation colonists' weakened loyalty to the settlement, spelled disaster for Plymouth's continued independence. When in 1691 the Puritan-dominated Massachusetts Bay Colony received its second charter, Plymouth was included within the Bay Colony's boundaries. The Pilgrims' colony slipped without a ripple into the larger jurisdiction. By then the erosion in original purposes and in piety was so advanced that Governor Bradford's successors were at least relieved that the government would remain in the hands of religious men—even if they were not of the Separatists' own persuasion.

William Bradford's "sweet communion" in its fullest form had depended for its success on deeply shared aspirations and on isolation from the corrupting influence of the changing outside world. But as towns and churches multiplied to accommodate the waves of new settlers, life in Plymouth eventually came to be shaped by new generations who did not share their ancestors' unshakable faith. Lacking all instinct for power, and tolerant of the errors of others in their humble pursuit of personal piety, the Pilgrims responded to the changes as they always had—by retreating from the world rather than by trying to reform it. They were incapable of perpetuating the community they had built, and their impact on American life was confined to the realm of ideas. Their unselfish pursuit of an unattainable ideal, and their rejection of wealth, power, comfort, and self-glory in favor of deeper, spiritual rewards, are part of America's collective memory and essential culture. But although the Pilgrims' model of life has been emulated in various ways throughout American history, it has never been dominant. Far more vital in American culture has been the very different legacy of the Puritans.

The Puritans: Power in the Service of God

The Puritans shared with the Pilgrims a desire for a direct religious experience free from an elaborate church organization. The two groups also shared certain theological views and a stubborn moral dignity.* But the Puritans, in America as in England, were proud and driving, and as demanding of themselves as they were of the world about them. They sought power—not for its own sake, to be sure, but for Christian purposes—and they sought it untiringly, intolerantly, and successfully.

The decisions that brought the Puritans to America were made in stages during a hectic three-year period in the late 1620s. By this time relations had deteriorated badly between the English government and church on the one hand, and the Puritans, who sought sweeping internal church reform, on the other. In 1628 a group of about ninety active nonconformists, deeply troubled by the repressive steps of the English government and church against dissidents, and well aware of the value of overseas settlements as refuges for people of their persuasion, formed the New England Company. They obtained a land patent covering most of present-day Massachusetts and New Hampshire, and sent out an advance party to rebuild a small settlement on Cape Ann, north of Boston, that had recently been abandoned by a Puritan fishing company. In 1629, increasingly concerned about the future of nonconformity, they sought and obtained a crown charter that created the Massachusetts Bay Company. This elaborate document empowered the company not only to trade and settle within the lands already given to the New England Company, but also "to govern and rule all of His Majesty's subjects that reside within the limits of our plantation." The charter proved to be a legal bulwark behind which a powerful social movement could organize and develop.

The new corporation quickly demonstrated its efficiency. Within weeks of its creation it sent off five vessels bearing more than two hundred settlers to join the advance party that was by then living in thatched cottages on the shores of Cape Ann. But far greater enterprises were stirring. In the spring and summer of 1629, conditions in England continued to worsen for critics of the Church of England. The Puritans also learned of the defeat of Protestant forces in the international war then raging in Europe. Moreover, the English king, Charles I, dissolved Parliament, and with this action all hope of political remedies seemed lost. On top of all this, an economic depression was creating great distress in the very districts of England that were most prone to religious dissent.

The Great Migration. In this atmosphere of social, political, and economic panic in the spring and summer of 1629, Puritans of experience, ability, and established position turned their thoughts not merely to creating

---

*For Puritanism as a religious movement, see chapter 3, pp. 79–82.

GOVERNOR JOHN WINTHROP
The leader of Puritan New England in its heroic age, a devout, able, and strong-willed leader, Winthrop directed his energies and talents to creating a pure version of the Church of England and a society directed to God's will. The set jaw, full but tightly drawn lips, and raised brows suggest intense self-discipline and resolution.

a religious refuge for their fellow Puritans, but to their own personal escape from England to a world apart, a safe, fresh, and uncorrupted world. Within six months of the creation of the Massachusetts Bay Company, a coalition of merchants, landed gentlemen, lawyers, and minor officials, alienated from their own society, turned to the company. They found in it a means of escaping from England and of serving their own—and Puritanism's—higher purpose.

Only some of the gathering group of substantial Englishmen who were thus attracted to Massachusetts Bay had been directly involved in the company before. Chief among the newcomers was John Winthrop, an intensely pious, well-connected forty-one-year-old Puritan landowner and lawyer who had recently been dismissed from his government position. Faced suddenly with unemployment and with the prospect of continuing harassment, and convinced that England was being overwhelmed by corruption, he came to see the hand of God in the work of the Massachusetts Bay Company. No mild and passive Pilgrims, Winthrop

and the other leaders of the Massachusetts Bay Colony were men of affairs, self-confident, determined, and used to exercising authority. But their love of action in the ordinary world was disciplined by a strong religious commitment. Unlike the Pilgrims, they did not want to separate from the Church of England: they wanted to seize control of it, cleanse it of its corruption, and reconstruct it in a pure and unadorned form. If they could not succeed in England, they would try again in New England. And far from withdrawing from society, they sought to seize and transform that, too. By persuasion if possible but by force if necessary, they hoped to create a society likely to gain God's approval. They were separatists only with respect to the English state, not with respect to the Church of England. Their goals became clear in the conclusion they reached at a momentous secret meeting in Cambridge, England, late in August 1629.

The twelve leaders who assembled at Cambridge pledged themselves "ready in our persons" to join the migration to New England, taking with them their families and whatever supplies they could gather, and "to inhabit and continue in New England." But they agreed to this plan only on condition that the company officially transfer itself—its charter, and the government—to the colony. Three days later the company agreed—in effect, voting itself out of existence as a commercial organization and transforming itself into the basis of a simple civil government. In October 1629 Winthrop was elected governor, and five months later, in March 1630, the great Puritan migration began. Before the year was over, a fleet of seventeen ships had carried well over 1,000 settlers to Massachusetts. In all during the years of the Puritan exodus (1630–43), some two hundred vessels transported more than 20,000 Englishmen to the Bay Colony.

No one community could contain all these settlers. The original settlement, Salem on Cape Ann, became a staging area for groups moving south along the coast. First Charlestown and then Boston became the central settlement. From Boston, groups moved on quickly to settle a ring of satellite towns immediately around the bay. Subsequently other parties founded a secondary ring of towns some twenty or thirty miles inland—among them, Haverhill, Concord, and Sudbury. Finally, beginning in 1636, small migrating groups of Puritans broke contact altogether with the central settlement around Boston and established an independent cluster of towns on the Connecticut River, more than one hundred miles from Boston. These towns included Hartford, Wethersfield, and Windsor. By banding together politically, they became the colony of Connecticut, which formed its own government in 1639 and was chartered by the crown in 1662.

Francis Higginson, a Puritan clergyman, was deprived of his pulpit in 1627. Facing legal prosecution, in 1629 he joined the first wave of the Great Migration and was chosen teacher of the church at Salem. His account of the New England settlement, *New-England's Plantation*, was published in London in 1630, the year of his death.

Francis Higginson Describes the "Aire of New-England" (1630)

THE Temper of the Aire of *New-England* is one speciall thing that commends this place. Experience doth manifest that there is hardly a more healthfull place to be found in the World that agreeth better with our English Bodyes. Many that haue beene weake and sickly in old *England*, by comming hither haue beene thoroughly healed and growne healthfull and strong. For here is an extraordinarie cleere and dry Aire that is of a most healing nature to all such as are of a Cold, Melancholy, Flegmatick, Reumaticke temper of Body. None can more truly speake hereof by their owne experience then my selfe. My Friends that knew me can well tell how verie sickly I haue been and continually in Physick, being much troubled with a tormenting paine through an extraordinarie weakenesse of my Stomacke, and aboundance of Melancholicke humors; but since I came hither on this Voyage, I thanke God I haue had perfect health, and freed from paine and vomitings, hauing a Stomacke to digest the hardest and coursest fare who before could not eat finest meat; and whereas my Stomacke could onely digest and did require such drinke as was both strong and stale, now I can and doe oftentimes drink *New-England* water verie well; and I that haue not gone without a Cap for many yeeres together, neither durst leaue off the same, haue now cast away my Cap, and doe weare none at all in the day time: and whereas beforetime I cloathed my selfe with double cloathes and thicke Wastcoats to keepe me warme, euen in the Summer time, I doe now goe as thin clad as any, onely wearing a light Stuffe Cassocke vpon my Shirt and Stuffe Breeches of one thicknesse without Linings. Besides, I haue one of my Children that was formerly most lamentably handled with sore breaking out of both his hands and feet of the Kings-Euill, but since he came hither he is verie well ouer hee was, and there is hope of perfect recouerie shortly, euen by the verie wholesomnesse of the Aire, altering, digesting and drying vp the cold and crude humors of the Body: and therefore I thinke it is a wise course for all cold complections to come to take Physicke in *New-England*: for a sup of *New-Englands* Aire is better then a whole draft of old *Englands* Ale.

Church and Community.

The Puritans fanned out into towns all over New England with remarkable speed. This spreading-out was remarkable even more for the degree to which it carried forward the Puritans' purposes. The colonists did not scatter randomly. Instead, there was a well-organized multiplication of church societies that became political bodies and land corporations as soon as they were founded. Groups that wished to establish towns sought the approval of the colony's legislature, the General Court. Once granted, this approval carried with it the legal right to create a limited governmental jurisdiction—a town—and to send representatives to the General Court. It also embraced control over a large parcel of land—a township—that was to be divided up among the original heads of households in proportion to their wealth or status. Consequently town founders not only owned their individual shares of land, but also collectively controlled the undistributed land. As the founding members of their local church, the same men dominated the vital area of religion. They also constituted the initial voting membership of the town's political assembly (the "meeting"), which regulated the everyday affairs of the community.

The founders' rights were not automatically granted to others who later joined the town. Therefore it was the town founders and their direct heirs who controlled all the main spheres of life. Their power was not resented, at least in the early years. Later there would be opposition and factionalism as newcomers found their way into these small farming villages and as the Puritans' fierce passion to reform the world faded into mere repressive austerity. But while the fires of the original faith burned brightly, and while the Puritans still thought in terms of reforming the world rather than rejecting it, these villages—oligarchic in form, but democratic for those who enjoyed full rights of participation—remained cohesive bodies closely bound into the overall colony.

The unity of the Massachusetts colony—the "Bible Commonwealth"—as a whole is remarkable when one considers the rapid and wide dispersal of the settlers. This unity reflected not only a deep general commitment to a particular way of life and to certain beliefs, but also the founders' skill in self-government and their refusal to tolerate dissent.

The Massachusetts charter had simply created a commercial organization: it contained no provision for an independent civil government. However, the structure of the Massachusetts Bay Company was in fact similar to that of a self-governing English town, and the government that developed in Massachusetts emerged along the lines of that model. John Winthrop, the Massachusetts Bay Company's chosen leader, became the colony's governor. The seven or eight members of the company's board of directors who had

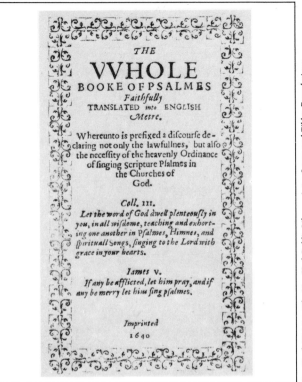

TITLE PAGE OF THE BAY PSALM BOOK
The Bay Psalm Book was one of the first publications of the Puritans' printing press set up in Cambridge in the fall of 1638, a time when Puritan writings were being suppressed by the censors in England.

come to Massachusetts formed the council of magistrates (the governor's assistants and advisers). The adult male heads of household were the "freemen," or voters, necessary to complete the membership of the transformed General Court. Soon a permanent government along these lines was established and the basic rules for its procedures were set down in writing. In 1632 the freemen were given the power to choose not only the governor's assistants, but also the governor himself, and the deputy governor. In 1634 it was agreed that taxes could be levied on the towns only by vote of the entire General Court and that in the future the entire body of freemen need not assemble in person for General Court meetings; instead, the freemen could select representatives. These representatives—two or three from each town—had the authority to make laws, grant land, levy taxes, and transact whatever other business might come before the General Court.

Thus a civil government evolved from the organization of a commercial corporation. It was quickly completed. Since the representatives to the General Court (called deputies) met together with the council of magistrates, they could conclude no business without the magistrates' approval. Hence the representatives had no distinct voice of their own and no incentive to develop their own rules and procedures. This problem was overcome by 1644. In a sensational case that pitted popular emotions against strict legality, the magistrates vetoed the proposals of the more numerous representatives. A great uproar resulted, and the two groups drew apart to form two separate houses. This division proved to be permanent. Each house now could express itself independently, although the agreement of both was needed to enact laws. The lower house thereupon organized itself separately, electing a Speaker and working out parliamentary rules, a committee system, and other procedures modeled on those of the English House of Commons.

During these same years the colony set up a court system, which it largely copied from the local court system of England, and established a code of laws. This code, *The Lawes and Libertyes* of 1647, expressed not only the English common law in terms appropriate for life in the wilderness, but also the Puritans' devotion to the precepts of the Bible.

Puritan Control and Dissent.

Massachusetts remained a Bible commonwealth despite all the secular pursuits that were undertaken: clearing the wilderness; organizing towns, courts, and a general government; and expanding coastal and transatlantic commerce. Puritan domination was legally secured not by the clergy's control of the government—in fact, the clergy did not hold public office—but by the fact that only church members could vote. This rule was introduced in 1631. As a result of this measure, the colony's central government would continue to represent primarily those loyal to the original Puritan purposes, no matter how the town populations might change, how the sources of immigration might shift, or how the people themselves might drift away from the church.

This arrangement was not challenged, for it expressed a broad consensus in the founding generation of Massachusetts. The opposition to the Puritan leadership that did arise in these early years challenged not the basic religious character of the Puritan colony, but specific points of doctrine. It resulted not from a lack of religious commitment, but from an excess. Such opponents of the Puritan regime as Anne Hutchinson and Roger Williams were even more fanatical in their pursuit of religious truth, more relentless in their theology, and more single-minded in their beliefs than were the Puritan leaders themselves. In one way or another they went to extremes on religious issues that the colony's leaders felt obliged to keep in balance.

Anne Hutchinson challenged the Puritan leaders

within a few years of the founding of the Bay Colony. She was passionate and rigid in her convictions and brilliant in her arguments. "Justification"—the mysterious gift of divine grace, by which a sinful person becomes one of God's elect—was for her all that essentially mattered in religion. "Sanctification"—that is, moral conduct, Christian behavior, piety, even prayer—was to her only the dry outer shell of religion. Rejecting "works" and in the end all worldly discipline and responsibility, she stood only for the "ravishment" of the soul by God. The band of followers she gathered constituted a church within a church; the Puritan leaders felt that unless they defeated her, they would destroy themselves by tolerating her. But she was not disposed of easily. In 1637, when the General Court tried her, a group of ministers was brought in to assist in the prosecution. In the dramatic trial that followed, she held them off with astonishing skill and defended herself learnedly and wittily. But at last, in exhaustion and perhaps also in exaltation, she blurted out that her knowledge of God was "an immediate revelation"—that is, free of all institutions, independent of all earthly authority. This was the worst heresy, condemned as "antinomianism," an arrogance of such dimensions that the General Court could safely and in good conscience banish her from the colony and silence her followers.

Roger Williams, a minister at Salem, Massachusetts, was more learned and more respectable than Anne Hutchinson, but he was at least as "divinely mad" as she, and as passionate in his beliefs. He could never accommodate himself to what he regarded as the halfway reforms of the nonseparatist Puritans who had established Massachusetts Bay Colony, nor could he accept the colony's unique constitutional foundation. Not only did he attack the validity of the colony's charter, but he challenged the mingling of church and state that was the essence of the "Bible Commonwealth." Civil officials, he insisted, should have power only over individuals' civil affairs and outward behavior, not over matters of conscience and religion. Only in later years in England and in banishment in Rhode Island did Williams develop the doctrine of religious toleration for which he would become famous. But in Massachusetts he was already heading in the direction of toleration, and the mere approach to this position was intolerable to the rulers of the colony. Moreover Williams condemned the colony's churches for their refusal to break completely with the polluted Church of England. Church *reform*, he insisted, was not enough; purification was not enough. *Perfection* was the goal—a church of absolute purity, even more pure than the church of the Separatists in Plymouth Colony. This kind of church was not to be had in Massachusetts. The Bay Colony's leaders realized that Williams was a fine intellect and a true Christian in his

RICHARD MATHER
Founder of a virtual dynasty of New England preachers and intellectuals, Mather is shown here in a woodcut by John Foster (c. 1670), which is probably the first print made in British America. Mather preached an austere Calvinism in Massachusetts for thirty-four years. In the background, notes taken on sermons heard in Boston by a spiritually tormented merchant, Robert Keayne. Convicted of overcharging and hence of greed and unchristian behavior, Keayne fell into an agony of protest and self-recrimination, which he expressed in an extraordinary 50,000-word will.

way. They tried to correct him, but when they failed they reluctantly banished him too from the colony.

Later there would be other deviants from the Puritan way, other challengers, who were either silenced or ejected from the colony. Some of these religious dissidents moved south to Narragansett Bay in what is today Rhode Island. Here, Roger Williams, certain followers of Anne Hutchinson, a few Quakers, and other religious outcasts from Massachusetts attempted to form communities in which they would be completely free to pursue their own special version of truth. But the scattered Narragansett villages were torn by discord. They splintered and regrouped repeatedly, and only in the late 1640s did four or five stable communities emerge. Although the prosperous merchants who founded and dominated Newport were the most worldly of the Rhode Islanders, it was Roger Williams, the founder of Providence, who recognized that only a confederation of the towns—their union for a common purpose—and legal authorization from England would preserve the freedom of these tiny refugee settlements. And it was he who secured the refugee towns' independence by extracting from the English government in 1644 a patent creating "The Incorporation of Providence Plantations." But only in 1663 did Williams finally obtain a crown charter that legalized the permanent existence of the colony of Rhode Island.

Connecticut and Rhode Island were both products of the Massachusetts Bay Colony. Connecticut was a reproduction of the Puritans' culture; Rhode Island was a rejection of it. Together the central Puritan colony and its satellites to the west, south, and north formed the most vigorous transplantation of English life anywhere in the Western Hemisphere. At the heart of Puritan New England lay the determination to wipe out the corruptions of an old and oppressive world and to create a new Jerusalem, in which power would not be rejected or despised, but mobilized and devoted to the service of the Lord.

A Catholic Refuge on the Chesapeake

Religion was a pervasive force in the establishment of English overseas settlements, and America profited greatly by England's willingness to allow its colonies to become refuges for religious minorities. These points can be seen with special clarity in the founding of Maryland.

In this case the refugees were not radical Protestants but Roman Catholics, a group that the Church of England regarded as even more obnoxious than Protestant extremists. The dynamic force in launching the

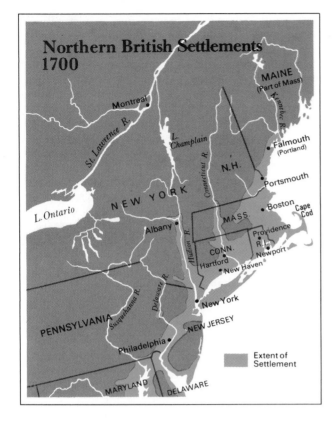

Northern British Settlements 1700

Extent of Settlement

Maryland colony was a single family, the Calverts, who were ennobled in 1625 as the Lords Baltimore. The Calverts, well connected with the rulers of England, were recent converts to Catholicism. They had long been involved in overseas enterprises. In 1628–29 the first Lord Baltimore had traveled to the Chesapeake to investigate a possible place of refuge for English Catholics, and upon his return he began the elaborate process of obtaining the necessary royal charter. He died just as the charter was being approved, and his twenty-six-year-old son, Cecilius Calvert, the second Lord Baltimore, carried out his father's project.

The key to much of what subsequently happened lies in the terms of the remarkable charter that was issued to the young Lord Baltimore in 1632 and in the use that the Calvert family made of the powers it bestowed. The charter granted Lord Baltimore the entire territory from the Potomac River north to the latitude of present-day Philadelphia and west hundreds of miles to the Appalachian sources of the Potomac. The charter also gave him extensive governmental powers: the colony's government was his to shape as he chose.

Significantly, the outmoded idea of creating a system of feudal relationships through land grants appealed to Lord Baltimore. In this case, as in so many others, the barrenness and openness of America challenged people's imaginations and inspired them to project their desires and fantasies in plans for new communities.

Toleration and Proprietary Plans. Success came quickly at first. The young Lord Baltimore, who was the proprietor (overlord) of Maryland until his death in 1675, sent his brother Leonard to the colony as governor. Leonard Calvert took with him detailed instructions on the management of the colony. Lord Baltimore had made it clear that Maryland was to be a Catholic refuge. But he knew that Catholics could survive in the English world only as a tolerated minority; they were in no position to impose their will on others. Further, he knew that the success of the colony would depend on the flow of immigrants into it, and most of these prospective settlers would be Protestants. At the very start, therefore, Lord Baltimore prohibited discrimination of any sort against Protestants. He also forbade Catholics from engaging in public controversies over religion. They were ordered to make every effort to live at peace not only with the Virginians to the south, but also with the Puritans and Dutch to the north.*

These conditions were all necessary and realistic. Fantasy entered Lord Baltimore's thinking only as he contemplated his personal proprietorship of the land, and his extensive powers of government. How was he to use his vast domain and these extensive powers? Feudalism, and its economic foundations in manorialism, provided a model of sorts for the Calverts to follow. Thus proprietary manors (landed domains) of 6,000 acres, complete with private law courts, were created and reserved for the blood relatives of the Lord Proprietor. Ordinary manors were limited to 3,000 acres. It was expected that tenants would settle on these manors and that their labor would produce the rents and money dues necessary to support the lords. The rest of the population would be landowning farmers and their dependents, all appropriately submissive to the domination of the provincial nobles. It was a rational but hopelessly unrealistic design, yet it nevertheless helped shape the community that developed in Maryland.

In 1632 the Calverts set up on the outskirts of London a recruiting office for settlers, advertised their colony (but not their religion) widely, and convinced more than two hundred settlers to join the first expedition. The prospective colonists arrived in the Chesapeake in March 1634, in good time for the year's planting and well equipped to survive the inevitable rigors of the first winter in a new colony. The Calverts located their main settlement, St. Mary's, on a creek just north of the Potomac River. There they constructed a

---

*For religious toleration in Maryland, see chapter 3, p. 78.

CECILIUS CALVERT, SECOND LORD BALTIMORE
(1605–75)

Baltimore, who devoted his life to developing the colony that his father had planned, was never able to visit Maryland himself, governing instead through deputies. He is pictured here with his grandson, who had been born in Maryland and died at the age of fourteen, holding a "new map of Maryland" ("*Nova Terrae-Mariae Tabula*") dated 1635 and attended by a handsomely dressed black servant. The boy's father, Charles, governor since 1661, succeeded as proprietor and third Lord Baltimore upon Cecilius' death in 1675.

palisaded fort similar to that of early Jamestown. After the first winter in the fort it became clear that the colony would have supplies sufficient for its survival and that the neighboring Indians were friendly. The distribution of land and the spreading-out of the population then began.

Distribution of Land. As planned, the proprietor's relatives were given title to 6,000-acre tracts, and lesser manors were distributed to other persons. The recipients of manors also received rights to private law courts and other privileges. In turn, the manorial lords and the proprietor himself began selling pieces of land to those who could afford to pay for them. Other property was rented out. Manorial lords reserved farms on their tracts for their own use ("demesne" farms) and retained all the undivided property. But none of the manorial arrangements survived. The settlement of

the countryside was in fact shaped by virtually the same forces already at work in Virginia.

As in Virginia, the primary cash crop in Maryland was tobacco, and the central difficulty in expanding production was similarly the shortage of labor. Every effort was made to stimulate the importation of laborers for the farms that spread out from several centers on the mainland and on the eastern shore of Chesapeake Bay. A series of laws required prospective manorial lords to import at first five workers, then ten, then twenty. Virginia's headright system was introduced in Maryland in 1640, and independent householders who settled in the colony received special land grants for themselves and the members of their families. The population rose rapidly, partly because transatlantic migration continued and partly because the availability of fresh tidewater land attracted farmers from Virginia and other neighboring areas. By 1660 the population had probably reached 8,000 and was beginning to grow by natural increase.* The colony had more than 13,000 inhabitants in 1670. A contemporary map identified 823 cultivated farms in the colony, scattered through a strip of settled territory along the lower shores of Chesapeake Bay and the banks of the major rivers.

By 1670—forty years after the initial settlement— it was clear that Maryland had become something different from the feudal-manorial regime that Lord Baltimore had envisioned. Maryland was dominated by a landholding oligarchy with an almost monopolistic control of public offices. The rulers were set off from the bulk of the population by their Catholic religion as well as by their wealth and power.

In the earliest years the grants of large estates had meant little because the labor shortage allowed the cultivation of only small segments of these properties. As a result indentured servants were brought in on generous terms, and freed servants easily acquired land and established themselves as independent farmers. But property values rose as the more fertile and accessible land came under cultivation and as a growing population competed more intensely for the best of the undistributed land. Freed servants now found it more difficult to establish independent property-owning households. Increasingly they tended to serve, for a time at least, as tenants; and their labor further raised the value of the land they worked. Landlords, of course, benefited greatly. In this situation the original "manorial" grants became more and more valuable simply as land, quite apart from the legal privileges that were supposed to accompany them. The original grantees and their heirs—especially those closely re-

---

*Natural increase means the predominance of births over deaths in accounting for a rising population—as opposed to population increase caused by immigration.

lated to the Calverts—found themselves not manorial lords, but well-to-do landowners in a world of tobacco farms. The properties they controlled were valuable both for the rents they could produce and for the sale price they could ultimately command in a rising land market.

The same men controlled the central offices in Maryland's government, which remained in Lord Baltimore's power except during the years 1655–58. Baltimore filled these offices with members of his own family and their close associates, most of whom were Catholics. As in Virginia, the governor's council quickly became the central governing body. But in Maryland membership on the council was less the result of having achieved local prominence than of being a personal ally or a relative of the proprietor. Therefore the earliest political struggles in Maryland were not between the governor and the council (as they were in Virginia), but rather between the governor and council on the one hand and the local representatives on the other. Fiercely competitive politics was part of Maryland life almost from the first years of settlement.

Governor Leonard Calvert had instructions to convene an assembly of freemen and to submit all laws to it for approval. But he retained the right to summon, adjourn, and dismiss the assembly, and he alone could initiate legislation. The proprietor in England, Baltimore, reserved the power to veto any action taken by the assembly. The first full meeting of the assembly in 1638 was, like the first assembly meetings of Massachusetts and Virginia, a confused affair. Any freemen who chose to appear were seated. From the outset the representatives sought to free themselves from control by the proprietor's friends on the council. Thus they insisted that the assembly model itself on the House of Commons, adopt parliamentary rules, and take over the power of convening and adjourning. Gradually the representatives won these demands, although the proprietor never gave up the theoretical rights granted in the charter. While civil war between the king and the supporters of Parliament raged in England in 1640–49, the Maryland assembly took advantage of the confusion to seize the power of initiating legislation. The representatives also forced the proprietor to allow them to meet independently of the council. Thereafter the representatives formed a separate lower house of the assembly.

By 1650 the political structure of seventeenth-century Maryland was fully evolved. The colony was governed by an absentee proprietor and by his resident governor and appointed council. Almost all of these leaders were Catholics. Together they monopolized the important public offices and the profits of officeholding, and they were also the major landlords. But the majority of the population, largely Protestant, had a legitimate voice in government through the lower house. In the assembly and outside it, the people fought continuously to force the proprietor and his followers to give up their special privileges. By the middle of the seventeenth century, in no other colony was politics so sophisticated and so bitter as it was in the colony that at first had been planned as an oasis of manorial harmony.

The Failure of the Dutch

The founding of the colony that was later known as New York differed radically from the pattern of the other British colonies. The Dutch, not the English, established this colony, and originally it was not conceived of as a community at all. From the start its population was culturally diverse. No legal system was effectively established, and no government evolved that was comparable to the assemblies of Virginia and Maryland and to the General Court of Massachusetts Bay.

New Netherland, as the colony was called until the English conquered it in 1664, was an almost accidental creation of the Dutch West India Company. This complex commercial organization, which had been founded in 1621 and had its headquarters in Amsterdam, was concerned chiefly with its trading forts on the Amazon River and its establishments in West Africa and Brazil as well as in North America. The company originally had no intention of creating a colony on the North American mainland. Its officials wished simply to exploit the fine fur supply and other resources of the Middle Atlantic region that had been revealed by Henry Hudson's explorations in 1609 and thereafter by the voyages of a short-lived Dutch fur-trading company.

New Amsterdam. In 1624 the Dutch West India Company sent thirty Dutch and Walloon (French-speaking Belgian) families to begin settlements at Fort Orange and Esopus on the upper Hudson River and at several points on the Delaware River. Supplies, equipment, and a total of perhaps two hundred people followed in 1625. In that year too a blockhouse (a sturdy fortification) was built at the tip of Manhattan Island, which lies at the mouth of the Hudson River, to protect Dutch shipping and to serve as a convenient transfer point for shipments to and from the Hudson and Delaware river posts. The next year, 1626, colonists set about building a village around the blockhouse on Manhattan Island—windmills to power the sawing of wood and grinding of corn, and about thirty log houses spread along the west side of the island. At the same time, an ambitious company official, Peter Minuit, purchased the whole island from the native Manhates Indians. He began to consolidate the main force of the scattered Dutch settlers in this central village, called

NEW AMSTERDAM, 1643
One of the earliest views of the Dutch port that became New York City. Although the scene is compressed, the main features—the city tavern and the church within the fort—are identifiable.

Fort Amsterdam or New Amsterdam. Minuit withdrew some of the settlers from the distant and exposed posts on the upper Hudson and the Delaware and left only skeleton forces there to channel furs to New Amsterdam and to defend the Dutch claims. The population of New Amsterdam grew slowly, reaching only 450 in 1646 and perhaps 1,500 in 1664.

By midcentury the village of New Amsterdam consisted of the original blockhouse and windmills and a number of houses, all enclosed within a palisade, or wall, along what is now known as Wall Street. The whole compound was surrounded by a canal. Scattered in the open area beyond the wall and canal were about fifty small farms, called *bouweries*. In 1650 the village of New Amsterdam was a frontier community in which people of all sorts mingled, traded, and brawled. Men and women of many nationalities—Dutch, Walloons, French, English, Portuguese, Swedes, Finns, and Brazilian blacks—flocked to the settlement, looking for a chance to profit from trading in furs, manufactured goods, produce, and land. There were reports that eighteen different languages were in use, and that virtually every religious persuasion from Catholicism to Anabaptism was rep-

resented. It was as quarrelsome and disorderly a village as could be found in North America—and it was neglected by the company that had sponsored the settlement and that remained legally responsible for its welfare.

The company never doubted that potential profits in North America lay only in the fur cargoes that came in from the posts along the Hudson, Delaware, and Connecticut rivers. The directors had no intention of throwing money away, as the officials of the Virginia Company had done, in the vain hope of establishing a populous and prosperous agricultural and industrial community. They made no serious efforts to populate the colony until it was too late, nor did they have available for that purpose as mobile a population as the English colonizers had had. The company's directors imposed high import and export duties on the colonists and taxed the settlements heavily in order to squeeze a profit from them. Yet the profits that were made from the Dutch colony were not made by the company, which never recovered its initial investment. Nor did the ordinary settlers benefit; they continued to live only a little above the subsistence level in these early years. Only a few Dutch middlemen in

New Amsterdam profited. These enterprising merchants and artisans cooperated with the resident company officials to manipulate for their own benefit the monopolized sale of goods and supplies as well as the prices offered for furs and surplus farm products.

Contention and Indian Wars.

At least one of the company's directors in the Netherlands, however, had a broader vision of the colony's future, and his strenuous efforts made a difference. Kiliaen Van Rensselaer, a wealthy Amsterdam jeweler, argued for the creation of large-scale private agricultural estates like the proprietary manors in Maryland. These farming establishments, he claimed, would not only help stabilize the colony, but also provide food, cattle, and necessary supplies for the Dutch ships heading for the West Indies and elsewhere in the Western Hemisphere. His efforts resulted in the Charter of Freedoms and Exemptions, issued by the company and confirmed by the Dutch government in 1629. This charter authorized the creation of "patroonships," large estates that would be financed by groups of investors. The investors would share in the profits but not in the management of these plantations, which would be controlled solely by the "patroons," the estate proprietors.

Ten of these investment groups were created. However, only the patroonship of Rensselaerswyck, which was situated on both sides of the Hudson surrounding Fort Orange (present-day Albany), developed in the form that had been provided for in the charter, and survived to the end of the seventeenth century. Van Rensselaer, the patroon, sent to this huge estate a flow of goods, cattle, and equipment. At his own expense he also dispatched farmers and other workers to populate the land. By 1655 he had leased sixteen farms on the estate and had developed his personal manor efficiently despite all the confusions and difficulties of managing the property through deputies. And although it is doubtful that in the end Van Rensselaer recovered his heavy investment in the estate, he did establish a prosperous agricultural community on the upper Hudson.

On the whole, however, the province of New Netherland remained (as a contemporary wrote) "a wild country." It was ill organized, ill managed, and contentious. The continuing disorder was partly the result of the uncontrolled multiplication of thinly populated villages that were poorly organized and incapable of defending themselves. They appeared on all sides: on upper Manhattan Island (New Haarlem); across the Harlem River in present-day Westchester County, New York, and across the Hudson in present-day Bergen County, New Jersey; on Staten Island; and especially on Long Island, where five Dutch towns had appeared by the 1640s. The confusion in these border towns was worsened by trouble with the neighboring English who had moved into New Netherland from the surrounding colonies. These immigrants had been attracted by the company's offer of freedom of worship, local self-government, and free land that would remain tax-exempt for ten years. Although the English settlers helped populate the company's lands, they created difficult administrative problems for the Dutch officials. In addition, these alien and discontented groups began to agitate against the Dutch rule and to call for English conquest of the border areas and even of the whole colony. So acute were these border conflicts that New Netherland and the New England colonies finally drew up a formal treaty. The Treaty of Hartford (1650) set the Dutch-Connecticut boundary ten miles east of the Hudson River and eliminated Dutch claims beyond that line. But the New Englanders who had settled on Long Island continued to resist the Dutch authorities. To the south, on the Delaware River, Maryland colonists challenged the Dutch openly. In the years preceding the English conquest of New Netherland, the English settlers in the border areas moved to open revolt.

None of these difficulties was eased by skillful management on the part of the Dutch officials or by the effectiveness of the colony's political institutions. Of the directors-general (governors) who had been sent over by the company, only Peter Minuit (1626–31) was reasonably capable. His two immediate successors were hopelessly inefficient, and they made more enemies than friends in the colony. Both were finally removed from office in response to repeated charges that they were ruining the colony by their arrogance, corruption, laziness, and constant drunkenness. The second of them, Willem Kiefft (1638–47), personally began a savage war against the neighboring Indians.

This war began in 1642 after a number of Indian raids on outlying farms. In retaliation 110 unsuspecting and peaceful Indians who were encamped near New Amsterdam were slaughtered. This butchery was so brutal that even contemporary observers were shocked ("Some came running to us from the country having their hands cut off; some lost both arms and legs; some were supporting their entrails with their hands, while others were mangled in other horrid ways, too horrid to be conceived"). The tone was thus set for a conflict that tore New Netherland apart for three years. Finally the Dutch hired a veteran English Indian fighter, Captain John Underhill, who led 150 men in a midnight raid on an Indian village. Some 500 Indians were shot or burned alive in Underhill's victory. The Dutch and the Indians concluded a peace treaty in 1646, but it was the result only of mutual exhaustion and fear of annihilation. When the next and last director-general, Peter Stuyvesant,

PETER STUYVESANT, c. 1660
Director-general of New Amsterdam for seventeen years, this storming, peg-legged war veteran swore he would die before surrendering New Amsterdam to the English, but in fact he gave up the fort quietly in 1664 and retired peacefully to his farm in New York City. It had become his home, and there he died in 1672.

arrived in 1647, New Netherland was badly reduced in size, hard-pressed by its competitive neighbors, and virtually abandoned by the failing company.

Stuyvesant, formerly the governor of the Dutch West Indies island of Curaçao, was commissioned to supervise all Dutch interests in the Caribbean as well as to rule New Netherland. He was a bitterly stubborn man, given to fits of rage, and the company had granted him almost dictatorial powers. Stuyvesant made savage efforts to wipe out all dissent from the official religion of the colony, Reformed Calvinism.* But he made little headway in solving the colony's mutiplying problems. In 1654 the Dutch West India Company finally went bankrupt. All that remained in New Amsterdam were a few wharves and bridges, a neglected fort, and a run-down town hall and market area. In 1655 the Indians took delayed vengeance and launched a new campaign of terror on the faltering and battered settlements. The colony's feeble re-

*For religion in New Netherland, see chapter 3, pp. 78–79.

sources were drained still further in the effort to survive. At the same time, the English settlers in Connecticut laid plans to seize New Netherland, and began more determined encroachments on Dutch-claimed territory. By 1664 the Dutch colony as a whole was helpless, and an English fleet conquered New Amsterdam easily. In their desolation the Dutch settlers could now only look to the new English authorities with hopes that had never been stirred by the Dutch West India Company or by such storming, hard-drinking martinets as Willem Kiefft and Peter Stuyvesant.

Royal Rewards: Carolina and the Jerseys

By the 1640s—within a single generation of the chartering of the Virginia Company—large-scale, permanent colonies with a total population of more than 50,000 had been established along Chesapeake Bay and the rivers of northern Virginia, at the mouth and along the banks of the Hudson River, and in central and southern New England. But no one had yet made a claim to two great territories that bordered these earliest European settlements: the mid-Atlantic region between New Netherland and Maryland, and the land south of Virginia, as far as the Spanish settlement at St. Augustine, Florida. The settlement of these two major coastal regions—out of which would eventually be carved Pennsylvania, New Jersey, North and South Carolina, and Georgia—took place in circumstances very different from those operating in the settlement of the first colonies. Yet in these later colonies the same pattern prevailed: high hopes and imaginative designs, followed by failure and disillusionment and then by the slow emergence of communities in unexpected forms.

Before these territories were settled, however, the political world in England had been transformed. In the two decades after 1640, England was convulsed by a civil war, by the execution of Charles I and the exile of Charles II, and by the creation of Oliver Cromwell's republican regime, which in the end became an autocratic "protectorate." In the midst of these domestic convulsions, England engaged in two international wars: with the Dutch in 1652–54, largely fought at sea, and with Spain in 1656–59, mainly fought in the Caribbean. By 1658, when Cromwell died and was briefly succeeded as "lord protector" by his son, England was exhausted by the turmoil and was eager for stability and reconciliation. Disillusioned defectors from the republican regime turned to Charles I's son, who had spent many years in exile. The son, Charles II, was welcomed back to England by Parliament in May 1660, having declared amnesty for all, promised liberty of conscience, and recognized existing land titles.

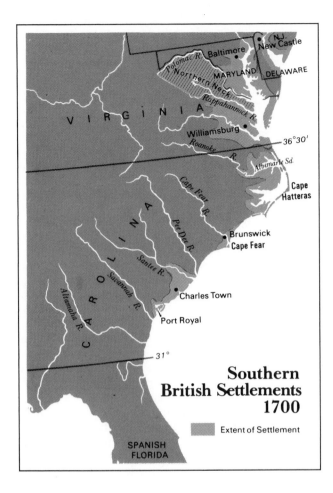

Southern British Settlements 1700

Extent of Settlement

The Carolina Charter. The main flow of colonization had been interrupted during the tumultuous 1640s and 1650s, but it was quickly resumed in the reign of the enterprising Charles II (1660–85). While still in exile in France, he and his followers, deprived of all other properties and prospects, had eyed the colonies as a rich field for profit. In 1649 the exiled king had rewarded the loyalty of seven of his close followers with the proprietorship of the Northern Neck of Virginia, a domain of 5 million acres between the Potomac and Rappahannock rivers. Once the monarchy had been reestablished in England, the royal court turned its attention more fully to the colonies. In the competitive, high-spirited atmosphere of Charles II's court, the most powerful of his followers joined forces to promote the colonization designs of a well-connected royalist, Sir John Colleton.

The exceptionally enterprising Colleton was the owner of a plantation on Barbados, the most profitable of England's Caribbean islands. He knew that the growth of large-scale slave plantations on Barbados was displacing an increasing number of land-hungry English farmers who had settled on that island. He also knew that Virginians and a few New Englanders were already attempting small experimental settlements in the lands just south of Virginia. Colleton proposed to advance the settlement of this region, and he quickly drew into his enterprise seven of the most powerful figures in England. Among them were his kinsman the Duke of Albemarle, who had managed Charles II's return to the throne; the Earl of Clarendon, Charles II's chief minister; Lord Berkeley, the brother of the governor of Virginia; and above all Sir Anthony Ashley Cooper, who as the Earl of Shaftesbury would become an important political power. These imaginative and ambitious men found Colleton's proposal irresistible: no funds, time, or effort seemed to be required of them. Since settlement was already proceeding by spillovers from the older colonies, the proprietors had merely to design a system of government and land distribution, open a land office, appoint officials, and collect the rents.

The charter of Carolina that was issued to the eight partners in 1663 (extended in 1665) granted them title to all the land lying between Virginia and northern Florida and across the continent from sea to sea, with full rights to govern it. The direct management of this immense territory did not interest them; they were not territorial imperialists who wished to acquire and govern more and more land. Rather, they had their eyes on the commercial possibilities of three tiny spots on the coastal fringe. The first was a northern settlement safe behind the long spits of land that formed Albemarle Sound. The second was a middle settlement at the mouth of the Cape Fear River, where a cluster of New Englanders had already gathered. The third was a community at Port Royal in the deeper South, close to what would later become Georgia. The proprietors hoped that three well-populated, land-buying, rent-paying communities would develop from these sites. They therefore divided the grant into three huge counties that centered on these projected settlements. Then, in "A Declaration and Proposals to All That Will Plant in Carolina," they designed governments that were patterned after those of the older English colonies, with veto powers retained by the proprietors. They guaranteed both freedom of religion and a system of land distribution based on headrights of various dimensions. Large estates were reserved for the proprietors themselves in every settlement.

It was a typical project of enthusiastic colonial entrepreneurs, and it was typically unrealistic. The few Virginians who had been living around Albemarle Sound in the proposed northernmost settlement were riled enough by the proprietor's actions to organize an assembly to protest the terms of land allotment. But their settlement, from which would eventually develop the colony of North Carolina, was isolated from transoceanic commerce by coastal sand dunes and yielded not a penny of profit. And nothing, it seemed, could induce settlers in any numbers to remain on the swampy, sandy coastal land of Cape Fear, the proposed middle settlement, which was surrounded by hostile Indians. By 1669 the entire enterprise of Carolina was on the verge of extinction, when Ashley suddenly took it over and rescued it from failure—although not in the way he had planned.

With the assistance of the philosopher John Locke, who was his secretary, physician, and legal adviser, Ashley reorganized the undertaking. He decided that funding would have to come from the sponsors themselves, that settlers would have to be sent directly from England, and that the focal point of colonization would be the third, most southerly location, Port Royal, the site that the settlers from Barbados most favored. With new capital that had been raised from the original proprietors, Ashley was able to send out from England three vessels with about a hundred colonists and a large supply of equipment. He instructed the fleet to sail by way of Barbados, where it was to take on new supplies and settlers, but the expedition suffered misfortunes of every kind. Only a handful of colonists survived to establish a settlement, which they located not where one had been planned, but much farther inland, out of the reach of the Spanish. In 1670 that community, isolated from principal transportation routes, was still only a fort surrounded by a few small subsistence farms. More vessels followed, however, especially from Barbados, and the leaders undertook a search for town sites suitable for the grand design of land distribution that the proprietors had drawn up. One of the promising sites they discovered, never considered by the proprietors, was Oyster Point, where the Ashley and Cooper rivers meet, some sixty miles north of the original Port Royal. Gradually the superior attractions of this location, safe from coastal raids yet open to ocean commerce and at the hub of a network of river routes into the interior, prevailed over the proprietors' original plans for concentrated settlements. Family groups and individual farmers from the older mainland settlements and from Barbados began to move into this unplanned center of the colony and to establish claims to the rich land along the riverbanks. By 1683 Oyster Point had been renamed Charles Town (a century later it would be called Charleston), and its population of a thousand had become the center of a quickly growing colony. It was altogether different from the community at Albemarle, three hundred miles to the north. It was also totally different from anything that the Carolina proprietors had contemplated.

Fundamental Constitutions. Ashley's and Locke's hopes and plans for Carolina after the reorganization of 1669 were described in great detail in one of the most remarkable documents of the age, the "Fundamental Constitutions of Carolina," which the two men wrote in collaboration. It presented an elaborate blueprint for a hierarchical manorial world that was to be dominated by three orders of nobility—proprietors, "landgraves," and "caciques." In this intricate utopian system landowners were to be magistrates; laws were to be made by a Council of Nobles, and law courts were to be maintained by the owners of manors. But this plan—like the Calverts' earlier scheme for Maryland—was a dream that could never be put into effect. The government that in fact emerged in the first decades of settlement soon came to resemble that of the other proprietary colonies. In the eighteenth century, when the original Carolina charter was annulled, the colony's public institutions easily fell into the standard pattern of royal governments. Yet although the romantic notions in Ashley and Locke's "Constitutions" never took hold, some of the document's provisions did become effective and helped shape the emerging community. The provisions that survived were those that conformed to patterns of life that were in fact developing in America.

One of these provisions was for religious toleration, which the original Carolina charter had also established, and which contributed significantly to the development of the Carolinas. Another enduring provision of the "Constitutions" made the naturalization of aliens extremely simple. Further, the "Constitutions" required that two-fifths of all the land in each county be granted in large estates to the nobility—a ruling that paved the way not so much for the creation of a landed nobility as for large-scale land speculation. Finally, the "Constitutions" established the rule of English law and outlined a structure of local administration similar to that of England. These latter provisions would remain fundamental to the distinctive variant of British society that was developing at the end of the seventeenth century in the southern part of the Carolina grant.

Carolina: Society and Economy. Unusual communities were springing up elsewhere in mainland British America, but the settlement that in time would become South Carolina was truly exotic. Its quickly growing population—still a mere 5,000 to 7,000 by the end of the seventeenth century—was peculiarly complex. It included not only New Yorkers, Puritan New Englanders, and Virginians, but also more than five hundred English Presbyterians and Baptists and also a group of Presbyterian Scots. Moreover, from the colony's earliest years, and increasingly after 1685, the

A D V E R T I S E M E N T,

To all Tradeſ-men, Husbandmen, Servants and others who are willing to Tranſport themſelves unto the Province of New-Eaſt-Jerſy *in* America, *a great part of which belongs to* Scots-men, *Proprietors thereof.*

Whereas ſeveral Noblemen, Gentlemen, and others, who (by undoubted Rights derived from His Majeſty, and His Royal Highneſs) are Intereſted and concerned in the Province of *New-Eaſt-Jerſie,* lying in the midſt of the *Engliſh* Plantations in *America,* do intend (God-willing) to ſend ſeveral Ships thither, in *May,* June, and *July* enſuing, 1684. from *Leith, Montroſs, Aberdeen* and *Glaſgow.* Theſe are to give notice to all Tradeſ-men, Huſbandmen and others, who are willing and deſirous to go there, and are able to Tranſport themſelves and Families thither , upon their own Coſt and Charges, to a pleaſant and profitable Countrey, where they may live in great Plenty and Pleaſure, upon far leſs Stock, and with much leſs labour and trouble then in *Scotland,* that as ſoon as they arrive there, they ſhall have conſiderable quantities of Land, ſet out Heretably to themſelves and their Heirs for ever, for which they ſhall pay nothing for the firſt four or five years, and afterwards pay only a ſmall Rent yearly to the Owners and Proprietors thereof, according as they can agree. And all Tradeſ-men, Servants, and others, ſuch as, Wrights, Coupers, Smiths, Maſons, Millers, Shoe-makers, &c. who are willing to go there, and are not able to Tranſport themſelves, that they ſhall be carried over free, and well maintained in Meat and Clothes the firſt four years, only for their Service, and thereafter they ſhall have conſiderable quantities of Land, ſet out to themſelves and their Heirs for ever , upon which they may live at the rate of Gentlemen all their lives, and their Children after them: Their ordinary Service will be cutting down of Wood with Axes, and other eaſie Husband-Work, there being plenty of Oxen and Horſes for Plowing and Harrowing, &c. Let therefore all Tradeſ-men, Husband-men, Servants, and others who incline to go thither, and deſire further Information herein, repair themſelves to any of the Perſons underwritten, who will fully inform them anent the Countrey , and every other thing neceſſary , and will anſwer and ſatisfie their Scruples and Objections, and give them all other Incouragements according to their ſeveral abilities and capacities; viz.

At *Edinburgh* let them apply themſelves to the Lord Theſaurer-Deput, the Lord Regiſter, Sir *John Gordon,* Mr. *Patrick Lyon,* Mr. *George Alexander,* Advocates, *George Drummond* of *Blair, John Swintoun, John Drummond, Thomas Gordon, David Falconer, Andrew Hamilton,* Merchants ; at *Brent-Iſland* to *William Robiſon* Doctor of Medecine; at *Montroſs,* to *John Gordon* Doctor of Medecine, *John Fullerton* of *Kinaber,* and *Robert* and *Thomas Fullertons* his Brothers ; in the Shire of the *Mearns,* to *Robert Barclay* of *Urie,* and *John Barclay* his Brother ; at *Aberdeen,* to *Gilbert Moleſin, Andrew Galloway, John* and *Robert Sandilands, William Gerard* Merchants ; in the Shire of *Aberdeen,* to *Robert Gordon* of *Clunie,* and *Robert Burnet* of *Lethanty* ; in the Shire of *Pearth* to *David Tiſbach* of *Monyvard* and Captain *Patrick Macgreiger* ; In *Merſ* Shire, to *James Johnſton* of *Spotſwood* ; At *Keſo,* to *Charles ormiſton* Merchant ; In the *Lews,* to *Kenith Mackenzie* younger of *Kildin:* And if any Gentleman or others be deſireous to buy or purchaſe any ſmall ſhares or portions of Land in the ſaid Province, they may repair to any of the foreſaid Perſons, who will direct them how they ſhall be ſerved, providing they do it timouſly, becauſe many more Perſons are daily offering to buy, then can be gotten well accommodated.

French Protestants known as Huguenots had been induced to immigrate to South Carolina from the Netherlands, where they had taken refuge after being expelled from France; and by 1700, at least five hundred Frenchmen were settled in the colony. But from the start the dominant element was the settlers from the West Indies: several thousand tough, experienced frontier farmers who had been displaced by the growth of the plantation economy in the sugar-producing islands, and who were determined to prosper in this hot, fertile, unexplored land.

The West Indian settlers were well acquainted with the production of semitropical crops and took an experimental approach to agriculture. They also knew how to run a slave labor system. Thus they were able to help the colony through the typical "starving times" of the early years and to lead it in the search for commercially profitable crops. The first marketable products were familiarly British and held no great promise: timber, cattle, and foodstuffs, all of which had to be exchanged for sugar in the West Indies, which in turn could be sold in the British markets. But gradually more exotic and more lucrative possibilities became clear. The first was the fur trade, which remained a crucial element in the economic and social life of South Carolina for half a century. As early as the 1680s pack horses could be seen hauling into Charles Town and the other coastal villages animal skins that had been bought through a series of exchanges with traders and Indian hunters ranging deep in the interior. The Carolina fur traders were anything but squeamish. Not limiting themselves to tracking down animals, they also overpowered and brought back human captives: troops of Indians taken from hostile tribes, who were sold into slavery at home and abroad.

Slavery was a basic fact of life from the earliest days of South Carolina. Africans, West Indian blacks, and Indians alike were enslaved. There is evidence that in the arduous early years, when basic survival was at stake, whites and blacks, freemen and slaves, worked together—"slaved" together—in conditions of relative equality. But by the 1690s, the condition of the blacks was reduced to one of absolute degradation. At this time the first successful experiments were made in rice cultivation, which along with indigo* production and the fur trade would ultimately be the basis of South Carolina's economy. These industries required an ever-increasing work force of slaves. As early as 1708 blacks outnumbered whites in South Carolina, and by then the colony's "black code," based on the savage slave laws of Barbados, had been drawn up and was rigorously enforced.

These were the results of the enterprise of Charles II's courtiers who had been granted the great gift of Carolina in 1663. By the beginning of the eighteenth century, South Carolina's survival was assured. The colony would prosper and grow—but not as the utopia of balanced social orders of which Locke and Ashley had dreamed. Rather, it was a competitive world of rice plantations, brutal race relations, land speculation, and commerce. As their fortunes rose, its most prominent families were increasingly eager for leisure and the grace of life; but even more than the leaders of the other colonies, they were directly exposed to the wildness of the frontier and the savagery of chattel slavery.

Settlement of the Jerseys.

The Jerseys were founded at the same time as the Carolinas, and under similar circumstances. In 1664 Lord John Berkeley and Sir George Carteret—both of whom were also among the proprietors of Carolina—were granted a tract of approximately 5 million acres between the Delaware and Hudson rivers by the Duke of York, overlord of the territory just conquered from the Dutch. But although these first proprietors of what is now called New Jersey issued grandiose plans modeled on the first Carolina designs, they had even less interest in managing this province than they had in governing the Carolinas. The proprietors' powers and claims almost immediately dissolved into a confusing maze of divisions and subdivisions that left New Jersey open to largely unregulated settlement.

In 1674 Berkeley sold his rights to a group of English Quakers. This transaction set in motion a bewildering exchange of shares, in the course of which, in 1676, New Jersey was formally divided into two provinces, East Jersey and West Jersey. In East Jersey Carteret's heirs attempted vainly to organize a coherent government out of the scattered settlements that had been founded by squatters. Meanwhile, amid paralyzing legal complications, the new Quaker proprietors of West Jersey tried to establish a refuge for their fellow Quakers who were being persecuted in England and New York. In 1677 the Quaker leaders, among

*Indigo is a blue dye obtained from various plants.

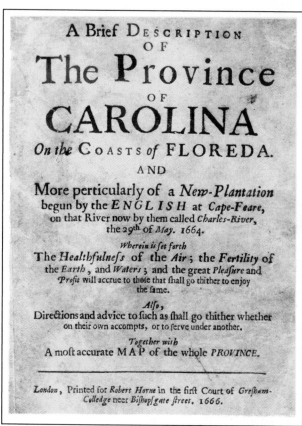

them William Penn, issued an extraordinarily liberal and humane document, "The Concessions and Agreements of the Proprietors, Freeholders, and Inhabitants of . . . West New Jersey in America." This document guaranteed a democratically elected popular assembly; absolute freedom of conscience, among other individual rights; and adult male participation in both local and provincial government. In the early 1680s the first West Jersey assemblies attempted, with uneven success, to enact these provisions into law. But although groups of settlers appeared and began the cultivation of West Jersey, the Quakers' interests in colonization soon shifted to Pennsylvania. West Jersey thereafter followed the pattern already set in East Jersey, where control was in the hands of land speculators interested primarily in the financial value of the proprietors' claims. The mixture of peoples in East Jersey became even more complex when Scottish entrepreneurs led a migration of Scots Presbyterians into the province. Gradually, as farms and towns were built in both East and West Jersey, a familiarly English pattern of local government emerged, in which the proprietors played only a minor role. Yet the proprietors retained title to the undistributed land, even when the crown took temporary control of the two governments between 1688 and 1692 and permanent control in 1702. In that year East Jersey and West Jersey were rejoined to form the single crown colony of New Jersey.

By 1702 the territory that the Duke of York had so casually bestowed on his two followers contained a population of approximately 14,000, almost all of whom lived on one-family farms of between 50 and 150 acres. The ethnic and religious diversity was extraordinary, even for a British North American colony. Only New York had a more complex population, and there a single group, the Dutch, predominated. In New Jersey no one group was dominant. There were Africans, West Indians, Dutch, Germans, French, English, Scots, and Irish. Religious groups in the colony included Congregationalists, Baptists, Quakers, Anglicans, Presbyterians, Huguenots, and Dutch and German Reformed. The colony had no particular cultural character or social organization, and its mixed farming economy was in no way distinctive in the agricultural world of the northern colonies.

Pennsylvania: A Godly Experiment and a Worldly Success

Of all the colonies perhaps Pennsylvania most vividly shows the contrast between soaring aspirations and modest accomplishments. The vividness of the contrast was in part a consequence of the speed with which everything happened in Pennsylvania, as well as a reflection of the fame of the original plans and the force of the original hopes. The contrast also reflected the mixture of conflicting elements in William Penn's personality.

Quaker Immigrants. The founding of Pennsylvania was the accomplishment of one of the most radical religious sects of the seventeenth century, the Quakers. As religious extremists, they had suffered severe persecution during their thirty years of existence as a group before the founding of Pennsylvania. The Quakers devoted themselves to finding the divine "inner light" within each soul and practiced their religion without the burdens of church, clergy, and formal ritual. They were proud and courageous people who defied state authority to the point of refusing to take ordinary oaths of loyalty. They advocated absolute freedom of conscience and were pacifists and political reformers.

By 1680 there were some 50,000 Quakers in Britain, largely among the poorest people, and smaller numbers were scattered through continental Europe and North America. In the late 1670s the English government, fearful of Catholic conspiracies and hoping to protect the established Church of England, had launched savage attacks on all religious dissidents, especially such extremists as the Quakers. Some 1,400 of these gentle but determined nonconformists were thrown into jail, and they were fined heavily for attending Quaker meetings (religious services) and for failing to attend Church of England services. If they could not pay these fines (and most could not), their goods—including their means of earning a living—were seized and either destroyed or carted away. This treatment severely injured the Quakers, not only economically, but also spiritually: as they regarded work a divine calling, their inability to pursue their occupations was a further obstacle to their achievement of a full religious life.

William Penn was the well-educated son of one of England's most influential naval officers and a familiar, respected figure at the court of Charles II. But he had joined the Quakers as a young man, and he suffered his share of religious persecution. His outlook was curiously complex. Convinced of the truth of the Quakers' teachings, he brought to the movement great energy, high-level contacts, a lawyer's shrewdness in argument, and a businesslike approach to the endless controversies in which the group was embroiled. He was a radical in religion and also in politics: he sought every means of protecting the individual from arbitrary governmental power and believed that government existed to improve the welfare of the masses. But he remained an aristocrat all his life. Despite being a political reformer and a religious extremist, he was also a monarchist. He continued to believe that well-educated and highly placed men should have the decisive voice in public affairs, and he managed to keep contact with the sources of political favors at Charles II's court despite the suffering he had to endure because of his Quaker views.

Why Charles II granted vast territories in America to this outspoken religious dissident has never been fully explained. No doubt one factor was the crown's long-standing debt to Penn's father. The king may also have thought the grant a convenient way to get rid of the Quakers. But Penn's personal relationship with the royal family was probably the decisive factor, and of that very little is known. In any case, in 1681 Charles II bestowed on Penn the last unassigned portion of the North American coast south of Massachusetts. The grant included the entire area between New York and Maryland, stretching west almost three hundred miles from the New Jersey border at the Delaware River—a total of 29 million acres, almost the size of England.

Penn was the outright owner of this territory. Furthermore, he had been granted the authority to form a government, to appoint most public officials, and to make laws subject only to the approval of an assembly of freemen and the crown's right of veto. The charter

THE CITY OF PHILADELPHIA.

WILLIAM PENN'S MAP OF PHILADELPHIA, c. 1681

specified that England's commercial regulations* be observed, but otherwise Penn was free to govern as he wished. He immediately drew up a Frame of Government—the first in a series of such documents, as it turned out. It was a strange work. In part it was a code of moral principles, including absolute freedom of worship and conscience. It was also a detailed plan for a very traditional civil administration, reformed to satisfy Quaker ideals—and a blueprint for a remarkably *un*democratic government. A governor and a large council were to initiate and execute all laws, which the assembly (elected only by property owners) might accept or reject, but not amend. Thus, amid striking statements of private and public morality, and appeals to humanity and decency, Penn gave power not to the people at large, but to their "natural" rulers. However, unlike the Calverts in Maryland, he never thought of himself as a feudal overlord. From this fusing of benevolence and paternalism Penn expected a community of brotherly love to emerge— tolerant, free, secure, and above all peaceful. With these hopes in mind he turned with passion and skill to making his dreams come true.

In the end Penn was deeply disillusioned. Simply maintaining the legal title to his colony was an endless struggle, and his relations with the settlers were profoundly embittering. His efforts to bring settlers to

Pennsylvania, however, were extraordinarily successful, especially at the start.

Growth of the Colony.

Pennsylvania was the best advertised of all American colonies. Recruitment pamphlets urging emigration to Pennsylvania circulated throughout Britain and, in translation, in western Europe. A central "city of brotherly love," Philadelphia, was founded at an excellent site at the junction of the Delaware and Schuylkill rivers, and a well-designed street plan was laid out. A generous system of land distribution was set up. Land along the Delaware River south of Philadelphia was added to Pennsylvania by the Duke of York to ensure the colony's access to the sea. Quaker merchants contributed heavily to meet the colony's expenses, and within a year an assembly met and composed a "Great Law" that served as a temporary code of legislative and administrative principles and procedures. Above all, settlers arrived in large numbers.

By 1682, when Penn visited the province, the population was already 4,000—a remarkable swarming of people within a few months. There were Dutch, Swedes, and Finns from earlier settlements on the Delaware River; West New Jerseyites; a large and influential influx of Welsh Quakers; Germans from the Rhineland who settled Germantown, near Philadelphia; and above all English Quakers who flocked to the refuge Penn had provided for them. Fifty vessels brought 3,000 more settlers in 1683. By 1700 the

---

*For the growth of England's commercial legislation, see chapter 4, p. 87.

colony's population was a remarkable 21,000. But by then Penn knew all the difficulties that his proprietorship entailed.

He was embroiled in a bitter struggle with Lord Baltimore over Pennsylvania's southern boundary. (This dispute would be finally settled only with the drawing of the Mason-Dixon line on the eve of the American Revolution.) He was faced with stiff resistance to his authority by the settlers in the newly acquired "lower counties," a district that would ultimately form the state of Delaware; in 1701 he was forced to allow the dissidents to establish their own assembly. Penn was unfortunate in his choice of deputy governors and suffered from their inefficiency. Above all, his concept of government evoked fierce opposition, led by some of the most deeply committed Quakers among the settlers.

From the beginning the colonial leaders had insisted that the representatives—not Penn or his deputy governors—have the deciding voice in government. The house of representatives seized the power of initiating legislation, and in 1696 it forced Penn to agree to its action. Against Penn's will it insisted on amending the bills that he presented, and it challenged his title to the undistributed land. Bitter struggles continued year after year in the 1690s, until finally Penn agreed to an altogether new Frame of Government. Written in 1701 by a joint committee of the council and the house, this charter of liberties marked the final defeat of Penn's political ideals. It would serve as Pennsylvania's constitution until the Revolution. The new Frame of Government completely eliminated the council from the legislative process, thus making the Pennsylvania assembly the only unicameral (one-house) legislature in British America. The king could still veto legislation, but Penn could not, and the inhabitants were freed from any special allegiance to Penn or his descendants. What remained beyond dispute were the founder's and his heirs' title to the undistributed land, and their authority to appoint the resident governors. All other powers that had been granted to the Penn family in the charters were either abolished or challenged. This resistance to Penn's authority did not stem from a democratic, populist majority of the population. Rather, it came from an oligarchy of Quaker politicians and representatives who had been elected on a limited franchise—a quarrelsome, opinionated, ambitious clique that would dominate the colony's politics for the next half-century.

Penn had lost control of the province. But although Pennsylvania had failed to develop into the utopia of its founder's dreams, it was a fabulous worldly success. Its politics were contentious, but it was populous and prosperous from the start, open and attractive to all. Pennsylvania was the distribution center for a mass population of laborers, but also a center of provincial high culture. Within a single generation the colony became the dynamic heart of British North America. With a sure instinct, the eager seventeen-year-old Benjamin Franklin left Boston to seek his fortune in Philadelphia in 1723. William Penn was only five years dead then, but his City of Brotherly Love had become a vigorous, thriving community of 10,000 persons, a vital part of a colonial world that was evolving in unexpected ways.

CHRONOLOGY

1607 Virginia Company of London establishes settlement at Jamestown.

1609 Pilgrims flee to Holland to avoid religious persecution.

1609 Second charter of Virginia Company.

1612 Third charter of Virginia Company.

1619 First Africans arrive in Virginia. First North American representative assembly meets in Virginia.

1620 Mayflower Compact signed; Pilgrims establish Plymouth Colony.

1621 Dutch West India Company chartered.

1622 Indian rebellion in Virginia.

1624 Virginia Company charter annulled; English crown takes control of Virginia. First settlements in New Netherlands.

1625–49 Reign of Charles I.

1626 Dutch settle Manhattan.

1629 Massachusetts Bay Company chartered.

1630 Puritan emigration from England begins; continues until 1643.

1632 Cecilius Calvert, Lord Baltimore, receives charter for Maryland colony.

1634 First settlements in Maryland.

1635 Roger Williams banished from Bay Colony.

1636 Harvard College founded. First permanent English settlements in Connecticut and Rhode Island.

1638 Anne Hutchinson convicted of heresy in Massachusetts; flees to Rhode Island.

1639 Fundamental Orders adopted in Connecticut.

1642 Basic literacy law passed in Massachusetts Bay.

1642–48 Civil war in England.

1643 Confederation of New England colonies.

1644 Rhode Island receives patent.

1647 Law requiring towns to maintain schools passed in Massachusetts Bay Colony.

1649 Northern Neck of Virginia granted to courtiers in exile.

1663 Carolina charter granted to eight proprietors; Rhode Island granted charter.

1664 English conquest of New Netherland; grant of New Jersey to two proprietors.

1681 Charles II issues Pennsylvania charter to William Penn.

SUGGESTED READINGS

There have been two efforts to summarize the English background of seventeenth-century colonization: Wallace Notestein, *The English People on the Eve of Colonization, 1603–1630* (1954), and Carl Bridenbaugh, *Vexed and Troubled Englishmen, 1590–1642* (1968). But more revealing than either of these general descriptions, which are based largely on literary sources, are studies that have nothing to do with colonization directly but make clear the disarray, mobility, and vitality of English society that underlay the extraordinary exodus of English men and women overseas: Peter Laslett, *The World We Have Lost* (1965); Peter Clark and Paul Slack, eds., *Crisis and Order in English Towns 1500–1700* (1972); John Patten, *English Towns, 1500–1700* (1978); and the writings of W. G. Hoskins on English local history, most of which are listed in his *Local History in England* (1959). The best introduction to the economic history of pre-industrial England is Charles Wilson, *England's Apprenticeship, 1603–1763* (1965), two-thirds of which is on the seventeenth century.

The most comprehensive survey of the native North American population is the massive Volume 15 (1978) of the Smithsonian Institution's new series, *Handbook of North American Indians*. This volume, subtitled *The Northeast*, summarizes the available information—historical, anthropological, and archaeological—concerning all the native tribes from Maine to North Carolina and west to the Great Lakes. Writings on the extremely difficult subject of the size, distribution, and structure of the Indian population are listed in H. F. Dobyns, *Native American Historical Demography* (1976), to which should be added S. F. Cook, *The Indian Population of New England in the Seventeenth Century* (1976), and several of the contributions to the *Handbook*, cited above. There are detailed accounts of the conflicts of races for only a few of the seventeenth-century colonies: Allen W. Trelease, *Indian Affairs in Colonial New York: The Seventeenth Century* (1960); Alden W. Vaughan, *New England Frontier: Puritans and Indians, 1620–1675* (1975); Douglas E. Leach, *Flintlock and Tomahawk: New England in King Philip's War*

(1958); Nancy O. Lurie, "Indian Cultural Adjustment to European Civilization," in James M. Smith, ed., *Seventeenth-Century America* (1959); Stephen S. Webb, *1676: The End of American Independence* (1984); and Francis Jennings, *The Invasion of America* (1975). Jennings's book is a bitter outcry against the wrongs done the North American Indians by the Puritans (and in this, a criticism of Vaughan's more even-handed treatment) and a boiling polemic against historians' characterization of the Indians as sparse in numbers, hostile to Europeans, savage, heathen, and unsophisticated in agriculture, trade, and politics. What the Indians *were*, aside from victims of Puritans and mythologizing historians, does not emerge.

The most detailed and comprehensive single narrative of the English settlements in the seventeenth century is Charles M. Andrews, *The Colonial Period of American History* (Vols. I–III, 1934–37), which concentrates on constitutional history and the development of public institutions. A more up-to-date and broad-ranging account of the planting and early growth of the southern colonies is Wesley F. Craven, *The Southern Colonies in the Seventeenth Century, 1607–1689* (1949). The settlement stories are retold in briefer scope in John E. Pomfret, *Founding the American Colonies, 1583–1660* (1970), and Wesley F. Craven, *The Colonies in Transition, 1660–1713* (1968), both of which contain extensive bibliographies. There are excellent essays on local government in the colonies in Bruce C. Daniels, ed., *Town and County* (1978).

On the founding of Virginia, there are, besides the relevant chapters of Andrews's *Colonial Period*, Vol. I, and Craven's *Southern Colonies*, a detailed narrative of public events in Richard L. Morton, *Colonial Virginia* (2 vols., 1960); a short summary in Alden T. Vaughan, *American Genesis* (1975); an account of the high culture of the initiators of settlement, in Richard B. Davis, *George Sandys* (1955); biographies of Pocahontas and John Smith by Philip L. Barbour; and two collections of documents: L. G. Tyler, ed., *Narratives of Early Virginia, 1606–1625* (1907), and Warren M. Billings, ed., *The Old Dominion in the Seventeenth Century . . .* (1975). Sigmund Diamond's essay, "From Organization to Society: Virginia in the Seventeenth Century," *American Journal of Sociology*, 63 (1958), 457–75,[†] interprets the founding as the transformation of a quasi-military organization into a fully formed society of multiple relationships. Bernard Bailyn, "Politics and Social Structure in Virginia," in Smith, ed., *Seventeenth-Century America*, pp. 90–115,[†] considers the development of politics in its relation to the evolving social structure. Edmund Morgan considers the human cost of the colony's success in terms of the exploitation of labor in "The First American Boom: Virginia 1618–1630," *Wm. and Mary Q.*, 18 (1971), 169–98, a topic discussed in a broader context in his *American Slavery, American Freedom* (1975).

The labor problem in Virginia involves the difficult question of the origins of chattel slavery. The modern debate on that question was initiated and framed by a brilliant article by Oscar and Mary F. Handlin, "Origins of the Southern Labor System," *Wm. and Mary Q.*, 7 (1950), 199–222,[†] reprinted as chap. 1 of Oscar Handlin's *Race and Nationality in American Life* (1957). The Handlins' view is that chattel slavery in British America was a unique institution, different from slavery elsewhere; that the concept of "slavery" in its American meaning was created in the seventeenth-century

Chesapeake; and that it arose as a legal condition, in response not so much to race prejudice as to an effort to attract voluntary white labor by debasing the condition of involuntary black labor. A more recent study is Russell Menard, "From Servants to Slaves," *Southern Studies*, 16 (1977), 355–90. For differing views, emphasizing race prejudice, the fear of foreignness, and religious differences, see Winthrop Jordan, *White over Black* (1968), Part I,[†] and Carl N. Degler, "Slavery and the Genesis of American Race Prejudice," *Comparative Studies in History and Society*, 2 (1959), 49–66. For a listing of recent writings on the subject, see Vaughan, *American Genesis*, p. 198.

On the Pilgrims and Plymouth, see George D. Langdon, Jr.'s general account, *Pilgrim Colony* (1966), and John Demos's social analysis, *A Little Commonwealth* (1970). George F. Willison's *Saints and Strangers* (1945) is a breezy, amusing interpretation. Bradford's great history, *Of Plymouth Plantation*, is available in a modern edition prepared by Samuel E. Morison (1952).

On the founding and early development of the Puritan colonies in New England, see, besides Andrews's chapters in *The Colonial Period*, Edmund S. Morgan's short biography of John Winthrop, *Puritan Dilemma* (1958); Darrett Rutman's *Winthrop's Boston* (1965); Samuel E. Morison's *Builders of the Bay Colony* (1930); Raymond P. Stearns, *The Strenuous Puritan: Hugh Peter* (1954); and above all, Winthrop's own *Journal . . . 1630–1649* (J. K. Hosmer, ed., 2 vols., 1908). For a theatrical and psychological account of Anne Hutchinson's career, see Emery Battis, *Saints and Sectaries* (1962), and on Roger Williams there are books by S. H. Brockunier, Perry Miller, and Edmund S. Morgan. On seventeenth-century Connecticut, besides Andrews, see Isabel M. Calder, *The New Haven Colony* (1934), and Mary J. A. Jones, *Congregational Commonwealth* (1968). On Rhode Island, see Sydney V. James, *Colonial Rhode Island* (1975), and on Maine and New Hampshire, Charles E. Clark, *The Eastern Frontier* (1970), Part I.

Maryland is well covered in Andrews's and Craven's general books, but in the case of New York the general accounts should be supplemented by Thomas J. Condon, *New York Beginnings* (1968); Van Cleaf Bachman, *Peltries or Plantations* (1969); and the early chapters of Michael Kammen, *Colonial New York* (1975). M. Eugene Sirmans, *Colonial South Carolina* (1966), and Peter H. Wood, *Black Majority* (1974), are essential on South Carolina. Hugh T. Lefler and Albert R. Newsome, *North Carolina* (1954), is a good summary of that colony's early history. Wesley F. Craven, *New Jersey and the English Colonization of North America* (1964), is the best short book on that colony, though there are a number of more detailed studies by John E. Pomfret. The most recent history of the founding of Pennsylvania is Edwin B. Bronner's *William Penn's "Holy Experiment"* (1962); on the colony's early political history, see Gary B. Nash, *Quakers and Politics . . . 1681–1726* (1968). Catherine O. Peare, *William Penn* (1957), narrates the essential facts of the founder's life in a somewhat exclamatory fashion; Mary M. Dunn, *William Penn, Politics and Conscience* (1967), is an excellent study of Penn's ideas and religious beliefs.

[†]See first footnote on p. 27.

3 Europe in the Wilderness: American Society in the Seventeenth Century

By 1700 communities of Europeans had been established on the North American mainland by many kinds of colonizers—commercial companies, religious organizations, individual entrepreneurs, and circles of courtiers. These colonies formed an almost continuous line of settlements along the Atlantic coast from New Hampshire to South Carolina and stretched inland as much as a hundred miles to the first falls of the coastal rivers. The population of these settlements totaled some 250,000 persons of European and African birth or descent, most of them English-speaking. But settlers were not spread evenly through this broad area. They clustered along river valleys to take advantage of fertile soil and easy lines of communication. Large pockets of land remained unsettled. Even in the oldest communities of Massachusetts and Virginia, this was still a frontier world, fundamentally shaped by its continuing encounter with the wilderness. Yet there were areas that were populated by the native-born children of native-born parents—a third generation in America. For them, home was the colony, however much they might realize that their ancestors had come from a greater "home" overseas. Although they did not think of themselves as "American," they lived settled lives in communities familiar to them from birth, and these were communities whose distinctive characteristics were becoming clear.

Immigration continued in all areas, although least in New England. Newcomers to the colonies in 1700 no longer faced the bewildering disorder that earlier settlers had known. But neither did they find themselves in communities quite like any seen before. There were great variations from one region or one settlement to another; but despite the differences, common elements of a reordering of European life could be found everywhere.

This reordering of social life was not the result of design, planning, or intent. As we have seen, there was an abundance of planning—elaborate designs and soaring dreams. But none of the original plans had been fulfilled. All had been quickly destroyed or had slowly dissolved upon contact with the harsh reality of life in America. The deviations from European life that had developed in the colonies by 1700 were products of the impact of circumstance upon the culture of essentially conservative immigrants. Most of these settlers sought personal satisfactions, personal freedoms, and security within the familiar patterns of life. Many felt that the changes that did take place were backward, not forward, steps. Change was resisted more often than it was pursued. Only later would the alterations in community life be seen as advances toward an ideal—the ideal, expressed in the goals of the American Revolution, of a freer, more fulfilling way of life.

Population Growth and Structure

American society in the seventeenth century was shaped in large part by demographic characteristics. Because the first American population consisted of immigrant settlers, and because life in the colonies was known to be harsh, the society that resulted was no evenly balanced re-creation of the European social structure. The upper classes of traditional society were absent from the start. There were no nobles, who composed the ruling class in Europe. There were few of what might loosely be called aristocrats, and few who had been landowning gentlemen; there were even few of what we would today call upper-middle-class professionals. In 1700, just as at present, society's leaders and well-established people did not easily tear up their roots, migrate, and struggle to secure themselves in an undeveloped land.

The Free Population. Most of the free population in mainland North America was recruited from the lower working population of England and the Netherlands. Generally these people did not come from the lowest class—that of penniless vagrants and social outcasts.

60

ALICE MASON, 1670

This forthright, unpretentious portrait by an unknown artist illustrates not only the appearance of children in the seventeenth century, but attitudes toward children and childhood. While parents did not consider children to be simply miniature adults, as the dress and appearance of this child suggests, and while they were aware that the individual's understanding develops gradually, they had no concept of childhood as such. They expected children to behave like adults, to be fully capable of religious experience, and to take complete responsibility for their actions at what seems now to be very early ages.

Rather they were farm workers, industrial laborers, and artisans. In the lists of immigrants compiled at the time, the two most commonly mentioned occupations were "yeoman," or "husbandman" (a farm worker, usually with some degree of independence), and artisan, or tradesman. Outside New England, between one-half and two-thirds of all white immigrants were indentured servants: persons who were bound, for four years or more, to serve their masters faithfully in exchange for transatlantic passage, care, and protection. On gaining their liberty they received "freedom dues," which often included a small piece of land. Approximately 1,500 of these indentured servants, bound in various conditions of servitude, arrived in the Chesapeake region yearly between 1630 and 1700; more than 100,000 had come by 1700.

Further, the free population in America by 1700 was unusually mobile. The population was originally recruited, and continued to be recruited, from groups that were already on the move in the mother country. For them resettlement in America was not a unique experience but a second or third uprooting. And institutional and legal restraints on mobility—important factors in traditional European life—scarcely existed at all outside New England. In most parts of America, people were free to move wherever they wished. The large majority of the indentured servants in the Chesapeake survived servitude and eventually entered the community as free people, able to seek security, profit, or congenial surroundings as they desired.

More important still, the free population of the northern colonies in the seventeenth century—and of the southern colonies after about 1700—grew unusually quickly. In this era most European populations were hardly growing at all, but the population increase in the fastest-growing American communities may have reached the extraordinary rate of 5 to 6 percent a year. In New England, once the initial immigration was completed, the population grew during the seventeenth century at an average rate of 2.6 or 2.7 percent a year, a statistic that shows that, quite aside from further immigration, the settled population was doubling approximately every twenty-seven years. On the other hand, until the 1650s Virginia and Maryland seem to have remained deathtraps of disease. A random list of ninety-nine adults (mostly men) who transacted business in a Virginia court shows an average age of death of forty-eight between 1637 and 1664. The life expectancy for women aged twenty in the same region was only forty. In Maryland the population began to grow on its own, independently of immigration, only in the 1680s; before then only the constant flow of immigrants accounted for population growth, and these immigrants were highly vulnerable to the diseases common in the Chesapeake region. But the death rate in the Chesapeake colonies fell rapidly in the later seventeenth century. This drop occurred as the proportion of native-born persons in the population—who early in life had developed immunities to the prevalent diseases—increased. By the late seventeenth century the population of Virginia was growing rapidly, supplemented by constant immigration. It stood at 8,000 in 1644, quadrupled to 32,000 in the next thirty years, and more than doubled again in the next thirty years, to reach an estimated 75,600 in 1704.

Whatever else may be said about the spectacular population growth, this phenomenon meant that all other social changes were intensified by sheer population pressure.

How can this extraordinary growth rate be explained? Not, apparently, by an unusual birthrate. The birthrates available for selected American communities are similar to those in French and English villages of this period. The root of the difference apparently lies in the lower death rate in the American colonies, once the initial "starving times" were over and once the deadly "seasoning" times in the southern colonies came to an end. In Plymouth, Massachusetts, the life expectancy of men who survived to the age of twenty-one was 69.2 years. In Andover, Massachusetts, the average age of death of the first settlers was 71.8 years; for their sons the average was 65.2. The life expectancy at birth for males in seventeenth-century Andover was longer by 12.6 years than it would be for men in England two hundred years later.

This rapidly growing population was also unusual in its age structure, which is associated with population growth. The American population was youthful. Most of the tens of thousands of indentured servants were between eighteen and twenty-four years of age when they arrived. In Bristol, Rhode Island, 54 percent of the population were children; in seventeenth-century England the equivalent figure was 42.6 percent. Because of its youthful composition, the American population was less vulnerable to the ravages of disease than a population more evenly distributed by age would have been. The survival rate also reflects a higher proportion of women in their childbearing years (between fifteen and forty-five), as well as a younger average age at marriage, at least in the northern colonies, especially for women. In England, where 15 percent of the population were servants who usually could marry only in later life, if at all, and where socioeconomic circumstances made it difficult for those without an inheritance to establish a household, it appears that the average age at first marriage was twenty-eight for men and twenty-four for women. In one Massachusetts community that has been closely studied, Dedham, the equivalent figures are 25.5 and 22.5. In Plymouth, Massachusetts, the average age at first marriage for women at the end of the seventeenth century was 22.3; in Bristol, Rhode Island, before 1750, the average age for women's first marriages was 20.5. As a result of these younger marriages, women commonly bore children from their very early twenties until their mid-forties. Younger marriages also ensured a higher survival rate of children because in preindustrial societies the offspring of younger marriages seem to have been more resistant to disease.

Finally, sex ratios in the emerging American communities differed from those of the parent communities in Europe. In England through these years, as in most settled societies, there were more women than men. (The figures in England for the period 1574–1821 are 91.3 men to every 100 women.) In the early years of American settlement, the figures are wildly inverted. In Virginia in 1625, more than 75 percent of the settlers were men, and by midcentury the proportion was still grossly unequal at approximately six to one.

Even in New England, where the immigration of entire families was more common, there were three men to every two women in the middle of the seventeenth century (a ratio reached in Virginia only in 1700); and although the proportion of men to women tended to equalize over the course of the century, the traditional preponderance of women was by no means reached by 1700.

The Black Population. These data pertain to the free white population; there are no such precise figures for the growing black population. We know only that of the 250,000 inhabitants of British North America in 1700, perhaps 10 percent were blacks, and almost all of them were slaves. Most had arrived from Barbados or elsewhere in the West Indies. Only in 1674 did the Royal African Company bring the first contingent directly from Africa, but thereafter shipments of African slaves rose steadily. This increase paralleled a decline in the flow of white indentured servants from Britain, which was the result of changes in the English labor market and of the growing attractions of the nonplantation colonies. The decisive turning point—a landmark in American history—was in the mid-1680s, when black slaves for the first time outnumbered white servants in the southern labor force. In 1698 the Royal African Company lost its monopoly, and a flock of small operators entered the grim but profitable trade in human lives. This development opened the floodgates: 10,000 slaves arrived in the Chesapeake colonies in the years 1698–1709.

In seventeenth-century America, however, the number of blacks was still small. Partly for that reason, the blacks lived lives of extreme degradation on the southern plantations. Family life—any kind of dignified existence—was impossible for the slave population, whose members, predominantly male, had been torn from their homes and brutalized in the utterly alien world of the South. Disease devastated infants and childbearing women, and plantations were so small, isolated, and primitive that the only tasks to be done were the most degrading kinds of field labor. Often slaves lived not even in small huts or sheds, where they might have maintained a semblance of family life or familiar culture, but in laborers' barracks. A measure of relief would come only a generation later, when the American-born black population was settled long enough to develop a more balanced sex ratio. By that time too, plantation life had evolved to the point where the need for artisanship and household help allowed some of the slaves to escape the worst kind of field drudgery. Furthermore, by then stable communities of blacks had arisen that were large enough to nourish a distinctive subculture, blending African and American traditions—a subculture that would persist and flourish and in the end

By the late seventeenth century, Virginia's black population was not only increasing rapidly, but also being forced into chattel slavery. Harsh laws such as the following were enacted to control blacks' movements and to prevent their insubordination.

An Act for Preventing Insurrections Among Slaves (1680)

WHEREAS the frequent meeting of considerable numbers of negroe slaves under pretence of feasts and burialls is judged of dangerous consequence; for prevention whereof for the future, *Bee it enacted by the kings most excellent majestie by and with the consent of the generall assembly, and it is hereby enacted by the authority aforesaid*, that from and after the publication of this law, it shall not be lawfull for any negroe or other slave to carry or arme himselfe with any club, staffe, gunn, sword or any other weapon of defence or offence, nor to goe or depart from of his masters ground without a certificate from his master, mistris, or overseer, and such permission not to be granted but upon perticuler and necessary occasions; and every negroe or slave soe offending not haveing a certificate as aforesaid shalbe sent to the next constable, who is hereby enjoyned and required to give the said negroe twenty lashes on his bare back well layd on, and soe sent home to his said master, mistris or overseer. *And it is further enacted by the authority aforesaid* that if any negroe or other slave shall presume to lift up his hand in opposition against any christian, shall for every such offence, upon due proofe made thereof by the oath of the party before a magistrate, have and receive thirty lashes on his bare back well laid on. *And it is hereby further enacted by the authority aforesaid* that if any negroe or other slave shall absent himself from his masters service and lye hid and lurking in obscure places, comitting injuries to the inhabitants, and shall resist any person or persons that shalby any lawful authority be imployed to apprehend and take the said negroe, that then in case of such resistance, it shalbe lawfull for such person or persons to kill the said negroe or slave soe lying out and resisting, and that this law be once every six months published at the respective county courts and parish churches within this colony.

help to shape the national culture of the American people.

Economic Instability

In the American society that had emerged by 1700, economic life, social organization, and the practice of religion varied greatly from region to region and from colony to colony. But a common characteristic ran through all these major areas of life. There was a glaring difference between the realities of American life and the colonists' assumptions, ideals, and expectations. In studying each of these areas, one should start by isolating the colonists' assumptions and expectations—the ideals by which they would instinctively measure reality. Against this background the unique features of American life stand out most sharply. And in this context one can most clearly assess the impact of these features on the inner experiences of settlers seeking to re-create a familiar and controllable world.

Assumptions and Expectations.

The dominant view of economic life that the colonists brought with them was that of a stable system through which a more or less constant supply of goods and services flowed for the benefit of a population with relatively unchanging needs and desires. In such a system the object of individual effort was to achieve security and to help preserve the system's organization. If difficulties arose, they were assumed to be disturbances in the established relations among the producers, distributors, and consumers; and remedies were sought that would bring these elements back to their established and proper proportions. The object of primary concern was the consumer, not the producer—and a consumer of fixed, not growing, wants. It was assumed that controls were necessary to keep the economy in proper working order, especially to prevent greed or accidents from disturbing the system. And these controls did not necessarily have to be only those of the state. Lesser bodies that stood between the individual and the state, such as guilds and municipal governments, were assumed to be proper agencies of economic regulation.

These were the ordinary assumptions and ideal expectations of the colonists, who were still close to late medieval culture, still far removed from the modern world of dynamic economic systems in which an ever-rising production and the manipulation of consumption are essential to success. How well did the developing colonial economies conform to these traditional assumptions? Both the northern and the southern colonial economies violated these expectations on every point. Because expectations were violated, a sense of jarring disorder arose, and it prevailed until the American economic system became established and familiar—and until Americans learned to accommodate themselves to the instability that lay at the heart of this new system.

New England's Economy.

In New England there had originally been little desire to create a commercial system that would link the Bay Colony's small port towns to an intricate network of Atlantic commerce and involve the Puritans in the greater world they had left behind. The original goal had been economic self-sufficiency: the Puritans had expected that the "Bible Commonwealth" would have the best chance of remaining free of corruption and contamination by being self-sufficient. But by the late 1650s circumstances had led the Puritans to create the uniquely complex economic system, closely involved with Atlantic commerce, that would continue essentially unchanged until the American Revolution.

Once the original settlers had exhausted their capital, their unsuccessful efforts to maintain the Bay Colony's economic independence took two main forms. First, Puritan entrepreneurs, with the active support of the colony's government, sought to produce locally the supplies that were needed by the colonists. The manufacture of iron goods and cloth was the key. An elaborate scheme that was launched by John Winthrop, Jr., the governor's son, resulted in the establishment of a complete ironworks at Saugus, Massachusetts. The project involved tremendous efforts by a few devoted entrepreneurs, the investment of more than £12,000 by English businessmen, and the General Court's gifts of land, tax exemption, and a monopoly of the local markets. But the Saugus Works flourished only briefly and then collapsed into bankruptcy, the victim of a destructive squeeze between inescapably high costs and low income.

The colony's effort to establish a local cloth industry was similarly ineffective. A Massachusetts law of 1656 hopefully but quite unrealistically ordered all idle persons to busy themselves with spinning and weaving; and it assessed every family an amount of cloth in proportion to the number of available "spinners" in the household. But there were no "idle hands" in the labor-short Bay Colony. Every available "hand" could find more than enough employment in the fields surrounding the newly established towns. There was no effective response to the government's demands and appeals.

But if neither of the two basic industrial manufactures—iron goods and cloth—could be locally produced, some kind of self-sufficiency might yet be achieved through the discovery of a small, lightweight, and highly valuable commodity that might be

SAUGUS IRONWORKS
In this restoration of the works as they existed in 1650, the
forge is at the left, the rolling and slitting mill at the right.

exchanged directly in England for the needed goods.
For a few years in New England's early economic history, it seemed as though this sort of commodity
would be the ultimate solution. The settlers found
a rich supply of fur-bearing animals in the coastal
region and just beyond, and they began a quick exploitation of this highly profitable resource. The easily
available beavers, otters, and raccoons were taken by
the hundreds, and their pelts were shipped back to
England in direct exchange for manufactured goods.
But furs proved to be a limited resource. The animals
reproduced themselves far more slowly than they
were killed, and by the 1650s trappers had exhausted
the supply in the immediate coastal region. The New
Englanders then pressed westward to the Hudson but
were blocked by the Dutch from contact with fur
sources in the Great Lakes region and what is today
northern New York. Some furs continued to flow into
Boston from trading posts on the Maine coast and on
the upper Connecticut River; but after a decade of
wonderful promise, the idea of basing New England's
economy on the fur trade faded.

After this failure to create economic independence
or to establish a direct exchange with England, a generation of small merchants in the Bay Colony worked
out a system of exchanges throughout the Atlantic
world that would produce the needed imports of manufactured goods. As New England's population multiplied, foodstuffs, fish, and timber products grew increasingly available, and the commercial possibilities
they created became clear. These products could not
be sold in England, which itself produced them, but in
Catholic Europe—France, Spain, and the "Wine
Islands" of Madeira, the Azores, and the Canaries.
These markets could use all the fish that could be sent;
and the West Indies could absorb not only fish and
other food supplies needed to feed the labor force, but
also building timber, and horses to help work the
sugar mills. From the West Indies in turn, sugar products could be obtained for sale elsewhere in America
and in the English markets; and from Madeira, the
Azores, and the Canary Islands, wine could be pro-
cured for sale in the Atlantic ports. And other contacts
could be made. Tobacco could be picked up in the
Chesapeake, fish in Newfoundland, and various agricultural products in New York and later in Pennsylvania. An intricate circuit of exchanges could be
created—horses and fish for sugar, and sugar for bills

certainty and inescapable risks. All factors combined to make this commercial world dynamic and unpredictable.

In the first place, the local production of salable commodities was unreliable and irregular. Not only were there ordinary crop failures, but on the backcountry farms that were just coming under cultivation, production was unreliable. Even less reliable were the West Indian and Atlantic island markets, which might easily be glutted by a few shipments and from which it was impossible to obtain reliable market information before cargoes were sent. Further, this commerce was managed not by a few big firms whose decisions and agreements might stabilize the system, but by many small and highly competitive merchants. Finally, it was virtually impossible for any of these small merchant entrepreneurs to specialize, if only because a chronic money shortage made it necessary for them to pay for goods by bartering other goods. Thus every merchant had to be prepared to sell—or barter—almost any commodity at any time in any market he could find.

As a result of these conditions, it was nearly impossible to match available goods to available markets. Between the initial shipment of goods and their arrival at an ultimate destination, the entire commercial picture could change. Merchants operated largely in the dark and were victims of sudden gluts, unpredictable shortages, and vicious price fluctuations. Trade patterns did not follow any fixed geometrical form. There was no rigid "triangular" trade in the seventeenth century or later. There were only constantly shifting polygons that formed and re-formed as merchants undertook what were in effect peddling voyages up and down the North American coast and in the Caribbean and Atlantic commercial lanes.

Overseas trade proved to be a highly competitive, risky business in which success was the result of speculative venturing, intelligent risk taking, and driving entrepreneurship. The principle of success was not the completion of safe, carefully planned exchanges, but the almost limitless accumulation of exchanges of all sorts of commodities in a great variety of markets. It was a dynamic system that was propelled by powerfully expansive forces.

For more than a century this commercial system provided the northern colonies with essential goods and helped produce the material basis for a flourishing provincial culture. And from this system important social consequences flowed. In this commercial world there could be no hard and clear definition of a merchant "class." The situation encouraged the participation of newcomers, starting with very little—men who would have been rejected as interlopers in English commercial towns. There were no effective institutional barriers that might confine the group.

Library of Congress

COD FISHING ON THE GRAND BANKS AND THE NORTH AMERICAN SHORE

This French print of 1705 shows all stages of the fishing industry, from catching the fish (C) to gutting and scaling (F,G) and drying and packing (V,Q). Fish at the upper left are being carted away for salting (L), and the press at lower left (R) is extracting oil from the cod livers, the waste draining into the tub (S), the oil into the barrel (T).

of exchange,* wine, tobacco, or locally produced goods.

These exchanges might go on for months or even years before they reached their conclusion—the establishment of credits with some merchant in a leading British port. These credits would finance the purchase of manufactured goods to be imported for profitable sale in the colonies. The profits would in turn make possible bigger shipments in the next cycle, and perhaps investment in shipbuilding as well.

So the commercial system evolved in New England, to be re-created with variations in all the northern colonies. Each colony's system was distinctive, but all were interlocked and had common characteristics. These flows of commodities were not stable and easily controllable. They were highly unstable, driven by un-

---

*A bill of exchange is an order written by a merchant, authorizing the bearer to receive payment from an associated merchant.

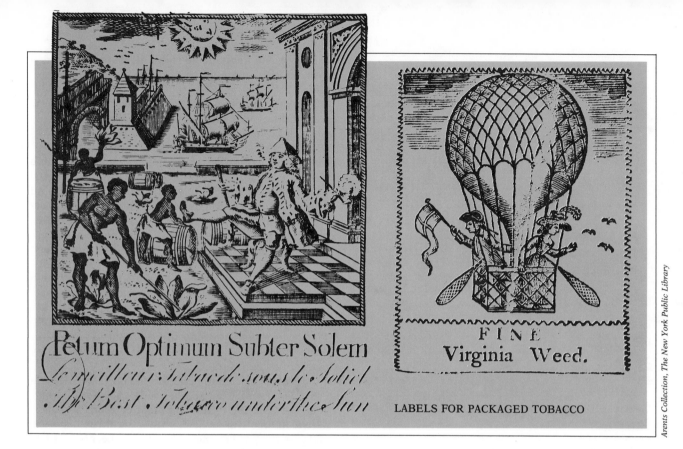

Petum Optimum Subter Solem

Le meilleur tabac sous le Soleil

The Best Tobacco under the Sun

FINE
Virginia Weed.

LABELS FOR PACKAGED TOBACCO

Neither guilds nor municipal corporations developed to restrict the merchant community or to regulate its activities. Anyone's contribution to the struggling commercial economy was valuable, and the government intervened only to stimulate innovation, not to limit it. A dynamic, unstable, unpredictable, yet successful commercial system produced a fluid merchant group, continually recruiting newcomers from among successful tradesmen and farmers, and seeking security and wealth in a system whose essence was risk.

The Southern Economy. The economic system that developed in the Chesapeake region was no less risky, competitive, and unstable. It centered on the production and marketing of a single staple crop, tobacco. The details are of course altogether different from those of the northern commercial system, but here too success was not won by sharing in regular production and a stable process of distribution. Rather, to be successful one had to contend with runaway cycles of production and a lurching, unpredictable distribution system. And in the South as in the North, a dynamic economy produced uncontrollable social consequences.

Originally there had been little enthusiasm for producing tobacco, which in the early seventeenth century was considered harmful to health and was associated with general immorality. King James I of England in 1604 wrote a pamphlet condemning smoking, entitled *A Counterblaste to Tobacco*, and during his reign tobacco pipes were used as door signs of brothels. But then as now, however harmful it was to health, tobacco sold—and it sold extremely well in England, originally as an expensive import from Spain. Once Americans began to sell tobacco in England, they worked hard to exploit the market, and they quickly flooded it. By the late 1630s the price of tobacco had dropped sharply, to a point less than the cost of production. There was a mild recovery of prices in the early 1640s, but prices collapsed again in the 1660s as production rose even further in the Chesapeake colonies. By the end of the century, prices were still low, and a pattern of recoveries and collapses had emerged that would persist throughout the colonial period.

The low prices and the uncontrollable cycles were symptoms of deep problems in the tobacco economy. The primary problem was overproduction. By the end of the 1630s—little more than a decade after the first marketable crop had reached England—the Chesapeake colonies were producing 1.5 million pounds of tobacco a year. By 1700 the figure had risen to about 38 million pounds annually. In addition, the Chesapeake industry suffered from serious competition. Spain continued to export the best-quality crop,

which commanded the highest prices, and the Caribbean islands also shipped sizable amounts. There were competitors too in England itself: tobacco was a well-established crop in the county of Gloucestershire. To compound the troubles further, as production rose American tobacco deteriorated in quality, and the middlemen assumed that it would sell at the lowest prices. Perhaps even more important were the technical difficulties of marketing this product of scattered Chesapeake farms.

The tobacco specialists who appeared quickly within the London merchant community worked out a marketing procedure that survived for a century. In this "consignment" system the English merchants acted primarily as selling agents. The Maryland and Virginia tobacco planters sent their crops to these merchants, usually on the merchants' vessels, for sale through them in the English and European markets. The English merchants lent money to the tobacco farmers to cover all the necessary charges—freight, fees, taxes, storage, and so on. They repaid themselves, with profit, when the crop was sold. In addition, they provided goods to the planters that they charged against the eventual tobacco sales, and so became the planters' bankers and creditors as well as their merchandisers. There was a rough efficiency in this system, but it victimized the tobacco planters by involving them in endless debt cycles. Any given crop was in effect mortgaged long before it was sold. Further, the planters had no control whatever over the sale of their crops; they had no choice but to rely on the merchants' goodwill. Finally, the system made it impossible ever to adjust production to demand. Often two years would go by between shipment and news of eventual sale, by which time several new crops would have been produced and shipped. The net result of the system was constant debts and an unmanageable rigidity in the economic process that governed the planters' lives.

As if overproduction, keen competition, deteriorating quality, and a rigid marketing system were not enough, there was the all-important problem of breaking into the markets of continental Europe. England could absorb relatively little of the enormous production of the Chesapeake region. Of the approximately 38 million pounds of tobacco exported to England in 1700, 25 million pounds were reexported to the continent. Thus these ultimate European markets were crucial to the prosperity of the American tobacco farmers.

At first the continental countries banned American tobacco altogether. Later they imposed high duties, and finally they established government-controlled or government-owned-and-operated monopolies of imports. These monopolies determined how much tobacco would be imported, what grades would be accepted, and what prices would be charged. As this system matured and the political complexities of tobacco marketing in Europe multiplied, Dutch middlemen became increasingly important in sending the commodity to the ultimate European markets. And so still another burden was added to the already complicated trade.

These were the problems that developed in the seventeenth century as the southern economy took shape. Throughout the century strong efforts were made to overcome them, with only partial success. The English government taxed Spanish tobacco out of the English markets and eliminated tobacco raising in Gloucestershire. At the same time, the West Indian producers withdrew from the increasingly competitive tobacco business. But Dutch shippers were shrewd competitors, and until the end of the seventeenth century they remained effective participants in the shipping trade.* And neither the English government nor the colonial governments could force individual American tobacco growers to limit their production. Quite the contrary. Most planters were convinced that the more they produced, the greater would be their income. Consequently production continued to expand, and so too did the area of land under cultivation.

The social consequences of this risky and unstable economy were far-reaching. The area of settlement was continually extended without regard for the Indians, who were driven back behind ever-expanding frontiers. As the planters pressed deeper into the interior in search of fresh lands, they forced even the friendly Indians into hostility. There were frontier

*Dutch competition ended because of the enforcement of England's navigation acts; for the navigation acts, see chapter 4, p. 87.

skirmishes long before the full-scale race war broke out that touched off Bacon's Rebellion in 1676.*

Further, the tobacco economy generated a desperate need for a large labor force. Hired or indentured servants were never available in sufficient numbers, and as a result the tobacco farms remained relatively small (an average of 250 acres). Slavery was an obvious solution to the labor problem, even if its capital costs were greater than those of a free-labor system. By the end of the seventeenth century, it was clear that the demands of the tobacco economy were constantly enlarging the slave labor force and thereby worsening one of the greatest evils of American life.

Finally, the tobacco economy eliminated the possibility that an urban society would develop south of Pennsylvania. The way in which the tobacco trade was organized prevented local merchants from developing into independent entrepreneurs, because the commercial processes were provided for in England. As a consequence the secondary activities (shipbuilding, service trades, brokerage, and shopkeeping) that ordinarily develop around "entrepreneurial headquarters" were frustrated from the start. On the eve of the American Revolution, Williamsburg, Virginia, had a total population of only 2,000; and even that small population was largely the result of the Virginia colonial government's residence in the town. Baltimore and Norfolk, each with a population of 6,000, developed not in the heart of the tobacco country, but at the borders of more varied economies.

*For Bacon's Rebellion, see chapter 4, pp. 98–99.

Social Instability

No aspect of community life came under more intense pressure than did social organization. The mentality of the generation that settled in America in the years before 1660 was still close to that of late-sixteenth-century Englishmen of Queen Elizabeth I's time. Both the Elizabethans and their colonizing descendants assumed that society was not a miscellaneous collection of people who were pursuing their separate goals and relating to each other haphazardly. Rather, Elizabethans and the first American settlers thought of society as a disciplined organism, a fabric closely "knit together," as they liked to say. The overall character of society, they thought, was more important than any of the separate parts that composed it. Specifically, they assumed that society would display at least three essential characteristics.

First, they expected that the parts of a community would complement each other and fit together harmoniously to compose the "commonwealth" as a whole. Second, they believed that the structure of society would be essentially hierarchical—that is, organized into distinct levels of inferiority and superiority. These levels did not reflect what we today call "class," but rather status and dignity—characteristics that were related to occupation and wealth but not defined by them. Third, they assumed that the hierarchy of society was a unified structure in which people of superior status in one aspect of life would be superior in all other aspects as well. Thus the rich would be politically powerful, well educated, and

NEW ENGLAND HOUSES OF THE SEVENTEENTH CENTURY

Near left, the Ironmaster's House, Saugus, built in the 1630s and enlarged twenty years later, is an exceptionally imposing residence for the period. The ordinary workers at Saugus lived in thatch-roofed cottages even simpler than the houses in Plymouth (p. 37). Far left, the Paul Revere house in Boston, 1680. The overhanging second story and heavily leaded casement windows are typical of the substantial artisans' houses of the time.

dignified. Leadership in public and private affairs would belong to the highborn, the firstborn—the natural leaders, who had the social superiority that was necessary to rule.

Elizabethans believed that these were the characteristics of all well-organized societies, and those who came to America had no intention of changing or rejecting such fundamental notions. But in fact the world that emerged in mainland North America did not conform to these ideals. To be sure, there was no total breakdown, once the horrors of the "starving times" were overcome. There was no instant transformation into a different kind of life. But from the first years of settlement, there were sharp stresses and strains that made social life in the colonies tense, strange, and difficult.

The sources of these problems were obvious. The colonists were well aware that the political and economic leadership of the communities was being taken over by people who, although capable of dealing with the harsh circumstances of life in America, lacked the traditional social qualities of command. These qualities included a sense of natural superiority, habitual dignity, and personal authority. As a result, the respect due to the leading figures was not automatically forthcoming. Political and economic leaders were vulnerable to criticism and were challenged in ways their social superiors would not have been.

Puritanism and Social Order.

In New England this general problem was compounded in a special way. Within the Puritans' distinctive status system, purity of religion,

piety, and upright behavior were decisive factors in establishing differences among individuals. At the same time, every effort was made to keep alive the traditional social structure. For example, it was agreed that in the newly established townships, persons of wealth, position, and professional training should receive the larger allotments of land. Even so vague a distinction as "ability" was materially rewarded. But the conflict with religious values could not be avoided.

At least the problem was clearly understood. One of the Puritans' most influential English leaders, Lord Say and Sele, considered joining the Great Migration in 1636; but he paused. Was it not true, he wrote the Reverend John Cotton in Boston, that men could vote in Massachusetts simply by being accepted into the church, no matter what their social status? If so, what certainty was there that people like himself would be able to play their proper roles? Cotton tried to reassure him. Everyone knew that "monarchy and aristocracy are both of them clearly approved and directed in scripture" and that God never considered democracy "a fit government either for church or commonwealth." So His Lordship need have no fear of finding New England a world turned upside down. Still, Cotton had to admit, the Puritans *were* committed to the service of the Lord: in the end religious considerations would and *should* prevail. For is it not better, he asked, "that the commonwealth be fashioned to the setting forth of God's house, which is his church, than to accommodate the church frame to the civil state?" The noble lord read the message correctly

JOHN FREAKE AND HIS WIFE ELIZABETH AND CHILD, 1674
Freake was one of the successful merchants who arrived in Boston well after the original Puritan migration and brought with him a "corrupting" luxuriance of style. His buttons are silver, his collar fine lace, his sleeves puffed muslin, and his gold brooch studded with precious stones. His wife's embroidered petticoat is carefully revealed.

and stayed home. The Bay Colony's turmoil in the founding years continued to reflect the strange confusion and the mingling of religious and social distinctions.

Social Structure and Family Life.

Everywhere in the colonies there were difficulties and confusions in maintaining a traditional social order in the raw wilderness world. On the farms in the northern, middle, and southern colonies alike, it was physically impossible to maintain the expected differences in styles of life—differences not merely between masters and servants who labored side by side, but between field workers on the one hand and preachers, teachers, and doctors on the other. Laboring together day after day, masters and servants found their lifestyles approaching each other until the differences rested only on a legal formality, a scrap of paper that established the servants' dependency. Because there was little material difference in the status of master and servant, the force of this formal difference grew weaker with time. There were few luxuries anywhere, and nowhere was there the material basis for leisure. The few people with professional training lived far more primitive lives than their education and occupational role would traditionally have assured them.

The problems of maintaining traditional status differentiation were especially dramatic in the towns.

Throughout the seventeenth century there were constant complaints that the free workers—the handicraftsmen, shipwrights, carpenters, shoemakers, and tailors—had lost all respect for traditional roles and social distinctions. It was commonly said that they demanded astronomical wages and that their pretense of social superiority was unbearable. They flaunted their prosperity outrageously and aped their superiors in ways that offended all sense of decency and social order. By eliminating the causes of this alleged misbehavior or by limiting its effects, the authorities made every effort to contain the social disorder that the free workers were creating. Occasionally, when the problem became acute, the colonial assemblies voted to keep wages down in order to restrict the workers' ambitions and to protect the public against their apparent greed. But such laws could not be enforced. The workers' services were indispensable; people would pay almost any price they demanded. And the workers' arguments were convincing too: costs, they said, were rising; they had expenses to meet. Let prices be fixed if wages were. But price fixing was as futile as wage fixing, and what a later generation would call "escalator clauses" were tried with only temporary effect on the demands and behavior of the free, self-employed workers.

By 1660 the effort to eliminate the source of the workers' extravagance had clearly failed. The colonial assemblies resorted to the idea of disciplining behavior itself—trying to confine dress and social interaction to appropriate forms of decency. Laws restricted the wearing of fine clothing, limited display, and lectured the supposedly disordered population on the confusion of the times. A law to this effect that was passed in the Massachusetts Bay Colony in 1651 is perhaps the most eloquent testimony of the age to the founders' widespread sense of disarray. The General Court declared its

utter detestation and dislike, that men or women of mean [low] condition should take upon them the garb of gentlemen, by wearing gold or silver lace, or buttons, or points at their knees, or to walk in great boots, or women of the same rank to wear silk or tiffany hoods or scarves which, though allowable to persons of greater estates or more liberal education, yet we cannot but judge it intolerable in persons of such like [low] condition.

The times were deeply disordered, the legislature declared, and therefore it ordered

that no person within this jurisdiction, . . . whose visible estates shall not exceed the true and indifferent value of £200 shall wear any gold or silver lace, or gold and silver buttons, or any bone lace above 2 shillings per yard, or silk hoods or scarves, upon the penalty of 10 shillings for every such offense.

And then, in a devilishly clever provision, the General Court decreed that if the town selectmen found anyone they judged "to exceed their ranks and abilities in the costliness or fashion of their apparel," they were to increase the offender's tax rate to the level of wealth he or she pretended to. But the General Court added—in an afterthought that brilliantly illuminates the unstable social landscape—that the law would *not* apply to any of the colony's magistrates or their families, to any regular military officers or soldiers on active duty, or to anyone else "*whose education and employment have been above the ordinary degree, or whose estates have been considerable, though now decayed.*"

"*Though now decayed*"—the phrase echoes an extreme sense of disordered change, of a decline of standards. And in no aspect of life was this more profoundly felt than in the family. Here, it was thought, the erosion and disorder went deepest. Puritan lawmakers repeatedly denounced the loosening of family ties and the defiance of authority in this most intimate and fundamental of all social units. Repeatedly they commanded parents to do their duty to their children and to themselves, and they ordered children to obey their parents and fulfill their family obligations. The laws grew harsher as the years went by. In New Hamp-

shire, Massachusetts, and Connecticut, laws were passed that revived the biblical provision that children who struck or cursed their parents were to be put to death. (These laws were invoked at least once, although they were never carried out.) In Massachusetts, church members called tithingmen were made responsible for the good behavior of groups of ten families. A meeting of church leaders in 1679 blamed the evils of the time on "defects of family government" and ordered the tithingmen to increase their efforts to reinforce the failing discipline of weak-willed parents.

Of course, family life was not really being destroyed. On the surface, at least, the institution of the family was little weaker at the end of the century than it had been at the start. But something *had* happened. There *were* problems—and those problems, if properly understood, help explain the outcries, the sense of disarray, and the efforts to remedy what many felt to be a disastrous decline in the traditional good order of family life.

To understand these problems, it is necessary to note that in the seventeenth century, families were considered to be the basic model of all social order. People believed that at this primary level all order began, and all patterns of inferiority and superiority took shape. The political commonwealth was only an enlargement of the family. Rulers were conceived of as patriarchs whose dominance as heads of the commonwealth was justified by God, the father of all. These ideas were a cliché of the age, but—like most clichés that pass unchallenged—they were essentially realistic. For most Englishmen experienced a larger, more highly structured, more complex, and more disciplined family unit than now exists in the Western world. The reason is not that the nuclear family—parents and children—was significantly larger than it is today. In seventeenth-century England most completed families contained only two or three children, although many more were born and died young. The sense of complexity, structure, and discipline grew from the fact that the word *family* meant or implied the *household*—all those who lived together under one roof. Almost all Englishmen at some time in their lives had experienced the household-family as a complex and disciplined institution. For servants were traditionally considered part of this artificially extended family, and servitude was remarkably widespread. About a third of all English families had servants. At any one time, between 10 percent and 15 percent of the entire English population were serving in someone else's household—and serving not merely as day workers who exchanged limited services for wages, but as family members who were committed to total employment in exchange for maintenance, protection, and to some extent education. In addition, free children of other families circulated as guests, often for long peri-

Puritan John Winthrop kept a journal, recording daily events and reflections on the state of his soul. Winthrop's high position and keen intelligence have made his *Journal* and his correspondence with his wife important historical sources. Here he reveals a characteristic seventeenth-century attitude toward women.

John Winthrop Defines a Woman's Place (1645)

MR. Hopkins, the governor of Hartford upon Connecticut, came to Boston, and brought his wife with him, (a godly young woman, and of special parts,) who was fallen into a sad infirmity, the loss of her understanding and reason, which had been growing upon her divers years, by occasion of her giving herself wholly to reading and writ-ing, and had written many books. Her husband, being very loving and tender of her, was loath to grieve her; but he saw his error, when it was too late. For if she had attended her household affairs, and such things as belong to women, and not gone out of her way and calling to meddle in such things as are proper for men, whose minds are stronger, etc., she had kept her wits, and might have improved them usefully and honorably in the place God had set her. He brought her to Boston, and left her with her brother, one Mr. Yale, a merchant, to try what means might be had here for her. But no help could be had.

ods, in more affluent households or even in households of equivalent social position. As a result, at least 45 percent of all English people lived in households of six or more members. Consequently most people, at least in their youth, had experienced families as complex, and to some extent patriarchal, units.

In traditional settings material circumstances reinforced and helped preserve these household-families. Young people found it difficult to break away and establish new independent households. For in such a predominantly agricultural world, economic independence was made possible largely by the purchase or long-term lease of plots of farmland. It was extremely difficult to make such transactions in the absence of available public land. As a result, many servants had to remain in service beyond the time of their contractual obligations. Marriages were delayed because married couples were expected to live in their own establishments, not within other households. Family discipline developed naturally and remained a familiar, accepted fact of life.

In contrast, in the colonies of seventeenth-century America, these material reinforcements of traditional family life were either greatly weakened or eliminated. Land was far more freely available than in England, and therefore the establishment of an independent household was relatively easy economically, although it involved the difficult physical work of clearing a new farm. Under these circumstances, it is remarkable not that the average age of first marriage fell, but that it did not fall even lower and faster than it did, and that there was not more pressure against traditional family organization than in fact there was.

But the availability of land was only one of the factors that weakened the reinforcements of traditional family life in the colonies. The acute and continuing labor shortage, which shifted the dependency relations within the family and household, meant that parents and masters depended on their children and servants as never before. They needed them, sometimes desperately, to provide critically necessary labor. In this sense the parents became dependents—but not only in this sense. For the young learned more rapidly than their seniors to cope with the unfamiliar environment. The young adapted to change more easily, and in the end they inevitably became their elders' lifelines to the world. In effect they became their parents' teachers, despite the unquestioned and continuing assumption of parental superiority.

In the Chesapeake region through most of the seventeenth century, the fearful death rate greatly increased the common disorder of family life. Here only half the children born would live to age twenty, and two out of three marriages were broken by the premature death of one of the partners (more often the husband). Family and household life was therefore chaotic. Widows, left with several children in a rough frontier society where there were many more men than women, remarried quickly, if only for survival. Often their husbands brought children from earlier marriages, and households were crowded with half-siblings and stepchildren. Wives acquired greater importance and authority than was customary for the age. And there were orphan children everywhere.

The consequences of the tensions and of the widespread disarray ran deep. Gradually the law responded to these altered circumstances. Primogeniture—the legal requirement that real estate be inherited only by the eldest son so that the family property would remain intact—was commonly ignored where land was plentiful. The usual practice was to divide property among the members of a family, perhaps with double portions for the wife and the eldest son. Orphan courts appeared in the South to protect children who were otherwise uncared for. And the law became more responsive to the interests of women. In Massachusetts, laws were passed that prohibited a husband from striking his wife—"unless it be in his own defense." North and south, women acquired new rights to own, administer, and legally protect property; to conduct business; and to represent themselves in court. And the courts treated them more fairly in divorce proceedings. In general, women enjoyed a higher social status in seventeenth-century America than they did in England, where the traditionally severe subordination of females, which had been inherited from the medieval past, continued largely unchanged.

The legal position of indentured servants also improved. In some places the severity of punishment was limited by law; in others, working conditions were improved. In all the colonies every effort was made to use the law to keep servants at work despite the liberating forces that surrounded them. A case is recorded in which a servant ran away after being punished for attempting to rape his master's ten-year-old daughter—the suit was filed not to punish the culprit, but to get him back and to force him to complete his term of service! Everywhere the conditions of contractual obligations grew lighter as the ease of transition to personal freedom was recognized.

Social order was not destroyed in the seventeenth-century colonies, nor was the world transformed. But on this western fringe of European civilization, society had acquired new instabilities, along with new freedoms for traditionally subordinated elements in the nonslave population. In calmer years and in more settled circumstances, some of these changes would fade back into more traditional forms, but most would become part of a permanently altered way of life.

Religion

Religion inevitably played a major role in the larger social changes in early America, for the colonists' culture was basically Christian. The churches were still the preeminent cultural institutions, as well as vital social agencies. Everywhere in Western civilization, the seventeenth century was a period of intense religious controversy as individuals and whole nations struggled savagely over differences in religious opinion. Yet a few basic ideas were shared by almost all religious groups—presumptions that illuminate the history of religion in early America particularly well.

Except for the most extreme radicals, Christians generally assumed that there was one true religion and that differences of belief should not be encouraged. Seventeenth-century Christians disagreed over what doctrines were orthodox, but most assumed that *some* doctrines were absolutely right and others wrong. Efforts to eliminate or at least strongly discourage heresy and to extend orthodoxy were therefore accepted as legitimate. Most Christians also thought that religion was not simply a spiritual matter or something of concern only to the church. They believed that governments should have a major responsibility for supervising religion and enforcing correct belief. Finally, when migration to the New World began, most people assumed that colonial churches would be organized along familiar European lines and would fit into some larger pattern of religious institutions. No one expected that the churches established in distant North America would become institutions with special characteristics.

The history of religion in the first two or three generations of colonial America can be seen as the story of the violation of these assumptions, and of the struggle to retain them in the face of adversity. Of course, Christianity survived in more or less familiar outward form. However, significant changes occurred —not because the leaders (except in New England) wanted change, but because they had to adapt to difficult circumstances. The churches did not fully accept and incorporate these changes until the eighteenth century. But the seeds of what later grew into America's distinctive pattern of religious denominations were planted in the seventeenth century.

The Anglican Church in Virginia.

The way in which circumstances shaped the development of Christianity in America is best illustrated by the history of the Church of England, the Anglican church, in Virginia. Here the sense of orthodoxy was strong, and here no doctrinal conflicts or pressures for reform existed. In Virginia stronger attempts were made to re-create the traditional English church institutions than in any other colony, and here hopes of maintaining these traditions met with particularly severe disappointment.

The Virginia Company—as well as the English government, when it took over direct control of Virginia in 1624—assumed that the settlers would simply reproduce the Church of England in its established form in the colony. But there were serious problems from the start, most of which grew out of the difficulty of putting the new church institutions on a workable financial foundation. In England churches were usually supported by gifts of income-producing property donated by patrons. In Virginia the company (and later the English government) served as patron to the newly created parishes. In 1618 the company set aside as church land one hundred acres (which the English government later increased to two hundred acres) in each of the "boroughs" into which Virginia was divided.* Tenants were to be settled on this land, and the rent they paid was to support a minister and maintain the local church. However, every free man in Virginia wanted to own property, not to rent it, and thus it proved difficult to find tenants. Yet without someone to rent the land, it was worthless. Two alternative means of supporting the church remained. First, the ministers themselves could become almost full-time, self-supporting farmers on the church land, and produce the expected income. But this prospect discouraged the recruitment of well-trained clergy: no self-respecting minister in England had to live in such a manner. The second alternative was to put the financial support of Virginia's ministers on a new basis—taxation. The Virginia Company anticipated this solution when it ordered parish members to supplement whatever income the church land produced until a sum of £200 a year was available to pay the minister and maintain the church. Supplements of this kind quickly became common, and then universal. It was soon standard practice for the governing body of the parish, the vestry, to vote an annual tax for support of the church.

Once taxation was made the financial basis of the

*For the boroughs, see chapter 2, p. 35.

church, the physical size of the parish became a major problem. Virginia was thinly populated. If the parish included as many people as was customary in England, its territory would be so large that proper ministrations would be impossible. On the other hand, if the parish area remained small, so that members could gather easily and the minister could keep in close touch with them, there would be too few members, and the cost per person of maintaining the church would be extremely high. In practice, because of Virginia's underdeveloped and struggling economy, parishes remained unworkably large. Furthermore, because of differences in population density and wealth, there were great variations in the support of the clergy.

The dilemma of how to finance the church was officially recognized by the end of the first generation of settlement in Virginia. In 1662 the colony's assembly tried to make all church salaries uniform at £80 a year. But this figure had to be translated into set amounts of tobacco, which served as a substitute for money in early Virginia. When the market value of tobacco fell, so did the real worth of the ministers' salaries. Because they were paid in tobacco, the ministers were in any case at the mercy of local variations in quality—and they were also dependent upon the goodwill of the parish members, who selected the tobacco they were to receive.

This simple but fundamental economic problem had extremely important consequences for the clergy and indeed for religion in general. By English standards almost all of Virginia's ministers were grossly underpaid, and they had to work under what Englishmen considered next-to-impossible conditions. Further, they were stripped of economic independence because of their reliance on annual gifts of the parish. Nor were their jobs secure. In England the patrons (or their descendants) who gave the parish church income-producing land also nominated ministers for lifetime appointments as rectors, and the bishops confirmed them in office. In Virginia the place of the patrons was taken by the vestries—self-perpetuating bodies that were made up of the leading members of the parish. The church officials in England instructed the vestries to present their nominees to the governor of Virginia, who in turn would formally appoint these candidates as ministers. But in most cases the vestries refused to nominate; only 10 percent of the Virginia clergy in the seventeenth century were ever formally appointed by the governor. The vestries gave as the reason for the scarcity of nominees the fact that available candidates were of such low quality that they did not deserve lifetime appointments.

Thus a vicious circle existed. The vestries named few candidates for permanent positions because they felt that the general quality of the clergy was too low

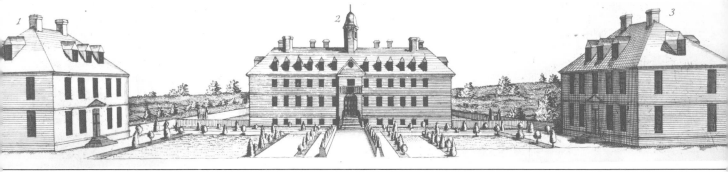

COLLEGE OF WILLIAM AND MARY, PICTURED IN THE 1730s
Founded in large part to educate Virginians for the Anglican ministry, it was built to the plans of Christopher Wren. The central building was erected by the end of the century but had to be rebuilt after a fire of 1705.

to justify the confidence and respect implicit in a nomination. But the vestries' refusal to nominate for permanent positions was one reason why well-qualified candidates were reluctant to settle in Virginia. Although there had been many excellent young clergymen in Virginia in the colony's early years, there were very few by the end of the seventeenth century. Recruitment seemed to come from the bottom of the barrel. The problem of course was noticed by the English church authorities, who sent over missionaries in an effort to remedy matters. Later, missionary work was undertaken by the Society for the Propagation of the Gospel in Foreign Parts, which was founded in England in 1701. A series of proposals to improve conditions resulted, including one that led to the chartering of the College of William and Mary in 1693, to provide a means of educating Virginians locally for the ministry. But it was extremely difficult to improve the situation. By 1724 the reputation of the clergy in Virginia had fallen so low that the following almost farcical proposals were included in a broad plan of reform that was submitted to the bishop of London, who had jurisdiction over the church in the American colonies:

And to prevent the scandals of bad life in the clergy, let it be enacted that whatsoever minister shall be found guilty of fornication, adultery, blasphemy, ridiculing of the Holy Scriptures, or maintaining . . . any doctrine contrary to the 39 Articles shall . . . lose his living [income] and be suspended from all exercise of the ministerial function for three years. . . . And because drunkenness is one of the most common crimes and yet hardest to be proved . . . let it be enacted that the following proof shall be taken for a sufficient proof of drunkenness, viz., first, let the signs of drunkenness be proved such as sitting an hour or longer in the company where they were a drinking strong drink and in the meantime drinking of healths

or otherwise taking his cups as they came around like the rest of the company; striking, challenging, threatening to fight, or laying aside any of his garments for that purpose; staggering, reeling, vomiting, incoherent, impertinent, obscene, or rude talking. Let the proof of these signs proceed so far till the judges conclude that the minister's behavior at such time was scandalous, indecent, and unbecoming the gravity of a minister.

The worsening quality of the clergy was one aspect of the general change taking place in the Church of England in Virginia. Another development, in the long run equally important, was the collapse of the church's hierarchical structure—that is, its chain of command, extending from the bishops down to the parish clergy—which was an essential aspect of the Church of England. This breakdown occurred because Virginia was so distant from the higher controls in England, and also because the vestries in Virginia had gained absolute power over the parishes. Officially the church in Virginia was part of the Church of England, which was governed by bishops and archbishops. But in practice the Virginia church was a congregational institution, with each parish responsible for its own affairs.

Furthermore, the practice of religion in Virginia was greatly simplified, even secularized to some extent. Since few ministers could reach all areas of their large parishes, ordinary church members, called lay readers, were appointed to fulfill certain ministerial duties. The general simplicity of life and the lack of funds meant that the church sacraments were administered without what the Church of England regarded as the proper ritual, minister's robes, and communion vessels. The dead were buried in private cemeteries more often than in parish burial grounds. Holy days were neglected, and marriages were performed in private residences without the participation of ministers.

Finally, the church in Virginia came to play a far less significant role as the regulator of community morals than did the Anglican church in England, which maintained a system of church courts. In Virginia the same people were often members of the vestry and the local civil court. In view of the weakness of the church, it seemed more reasonable for persons who were accused of moral offenses to be brought before the civil courts than before church courts. Vital statistics—the records of births, baptisms, marriages, and deaths—likewise came to be kept by the civil courts rather than by the weak parish organizations.

No one, of course, doubted that the Church of England had been established in Virginia, but it was a strange establishment indeed. Conditions had led the church as an institution toward what might be called nonseparating Congregationalism—the position adopted in New England—not as a matter of doctrine, but as a matter of social and institutional fact.

Toleration in Catholic Maryland.
Geographical, social, and economic conditions were similar in Maryland and Virginia, and Maryland's religious institutions would have been similar to Virginia's except for two basic facts. First, the government of Maryland was controlled by a Catholic proprietor who wanted the colony to be a place of refuge for English Catholics. Second, the colony would be successful only if it attracted an adequate number of settlers, but the great majority of the potential settlers of Maryland were Protestants. Thus the proprietor had to treat religious matters very carefully.

At first the proprietary family, the Calverts, gave the colony's governors instructions that, they thought, would satisfy both the Catholic and the Protestant settlers. They ordered government officials to give no offense to Protestants because of their religion. Catholicism was to be practiced as privately as possible, and all Christians were to be allowed to worship in any form they wished. But this vague, pragmatic liberalism satisfied neither side. The Jesuit priests who had accompanied Maryland's first Catholic settlers demanded that the colony be much more openly Catholic, and Protestant Marylanders rebelled against the colony's Catholic proprietor during the early years of the English Civil War of the 1640s. To stabilize the situation in the face of these conflicting pressures—as well as to protect Maryland's status as a chartered colony—in 1649 the Calverts issued their famous Act Concerning Religion.

Although this document was remarkably liberal for the seventeenth century, it did not provide for full religious freedom. In fact it began by ordering the death penalty for non-trinitarian Christians (those who denied that God was a Trinity of Father, Son, and Holy Spirit) who insisted on professing their religion in Maryland. But the Act Concerning Religion went on to say that in order to ensure public tranquility—and for that reason only—all Christians who accepted the Trinity were guaranteed the right to profess and practice their religion freely.

This document remained in effect for the rest of the seventeenth century. It offered no challenge to what most people of the era thought to be correct Christian doctrine. It contained no hint of the principle of the separation of church and state, or of freedom of conscience and worship as good in themselves —no hint of the soaring ideals of liberty of thought and conscience that would later inspire Thomas Jefferson's great Act for Establishing Religious Freedom. The Calverts' act kept toleration as narrow as possible. It offered religious freedom only to those groups that it was necessary to tolerate: Catholics, Anglicans, and moderate Protestant dissenters. Yet, although it was quite limited and pragmatic, the act represented a significant advance over the policies that were typically followed by European governments of the time. It also fitted in well with the decentralized kind of church organization that was developing in Maryland. For just as in Virginia, in Maryland the churches had to be supported by taxes—and so they came under the full control of local authorities, generally the vestries. This local control, as well as the official toleration of Catholics and of moderate Protestants, meant that a multi-denominational Christianity was emerging in Maryland, whose form was essentially congregational.

The Dutch Church in New York.
A decentralized church system emerged in an even more extreme form in New York—or, as the Dutch called it, New Netherland. Here, the original Dutch settlers assumed that the national church of the Netherlands, officially known as the Dutch Reformed Calvinist church, would be recreated in America and would be supervised by the church's ruling body in Amsterdam. But their expectations were not fulfilled. From the colony's earliest years its religious life was quite complex, and there were no effective controls from the home country. The policy of the Dutch West India Company, which controlled New Netherland, was to permit *private* worship of any kind, as long as the Dutch Reformed church was officially recognized and was supported by taxes paid by all the colony's residents. Besides Dutch Calvinists, Jews, and the members of many radical sects, New Netherland's population included Lutherans, who insisted on the right to *public* worship. The Lutherans' demands led to their severe persecution by the colony's governor, Peter Stuyvesant. But the challenge they raised continued to generate fierce arguments until after the English conquered

SYMBOLISM ON PURITAN GRAVESTONES
Folk art (see color section) was never absent from the colonies. In Puritan New England it took particularly imaginative form in the portrayal of death, sin, and salvation in gravestone carvings. In this stone panel of 1692, a naked imp of the underworld carries both Time's hourglass and Death's dart.

the Dutch colony. Then, in 1665, the qualified voters, called freeholders, of each community were ordered to choose a single Protestant denomination that would become the local established church. Once chosen, this church would be supported by general taxation, although members of other faiths could worship privately.

Under this "local option" plan adopted in 1665, the Dutch Reformed church remained dominant, of course, because most of the colonists were of Dutch background and sought to perpetuate their religious heritage and mode of worship. But in New York, as in Virginia and Maryland, settlements were widely scattered. It was extremely difficult to recruit qualified clergymen, and ministers found it impossible to keep in regular contact with all the members of their congregations. New York's solution was similar to Virginia's and Maryland's: ordinary members of the congregations presided when ministers could not be present to fulfill their duties. The outward quality of religious life declined drastically. Worse still, after they had conquered New York, the English regarded the Dutch Reformed church as a branch of an alien national church. How did this American branch relate to the home church body in the Netherlands? If the

Dutch settlers in New York fully acknowledged the supremacy of the Dutch Reformed church, they would in effect be challenging the supremacy of the English crown; if they did not make that challenge, they would not be entirely true to their own faith. This dilemma could not be resolved, but it might be endured if the issue was never pressed.

New England Puritanism. In view of these unexpected developments elsewhere in the colonies, the outward form of religion that was established in New England may not, perhaps, be considered unique. Everywhere in colonial America, the hierarchy of church organization had failed to take shape, ritual had become simplified, the church's role in dispensing the sacraments had been reduced, and members of the congregations shared the pulpits with ordained ministers. But in most colonies these adaptations had resulted in response to the conditions of life in America, not to doctrine or belief or intent. In New England, however, the same developments were based on religious doctrine and had been intended from the start.

The development of New England's decentralized church system was part of a general plan of religious reform that was pursued almost fanatically and fortified by a theological outlook that was constantly being refined by men of subtle mind and great intellectual energy. But Puritanism was not simply an intellectual system, and it did not satisfy the needs of theologians alone. It was a social movement as well as an intellectual movement, and in both New England and Old England it performed an important social function.

New England Puritanism was one specific offshoot of a broad movement in late-sixteenth-century England that challenged the religious conservatism of the Church of England under Elizabeth I. Those who eventually came to be known as Puritans felt that England's break with the Roman Catholic church in Henry VIII's time had not gone far enough. Puritan reformers and conservative Anglican churchmen did not disagree on central points of theology. Both sides believed in predestination—that is, the idea that human salvation depended not on an individual's efforts, but on the mysterious decisions of God alone. The differences between the Puritans and the conservatives of the Church of England concerned the nature and function of the church as an institution.

Debate over the nature of the church focused on how effective the church could be in assisting people in their search for salvation. The Anglican churchmen, like their Roman Catholic counterparts, believed that the church could help bridge the gap between the world of ordinary, physical humanity and that of men in a state of God's grace. The Church of England in-

Photos by Arthur B. Mazmanian from his book The Structure of Praise, © The Beacon Press

FIRST PARISH MEETING HOUSE, HINGHAM, MASS., 1681
This famous building, whose exterior is largely the work of the eighteenth century, retains much of the original seventeenth-century interior. Lacking models for the spacious but austere building they had in mind, and spurning all architectural embellishments, the ship carpenters hired for the occasion simply built a ship's keel in reverse to form the interior roof.

sisted that there was not a total and absolute difference between ordinary physical existence and true holiness, a difference bridgeable only by God's gift of spiritual rebirth. It maintained that qualified priests performing the church's rituals could assist in the great search for salvation. The Puritans disagreed. For them the gap between ordinary natural existence on the one hand, and holiness, or "grace," on the other, was absolute and total. This gap could not be closed by human efforts of any kind, but only by God, if he chose to enter into direct contact with an open, willing soul—a contact, the Puritans believed, that could be facilitated through study of the Bible, which contained God's actual words. The Puritans considered the church's institutions and rituals to be mere outward "works" that interfered with the central experience of religion. For them the essence of religion was an individual's struggle for contact with a mysterious God.

Puritans and conservative Anglicans also differed over the question of whether the members of God's church were "visible"—that is, whether those Christians who had been saved could be identified in this life. Orthodox Anglicans felt that it was impossible to tell truly which persons God had saved and which he had not. The church therefore existed for everyone, in the hope that it would help some achieve a better life and would be a natural home for those whom God had already chosen for salvation as his "elect." For Anglicans, therefore, the membership of the "visible" church (that is, the actual institutions of the church) should include the whole of society. People should be born into the church as a fact of life. The Puritans completely rejected this idea. They felt that it was possible—although difficult—to identify the elect by using various tests and signs. Therefore they believed that church membership could and should be limited to those who were saved: the church should be a "gathering of saints," a congregation of the visibly saved members. As far as possible, the visible church should be the same as "God's church" of the elect. Thus not everyone in society should be a church member.

These key issues defined the protest movement of the late sixteenth century that in the broadest sense was Puritanism. But Puritanism in this broadest sense includes a wide range of positions on the question of the church's relation to society. The Puritans who established the Bay Colony in Massachusetts believed with the others that church membership should be limited to the elect, but they also thought that the church (even though it excluded many people in the community) should control society as a whole and should create conditions favorable to the search for salvation. They believed that the visibly saved church members—the "saints"—must somehow be active and controlling in the affairs of those who had not been saved.*

Puritans in England and New England alike discussed endlessly how such a program could be put into effect. But in early-seventeenth-century England the Congregational Puritans were wholly engaged simply in the struggle to survive in the face of the hostility of the Anglican church. In Massachusetts and Connecticut, however, they were protected by charters giving them self-government, as well as by distance from England, and they therefore had the opportunity to put into practice their view of how the church should be organized. Believing very strongly that the "visible church" must consist only of God's elect, they concentrated their attention on the process of becoming full church members. In England only deeply committed and utterly sincere people were willing to run the risks of belonging to the persecuted Congregationalist Puritan groups. In New England, however, the situation was completely different. Here, the Congregationalist leaders held all the powers; they *were* the government, and the communities' available resources and power were at their disposal. Where the Congregational church was fully established and where social rewards were attached to membership in the church, entry into full church membership became an important issue for the society. Therefore the church leaders had to devise procedures that allowed everyone to apply for membership but that permitted only those persons to join who demonstrated their superior spirituality.

Candidates for membership in the New England churches were required to make a public "profession"—that is, to give an account before the entire congregation of how God had saved them, and in that way to justify their membership in the church. They were then publicly interrogated by ministers and experienced members of the congregation. Often this formal questioning was sophisticated and intense: the truthfulness of a candidate's public statement could be challenged, and he had to respond to all challenges. If his "profession" and defense were successful, church membership was conferred through a formal ritual of acceptance.

Joining the church was thus no casual matter. Gaining entrance to the church was the central event in the religious life of the Puritan communities. The later history of the church in New England would be shaped by what happened to these procedures.*

Besides defining the process of joining the church, the other major problem that faced the New England Puritan community was that of justifying the rule of the "saints" to those people who were not church members. The *intellectual* justification of the rule of the elect was never in doubt. A central Puritan idea was the doctrine of the "covenant"—the agreement between God and the saved. According to this doctrine, the saved were obliged to do what they could to help those who were not saved to attain salvation—to expose ordinary people to the truth contained in the Bible, to remove obstacles to their salvation, and to urge them to seek salvation. But intellectual justifications for an elite minority's rule over a majority are never enough to maintain control over an entire society for any extended period of time. Yet there is every reason to believe that the mass of the settlers, most of whom were not church members, accepted—indeed, welcomed—the rule of the saints.**

To understand in psychological and sociological terms the reasons for the Puritans' success, it is necessary to know what kinds of people joined the Great Migration. The mass of the settlers were farmers and artisans who were drawn from two regions of England, East Anglia and the West Country. These regions were the chief centers not only of English Puritanism but also of the seventeenth-century English cloth industry. They were hard hit by severe economic troubles in the 1620s and 1630s: great discontent and social unrest were created by crop failures and by an extended economic depression in the cloth industry. Under these troubled conditions, Puritanism gained many followers. Puritan teachings offered a convincing *moral* explanation of what was happening in the lives of the frightened, uprooted people of these two regions. The Puritans' social views were not modern—the Puritans were basically medieval in their suspicion of trade and moneymaking. They feared the effects of greed and urged that individuals put the welfare of the community above their own ambitions. It is true that the personality traits encouraged by Puritanism—diligence, accountability, self-denial, and the careful use of every God-given moment

*See chapter 5.

**We do not know exactly how many New Englanders reached full church membership during the first two generations after settlement. One historian estimates that 47 percent did, but this figure is probably too high. In any case, the majority of New England's seventeenth-century population remained outside the church and thus under the rule of the saints.

*Unlike the Pilgrims of Plymouth Colony, the Puritans who settled Massachusetts Bay Colony were not separatists and did not consider themselves *formally* withdrawn from the Church of England.

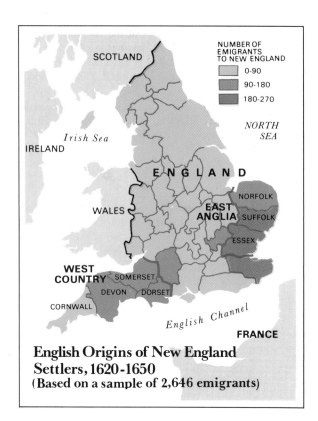

English Origins of New England Settlers, 1620-1650
(Based on a sample of 2,646 emigrants)

NUMBER OF EMIGRANTS TO NEW ENGLAND
0-90
90-180
180-270

toward the welfare of the entire group. Greed and self-satisfaction were *not* good things in themselves, and they should be strictly controlled.

The thousands of "unsaved" people who joined the Great Migration found in Puritanism not tyranny, but a source of the security for which they longed. In England they had been uprooted and buffeted by economic distress and social change. They found in New England a society that officially restrained economic activity and explained the mysterious workings of the marketplace in familiar moral language. Moreover, ordinary people were glad to find in the close-knit New England village communities a system of group controls that would effectively eliminate the threat of arbitrary economic fluctuations. Thus New England promised—and in many ways created—the kind of security that was one of the chief goals of life of early-seventeenth-century Englishmen.

By the end of the seventeenth century, however, Puritanism was losing its power. The third generation of New Englanders, American natives who had been born to relative security, lost touch with the original aims of the Great Migration. But for more or less two generations, Puritanism had been a comfort, not an affliction. Ordinary victims of social change had found it a source of security that was otherwise unattainable.

No more in religion than in social organization or economic life was this a world transformed. Changes were still in motion. Everywhere in New England's small but rapidly growing communities, there were instabilities, uncertainties, and transitions. The changing world of Puritan New England had not yet settled into permanent new forms.

of time—eventually helped stimulate capitalism. But the seventeenth-century Puritans were not thinking in terms of a competitive, capitalistic economy. They believed that diligence and self-denial should be directed

SUGGESTED READINGS

There is no single comprehensive and detailed history of American society in the seventeenth century. The subject has only recently been conceived of in the terms discussed in this chapter, and the student must draw for details on a scattering of publications. This is especially true of the first topic discussed in this chapter: population. There has recently been a burst of interest in historical demography, especially for the seventeenth century, in large part stimulated by innovating studies of the French and English populations of the same period. Their influence on early American history is summarized in Philip J. Greven, Jr., "Historical Demography and Colonial America," *Wm. and Mary Q.*, 24 (1967), 438–54. Of the older publications, the compilation of contemporary population estimates in Evarts B. Greene and Virginia D. Harrington, *American Population Before the Federal Census of*

1790 (1932), is still essential. The new writings, based on statistical analysis of small communities, originally concentrated on New England; the most recent and most elaborate of these studies relate to the Chesapeake region. A summary of New England's extraordinary growth rate appears in Daniel S. Smith, "The Demographic History of Colonial New England," *Journal of Economic History*, 32 (1972), 165–83. Other important writings on population growth in the North are Philip J. Greven, Jr., *Four Generations . . . Andover, Massachusetts* (1970); John Demos, "Notes on Life in Plymouth Colony," *Wm. and Mary Q.*, 22 (1965), 264–86;[†] and the same author's *A Little Commonwealth* (1970). The contrasting high death rate in the earliest years in Virginia and the eventual recovery and rapid growth of population there too are discussed in Edmund S.

Morgan, *American Slavery, American Freedom* (1975). Most of these studies reveal the distorted age structure and sex ratio in the settlement years, but there is important additional information on both in John Demos, "Families in Colonial Bristol, R. I. . . . ," *Wm. and Mary Q.*, 25 (1968), 40–57; in Irene W. D. Hecht, "The Virginia Muster of 1624/5," ibid., 30 (1973), 65–92; and in Herbert Moller's occasionally fanciful "Sex Composition and Correlated Culture Patterns of Colonial America," ibid., 2 (1945), 113–53. On migration to early New England, see T. H. Breen and Stephen Foster, "Moving to the New World," in *Puritans and Adventurers* (1980); Charles Banks, *Planters of the Commonwealth* (1930); and David G. Allen, *In English Ways* (1981). On the spread of population, see Lois K. Mathews, *The Expansion of New England* (1909), chaps. 2–3. On the Chesapeake area, see A. C. Land et al., eds., *Law, Society, and Politics in Early Maryland* (1977); T. W. Tate and D. L. Ammerman, eds., *The Chesapeake in the Seventeenth Century* (1979); Gloria L. Main, *Tobacco Colony* (1982); and Paul Clemens, *The Atlantic Economy and Colonial Maryland's Eastern Shore* (1980). Essays in J. M. Smith, ed., *Seventeenth-Century America* (1959), and Wesley F. Craven, *White, Red, and Black* (1971), are also useful.

Two useful sketches of the overall development of the early American economy are Stuart Bruchey, *Roots of American Economic Growth, 1607–1861* (1965), and George R. Taylor, "American Economic Growth Before 1840," *Journal of Economic History*, 24 (1964), 427–44. The world context of American commercial development is well presented in Ralph Davis, *Rise of the Atlantic Economies* (1973).

The growth of the commercial economy in early New England is traced in Bernard Bailyn, *The New England Merchants in the Seventeenth Century* (1955), and in Bernard and Lotte Bailyn, *Massachusetts Shipping, 1697–1714* (1959). The psychological turmoils of a Puritan merchant, caught between entrepreneurial and religious impulses, emerge in Bailyn, ed., *The Apologia of Robert Keayne* (1965). Curtis P. Nettels, *The Money Supply of the American Colonies Before 1720* (1934), covers aspects of American and Atlantic commerce as well as monetary history. For a social description of the emerging port towns, see Carl Bridenbaugh, *Cities in the Wilderness* (1938).

Aspects of the southern economy are described in Lewis C. Gray, *History of Agriculture in the Southern United States to 1860* (2 vols., 1933), and there is still value in Philip A. Bruce's *Economic History of Virginia in the Seventeenth Century* (2 vols., 1896). The master historian of the tobacco economy, however, is Jacob M. Price; it is from his writing particularly that one learns of the worldwide commercial network that shaped the lives of the Chesapeake farmers. In his *The Tobacco Adventure to Russia . . . 1676–1722* (*Transactions of the American Philosophical Society*, 1961), Price traces the failure of the London tobacco merchants to market Chesapeake tobacco in Russia, an effort that, if it had succeeded, would have transformed the economy and society of the American South. Price discusses the French-American tobacco trade in *France and the Chesapeake* (2 vols., 1973).

Traditional ideals of social organization are depicted in E. M. W. Tillyard, *Elizabethan World Picture* (1943), and in Gordon J. Schochet, *Patriarchalism in Political Thought* (1975); the latter has an excellent chapter on the ideals and actuality of the family in seventeenth-century England, a subject discussed at length by Peter Laslett in *The World We Have Lost* (1965) and in his introduction to *Household and Family in Past Time* (1972). Many of the new community-demographic studies cited above, particularly those of Greven and Demos, make clear the difficulty of maintaining traditional forms in the wilderness setting. See also Sumner C. Powell, *Puritan Village* (1963), and Edmund S. Morgan, *Puritan Family* (1944). Kenneth A. Lockridge, *New England Town: Dedham . . .* (1970), locates the disarray only at the end of the seventeenth century. On social mobility there are several important writings: William A. Reavis, "The Maryland Gentry and Social Mobility, 1637–1676," *Wm. and Mary Q.*, 14 (1957), 418–28; Russell R. Menard, "From Servant to Freeholder," ibid., 30 (1973), 37–64;[†] Linda A. Bissell, "From One Generation to Another," ibid., 31 (1974), 79–110; and Menard et al., "Opportunity and Inequality," *Maryland Historical Magazine*, 69 (1974), 169–84. The political consequences of social mobility and conflict are depicted in Bernard Bailyn, "Politics and Social Structure in Virginia,"[†] in James M. Smith, ed., *Seventeenth-Century America* (1959). On the altered role of women in seventeenth-century America, see Roger Thompson, *Women in Stuart England and America* (1974); on children and childhood, see Linda A. Pollock, *Forgotten Children . . . 1500 to 1900* (1983). Philip Greven has sketched the history of child rearing in early America in terms of shifting patterns of family life, religious experience, and self-identity in *The Protestant Temperament* (1977).

On religion, Sydney E. Ahlstrom, *Religious History of the American People* (1972), surveys generally the European background as well as the transplantation of European institutions, ideas, and beliefs to the North American continent. For a thoughtful overall interpretation, see Sidney E. Mead, *The Lively Experiment* (1963). For the seventeenth century, the subject has been dominated by the prolific scholarship on Puritanism. The master scholar in that subject has been Perry Miller. His two-volume *New England Mind* (*The Seventeenth Century*, 1939; *From Colony to Province*, 1953); his essays, collected in *Errand into the Wilderness* and *Nature's Nation* (1967); and his and Thomas H. Johnson's anthology of sources, *The Puritans* (1938), have made New England Puritanism one of the most absorbing subjects of modern historiography. Miller's books set in motion a flood of writing on Puritanism, which is surveyed in Michael Mc-Giffert, "American Puritan Studies in the 1960s," *Wm. and Mary Q.*, 27 (1970), 36–67. The closest approach to a new general interpretation of Puritan thought since Miller's *New England Mind* is Charles E. Hambrick-Stowe, *The Practice of Piety* (1982), which emphasizes devotional practice. Among the many other important writings on Puritanism are David D. Hall, *The Faithful Shepherd* (1972); Alan Simpson, *Puritanism in Old and New England* (1955); and Edmund S. Morgan, *Visible Saints* (1963). Sacvan Bercovitch, *The Puritan Origins of the American Self* (1975), shows the enduring impact of Puritan ideals on American self-imagery and culture.

No other religious community of the seventeenth century has received even remotely comparable study. On Anglicanism, see George M. Brydon *Virginia's Mother Church* (1947); Elizabeth H. Davidson, *Establishment of the English Church in the Continental American Colonies* (1936); and Parke Rouse, Jr., *James Blair of Virginia* (1971). On the Catholics, see John T. Ellis, *Catholics in Colonial America* (1965); on the Dutch Reformed, Frederick J. Zwierlein, *Religion in New Netherland* (1910); and on the Baptists, William G. McLoughlin, *New England Dissent, 1630–1833* (2 vols., 1971).

[†]See first footnote on p. 27.

4 Elements of Change, 1660–1720

Thus, the founding of British North America is the story of the efforts of private groups and individuals to profit in some way from the exploitation of the North American continent. The leading organizers of settlement had various motives. For some, the predominant goals were economic; for others, they were religious. For most, however, religious, economic, and patriotic interests were combined, stimulated by discontent at home, the lure of adventure, and the hope of improved fortunes in a new, open land. The scattering of privately organized settlements in British North America, some of them protected in their independence by royal charters, had developed without any overall plan or general organization. By 1660 there was little sense on either side of the Atlantic that these settlements together formed an effective empire.

In the two generations that followed the restoration of the Stuarts to the throne of England (1660), there were determined efforts to draw these scattered colonial settlements into an overall governmental organization, to impose regulation and control of some sort over this miscellaneous collection of towns, villages, and farms. The way this was done, and the way in which these efforts at regulation interacted with the natural growth and maturing of the American communities, permanently affected the character of American life.

Empire

Three interest groups, dominant at the Restoration court of Charles II (1660–85), account for the extension of the authority of the English government to America. The first of these was the courtiers, the most active of them the proprietors of the new colony of Carolina (named for Charles II), who had helped restore Charles to the English throne and remained his key advisers. Their stake in America deepened as the possibilities of making a profit from the settlements became more realistic. And to advance their interests in the colonies,

most of these courtiers were willing to help create and serve in an appropriate administrative system.

A second and ultimately more influential group was that of the merchants and their allies in the English government who marketed American products and sold manufactured goods to the colonists. These merchants knew that an important part of the British economy would in time be involved in the colonies. Therefore, they became the leaders in the growing movement to assert greater English control over the American settlements, for the sake of trade and England's economic prosperity.

A third influential pressure group was the royal family itself—particularly Charles's brother James, the duke of York, and his personal following. James became proprietor of New York when it was seized from the Dutch in 1664. An expert in naval affairs and an unusually forceful administrator, James made it clear soon after the Stuart restoration that he would be a leading figure in designing an empire out of the scattered American settlements.

It was the combination of these three groups—courtiers, merchants, and the royal family, particularly James—all with stakes in the colonies, that accounts for the creation of the British Empire at the end of the seventeenth century. Their goals were not identical, and there was no coordinated planning, but their interests converged in efforts at three levels.

Administration. Together they created, through a fumbling, pragmatic process of evolution, a network of administrative controls. Immediately after the Restoration, the Privy Council began appointing committees of its own members, and occasionally of outside experts, to deal with colonial problems as they arose. Soon, in 1675, enough important business came before these committees that a permanent committee of the Privy Council, called the Lords of Trade, was appointed. This committee met irregularly and had an inadequate staff, but it served as a forerunner of the

National Portrait Gallery, London

JAMES II AT THE TIME OF HIS ACCESSION
James's stubborn insistence on imposing a Catholic regime on a Protestant nation and his autocratic disregard of political realities led to his downfall in the Glorious Revolution (1688) and to a great advance in British liberalism.

better-organized permanent supervisory body, the Board of Trade and Plantations, which was created in 1696.

The Board of Trade was an independent agency of eight high state officials and eight paid members. It remained the central pivot of the British imperial administration throughout the eighteenth century. But it had notable weaknesses. First, the range of its activities was unrealistically broad. Besides colonial matters, it was expected to supervise all the trade of Great Britain, the British fishing industry, and the care of the poor throughout Britain. In dealing with the colonies it was given special responsibility for reviewing all royal appointments in America and all laws that the colonists enacted for themselves. Yet despite these broad responsibilities, the board's actual power proved to be severely limited. Other, better-established branches of the British government took over control of some aspects of colonial affairs, and the board's power failed to mature.

The greatest conflict lay between the Board of Trade and the secretary of state for the Southern Department. This secretary of state was one of the chief executive officers of the government, with particular responsibility for international relations. Although this responsibility included the affairs of the Western Hemisphere, the secretary of state's main attention was focused on Europe—especially on the glittering court of Louis XIV of France. Nevertheless, by 1704 the secretary of state for the Southern Department successfully challenged the Board of Trade for executive authority over the colonies. As a result, a fundamental weakness arose at the heart of the British overseas administration. The Board of Trade remained an information-gathering body, in charge of the flow of information between the colonies and the mother country, but it had no power to enforce regulations, make appointments, or otherwise control events. It could advise, counsel, and admonish; but *orders* came from the secretary of state's office, which might or might not be acting on the basis of the Board of Trade's stores of information. Moreover, the secretary of state tended to view colonial affairs from the standpoint not of trade, but of western European diplomacy.

Administrative confusion did not stop there. Almost every major branch of the British government discovered that it had an interest in the colonies, and managed to assert control over some sphere. The Treasury took over the colonial customs administration. The Admiralty successfully claimed jurisdiction over the North American sources of timber and other products vital to the British navy. It also patrolled the coastal waters to enforce the growing body of commercial regulations. The War Office took charge of army operations on the North American mainland during the many years when European international conflicts spilled over to the colonial territories. The army's contracting, like that of the navy, powerfully influenced the economic development of the colonies, and British strategic planning involved American manpower as well. Weaving through all of these ill-assorted jurisdictions was the legitimate authority of such important British officials as the attorney general, the solicitor general, and the various auditors and collectors of royal revenues.

By the early eighteenth century an imperial administration had taken shape in the British world. But it was very different in structure from that of the Spanish American empire. There was no British equivalent of Spain's Council of the Indies—a central authority that combined information gathering and executive authority and drew together all other governmental agencies that had an interest in colonial matters. British imperial administration was a maze of conflicting offices, with overlaps in jurisdiction and significant gaps in authority. As a result, there was a minimum of effective central control.

Yet this administrative inefficiency was not disastrous for Britain. The British Empire did not need tight administrative control before 1760. The colonies could largely be left alone, as long as certain minimal expectations were met, mostly centering on the regulation of commerce.

Mercantilism and Trade Regulation.

Britain's was a mercantilist empire. It arose as an extension of England's commercial growth. Its basic principles of economic organization were derived from mercantilism, a name modern historians have given to the age-old doctrine that the state must regulate economic activity for the public welfare. In seventeenth-century Europe most governments accepted mercantilist ideas, and the continent was torn by intense commercial rivalries among the great powers.

The mercantilists who designed the economic policy of the British Empire made two basic assumptions. First, they believed that the world consisted of competing nation-states. Second, they assumed that there was a fixed amount of wealth available in the world economy. Mercantilists therefore advocated the regulation of commerce by the government in order to make the state economically self-sufficient and, by maintaining a favorable balance of trade, to avoid becoming dependent on rival nations. Colonies were of fundamental importance in this competition among nations. English mercantilists pointed out that if Britain did not obtain necessary products from its own colonies, it would have to buy them from other nations; and thus its wealth would be drained off by rival states. Therefore, every effort had to be made to direct the flow of valuable colonial products to Britain alone. Further, Britain had to monopolize the sale of manufactured goods to the colonies, for every purchase of goods from a rival state meant some small drain on the nation's wealth.

To put these ideas into effect, Parliament passed the famous navigation acts in the years after the Restoration. Under the first of these acts, which was passed in 1660, only British subjects could ship and market colonial goods. It was decreed that England alone would enjoy the profits of shipping colonial goods and of reexporting them to other nations. Further, a special list was prepared of "enumerated" commodities—those that the colonies could ship only to England or to British colonial ports. The basic list included all the goods that England would otherwise have had to buy from competing imperial powers, principally France, Spain, and the Netherlands: sugar, tobacco, cotton, indigo, ginger, certain dyes, and special wood products. Later, other commodities were added to the original list: rice and molasses in 1704, naval stores in 1705 and 1729, and copper and furs in 1721.

The act of 1660 was the basic law governing colonial trade. Two other acts completed the pattern of mercantilist regulation. First, the so-called Staple Act of 1663 gave England a monopoly of the sale of European manufactured goods to the American colonies. European goods, the law stated, could not be shipped directly to America from Europe, even if the ships that carried them were British. These goods would first have to be sent to England and unloaded there, and then could be reshipped to the colonies. Under this law the English Treasury would collect valuable customs duties, and at the same time foreign merchants would be put at a disadvantage. Certain exceptions were made. Salt was exempted because it was necessary for American industry. Servants, horses, and provisions from Scotland and Ireland, as well as wines from the Portuguese islands of Madeira and the Azores, were all exempted because they involved no competition with English production. Finally, the third act, a supplementary law of 1673, tried to plug the gaps that had been created by the wording of the earlier legislation. This quite technical law caused endless confusion.

Thus, out of the converging interests of courtiers, merchants, and the royal family had come the foundations of an imperial system. This system operated at three levels: as an administrative apparatus, as a doctrine (mercantilism), and as a set of commercial regulations. By 1700 the British Empire was of world importance, but it was ineffectively governed by a poorly coordinated jumble of agencies. Colonial rule was also limited by the theory of mercantilism, which demanded not the direct governing of the colonies in depth, but only the regulation of their external trade. Finally, colonial rule was limited by the complexity of British commercial laws and by the great difficulty of enforcing these laws 3,000 miles from home. By the early eighteenth century no one could doubt that the American colonies were part of an empire. But neither could anyone think of the poorly managed, superficial colonial administration as a centralized empire. The passion for territorial rule was not there, nor the drive of royal ambition.

James II and the Dominion of New England.

The limits of the British imperial system become particularly clear when one considers the efforts that were undertaken in the late seventeenth century to make the empire more powerful than it was—more effective than it ever in fact became. For there was one person at the center of the English government who did have ambitions similar to those of the continental European monarchs and who also had the instincts of an able administrator and a group of close followers capable of managing an efficient system of government.

This man was the duke of York, who eventually became James II (1685–88). His urge to expand and deepen the controls of empire can be traced back to his childhood training as a military leader at the court of the powerful king of France, and to his desire, during the Stuarts' exile between 1649 and 1660, to exercise the power that had been denied him. He finally got his chance to exert authority when his brother, Charles II, returned to the throne. As lord high admiral with a loyal following of war-seasoned officers, James took command of military garrisons all over England and put those power-hungry veterans in charge of them. For him the colonial world was only an extension of England, another place where he could reward his followers. Soon these men turned up as governors and other high officials in the Caribbean and North American governments. James's base on the mainland of North America was New York, which he ruled as proprietor from the time it was captured from the Dutch. Slowly he expanded this center into a larger imperial dominion. His efforts coincided with the more general efforts that the English government was undertaking in the late seventeenth and early eighteenth centuries to cut back on the powers of the private jurisdictions that had been created in the early years of colonization.

Progress toward the goal of restricting the chartered colonies' authority was slow, erratic, and in the end incomplete. Virginia had become a crown colony when the Virginia Company failed in 1624; New York became a crown colony when its proprietor, James II, acceded to the throne of England in 1685. In 1680 New Hampshire was separated from Massachusetts with little difficulty and was given a royal governor. But in the other colonies the charters created serious problems, and they had to be attacked directly. Between 1684 and 1691 the crown confiscated the charters of Massachusetts, Connecticut, Rhode Island, New Jersey, Pennsylvania, Maryland, and Carolina. The king's grand but ill-fated plans began to unfold during these early years of his campaign against the chartered colonies.

James II's ultimate ambition seems to have been to create two centralized viceroyalties in America that would be ruled by crown-appointed governors and councils. Apparently the boundary between the two viceroyalties was to have been drawn westward from the Delaware River along the fortieth parallel—the division between the grants that had been given to the two Virginia companies at the beginning of the seventeenth century. During his short and tumultuous reign James focused his attention on the northern section, which became known as the Dominion of New England.

In a legal sense, the Dominion came together easily after 1685. To the core colony of New York were added New Hampshire, Massachusetts, Connecticut, Rhode Island, and New Jersey as each of these

colonies' charters was annulled or suspended. James sent over Edmund Andros, one of his closest allies and a former military associate, to rule the Dominion. Andros had already served James well in several other positions, particularly as governor of New York from 1674 to 1681. To assist Andros at his headquarters in Boston, James appointed a royal council, on which the majority of seats were held by merchants who had recently arrived in America and who had been struggling with little effect against the Puritan establishment. Together, Andros and the new royal council moved to create a centralized system of government similar to that of the Spanish in Latin America.

To the horror of the Puritans throughout New England, Andros declared toleration for all religious groups and confiscated Boston's Old South Church for use by the Church of England in conducting its services. Equally offensive to the colonists was his disregard of the ancient principles of English self-government. By mere executive declaration he continued collecting taxes that had originally been levied by the colony's representative General Court. The colonists were even more outraged by his land policy. He commanded that all town lands be regranted in the king's name, and that holders of these grants pay annual taxes ("quitrents") to the crown; also, the towns' undistributed lands (which were held in common by all town members) were to come under the council's control. And to complete the destruction of local authorities' powers, he ordered the town meetings to limit themselves to electing officials who would help collect taxes.

Andros's efforts never extended beyond Massachusetts; in fact, they scarcely reached beyond Boston and the coastal towns. But their implications were widely known, and they stimulated ferocious opposition. In the town of Ipswich, his tax policy provoked an open rebellion, led by the outspoken Reverend John Wise, who was imprisoned along with four of his followers. Resistance grew among the Puritan leaders and the landholders throughout New England.

Meanwhile, in England, James II's high-handed policies led to his downfall. In the Glorious Revolution of 1688–89, Parliament overthrew James and recognized as his successors William III and the latter's wife Mary, James II's daughter. Andros's royal regime in Boston had become so universally hated and so isolated that a rebellion against it in April 1689 took place almost without a struggle. Andros and his closest allies were imprisoned.

All of James's colonial plans disappeared with his fall from power. English imperial ambitions had reached their high tide and had receded. The more permanent forms of Anglo-American relations emerged as the colonial charters were restored, although with qualifications. There was a return to the limited and superficial empire that had existed long before 1685, modified by the reduction of chartered privileges in several colonies. East and West Jersey were reunited into the single royal colony of New Jersey in 1702. In Carolina a popular rebellion against the proprietors in 1719 and constant pressure against them in England led in 1729 to the formal separation of North and South Carolina into two royal colonies. (Only one aspect of the Carolinas' proprietary origins remained: the diplomat and politician the Earl Granville, heir of Sir George Carteret, one of the original eight proprietors, retained his ancestor's shares. When it was consolidated in 1745, his inheritance, the so-called Granville District, gave him title to the undistributed land of fully half of North Carolina, on which lived perhaps two-thirds of the colony's population.) The charters of Pennsylvania and Maryland were restored to the Penn and Calvert families; but in both cases the selection of the governor had to be approved by the crown, and all legislation was subject to review by the crown's legal officers.

The British-American Empire.

In its decentralization and inefficiency Britain's empire was far different from Spain's; but it was still a visible, extensive empire. By the early eighteenth century its visibility appeared most dramatically to Americans not so much in law enforcement or in new institutions as in the increasing number of officials sent to America to manage the new system. In most port towns there were customs collectors, appointed by the Treasury, who brought with them small teams of assistants. There were auditors and surveyors of the king's revenues. And there were officers of the vice-admiralty courts that had been created in 1696 as subordinate agencies of the admiralty court system that in Britain held jurisdiction over maritime law. The judges and clerks of these "prerogative" courts (operating without juries and under rules different from those of the common-law courts) were part of an imperial presence. So too— although indirectly, and for the limited purpose of enforcing the navigation laws—were the governors and lieutenant governors of all the royal colonies.

The importance of these officials, most of whom were newcomers to America at the end of the seventeenth century, cannot be exaggerated. They represented—indeed, they embodied—the empire. The way they approached their work, the attitudes they brought to Anglo-American relations, and the ways in which they related to the local communities became matters of importance in the lives of the American people. They affected not only the day-to-day workings of government, but also the popular image of government and of political authority more generally.

These officials were not efficient imperial bureau-

LORD CORNBURY, GOVERNOR OF NEW YORK, IN FEMALE DRESS
Of Lord Cornbury, a cousin of Queen Anne, an eighteenth-century historian wrote that he used "to dress himself in a woman's habit and then to patrol the fort in which he resided. Such freaks of low humor exposed him to the universal contempt of the people." His avarice led the Assembly to assert its control over tax revenues, and his zealous Anglicanism resulted in broader religious toleration.

crats, and they were seldom committed to promoting the strength of the empire. Their offices were minor parts of the patronage system of the English government. Hence these offices were seen as a kind of private property that political leaders doled out to their deserving followers. Appointees were expected to profit by their positions through the fees, gifts, and various benefits they received, as well as through their salaries. Appointments were made almost randomly with respect to administrative ability or interest in public affairs. What counted were political connections and the applicants' capacity to force their patrons to reward loyalty and previous service.

At times the appointments, even those at the highest levels, were bizarre. The governor of New York from 1701 to 1708 was a greedy transvestite, Lord Cornbury, a member of the powerful Clarendon family. He traipsed around the colony in women's clothes and squeezed profit from anything he could lay his hands on. The governor of Virginia from 1705 to 1737 was the earl of Orkney, who never had the slightest intention of setting foot in America, and never did. He had been a war companion of King William III and was the leading infantry commander of the duke of Marlborough. Orkney's appointment was also a reward for somewhat less heroic service: he had made what may have been a supreme sacrifice by marrying William III's mistress, Elizabeth Villiers.

Orkney's career as the absentee governor of Virginia is revealing in many ways. The official salary of the position was £2,000 a year. Orkney in effect sold the office for £1,200 to a series of lieutenant governors who served in his place, with the understanding that they were entitled to make as much out of the job as they could. As it happened, Orkney selected some able men. In 1706 he appointed Robert Hunter—who, because of accidents at sea and his wife's connections, ended up as the governor not of Virginia, but of New York, a post he filled with distinction. Alexander Spotswood, appointed in 1709, and William Gooch, appointed in 1727, were also capable officials. These three men had in common only the fact that they all had fought as army officers under Orkney and Marlborough. No less than nine veterans of Marlborough's famous victory in the battle of Blenheim (1704) received colonial governorships for their services.

Under these conditions it is hardly surprising that colonial offices were occasionally filled by grasping deviants like Cornbury or by psychological cripples like Sir Danvers Osborn, who hanged himself in a fit of melancholy a week after his arrival in New York to serve as that colony's governor. Nor is it surprising that lesser posts were frequently held by altogether unqualified hacks. What is remarkable is that some appointees were in fact conscientious and honest, and dutifully sought to serve the interests of the empire and of the local population.

Still, it is the randomness of these appointments and the disregard of the incumbents' ability and experience, and hence the arbitrariness of the system, that had the deepest effect on American life. The consequences were profound.

First, these appointments to offices in the colonies served to increase the existing superficiality of the British imperial system. Officeholders, always insecure in tenure, realized that the same arbitrary movements of the patronage system that had put them in office could easily remove them. Sooner or later, they knew, they would be replaced by men who were closer to the levers of power, although not necessarily more qualified. Consequently, incumbents were quite open to compromises and quite vulnerable to local pressures. If the situation required speed in making a profit from office, they would be quick about it—at the expense of the strict execution of their duties if need be.

Further, as it emerged in these formative years, British officialdom gave Americans the sense that government was far from being a seamless web that united high and low through a series of responsible links. Instead, they learned to see it as essentially a structure that was composed of two antagonistic levels: local, internal government that expressed the dominant interests of the local community; and a superior, external authority that was by nature hostile to local interests. Often the external power became identified with executive authority, and the local and benevolent authority with legislative power. This sharp distinction between the functions of government was extraordinary for the time, and it was destined to have a continuing importance in American history.

An even more general consequence of the character and behavior of British officialdom was the growth among politically active Americans of a kind of anti-authoritarian cynicism about all government. These officeholders represented a nation that was revered by most colonists; but in themselves these officers were often incompetent, poor, and arrogant, a bad enough combination made worse by their easy corruptibility. Americans could only wonder whether the government these officials represented deserved automatic obedience.

Beyond all of this lay the sense, as the imperial officialdom developed, that the social and political worlds were far from unified—that there was a gap between social and political leadership at the highest level. The native-born social leaders of the colonies did not represent the state. In fact, when local leaders competed with outsiders for high office in their own colonies, they competed on unequal terms, and their failures were embittering. Thus William Byrd II, a second-generation American who spent fifteen years being educated and making contacts in England before taking over the family property in Virginia, failed in his bid to buy the lieutenant governorship of his native colony from Orkney. Byrd spent years struggling with his successful rival, Spotswood, who had no original stake in the colony and no knowledge of it when he arrived on the scene. Byrd finally acquired a seat on the colony's council, but only after years of diligent effort.

These consequences of the growth of officialdom were especially important because they coincided with the natural emergence of local elites in the mainland colonies. The dominance of these local leaders within the maturing American communities could not be doubted, and their demands for recognition—in politics as well as in other spheres of life—could not easily be ignored.

Anglo-American Aristocracy

The rise of a provincial aristocracy toward the end of the seventeenth century and in the early eighteenth century was the result of the exploitation, by skillful, energetic, and ambitious men, of opportunities that suddenly became available. These opportunities were created by basic developments in social and economic life.

Land as the Basis of Aristocracy.

In the colonies as in England, the ownership or control of land was the material basis for most social distinctions. In the thirty years that bridged the end of the seventeenth century, 1690–1720, there was a significant shift in this basic relationship in the American colonies. Between these two dates the land area under active cultivation remained approximately the same because of Indian wars and the difficulty of overcoming natural barriers in the way of westward expansion. But during these same years the population more than doubled: it rose from approximately 210,000 to 460,000. Land was still far easier to acquire in the colonies than it was in England; but the increasing population pressure created significant changes in social relations and in itself accounts for the rise of new social elites.

In New England the emergence of a landowning aristocracy in the long-settled towns was marked by dramatic conflicts almost everywhere. In its original form the New England town had been a kind of democracy of male heads of households, all of whom were full church members, voting members (freemen) in the town meeting, and landowners with shares in the undivided land. As time passed, migration among towns grew and immigration into the colonies continued. Questions arose as to how newcomers would share in these original privileges. Certain answers came quickly. Access to membership in the church was controlled by a procedure that was calculated to make the entry of newcomers possible but still highly selective. Access to participation in the town meeting was less easily determined, but in the end the meeting was opened to all respectable male inhabitants. There was no easy way, however, to resolve the question of control of the undivided land. The heirs of the original grantees had no desire to share their inheritances with newcomers, and they closed ranks against the claimants.

Without originally intending to do so, these second- and third-generation colonists began to form exclusive groups of landholders. Challenged in the town meeting by those who were excluded from sharing in the common land, they drew apart and met separately, only to have their rights to the undivided land challenged at law. In certain towns they sought compromises—often dismissed as bribes—by allo-cating plots of land to the more prominent opponents or to those with special claims. Most often, confrontation could not be avoided. The challenges were decided by the General Court, which, after a period of uncertainty, favored the heirs of the original grantees.

As a result, the fortunate heirs not only continued to enjoy the increasingly valuable property, but also shared control of the still undivided common land. With this inherited capital, they were in the best possible position to build fortunes out of real estate. Those who were shrewd or enterprising enough to take full advantage of the available opportunities broadened their operations from small local transactions to large-scale land speculation. Some moved into trade after making money at commercial farming; the more industrious engaged in both commerce and farming. The most successful landowners in Connecticut became known as River Gods because of their valuable property along the colony's main waterway, the Connecticut River. Everywhere in New England, land claims proved to be a rich source of money, prestige, and power.

The same was true in the South. But there, as tobacco cultivation spread westward, profits from the land were intimately bound up with the problem of labor, and that increasingly meant slavery. It was in the later seventeenth century that slavery first emerged as a critical problem in southern society. Its spread, and the growth of the black population, created a great revolution in social relations as well as in the economy. Not only did slavery introduce a major element into the American population; it also became a basic source of social stratification among the whites. The logic of this development quickly became clear.

Profits from tobacco production were small and at times nonexistent. Therefore it seemed increasingly important to plant *extensively*. Land was available for expansion, but labor was not. The immigration of white indentured servants from England declined sharply after 1660 because of a slowing of England's population growth and an improved English labor market, especially in the London area. Slaves alone, it seemed, provided an answer to the labor problem. And slaves were increasingly available as the British slave trade entered a period of expansion and increasing efficiency.

Slaves *in the long run* were cheap. Their upkeep, averaged over a lifetime of labor, was perhaps £1 per year, as opposed to an indentured servant's annual maintenance cost of £2–£4. But if slaves were cheaper in the long run, they were more costly in the short run because they required a higher initial investment. And costs were rising constantly. Average slave prices doubled between 1660 and 1750, and by the time of the American Revolution they tripled. In 1700 a newly

Charleston Library Society

INDIGO CULTURE IN SOUTH CAROLINA
The plants of the blue dyestuff are being carried to fermenting vats, and the resulting liquid flows down the sluice at left into containers.

imported "prime field hand" cost £20 in Virginia; in 1750, £30. Nevertheless, the number of slaves continued to rise as their importance in the expanding tobacco culture became clearly understood. An estimated 20,000 slaves were brought to British North America in the two decades after 1700; 50,000 arrived in the subsequent two decades. In 1715 blacks formed a quarter of Virginia's total population; by the 1730s, 40 percent. In South Carolina blacks outnumbered whites by 1708; by 1720 the ratio was almost two to one, and the black population was growing at a faster rate than the white.

The growth of the slave labor force, which made possible a significant increase in tobacco cultivation and eventually in rice and indigo production, created a deepening social distinction within the white population. Capital was critical here: profits depended on the extent of cultivation, and that in turn depended on slave labor, which required high capital outlays. The white population became sharply divided into those who had capital available or could acquire it, and those who did not. Those with greater assets formed a new class of "great planters" in a society that as late as 1700 consisted almost entirely of small and medium-sized farm operations. For example, in Lancaster County in northern Virginia in 1716, a majority of taxpayers owned slaves, but few had more than 2 or 3;

only four owned more than 20; one, however—Robert Carter—had 126. Carter was a landowner and above all a land agent and speculator, the son of a settler who in 1649 had brought capital with him and had accumulated the land claims of no less than five wives. At his death in 1732, Carter was said to possess 300,000 acres of land and £10,000 in cash. In a world of steeply rising land values, capital and inherited land claims determined who would succeed and who would not. Those who succeeded would live like princes on the land—bourgeois, enterprising princes, to be sure, desperately concerned with markets, prices, and the humblest details of farming—but princes nevertheless.

Trade as the Basis of Aristocracy. In the main commercial centers the merchant community as a whole remained open—free of the formal limitations of guilds and of other artificial barriers to entrance. Nevertheless, significant differences within the merchant group appeared toward the end of the seventeenth century and increasingly in the early eighteenth century. A merchant aristocracy of sorts began to appear.

As the commercial system settled into a complex pattern of oceanic routes covering the North Atlantic basin, certain portions of the network proved crucial and dominated the others. It became more and more difficult to enter the trade of this primary route, and the colonial merchants who controlled it developed into powerful figures. As imports from England increased, and as the handling of ever larger quantities of colonial products made greater demands on colonial entrepreneurs, the English specialists in North American trade began to concentrate their shipments to a few ports and to a relatively few merchants. They sought commercial correspondents in America who could be relied on to send payments quickly, either in good bills of exchange or in salable commodities. The American merchants who became involved in these primary circuits of trade, through which flowed the all-important "dry goods" (primarily iron products and textiles), had a growing advantage over competitors. The main profits of the commercial system tended to go to these major importers, while the smaller merchants, confined to local routes, fell more and more clearly into subordinate roles.

Thus a merchant aristocracy of sorts developed in the large port towns. Its members were the dominant entrepreneurs who had gained direct contact with the English merchants and were in control of the critical colonial exports. It was an aristocracy that was still limited in affluence, changing in membership, and insecure; but it was a visible elite nevertheless, whose fortunes depended on the primary flows of commerce.

Political Influence as the Basis of Aristocracy.

Native elites thus arose in America on the basis of economic changes: in the ownership of land in New England, in the expansion of the tobacco economy in the Chesapeake region, and in the maturing of commerce in the main centers in the North. But the forces behind this rise of American elites were not merely economic; they were political as well. As the colonial governments took firm shape in the middle and later years of the seventeenth century, the value of political patronage and the yields of officeholding became unmistakably clear. The possibilities were first seen in Virginia, where what might be called the first American "court house gang" formed during the long governorship of Sir William Berkeley (1642–52, 1659–77).

The appointments that Berkeley could make gave him power over many aspects of the colony's life. He appointed justices of the peace, sheriffs, and tax collectors. He also nominated members of the council, who not only enjoyed considerable prestige, but also benefited materially from the privileges that were available to them. During the twenty-nine years of his administration, Berkeley used his power of appointment to create a clique of loyal officials, to whom he channeled these benefits. Similarly a little group of rich and influential men developed around the proprietors' associates in Maryland.

But it was in New York, not in Virginia or Maryland, that the possibilities of becoming wealthy

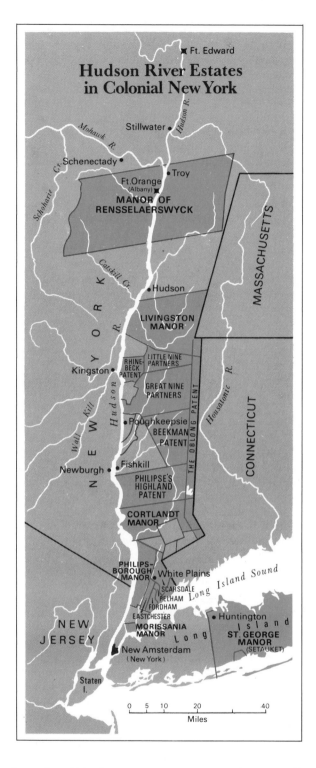

through political connections were most dramatically revealed. A new landowning elite was created in New York almost overnight in the 1690s, largely through the actions of a single governor who was attempting to make his fortunes and the fortunes of his followers as quickly as possible. In New York's tumultuous and competitive politics at the end of the seventeenth century, the ruthless partisanship of Governor Benjamin Fletcher (1692–97) was extraordinarily effective. Fletcher himself was personally greedy, and he was surrounded by a corrupt gang of petty plunderers whom he had brought over from England. Like his successor Cornbury, Fletcher proceeded to buy the loyalty of the dominant group of local influential men by bestowing on them enormous grants of land and by confirming other grants that had previously been made.

Fletcher did not invent this procedure. One patroonship from the Dutch period had survived and in fact flourished—Rensselaerswyck, a manor of close to a million acres on both sides of the Hudson surrounding present-day Albany. Several other great estates had been granted subsequently, and of these the most important was Livingston Manor. This grant of 160,000 acres had been extracted from the government of the Dominion of New England by Robert Livingston, a particularly clever politician of Scottish, English, and Dutch ancestry. Livingston, Fletcher remarked, had begun as "a little bookkeeper" but had "screwed himself into one of the most considerable estates in the province, . . . never disbursing sixpence but with the expectation of twelve." Fletcher himself fed the appetites of just such sharp-eyed opportunists and hustling politicians scrambling in the bonanza land grab of late-seventeenth-century New York. The estates he handed out in Dutchess and Westchester counties varied in size and in legal and political privileges, but almost all exceeded 100,000 acres. Some grants were literally open-ended: commonly stretching for sixteen miles along a riverbank, they ran back indefinitely into the unsurveyed countryside.

Profits from the French Wars.

The results of political influence were not limited to landholding: politics also affected the development of trade and the establishment of the merchant leadership. For at the end of the seventeenth century, government contracting—political in its essence—became a prime source of economic advancement. The colonies were involved in both of the international wars in which England fought during these years. The first was the inconclusive War of the League of Augsburg (1689–97), in which England led a coalition of European states resisting France's effort to dominate central Europe. The second was the War of the Spanish Succession (1702–13), a more decisive conflict, in which England and the Netherlands joined to block the French king Louis XIV's claim to the crown of Spain.

Both of these European wars led to hostilities between the English colonies and the French settlements in southern Canada. The slow-growing French colony of New France had been settled at the same time as the English colonies. But the growth of New France had been limited by religious restrictions on immigration, by rigid systems of land distribution and of social relations, and by a tightly controlled colonial bureaucracy. Its population was only 6,000 in 1660 and perhaps 15,000 in 1700. Nevertheless, from the beginning the French had been aggressive fur traders, trappers, and fishermen, and for years there had been minor clashes between them and the English settlers, especially in Nova Scotia. These clashes escalated into savage border warfare and extended struggles for inland territories during the two international wars that spanned the years 1689–1713. Both wars involved the English colonists economically as well as militarily.

In the first war, of 1689–97, which was known in the colonies as King William's War, the French and their Indian allies fought the English for control of Hudson Bay and in 1690 attacked the exposed northern borders of English settlement in devastating raids on an arc of towns from Portland, Maine, to Schenectady, New York. The British and American forces concentrated on capturing the French fortress of Port Royal in Nova Scotia, which Massachusetts troops took but then lost in 1690–91. An elaborate Anglo-American attack on the center of French Canada failed miserably.

The same pattern was repeated in the second of these wars, that of 1702–13, which the American colonists knew as Queen Anne's War. Once again the Maine settlements were raided by the French and Indians, and Deerfield, Massachusetts, was destroyed. In retaliation the colonists burned down French villages in Nova Scotia and attacked Port Royal twice before finally taking it. Far to the south a force of Carolinians and Indians burned the Spanish town of St. Augustine, Florida, and destroyed the string of Spanish missionary outposts that linked the Spanish coastal settlements to French Louisiana. The war ended in 1713 with the Treaty of Utrecht, whose main terms marked a significant victory in Europe for Britain. In the Western Hemisphere, Britain obtained permanent title to Newfoundland, Nova Scotia, and Hudson Bay, although not all the boundaries were clear. The British also won a thirty-year contract to supply Spanish America with 4,800 slaves and a cargo of goods annually.

The American efforts in these European wars had made great demands on the fragile American economies and had accounted for significant inflows of money. Troops had to be mobilized, housed, transported, and fed. Ships had to be built, equipped, and manned. Native sources of naval supplies had to be exploited. The management of these efforts during the two decades of war fell into the eager hands of a few colonial merchants. Some were experienced in the

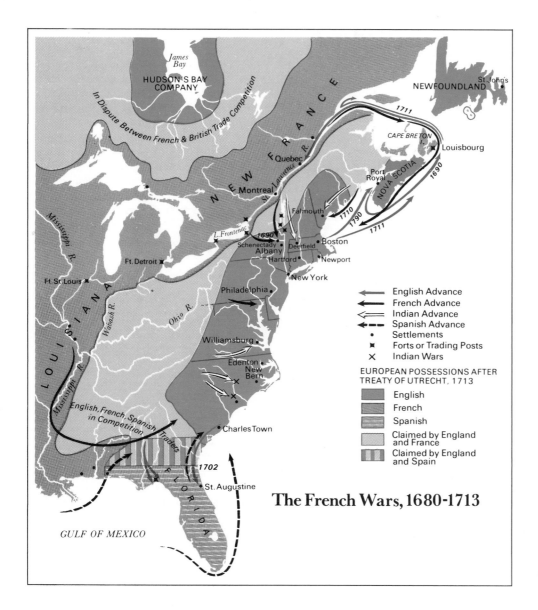

The French Wars, 1680-1713

Map legend:

- English Advance
- French Advance
- Indian Advance
- Spanish Advance
- • Settlements
- ✶ Forts or Trading Posts
- ✕ Indian Wars

EUROPEAN POSSESSIONS AFTER TREATY OF UTRECHT, 1713
- English
- French
- Spanish
- Claimed by England and France
- Claimed by England and Spain

business of supplying war materiel. Andrew Belcher, once an innkeeper in Cambridge, Massachusetts, had made his first success in trade as a supplier to the Massachusetts government during King Philip's War (1675–76), a brief and bloody clash between the colonists and the local Indians. In the international conflicts that followed, Belcher became the colony's principal military contractor. With the profits he made, he established a family that would rise to the governorship and to other important offices and would enjoy grand tours of Europe and the acquaintance of monarchs. The Faneuil family, Huguenot refugees from France, also established itself partly through wartime contracting. In New York another Huguenot, Stephanus DeLancey, and the Schuyler brothers in Albany used government contracting as a

major source of profits. Through the contracting business, political in its origins, these merchants established families as important in New York as the Belchers and Faneuils were in Massachusetts.

The Limits of Social Distinction. Thus in these many ways toward the end of the seventeenth century, the situation made possible the growth of American elites—a leadership group that was distinguished by wealth or substantial claims to wealth, by political influence, and by a superior style of life. But if these elites constituted an aristocracy, it was a limited aristocracy indeed. The limitations of their distinctions, the basic weakness of their positions, and the instability of their membership were as important as the eminence they had achieved.

VAN CORTLANDT MANOR HOUSE, CROTON-ON-HUDSON, NEW YORK
The manor, granted to Stephanus Van Cortlandt in 1697, originally included 86,123 acres. The restored manor house, shown here, was built around an even simpler structure by Stephanus's grandson, Pierre, over a period of years beginning in 1749.

Courtesy of Sleepy Hollow Restorations, Tarrytown, New York

To begin with, they formed no "class"—that is, no body with group interests, known and recognized, that were more important than individual or family concerns. These striving merchants, hustling land speculators, and hard-pressed planters were driven by personal, local, and immediate interests. They did not identify themselves with the stable concerns of a particular social group that had existed before them and would exist after them—a group that each individual member recognized as essential to his own welfare. Their interests were their own. Only occasionally and erratically did they merge their concerns with those of other men in similar situations, forming common commitments and a joint program of public action.

Further, these emerging elites were distinguished from most of their contemporaries only by their wealth. In education, in race, in ancestry, in cultural outlook, in speech, and in personal style, they were largely indistinguishable from the hundreds of others who competed with them openly. They had simply achieved wealth—but wealth in the American colonies was remarkably fragile and insecure. There was almost no way to invest a fortune securely. "Urban" properties provided perhaps the steadiest yields but were limited in scale and availability. Most capital was tied up in daily trading or farming operations or in land that had been bought on speculation. Momen-

tary upsets could be disastrous, and bankruptcies were common. Repeatedly men rose from obscurity only to disappear back into the population at large.

Even if an individual's wealth remained secure, it could provide no institutional protection for the distinctions he had won. No legal barriers or institutions existed to protect the fragile American aristocracy—no nobility, no House of Lords, no legal institution of any kind in which membership, once achieved, could be passed on from generation to generation. The colonial councils were political bodies; although membership in them bestowed enviable status, seats could not be inherited (in contrast to membership in certain political institutions in Europe, which could be inherited). Membership in the colonial councils remained open not merely to ambitious local competitors—merchants, farmers, and landowners—but also to officials sent from abroad.

Of all the limitations in the distinctions of the new elites, however, the most striking was the lack of a visible distance between them and the bulk of the population from which they had emerged. In the short time in which these men had risen, they had not been able to create for themselves a world that was set far apart from the world of ordinary prosperous people. They built manor houses, town houses, and plantation "seats" (residential estates) that had some style, and they made other efforts to establish the outward forms of a superior way of life. But as yet their material achievements were relatively modest—lavish, perhaps, by the standards of frontier tobacco farmers and petty shopkeeper-merchants, but not at all comparable to the magnificent establishments of European aristocrats. The Van Cortlandts' manor house on their estate on the Hudson was a modest one-and-a-half-story wooden building, a pleasant farmhouse that had been improved for middle-class comfort; an affluent country gentleman in early-eighteenth-century England would hardly have considered it a suitable residence. "Westover," the Byrds' estate in Virginia, was more elegant and more substantial, with pretentions to a higher, more sophisticated style in its carved interior woodwork and up-to-date exterior brick façades. But much of its ultimate beauty was acquired gradually, in successive additions and refinements. In its original form it was a square house of eight main rooms, and like so many other proud houses of the time it was solidly middle class. The most elegant and famous house in Boston in this period also seemed an immense achievement by the standards of the place and time. But this house, built by the merchant John Foster between 1689 and 1692 and destined to be inherited by the Hutchinson family, would have been indistinguishable from the ordinary town houses of prosperous tradesmen in any of the major cities of Europe. There was nothing in America to compare with the great urban residences and magnificent country houses of Europe's very rich, or even fairly rich.

The heights that the Van Cortlandts, the Hutchinsons, the Belchers, and the Byrds achieved were within the reach of many, and never free from competition. At the same time, the ordinary people in the colonies enjoyed a remarkably high level of general well-being. To be sure, there was poverty in early-eighteenth-century America, as there has been in almost every society that has ever existed; but among the ordinary free population there was a degree of affluence that was unique for the time. Land remained available, even if it was increasingly difficult for freed servants to rise to full independence and public influence. Entrance to wholesale trade, although more difficult than before, remained open to competition. If there were a few great landlords, there were a great many independent farmers. If there were a few merchants who had suddenly become quite rich, there were many others who had some share in the profits of trade. During Queen Anne's War one-third of the entire adult male population of Boston (544 individuals) were part owners of some seagoing vessel. And no fewer than 207 of these investors—12 percent of the adult male population of the town—called themselves merchants.

Rebellion: The Measure of Social Strain

It is the sudden emergence of these new elites—proud but still striving and well within the range of rivals close behind—that explains the intensity of the rash of rebellions that broke out in the American colonies in the late seventeenth century. These rebellions are very small events in the scale of Western history, but they are extremely revealing within the context of the rapidly maturing Anglo-American society. They show the inner strains and tensions of communities whose social structure was still forming and in which no group's dominance and no individual's eminence were safe from effective competition.

There were five outbreaks, and their dates are significant:

Virginia	Bacon's Rebellion	1676
Carolina	Culpeper's Rebellion	1677
Massachusetts	Rebellion against Andros and the Dominion of New England	1689
New York	Leisler's Rebellion	1689
Maryland	The Protestant Association	1689

The origins of three of these rebellions—those in Massachusetts, New York, and Maryland—coincided with the arrival in the colonies of news of the Glorious Revolution of 1688 in England. In all three cases the rebels explicitly associated themselves with that uprising in England, which forced James II into exile and destroyed the threat of his authoritarian rule. But the parallels between these American uprisings and the Glorious Revolution are superficial, although not altogether fanciful. The revolution in England deposed a king and showed that sovereignty lay not in a monarch appointed by God, nor in popular mobs, but rather in Parliament and the consensus of political and social leaders. Further, in England the supremacy of law—the statutes that were enacted by Parliament and the common law that had come down through the ages—had been placed above any action of the crown, and judges had been made independent of the monarch's wishes. Finally, Parliament had declared that it had an independent existence: its elections and its sessions were fixed on regular schedules, free of dictation by the crown. None of these basic accomplishments of the Glorious Revolution was duplicated in America. Sovereignty was in no way an issue in the colonial upheavals. The American governors retained the arbitrary powers that were eliminated in England. American judges remained subordinate to the crown's will, and

the existence and convening of the representative assemblies remained subject to executive decree.

The colonial revolts differed greatly in their immediate causes. But whatever the colonists' original motivations, once under way their uprisings expressed the strains within communities in which social controls and political dominance were both subjects of controversy, objects of challenge and of continuous struggle.

Bacon's Rebellion. In a period of economic distress, Bacon's Rebellion began as an unauthorized war against the Indians on Virginia's northwestern frontier. Governor Berkeley's policy had been to stabilize the boundaries between Indians and whites and to protect the native Americans from land-hungry settlers. Although it was a sincere attempt to deal with a difficult problem, it was also a conservative policy that favored the well-established farmers, and especially Berkeley's supporters and beneficiaries. As such, it was offensive to newcomers like Nathaniel Bacon and the latter's chief ally, Giles Bland. Bacon had quarreled with the governor and had been denied the monopoly of the Indian trade he sought; Bland, who had arrived in the colony in 1671 as a customs collector, had been fined by the governor for "barbarous and insolent behaviors," then arrested, and finally dismissed from his post.

Around Bacon and Bland an opposition group gathered that was increasingly resentful of the benefits that Berkeley's clique had acquired. The challengers demanded land without regard to the rights or needs of the border Indians, who were being squeezed between the double pressure of rival tribes behind them and white settlers before them. A violent clash between the Indians and the settlers in the border area that Bacon sought to control provided an excuse to launch a full-scale war. This conflict became a civil war in 1676 when Berkeley repudiated Bacon and his allies and tried to bring them to justice. Having suppressed the border Indians in bloody battles, the rebels turned back upon the colony. They seized the government, defeated and scattered Berkeley's forces, and burned Jamestown to the ground. But they could not sustain the revolt. Bacon died of exposure and exhaustion in the midst of a confused military campaign. Deprived of his leadership, the rebellion faded out, and Bacon's chief allies were soon hanged for treason.

But in all this turmoil the Baconites' voice rose loud and clear. Who are these men "in authority and favor," they demanded to know in their "Manifesto," to whose hands the control of the country's wealth had been committed? Note, they cried,

the sudden rise of their estates compared with the mean quality in which they first entered the country, . . . and let us see whether their extractions and education have not been vile, and by what pretense of learning and virtue they could [enter] so soon into employments of so great trust and consequence; let us . . . see what sponges have

sucked up the public treasure and whether it hath not been privately contrived away by unworthy favorites and juggling parasites whose tottering fortunes have been repaired and supported at the public charge.

But these challengers were themselves challenged. For another element in the upheaval was the discontent among the ordinary settlers over the *local* privileges of some of the newly risen, powerful men in the counties—the Baconites—who had attacked the privileges of Governor Berkeley's inner clique. The ordinary settlers expressed their grievances in the laws of "Bacon's Assembly," which met in 1676. At both the local and the central levels, the rebellion thus challenged the stability of newly secured authority.

The wave of rebellion in Virginia, which had risen suddenly and spread quickly, soon subsided. By the end of the seventeenth century, the most difficult period of adjustment had passed: the colonists generally accepted the fact that certain families were indeed distinguished from others in riches, in dignity, and in access to political authority—and were likely to remain so. There had never been a challenge to British supremacy or to the idea that some people would inevitably be "high and eminent in power and dignity; others mean and in subjection." Protests and upheavals had resulted from the discomforts of discovering *who* in fact was "high" and who was "mean," and what the particular consequences were of "power and dignity."

Culpeper's Rebellion.

More confused than Bacon's Rebellion was the almost comic-opera uprising that took place in 1677 in Albemarle, the northern sector of Carolina. There some 3,000 farmers struggled to survive in the swampy, sandy coastal lands and to profit from smuggling tobacco with the help of a few enterprising New England merchants. When the Carolina proprietors' clique—men no less hard-drinking, ill-tempered, and profiteering than their opponents—attempted to collect customs duties, they were attacked by a gang of rivals. The leader of this gang, a belligerent malcontent named John Culpeper, accused the clique of corruption and treason. Culpeper seized the government, jailed his enemies, and sent charges against them to England. After endless confusion and an almost farcical series of attacks between the two groups, the Carolina proprietors managed to restore order. But the rebellion died slowly, partly because the legal proceedings in England were drawn out over a long period, and even more because there was ongoing uncertainty over who had legitimate leadership in the rough, tumultuous backwoods community.

Leisler's Rebellion.

In New York the struggle between an emerging group of influential men and a resentful opposition was clearer than it was in the South; and it was also more bitter and had more permanent political consequences.

When word of the Glorious Revolution arrived in New York, the colony's lieutenant governor, Francis

Nicholson, decided to strengthen Manhattan's garrison with militia troops. One of the militia captains was a well-to-do, quarrelsome merchant, Jacob Leisler. Relations between the militia and Nicholson's regular troops grew difficult, then explosive, especially because Nicholson's legal status was unclear after the king who had appointed him, James II, had been deposed. In June 1689 the militia, led by Leisler, seized the fort at Manhattan in the name of the new English monarchs, William and Mary. Nicholson sailed for England. In December a message from William III arrived, instructing the chief officer of New York's government to retain his post. Leisler, in control of the fort, received this message and interpreted it as being addressed officially to himself as the colony's acting governor. He drew around him what was at first a large group of supporters, who proceeded to parcel out the colony's offices and run the government, including its feeble effort in King William's War. In 1691 a new, officially appointed royal governor arrived, Henry Sloughter, whose name later proved to be appropriate. Sloughter demanded that Leisler surrender the city and the government. Leisler's support had steadily eroded in two years of erratic rule, and he scarcely controlled any of the colony outside the city walls. Nevertheless, he refused to give up. Sloughter's superior power prevailed. Leisler and his followers surrendered; and after a legally dubious trial he and his chief assistant, his son-in-law Jacob Milbourne, were hanged for treason and their property was confiscated.

But these savage sentences, which Parliament legally annulled in 1695, hardly ended the struggle. By the time Leisler's regime had ended, the political leadership of the colony was broken into two violently opposing parties, the Leislerians and the anti-Leislerians. Thereafter the two parties alternated in power as successive governors arrived, each side attempting literally to annihilate the other when the opportunity arose—or failing that, to crush the opposition politically so that it would never regain power. Again, the social background of the turmoil is crucial. Behind the see-sawing political conflict in New York lay a background struggle that had been under way since the English had conquered the colony from the Dutch. In the years that followed the English takeover, an Anglo-Dutch leadership group had taken form under governors sent to the colony by the duke of York. The colony's official patronage had come to center on this small group of families, whose ultimate rewards would come in the land grants of Benjamin Fletcher. Gradually this Anglo-Dutch clique—the Bayards, Van Cortlandts, Philipses, Livingstons, and Schuylers—had made arrangements that satisfied its members' interests. They had gained a monopoly of

PETER SCHUYLER, MAYOR OF ALBANY, 1686–94, BY NEHEMIAH PARTRIDGE
Also for many years chief English negotiator with the Indians, Schuyler is pictured here in 1718, eight years after he took four Iroquois chiefs to London where they were received with honor by Queen Anne.

the milling and exporting of flour for New York City, in effect giving them control of that vital industry; a New York City monopoly of shipping on the Hudson; and an Albany monopoly of the colony's Indian trade.

The Anglo-Dutch clique had thus gained control of the colony's offices, and its members had also begun to control New York's economy. But those excluded from power had grown increasingly resentful. Gradually a combination of alienated factions had taken shape. This opposition was led by the merchants (especially those of Dutch origin) who had been denied access to these privileges. It included the city artisans, who were indirectly the victims of the monopolies, and the Long Island townsmen, most of whom had migrated from Connecticut. Increasingly, Jacob Leisler had assumed the leadership of this rising discontent. Leisler had fought the Anglo-Dutch leaders on several issues, had been jailed in a religious controversy in Albany, had thereafter refused to pay customs duties, and had defied all efforts to bring him to court. His associates had had similar careers.

This group of alienated, resentful, and enterprising men—many of whom had been in positions of authority under the Dutch—had sparked the opposition to Nicholson and turned it into a rebellion against the new Anglo-Dutch establishment. In principle, Leisler and his followers were no more "democrats" than were the Baconites in Virginia. But they found in the language of the Glorious Revolution a "Protestant" program—against monopolies, against arbitrary power, in favor of open access to benefits and a broad sharing of them—that served their own interests well.

The Protestant Association.

In Maryland, resentment had been building for a long time against the domination of the colony by the Calverts and their Catholic associates. This resentment had erupted into open violence as early as 1676 in an obscure rebellion in Calvert County. When news of the Glorious Revolution arrived, the same group of insurgents, further antagonized by a particularly obnoxious governor, led 250 settlers to seize the colony's government. Calling themselves the Protestant Association, the rebels issued a declaration condemning the proprietor's party for excessive fee taking, for resisting royal authority, and for arbitrary taxation. They also identified telltale signs of a secret papal plot, and they petitioned the crown to take over the colony's government from the Calverts, which was promptly done.

Only in 1715 was control of Maryland restored to the Calvert family, whose members by that time had turned Protestant. By that time too, Maryland had been drawn into the general pattern of colonial governance: the crown had to approve executive appointments and the colony's legislation. The rebellion in Maryland had been the product of the instability created by the conflict of opposing groups in the col-

ony. Although the proprietors' clique thereafter still dominated the executive branch of the colony's government, it could no longer block the advance of the planter aristocracy or ignore the legislative assembly, whose influence was built into the government.

The Downfall of Andros.

Although in Massachusetts there were special, local factors in the rebellion that took place, there was also an underlying conflict similar to that found in other colonies. The characteristic struggle of social groups had been delayed in the Bay Colony by the continuing dominance of the Puritan regime, protected by the original Massachusetts charter. But when the colony's charter was taken away by the English government in 1684 and the Dominion of New England was established, the pattern already seen in the other colonies quickly developed. Almost immediately, the favors of patronage and power began to flow to a small group of speculators and merchant insiders. Some of those who were favored had come over with Andros; some of them were ambitious native-born Americans who were drawn to the newly established group. For four years the members of this clique collected numerous privileges—and in the process generated resentment among others that found expression in an uprising made especially bitter by the Puritan outrage that fueled it.

These rebellions were obscure and confused events—especially those in New York, Maryland, and Massachusetts, where the insurgents claimed association with the successful revolutionaries in England. Everywhere the rebels sought to identify themselves with the struggle for English liberty and against various forms of tyranny. None, however, questioned the basis of public authority; all submitted to legitimate royal power when it appeared; and none fought for the full range of liberties that were achieved by the Glorious Revolution—liberties that were spelled out in the English Bill of Rights of 1689 and the Act of Settlement of 1701, which concluded the revolution in England. The American rebels did not question the nature, structure, and essential character of government; rather, they challenged the personnel of government—those in control. In short, the issue was not a question of "what?" or "how?" but one of "who?" Enclosed in their provincial world, the rebels sought, above all, fairness in the actions of government that properly reflected the balance of society as it had emerged from a period of rapid growth and change.

Provincial Culture

These uprisings of the late seventeenth century were not only relatively obscure events in the scale of West-

Sarah Kemble Knight (1666–1727) was the wife of a Boston merchant. She herself pursued an active business career, in 1704–05 journeying overland alone from Boston to New York and back. Her diary is full of amusing and shrewd comments on the people and towns she encountered.

Sarah Kemble Knight Describes New York City (1704)

THE Cittie of New York is a pleasant, well compacted place, situated on a Commodius River wch is a fine harbour for shipping. The Buildings Brick Generaly, very stately and high, though not altogether like ours in Boston. The Bricks in some of the Houses are of divers Coullers and laid in Checkers, being glazed look very agreeable. The inside of them are neat to admiration, the wooden work, for only the walls are plasterd, and the Sumers and Gist are plained and kept very white scowr'd as so is all the partitions if made of Bords. The fire places have no Jambs (as ours have) But the Backs run flush with the walls, and the Hearth is of Tyles and is as farr out into the Room at the Ends as before the fire, wch is Generally Five foot in the Low'r rooms, and the peice over where the mantle tree should be is made as ours with Joyners work, and as I supose is fasten'd to iron rodds inside. The House where the Vendue was, had Chimney Corners like ours, and they and the hearths were laid wth the finest tile that I ever see, and the stair cases laid all with white tile which is ever clean, and so are the walls of the Kitchen wch had a Brick floor. They were making Great preparations to Receive their Govenor, Lord Cornbury from the Jerseys, and for that End raised the militia to Gard him on shore to the fort.

They are Generaly of the Church of England and have a New England Gentleman for their minister, and a very fine church set out with all Customary requsites. There are also a Dutch and Divers Conventicles as they call them, viz. Baptist, Quakers, & c. They are not strict in keeping the Sabbath as in Boston and other places where I had bin, But seem to deal with great exactness as farr as I see or Deall with. They are sociable to one another and Curteos and Civill to strangers and fare well in their houses. The English go very fasheonable in their dress. But the Dutch, especially the middling sort, differ from our women, in their habitt go loose, were French muches wch are like a Capp and a head band in one, leaving their ears bare, which are sett out wth Jewells of a large size and many in number. And their fingers hoop't with Rings, some with large stones in them of many Coullers as were their pendants in their ears, which You should see very old women wear as well as Young.

They have Vendues very frequently and make their Earnings very well by them, for they treat with good Liquor Liberally, and the Customers Drink as Liberally and Generally pay for't as well, by paying for that which they Bidd up Briskly for, after the sack has gone plentifully about, tho' sometimes good penny worths are got there. Their Diversions in the Winter is Riding Sleys about three or four Miles out of Town, where they have Houses of entertainment at a place called the Bowery, and some go to friends Houses who handsomely treat them. Mr. Burroughs cary'd his spouse and Daughter and myself out to one Madame Dowes, a Gentlewoman that lived at a farm House, who gave us a handsome Entertainment of five or six Dishes and choice Beer and metheglin, Cyder, & c. all which she said was the produce of her farm. I believe we mett 50 or 60 slays that day—they fly with great swiftness and some are so furious that they'le turn out of the path for none except a Loaden Cart. Nor do they spare for any diversion the place affords, and sociable to a degree, they'r Tables being as free to their Naybours as to themselves.

ern history; they were also—significantly—provincial events. And as such they were characteristic of early-eighteenth-century Anglo-American culture. That culture had changed greatly in its relations to the English culture from which it had developed.

In the early seventeenth century the new English settlements in America may have been small, distant, and isolated, but they had been part of a vital movement prominent in western European life. The key figures in the American colonies were products of the European world. In America they were isolated physically but not psychologically, intellectually, or spiritually. They never lost the sense of being involved in something that mattered in an important way to the world they had left behind. They felt that they could easily return to that world; and when they did return, they found themselves enhanced, not diminished, by having spent time in the exotic American frontier land. Thus George Sandys, an English poet, traveler, and scholar (and the son of the archbishop of York), easily slipped back into English literary circles after his stay in Virginia, having made good progress on his translation of Ovid's *Metamorphoses*. So Roger Williams returned to England from America to join the Council of State during the English Civil War. And John Winthrop's nephew George Downing, who had been sent to Harvard College for his education, became the chief intelligence officer to Oliver Cromwell, the head of England's revolutionary government in the 1650s; ultimately knighted, Downing in 1657 became England's ambassador to the Netherlands. The American settlements had thus been relevant and vital to some of the most forward-looking minds of the time.

By 1700 circumstances had changed drastically. As the colonies had grown, they had grown apart, into a separate world of their own. The colonial world was still connected with the greater world beyond, but it was fundamentally removed from it. The success or failure of the colonists' daily affairs no longer mattered in England, as they once had. The settlers no longer made news in the larger world; they listened for it, intently, from abroad, and they imitated as best they could foreign styles of thought, ways of living, and patterns of behavior. They knew themselves to be provincials in the sense that their culture was not self-contained; its sources and superior expressions were to be found elsewhere than in their own land. They must seek the higher forms of their culture from afar; they must be acquired and maintained according to standards externally imposed, in the creation of which the colonists had not shared. The most cultivated of them read much, and they read purposefully, determined to retain contact with a world greater than their own. The diary of William Byrd II, with its record of daily stints of study, testifies to the virtues of regu-

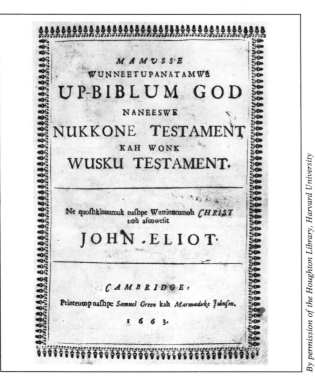

TITLE PAGE OF THE REVEREND JOHN ELIOT'S ALGONQUIAN TRANSLATION OF THE BIBLE
A work of 1200 pages, the Indian Bible was part of Eliot's great, and failing, missionary effort to convert the native Americans to Protestant Christianity. At the height of his success, before King Philip's War, he had established fourteen self-governing communities of "praying Indians."

By permission of the Houghton Library, Harvard University

fall too far behind. And to those in England who were concerned with the spreading of Christianity, he sent back the Indian-language translation of the Bible by the Massachusetts minister John Eliot, and two essays written in Latin by Indian students at Harvard. But these were failing efforts. In the end loneliness and isolation overcame Winthrop. By the time of his death in 1676, he was venerated in the villages along the Connecticut River—themselves changing like autumn leaves from vital, experimental religious communities to sere, old-fashioned backwoods towns. But he was forgotten by the greater world in England. His sons, however, provincial land speculators and petty politicians, had no such memories as their father had had, and no such aspirations; they suffered, therefore, none of his disappointments. They were native to the land, and their cultural horizons had narrowed to its practical demands.

The silent drama of a high culture being transplanted to America and becoming permanently provincial was played out most vividly in the field of education. For in its broadest sense, education, more than any other social process, liberates people from narrow local origins and brings them into contact with larger worlds and broader horizons. Education is perhaps the most sensitive index of the changing character of American life as it developed in the transitional years of the late seventeenth century. It is also one of the most difficult subjects to interpret. For there were great accomplishments in colonial education, but there were also great defeats; soaring ambitions, but serious neglect.

Education. Certain things, however, are clear. In New England the founding generation made a remarkable effort not only to perpetuate education as it was then known, but to improve it. They wanted to spread it more widely and more effectively throughout the entire population than it had been extended even in England, where formal education was extraordinarily widespread for the time. The Puritans' efforts in education stemmed primarily from their religious convictions—specifically, from their insistence that every person, saint or sinner, have personal access to the Holy Scriptures, which meant that everyone must be able to read. But the ability to read was only the beginning, for to the Puritans the truly religious person was a student not only of the Bible, but also of commentaries on the Bible, including those enormously long, intricate sermons preached from every pulpit in the land. Keeping alive this biblical culture among the entire population required that much more schooling be provided than was considered normal by Elizabethan Englishmen, who assumed that the goal of formal education was training in vocational roles. For the

larity and effort in maintaining standards of civilization set abroad.

This basic transformation can be seen particularly well in the later career of John Winthrop, Jr., the gifted and learned son of the first governor of Massachusetts Bay Colony. John, Jr., was educated at Trinity College, Dublin, and in London at the lawyers' Inner Temple. As a young man he had helped manage an English overseas military expedition, and he had traveled in the Mediterranean and Middle East. He was a physician, an amateur scientist, and an imaginative entrepreneur, and for eighteen years he served as governor of Connecticut. He struggled to maintain contact with the Royal Society in London, of which he was the first American member. There was "a current of loneliness, almost pathos," the younger Winthrop's most recent biographer writes, "in his anxiety to stay in touch." He wrote letter after letter to the society's secretary. He sent over scientific specimens—rattlesnake skins, birds' nests, plants, crabs, strange pigs. He studied the society's *Transactions* so as not to

Puritans there was only one important vocation, and that was spiritual. Although true salvation was in the end a God-given grace, the preparation for grace—the opening of the mind and soul to such a possibility—required education, knowledge, and will.

It was not this central religious commitment alone, however, that led the Puritans to their remarkable efforts in education. Partly too they were driven by a sense that in their wilderness situation the family, which traditionally had carried so much of the burden of transmitting culture from one generation to the next, had weakened and was failing in its duties. This fear bore heavily on the minds of the founding elders.* They looked ahead and noted that if extraordinary precautions were not taken in time, they would leave behind not a "Bible Commonwealth," but a society of rural barbarians. If family discipline were loose, if parents did not take their responsibilities seriously, the government would have to provide for the future.

When they founded the New England colonies, the Puritans therefore hoped not merely to provide education, but to extend it. Instinctively they relied on the willingness of people voluntarily to establish and support facilities for formal education. They knew that in England numerous primary and secondary schools had recently been founded by private donations—by gifts from such institutions as guilds and universities and even more often from individual donors. Such gifts were usually in the form of grants of land to support a school. In the first fifteen years after settlement, a number of relatively rich inhabitants in six New England towns *did* attempt to establish schools by making such traditional grants of land. But the land was wild and tenants were scarce; and gifts of land were worthless if they produced no rents. Other ways of financing education would have to be found. Instead of pleading with the rich, the government would have to command. The towns ordered the wealthy to volunteer their help, and later some of the towns' undivided common land was set aside for the support of schools. But the hoped-for income could not be raised for lack of reliable tenants. In the end, there remained only one resource: taxation. It began as a supplement to private gifts and ended as almost the sole and universal basis of elementary education.

In the 1640s, after struggling for more than ten years with the problem of financing education, the Puritans decisively enacted what would become two famous laws. In 1642 the Massachusetts General Court ordered all parents and ministers to assume responsibility for the "calling and employment of their children, especially of their ability to read and understand

*For pressures on family life in the seventeenth century, see chapter 3, pp. 72–75.

the principles of religion and the capital laws of this country." Five years later, in 1647, the legislature ruled that all towns of fifty families must provide for the maintenance of elementary schools, and all towns of one hundred families must support secondary (Latin grammar) schools. These laws became models for the rest of Puritan New England. Connecticut enacted similar provisions in 1650, and Plymouth did so in two stages, in 1658 and 1677. Wherever these laws remained on the books, they were innovative and creative. But they are easily misunderstood.

The laws of the 1640s did *not* provide for public education as it has been known since the nineteenth century. No strict distinction between "private" and "public" existed in the seventeenth century. Neither of these laws specified that "public" money would be the financial basis of a community's schools; neither made formal schooling obligatory at any level. What the laws *did* do was, first, to establish a minimum level of educational accomplishment (not schooling) by spelling out the obligations of parents toward their children and of masters toward their servants, and by reinforcing these obligations with threats of fines and of removing children to other households. Second, the laws required that, at both the elementary and the secondary level, schooling be made universally *available* to those who wished to take advantage of it. Third, the laws established a community-wide obligation to support formal institutions of education without reference to the benefits any individual or family derived from these schools. Finally, the laws made clear that the government's role in the area of education would not be merely supplementary or supportive or supervisory, but positive and compelling.

All the provisions written into these innovative American laws on education were highly creative. But these famous laws stand at the beginning, not at the end, of the historical development of education in Puritan New England. The question is not merely what was hoped for or what was provided for, but what happened to these hopes and these provisions in later years. What effect did these remarkable provisions have on the lives of the people?

By the end of the seventeenth century, it was clear that the hopes of the Puritans were not being evenly and satisfactorily fulfilled. Many towns failed to provide for schools and were fined. Later amendments to the laws complained of continuing neglect of education by masters, parents, and towns. The old fears that New England's younger generation would grow up without a proper education not only remained, but seemed to grow more intense. In 1671 Massachusetts doubled the fines on towns that neglected to maintain grammar-school instruction. In a sermon in 1689, Cotton Mather, the third-generation member of a great line of ministers and the self-appointed guardian of the old Puritan hopes, bemoaned his people's fate. He doubted, he declared, whether New England suffered "under an iller [worse] symptom than the too general want of education in the rising generation." If not overcome, this neglect would "gradually and speedily dispose us to that sort of Creolean degeneracy observed to deprave the children of the most noble and worthy Europeans when transplanted into America."

But even Mather's authoritative voice could not halt the movement of change. In 1718 the General Court, again increasing the delinquency fines, condemned the "many towns that not only are obliged by law but are very able to support a grammar school, yet choose rather to incur and pay the fine and penalty than maintain a grammar school." As settlements spread throughout the countryside, as contact with the centers of high culture grew thin, and as the original Puritan enthusiasms cooled, people increasingly tended to favor modifying the law or adjusting it to the realities of everyday life. The laws remained on the books, and the colonial magistrates sought to enforce them, but sometimes there was outright evasion. A town would obey by hiring a teacher who knew no Latin, telling him to teach the subject "as far as he was able." More commonly, a new institution was used, the "moving school," which satisfied the law by providing a schoolmaster and his equipment but distributed his services on a circuit through the town's lands in proportion to the spread of population. Thus Gloucester, Massachusetts, had a Latin grammar school, but the teacher and his books moved about in a cycle of three years, settling in seven places in the following monthly proportions: 9, 7, 5-1/2, 5-1/2, 4-1/2, 3, 1-1/2. Even the most remote corner of the township had contact with the "moving school," but it was available for children in that most isolated area only one and a half months every three years.

Finally, by the mid-eighteenth century the towns found a permanent solution: the district school. The towns were now formally divided into school districts, each district drawing its proportionate share of the available funds and using the money as the local school committee decided. Schools thus existed in almost every town, although variations were great. For the management of the schools was now entirely in local hands, and some localities were limited, isolated places, incapable of and uninterested in rising above their narrow horizons. Some schools were excellent, some poor, some dismal. Often the Latin grammar school proved to be a one-room schoolhouse in which children of all ages were taught at their own levels. Uniformity was lost, but there was no "Creolean degeneracy" that Mather had feared. New England in fact emerged in the eighteenth century still a literate

LT. GOV. WILLIAM STOUGHTON OF MASSACHUSETTS
In the background is the building that this dour, wealthy, old-fashioned Puritan gave to his alma mater, Harvard, in 1699. It was the first American college building donated by an alumnus.

culture, still open to a high level of cultural attainment.

All of this was a flame, sparked by the original creators of the "Bible Commonwealth," that sputtered at times but never went out. It is a remarkable accomplishment when it is contrasted with the slow and irregular development of education elsewhere in the colonies, where the churches and a few generous individuals sought to provide for schooling. In 1671 Governor Berkeley of Virginia wrote about his colony, "I thank God there are no free schools nor printing," these being sources, he declared, of "disobedience and heresy and sects." By 1689 there were still only six schools of various kinds in Virginia. In that same year Maryland had one school. New York, mainly through the efforts of the Dutch church, may have had eleven.

View of Savannah, 1734.

Embellishing the Wilderness

*T*he European settlement of North America was an intrusion into the wilderness, a struggle to impose the familiar forms of an advanced civilization upon an environment that was almost totally unredeemed from its natural, uncultivated state. The awareness of this struggle was as vivid to those who settled the last British colony, Georgia, and who pictured Savannah in 1734 as a tiny clearing at the edge of a vast forest as it had been to the settlers of Virginia a century and a quarter earlier. The struggle took its toll. Not only were there significant modifications in the conduct of everyday life—regressions and simplifications, it seemed—but at the margins there were complete surrenders to the wilderness. There were always frontiersmen who spent months drifting from one isolated primitive encampment to another, and emerging from time to time to buy with animal skins what they needed for survival and to

Massachusetts press cupboard, late seventeenth century.

tell remarkable tales of worlds beyond the mountains and the swamps. But these wandering semiprimitives were rare in British America—much rarer than they were in French Canada, where half-savage trappers and woodsmen (the famous *coureurs de bois* who roamed the wilderness for years at a time) formed a significant part of the population.

From the beginning British America was a bourgeois society. The wilderness exerted no fatal seduction; it proved to be a challenge to the arts of cultivation, to the nesting instinct, to the impulse to domesticate and to embellish. Beauty, in European terms, was sought from the start, transferred at first from "home" and then imitated, however crudely, by local craftsmen. The artifacts of daily living had to be made from materials that lay at hand, by men whose task it was to provide the necessities of life, not the refinements. But although the products were often rough, they were rarely primitive. Occasionally, even in the earliest years, some striking embellishment, some special grace of line, balance, or proportion, some flash of vivid and harmonious color, emerged to mark the point at which craft turned to art.

So furniture was crafted in the seventeeth century from local woods, its bare, hard surfaces as uncomfortable as they were serviceable and durable; but sometimes even in the earliest years the furniture was embellished too, with a conscious style, decorated and beautified. Spindled oak pieces like the Ipswich, Massachusetts, press cupboard were stained with vegetable dyes to give them tone, and their ornaments painted black to simulate ebony; the result was a complex, dappled black-brown surface. Later such embellishments grew more sophisticated, as the Queen Anne chair reveals; and by the early 1700s japanned highboys

Spindled chair, 1640–1660.

Queen Anne chair from Philadelphia.

were being produced with structural designs in classical modes and oriental scenes in brilliant color. Quite independently the Dutch in New York and the Germans in Pennsylvania developed from their own folk traditions a distinctive pattern of decoration. And everywhere craftsmen learned to produce not only beautifully designed wooden furniture in contemporary styles, but upholstered pieces that were colorful as well as solid and comfortable.

Textile embellishments took many forms, from embroidered chair seats and petticoat borders to crewel bed hangings and draperies. And the skill of the silversmiths developed quickly too. By the end of the seventeenth century, intricately designed and handsomely worked silver bowls, tankards, coffeepots, and sugar boxes were seen on tables in the South as in the North. Craftsmen like John Coney were creating objects in silver that would delight their users and viewers for generations to come.

(*Far left*) Sugar box, by John Coney, 1680–1690. *Courtesy, Museum of Fine Arts, Boston, Elliot Fund*

(*Left*) Silver tankard, late seventeenth century. *Courtesy, Museum of Fine Arts, Boston. Gift of Mr. and Mrs. Dudley Pickman*

(*Left*) Japanned chest, early eighteenth century. *Courtesy, Metropolitan Museum of Art, Purchase 1940, Joseph Pulitzer Bequest*

(*Below*) Crewel petticoat border, mid-eighteenth century. *Courtesy, Museum of Fine Arts, Boston. Gift of Mrs. J. R. Churchill*

Bed hangings, c. 1745.

Glass sugar bowl, late eighteenth century.

Doorway of Fowler Tavern, mid-eighteenth century, Westfield, Massachusetts. ▶

Everyday life was visibly enhanced—not transformed into a wonder world of aristocratic ostentation, but simply embellished, decorated, elevated above mere praticality. Clock faces and inlaid rifle stocks became minor works of art; clock cases and gun grips were fashioned of beautifully worked wood. Door frames were improved by conscious imitation of metropolitan models. Glassware evolved in unexpected forms, and metal workers produced weathervanes that had the animated beauty of modern mobiles.

Colonial Williamsburg Foundation

Raleigh Tavern, Williamsburg, Virginia.

Siteman/Stock, Boston

The wilderness remained—a threat to European civilization and a constructive challenge to creativity in a people conscious both of the simplicity of their lives and of the richness of their cultural heritage. Young men like Jefferson grew up in a borderland world, looking out from Queen Anne rooms of spare elegance onto a wild, uncultivated land.

COLLEGE	COLONY	FOUNDED
Harvard College	Massachusetts	1636
College of William and Mary	Virginia	1693
Yale College	Connecticut	1701
College of New Jersey (Princeton University)	New Jersey	1746
College of Philadelphia (University of Pennsylvania)	Pennsylvania	1754
King's College (Columbia University)	New York	1754
College of Rhode Island (Brown University)	Rhode Island	1764
Queen's College (Rutgers University)	New Jersey	1766
Dartmouth College	New Hampshire	1769

The Colleges. In New England the remarkable development of education at the elementary and secondary levels was in part the result of the reinforcement it received from higher education, which too became closely bound to the immediate needs of these provincial communities.

There can be little doubt about the Puritans' primary reason for founding in 1636 the institution that became Harvard College (named after its first private benefactor, John Harvard). They dreaded, they said, "to leave an illiterate ministry to the churches when our present ministers shall lie in the dust." There were other motives too. Some Puritans hoped that the institution would help spread Christianity to the Indians by training preachers who would go out to deliver the word. But although the gospel mission failed miserably amid the general breakdown of relations between Indians and whites, the effort to maintain a college primarily for training preachers and secondarily for educating gentlemen in the liberal arts took root and flourished. Harvard College was a stable institution by the time the second English colonial college, William and Mary, was chartered in 1693 as part of the effort to improve the quality of the Anglican ministers in Virginia. Through its graduates, Harvard College exerted a great influence; and its continued existence, written into the terms of the Bay Colony's second charter of 1691, was firmly guaranteed.

Yet like so much else in American life, this college, and those that would follow it, became something different from the models on which they were based. The Puritan founders had intended to create an institution similar to the English college—a residential establishment that would be owned and directed by the tutors and professors who lived and taught there. But the colonial colleges did not develop in that way. Instead, the ownership of a college's property, and ultimately its government, came to rest not with the teachers, but with boards of trustees outside the educational process. These trustees hired the teachers and supervised the work of the college on behalf of the founding community. This development arose from the central motivation for the founding of the college: the community's desire to ensure a continuing supply of educated ministers and to advance learning in the American wilderness. Later in American history, the nature of the communities that founded colleges would shift. Colleges would be founded by religious denominations serving their particular concerns, and by state governments recognizing the need for experts in technical fields and seeking to provide for the public's general education. But ever since the establishment of the first college in 1636, the motivation and the resources have come from groups outside the teaching profession. The governance of higher education has reflected the insistence by these groups that the colleges fulfill these community mandates.

In this sense all the American colleges and universities have been community schools—products not so much of the world of education and learning as of desires and decisions of the community at large. Control has therefore rested with the founding communities; and as, in the colonial period, the horizons of the communities narrowed, the mandates of the colleges narrowed too. Educated ministers were indeed trained, and higher education was indeed made generally available, not only in Massachusetts, Virginia, and Connecticut, but also in New Jersey, Pennsylvania, New York, Rhode Island, and New Hampshire. Through the institutions of higher education, the pursuit of learning and the cultivation of the arts were advanced and passed on from generation to generation. But the primary reason for their foundation was not so much a love of learning for its own sake as it was the local concerns of communities with limited horizons—communities that were determined to sustain their founders' commitments to serving local, provincial needs.

1660	Restoration of Stuart monarchy (Charles II, 1660–85).
	Basic navigation law, monopolizing colonial trade and shipping for Britain, passed by Parliament; includes "enumeration" clause.
1662	Massachusetts Bay ministers sanction the Halfway Covenant.
	Colony of Connecticut chartered by crown.
1663	New royal charter issued to Rhode Island.
	New navigation act (Staple Act) passed, channeling colonies' importation of European goods through England.
	Charter of Carolina given to eight courtiers.
1664	England conquers New Netherland, which becomes proprietary colony of Duke of York.
	New Jersey charter issued to two courtiers.
1665	Duke's Laws for New York promulgated.
1669	Fundamental Constitutions of Carolina issued.
1673	New navigation act imposes "plantation duties."
1675	Lords of Trade appointed as committee of Privy Council.
1675–76	King Philip's War in New England.
1676	Bacon's Rebellion in Virginia.
	New Jersey divided into East and West New Jersey.
1677	West New Jersey's Concessions and Agreements issued.
	Culpeper's Rebellion in Carolina.
1680	New Hampshire given royal charter.
1681	Pennsylvania charter granted to William Penn; first settlements in 1682.
1684	Massachusetts Bay charter annulled by crown (charters of Connecticut, Rhode Island, New Jersey, Pennsylvania, Maryland, and Carolina abrogated in following years, to 1691).

1685–88	Duke of York becomes James II; his accession makes New York a royal colony.
1686	Dominion of New England established.
1688	Glorious Revolution in England drives out James II in favor of William and Mary.
1689	Successful rebellion in Boston against Dominion of New England.
	The Protestant Association in Maryland rebels.
1689–91	Leisler's Rebellion in New York.
1689–97	King William's War (colonial phase of Europe's War of the League of Augsburg).
1691	Massachusetts Bay Colony gets new charter.
1692	Witchcraft hysteria in Salem, Massachusetts; twenty "witches" executed.
1693	College of William and Mary founded.
1696	English government establishes Board of Trade and Plantations.
	Passage of comprehensive navigation act, extending admiralty court system to America.
1699	Woolen Act passed by Parliament.
1701	Yale College founded.
	New and permanent Frame of Government adopted in Pennsylvania.
1702–13	Queen Anne's War (colonial phase of Europe's War of the Spanish Succession) concluded in Treaty of Utrecht.
1702	East and West New Jersey formed into single royal colony.
1702–14	Reign of Queen Anne.
1708	Saybrook Platform adopted in Connecticut.
1714–27	Reign of George I, beginning Hanoverian dynasty.
1719	Rebellion against proprietors in Carolina.

The fullest account of the origins of the British imperial system, in both theory and institutions, is Charles M. Andrews, *The Colonial Period of American History*, IV (1938). On the theory of empire, see in addition Richard Koebner, *Empire* (1961), chap 3; on the all-important customs administration in the colonies, Thomas C. Barrow, *Trade & Empire* (1967); and on the difficulty in the late seventeenth century of imposing regulations on the scattered settlements, Michael G. Hall, *Edward Randolph and the American Colonies* (1969). On the influence of the Duke of York (James II) and his entourage on the evolution of empire and the importance of his and his lieutenants' military background, see Stephen S. Webb, ". . . The Household of James Stuart in the Evolution of English Imperialism," *Perspectives in American History*, 8 (1974), 55–80. On the patronage sources of colonial appointments and other aspects of the politics of the early empire, see Webb's "Strange Career of Francis Nicholson" and "William Blathwayt, Imperial Fixer," *Wm. and Mary Q.*, 23 (1966), 513–48; 26 (1969), 373–415—a subject presented in full in Webb's *The Governors-General* (1979). On James II's ill-fated effort to organize a territorial government, see Viola F. Barnes, *The Dominion of New England* (1923).

The emergence of a native Anglo-American aristocracy is traced generally, in the case of Virginia, in Bernard Bailyn, "Politics and Social Structure in Virginia,"[†] James M. Smith, ed., *Seventeenth-Century America* (1959), and Louis B. Wright, *First Gentlemen of Virginia* (1940); in the case of commerical New England, in Bernard Bailyn, *New England Merchants in the Seventeenth Century* (1955); in the case of New York, in Thomas Archdeacon, *New York City, 1664–1710* (1976); and in the five main port towns, in Carl Bridenbaugh, *Cities in the Wilderness* (1938). The origins of rural aristocracies in New England, rooted in the shifting relations between population and land, are described in Roy H. Akagi, *The Town Proprietors of the New England Colonies* (1924), and probed analytically in Richard L. Bushman, *From Puritan to Yankee* (1967), and in the individual community studies listed in the references to chapter III. For case studies of the emergence of the southern aristocracy, see the essays on social mobility in the Chesapeake area cited for the previous chapter; Louis B. Wrights's edition of Byrd's diaries and literary writings; and Richard B. Davis, ed., *William Fitzhugh and His Chesapeake World, 1676–1701* (1963). The political aspects of a rising aristocracy are analyzed in the case of New York in Patricia U. Bonomi, *A Factious People* (1971), chaps. 2, 3; in Archdeacon's *New York City*; and in Lawrence H. Leder, *Robert Livingston* (1961).

The late-seventeenth-century wars (the subject of Francis Parkman's dramatic classics, *Count Frontenac and New France Under Louis XIV*, 1877; and *A Half-Century of Conflict*, 1892) are sketched briefly in Howard H. Peckham, *The Colonial Wars, 1689–1762* (1964); their significance for the development of Anglo-American politics, trade, and society is suggested in G. M. Waller, *Samuel Vetch, Colonial Enterpriser* (1960).

The colonial rebellions of the late seventeenth century are described, insofar as they relate to the English rebellion against James II, in David S. Lovejoy, *The Glorious Revolution in America* (1972). But as social events these uprisings are to be associated with Bacon's Rebellion, which is described generally in Wilcomb E. Washburn, *The Governor and the Rebel* (1957), and analyzed in social terms in Bailyn, "Politics and Social Structure"[†]; in Wesley F. Craven, *Southern Colonies in the Seventeenth Century* (1949); and in Edmund Morgan, *American Slavery, American Freedom* (1975). Stephen S. Webb, *1676: The End of American Independence* (1984), sees the rebellion as an "imperial revolution" that led to the imposition of royal rule over the once semi-independent colonies. For the social background of Leisler's Rebellion, see Archdeacon's book cited above and Jerome R. Reich, *Leisler's Rebellion* (1953), which exaggerates the "democratic" impulses of the rebels. On Boston's rebellion, see Barnes, *Dominion of New England*. The most exhaustive study of the social background of any of these rebellions, however, is Lois G. Carr and David W. Jordan, *Maryland's Revolution of Government 1689–1692* (1974).

The deepening provincialism of American culture in the late seventeenth century emerges in the colonists' writings, analyzed in the opening chapter of Kenneth S. Lynn, *Mark Twain and Southwestern Humor* (1959); in the careers of third-generation Anglo-Americans such as the Winthrops (Richard S. Dunn, *Puritans and Yankees*, 1962, Bk. III) and the Mathers (Robert Middlekauff, *The Mathers*, 1971, Bk. III); in travelers' accounts (Jasper Danckaerts [1679–80], pub. 1867; the Frenchman Durand [1687], pub. 1923; Sarah Knight [1704], latest pub. 1972); and above all in education.

For a comprehensive, detailed, and broadly conceived account of early American education, see Lawrence A. Cremin, *American Education: The Colonial Experience, 1607–1783* (1970), parts I–III; for a general interpretation of the social role of colonial education, see Bernard Bailyn, *Education in the Forming of American Society* (1960); and for the deepening localization of standards, described in the text, Harlan Updegraff, *Origin of the Moving School in Massachusetts* (1907). Robert Middlekauff has traced the persistence of the classical tradition in the face of provincial difficulties in *Ancients and Axioms* (1963). James Axtell, *The School upon a Hill* (1974), shows through education in the broadest sense how New England's culture was transmitted across the generations.

On the origins of higher education, see Samuel E. Morison's magisterial works, *The Founding of Harvard College* (1935) and *Harvard College in the Seventeenth Century* (2 vols., 1936), both summarized in his *Three Centuries of Harvard: 1636–1936* (1936). Although these learned and readable books remain fundamental, Morison's general interpretation has been challenged: by Winthrop S. Hudson, "The Morison Myth Concerning the Founding of Harvard College," *Church History*, 8 (1939), 148–59, and by Jurgen Herbst, *From Crisis to Crisis* (1982), in which parallels are drawn between Harvard, Yale, and William and Mary on the one hand and the "*gymnasia illustria*, academies, or *Gelehrtenschulen* on the Continent" on the other. Yale's origins are detailed in Richard Warch, *School of the Prophets: Yale College, 1701–1740* (1973), and William and Mary's in Parke Rouse, Jr., *James Blair of Virginia* (1971). All aspects of education and artistic expression are discussed in Richard B. Davis, *Intellectual Life in the Colonial South, 1585–1763* (3 vols., 1978).

[†]See first footnote on p. 27.

5 American Society in the Eighteenth Century

The end of the War of the Spanish Succession in 1713 and the creation of a stable political regime in England under Sir Robert Walpole, prime minister from 1721 to 1742, introduced a period of great expansion in all spheres of Anglo-American life. In the two generations that followed the war, the American settlements, despite minor involvements in other international conflicts and repeated cycles of commercial recession, grew so rapidly and matured so fully that they came to constitute an important element in British life and in the life of the Atlantic world generally. From scattered seventeenth-century foundations the colonies, even as they were drawn more and more elaborately into the ill-organized structure of the British Empire, were becoming increasingly distinctive, although outwardly they sought to conform to traditional European ways of life. During this period they acquired characteristics that would remain permanent features of American society.

The New Population: Sources and Impact

Fundamental to all aspects of eighteenth-century American history was the phenomenal growth of the population. By 1700 the population was approximately 250,000; by 1775 it had grown tenfold, to 2.5 million, which was more than a third the size of the population of England and Wales (6.7 million). A fifth of the American people were black, almost all of them slaves. Nine-tenths of the slaves lived south of Pennsylvania. They constituted two-fifths of the population of Virginia and almost two-thirds of the population of South Carolina.

By the 1760s the settled areas formed an almost unbroken line down the coast from Maine to Florida, and they reached deep into the interior. In New England, groups moving up the Connecticut River and the coastal streams penetrated into New Hampshire and Vermont. In New York, settlements spread through the rich Hudson, Mohawk, and Schoharie valleys, and in Pennsylvania and the Carolinas they extended back to the Appalachians. In a few places, especially southwestern Pennsylvania, the Appalachian mountain barrier had been breached by frontiersmen who were actively opening fresh lands to cultivation in Indian territories.

The population was almost entirely rural. Of the towns, the most populous was Philadelphia, with approximately 35,000 inhabitants. The five largest communities (Philadelphia, New York, Boston, Charleston, and Newport, Rhode Island) had a combined population of 90,000—3.6 percent of the total population. Fifteen smaller towns, ranging from New Haven, Connecticut (with 8,000), to Savannah, Georgia (with 3,200), account for another 77,500. But very few of the total town population of approximately 167,500 lived in circumstances that can be called "urban" in a modern sense.

The rapid increase in the size of the population—it almost doubled every twenty-five years—was in large part the result of natural growth, that is, the excess of births over deaths. But new flows of immigration also contributed to population growth. The basic recruitment from England continued, although at a reduced rate, and between 250,000 and 300,000 Africans were imported. New groups also began to arrive in significant numbers. Religious persecution in France led to the immigration of several thousand Huguenots (forced to flee from France after 1685, when the tolerant Edict of Nantes was revoked); and from Scotland came groups of Jacobites (those faithful to the exiled James II and his son) after their military defeat by the English in 1715. But the main new flows of immigration came from two quite different sources, which together supplied approximately 20 percent of the total American population when the first national census was taken in 1790.

The Irish. The first new source was Ireland—not Catholic Ireland but Protestant northern Ireland, which had been the first overseas colony of the English people.

Foreground: Library of Congress. Background: Penn. Museum and Historical Commission, Harrisburg.

GERMAN PIETIST EMIGRANTS

The man carries in one hand the orthodox Lutheran "Augsburg Confession" and in the other Johann Arndt's classic of pietistic devotion, *Vom Wahren Christentum* (1605; republished in Philadelphia in 1751). His pack bears the motto, "God is with us in need," hers, "God has done great things for us"; and between the two in the original print was the caption "Nothing but the gospel drives us into exile. Though we leave the fatherland, we remain in God's hand." In the background is a German servant's indenture dated 1736, a year in which a large number of Salzburg emigrants, such as the two depicted here, were fleeing religious persecution.

The efforts of the English in the early seventeenth century to colonize a great "plantation" in Ulster, the six northern counties of Ireland, had attracted to that region a large migration from Scotland, where social and religious conditions throughout the seventeenth century were unsettled. By 1715 perhaps 150,000 Scots had crossed the Irish Sea to settle on Irish estates, where rents were originally low. During the eighteenth century there was a large migration of these "Scotch-Irish" Presbyterians to America. We do not know exactly how many came, but the best estimate is a yearly average of 4,000 through most of the century, totaling nearly a quarter of a million. It was said by Ireland's greatest historian, W. E. H. Lecky, that the loss of so many Irish Protestants to America in the eighteenth century ended forever the hope of balancing the religious communities on that tormented island.

The Germans. The other new source of the American population was the upper Rhine Valley in southwestern Germany. This region, especially the area known as the Rhenish Palatinate, had been badly ravaged in the religious wars of the seventeenth century and then, in 1688–89, devastated by French armies. In addition, Catholic princes had begun to persecute the region's increasingly numerous Protestant sects. Further troubles beset the area in 1708 and 1709, when crop disasters reduced much of the population to beggary. A new English naturalization law enacted at this time made England an attractive refuge, and a movement of peoples into British territory began that ended in furnishing a major component of the American population. As early as the 1680s William Penn had begun recruiting settlers in the Rhineland, and the greatest number of German-speaking settlers came to his colony. These "Pennsylvania Dutch" (from *Deutsch*—that

German Settlements in
18th-Century America

is, Germans, not Hollanders) composed one-third of Pennsylvania's population by 1775. The census of 1790 showed almost as many German-born or German-descended Americans (9 percent of the nation's population) as there were Scotch-Irish, and the German influence was at least as important in the development of American society.

Attitudes of the New Immigrants.

In the end numbers alone do not account for the importance of migrations like these. More significant are the attitudes, aptitudes, and ambitions of the immigrants, and their influence on the development of the community's life. In the case of the Scotch-Irish and the Germans, the impact was profound. Both groups were alienated from civil and church authority; both were hostile to all establishments, stubborn in defense of their rights, and eager to gain economic security. Both contributed powerfully to the shaping of American social and political life.

For the Scotch-Irish, resentment, if not hatred, of the English establishment had long been a way of life.

Britain had excluded Irish products from sale elsewhere in British territory and thereby had crippled Ireland's economic growth. Further, the Anglo-Irish landlords, mainly absentees, had increased rents whenever leases fell due. Moreover, the Scotch-Irish, being Presbyterians, were outside the official Anglican church, hence "nonconformist"; as such they were victimized by the Anglican religious establishment, which they had to support by paying special taxes. In 1704 a religious test excluded Presbyterians from all public offices, and marriages performed in their churches were declared invalid. As a result of this harassment, the first wave of Scotch-Irish immigrants, arriving in Boston and in the Delaware ports between 1717 and 1720, carried with it a burning resentment of the English establishment in all its forms. Those who followed, attracted by enthusiastic letters from America promising "liberty and ease as the reward of . . . honest industry," freedom from escalating rents, and access to public office, shared these attitudes in varying degrees and carried these resentments throughout the colonies.

The Germans had no natural affinity with the British establishment and no political contacts to help protect them in this exploitative world. Further, since they were aliens, their legal position was weak. Before 1740 they could become British subjects only through specific deeds of "denization" (grants of residency) or through naturalization conferred by the colonial governments. Generous rights were bestowed by such actions, but they could be revoked, and they did not bind the *British* government. Hence locally naturalized Germans could not qualify as "British" subjects under the navigation acts, and naturalization by one colony was not automatically recognized in the other colonies. Many of these problems were eliminated by Parliament's general Naturalization Law of 1740, which permitted aliens who had resided continuously for seven years in any of the British colonies to become naturalized subjects of all colonies. But naturalization by this process was time-consuming. Moreover, it excluded Catholics; it involved an oath offensive to Jews, Quakers, and certain other Protestants; and it did not carry over fully to England itself, where naturalized colonists were not automatically entitled to own land or to hold crown office.

Alienated from, if not actively hostile to, the British government, these Scotch-Irish and German newcomers had little reason to feel close to the colonial governments either, or to the groups that dominated these governments. They often settled in backcountry areas remote from the colonial capitals; sometimes they did not even know which colony they belonged to as they moved through the hinterland. Often they settled an area before the arrival of the local government, whose agents therefore appeared as exploiters. And in addition, the immigrants were often deliberately victimized, not merely by land speculators and managers of the infamous trade in "redemptioners" (those who found upon their arrival that they had to sell their labor for a term of years to pay for their transportation), but almost officially by the colonial governments themselves.

The Blacks and Slavery.

If the Scotch-Irish and the Germans were alienated in various ways from the Anglo-American establishment, they at least had access to the processes of law and ultimately of politics by which to express their grievances. For the black population there were no possibilities of relief and assimilation. Their separateness was rigidly fixed by the alienation of race and by the debasement of slavery.

We do not fully know—and probably never will know—how this large population of black people accommodated themselves to North American life, the fearful human cost of that accommodation, and the character of their resistance to the brutal system that dominated their lives. There are no documents that

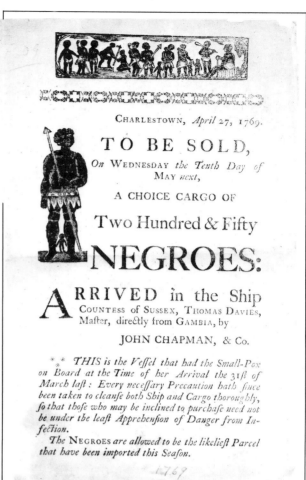

CHARLESTOWN, *April* 27, 1769.

TO BE SOLD,

On WEDNESDAY the *Tenth Day of* MAY next,

A CHOICE CARGO OF

Two Hundred & Fifty

NEGROES:

ARRIVED in the Ship COUNTESS of SUSSEX, THOMAS DAVIES, Master, directly from GAMBIA, by

JOHN CHAPMAN, & Co.

** *THIS is the Vessel that had the Small-Pox on Board at the Time of her Arrival the* 31st *of* March last: *Every necessary Precaution hath since been taken to cleanse both Ship and Cargo thoroughly, so that those who may be inclined to purchase need not be under the least Apprehension of Danger from Infection.*

The NEGROES *are allowed to be the likeliest Parcel that have been imported this Season.*

1769

American Antiquarian Society

directly record the blacks' feelings and the intimate details of their personal lives. But from the indirect evidence that has been assembled, one catches glimpses not only of degradation, but also of bewildering ambiguities and paralyzing tensions in human relations. There were also heroic efforts to maintain some measure of human dignity.

As it developed in the eighteenth century, slavery had many shadings and variations. Only 10 percent of the slave population lived north of Maryland, constituting a mere 4 to 5 percent of the population of the northern colonies. Slaves were spread thinly throughout the North; their highest concentration in that region was in New York City, where they may have formed as much as 17 percent of the population. Slaves in the North worked side by side with white field servants in the countryside and as laborers in the towns. They mingled with the poorest elements among the whites, formed stable families, and even managed to accumulate small sums on the side when they were "hired out" by their masters to work for

VIRGINIA TOBACCO WHARF
This realistic dockside scene in the Chesapeake tobacco country is a decorative design from the first accurate map of Virginia (1751) made by Joshua Fry and Peter Jefferson, Thomas's father, who was a surveyor as well as a planter.

others. These northern blacks—field hands, town laborers, and factory workers—were mostly native-born Americans, and they formed part, although a severely deprived part, of the general Anglo-American world.

The opposite was true of the tens of thousands of transplanted Africans (a third of all the North American blacks) who lived in the Carolinas and Georgia. The worst conditions were those on the fearful rice and indigo plantations of South Carolina. There, in tropical heat, laboring half the year knee-deep in the muck of the rice fields, the slaves lived unspeakably wretched lives. They were utterly isolated from the dominant society and alienated from the roots of their own culture. The death rate in this disease-ridden environment was appalling, and the black population increased only because of the continuous addition of new arrivals—thousands upon thousands of newly enslaved Africans who had survived the 15–20 percent death rate on the transatlantic voyage and had been sold like animals in the great Charleston slave market. On these isolated plantations in the Deep South, the blacks' culture remained closer to that of West Africa than it did anywhere else in British North America.

The tobacco plantations of the Chesapeake region, on which more than half of the black population lived, were quite different. By the 1760s some of the plantations had become large enough to support slave quarters that constituted well-organized communities. Family life was relatively stable, and the population grew by natural increase. Further, the need for house servants and artisans of all kinds relieved a sizable percentage of the black population from the worst kind of field work. Here, in this long-established tobacco world, where black kinship groups of second- and third-generation American natives spread across groups of plantations, a stable Afro-American culture, distinctive in religion, folk art, and social patterns, developed most fully. But the decency of the slaves' lives, where it existed at all, was extremely superficial. However assimilated they may have been in the North, and however involved they may have been in kinship networks in Virginia and Maryland, slaves everywhere were debased by the bondage that confined them. Humane masters might create plantations resembling biblical patriarchies, and wise masters might discover the economic value of allowing blacks to enjoy a little leisure and independent activity, as well as the dignity of family life. But everywhere brutality was never far below the surface. And everywhere there was resistance of some sort.

On the plantations in the South, untrained slaves fresh from Africa were most often sent off to outlying plots of land, where they spent their lives in unending field work. Frequently they still bore the ritual face scars of their earlier life in African tribes, where they had learned companionship and cooperation, and where they had thought of time not in terms of hourly

The New Population: Sources and Impact **115**

routines but of seasonal cycles. Thus they found it extremely difficult, at times impossible, to adjust to the grueling labor. Some ran off in the hope of returning to Africa or of setting up villages to re-create the life they had known. In the early years a few found refuge in "maroon" (fugitive) encampments in the Carolina swamps and deep in frontier forests; but most of the runaways were returned—exhausted, half-starved, and in rags after long exposure in the woods and swamps—to continue their inescapable "seasoning." In time, however, these field hands found effective means of resistance, not in hopeless efforts to escape, but in deliberately slowing down in their work, in wasting equipment, in damaging crops, and in silently disobeying. Their rebelliousness, directed at the plantation and only occasionally at their overseers or master, could have no long-term results, but at least it gave immediate relief to their feelings.

More complex and more self-damaging was the resistance of the American-born slaves employed as personal servants in and around the planters' houses. Enclosed within households of patriarchal discipline, they were forced into continuous close contact with their masters, who were made tense and insecure by the blacks' constant presence, and whose domestic lives were poisoned by the helpless availability of slaves of both sexes. Commonly the slaves perfected techniques of petty harassment that increased their masters' insecurity. Convenient personality disguises (the seemingly obedient "Sambo") minimized for slaves the likelihood of clashes with masters whose tensions could be released in sadistic rages.

The most openly rebellious of the eighteenth-century slaves were the most thoroughly assimilated and highly skilled artisans, whose talents gave them a measure of independence and who could deal with the environment as effectively as the whites. They were the most likely to survive as fugitives, and the most capable of easing their everyday burdens by shrewd manipulation. Closest to the white man's world, these skilled workmen understood the full meaning of their bondage; and although they lived more comfortably than the majority of blacks, they may have suffered even more. Everywhere slavery meant profound degradation and constant fear—for the whites as well as for the blacks.

A Maturing Economy and a Society in Flux

The single most distinctive fact of the American economy as a whole in the eighteenth century was the broad spread of freehold tenure—the outright ownership of land—throughout the free population. In contrast, all the land in England in the mid-eighteenth century was owned by only one-tenth of all heads of household. Between 20 percent and 25 percent of England's land was owned by 400 great landlords, representing a mere 3/100 of 1 percent of all families. More than 80 percent of this land was worked by tenants, whose rent constituted the income upon which the landowners lived. The social experience of the great majority of the English people was based on tenancy; it shaped the structure of English society and the organization of politics, for both rested on the existence of a leisured aristocracy supported by the income that others produced from the land. And the force behind all agrarian enterprise was the unspoken assumption that the more land one owned, the greater one's income would be, an assumption based on the scarcity of arable land relative to the available labor.

The situation in the American colonies was entirely different. From the beginning the great attraction had been the availability of free land, and that attraction had not proved false. Although there were important regional variations, the large majority of the nonslave farm workers owned the land they worked, even if only at the end of their working lives and even if not in the form and amount they desired. This dominant fact of eighteenth-century American life created conditions altogether different from those that existed elsewhere. How unusual the resulting situation was may perhaps best be seen by examining the apparent *exceptions*—situations in which a re-creation of the traditional life of landlords would appear to have taken place.

The Great Landowners. The population growth and the resulting increase in land values led the descendants of the seventeenth-century proprietors to cash in, if possible, on their claims to large tracts of land. Four such claims were particularly imposing. The Penn family claimed the undistributed land of Pennsylvania. The Calvert family asserted its rights to Maryland's unsettled land. Earl Granville, the heir of Sir George Carteret, took up his right to one share of the original Carolina grant, a claim that was calculated to cover most of the northern half of the present state of North Carolina. And Lord Fairfax was the heir to the Northern Neck of Virginia, the 5 million acres between the Potomac and the Rappahannock rivers that had originally been granted by Charles II in 1649. By the mid-eighteenth century these colossal properties were no longer wild lands, but territories being opened to cultivation, and they were suddenly becoming valuable to their owners. But with the exception of Fairfax, who lived in Virginia after 1753, none of these great landowners was a resident landlord, and none was personally engaged in managing and developing landed estates worked by permanent tenants in the familiar European pattern. The landlords' greatest profits came less from steady rents than from sales in rising land markets.

PETER MANIGAULT AND HIS FRIENDS
Manigault (1731–73) was a Charleston, South Carolina, lawyer, merchant, and plantation owner, educated in England, who served in the colony's Assembly for many years, as Speaker after 1765. A collector of furniture, silver, and books, he was a classical scholar, a politician, and—as this cartoon of 1760 shows—a bon vivant as well.

The operations of these great proprietary land-owners were not essentially different from those of lesser land speculators throughout the colonies. Because the lands were originally wild, the owners had the choice either of making a high capital investment to clear the land, to erect buildings on it, and otherwise to make it rentable at a profit; or of renting it out at low or no rent, and benefiting from the increased value created by the labor of tenants as they worked the land. The former of these choices was distinctly uneconomic: many other kinds of investments were more profitable than preparing wild land for lucrative rentals. The best strategy was to rent the land cheaply to tenants who would open it to cultivation and who looked forward eventually to buying the land themselves. Profits from such land sales, based on the initial labor of tenants, could be huge, and also continuous, since the purchasers often bought the farms from the original landowners on loans secured by mortgages on the land itself.

In a few places in the colonies, however, there were landowners who *did* seek to establish themselves as landlords in the traditional sense, and they encountered sharp and at times even violent opposition. On a few estates along the Hudson River, and in New Jersey to a lesser extent, many of the traditional forms of landlordism were re-created: high perpetual rents, incidental taxes and fees, and insecurity of tenure. These burdens could be enforced because the landlords had political influence, because their land claims were carefully protected in law, and because they controlled the courts through which tenants would normally have sought relief. But in the end there was no

re-creation of a traditional landlord system. Such a system produced more trouble than could easily be handled. Many of the tenants simply refused to accept the burdens. They protested continually, and they resorted to all sorts of devices to destroy the landlords' control. From Indians or from New England land speculators, they commonly acquired dubious titles to the land they worked, and they sought to validate these claims legally.

By the 1750s the situation on the tenanted estates in eastern New York and in New Jersey was explosive. The tenants refused to pay rents and duties; and when the courts tried to extract the payments due, the tenants rose up in armed rebellion. The climax came in 1766 in a wave of rioting. Tenants simply renounced their leases and refused to get off the land when ordered to do so. In Westchester County in New York, rebellious farmers formed mobs, opened the jails, and stormed the landlords' houses. It took a regiment of regular troops with militia auxiliaries to put down the uprising. Yet even after the rebellion had been forcibly put down, tenancy could not be uniformly enforced. Many of the farmers simply moved off to the nearest vacant land. One of their chief destinations was Vermont, which as a result of this exodus from the Hudson River estates, and of a parallel migration of discontented New Englanders, was opened to settlement for the first time.

Plantations in the South. As an exception to the general American pattern of landownership, landlordism on the Hudson River estates could be maintained only with great difficulty. A more glaring exception to the

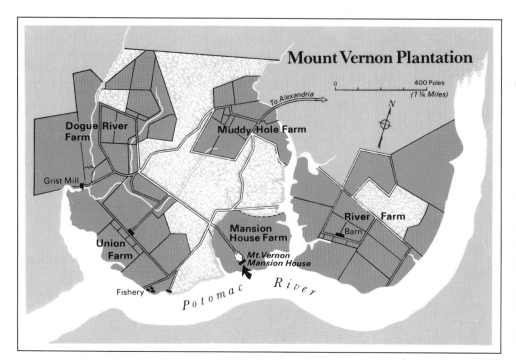

Mount Vernon Plantation

0   400 Poles
          (1¼ Miles)

To Alexandria

Dogue River Farm

Muddy Hole Farm

Grist Mill

River Farm

Barn

Union Farm

Mansion House Farm

Mt. Vernon Mansion House

Fishery

Potomac River

MOUNT VERNON PLANTATION, ABOUT 1787

The plantation, which occupied about 10,000 acres, consisted of four working farms and the mansion house property. It was a largely self-sufficient community, containing, besides the slave quarters and agricultural buildings on the farms, a coach house and stables, a smoke house, a spinning house, a spring house, a wash house, carpenter's, tailor's, shoemaker's, and blacksmith's shops, and vegetable gardens.

rule of freehold tenure was in the South, where plantations worked by slave labor would seem, in some measure at least, to have created the economic basis of a landed aristocracy. But the southern aristocrats of the eighteenth century lived in a completely different world from that of the English gentry and aristocracy whose lifestyle they tried to emulate. There *were* large estates in the South, although not many: in Maryland only 3.6 percent of all estates were worth over £1,000. And these large estates did support an aristocracy of sorts. But the plantation estates in the South were far different from the tenanted estates of the English aristocracy, quite aside from the obvious fact that the labor force was composed of slaves rather than of legally free tenants.

An English estate was not a single unit of production: it was a combination of many separately producing farms managed by individual tenants. A plantation in the eighteenth-century American South, on the other hand, *was* a single unit of production—a large, unified agricultural organization under a single management. The whole enterprise was operated as a unit in directing labor and in planning production. From these basic conditions flowed the central characteristics of the life of the southern gentry.

The eighteenth-century southern planters were not leisured landlords living comfortably on profits produced by others, any more than the seventeenth-century plantation owners had been. They

were closely involved in the process of crop management, land use, and labor direction, and they thus became active producers of their own income. Even if overseers were the immediate supervisors of work on the plantations, the planters discovered at their cost that they themselves had to exercise managerial responsibility. The eighteenth-century British politician and political thinker Edmund Burke said that the basis of any true aristocracy was "uncontending ease, the unbought grace of life." But a glance at such vivid documents as the diaries of the Virginia planter Landon Carter shows the worried concerns of hardpressed agrarian businessmen, absorbed in ledgers, profit margins, and the endless difficulties of farm production and labor management. The plantation owners did attain a certain graciousness in style of living. But that elegance was a light veneer over a rough-grained life of land dealing, of physically caring for and disciplining a partially dehumanized and potentially rebellious slave labor force, and of trying to make a profit in a commercial world over which the planters could exercise little influence.

Plantations in the South differed from European estates in that an increase in the size of the unit of ownership did not increase the income available to the owner. The larger the plantation, the more exposed the owner was to economic dangers, and the more uncertain the profits he might earn; for the larger the estate, the greater the fixed costs of maintaining slaves

ISAAC ROYALL, JR., AND HIS FAMILY, BY ROBERT FEKE (1741)

This painting, one of the earliest by the self-taught American painter Feke and one of the earliest group portraits painted in America, shows (right to left) Royall, his wife and child, his sister-in-law, and his sister. Royall, then twenty-two years old, had inherited a fortune from his father, an Antiguan sugar planter who moved to Massachusetts in 1732 and settled his family on a handsome estate in Medford. The younger Royall, who served on the Massachusetts Council for over twenty years, was a loyalist during the Revolution; his estate was confiscated, and he died in England in 1781.

Harvard University Law School Collection

and equipment. These expenses remained constant or increased no matter what the marketing situation might be, and in bad years debts could rise drastically. Indeed, once started, a marketing depression tended to deepen rapidly and uncontrollably as unsold goods carried over from one season to the next, enlarging the glut to catastrophic size.

In such periods of downturn, the planter, far from enjoying the "unbought grace of life," struggled desperately to cut overhead costs or otherwise compensate for the marketing losses. Some concentrated on attaining self-sufficiency in the production of food and clothing so that indebtedness would not mean actual impoverishment. Others turned to crop diversification. Starting on the eastern shore of the Chesapeake in the 1720s and continuing west rapidly, planters began converting to the production of grains and livestock, although the emphasis on tobacco production remained. Still other planters took what benefit they could from a new form of marketing introduced by Scottish entrepreneurs, whose investments in the southern American economy in the eighteenth century were a significant development.

The Scottish merchants and bankers, principally in Glasgow, concentrated on developing the interior of the Chesapeake region. In this backcountry the units of tobacco production tended to be smaller than they were in the coastal regions, there was very little capital to start with, and there was no direct contact with

ocean shipping. The old consignment system of marketing tobacco was therefore inappropriate for the development of this region.* In an effort to reduce freight charges and to increase efficiency, the Scottish firms established stores in the backcountry. The agents, or "factors," who managed these stores bought tobacco crops outright, stored them, and in the end shipped them to central distribution points where vessels sent from Scotland could take up cargoes as fast as they could load.

From the merchants' point of view, this system had the advantage of eliminating the waiting time that vessels otherwise would have in collecting a cargo. Hence it provided a considerable reduction in shipping costs. For the tobacco growers it offered somewhat greater control, since they could oversee the actual sale of their crops without having to account for the complexities of the European tobacco markets. Like the tidewater planters, these inland tobacco growers also accumulated debts to the merchants, but their debts were less for consumer goods than for items needed for production: they took the form of loans for the purchase of slaves, equipment, and the other costs of initiating production. In organizing this trade and in making these investments, the Scots became the financiers of the development of the western tobacco lands. It was estimated that in

*For the consignment system, see chapter 3, p. 69.

SEA CAPTAINS CAROUSING IN SURINAM, BY JOHN GREENWOOD (1758)
Surinam (Dutch Guiana) on the northern coast of South America was a favorite port of call for American merchants who exchanged horses and tobacco there for sugar products. Greenwood, a Bostonian who lived in Surinam, painted in the faces of several well-known Rhode Island merchants.

1765, Glasgow firms had £500,000 of credits outstanding in the Chesapeake region. And by then their "factors" had become prominent figures—usually unpopular figures—in the region's society.

In none of this was there a reproduction of the economic basis of a traditional landlord class. In all areas and in every subcategory of the agricultural economy, something new had evolved, and what appeared to be traditional was not. The few vast properties of the heirs of the original proprietary families were not tenanted estates, but rather the assets of personal land companies whose greatest profits came from the sale of the land. The southern planters did not form a leisured aristocracy, but rather were active, hard-pressed farm and labor managers whose profits were as likely to be lowered as to be raised by an increase in their holdings. In this world of widespread freehold tenure, attempted re-creations of traditional landlord systems led not to reliable incomes and a life of agrarian ease, but rather to controversy, or even violent conflict. It is true that there were peaceable tenants in many areas. But tenancy was not the normal, permanent pattern of life for those who worked the land. In most areas it was an exceptional and often temporary condition, and its economic function was ordinarily different from what it traditionally had been in Europe. Above all, land speculation—the use of land as a salable commodity rather than as a source of steady income—was an almost universal occupation in rural America.

The World of Commerce.

The commercial sector of the economy was equally distinctive. Its focus lay in the larger port towns, comparable in size to the second- and third-rank English provincial cities. Except for Boston, whose population was stable at around 16,000, all of these towns continued to grow quickly. Although visitors often noted their outward resemblance to such cities as Edinburgh and Bristol, they also observed some of the differences, which resulted from the fact that the American towns were products of a frontier economy. In all these towns there was, of course, a laboring population, but most of the urban workers were self-employed artisans or workmen in small-scale, often family-sized, businesses. There was a small though growing number of casual laborers—dock hands, workers in shipbuilding enterprises, and others—who picked up what employment they could in menial tasks around the towns. They formed a volatile element in these communities, and they suffered in times of depression. But there is no evidence of mass poverty. The number of those who received charity increased, but it never approached the figures of the dependent poor in Europe. In England at times one-third of the population was impoverished; and in the cities, where beggars crowded the cellars and attics,

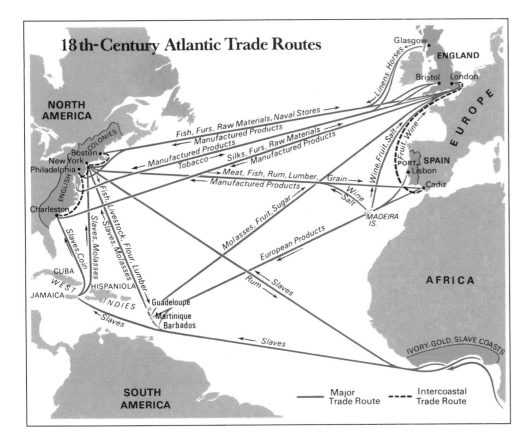

18th-Century Atlantic Trade Routes

massed in back alleys, and overwhelmed the charitable institutions, another third was poor enough to be rendered destitute by the repeated economic crises. But Philadelphia did not even build an almshouse until 1732; New York built one only in 1736. Before 1760 rarely were more than one hundred people supported by poor relief in Philadelphia. At no time during those years did as much as 1 percent of the population of New York and Philadelphia receive charity in any form.

A series of detailed statistical studies of the British mainland North American colonies in the 1700s reveals a level of living that, the author has written, "was probably the highest achieved for the great bulk of the population in any country up to that time." That situation was as true in the towns as in the countryside. Although a relatively small part of the urban population controlled an increasing proportion of the total wealth, and although the gap between rich and poor deepened, "the fact remains that not only were the rich getting richer but the poor were too, albeit at a slower rate." There was poverty in the pre-Revolutionary towns, but no mass starvation. There were riots, but no "bread riots" such as frequently broke out in European towns at times of food shortages and high prices. The "mobs" that became highly visible were not spear-

heads of a desperate proletariat inflamed by utopian aspirations and seeking to transform the structure of society. Rather, they were crowds of young apprentices, dock workers, and seamen temporarily idle between voyages, usually led by lesser merchants or independent craftsmen.

These conditions are not surprising, for the society of the commercial towns retained the characteristics of a pioneer world. Because labor was still relatively scarce, wages remained high enough to make small savings possible. Day laborers in Boston were paid twice as much as their counterparts in London. Furthermore, in the typical small-scale enterprise the distance between employer and employee remained narrow, both objectively (in terms of lifestyle and function) and subjectively (in terms of feelings of superiority or alienation). The typical artisan worked closely with his employer, and their activities were not unbridgeably different. Labor troubles were quite unlike those in modern society. Strikes were not protests by urban workers against conditions or wages. They were either protests by master workers, employers, and independent artisans against price levels set by the community for the sale of their products, or else they were efforts to stop widespread infiltration by outsiders into licensed trades. Town workers period-

BALTIMORE IN 1752
Aquatint by William Strickland, done in 1817 after a sketch made by John Mole, Esq., in 1752.

ically experienced hardships because of changes in the economy, which lurched through repeated phases of boom and bust, but there was no permanently alienated "proletariat."

The urban communities were dominated by the merchants, who in this period became important figures throughout the Atlantic world. Two conflicting tendencies shaped the development of the merchant group. During the early and middle years of the eighteenth century, there were forces that tended to limit and stabilize the mercantile leadership—to make of these leading figures an elite merchant aristocracy. But at the same time other forces, related to the deepest elements of the developing economy, were tending to upset the dominance of all would-be merchant elites.

In part, political stability in England created a significant degree of stability in the early-eighteenth-century merchant group. The secure arrangement of politics, patronage, and influence devised by the prime minister Robert Walpole in the 1720s helped stabilize the organization of Atlantic commerce, which was involved with politics and government contracting. At the same time, specialization increased within the English merchant establishment throughout the period, and the specialist wholesalers who controlled shipments to the colonies restricted their trade to selected American associates. And there were also technical improvements in trade and finance, particularly the development of marine insurance, that helped make possible a growing concentration of commercial capital and entrepreneurial control.

All these developments, along with the general fact that large operators could create economies of scale, tended to produce elitist characteristics within the commercial community. Yet despite the emergence of dominant groups, the merchant community as a whole, and commerce as a whole, remained highly competitive and changeable in membership. For, first, as raw frontier areas matured into settled agricultural producing regions, successful farmers branched out into marketing, becoming inland traders and ultimately merchants. Prosperous market farmers, particularly those located at transfer points on the rivers or inland trade routes, parlayed their advantages in goods and location into trading operations and drifted into commercial pursuits, often combined with land speculation.

But it was not only a matter of old settled areas producing surpluses from which market farmers could build careers in commerce. Wholly new hinterlands developed almost overnight, and from them emerged new men who proved effective competitors indeed.

In 1720 the chief agricultural producing areas

were located northeast of the Hudson River and in the Chesapeake region. Thereafter the area between the Hudson River and Chesapeake Bay became the dominant agricultural region. Into the swiftly growing port of Philadelphia poured surplus goods, chiefly grain, from the Pennsylvania backcountry, from New Jersey, and from parts of Maryland; and this flow enriched a new merchant aristocracy in Philadelphia, many of whose members were Quakers. By the 1760s the value of their trade with England exceeded that of all of New England. Similar developments took place in other regions. Within only ten years in the 1740s and 1750s, Baltimore rose from a wilderness village to a thriving urban center serving the marketing needs of a new backcountry area, and within a single generation Baltimore's merchants became important figures in the commercial world.

The result of all these movements in agriculture and trade was a highly dynamic mercantile world. Conditions had made possible the stabilization of a merchant leadership group. But the rapid development of the economy in long-settled areas and the constant opening of new areas of agricultural production created a steady recruitment of new merchants and a continuous competition between established figures and newcomers. There was a widespread sense that certain merchant families, established by the 1760s for two, three, or even four generations, were forming an elite; but there were always new faces, new families, capable of taking the same successful risks that had once served to establish the older families.

Religion: The Sources of American Denominationalism

The tensions within the commercial world were moderate compared with those that developed in religion. Because American culture in the mid-eighteenth century was still largely religious in its orientation, these tensions lay at the heart of the social world everywhere in the colonies, north and south, seaboard and inland.

The central event in the history of religion in America in the eighteenth century was the Great Awakening, a series of outbreaks of revivalism in the late 1730s and the 1740s. The Great Awakening roared through the colonies like a sheet of flame and left behind it a world transformed. In part this wave of passionate evangelicalism was a typical expression of a general religious movement that swept through much of the Western world in the eighteenth century. The Great Awakening coincided with an outpouring of Anglican evangelicalism—which would become Method-

ism—in England and Wales, and with a wave of Pietism in the German-speaking world. There were direct connections between the American revivalists and their European counterparts; but there was also something unique in the American evangelical movement, and it produced quite distinctive results.

Religion and Society in New England. In New England the background and sources of the Awakening came closest to the European pattern of such evangelical waves. By the early eighteenth century the Congregationalist churches had experienced the draining away of inner fervor and of emotional commitment that is typical of all long-established churches and that characteristically produces searchings for religious renewal and outbursts of evangelical enthusiasm. It is paradoxical that this waning of religious fervor should have happened, since Puritan Congregationalism had itself originated as a protest against a formal church establishment, the Church of England, and contained two essential characteristics that distinguished it from any established church. First, membership in the Congregationalist churches was not an automatic consequence of physical birth: that is, people were not "born into" the church. Rather, membership resulted from individual acts of voluntary commitment based on an inner experience. Second, church institutions in New England had been decentralized into Congregational units.

These original characteristics of New England Puritanism did not survive unchanged into the eighteenth century. By the mid-seventeenth century the New England churches had faced a crisis that arose from the failure of the second and third generations to duplicate the spiritual experiences of the founders and to join the churches through an act of saving grace. The founders' children had been baptized in the church because their parents had been members and it was felt that ultimately they too would experience a conversion. But until that "calling" came, these children could not become full members. In fact, many were never converted. Should, then, the children of these baptized but unconverted persons also be baptized?

This was the agonizing problem that had faced the Puritans in the mid-seventeenth century. If the answer had been Yes, then the church as a body of converted Christians would have been destroyed. But if the answer had been No, then, as conversions became fewer and fewer, the church would have grown apart from the society as a whole; it would have become a mere sect, without the basis for social control that was so fundamental a part of Puritan life. The solution came from a convention of ministers that met in 1657, whose decision was confirmed by a synod of 1662. The arrangement that was devised became known as the Halfway Covenant. Unconverted members *could* transmit membership in the church automatically to their children, but only a *halfway* membership. These children would be baptized, but they would not be offered the sacrament of communion, nor would they be entitled to vote as members of the church. As halfway members, they would be required to make a public pledge to obey the rulings of the church and to bring up their children as proper Christians. Still, they were members, if only partial, and the distinction between them and the full members who sat with them in church week after week was thin and grew thinner and more technical as the years passed.

The Halfway Covenant was an unstable compromise that deeply eroded the Puritans' original concept of the church as a body of proven saints. Conservatives and liberals alike found the halfway distinction illogical and unmanageable. Both factions turned to baptizing all, and sought to bring everyone to communion who was willing to accept it.

It was partly in an effort to control such permissive innovations that the more orthodox Puritan churches moved toward centralization of church government and away from congregational autonomy. In Massachusetts regional associations of ministers were formed, which sought to impose certification and disciplinary powers over the clergy and over the general management of church affairs. Although an attempt to give these organizations legal force was defeated in 1705, informal communication among the churches was strengthened. In Connecticut a parallel effort succeeded completely. There, the so-called Saybrook Platform of 1708 became public law. County "consociations" of the Congregationalist churches with disciplinary powers were created, together with regional associations of ministers and a colonywide general association of delegates of the ministers.

By all of these developments—a slackening in religious fervor, a growing identity of church and society, and the spread of general controls over originally independent congregations—the Puritan churches increasingly approached the condition of a formalized church establishment. But the process had obvious limits. In the eyes of British law, Congregational churches were nonconformist, and therefore they could never have the full sanction of law behind them. In New England the Anglican church (here, paradoxically, a "dissenting" body) led all opposition groups in demanding that its members enjoy the privileges granted to nonconformists in England. And in this the opposition groups were successful. In the 1720s Anglicans, Quakers, and Baptists gained full rights of worship in Congregationalist New England and of using their church taxes to support their own churches. Members of these groups were free, too, to hold office and to attend all institutions of learning. But they still remained *tolerated* groups, obliged to register with the authorities. No one was free of the obligation to support religion, and no group but these three was allowed the privileges of dissent.

New England Congregationalism was thus an establishment, but it was a loose establishment, in which religion as an inner experience tended to fade, and in which formal observance and institutional ritual had grown increasingly important. Less and less did the churches satisfy people's inner yearnings; more and more were these churches vulnerable to the charge of excessive formalism and of a deadening complacency.

Religion and Society South of New England.

In the other colonies the churches were even less capable of satisfying the deeper needs of their societies, which were still generally religious. In Virginia the Church of England had long been unable to serve the needs of the community, and the situation there was now worsened by the church's uncertain relationship to the new settlers, almost all non-Anglicans, who had moved into the backcountry in the 1720s and 1730s. Maryland too, after 1702, had an established Anglican church, but the Anglican community in that colony was numerically small, and its hold on the population at large was even looser than that of the Church of England in Virginia.

Elsewhere religious institutions were so chaotic and so volatile that they can hardly be clearly described. There were Anglican establishments of sorts in the Carolinas and Georgia—the latter colony having been settled in 1732 by Anglicans as a refuge for England's paupers and as a buffer against Spanish Florida. But nonconformists were welcomed in these colonies, and little effort was made to regulate religious life as a whole, which in many areas was overwhelmingly non-Anglican. Pennsylvania, Rhode Island, and New Jersey had no established churches at all. In Pennsylvania and Rhode Island the very idea of an established church ran against the principles of the influential Quakers. In New Jersey the religious diversity was so extreme and the Anglican community so small that no agreement on a privileged religion could be reached. And in New York, where non-Anglicans outnumbered Anglicans by at least fifteen to one, the only flourishing Anglican institution was New York City's Trinity Church, which Governor Fletcher had endowed with an independent source of income.

Amid the institutional confusion of religion in eighteenth-century America, the overwhelming fact was that the dominant churches, no matter what their definition, were failing to minister effectively to the needs of a people for whom religion continued to be a primary emotional and cultural experience. It is significant that the most vigorous branch of the Church of England in eighteenth-century America was its missionary organization, the Society for the Propagation of the Gospel in Foreign Parts, or SPG. Originally formed to bring Christianity to the Indians, it had instead devoted itself to guaranteeing the survival of the Anglican church in America and strengthening it in every possible way. Under its first leader, the Reverend Thomas Bray (1656–1730), the SPG launched missionary expeditions to likely points throughout the colonies, helped maintain existing parishes and establish new ones, and functioned as the Anglican church's only effective organization above the parish level.

The Great Awakening.

Into this ill-served, parched, and questing religious world the fervor of the Great Awakening fell like a blazing torch. The revival did not begin all at once. There were early stirrings in the Connecticut River valley, touched off by the remarkable young minister of Northampton, Massachusetts, Jonathan Edwards.

He was heir to a famous ecclesiastical tradition. Edwards's grandfather had been the influential "Pope" Solomon Stoddard of Northampton, whom he eventually succeeded. From the time of his graduation from Yale at the age of seventeen, Edwards had devoted himself to the central philosophical and theological problems of the age. While preaching and fulfilling his other duties as a minister, he worked out a system of ideas so subtle and so original that it has established him as one of the most powerful thinkers of the eighteenth century. His chief professional task, however, was more ordinary: it was to bring the sinful to a knowledge of God and to the experience of spiritual rebirth. Stoddard had stirred local revivals in the 1720s; in 1734 and 1735 Edwards, to his own great surprise and gratification, suddenly found his own people responding overwhelmingly to his carefully reasoned sermons on justification by faith. Northampton was overcome with religious enthusiasm. Dozens of once complacent parishioners experienced tumultuous passions of religious rebirth.

Word of the God-inspired revival spread swiftly through the farming hamlets of the Connecticut River valley and then eastward along Long Island Sound, touching off similar outbreaks as it went. By the time Edwards published an account of his local revival, his *Faithful Narrative of the Surprising Work of God* (1737), the wave had passed, but already the surge of religious fervor had become famous throughout the colonies and in Great Britain as well. It had inspired ministers everywhere to new efforts in bringing sinful people to

JONATHAN EDWARDS, BY JOSEPH BADGER
Painted a few years before Edwards was expelled from his Northampton pulpit for insisting on conversion as a basis for church membership and for attempting to discipline children of leading families. After seven years as a missionary to the Indians, Edwards was chosen president of the College of New Jersey (Princeton) but died after a few months in office, at the age of fifty-five.

an experience of God's grace, and it had created a great sense of expectation that some vast outpouring of religious zeal—perhaps even the actual establishment of God's Kingdom on earth—was about to take place. Such anticipation was spilling over into fulfillment by 1740. In that year George Whitefield, the brilliant English preacher who had already stirred successful revivals on two tours through the middle and southern colonies, appeared in New England. It was Whitefield, following in the wake of Edwards's revival, who finally threw open the floodgates and let loose an outpouring of soul-shaking evangelicalism that flooded New England for four tumultuous years.

Whitefield's tour of New England was spectacular. In Boston he preached first to hundreds who jammed the churches until they could hold no more, and then to thousands at open-air meetings. The young, impassioned orator deeply stirred listeners used to hearing scholarly sermons read to them from carefully prepared texts. He was equally successful in

GEORGE WHITEFIELD PREACHING, BY JOHN WOLLASTON (1741, WHEN WHITEFIELD WAS 27)
He appeared, a Connecticut farmer recalled, "almost angelical; a young, slim, slender youth before thousands of people with a bold, undaunted countenance, . . . he looked as if he was clothed with authority from the Great God, . . . and my hearing him preach gave me a heart wound." "What a spell he casts over an audience," Jonathan Edwards's wife wrote, "by proclaiming the simplest truths of the Bible. I have seen upwards of a thousand people hang on his words with breathless silence, broken only by an occasional half-suppressed sob."

National Portrait Gallery, London

ligion that was deeply experienced rather than intellectual and doctrine-bound. Tennent's tour through southern New England lasted three months in the fall and winter of 1740–41. This was a time of mass excitement, profound emotional upheaval, and inner transformation.

Elsewhere too the revival continued its blazing progress. It tore through the Presbyterian and Dutch Reformed communities of the middle colonies, splitting them into conservative and evangelical wings. The "New Side" evangelical Presbyterians of Pennsylvania and New Jersey formed their own governing body in 1741 and sent out traveling preachers to invade districts dominated by the conservative "Old Side." These revivalist Presbyterians moving southward from Pennsylvania had the greatest impact in Virginia; in Hanover County in that colony, their most successful preacher, Samuel Davies, produced the most important of the southern revivals. In the process Davies spurred the Anglican authorities to take repressive measures against nonconformity by fining preachers who had no official license to preach. Even more influential in the southern colonies were the evangelical Baptists. They reached out more effectively than any other church or sect to the unchurched common people in the backcountry, especially the new settlers on the southern frontier. And at the end of the colonial period, evangelicals within the Church of England, led by the Reverend Devereux Jarratt, who would soon organize the Methodist church, also began to share in the work of extending the Awakening to the settlers on the expanding frontier.

Effects of the Great Awakening.

Such was the greatest event in the history of religion in eighteenth-century America. Its effects were more revolutionary by far than those of the parallel developments in Europe—Pietism in Germany, and Methodism in England and Wales. The differences are revealing. The revivals in America were not, as elsewhere, distinctively lower-class movements that gave new voice to the aspirations of the socially deprived. Nor were they limited to any particular geographical group: they were as successful in the large towns as in the countryside. Their impact could not be confined. At least four areas of American social life were irreversibly affected by the great revivalist wave.

First, the authority and status of the clergy were permanently weakened. The revivalists cared little for offices, formal status, education, learning, or even, within reasonable limits, outward behavior. For the revivalists, qualification for religious leadership was gained only by force of inner experience and by the ability to unlock parishioners' spiritual aspirations. It followed naturally that the revivalists would challenge the authority of established educational institu-

a series of meetings in northern New England, and then in the West. In Northampton his preaching was so moving that Jonathan Edwards, Whitefield reported, "wept during the whole time of exercise." After stops south in the Connecticut River valley towns that had already experienced the revival, Whitefield ended his tour in New York.

His preaching, Whitefield correctly reported, had made a significant impact in the North. So too did the preaching of the second great leader of the Awakening, Gilbert Tennent. For a decade this second-generation Scotch-Irish minister had led the "New Light" (evangelical) party within the growing Presbyterian communities of New Jersey and New York. He had been educated in his father's "Log College" in Neshaminy, Pennsylvania, which had been devoted to spreading the principles of "experimental" religion—that is, re-tions like Yale and Harvard, whose methods of training ministers seemed to them dry and merely intellectual. The government of Connecticut became alarmed at the progress of the Great Awakening and barred from the ministry anyone not trained at Yale, Harvard, or a foreign Protestant university; but the Presbyterian "New Lights" responded not only by setting up their own church organization, but also, in 1746, by creating a new college. This institution, the College of New Jersey, later renamed Princeton, was intended to emphasize religion of the emotions, of the spirit, as well as of the mind. Rutgers, Brown, and Dartmouth were also founded in response to the revival movement. For the Awakening, which challenged all preachers to justify their authority by their own spiritual gifts and by their power to reach into other souls, could not tolerate merely formal qualifications of any kind.

Second, the Awakening tended to destroy the identification of churches with specific territorial boundaries. The revivalists believed that their call extended not only to the few people who had employed them as preachers, but to anyone anywhere who would heed their word, and especially to all those whose ministers were unconverted. They therefore naturally became "itinerants," wandering ministers who moved into established congregations. If welcomed, they preached officially as visiting ministers; if not, they set up in barns or open fields and preached to anyone who would listen. The official churches angrily protested against such invasions, and "itineracy" became one of the central controversies of the revival. But it could not be stopped, and where it occurred it tended to free the churches from specific territorial foundations—to release them into a universe of competing groups.

Related to this was a third effect of the Awakening: nothing less than the near destruction of institutional religion as the organizing framework of small-group society. For throughout the new settlements, and at all times on the disorganized frontiers, the church had provided a vital center for society itself. When the Awakening hit the more vulnerable communities, a series of splits frequently occurred. A split-off of a "New Light" faction from a stubborn "Old Light" majority could severely rupture a community; and even if the splinter group eventually returned, it would be more or less free of general control. Often there was no point at which the disintegration could be stopped. Whole units simply disappeared in the course of successive splinterings, ending in a mere cluster of family-sized factions, free of all constraints of church organization.

Finally, the Awakening put unsupportable pressures on what remained of church-state relations, not in doctrine, but in practice. The revivalists did not consider their beliefs to be unorthodox; quite the contrary. They claimed that they alone represented the true orthodoxy in Protestant Christianity and denounced the established churches for their deviations. In doing so they created new grounds for challenging the practical right of any church to claim a privileged place in the eyes of the law. They thereby moved closer to thinking that the very notion of an established church was false, and that the only safe and correct course was to deny all state privileges to any religious group.

Denominationalism. Religion in America acquired a new character as a result of the developments that had been in motion from the time of the first English settlements in North America, developments that had been greatly intensified by the Great Awakening. American religion became essentially voluntaristic— that is, an activity that one was free to join or not to join. Such voluntarism came to apply even to the older established churches, whose official doctrines assumed a close bond between church and society, enforced by the state. Organized religion in America had also developed an emphasis on persuasion as its essential activity. The churches, lacking the sanction of the state to guarantee membership, as well as secure institutional structures and effective group discipline, swung their efforts toward promotion and outward activity and away from the purification of doctrine and the maintenance of internal order. Finally, the role of individual decision shifted. In traditional societies involvement with a dominant religion was automatic, and it was a momentous decision to break with the religious association into which one had been born. As a consequence, religious indifference could go hand in hand with extensive though merely formal church membership. In the colonies the opposite became true: to do nothing was likely to mean having no religious affiliation at all, and the momentous decision involved joining, not withdrawing from, a religious association. As a result, broad waves of religious enthusiasm could go hand in hand with low church membership.

By the end of the colonial period, these characteristics were taking on a patterned and stable form, which would later be called Denominationalism. Products of the fundamental realities of colonial life, these characteristics would find expression in theory, law, and formal doctrine during the American Revolution and in the years that followed.

The Origins of American Politics

A key to understanding much in pre-Revolutionary America is the gap that developed between expectation and reality. This discordant pattern was

As the following account, written by a Connecticut farmer, makes clear, George Whitefield seemed almost an angel sent from God to summon Christians in the Great Awakening.

NOW it pleased God to send Mr Whitefield into this land; and my hearing of his preaching at Philadelphia, . . . and many thousands flocking to hear him preach the Gospel; and great numbers were converted to Christ; I felt the Spirit of God drawing me by conviction; I longed to see and hear him. . . . I heard he was come to New York and the Jerseys and great multitudes flocking after him under great concern for their Souls which brought on my Concern more and more hoping soon to see him but next I heard he was at long Island; then at Boston and next at Northampton; then on a Sudden, in the morning about 8 or 9 of the Clock there came a messenger and said Mr Whitfield preached at Hartford and Weathersfield yesterday and is to preach at Middletown this morning at ten of the Clock, I was in my field at Work, I dropt my tool that I had in my hand and ran home to my wife telling her to make ready quickly to go and hear Mr Whitfield preach at Middletown, then run to my pasture for my horse with all my might; fearing that I should be too late; having my horse I with my wife soon mounted the horse and went forward as fast as I thought the horse could bear, and when my horse got much out of breath I would get down and put my wife on the Saddle and bid her ride as fast as she could and not Stop or Slack for me except I bad her and so I would run untill I was much out of breath; and then mount my horse again, and so I did several times to favour my horse; we improved every moment to get along as if we were fleeing for our lives; all the while fearing we should be too late to hear the Sermon, for we had twelve miles to ride double in little more than an hour and we went round by the upper housen parish and when we came within about half a mile or a mile of the Road that comes down from Hartford weathersfield and Stepney to Middletown; on high land I saw before me a Cloud or fogg rising; . . . I heard a noise something like a low rumbling thunder and presently found it was the noise of Horses feet coming down the Road and this Cloud was a Cloud of dust made by the Horses feet; . . . when I came within about 20 rods of the

Road, I could see men and horses Sliping along in the Cloud like shadows and as I drew nearer it seemed like a steady Stream of horses and their riders. . . . We went down in the Stream but heard no man speak a word all the way for 3 miles but every one pressing forward in great haste and when we got to Middletown old meeting house there was a great Multitude it was said to be 3 or 4000 of people Assembled together; we dismounted and shook of our Dust; and the ministers were then Coming to the meeting house; I turned and looked towards the Great River and saw the ferry boats Running swift backward and forward bringing Over loads of people and the Oars Rowed nimble and quick; every thing men horses and boats seemed to be Struggling for life; the land and banks over the river looked black with people and horses all along the 12 miles I saw no man at work in his field, but all seemed to be gone— When I saw Mr. Whitfield come upon the Scaffold he lookt almost Angelical; a young, Slim, slender youth before some thousands of people with a bold undaunted Countenance, and my hearing how God was with him every where as he came along it Solemnized my mind; and put me into a trembling fear before he began to preach; for he looked as if he was Cloathed with Authority from the Great God; and a sweet sollome solemnity sat upon his brow And my hearing him preach, gave me a heart wound; By Gods blessing: my old Foundation was broken up, and I saw that my righteousness would not save me.

more extreme and had greater consequences in politics and government than in any other area of life. Not only did the discrepancy between theory and expectation on the one hand and reality on the other shape the character of American public life; it also laid the basis for the transformation of the relations between Britain and the colonies.

The Structure of British Politics.

All formal notions of public life in the British world rested on the belief that the British political system of the mid-eighteenth century was the freest and best that existed. And the colonial governments and political systems, it was also believed, were more or less imperfect copies of the world-famous British model.

In theory, the heart of the unwritten British constitution was balance. From classical antiquity had come the notion, reaffirmed in the Renaissance and in seventeenth-century England, that there were three pure forms of government. Any one of these, if properly maintained, could serve the people well; but all three tended to degenerate into evil forms that created oppression. Thus monarchy, rule by one person, tended to degenerate into tyranny; aristocracy, rule by a few, became oligarchy (corrupt government by a group of self-serving, all-powerful leaders); and democracy, the rule of the whole political population, declined into the rule of the mob. The challenge to political thinkers had long been the problem of devising a balance among these forms that would stabilize government and bring the degenerative processes to a halt. The British constitution, it was generally agreed, had achieved precisely such a stable balance of pure forms. This balance was embodied in the competition among the crown (monarchy), the House of Lords (aristocracy), and the House of Commons (democracy). This theory was almost universally believed to explain the stability and freedom that Britain had attained.

Yet the theory was misleading as a description of the actual working of the British government. The balance of these three elements was more apparent than real. In theory, each element stayed in its proper sphere; in practice, each thoroughly infiltrated the others' spheres. Moreover, each element functioned differently from the idealized description. In fact, the source of the political stability of mid-eighteenth-century Britain did not lie in the supposed balance of these three elements, a balance that Americans sought to emulate. Rather, stability came from two sets of special conditions, both highly relevant to an understanding of the unique form of politics that developed in eighteenth-century America.

The main underlying condition that made Britain's stability possible was the fact that the great constitutional issues of the seventeenth century had been settled in the Glorious Revolution of 1688. These issues had centered on the extent of the crown's authority and on the problem of the relationship between church and state.

First, as to the crown's authority, Parliament had concluded the Glorious Revolution by stipulating that the monarch could neither create courts without a law approved by Parliament nor dismiss judges without Parliament's formally indicting them for misconduct —that is, without a formal impeachment. Furthermore, the monarch could not impose taxes, maintain a standing army in peacetime, or engage in wars for foreign territory without Parliament's consent. The crown had also been forced to agree not to limit unduly or to extend the existence of a Parliament or interfere with its regular meetings. Parliamentary elections and convenings were put on a regular calendar schedule. In addition, at least after 1707, it was understood that the monarch would not veto acts of Parliament.

Second, as to the church-state relationship after the Glorious Revolution, the Church of England continued to be the established church and, as such, to enjoy the privileges and benefits of the state; and all persons who did not openly reject it were considered to be among its members. But the desire for an enforced uniformity was abandoned. Dissent was tolerated, although it was penalized. The great majority of nonconformists were permitted to worship as they pleased; they enjoyed almost full civil rights, and in the course of the eighteenth century they gained most political rights as well.

These underlying conditions made political stability possible in Britain. The stability that was actually attained was the result of the informal agreement worked out between the crown and the House of Commons. A working relationship between the two was achieved by a set of rules of operation so fundamental that they constituted, in effect, a private, informal constitution. Under these rules the ministry acted in the crown's behalf to discipline and manipulate the House of Commons, in part by managing elections to the House through the control or outright ownership of easily dominated election districts and "rotten boroughs,"* and in part by distributing crown favors (patronage) to the members so as to ensure safe majorities on controversial issues. In the mid-eighteenth century about 200 of the 558 members of the House of Commons held crown appointments or gifts of one sort or another, and another 30 or 40 were more loosely tied to the government by awards of profitable contracts. A varying number of other members was bound to the administration less directly, particularly by the gift or

*For a discussion of rotten boroughs and the unreformed House of Commons in general, see chapter 7, pp. 179–80.

promise of one or more of the 8,000 excise (tax-collecting) offices that were available for distribution.

Together with the settlement of the main policy questions—those of the crown's powers and of the church-state relationship—it was this use of "influence" in managing elections and in controlling votes in the two houses of Parliament that explains the stability of English political life in the mid-eighteenth century. There were certain underlying technical conditions for such stabilizing control. The ministry had to have at its command an abundance of patronage that it could distribute. The electorate had to be small, for the larger the voting population, the greater the difficulty of controlling it. And the system of representation had to be unrelated to the shift and growth of the population and not closely bound to the wishes of a broad electorate.

Differences in the Colonies.

All these conditions existed in eighteenth-century Britain, but none of them existed in anything like the same measure in the mainland colonies of British North America. Yet the similarity between the British government and the separate colonial governments was a basic principle of political thought in eighteenth-century America. Ever since the rise of bicameral (two-chamber) legislatures in the colonies during the seventeenth century, the assumption had grown that the colonial governments were miniatures of the British government. Dr. William Douglass of Boston explained in his *Summary, Historical and Political . . . of the British Settlements in North America* (1749–51) that by the governor's

representing the King, the colonies are monarchical; by the Council, they are aristocratical; by a House of Representatives or delegates from the people, they are democratical: these three are distinct and independent of one another . . . the several negatives being checks upon one another. The concurrence of these three forms of government seem to be the highest perfection that human civil government can attain to in times of peace.

Such irregularities and exceptions as there were in the American replicas of the perfect British government, Douglass said, "doubtless in time will be rectified."

But while in Britain the mixed and balanced constitution produced a high degree of political harmony, similar institutions in the colonies produced the opposite. Conflict, so intense at times that it could lead to the total paralysis of government, was common in American politics. First, there was contention between the branches of government—between the executive on the one hand and the legislatures on the other. But it was not only a matter of conflict between branches of government. There was also factionalism that went beyond institutional boundaries and at times reduced the politics of certain colonies to an almost hopeless chaos of competing groups. Some were personal groups—small clusters of relatives and friends that rose suddenly at particular moments and faded quickly, merging into other equally unstable arrangements. Others were economic, regional, and more generally social interest groups; and some of these quickly rose and fell, while some were durable, persisting through a generation or more, although they were never highly organized, were only occasionally active, and were continually changing in their membership. There also were a few groups formed to defend and advance programs that went beyond immediate personal and group interests. Most of these competing groups were vocal and difficult to control. It is true that in certain colonies at certain times, political life attained the hoped-for balance and tranquility. But most eighteenth-century governors at one time or another echoed the weary question and the anguished plea of William Penn to the political leaders of the City of Brotherly Love soon after it was founded: "Cannot more friendly and private courses be taken to set matters right in an infant province? . . . For the love of God, me, and the poor country, be not so *governmentish!*"

But Pennsylvania remained, in Penn's words, "noisy and open in [its] dissatisfactions," and so did most of the other colonies during the three generations that preceded the Revolution. For beneath the apparent similarities in the formal systems of government in Britain and America, there were basic differences in the informal structure of politics. The similarities in government were superficial; the differences in politics were so profound as to make the colonies seem almost the reverse of the universally admired British model.

The political settlement that had been made in England at the end of the Glorious Revolution had not extended to the colonies. In all but the chartered colonies of Rhode Island and Connecticut, the governors had the executive authority to veto legislation, which could also be disallowed by the Privy Council or the proprietors in Britain. In addition, the royal governors had the authority to delay sittings of the lower houses of the colonial assemblies and to dissolve them at will, and they quickly became accustomed to using those powers. As a result, the lower houses were as dependent on executive wishes for their existence as the House of Commons had been before the mid-seventeenth century. Nor was the judiciary in the colonies protected as it was in Britain. Judges at all levels, from justices of the peace to the chief justices of the supreme courts, were appointed by nomination of the governors and dismissed by the executives' wishes. Similarly, the governors in all but the three chartered colonies (Massachusetts, Rhode Island, and Connecticut) could create courts without the agreement of the legislature. Indeed, the governors did so repeatedly,

especially chancery courts, in which there were no juries and which were concerned with such unpopular matters as collecting arrears of quitrents. Associated with these "prerogative courts" in the colonists' minds were the vice-admiralty courts, also without juries, which decided maritime cases and had broader jurisdiction than did the equivalent courts in England. Lesser powers that had been eliminated in Britain were also given to the executive in America: power over the election of the Speakers of the House; power over church appointments; power over fees.

It was primarily in the more important areas—vetoing colonial legislation, dismissing and dissolving legislative bodies, and firing judges and creating courts—that the legal power of the executive was felt by the colonists to be most threatening and a source of danger to liberty and to the free constitution. But even more than the greater power of the executive, an array of other circumstances distinguished the American colonial governments from the British government. These factors radically reduced and sometimes eliminated the "influence" by which the executive in England disciplined dissent and conflict in the political community and maintained its supremacy in government.

To begin with, the colonial executives lacked the flexibility they needed for successful political maneuver. The royal governors arrived in the colonies with instructions that spelled out their duties in great detail and left no room for compromise. Thus in some of the most controversial and sensitive public issues, the executive was politically immobilized. Further, in the colonies there was nothing to match the powerful political weapons that the British government had at its disposal and that were so essential to governing. Very little political patronage—gifts of public office, contracts, honors, or other benefits of government—was available to the colonial governors by which to buy off opposition and maintain their dominance over the legislatures. Furthermore, the American electoral system was not like the highly irregular, corrupt, and hence easily manipulated British system.

There were no rotten boroughs in the colonies. No assembly seats were owned outright by the government, and there were no defunct constituencies that the administration could easily manipulate. In Britain the House of Commons was frozen in composition throughout the eighteenth century, but most of the colonial assemblies had been created on the principle of so many delegates per unit of local government, and the number of such units was continually expanding as settlement spread. By the mid-eighteenth century the governors, fearing a total loss of their influence in the legislatures, tried to stop the multiplication of election districts. But the governors' efforts to keep the legislatures from growing involved them in serious political struggles, so normal had the expectation by this time become that assemblies would continue to expand with the spread of settlement. It scarcely matters that by enlightened twentieth-century standards the distribution of seats in the colonial legislatures was occasionally disproportionate to the population. What is important is that by normal eighteenth-century standards apportionment was remarkably well adjusted to the growth and spread of population and thus insensitive to pressure from embattled governors.

Other practices created additional problems for the governors. From the earliest years of settlement, it had been common in Massachusetts for towns to instruct their representatives on how to vote in the General Court on controversial issues. This practice continued irregularly in the eighteenth century. It was used when localities were committed to particular views that they wished their representatives to defend no matter what influence was brought to bear against them. Elsewhere too, representatives were instructed on delicate issues. Often when delegates were not instructed, they themselves postponed acting until—as in New York in 1734—"they had taken the sentiments of their constituents." Further, delegates were often required to be residents of the communities they represented at the time of their incumbency—something that was not required in eighteenth-century Britain and indeed is still not required there. Residential requirements were not universal in eighteenth-century America, but they were common enough to contribute measurably to the weakening of "influence." The result, wrote the eighteenth-century historian William Smith, was that the assemblies seemed to be composed "of plain, illiterate husbandmen, whose views seldom extended farther than to the regulation of highways, the destruction of wolves, wildcats, and foxes, and the advancement of the other little interests of the particular counties which they were chosen to represent."

But of all the underlying factors that distinguished politics in America from the British model, perhaps the most dramatic was the sheer number of those who could vote. Originally there had been no plan or desire to permit large numbers of men to vote. Most colonies sought to do no more than re-create, or adapt with minor variations, the property qualification that had prevailed in English county districts for three centuries. That requirement was the forty-shilling freehold qualification, the ownership of real estate worth forty shillings a year in rents. But if this was a restrictive qualification in England, it permitted a great many men to vote in the colonies, where freehold tenure was widespread among the white population. So ineffective was this traditional franchise definition that most colonies went on to create more elaborate restrictions. But the effect everywhere was

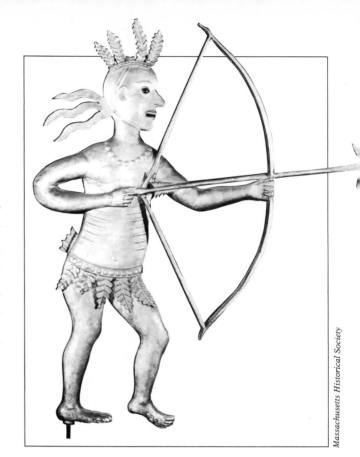

WEATHERVANE, BY SHEM DROWNE (MID-EIGHTEENTH CENTURY)
Swiveling atop the cupola of the Massachusetts Province House with its glass eyes flashing in the sun, this 4½-foot gilded weathervane was the work of an untutored craftsman. The visual and symbolic effect of the almost life-sized American archer swinging vigilantly year after year over the residence of the royal governors, always aiming an arrow to fly with the wind, was striking. It "bedazzled the eyes of those who looked upward," Nathaniel Hawthorne wrote in a story inspired by Drowne, "like an angel of the sun."

to broaden the voting population rather than restrict it. To the disgusted governor Thomas Hutchinson in Massachusetts, it seemed that "anything with the appearance of a man" was allowed to vote.

One can safely generalize the situation in the various colonies by saying that 50 to 75 percent of the adult male white population was entitled to vote. This was far more than could do so in Britain—and, it seems, also far more than wished to do so in the colonies themselves. Apathy in elections was common. Yet however neglected, the widespread right to vote was potentially a powerful weapon, certain to work against the ability of colonial governors to control elections and the voting in the assemblies.

The Pattern of Colonial Politics. Overall, early American politics was a patchwork of contradictions. There was a firmly rooted belief that the colonial constitutions corresponded in their essentials to the English model of mixed government. That assumption was violated, however, by two factors. First, it was believed that too much power was exercised by the governors. Second, in the colonies there were none of the devices by which in Britain the executive maintained discipline, control, and stability in politics. Swollen claims and shrunken powers, especially when they occur together, are always sources of trouble, and the political turmoil that resulted from this combination can be traced through the history of eighteenth-century American politics.

But the structure of American politics in the eighteenth century is not wholly revealed in this. The nature of leadership was also a source of controversy. Americans, like all Britons—indeed, like all Europeans of the eighteenth century—assumed that political leadership was only one of a number of expressions of leadership in a society. They believed that those who were superior in one sphere would attain and exercise superiority in other spheres as well. Hence in a society of ranked "dignities" (if not classes), political leadership was expected to rest with the natural social leaders of the community. And so indeed it was in America—in *some* of the colonies, in *certain* respects, at *certain* times.

In Virginia, in the three generations that followed Bacon's Rebellion, a hierarchy of the plantation gentry emerged in stable form, dominated by social and economic leaders whose roots could be traced back to the 1650s and whose preeminence in politics was largely unquestioned. So too in Connecticut, a landed gentry of "ancient" families consolidated its control in the early eighteenth century and came to dominate the political life of the colony. But even in these extreme examples there were signs of trouble to come. In Virginia, settlement expanded in the west, where potentially powerful new men with distinctive religious interests established themselves. In Connecticut the danger sign was the growth of religious radicalism, especially in the eastern counties, which were already disturbed as a result of a poor agricultural economy and a frustrated desire for the expansion of settlement.

Yet Virginia and Connecticut were colonies of the greatest stability. In most of the colonies, the identity of the natural political leaders remained as it had been in the late seventeenth century—a matter of controversy, at times the source of political struggles. New figures appeared overnight everywhere in the colonies, and always there were alien elements introduced into the top of the political hierarchy in the form of officials sent from England in positions of high authority.

These were the shaping elements of those "noisy dissatisfactions" that so plagued the tranquility of governors in eighteenth-century America. The politi-

Colonial Williamsburg Foundation

THE VIRGINIA HOUSE OF BURGESSES
As in the British House of Commons, the speaker's chair and table separated the facing benches. Both the smallness of the room and the closeness of the seating arrangements encouraged intimate discussion.

cal system was full of conflict—a factional system in which the will and dignity of the ill-organized imperial state were openly attacked by opposition groups. American politics was freely competitive—the very opposite of the immobile, bureaucratized state system that prevailed in the Spanish-American colonies.

Such was American society in the eighteenth century. It was a strange society, caught between traditional institutions and ways of thinking on the one hand, and unexpected circumstances on the other. Its population, drawn from many sources in Europe, Africa, and the West Indies, lived in communities that did not recognize cultural pluralism or conceive of ways by which an alien race could coexist with the dominant British element except in constant conflict or absolute subjection. While one-fifth of the population was held in slavery and enjoyed no more of the world's goods than well-cared-for animals, the rest enjoyed a level of affluence unknown to any other large population in the Western world. Social institutions that presumed a stable and well-ordered population were subjected to extreme pressures of population growth and mobility. Land was widely distributed in freehold tenure, although efforts were repeatedly made to re-create a traditional landlord class. Tenancy, however, was just as likely to foster land speculation as to provide income for a leisured landed gentry. Transoceanic commerce was increasingly dominated by a merchant class tied securely to a traditional mercantile elite in Britain, but the established merchants always had to contend with competition they could never eliminate, generated by the swift, uneven growth of an uncontrolled economy. Religious organization, still traditional in concept and doctrine, was so deeply eroded by altered circumstances that it seemed transformed even before the Great Awakening. And the Great Awakening reduced what remained of familiar forms of religion to an almost unrecognizable disorder. Politics was an open competition for place, profit, and power. But it was fought out within a culture that condemned factionalism as seditious and that assumed that the state was in some sense sanctified and above mere factional contention.

It was a strange world, full of contradictions, but it was moving toward a resolution of its most glaring inconsistencies.

SUGGESTED READINGS

The most valuable survey of American society in the 1700s remains James T. Adams, *Provincial Society, 1690–1763* (1927); although out of date on certain matters, it touches on all major topics, includes a great deal of basic information, and conceives of society in structural terms. Lawrence H. Gipson, *British Empire Before the American Revolution*, vols. II and III (1936), provides a comprehensive description from literary sources of the colonies in the years 1748–54; volumes IV and V (1939–1942) survey the frontier areas in dispute with Spain and France and also the Caribbean colonies. An effort to bring together into a general picture the recent findings on social organization is James A. Henretta, *The Evolution of American Society, 1700–1815* (1973), chaps 1–4. Daniel J. Boorstin's *The Americans: The Colonial Experience* (1958) is particularly valuable for its analysis of the professions in colonial America. Max Savelle, *Seeds of Liberty* (1948), is a survey of intellectual history and the fine arts.

On the eighteenth-century population, see Robert V. Wells, *The Population of the British Colonies in America Before 1776* (1975), which analyzes the surviving censuses. Of the new immigrations, the Irish are described in R. J. Dickson, *Ulster Immigration to Colonial America* (1966), and Wayland F. Dunaway, *The Scotch-Irish of Colonial Pennsylvania* (1944); the Germans in Albert B. Faust, *The German Element in the United States* (2 vols., 1909), F. R. Diffenderfer, *The German Immigration . . .* (1900), and Gillian L. Gollin, *Moravians in Two Worlds* (1967); the Scottish in Ian C. C. Graham, *Colonists from Scotland* (1956); and the Huguenots in Jon Butler, *The Huguenots in America* (1983). For a summary of all of these population movements, see Thomas J. Archdeacon, *Becoming American* (1983), chap. 1. The influx of indentured servants from Britain is analyzed in David W. Galenson, *White Servitude in Colonial America* (1981); and Abbot E. Smith, *Colonists in Bondage* (1947). On the legal incorporation of foreign peoples into British America, see James H. Kettner, *The Development of American Citizenship, 1608–1870* (1978).

A detailed picture of the life of the black population and of slavery in the eighteenth century has only recently begun to appear and is still incomplete. An attempt to summarize the recent writing is Ira Berlin, "Time, Space, and the Evolution of Afro-American Society on British Mainland America," *American Historical Review*, 85 no. 1 (February 1980), 44–78. There are useful articles devoted entirely to colonial slavery in *Wm. and Mary Q.*, 35 (1978), no. 2; and *Southern Studies*, 16 (1977), no. 4. Peter Wood, *Black Majority* (1974), is an excellent account of slavery in South Carolina to 1739; Gerald W. Mullin, *Flight and Rebellion* (1972), traces slave resistance in Virginia. Two articles by Allan Kulikoff on slavery in the Chesapeake region are also useful: *Journal of Southern History*, 45 (1979), 513–40; and in A. C. Land et al., eds., *Law, Society, and Politics in Early Maryland* (1977). Winthrop D. Jordan, *White over Black* (1968), parts I, II, scrutinizes white attitudes toward blacks. On the slave trade, see Philip D. Curtin, *The Atlantic Slave Trade* (1969), and H. A. Gemery and J. S. Hogendorn, eds., *The Uncommon Market* (1979).

On landowning and agriculture, see Lewis C. Gray, *History of Agriculture in the Southern United States to 1860* (2 vols., 1933), and Percy W. Bidwell and John I. Falconer's parallel book on the North. A broad survey of the opening of new frontier lands in the tradition of Frederick Jackson Turner is Ray A. Billington, *Westward Expansion* (1949), chaps. 5–8, which contains an exhaustive bibliography of writings on the westward movement. A case study of the opening of new townships in New England, contradicting the Turner view on many points, is Charles S. Grant, *Democracy in the Connecticut Frontier Town of Kent* (1961). On the New England towns, see Edward M. Cook, Jr., *The Fathers of the Towns* (1976), and Michael Zuckerman, *Peaceable Kingdoms* (1970). On settlements in Pennsylvania, see James T. Lemon, *The Best Poor Man's Country* (1972); on land utilization in North Carolina, Harry R. Merrens, *Colonial North Carolina* (1964); on land and population in Virginia, Carville V. Earle, *The Evolution of a Tidewater Settlement System* (1975).

Of the exceptions to freehold tenure discussed in this chapter, there is an excellent essay on the old proprietary estates: Rowland Berthoff and John M. Murrin, "Feudalism, Communalism, and the Yeoman Freeholder . . . ," Stephen G. Kurtz and James H. Hutson, eds., *Essays on the American Revolution* (1973). On tenancy, see Willard F. Bliss, "Rise of Tenancy in Virginia," *Virginia Magazine of History and Biography*, 58 (1950), 427–41; Clarence P. Gould, *Land System in Maryland, 1720–1765* (1913); Gregory A. Stiverson, *Poverty in a Land of Plenty* (1977); Sung Bok Kim, *Landlord and Tenant* in *Colonial New York* (1978); and Patricia U. Bonomi, *A Factious People* (1971), chap. 6. Plantation life and the harassed role of the large planters are vividly revealed in Jack P. Greene, ed., *Diary of Colonel Landon Carter* (2 vols., 1965), and interpreted in Daniel Blake Smith, *Inside the Great House* (1980). The condition of ordinary planters is described in Aubrey C. Land, "Economic Behavior in a Planting Society . . . ," *Journal of Social History*, 33 (1967), 469–85, and "Economic Base and Social Structure . . . ," *Journal of Economic History*, 25 (1965), 639–54.[†] Rhys Isaac, *The Transformation of Virginia 1740–1790* (1982), contains an interpretation of Virginia society and culture viewed as an anthropologist would view a strange and alien world whose "meanings" are not what the people of the time thought they were, but what the historian interprets them to be. On the role of the Scottish merchants in transforming the marketing of tobacco, see Jacob M. Price, "The Rise of Glasgow in the Chesapeake Tobacco Trade, " *Wm. and Mary Q.*, 11 (1954), 179–99, and T. M. Devine, *The Tobacco Lords* (1975). On marketing in general, see Price's "Economic Growth of the Chesapeake and the European Markets, 1697–1775," *Journal of Economic History*, 24 (1964), 496–511, and *France and the Chesapeake* (2 vols., 1973).

On commerce generally, besides Emory R. Johnson et al., *History of Domestic and Foreign Commerce* (1915), see James F. Shepherd and Gary M. Walton, *Shipping, Maritime Trade, and the Economic Development of Colonial North America* (1972), a technical study with elaborate statistics on 1768–72. Arthur L. Jensen, *Maritime Commerce of Colonial Philadelphia* (1963), is an excellent account. Richard Pares, *Yankees and Creoles* (1956), and Richard B. Sheridan, *Sugar and Slavery . . . the British West Indies, 1623–1775* (1974), cover the Caribbean trade; on the timber trade and fisheries, see Joseph J. Malone, *Pine Trees and Politics* (1964), and Harold A. Innis, *The Cod Fisheries* (1940). Perhaps the best insight into the working of commerce is provided by studies of individual merchants. There are accounts of the Hancocks of Boston by W. T. Baxter, of the Beekmans of New York by Philip L. White, of the Pepperrells of Maine and New Hampshire by Byron Fairchild, and of the Browns of Rhode Island (a particularly vivid example of social and occupational mobility) by James B. Hedges. Life in the port towns is described in Carl Bridenbaugh, *Cities in the Wilderness* (1938), *Cities in Revolt* (1955), and *Rebels and Gentlemen* (1942); and in Gary B. Nash, *Urban Crucible* (1979). Alice H. Jones has published a masterful interpretation of American affluence on the eve of the Revolution in her *Wealth of a Nation to Be* (1980).

Eighteenth-century religion is summarized in Sydney E. Ahlstrom, *Religious History of the American People* (1972), Part III. Sidney E. Mead, *The Lively Experiment* (1963), traces the development of American denominationalism. Major religious currents in New England are described in Perry Miller, *New England Mind: From Colony to Province* (1953); Robert G. Pope, *The Half-Way Covenant* (1969); Robert Mid-

dlekauff, *The Mathers* (1971); Ola Winslow, *Meetinghouse Hill* (1952); and James W. Jones, *The Shattered Synthesis* (1973). There is a large literature on the Great Awakening, much of it brought together into a single brief book, J. M. Bumsted and John E. Van de Wetering, *What Must I Do to Be Saved?* (1976), which contains a good bibliography. The major works are: Edwin S. Gaustad, *Great Awakening in New England* (1957); Wesley M. Gewehr, *Great Awakening in Virginia* (1930); Chares H. Maxson, *Great Awakening in the Middle Colonies* (1920); Richard L. Bushman, *From Puritan to Yankee* (1967); C. C. Goen, *Revivalism and Separatism* (1962); and William G. McLoughlin, *New England Dissent* (2 vols., 1971). Excellent also on the complicated awakenings in the middle colonies are Leonard J. Trinterud, *Forming an American Tradition . . . Presbyterianism* (1949), and Martin E. Lodge, "The Crisis of the Churches in the Middle Colonies, 1720–1750," *Pennsylvania Magazine of History and Biography*, 95 (1971), 195–220. There are biographies of Jonathan Edwards by Perry Miller (1949), Ola E. Winslow (1940), and Edward H. Davidson (1968); of Whitefield, by Stuart C. Henry (1957); and of the important Baptist leader Isaac Backus, by William G. McLoughlin (1967). Evarts B. Greene, *Religion and the State* (1941), and William G. McLoughlin, "Isaac Backus and the Separation of Church and State," *American Historical Review*, 72 (1968), 1392–1413, show the colonial origins of American church-state relations.

The operation of the imperial government is described in Leonard W. Labaree, *Royal Government in America* (1930), and Jack P. Greene, *The Quest for Power* (1963); but politics, though intimately related to government, is a different matter. Bernard Bailyn, *Origins of American Politics* (1968), is an effort at a general interpretation, stressing the relations between formal and informal organizations and between political activities and political beliefs. The role of colonial offices in the British patronage system is explained from the British point of view in James A. Henretta, "*Salutary Neglect*" (1972), and in Alison G. Olson and Richard M. Brown, eds., *Anglo-American Political Relations, 1675–1775* (1970), and from the American point of view in Stanley N. Katz, *Newcastle's New York* (1968). Michael Kammen, *Empire and Interest* (1970), is an imaginative effort to show the changing ways in which the British political system accommodated the interests of economic and political groups in Britain and America.

Of the many thorough studies of the politics of individual colonies, several are outstanding; see especially Bonomi, *A Factious People;* Robert Zemsky, *Merchants, Farmers, and River Gods* (1971); Charles Barker, *Background of the Revolution in Maryland* (1940); and M. Eugene Sirmans, *Colonial South Carolina* (1966). J. R. Pole, *Political Representation* (1966), covers both England and America throughout the eighteenth century.

[†]See first footnote on p. 27.

6 The Enlightenment's New World

In 1760 the young George III ascended the throne of Great Britain. Like Britons everywhere, Americans joined in the celebrations enthusiastically. Along with the people of Britain, the nonslave population of the colonies enjoyed the freest political conditions in the Western world, and the colonists shared, although unevenly, in Britain's rising prosperity. Moreover, the American colonists had participated in Britain's recent military victories over its perennial enemy, France. The colonists now felt a sense of release from the pressure of war on their frontiers, and they were aware as never before of the richness of the land that lay to the west. They glimpsed a future that could be free and prosperous beyond all earlier expectations. In 1759 the Boston preacher Jonathan Mayhew wrote that one could easily imagine in British North America "a mighty empire (I do not mean an independent one) in numbers little inferior perhaps to the greatest in Europe, and in felicity to none." One could picture, he continued, cities "rising on every hill . . . happy fields and villages . . . [and] religion professed and practiced throughout this spacious kingdom in far greater purity and perfection than since the times of the apostles."

In varying degrees, many others shared Mayhew's optimism about America's prospects as part of the British world. But beneath the glowing surface there were tensions—dark undertones in Anglo-American relations. These tensions had been building through all the years of mutual growth and accommodation, but they had no predictable or inevitable outcome. They could as reasonably have grown into a pattern of stable and peaceable relations as become sources of serious disruption. The future would depend on the ability of men in power to understand and manage the complex problems that faced them. In retrospect, however, one thing is clear. These antagonisms, rooted at three levels in the subsoil of Anglo-American life, were like buried traps: to ignore them was to risk disaster.

"Rule Britannia"

At the most obvious level were the antagonisms generated by the war efforts of the mid-eighteenth century.

War of Jenkins' Ear. During the years after 1713, Britain fought three wars with European powers, and the colonies were involved in varying degrees in all of them. The first, the so-called War of Jenkins' Ear (1739–42), was fought with Spain over trading rights in the Caribbean and Central America.

In the peace treaty of 1713 that had ended the War of the Spanish Succession, Britain had been granted the privilege of selling a limited number of slaves and a specified quantity of goods in the Spanish West Indies. The legitimate presence of British trading vessels in these otherwise closed markets had encouraged smuggling, which was countered by mutual rights of search. Spain's brutal handling of shipboard searches had been no more improper or illegal than British smuggling, but it had outraged British public opinion. When a certain Captain Robert Jenkins presented to a parliamentary committee one of his ears, which he said had been cut off by the Spanish seven years earlier as a punishment for smuggling, Parliament demanded a war of revenge for such atrocities. The head of the government, Robert Walpole, wished to avoid a conflict but could not refuse.

The war, which spread over a wide area, was fought at first in the Western Hemisphere. A makeshift army of South Carolina and Georgia troops invaded Spanish Florida but failed to capture St. Augustine or to relieve the pressure on the southern frontier, and the action turned to the Caribbean. There the main effort was an assault in 1740 on the Spanish town of Cartagena, on the coast of what is today Colombia. For this campaign an American regiment of 3,500 men was recruited, serving under British commanders. Most of the money for the expedition was also raised in America. But the campaign was a ghastly failure. A hope-

lessly slow and poorly mounted attack on Cartagena's fort led to the butchery of the American troops, followed by an epidemic of yellow fever and a loss of supplies. After further failures in Cuba, the remains of the expedition staggered home. The losses were shocking. Only 600 Americans survived, and they brought back with them a bitter resentment of the callousness, incompetence, and arrogance of the British military commanders. Years later Americans still recalled the agonies their countrymen had endured in this senseless campaign, and the appalling waste of lives and goods.

King George's War.

In 1740 the Spanish war had broadened into a general European conflict when Prussia seized the province of Silesia from Austria. To maintain the balance of power, Britain went to Austria's aid, and France joined Spain—already at war with Britain. The British feared above all that a single continental power would control Europe, and so in 1742 they made peace with Spain, and in 1744 declared war on France. This complicated series of struggles was known in Europe as the War of the Austrian Succession (1740–48) and in America as King George's War (1744–48). The agreement that ended the war, the Treaty of Aix-la-Chapelle, was merely a truce to allow the combatants to recuperate. In accepting the treaty the British abandoned an important American victory and thus created another source of resentment between Britain and the colonies.

The focus of conflict in the Western Hemisphere during King George's War was the French naval station at Louisbourg. This was a massive fortification on Cape Breton Island, just north of Nova Scotia. Louisbourg guarded the entrance to the St. Lawrence River, sheltered French privateers, and controlled the rich fishing waters between mainland North America and Newfoundland. When Governor William Shirley of Massachusetts heard that Louisbourg's garrison was undermanned and in poor spirits, and that its fortifications were in disrepair, he rallied support from the Massachusetts merchant community and persuaded the General Court to finance an expedition to capture the fortress. Equipment and troops were gathered from all over New England and from colonies as far south as Pennsylvania. Arrangements were made for British naval support under a New Yorker, Commodore Peter Warren, and the troop command was given to a popular Maine merchant and militia colonel, William Pepperrell.

As the transports, warships, supplies, and men gathered in Boston, the campaign, in the aftermath of the Great Awakening, took on the air of a festive crusade. Ministers preached fire and destruction to the French Catholics and their Indian allies. In April 1745, 4,000 New England troops landed safely near Louisbourg, turned captured French cannons against the

SIR WILLIAM PEPPERRELL, 1747, BY JOHN SMIBERT
Pepperrell is posed on a hill overlooking Louisbourg, to which he points and into which two cannonballs are gracefully falling. An engraving of this painting of the popular hero was promptly made for wide distribution.

central fortification, and attacked. The assault came not from the sea (as the French had expected), but by weakly defended land approaches. The French held off the attackers through all of April and May while the New Englanders—who were not soldiers but undisciplined farmers, fishermen, and town workers—bumbled and stumbled their way to control of the harbor islands. Just as Warren was preparing to land an untrained amphibious force to take the partly demolished fortress, the French surrendered. They were hopelessly outnumbered and lacked food supplies and naval support. On June 17 the "Gibraltar of the New World" was handed over to Pepperrell.

For New England, indeed for all of America, it was a glorious victory. Warren, who made a fortune from his capture of French merchant ships, was promoted to admiral; Pepperrell was knighted. But the war was far from over. Disease decimated the troops occupying Louisbourg, and the frontiers from Maine to New York were set aflame in savage raids. Border garrisons in Vermont, western Massachusetts, and New York were attacked, captured, retaken, and attacked again. Mas-

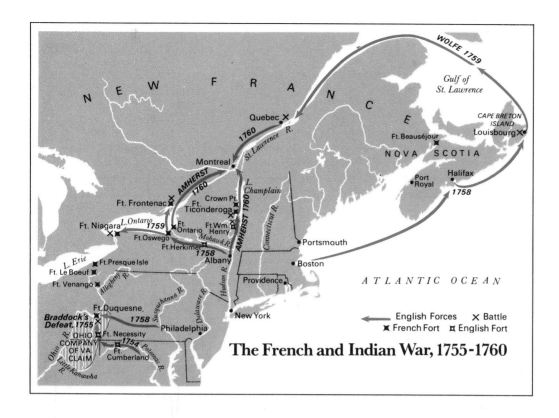

The French and Indian War, 1755-1760

Legend:
- ← English Forces
- ✕ Battle
- ✖ French Fort
- ⬚ English Fort

sachusetts, which had been promised repayment by Parliament for its expenses in capturing Louisbourg, planned a massive assault on Quebec but then abandoned it when news arrived of a large French expedition moving to recover Louisbourg. That French fleet was scattered by storms and swept by disease, and it never made contact with the fortress; another French fleet on the same mission was captured by Warren. But the border raids continued and spilled over into Nova Scotia. The war degenerated into random violence. Isolated towns and farmhouses were burned and their inhabitants slaughtered, even though such butchery could make no possible difference in the end. Prisoners were taken and then exchanged. Grand campaigns were hatched with Indian allies but then, for reasons that could not be clearly explained, dissolved before any action could be taken. Spain's raids on several forts along the coast of the southern British mainland colonies were equally inconclusive and equally ill designed to affect the outcome of the war.

Beyond the capture of Louisbourg, nothing substantial had been accomplished when in December 1748 news arrived that peace had been concluded in Europe. It brought relief from bloodshed; but in exchange for the return of Madras in India, which France had taken, England returned Louisbourg, the symbol of American military pride, to the French. Five hundred Americans had died in action to accomplish nothing, and twice that many had been killed by disease,

exposure, and accidents. The return of Louisbourg would be recalled along with bitter memories of the Cartagena expedition—and with memories of another famous episode in King George's War.

In 1747 the "press gangs" of the British naval commander, Charles Knowles, had attempted to seize likely recruits for the royal navy on the streets of Boston.* But Boston, he discovered, was not London. To his amazement, his men were fought off by an angry mob in one of the most violent town riots in the pre-Revolutionary years. The townsmen's rampage against this flagrant although traditional violation of civilian rights lasted for four days and remained a living memory for a generation to come.

The French and Indian War. The third and last of these pre-Revolutionary wars in part followed the pattern of the others. This time, however, America was the central theater of war, not a marginal one. And this time the military outcome was conclusive, and the resentment generated between Britain and the colonies was much greater.

The conflict that in America was called the French and Indian War was known in Europe as the Seven Years' War; it lasted from 1756 to 1763. As was true of earlier eighteenth-century wars, Britain became in-

*"Press gangs" were frequently and legally used in the 1700s to round up the manpower needed for naval vessels.

FRANKLIN'S SNAKE DEVICE, 1754
This famous emblem, first published by Franklin just before the meeting of the Albany Congress, was reprinted with variations throughout the colonies and became a symbol of resistance to Britain in the years preceding the Revolution.

volved in order to maintain the balance of power in Europe, which the British government thought was threatened by the aggressive policies of France. This time Britain's ally in continental Europe was Prussia, and France's allies were Austria and Russia. The Seven Years' War was also a struggle for supremacy overseas—not only in the Western Hemisphere, but in Asia and Africa as well.

In America the immediate cause of the conflict was a series of clashes between French army units on the one hand and Virginians on the other. The French units were trying to secure the Ohio River valley for France by establishing a string of forts there. The Virginians had claims to this territory going back to the original charter, and these claims were now being advanced by a powerful group of land speculators. The French repulsed the Virginians' efforts to set up a British fort at the strategic junction of the Ohio, Allegheny, and Monongahela rivers (the site of present-day Pittsburgh). Early in 1754 the French established their own Fort Duquesne there. A small British force under the twenty-two-year-old Major George Washington failed to dislodge the French and was itself defeated at a stockaded encampment called Fort Necessity.

The colonies anticipated a conflict larger than any of the previous wars. Shortly after the engagement at Fort Necessity, the representatives of seven colonies met at Albany, New York, to try to work out defense plans among themselves and with their Indian allies. But this effort did not succeed. While in principle the delegates adopted Benjamin Franklin's proposal for a political and military union of the colonies, they could not convince a single colonial assembly to ratify a suggested plan for a general government of all the colonies. Meanwhile the British government moved ahead with a design for a large-scale war that involved dispatching a sizable army to America, enlisting colonial troops, and collecting quantities of provisions and equipment in America. Early in 1755 the British commander, Major General Edward Braddock, arrived with the first regiments. He was an arrogant disciplinarian with little sympathy for difficult colonials and no sense of how to handle them. Even before war was formally declared in May 1756, Braddock fought the first engagement of the conflict in the wilderness of western Pennsylvania. Once declared, the conflict spread quickly to all points of contact among the major European powers—not only in Europe, America, and the Caribbean, but also in Africa, India, and the Philippines.

For two years the British suffered defeat after defeat. Braddock's army, moving west to eliminate Fort Duquesne, fell into confusion at its first, accidental contact with the enemy and was almost annihilated by a small French and Indian force hidden along the sides of the road. There were 1,000 casualties in an army of 1,400; only 23 of 86 officers survived. Washington, who helped lead the pell-mell retreat, buried Braddock in the road to keep his grave from being discovered. To the north the British had to retake Nova Scotia, whose boundaries were disputed and whose French-speaking inhabitants, the Acadians, were either pro-French or unreliably neutral. Thereafter, 6,000 of the Acadians were rounded up and deported south to the thirteen colonies. But although this action isolated Cape Breton Island and its fortress, Louisbourg, the effort by the new British commander in chief, Lord Loudoun, to capture that stronghold in 1757 failed. So too did Governor Shirley's ambitious attempt to force the French out of the arc of forts that formed the northwest boundary of the British colonies. Instead of the British taking the two French forts, Frontenac and Niagara, on Lake Ontario, the French, under the able commander Montcalm, captured the British fort, Oswego, on the eastern side of Lake Ontario. Secure at Crown Point on Lake Champlain, the French moved deeper into New York by establishing Fort Ticonderoga, ten miles to the south on Champlain. In August 1757 they seized Fort William Henry even farther to the south, on Lake George, capturing 2,000 British troops along with it. Later the French on the western American frontier penetrated northern New York as far as Fort Herkimer on the Mohawk River, murdering noncombatant German farmers along the way. The whole of central New York and western New England was exposed; Albany seemed doomed. In Europe, meanwhile, the allied armies of France and Austria overran Britain's dependent state, Hanover,* and threatened Britain's ally, Prussia.

It was at this absolute low point in British fortunes that the planning of the great British statesman William Pitt began to have its effect. Pitt was a strange, brilliant, imaginative, and neurotic war minister. Appointed secretary of state in 1757, he possessed a vision of imperial greatness that was unique for the time. He also intended to fight what today would be called a total war. He demanded huge government expenditures, heavy subsidies for the Euro-

pean allies to neutralize the continental theater of war, and large commitments by the colonies, to be financed by Parliament. Pitt planned an American army of 24,000 British regulars and 25,000 colonial troops—a very large force for the time.

Passing over established but ineffective generals in favor of younger and more energetic commanders, Pitt launched a series of efforts to break the arc of French forts north and west of the mainland colonies. The first of his plans—an attack on Ticonderoga in July 1758—failed miserably. But that was his only failure. Later the same month, a force of 9,000 regular army troops and 500 colonials under the young general Jeffrey Amherst and the thin, sickly, but tigerish brigadier James Wolfe, only thirty-one years old, took Louisbourg. A month later a swift British raid overran the critical supply depot of Fort Frontenac, the link between the St. Lawrence River and the French posts farther to the west and south. With the capture of Fort Frontenac, the British gained control of Lake Ontario. In November 1758 a mixed force led by three excellent commanders, including Colonel Washington, finally avenged Braddock's defeat by seizing Fort Duquesne from the French, thereby securing British control of the entire upper Ohio River valley.

By early 1759, the year of Britain's greatest victories, the iron ring around the northern British colonies had been broken at three critical points. In the east, Louisbourg and Nova Scotia were in British hands; in the west Fort Frontenac and Lake Ontario were secured; and in the south Fort Duquesne had been captured. Successes had also been won in India, in Africa, and at sea. Then Pitt, riding the crest of great popularity at home, planned the kill. Canada was to be sealed off in the far west by the capture of Fort Niagara; General Amherst was to invade Canada by way of Lake Champlain and the St. Lawrence River valley; and Wolfe was to take Quebec in an amphibious expedition moving west up the St. Lawrence River. For all of this, a fortune in supplies, transports, and firearms, in addition to three large armies with substantial naval support, was required.

Somehow these great demands were met. In July 1759 Fort Niagara, which linked New France with the far west, was captured. At the same time, the French withdrew from Ticonderoga and Crown Point, leaving them to Amherst. By the time his troops had rebuilt these forts, it was too late for Amherst to proceed with the planned thrust into Canada from the south. But Wolfe, in one of the best-organized, most daring, and luckiest exploits in British military history, succeeded in his assigned task in Pitt's strategy.

Moving almost 10,000 men in more than 200 warships and transports through the St. Lawrence to Quebec without serious loss, Wolfe fumbled for more than

*Hanover was the small state in northern Germany whose rulers, beginning with George I in 1714, occupied the British throne. Hanover was governed independently of Great Britain.

A VIEW OF THE TAKING OF QUEBEC, SEPTEMBER 13, 1759
The debarking of the troops, their dislodging of the French defenders, and the final battle on the Plains of Abraham are shown.

seven weeks, seeking a way to attack the heavily fortified city, which had been built atop cliffs rising 150 feet above the St. Lawrence. Finally, on the night of September 12, 1759, he led 4,500 men up the cliff along a diagonal roadway he had discovered. A battle began on the Plains of Abraham, just west of the city. The French did not wait for reinforcements but charged the carefully arranged British troops rather wildly. They were met with a disciplined and efficient barrage that broke their ranks, and they were driven from the field defeated. Among the relatively few British casualties (60 dead, 600 wounded) was Wolfe; among the French, Montcalm. On September 17 Quebec surrendered. A year later, Amherst's army moved north and east from the lakes, converged on Montreal, and, with the aid of British troops sent from Quebec, forced the French governor to surrender the whole of New France.

The war ended in 1763. In the final peace treaty Britain gained undisputed possession of all of North America east of the Mississippi River except for New Orleans, including all of Nova Scotia and all of Canada. Spain, which had entered the war on the French side in 1762, was forced to give Florida to Britain in exchange for the return of Cuba, captured by a British

expedition in 1762. Spain's compensations were New Orleans and the vast lands west of the Mississippi, which France had rashly pledged to Spain as a reward for its entry into the war. Britain had won a great military triumph, and its gains in North America were matched by other British successes all over the world.

But there were serious hidden costs in the British victory. The most obvious was the huge debt that Britain had acquired in fighting the war. This financial burden set off a political reaction in Britain against grand and costly overseas adventures and eventually forced the government of George III to consider new forms of taxation. A less obvious cost was the immediate effect of the war on Anglo-American relations. On the one hand Americans rejoiced in the victory: for the first time in their history, they were relieved of the threat that the French and Spanish would stir up the Indians to attack the frontiers. But in the course of the war, they had learned to fear the presence of large professional armies, and they insisted that the only military forces compatible with liberty were militias. They learned, too, something that they had not fully realized before: although they were British, they were somehow a separate people, yet not an inferior people as the army commanders under whom they fought seemed so often to assume. For through all these wars—from the catastrophe at Cartagena to the triumph on the Plains of Abraham—they experienced the arrogance, the indifference, and often the stupidity of an officer class that was a traditional part of European life but was alien, abrasive, and in the end intolerable in America.

Above all, Americans resented the imperial regulations—some of them newly devised, some newly enforced during the French and Indian War. As part of his program for a total national effort, Pitt sought to eliminate all violations of the navigation acts, all smuggling, and indeed all commercial contact with the enemy that might bolster the enemy's economy or help supply enemy troops. It was not an altogether new effort. As early as 1756, the Privy Council had ordered the colonial governors to enforce the laws strictly and to eliminate the trade with the enemy that was well known to be taking place in neutral ports. In pursuit of these goals and in support of the efforts of the customs officials, the highest colonial courts had issued writs of assistance to customs officers—general warrants authorizing the officers to command court officials to assist them in searching for smuggled goods. Such writs of assistance were granted by the high court of Massachusetts in 1755, 1758, 1759, and 1760, and they were valid through the lifetime of the reigning king. They served their purpose well, but they were deeply resented by the merchant community, which was determined to seek relief when the opportunity arose.

Pitt's insistence on enforcing the letter of the law raised all these efforts to a new level. In the course of his brief but powerful ministry (he was forced to resign in 1761), he issued strict orders that closed the loopholes in the regulations, brought the complex rules together into a unified whole, and imposed responsibility for negligence. Governors were drawn directly into the business of imperial law enforcement, and the navy became a more effective police arm than ever before. All this made conflict likely. Well before 1763 certain colonial merchants and politicians who were antagonistic to the imperial establishment were beginning to question the value of the connection with Britain, of which they seemed to be the victims.

Yet all of this was only the tip of an iceberg. Attempts to enforce the mercantilist system during the last colonial war stirred up public controversy over other conflicts in imperial relations that had hitherto been submerged.

The Alienation of the State

Long before Pitt became involved in public affairs, three problems had arisen in Anglo-American relations that had not been solved but merely put off,

patched up with makeshift solutions, and then ignored. They could be ignored because they had developed largely as a consequence of the mercantilist system, and as long as that system was not rigidly enforced the pressure of these problems was slight. The problems remained, nevertheless, and there was a price to be paid for evading and neglecting them. Even in their moderate form they created a distance, an alienation, between Britain and America. That alienation was as much a part of the Anglo-American world in 1760 as the universal rejoicing for the new British monarch, the young George III.

Smuggling and the Balance of Payment. The first of these problems arose from the fact that the rapidly increasing American population created an expanding market for British goods that was not matched by an equivalent growth of a market within Britain itself for the products that the colonies could sell. By the 1730s American consumption of British goods rose well beyond the colonists' capacity to pay for them through direct exchanges with Britain. By the late 1760s the colonists were running a trade deficit with Britain of £1,800,000 a year, more than 90 percent of it incurred by the northern and middle colonies.

The deficit had largely been made up by "invisible earnings" (such as shipping services) and by the profits of trade with southern Europe and the West Indies. The West Indies trade was particularly important in keeping the colonies from falling into debt. Exchanges with the *non-British* islands in the West Indies—especially with the French sugar-producing islands of Guadeloupe, Martinique, and Santo Domingo—had become a vital part of that trade. Dealings with the French islands, where the American merchants could buy cheaply and sell at unusually high rates, were particularly important in making up the deficits in payments to Britain and thus in keeping the commercial colonies solvent. But that trade was increasingly resented by the British West Indian planters and their merchant associates in Britain. They recognized that the more successful this foreign trade was, the higher the cost of provisions would be on their own plantations and the lower the price they could obtain for their own products.

The issue flared up as early as 1730. The British planters and merchants moved to protect themselves against French competition by seeking to establish high duties on foreign sugar products imported into the mainland colonies. The American merchants and the colonial agents in London rose in opposition, claiming that such duties were more than the trade could bear and that they would wreck the Anglo-American commercial system and bankrupt the northern colonies. A fierce debate raged in the press and in the House of Commons. But there was no question of

SUGAR CANE AND THE ART OF MAKING SUGAR, FROM A PRINT OF 1749

the result, given the power of the West Indian lobby in London. In 1733 Parliament passed the so-called Molasses Act, which imposed prohibitively high import duties on foreign sugar products.

The problem as it existed in 1760 had thus been created in 1733. Passage of the Molasses Act set in motion the development of a network of illegal importations. Customs officers in the North American ports were systematically bribed. They became accustomed to ignoring the strict letter of the law and to settling for a certain percentage of the legal dues. Techniques for smuggling were perfected, and gradually a large part of the northern commercial economy developed a stake in the systematic breaking of the law—law that seemed arbitrary, the product of a distant, alien, and hostile government.

Conflict over Manufactures.   A similar sense of alienation developed from the second problem in Anglo-American economic relations that arose during these years. The mercantile system was based on the assumption that colonial areas were producers of exotic goods and raw materials and that they were consumers, not producers, of finished goods. It was expected that large-scale manufacturing would be confined to the home country, and the law reflected

that assumption by prohibiting the manufacture of certain basic goods in the colonies. English statutes from the end of the seventeenth century forbade the export from England of machines or tools used in the clothing industry. The Woolen Act (1699) prohibited the export of American wool or woolen products from any one colony to another. A law of 1718 forbade the free emigration of skilled artisans from Britain, and the Hat Act (1732) barred the exportation of American-made hats from the colony where they were manufactured.

Yet increasingly as the American economy developed, investments in manufactures seemed attractive and proved to be lucrative as small accumulations of capital appeared in various areas. The sums were not large by English standards, but Americans who acquired surplus capital were inclined to invest it in manufactures. For other outlets were limited. Some profits could be plowed back into the expansion of commercial enterprise. Surpluses could also be invested in urban properties, in land speculation, in English government bonds, in personal loans, or in equipment for business. But most such investments were limited to face-to-face transactions; there were no investment institutions that could broaden the range and size of the money market. In a society not prone to extravagant consumption, those who controlled the slowly growing surplus turned more and more to investing in manufactures. Adverse conditions—a continuing labor shortage, a poor overland transportation system, and limited markets—restricted what could be done. But wherever these difficulties were to some degree overcome, the results were impressive.

In shipbuilding the problems of both transportation and markets were eliminated, since England had a continuous and heavy need for merchant vessels. By the late colonial period almost 40 percent of all British-owned merchant vessels were built in the thirteen colonies. About 100 vessels were sold to Britain annually, worth at least £140,000. Iron production presented greater difficulties, which were only partly overcome by dispersal into small producing units and by the use of slave labor. Nevertheless, iron production too rose remarkably, not only in the large Principio works in Maryland and the Hasenclever plants in New Jersey, but also in dozens of smaller establishments scattered throughout the colonies. At the end of the colonial period there were 82 blast furnaces and 175 forges in the colonies (more than existed in England and Wales), and they produced 30,000 tons of crude iron a year. This was less than half of Britain's output, but it was an imposing achievement nevertheless.

Of the products manufactured in the colonies, only ships and rum were produced in such quantities that the colonists' needs were filled. But the manufacture of other goods was increasing steadily, and British authorities recognized the danger that this growth posed to the principles of mercantilism. Britain's restrictive legislation grew more elaborate. In 1750 the colonies' manufacture or export of specific textiles was outlawed. And in that year too the most famous restrictive law, the Iron Act, was passed. Although it removed duties on the importation of pig iron and bar iron into Britain, this act prohibited the erection of finishing plants for iron goods in all the colonies.

It is difficult to gauge the effect of these laws in economic terms. There was never a large amount of surplus wealth available in the colonies for investment in manufactures. And other factors besides restrictive laws tended to impede industrial growth. But in the less measurable area of attitudes toward the government that passed such laws, restrictive legislation had a significant impact. It further heightened the colonists' awareness of hostile interests in the government "at home" and deepened Americans' feelings of hostility and alienation.

Currency and Banking. The same kind of hostility and alienation resulted from the handling of the money problem, which remained a major issue through most of the mid-eighteenth century. The problem was created by the virtual absence of specie, or coined money, in America as a medium of exchange. The coinage of money was a prerogative of the king and hence was prohibited in the colonies after the confiscation of the original Massachusetts charter in 1684. (Massachusetts had been minting a coin, the "pine tree shilling," during the seventeenth century.) In the eighteenth century the colonists made every effort to attract Spanish coin to the British colonies, but the negative balance of trade made these efforts unsuccessful. The solution was paper money—unusual in the eighteenth century—which entered the American economy in two ways.

The first form of paper money was bills of credit that were issued by the colonial governments to repay debts the governments owed to merchant contractors. Massachusetts began this practice in 1690, and between 1690 and 1760 almost every other colony did the same. These bills were in effect IOUs to be redeemed eventually by the governments. Since they were declared legally valid as payment for taxes, they entered into general circulation, and their value was maintained by the expectation that the governments would eventually redeem them. But these bills were generally not made full legal tender (that is, valid payment of all debts, public and private), and they continued to be thought of as wartime expedients. The quantity available depended less on the needs of the economy than on the occasional demands for public expenditure.

The second form of paper money was the bills issued by land banks, which were in effect public loan agencies. These banks were created to issue money to individuals at 5 percent interest. The loans were repayable gradually, and they were secured against default by mortgages on land or other real estate. By 1750 land banks existed in every colony except Virginia, and their success was striking. They injected a badly needed flow of currency into the colonies' economies. They reduced taxation through the income produced from the interest on the loans. They created a source of low-interest credit needed for agricultural development. And they built up purchasing power that may have helped soften the effects of periodic depressions. Further, unlike bills of credit, the land banks put funds at low interest directly into the hands of the farmers; bills of credit went first to the merchants, who in turn lent to the farmers at higher rates of interest. Both forms of paper money, however, provided a needed medium of exchange and, despite their experimental character, were on the whole successful. Bills of credit were especially sound in the middle colonies, where both merchants and officials backed the issues and limited them carefully.

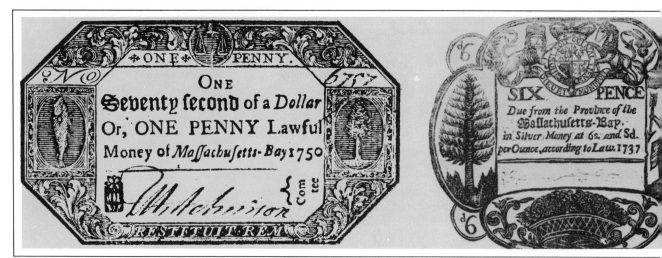

COLONIAL PAPER MONEY

The Massachusetts paper penny bears the signature of Thomas Hutchinson, the future loyalist governor, then a member of a committee in charge of issuing bills of credit. The issue of 1750 was a victory for Hutchinson's hard money policy. Based on £180,000 of silver that Parliament sent in repayment of wartime expenses, it replaced all of the colony's inflated currency in circulation.

But in parts of New England and the South, too much paper money was issued, and its value depreciated seriously. In these areas creditors feared that they would be repaid in paper money that had lost value since the time the debts had been incurred. The English merchants were even more apprehensive. They feared severe losses if their credit were in any way affected by the cheapening of the currency. Together, creditors in the colonies and in England pressured the British government to send the colonial governors strict orders not to allow bills to be issued as full legal tender and to insist that the colonial currency laws state clearly when these bills would be redeemed. The governors were to make sure that these requirements were honored to the letter.

Such tight controls were difficult to enforce, however, and a crisis arose in New England in the 1730s. Rhode Island's bills flooded the region (that colony issued £100,000 worth of paper bills in 1733 alone), and Boston merchants refused to honor them. But the pressure for more issues continued, and in 1739 a group of Massachusetts merchants formed a *private* land bank, which was authorized by the General Court to issue £150,000 worth of bills at 3 percent interest. Many members of the business community were greatly alarmed at this development, especially because debtors were allowed to repay in commodities of uncertain value. The opponents of the land bank formed what was called a silver bank, which would issue notes redeemable in silver, not in commodities. The two groups fought bitterly, and in the end the governor and council declared the land bank's bills

invalid, although £50,000 had already been placed in circulation. The leading land bankers organized public protests, which became riotous. There were arrests and jailings, and in the end the British government adopted repressive measures. In 1741 the so-called Bubble Act, already in force in Britain, was extended to the colonies: it outlawed all joint-stock companies not authorized by Parliament. In effect, this measure outlawed all private banks. Years of litigation followed in Massachusetts, as creditors who had already accepted payment in the bank's bills demanded repayment in valid money. It was the worst upheaval in the Bay Colony between the establishment of the Dominion of New England in the 1680s and the early years of the Revolution. The father of Samuel Adams, the man who would be a leader of the Revolution in Massachusetts, was one of the local officials removed from office for continuing to support the land bank.

But the more traditional *public* land banks remained in existence, and the value of their issues continued to fluctuate. In Massachusetts paper money was discounted from par (face value) at a ratio of nine to one. In Rhode Island nine issues of paper money were in circulation in 1750, representing a par value of £465,000, and in addition there was £60,000 worth of bills of credit legally available. But by then more comprehensive legislation was being drafted. In 1751 Parliament passed the Currency Act, which applied only to the New England colonies. Under this act no new land banks could be created in New England; no paper money could thereafter be made full legal tender; all bills were to be withdrawn from circulation on the strict schedule that had been specified at the time of issue; and bills could be issued to pay for government expenses only if provisions were made for their redemption out of tax revenues within two years.

Although the Currency Act applied only to New England, it constituted a warning and a threat to all colonial governments against allowing any looseness in the management of paper money. Orders from London severely restricted the use of this currency in all the colonies. But paper money had become an essential part of the American economy, and those who issued it were by no means wildcat inflationists. Every knowledgeable merchant knew the value of sound paper money, and many, like Benjamin Franklin, correctly saw that its controlled expansion could be a stimulus to the entire economy.

In this case, as in the case of the prohibitive taxation of the trade with the foreign West Indies and in the case of the restriction of American manufactures, the action of the British government was seen by Americans as not merely unfairly competitive, but hostile. The legislation and orders seemed arbitrary and unreasonable—impositions that called into question the grounds of loyalty. To obey such laws as these was a form of humiliation at the hands of a government that seemed distant, alienated from the people it governed and unresponsive to their needs.

The American and the Enlightenment

Thus tensions arose between Britain and the colonies as a result of their uneasy collaboration in wartime and of the resentments created by Britain's seemingly arbitrary and hostile legislation. These were problems largely of policy and management. Potentially, at least, they could be controlled by wise political action. A deeper and less manageable source of distance and alienation between Britain and America lay in the area of cultural perceptions—the sense Americans had of who they were in relation to the other peoples of the world, of what their life was like, and of who, in contrast, the British were within the same set of considerations. These attitudes and perceptions are facts that in the end are as important as battles, laws, and political campaigns. But they are more difficult to establish, to measure, and to describe.

Through the two generations of growth and expansion that preceded the accession of George III, Americans had gradually acquired a sense of themselves as a separate people—separate not in law or politics or constitution, but rather in character and culture. It was a complex image composed of many strands, and it could be seen as positive or negative depending on the context or point of view. It was an image of a simple, rustic, innocent, uncorrupted, and unsophisticated people, an appropriate self-image for a colonial people, perhaps, but no simple reflection of reality. For it was, first, a blending of several intellectual traditions and influences. It was in addition a reflection of the ideas and attitudes of eighteenth-century Europe's most enlightened thinkers; and it was, finally, a product of certain specific political ideas of great potential.power.

The origins of this image can be traced back to the ambiguous picture of the American Indians that Europeans formed soon after their first contact with the Western Hemisphere. This picture combined simplicity and savagery, vigor and barbarism, innocence and paganism. By the eighteenth century this mingled image began to be applied as much to the Creoles—that is, North Americans of European descent—as to the Indians, whom the English had long since come to think of as hopelessly savage, if not satanic. This transfer of traits from the native Americans to the colonists of European background was facilitated by the common belief that the colonists had deliberately copied various practices and skills from the Indians and as a result had acquired from them certain peculiar characteristics. Infants strapped to boards, for example, were thought to develop like Indians whatever their race or culture. American women, like Indian women, were believed to be taller than European women and to suffer fewer miscarriages. This notion was reinforced by the "scientific" arguments of the environmentalists, an influential group of continental European thinkers who held that life in all its forms was shaped by the material conditions in which it was lived. From this point of view, it seemed reasonable to believe that what was true of the Indians in the great American laboratory of nature would eventually apply, if it did not already, to the colonists too.

But more practical and immediate influences were also at work detailing the Americans' simplicity, innocence, and rural virtues. The image of the American colonists—their own view of themselves as well as the view that others had of them—was also shaped by the recruiting propaganda that had circulated throughout Europe and America for more than a century. All of these publications had stressed the wonders of a simple, loosely institutionalized, benign society where land was free, where government scarcely existed, and where religion was practiced in absolutely uncontested freedom.

Perhaps the greatest influence of all in spreading the image of British North America as a land of simple, innocent, independent, and virtuous folk was the widespread knowledge of the kinds of people who had in fact gone there. Europeans knew that the settlers of America had been self-respecting servants, ambitious artisans, sturdy yeoman farmers, Puritans, and—

"A VIEW OF THE HOUSE OF EMPLOYMENT, ALMS-HOUSE, PENNSYLVANIA HOSPITAL, & PART OF THE CITY OF PHILADELPHIA," 1767

above all, and most sensationally—Quakers. The symbolic importance of the Quakers to the world at large was overwhelming. In the seventeenth century they had been thought of principally as exotic radicals. They were famous throughout Britain and France for their fanatical independence of mind and for their absolute refusal to respect mere earthly authorities (hence their practice of addressing people of all ranks with the familiar "thee" and "thou"). In the more tolerant atmosphere of the early eighteenth century, the Quakers' reputation had shifted from that of defiant and fanatical seekers of religious freedom to that of gentle advocates of pacifism, toleration, simplicity in religion, and ordinary human rights in the face of aristocratic and authoritarian power. These traits had attracted Voltaire, the best known of the enlightened thinkers of the eighteenth century, to the Quakers during his stay in England from 1726 to 1729, and had led him to praise them extravagantly again and again.

For Voltaire, the Quakers as a group were the embodiment of civic virtue. And, he believed, the essence of their virtue could be seen in Pennsylvania, where their dreams and the dreams of all humanity, he thought, had reached fulfillment. Here, Voltaire stated, an enlightened republican lawgiver had created a human paradise. Philadelphia, he wrote in one of his *Philosophical Letters* (1734), was so prosperous that people flocked to it from all over America. Penn's laws were so wise that not one of them had ever been changed. The Indians had been won over to friendship; there was equality and religious freedom without priests; and there was peace everywhere. "William Penn might glory," he wrote, "in having brought down

upon the earth the so much boasted golden age, which in all probability never existed but in Pennsylvania."

The world, it seemed, agreed with Voltaire. Montesquieu, perhaps the most widely respected and influential political analyst of the age, called Penn the greatest lawgiver since classical antiquity. The French *Encyclopédie*, the monumental collection of enlightened ideas published in the mid-eighteenth century, included Penn among the cultural heroes of Europe. And in addition to all of this, every informed person in the Western world knew something about Pennsylvania and about America in general through the extraordinary figure of Benjamin Franklin.

Franklin and the Image of America. Franklin, the most celebrated American of the eighteenth century and one of the most famous and influential Americans who has ever lived, was born in Boston in 1706, the son of a candle- and soap-maker. At the age of seventeen he ran away to Philadelphia, where he eventually prospered as a printer and an organizer of printing businesses in several colonies. At the age of forty-two he retired from business to devote himself to public causes, to writing, and to scientific experimentation. He corresponded with English scientists and intellectuals, particularly Peter Collinson, a Quaker merchant and a member of the Royal Society, on the problems of electricity. It was in the form of letters to Collinson that he published the results of his studies, *Experiments and Observations on Electricity* (1751). This book was one of the great sensations of the eighteenth century. Before 1800 it went through five editions in English, three in French, one in Italian, and one in German, and it

28   LETTERS *concerning*

different perfuafion, embrac'd him tenderly. *William* made a fruitlefs exhortation to his father not to receive the facrament, but to die a Quaker; and the good old man intreated his fon *William* to wear buttons on his fleeves, and a crape hatband in his beaver, but all to no purpofe.

WILLIAM PEN inherited very large poffeffions, part of which confifted in crown-debts due to the vice-admiral for fums he had advanc'd for the fea-fervice. No monies were at that time more fecure than thofe owing from the king. *Pen* was oblig'd to go more than once, and *Thee* and *Thou* king *Charles* and his minifters, in order to recover the debt; and at laft inftead of fpecie, the government invefted him with the right and fovereignty of a province of *America*, to the fouth of *Maryland*. Thus was a Quaker rais'd to fovereign power. *Pen* fet fail for his new dominions with two fhips freighted with Quakers, who follow'd his fortune. The country was then call'd *Penfilvania* from *William Pen*, who there founded *Philadelphia*, now

the ENGLISH NATION.   29

now the moft flourifhing city in that country. The firft ftep he took was to enter into an alliance with his *American* neighbours; and this is the only treaty between thofe people and the Chriftians that was not ratified by an oath, and was never infring'd. The new fovereign was at the fame time the legiflator of *Penfilvania*, and enacted very wife and prudent laws, none of which have ever been chang'd fince his time. The firft is, to injure no perfon upon a religious account, and to confider as brethren all thofe who believe in one God.

HE had no fooner fettled his government, but feveral *American* merchants came and peopled this colony. The natives of the country inftead of flying into the woods, cultivated by infenfible degrees a friendfhip with the peaceable Quakers. They lov'd thefe foreigners as much as they detefted the other Chriftians who had conquer'd and laid wafte *America*. In a little time, a great number of thefe favages (falfely fo call'd) charm'd with the mild and gentle difpofition

30   LETTERS *concerning*

pofition of their neighbours, came in crowds to *William Pen*, and befought him to admit them into the number of his vaffals. 'Twas very rare and uncommon for a fovereign to be *Thee'd* and *Thou'd* by the meaneft of his fubjects, who never took their hats off when they came into his prefence; and as fingular for a government to be without one prieft in it, and for a people to be without arms, either offenfive or defenfive; for a body of citizens to be abfolutely undiftinguifh'd but by the public employments, and for neighbours not to entertain the leaft jealoufy one againft the other.

WILLIAM PEN might glory in having brought down upon earth the fo much boafted golden age, which in all probability never exifted but in *Penfilvania*. He return'd to *England* to fettle fome affairs relating to his new dominions. After the death of king *Charles* the fecond, king *James*, who had lov'd the father, indulg'd the fame affection to the fon, and no longer confider'd him as an obfcure Sectary, but as a very great man,

THE EUROPEAN IMAGE OF AMERICA: VOLTAIRE ON PENNSYLVANIA AND THE QUAKERS

Voltaire's account of Anglo-American life, which first appeared in English translation in 1733, was published in France in 1734 as *Lettres Philosophiques* and was promptly condemned to be burnt by the hangman as "likely to inspire a license of thought most dangerous to religion and civil order." The book nevertheless circulated widely. This passage on Penn as a great lawgiver, on Pennsylvania as a utopia, and on the Quakers as humble people of civic virtue and peace was taken over almost verbatim into the great French *Encyclopédie* (1751–80), the massive summary of European liberal thought, and hence entered the mainstream of the Enlightenment.

raised Franklin to the highest ranks among Western thinkers. The Count de Buffon, the greatest French naturalist of the age, himself arranged for the French edition; Denis Diderot, the editor of the *Encyclopédie*, declared Franklin to be the very model of the modern experimental scientist.

And who was Franklin? A simple, unsophisticated product of the primitive society of British North America—yet he had outdone the most sophisticated intellectuals of Europe in their own fields of endeavor. The implications were sensational. In the context of the great wave of reform thinking that is called the Enlightenment, Franklin's mere existence as a successful intellectual conveyed a powerful message. It reinforced the arguments of reformers everywhere and demonstrated conclusively the validity of their challenge to the establishment.

Although Enlightenment thought was complicated in its details, in its essence it was clear and simple. At its heart lay discontent with the condition of life as it was known in Europe, and a general approach to improvement. All enlightened thinkers in one way or another pictured human life as good—or if not as good, then at least as capable of great improvement and of far more happiness than was commonly experienced. The evils of the world that reduced people to misery were seen mainly as artifacts, things that men and women themselves had created. To Voltaire, the chief evils of life were the great public institutions, especially the church and a corrupt and dogmatic priesthood. To the physiocrats, the French economic reformers who believed that agriculture alone produced wealth, the great evil was the irrational controls on agricultural production and mar-

BENJAMIN FRANKLIN, BY ROBERT FEKE, AND "POOR RICHARD'S ALMANAC"
The portrait was painted about the time of Franklin's retirement from business. Thirty years later Franklin's image was completely transformed (see opposite).

Fogg Art Museum, Harvard University

Poor Richard, 1733.

AN

Almanack

For the Year of Christ

1733,

Being the First after LEAP YEAR:
And makes *since the Creation*   Years
By the Account of the Eastern *Greeks*   7241
By the Latin Church, when ☉ ent. ♈   6932
By the Computation of *W.W.*   5742
By the *Roman* Chronology   5682
By the *Jewish* Rabbies   5494

Wherein is contained

The Lunations, Eclipses, Judgment of the Weather, Spring Tides, Planets Motions & mutual Aspects, Sun and Moon's Rising and Setting, Length of Days, Time of High Water, Fairs, Courts, and observable Days.

Fitted to the Latitude of Forty Degrees, and a Meridian of Five Hours West from *London*, but may without sensible Error, serve all the adjacent Places, even from *Newfoundland* to *South-Carolina*.

By *RICHARD SAUNDERS*, Philom.

PHILADELPHIA:
Printed and sold by *B. FRANKLIN*, at the New Printing Office near the Market.

The Third Impression.

The Historical Society of Pennsylvania

FRANKLIN, THE ENLIGHTENMENT'S PHILOSOPHER

Left, this engraving by Augustin de Saint Aubin, based on a drawing by Charles Cochin, was made in early 1777 shortly after Franklin arrived in France to represent the United States. It expresses perfectly the image of Franklin as nature's philosopher and as the embodiment of Enlightenment ideals. Right, the popularization of Franklin's image. A box cover, probably of the nineteenth century, showing the great triumvirate of the Enlightenment—"The Light of the Universe"—Voltaire, Rousseau, and Franklin.

keting that the European governments imposed. To John Locke, the primary evil was the arbitrary, authoritarian state. To Jean-Jacques Rousseau, the primary evil was civilization itself. For all, the cruelties and miseries of life were products of institutions and practices that people themselves had made. The solution was to reform these structures so that human nature would be released to attain the happiness of which it was capable.

But there were powerful counter-arguments to these visions of the Enlightenment. The great imposing institutions—the state, the church, the regulated economy, and the social structures that gave power to a hereditary aristocracy—were, after all, the guardians of social order and stability. They were also the carriers of high culture and the sponsors of the finest human achievements. To eliminate or change them radically might create not freedom, but anarchy; not a higher civilization, but barbarism. To answer these arguments, the enlightened thinkers needed to be able to point to an example of civilized simplicity—a Christian society free of the hindrances of rigid and powerful institutions, a society in which reason had been used in shaping public institutions and in which, despite the simplicity of life, high culture was maintained and advanced. They found the example they wanted in British North America generally, in Pennsylvania more specifically, and above all in the figure of Franklin—apparently an untutored genius, a simple and unaffected but accomplished man of science, letters, and statecraft. If Franklin had never existed, it

would have been necessary for the philosophers of the Enlightenment to invent him. Franklin understood this perfectly, shrewdly played upon it, and expressed it most clearly in his *Autobiography*, which he wrote in the later years of his life.

To much of the Western world, Franklin *was* America; he was *the* American. Caught up in the imagery of simplicity and natural gifts demanded by Enlightenment aspirations, Franklin demonstrated the meaning of the New World to the Old. He thereby helped shape Americans' self-awareness, as well as Europe's perception of the provincial society beyond the sea.

America and the Grounds of Political Freedom. Inevitably Franklin played up the theme of the social and moral grounds of political freedom, for it was in this area that American self-imagery came into its sharpest focus and acquired its greatest relevance for everyday affairs. Informed people universally agreed that in the end the success of Britain's famous unwritten constitution—indeed, the success of any constitution that protected the people's liberties—depended on the virtue of the politically active population. Eternal vigilance was needed to maintain in government the balance of forces that prevented the misuse of power. Freedom from oppression rested on the ability of the people to resist the encroachments of a privileged and arrogant aristocracy; it also required the aristocracy to resist the temptations of profit and power and to use its privileges for the good of the entire society. If the people's will to protect their own liberties weakened, or if the British aristocracy gave in to laziness and self-indulgence as had the aristocracies of continental Europe, freedom would be destroyed by the predictable growth of arbitrary power.

The signs, for Americans of the late colonial period, were worrisome. Repeatedly the colonists found reason to question the moral qualities of English society, to doubt the independence of "the democracy" in Britain and the impartiality and responsibility of the British aristocracy. American visitors to England sent back disturbing reports. John Dickinson of Pennsylvania, in England in the election year 1754, wrote home that he was "filled with awe and reverence" by his contact with scenes of ancient greatness and by the sophistication and variety of life in London. But he was also shocked by the corruption of English politics. More than £1 million, he reported to his father, was spent in efforts to manipulate the election.

If a man cannot be brought to vote as he is desired, he is made dead drunk and kept in that state, never heard of by his family or friends till all is over and he can do no harm. The oath of their not being bribed is as strict and solemn as language can form it, but is so little regarded that few people can refrain from laughing while they take it. . . . Bribery is so common that it is thought there is not a borough in England where it is not practiced. . . . We hear every day in Westminster Hall leave moved to file information for bribery, but it is ridiculous and absurd to pretend to curb the effects of luxury and corruption in one instance or in one spot without a general reformation of manners, which everyone sees is absolutely necessary for the welfare of the kingdom. Yet Heaven knows how it can be effected. It is grown a vice here to be virtuous.

This was not simply provincial prudery. English writers too deplored the loss of virtue, warning of its implications for politics, and their voices were clearly heard in America. James Burgh's *Britain's Remembrancer* (1746) denounced "our degenerate times and corrupt nation." The British people, he said, were wallowing in "luxury and irreligion . . . venality, perjury, faction, opposition to legal authority, idleness, gluttony, drunkenness, lewdness, excessive gaming, robberies . . . a legion of furies sufficient to rend any state or empire . . . to pieces." Burgh's pamphlet was reprinted first by Franklin in 1747, then by another Philadelphia printer in 1748, and again in Boston in 1759. So too Dr. John Brown's blistering attack on English corruption, *An Estimate of the Manners and Principles of the Times* (1757), found an eager audience in America—an audience convinced of the superiority and virtue of its own uncorrupted manners and of its own moral capacity to satisfy the demands of freedom if freedom were ever challenged.

So the American people entered the age of George III. Their prospects were excellent despite the troubles that lay beneath the surface of Anglo-American life and the doubts they had about the moral quality of the British people and the responsibility of the British leaders. Conscious of their characteristics as a colonial people—provincial but vigorous, unsophisticated but uncorrupted, quarrelsome but free, undeveloped in all the main institutions of society but more prosperous than any large group in the Western world—they saw themselves growing powerful and mature as part of an enriching imperial connection.

CHRONOLOGY

1727–60 Reign of George II.

1729 Separate royal colonies, North and South Carolina, created.

1732 Georgia established as buffer against Spanish and as philanthropic effort to relocate England's paupers.

1733 Molasses Act restricts colonial importation of sugar goods from French West Indies.

1734–35 Jonathan Edwards touches off evangelical revival in Northampton, Massachusetts, and throughout Connecticut River valley.

1735 New York jury acquits John Peter Zenger of charge of seditious libel on ground that printing truth can be no libel.

1739–40 George Whitefield tours America and ignites major phase of Great Awakening.

1739–42 War of Jenkins' Ear, fought with Spain principally in Caribbean and Central America.

1740–41 Private land bank created in Massachu-setts; outlawed by Parliament.

1744–48 King George's War (colonial phase of Europe's War of the Austrian Succession, 1740–48); concluded in Treaty of Aix-la-Chapelle.

1745 New England troops take fortress of Louisbourg on Cape Breton Island (returned to France at end of war).

1750 Iron Act, limiting production of finished iron goods in colonies, passed by Parliament.

1751 Currency Act, restricting issuance and currency of paper money in New England colonies, passed by Parliament.

Publication of Franklin's *Experiments and Observations on Electricity*.

1754 Albany Congress and Plan of Union.

1754–63 French and Indian War (colonial phase of Europe's Seven Years' War, 1756–63).

1759 Quebec falls to British army.

1760 George III accedes to throne.

SUGGESTED READINGS

The eighteenth-century colonial wars were the subject of Francis Parkman's most dramatic narratives—still immensely readable—in his nine-volume series, *France and England in North America*. His *Half-Century of Conflict* (2 vols., 1892) covers King George's War, and his *Montcalm and Wolfe* (2 vols., 1884) the French and Indian War. A modern, technical, scholarly work covering the same ground in greater detail but lacking Parkman's narrative style is Lawrence H. Gipson's *British Empire Before the American Revolution*, vols. VI–VIII (1946–53). On the British army in pre-Revolutionary America, see John Shy, *Toward Lexington* (1965), chaps. 1–3. Howard H. Peckham, *The Colonial Wars, 1689–1762* (1964), provides a brief introduction to the whole subject.

On the three problems of Anglo-American relations discussed in the second section of the chapter, the balance of payments and commerce with the West Indies are discussed in James F. Shepherd and Gary M. Walton, *Shipping, Maritime Trade, and the Economic Development of Colonial North America* (1972), esp. App. IV; Richard B. Sheridan, "The Molasses Act and the Market Strategy of the British Sugar Planters," *Journal of Economic History*, 17 (1957), 62–83, and *Sugar and Slavery* (1974); Richard Pares, *Yankees and Creoles* (1956), and *War and Trade in the West Indies, 1739–1763* (1936); and Thomas C. Barrow, *Trade and Empire* (1967). On manufactures: Victor S. Clark, *History of Manufactures in the United States* (3 vols., 1929); Eleanor L. Lord, *Industrial Experiments in the British Colonies . . .* (1898); Curtis P. Nettels, "The Menace of Colonial Manufacturing, 1690–1720," *New England Quarterly*, 4 (1931), 230–69; Arthur

C. Bining, *British Regulation of the Colonial Iron Industry* (1933); Shepherd and Walton, *Shipping* (cited above), esp. App. VI. And on the money supply and banks, see E. James Ferguson, "Currency Finance . . . ," *Wm. and Mary Q.*, 10 (1953), 153–80; Theodore G. Thayer, "The Land Bank System in the American Colonies," *Journal of Economic History*, 13 (1953), 145–59; Andrew M. Davis, *Currency and Banking in . . . Massachusetts Bay* (2 vols., 1901); Richard A. Lester, *Monetary Experiments . . .* (1939); and George A. Billias, *Massachusetts Land Bankers of 1740* (1959).

On cultural relations between the colonies and Europe, see, besides the Boorstin and Savelle books cited for chapter 5, Michael Kraus, *The Atlantic Civilization: Eighteenth-Century Origins* (1949); Sacvan Berkovitch, *The Puritan Origins of the American Self* (1975); Durand Echeverria, *Mirage in the West . . . the French Image of American Society to 1815* (1957); Howard M. Jones, *O Strange New World* (1964); and Bernard Bailyn, *Ideological Origins of the American Revolution* (1967), chaps. 2–3. On Franklin's extraordinary role in cultural relations between Europe and America, see Alfred O. Aldridge, *Franklin and His French Contemporaries* (1957); Antonio Pace, *Franklin and Italy* (1958); I. Bernard Cohen's edition, *Benjamin Franklin's Experiments* (1941) and his *Franklin and Newton* (1956); and Charles C. Sellers, *Benjamin Franklin in Portraiture* (1962). The full standard biography is Carl Van Doren, *Benjamin Franklin* (1938); a shorter but well-rounded account is Verner W. Crane, *Benjamin Franklin and a Rising People* (1954). Ronald W. Clark's biography (1983) concentrates on Franklin's early career and his achievements in science.

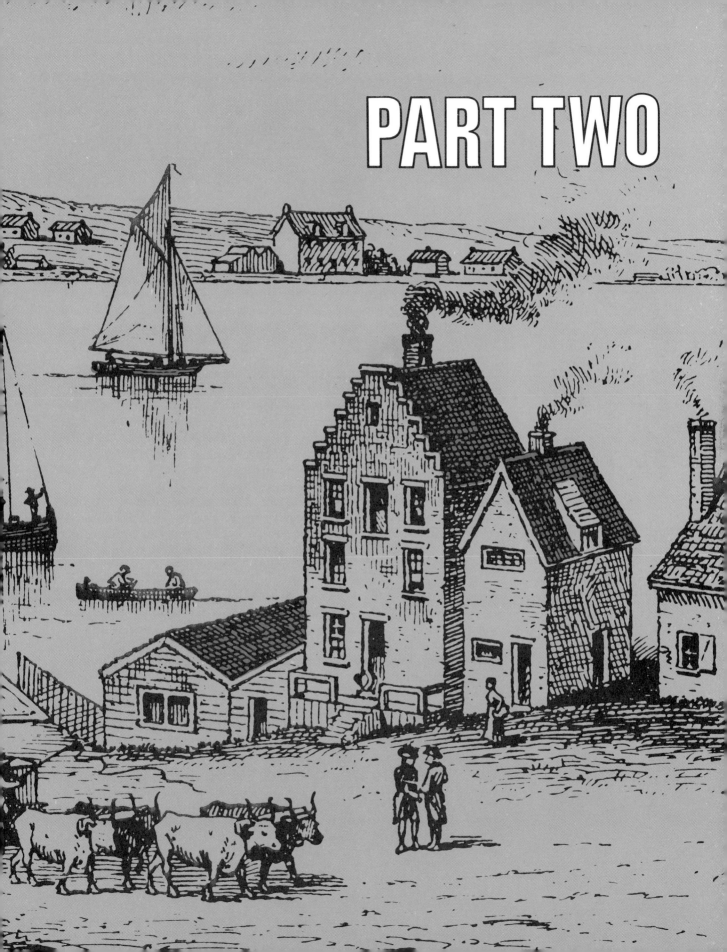

PART TWO

FRAMING THE REPUBLIC, 1760–1820

Gordon S. Wood

*T*he American Revolution is the single most important event in American history. Not only did it create the United States, but it defined most of the persistent values and hopes of the American people. The noblest ideals of Americans—the commitments to freedom, equality, constitutionalism, and the well-being of ordinary people—were first defined in the Revolutionary era. The Revolution gave Americans the belief that they were a people with a special destiny to lead the world toward liberty. The Revolution, in short, gave birth to whatever ideology Americans as a whole have had. The United States was the first nation in the modern world to make political and social principles the foundation of its existence. A society that was composed of so many different races and of people from so many different places could not be a nation in any traditionally understood sense of the term. It is the Revolutionary experience and the ideals and beliefs flowing from it that have held Americans together and made them think of themselves as a single people.

The origins of such a great event lie deep in America's past. A century and a half of dynamic developments in the British mainland colonies of North America had fundamentally altered inherited European institutions and patterns of life and had created the basis for a new society. Suddenly in the 1760s Great Britain thrust its imperial power into the changing world of North America with a thoroughness that had not been felt in a century. Its policies touched off a crisis within the loosely organized empire, and American resistance turned into rebellion. As the colonists searched for a way to make sense of the unique qualities of their society, this rebellion became for them a justification and idealization of American life as it had gradually and unintentionally developed over the previous century and a half. In this sense, as John Adams later said, "The Revolution was effected before the war commenced." It was a change "in the minds and hearts of the people."

But this change was not the whole American Revolution. The Revolution was also part of the great transforming process that carried America into modernity. By 1760 the difficult circumstances of life in the North American wilderness had fundamentally altered the institutions and lives of the colonists. But along with powdered wigs and knee breeches, mid-eighteenth-century society still retained many traditional habits of behavior and social relationships. These traditional patterns of

Overleaf: The Brooklyn Ferry, c. 1790.
The Bettmann Archive, Inc.

156

life separated colonial America from the more rapidly changing, bustling, individualistic world of the early nineteenth century. Much had changed by 1760, but more remained to be changed.

Although the Revolution began as a political and constitutional struggle, its deepest roots and its most far-reaching results were social. The Revolution released and intensified forces that, by the early years of the nineteenth century, helped create a society unlike any that had existed before. The society that emerged from the Revolution was almost as different from the America of 1760 as colonial America had been from eighteenth-century England.

The Revolution's origins went back to the seventeenth-century settlements, and its consequences are still felt by the American people. Yet the Revolution itself took place essentially between 1760 and 1820. Some Americans thought that the Revolution was over in 1776 with the Declaration of Independence and the creation of new state governments. Others believed that the Revolution ended only with the reconstruction of the national government in 1787. Still others thought it was not finished until the new central government gathered strength and energy in the 1790s. Yet many other Americans saw these later centralizing developments—the creation of a strong national government—as a betrayal of the original Revolution and thus sought to recover the spirit of 1776. For them the election of Thomas Jefferson as president of the United States in 1800 was the real fulfillment of the Revolution, a fulfillment that required confirmation in another war against Great Britain in 1812.

By the end of that second war against Britain, the central impulses of the Revolution had run their course. At last the future and stability of the Republic seemed secure. Democracy and equality were no longer issues to be debated; they had become articles of faith to be fulfilled. The ideological antagonisms that the Revolution had aroused had finally petered out. In 1760 the colonists were provincial Britons living on the edges of civilization; by 1820 they were Americans leading what they thought was a world revolution on behalf of liberty. In place of a collection of little more than 2 million monarchical subjects huddled along the Atlantic coast, America by 1820 had become a huge, expansive nation of nearly 10 million republican citizens, active, energetic, and filled with the great possibilities that lay before them.

7 Sources of the Revolution

In 1763 Great Britain straddled the world with the greatest and richest empire since the fall of Rome. From India to the Mississippi River, its armies and navies had been victorious. The Peace of Paris that concluded the Seven Years' War—or the French and Indian War, as the Americans called it—gave Britain undisputed dominance over the northern and eastern half of North America. From the defeated powers, France and Spain, Britain acquired huge chunks of territory in the New World—all of Canada, East and West Florida, and millions of fertile acres between the Appalachian Mountains and the Mississippi River. France turned over to Spain the territory of Louisiana in compensation for Spain's loss of Florida; and thus this most fearsome of Britain's enemies removed itself altogether from the North American continent.

Yet at the moment of Britain's supremacy there were powerful forces at work that would soon, almost overnight, change everything. In the aftermath of the Seven Years' War, British officials found themselves having to make long-postponed decisions concerning the colonies that set in motion a chain of events that ultimately shattered the empire.

The Changing Empire

Ever since the formation of the British Empire in the late seventeenth century, royal officials and bureaucrats had been interested in reforming the awkwardly imposed imperial structure and in expanding royal authority over the American colonists. But most of their schemes had been blocked by English ministries more concerned with the patronage of English politics than with colonial reform. These ministries were anxious to keep troublesome colonial issues out of Parliament, where they might be readily exploited by opposition politicians. Under such circumstances, the empire had been allowed to grow haphazardly, without much control from London. People from all countries had been allowed to settle in the colonies, and land had been given out freely.

Although few imperial officials had ever doubted that the colonies were supposed to be inferior to the mother country and dependent upon it, in fact the empire had not worked that way. The relationship that had developed reflected the irrational and inefficient nature of the imperial system—the variety of offices, the diffusion of power, and the looseness of organization. Even in trade regulation, which was the empire's main business, inefficiency, loopholes, and numerous opportunities for corruption prevented the imperial authorities from interfering substantially with the colonists' pursuit of their own economic and social interests.

By the middle of the eighteenth century, however, new circumstances began forcing changes in this irrational but working relationship. The British colonies—there were twenty-two of them in the Western Hemisphere in 1760—were becoming too important to be treated as casually as the mother country had treated them in the first half of the eighteenth century. Dynamic developments throughout the greater British world demanded that England pay more attention to its North American colonies.

Population Growth and Movement. The most basic of these developments were the growth and movement of people. In the middle decades of the eighteenth century, the population throughout the whole English-speaking-world—in Britain and the colonies alike—was increasing at unprecedented rates and redistributing itself in massive movements of people. During the 1740s the population of England, which had hardly grown at all for half a century, suddenly began to increase. The populations of Ireland and Scotland had been rising steadily since the beginning of the eighteenth century. The population of the North American colonies was growing even faster—virtually exploding—and had been doing so almost since the beginning of the settlements. Indeed, the North American colonists continued to multiply more rapidly than any other people in the Western world. Between

158

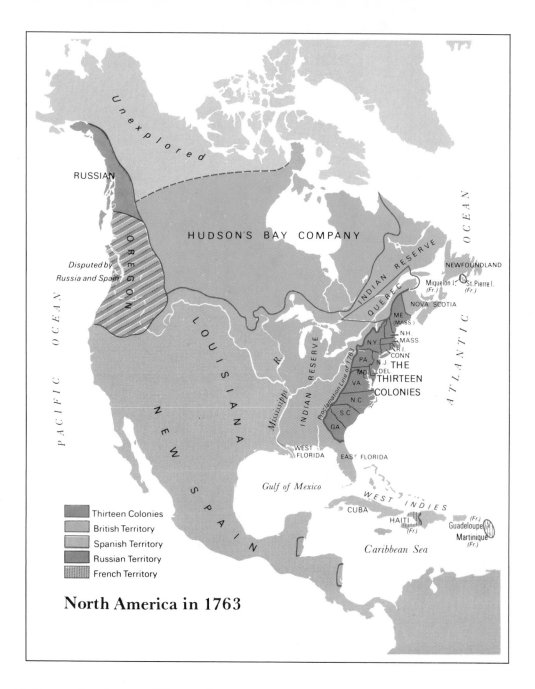

North America in 1763

Thirteen Colonies
British Territory
Spanish Territory
Russian Territory
French Territory

1750 and 1770 they doubled in number, from a million to more than 2 million, and thereby became an even more important part of the British world. In 1700 the American population had been only one-twentieth of the British and Irish populations combined; by 1770 it was nearly one-fifth, and such far-sighted colonists as Benjamin Franklin were predicting that sooner or later the center of the British Empire would shift to America.

Everywhere the expanding British population was in motion, moving from village to village and from continent to continent. In Britain growing numbers of migrants in a few decades created the new industrial cities of Birmingham, Manchester, and Leeds and made London the largest urban center in the Western world. A steady stream moved from the British Isles across the Atlantic to the New World. The migration of Protestant Irish and Scots that had begun early in the century increased after the French and Indian war. Between 1764 and 1776 some 125,000 people left the British Isles for the American colonies. From the colonial port towns, particularly Philadelphia, British migrants and Germans from the Rhine Valley joined with increasing numbers of uprooted colonists to spread over half a continent, along a variety of routes.

For nearly a century and a half the colonists had been confined to a several-hundred-mile-wide strip of territory along the Atlantic coast. But in the middle decades of the eighteenth century, the pressures of increasing population density began to be felt. Overcultivated soil in the East was becoming depleted. Particularly in the Chesapeake areas the number of tenants was visibly growing. Older towns now seemed overcrowded, especially in New England, and young men coming of age could no longer count on obtaining pieces of land as their fathers had done. Throughout the colonies more and more people were on the move; many were drifting into the small colonial cities, which were ill equipped to handle them. By 1772 in Philadelphia, the percentage of poor was eight times greater than it had been twenty years earlier, and almshouses were being constructed and filled as never before. Most of these transient poor, however, saw the cities only as way stations in their endless search for land on which they might re-create the stability they had been forced to abandon.

With the defeat of the French, people set out in all directions, eager to take advantage of the newly acquired land in the interior. In 1759 speculators and settlers moved into the area around Lake Champlain and westward along the Mohawk River into central New York. Between 1749 and 1771 New York's population grew from 73,348 to 168,007. Tens of thousands of colonists and new immigrants pushed into western Pennsylvania and southward into the Carolinas along routes on each side of Virginia's Blue Ridge. Along these roads strings of towns—from York, Pennsylvania, to Camden, South Carolina—quickly developed to service the travelers and to distribute produce to distant markets. The growth of settlement was phenomenal. In Pennsylvania twenty-nine new localities were created between 1756 and 1765—more in these few years than in the colony's entire previous history. North Carolina increased its population sixfold between 1750 and 1775 to become the fourth-largest colony.

New frontiers appeared everywhere simultaneously throughout British North America. By the early 1760s hunters and explorers such as Daniel Boone began opening up paths westward through the Appalachians. Settlers, mostly small farmers, soon followed. Some moved southward to the valley of the Holston River and to the headwaters of the Cumberland and Tennessee rivers, and others spread northwest into the Ohio Valley and the Kentucky basin. Some drifted down the Ohio and Mississippi rivers to join overland migrants from the southern colonies

in the new province of West Florida, and thus completed a huge encirclement of the new western territory.

During the decade and a half before Independence, New England throbbed with movement. New towns were created by the founding of new settlements and the division of existing ones. By the early 1760s the number of transients drifting from town to town throughout the region multiplied dramatically, in some counties doubling or even more than tripling the numbers of the previous decade. Many farmers gave up searching for opportunities within established communities and set out for distant places on the very edges of the expanded empire. Massachusetts and Connecticut colonists trekked not only to northern New England and Nova Scotia, but to areas as far away as the Susquehanna River in Pennsylvania and the lower Mississippi River. Indeed the largest single addition to the population of West Florida came from the settlement of four hundred families from Connecticut in 1773–74. In the late 1760s the migration of people from Connecticut to the Wyoming Valley in Pennsylvania was so massive that Connecticut in 1774 annexed these Pennsylvania settlements and made them part of one of the province's counties. Between 1760 and 1776 some 20,000 people from southern New England moved up the Connecticut River into New Hampshire and into what would later become Vermont. In that same period migrants from Massachusetts streamed into Maine and founded 94 towns. A total of 264 new towns were established in northern New England during the years between 1760 and 1776.

British and colonial authorities could scarcely comprehend the meaning of this enormous explosion of peoples in search of land. The colonists, one astonished official observed, were moving "as their avidity and restlessness incite them. They acquire no attachment to place: but wandering about seems engrafted in their nature; and it is a weakness incident to it that they should forever imagine the lands further off are still better than those upon which they are already settled." Land fever infected all levels of society. While Ezra Stiles, a minister in Newport, Rhode Island, and later the president of Yale University, bought and sold small shares in places all over New England and in Pennsylvania and New York, more influential figures like Benjamin Franklin were concocting huge speculative schemes in the vast unsettled lands of the West.

All this movement had far-reaching effects on American society and its place in the British Empire. The fragmentation of households, churches, and communities increased, and the colonial governments lost control of the mushrooming new settlements. In the backcountry, lawlessness and vagrancy became common, and disputes over land claims and colonial

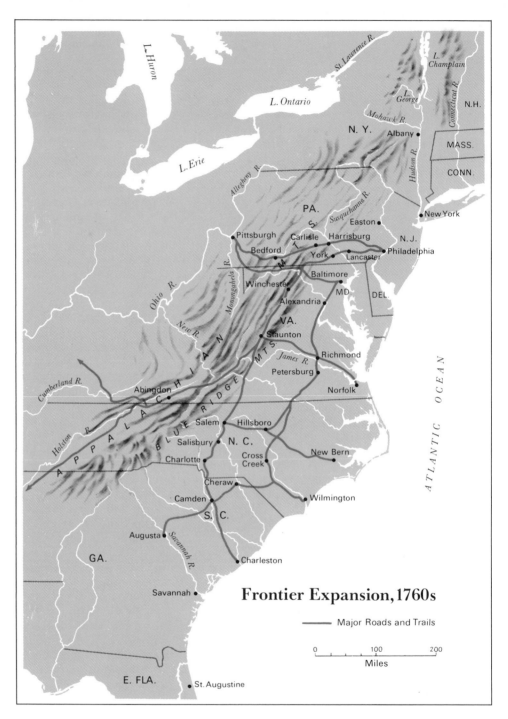

Frontier Expansion, 1760s

——— Major Roads and Trails

0   100   200

Miles

boundaries increased sharply. But the most immediate effect of this rapid spread of people—and the effect that was most obvious to imperial officials in the 1760s—was the pressure that the migrations placed on the native Americans.

Indians. At the beginning of the Seven Years' (or French and Indian) War, the problem of the native

Americans in the West compelled the British government for the first time to take over from the colonies the direct control of Indian affairs. Two British officials, one each for the northern and southern regions, now had the task of pacifying tribes of Indians, whom one of the superintendents described as "the most formidable of any uncivilized body of people in the world." New England had few Indians left, but in

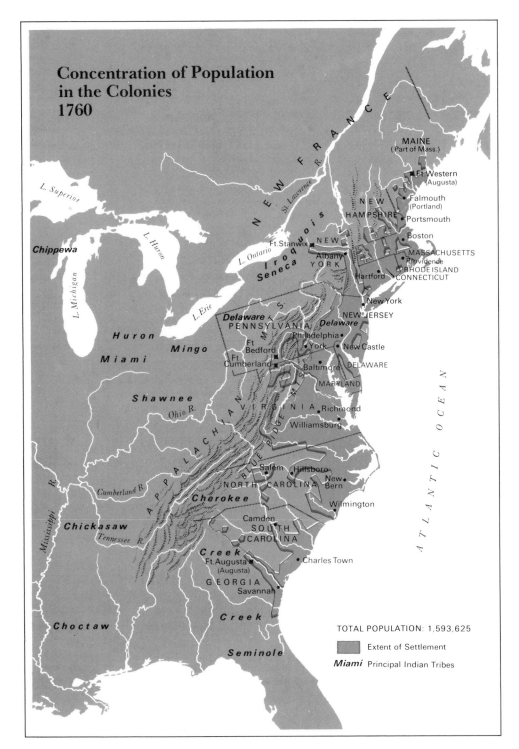

Concentration of Population in the Colonies 1760

MAINE
(Part of Mass.)

Ft Western
(Augusta)

Falmouth
(Portland)

Portsmouth

Boston

NEW
HAMPSHIRE

Ft.Stanwix

NEW

MASSACHUSETTS

Albany

Providence

YORK

RHODE ISLAND

Hartford

CONNECTICUT

New York

NEW JERSEY

Delaware

PENNSYLVANIA

Delaware

Philadelphia

Ft.
Bedford

York

New Castle

Ft.
Cumberland

Baltimore

DELAWARE

MARYLAND

VIRGINIA

Richmond

Williamsburg

Salem

Hillsboro

NORTH CAROLINA

New
Bern

Wilmington

Camden

SOUTH
CAROLINA

Ft.Augusta
(Augusta)

Charles Town

GEORGIA

Savannah

Chippewa

Huron

Mingo

Miami

Shawnee

Cherokee

Chickasaw

Creek

Choctaw

Creek

Seminole

Iroquois

Seneca

Delaware

L. Superior

L. Huron

L. Michigan

L. Ontario

L. Erie

St. Lawrence

NEW FRANCE

Ohio R.

Cumberland R.

Tennessee R.

Mississippi R.

APPALACHIAN MTS.

BLUE RIDGE MTS.

ATLANTIC OCEAN

TOTAL POPULATION: 1,593,625

Extent of Settlement

Miami Principal Indian Tribes

New York there were 2,000 warriors, mostly fierce Senecas, left from the once-formidable Six Nations of the Iroquois. In the Susquehanna and Ohio valleys dwelled a variety of tribes, mostly Delawares, Shawnees, Mingos, and Hurons, who claimed about 12,000 fighting men. On the southern frontiers the Indian presence was even more forbidding. From the Carolinas to the Yazoo River were some 14,000 warriors, mainly Cherokees, Creeks, Chocktaws, and Chickasaws. Altogether this native American population formed an imposing barrier to British western expansion.

"OUTEWAS INDIAN, 1759," BY GEORGE TOWNSHEND
The story of Indian-white relations in North America is a
tragic one. Already by the middle of the eighteenth century,
many of the Indian tribes had become dependent on the white
man's goods, including tools, weapons, and liquor. Thus not
only were the Indians losing their lands to the whites, but they
were inadvertently collaborating in the corruption and destruction of their culture.

National Portrait Gallery, London

After French authority had been eliminated from
Canada and Spanish authority from Florida, the native Americans were no longer able to play one European power off against the other. Britain now had sole
responsibility for regulating the profitable fur trade
and for maintaining peace between whites and Indians. The problems were awesome. Not only were
many whites prepared to use brandy and rum to
achieve their aims, but they had conflicting interests.
Traders competed among themselves: some favored
regulation of the fur trade, although most did not. But

all traders favored the establishment in the West of
Indian reservations that settlers would not be permitted to invade, and they drew upon the support of humanitarian groups who were concerned with the
Indians' fate. Land speculators, however, wanted to
push back the Indians and open the West for settlement. Confused, lied to, and cheated of their land
and their furs by greedy white traders and land-
hungry migrants, the Indians retaliated with atrocities and raids. Some tribes attempted to form coalitions and wage full-scale war.

Thus the end of the Seven Years' War did not end
violence on the frontier. From the devastating Cherokee War of 1759–61 in South Carolina to the assault
on the Shawnees in 1774 by Lord Dunmore, the royal
governor of Virginia, British officials repeatedly had
to resort to troops to put down the Indians' revolts
over white encroachments on their lands and to curb
the dishonest practices of the traders. The biggest Indian uprising of the period occurred in 1763 following
the British takeover of the former French forts in the
West. In just a few weeks Indians from several tribes
that had joined under the leadership of an Ottawa
chief named Pontiac surprised and destroyed all but
three of the British posts west of the Appalachians.
Before they were defeated by British troops, the angry
warriors had penetrated eastward into the backcountry of Pennsylvania, Maryland, and Virginia and
had killed more than 2,000 colonists. It is no wonder
that many royal authorities in the 1760s concluded
that only the presence of regular troops of the British
army could maintain peace in the American borderlands of the empire.

Backcountry Disorder. The rapid growth and spread of
people in the mid-eighteenth century affected more
than white-Indian relations on the frontier. Thousands
of migrants flowed into the backcountry, beyond the
reach of the colonial governments. These backcountry
settlers were so distant from authority that sometimes
vigilante groups had to be relied on to impose order. In
the 1760s backcountry people in South Carolina organized vigilante "Regulators" to put down roving
gangs of thieves, but illegal posses of this kind often
turned raiders themselves. By the early 1770s the
Green Mountain Boys of Vermont, under the leadership of Ethan Allen and his brother, were terrorizing
all who submitted to New York's jurisdiction, and
Connecticut Yankees were fighting Pennsylvanians for
control of the settlements along the Susquehanna
River. Sometimes frontiersmen in these trans-
Appalachian areas had to form compacts of government for their raw societies, which often consisted of
little more than "stations"—primitive stockaded forts
surrounded by huts.

JOSEPH BRANT (1742–1807)
This chief of the Mohawks was educated by English Indian Superintendent Sir William Johnson, sent to London, and presented to the Court. He fought effectively on the British side during the Revolution. As an Anglican convert he translated the New Testament and the Prayer Book into his native tongue.

Everywhere in the backcountry the sudden influx of people weakened the legitimacy of existing authority. In the rapidly growing interiors of both Pennsylvania and North Carolina, settlers in the 1760s rose in arms against what they believed was exploitation by remote eastern governments. In western Pennsylvania Scotch-Irish settlers led by the Paxton Boys rebelled against the Quaker-dominated, pacifist-minded colonial legislature, in which they were underrepresented. In 1763–64 they killed Indians who were under the government's protection and then marched on Philadelphia. The rebels turned back only after mediation by Benjamin Franklin and the promise of a greater voice in the colonial assembly. In North Carolina not only was the backcountry underrepresented in the provincial legislature, but its local government was under the corrupt management of officials and lawyers from the eastern part of the colony. In 1767 a group of western vigilantes, assuming the familiar title "Regulators," erupted in violence. They took over the county courts and petitioned the North Carolina government for greater representation, lower taxes, and local control of their affairs. Two thousand of these "Regulators" were dispersed by the North Carolina governor and his force of eastern militia at the so-called battle of the Alamance in 1771. But royal officials could not so easily dispel the deeply rooted fears among many Americans of the dangers of unfair representation and distant political power. Indeed, these Westerners were only voicing toward their own colonial governments the same attitudes that Americans in general had about British power.

Economic Expansion. All these consequences flowing from the increased numbers and movement of people in North America were bound to raise Britain's interest in its colonies. But population pressures were not the only factor in the reshaping of British attitudes toward the colonies and in the transforming of American society. Equally important was the related expansion of the Anglo-American economy that took place in the middle years of the eighteenth century.

By 1750 the immediate origins of what would soon become the Industrial Revolution were already visible in Britain. British imports, exports, and industrial production of various sorts—all the major indicators of economic growth—were rapidly rising. Americans were deeply involved in this sudden British economic expansion, and by the 1760s they were feeling its effects everywhere.

In the years after 1745, colonial trade with Great Britain grew dramatically and became an increasingly important segment of the English and Scottish economies. Nearly half of all English shipping was engaged in American commerce. The North American mainland was absorbing 25 percent of English exports, and Scottish commercial involvement with the colonies was growing even faster. From 1747 to 1765, the value of colonial exports to Britain doubled, from about £700,000 to £1,500,000, while the value of colonial imports from Britain rose even faster, from about £900,000 to more than £2 million. For the first time in the eighteenth century, Britain's own production of foodstuffs could not meet the needs of its suddenly rising population. By 1760 Britain was importing more grain than it exported.

This increasing demand for foodstuffs—not only in Great Britain, but in southern Europe and the West Indies as well—meant soaring prices for American exports. Between the 1740s and the 1760s, the price of American wheat that was exported to the Caribbean increased nearly 60 percent, flour 54 percent, and pork 48 percent. Even tobacco prices went up 34 percent in the same period. Seeing the greater demand and rising prices for American exports, more and more ordinary farmers began to produce foodstuffs and other goods for distant markets. By the 1760s remote trading centers in the backcountry such as Staunton, Virginia, and Salisbury, North Carolina, were shipping large quantities of tobacco and grain eastward to the sea along networks of roads and towns. Port cities like Baltimore, Norfolk, and Alexandria grew up almost overnight to handle this swelling traffic.

Soaring prices for agricultural exports meant rising standards of living for more and more Americans. It was not just the great planters of the South and the big merchants of the cities who were getting richer. Now ordinary Americans were also buying luxury items that traditionally had been purchased only by the well-to-do—items that were increasingly called conveniences and that ranged from Irish linen and lace to matched sets of Wedgwood dishes.

Although nineteen out of twenty Americans were still engaged in agriculture, the rising levels of taste and consumption drew more colonists into manufacturing—at first, mostly the production of crude textiles and shoes. Transportation and communications rapidly improved as roads were built and regular schedules established for stagecoaches and packet boats. In the 1750s the post office, under the leadership of Benjamin Franklin, the colonial deputy postmaster general, instituted weekly mails between Philadelphia and Boston and cut delivery time in half, from six to three weeks. The growing populaton, better roads, more reliable information about markets, and the greater variety of towns all encouraged domestic manufacturing for regional and intercolonial markets. By 1768 colonial manufacturers were supplying Pennsylvania with 8,000 pairs of shoes a year. Areas of eastern Massachusetts were becoming more involved in manufacturing: in 1767 the town of Haverhill, with fewer than three hundred residents, had forty-four workshops and nineteen mills. By this date many colonial artisans and would-be manufacturers were more than eager to support associations to boycott English imports.

But most colonists still preferred British goods. Since the mid-1760s Americans were importing from Britain about £500,000 worth of goods more than they were exporting to the mother country, and thus they continued to be troubled by a trade deficit with Britain. Part of this deficit in the colonists' balance of payments with Britain was made up by the profits of shipping, by British wartime expenditures in America, and by increased sales to Europe and the West Indies. But a large part was also made up by the extension to the colonists of large amounts of English and Scottish credit. By 1760 colonial debts to Britain amounted to £2 million; by 1772 they had jumped to more than £4 million. After 1750 a growing proportion of this debt was owed by colonists who earlier had been excluded from direct dealings with British merchants.

"ATTEMPT TO LAND A BISHOP IN AMERICA"
By 1768 proposals for establishing an Anglican bishop in America had become identified with British efforts to deprive the colonists of their liberties.

Small tobacco farmers in the Chesapeake gained immediate access to British credit and markets through the spread of Scottish "factors" (stores) in the backcountry of Virginia and Maryland.* By 1760 it was not unusual for as many as 150 petty traders in a single port to be doing business with a London merchant company.

These demographic and economic forces undermined the traditional structure of colonial society. The ties of kinship and patronage that held people together, which had never been strong in America, were now further weakened. Even in Virginia, one of the most stable of the colonies, the leading plantation owners found their authority challenged by small farmers who had been cut loose from older dependent economic relationships. During the middle decades of

*For the Scottish "factors," see chapter 5, p. 119.

the eighteenth century, ordinary people in Virginia left the official Church of England in growing numbers. They formed new evangelical religious communities that rejected the high style and luxury of the dominant Anglican gentry. Within a few years succeeding waves of New Light Presbyterians, Separate Baptists, and finally Methodists swept up new converts from among the common farmers of the Chesapeake region. Between 1769 and 1774 the number of Baptist churches in Virginia increased from seven to fifty-four.

The Virginia gentry blamed the growth of religious dissent on the long-existing incompetence of the Anglican ministers. In turn the ministers accused the lay vestries, which were composed of Anglican gentry, of not supporting them. Amid these mutual accusations the Virginia House of Burgesses passed acts in 1755 and 1758 that fixed at two pence a pound the standard value of tobacco used to meet debts and public obligations. Since tobacco prices were rising rapidly, these so-called Two Penny Acts penalized creditors and those public officials (including ministers) who were used to being paid in tobacco. British merchants and the ministers of the Virginia established church protested and were able to get the king's Privy Council in England to veto the Burgesses' 1758 act. In 1763 a rising young lawer, Patrick Henry, first made his reputation in a court battle over one of the Virginia ministers' legal suits for the recovery of wages lost by the Two Penny Act. In his defense of the Virginia planters against this "Parson's Cause," Henry argued that, because the king had disallowed the act, he "from being the father of his people [has] degenerated into a Tyrant, and forfeits all rights to his subjects' obedience." In similar ways in all the colonies, local and imperial authority was being placed under increased pressure.

It is doubtful whether anyone anywhere in the mid-eighteenth century knew how to control the powerful social and economic forces at work in the Anglo-American world. Certainly the flimsy administrative arrangement that governed the British Empire was unable to manage this dynamic world. By mid-century many British officials realized that some sort of overhaul of this increasingly important empire was needed. But few understood the explosive energy and the sensitive nature of the people they were tampering with. The British Empire, Benjamin Franklin warned, was like a fragile Chinese vase that required delicate handling indeed.

The Reorganization of the Empire

After 1748 various imperial reforms were in the air. The eye-opening experience of fighting the Seven Years' War amid the colonists' evasion and corruption of the navigation laws had provoked William Pitt and other royal officials into vigorous though piecemeal reforms of the imperial system. But these beginnings might have been suppressed, as others had been, if it had not been for the enormous problems that were created by the Peace of Paris, which ended the Seven Years' War in 1763.

The most immediate of these problems was the reorganization of the territory that had been acquired from France and Spain. New governments had to be organized. The Indian trade had to be regulated, land claims had to be sorted out, and something had to be done to keep the conflicts between land-hungry white settlers and the restless native Americans from exploding into open warfare.

Even more disturbing was the huge expense confronting the British government. By 1763 the war debt totaled £137 million; its annual interest alone was £5 million, a huge figure when compared with an ordinary yearly British peacetime budget of only £8 million. There was, moreover, little prospect of military costs declining. Since the new territories were virtually uninhabited by Englishmen, the government could not rely on its traditional system of local defense and police to preserve order. Lord Jeffrey Amherst, commander in chief in North America, estimated that he would need 10,000 troops to keep the peace among the French and Indians and to deal with squatters, smugglers, and bandits. Thus at the outset of the 1760s, the British government made a crucial decision that no subsequent administration ever abandoned— the decision to maintain a standing army in America. This peacetime army was more than double the size of the army that had existed in the colonies before the Seven Years' War, and the costs of maintaining it quickly climbed to well over £400,000 a year.

Where was the money to come from? The landowning gentry in England felt pressed to the wall by taxes; a new English cider tax of 1763 actually required troops to enforce it. Meanwhile, returning British troops were bringing home tales of the prosperity Americans were enjoying at the war's end. Under the circumstances it seemed reasonable to the British government to seek new sources of revenue in the colonies and to make the navigation system more efficient in ways that royal officials had long advocated. A half-century of "salutary neglect" had come to an end.

George III and British Politics.
Disruptions within the delicate balance of the empire were therefore inevitable. But the coming to the throne in 1760 of a new monarch, the young and impatient George III, worsened the changing Anglo-American relations. George III was only twenty-two years old at the time, shy and inexperienced in politics. But he was stubbornly determined to rule personally, in a manner distinctly

GEORGE III (1738–1820), BY BENJAMIN WEST

George III had one of the longest reigns in English history. He was sincere but slow-witted, and suffered from a hereditary disease that eventually caused him spells of madness. The artist, Benjamin West, was an American who became in 1772 historical painter to the king and later president of the Royal Academy.

NORTH (1732–92)

North was the first political leader George III found who could organize a stable government. He had the political skills to manage the House of Commons, but he had no knowledge of waging war. Despite his repeated talk of resigning, he lasted as prime minister from 1770 to 1782.

different from that of George I and George II, the first of the Hanoverian kings. After the disastrous failure in 1745–46 of the Stuart heir, "Bonnie Prince Charlie," to reclaim the English throne, the Whigs' repeated cry that they were the only real defenders of the Hanoverian crown against the Tories and the Stuarts tended to lose its power and meaning.* By 1760 George III felt little of the loyalty to the old Whigs that his grandfather and great-grandfather had felt. Instead, influenced by his inept Scottish tutor and

---

*In eighteenth-century British politics the Whigs, especially under the leadership of Sir Robert Walpole (1721–42), were those who controlled the crown offices; they upheld the supremacy of Parliament and the 1714 settlement of the British crown on George I and the Hanoverian line of kings. The Tories were good royalists and good believers in nonresistance to legitimate authority; they tended to look backward to an earlier time when the king and the Church of England together dominated English life. Because after 1714 many of the Tories were suspected of being supporters of the Stuart line (the so-called Jacobites), the Tories were effectively excluded from crown offices through the reigns of George I (1714–27) and George II (1727–60).

"dearest friend," Lord Bute, George aimed to purify English public life of its corruption and factionalism. He wanted to replace former Whig-Tory squabbling and party intrigue with duty to crown and country. The results of George's good intentions were the greatest and most bewildering fluctuations in English politics in a half-century—all at the very moment the long-postponed reforms of the empire were to take place.

Historians no longer depict George III as a tyrant seeking to undermine the English constitution by choosing his ministers against Parliament's wishes. But there can be little doubt that men of the time felt that George III, whether he intended to or not, was violating the political customs of the day. When he chose Lord Bute, his Scottish favorite, who had little strength in Parliament, to head his government, thereby excluding such Whig ministers as William Pitt and the Duke of Newcastle, who did have political support in Parliament, the new king may not have been acting unconstitutionally; but he certainly was violating customary political realities. Bute's retirement in 1763 did little to ease the opposition's fears that the king was seeking the advice of Tory favorites "behind the curtain" and was attempting to impose decisions upon the leading political groups in Parliament rather than governing through them. By diligently attempting to shoulder what he thought was his constitutional responsibility for governing in his own stubborn, peculiar way, George III helped to increase the political confusion of the 1760s.

A decade of short-lived ministries in the 1760s contrasted sharply with the stable and long-lasting Whig governments of the previous generation. It almost seemed as if the stubborn king trusted no one who had Parliament's support. After Pitt and Newcastle had been dismissed, and after Bute had failed, the king in 1763 turned to George Grenville, Bute's protégé, only because he found no one else acceptable to be his chief minister. Although Grenville was responsible for the first wave of colonial reforms, his resignation in 1765 resulted from a personal quarrel with the king and had nothing to do with colonial policy. Next, a government was formed by Whigs who were connected with the Marquess of Rockingham and for whom the great orator and political thinker Edmund Burke was a spokesman; but this Whig coalition never had the King's confidence, and it lasted scarcely a year. In 1766 George at last called upon the aging Pitt, now Lord Chatham, to head the government. But Chatham's illness (gout in the head, critics said) and the bewildering parliamentary factionalism of the late 1760s turned his ministry into a hodgepodge that Chatham scarcely ruled at all.

By 1767 no one seemed to be in charge. Ministers shuffled in and out of offices, exchanging positions and following their own inclinations even against their colleagues' wishes. Amid this confusion only Charles Townshend, chancellor of the exchequer, gave any direction to colonial policy, and he died in 1767. Not until the appointment of Lord North as prime minister in 1770 did George find a politician whom he trusted and who also had Parliament's support.

Outside of Parliament, the huge portion of the British nation that was excluded from active participation in politics was stirring as it never had before. Ireland was restless under Britain's continual interference in its affairs. Political corruption and Parliament's failure to extend either the right to vote or representation created widespread resentment and led to many calls for reform. Mob rioting in London and elsewhere in England increased dramatically in the 1760s. In 1763 George III noted that there were "insurrections and tumults in every part of the country." The situation was worse at the end of the decade. Lord North was attacked on his way to Parliament; his coach was destroyed and he barely escaped with his life. Rioting had long been common in England, but many of the popular uprisings of the 1760s were different from those in the past. Far from being limited to particular grievances such as high bread prices, much of the rioting was now directed toward the whole political system. The most important crowd leader was John Wilkes, one of the most colorful demagogues in English history. Wilkes was a member of Parliament and an opposition journalist who in 1763 was arrested and tried for seditiously libeling George III and the government in No. 45 of his newspaper, the *North Briton*. Wilkes immediately became a popular hero, and the cry "Wilkes and Liberty" spread on both sides of the Atlantic. The House of Commons ordered the offensive issue of the newspaper publicly burned, and Wilkes fled to France. In 1768 he returned and was several times elected to the House of Commons; but each time Parliament denied him his seat. London crowds, organized by substantial shopkeepers and artisans, found in Wilkes a symbol of all their pent-up resentments against Britain's corrupt and oligarchic politics. The issue of Wilkes helped to bring together a radical reform movement that shook the foundations of Britain's narrow governing class.

Thus in the 1760s and early 1770s, the British government was faced with the need to overhaul its empire and gain revenue from its colonies at the very time when the political situation in the British Isles was more chaotic, confused, and disorderly than it had been since the early eighteenth century. No wonder that it took only a bit more than a decade for the whole shaky imperial structure to come crashing down.

The Proclamation of 1763 and the West.

The government began its reform of the newly enlarged empire by issuing the Proclamation of 1763. This crown proclamation created three new royal governments—East Florida, West Florida, and Quebec—and enlarged the province of Nova Scotia. It turned the vast trans-Appalachian area into an Indian reservation and prohibited all private individuals from purchasing Indian lands. The aim was to maintain peace in the West and to channel the migration of people northward and southward into the new colonies. There, it was felt, the settlers would be in closer touch with both the mother country and the mercantile system—and more useful as buffers against the Spanish and the remaining French.

But circumstances destroyed these royal blueprints. Not only were there bewildering shifts of the ministers in charge of the new policy, but news of Pontiac's Indian rebellion in the Ohio Valley in 1763 forced the government to rush its program into effect. The demarcation line along the Appalachians that closed the West to white settlers was hastily and crudely drawn, and some colonists suddenly found

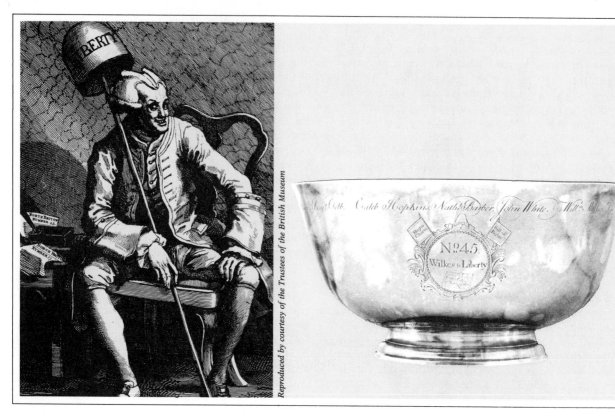

AN ENGLISH RADICAL

John Wilkes, depicted here in an etching by William Hogarth, was the most popular hero of the age in the Anglo-American world. Although a gentleman himself, he came to symbolize for middling and lowly sorts of people all their pent-up hostilities toward established authority. Note the references in the etching to Wilkes's *North Briton* Number 45 and Number 17. Silver bowl by Paul Revere (1735–1818), Boston, 1768. Note the engraving No. 45, Wilkes and Liberty.

themselves living in the Indian reservation. The new trading regulations and sites were widely ignored and created more chaos in the Indian trade than had existed earlier. So confusing was the situation in the West that the British government could never convince the various contending interests that the Proclamation was anything more than, in the words of George Washington, who had speculative interests in western lands, "a temporary expedient to quiet the minds of the Indians." Scores of speculators and lobbyists pressured the unsteady British governments to negotiate a series of Indian treaties shifting the line of settlement westward. But each modification only whetted the appetites of the land speculators and led to some of the most grandiose land schemes in modern history. The climax of this speculative frenzy was reached in 1769, when a huge conglomerate, the Grand Ohio Company, whose membership involved prominent figures on both sides of the Atlantic, petitioned the crown for the rights to millions of acres in the Ohio Valley.

In the Quebec Act of 1774, the British government, with Parliament's help, finally tried to steady its dizzy western policy. This act transferred to the province of Quebec the land and the control of the Indian trade in the huge area between the Ohio and Mississippi rivers and allowed Quebec's French inhabitants French law and Roman Catholicism. As enlightened as this act was toward the French Canadians, it managed to anger all American interests—speculators, settlers, and traders alike. This arbitrary alteration of provincial boundaries threatened the security of all colonial boundaries and frightened American Protestants into believing that the British government was trying to erect a hostile Catholic province in the North and West.

The Sugar and Stamp Acts. The new colonial trade policies were more coherent than Britain's western policy, but no less dangerous in American eyes. The Plantation Act, or Sugar Act, of 1764 was clearly a major successor to the great navigation acts of the late seventeenth century. The series of regulations that it established were designed to tighten the navigation system and in particular to curb the colonists' smuggling and corruption. Absentee customs officials were ordered to return to their posts and were given greater authority and protection. The jurisdiction of the vice-admiralty courts in customs cases was broadened.* The navy was granted greater power in inspecting American ships. The use of writs of assistance (or search warrants) was enlarged. To the earlier list of "enumerated" colonial products that had to be exported directly to Britain, such as tobacco and sugar, were added hides, iron, timber, and others.** And finally the requirements of American shippers for posting bonds and for obtaining certificates of clearance were so greatly increased that nearly all colonial merchants, even those involved only in the coastwise trade, found themselves enmeshed in a bureaucratic web of bonds, certificates, and regulations.

To these frustrating rigidities that were now built into the navigation system were added new customs duties, which raised the expenses of American importers in order to increase British revenue. The Sugar Act imposed duties on foreign cloth, sugar, indigo, coffee, and wine imported into the colonies, and eliminated the refunds of duties that had been previously made in England on foreign goods reexported to America. Most important, the Sugar Act reduced the supposedly very high duty of sixpence a gallon on foreign molasses, set by the Molasses Act of 1733, to threepence a gallon; in 1766 the duty was further reduced to one penny a gallon on all molasses. The government assumed that with the smaller duty it would be cheaper for American merchants to import molasses legally than to resort to smuggling and bribery. The lower duty would thus earn money for the crown.

These British reforms, which threatened to upset the delicately balanced patterns of trade that had been built up in the previous generations, could be regarded as part of Britain's traditional authority over colonial commerce. But the next step in Britain's new imperial program could not be thus regarded; it was radically new. Grenville's ministry, convinced that the customs reforms could not bring in the needed revenue, was determined to try a decidedly different method of getting at American wealth. In March 1765 Parliament by an overwhelming majority passed the Stamp Act, which levied a tax on legal documents, almanacs, newspapers, and nearly every form of paper used in the colonies. Like all duties the tax was to be paid in British sterling, not in colonial paper money. Although stamp duties had been used in England since 1694 and in several colonies in the 1750s, this parliamentary tax, which directly touched Americans' everyday affairs, exposed the nature of political authority within the empire in a way no other issue in the eighteenth century ever had.

American Resistance

The atmosphere in the colonies could not have been less receptive to these initial efforts by the British government to reorganize the empire. In the early 1760s, with the curtailing of wartime spending, the commercial boom collapsed. Between 1760 and 1764 American markets were glutted with unsold goods. At the same time, bumper tobacco crops (in part the result of new independent producers) drove tobacco prices down by 75 percent. These developments threatened the entire credit structure, from London and Scottish merchant companies to small farmers and shopkeepers in the colonies. As a result business failures and bankruptcies multiplied. The collapse was worsened by the large number of small merchants who had entered the market during the boom in the previous decade.

It is not surprising that the victims of the collapse sought to blame their shifting fortunes on the distant government in England. In fact the British government's response to the financial crisis could not have been more clumsy and irritating to the Americans. In 1764 Parliament passed a new Currency Act, which extended to all the colonies the 1751 prohibition against New England's issuing of paper money as legal tender. This sweeping and simpleminded attempt to solve a complicated problem was only one of the many ways in which British power in these years brought to the surface the deep-rooted antagonisms between the colonies and England.

The Sugar Act, coinciding with this postwar depression, created particularly severe problems for all those who depended on trade with the French and Spanish West Indies. The colonists feared that an added duty on foreign molasses would make it too expensive to import. Yet without foreign sugar products the northern rum industry would be ruined, the export trade in fish and foodstuffs to the Caribbean would be curtailed, and America's ability to pay for its British imports would be endangered. These fears, together with hostility to all the new trade regulations accompanying the Sugar Act, stirred up opposition and provoked the first deliberately organized intercolonial protest. In 1764 the assemblies of eight colonies drew up and endorsed formal petitions claiming that the Sugar Act was causing economic injury, and sent them to the royal authorities in England.

Britain's next step, however—Grenville's stamp

*For the vice-admiralty courts, see chapter 5, p. 131.

**For the "enumerated" colonial goods, see chapter 4, p. 87.

PATRICK HENRY (1736–99)
Unlike most of the other Revolutionary leaders, Henry left almost no writings. What he did leave were vivid memories of his impassioned oratory. He introduced to the political world of the Virginia gentry the fervor and style of an evangelical preacher.

tax of 1765—excited not a protest, but a firestorm that swept through the colonies with amazing force. This parliamentary tax, however justifiable it may have been in fiscal terms, posed such a distinct threat to the colonial legislatures' jurisdictions and the colonists' liberties that Americans could no longer contain their opposition within the traditional channels of complaints and lobbying.

When word reached America that Parliament had passed the Stamp Act without even considering any of the colonial petitions against it, the colonists reacted angrily. Merchants in the principal ports formed protest associations and pledged to stop importing British goods in order to bring economic pressure on the British government. Newspapers and pamphlets, the number and like of which had never appeared in America before, carried articles that seethed with resentment against what one New Yorker called "these designing parricides" who had "invited despotism to cross the ocean, and fix her abode in this once happy land." At hastily convened meetings of towns, counties, and legislative assemblies, the colonists' anger boiled over into fiery declarations.

This torrent of angry words could not help but bring the constitutional relationship between Britain and its colonies into question. In the spring of 1765, the Virginia House of Burgesses adopted a series of resolves denouncing the parliamentary taxation and asserting the colonists' right to be taxed only by their elected representatives. These resolves were introduced by Patrick Henry, who at age twenty-nine had just been elected to the legislature. Henry had made a name for himself in a county courthouse two years earlier during the Parson's Cause, the legal suits over the payment of Anglican ministers. Now, in the more dignified setting of the House of Burgesses, Henry dared to repeat his earlier challenge to crown authority. He declared that, just as Julius Caesar had had his Brutus and King Charles I his Oliver Cromwell, so some American would undoubtedly stand up for his country. The Speaker of the House stopped him for suggesting treason; and some of his resolves (including one proclaiming the right of Virginians to disobey any law that had not been enacted by the Virginia assembly) were too inflammatory to be accepted by the legislature. Nevertheless, colonial newspapers printed the resolves as though they had all been endorsed by the Virginia assembly, and many Americans were convinced that Virginians had virtually asserted their legislative independence from Great Britain.

Henry's boldness was contagious. The Rhode Island assembly declared the Stamp Act "unconstitutional" and authorized the colony's officials to ignore it. In October 1765 thirty-seven delegates from nine colonies met in New York in the Stamp Act Congress and drew up a set of formal declarations and petitions denying Parliament's right to tax them. But as remarkable as this display of colonial unity was, the Stamp Act Congress, with its opening acknowledgment of "all due Subordination to that August Body the Parliament of Great Britain," could not fully express American hostility.

Ultimately it was violence that destroyed the Stamp Act in America. On August 14, 1765, a crowd tore apart the office and attacked the home of Andrew Oliver, the stamp distributor for Massachusetts. The next day Oliver promised not to enforce the Stamp Act. Twelve days later a mob burned down the home of the person who seemed to be responsible for defending the Stamp Act in Massachusetts, Oliver's brother-in-law, Lieutenant Governor Thomas Hutchinson. As news of the rioting spread to other colonies, similar violence and threats of violence spread with it. From Newport, Rhode Island, to Charleston, South Carolina, local groups organized for resistance. In many places fire and artillery companies, artisan associations, and other fraternal bodies formed the basis for these emerging local organizations, which commonly called themselves Sons of Liberty. Led mostly by members of the middle ranks—shopkeepers, printers, master mechanics, small merchants—these Sons of Liberty burned effigies of royal officials, forced stamp agents to resign, compelled businessmen and

On August 26, 1765, a week and a half after the riot that forced Massachusetts stamp distributor Andrew Oliver to resign, a Boston mob attacked the homes of several members of the gentry. Josiah Quincy (1744–75), a young lawyer, set down his reactions in his diary.

Josiah Quincy, Jr., Deplores the Stamp Act Riot (1765)

*T*HE destructions, demolitions, and ruins caused by the rage of the Colonies in General—perhaps too justly inflamed—at that singular and ever-memorable statute called the Stamp Act, will make the present year one of the most remarkable eras in the annals of North America. And that peculiar inflammation, which fired the breasts of the people of New England in particular, will always distinguish them as the warmest lovers of liberty; though undoubtedly, in the fury of revenge against those who they thought had disclaimed the name of sons, for that of enslavers and oppressive tax-masters of their native country, they committed acts totally unjustifiable.

The populace of Boston, about a week since, had given a very notable instance of their detestation of the above unconstitutional Act, and had sufficiently shown in what light they viewed the man who would undertake to be the stamp distributor. But, not content with this, the last night they again assembled in King's Street; where, after having kindled a fire, they proceeded, in two separate bodies, to attack the houses of two gentlemen of distinction, who, it had been suggested, were accessories to the present burthens; and did great damage in destroying their houses, furniture, &c., and irreparable damage in destroying their papers. Both parties, who before had acted separately, then unitedly proceeded to the Chief-Justice's house, who, not expecting them, was unattended by his friends, who might have assisted, or proved his innocence. In this situation, all his family, it is said, abandoned the house, but himself and his eldest daughter, whom he repeatedly begged to depart; but as he found all ineffectual, and her resolution fixed to stay and share his fate, with a tumult of passions only to be imagined, he took her in his arms and carried her to a place of safety, just before the incensed mob arrived. This filial affection saved, it is more than probable, his life. Thus unexpected, and nothing removed from the house, an ample field offered to satiate, if possible, this rage-intoxicated rabble. They beset the house on all sides, and soon destroyed every thing of value. . . . The destruction was really amazing; for it was equal to the fury of the onset. But what above all is to be lamented is the loss of some of the most valuable records of the country, and other ancient papers; for, as his Honor was continuing his history, the oldest and most important writings and records of the Province, which he had selected with great care, pains, and expense, were in his possession. This is a loss greatly to be deplored, as it is absolutely irretrievable.

FRONT AND BACK OF A PRIVATELY MINTED TOKEN HONORING WILLIAM PITT, 1766, AND THE REPEAL OF THE STAMP ACT

judges to carry on without stamps, developed an intercolonial network of correspondence, and generally enforced nonimportation and managed antistamp activities throughout the colonies.

British Reaction. In England the Rockingham Whigs (who had been critical of the policies of George III and Grenville) were now in charge of the ministry, and the government was prepared to retreat. Not only were these Whigs eager to disavow Grenville's policies, but they had close connections with British merchants who had been hurt by American economic boycotts. In February 1776 Parliament repealed the Stamp Act. Yet British anger over the rioting in the colonies, and the constitutional issue that had been raised by colonial protests, forced the Rockingham Whigs to couple the repeal with a Declaratory Act stating that Parliament had the right to legislate for the colonies "in all cases whatsoever."

Despite the British government's attempt to offset its repeal of the Stamp Act by this declaration of parliamentary supremacy, after 1765 the imperial relationship and American respect for British authority—indeed, for all authority—would never be the same. The crisis over the Stamp Act aroused and unified Americans as no previous political event ever had. It stimulated bold political and constitutional writings throughout the colonies, deepened the colonists' political consciousness and participation, and produced new forms of organized popular resistance. In their mobs the people learned that they could compel both the resignation of royal officials and obedience to other popular measures. Through "their riotous meetings," Governor Horatio Sharpe of Maryland observed in 1765, the people "begin to think they can by the same way of proceeding accomplish anything their leaders may tell them they ought to do."

The British government could not rely on a simple declaration of parliamentary supremacy to satisfy its continuing need for more revenue. Since the colonists evidently would not stomach a "direct" and "internal" tax like the stamp tax, British officials concluded that the government would have to gather revenue through the more traditional "indirect" and "external" customs duties. After all, the colonists were already paying duties on molasses, wine, and several other imported products as a result of the Sugar Act. Consequently in 1767, led by Chancellor of the Exchequer Charles Townshend, Parliament imposed new levies on glass, paint, paper, and tea imported into the colonies. Although all the new customs duties, particularly the lowered molasses duty of 1766, began bringing in an average yearly revenue of £45,000—in contrast to only £2,000 a year collected before 1764—the yearly sums that were raised were scarcely a tenth of the annual cost of maintaining the army in America.

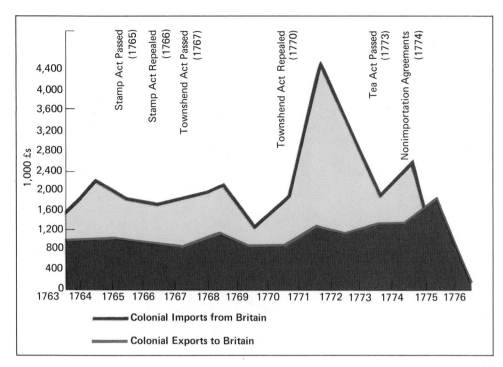

TRADE BETWEEN THE COLONIES AND BRITAIN, 1763–1776

Convinced that something more drastic had to be done, the British government reorganized the executive authority of the empire. In 1767–68 the government created the American Board of Customs, located in Boston and reporting directly to the Treasury. It also established three new superior vice-admiralty courts—in Boston, Philadelphia, and Charleston—to supplement the one already in operation in Halifax, Nova Scotia. In belated recognition of the importance of the colonies, it created a new secretaryship of state exclusively for American affairs, an office that would cap the entire structure of colonial government. At the same time, the government decided to economize by pulling back much of its army from its costly deployment in the West and by closing many remote posts. The army was now to be stationed in the coastal cities, where, according to Parliament's Quartering Act of 1765, the colonists would be responsible for its housing and supply. Not only did this withdrawal of the troops eastward away from the French and Indians contribute to the chaos in the western territory, but the concentration of a standing army in peacetime amid a civilian population blurred the army's original mission in America and raised the colonists' fears of British intentions.

By 1768 there was a new determination among royal officials to put down the unruly forces that seemed to be loose. Amid the ministerial squabbling of the late 1760s, some officials were suggesting that

British troops be used against American rioters. Revenue from the Townshend duties was earmarked for the salaries of royal officials in the colonies so that they would be independent of the colonial legislatures. The colonial governors were instructed to maintain tighter control of the assemblies and not to agree to acts that would increase popular representation in the assemblies or the length of time the legislatures sat. Royal officials toyed with more elaborate plans for remodeling the colonial governments: some proposed that the Massachusetts charter be revoked; others, that royal councils be strengthened. Some even suggested introducing a titled nobility into America to sit in the colonial upper houses.

The Townshend Crisis in America. In the atmosphere of the late 1760s, these measures and proposals were not simply irritating; they were explosive. After the Stamp Act crisis, American sensitivities to all forms of English taxation were thoroughly aroused. With the passage of the Townshend duties, the earlier pattern of resistance reappeared and expanded. Pamphleteers and newspaper writers again leapt to the defense of American liberties. The cultivated Philadelphia lawyer John Dickinson, in his *Letters from a Farmer in Pennsylvania* (1767–68), the most popular pamphlet of the 1760s, rejected all parliamentary taxation. According to Dickinson Parliament had no right to impose either "internal" or "external" taxes levied for the sole

WILLIAM JACKSON,

an *IMPORTER*; at the

BRAZEN HEAD,

North Side of the TOWN-HOUSE,

and *Oppofite the Town-Pump,* i

Corn-hill, BOSTON.

It is defired that the Sons and
Daughters of *LIBERTY,*
would not buy any one thing of
him, for in fo doing they will bring
Difgrace upon *themfelves,* and their
Pofterity, for *ever* and *ever,* AMEN.

SAMUEL ADAMS, BY JOHN SINGLETON COPLEY
Of all the American leaders, Sam Adams came closest to being
a professional revolutionary, selflessly devoted to the cause. As
"one of Plutarch's men," Adams took seriously the spartan
severity of classical republicanism.

purpose of raising revenue. He called for the revival of
the nonimportation agreements that had been so effective in the resistance to the Stamp Act. Following
Boston's lead in March 1768, merchants in colonial
ports again formed associations to boycott British
goods. Despite much competition among different
groups of merchants and jealousy among the ports, by
1769–70 these nonimportation agreements had cut
British sales to the northern colonies by nearly two-
thirds. The wearing of homespun cloth was encouraged, and in New England villages "Daughters of
Liberty" held spinning bees. By now more Americans
were involved in the resistance movement. Extralegal
groups and committees, usually but not always restrained by popular leaders, emerged to intimidate
tobacco inspectors in Maryland, punish importers in
Philadelphia, mob a publisher in Boston, or harass
customs officials in New York.

Nowhere were events more spectacular than in
Massachusetts. There the situation was so inflammatory that every move triggered a string of explosions that widened the gap between the colonists
and royal authority. Forty-six-year-old Samuel Adams, with his puritanical zeal, organizational skill,
and deep hatred of crown authority, soon became a
dominant political figure. It was later said that 1768
was the year Adams decided on independence for
America. Given the events in Massachusetts during
that year, it is easy to see why.

In February 1768 the Massachusetts House of
Representatives issued to the other colonial legislatures a "circular letter" that denounced the Townshend duties as unconstitutional violations of the
principle of no taxation without representation. Lord
Hillsborough, the secretary of state of the newly
created American Department and a hard-liner on
controlling the colonies, ordered the Massachusetts
House to revoke its circular letter. When the House
defied this order by a majority of 92–17 (thereby en-
shrining the number 92 in patriot rituals), Governor
Francis Bernard dissolved the Massachusetts assembly. With this legal means for dealing with grievances
silenced, mobs and other unauthorized groups in the
colony broke out in violence. Boston, which was rapidly becoming a symbol of colonial resistance, ordered
its inhabitants to arm and called for a convention of
town delegates—a meeting that would have no legal
standing. Attacked by mobs, customs officials in Bos-

"THE BOSTON MASSACRE" ENGRAVED BY PAUL REVERE

This print was scarcely an accurate depiction of the "Massacre." It aimed for rhetorical and emotional effect and became perhaps the most famous piece of antimilitary propaganda in American history.

ton found it impossible to enforce the navigation regulations and pleaded for military help. When a British warship arrived at Boston in June 1768, customs officials promptly seized John Hancock's ship *Liberty* for violating the trade acts. Since the wealthy Hancock was prominently associated with the resistance movement, the seizure was intended to be an object lesson in royal authority. Its effect, however, was to set off one of the fiercest riots in Boston's history.

Hillsborough, believing that Massachusetts was in a state of virtual anarchy, dispatched two regiments of troops from Ireland. They began arriving in Boston on October 1, 1768, and their appearance marked a crucial turning point in the escalating controversy: for the first time the British government had sent a substantial number of soldiers to enforce British authority in the colonies. By 1769 there were nearly 4,000 armed redcoats in the crowded seaport of 15,000 inhabitants. Since the colonists shared traditional English fears of standing armies, relations between townspeople and soldiers deteriorated. On March 5, 1770, British troops fired upon a threatening crowd and killed five civilians. The "Boston Massacre," especially as it was depicted in Paul Revere's engraving, aroused

American passions and inspired some of the most sensational rhetoric heard in the Revolutionary era.

This resort to troops to quell disorder was the ultimate symptom of the ineffectiveness of the British government's authority, and many Britons knew it. The use of force, it was argued in Parliament and in the administration itself, only destroyed the goodwill on which the colonists' relation to the mother country must ultimately rest. Indeed, throughout the escalation of events in the 1760s, many British ministers remained confused and uncertain. "There is the most urgent reason to do what is right, and immediately," wrote Lord Barrington to Governor Bernard in 1767, "but what is that right and who is to do it?" English officials advanced and retreated, pleaded and threatened in ever more desperate efforts to enforce British authority without aggravating the colonists' hostility. In the winter of 1767–68, the British responded to the disorder in Massachusetts with a series of parliamentary resolutions and addresses to the king, in which they condemned Massachusetts's denial of parliamentary supremacy and threatened to bring the colonial offenders to England for trial. Yet strong minority opposition in the House of Commons and the ministry's unwillingness to bring on further crises made these resolutions empty gestures: the government was now only waging what one Englishman called "a paper war with the colonies."

By the end of the 1760s, British plans for reorganizing the empire were in shambles. Colonial legislatures and royal governors were at loggerheads. Colonial papers daily denounced Britain's authority, and mobs were becoming increasingly common in the countryside as well as in city streets. Customs officials, under continuous intimidation, quarreled with merchants, naval officers, and royal governors. The customs officials' entanglement in local politics made efficient or even-handed enforcement of the trade acts impossible. What enforcement there was thus appeared arbitrary and discriminatory, and drove many merchants, such as the wealthy South Carolinian Henry Laurens, who had earlier been contemptuous of the Sons of Liberty, into bitter opposition.

The financial returns to the British government from the customs reforms seemed in no way worth the costs. By 1770 less than £21,000 had been collected from the Townshend duties, while the loss to British business because of American nonimportation movements during the previous year was put at £700,000. It was therefore not surprising that the British government now abandoned the hope of securing revenue from the duties and labeled the Townshend program, in Lord Hillsborough's words, "contrary to the true principles of commerce." In 1770, after years of chaos in the British government, the reorganization of the king's ministry under Lord North prepared the way for repeal of the Townshend duties. Only the duty on tea was retained, to serve, as Lord North said, "as a mark of the supremacy of Parliament, and an efficient declaration of their right to govern the colonies."

Yet the stabilization of English politics that came with the formation of North's ministry and the repeal of the Townshend duties could scarcely undo what had already been done. Whatever ties of affection had earlier existed between the colonists and Great Britain were fast being destroyed by irritation and suspicion. Many Americans were coming to believe that their interests and their hopes, their rights and their liberties, were threatened by British power. Although politicians on both sides of the Atlantic were by the early 1770s calling for a return to the conditions that had existed before 1763, going back was clearly no longer possible.

For two years there was a superficial tranquility. Then the struggle began again. In 1772 Rhode Islanders, angry at the heavy-handed enforcement of the navigation acts, boarded the British naval schooner *Gaspée*, which had run aground in Narragansett Bay, sank it, and wounded its captain. A royal commission, empowered to send all suspects to England for trial, was dispatched from England to inquire into the sinking. This authority seemed to fulfill earlier British threats to bypass regular judicial procedures, and it provoked Virginia into calling for the creation of legislative committees of correspondence, to which five assemblies responded.

Under Boston's and particularly Samuel Adams's leadership, Massachusetts towns had already begun organizing committees of correspondence. In the fall of 1772 Bostonians published a fiery document, *The Votes and Proceedings* of their town meeting, which listed all the British violations of American rights. These included taxing and legislating for the colonists without their consent, introducing standing armies in peacetime, extending the powers of vice-admiralty courts (which did not use jury trials), restricting colonial manufacturing, and threatening to establish Anglican bishops in America. The publication was sent to the 260 towns of Massachusetts, and more than half responded positively in the greatest outpouring of ordinary local opinion the resistance movement had yet seen. By the end of 1773, independence was being discussed freely in colonial newspapers. Since the North government was determined to uphold the sovereignty of Parliament, an eventual confrontation seemed unavoidable.

The Climax: The Tea Act and the Coercive Acts.

In 1773 Parliament provided the occasion for a confrontation, by granting the East India Company the exclusive privilege of selling tea in America. Although the North government intended this Tea Act only to be a means of saving the East India Company from bankruptcy, it set off the final series of explosions. For the act not only allowed colonial radicals to draw attention once again to the unconstitutionality of the existing tax on tea, but it also permitted the company to grant monopolies of selling tea to particular colonial merchants—a provision that angered those American traders who were excluded. The Tea Act spread an alarm throughout the colonies. In several ports colonists stopped the ships from landing the company's tea. When tea ships in Boston were prevented from unloading their cargoes, Governor Thomas Hutchinson, whose merchant family had been given the right to sell tea, refused to allow the ships to leave without landing the tea. In response, on December 16, 1773, a group of patriots disguised as Indians dumped about £10,000 worth of tea into Boston harbor. "This is the most magnificent movement of all," exulted John Adams, an ambitious young lawyer from Braintree, Massachusetts. "This destruction of the tea is so bold, so daring, so firm, intrepid, and inflexible, and it must have so important consequences, and so lasting, that I can't but consider it an epocha in history."

Adams was right. To the British the Boston Tea Party was the ultimate outrage. Angry officials and many of the politically active people in Great Britain clamored for a punishment that would squarely confront America with the issue of Parliament's right to legislate for the colonies. "We are now to establish our authority," Lord North told the House of Commons, "or give it up entirely." In 1774 Parliament passed a succession of laws that came to be known as the Coercive Acts. The first of these closed the port of Boston until the destroyed tea was paid for. The second altered the Massachusetts charter and reorganized the government: council members were now to be appointed by the royal governor rather than elected by the legislature, town meetings were restricted, and the governor's power of appointing judges and sheriffs was strengthened. The third act allowed royal officials who had been charged with capital offenses to be tried in England or in another colony to avoid a hostile jury. The fourth gave the governor power to take over private buildings for the quartering of troops instead of using barracks. At the same time, Thomas Gage, commander in chief of the British army in America, was made governor of the colony of Massachusetts.

These Coercive Acts were the last straw. They convinced Americans once and for all that Parliament had no more right to make laws for them than to tax them.

The Imperial Debate

The colonists had been groping toward this denial of Parliament's power from the beginning of the controversy. For a decade they had been engaged in a re-markable constitutional debate with the British over the nature of the empire. This debate exposed for the first time just how divergent America's previous political experience had been from that of the mother country. By the 1770s the colonists had arrived at a very different understanding of the empire from most Englishmen.

Virtual Versus Actual Representation. With the passage of the Stamp Act, Parliament's first unmistakable tax levy on Americans, American intellectual resistance was immediately raised to the highest plane of principle. "It is inseparably essential to the freedom of a people, and the undoubted rights of Englishmen," the Stamp Act Congress declared in 1765, "that no taxes should be imposed on them, but with their own consent, given personally, or by their representatives." And since "the people of these colonies are not, and from their local circumstances, cannot be represented in the House of Commons in Great Britain," the colonists would be represented and taxed only by persons who were known and chosen by themselves and who served in their respective legislatures. This statement defined the American position at the outset of the controversy, and despite subsequent confusion and stumbling the colonists never abandoned this essential point.

Once the British ministry sensed a stirring of colonial opposition to the Stamp Act, a number of English government pamphleteers set out to explain and justify Parliament's taxation of the colonies. Although the arguments of these writers differed, they all eventually agreed that Americans, like Englishmen everywhere, were subject to acts of Parliament through a system of "virtual" representation. These writers argued that it was this concept of virtual representation, as distinct from actual representation, that gave Parliament its supreme authority—its sovereignty. One government pamphleteer wrote that even though the colonists, like "nine-tenths of the people of Britain," did not in fact choose any representative to the House of Commons, they were undoubtedly "a part, and an important part of the Commons of Great Britain: they are represented in Parliament in the same manner as those inhabitants of Britain are who have not voices in elections."

During the eighteenth century the British electorate made up only a tiny proportion of the nation; probably only one in six British adult males had the right to vote, compared with two out of three in America. In addition Britain's electoral districts were a confusing mixture of sizes and shapes left over from past centuries. Some of the constituencies were large, with thousands of voters, but others were virtually in the pocket of a single great landowner. Many of the electoral districts had few voters, and some so-called rotten boroughs had no inhabitants at all. One town, Dunwich, continued to send representatives to Parliament even though it had long since slipped into the North Sea. At the same time, some of England's largest cities, such as Manchester and Birmingham, which had grown suddenly in the mid-eighteenth century, sent no representatives to Parliament. Although radical reformers, among them John Wilkes, increasingly criticized this political structure, parliamentary reform was slow in coming and would not begin until 1832. Many Englishmen justified this hodgepodge of representation by claiming that each member of Parliament represented the whole British nation, and not just the particular locality he came from. (In 1774 Edmund Burke, the famous political philosopher and member of Parliament, offered the classic expression of this concept of virtual representation.) According to this view, virtual representation in England was proper and effective not because of the process of election, which was incidental, but rather because of the mutual interests that members of Parliament were presumed to share with all Englishmen for whom they spoke—including those, like the colonists, who did not actually vote for them.

The Americans immediately and strongly rejected these British claims that they were "virtually" represented in the same way that the nonvoters of cities like Manchester and Birmingham were. In the most notable colonial pamphlet written in opposition to the Stamp Act, *Considerations on the Propriety of Imposing Taxes* (1765), Daniel Dulany of Maryland admitted the relevance in England of virtual representation, but he denied its applicability to America. For America, he wrote, was a distinct community from England and thus could hardly be represented by members of Parliament with whom it had no common interests. Others pushed beyond Dulany's argument, however, and challenged the very idea of virtual representation. If the people were to be properly represented in a legislature, many colonists said, they not only had to vote directly for the members of the legislature but had to be represented by members whose numbers were proportionate to the size of the population they spoke for. What purpose is served, asked James Otis of Massachusetts in 1765, by the continual attempts of Englishmen to justify the lack of American representation in Parliament by citing the examples of Manchester and Birmingham, which returned no members to the House of Commons? "If those now so considerable places are not represented, they ought to be."

In the New World, electoral districts were not the products of history that stretched back centuries, but rather were recent and regular creations that were related to changes in population and the formation of new towns and counties. As a consequence many Americans had come to believe in a very different kind

"THE BRUTAL TREATMENT OF JOHN MALCOMB"
This print from a London paper shows John Malcomb, commissioner of customs at Boston, being tarred and feathered in 1774 for trying to collect customs duties. Note the number "45" on the patriot's hat, a symbol of liberty since John Wilkes's imprisonment for printing the *North Briton* No. 45.

of representation from that of the English. Their belief in "actual" representation made election not secondary but central to representation. Actual representation stressed the closest possible connection between the local electors and their representatives. For Americans it was only proper that representatives be residents of the localities they spoke for and that people of the locality have the right to instruct their representatives. Americans thought it only fair that localities be represented in proportion to their population. In short the American belief in actual representation pointed toward the fullest and most equal participation of the people in the process of government that the modern world had ever seen.

The Problem of Sovereignty. Yet while Americans were denying Parliament's right to tax them because they were not represented in the House of Commons, they knew that Parliament had exercised some authority over their affairs during the previous century. They therefore tried to explain what that authority should

JOHN DICKINSON'S "THE PATRIOTIC AMERICAN FARMER"

In the 1760s Dickinson was the most famous patriot-writer in all America. But by 1776 his unwillingness to endorse American independence diminished his reputation, which posterity has not yet restored.

be. What was the "due subordination" that the Stamp Act Congress admitted Americans owed Parliament? Could the colonists accept parliamentary legislation but not taxation—"external" customs duties for the purpose of regulating trade, but not "internal" stamp taxes for the purpose of raising revenue? In his famous *Letters from a Farmer in Pennsylvania*, John Dickinson rejected the idea that Parliament could rightly impose "external" or "internal" taxes and made clear that the colonists opposed *all* forms of parliamentary taxation. Dickinson recognized nevertheless that the empire required some sort of central regulatory authority, particularly for commerce, and conceded Parliament's supervisory legislative power so far as it preserved "the connection between the several parts of the British empire." The empire, it seemed to many colonists, was a unified body for some affairs but not for others.

To counter all of these halting and fumbling efforts by the colonists to divide parliamentary authority, the British offered a simple but powerful argument. Since they could not conceive of the empire as anything but a single, unified community, they found absurd and meaningless all these American distinctions between trade regulations and taxation, between "external" and "internal" taxes, and between separate spheres of authority. If Parliament even "in one instance" was as supreme over the colonists as it was over the people of England, wrote a sub-cabinet official, William Knox, in 1769, then the Americans were members "of the same community with the people of England." On the other hand, if Parliament's authority over the colonists was denied "in any particular," then it must be denied in "all instances," and the union between Great Britain and the colonies must be dissolved. "There is no alternative," Knox concluded; "either the colonies are part of the community of Great Britain or they are in a state of nature with respect to her, and in no case can be subject to the jurisdiction of that legislative power which represents her community, which is the British Parliament."

What made this British argument so powerful was its basis in the widely accepted doctrine of sovereignty—the belief that in every state there could be only one final, indivisible, and uncontestable supreme authority. This was the most important concept of eighteenth-century English political theory, and it became the issue over which the empire was finally broken.

This idea that, in the end, every state had to have one single supreme undivided authority had been the basis of the British position from the beginning. The British expressed this concept of sovereignty officially in the Declaratory Act of 1766, which, following the repeal of the Stamp Act, affirmed Parliament's authority to make laws binding the colonists "in all cases whatsoever." But now in the early 1770s, the implications of this argument were drawn out fully. In 1773 Massachusetts Governor Thomas Hutchinson was provoked into directly challenging the radical movement and its belief in the *limited* nature of Parliament's power. In a dramatic and well-publicized speech to the Massachusetts legislature, Hutchinson attempted once and for all to clarify the central constitutional issue between America and Great Britain and to show the colonists how unreasonable their views were. "I know of no line," he declared, "that can be drawn between the supreme authority of Parliament and the total independence of the colonies, as it is impossible there should be two independent legislatures in one and the same state."

By 1773 many Americans despaired of trying to divide what royal officials told them could not be divided. The Massachusetts House of Representatives had a simple answer to Hutchinson's position. If, as Governor Hutchinson had said, there was no middle ground between the supreme authority of Parliament and the total independence of the colonies from Parliament, the House members felt that there could be no doubt that "we were thus independent." The logic of sovereignty therefore forced a fundamental shift in the American position. By 1774 the leading colonists, including Thomas Jefferson and John Adams, were arguing that only the separate American legislatures were sovereign in America. According to this argument Parliament had no final authority over America, and the colonies were connected to the empire only through the king. The most the colonists would concede was that Parliament had the right to regulate their external commerce—"from the necessity of the case, and a regard to the mutual interest of both countries," as the Declarations and Resolves of the First Continental Congress put it. But the British government remained committed to the principle of the Declaratory Act, which no leader of the Revolution could any longer take seriously.

It was now only a matter of time before these irreconcilable positions would be brought to the point of conflict.

CHRONOLOGY

1760	George III accedes to throne.
1763	Treaty of Paris ends Seven Years' War between Great Britain, and France and Spain.
	Pontiac's rebellion, uprising of Indians in Ohio Valley.
	Proclamation line drawn along Appalachians by British forbids settlement in West by whites.
	Parson's Cause, resulting from efforts by Anglican clergy in Virginia to recover salaries lost from Two Penny Acts.
	Paxton uprising by Scotch-Irish settlers in western Pennsylvania.
1764	Sugar Act passed by Parliament, reducing duty on foreign molasses.
	Currency Act prohibits issues of legal-tender currency in the colonies.
	Brown University founded.
1765	Stamp Act passed.
	Stamp Act Congress meets in New York.
1766	Stamp Act repealed by Parliament, which adopts Declaratory Act asserting its authority to bind the colonies "in all cases whatsoever."
	Antirent riots by tenant-farmers in New York.
1767	Townshend duties passed.
	American Board of Customs established.
	John Dickinson's *Letters from a Farmer in Pennsylvania*.
	Organization of the Regulators in back-country of South Carolina.

1768	Secretary of State for the Colonies established in England—first executive department with exclusively colonial concerns.
	Circular letter of Massachusetts House of Representatives.
	John Hancock's ship *Liberty* seized.
	British troops sent to Boston.
1769	American Philosophical Society reorganized, with Benjamin Franklin as president.
1770	Lord North's ministry formed. Townshend duties repealed, except for duty on tea.
	Boston Massacre.
1771	Benjamin Franklin begins his *Autobiography*.
	Battle of the Alamance, North Carolina, between western Regulators and eastern militia led by the governor.
1772	British schooner *Gaspée* burned in Rhode Island.
	Boston Committee of Correspondence formed.
1773	Tea Act imposed.
	Boston Tea Party.
1774	Coercive Acts.
	Continental Congress meets in Philadelphia.
	Galloway's Plan of Union.
	Continental Association.

SUGGESTED READINGS

A convenient guide to the historical literature on the American Revolution can be found in Jack P. Greene, ed., *The Reinterpretation of the American Revolution, 1763–1789* (1968). Although there are many short accounts of the Revolution, including Edmund S. Morgan, *The Birth of the Republic, 1763–1789* (1956), and Robert Middlekauff, *The*

Glorious Cause: The American Revolution, 1763–1789 (1982), the student ought to begin with R. R. Palmer's monumental *The Age of the Democratic Revolution: A Political History of Europe and America, 1760–1800* (2 vols. 1959, 1964), which places the American Revolution in a Western perspective. Stephen G. Kurtz and James H. Hutson, eds., *Essays on the*

American Revolution (1973); Alfred F. Young, ed., *The American Revolution* (1976); and the five volumes from the Library of Congress, *Symposia on the American Revolution* (1972–76), are collections of original essays on various aspects of the Revolution.

Among the early attempts to treat the coming of the Revolution from an imperial viewpoint, George Louis Beer, *British Colonial Policy, 1754–1765* (1907), is still informative. Charles M. Andrews summarized his ideas on the causes of the Revolution in *The Colonial Background of the American Revolution* (1931). The most detailed narrative of the political events leading up to the Revolution, written from an imperial perspective, is Lawrence H. Gipson, *The British Empire Before the American Revolution* (15 vols., 1936–70). Gipson has summarized his point of view in *The Coming of the Revolution, 1763–1775* (1954). Merrill Jensen, *The Founding of a Nation* (1968), is the fullest single volume of the pre-Revolutionary years written from an American perspective; it is especially rich in its description of the factional struggles within the separate colonies. An ingenious but sound study that combines the views of a British and an American historian on the causes of the Revolution is Ian R. Christie and Benjamin W. Labaree, *Empire or Independence, 1760–1776* (1976).

The appropriate chapters of James A. Henretta, *The Evolution of American Society, 1700–1815* (1973), discuss American society on the eve of the Revolution. Jackson T. Main, in *The Social Structure of Revolutionary America* (1965), has attempted to describe the distribution of wealth and the nature of "classes" in American society. Rhys Isaac, *The Transformation of Virginia, 1740–1790* (1982), uses anthropological techniques to describe popular challenges to the Virginia aristocracy. Carl Bridenbaugh, *Cities in Revolt* (1955), attributes the Revolutionary impulse to the cities. Gary B. Nash, *The Urban Crucible: Social Change, Political Consciousness, and the Origins of the American Revolution* (1979), stresses urban class conflict in bringing on the Revolution. A brief but stimulating overview of the mid-eighteenth-century Atlantic world in motion is Bernard Bailyn, "1776: A Year of Challenge—a World Transformed," *The Journal of Law and Economics,* XIX (1976). The extent of westward migration is ably recounted in Jack M. Sosin, *Revolutionary Frontier, 1763–1783* (1967). Carl Bridenbaugh, *Mitre and Sceptre* (1962), describes the growth of Anglicanism and the effort to establish an American episcopacy in the decades leading up to the Revolution. For the American reaction to these efforts, see Charles W. Akers, *Called unto Liberty: A Life of Jonathan Mayhew, 1720–1766* (1964).

The opening years of the reign of George III have been the subject of some of the most exciting historical scholarship in the twentieth century—largely the work of Sir Lewis Namier and his students. Namier and his followers have exhaustively demonstrated that George III was not seeking to destroy the British constitution, as nineteenth-century historians had argued, and that in 1760 party government with ministerial responsibility to Parliament lay very much in the future. Namier's chief works include *The Structure of Politics at the Accession of George III* (2d ed., 1957), and *England in the Age of the American Revolution* (2d ed., 1961). For detailed studies of British politics in the Revolutionary era, see P. D. G. Thomas, *British Politics and the Stamp Act Crisis* (1975); Paul Langford, *The First Rockingham Administration: 1765–1766* (1973); John Brooke, *The Chatham Administration, 1766–1768* (1956); and Bernard Donoughue, *British Politics and the American Revolution: The Path to War, 1773–1775*

(1964). The best biography of George III is John Brooke, *King George III* (1972). An excellent summary of British politics is George H. Guttridge, *English Whiggism and the American Revolution* (2d ed., 1963); but for a more recent study that reconciles the Whig and Namierite interpretations, see John Brewer, *Party Ideology and Popular Politics at the Accession of George III* (1976).

Other important studies of British imperial policy in the period 1760–1775 include Jack M. Sosin, *Whitehall and the Wilderness . . . 1763–1775* (1961); Michael Kammen, *A Rope of Sand: The Colonial Agents, British Politics, and the American Revolution* (1968); and Franklin B. Wickwire, *British Subministers and Colonial America, 1763–1783* (1966). On the military in America, see John Shy, *Toward Lexington: The Role of the British Army in the Coming of the American Revolution* (1965), and Neil R. Stout, *The Royal Navy in America, 1760–1775* (1973).

On American resistance, see especially Edmund S. Morgan and Helen M. Morgan, *The Stamp Act Crisis* (1953), which emphasizes the colonists' appeal to constitutional principles. Pauline Maier, *From Resistance to Revolution* (1972), stresses the limited and controlled character of American opposition. But see Dirk Hoerder, *Crowd Action in Revolutionary Massachusetts, 1765–1780* (1977). Oliver M. Dickerson, *The Navigation Acts and the American Revolution* (1951), argues that Americans accepted the navigation system until "customs racketeering" was introduced in the late 1760s. For a more balanced view of the navigation system, see Thomas C. Barrow, *Trade and Empire: The British Customs Service in Colonial America, 1660–1775* (1967).

On other irritants and incidents in the imperial relation, see Joseph A. Ernst, *Money and Politics in America, 1755–1775* (1973); Carl Ubbelohde, *The Vice-Admiralty Courts and the American Revolution* (1960); M. H. Smith, *The Writs of Assistance Case* (1978); Hiller Zobel, *The Boston Massacre* (1970); Benjamin W. Labaree, *The Boston Tea Party* (1964); and David Ammerman, *In the Common Cause: American Response to the Coercive Acts of 1774* (1974). Arthur M. Schlesinger, *The Colonial Merchants and the American Revolution, 1763–1776* (1918), traces the responses of an important social group.

Among the many local studies of American resistance are Carl Becker, *The History of Political Parties in the Province of New York, 1760–1776* (1909); David S. Lovejoy, *Rhode Island Politics and the American Revolution, 1760–1776* (1958); Theodore Thayer, *Pennsylvania Politics and the Growth of Democracy, 1740–1776* (1954); Richard Ryerson, *The Revolution Is Now Begun: The Radical Committees of Philadelphia, 1765–1776* (1978); Patricia Bonomi, *A Factious People: . . . New York* (1971); Jere R. Daniel, *Experiment in Republicanism: New Hampshire Politics and the American Revolution, 1741–1794* (1970); Richard D. Brown, *Revolutionary Politics in Massachusetts* (1970); Stephen E. Patterson, *Political Parties in Revolutionary Massachusetts* (1973); and Ronald Hoffman, *A Spirit of Dissension: Economics, Politics, and the Revolution in Maryland* (1973). For biographies of some leading Revolutionaries, see John C. Miller, *Sam Adams* (1936); Richard R. Beeman, *Patrick Henry* (1974); Merrill Peterson, *Thomas Jefferson and the New Nation* (1970); Eric Foner, *Tom Paine and Revolutionary America* (1976); Peter Shaw, *The Character of John Adams* (1976); and John R. Howe, Jr., *The Changing Political Thought of John Adams* (1966).

On the imperial debate see Bernard Bailyn, *The Ideological Origins of the American Revolution* (1967), and Randolph G. Adams, *Political Ideas of the American Revolution* (1922).

8 Independence and War

By 1774, within the short span of a decade following the introduction of the imperial reforms, Americans who had celebrated George III's coronation were in virtual rebellion against Great Britain. During the two years after the Coercive Acts of 1774, events moved rapidly, and reconciliation between Britain and its colonies became increasingly unlikely. By this time the crisis had become something more than a simple breakdown in the imperial relationship. The colonists' extraordinary efforts to understand what was happening transformed their resistance and ultimately their rebellion into a world-shattering revolution. The Americans' 1776 Declaration of Independence turned their separation from Britain into an event that Americans thought rivaled anything that had happened before in history. Americans saw themselves striving not only to make themselves free, but also to bring freedom to the whole world. To do so, however, they would have to wage war against the greatest power of the eighteenth century.

The Coming of Independence

The Coercive Acts of 1774 provoked open rebellion in America. Whatever royal authority was left in the colonies now dissolved. Many local communities, with a freedom they had not had since the seventeenth century, attempted to put together new popular governments from the bottom up. Mass meetings that sometimes attracted thousands of aroused colonists endorsed resolutions and called for new political organizations. Committees of different sizes and various names—committees of safety, of inspection, of merchants, of mechanics, of Fifty-One, of Nineteen, of Forty-Three—competed with one another for political control. In the various colonies royal government was displaced in different ways, depending on how extensive and personal previous royal authority had been. In Massachusetts, where the crown's authority had reached into the villages and towns through the royally appointed justices of the peace, the displacement

was greater than in Virginia, where royal influence had scarcely touched the control of the counties by the powerful landowners. But everywhere there was a fundamental transfer of authority that opened new opportunities for new men to assert themselves.

By the end of 1774 in many of the colonies, local associations were controlling and regulating various aspects of American life. Committees manipulated voters, directed appointments, organized the militia, managed trade, intervened between creditors and debtors, levied taxes, issued licenses, and supervised or closed the courts. Royal governors stood by in helpless amazement as new informal governments gradually grew up around them. These new governments ranged from town and county committees and the newly created provincial congresses to a general congress of the colonies—the First Continental Congress, which convened in Philadelphia in September 1774.

The First Continental Congress. In all, fifty-five delegates from twelve colonies (all except Georgia) participated in the First Continental Congress. Some colonists, and even some royal officials, hoped that this Congress might work to reestablish imperial authority. Those who were eager to break the bond with Great Britain, however, won the first round. Led by the cousins Samuel and John Adams from Massachusetts, and by Patrick Henry and Richard Henry Lee from Virginia, the Congress endorsed the fiery Resolves of Suffolk County, Massachusetts, which recommended outright resistance to the Coercive Acts. But the Congress was not yet ready for independence. It came very close—failing by the vote of a single colony—to considering further and perhaps adopting a plan of union between Britain and the colonies, which had been proposed by Joseph Galloway, leader of the Pennsylvania assembly and spokesman for the conservative congressional delegates from the middle colonies. Galloway's plan was radical enough: it called for the creation of a grand colonial council along the lines that the Albany Congress had proposed in 1754. Laws passed by either

the American grand council or the British Parliament were to be subject to mutual review and approval.

By 1774, however, it was unlikely, even if Galloway's plan had been adopted, that the Congress could have reversed the transfer of authority that was taking place in the colonies. In the end the Continental Congress simply recognized the new local authorities in American politics and gave them its blessing by establishing the Continental Association. This continent-wide organization put into effect the non-importation, nonexportation, and nonconsumption of British goods that the Congress had agreed on. Committees in all the counties, cities, and towns were now ordered by the Congress "attentively to observe the conduct of all persons," to condemn publicly all violators as "enemies of American liberty," and to "break off all dealings" with them.

Thus with the Congress's endorsement through the Association, the local committees, speaking in the name of "the body of the people," proceeded with the political transformation that was taking place. Groups of men, from a few dozen to several thousand, marched through villages and city streets searching out enemies of the people. Suspected enemies were often forced to take back unfriendly words or designs against the public, to sign confessions of guilt and repentance, and to swear new oaths of friendship to the people. In all the colonies there were signs of an emerging new political order.

The Popularization of Politics.

These remarkable political changes were not simply the product of the colonists' resistance to British imperial reform. Britain's attempts to reorganize its empire took place not in a vacuum, but in complicated, highly charged situations existing in each colony. In some cases these local political conditions had as much to do with the escalation of the controversy between the colonies and the mother country as did the steps taken by the British government 3,000 miles away. Everywhere in the 1760s members of the colonial gentry were eager to exploit popular resentment against the British reforms in order to gain local political advantage—with, however, little understanding of the ultimate consequence of their actions.

In New York, for example, political factions that were led by the well-to-do Livingston and DeLancey families vied with each other in whipping up opposition to the imperial legislation and in winning the support of popular extralegal groups such as the Sons of Liberty. Thus these gentry generally helped expand the rights and participation of the people in politics—not with the aim of furthering electoral democracy, but only for the tactical purpose of gaining control of the elective assemblies. While this sort of unplanned popularization of politics had gone on in the past, particularly in urban areas, the inflamed atmosphere that the imperial crisis generated gave it a new cutting edge with new and unpredictable implications.

In colony after colony local quarrels, often of long standing, became so entangled with imperial antagonisms that they reinforced one another in a spiraling momentum that brought all governmental authority into question. Even those colonial authorities that were not directly controlled by Great Britain, such as the proprietary governments of Pennsylvania and Maryland, were victimized by the imperial crisis. Thus in Maryland in 1770, a proclamation by the proprietary governor setting the fees that were paid to government officials seemed to violate the principle of no taxation without representation that had been made so vivid by the imperial debate. This executive proclamation provoked a bitter local struggle that forced Daniel Dulany, a wealthy member of the colony's council and former opponent of the Stamp Act, into defending the governor. In the end the controversy destroyed the governor's capacity to rule and made Dulany a loyalist to the British cause.

By the 1770s all these developments, without anyone's clearly intending it, were revealing a new kind of politics in America. The rhetoric of liberty now quickened long-existing popular political tendencies. Ordinary people were no longer willing to trust only wealthy and learned gentlemen to represent them in government. Various artisan, religious, and ethnic groups now felt that their particular interests were so distinct that only people of their own kind could speak for them. In 1774 radicals in Philadelphia demanded that seven artisans and six Germans be added to the revolutionary committee of the city. Americans today are used to such "coalition" and "interest-group" politics, but their eighteenth-century counterparts were not. Educated gentlemen such as the prominent Oxford-trained landowner William Henry Drayton of South Carolina therefore complained of having to participate in government with men who knew only "how to cut up a beast in the market" or "to cobble an old shoe": "Nature never intended that such men should be profound politicians, or able statesmen." In 1775 the royal governor of Georgia noted in astonishment that the committee in control of Savannah consisted of "a Parcel of the Lowest People, chiefly carpenters, shoemakers, Blacksmiths etc. with a Jew at their head." In some colonies politicians called for an expanded suffrage, the use of the ballot rather than the customary oral voting, the opening of legislative meetings to the public, the printing of legislative minutes, and the recording of votes that were taken in the legislatures. All these proposals involved enlarging the political arena and limiting the power of those who clung to the traditional ways of private arrangements and personal influence.

Everywhere in the colonies "incendiaries" (as royal officials called them) used fiery popular rhetoric and competed openly for political leadership. More and more "new men" took advantage of the people's resentments of the British regulations and actively campaigned for popular election in order to bypass the traditional narrow and patronage-controlled channels of politics. The political atmosphere in America was now charged as never before with both deep animosities and new hopes for bettering the world. Americans told themselves they were "on the eve of some great and unusual events," events that "may form a new era, and give a new turn to human affairs."

Men who, like Thomas Hutchinson, had been reared in the old ways and had benefited from them stood bewildered and helpless in the face of these popularizing developments. They possessed neither the psychological capacity nor the political sensitivity to understand—let alone to deal with—this popular politics and the moral outrage and fiery zeal that lay behind it. They intrigued and schemed, and they tried to manipulate those who they thought were the important people in the opposition. (In 1768, for example, John Adams was offered the office of advocate-general in the Massachusetts admiralty court.) When they could not buy them off, they accused those individuals of demagoguery or ridiculed them as upstarts. Frightened by the increased violence, they struck out furiously at the kinds of popular politics they believed were undermining authority and causing the violence. Traditional and prudent men of this sort could not accept a new and different world, and soon they either fell silent or became loyalists, determined to remain faithful to the king and to support the society that had bred them.

The Declaration of Independence

By the beginning of 1775, the British government was already preparing for military action. In February Lord North got Parliament to pass what he regarded as a conciliatory measure. He proposed that any colony contributing its proportionate share to the common defense would not be subject to parliamentary taxation. But since the British government had done nothing to resolve the issues that had been raised by the Coercive Acts and by the declarations of the Continental Congress, the colonists regarded North's efforts at reconciliation as an underhanded attempt to divide them. By this date North's supporters and the king himself saw no choice but force to bring the colonists back into line. As early as November 1774,

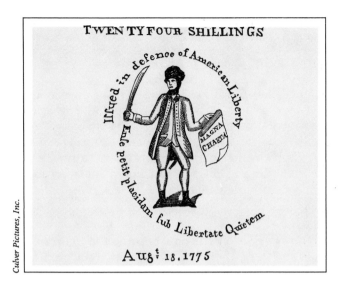

MASSACHUSETTS PAPER MONEY, 1775

George III had told North that "blows must decide whether they are to be subject to the Country or Independent." The British government thus built up its army and navy and began restraining the commerce first of New England and then of the other colonies.

The Second Continental Congress.
In May 1775 delegates from the colonies met in Philadelphia for the Second Continental Congress, to take up where the first Congress had left off. Outwardly the Congress continued the policy of resolves and reconciliation. In July, at the urging of John Dickinson, the Congress approved the Olive Branch Petition, which claimed loyalty to the king and humbly asked him to break with his "artful and cruel" ministers, whom the Congress blamed for the oppressive measures. At the same time the Congress issued the Declaration of the Causes and Necessities of Taking Up Arms (largely the work of Dickinson and Thomas Jefferson), in which the colonies denied that they had any "ambitious design of separating from Great Britain, and establishing independent states." As this superb summary of the American case against Britain demonstrated, the time for paper solutions had passed.

In April 1775 fighting had broken out in Massachusetts. The British government had long assumed that Boston was the center of the disturbances in America: the collapse of colonial resistance would follow simply from isolating and punishing the port. The Coercive Acts of 1774 had rested on this assumption, and the British military actions of 1775 were simply a logical extension of the same assumption. The British government, thinking that it was dealing only with mobs led by a few seditious instigators, therefore or-

Jonathan Sewall (1728–96) was a Massachusetts attorney and a close friend of John Adams. But after Sewall received several crown appointments in the 1760s, the paths of their careers diverged, and Sewall became a government supporter. These observations, written to the governor of Canada a month or so after Lexington and Concord, reveal a common loyalist astonishment over a rebellion that seemed to have no justifiable causes.

Jonathan Sewall Condemns the Drive Toward Independence (1775)

IT is now become too plain to be any longer doubted, that a Union is formed by a great Majority, almost throughout this whole Continent, for opposing the Supremacy, and even the lowest Degree of legislative Jurisdiction, of the British Parliament, over the British Colonies—that an absolute unlimited Independence, is the Object in View—and that, to obtain this End, preparations for War are made, and making, with a Vigor, which the most imminent Dangers from a foreign Enemy, could never inspire. It should seem astonishing, that a Country of Husbandmen, possessed every one, almost, of a sufficient Share of landed property, in one of the finest Climates in the World; living under the mildest Government, enjoying the highest portion of civil and religious Liberty that the Nature of human Society admits, and protected in the Enjoyment of these, and every other desirable Blessing in Life, upon the easiest Terms, by the only Power on Earth capable of affording that protection—that a people so scituated for Happiness, should throw off their rural Simplicity, quit the peaceful Sweets and Labours of Husbandry, bid open Defiance to the gentle Intreaties and the angry Threats of that powerful parent State which nursed their tender Years, and rush to Arms with the Ferocity of Savages, and with the fiery Zeal of Crusaders!—and all this, for the Redress of Chimerical Grievances—to oppose a claim of Parliament, made explicitly, exercised uniformly over, and quietly acquiesced in by, the Colonies from their earliest Origin! It is, I say, so truly astonishing, so entirely out of the Course of Nature, so repugnant to the known principles which most forceably actuate the human mind, that we must search deeper for the grand and more hidden Spring which causes so wonderful a movement in the Machine. And this, in my Opinion, is no other than that ancient republican independent Spirit, which the first Emigrants to America brought out with them; and which the Forms of Government, unhappily given to the New England Colonies, instead of checking, have served to cherish and keep alive. This is the Seed, which, being planted together with the Colonies, early took deep root; and being nourished by the Beams of civil and

ecclesiastical Government, though, at some Seasons, it has appeared withered and almost dead, yet accidental Causes, like Showers in the natural World, have, from Time to Time, revived and given it fresh Growth; but never before, with that Luxuriance with which we now see it spread. The immediate Causes, which brought it to its present Enormity, lie obvious to every observing Eye here; they originated in the disappointed Ambition of one Man, of great Influence and no principle of publick or private Virtue—the Occasion did not escape the Notice of those watchful turbulent Spirits which are ever to be found in all Governments partaking of Democracy; by the help of the single Word, *Liberty*, they conjured up the most horrid Phantoms in the Minds of the common people, ever, an easy prey to such specious Betrayers—the Merchants, from a Desire of a free and unrestrained Trade, the sure and easy Means of arriving at a Superiority in Wealth, joined in Bubbling the undiscerning Multitude—the Clergy, from that restless Spirit and Lust of Dominion, which, with a melancholy Notoriety, mark the Character of the priesthood in all Ages and Nations; from a genuine republican Temper, and from a rooted Enmity against the Church of England, opined, as Leaders of the pack, upon those never failing Topics of Tyranny and Popery—the simple unmeaning Mechanics, peasants and Labourers, who had really no Interest in the Matters of Controversy, hoodwinked, inflamed and goaded on by their Spiritual Drivers, fancied they saw civil and religious Tyranny advancing with hasty Strides; and by the Help of kindred Spirits on the other Side [of] the Atlantic it has at length spread through the Continent.

dered its commander in Massachusetts, General Gage, to arrest the rebel leaders, to break up their bases, and to reassert royal authority in the colony. On April 18–19 Gage's army attempted to seize rebel arms and ammunition stored at Concord, a town northwest of Boston. Colonial scouts, including the silversmith Paul Revere, rode ahead of the advancing redcoats, warned patriot leaders John Hancock and Samuel Adams to flee, and roused the farmers of the countryside—the minutemen—to arms. No one knows who fired first at Lexington, but shots between the colonial militia and British troops were exchanged there and later at Concord, where the British found only a few supplies. During their long march back to Boston, the strung-out British columns were repeatedly harassed by patriot militia. By the end of the day, 273 redcoats and 95 patriots had been killed, wounded, or lost, and the countryside was aflame with revolt. From positions in Charlestown and Dorchester, the colonists quickly surrounded the besieged British in Boston and thus raised doubts that police action would be enough to quell the rebellion.

Two months later, in June 1775, British soldiers attempted to dislodge the American fortification on a spur of Bunker Hill in Charlestown, overlooking Boston. The British assumed, as one of their generals, John Burgoyne, put it, that no numbers of "untrained rabble" could ever stand up against "trained troops." Under General William Howe British forces attempted a series of frontal assaults on the American position. These attacks were eventually successful, but only at the terrible cost of 1,000 British casualties—more than 40 percent of Howe's troops. At Bunker Hill—the first formal battle of the Revolution—the British suffered their heaviest losses in what would become a long and bloody war.

When news of the fighting reached Philadelphia, the Second Continental Congress had to assume the responsibilities of a central government for the colonies. The Congress created a Continental army, appointed George Washington of Virginia as commander, issued paper money for the support of colonial troops, and formed a committee to negotiate with foreign countries.

By the summer of 1775, the escalation of actions and reactions was out of control. On August 23, George III, ignoring the colonists' Olive Branch Petition, proclaimed the colonies in open rebellion. In October he publicly accused them of aiming at independence. By December the British government had declared all American shipping liable to seizure by British warships. As early as May 1775, American forces had captured Fort Ticonderoga at the head of Lake Champlain. Out of a desire to bring the Canadians into the struggle against Britain, the Congress ordered makeshift forces under Richard Montgomery and Benedict Arnold to invade Canada, but the colonists were badly defeated in Quebec in the winter of 1775–76. With all of this fighting between Britain and its colonies taking place, it was only a matter of time before the Americans formally cut the remaining ties to Great Britain. Although no official American body had as yet endorsed independence, the idea was obviously in the air.

It was left to Thomas Paine, a onetime English corsetmaker and schoolmaster and twice-dismissed excise officer who had only arrived in the colonies in late 1774, to express in January 1776 the accumulated American rage against George III. In his pamphlet *Common Sense* Paine dismissed the king as the "Royal Brute" and called for American independence immediately. *Common Sense* was the most incendiary and popular pamphlet of the entire Revolutionary era; it went through twenty-five editions in 1776 alone. In it Paine rejected the traditional and stylized forms of persuasion designed for educated gentlemen and reached out for new readers among the artisan- and tavern-centered worlds of the cities. Unlike more genteel writers, Paine did not decorate his pamphlet with Latin quotations and learned references to the literature of Western culture, but instead relied on his readers' knowing only the Bible. Although Paine was criticized for using ungrammatical language and coarse imagery, he showed the common people, who in the past had not been very involved in politics, that fancy words and Latin quotations no longer mattered as much as honesty and sincerity and the natural revelation of feelings.

In the early spring of 1776, the Congress threw open America's ports to the world and prepared for independence. On July 4, 1776, the delegates formally approved the Declaration of Independence, a thirteen-hundred-word document largely written by the graceful hand of Thomas Jefferson of Virginia. In the Declaration the king, who was now regarded as the only remaining link between the colonists and Great Britain, was held accountable for every grievance that the Americans had suffered since 1763. The reign of George III, Americans declared "to a candid world," was "a history of repeated injuries and usurpations, all having in direct object the establishment of an absolute Tyranny over these States."*

The Declaration of Independence was a brilliant expression of Enlightenment ideals—ideals that still reverberate powerfully in the lives of Americans and other peoples today. "That all men are created equal; that they are endowed by their Creator with certain inalienable rights; that among these are life, liberty,

*For the full text of the Declaration of Independence, see Appendix.

THOMAS PAINE, BY JOHN WESLEY JARVIS
Paine was probably the first detached "intellectual" in American history. He belonged to no country, lived by his pen, and saw his role as the stimulator of revolutions.

and the pursuit of happiness"—these "truths" seemed "self-evident" even to an eighteenth-century American society that was divided by classes and by the glaring contradiction of black slavery. Jefferson later recalled that his draft of the Declaration aimed "not to find out new principles, or new arguments, never before thought of," but rather "to place before mankind the common sense of the subject, in terms so plain and firm as to command their assent." The Declaration of Independence set forth a philosophy of human rights that could be applied not only to Americans, but to peoples everywhere. It was essential in giving the American Revolution a universal appeal.

An Asylum for Liberty

It was a strange revolution that Americans had begun, one that on the face of it is not easily comprehended. A series of trade acts and tax levies does not seem to add up to a justification for independence. And although by 1776 most Americans agreed with John Adams that they were "in the very midst of a revolution, the most complete, unexpected and remarkable of any in the history of nations," their revolution has always

"THE DECLARATION OF INDEPENDENCE," BY JOHN TRUMBULL
The committee that drafted the Declaration of Independence included, from left to right, John Adams, Roger Sherman, Robert R. Livingston, Thomas Jefferson, and Benjamin Franklin.

seemed to have had an unusual conservative cast to it.

Throughout the imperial crisis American patriot leaders insisted that they were rebelling not against the principles of the English constitution, but on behalf of them. In order to express continuity with the great struggles for political liberty in England, they invoked historic English party designations and called themselves "Whigs," and branded the supporters of the crown "Tories." By emphasizing that it was the letter and spirit of the English constitution that justified their resistance, Americans could easily believe that they were simply preserving what Englishmen had valued from the beginning of their history.

Yet the colonists were mistaken in believing that they were struggling only to return to the essentials of the English constitution. The historical traditions of that constitution were not the principles that were held by English officials in the mid-eighteenth century. In fact, the Americans' principles were, as the Tories and royal officials tried to indicate, "revolution principles" outside the mainstream of English thought. Since the colonists seemed to be reading the same literature as other Englishmen, they were hardly

aware that they were seeing the English tradition differently. Despite their breadth of reading and references, however, they concentrated on a set of ideas that ultimately gave them a peculiar conception of English life and an extraordinarily radical perspective on the English constitution they were so fervently defending.

The Country Tradition of Opposition. The heritage of liberal thought that the colonists drew upon was composed not simply of the political treatises of notable philosophers like John Locke but also of the writings of such influential eighteenth-century pamphleteers as John Trenchard and Thomas Gordon. Indeed, many of England's leading intellectuals, such as Alexander Pope and Jonathan Swift, wrote in the first half of the eighteenth century out of a deep and bitter hostility to the great political, social, and economic changes they saw taking place around them. These critics thought that traditional values were being corrupted and that England was being threatened with ruin by the general commercialization of English life, as seen in the rise of such institutions as the Bank of England, powerful stock companies, stock markets, and the huge public debt. Believing that the crown was ultimately responsible for these changes, such writers championed a so-called country opposition to the deceit and luxury of the "court," which they associated with the crown and its networks of influence.

This country opposition had a long and complicated history in England. It stretched back at least to the early seventeenth century, to the Puritan opposition to the established church and the courts of the early Stuart kings, James I and Charles I. The English Civil War of the mid-seventeenth century can in part be understood as an uprising of the local gentry, representing the counties or the "country" of England in the House of Commons, against the court surrounding the Church of England and the king. Such localist and grassroots opposition to the far-removed central authorities was a recurring theme in English history, as it would continue to be in American history.

In the eighteenth-century Anglo-American world, writers in this country-opposition tradition were especially fearful that executive or state power—particularly as it operated under the ministries of Sir Robert Walpole—was corrupting Parliament and English society. Throughout the first half of the eighteenth century, these defenders of political liberties made ringing proposals to reduce and control what seemed to be the enormously expanded powers of the crown. Their goal was to recover the rights of the people and the original principles of the English constitution.

Many of the reforms they proposed were ahead of their time for England—reforms that advocated the right to vote for all adult males and not just the well-to-do property holders, more liberty for the press, and greater freedom of religion. Other suggested reforms aimed at prohibiting salaried government puppets ("placemen") from sitting in the House of Commons, at reducing the public debt, and at obtaining such popular rights as equal representation for more people, the power to instruct members of Parliament, and shorter Parliaments. All these reform proposals combined into a widely shared conception of how political life in England should ideally be organized. In this ideal nation the parts of the constitution would be independent of one another, and members of Parliament would be independent of any "connection" or party. In other words there would exist a political world in which no one would be controlled by anyone else.

The American colonists had long felt the relevance of these "country" ideas more keenly than the English themselves. These ideas had not only explained the simple character of American life in contrast with the sophistication of England. They had also justified the colonists' antagonism to royal power. In the conflicts between the colonial assemblies and the royal gover-nors in the first half of the eighteenth century, Americans had invoked these ideas off and on. Now, however, in the years after 1763, the need to explain the growing controversy with Britain gave this country-opposition ideology a new and comprehensive importance. It not only prepared the colonists intellectually for resistance, but also offered them a powerful justification of their many differences from a decayed and corrupted mother country.

A Conspiracy Against Liberty.

These inherited ideas contained an elaborate set of rules for political action by the people. How were the people to identify a tyrant? How long should the people put up with abuses? How much force should they use? The answers to these questions came logically as events unfolded, and led the colonists almost irresistibly from resistance to rebellion. Step by step the colonists became convinced that the obnoxious efforts of crown officials to reform the empire were not simply the result of insensitivity to unique American conditions or mistakes of well-meant policy. Instead Americans saw these as the intended consequences of a grand tyrannical design. In Thomas Jefferson's words the British reforms were nothing less than "a deliberate systematical plan of reducing us to slavery."

America, the colonists believed, was the primary object of this tyrannical conspiracy, but the goals of the conspiracy ranged far beyond the colonies. Americans were involved not simply in a defense of their own rights, but in a worldwide struggle for the salvation of liberty itself. The crucial turning point came in the late 1760s. Americans earlier had read of the prosecution of the English radical John Wilkes for criticizing His Majesty's government in his *North Briton* No. 45 and had made Wilkes and the number 45 part of their political symbolism. Then in 1768 Wilkes's four successive expulsions from the House of Commons, despite his repeated reelection by the voters of Middlesex, outside London, for many Americans marked the twilight of representative government in Great Britain. Everywhere liberty seemed to be in retreat before the forces of tyranny. The struggles of "sons of liberty" in Ireland to win constitutional concessions from Britain were suppressed. The attempts of the freedom fighter Pascal Paoli and his followers to establish the independence of Corsica from France ended in failure. As Americans learned of these setbacks, they became convinced that America was the only place where a free popular press still existed and where the people could still elect representatives who spoke for them and them only.

By 1776 their picture of the immense struggle they were involved in was complete. And they could respond enthusiastically, as lovers of humanity and

THE BATTLE OF CONCORD, MASSACHUSETTS
In their march to and from Concord on April 19, 1775, 73 British soldiers were killed and 200 wounded out of a total force of 1800. Of the nearly 4,000 colonial militia who fought sometime during the day, 49 were killed and 46 were wounded.

haters of tyranny, to the passionate appeal of Thomas Paine's *Common Sense* to stand forth for liberty:

Every spot of the old world is overrun with oppression. Freedom hath been hunted round the globe. Asia and Africa have long expelled her. Europe regards her like a stranger, and England hath given her warning to depart. O! receive the fugitive, and prepare in time an asylum for mankind.

The War for Independence

However necessary were ideas such as Paine's in making events meaningful and in mobilizing people into revolution, ideas by themselves could not achieve independence. Once Britain had determined to enforce its authority with troops, Americans knew that they had to take up arms to support their beliefs. For over a year before the Declaration of Independence, American and British forces had been at war. It was a war that would go on for nearly eight years—the longest conflict in American history until the Vietnam War two centuries later.

The war for independence passed through a series of distinct phases, growing and widening until what had begun in British eyes as a breakdown in governmental authority in a section of the empire became a worldwide struggle. For the first time in the eighteenth century, Great Britain found itself diplomatically isolated; at one point in 1779 it was even threatened with French invasion. The war for American independence thus eventually became an important episode in Britain's long struggle with France for global supremacy, a struggle that went back a century and would continue for another generation into the nineteenth century.

The War in the North, 1775–1776. British troops had suffered heavy losses in their first clashes with the American militia in Massachusetts in the spring of 1775—at

Lexington and Concord and especially in the bloody battle of Bunker Hill. This initial experience convinced the British government that it was not simply dealing with a New England mob, and it swept away almost every objection the members of the ministry had to a conquest of the colonies. The appointment of generals by the Second Continental Congress, the organization of a Continental field army under George Washington in the summer of 1775, and the American invasion of Canada only confirmed the British government's realization that it was now involved in a military rather than a police action. This new understanding of what Britain was up against dictated a conventional eighteenth-century military policy of maneuver and battle.

This change of strategy required that the British evacuate Boston and transfer their main forces to New York, with its presumably more sympathetic population, its superior port, and its central position. Accordingly, in the summer of 1776 Sir William Howe, who replaced Gage as commander in chief of the British army in North America, sailed into New York harbor with a force of more than 30,000 men. Howe aimed to cut New England off from the other rebels and to defeat Washington's army in a decisive battle. He was to spend the next two frustrating years trying to succeed at this plan.

On the face of it, a military struggle seemed to promise all the advantage to the British. Britain was the most powerful nation in the world with a population of about 11 million, compared with only 2.5 million colonists. The British navy was the largest in the world, with nearly half its ships initially committed to the American struggle. The British army was a well-trained professional force, having at one point in 1778 nearly 50,000 troops in North America alone; and more than 30,000 hired German mercenaries were added to this force during the war. To confront this military might the Americans had to start from scratch. Eventually they created a small Continental army, numbering at times less than 5,000 troops, supplemented by state militia units of varying sizes. In most cases inexperienced, amateur officers served as the American military leaders. For example, the commander in chief, Washington, had been only a regimental colonel on the Virginia frontier and had little firsthand knowledge of combat. Not surprisingly, then, most British officers thought that the Americans would be no match for His Majesty's troops. A veteran of many North American campaigns told the House of Commons in 1774 that with 5,000 regulars he could easily march from one end of the country to the other.

Yet this contrast of numbers was deceptive. The British disadvantages were immense and perhaps overwhelming—even at the beginning, when they had

GEORGE WASHINGTON, BY CHARLES WILLSON PEALE
Washington's genius lay not in his military expertise in the field, but in his coolness, determination, and extraordinary political skills. Although he lost most of his battles, he never lost the support of his officers or the Congress.

the greatest opportunities to put down the rebellion. Great Britain had to carry on the war 3,000 miles across the Atlantic with consequent problems of communications and logistics. It also had to wage a different kind of war from any other it had fought in the eighteenth century. A well-trained army might have been able to conquer the American forces, but, as one French officer observed at the end, America itself was unconquerable. The great breadth of territory and the wild nature of the terrain made conventional maneuverings and operations difficult and cumbersome. The fragmented and local character of authority in America inhibited decisive action by the British. There was no nerve center whose capture would destroy the rebellion. In these circumstances the Americans' reliance on amateur militia forces and the weakness of their organized army made them more dangerous than if they had had a trained professional army. The British never clearly understood what they were up against—a revolutionary struggle involving wide-

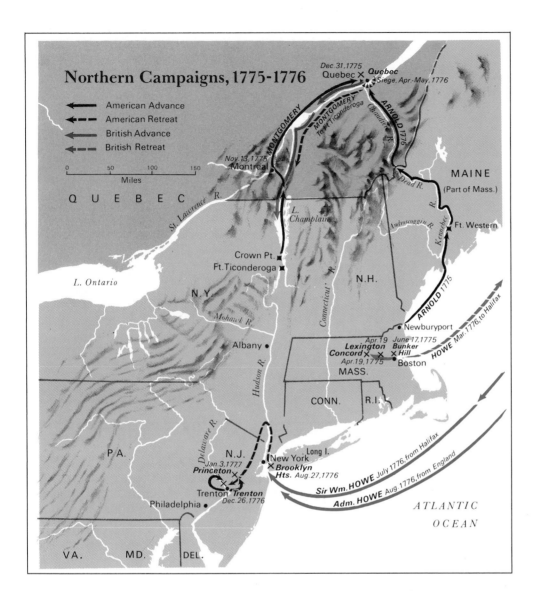

Northern Campaigns, 1775-1776

American Advance
American Retreat
British Advance
British Retreat

Miles
0   50   100   150

QUEBEC
L. Ontario
L. Champlain
St. Lawrence R.
Montreal *Nov. 13, 1775*
Crown Pt.
Ft. Ticonderoga
MONTGOMERY
Ticonderoga
Dead R.
Chaudière R.
ARNOLD 1776
Quebec *Dec. 31, 1775*
Quebec Siege, Apr.-May, 1776
MAINE (Part of Mass.)
Kennebec R.
Androscoggin R.
Ft. Western
N.H.
N.Y.
Mohawk R.
Albany
Hudson R.
Connecticut R.
Newburyport
ARNOLD 1775
Lexington *Apr. 19* Bunker *June 17, 1775*
Concord   Hill
Apr. 19, 1775 Boston
MASS.
HOWE Mar. 1776, to Halifax
CONN.   R.I.
PA.
Delaware R.
N.J.
Jan. 3, 1777
Princeton
Trenton *Trenton*
Dec. 26, 1776
New York
Long I.
Brooklyn Hts. Aug. 27, 1776
Sir Wm. HOWE July 1776, from Halifax
Adm. HOWE Aug. 1776, from England
Philadelphia
ATLANTIC OCEAN
VA.   MD.   DEL.

spread support in the population. Hence they continued to underestimate the staying power of the rebels and to overestimate the strength of the loyalists. And in the end independence came to mean more to the Americans than reconquest did to the English.

From the outset the English objective could never be as simple and clear-cut as the Americans' desire for independence. Conquest by itself could not restore political relations and imperial harmony. Many people in England were reluctant to engage in a civil war, and several officers actually refused on grounds of conscience to serve in America. Although the British ministry and most members of Parliament were intent on subjugating America by force, the British commanders appointed in 1775 never shared this overriding urge for outright coercion. These commanders—Sir William Howe and his brother Admiral Richard, Lord Howe, who was in charge of the navy—saw themselves not simply as conquerors, but also as peacemakers. They interrupted their military operations with peace feelers to Washington and the Continental Congress, and they tried to avoid plundering and ravaging the American countryside and ports out of fear of destroying all hope for reconciliation. This "sentimental manner of waging war," as Lord George Germain, head of the American Department, called it, weakened the morale of British officers and troops and left the loyalists confused and disillusioned.

The Howes' policy was not as ineffectual initially as it later appeared. After defeating Washington at

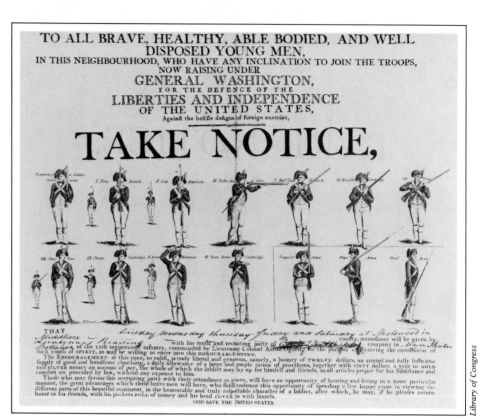

CONTINENTAL ARMY RE-CRUITING POSTER, OFFER-ING A BOUNTY OF TWELVE DOLLARS FOR ENLISTMENT

Brooklyn Heights on Long Island in August 1776 and expelling him from New York City, General Howe drove Washington into pell-mell retreat southward. Instead of pursuing Washington across the Delaware River, Howe resorted to a piecemeal occupation of New Jersey. He extended his lines and deployed brigade garrisons at a half-dozen towns around the area with the aim of gradually convincing the rebels that the British army was invincible. Loyalist militiamen emerged from hiding and through a series of ferocious local struggles with patriot groups began to assume control of northern New Jersey. Nearly 5,000 Americans came forward to accept Howe's offer of pardon and to swear loyalty to the crown. American prospects at the end of 1776 were as low as they ever would be during the war. These were, as Thomas Paine wrote, "times that try men's souls."

The Howes' policy of leniency and pacification, however, was marred by plundering by British troops and by loyalist acts of vengeance against the rebels. But even more important in undermining the British successes of 1776 were Washington's brilliant strokes in picking off two of General Howe's extended outposts, at Trenton on December 26, 1776, and at Princeton on January 3, 1777. With these victories Washington forced the British to withdraw from the banks of the Delaware and to leave the newly formed bands of loyalists to fend for themselves. American morale soared, oaths of loyalty to the king declined, and patriot militia regained local control in areas that had been vacated by the withdrawing British troops. The British again had to reconsider their plans.

Burgoyne and Saratoga, 1777.

The British strategy for 1777 involved sending an army of 8,000 under General John Burgoyne southward from Canada by way of Lake Champlain to recapture Fort Ticonderoga. Near Albany Burgoyne was to join a secondary force under Lieutenant Colonel Barry St. Leger, moving eastward through the Mohawk Valley, and General Howe, advancing northward from New York City through the Hudson Valley. The ultimate aim of the campaign was to isolate New England and break the back of the rebellion. It was assumed in England that General Howe would join with Burgoyne. But Howe continued to believe that there was widespread loyalist support in the middle states and decided to capture Philadelphia, the seat of the Continental government. He moved on Philadelphia by sea and after much delay landed at the head of Chesapeake Bay in late August 1777. Washington, believing that he should not give up the Continental capital without a struggle, confronted Howe at Brandywine and later at Germantown. He

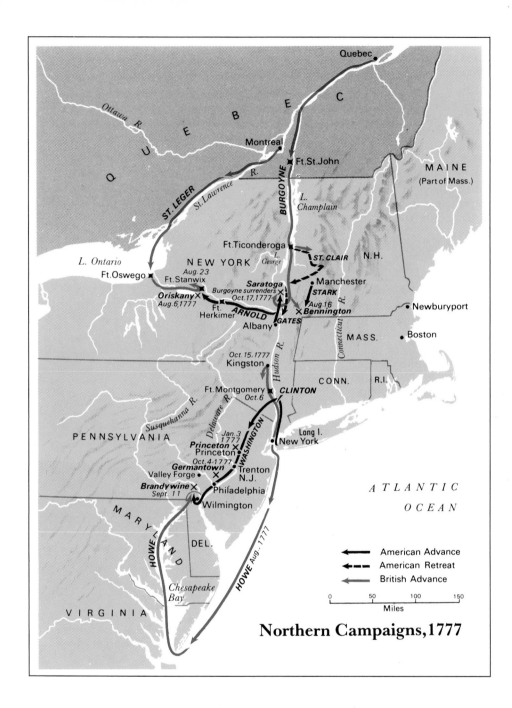

Northern Campaigns, 1777

was defeated in both battles. But his defeats were not disastrous: they proved that the American army was capable of organized combat, and they prevented Howe from moving north to help Burgoyne. Howe's capture of Philadelphia demonstrated that loyalist sentiment reached only as far as the British army could advance, and it scarcely justified what happened to Burgoyne's army in the north.

After St. Leger's force was turned back at Oriskany, New York, in the summer of 1777, Burgoyne and his huge slow-moving army from Canada increasingly found their supply lines stretched thin and their flanks harassed by patriot militia from New England. While Burgoyne's slow advance gave the American forces in the Hudson Valley needed time to collect themselves, the British army was diminishing. When 900 of Burgoyne's men attempted to seize supplies from a patriot arsenal in Bennington, Vermont, they were defeated by 2,000 New England militia under John Stark. Another 900 British redcoats were detached to garrison Ticonderoga. Burgoyne decided to press on. On September 13–14 he crossed to the west side of the Hudson River, cutting off communications with his rear. When he reached Saratoga, he confronted a growing American force of more than 10,000 men under General Horatio Gates. Two bloody battles convinced Burgoyne of the hopelessness of his situation, and in October 1777 he surrendered his entire army to the Americans.

Saratoga was the turning point. It suggested that the reconquest of America might be beyond British strength. It brought France openly into the struggle. And it led to changes in the British command and a fundamental alteration in strategy.

From the beginning of the rebellion, France had been secretly supplying money and arms to the Americans in the hope of avenging its defeat by Britain in the Seven Years' War. Benjamin Franklin had gone to Paris in 1776 to serve as the unofficial American ambassador. By 1777 French ports had been opened to American privateers, and French officers were joining Washington's army. It seemed only a matter of time before France would recognize the new republic. The British ministry realized at once the significance of Burgoyne's surrender, and by appointing the Carlisle Commission early in 1778 made new efforts to negotiate a settlement. The British government now offered the rebels a return to the imperial status before 1763—indeed, everything that the Americans had originally wanted. These British overtures, which Franklin skillfully used in Paris to play on French fears of an Anglo-American reconciliation, led the government of King Louis XVI in February 1778 to sign two treaties with the United States: one a commercial arrangement, the other a military alliance that was pledged to American independence. In 1779 Spain became allied with France in the hope of recovering earlier losses from England, especially Gibraltar. And in 1780 Russia formed the League of Armed Neutrality, which nearly all the maritime states of Europe eventually joined. For the first time in the eighteenth century, Britain was diplomatically isolated.

The War in the South, 1778–1781.

After 1778 putting down the rebellion became secondary to Britain's global struggle with France and Spain. The center of the war effort in America shifted seaward and southward as Britain sought to protect its possessions in the West Indies. General Howe was replaced by Sir Henry Clinton, and a more ruthless policy was adopted, including the bombardment of American ports, and raids on the countryside. The British abandoned Philadelphia and assumed a defensive position in New York and Rhode Island. Concentrating their forces in the West Indies, they now aimed to secure military control of ports in the American South, restore civil royal government

Library of Congress

HORATIO GATES (1728–1806)
This lowborn former officer in the British army was appointed Washington's adjutant-general in 1775. After his victory at Saratoga, some members of Congress and several officers, including General Thomas Conway, thought about replacing Washington with Gates. These suggestions, which became known as the "Conway Cabal," were stifled by Washington's political shrewdness.

with loyalist support, and then methodically move the army northward as a screen behind which local loyalists would gradually pacify the rebel territories. This strategy was based on the assumption that the South, with its scattered, presumably more loyalist population living in fear of Indian raids and slave uprisings, was especially vulnerable to the reassertion of British authority.

At the end of 1778, the British captured Savannah. On May 12, 1780, with the surrender of General Ben-

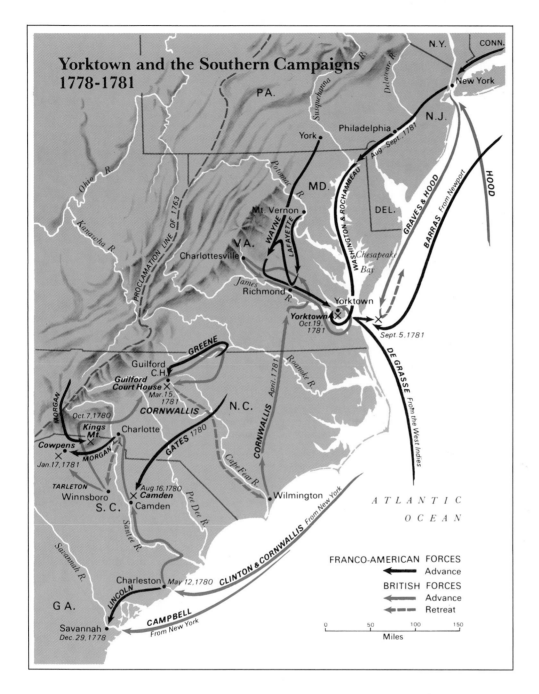

Yorktown and the Southern Campaigns
1778-1781

FRANCO-AMERICAN FORCES
→ Advance

BRITISH FORCES
→ Advance
⇢ Retreat

0   50   100   150
Miles

jamin Lincoln and an American army of 5,500, the British took Charleston. It was the greatest American loss of soldiers in the entire war. A new, hastily assembled American southern army under General Gates—the victor at Saratoga—rashly moved into South Carolina to stop the British advance. On August 16, 1780, at Camden, South Carolina, Gates suffered a devastating defeat, which destroyed not only his new American army but his military reputation as well. But the British were not able to consolidate their gains and

give the loyalists the military protection they needed to pacify the countryside. Loyalist retaliations against patriots for past harsh treatment, along with British plunder of the backcountry, particularly by Colonel Banastre Tarleton, drove countless Georgians and Carolinians into support of the Revolution. Colorful leaders such as Francis Marion, "the Swamp Fox," organized bands of patriots outside of the regular army to harass the loyalists and the British forces. The war in the South became a series of guerrilla skirmishes.

JOHN TRUMBULL'S "SURRENDER OF LORD CORNWALLIS"
General Benjamin Lincoln of Massachusetts leads the surrendered British troops between the French and American forces. Rochambeau and Washington, the two allied commanders in chief, are on horseback to the rear. Lafayette is the second figure from Washington's left. To Lafayette's immediate left is Baron von Steuben, the Prussian army captain who in 1778 was made a major-general in the Continental Army.

Now in command of the British forces in the South, Lord Cornwallis was impatient with the gradual policy of pacification. He was eager to demonstrate British strength by dramatically carrying the war into North Carolina. With his army constantly bedeviled by patriot guerrillas, he had just begun moving northward when he learned of the destruction of his left flank at King's Mountain on October 7, 1780. The news forced him to return to South Carolina. In the meantime the Americans had begun organizing a third southern army under the command of a thirty-eight-year-old ex-Quaker from Rhode Island, Nathanael Greene, recently quartermaster general of the Continental army. Shrewdly avoiding direct confrontation with Cornwallis, Greene compelled the British to divide their forces. On January 17, 1781, at Cowpens in western South Carolina, a detached corps of Greene's army under Daniel Morgan defeated "Bloody" Tarleton's Tory Legion and changed the course of British strategy in the South. Cornwallis cut his ties with his base in Charleston and set out after the elusive American army. After an indecisive battle with Greene at Guilford Courthouse on March 15, 1781, Cornwallis's tired and battered soldiers with-

drew to Wilmington on the North Carolina coast with the intention of moving the seat of war northward into Virginia. Thus ended the British experiment with a thorough program of pacification. During the spring and summer of 1781, patriot forces regained control of the entire Lower South except for a narrow strip between Charleston and Savannah.

Although raids by British forces in the summer of 1781 frightened Virginians and humiliated Governor Thomas Jefferson, Cornwallis could not convince his commander in chief, Clinton, in New York to make Virginia the center of British military operations. The haggling between the two generals enabled the Americans to bolster their Virginian troops under the command of the dashing French nobleman, the Marquis de Lafayette, who had been in the struggle since 1777. Cornwallis's withdrawal to the Virginia coast and his eventual isolation at Yorktown gave the combined American and French army of nearly 17,000 men under Washington and the Comte de Rochambeau the opportunity it was looking for. The French fleet under Admiral de Grasse moved into Chesapeake Bay and blocked Cornwallis's planned escape by sea. Thus surrounded and bombarded at Yorktown, Cornwallis was

Illumination.

COLONEL TILGHMAN, Aid de Camp to his Excellency General WASHINGTON, having brought official acounts of the SURRENDER of Lord Cornwallis, and the Garrifons of York and Gloucefter, thofe Citizens who chufe to ILLUMINATE on the GLORIOUS OCCASION, will do it this evening at Six, and extinguifh their lights at Nine o'clock.

Decorum and harmony are earneftly recommended to every Citizen, and a general difcountenance to the leaft appearance of riot.

October 24, 1781.

BROADSIDE OF OCTOBER 24, 1781, INVITING AMERICANS TO LIGHT CANDLES IN THEIR WINDOWS IN CELEBRATION OF CORNWALLIS'S DEFEAT

PRELIMINARY PEACE NEGOTIATIONS WITH GREAT BRITAIN, BY BENJAMIN WEST
Although he was history painter to George III, the American-born Benjamin West actually toyed with the idea of painting the great events of the American Revolution. But this unfinished picture of the peace negotiators was the only one he attempted. The picture includes John Jay, John Adams, Benjamin Franklin, Temple Franklin (Franklin's grandson and secretary to the delegation), and Henry Laurens, who did not sign the final treaty.

forced to surrender his army of 8,000 troops to Washington in October 1781. Britain's policy since 1778 of spreading its control along the entire Atlantic coastline had depended on maintaining naval superiority; and when this superiority was temporarily lost in 1781, the entire plan collapsed. Although the war dragged on for several months, everyone knew that Yorktown meant American independence.

The Peace Treaty. Nevertheless, the peace still had to be won. The main objective of the new nation—independence from Great Britain—was clear and straightforward. But this objective and others concerning America's territorial boundaries and its rights to the Newfoundland fisheries had to be reconciled with the aims of America's ally, France, and with those of France's ally, Spain, which had been at war with Great Britain since 1779. The United States and France had pledged in 1778 not to make a separate peace with Britain. But since France was bound to Spain against Britain until Gibraltar was recovered,

there was great danger of American interests getting lost in the maneuverings of the European powers. Despite the desire of France and Spain to humiliate Britain, neither monarchy really wanted a strong and independent American republic. Spain in particular feared the spread of republicanism among its South American colonies and sought to protect its interests in the Mississippi Valley.

Although Franklin, John Adams, and John Jay, the American negotiators in Europe, were only "militia diplomats," in Adams's words, they wound their way through the intricate problems of international politics with professional diplomatic skill. Despite instructions from the Continental Congress to do nothing without consulting France, the American diplomats decided to negotiate with Britain alone. By hinting at the possibility of weakening the Franco-American alliance, they persuaded Great Britain to recognize the independence of the United States and to agree to much more generous boundaries than the French and particularly the Spanish had been willing to support. On the west, United States territory reached to the Mississippi River; on the south, to the thirty-first parallel; and on the north, roughly to the present boundary with Canada. The American negotiators then presented this preliminary Anglo-American treaty to France and persuaded the French to accept it by suggesting that the allies must conceal their differences from their enemies. The prospect of American peace with Britain now compelled Spain to abandon its demands for Gibraltar and to settle for the Mediterranean island of Minorca (lost to Britain early in the eighteenth century) and for East and West Florida. In the final treaty, signed in Paris on September 3, 1783, the United States, by shrewdly playing off the mutual fears of the European powers, gained both independence and concessions that stunned the French and indeed all Europeans.

CHRONOLOGY

1774 Coercive Acts.
Continental Congress meets in Philadelphia.
Galloway's Plan of Union.
Continental Association.

1775 Battle of Lexington and Concord.
Fort Ticonderoga taken by American forces.
Second Continental Congress meets in Philadelphia.
George Washington appointed commander in chief of Continental army.
Battle of Bunker Hill.
Congress adopts its "Declaration of the Causes and Necessities of Taking Up Arms."
George III proclaims colonists in open rebellion.
American forces fail to take Quebec; General Montgomery killed.
Pennsylvania Quakers form first antislavery society in world.

1776 Thomas Paine's *Common Sense*.
British troops evacuate Boston.
Congress calls on colonies to suppress all crown authority and establish governments under authority of the people.
Declaration of Independence.
Battle of Long Island, New York; Americans defeated by General Howe.
British take New York City.
Battle of Trenton.
New Hampshire, New Jersey, Pennsylvania, Delaware, Maryland, Virginia, North Carolina, and South Carolina write state constitutions.
Rhode Island and Connecticut change their colonial charters.

1777 Battle of Princeton.
Battle of Brandywine, Pennsylvania; Washington defeated.

British occupy Philadelphia.
Battle of Germantown, Pennsylvania; Howe repulses Washington's attack.
Burgoyne surrenders at Saratoga.
Articles of Confederation adopted by Continental Congress, but not ratified by all states until 1781.
Washington retires to Valley Forge for winter.
New York and Georgia write state constitutions.

1778 United States concludes military alliance and commercial treaty with France. First and only military alliance by United States until North Atlantic Treaty Organization, 1949.
British evacuate Philadelphia.
Battle of Monmouth, New Jersey. Although outcome indecisive, Washington's troops stand up to British regulars.
British seize Savannah, Georgia.

1779 Spain enters the war against Britain.
George Rogers Clark captures Vincennes and ends British rule in Northwest.

1780 Americans surrender 5,500 men and the city of Charleston, South Carolina.
Battle of Camden, South Carolina; Gates defeated by Cornwallis.
Battle of King's Mountain, South Carolina; British and Tories defeated.
Creation of Massachusetts constitution.

1781 Battle of Cowpens, South Carolina; British under Tarleton defeated by Morgan.
Battle of Guilford Courthouse, North Carolina; outcome indecisive, but Cornwallis withdraws to coast.
Cornwallis surrenders to Washington at Yorktown, Virginia.

1783 Treaty of Peace with Britain signed.

SUGGESTED READINGS

Modern interest in the ideas of the Revolution dates back to the 1920s and 1930s with the studies of constitutional law and natural rights philosophy by Carl Becker, *The Declaration of Independence* (1922); Charles H. McIlwain, *The American Revolution: A Constitutional Interpretation* (1923); William S. Carpenter, *The Development of American Political Thought* (1930); and Benjamin F. Wright, Jr., *American Interpretations of Natural Law* (1931). While these books emphasized formal political theory, others explicitly treated the ideas as propaganda. See Philip Davidson, *Propaganda and the American Revolution, 1763–1783* (1941); and Arthur M. Schlesinger, *Prelude to Independence: The Newspaper War on Britain, 1764–1776* (1958).

In the 1950s serious attention was paid to the determinative influence of ideas in Clinton Rossiter, *Seedtime of the Republic* (1953); and especially in Edmund S. Morgan and Helen M. Morgan, *The Stamp Act Crisis* (1953). The Morgan book focuses on parliamentary sovereignty.

Only in the 1960s, however, did historians comprehend the Revolutionary ideas as ideology and begin to recover the distinctiveness of the late-eighteenth-century world. The starting point now for analyzing the ideology of the Revolution—as a configuration of ideas giving meaning and force to events—is Bernard Bailyn, *The Ideological Origins of the American Revolution* (1967). Bailyn's book, which appeared initially as the introduction to the first of a four-volume edition of *Pamphlets of the American Revolution, 1750–1776* (1965–   ), was partly based on the rediscovery of the radical Whig tradition by Caroline Robbins, *The Eighteenth-Century Commonwealthmen* (1959). J. G. A. Pocock, *The Machiavellian Moment* (1975); J. R. Pole, *Political Representation in England and the Origins of the American Republic* (1966); Trevor H. Colbourn, *The Lamp of Experience: Whig History and the Beginnings of the American Revolution* (1965); and Isaac F. Kramnick, *Bolingbroke and His Circle* (1968), have further contributed to an understanding of the sources of the Revolutionary tradition. Pauline Maier, *From Resistance to Revolution* (1972), details the escalation of American fears of British policy between 1765 and 1776.

The loyalist reaction is analyzed in William H. Nelson, *The American Tory* (1961); Robert M. Calhoon, *The Loyalists in Revolutionary America: 1760–1781* (1973); and Bernard Bailyn, *The Ordeal of Thomas Hutchinson* (1974). A vitriolic account by a loyalist of the causes of the Revolution is Peter Oliver, *Origin and Progress of the American Rebellion*, ed. Douglass Adair and John A. Schutz (1961).

On the military actions of the Revolutionary War, the best brief account is Willard M. Wallace, *Appeal to Arms* (1951). Don Higginbotham, *The War of American Independence* (1971), and John Shy, *A People Numerous and Armed: Reflections on the Military Struggle for American Independence* (1976), best appreciate the unconventional and guerrilla character of the war. Two books edited by George A. Billias, *George Washington's Generals* (1964) and *George Washington's Opponents* (1969), contain excellent essays written by various historians on the military leaders of both sides. Eric Robeson, *The American Revolution in Its Political and Military Aspects, 1763–1783* (1955), has some penetrating chapters on the conduct of the war. For naval operations, see Gardner W. Allen, *A Naval History of the American Revolution* (2 vols., 1913). The fullest account of British strategy is Piers Mackesy, *The War for America, 1775–1783* (1964). On the British commanders in chief, see Ira Gruber, *The Howe Brothers and the American Revolution* (1972), and William Willcox, *Portrait of a General: Sir Henry Clinton in the War of Independence* (1964). Paul H. Smith, *Loyalists and Redcoats* (1964), describes British attempts to mobilize the loyalists. A particularly imaginative study is Charles Royster, *A Revolutionary People at War: The Continental Army and American Character, 1775–1783 (1979)*.

On diplomacy the standard account is Samuel Flagg Bemis, *The Diplomacy of the American Revolution* (1935). See also William C. Stinchcombe, *The American Revolution and the French Alliance* (1969). Richard B. Morris, *The Peacemakers* (1965), is a full study of the peace negotiations.

9 Republicanism

A military victory over Great Britain may have been essential for the success of the Revolution, but for Americans it was scarcely the whole of the Revolution. Although the Revolution had begun as a political crisis within the British Empire, by 1776 it was no longer merely a colonial rebellion. The imperial debate had released a flood of American writings that ultimately made the Revolutionary era the most creative period in the history of American political thought. From 1775, when independence and hence the formation of new governments became imminent, and continuing throughout the war, nearly every piece of writing about the future was filled with extraordinarily visionary hopes for the transformation of America. Americans had come to believe that the Revolution meant nothing less than the remaking of eighteenth-century politics and society—a remaking that was summed up in the concept of republicanism.

Republican Idealism

This republicanism was in every way a radical ideology—as radical for the eighteenth century as Marxism was to be for the nineteenth century. It meant more than simply eliminating a king and establishing an elective system of government. It added a moral, idealistic, and indeed utopian dimension to the political separation from Britain—a dimension that promised a fundamental shift in values and a change in the very character of American society.

Republicanism intensified the radicalism of the "country" ideology that Americans had borrowed from opposition groups in English society, and linked it with older and deeper European currents of thought that went back to antiquity. Indeed, classic republican ideas had their ultimate origin in ancient Greece and Rome. They had been revived by Renaissance writers, particularly by the early-sixteenth-century Italian philosopher Niccolò Machiavelli, and had been carried into seventeenth-century English thought by such writers as James Harrington, the poet John Milton,

and Algernon Sidney. It was under the influence of these classical republican ideas that England in the seventeenth century had executed its king, Charles I, and had tried its brief experiment in republicanism, the Commonwealth (1649–53). By the eighteenth century these classical republican ideals had spread through western Europe; indeed they had become a kind of counterculture for many dissatisfied Europeans. In countless writings and translations eighteenth-century European and English intellectuals evoked the utopian image of an earlier Roman republican world of simple farmer-citizens enjoying liberty and rural virtue. They viewed this idealized ancient world as an alternative to the sprawling monarchies, with their hierarchies, luxury, and corruption, that they had come to despise in their own time.

In the excitement of the Revolutionary movement, these classical republican values came together with the long-existing image of Americans as simple liberty- and equality-loving people to form one of the most coherent and powerful ideologies the Western world had yet seen. Many of the ambiguities Americans had felt about the rural, provincial character of their society were now clarified. What some people had seen as the crudities and limitations of American life could now be viewed as advantages for republican government. Independent American farmers who owned their own land were no longer regarded as primitive folk living on the edges of European society and in the backwaters of history. Rather, they were now perceived as citizens naturally equipped to realize the republican values that intellectuals had advocated for centuries.

Independent Citizens. Inevitably the new American states in 1776 became republics. Everyone knew that these new republics with their elective systems had not only political but also moral and social significance. Republicanism struck directly at the traditional society, in which heredity, patronage, and dependency were essential. Republican liberals believed that the social

VENERATE THE PLOUGH

Library of Congress

evils of the Old World—entrenched privilege, inflated aristocracy, and ever-present poverty—all flowed from the abuses of government. Therefore they aimed to reduce, if not destroy, government's overarching power. They were determined that government would no longer be able to squeeze money from the people, create titles of distinction, grant monopolies, shore up religious establishments, give out offices, and do all those other things that ate away at the moral vitality of the people. In place of strong government, republicanism promised a society in which relations would be based on natural merit and the equality of independent citizens who were linked to one another in affection and harmony. Although republicanism was based on individual property holding, it rejected a narrow, selfish individualism and stressed a morality of social cohesion and devotion to the common welfare. Several of the states—Massachusetts, Pennsylvania, and Virginia—in 1776 even adopted the name "commonwealth" to express better this new dedication to the public good.

These new republican communities of independent citizens were an inspiring ideal. But history had shown republics to be the most unstable kind of state, highly susceptible to faction and internal disorder. Theorists thus concluded that republics had to be small in territory and of essentially uniform character. The only existing European republican models—the Netherlands, and the Italian and Swiss city-states—were small and compact. According to the best political science of the day, when a large country attempted to establish a republic, as England had tried to do in the seventeenth century, the experiment was sure to end in some sort of dictatorship, like that of Oliver Cromwell. Unlike monarchies, whose executive power and numerous dependent ranks maintained public order even over a large and diverse population, republics

had to be held together from below, by the people themselves.

The Need for Virtue. Republicanism was radical precisely because it demanded an extraordinary degree of moral virtue—unselfish devotion to the public good—in the people. If only the society could be organized so as to allow the moral strength of people to express itself, then there would be little need for excessive central or royal government. But if the society developed in such a manner as to lessen the people's virtue, if the people became selfish and luxury-loving as the ancient Romans had, then the society would lose its ability to keep the republic alive and the degeneration of the republican state into a monarchy or dictatorship would be inevitable.

Americans, however, believed themselves to be naturally virtuous and thus ideally suited for republican government. Did they not possess the same hardy equality-loving character that the ancient republican citizens of Greece and Rome had had? Were not the remarkable displays of popular order in the face of disintegrating royal government in 1774–75 evidence that the American people would obey their governments without coercion? The Revolutionary leaders appealed to the American people to act patriotically, telling them, as Samuel Adams did, that "a Citizen owes everything to the Commonwealth." The citizen was, in fact, as the Philadelphia physician Benjamin Rush said, "public property. His time and talents—his youth—his manhood—his old age—nay more, life, all belong to his country."

In short, republican citizens had to be patriots, and patriots were not simply those who loved their country but those who were free from the control of others. As Jefferson wrote in his *Notes on Virginia*, "Dependence begets subservience and venality, suffocates the germ of virtue, and prepares fit tools for the designs of ambition." Hence the sturdy independent yeoman-farmers, Jefferson's "chosen people of God," were regarded as the most incorruptible and the best citizens for a republic.

The individual ownership of property, especially land, was essential for a republic, both as a source of independence and as evidence of a permanent attachment to the community. Those who were propertyless and dependent, like women and servants, thus could justifiably be denied the vote because they could have no wills of their own. In Europe corruption and dependency were thought to be common because only a few people possessed property. But, as one Carolinian wrote in 1777, "the people of America are a people of property; almost every man is a freeholder." Jefferson was so keen on this point that he proposed in 1776 that the new commonwealth of Virginia grant fifty acres of land to every citizen who did not have that many.

FRONTIER FARM IN 1793

Even at the end of the eighteenth century, many American farmers continued to grow their crops Indian style, girdling and burning trees, planting between tree stumps, and allowing the fields to revert to forest when their fertility gave out. Such wasteful and shifting methods of agriculture shocked foreign observers but made sense where land was so abundant.

Equality. At the heart of this republican emphasis on virtue and independence lay equality, the most powerful and influential concept in American history. Equality was the necessary basis for the anticipated harmony and public virtue of the New World. Many felt that the endless squabbling over position and rank and the bitter factional politics in the colonies had been the result of the artificial inequality of colonial society. This inequality, republicans said, had been created and nourished largely through the corrupting influence and patronage of the British crown. In a republic individuals were no longer doomed to be what their fathers had been. Ability, not birth, was what mattered. But republican egalitarianism did not mean the elimination of distinctions. Republics would still have an aristocracy, said Jefferson, but it would be a natural, not an artificial, one. A republican elite would resemble not the luxury-loving, money-mongering lackeys of the British court, but the stern and disinterested heroes of antiquity—men like George Washington, who seemed to Americans to embody perfectly the classical ideal of a republican leader.

Obviously these ideals of Revolutionary republicanism could not be wholly fulfilled. Much of republicanism's emphasis on the common good contradicted the surging individualism of American life. Yet whatever the practical results, republicanism as it was idealized by Jefferson's generation colored the entire Revolutionary movement. Eventually it would come to shape much of what Americans believe and value.

State Constitution Making

"How few of the human race have ever enjoyed an opportunity of making an election of government," rejoiced John Adams, like many others in 1776. Indeed, it was in the spirit of being able to control their own destinies that the Revolutionaries approached the immense task ahead of them. They knew very well that the entire world was watching to see how they would put their republican ideals into practice when they established governments for the new country. Their investigations into the abuses of power and the protection of liberty that had begun during the imperial debate now shaped the new constitutions they formed.

From the time royal authority had begun to disintegrate, Americans began thinking about creating new governments. During the summer of 1775, Samuel Adams and John Adams of Massachusetts, together with the Virginia delegation to the Continental Congress, led by Richard Henry Lee, worked out a program of independence. They made plans to negotiate foreign alliances, to create a confederation—a union for common purposes—and, most important, to establish new state governments. The climax of their efforts came with the congressional resolutions of May 1776, advising the colonies to adopt new governments "under the authority of the people" and declaring "that the exercise of every kind of authority under the . . . Crown should be totally suppressed." Even before the Declaration of Independence, the Congress had created a committee to form a confederation, and some of the states—New Hampshire, South Carolina, and Virginia—had begun working on new constitutions. With the May resolves and the Declaration of Independence, the other states also began to form new governments. By the end of 1776, new constitutions had been adopted in New Jersey, Delaware, Pennsylvania, Maryland, and North Carolina. Because they were corporate chartered colonies, Rhode Island and Connecticut were already republics in fact, and they simply confined themselves to eliminating all mention of royal authority in their existing charters. War conditions forced Georgia and New York to delay their constitution making until 1777. Massachusetts had recovered its old charter, which the British had abolished, and was busy preparing to write a more permanent constitution.

In 1776–77 Americans concentrated much of their attention and energy on establishing these new state constitutions. The states, not the central government or the Congress, were to test the Revolutionary hopes. In fact, forming new state governments, as Jefferson said in the spring of 1776, was "the whole object of the present controversy." For the aim of the Revolution had become not simply independence from British tyranny, but the prevention of future tyrannies.

Constitutions as Written Documents.

It was inevitable that Americans would draw up written constitutions. By the word *constitution* most eighteenth-century Englishmen meant not a written document, but the existing arrangements of government—that is, laws, customs, and institutions, together with the principles they embodied. Americans, however, had come to view a constitution in a different way. Ever since the seventeenth century they had repeatedly used their colonial charters as defensive barriers against royal authority. During the imperial debate wih Britain, they had been compelled to recognize that laws made by Parliament were not necessarily constitutional or in accord with fundamental principles of rightness and justice. If the constitutional principles were to be asserted against a too powerful government, then somehow they had to be lifted out of the machinery of day-to-day government and set above it. The Americans' new state constitutions would therefore have to be fixed plans—written documents, as the English constitution never had been—outlining the powers of government and specifying the rights of citizens.

Fear of Executive Power.

As they wrote these new state constitutions, the Americans set about to institutionalize all that they had learned from their colonial experience and the recent struggle with England. Although they knew they would establish republics, they did not know precisely what forms the new governments should take. Their central aim was to prevent power, which they identified with the rulers or governors, from encroaching upon liberty, which they identified with the people or their representatives in the legislatures. This aim was basic to the Anglo-American "country" ideology. Only the Americans' deep fear of executive power can explain the radical changes they made in the authority of their now elected governors.

In their desire to root out tyranny once and for all, the members of the state congresses who drafted the new constitutions reduced the elected governors' powers to a pale reflection of those that had been exercised by the royal governors. No longer would governors have the authority to create electoral districts, control the meeting of the assemblies, veto legislation, grant lands, establish courts of law, issue charters of incorporation to towns, or—in some states—pardon crimes. All the new state governors were surrounded by controlling councils whose members were elected by the assemblies. These governors were to be elected annually (generally by the assemblies), limited in the number of times they could be reelected, and subject to impeachment.

However radical these changes in executive authority may have been, many Americans believed that they did not get to the heart of the matter. They did not destroy the most subtle and dangerous source of despotism—the executive's power of appointment to office. Since in a traditional, monarchical society the distribution of offices, honors, and favors affected the social order, American republicans were determined that their governors would never again have the capacity to dominate public life. Exclusive control over appointments to executive and judicial offices was now taken from the traditional hands of the governors and shared with the legislatures. This change in the new state constitutions of 1776 was justified by the familiar principle of "separation of powers." The idea behind maintaining the executive, legislative, and judicial parts of the government separate and distinct was not to protect each power from the others, but to keep the judiciary and particularly the legislature free from executive manipulation—the very kind of manipulation that, Americans believed, had corrupted the English Parliament. Hence the new constitutions absolutely barred all executive officeholders and those receiving government salaries from sitting in the legislatures. As a consequence, parliamentary cabinet government of the kind that existed in England was forever prohibited in America, and constitutional development moved off in a direction independent of Great Britain—a direction that American government still follows.

Strengthening of the Legislatures.

The powers and rights that the new state constitutions of 1776 took from the governors were granted to the legislatures. This action marked a radical shift in the responsibility of government. In English history the "government" had traditionally been identified mainly with the executive. Representative bodies had generally been confined to voting taxes and passing corrective legislation on special occasions. But the new American state legislatures, in particular the lower houses of the assemblies, were no longer merely to be secondary units of governmental power or checks upon it. They were now given powers that had formerly been reserved for the magistrates—the executive and judicial leaders of government. These powers included the making of alliances and the granting of pardons.

To ensure that the state legislatures fully embodied the people's will, the ideas and experiences behind the Americans' view of representation were now drawn out and implemented. The Revolutionary state constitutions put a new emphasis on actual representation and explicit consent. They did so by creating equal electoral districts, requiring annual elections, enlarging the suffrage, imposing residence requirements on both electors and the persons elected, and granting constituents the right to instruct their representatives. The royal governors' former attempts to resist extending representation to newly settled areas was now dramatically reversed. Towns and counties, particularly in the backcountry, were granted either new or additional representation in the state legislatures. Thus Americans belatedly recognized the legitimacy of the western uprisings of the 1760s. Some of the new constitutions even explicitly stated the principle that population was the basis of representation. Five states wrote into their constitutions specific plans for periodic adjustments of their representation, so that (as the New York constitution of 1777 stated) it "shall for ever remain proportionate and adequate."

In light of what would happen in the coming decade, the Revolutionaries' confidence in 1776 in their representative legislatures was remarkable. Except for some dissatisfied Tories, few people expected these state legislatures to become tyrannical—in the Whig theory of politics, it did not seem possible for the people to tyrannize over themselves. Of course the people were apt to be rowdy or impatient; hence the republics needed not only governors, but also upper houses in the legislature to counterbalance the popular lower houses of representatives. All the states except Pennsylvania, Georgia, and the new state of Vermont therefore provided for upper houses, or senates, the designation taken from Roman history. The senators in these bicameral, or two-chamber, state legislatures were not to be a legally defined nobility but the wisest and best members of the society, who would revise and correct the well-intentioned but often careless measures of the people represented in the lower houses.

This Revolutionary state constitution making was an extraordinary achievement. Nothing quite like it had occurred before in modern history. Foreign intellectuals considered the new American state constitutions concrete realizations of Enlightenment ideas. In the decade following Independence the state constitutions were translated, published, and republished in France and other European countries, and their features were eagerly examined and debated. More than anything else in 1776, these new written state constitutions gave people everywhere a sense that a new era in history was beginning.

The Articles of Confederation

At the same time that the Revolutionaries were creating their state constitutions, they also set up a central government. Yet in marked contrast to the rich and exciting public explorations of political theory accompanying the formation of the state constitutions, there was little discussion of the plans for a central government. In 1776 most people's loyalties were still concentrated on their particular provinces. The Declaration of Independence, drawn up by the Continental Congress, was actually a declaration by "thirteen united States of America" proclaiming that as "Free and Independent States, they have full Power to levy War, conclude Peace, contract Alliances, establish Commerce, and to do all other Acts and Things which independent States may of right do." Despite all the talk of union, few Americans in 1776 could con-

OFFICIAL COPY OF THE ARTICLES OF
CONFEDERATION, PUBLISHED IN 1777

ceive of creating a single full-fledged Continental republic.

Still, the Congress needed some legal basis for its authority. Like the various provincial conventions, it had been created in 1774 simply out of necessity, and it was exercising an extraordinary degree of political, military, and economic power over Americans. It had adopted commercial codes, established and maintained an army, issued a Continental currency, laid down a military law code, defined crimes against the Union, and negotiated abroad. With the approach of Independence it was obvious to many leaders that a more permanent and legitimate union of the states was necessary. Although a draft of confederation was ready for consideration by the Congress as early as mid-July 1776, not until November 1777, after heated controversy, did the Congress present a document of union to the states for each of them to approve or reject. It took nearly four years, until March 1781, for all the states to accept this document and thereby legally establish the Articles of Confederation.

The Nature of the Union. The Articles created a confederation, "The United States of America," that was essentially a continuation of the Second Continental Congress. Delegates from each state were to be sent annually to the Congress, and each state delegation was to have only a single vote. In Article 9 the Congress was granted authority to control diplomatic relations, requisition soldiers and money from the states, coin and borrow money, regulate Indian affairs, and settle disputes between the states. Although a simple majority of seven states was needed to settle minor matters, a larger majority, nine states, was required to resolve important issues, including engaging in war, making treaties, and coining and borrowing money. There was no real executive, but only congressional committees with fluctuating memberships.

The Union was stronger than many people expected. The states were specifically forbidden to conduct foreign affairs, make treaties, and declare war. The citizens of each state were entitled to the privileges and immunities of the citizens of all states. All travel restrictions and discriminatory trade barriers between the states were eliminated. The judicial proceedings of each state were honored by all the states. These provisions, together with the substantial powers granted to the Congress, made the United States of America as strong as any similar republican confederation in history. The Articles marked a big step toward a genuine national government.

Nevertheless, the Americans' fear of distant central authority, intensified by century of experience in the British Empire, left no doubt that this Confederation would remain something less than a full national government. Under the Articles the crucial powers of commercial regulation and taxation—indeed, all final lawmaking authority—remained with the states. Congressional resolutions continued to be, as they had been under the Continental Congress, only recommendations; the states, it was assumed, would enforce them. And should there be any doubts of the decentralized nature of the Confederation, Article 2 stated bluntly that "each State retains its sovereignty, freedom and independence, and every power, jurisdiction, and right, which is not by this confederation expressly delegated to the United States, in Congress assembled."

The phrase "United States of America" thus possessed a literal meaning that is hard to appreciate today. The Confederation, based on the equal representation of each state, was more like a treaty among closely cooperating sovereign states than a single government. It was intended to be and remained, as Article 3 declared, "a firm league of friendship" among states jealous of their individuality. Not only ratification of the Articles of Confederation, but any subsequent changes in them, required the consent of all states.*

State Rivalries and the Disposition of the Western Lands. The local self-interests of the states prolonged the congressional debates over the adoption of the Articles

*For the Articles of Confederation, see Appendix.

State Claims to Western Lands and Cessions

Western Claims

Western Reserve, Ceded 1800

and delayed the required unanimous ratification until 1781. The major disputes—over representation, the share each state should contribute to the Union, and the disposition of the western lands—involved concrete state interests. Virginia and other populous states argued for proportional representation in the Congress, but these larger states had to give way to the smaller states' determination to maintain equal representation. The original draft of the Articles provided that each state's financial contribution to the general treasury would be based on its population, including slaves. Strong opposition from the southern states, however, forced the Congress to shift the basis for a state's financial contribution to the value of its land. This change was made against the wishes of the New England states, where land values were high.

The states' rivalries were most evident in the long controversy over the disposition of the western lands between the Appalachian Mountains and the Mississippi River. The Articles sent to the states in 1778 for ratification gave the Congress no authority over the unsettled lands of the interior, and this omission delayed their approval. States like Virginia and Massachusetts with charter claims to this western territory wanted to maintain control over the disposal of their land. But states without such claims, like Maryland and Rhode Island, wanted the western land pooled in a common national domain under the authority of the Congress. By March 1779, however, all but Maryland had ratified the Articles. Maryland, under the influence of land speculators, refused to join the Union until all the states had ceded their western lands to the central government. When Virginia, the state with charter rights to the largest amount of western territory, finally agreed on January 2, 1781, to surrender its claims to the United States, the way was prepared for other land cessions and for ratification of the Articles of Confederation by all the states. But the Confederation had to promise, in return for the cession of claims by Virginia and the other states, that this huge national domain in the West would "be settled and formed into distinct republican states."

Ordinances for the West.

The Congress drew up land ordinances in 1784 and 1785, and in 1787 it adopted the famous Northwest Ordinance. This act acknowledged —as the British had not done in the 1760s—the settlers' destiny in the West. The land ordinances of 1784 and 1785 provided for the land north of the Ohio River and west of the Appalachians to be surveyed and formed into townships of six miles square along lines running east-west and north-south. Each township was to be divided into thirty-six numbered lots (called sections) of 640 acres each. The Confederation favored speculators and large groups by providing for the sale of the land by auction and by requiring that a section was to be the smallest unit purchased, at a price of no less than a dollar an acre. In each township the Congress retained four sections for future sale and set aside one other for the support of public education. The Ordinance of 1787 dealt with the political organization of the Northwest. It guaranteed to the settlers basic political and legal rights and arranged for the area to be divided into not less than three nor more than five territories. When a territory reached a population of 60,000, it was to be admitted to the Union on equal terms with the existing states.

Outside of winning the war, these remarkable ordinances were the Confederation's greatest achievement. They solved at a stroke the problem, which Britain had been unable to solve, of relating "colonies" or other dependencies to the central government. In succeeding decades the Land Ordinance of 1785 and the Ordinance of 1787 remained the bases for the surveying, sale, and political evolution of America's western territories. Settlers could leave the older states with the assurances that they were not losing their political liberties and that they would be allowed eventually to form new republics as sovereign and independent as the other states in the Union. Thus even the organization of this great national landed resource by the Congress was immediately devoted to the dispersion of central authority through the anticipated creation of more states—the only political units most Americans seemed to value.

Republican Society

At the same time that Americans were trying to establish new governments and constitutions, disturbing changes in American society were taking place. To be sure, there was no immediate collapse of the social order and no abrupt and wholesale destruction of familiar social institutions. But everywhere there were alterations in the way people related to government, to the economy, and to each other. Many of these changes were the results of deeply rooted forces long in motion, some dating back to the beginning of the colonial period. But others were the recent and direct results of the Revolution itself.

The Departure of the Loyalists.

One sudden effect was the departure of tens of thousands of loyalists—or Tories, as the patriots called them. The loyalists may have numbered close to half a million, or 20 percent of white Americans. Nearly 20,000 of them fought for the crown in the regiments of His Majesty's army, and thousands of others served in local loyalist militia bodies. As many as 60,000 to 80,000 loyalists, it is estimated, left America during the Revolution for Canada and Great Britain, although many of these returned after the war and were reintegrated into American society. Although the loyalists came from all ranks and occupations, a large proportion belonged to the upper political and social levels. Many had been officeholders and overseas merchants involved in government contracting; in the North, most were Anglicans. Their regional distribution was likewise uneven. The loyalists were a tiny minority in New England and Virginia; but in western frontier areas, where hostility to eastern encroachment went back to pre-Revolutionary times, they were numerous. The loyalists also made up a considerable part of the population in the regions of New York, New Jersey, Pennsylvania, and the Deep South where the British army offered them protection. Their flight, displacement, and retirement created a vacuum at the top of society that was rapidly filled by patriots. The effects were widespread. Crown and Tory property and lands valued at millions of pounds were confiscated by the Revolutionary governments and almost immediately thrown onto the market. The resulting speculation contributed to the sudden rise and fall of fortunes during the Revolutionary years.

Economic Effects of the Revolution.

Economic disruptions created most of the social disorder. Suddenly Americans found themselves outside the protective walls of the British mercantile empire that had nurtured their commercial life for more than a century. Exports dropped drastically. Traditional markets in Britain, and especially in the British West Indies, were closed. Bonuses or bounties that formerly had been paid on particular colonial products were now gone. Colonial ships could no longer be sold to Britain, and prewar sources of credit were upset. These changes were devastating to particular groups and individuals, but

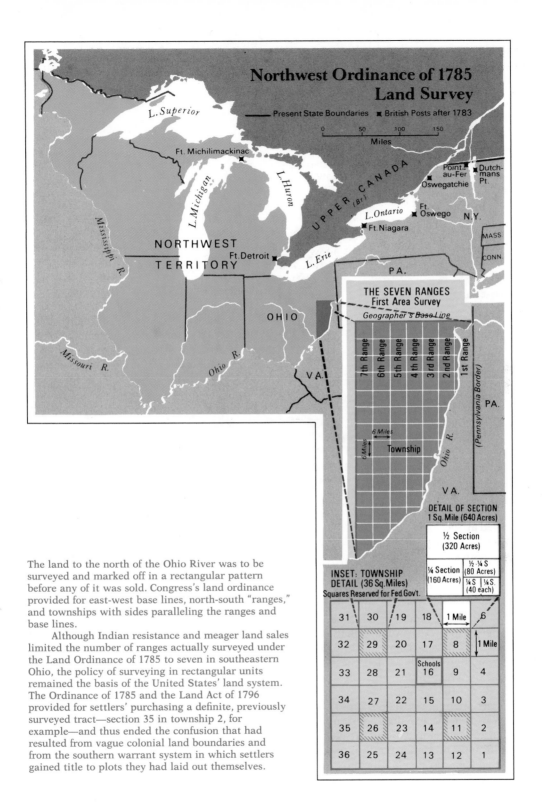

Northwest Ordinance of 1785 Land Survey

—— Present State Boundaries ■ British Posts after 1783

0   50   100   150
Miles

L. Superior

Ft. Michilimackinac

L. Michigan

L. Huron

UPPER CANADA (Br.)

Point-au-Fer
Oswegatchie
Dutch-mans Pt.

L. Ontario
Ft. Oswego
Ft. Niagara

N.Y.

MASS.

CONN.

NORTHWEST TERRITORY

Ft. Detroit

L. Erie

Mississippi R.

Missouri R.

Ohio R.

OHIO

V.A.

PA.

THE SEVEN RANGES
First Area Survey

Geographer's Base Line

7th Range | 6th Range | 5th Range | 4th Range | 3rd Range | 2nd Range | 1st Range

(Pennsylvania Border)

PA.

6 Miles

6 Miles   Township

Ohio R.

V.A.

DETAIL OF SECTION
1 Sq. Mile (640 Acres)

½ Section (320 Acres)	
¼ Section (160 Acres)	½ -¼ S (80 Acres)
	¼ S (40 each)

INSET: TOWNSHIP DETAIL (36 Sq. Miles)
Squares Reserved for Fed Gov't.

31	30	19	18	1 Mile	6
32	29	20	17	8	1 Mile
33	28	21	Schools 16	9	4
34	27	22	15	10	3
35	26	23	14	11	2
36	25	24	13	12	1

The land to the north of the Ohio River was to be surveyed and marked off in a rectangular pattern before any of it was sold. Congress's land ordinance provided for east-west base lines, north-south "ranges," and townships with sides paralleling the ranges and base lines.

Although Indian resistance and meager land sales limited the number of ranges actually surveyed under the Land Ordinance of 1785 to seven in southeastern Ohio, the policy of surveying in rectangular units remained the basis of the United States' land system. The Ordinance of 1785 and the Land Act of 1796 provided for settlers' purchasing a definite, previously surveyed tract—section 35 in township 2, for example—and thus ended the confusion that had resulted from vague colonial land boundaries and from the southern warrant system in which settlers gained title to plots they had laid out themselves.

"THE TONTINE COFFEE HOUSE," BY GUY FRANCIS, 1797

During the Revolution, fire had ravaged much of the commercial section of New York. In the following years New York's merchants enlarged the harbor facilities and rebuilt the business district, including this busy corner of Wall and Water streets. By 1797 New York had surpassed rival Philadelphia in both imports and exports.

overall the results of the break from Britain were beneficial and stimulating. Simply by destroying old encrusted habits and relationships, the Revolution released new energies.

The South suffered the greatest upheavals from the war. Not only did it lose established markets for its tobacco and other cash crops, but the British freed tens of thousands of its slaves to fight for the crown; at the end of the war, the British settled these former slaves in Canada, the West Indies, and other parts of the world. Indeed, the British army was perhaps the greatest single instrument of emancipation in America until the Civil War. But these dislocations only accelerated an agricultural diversification that had begun before the Revolution. The Upper South in particular recovered rapidly. Tobacco production in the 1780s equaled prewar levels, and it involved many new participants and new marketing arrangements.

Within the merchant communities in the North, divisions that had been apparent before the Revolution now widened, and merchants who had previously been on the fringe of economic activity found new opportunities at the center of things. In Massachusetts, provincial families like the Higginsons, Cabots, and Lowells moved into Boston and quickly formed the basis of a new Massachusetts elite. The same process was duplicated less notably but no less importantly elsewhere. New merchants pushed out in all directions in search of fresh markets, not only into the restricted colonial areas of the West Indies and South America, but also throughout Europe and even as far away as China.

Postwar trade with Great Britain quickly reached its earlier levels. By the 1780s the overall figures show an amazing recovery of commerce. Yet gross statistics do not do justice to the extent of change that was involved. In all the states there were new sources of supply, new commercial patterns, and new and increased numbers of participants in the market. Although exports soon surpassed their prewar levels, they now represented a smaller part of America's total economic activity. The wartime collapse of British imports had encouraged domestic manufacturing; and although the purchase of British goods resumed with

"VIEW OF BRIDGE OVER CHARLES RIVER," 1789
Building a bridge across the Charles River and linking Boston with Cambridge, Massachusetts, in the 1780s was only one of many such encouragements to internal commerce in post-Revolutionary America. This chartered toll bridge was the one later challenged by a rival bridge, a challenge that eventually resulted, in 1837, in one of the great Supreme Court decisions of American history.

the return of peace, societies were now formed to promote protective legislation for American manufacturing. Already the economy was beginning to turn inward: a remarkable spread of interstate and interregional trade would soon generate demands for new roads and canals. In these changing circumstances towns without hinterlands to exploit began a relative decline. Newport, Rhode Island, for example, had been a flourishing colonial port. But without an inland area for supply and marketing, it rapidly slipped into insignificance.

The Revolutionary War itself was both a disruptive and a creative force. It touched nearly everyone in one way or another. Like all wars, it destroyed familiar channels of trade and produced new sources of wealth. During the eight long years of the war, perhaps as many as 100,000 men bore arms in the Continental army and the state militias. All these soldiers had to be clothed, fed, housed, armed, and moved about. Thus for years the Congress and the state governments were involved in gigantic mobilization efforts that had powerful and far-reaching effects on the

American economy. Hundreds of military and government officials, ranging from quartermasters and commissary generals down to a variety of local purchasing agents, bought millions of dollars' worth of goods, from food and wagons to blankets and uniforms—anything and everything needed to wage war. Some military supplies were imported from abroad; but because of the scarcity of foreign credit and the British blockade of American shipping, most goods had to be grown or made by Americans. Consequently American farmers and artisans were drawn into producing for these huge new government markets on a scale never before experienced in America. Although in the past Americans had thought of commerce mostly in terms of international or overseas trade, as a result of this wartime experience they now began to realize the tremendous significance of trading with each other in their own domestic markets. Therefore military purchasing agencies became important new centers of economic activity and breeding grounds for both petty entrepreneurs and powerful postwar capitalists. Moreover, countless farmers and artisans became

Fogg Art Museum, Harvard University

NICHOLAS BOYLSTON, BY JOHN SINGLETON COPLEY, 1760
Boylston represented those wealthy and fashionable circles surrounding royal authority that ambitious men like John Adams simultaneously admired and resented. "Dined at Mr. Nick Boylstones . . . ," Adams in 1766 confided to his diary with wide-eyed excitement. "An elegant dinner indeed! Went over the house to view the furniture, which alone cost a thousand pounds sterling. A seat it is for a noble man, a prince, the turkey carpets, the painted hangings, the marble tables, the rich beds with crimson damask curtains and counterpanes, the beautiful chimney clock, the spacious garden, are the most magnificent of any thing I have ever seen."

used to the idea that they could expand their productivity and their wealth by working harder and selling goods in impersonal domestic markets. No wonder that by the 1780s many ordinary Americans were enthusiastic about the possibility of raising their standard of living.

Because the Revolutionary states were reluctant to tax their citizens, and because the Congress did not even have the legal authority to tax, the American

governments had to rely on borrowing to pay for all the goods they needed for the war effort. But government borrowing could scarcely raise the needed sums. Both the Congress and the state governments therefore resorted to the extensive printing of noninterest-bearing paper currency. These bills of credit, which the governments promised to redeem by taxes at some future date, were given to citizens in payment for supplies and services.

The currency that was issued by the congressional and state governments eventually totaled nearly $400 million in paper value and led to a socially disintegrating inflation. By 1781 $167 of congressional paper money was worth only $1 in specie (gold and silver), and the depreciation of the states' bills was nearly as bad. While creditors, wage earners, and those on relatively fixed incomes were hurt by this inflation, many of those who were most active in the economy—those who bought and sold goods rapidly—were able to profit. These circulating government bills enabled countless commodity farmers and traders to break out of a simple barter economy and to specialize and participate more independently in the market than they had in the past. The war thus fundamentally altered the American economy.

Long-Range Social Change. These were the immediate social and economic effects of the war. But there were other, deeper, and more long-lasting forces that were greatly affected by the Revolution and by republicanism. Despite a slowing-down of immigration and the loss of tens of thousands of loyalists who emigrated, the population continued to grow. The 1780s saw the fastest rate of population growth of any decade in American history. This swelling population resumed its movement westward after being delayed for several years in the late 1770s by intermittent warfare against the British and Indians. By the early 1780s there were more than 20,000 inhabitants in the Kentucky territory; within a decade it had become more populous than most of the colonies had been at the time of the Revolution.

This spectacular growth and movement of people further weakened the traditional forms of social organization. Such a mobile population, one Kentuckian told James Madison in 1792, "must make a very different mass from one which is composed of men born and raised on the same spot. . . . They see none about them to whom or to whose families they have been accustomed to think themselves inferior." And the ideology of republicanism intensified these tendencies. In a republic, declared a writer in 1787 in the *American Museum* (the most important of several new American magazines that were founded in the postwar years), "the idea of equality breathes through the whole and every individual feels ambitious to be in a situation not inferior to his neighbour."

This republican equality became a rallying cry for people in the aspiring middle ranks who were now more openly resentful than before of those who presumed to be their social superiors. In 1783 Revolutionary army officers formed the hereditary Order of the Cincinnati, named after the legendary Roman republican leader Cincinnatus, who retired from war to take up his plow. Although Washington was asked to lead the organization, the Cincinnati aroused bitter hostility. Old patriots such as Samuel Adams thought that the order represented "as rapid a Stride towards an hereditary Military Nobility as was ever made in so short a Time." This sort of ferocious criticism forced the army officers to deny some of their pretensions, and the Cincinnati soon became just another one of the many pressure groups emerging in a country that, as the governor of South Carolina said in 1784, had gone "Society mad."

Some fervent equality-minded citizens attacked distinctions of all kinds, including membership in private social clubs and the wearing of imported finery. Gentlemen in some areas of the North found that the traditional marks of social authority—breeding, education, good manners—were becoming liabilities for political leadership. In this new republican society no one would admit being dependent on anyone else. Ordinary citizens now claimed the right to the titles— "Mr." and "Mrs."—that had once belonged only to the members of the gentry. Foreign visitors were stunned by the unwillingness of American servants to address their masters and mistresses as superiors and by the servants' refusal to admit that they were anything but "help." For many Americans, living in a free country meant never having to tip one's cap to anyone.

This growing egalitarianism did not mean that wealth was distributed more evenly in post-Revolutionary America. On the contrary: the inequality of wealth was greater after the Revolution than before. What it did mean was that the way people related to one another was being transformed. Relationships came to be based on money rather than on social position. Towns, for example, stopped assigning seats in their churches by age and status and began auctioning the pews to the highest bidders. Self-earned wealth gave men the independence that republicans celebrated; it seemed a more appropriate source of achievement than patronage or influence. For many Americans wealth soon became the sole means and—in the new republican society—the proper means of distinguishing one person from another.

By the end of the eighteenth century, the character of all sorts of former paternalistic dependencies was changing. Apprentices were no longer "children"

The Metropolitan Museum of Art, bequest of Susan W. Tyler, 1979

ELIJAH BOARDMAN, BY RALPH EARL, 1789
Boardman was a prosperous textile merchant of Connecticut. Although he was still eager to have himself pictured as a learned gentleman, he was equally eager, unlike wealthy pre-Revolutionary merchants, to show off the fact that he was a successful businessman dealing in bolts of cloth.

in the master's family; rather, they were considered trainees in a business that was now often conducted outside the household. Paternalism in labor relations was now replaced by impersonal cash payments, and journeymen moved more frequently from one master to another.* In many crafts both masters and journeymen saw themselves less as members of a common household and more as employers and employees.

*A journeyman was a craftsman who had ceased to be an apprentice but was not yet willing or able to set himself up as an independent master.

Eastern alarm over the prevalence of primitive and hard-drinking settlers in the new lands of the trans-Appalachian West helps explain the Northwest Ordinance of 1787 and its provision for initial authoritarian governments over the new territories. Until each territory reached a population of 5,000 adult males, it was to be ruled by a governor, secretary, and three judges appointed by Congress, with no elected legislature. This account was written by Dr. Benjamin Rush, a Philadelphia physician who often visited the Scotch-Irish frontier of Pennsylvania.

A Pennsylvania Citizen Describes Frontier Settlement (1786)

THE first settler in the woods is generally a man who has outlived his credit or fortune in the cultivated parts of the State. His time for migrating is in the month of April. His first object is to build a small cabbin of rough logs for himself and family. The floor of this cabbin is of earth, the roof is of split logs—the light is received through the door, and, in some instances, thro' a small window made of greased paper. A coarser building adjoining this cabbin affords a shelter to a cow, and pair of poor horses. The labor of erecting these buildings is succeeded by killing the trees on a few acres of ground near his cabbin; this is done by cutting a circle round the trees, two or three feet from the ground. The ground around these trees is then ploughed and Indian-corn planted in it. The season for planting this grain is about the 20th of May—It grows generally on new ground with but little cultivation, and yields in the month of October following, from 40 to 50 bushels per acre. After the first of September it affords a good deal of nourishment to his family, in its green or unripe state, in the form of what is called roasting ears. His family is fed during the summer by a small quantity of grain which he carries with him, and by fish and game. His cows and horses feed upon wild grass, or the succulent twigs of the woods. For the first year he endures a great deal of distress from hunger—cold—and a variety of accidental causes, but he seldom complains or sinks under them. As he lives in the neighbourhood of Indians, he soon acquires a strong tincture of their manners. His exertions, while they continue, are violent; but they are succeeded by long intervals of rest. His pleasures consist chiefly in fishing and hunting. He loves spirituous liquors, and he eats, drinks and sleeps in dirt and rags in his little cabbin. In his intercourse with the world, he manifests all the arts which characterize the Indians of our country. In this situation he passes

two or three years. In proportion as population increases around him, he becomes uneasy and dissatisfied. Formerly his cattle ranged at large, but now his neighbours call upon him to confine them within fences, to prevent their trespassing upon their fields of grain. Formerly he fed his family with wild animals, but these, which fly from the face of man, now cease to afford him an easy subsistence, and he is compelled to raise domestic animals for the support of his family. Above all, he revolts against the operation of laws. He cannot bear to surrender up a single natural right for all the benefits of government,—and therefore he abandons his little settlement, and seeks a retreat in the woods, where he again submits to all the toils which have been mentioned. There are instances of many men who have broken ground on bare creation, not less than four different times in this way, in different and more advanced parts of the State. It has been remarked, that the flight of this class of people is always increased by the preaching of the gospel. This will not surprise us when we consider how opposite its precepts are to their licentious manner of living. If our first settler was the owner of the spot of land which he began to cultivate, he sells it at a considerable profit to his successor; but if (as is oftener the case) he was a tenant to some rich landholder, he abandons it in debt; however, the small improvements he leaves behind him, generally make it an object of immediate demand.

Library of Congress

PLEDGE OF SOLIDARITY
This pledge of solidarity between worker and employer in 1795 represented the tradition of the past when journeymen and masters of a particular craft worked together in the same shop. Already, the interests of artisan employers and employees were becoming separate and distinct.

Their interests were more distinct and conflicting than they had been before; and they formed new class-conscious organizations to protect these interests. Between 1786 and 1816 at least twelve major strikes by various craftsmen occurred—the first major strikes by employees against employers in American history. Meanwhile, masters resorted more and more to the courts to enforce what had once been seen as a mutual and personal relationship.

The Destruction of Corporate Privilege. Many of the individual and face-to-face relationships that had characterized the older society gradually gave way to larger and more impersonal business associations. Although only a half-dozen business charters had been granted in the entire colonial period, corporate grants multiplied after the Revolution. The republican state legislatures created private banks, insurance companies, and man-

PAUL REVERE, BY JOHN SINGLETON COPLEY
Urban artisans and craftsmen like the silversmith Paul Revere were the most important urban social group that emerged into political consciousness during the Revolutionary era.

ufacturing concerns, and they licensed entrepreneurs to operate bridges, roads, and canals.

The states issued 11 charters of incorporation between 1781 and 1785, 22 between 1786 and 1790, and 114 between 1791 and 1795. Between 1800 and 1817 they granted nearly 1,800 corporate charters; Massachusetts alone had more corporations than existed in all of Europe. If one town had an incorporated bank, it seemed that every town wanted one, and the annually elected popular state legislatures, beset by hosts of new interests, were readily pressured into granting them.

This rapid creation of corporations typified the increasingly fragmented nature of the public interest under popularly elected governments. As far back as the Virginia Company at the time of the original settlements, chartered corporations had been instruments by which the government harnessed private enterprise to carry out such desirable public goals as founding a colony, maintaining a college, or building a bridge. In the new republican society, however, not only were these forms of legal privilege beginning to be regarded with suspicion, but it was no longer clear to whom the states ought to grant legal authority. So mistrusted was legal privilege in the egalitarian atmosphere of the early republic that these corporate monopolies could be justified only if the states made them available virtually to everybody. This practice, of course, destroyed their exclusiveness. If nearly everybody had access to the corporate powers granted by the states, then what had once been a privilege now became a right. And as rights, these corporate charters, even though they were issued by state legislatures, were immune from future legislative tampering. Eventually this view was endorsed by the United States Supreme Court in the *Dartmouth College* case of 1819.

In this famous case the Court decided that the charter of Dartmouth College, although it was originally granted by the New Hampshire legislature and had a public purpose, was a private contract that the legislature could not violate. The states in the post-Revolutionary years therefore not only parceled out their legal authority to individuals and groups in the society, but at the same time lost control of what they dispersed. Unexpected and disturbing as these disintegrating developments were to Jefferson and other devout republicans, they were only the logical consequence of the Revolution's promise to break up politically supported privilege in order to allow free rein to individual talent and energy.

The Betterment of Humanity

The republicanism of the Revolutionary era was not just exhilarating; it was contagious as well. Its optimistic liberalism, its promise of beginning everything anew, could not be confined to governmental reform or to the stimulation of manufacturing and commerce. Inevitably it spilled out into all areas of American life.

Following the Revolution there was a suddenly aroused enthusiasm for putting the humanitarian hopes of the Enlightenment into practice. Drawing upon the thoughts of the great seventeenth-century English philosopher John Locke, eighteenth-century liberals stressed the capacity of human nature to be shaped by experience and external circumstances. Placed in a proper republican environment, people could develop in healthy ways that the rigid Old World society had not permitted. From these enlightened assumptions flowed the reforming liberalism that would affect the Revolutionary era and all subsequent American history as well.

Educational and Social Reform. Since republicanism depended upon a knowledgeable citizenry, the Revolution immediately inspired educational efforts of every conceivable sort. American leaders formed numerous scientific organizations and medical societies and produced many scholarly magazines. Gentleman-scientists and amateur philosophers gave lectures and wrote essays on everything from raising Merino sheep to expelling noxious vapors from wells. They compiled geographical and historical studies of the states. And they prepared elaborate plans for educational structures ranging from elementary schools to a national university.

Although by 1776 there were only nine colleges in America, sixteen more had been founded by 1800. By the early nineteenth century, colleges—mostly religiously inspired and short-lived—were being created by the dozens. Yet in the decades immediately following the Revolution, most of the high hopes of the Revolutionary leaders for the establishment of publicly supported educational systems were not fulfilled, largely because of penny-pinching legislatures and religious jealousies. Even in New England, which had a long tradition of public education, privately supported academies sprang up in the post-Revolutionary years to replace the older town-supported grammar schools. Nevertheless, the republican ideal of the state's fundamental responsibility to educate all its citizens remained alive and was eventually realized in the educational reform movement of the second quarter of the nineteenth century.*

All social institutions were affected by this Revolutionary idealism. Americans grasped at the possibility that they might change their environment, even their natural environment, and thus their character. When the fast-growing cities were struck by epidemics of yellow fever, Americans cleaned the streets and built public waterworks for sanitation. If the heat and cold of America's climate were too extreme, they cleared forests and drained marshes—and congratulated themselves on having moderated the weather. They now regarded virtually every sort of social victim as salvageable. Societies for assisting widows, immigrants, debtors, and other distressed groups were formed in the cities. More charitable organizations were established in the decade and a half following Independence than in the entire colonial period. Jefferson and other Revolutionary leaders drew up plans for liberalizing the harsh penal codes inherited from the colonial period. Pennsylvania led the way in the 1790s by abolishing the death penalty for all crimes except murder. Instead of—as in the past—publicly punishing criminals by such bodily penalties as whipping, mutilation, and execution, that state began the experiment of confining criminals in private cells in penitentiaries that were designed to work on the criminals' minds.

*See chapter 13, pp. 314–17.

Colonial Williamsburg Foundation

"GIRL IN GREEN," c. 1790
Picturing a young girl with a book in her hand was new and unusual in eighteenth-century portraits. It suggested the changes taking place in the role women were expected to play.

The Family and Women. Republicanism even affected the transformation of the family that was taking place in many parts of the Western world at the end of the eighteenth century. In a republican society children could no longer be regarded simply as a means of making money for the family and bringing honor to it. Everyone in the family had to be treated individually and equally. Thus the new Revolutionary state governments repealed aristocratic colonial laws that had confined the inheritance of property to the eldest son (primogeniture) and to special lines of heirs (entail). Family-arranged marriages increasingly gave way to ties that were based on romantic love, and novelists

New York State Historical Association, Cooperstown, New York

ABIGAIL ADAMS, BY MATHER BROWN

Though unschooled, the wife of John Adams was a confident, intelligent and widely read woman. Occasionally she expressed her resentment at the circumscribed role allowed to women in the eighteenth century, playfully urging John in 1776 to "remember the ladies" in his plans for enhancing liberty. But generally she was very willing to sacrifice herself for her husband and to accept her femininity "as a punishment for the transgressions of Eve."

and others writing in the post-Revolutionary years stressed the importance of raising children to become rational and independent citizens.

Republicanism also raised the status of women. It was now said that women as wives and mothers had a special role: that of cultivating in their husbands and children the moral feelings—virtue and social affection—necessary to hold a sprawling and competitive republican society together. Although some American leaders, among them the physician and humanitarian Benjamin Rush, concluded that republicanism required women to be educated along with men, others feared that female education would lead only to vanity and an affected gentility. Besides, asked Timothy Dwight, president of Yale, if women were educated, "Who will make our puddings?"

At the same time that women were being urged to make themselves useful in a distinct domestic sphere, they were becoming more economically important

and independent. Economic developments made it possible for women to earn their own incomes by working in handicrafts at home, hence enabling them to purchase more and more luxury items and conveniences. Once they had gained increased independence by earning money at home, women found it easier to work outside the household, as factory workers and later as teachers. Although the development of a new sphere of domestic usefulness for women may seem a step backward by modern standards, it was at the time liberating, and it intensified the advance, which had begun in the colonial period, over the dependent, inferior position that women had traditionally held.

Antislavery. Perhaps the institution that was most directly and substantially affected by the liberalizing spirit of republicanism was slavery. To be sure, the enslavement of nearly half a million blacks was not ended at the Revolution, and in modern eyes this failure, amid all the high-blown talk of liberty and equality, becomes the one glaring and hypocritical inconsistency of the Revolutionary era. Nevertheless, the Revolution did suddenly and effectively end the social and intellectual climate that had allowed black slavery to exist in the colonies for more than a century without substantial questioning. The colonists had generally taken slavery for granted as part of the natural order of society and as one aspect of the general brutality and cheapness of life in those premodern and prehumanitarian times. Bondage and servitude in many forms had continued to exist in pre-Revolutionary America, and the colonists had felt little need to question or defend slavery any more than other forms of debasement. Now, however, republican citizenship suddenly brought into question all kinds of personal dependency. For the first time Americans were compelled to confront the slavery in their midst. They had to recognize that it was a deviation, a "peculiar institution," and that if they were to retain it they would have to explain and justify it.

Even before the Declaration of Independence, the colonists' struggle against what they called political "slavery" had exposed the contradiction of their toleration of chattel slavery. The initial efforts to end the contradiction were directed at the slave trade. In 1774 the Continental Congress urged the abolition of this trade, and a half-dozen states quickly complied. In 1775 the Quakers of Philadelphia formed the first antislavery society in the world, and soon similar societies were organized elsewhere, even in the South. During the war the Congress and the northern states, as well as Maryland, gave freedom to black slaves who enlisted in their armies. In various ways the Revolution worked to weaken slavery.

Rarely during the Revolution did anyone object to the traditional idea that women belonged in the home. But many now argued that the significance of what republican women did in the home was greatly enhanced. As this Columbia College commencement oration on "female influence" indicates, mothers were to be the teachers of republicanism.

LET us then figure to ourselves the accomplished woman, surrounded by a sprightly band, from the babe that imbibes the nutritive fluid, to the generous youth just ripening into manhood, and the lovely virgin. . . . Let us contemplate the mother distributing the mental nourishment to the fond smiling circle, by means proportionate to their different powers of reception, watching the gradual openings of their minds, and studying their various turns of temper. . . . Religion, fairest offspring of the skies, smiles auspicious on her endeavours; the Genius of Liberty hovers triumphant over the glorious scene. . . . Yes, ye fair, the reformation of a world is in your power. . . . Reflect on the result of your efforts. Contemplate the rising glory of confederated America. Consider that your exertions can best secure, increase, and perpetuate it. The solidity and stability of the liberties of your country rest with you; since Liberty is never sure, 'till Virtue reigns triumphant. . . . Already may we see the lovely daughters of Columbia asserting the importance and the honour of their sex. It rests with you to make this retreat [from the corruptions of Europe] doubly peaceful, doubly happy, by banishing from it those crimes and corruptions, which have never yet failed of giving rise to tyranny, or anarchy. While you thus keep our country virtuous, you maintain its independence.

American Women Are Urged to Practice Republican Virtue (1795)

THE OLD PLANTATION, c. 1774–94
"On Sundays," wrote a British visitor to the Chesapeake in 1774, "the slaves generally meet together and amuse themselves with Dancing to the Banjo. This musical instrument . . . is made of a Gourd something in imitation of a guitar, with only four strings. . . . Their Dancing is most violent exercise, but so irregular and grotesque. I am not able to describe it."

In the North, where slavery of a less harsh sort than existed in the South had been widespread but not deeply rooted in the society or economy, the institution was open to political pressure, and it slowly began to disappear. In the decades following the Revolution, most northern states moved to destroy slavery. By 1830 there were fewer than 3,000 slaves out of a northern black population of more than 125,000. The Revolutionary vision of a society of independent freeholders led the Congress in the 1780s to forbid slavery in the newly organized Northwest Territory between the Appalachians and the Mississippi River. The new federal Constitution of 1787 promised an end to the slave trade after twenty years—that is, in 1808—and many hoped that this action would cripple the institution of slavery.

In the South, however, despite initial criticism by Jefferson, Madison, and other enlightened social thinkers, slavery was too deeply entrenched to be abolished by legislative or judicial action. Southern whites who had been in the forefront of the Revolutionary movement and among the most fervent spokesmen for its liberalism now began to realize for the first time that the South was different from the rest of America. In the 1790s slave insurrections on the French West Indian island of Santo Domingo, together with the tales of horror brought by thousands of fleeing white refugees to American ports, created fears about the future stability of America's slave society. By this time the South had to live with a growing realization that the American claim that people everywhere had a right to seek their freedom meant *all* people, blacks as well as whites. Liberalism in the South was now on the defensive.

SUGGESTED READINGS

For a summary of the history writing covering the eighteenth-century tradition of republicanism, see Robert E. Shalhope, "Toward a Republican Synthesis: The Emergence of an Understanding of Republicanism in American Historiography," *Wm. and Mary Q.*, 3d. ser., 29 (1972). Studies emphasizing the peculiar character of this tradition include Bernard Bailyn, *The Ideological Origins of the American Revolution* (1967); J. G. A. Pocock, *The Machiavellian Moment* (1975); Franco Venturi, *Utopia and Reform in the Enlightenment* (1971); Gerald Stourzh, *Alexander Hamilton and the Idea of Republican Government* (1970); and Gordon S. Wood, *The Creation of the American Republic, 1776–1787* (1969). Garry Wills, *Inventing America: Jefferson's Declaration of Independence* (1978), stresses the importance of Scottish moral sense philosophy and the natural sociableness of people in Jefferson's thought. On the origins of the Americans' conception of the individual's relationship to the state, see James H. Kettner, *The Development of American Citizenship, 1608–1870* (1978). For the influence of antiquity, see Richard Gummere, *The American Colonial Mind and the Classical Tradition* (1963), and Meyer Reinhold, ed., *The Classick Pages* (1975). For the way in which many Europeans viewed the New World in the eighteenth century, see Durand Echeverria, *Mirage in the West* (1957).

The fullest account of state constitution making and politics is Allan Nevins, *The American States During and After the Revolution, 1775–1789* (1924). Elisha P. Douglass, *Rebels and Democrats* (1955), is important in emphasizing the radical and populist impulses in the states. Among the most significant of the state studies are Philip A. Crowl, *Maryland During and After the Revolution* (1943); Richard P. McCormick, *Experiment in Independence: New Jersey in the Critical Period, 1781–1789* (1950); Irwin H. Polishook, *Rhode Island and the Union, 1774–1795* (1969); Robert J. Taylor, *Western Massachusetts in the Revolution* (1954); and Alfred F. Young, *The Democratic Republicans of New York: The Origins, 1763–1797* (1967). Jackson T. Main, *The Sovereign States, 1775–1783* (1973), describes state affairs during the war. J. R. Pole, *Political Representation in England and the Origins of the American Republic* (1966), has some excellent chapters on state politics during the Revolutionary and immediate post-Revolutionary years. Merrill Jensen, in *The Articles of Confederation . . . 1774–1781* (1940) and *The New Nation . . . 1781–1789* (1950), describes the political and social conflicts within the Confederation government and stresses the achievements of the Articles. H. James Henderson, *Party Politics in the Continental Congress* (1974), emphasizes a sectional rather than a social division among the delegates to the national government. The best history of the Congress is Jack N. Rakove, *The Beginnings of National Politics* (1979).

The starting point for appreciating the social changes of the Revolution is the short essay by J. Franklin Jameson, *The American Revolution Considered as a Social Movement* (1926). The last two chapters of James A. Henretta, *The Evolution of American Society, 1700–1815* (1973), summarize the social effects of the war and the Revolution. J. Kirby Martin, *Men in Rebellion: Higher Government Leaders and the Coming of the American Revolution* (1973); Jackson T. Main, *The Upper House in Revolutionary America, 1763–1788* (1967); and Main, "Government by the People: The American Revolution and the Democratization of the Legislatures," *Wm. and Mary Q.*, 3d ser., 28 (1966), document the displacement of elites in politics during the Revolution. Chilton Williamson, *American Suffrage from Property to Democracy, 1760–1860* (1960), describes the expansion of voting rights. A neat account of Concord, Massachusetts, in the Revolution is Robert A. Gross, *The Minutemen and Their World* (1976).

A helpful survey of American social history is Rowland Berthoff, *An Unsettled People* (1971). But it has not replaced the encyclopedic History of American Life Series edited by Arthur M. Schlesinger and Dixon Ryan Fox. The two volumes covering the Revolutionary era are Evarts B. Greene, *The Revolutionary Generation, 1763–1790* (1943), and John Allen Krout and Dixon Ryan Fox, *The Completion of Independence, 1790–1830* (1944). Population developments are summarized by J. Potter, "The Growth of Population in America, 1700–1860," in David Glass and D. E. Eversley, eds., *Population in History* (1965). An important social history that goes well beyond its title is David J. Rothman, *The Discovery of the Asylum: Social Order and Disorder in the New Republic* (1971). *The Press and the American Revolution*, ed. Bernard Bailyn and John B. Hench (1980), is an important collection.

Two surveys of economic life are useful: Stuart Bruchey, *The Roots of American Economic Growth, 1607–1861* (1965), and Douglass C. North, *The Economic Growth of the United States, 1790–1860* (1961). To understand the interrelated nature of the social, economic, and political processes in this period, the student can find no better work than Oscar Handlin and Mary Handlin, *Commonwealth: A Study of the Role of Government in the American Economy: Massachusetts, 1774–1861* (rev. ed., 1969). It is especially important for its analysis of the changing nature of the corporation.

On the commercial effects of the Revolution, see Curtis P. Nettles, *The Emergence of a National Economy, 1775–1815* (1962), and Robert A. East, *Business Enterprise in the American Revolutionary Era* (1938). On the plight of the loyalists, see Wallace Brown, *The Good Americans* (1969), and Mary Beth Norton, *The British-Americans: The Loyalist Exiles in England, 1774–1789* (1972).

On the Enlightenment, see Henry May, *The Enlightenment in America* (1976), and Henry S. Commager, *Empire of Reason* (1977). The standard survey is Russel B. Nye, *The Cultural Life of the New Nation, 1776–1830* (1960). See also Joseph J. Ellis, *After the Revolution: Profiles of Early American Culture* (1979). A particularly important study of education is Carl F. Kaestle, *The Evolution of an Urban School System* (1973). See also Rush Welter, *Popular Education and Democratic Thought in America* (1962), and Douglas Sloan, *The Scottish Enlightenment and the American College Ideal* (1971). On women, see Mary Beth Norton, *Liberty's Daughters: The Revolutionary Experience of American Women, 1750–1800* (1980), Linda Kerber, *Women of the Republic: Intellect and Ideology in Revolutionary America* (1980), and Nancy Cott, *The Bonds of Womanhood* (1977). Benjamin Quarles, *The Negro in the American Revolution* (1961), is the best study of the contribution of blacks to the Revolution. On slavery and opposition to it, see Winthrop Jordan, *White over Black: American Attitudes Toward the Negro, 1550–1812* (1968), and David Brion Davis, *The Problem of Slavery in the Age of Revolution, 1770–1823* (1975). On the abolition of slavery in the North, see Arthur Zilversmit, *The First Emancipation* (1967).

10 The Federalist Age

The American Revolution, like all revolutions, could not fulfill every high hope of its leaders. Within a decade after the Declaration of Independence was signed, many Revolutionary leaders had come to doubt the way America was going. Not only were they eager to lessen the power of the state legislatures, but at the same time they were becoming increasingly aware that the Confederation Congress was too weak to accomplish its tasks, both at home and abroad. In the mid-1780s frustration with piecemeal changes in the Articles of Confederation came together with mounting concern over examples of democratic despotism and other political and social conditions in the states to produce a powerful momentum for drastic constitutional change. The result was the federal Constitution of 1787.

This new national Constitution, which replaced the Articles of Confederation, limited the authority of the states and created an unprecedented concentration of power at the federal level. Many Americans could only conclude that the new Constitution represented as radical a change as the Revolution itself. At last, in the eyes of some, the inauguration of a new federal government promised the harmony and stability that would allow America to become a great and glorious nation.

The Critical Period

For some Americans the 1780s had become a very critical period, a point at which the Revolution and the entire experiment in republicanism seemed to be in danger. The very success of the Revolution in opening up opportunities for economic prosperity to new and lower levels of the population helped to create a sense of crisis among certain members of the Revolutionary elite.

Too many ordinary people, some felt, were distorting republican equality, defying legitimate authority, and blurring those natural distinctions that all gentlemen, even republican gentlemen, thought essential for social order. Everywhere, even among the sturdy independent yeoman-farmers—Jefferson's "chosen people of God"—private interests, selfishness, and moneymaking seemed to be destroying social affection and public spirit—the very qualities of virtue that were required of republicans. The expressions of democratic despotism by the state legislatures seemed to be evidence that the people were too self-interested to be republicans. Some feared, therefore, that America was doomed to share the fate that had befallen the ancient republics, Britain, and other corrupt nations. Americans, Governor William Livingston of New Jersey concluded in 1787, "do not exhibit the virtue that is necessary to support a republican government." Many thought that this unrepublican character of the people was most clearly revealed in the behavior of the greatly strengthened state legislatures.

The Democratization of the State Legislatures. The radical changes in representation that accompanied the Revolution had democratized the state assemblies by increasing the number of members and by altering their social character. Men of more humble and more rural origins—and less educated than those who had sat in the colonial legislatures—now became representatives. In New Hampshire, for example, in 1765 the colonial house of representatives had contained only thirty-four members, almost all well-to-do gentlemen from the coastal region around Portsmouth. By 1786 the state's house of representatives had increased to eighty-eight members. Most of these were ordinary farmers or men of moderate wealth, and many were from the western areas of the state. In other states the change was less dramatic but no less important. It was reflected in the shifts (or attempted shifts) of many of the state capitals from their former colonial locations on the eastern coastline to new sites in the interior—from Portsmouth to Concord in New Hampshire, from New York City to Albany in New York, from Wil-

liamsburg to Richmond in Virginia, from New Bern to Raleigh in North Carolina, from Charleston to Columbia in South Carolina, and from Savannah to Augusta in Georgia.

Everywhere, electioneering and the open competition for office increased, along with demands for greater public access to governmental activities. The number of contested elections and the turnover of legislative seats multiplied. Assembly proceedings were opened to the public, and a growing number of newspapers (which now included dailies) began to report legislative debates. Self-appointed leaders, speaking for newly aroused groups and localities, took advantage of the enlarged suffrage and the annual elections of the legislatures (a radical innovation in most states) to seek membership in the assemblies. New petty entrepreneurs like Abraham Yates, a part-time lawyer and shoemaker of Albany, and William Findley, a Scotch-Irish ex-weaver of western Pennsylvania, bypassed the traditional hierarchy and vaulted into political leadership in the states.

Local Factionalism. Under these circumstances a number of the state legislatures could scarcely fulfill what many Revolutionaries in 1776 had assumed was their republican responsibility to promote the general good. In every state decisions had to be made about what to do with the loyalists and their confiscated property, about the distribution of taxes among the citizens, and about the economy. Yet with the general political instability, the common welfare in the various states was increasingly difficult to define. By the 1780s James Madison concluded that "a spirit of *locality*" in the state legislatures was destroying "the aggregate interests of the community." This localist spirit, he thought, was a consequence of having small districts and towns elect members of the state legislatures. Each representative, said Ezra Stiles, president of Yale College, was concerned only with the special interests of his electors. Whenever a bill was read in the legislature, "every one instantly thinks how it will affect his constituents."

Narrow-minded politics of this kind was not new to America. But the multiplication of economic and social interests in the post-Revolutionary years, along with the greater sensitivity of the enlarged popular assemblies to the conflicting demands of these interests, now dramatically increased its intensity and importance. Farmers in debt urged low taxes, the suspension of court actions to recover debts, and the printing of paper money. Merchants and creditors called for high taxes on land, the protection of private contracts, and the encouragement of foreign trade. Artisans pleaded for the regulation of the prices of agricultural products, the abolition of mercantile mo-

nopolies, and tariff protection against imported manufactured goods. And entrepreneurs everywhere petitioned for legal privileges and corporate grants.

All this political scrambling among contending interests made lawmaking in the states seem chaotic. Laws, as the Vermont Council of Censors said in 1786 in a common complaint, were "altered—realtered—made better—made worse; and kept in such a fluctuating position, that persons in civil commission scarce know what is law." As James Madison pointed out, more laws were enacted by the states in the decade following Independence than in the entire colonial period. Many of them were simply private acts for individuals or resolutions that satisfied minor grievances. But every effort by the legislatures to respond to the excited pleas and pressures of all the various groups alienated as many people as it satisfied and brought lawmaking itself into contempt.

By the mid-1780s many American leaders had come to believe that the state legislatures, not the governors, were the political authority to be most feared. Some of the legislatures were violating the individual rights of property owners through their excessive printing of paper money and their various acts on behalf of debtors. Furthermore, in all the states the assemblies pushed beyond the generous grants of legislative authority of the 1776 Revolutionary constitutions and were absorbing numerous executive and judicial duties. It began to seem that the legislative power of the people was no more trustworthy than the detested royal power had been. Legislators were supposedly the representatives of the people who annually elected them. But "173 despots would surely be as oppressive as one," wrote Jefferson in 1785 in his *Notes on Virginia*. "An *elective despotism* was not the government we fought for."

Revision of the State Constitutions. These growing fears of tyrannical legislatures forced many leaders to have second thoughts about their popularly elected assemblies. Indeed, the ink was scarcely dry on the Revolutionary state constitutions before some were suggesting that they needed to be revised. Beginning with the New York constitution in 1777 and proceeding through the constitutions of Massachusetts in 1780 and New Hampshire in 1784, constitution makers now sought a very different distribution of powers of government from that made in 1776.

Instead of placing all power in the legislatures, particularly in the lower houses, and draining all power from the governors, as the early state constitutions had done, these later constitutions strengthened the executives, senates, and judiciaries. The Massachusetts constitution of 1780 especially seemed to many to have recaptured some of the best characteristics of the English constitutional balance, which had been forgotten during the popular enthusiasm of 1776. The new Massachusetts governor, with a fixed salary and elected directly by the people, now assumed more of the independence and some of the powers of the old royal governors, including those of appointing to offices and vetoing legislation.

With the Massachusetts constitution as a model, reformers from other states worked to revise their constitutions. The popular legislatures were reduced in size, and their authority was curbed. Senates, or upper houses, were instituted where they did not exist, as in Pennsylvania, Georgia, and Vermont. In states where senates did exist, they were made more stable by lengthening their terms and by requiring higher property qualifications for their members. The governors were freed of their dependence on the legislatures, and they were given a clearer responsibility for government. And judges became independent guardians of the constitutions. By 1790 Pennsylvania, South Carolina, and Georgia had reformed their constitutions along these more conservative lines. New Hampshire, Delaware, and Vermont soon followed in the early 1790s.

At the same time that political leaders were trying to restrengthen the authority of governors, senators, and judges, they were also trying to limit the powers of the legislatures by appealing to the "fundamental law" that was presumably embodied in these written documents. Since many of the constitutions had been created by simple legislative act, it was not easy to draw a line between "fundamental" and ordinary law. At first several of the states had grappled with various devices to ensure that their constitutions remained "fundamental" law. Some simply declared their constitutions to be "fundamental"; others required a special majority or successive acts of the legislature for amending the constitution. But none of these measures proved effective against repeated legislative encroachments.

Out of these kinds of pressures, both logical and political, Americans gradually moved toward institutionalizing the belief that if the constitution was to be truly immune from legislative tampering, it would have to be created, as Jefferson said in 1783, "by a power superior to that of the ordinary legislature." For a solution Americans fell back on the institution of the convention. In 1775–76 the convention had been merely an ad hoc legislative assembly, lacking legal sanction but made necessary by the crown's refusal to call together the regular representatives of the people. Now, however, the convention became a special alternative institution representing the people and having exclusive authority to write or amend a constitution. When Massachusetts and New Hampshire came to write new constitutions in the late 1770s and early 1780s, the proper pattern of constitution making and constitution altering had become clear. Constitutions were formed by specially elected conventions and then submitted to the people for ratification.

With the idea growing that a constitution was fundamental law, immune from legislative changes, some state judges during the 1780s began cautiously moving in isolated cases to impose restraints on what the assemblies were enacting as law. In effect they said to the legislatures, as George Wythe, judge of the Virginia supreme court, did in 1782, "Here is the limit of your authority; and hither shall you go, but no further." These were the hesitant beginnings of what would come to be called judicial review.* But as yet many leaders were unwilling to allow appointed judges to set aside laws that had been made by the people represented in democratically elected legislatures. It appeared obviously unrepublican.

As vigorously as all these state reforms were tried in the 1780s, however, to many they did not seem sufficient. By the mid-1780s some reformers were thinking of shifting the arena of constitutional change from the states to the nation and were considering a modification of the structure of the central government as the best and perhaps only answer to America's political and social problems.

Domestic Weakness of the Confederation. Even before the Articles of Confederation were ratified in 1781, the experiences of war had exposed the weakness of the Congress and had encouraged some Americans to think about making changes in the central government. By 1780 the war was dragging on longer than anyone had expected, and the skyrocketing inflation of the paper money that was being used to finance it was unsettling commerce and business. Congressional delegates were barred from serving more than three years in any six-year period, and leadership in the Confederation was unstable and confused. The states were ignoring congressional resolutions and were refusing to supply their allotted contributions to the central government. The Congress stopped paying interest on the public debt. The Continental army was smoldering with resentment at the lack of pay and was falling apart through desertions and even outbreaks of mutiny. All these circumstances were forcing merchant and creditor interests, especially those that were centered in the mid-Atlantic states, to seek to add to the powers of the Congress. They tried to strengthen the Congress by broadly interpreting the Articles, by directly amending the Articles (which required the consent of all the states), and even by threatening military force.

*For judicial review, see chapter 11, pp. 267–70.

ROBERT MORRIS

Morris, a wealthy Philadelphia merchant, has been called "the financier of the Revolution." Land speculation in the 1790s ruined him, and he ended his career in debtor's prison.

A shift in congressional leadership in the early 1780s demonstrated the increasing influence of these concerned groups. Older popular radicals such as Richard Henry Lee and Arthur Lee of Virginia and Samuel Adams of Massachusetts were replaced by such younger men as James Madison of Virginia and Alexander Hamilton of New York. These new leaders were more interested in authority and stability than in popular liberty. Disillusioned by the Confederation's ineffectiveness, these nationalists in the Congress set about reversing the localist and power-weakening emphasis of the Revolution. They strengthened the regular army at the expense of the militia and promised pensions to the Continental army officers. They reorganized the departments of war, foreign affairs, and finance in the Congress and replaced the committees that had been running them with individuals.

The key man in the nationalists' program was Robert Morris, a wealthy Philadelphia merchant who was made superintendent of finance and virtual head of the Confederation in 1781. Morris undertook to stabilize the economy and to involve financial and commercial groups with the central government. He persuaded the Congress to recommend to the states that paper-money laws be repealed and to require that the states' contributions to the general expenses be paid in specie—gold or silver. And he sought to establish a bank and to make the federal government's bonds more secure for investors.

Carrying out this nationalist program depended on amending the Articles so as to grant the Confederation the power to levy a 5 percent duty on imports. Once the Congress had adequate revenues independent of the states, the Confederation could pay its debts and would become more attractive to prospective buyers of its bonds. Although Morris was able to get the Congress to charter the Bank of North America, the rest of the nationalists' economic proposals narrowly failed. Not only did the states ultimately refuse to approve the tax amendment, but many were slow in supplying money that had been requested of them by the Congress. Nor was the Congress able to get even a restricted authority to regulate commerce.

After the victory at Yorktown in October 1781 and the opening of peace negotiations with Great Britain, the states lost interest in the Congress. Some individuals became desperate. The prospect of the Congress's demobilizing the army without fulfilling its promises of back pay and pensions created a crisis that brought the United States as close to a military coup d'état as it has ever been. In March 1783 the officers of Washington's army, encamped at Newburgh, New York, on the Hudson River, issued an address to the Congress concerning their pay. They actually considered some sort of military action against the Confederation. Only when Washington personally intervened and refused to support a movement that was designed, he said, "to open the floodgates of civil discord, and deluge our rising empire in blood" was the crisis averted.

News of the peace treaty shattered much of the unionist sentiment that had existed during the war. By December 1783 the Congress, in Jefferson's opinion, had lost most of its usefulness. "The constant session of Congress," he said, "can not be necessary in time of peace." After clearing up the most urgent business, the delegates should "separate and return to our respective states, leaving only a Committee of the states," and thus "destroy the strange idea of their being a permanent body, which has unaccountably taken possession of the heads of their constituents."

Congressional power, which had been substantial during the war years, now began to disintegrate. The delegates increasingly complained of how difficult it was even to gather a quorum. The Congress could not even agree on a permanent home for itself: it wandered from Philadelphia to Princeton, New Jersey; to

Annapolis, Maryland; to Trenton, New Jersey; and finally to New York City. The states reasserted their authority and began taking over the payment of the federal debt that many had earlier hoped to make the cement of union. By 1786 nearly one-third of the Confederation's securities had been converted into state bonds, thus creating a vested interest among public creditors in the sovereignty of the individual states. Under these circumstances the influence of those, in Hamilton's term, "who think continentally" rapidly declined, and the chances of amending the Confederation piecemeal declined with them. The only hope of reform now seemed to lie in some sort of convention of all the states.

International Weakness of the Confederation.

In Europe the reputation of the United States dwindled as rapidly as did its credit. The Dutch and French would lend money only at extraordinary rates of interest. Since American ships now lacked the protection of the British flag, many of them were seized by corsairs from the Muslim states of North Africa, and their crews were sold as slaves. The Congress had no money to pay the necessary tribute and ransoms to these Barbary pirates.

It was even difficult for the new republican confederacy to maintain its territorial integrity in the late-eighteenth-century world of hostile empires. Britain refused to send a diplomatic minister to the United States and ignored its treaty obligations to evacuate its military posts in the Northwest, claiming that the United States had not honored its own commitments. The treaty of peace had specified that the Confederation would recommend to the states that loyalist property confiscated during the Revolution be restored, and that neither side would make laws obstructing the recovery of prewar debts. When the states flouted these treaty obligations, the impotent Confederation could do nothing.

Britain was known to be plotting with the Indians and encouraging separatist movements in the Northwest and in the Vermont borderlands, and Spain was doing the same in the Southwest. Spain in fact refused to recognize American claims in the territory between the Ohio River and Florida. In 1784, in an effort to influence American settlers moving into Kentucky and Tennessee, Spain closed the Mississippi River to American trade. Many Westerners were ready to deal with any government that could ensure access to the sea for their agricultural produce. As Washington noted in 1784, they were "on a pivot. The touch of a feather would turn them any way."

In 1785–86, John Jay, a New Yorker and the secretary of foreign affairs, negotiated a treaty with the Spanish minister to the United States, Diego de Gardoqui. By the terms of this agreement, Spain was opened to American trade in return for America's renunciation of its right to navigate the Mississippi for several decades. Out of fear of being denied an outlet to the sea in the West, the southern states prevented the necessary nine-state majority in the Congress from agreeing to the treaty. But the willingness of a majority of seven states to sacrifice western interests for the sake of northern merchants aroused long-existing sectional jealousies and threatened to shatter the Union.

Toward the Philadelphia Convention.

The Confederation's inability to regulate commerce finally brought about reform of the Articles. Jefferson, Madison, and other leaders with agrarian interests feared that if American farmers were prohibited from selling their surplus crops freely in Europe, not only would the industrious character of the farmers be undermined, but the United States would be unable to pay for manufactured goods imported from Europe, and would therefore be compelled to begin large-scale manufacturing for itself. These developments in turn would eventually destroy the farmer-citizenry on which republicanism was based and would create in America the same kind of corrupt, rank-conscious, and dependent society that existed in Europe.

Yet the mercantilist empires of the major European nations remained generally closed to the new republic in the 1780s. John Adams in Britain and Jefferson in France made strong diplomatic efforts to develop new international commercial relationships based on the free exchange of goods, but these efforts failed. The French were unwilling to take as much American produce as had been expected, and Britain effectively closed its markets to competitive American goods while recapturing American consumer markets for its own goods. The Confederation lacked the authority to retaliate with its own trade regulations, and several attempts to grant the Congress a restricted power over commerce were lost amid state and sectional jealousies. The Confederation Congress watched helplessly as the separate states attempted to pass conflicting navigation acts of their own. By the mid-1780s, for example, Connecticut was laying heavier duties on goods from Massachusetts than on those from Great Britain.

By 1786 these accumulated pressures made some sort of revision of the Articles inevitable. Virginia's desire for trade regulation led to a convention of several states at Annapolis, Maryland, in September 1786. Those who attended this meeting quickly realized that commerce could not be considered apart from other problems and called for a larger convention in Philadelphia the following year. After several states agreed to send delegates to Philadel-

THE OLD STATE HOUSE OF PENNSYLVANIA (UNTIL 1799), LATER CALLED INDEPENDENCE HALL
Both the Second Continental Congress and the federal Convention of 1787 met here. The tower was added in the middle of the eighteenth century to house the Liberty Bell.

By permission of the Houghton Library, Harvard University

phia, the Confederation Congress belatedly recognized the approaching convention and in February 1787 authorized it to revise and amend the Articles of Confederation.

Although by 1787 nearly all of America's political leaders agreed that some reform of the Articles was necessary, few expected what the Philadelphia Convention eventually created—a new Constitution that utterly transformed the structure of the central government and promised a radical weakening of the power of the states. The extraordinarily powerful national government that emerged from Philadelphia had far more than the additional congressional powers that were required to solve the United States' difficulties in credit, commerce, and foreign affairs. Given the Revolutionaries' loyalty to their states and their deep-rooted fears of centralized governmental authority, the formation of the new Constitution was a truly remarkable achievement. It cannot be explained simply by the obvious weaknesses of the Articles of Confederation.

In the end it was the problems within the separate states during the 1780s that made possible the constitutional reform of the central government. The confusing and unjust laws coming out of the state legislatures, Madison informed Jefferson in 1787, had become "so frequent and so flagrant as to alarm the most stedfast friends of Republicanism." These popular abuses by state legislatures, said Madison, "contributed more to that uneasiness which produced the Convention, and prepared the public mind for a general reform, than those which accrued to our national character and interest from the inadequacy of the Confederation to its immediate objects."

In 1786 a rebellion of nearly 2,000 debtor farmers who were threatened with foreclosure of their mortgaged property broke out in western Massachusetts. This rebellion, led by a former militia captain, Daniel Shays, confirmed many of these anxieties about state politics. The insurrection, which temporarily closed the courts and threatened a federal arsenal, occurred in the very state that was considered to have the best-

**DANIEL SHAYS AND
JACOBB SHATTUCKS**
Shays and Shattucks, former militia
officers, were leaders of the uprising
of aggrieved western Massachusetts
farmers in 1786. The farmers,
calling themselves "Regulators,"
protested the shortage of money and
the foreclosures of mortgages and
imprisonments for debt. Shays's
Rebellion had a powerful effect on
conservative leaders and helped
compel reform of the national
government.

balanced constitution. Although Shays's rebels were
defeated by militia troops, his sympathizers were victorious at the polls early in 1787. The newly chosen
state representatives soon enacted debtor relief legislation that added to the growing fears of legislative
tyranny.

Thus by 1786–87 the reconstruction of the central
government was being sought as a means of correcting
not only the weaknesses of the Articles, but also the
democratic despotism and the internal political
abuses of the states. A new central government, some
believed, could save both the Congress from the states
and the states from themselves. And new groups
joined those already working to invigorate the
national government. Urban artisans hoped that a
stronger national government would prevent competition from British imports. Southerners, particularly in Virginia, wanted to gain representation in the
national government proportional to their growing
population. And most important, members of the gentry up and down the continent momentarily submerged their sectional and economic differences in the
face of what seemed a threat to individual liberty from
the tyranny of legislative majorities within the states.
Creating a new central government was no longer simply a matter of cementing the Union, or of standing up
strong in foreign affairs, or of satisfying the demands
of particular creditor, merchant, and army interests.
It was now a matter, as Madison declared, that would
"decide forever the fate of republican government."

The Federal Constitution

The meeting of the Philadelphia Convention that
drafted the federal Constitution in the summer of 1787
was very much a revolutionary action. Yet such were
the circumstances and climate of opinion of the post-
Revolutionary years in America that the sudden calling of a constitutional convention and the creation of
an entirely new and different sort of federal republican government in 1787 seemed remarkably natural
and legitimate.

Fifty-five delegates representing twelve states attended the Philadelphia Convention. (Rhode Island,
which feared any national regulation of its trade,
refused to have anything to do with efforts to revise
the Articles.) Although many of the delegates were
young men—their average age was forty-two—most
were well educated and experienced members of
America's political elite. Thirty-nine had served in the
Congress at one time or another, eight had worked in
the state constitutional conventions, seven had been
state governors, and thirty-four were lawyers. One-
third were veterans of the Continental army, that
"great dissolvent of state loyalties," as Washington
once called it. Nearly all were gentlemen, "natural
aristocrats," who took their political superiority for
granted as an inevitable consequence of their social
and economic position. Washington was made president of the Convention. But some of the outstanding
figures of the Revolution were not present: Samuel

JAMES MADISON (1751–1836)
Madison was the greatest political thinker of the Revolutionary era and perhaps of all American history. His was the most critical and undogmatic mind of the Revolutionary leaders. More than anyone else, he formulated the theory that underlaid the new expanded republic of 1787.

Adams was ill; Thomas Jefferson and John Adams were serving as ministers abroad; and Richard Henry Lee and Patrick Henry, although selected by the Virginia legislature, refused to attend the Convention. "I smelt a rat," said Henry. The most influential delegations were those of Pennsylvania and Virginia, which included Gouverneur Morris and James Wilson of Pennsylvania, and Edmund Randolph, George Mason, and James Madison of Virginia.

The Virginia Plan. The Virginia delegation took the lead and presented the Convention with its first working proposal. This, the Virginia Plan, was largely the effort of the thirty-seven-year-old Madison, who more than any other person deserves the title "father of the Constitution." He was a short, shy, and soft-spoken man who habitually dressed in black. Madison had not trained for a profession, but he was widely read, possessed a sharp and questioning mind, and had devoted his life to public service. He understood clearly the historical significance of the meeting of the Convention; and it is because he decided to make a detailed private

record of the Convention debates that we know so much of what was said that summer in Philadelphia.

Madison's initial proposals for reform were truly radical. As he pointed out, they were not mere expedients or simple revisions of the Articles; they promised "systematic change" of government. Madison wanted to create a general government that would be not a confederation of independent republics but a national republic in its own right. It would exercise direct power over individuals and be organized as most of the state governments were organized, with a single executive, a bicameral legislature, and a separate judiciary.

This national republic would be superimposed on the states. The states, in John Jay's words, would now stand in relation to the central government "in the same light in which counties stand to the state of which they are parts, viz., merely as districts to facilitate the purposes of domestic order of good government." Thus the radical Virginia Plan provided for a two-house national legislature with the authority to legislate "in all cases to which the states are incompetent" and to veto, or negative, "all laws passed by the several states, contravening in the opinion of the national legislature, the articles of union." If the national government had the power to veto all state laws, Madison believed, it could then play the same role the English crown had been supposed to play in the British Empire—that of a "disinterested umpire" over clashing interests.

The New Jersey Plan. For many in the Philadelphia Convention, however, this Virginia Plan was much too extreme. Most delegates were prepared to grant substantial power to the federal government, including the right to tax, regulate commerce, and execute federal laws. But many refused to allow such a weakening of state authority as the Virginia Plan proposed. Opponents of the nationalists, led by the delegates from New Jersey, Connecticut, New York, and Delaware, countered with their own proposal, the New Jersey Plan (so-called because it was introduced by William Paterson of New Jersey). This plan essentially amended the Articles of Confederation by increasing the powers of the Congress, but at the same time it maintained the basic sovereignty of the states. With two such opposite proposals before it, the Convention approached a crisis in the middle of June 1787.

Provisions of the Constitution. During the debate that followed, the nationalists, led by Madison and Wilson, were able to retain the basic features of the Virginia Plan. Although the Convention refused to grant the national legislature a blanket authority "to legislate in all cases to which the separate States are incompe-

"Pat Lyon at the Forge" by John Neagle.

This new kind of republican portrait reveals just how far behind early-nineteenth-century America had left its patrician colonial hierarchy. Although Lyon by 1826 was a rich and prominent businessman, he wanted his portrait, as he said, to depict his humble origins as a blacksmith in Philadelphia, "at work at my anvil, with my sleeves rolled up and a leather apron on." The artist, John Neagle (1796–1865), was himself something of a self-made man. His father came from County Cork and his mother was a New Jersey yeoman's daughter. He managed, however, to marry the stepdaughter of the well-known and successful portrait painter, Thomas Sully (1783–1872).

As different as the new bourgeois leaders of the early republic were from the eighteenth-century gentry, they were much the same in wanting from art mainly pictures of themselves. By the 1820s many American intellectuals were still eagerly awaiting the long-predicted westward transit of the arts across the Atlantic.

"The Old House of Representatives" by Samuel F. B. Morse.

The symbol making of American neoclassical art reached its height with the various depictions of George Washington, who came to represent all the great republican virtues Americans ought to value. This oil painting on glass shows the great hero, no longer a man but a symbol, being borne to heaven in a dramatic apotheosis. Such pictures were supposed to fill viewers with awe and inspiration and make them conscious of their national identity.

The concept of art as high-minded moral instruction lingered into the new democratic age of the 1820s. Like earlier American artists, Samuel F. B. Morse (1791–1872) sought to escape from the vulgarity of painting portraits. Instead he wanted to "elevate and refine public feelings by turning the thoughts of his countrymen from sensuality and luxury to intellectual pleasures" by painting great historical subjects, like his *Old House of Representatives* (1821). The canvas measured nearly seven feet by twelve feet and cost Morse a year of labor. Although the painting was photographic in its meticulous detail, in its emphasis on classical sobriety, dignity, and decorum, it hopelessly idealized the brawling and rowdy House of Representatives that had emerged by the 1820s. Morse put the painting on tour, but the public would not pay to see its elected officials, and Congress would not buy it. In disillusionment Morse eventually turned to photography and the invention of the telegraph and the code that bears his name.

◀ Oil painting on glass, made in China.

Plan of Washington, D.C., 1791, by Pierre Charles L'Enfant *(Library of Congress)*; Great Seal of the United States of America, front and back; House of Representatives colonnade and design for female figure for the Capitol, drawn by Benjamin Latrobe, 1815 *(Library of Congress)*; Capitol building, east and west wings, drawn by W. Thornton, 1794 *(Library of Congress)*.

Excited by the new ideas about art, the Revolutionaries created a sudden outpouring of iconographic works. Statues and monuments were planned; plays, prints, and pageants were employed in support of the Revolution and the new republic. The Revolutionaries continually interrupted their constitution making and military campaigning to design all sorts of emblems and commemorative medals and to sit for long hours having their portraits painted for history's sake.

When compared with the later extravagant French Revolutionary achievement, under the direction of Jacques Louis David, of putting the arts into the service of republicanism, the American artistic efforts seem pale and feeble. But given America's provincialism and its lack of artists and artistic experience, the Revolutionaries' aims and accomplishments are astonishing. That a monumental city like Washington, D.C., with its sweeping scale, its huge boulevards, and its magnificent parks, could have been conceived and begun in the midst of a swampy wilderness is an extraordinary tribute to the neoclassical aspirations of the Revolutionary leaders.

Yet the classical spirit that inspired Washington, D.C.—the ancient place names, the Roman and Greek buildings, and the many emblems and devices—was being lost even as these things were being created. Soon few Americans would know the meaning behind the Latin mottoes and the Masonic pyramid and eye appearing on the Great Seal. Indeed, many of the cultural artifacts that Americans inherited from the Revolutionary and early republican eras remain only as awkward reminders of the brevity of America's classical age.

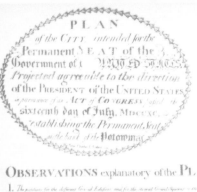

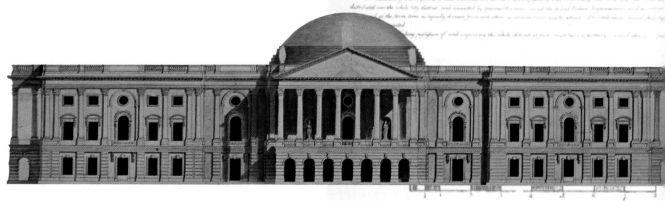

View of Richmond from Bushrod Washington's Island in the James River by Benjamin Henry Latrobe.

inspirational forms be used. He cursed the Georgian buildings of colonial Virginia as barbaric, and aimed, through a new symbolic architecture, "to improve the taste of my countrymen, to increase their reputation, to reconcile to them the respect of the world and procure them its praise." He wanted Americans to emulate a classical art that "has pleased universally for nearly 2000 years," even at the expense of functional requirements. In the 1780s Jefferson, writing from France, badgered his Virginia colleagues into erecting as the new state capitol a magnificent copy of the Maison Carrée, a Roman temple at Nîmes from the first century A.D., and thus almost singlehandedly introduced the classical style to American public buildings. In fact there was nothing like this use of a Roman temple anywhere in the world. No matter that Richmond was still a backwoods town with mud-lined streets. No matter that a model of a Roman temple was hard to heat and acoustically impossible. For Americans other considerations counted more. By 1820 Roman and Greek revival architecture had become the official style of public buildings in the new nation.

Detail of Virginia State Capitol.

"Battle of Bunker's Hill," by John Trumbull.

amusing a few rich aristocratic patrons; they would become philosophers instructing a whole society eager to uplift its taste and cultivate its manners.

John Singleton Copley (1738–1815) of Boston had longed to express these new ideas in his art, but the provinciality of colonial society had compelled him to devote his immense talent to painting portraits of the colonial gentry. In 1774, in frustration, he sailed for England. He left a moment too soon, for the Revolution changed everything.

John Trumbull (1756–1843), a member of a distinguished Connecticut family, quickly grasped that the Revolution was as much a cultural as a political event. He knew only too well that being an artist, "as it is generally practiced, is frivolous, little useful to society, and unworthy of a man who has talents for more serious pursuits. But, to preserve and diffuse the memory of the noblest series of actions which have ever presented themselves in the history of man"—that was a task that "gave dignity to the profession" and justified any gentleman's devotion.

Trumbull's use of the grand style and his attempt at an ennobling effect from history painting can be seen vividly in his *Battle of Bunker's Hill* (1786). Trumbull thought that he would make a fortune from the sale of engravings of his paintings of the Revolution, but, after an initial encouraging reception, subscriptions soon ceased. Early-nineteenth-century Americans were not much interested in history paintings, and Trumbull even had trouble getting Congress to pay for the huge commemorative scenes of the Revolution that he painted in the rotunda of the Capitol.

No one responded to neoclassical ideas about art with more enthusiasm than did Thomas Jefferson. Since architecture to Jefferson was "an art which shows so much," it was particularly important to the new republican nation that appropriate

"The Gore Children," c. 1753 by John Singleton Copley.

The Rising Glory of America

ate-eighteenth-century Americans of the gentry were confident that the United States would eventually exceed Europe in artistic grandeur and taste. Yet the fine arts had so long been associated with European court life and social decadence that many Americans thought them incompatible with republican simplicity and virtue. Hence any art that Americans developed would have to be a peculiarly republican one.

Americans found the sources for such a republican art in a revolutionary artistic movement that swept through Europe in the latter half of the eighteenth century. This movement, later called neoclassicism, sought to emulate the severe and rational standards of classical antiquity and to infuse art with new moral seriousness and idealistic virtue. Drawing its subjects from history, art would become an instrument for public reform and refinement. Artists would no longer be craftsmen

tent," it granted the Congress (in Article I, Section 8, of the Constitution) a list of enumerated powers, including the powers to tax, to borrow and coin money, and to regulate commerce. Instead of giving the national legislature the right to veto harmful state laws, as Madison wanted, the Convention forbade the states to exercise certain sovereign powers whose abuse had helped to create the crisis of the 1780s. In Article I, Section 10, of the final Constitution, the states were barred from carrying on foreign relations, levying tariffs, coining money, issuing bills of credit, passing *ex post facto* laws (which punished actions that were not illegal when they were committed), and doing anything to relieve debtors of the obligations of their contracts.*

In contrast to the Congress, which was given extensive fiscal powers, the state governments were rendered nearly economically impotent. Not only did the new federal Constitution prohibit the states from imposing customs duties—the eighteenth century's most common and efficient form of taxation—but it denied the states the authority to issue paper money, and thus succeeded in doing what the British government's various currency acts had earlier tried to do.

The Convention decided on a single strong executive. The president was to stand alone, unencumbered by an executive council except one of his own choosing—his group of cabinet officers. With command over the armed forces, with the authority to direct diplomatic relations, with power over appointments to the executive and judicial branches, and with a four-year term of office and perpetual eligibility for reelection, the president was a high official who, as Patrick Henry later charged, could "easily become a king."

To ensure the president's independence, he was not to be elected by the legislature, as the Virginia Plan had proposed. Since the framers of the Constitution believed that few presidential candidates in the future would enjoy wide popular recognition throughout the country, they provided for local elections of "electors," equal in number to the representatives and senators from each state. These electors would cast ballots for the president. If no candidate received a majority—which in the absence of political parties and organized electioneering was normally expected—the final selection from the five candidates with the most votes would be made by the House of Representatives, with each state delegation having one vote.

The Virginia Plan's suggestion of a separate national judiciary to hold office "during good behavior" was accepted without dispute. The structure of the

*For the Constitution, see Appendix.

ROGER SHERMAN, BY RALPH EARL
Well before the Revolution, Roger Sherman, who had begun as a cobbler, had become a lawyer, merchant, and substantial Connecticut official. He is best known for his introduction in the Philadelphia Convention of the "compromise" granting each state two senators.

national judiciary was left to the Congress to devise. However, the right of this judiciary to nullify acts of the Congress or of the state legislatures was as yet by no means clearly established.

The nationalists in the Convention reluctantly gave way on several crucial issues, particularly on the national legislature's authority to veto state legislation. But they fought longest and hardest to hold on to the principle of proportional representation in both houses of the legislature, and this dispute almost stalemated the Convention. It was decided at last that both taxation and representation, at least in the House of Representatives, would be based not on the states as such or on landed wealth, but on population, with the slaves each counting as three-fifths of a person. The nationalists like Madison and Wilson, however, wanted representation in the Senate also to rest on population. Any suggestion that the separate sovereignty of the states might be represented smacked too much of the Articles of Confederation. Hence the nationalists came to regard as a defeat the eventual adoption of the "Connecticut Compromise," by which each state was given two senators in the upper house of the legislature.

Thus Madison and Wilson lost the battles over the congressional veto of state laws and proportional representation in both houses. But the Federalists (as those who supported the Constitution came to call themselves) had won the war even before the Convention adjourned. Once the New Jersey Plan, which preserved the essentials of the Articles of Confederation, was rejected in favor of the Virginia Plan, the opponents of the Constitution, or Antifederalists, found themselves forced, as Richard Henry Lee complained, to accept "this or nothing."

The Articles of Confederation required that amendments be made by the unanimous consent of the state legislatures. But the delegates to the Philadelphia Convention decided to bypass the state legislatures and to submit the Constitution to specially elected state conventions for ratification. Approval by only nine of the thirteen states was necessary for the new government to take effect. This violation of earlier political principles was only one of many to which the Antifederalists objected.

The Federalist-Antifederalist Debate.

The federal government that was established by the Philadelphia Convention seemed severely to violate the ideals of 1776 that had guided the Revolutionary constitution makers. The new Constitution provided for a strong government, with an extraordinary amount of power given to the president and the Senate. It also created a single republican state that would span the continent and encompass all the diverse and scattered interests of the whole of American society—an impossible thing to expect of a republic, according to the best political science of the day.

During the debates over ratification in the fall and winter of 1787–88, the Antifederalists focused on these Federalist violations of the earlier Revolutionary assumptions. They charged that the new federal government resembled a monarchy in its concentration of power at the expense of liberty. Because the society it was to govern was extensive and heterogeneous, the Antifederalists asserted, the federal government would have to act tyrannically. Inevitably America would become a single consolidated state, with the individuality of the separate states sacrificed to a powerful government. And the source of this development, the Antifederalists argued, would be the logic of sovereignty. That powerful principle of eighteenth-century political science, on which the British had relied in the imperial debate, held that no society could long possess two legislatures: it must inevitably have one final, indivisible lawmaking authority. The Antifederalists argued that if the new national government was to be more powerful than the state governments—and if the Constitution was to be "the supreme law of the land"—then, according to the doctrine of sovereignty, the legislative authority of the separate states would eventually be annihilated.

Despite these formidable Antifederalist arguments, the Federalists did not believe that the Constitution repudiated the Revolution and the principles of 1776. In the decade since Independence had been declared, the political world had been transformed. Americans, it now appeared clear, had effectively transferred this final lawmaking authority, called sovereignty, from the institutions of government to the people at large.

In the years since the Revolution, many Americans had continued to act outside of all official institutions of government. During the 1780s they had organized various committees, conventions, and other extralegal bodies of the people in order to voice grievances and to achieve political goals. By so doing, they had continued a common practice of the Revolution itself. Vigilante actions of various kinds had done quickly and efficiently what the new state governments were often unable to do—control prices, prevent profiteering, and punish Tories. Everywhere people had extended the logic of "actual" representation and had sought to instruct and control the institutions of government. By 1787–88 all this activity by the people at large tended to give reality to the idea that sovereignty in America resided in the people, and not in any specific institution of government. Only by believing that sovereignty was held by the people outside of government could Americans make theoretical sense of their recent remarkable political inventions—their conception of a written constitution that was immune from legislative tampering, their special constitution-making conventions, and their unusual ideas of "actual" representation. This new concept of sovereignty residing in the people rather than in any institution of government now made the traditional logic of having ultimate power in one legislature or another irrelevant.

To meet the Antifederalist arguments against the Constitution, the Federalists were now determined to use this new understanding of the ultimate power of the people. True, they said, the Philadelphia Convention had gone beyond its instructions to amend the Articles of Confederation. It had drawn up an entirely new government, and it had provided for the new Constitution's ratification by special state conventions. But had Americans not learned during the previous decade that legislatures were not competent to create or change a constitution? If the federal Constitution were to be truly a fundamental law, then, argued the Federalists, it had to be ratified "by the supreme authority of the people themselves." Hence it

Courtesy of the New-York Historical Society, New York City

SILK BANNER OF THE PEWTERERS (DETAIL)
The pewterers, like other artisans, favored the new Constitution and in several cities in July 1788 joined in huge parades celebrating the new federal government. Such craftsmen were worried about imported foreign manufactures and believed that the new national government could better levy tariffs than could the separate states. Their support of the Constitution was important for ratification in several northern states.

was "We the people of the United States," and not the states, that ordained and established the Constitution.

By locating sovereignty in the people rather than in any particular institution, the Federalists could now conceive of what had previously been a contradiction in politics—two legislatures operating simultaneously over the same community. Thus they could answer the principal objection to the Constitution: the logic of legislative sovereignty. Only by making the people themselves the final lawmaking authority could the Federalists explain this emerging conception of federalism, that unique division of legislative responsibilities between the national and state governments that still amazes the world.

This new understanding of the relation of the society to government now enabled the Federalists to explain the expansion of a single republican state over a large continent of diverse groups and interests. The Federalists—especially Madison—took up the Scottish philosopher David Hume's radical suggestion that a republican government might operate better in a large territory than in a small one, and ingeniously used it to turn upside down the older assumption that a republic must be small and compact.

The Federalists argued that American experiences since 1776 had demonstrated that no republic could be made small enough to avoid the clashing of rival parties and interests. (Tiny Rhode Island was the most faction-ridden of all.) The extended territory of the new national republic was actually its greatest source of strength, Madison wrote in a series of publications, especially in his most famous piece, *The Federalist* No. 10.* In a large society, Madison concluded, there were so many interests and parties that no one faction could triumph, and thus the threat of tyranny by the majority would be eliminated. Furthermore, representatives to the national Congress would have to be elected from relatively large districts—a fact that Madison hoped would inhibit demagogic electioneering. If the people of a particular state—New York, for example—had to elect only ten men to the federal Congress, in contrast to the sixty-six they elected to their state legislature, they would be more likely to pass over ordinary men and to elect those who were experienced, well educated, and well known. In this way the new federal government would avoid the problems that had plagued the states in the 1780s.

The Antifederalists provided little match for the arguments and the array of talents that the Federalists gathered in support of the Constitution in the ratifying conventions that were held in the states throughout the fall, winter, and spring of 1787–88. Many Antifederalists were state-centered men with local interests and loyalties. They tended to lack the influence and education of the Federalists, and often they had neither social nor intellectual confidence. The Antifederalists had difficulty making themselves heard because they had very few influential leaders and because much of the press was closed to them; out of a hundred or more newspapers printed in the late 1780s, only a dozen supported the Antifederalists.

Many of the small states—Delaware, New Jersey, Connecticut, and Georgia—commercially dependent on their neighbors or militarily exposed, ratified immediately. The critical struggles took place in the large states of Massachusetts, Virginia, and New York. The Constitution was accepted in these states only by narrow margins and with the promise of future amendments. North Carolina and Rhode Island rejected the Constitution, but after New York's ratification in July 1788 the country was ready to go ahead and organize the new government without them.

The Federalist was a series of eighty-five essays in defense of the Constitution, published in New York in the winter of 1787–88. They were written under the pen name "Publius" largely by Madison and Alexander Hamilton, with five essays contributed by John Jay. The essays were quickly published as a book and became the most famous work of political philosophy in American history, labeled by Jefferson in 1788 as "the best commentary on the principles of government, which ever was written."

Most ordinary farmers who attended the state ratifying conventions in 1787–88 to consider the Constitution tended to oppose it. In the Massachusetts convention the delegate who spoke prior to this one was just such a farmer, and he had identified support for the Constitution with all those eastern "lawyers and men of learning, and moneyed men that talk so finely . . . to make us poor illiterate people swallow down the pill." This speaker, Jonathan Smith of Berkshire County, who rose in response, may have been a farmer, but he was also an established legislative politician who had been frightened by Shays's Rebellion. Note his studied effort to identify with the common farmers.

A Farmer Favors the Constitution (1788)

MR. President, I am a plain man, and get my living by the plough. I am not used to speak in public, but I beg your leave to say a few words to my brother plough-joggers in this house.

I have lived in a part of the country where I have known the worth of good government by the want of it. There was a black cloud [Shays's Rebellion] that rose in the east last winter, and spread over the west. . . . It brought on a state of anarchy and that led to tyranny. I say, it brought anarchy. People that used to live peaceably, and were before good neighbors, got distracted, and took up arms against government. . . . People, I say, took up arms, and then, if you went to speak to them, you had the musket of death presented to your breast. They would rob you of your property, threaten to burn your houses; oblige you to be on your guard night and day. Alarms spread from town to town; families were broken up; the tender mother would cry, O my son is among them! . . .

Our distress was so great that we should have been glad to snatch at anything that looked like a government. Had any person that was able to protect us come and set up his standard, we should all have flocked to it, even if it had been a monarch, and that monarch might have proved a tyrant. So that you see that anarchy leads to tyranny; and better have one tyrant than so many at once.

Now, Mr. President, when I saw this Constitution, I found that it was a cure for these disorders. It was just such a thing as we wanted. I got a copy of it and read it over and over. I had been a member of the convention to form our own state constitution, and had learnt something of the checks and balances of power; and I found them all here. I did not go to any

lawyer, to ask his opinion—we have no lawyer in our town, and do well enough without. I formed my own opinion, and was pleased with this Constitution. . . .

But I don't think the worse of the Constitution because lawyers, and men of learning, and moneyed men are fond of it. I don't suspect that they want to get into Congress and abuse their power. I am not of such a jealous make. They that are honest men themselves are not apt to suspect other people. . . .

Brother farmers, let us suppose a case, now. Suppose you had a farm of 50 acres, and your title was disputed, and there was a farm of 5000 acres joined to you that belonged to a man of learning, and his title was involved in the same difficulty. Would you not be glad to have him for your friend, rather than to stand alone in the dispute?

Well, the case is the same—these lawyers, these moneyed men, these men of learning, are all embarked in the same cause with us, and we must all swim or sink together. And shall we throw the Constitution overboard because it does not please us alike? Suppose two or three of you had been at the pains to break up a piece of rough land, and sow it with wheat—would you let it lie waste because you could not agree what sort of a fence to make? Would it not be better to put up a fence that did not please everyone's fancy, rather than not fence it at all, or keep disputing about it until the wild beasts came in and devoured it?

Some gentlemen say, don't be in a hurry; take time to consider; and don't take a leap in the dark. I say, take things in time—gather fruit when it is ripe. There is a time to sow, and a time to reap. We sowed our seed when we sent men to the federal convention. Now is the harvest; now is the time to reap the fruit of our labor. And if we won't do it now, I am afraid we never shall have another opportunity.

Despite the difficulties and the close votes in some states, the country's eventual acceptance of the Constitution was almost inevitable. The alternative was governmental chaos. Yet in the face of the great number of wealthy and influential people who supported the Constitution, what in the end remains extraordinary is not the political weakness and disunity of Antifederalism, but its strength. The fact that large numbers of Americans could actually reject a plan of government that was backed by George Washington and nearly the whole of the country's "natural aristocracy" said more about the changing character of American politics and society than did the Constitution's acceptance. It was indeed a sign of what was to come.

The Hamiltonian Program

The Constitution created only the outline of the new government. Americans still had to fill in the details of the government and make something of it. During the 1790s the government leaders—that is, the Federalists, who clung to the name used by the supporters of the Constitution—sought to build a large consolidated nation that few Americans had envisioned in 1776. The consequence of their efforts was to make the 1790s the most awkward decade in American history, a decade that bore little relation to what went on immediately before or after.

Because the Federalists stood in the way of democracy as it was emerging in the United States, everything seemed to turn against them. They despised political parties, yet parties nonetheless emerged, shattering the remarkable harmony of 1790 and producing one of the most divisive and passionate eras in American history. They sought desperately to avoid conflict with England, to the point of appearing to compromise the new nation's independence. But in 1812 the war with Great Britain that they sought to avoid had to be fought anyway. By the early nineteenth century Alexander Hamilton, the brilliant Federalist leader who more than anyone else pursued the heroic dreams of the age, was not alone in his despairing conclusion "that this American world was not made for me."

Organizing the Government. There was more consensus when the new government was inaugurated in 1789–90 than at any time since the Declaration of Independence. Regional differences were temporarily obscured by a common enthusiasm for the new Constitution. And the unanimous election of Washington as the first president gave the new government an immediate respectability. Washington, with his tall, imposing figure, Roman nose, and stern, thin-lipped face,

EDWARD SAVAGE'S "LIBERTY"
This 1796 engraving combines the two most important symbols of the early Republic, the goddess "Liberty" and the eagle, the latter representing power and unity. The print was very popular and for years appeared in a wide variety of adaptations, including embroidery. Note the liberty cap on the flagstaff in the background.

Library of Congress

was already at age fifty-eight an internationally famous classical hero. Like the Roman conqueror Cincinnatus, he had returned to his farm at the moment of military victory. He was understandably reluctant to take up one more burden for his country and thus risk shattering the reputation he had so painstakingly earned as commander in chief. Yet his deep sense of duty made refusal of the presidency impossible. He possessed the dignity, patience, and restraint that the untried but potentially powerful office needed at the outset. Despite the strong-minded, talented people around him—particularly Secretary of the Treasury Hamilton and Secretary of State Jefferson—Washington was very much the leader of his administration.

Madison, the government's leader in the House of Representatives, immediately sought to fulfill earlier promises to the Antifederalists and to quiet their fears by proposing amendments to the Constitution. He beat back Antifederalist efforts to change fundamentally the character of the Constitution and extracted from the variety of suggested amendments those that were least likely to drain the new government's energy. To the disappointment of some former Antifederalists, the ten amendments that were ratified in 1791—the amendments known collectively as the Bill of Rights—were mostly concerned with protecting from the federal government the rights of *individuals* rather than the rights of the *states*. They included the guarantees of freedom of speech, press, religion, petition, and assembly, as well as a number of protections for accused persons. Only the Tenth Amendment, which reserved for the states or for the people those powers not delegated to the United States, was a concession to the main Antifederalist fear.*

With the inauguration of Washington and the establishment of the new government, many Americans began to feel a sense of beginning anew, of putting the republican experiment on a new and stronger foundation. They talked of benevolence, glory, and heroism, and they foresaw the inevitable westward movement of the arts and sciences from Europe to the New World. The outlook was cosmopolitan, liberal, and humanitarian; America was entering a new age.

Yet despite all this optimism, the Americans of the 1790s never lost their Revolutionary sense of the novel and fragile nature of their boldly extended republican government. Except in the epic poems of a few excited patriots such as Joel Barlow and Timothy Dwight, America was far from being a consolidated nation in any modern sense. Already separatist movements in the West threatened to break up the new country. Some westerners even considered giving their allegiance to Spain in return for access to the Gulf of Mexico. The entire Mississippi River basin was open to exploitation by ambitious adventurers willing to sell their services to European nations. These included William Blount, a senator from Tennessee, and George Rogers Clark, a frontier hero during the Revolution. Fear of this kind of intrigue and influence led to the hasty admission of Vermont, Kentucky, and Tennessee

*For the first ten amendments, see Appendix.

into the Union during the 1790s. But the danger of splintering remained.

The Federalist aims and the conflicting passions they aroused can be properly understood only if one takes into account this context of uncertainty and awesome responsibility for the future of republican government. The very character of America's emerging republican state was at issue in the 1790s. The Federalist leaders sought to maintain the momentum that had begun in the late 1780s when the Constitution was formed. In place of the impotent confederation of chaotic states, they envisioned a strong, consolidated, commercial state that would be led by an energetic government composed of the best men in the society.

Many Federalists were interested in bolstering the dignity of the new republic by adopting some of the ceremony and majesty of monarchy. Led by Vice-President John Adams, some Federalists in the Senate tried to make "His Highness" the proper title for addressing the president. Because the future of the new republic was so unformed and doubtful, this issue seemed loaded with significance, and it occupied the Congress in a month of debate. The attempt to give the president a royal-sounding title failed, and the republican simplicity of "Mr. President" was adopted. But the Federalists did draw up elaborate rules concerning government receptions and the proper behavior at what soon came to be called the "republican court," located in New York and, after 1790, in Philadelphia. At the same time, plans were begun for erecting a monumental "federal city" as the permanent capital. Always strongly sensitive to the precedents being established, the Federalists also worked out the relations between the president and Congress. Before the end of the first session of Congress in 1789, the bare outlines of government that had been provided by the Constitution had been filled in. Congress created the executive departments of state, war, and treasury, as well as a federal judiciary consisting of the Supreme Court and a pyramid of lower courts.

Hamilton's Financial Program.

Alexander Hamilton, then thirty-five years old, was the moving force in the new government. As a military aide to Washington during the Revolutionary War, he had earned the president's admiration. In fact, despite his short stature, Hamilton impressed everyone who met him. Unlike Washington, he was quick-witted, excitable, and very knowledgeable about public finance. Born in the West Indies an illegitimate son of a Scottish merchant, Hamilton longed to enter and enjoy the polite world of the rich and wellborn. But despite his concern for the commercial prosperity of the United States, he cannot be regarded simply as a capitalist promoter of America's later business culture. He was willing to allow ordinary men their profits and property, but it

Library of Congress

ALEXANDER HAMILTON (1757–1804)
Hamilton is the most controversial of the Founding Fathers. Certainly he was the least taken with radical Whig ideology and the most adventurous and heroic. As Gouverneur Morris said, "He was more covetous of glory than of wealth or power." His talents, his energy, and his clear sense of direction awed his contemporaries, friends and enemies alike.

was fame and honor he wanted for himself and for his country. As the secretary of the treasury, he was now in a crucial position to put his ideas into effect.

Since British "country-opposition" groups had traditionally considered the treasury a source of political corruption, the first Congress regarded the new secretary of the treasury with some suspicion—and with good reason. The treasury was by far the largest department, with dozens of officers and well over 2,000 customs officials, revenue agents, and postmasters. Although Congress limited the capacity of these officials to engage in business and trade and to buy public lands and government securities, the treasury offices were an important source of patronage and influence. Hamilton, in fact, saw his role in eighteenth-century English terms—as a kind of prime minister to President Washington. Hamilton felt justified in meddling in the affairs of other departments and of Congress and in taking the lead in organizing and administering the government. He denied that he was creating a "court" party, but he set out to duplicate the great financial achievements of the early-eighteenth-century English governments

FIRST BANK OF THE UNITED STATES, PHILADELPHIA
Designed by an unsuccessful businessman from New Hampshire, Samuel Blodget, this building was essentially a three-story New England brick house with a classical portico, decorated, the *Gazette of the United States* reported excitedly, in the style of "Palmyra and Rome when architecture was at its zenith in the Augustan age."

that had laid the basis for England's stability and commercial supremacy.

Hamilton worked out his program in a series of four reports to Congress in 1790–91: on credit (including duties and taxes), on a national bank, on a mint, and on manufactures. Nearly everyone admitted that the new government needed to put its finances in order and to settle the Revolutionary War debts of the United States. Hamilton was determined to establish the public credit of the United States. In 1790 the amount owed to foreigners totaled $12 million, and no one had any quarrel with Hamilton's desire to pay this off in full. Of the domestic public debts—that is, the amount due Americans—the federal government owed $42 million, and the various state governments owed an estimated $25 million. In the boldest and most controversial part of his plan, Hamilton proposed that the United States government assume the obligation of paying all the state debts. But then instead of paying off either these assumed state debts or the Confederation's debts, he urged that the United States government "fund" them. That is, he wanted the new national government to collect into a single package all the federal and state bonds and loan certificates left over from the Revolutionary War and to issue new federal securities in their place with the same face value as the old debts. Although Hamilton, in order to maintain the value of the government's new bonds, had to promise to pay off the principal of the debt, he actually had no intention of doing so. Retirement of the public debt would only destroy its usefulness.

By these proposals Hamilton hoped to create a consolidated and permanent national debt that would strengthen America in the same way that the British national debt had strengthened Great Britain. Regular interest payments on the refunded debt were to be backed by the new government's revenues from customs duties and excise taxes. Indeed, more than 40 percent of these revenues in the 1790s went to pay interest on the debt. These interest payments not only would make the United States the best credit risk in the world, but would create a system of investment for American moneyed groups that had lacked the stable alternatives for speculation and investment that Europeans had.

Besides giving investors a secure stake in the new national government, these new bonds would become the basis of the nation's money supply. Not only would the securities themselves be negotiable instruments in business transactions, but Hamilton's program provided for their forming three-fourths of the privately subscribed capital of a new national bank that would be patterned on the Bank of England. This Bank of the United States and its branches (to be established in selected cities) would serve as the government's depository and fiscal agent and would act as a central control on the state banks, of which there were thirty-two by 1801. But most important, the Bank of the United States would create paper money.

The Bank would issue its notes as loans to private citizens, and these notes, along with those of the banks chartered by the states, would become the principal circulating medium of money for a society that lacked an adequate supply of specie, gold and silver coin. Above all, Hamilton wanted a paper money that would hold its value in relation to specie. By guaranteeing that the federal government would accept the Bank's notes at face value in payment of all taxes, holders of the notes would be less likely to redeem them in coin. The notes would pass from hand to hand without depreciating, even though only a fraction of their value was available in specie at any one time. Many American leaders continued to believe, as John Adams did, that "every dollar of a bank bill that is issued beyond the quantity of gold and silver in the vaults, represents nothing, and is therefore a cheat upon somebody." Nevertheless, these multiplying bank notes quickly broadened the foundation of the nation's economy.

In his final report, the report on manufactures, Hamilton laid out plans for eventually industrializing the United States. He and some other Federalists hoped to transform America from an agricultural nation into precisely the complicated and rank-organized country that agrarians like Jefferson and Madison feared. He proposed incentives and bounties for the development of large-scale manufacturing that would be very different from the small household industry that most Americans were used to. Yet because the Federalist government needed the revenue from customs duties on imported manufactures, and because most businessmen's energies were still absorbed in overseas shipping and land speculation, these proposals for stimulating manufacturing went unfulfilled. The rest of Hamilton's extraordinary financial program, however, was adopted by Congress early in the 1790s.

Hamilton's Political Program. As much as Hamilton and other Federalist leaders planned for and celebrated the commercial prosperity of the United States, their ultimate goals were more political than economic. Like many other Federalists, Hamilton had no faith in the idealistic Revolutionary hopes that American society could be held together solely by "virtue," by the people's willingness to sacrifice their private interests for the sake of the public good. Instead of virtue and the natural sociability of man, Hamilton saw only the ordinary individual's selfish pursuit of his own private happiness. Social stability therefore required the harnessing of this self-interest. The Federalists thus tried to use the new economic and fiscal measures to re-create in America traditional kinds of eighteenth-century "connections" that would knit the sprawling society together.

In effect, Hamilton sought to reverse the egalitarian thrust of the Revolutionary movement. He and other Federalists believed that the national government could influence and manipulate the economic and social leaders of the country. These leaders in turn would use economic self-interest to gain support for the new central government among the groups and individuals dependent upon them. Not only did the Federalists expect the new national financial program to draw people's affections away from the now economically weakened state governments, but they deliberately set out to "corrupt" the society (as eighteenth-century "country-opposition" writers put it) by tying people's interests to the central government. In local areas they built up a following among Revolutionary War veterans and among members of the Society of the Cincinnati, the organization of Revolutionary War officers. They appointed important and respectable local figures to the federal judiciary and other federal offices. They carefully managed the Bank of the United States and other parts of the national economic program. And in 1791 they had President Washington make an elaborate tour of the country in the manner of a king.

By 1793, through the shrewd use of these kinds of influence or "corruption" on key individuals, the Federalists had formed groups of "friends of government" in most of the states. The lines of connection of these centers of economic and political patronage ran from the federal executive through Congress down to the various localities. Thus was created a vested interest in what opponents called "a court faction"—the very thing that Madison in *The Federalist* No. 10 had believed unlikely in an expanded republic.

Hamilton ultimately believed, as he declared in 1794, that "government can never [be] said to be established until some signal display has manifested its power by military coercion." From the beginning many Federalists, including Secretary of War Henry Knox, regarded a cohesive militia and a regular army as "a strong corrective arm" necessary for the federal government to meet all crises "whether arising from internal or external causes." In 1791 the Federalists imposed a federal excise tax on whiskey—a profitable and transportable product for many inland grain farmers—to ensure that all citizens, however far removed from the seaports, felt the weight of the new national government. When in 1794 some western Pennsylvania farmers rebelled against this hated internal tax, they seemed to fall into the government's plans (as Madison charged) to "establish the principle that a standing army was necessary for enforcing the laws." The national government raised nearly 15,000 militia troops to meet this Whiskey Rebellion. This excessive show of force was essential, President Washington declared, because "we had given no testimony to the world of being able or willing to support our government and laws."

Dealing with external problems was not as easy as putting down internal rebellions. Both Great Britain and Spain maintained positions on the borderlands of the United States. There they traded and plotted with the Indians, who still occupied huge areas of the trans-Appalachian West. From its base in Canada, Britain encouraged the Indians to join forces and resist American encroachments. In the South, Spain, which held the Floridas, New Orleans, and the Louisiana territory, refused to recognize American boundaries, controlled navigation down the Mississippi River, and offered protection to the Creek and Cherokee Indians of the Southwest. Much of the diplomacy of the early Republic was devoted to the removal of these barriers to western expansion.

Major breakthroughs came in 1795. In 1790–91 the Indians of the Northwest had inflicted several defeats on American soldiers, mostly militia, in the area along the present boundary between Ohio and Indiana. The worst came in November 1791, with the annihilation of a motley collection of troops under the command of Arthur St. Clair, the territorial governor of the Northwest. These devastating defeats gave the Federalists the opportunity to overhaul the War Department and to create the regular standing army that many of them wanted. With a reorganized professional army, General Anthony Wayne in 1794 smashed the Indians at Fallen Timbers, near present-day To-

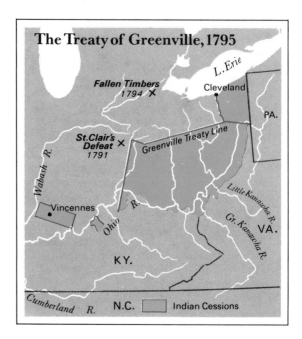

ledo, Ohio, and temporarily broke Indian resistance and British influence in the Old Northwest. In the Treaty of Greenville in 1795, the Indians ceded much of the Ohio territory to the United States. In turn, this cession now made inevitable Britain's evacuation of the Northwest posts it had been occupying since the Revolution. In a treaty negotiated by John Jay and ratified in 1795,* Britain finally agreed to get out of American territory.

In another treaty, negotiated by Thomas Pinckney in the same year, Spain finally recognized American claims to the Florida boundary and to navigation of the Mississippi River. Both Jay's Treaty and Pinckney's Treaty thus secured the territorial integrity of the United States in a way the diplomacy of the Confederation had been unable to do.

But the United States was still far from being a world power. Measuring American strength by European standards, the Federalists were strongly aware of the country's weakness in the world, and this awareness largely determined their foreign policy. Unlike England and France, the United States as yet lacked the essential elements that made a nation powerful and great—commercial strength and military might. Since to build the United States into a strong and prosperous nation rivaling the powers of Europe might take fifty years or more, the Federalists thought that the new nation had to buy time by maintaining harmonious relations with Great Britain.

Britain was the only power that could seriously

*For Jay's Treaty, see below, p. 248.

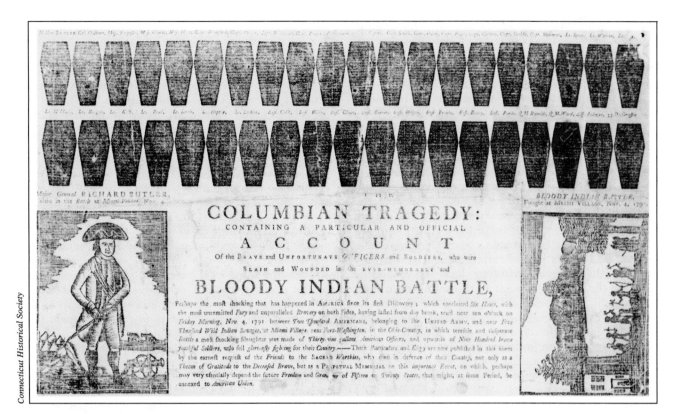

"BLOODY INDIAN BATTLE," 1791
In an effort to put down the native Americans who were trying to hold back the advancing white settlers in the Northwest, the U.S. government in 1791 sent General Arthur St. Clair against them with an army of 2,000 soldiers. At dawn on November 4, south of the Maumec River, the American force was surprised and overwhelmed by the Indians and suffered over 900 casualties. It was the worst defeat the native Americans ever inflicted upon the United States.

hinder American development. Duties on British imports supplied the national revenue on which Hamilton's entire financial program depended. Until the United States could stand up to Great Britain, the Federalists believed that the country ought to concentrate on acquiring or controlling the New World possessions of a weakened Spain and on dominating the Western Hemisphere. The Federalists' policy of reconciliation with Britain thus became another means toward the ultimate fulfillment of their grandiose dreams of American glory.

The Republican Opposition

Opposition to the Federalist program was slow in developing. Since the only alternative to the new national government was the prospect of disunity and anarchy, Alexander Hamilton and the Federalists were in a position to build up their system without great difficulty. During the first year of the new government (1789–90), James Madison acted as congressional leader of those who were eager to counteract Antifederalist sentiment and to build a strong and independent executive. Not only did Madison write President Washington's first inaugural address, but he argued for the president's exclusive power to remove executive officials, and worked hard to create a Treasury Department with a single head. Indeed, Hamilton, thinking of the cooperative atmosphere of 1787–88 in which he and Madison had written the *Federalist* papers, was so confident of Madison's nationalism and of the nationalism of the southern representatives in Congress that he felt betrayed when they did not unquestioningly support his program.

But Madison broke with the administration on the issues of refunding the debt and the federal government's assumption of the states' debts. On the refunding issue he urged that some sort of distinction be made between the original purchasers of the federal bonds and their present, often northern, speculative holders who had bought them cheaply. Madison was also convinced that national assumption of the existing state debts would penalize those states, particularly Virginia, that had already paid off a large portion of their debts. Yet in 1790 congressmen who were opposed to these measures were still capable of compromising for the sake of federal union. Jefferson, Madison, and other southern representatives were even willing to support national assumption of state debts in return for locating the new federal capital on the Potomac River on the border between Virginia and Maryland.

With the government's effort to charter the Bank of the United States in December 1790, the opposition began to assume a more strident and ideological character. Madison in the House of Representatives and Jefferson in the cabinet (as secretary of state) both urged a strict interpretation of the Constitution as a defense against what seemed to be the dangerous consolidating implications of Hamilton's program. They argued that the Constitution had not expressly granted the federal government the authority to charter a bank. Washington, after asking the opinions of his cabinet members on the constitutionality of the Bank, rejected Jefferson's view in favor of Hamilton's broad "construction," or interpretation, of the Constitution. Hamilton argued that Congress's authority to charter a bank was implied by the clause in the Constitution that gave Congress the right to make all laws "necessary and proper" to carry out its delegated powers. But this presidential decision in favor of the Bank did not quiet the opposition.

By 1791 a "republican interest" was emerging in Congress and in the country, with Madison and Jefferson as its spokesmen. By 1792 this "interest" had begun to form into a Republican "party." This Republican party now saw itself representing the "country opposition" of the people against the corrupt influence of the Federalist "court." It was the 1760s and 1770s all over again.

The Republican Party.

The Republican party was composed of and supported by a variety of social elements. Foremost were the southern landowners, who were becoming increasingly conscious of the distinctiveness of their section of the country and more and more estranged from the business world that Hamilton's system seemed to be promoting. Unlike Federalist gentlemen in the North, these members of the southern gentry retained the earlier Whig confidence in what Jefferson called the "honest heart" of the common man. Part of this faith in democracy that Jefferson and his southern colleagues shared came from their relative isolation from it. With the increasing questioning of black slavery in the North and throughout the world, small white farmers in the South found a common identity with large plantation owners. Most of the leading landowners therefore did not feel threatened by the democratic electoral politics that was eating away people's deference to "the better sort" in the North.

In the North, especially in the rapidly growing middle states, ambitious individuals and new groups without political connections were finding that the Republican party was a means by which they could challenge entrenched leaders. Therefore the Republican party in the North was very different from what it was in the South. In the South the Republican opposition to the Federalist program was largely the response of rural gentry who were committed to a nostalgic image of independent freeholding farmers. In the North, however, the Republican party was the political expression of new equality-minded social forces released and intensified by the Revolution—particularly ambitious artisans, tradesmen, and second- and third-level merchants who were resentful of the pretensions and privileges of the Federalist elites. These rising northern entrepreneurs were in fact the principal contributors to the very world the southern Republicans were coming to fear.

These diverse and ultimately incompatible sectional and social elements were brought together in a national Republican party by a comprehensive and common ideology. This Republican ideology, involving a deep hatred of overgrown central power and of the political and financial mechanisms that created such power, had been inherited from the English "country-opposition" tradition that had been sharpened and Americanized during the Revolutionary years. Now, during the 1790s, it was given a new and heightened relevance by the policies of the federal administration.

To those who deeply believed in country-Whig ideology, Hamilton's system threatened to re-create the kind of government and society that Americans had presumably destroyed in 1776. It was feared that such a society, based on patronage connections and artificial privilege and supported by executive power, would in time destroy the independence of the republican citizenry. Hamilton appeared to be another Sir Robert Walpole, using the new economic program to corrupt Congress and the country and to create a swelling army of "stock-jobbers and king-jobbers" (in Jefferson's words) in order to build up executive power at the expense of the people.*

Once the Republicans grasped this ideological pattern, all the Federalist measures fell into place. The high-toned pageantry of the "court," the aristocratic

---

*For Walpole's "system" in Great Britain, see chapter 8, p. 192.

I Jon^a Dayton. Speaker. | Congressional Pugilists | 2 Jon^a W. Condy. Clerk

He in a trice struck Lyon thrice
Upon his head, enrag'd sir,

Who seiz'd the tongs to ease his wrongs,
And Grifwold thus engag'd, sir.

Congress Hall.
in Philad^a Feb. 15 1798.

CARTOON LAMPOONING THE LYON-GRISWOLD TANGLE IN CONGRESS IN 1797
With the wrestling on the floor of the House of Representatives in 1797 between Republican Matthew Lyon of Vermont and Federalist Roger Griswold of Connecticut, followed by Lyon's "outrageous" and "indecent" defense (he was reported in the *Annals* of Congress to have said, "I did not come here to have my —— kicked by everybody"), some members concluded that Congress had become no better than a "tavern," filled with "*beasts*, and not gentlemen," and contemptible in the eyes of all "polite or genteel" societies.

The New York Public Library

talk of titles, the defense of corporate monopolies, the enlargement of the military forces, the growth of taxes, the reliance on the monarchical president and the aristocratic Senate—all these pointed toward a systematic plan, as Caroline County of Virginia declared in 1793, of "assimilating the American government to the form and spirit of the British monarchy." Most basic and dangerous of all was the Federalist creation of a huge perpetual federal debt, which, as George Clinton, the Republican governor of New York, explained, not only would poison the morals of the people through speculation, but would also "add an artificial support to the administration, and by a species of bribery enlist the monied men of the community on the side of the measures of the government. . . . Look to Great Britain."

The French Revolution. The outbreak of the French Revolution in 1789, and its subsequent expansion in 1792 into a European war pitting monarchical Britain against republican France, added to the quarrel Americans were having among themselves over the direction their society and government were taking. The meaning of the American Revolution, and the capacity of the United States to sustain its grand republican experiment, now seemed tied to the fate of Britain and France.

President Washington proclaimed America's neutrality in the spring of 1793. The United States quickly tried to take advantage of its position and to gain the warring countries' recognition of its neutral rights. Unable to control the seas, France threw open its empire in the West Indies to American commerce, and American merchants soon developed a profitable shipping trade between the French and Spanish West Indies and Europe. Britain retaliated by invoking what was called the Rule of 1756. This rule, which had been first set forth during the Seven Years' War, enabled British prize courts (that is, courts that judged the legitimacy of the seizure of enemy ships or goods) to deny the right of neutral nations in time of war to trade with ports in belligerent countries that had been closed to them in time of peace. During 1793 and 1794 Britain seized more than three hundred American merchant ships.

Although Washington had proclaimed the United States' neutrality, both the Federalists and their Republican opponents sought to favor whichever power—Britain or France—they thought would better promote American interests. The Federalists made strong attempts to overcome the natural sympathy most Americans had for France, their former ally in the Revolutionary War and now a sister republic. Citizen Genêt, the new French minister to the United States, in 1793 began arming privateers in the United States for use against the British and seemed to be appealing over the head of the government to the American people for support. These clumsy actions helped the Federalists win over many Americans who were otherwise sympathetic to the French Revolution. In addition, the Federalists recruited to their cause a growing number of Protestant ministers and conservative groups who were alarmed by the social upheaval and antireligious passion that they thought were being spread by the French Revolution. Britain seemed to the Federalists to be a bastion of stability in the midst of worldwide chaos. While the Republicans were calling for stiff commercial retaliation against Britain for its seizing of American ships and sailors and for its continued occupation of posts in the Northwest, the Federalists hoped to head off war with Britain by negotiation. In the spring of 1794, Washington appointed John Jay, chief justice of the Supreme Court, to be a special minister to Great Britain.

Jay's Treaty. The treaty that Jay negotiated with Britain in 1794 demonstrated both the Federalists' fears of France and their reliance on the British connection. In the treaty Britain finally agreed to evacuate the Northwest posts, to open parts of its empire to American commerce, and to set up joint arbitration commissions to settle the unresolved issues of prewar debts, boundaries, and compensation for illegal seizures. The United States was compelled to abandon principles concerning freedom of the seas and broad neutral rights that it had been supporting since 1776. In effect the treaty recognized the British Rule of 1756. Moreover, by granting Britain more favorable trade conditions than it gave to any other nation, the United States surrendered the power to make any future commercial discrimination against Britain, the one great weapon that the Republicans were counting on to weaken the former mother country's hold on American commerce.

The Republicans were greatly shocked and angered by the treaty. Jay was burned in effigy. When the Senate reluctantly ratified the treaty in 1795 after a bitter struggle, the Republicans in the House tried to prevent its implementation. Although the Republicans thought that Britain had conceded to the United States little more than peace, peace was enough for most Federalists. War with Britain, they thought, would be disastrous for America. It would end the imports of British goods and the customs revenues on which Hamilton's financial program depended and would only increase the influence of what the Federalist senator George Cabot of Massachusetts called "French principles [that] would destroy us as a society."

JOHN ADAMS (1735–1826)
Adams is perhaps the most neglected of the Founders; he certainly felt himself to be. He seemed to court unpopularity with his displays of jealousy, vanity, and pomposity. Yet as his diaries reveal, he was at heart vulnerable and amiable.

The Quasi-War with France. Washington's decision to retire from the presidency at the end of his second term created an important precedent for the future. The New Englander and vice-president John Adams was widely regarded as Washington's natural successor, but he was elected in 1796 by only a narrow margin of electoral votes, seventy-one to sixty-eight, over the Republican leader, Thomas Jefferson. Under the constitutional rule then in force, Jefferson as runner-up became vice-president.

Before Washington left office, with Hamilton's help he prepared his Farewell Address. By laying the basis for later American "isolationism," the address became one of the most important political documents in American history. In it Washington urged Americans "to steer clear of permanent alliances" with any foreign power. Republicans saw this neutralism as anti-French: they rightly thought that Washington was rejecting the idea that the United States and France were naturally linked in the common cause of bringing revolutionary republicanism to the world.

The Federalist government's pro-British policies as expressed in Jay's Treaty now drove the embattled French into a series of attacks on American shipping; they even refused to treat with the United States until the new American connection with Britain was broken. President Adams dealt with the crisis in 1797 by sending a special mission to France. The French government, using agents whom they designated as X, Y, and Z, tried to extort a payment from the American diplomats as a precondition for negotiations. This humiliating "XYZ Affair" further aroused American antagonism to France and led to the American revocation of the Franco-American treaties of 1778. In 1798 an undeclared "quasi-war" with France broke out on the seas. All this in turn created an opportunity for some extreme Federalists, led by Hamilton, to call for a strengthening of the central government once and for all.

As leader of the Republican party, Jefferson saw the world differently. Whether in or out of office, he never let the growing anti-French atmosphere weaken his faith in the cause of the French revolutionary republic. Although he supported the outward neutrality of the United States in the European war between Britain and France, he and other Republicans were bitterly opposed to Jay's Treaty; they were convinced that they could not remain impartial in the French revolutionary cause, on which "the liberty of the whole earth was depending." Jefferson was aware of the bloody excesses of the French Revolution, including the Reign of Terror, in which thousands of aristocrats, priests, and others were guillotined for political offenses; but his enthusiasm for the Revolution was not dampened. "Rather than it should have failed," he wrote in 1793, the year of the Terror, "I would have seen half the earth desolate; were there but an Adam and Eve left in every country, and left free, it would be better than it is now."

Because Federalists and Republicans alike were convinced that the very meaning of the United States as a republic was directly related to the conflict between Britain and France, some American public officials of both parties were led into extraordinarily improper diplomatic behavior during the 1790s. Hamilton as secretary of the treasury secretly passed on information about United States plans to the British government. Jefferson as secretary of state under Washington, his successor Edmund Randolph, and James Monroe as minister to France all indiscreetly tried to undermine the pro-British stand of the administration they were serving and came very close to becoming unwitting tools of French policy.

The Crisis of 1798–1799. In this inflamed atmosphere political passions ran as high as they ever have in American history. Every aspect of American life—business groups, banks, dance assemblies, even funerals—became politicized. People who had known each other their whole lives now crossed streets to avoid meeting. As personal and social ties fell apart, differences easily spilled into violence, and fighting broke out in the state legislatures and even in the Congress.

Amid these passions the political parties that emerged in the 1790s were unlike any later American parties. Although by 1796 the Federalists and the Republicans had organized to win the presidency for their respective candidates, Adams and Jefferson, both parties saw themselves in an increasingly revolutionary situation. The Federalists thought of themselves as the most enlightened and socially established members of the natural aristocracy, who were best able to carry out the responsibility of running the country. Thus they claimed that they were the government, not a "party." Parties, as Washington warned in his Farewell Address, were equivalent to factions and could lead only to sedition and the disruption of the state.

Although Jefferson and many other Republicans shared this traditional eighteenth-century abhorrence of parties, they considered that the extraordinary circumstances of the 1790s justified the formation of an organized opposition. The Republicans thought that the normal processes of American politics had become corrupted and poisoned by a Federalist government that had detached itself from the people. Hence it was necessary to create popular organizations of political opposition similar to those that the American Whigs had formed during the pre-Revolutionary crisis. Their goal in forming caucuses, corresponding committees, and Democratic-Republican societies was to band people together and use what they increasingly called "public opinion" to influence elections and counteract the influence of prominent Federalists in national politics. The extralegal opposition of the Republican party, they believed, would be a temporary but necessary instrument that would save the people's liberties from Federalist monarchism.

In mobilizing the people into political consciousness, nothing was more important than the press. Newspapers multiplied dramatically, from fewer than 100 in 1790 to more than 230 by 1800. By 1810 Americans were buying more than 22 million copies of 376 papers annually, the largest circulation of newspapers anywhere in the world. By the late 1790s these papers, many of them Republican, were lowering their prices and adopting eye-catching typography and cartoons in order to reach new readers. By popularizing political affairs as never before and

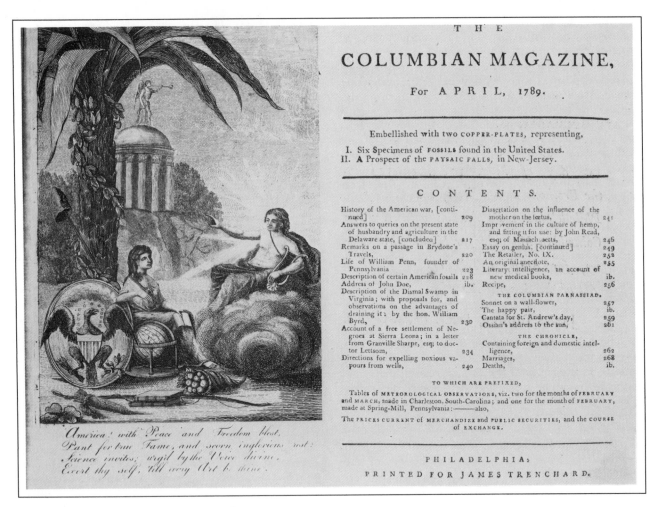

America: with Peace and Freedom blest,
Pant for true Fame, and scorn inglorious rest;
Science invites; urgd by the Voice divine,
Exert thy self, till every Art be thine.

PAGES FROM "COLUMBIAN MAGAZINE"
Between 1775 and 1795 twenty-seven learned and gentlemanly magazines like this one were begun, six more than in the entire colonial period. The creation of these new journals was a remarkable testimony to the cultural promise of the Revolution.

by relentlessly criticizing Federalist officials, the press seemed to be single-handedly shaping American political life.

Although the Federalists began to adopt some of what they called the "petty electioneering arts" of the Republican opposition, they were not comfortable with the new democratic politics. They saw themselves in traditional eighteenth-century terms as gentlemen leaders to whom ordinary people, if they were only left alone, would naturally defer. The Federalists attributed the difficulties and disorder of the 1790s to the influence of newspapers, demagogues, and extralegal political associations. Republican upstarts and factions, they believed, were stirring up the people against their natural rulers. They spread radical French principles, interfered with the electoral proc-

ess, and herded the people, including recent immigrants, into political activity. New kinds of writers and publishers, including the former indentured servant and now congressman and editor Matthew Lyon of Vermont, were reaching out to influence an audience as obscure and ordinary as themselves. Through the coarse language and slander of their publications, thought the Federalists, these writers and editors were destroying the governing gentry's personal reputation for character on which popular respect for the entire political order was presumably based.

By the late 1790s, amid an economic depression and the "quasi-war" with France, all these Federalists' fears climaxed in their desperate repressive measures of 1798. These measures more than anything else have tarnished the historical reputation of the Federalists.

In control of both the presidency and Congress, the Federalists contemplated various plans for strengthening the Union. They sought to broaden the power of the federal judiciary, to increase the transportation network throughout the country, and to enlarge the army and navy. Above all, the Federalists aimed to end the Republicans' political exploitation of new immigrants and to stop the flow of Republican literature that was poisoning the relations between the rulers and the ruled.

In 1798 the Federalist-dominated Congress passed the Alien and Sedition Acts. These acts lengthened the naturalization process for foreigners, gave the president extraordinary powers to deal with aliens, and provided the central government with the authority to punish as crimes seditious libels—derogatory remarks tending to incite disobedience to the law—against federal officials. At the same time Congress ordered the immediate enlistment of a new regular army of 12,000 and laid plans for provisional armies numbering in the tens of thousands. Washington was to be called out of retirement as commander in chief of the new army, but Hamilton was to be actually in command. Presumably all these measures were designed to meet the threat of a French invasion, but some people believed that their purpose was actually to deal with domestic disorder in the United States. When the United States army quickly suppressed an armed rebellion of several northeastern Pennsylvania counties, led by John Fries, in protest against the new federal tax on houses, land, and slaves, the advantages of federal strength were confirmed in some Federalist eyes.

For their part, the Republicans in 1798–99 thought the very success of the American Revolution was at stake. In response to the Federalist repression, particularly the Alien and Sedition Acts, the Virginia and Kentucky legislatures issued resolutions that were drawn up by Madison and Jefferson respectively. These resolutions proclaimed the right of the states to judge the constitutionality of federal acts and to interpose themselves between the citizenry and the unconstitutional actions of the central government. Although the other states declined to support Virginia and Kentucky, the stand taken by these two states opened a question about the nature of the Union that would trouble the country for many decades, leading up to the Civil War.

By the end of the 1790s, several developments brought a measure of reconciliation. Both Madison and Jefferson were unwilling to resort to force to support their resolutions. British Admiral Horatio Nelson's naval victory over the French at the Battle of the Nile in October 1798 lessened the threat of a French invasion of either England or America. But most important in calming the crisis was the action of President John Adams.

Adams's presidency had been contentious, and he was never in command of his own cabinet, let alone the government. This short, puffy, and sensitive man, who wore his heart on his sleeve, was much too honest, impulsive, and independent-minded to handle the growing division among the Federalists over the military buildup. But he had an abiding fear of standing armies and a stubborn courage. In 1799, against the wishes of his advisers, he decided to send another peace message to France despite the humiliating failure of his earlier effort in the XYZ Affair. France, now headed by First Consul Napoleon Bonaparte, who would soon make himself emperor, agreed to make terms and in 1800 signed an agreement with the United States that brought the quasi-war to a close.

Adams's independent action fatally divided the Federalist leadership between the moderates who supported the president and the High Federalists who supported Hamilton. This split crippled Adams's chances of winning the presidential election of 1800. Adams, always ready to bemoan his country's neglect of his achievements, considered his decision to negotiate with France "the most disinterested, most determined and most successful of my whole life." His controversial decision ended the war crisis and undermined the attempts of the extremist Federalists to strengthen the central government and the military forces of the United States. Although the worst was over, that was not yet clear to everyone at the time. In 1800 the British ambassador still thought the "whole system of American Government" was "tottering to its foundations."

CHRONOLOGY

1781 Articles of Confederation ratified.
Congress establishes Bank of North America.

1782 Fall of Lord North's ministry.

1783 Newburgh conspiracy of American army officers.
Society of the Cincinnati founded.
Pennsylvania Evening Post, first daily newspaper in the United States, begins publication.
Treaty of Peace with Britain signed.

1785 Land Ordinance for Northwest Territory adopted by Congress.

1786 Jay-Gardoqui Treaty; rejected by Congress.
Virginia Act for Establishing Religious Freedom.
Shays's Rebellion in western Massachusetts.
Annapolis Convention; adopts plan to meet in Philadelphia to revise Articles of Confederation.

1787 Federal Constitutional Convention meets in Philadelphia and drafts Constitution.
Northwest Ordinance enacted by Congress.
The Federalist papers begun by Madison, Hamilton, and Jay.

1788 Ratification of United States Constitution by all states except Rhode Island and North Carolina.

1789 First session of Congress meets.
Washington inaugurated as first president.
Capitol at Richmond, Virginia, built from model of Maison Carrée supplied by Jefferson.
Outbreak of French Revolution.

1790 Hamilton's Report on Public Credit; Funding Bill; Assumption Bill.
Father John Carroll made first Roman Catholic bishop of United States with see in Baltimore.

1791 Bank of the United States established.
First ten amendments to Constitution (Bill of Rights) adopted.
Defeat of General Arthur St. Clair by Ohio Indians.

1793 Execution of Louis XVI of France; outbreak of European war.
Washington inaugurated for second term.
Proclamation of Neutrality by Washington.
Citizen Genêt Affair.
Samuel Slater erects first U.S. cotton mill, at Pawtucket, Rhode Island.
Eli Whitney applies for patent on cotton gin.
Yellow fever epidemic in Philadelphia.

1794 Whiskey Rebellion in western Pennsylvania.
Battle of Fallen Timbers, Ohio; General Anthony Wayne defeats Indians.
Philadelphia-Lancaster turnpike completed.

1795 Jay's Treaty with Britain.
Treaty of Greenville, between United States and Indians of Northwest.
Pinckney's Treaty with Spain.

1796 Washington's Farewell Address, warning against foreign entanglements and domestic factionalism.
John Adams elected president.

1798 XYZ Affair reported by Adams to Congress.
Quasi-war with France on high seas.
Alien and Sedition Acts enacted by Federalists in Congress.
Virginia and Kentucky resolutions.
Eleventh Amendment to Constitution ratified.

1799 *American Review and Literary Journal*, first quarterly literary review in America, established by the novelist Charles Brockden Brown.
Fries uprising in Pennsylvania.

SUGGESTED READINGS

John Fiske, *The Critical Period of American History* (1888), popularized the Federalist view of the Confederation for the nineteenth century. Merrill Jensen, *The New Nation* (1950), minimizes the crisis of the 1780s and explains the movement for the Constitution as the work of a small but dynamic minority. E. James Ferguson, *The Power of the Purse . . . , 1776–1790* (1961), also stresses the nationalists' efforts to strengthen the Confederation. Clarence L. Ver Steeg, *Robert Morris, Revolutionary Financier* (1954), is the major study of that important figure. Forrest McDonald, *E. Pluribus Unum: The Formation of the American Republic, 1776–1790* (1965), describes the commercial scrambling by the Americans in the 1780s. The best account of the army and the Newburgh Conspiracy is Richard H. Kohn, *Eagle and Sword: The Federalists and the Creation of the Military Establishment in America, 1783–1802* (1975). Frederick W. Marks III, *Independence on Trial* (1973), analyzes the foreign problems contributing to the Constitution. The best short survey of the Confederation period is still Andrew C. McLaughlin, *The Confederation and the Constitution, 1783–1789* (1905).

Charles Beard's *An Economic Interpretation of the Constitution* (1913) sought to explain the Constitution as something other than the consequence of high-minded idealism. It became the most influential history book ever written in America. Beard saw the struggle over the Constitution as a "deep-seated conflict between a popular party based on paper money and agrarian interests and a conservative party centered in the towns and resting on financial, mercantile, and personal property interests generally." While Beard's particular proof for his thesis—that the Founders held federal securities that they expected would appreciate in value under a new national government—has been demolished, especially by Forrest McDonald, *We the People* (1958), his general interpretation of the origins of the Constitution still casts a long shadow. Jackson T. Main, *Political Parties Before the Constitution* (1974), finds a "cosmopolitan"-"localist" split within the states over the Constitution. Gordon S. Wood, *The Creation of the American Republic, 1776–1787* (1969), working through the ideas, discovers a similar social, but not strictly speaking a "class," division over the Constitution.

For a different emphasis on the origins of the Constitution, see Robert E. Brown, *Reinterpretation of the Formation of the American Constitution* (1963), and Benjamin F. Wright, Jr., *Consensus and Continuity, 1776–1787* (1958). The best history of the Convention is still Max Farrand, *The Framing of the Constitution of the United States* (1913), which sees the Constitution as "a bundle of compromises" designed to meet specific defects of the Articles. Irving Brant's third volume of his biography of *James Madison* (6 vols., 1941–61) has a sure-footed description of the Convention.

Max Farrand, ed., *The Records of the Federal Convention of 1787* (4 vols.; 1911, 1937); and Jonathan Elliot, ed., *The Debates in the Several State Conventions on the Adoption of the Federal Constitution* (5 vols., 1876), are collections of the important documents. Jacob Cooke, ed., *The Federalist* (1961), is the best edition of these papers. Two sympathetic studies of the Antifederalists are Jackson T. Main, *The Antifederalists . . . , 1781–1788* (1961); and Robert A. Rutland, *The Ordeal of the Constitution* (1966). See also Robert A. Rutland, *The Birth of the Bill of Rights, 1776–1791* (1955). The papers of the Founders—Jefferson, Franklin, Hamilton, John Adams, Madison, and others—are currently being published in mammoth scholarly editions.

Politics in the 1790s is ably summarized in John C. Miller, *The Federalist Era, 1789–1801* (1960). Richard Buel, Jr., *Securing the Revolution: Ideology in American Politics, 1789–1815* (1972), however, better recaptures the distinctiveness of the age and the problematical character of the new national government. John C. Miller, *Alexander Hamilton, Portrait in Paradox* (1959), is the fullest biography; but

Gerald Stourzh, *Alexander Hamilton and the Idea of Republican Government* (1970), better places this leading Federalist in an eighteenth-century context. In this respect, see also the collected essays of Douglass Adair, *Fame and the Founding Fathers* (1974). A concise study is Forrest McDonald, *The Presidency of George Washington* (1974). For single-volume biographies of Washington, see Marcus Cunliffe, *George Washington: Man and Monument* (1958), and James Thomas Flexner, *Washington: The Indispensable Man* (1974). See also Garry Wills, *Cincinnatus: George Washington and the Enlightenment* (1984).

Leonard D. White, *The Federalists: A Study in Administrative History* (1948), is the standard account of the creation of the governmental bureaucracy. See also Carl Prince, *The Federalists and the Origins of the U.S. Civil Service* (1978). Lisle A. Rose, *Prologue to Democracy* (1968), describes the formation of Federalist influence in the South during the 1790s. Richard H. Kohn, *Eagle and Sword: The Federalists and the Creation of the Military Establishment in America, 1783–1802* (1975), is important for understanding the Federalist goals. On foreign policy, see Samuel Flagg Bemis, *Jay's Treaty* (1923) and *Pinckney's Treaty* (1926). Jerald A. Combs, *The Jay Treaty* (1970), is broader than its title would suggest. A good survey is Lawrence S. Kaplan, *Colonies into Nation: American Diplomacy, 1763–1801* (1972).

Much of the literature on the history of the 1790s treats the opposition of the Republicans as ordinary party activity. See William N. Chambers, *Political Parties in a New Nation . . . , 1776–1809* (1963), and Noble E. Cunningham, Jr., *The Jeffersonian Republicans: The Formation of Party Organization, 1789–1801* (1957). Notable exceptions are Richard Buel, Jr., *Securing the Revolution* (1972); Lance Banning, *The Jeffersonian Persuasion* (1978); and Ronald Formisano, *The Transformation of Political Culture: Massachusetts Parties, 1790s–1840s* (1983). See also John Zvesper, *Political Philosophy and Rhetoric: A Study of the Origins of American Party Politics* (1977). On the formation of extralegal organizations, all we have is Eugene P. Link, *Democratic Republican Societies, 1790–1800* (1942). There are a number of studies of the growth of the Republican party in the separate states. See especially Paul Goodman, *The Democratic Republicans of Massachusetts* (1964); Alfred F. Young, *The Democratic Republicans of New York* (1967); Sanford W. Higgenbotham, *The Keystone in the Democratic Arch: Pennsylvania Politics 1800–1816* (1952); Carl E. Prince, *New Jersey's Jeffersonian Republicans* (1967); and Norman K. Risjord, *Chesapeake Politics, 1781–1800* (1978). On the Whiskey Rebellion, see Leland D. Baldwin, *Whiskey Rebels* (1939).

On the foreign crisis of the late 1790s, see Alexander De Conde, *The Quasi-War: Politics and Diplomacy of the Undeclared War with France, 1797–1801* (1966). Manning J. Dauer, *The Adams Federalists* (1953), captures some of the desperation of the Federalists in 1798. The fullest study of the Alien and Sedition Acts is James Morton Smith, *Freedom's Fetters* (1956); but for a proper appreciation of the special eighteenth-century context in which freedom of speech and of the press has to be viewed, see Leonard W. Levy, *Legacy of Suppression* (1960). Stephen G. Kurtz is solid on *The Presidency of Adams . . . , 1795–1800* (1957).

11 The Jeffersonian Revolution

The Federalist world had been born in reaction to the popular excesses of the Revolution, and it could not endure. It ran too much against the grain of fast-moving social developments. The Federalists of the 1790s refused to recognize that the people's position in American politics was no longer a debatable issue. Convinced that people feared disunion so much that almost any sort of strong national government within a republican framework would be acceptable, the Federalists tried to revive some of the energy and authority of executive government that had been lost in the turbulence of the Revolution. America was increasingly prosperous, and the Federalists counted on this prosperity to justify both their program and their reliance on rule by a traditional gentlemanly elite. But they were so out of touch with the rapid developments of American life, and their program was so counter to the basic principles of American republican ideology, that they provoked a second revolutionary movement that threatened to tear the Republic apart.

Only the electoral victory of the Republicans in 1800 ended this threat and brought, in the eyes of many Americans, the entire revolutionary venture of two and a half decades to successful completion. Indeed, "the Revolution of 1800," as the Republican leader and third president of the United States, Thomas Jefferson, described it, "was as real a revolution in the principles of our government as that of 1776 was in its form."

The Revolution of 1800

Thomas Jefferson was an unlikely popular radical. He was a well-connected and highly cultivated southern landowner who never had to scramble for his position in Virginia. The wealth and leisure that made possible his great contributions to liberty were supported by the labor of a hundred or more slaves. He was tall, gangling, red-haired; and unlike his fellow Revolutionary John Adams, whom he both fought and be-friended for fifty years, he was reserved, self-possessed, and incurably optimistic. He disliked personal controversy and was always charming in face-to-face relations with both friends and enemies. But at a distance he could hate, and thus many of his opponents concluded that he was two-faced. He was undeniably complicated. He mingled the most lofty visions with astute back-room politicking. He was a sophisticated man of the world who loved no place better than his native Virginia. This complex slave-holding aristocrat became the most important apostle for democratic idealism in American history.

Thomas Jefferson's narrow victory in the presidential election of 1800 confirmed the changing course of national developments. Jefferson received seventy-three electoral votes to the sixty-five of the Federalist candidate, John Adams, who was opposed by the Hamiltonians within his own party. For a moment even that close victory was in doubt. Because the Constitution did not state that the electors had to distinguish between their votes for president and those for vice-president, both Jefferson and the Republican vice-presidential candidate Aaron Burr had received the same number of electoral votes. Thus the election was thrown into the House of Representatives. After thirty-five deadlocked ballots, Hamilton and other Federalist leaders allowed Jefferson, the acknowledged Republican leader, to become president. They preferred Jefferson to Burr and thought that they had assurances from Jefferson that he would continue Federalist policies.* To avoid a repetition of this electoral impasse, the country adopted the Twelfth Amendment to the Constitution, which allowed the electors to designate their presidential and vice-presidential choices separately in their ballots.**

---

*This was one of the causes of the feud between Burr and Hamilton that led to a duel between the two men in 1804, in which Hamilton was killed.

**For the Twelfth Amendment, see Appendix.

254

In this confused electoral maneuvering it is difficult to see the bold and revolutionary character of Jefferson's election. It was one of the first popular elections in modern history that resulted in the peaceful transfer of power from one "party" to another. At the outset Jefferson himself struck a note of conciliation: "We are all republicans—we are all federalists," he said in his inaugural address. Many Federalists were soon absorbed into the Republican cause. And the Republican administration did subsequently deviate from strict Republican principles. Thus the continuities are impressive, and the Jeffersonian "revolution of 1800" has blended nearly imperceptibly into the main democratic currents of American history. However, when compared to the consolidated state that the Federalists tried to build in the 1790s, what the Republicans did after 1800 proved that a real revolution—as real as Jefferson said it was—took place.

Government Without Power.

Believing that most of the evils afflicting humanity in the past had flowed from the abuses of political establishments, the Republicans in 1800 deliberately set about to carry out what they rightly believed was the original aim of the Revolution: to reduce the overawing and dangerous power of government. They wanted to form a national republic that would be based on the country-opposition ideology and modeled on the Revolutionary state governments of 1776. They envisioned a central government whose authority would resemble that of the old Articles of Confederation more than that of the European

"Architecture," Thomas Jefferson once said, "is my delight,
and putting up and pulling down one of my favorite
amusements." Even as a young man, Jefferson was
absorbed in designing and building his home at Monticello.
He went at architecture with a mathematical precision; no
detail of building—from the chemistry of mortar to the
proper technique of laying bricks—was too insignificant for
his attention.

Portrait by R. Peale. Courtesy of the New-York Historical Society, New York City

Massachusetts Historical Society

type of government the Federalists had thought essential. In fact, they wanted to create a general government that would rule without the traditional characteristics of power.

From the outset Jefferson was determined that the new government would lack even the usual rituals of power. At the very beginning he purposefully set a new tone of republican simplicity that was in sharp contrast to the stiff formality and regal ceremony with which the Federalists, in imitation of European court life, had surrounded the presidency. The Federalist presidents, like the English monarchs, had personally delivered their addresses to the legislature "from the throne," but Jefferson chose to submit his in writing. Unlike Washington and Adams, he made himself easily accessible to visitors, all of whom, no matter how

distinguished, the British government's representative to the United States reported, he received "with a most perfect disregard to ceremony both in his dress and manner." Much to the shock of foreign dignitaries, at American state occasions Jefferson replaced the protocol and distinctions of European court life with the egalitarian rules of what he called "pell-mell."

Although Jefferson's dignity and gentlemanly tastes scarcely allowed any actual leveling in social gatherings, his transformation of manners at the capital harmonized with changes that were occurring in American society. For the Republican revolution soon brought to the national government men who, unlike Jefferson, did not have the outward manner of gentlemen, who did not know one another, and who were decidedly not at home in polite society. During the

EARLIEST-KNOWN ENGRAVED VIEW OF WASHINGTON, D.C.

In the early nineteenth century Washington, D.C., the nation's capital, was such a primitive, desolate village that, as a British diplomat remarked, "one may take a ride of several hours within the precincts without meeting with a single individual to disturb one's meditations." Its streets were muddy and filled with tree stumps, its climate was swampy and mosquito-infested, and its unfinished government buildings stood like Greek temples in a deserted ancient city.

early years of the nineteenth century, life in the national capital became steadily vulgarized by the growing presence in drawing rooms of muddy boots, unkempt hair, and the constant chawing and spitting of tobacco.

Even the removal of the national capital in 1800 from Philadelphia, the bustling intellectual and commercial center of the country, to the rural wilderness of the "federal city" on the Potomac accentuated the transformation of power that was taking place. It dramatized the Republicans' attempt to separate the national government from close involvement in the society and their aim to erect the very kind of general government that Hamilton, in *The Federalist* No. 27, had warned against, "a government at a distance and out of sight" that could "hardly be expected to interest the sensations of the people." The new and remote capital, Washington, D.C., utterly failed to attract the population, the commerce, and the social and cultural life that were needed to make it what its original planners had boldly expected, the Rome of the New World. By 1820 Washington was an out-of-the-way village of less than 10,000 inhabitants whose principal business was keeping boardinghouses. Situated in a marsh, the federal city fully deserved the gibes of the visiting Irish

poet Thomas Moore:

> *This embryo capital*
> *where Fancy sees*
> *Squares in Morasses,*
> *obelisks in trees.*

Political Reform. The Republicans in fact meant to have an insignificant national government. The federal government, Jefferson declared in his first message to Congress in 1801, was "charged with the external and mutual relations only of these states." All the rest—the "principal care of our persons, our property, and our reputation, constituting the great field of human concerns"—was to be left to the states. Such a limited national government required turning back a decade of Federalist policy. The Sedition Act of 1798 was allowed to lapse; a new, liberal naturalization law was adopted; and strict economy was ordered, to root out Federalist corruption.

The inherited Federalist governmental establishment was minuscule by modern standards and was small even by eighteenth-century European standards. In 1801 the headquarters of the War Department, for example, consisted of only the secretary, an accountant, fourteen clerks, and two messengers. The attorney general did not have even a clerk. Nevertheless, in Jefferson's eyes, this tiny federal bureaucracy had become "too complicated, too expensive," and offices under the Federalists had "unnecessarily multiplied." Thus the roll of federal officials was severely cut back. All tax inspectors and collectors were eliminated. The diplomatic establishment was reduced to three missions—in Britain, France, and Spain. The Federalist dream of creating a modern army and navy in imitation of Europe disappeared, and the military budget was cut in half. The army, stationed in the West, was left with 3,000 regulars and only 172 officers. The navy had but a half-dozen frigates, and by 1807 these were replaced with several hundred gunboats, which were designed only to defend the coast and to deal with the Barbary pirates in the Mediterranean. The benefits of a standing military establishment, the Jeffersonians believed, were not worth the cost either in money or in the threat to liberty that this kind of establishment posed.

Since Hamilton's financial program had formed the basis of the heightened political power of the federal government, it above all had to dismantled. All the internal excise taxes the Federalists had designed to make the people feel the energy of the national government were eliminated. For many citizens the federal presence was now reduced to the delivery of the mails.

Although Jefferson's extremely able secretary of the treasury, Albert Gallatin, persuaded the reluctant president to keep the Bank of the United States, the government was under continual pressure to reduce the Bank's influence. The growing numbers of state banking interests resented the privileged and restraining authority of the national Bank. Eventually, in 1811, state bankers, along with southern landowners, who hated all banks, prevented a renewal of the Bank's charter. The federal government then distributed its patronage among twenty-one state banks and thus effectively diluted its authority to control either the society or the economy. It was in fact the proliferation of these state-chartered banks and their issuing of notes that enabled the states to have paper money after all, despite the Constitution's prohibition against the states' issuing bills of credit.

Precisely because Hamilton had regarded the permanent federal debt as a principal source of support for the federal government, the Republicans were determined to pay off the debt—and quickly. By 1810 the federal debt had been reduced to nearly half of the $80 million it had been when the Republicans took office. Jefferson's lifelong desire to reduce the government's debt was not simply a matter of prohibiting a present generation from burdening its descendants. He wanted also to destroy what he considered an insidious and dangerous instrument of political influence. His aim was to create a new kind of government, one without privilege or patronage.

Perhaps nothing illustrates Jefferson's radical conception of government better than his problems with patronage. Jefferson was reluctant to dismiss or appoint men to office for political reasons. But not all Republicans took his dislike of using patronage as seriously as he did, and many Republicans hesitated to join a government in which they would have no sources of influence. Time and again Jefferson found himself caught between his conscientious determination to avoid anything resembling Hamilton's political patronage, or "corruption," and the pressing demands of his fellow Republicans that he give them a share in the government and oust the enemy. Once the Federalists were replaced by Republicans, however, there was no further need for Republicans to compromise on this issue; and removals from office for political reasons came to an end. By the end of the administrations of Jefferson's Republican successors, James Madison (1809–17), James Monroe (1817–25), and John Quincy Adams (1825–29), the holders of government appointments had become a permanent officialdom of men grown old in their positions. Until the Jacksonian revolution of 1828, patronage as a means of influence in government virtually ceased.

Republican Politics.
Jefferson was able personally to direct Congress and the Republican party to an extraordinary degree. He used a combination of this initial patronage and some improvised forms of political influence—in particular, his nightly legislative dinner parties and his use of confidential legislative agents. Yet Jefferson's personal strength and his notable achievements as president cannot hide the remarkable transformation in the traditional meaning of government that the Republican revolution of 1800 created. During the opening three decades of the nineteenth century, particularly after Jefferson retired from the presidency, the United States government was weaker than at any other time in its national history.

The alignments of politics became increasingly confused. The Federalists in 1800–1801 surrendered the national ruling authority without a fight. Because the Federalist leaders considered themselves gentlemen for whom politics was not an exclusive concern, they were prepared to retire to their businesses and private lives and await what they assumed would soon be the people's desperate call for the return of the "wise and good" and the "natural rulers." But the popular reaction against the Republican revolution did not come. Some, like John Jay and John Adams, retired to their country estates. Others, like John Quincy Adams, the son of the former president, eventually joined the Republican movement. Others, like Robert

Goodloe Harper of South Carolina, clung to their principles and their minority status in politics. And still others, like Timothy Pickering, secretary of state under John Adams, dreamed of revenge and encouraged separatist plots in New England. But as a national party, Federalism slowly withered under the relentless democratization of American society.

Although the Federalists and Republicans continued to compete for election and worked successfully to increase voter participation, neither was a party in any modern sense; that is, neither recognized the other as a necessary and permanent part of the political process. It is therefore probably anachronistic to call their electoral competition "the first party system," as some historians have done. Although the Federalists continued to put up presidential candidates, their electoral strength was generally very weak and was confined primarily to New England. By 1807 even in Massachusetts there were more Republican than Federalist congressmen. During the administration's Republican crises over foreign policy and the embargo in 1808–09 and the War of 1812, the Federalists did manage to rally and to win major victories—not only in New England, but also in New York, Maryland, and Delaware. But elsewhere the Federalists' power at the polls rarely approached that achieved in 1800, and the party slowly declined. It was much too tainted with aristocracy and New England sectionalism to persist as a national party. By 1820 it was too weak even to nominate a presidential candidate.

While the declining Federalist gentlemen regarded themselves less as a party than as rightful rulers who had been driven from power, the Republicans saw themselves as leaders of a revolutionary movement and were eager to incorporate the bulk of the opposition into their fold. Only as long as the Federalists posed a threat to the principles of free government could the Republicans remain a unified party. Thereafter, as the possibility of a Federalist comeback faded, the Republican party gradually fell apart. A variety of Republican factions and groups arose in Congress and in the country. These were organized around particular individuals (the "Burrites," the "Clintonians"), around states and sections (the "Pennsylvania Quids," the "Old Republicans" of Virginia), and sometimes around ideology ("the Principles of '98," the "Invisibles," the "War Hawks"). Individual politicians continued to pride themselves on their independence from influence of any sort, and *party* remained a disrespectful word. In fact, until the Jacksonian era nothing approaching a stable party system developed in Congress.

By the end of Jefferson's presidency in 1809, the balance of governmental power had slipped to Congress, which was unequipped to exercise it. Because of the great increase in the size of Congress and its growing disintegration into diverse voting blocs, neither Madison nor Monroe was able to use any of the personal charm and influence that Jefferson had used. By 1808 caucuses of Republicans within Congress had taken over nomination of the party's candidates for the presidency, and Republican presidential aspirants soon became dependent on the legislature in the way governors in the Revolutionary state constitutions of 1776 had been.

With Jefferson's private blessing, Secretary of State James Madison was able to secure the Republican nomination in 1808 and again in 1812 against only some divided opposition. But in 1816, Madison's secretary of state, James Monroe, had to contend strenuously with Secretary of War William H. Crawford of Georgia for the nomination. By the early 1820s Secretary of State John Quincy Adams, Secretary of War John C. Calhoun, and Secretary of the Treasury Crawford were all feuding with one another and seeking support in Congress for the presidential nomination. If such political realities did not dictate that presidents defer to the legislature, Republican ideology did. Except in foreign affairs, presidents Madison and Monroe, the second and third members of the so-called Virginia Dynasty, considered that Congress had the right to determine the public will, free of executive influence.

As Congress gathered up the power draining away from the executive in the Madison and Monroe administrations (1809–25), it sought to organize itself into committees in order to initiate and supervise policy. But the rise of the committee system only further fragmented the government into contending interest groups. The executive authority itself broke apart into competing departments, with each member of the cabinet seeking his own support in Congress and becoming a rival of the president. Congress now fought with the president for control of the cabinet and connived with executive department heads behind the president's back. At one point Congress actually forced Madison to accept a secretary of state who was plotting against him, and its meddling drove Monroe into bitter hostility against his secretary of the treasury, with whom he stopped speaking. Until the congressional caucus system of presidential nomination collapsed in 1824 and a new kind of democratic presidency emerged in 1828 with the election of Andrew Jackson, the energy of the national executive remained weak.

But despite this concentration on strict republican principles, by the second decade of the nineteenth century many Americans sought to reclaim and reenact some of the abandoned Federalist measures. A new generation of politicians, less attached to the ideology

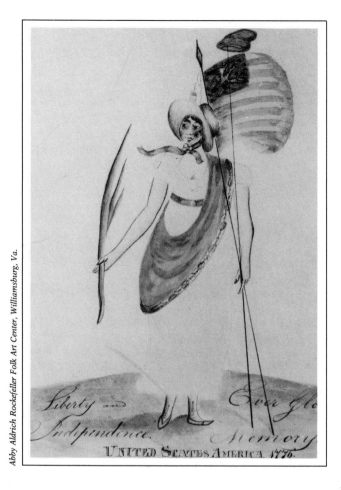

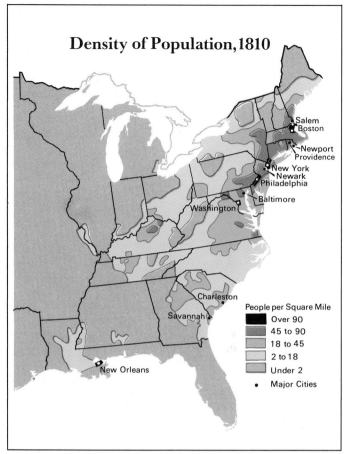

and fears of the eighteenth century and with none of Hamilton's dream to create a consolidated state in the European manner, now began urging a new national bank, protective tariffs, and a federally sponsored system of "internal improvements"—canals, turnpikes, and the like. By 1814 the nation had grown faster than anyone had expected, and new states, new interest groups, and new outlooks had to be taken into account. By then it was becoming clear that the future of the country lay in the West.

An Empire of Liberty

While Hamilton and the Federalists had looked eastward across the Atlantic to Europe for their image of the destiny of the United States, the Republicans from the beginning had had their eyes on the West. Only by moving westward, Jefferson thought, could Americans maintain their republican society of independent yeoman-farmers and avoid the miseries of the concentrated urban working classes of Europe. Jefferson was indeed the most expansion-minded president in Amer-

ican history. He dreamed of Americans with republican principles eventually swarming over the continent and creating an "empire of liberty." Yet even Jefferson did not anticipate how suddenly and chaotically Americans would scatter westward.

The population grew from almost 4 million in 1790 to more than 7 million in 1810 and nearly 10 million by 1820, and much of it was moving west. By the 1790s the population in some of the tidewater counties of the Chesapeake region was declining. The advance over the Allegheny Plateau that had been a trickle before the Revolution and had swelled during the 1780s now became a flood. Within a single generation after the Revolution, more territory was occupied than during the entire colonial period. By 1810 westward-moving Americans had created a great triangular wedge of settlement reaching to the Mississippi River. The northern side of the triangle ran from New York along the Ohio River, the southern side extended from east Georgia through Tennessee, and the two sides met at the tip of the wedge at St. Louis. Within this huge triangle of settlement, people were

UNDER MY WINGS EVERY THING PROSPERS

VIEW OF NEW ORLEANS, 1803
"There is on the globe one single spot, the possessor of which is our natural and habitual enemy," said President Jefferson in 1802. "It is New Orleans, through which the produce of three-eighths of our territory must pass to market." It was the American desire to control this port that led to the Louisiana Purchase.

distributed haphazardly, and huge pockets remained virtually uninhabited.

National leaders had expected westward migration, but not the way it happened. The carefully drawn plans of the 1780s for the orderly surveying and settlement of the West were simply overwhelmed by the massive and chaotic movement of people. Many settlers ignored land ordinances and titles, squatted on the land, and claimed rights to it. For decades beginning in 1796, the federal government steadily lowered the price of land, reduced the size of purchasable tracts, and relaxed the terms of credit in ever more desperate efforts to bring the public land laws into line with the speed with which the West was being settled. There was more land than people could use, and still they kept moving. Some moved three and four times in a lifetime. Speculators and land companies that had counted on land values rising through neat and orderly settlement, as in colonial days, were now wiped out. Many of the most prominent and wealthy Revolutionary leaders, including Robert Morris, the financier

of the Confederation, Henry Knox, Washington's secretary of war, and James Wilson, justice of the Supreme Court, speculated heavily in land and ended their careers in bankruptcy. Even Washington died with his estate tied up in speculative land that no one would pay for.

The Louisiana Purchase. Nothing in Jefferson's administration contributed more to this astonishing expansion than his sudden acquisition in 1803 of the entire territory of Louisiana. This territory extended from the Mississippi River to the Rocky Mountains, and its acquisition doubled the size of the United States. For decades Jefferson and other American leaders had foreseen that the young and thriving nation would expand naturally and "piece by piece" would take over the feebly held Spanish possessions in North America. Some even thought that British-held Canada would eventually pass to the United States. When the Revolutionary War ended in 1783, Jefferson was already dreaming of explorations to the Pacific. And when he

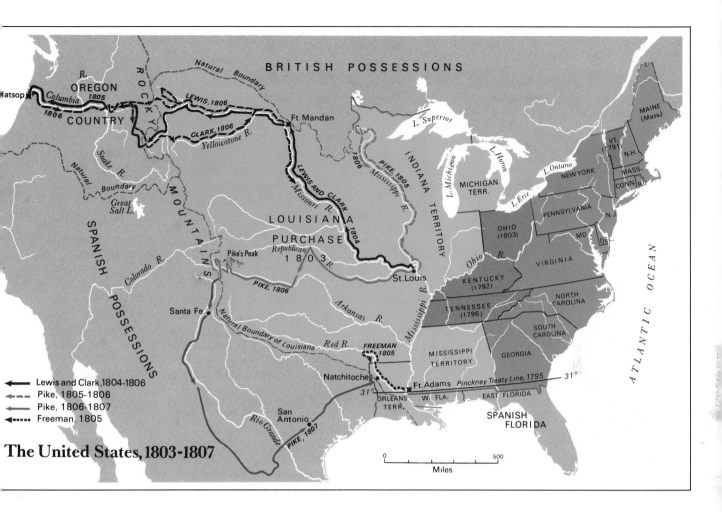

The United States, 1803-1807

Lewis and Clark, 1804-1806
Pike, 1805-1806
Pike, 1806-1807
Freeman, 1805

became president, well before he had any inkling that America would purchase all of Louisiana, he laid plans for scientific—and also military and commercial—expeditions into the foreign-held trans-Mississippi West. The most famous of these expeditions was that of Lewis and Clark, eventually undertaken in 1803–06.

In 1800 these dreams of expansion were suddenly placed in doubt when, in the Treaty of San Ildefonso, a weak Spain ceded back to a powerful France the territory of Louisiana, including New Orleans, that France had once held west of the Mississippi River. The livelihood of the western farmers depended on the free navigation of the Mississippi, and Jefferson was determined to maintain it. He immediately began strengthening fortifications in the West and preparing for the worst. "The day that France takes possession of New Orleans," he informed the American minister to France, Robert Livingston, in April 1802, "we must marry ourselves to the British fleet and nation." This prospect of an American-British alliance threatened

the French. Napoleon Bonaparte—soon to become Emperor Napoleon I—was already calculating the difficulties of reestablishing the French empire in the New World if war should break out again in Europe. As a result, in 1803 the French government decided to sell to the United States not just New Orleans, which Jefferson had sought to purchase, but all of Louisiana, for $15 million.

Jefferson hesitated over what to do. He feared that the purchase of Louisiana by the federal government would exceed the limited powers that had been granted to the government by the Constitution. He considered amending the Constitution in order to acquire this new territory. But finally and regretfully, under intense pressure, he allowed his constitutional scruples to be passed over in silence. Despite the fact that the Louisiana Purchase fulfilled his grandest dreams for America, Jefferson's agonized decision did not suggest that he was conceding in any way to a broad Federalist interpretation of the Constitution.

The Lewis and Clark expedition (1804–06) was the greatest expedition of exploration in American history. Lewis and Clark led a party of fifty from St. Louis to the Pacific with instructions from President Jefferson to keep detailed records of everything they saw, including the various tribes of Indians. As Nicholas Biddle, the first editor of the expedition's journals, later told Clark, "[Because] in our towns, and in Europe too . . . we know nothing of Indians, every little matter is a subject that excites curiosity." The Ricaras (modern name Arikaras) were remnants of the Pawnees. Their three villages, on the southwestern bank of the Missouri, contained 500 warriors and a total population of 2,600.

*T*HE weather was this day fine, and as we were desirous of assembling the whole nation at once, we . . . invite[d] the chiefs of the two upper villages to a conference. They all assembled at one o'clock, and after the usual ceremonies we addressed them in the same way in which we had already spoken to the Ottoes and Sioux. . . . The air-gun was exhibited, very much to their astonishment, nor were they less surprised at the color and manner of York [Clark's black servant]. On our side we were equally gratified at discovering that these [Indians] made use of no spirituous liquors of any kind, the example of the traders who bring it to them, so far from tempting, having in fact disgusted them. Supposing that it was as agreeable to them as to the other Indians, we had at first offered them whisky; but they refused it with this sensible remark, that they were surprised that their father should present to them a liquor which would make them fools. . . .

We went . . . to the house of the chief of the second village, where we found his chiefs and warriors. They made us a present of about seven bushels of corn, a pair of leggings, a twist of their tobacco, and seeds of two different species of tobacco. The chief then delivered a speech expressive of his gratitude for the presents and good counsels which we had given him; his intention of visiting his great father, but for fear of the Sioux; and requested us to take one of the Ricara chiefs up to the Mandans and negotiate a peace between the two nations. To this we replied in a suitable way. . . .

The . . . villages . . . are the residence of a nation called the Ricaras. . . . The Ricaras are tall and well proportioned, the women handsome and lively, and as among other savages to them falls all the drudgery of the field and the labors of procuring subsistence, except that of hunting. Both sexes are poor, but kind and generous, and although they receive with thankfulness what is given to them, do not beg as the Sioux did. . . .

Lewis and Clark Encounter the Plains Indians

These women are handsomer than the Sioux; both of them are, however, disposed to be amorous and our men found no difficulty in procuring companions for the night by means of the interpreters. These interviews were chiefly clandestine, and were of course to be kept a secret from the husband or relations. The point of honor indeed is completely reversed among the Ricaras; that the wife or the sister should submit to a stranger's embraces without the consent of her husband or brother is a cause of great disgrace and offense, especially as for many purposes of civility or gratitude the husband and brother will themselves present to a stranger these females, and be gratified by attentions to them. The Sioux had offered us squaws, but we having declined while we remained there, they followed us with offers of females for two days. The Ricaras had been equally accommodating; we had equally withstood their temptation; but such was their desire to oblige us that two very handsome young squaws were sent on board this evening, and persecuted us with civilities. The black man York participated largely in these favors; for, instead of inspiring any prejudice, his color seemed to procure him additional advantages from the Indians, who desired to preserve among them some memorial of this wonderful stranger. Among other instances of attention, a Ricara invited him into his house and, presenting his wife to him, retired to the outside of the door; while there one of York's comrades who was looking for him came to the door, but the gallant husband would permit no interruption until a reasonable time had elapsed.

The Ricara lodges are in a circular or octagonal form, and generally about 30 or 40 feet in diameter. They are made by placing forked posts about six feet high round the circumference of the circle; these are joined by poles from one fork to another, which are supported also by other forked poles slanting from the ground; in the center of the lodge are placed four higher forks, about 15 feet in length, connected together by beams; from these to the lower poles the rafters of the roof are extended so as to leave a vacancy in the middle for the smoke; the frame of the building is then covered with willow branches, with which is interwoven grass, and over this [is placed] mud or clay; the aperture for the door is about four feet wide, and before it is a sort of entry about ten feet from the lodge. They are very warm and compact.

They cultivate maize or Indian corn, beans, pumpkins, watermelons, squashes, and a species of tobacco peculiar to themselves. Their commerce is chiefly with the traders, who supply them with goods in return for peltries, which they procure not only by their own hunting, but in exchange for corn from their less civilized neighbors. The object chiefly in demand seemed to be red paint, but they would give anything they had to spare for the most trifling article. One of the men to-day gave an Indian a hook made out of a pin, and received in return a pair of moccasins.

His hesitation only showed the extreme seriousness with which he took his strict construction of the Constitution.

The purchase of Louisiana was the most popular and important event of Jefferson's presidency. It ended the long struggle for control of the Mississippi River's outlet to the sea. It also, as Jefferson exulted, freed America from Europe's colonial entanglements and prepared the way for the eventual dominance of the United States in the Western Hemisphere. Its most immediate consequence, however, was to raise new fears of the country's splitting apart. The borders of the new territory were so vague, the Spanish hold on Mexico and the Floridas so weak, and the rough and unruly frontier inhabitants so captivated by the dreams of America's continued expansion that adventurers, filibustering expeditions,* and rumors of plots and conspiracies flourished throughout the South and the West.

The Burr Conspiracy.

The most grandiose of these schemes was that of 1806–07. It involved Aaron Burr, Jefferson's former vice-president, and (until he turned state's evidence) General James Wilkinson, commanding general of the United States Army. Wilkinson was secretly in the pay of the Spanish government and was one of the most unscrupulous and skillful adventurers in American history. In the summer of 1806, Burr and sixty men floated in flatboats down the Ohio and Mississippi rivers toward New Orleans to make contact with the Spanish. When Burr learned that Wilkinson had denounced him, he fled toward Florida, probably on his way to Europe, but he was captured and brought east to be tried for treason. Although Burr was acquitted because no overt act of treason could be consitutionally proved, he undoubtedly had had in mind some sort of conspiracy, involving a number of American civil and military officials, directed toward an attack on Mexico or a separation of the western areas of the United States.

These kinds of activities and the danger of the country's splintering caused Congress to incorporate into the Union as fast as possible the underdeveloped frontier territories of Ohio (1803), Louisiana (1812), Indiana (1816), Mississippi (1817), Illinois (1818), and Alabama (1819). These new western states were firmly Republican, and they created constitutions that were more democratic than those of the older eastern states. Most provided for weak executives, white male suffrage, annually elected legislatures, no property qualifications for officeholders, and popular election for a host of officials, including judges.

Indians.

The native Americans in these western territories were no match for the hordes of advancing settlers. By 1800 Ohio had 45,000 inhabitants; by 1810 it had more than 230,000 and was already bursting its boundaries. Although the Greenville Treaty of 1795 had drawn a definite line between Indians and whites, most Americans, including President Jefferson, assumed that the vast Indian hunting grounds between the Ohio and Mississippi rivers must sooner or later belong to the advancing Americans. Jefferson expected the native Americans willingly to cede their lands to the United States and either become farmers and share the blessings of republican civilization or move west beyond the Mississippi.

American pressure on the Indians to surrender their lands was immense, and under presidents Jefferson and Madison fifty-three treaties of land cession were made. Finally in 1805 the Shawnee chief Tecumseh and his brother The Prophet attempted to halt this steady American encroachment by forming an Indian confederacy. This tribal effort at organized resistance was broken by the governor of the Indiana Territory, General William Henry Harrison, in a battle between six hundred Indians and a mixed force of a thousand American army troops and Kentucky frontiersmen at Tippecanoe in 1811. Sporadic Indian fighting and raiding in the Old Northwest continued, however, but it did not stop the wave of settlers. By 1815 the Indiana Territory had nearly 60,000 settlers.

In the southwestern territories the Indian presence was even more formidable. Still, by 1810 the Mississippi Territory (much of present-day Alabama and Mississippi) had more than 40,000 people, including 17,000 slaves, mainly clustered along the Mississippi River counties south of Natchez, which was fast becoming a bustling trade center. In 1810 the Territory of Orleans (modern Louisiana) had more than 76,000 inhabitants, more than half of whom were slaves. New Orleans, with its mixture of Spanish, French, and other nationalities in a population of more than 10,000, was by far the largest and most flamboyant city of the Mississippi Valley and was on its way to becoming one of the greatest ports of the country. By 1810 pioneers were rapidly pushing beyond the Mississippi River into what are now the states of Arkansas and Missouri, leaving behind huge pockets of native Americans—Creeks in Georgia and Cherokees in Tennessee. By 1815 the Missouri Territory had more than 20,000 people.

All the while, eastern Federalists expressed alarm at this expanding "empire of liberty." With their vision of the United States as a homogeneous and integrated

---

*In nineteenth-century America *filibustering* meant stirring up or attempting to carry out revolutions in Central American or Caribbean nations. Those who led expeditions for this purpose were called filibusters.

TECUMSEH (c. 1768–1813)

Tecumseh, a Shawnee chief, was perhaps the most extraordinary Indian leader in American history. Together with his brother, The Prophet, he attempted in the early nineteenth century to organize a huge confederation of Indians in the Northwest. The Indians were to refuse to cede any more lands to the Americans and were to abandon the white man's ways and goods. But after the battle of Tippecanoe in 1811, organized Indian resistance gave way to sporadic warfare. Tecumseh was killed fighting for the British at the battle of the Thames (1813).

nation-state like those of Europe, the Federalists found it inconceivable that such a gigantic republic could long hold together. To the Republicans, however, who thought of the United States as a loosely bound confederation of states, the huge expanse of territory posed no problems. "Who can limit the extent to which the federative principle may operate effectively?" asked Jefferson in his second inaugural address. Jefferson always conceived of his "empire of liberty" in terms of like principles, not of like boundaries. At times he was remarkably indifferent to the possibility that a western confederacy might break away from the eastern United States. What did it matter? he asked in 1804. "Those of the western confederacy will be as much our children and descendants as those of the eastern."

The Federalists called this idea of a nation bound

together only by principles "a most visionary theory," and they believed that the consequence would eventually be anarchy. But Republicans considered that Americans were creating new bonds of social cohesion—not the patronage and coercion of the Federalists, and not even the virtue of classical republicanism, but, as Jefferson said, "that progress of opinion which is tending to unite them in object and in will."

The Origins of Judicial Review

At the time of Jefferson's election in 1800, no institution of the national government was more detested by the Republicans than the judiciary. The appointed federal judges were less susceptible to popular rule than were other government officials, and during the 1790s the Federalists had consciously tried to strengthen the federal courts in order to extend the central government's presence among the people. Since there was not a single Republican judge in the entire national judiciary during the 1790s, Republican newspaper editors had often been brought before the federal courts on charges of sedition. Moreover, Federalist land speculators with interests that spanned state lines had used the more sympathetic federal courts to resolve their conflicting claims, often to the anger of Republican-controlled state courts. Even after the Federalists had lost the election of 1800, the lame-duck Congress dominated by Federalists had passed a new judiciary act creating a system of circuit courts and broadening the jurisdiction of the federal courts. And before surrendering the presidency to Jefferson, John Adams had hastily appointed a number of judges, including John Marshall as chief justice of the United States. Jefferson was convinced that "the remains of federalism" had "retired into the judiciary as a stronghold . . . , and from that battery all the works of republicanism are to be beaten down and erased."

To complete "the revolution," therefore, as a fellow Virginian told Jefferson, "the enemy" had to be routed from "that strong fortress." After a bitter debate in Congress, the Republicans repealed the Federalist Judiciary Act of 1801. They thus destroyed the newly created circuit courts and for the first and only time in United States history revoked the tenure of federal judges as well. In order to bring the entire judicial establishment under greater congressional control, some Republicans proposed amending the Constitution. Others, however, fixed on impeachment for "high crimes and misdemeanors" as the best constitutional device for removing obnoxious Federalist judges. The Republicans in the House of Representatives first impeached and the Senate then convicted John Pickering, an alcoholic and insane judge of the federal district court of New Hampshire, even though he had committed no crimes or misdemeanors.

Having thus broadly interpreted the criminal meaning of impeachment, the most rabid Republicans, under the leadership of John Randolph of Virginia, next attempted to bring down Supreme Court Justice Samuel Chase, the most overbearing Federalist on the Court. However, this perversion of the impeachment process into a means of simply removing unpopular judges from office was too much for some Republicans. Although a majority of the Senate in 1805 found Chase guilty, the Republicans could not muster the necessary two-thirds majority. Not only did Chase's acquittal hurt Randolph's reputation, driving him to the extremist edges of the Republican party, but it ended any further direct assault by the Republicans on the national judiciary.

Marbury v. Madison.

In the meantime John Marshall, who was to become the most important chief justice of the Supreme Court in American history, used his position to drain some of the bitterness from the controversy over the judiciary. During his long career (1801–35), which spanned the administrations of five presidents, he laid the foundations both for the Court's eventual independence and for the constitutional supremacy of the national government over the states.

In 1801, however, the Court was very weak. Although Marshall solidified the Court by making one justice's opinion (usually his own) stand for the decision of the whole Court, he had to move very cautiously. Many Federalists urged him to confront the Republicans head-on by declaring unconstitutional Congress's repeal of the Judiciary Act of 1801. But Marshall chose to act indirectly. In the case of *Marbury v. Madison* (1803), the Marshall Court decided that Marbury, one of the "midnight judges" whom President Adams had appointed as his own term was ending, was entitled to his commission, which Secretary of State Madison had withheld. Yet if unenforced by the president, such a bold decision would obviously have discredited the Court. Marshall avoided a losing clash with the executive by going on to state that, although Marbury deserved his commission, the Court had no authority to order the president to grant it. He ruled that the provision of the earlier, Federalist-enacted Judiciary Act of 1789, which had given the Supreme Court such original authority, was unconstitutional. Thus Marshall indirectly asserted the Court's role in overseeing the Constitution without the serious political repercussions involved in openly opposing the Republicans. Since the American people regarded their written Constitution as "the fundamental and paramount law of the nation," wrote Marshall for the Court, then it followed that "a law re-

JOHN MARSHALL (1755–1835), BY CEPHAS THOMPSON
Marshall is the most famous Chief Justice of the Supreme Court in American history. During his long tenure on the Court from 1801 to his death, this Virginia Federalist participated in more than 1,000 decisions, writing over half himself. In effect Marshall created for America what came to be called constitutional law and transformed the meaning and role of the Supreme Court.

The Bettmann Archive, Inc.

pugnant to the Constitution," such as part of the Judiciary Act of 1789, "is void; and that courts, as well as other departments, are bound by that instrument."

Although Marshall's decision in *Marbury* v. *Madison* has since taken on immense historical significance as the first assertion by the Supreme Court of its right to declare acts of Congress unconstitutional, few in 1803 saw its far-reaching implications. This right of judicial review was nowhere explicitly recognized in the Constitution. To be sure, some, like Hamilton in *The Federalist* No. 78, had tried to justify this ultimate judicial authority by invoking the supremacy of the Constitution as created by the sovereignty of the people and as protected by the courts. But it was by no means established in American culture at the end of the eighteenth century.

By asserting in the *Marbury* decision that the Supreme Court had a right and a duty to declare what the fundamental law was, Marshall obviously drew upon this earlier thinking. But he did not say that the Court was the only part of the national government that had this right and duty. Indeed, Marshall's assertion of judicial authority in the *Marbury* decision was limited and ambiguous. It implied that the other branches of the government had an equal obligation, along with the courts, to interpret the law in accord with the Constitution. Jefferson certainly believed that the executive and the legislature had the same ultimate right as the judiciary to interpret the Constitution, and he always explicitly denied the "exclusive" authority of the judiciary to decide what laws were constitutional. Such a monopoly of interpretative power, he said in 1804, "would make the judiciary a despotic branch." *Marbury* v. *Madison* in fact marked the only time in Marshall's long tenure in which the Supreme Court declared an act of Congress unconstitutional.

Constitutional Nationalism.

What the Marshall Court did do in its long career was declare a large number of *state* judicial interpretations and *state* laws invalid because they violated the federal Constitution. In a series of decisions beginning with *United States* v. *Peters* (1809) and proceeding through *Martin* v. *Hunter's Lessee* (1816) and *Cohens* v. *Virginia* (1821), the Supreme Court established its right to review and reverse decisions of state courts involving interpretations of federal law and the federal Constitution. At the same time, following the first test in *Fletcher* v. *Peck* (1810), the Court overturned a series of state laws that interfered with private contracts and hence violated the Constitution.

Marshall, however, was not content merely with these negative restraints on the states' powers. He sought positively to enhance the supremacy of the national government. In the greatest decision of his career, *McCulloch* v. *Maryland* (1819), Marshall upheld the right of Congress to charter a national bank even though that right was not specifically mentioned in the Constitution. The power to charter a bank, said Marshall, was implied by the "necessary and proper" authority that the Constitution granted to Congress to carry its delegated powers into effect. Hence the attempt by the Maryland legislature to destroy the Bank of the United States by taxation was unconstitutional. No decision of Marshall's was more important to the future of America, and none asserted the supremacy of the Constitution more clearly. By 1820 the Court had already become—even for James Madison—something resembling that "disinterested umpire" that in 1787 he had wanted the entire federal government to be.

The Manipulative Tradition of American Law.

Yet as important as Marshall's decisions were in establishing the Supreme Court's final authority over the states to interpret the Constitution, they do not by themselves explain the origins of the extraordinary authority that has been wielded by all American judges. Judicial review has deeper roots than simply the Marshall court. Nineteenth-century Americans inherited from the colonial period an unusually manipulative attitude toward law. Since the colonists had derived their law haphazardly both from their colonial legislature and courts and from various English sources, they tended to equate law not with what English judges and legal authorities said it was, but with what made sense in America's local circumstances. Time and again eighteenth-century Americans had justified minor deviations and irregularities in their laws in the name of reason, justice, or utility. They thus developed a particularly pragmatic attitude toward law that became stronger in the decades that followed the Revolution.

In the emerging business society of early-nineteenth-century America, the desired predictability of law came not from strict adherence to the decisions of the past, but rather from rapid adaptability to changing commercial circumstances. To mold the law to fit the needs of America's expanding enterprise, both state and federal judges increasingly abandoned the customs and technicalities of the inherited English common law and replaced them with useful and prudent regulations. The idea of the sovereignty of the people that had been emphasized by Revolutionary ideology only confirmed and further justified the independent manipulative power of the judges; the judges were now seen as just another kind of agent of the people with a responsibility equal to that of the legislatures or executive to carry out the people's will. By the second decade of the nineteenth century, American law was coming to be thought of as a man-made creative instrument of social policy. And under fast-moving economic pressures, judges were becoming the chief agents of legal change. The judicial interpretative power that from the beginning was present in the flexibility of American law was now starkly revealed and greatly expanded.

Despite continued efforts in the early nineteenth century to weaken this remarkable judicial authority, law in America maintained its flexible quality. Although judges continued to deny that they made law in the way legislatures did, it was obvious that they did something more than simply discover it in the precedents and customs of the past. Law in America, rooted in the consent and sovereignty of the people, was designed to serve the needs of that people; and when it did not, it was the obligation of judges to interpret it in such a way that it did. In fact, if neither legislatures nor judges could act fast enough to shape the law to changing circumstances, then, some Americans thought, the people themselves, in extralegal groups and "mobs," had the right to take the law into their own hands and mold it as their situation demanded. The uniquely American practices of judicial review and vigilantism were actually two sides of the same legal coin.

Republican Religion

Although politics and constitutionalism dominated the Revolutionary era, most ordinary Americans still conceived of the world in religious terms. Hence the Revolution and even republicanism had a religious dimension. Indeed, the Revolution marked an important point in the history of American religion. It endorsed the Enlightenment's faith in liberty of conscience, cut the already weak connection between church and state, and advanced America into a religious world of competing denominations that was unique to Christendom.

Religious Liberty in the Revolution.
From the outset of the Revolutionary controversy, Americans had argued that the dark forces of civic tyranny and religious tyranny were linked. All the new Revolutionary constitutions of 1776 in some way affirmed religious freedom. Yet the constitutional declarations "that all men have a natural and unalienable right to worship Almighty God according to the dictates of their own consciences" did not necessarily mean that the government would abandon its traditional role in religious matters. To be sure, the official establishment of the Church of England that existed in several of the colonies was immediately eliminated. But the Maryland, South Carolina, and Georgia Revolutionary constitutions authorized their state legislatures to create in place of the Anglican church a kind of multiple establishment of a variety of religious groups, using tax money to support "the Christian religion."

Virginians especially were divided over the meaning of their 1776 declaration of religious liberty. Liberals like Jefferson and Madison joined growing numbers of Presbyterian and Baptist dissenters to oppose the Anglican clergymen and landowners in a fierce but eventually successful struggle for the complete disestablishment of the Church of England. In 1786 this Virginia struggle was climaxed by the passage of Jefferson's memorable Act for Establishing Religious Freedom. Many of the states, however, retained some vague or general religious qualifications for public office, and both Connecticut and Massachusetts continued to recognize the modified but still official status of the Congregational church.

In short, unlike the church in Europe, the American churches, developing as they had in the colonial period, perceived no threat from revolution or republicanism. Except for the Anglicans, Protestant ministers were in the forefront of the Revolutionary movement. In fact, it was the clergy who made the Revolution meaningful for most common people. For every gentleman who read a scholarly pamphlet and delved into Whig theory and ancient history for an explanation of events, there were dozens of ordinary people who read the Bible and looked to their ministers for an interpretation of what the Revolution meant. Evangelical Protestantism blended with republicanism in a common effort to rid America of sin and luxury and to build a new society of goodness and virtue.

Despite these hopes, however, the immediate effect of the Revolution on church organization was devastating. The Revolutionary War destroyed churches, scattered congregations, and led to a sharp decline in church membership. By the 1790s perhaps only one in twenty Americans was affiliated with a church. The earlier revivalistic enthusiasm receded under the pressure of a spreading religious rationalism, called deism, which sought to substitute nature and reason for revelation, and the science of Sir Isaac Newton for the mysteries of traditional Christianity. In 1784, the Vermont Revolutionary Ethan Allen published his book *Reason the Only Oracle of Man*, which boldly attacked the Bible and the clergy and defended natural religion. This was followed by other works, such as Thomas Paine's *Age of Reason* (1794) and the French Comte de Volney's *Ruins of Empire* (1791), which, together with Elihu Palmer's attempts to organize deistic societies among urban workingmen in the 1790s, frightened many religious leaders into concluding that republicanism was breeding disbelief in traditional Christianity.

As long as the enlightened deism of Jefferson and other Revolutionary leaders had been confined to the drawing rooms of the gentry and was not publicized, it had posed little threat to traditional Protestantism. But the spreading of rational and natural religion among ordinary people at the time of the French Revolution alarmed American clergymen, particularly those of the older Calvinist churches. These ministers thus began a countermovement on behalf of orthodox Christianity. For many people, rational deism became so deeply identified with the anti-Christian excesses of the French Revolution and hence with the Republican party that even Hamilton toyed with the idea of enlisting Christianity on behalf of the politically beleaguered Federalists. In the end this countermovement by conservative Congregationalists and Presbyterians in the 1790s went beyond its creators. It became an eastern version of the revivalism that had continued throughout the South and West during the Revolutionary era, and it eventually fused into the early-nineteenth-century evangelical movement that is known as the Second Great Awakening.

LEMUEL HAYNES, 1753–1833, FIRST BLACK MINISTER OF THE CONGREGATIONAL CHURCH IN AMERICA
Haynes fought in the Revolutionary War, and after he was ordained in 1785 he became a minister in Rutland, Vermont, where he remained for thirty years. He was one of the first blacks to protest in writing against slavery.

The Second Great Awakening.

The Second Great Awakening was a radical expansion and extension of the earlier eighteenth-century revivals. It did not simply intensify the religious feeling of existing church members. More important, it mobilized unprecedented numbers of people who previously had belonged to no church and made them members of religious groups. By popularizing religion as never before and by extending Christianity into the remotest areas of America, this great revival marked the beginning of the republicanizing and nationalizing of American religion. Thousands upon thousands of ordinary people found in evangelical religion new sources of order and community.

In the decades following the Revolution, the various Protestant churches reorganized themselves nationally and entered a period of denominational rivalry. Among the gentry the number of college graduates willing to enter the ministry was declining, and the older Calvinist churches—the Presbyterians and Congregationalists—were forced to form separate colleges and seminaries for the professional education of ministers. They also had to recruit increasing numbers of ministers from lower social levels. The newer denominations—the Methodists and the Baptists—recruited their preachers even more informally. Rejecting the idea of a settled and learned ministry, this new breed of preachers was more capable than the ministers of the older churches of speaking the language of the common people it sought to convert. By 1820 the Baptists and Methodists had become the largest denominations in America.

Although evangelism spread throughout America, it was most successful in the West, where the dynamic process of revivalism was better able to deal with a mobile population than were the traditional churchly institutions. In the first twelve years of the nineteenth century, the Methodists in Tennessee, Kentucky, and Ohio grew from less than 3,000 to well over 30,000. In the short period between 1800 and 1802, the Baptists in Kentucky alone increased from 4,700 to 13,500. In these fast-growing new territories, the need for some kind of community, however loose and voluntary, among isolated men and women was most intense.

And there the need for building barriers against barbarism and sinfulness was most keenly felt.

In the summer of 1801 at Cane Ridge, Kentucky, unbelievable numbers of these Westerners, together with dozens of ministers of several denominations, came together in what some thought was the greatest outpouring of the Holy Spirit since the beginning of Christianity. Crowds that were estimated at 12,000–15,000 participated in a week of frenzied conversions. The heat, the noise, and the confusion were overwhelming. Ministers shouted sermons from wagons and tree stumps; people fell to the ground moaning and wailing in remorse, and they sang, laughed, barked, rolled, and jerked in excitement. This gigantic camp meeting at Cane Ridge immediately became the symbol of the promises and the excesses of the new kind of evangelical Protestantism spreading throughout the South and West. Although the conservative Presbyterians and Congregationalists in the East did not hold camp meetings, they too were compelled to adopt some of the new revivalistic methods. By 1820 there were already clearly revealed a number of basic, interrrelated characteristics of American religious life whose roots went back to the colonial period and which underlay the emerging Evangelical Age.

Evangelical Denominationalism.

First, the number of religions multiplied, and any lingering sense that there was one true religion disintegrated. What was left of the official establishment of Congregationalism was eliminated in Connecticut in 1818 and in Massachusetts in 1833. American religions became denominations and abandoned once and for all the traditional belief that any of them could be the true and exclusive church for the society. Each religious association, called or *denominated* by a particular name, now saw itself simply as one limited and imperfect representative of the larger Christian community. Each denomination was equal to and in competition with the others. No other society in the world had ever conceived of religion in this way.

By abandoning all expectation of maintaining any special identity with the society, religion in America became an entirely personal and voluntary affair in which individuals who wished to could bring about their own salvation. Even the Calvinists, who believed that God had already chosen those who were to be saved, nevertheless managed to stress the responsibility of each individual for his or her own conversion. Sin was no longer thought of as inherent in human beings but as a kind of failure of individual will. Thus each person was fully capable of eliminating sin through his or her individual exertion. With such an assumption the numbers who could be saved were no longer limited by God's election, and all the

denominations began to sound remarkably like the new denomination, the Universalists, who democratically promised salvation for everyone.

Since religion was now clearly personal and voluntary, people were free to join and change religious associations whenever they wished. Consequently the churches were less capable than they had been in the eighteenth century of reflecting the variety of social ranks within their own community. Particular denominations were identified with particular social classes. For example, the Episcopalians (as the Anglicans were now known) and the Unitarians (liberal Congregationalists) became largely the preserve of social elites. If the role of the denominations was to contend with one another for souls in the religious marketplace, then it was important that each denomination be as united, tightly organized, and homogeneous in its membership as possible. Dissenters were thus allowed to go their separate ways without the struggles that had marked earlier American religious life. The result was a further splintering of religion and the multiplying of new, unique religious groups, like the Stonites and Campbellites, with no connection whatever to the Old World.

The divisive effects of this fragmentation were offset by a curious blurring of theological distinctions among the competing denominations. Some extreme evangelicals urged the creation of a simple Christian religion based only on the gospel. In the name of the Revolution, they denounced all the paraphernalia of organized Christianity, including even the ministry, and claimed the right of each individual to be his own theologian. Within a few decades some of these fundamentalist Christians came together as the Disciples of Christ, which soon emerged as the third-largest Protestant religious group in nineteenth-century America.

Despite the competition among them, all the denominations identified themselves with the nation and worked to unify American culture under evangelical Protestantism. Clergymen were determined to prove that America's separation of church and state would not result in the infidelity and religious neglect that most Europeans expected. Evangelicals emphasized over and over that America, although without a state-supported church, was nonetheless a nation of God. Throughout the early nineteenth century, religious groups resisted the secularizing effects of the Enlightenment and the First Amendment, which had forbidden the federal government from establishing any religion. Instead, they urged the Republic to recognize its basis in Christianity by providing chaplains in Congress, proclaiming days of fasting and prayer, and ending mail delivery on the Sabbath. Ministers, said Nathaniel William Taylor of Connecticut, the

I. N. Phelps Stokes Collection, The New York Public Library

BUILDING THE FRIGATE "PHILADELPHIA"
All seven of the frigates of the United States Navy that fought the War of 1812 were built in the 1790s, when war with France threatened. The Federalists also wanted to build some ships of the line, which had more decks and nearly twice as many guns as frigates. Although the Federalists acquired timber and six navy yards, the accession of the Republicans in 1801 ended their plans for enlarging the Navy.

most important theologian of the Second Great Awakening, had no intention of creating a new church establishment or of denying the rights of conscience. "We only ask for those provisions in law . . . in behalf of a common Christianity, which are its due as a nation's strength and a nation's glory."

By 1800 the fate of Christianity and the fate of the nation were tied together by a belief in millennialism. Many evangelical ministers had come to believe that America was leading humanity into the millennium—the earth's final thousand years of glory and happiness before the Second Coming of Christ and the Day of Judgment that had been predicted in the Bible. The hopes of these ministers focused on contemporary historical events occurring in America as signs of the approaching age of perfection. The millennium thus became more than a vague promise of Christian theology; it was to be an actual phase in the history of the American republic. Every advance in America's worldly progress—even new inventions and canals—was interpreted in millennial terms. By giving the millennium such a concrete temporal and material char-

acter and by identifying the Kingdom of God with the prospects of the United States, the Protestant ministry contributed greatly to nineteenth-century Americans' growing sense of mission. By improving and prospering, the United States—it was thought—was destined to redeem the world.

Republican Diplomacy

The dramatic culmination of the Republican revolution of 1800 came in the War of 1812. It was an unusual war, a war on which the entire experiment in free government seemed to rest. It was a war that few wanted but that many had made inevitable. It was a war that in the end solved nothing but that was widely regarded as a glorious American victory.

The origins of the War of 1812 lay in the American principles of foreign relations that were first expressed at the time of the Revolution. The American Revolution had been centrally concerned with power—not only power within a government, but power

Republican Diplomacy   **273**

among governments in their international relations. Throughout the eighteenth century, liberal intellectuals had looked forward to a rational world in which corrupt monarchical diplomacy and secret alliances, balances of power, and dynastic conflicts would be eliminated. In short, they had dreamed of nothing less than an end of war and a new era of peace based on natural commercial relations among nations. If the people of the various nations were left alone to exchange goods freely among themselves, it was believed, then international politics would become republicanized and pacified.

Suddenly in 1776, with the United States isolated outside the European mercantile empires, the Americans had an opportunity and a need to put into practice these liberal ideas about international relations and the free exchange of goods. Thus commercial interest and Revolutionary idealism blended to form the basis for American thinking about foreign affairs that lasted until well into the first half of the twentieth century. America first expressed these principles during discussions over the proposed treaty with France at the time of Independence. Many in the Congress in 1776 attempted to work out a model treaty that would be applied to France and eventually to other nations—a treaty that would avoid the traditional kinds of political and military commitments and focus instead on exclusively commercial connections. Although in the treaties of 1778 with France the United States was unable to implement its desired commercial plan—and in fact had to settle for a customary European kind of military alliance—many Americans never lost their enlightened hope that international politics might be transformed by new liberal commercial relationships.

By the 1790s, however, the Federalists had rejected many of these Revolutionary enlightened dreams for international relations. Hamilton in particular denied the liberal assumptions that republics were naturally peaceful and that commerce was an adequate substitute for the power politics of traditional diplomacy. He put no stock in the idealistic Republican conviction that Britain's great power could be dealt with solely by a policy of commercial discrimination and economic coercion.

The Republicans therefore emerged as the preservers of the visionary principles of diplomacy that were identified with the Revolution of 1776. In contrast to the Federalists, who thought that the only way to prepare for war was to build up the government and armed forces in a European manner, the Republicans believed that the United States did not need, nor could safely afford, enlarged national power and a traditional army and navy. It did not even need an elaborate diplomatic establishment: some Republicans in the 1790s urged eliminating all American diplomatic posts except those in London and Paris; others favored replacing the entire American representation abroad with consuls, who were all that were required to handle matters of international trade. At times Jefferson even talked wistfully of abandoning all international commerce so that the United States might "stand, with respect to Europe, precisely on the footing of China." More often, however, he and other Republicans saw American commerce not simply as something to be protected by national policy, as the Federalists did, but as a political weapon to be used as an alternative to war in the way the colonists had used nonimportation in the pre-Revolutionary crisis with Great Britain.

Republicans and the War in Europe. When the conflict between Britain and France resumed in 1803, the Republicans, now in control of the national government, at last had an opportunity to put their policies to a test. Since Britain was unable to oppose on land Napoleon's domination of the continent of Europe, it was determined to exploit its supremacy on the seas to blockade France into submission.

American commerce, once again caught between these two Goliaths, prospered magnificently. Ever since the outbreak of the European war in the early 1790s, American merchants had gained access to the European mercantile empires that had formerly been barred to them and had made the United States the largest neutral carrier of goods in the world. Between 1793 and 1807 American ship tonnage tripled, and the value of American exports increased fivefold. America's expanding wartime shipping between the Spanish and French possessions in the New World and Europe was particularly profitable. The value of this trade increased from $300,000 in 1790 to nearly $60 million by 1807. This commerce, however, violated the British Rule of 1756, which prohibited neutrals in time of war from trading within a mercantile empire closed to them in time of peace. To protect this carrying trade, therefore, American merchants developed a legal fiction. For example, by carrying goods from the French West Indies to American ports, unloading and paying duties on them, and then reloading and getting a rebate on the duties before taking them on to France, American traders broke their voyage and thus technically conformed to the British Rule of 1756. The British now resolved to put a stop to this reexport trade. The *Essex* decision of 1805, in which a British admiralty court held that enemy goods reexported in this fictitious manner were liable to seizure, opened the way to increased British attacks on American ships.

At the same time, Britain expanded its impressment, or forcible removal, of seamen from Amer-

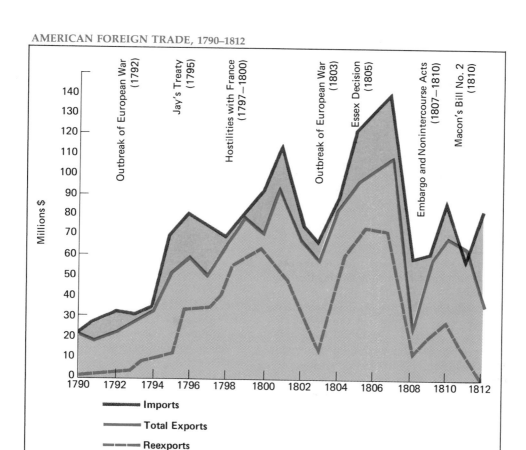

AMERICAN FOREIGN TRADE, 1790–1812

(Chart labels, left to right across the top:)
Outbreak of European War (1792)
Jay's Treaty (1795)
Hostilities with France (1797–1800)
Outbreak of European War (1803)
Essex Decision (1805)
Embargo and Nonintercourse Acts (1807–1810)
Macon's Bill No. 2 (1810)

(Y-axis: Millions $ — 0, 10, 20, 30, 40, 50, 60, 70, 80, 90, 100, 110, 120, 130, 140)

(X-axis: 1790, 1792, 1794, 1796, 1798, 1800, 1802, 1804, 1806, 1808, 1810, 1812)

▬▬ Imports

─── Total Exports

--- Reexports

ican vessels on the grounds that they were British subjects. Many of these seamen were deserters from the British navy; and since Great Britain refused to recognize the right of expatriation (or changing citizenship), which was an essential right for a nation of immigrants, conflict over the nationality of American seamen was inevitable. "This authorized system of kidnapping upon the ocean," as John Quincy Adams called it, continued until it was ended by the general European peace of 1815. It resulted in an estimated 10,000 sailors being forcibly taken from American ships. These provocative practices dissolved the cordial relations between Britain and America that had begun with Jay's Treaty in 1795.

Napoleon responded to the British blockade with commercial restrictions of his own—a "continental system" that was designed essentially to deprive England of markets in Europe. In his Berlin Decree of 1806, he ruled that any neutral vessel stopping at an English port would be denied access to all European ports under French control. The British retaliated by requiring all neutral ships trading in the blockaded zones of Europe to stop at British ports to secure licenses. Napoleon then countered with his Milan De-

cree of 1807, which declared that all neutral ships submitting to British search or entering British ports to secure licenses would be confiscated by the French. The net effect of these regulations by the warring parties was to render all neutral commerce illegal and liable to seizure by one power or the other. Although by 1807 the French were rigorously confiscating American ships in European ports, Britain's greater ability to capture American vessels (it was plundering about one of every eight American ships that put to sea) and its humiliating practice of impressment made Britain appear the greater culprit in American eyes. British regulations seemed to strike at the heart of American independence. "They assume the principle," said John Quincy Adams in 1808, "that we shall have no commerce in time of war, but with her dominion, and as tributaries to her."

The Jefferson administration's immediate response to the British seizures was the Nonimportation Act of 1806, which threatened a prohibition of certain British imports unless an Anglo-American agreement could be reached. Jefferson refused to send to the Senate for ratification a treaty with Britain that William Pinkney and James Monroe had negotiated in December 1806. Jefferson objected to the treaty not only because its commercial provisions scarcely went beyond Jay's Treaty in opening the British Empire to American trade, but, more important, because it did not renounce the British practice of impressment.

Almost immediately thereafter, in June 1807, the British man-of-war *Leopard* fired upon the American warship *Chesapeake* as it sailed out of Norfolk, Virginia. Several seamen were killed. The British then boarded the American ship and impressed four sailors, including three Americans who were alleged to be deserters from the British navy. Waves of patriotic indignation swept through the United States and brought Anglo-American relations to the breaking point. "Never since the battle of Lexington," said President Jefferson, "have I seen the country in such a state of exasperation as at present." Although the United States was emotionally primed for war, the Republican leaders were reluctant as yet to abandon their idealistic principles of diplomacy.

The Embargo. All the strains of idealism and utopianism in American Revolutionary thinking were now brought to a head with the Republicans' resort to a general embargo. In 1807 Congress passed a sweeping prohibition of all American shipping with the outside world. Jefferson was determined to see this "candid and liberal experiment" in "peaceful coercion" through to the end. From December 1807 to March 1809, in the face of mounting opposition (particularly from New England), Jefferson's government desperately stuck by its embargo policy. In fact, it used ever harsher measures to enforce it.

Although Britain and France showed few ill effects from this self-imposed stoppage of American shipping, American commerce was thrown into chaos. The American export and reexport trade, which between 1805 and 1807 had doubled to more than $108 million in value, suddenly fell to $22 million during 1808; and American imports declined in value from $138 million to $56 million. Some places were especially hard hit. Although many areas of the United States could fall back on their domestic overland and coastwise trade to replace losses in international commerce, the New England ports, such as Boston, Salem, and Providence, had relatively meager backcountries and unusually heavy investments in the carrying and reexport trade; these ports thus could not easily adjust to the embargo. Yet the economic effects of the embargo on the nation as a whole were far from disastrous. Not only did numerous loopholes and violations—especially toward the end of 1808—lessen the embargo's depressing impact on the economy, but America's growing reliance on its domestic manufactures and its internal markets was strengthened by the cutbacks in international trade.

Still, everywhere in the North but especially in New England, the embargo had the political effect of temporarily reviving Federalism. Hundreds of New England petitions flooded in on the government. Some New Englanders were on the verge of rebellion, and the Federalist governor of Connecticut claimed the right of his state to interpose its authority between the federal government and its citizens. Thus some sort of retreat from the embargo was inevitable. Hopeful of salvaging something from their policy of peaceful coercion, the Republicans on March 1, 1809, replaced the embargo with the Nonintercourse Act, which prohibited trade with France and Britain alone and provided that if either warring side canceled its blockade against American shipping, then nonintercourse would be maintained only against the other.

President Madison was just as determined as Jefferson had been to maintain this Republican experiment in commercial warfare. But difficulties in enforcing the Nonintercourse Act and growing governmental deficits from the loss of duties on trade forced the Madison administration to turn its commercial restrictions inside out. Macon's Bill No. 2, which passed Congress in May 1810, once again opened American shipping with both Britain and France, with the provision that if either side revoked its restrictions on neutral commerce, nonintercourse would be restored against the other. Signs of a change in Napoleon's policy against American shipping, coupled with Madison's eagerness to prove the workability of the experiment in peaceful coercion, led the Republican administration in March 1811 into a hasty invocation of nonintercourse against Great Britain.

If the United States had to go to war, the Republicans thought, then better to fight Britain, the country that from the beginning had symbolized resistance to the experiment in popular self-government. Despite some strong misgivings over Napoleon's dictatorship and some weak suggestions that America fight both belligerents simultaneously, it was virtually inconceivable that the Republicans would have gone to war against France. The threat of Federalist "monarchism" tied to Great Britain was still so real to Republicans that war with Britain became a necessary product of the Republican revolution of 1800, and thus of the original Revolution itself. "We are going to fight for the re-establishment of our national character," declared Andrew Jackson.

The War of 1812

War was declared in June 1812, and it was strictly a Republican party war. The congressional vote for war was solidly opposed by the Federalists, and it temporarily unified the splintered Republican party. A num-

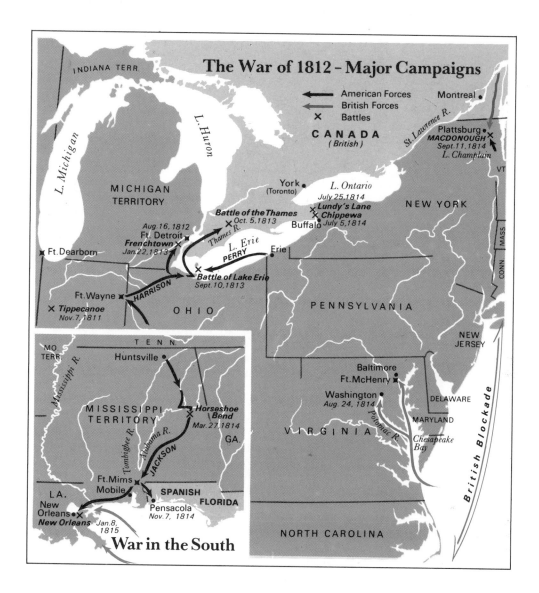

The War of 1812 – Major Campaigns

American Forces
British Forces
× Battles

INDIANA TERR.

CANADA (British)

Montreal

St. Lawrence R.

Plattsburg
MACDONOUGH
Sept. 11, 1814
L. Champlain

L. Huron

L. Michigan

MICHIGAN TERRITORY

York (Toronto)

L. Ontario
July 25, 1814

NEW YORK

VT

Battle of the Thames
Oct. 5, 1813

Lundy's Lane
Chippewa
July 5, 1814

Thames R.

Aug. 16, 1812
Ft. Detroit
Frenchtown
Jan. 22, 1813

L. Erie
PERRY

Buffalo

MASS

Ft. Dearborn

Erie

CONN

Ft. Wayne
HARRISON

Battle of Lake Erie
Sept. 10, 1813

PENNSYLVANIA

NEW JERSEY

× Tippecanoe
Nov. 7, 1811

O H I O

MO. TERR.

T E N N.

Huntsville

NEW YORK

Baltimore
Ft. McHenry

DELAWARE

British Blockade

Mississippi R.

MISSISSIPPI TERRITORY

Horseshoe Bend
Mar. 27, 1814

Washington
Aug. 24, 1814

MARYLAND

Tombigbee R.

Alabama R.

JACKSON

GA.

V I R G I N I A

Potomac R.

Chesapeake Bay

L. A.

Ft. Mims
Mobile

SPANISH
FLORIDA

New Orleans
New Orleans
Jan. 8, 1815

Pensacola
Nov. 7, 1814

NORTH CAROLINA

War in the South

---

ber of Republican congressmen who were newly elected in 1810, such as Henry Clay of Kentucky, Felix Grundy of Tennessee, and John C. Calhoun of South Carolina, were so eager to fight that they earned the label "War Hawks." Although many of the Republican congressmen came from areas that were far removed from the eastern trading ports, they represented farmers who were interested in commerce and in the marketing of their agricultural produce. Moreover, such backcountry dwellers tended deeply to resent British and Spanish scheming among the native Americans of the Northwest and Southwest, and they were convinced, especially by the recent battle with Tecumseh's Indians at Tippecanoe in November 1811, that the frontier would never be at peace until the British and Spanish bases in Canada and Florida were

eliminated. War offered them the opportunity to do just that.

Yet in the end the war came because the Republicans' foreign policy left no alternative. America had been engaged in a kind of war with both Britain and France since 1806. The actual fighting of 1812 was only the logical consequence of the failure of "peaceful coercion." Still, many Republicans hesitated to commit the United States to a traditional sort of military conflict. They realized, as Jefferson had warned in 1806, that "our constitution is a peace establishment—it is not calculated for war." War, they feared, would lead to a Hamiltonian enlargement of taxes, debt, military forces, and the executive branch. Far from saving the Jeffersonian revolution of 1800, war might ultimately destroy republican principles. Therefore, even

New York State Historical Association, Cooperstown, N.Y.

PERRY'S VICTORY ON LAKE ERIE
Oliver Hazard Perry (1785–1819) commanded a fleet of nine vessels built in Erie, Pa., to challenge British control of the Great Lakes in the War of 1812. During the battle on Sept. 10, 1813, Perry's flagship was disabled, and, as the painting depicts, he transferred to the *Niagara*. Then he sailed directly into the British line and destroyed the British ships, inspiring his famous dispatch: "We have met the enemy and they are ours."

as the Republicans moved inevitably toward war, many of them opposed all efforts to strengthen the government's capacity to wage it. For example, Nathaniel Macon of North Carolina reluctantly conceded the necessity of war, but like other Republicans he urged reduction of the navy and even abolition of the army, opposed raising taxes, and resisted all efforts to add two assistant secretaries to the War Department. Not only was the regular army cut back in favor of the militia, but the Bank of the United States, the government's chief financial agency, was allowed to expire in 1811 on the eve of hostilities. With such a deliberate lack of preparation, the war was bound to be very different from any known before.

The Invasions of Canada. Although woefully unprepared for war, many Americans in 1812 were confident of victory. Since two out of every three persons in Upper Canada (present-day Ontario) came from America, Canada seemed ripe for American "liberation." It

would be, said Jefferson, "a mere matter of marching." But the American militia campaigns against Canada in 1812 were all dismal failures. General William Hull surrendered his entire army at Detroit without a fight. William Henry Harrison, the hero at Tippecanoe, was then made commander of the northwestern army; but before he could get very far, part of his army was wiped out at Frenchtown, near Detroit, in January 1813.

In April 1813 invading Americans captured York (present-day Toronto), the capital of Upper Canada, and burned its public buildings. But within two months the American forces were in retreat once again. After Oliver Perry secured naval control of Lake Erie, Harrison finally defeated combined British and Indian forces on the Thames River north of Lake Erie in October 1813. Although this victory broke up the Indian confederacy, American leaders thought it was too far west to have any strategic significance and did not follow it up. During the summer of 1814, Americans tried to invade Canada again but withdrew after several tough but indecisive battles in the Niagara region. After two years of repeated forays, the American position on the Canadian frontier remained what it had been at the beginning.

On the sea American frigates, including the U.S.S. *Constitution*, initially won some notable single-ship engagements, and American privateers, the naval equivalent of the militia, captured more than 1,300 British merchant vessels. Eventually, however, Britain's great naval superiority made itself felt: by 1813 most of the American warships were bottled up in their ports and American commerce was effectively blockaded. When Napoleon abdicated early in 1814, Britain was able to concentrate its military attention on America. It planned several major assaults: one was designed to move down the Lake Champlain route that Burgoyne had followed in the Revolutionary War, and another was aimed at New Orleans. During the summer of 1814, a British marauding force landed in Chesapeake Bay, entered Washington, and burned the Capitol building and the White House. The government's credit collapsed and the nation's finances were thrown into chaos. Without a national bank the government was unable to transfer funds across the country or pay its mounting bills.

The Treaty of Ghent. Despite these humiliating circumstances, however, the American peace commissioners who had been sent to negotiate with the British in August 1814 in Ghent, Belgium, were unwilling to make any concessions. The British, learning that their invasion from Canada had turned back as a result of an American naval victory on Lake Champlain in September 1814, and increasingly anxious about the shifting situation in Europe, came to realize once again that a decentralized government and a spacious continent were not easily conquered. The peace that was signed on Christmas Eve, 1814, restored the status quo as it was before the war and said nothing about impressment and maritime rights. Andrew Jackson's smashing victory over the British invasion at New Orleans at the beginning of 1815 came after the treaty was signed, and clinched it. Although the Americans had gained nothing tangible from the peace, the war was widely and rightly regarded as a great success for the Republican party and the nation.

The Hartford Convention and the End of the Federalists.

The peace effectively destroyed Federalism as a national movement. The northeastern Federalists had repeatedly obstructed the war, refusing to comply with federal militia call-ups and discouraging loans to the United States government. Some New England extremists talked of separating from the Union. Other Federalists were convinced that the Republican failures in the war would justify their opposition and that a disillusioned people would catapult the Federalists back into national dominance.

Hence the Federalist convention that met in Hartford, Connecticut, at the end of 1814 was hopeful for the future; it rejected secession and contented itself with proposing a series of amendments to the Constitution. These amendments were designed to curb the power of the South in the federal government by eliminating the three-fifths representation of slaves; to prevent the admission of new states, future embargoes, and declarations of war without a two-thirds majority of Congress; and to end Virginia's dominance of the executive by prohibiting the president from serving two terms and the same state from providing two presidents in succession. But the national exuberance following the Treaty of Ghent and Jackson's victory discredited these Federalist hopes and led to the enthusiastic election in 1816 of still another Republican and Virginian president, James Monroe. The Republicans' remarkable experiment in governing a huge country and fighting a war without the traditional instruments of power was thus vindicated.

Although the war seemed to settle nothing, actually it settled everything. "Notwithstanding a thousand faults and blunders," John Adams told Jefferson in 1817, Madison's administration had "acquired more glory, and established more Union than all his three predecessors, Washington, Adams, Jefferson, put together." The Revolution, which had begun nearly a half-century earlier, at last seemed to be over and to have succeeded. The Federalist attempt to build a strong central government had been halted. The new national government that the Republicans had created was unlike any other government known to the age. Its capital was isolated from the main social and economic centers of the country; its influence was diffused throughout a rapidly expanding geographical sphere; and its effect on the daily lives of its citizens was negligible.

By 1818 Jefferson was exultant. "Our government," he wrote to his old French ally, the Marquis de Lafayette, "is now so firmly put on its republican tack, that it will not be easily monarchised by forms." The War of 1812 and the disgrace of the Federalists, he said, had ended the need for his revolutionary party, and had in fact resulted in the "complete suppression of party." In the new so-called Era of Good Feelings, symbolized by Monroe's uncontested reelection to the presidency in 1820, the ideological passions and divisions that had been aroused by the Revolution could at last subside. Americans could begin celebrating their own common national identity.

CHRONOLOGY

1800	Washington, D.C., becomes capital.
	Library of Congress established.
	Convention of 1800, supplanting treaties of 1778 with France.
	Thomas Jefferson elected president.
1801	Plan of Union between Presbyterians and Congregationalists to bring religion to frontier.
	War with Barbary states.
	Cane Ridge, Kentucky, revival meeting.
	John Marshall becomes chief justice.
1802	Republican Congress repeals Judiciary Act of 1801.
1803	*Marbury* v. *Madison*, Supreme Court upholds right of judicial review.
	Louisiana Purchase.
	War resumed in Europe.
	Lewis and Clark expedition begun.
1804	Hamilton killed by Vice-President Aaron Burr in duel.
	Impeachment of judges Pickering and Chase.
	Twelfth Amendment to Constitution ratified.
	Jefferson elected for second term.
1805	Pennsylvania Academy of Fine Arts

formed.

Essex decision by British prize court increases British seizures of American neutral ships.

1806 Monroe-Pinkney Treaty with Britain, which Jefferson refuses to send to Senate for ratification.

Burr conspiracy.

1807 *Chesapeake-Leopard* affair.

Embargo Act.

Robert Fulton's steamboat *Clermont* travels on Hudson River from Albany to New York City in 30 hours.

1808 Congress prohibits Americans from participating in African slave trade.

James Madison elected president.

1809 Embargo repealed; Nonintercourse Act passed, prohibiting trade with Britain and France.

1810 Macon's Bill No. 2 passed, restoring trade with Britain and France, but providing for trade restrictions to be reimposed on one of the powers if other should abandon its seizure of American ships.

Connecticut Moral Society formed to combat infidelity and drinking.

West Florida annexed by Madison.

American Board of Commissioners for Foreign Missions formed.

In *Fletcher* v. *Peck*, Supreme Court invalidates state law re *Yazoo* land claims because of impairment of contracts.

1811 Madison, believing Napoleon has removed restrictions on American commerce, prohibits trade with Britain.

Battle of Tippecanoe, Indiana, in which William Henry Harrison defeats Tecumseh and prevents formation of Indian confederacy.

Charter of the Bank of the United States allowed to lapse by Congress.

1812 Congress declares war against Britain.

Americans surrender Detroit to British.

Madison elected for second term.

1813 Battle of Lake Erie, in which Captain Oliver Perry defeats British naval forces.

Battle of the Thames, in which General Harrison defeats British and their Indian allies.

1814 Battle of Horseshoe Bend, Alabama; General Andrew Jackson defeats Creek Indians fighting for British.

British burn Washington, D.C.

Commander Thomas Macdonough defeats British fleet on Lake Champlain; invading British turned back at Plattsburgh, New York.

Hartford Convention of Federalist delegates from New England states meets.

Treaty of Ghent signed between United States and Great Britain.

1815 Battle of New Orleans; Jackson defeats British.

North American Review founded in Boston; soon becomes leading literary review in America.

1816 Second Bank of the United States chartered by Congress.

American Bible Society founded.

Protective tariff passed.

James Monroe elected president.

1817 Bonus Bill establishing fund for building roads and canals vetoed by Madison.

American Tract Society formed to circulate religious literature in the West.

Seminole War on Georgia-Florida border.

1818 General Jackson invades Florida to end Seminole War.

Rush-Bagot convention between Britain and United States establishes American fishing rights and boundary between United States and Canada.

1819 Commercial panic with many bank failures.

Adams-Onís Treaty signed between United States and Spain; Spain cedes Florida to the United States and recognizes the western limits of the Louisiana Purchase.

Dartmouth College case.

McCulloch v. *Maryland*.

1820 Missouri Compromise.

James Monroe reelected president.

SUGGESTED READINGS

The classic account of the Republican administrations is Henry Adams, *History of the United States of America During the Administration of Thomas Jefferson* [and] *of James Madison* (9 vols., 1889–1891). It is artful, but its obsession with the ironic turn of Jeffersonian policies subtly distorts the period. Marshall Smelser, *The Democratic Republic, 1801–1815* (1968), is a one-volume survey. Daniel Sisson, *The American Revolution of 1800* (1974), tries to recapture the radical meaning of Jefferson's election; but it does not succeed as well as James S. Young, *The Washington*

Community, 1800–1828 (1966), which despite an unhistorical focus rightly stresses the Republicans' fear of power. On the Republican party, see Noble E. Cunningham, Jr., *The Jeffersonian Republicans in Power: Party Operations, 1801–1809* (1963). Richard Hofstadter, *The Idea of a Party System: The Rise of Legitimate Opposition in the United States, 1740–1840* (1969), is a lucid essay that tries but does not quite break from the party conception of the secondary sources on which it is based. David Hackett Fischer, *The Revolution of American Conservatism: The Federalist Party in the Era of Jeffersonian Democracy* (1965), is an important book that compels a new look at the Republicans as well as the Federalists. A tough-minded study is Forrest McDonald's *The Presidency of Thomas Jefferson* (1976). See also James H. Broussard, *The Southern Federalists, 1800–1816* (1979). Howard B. Rock, *Artisans of the New Republic: The Tradesmen of New York City in the Age of Jefferson* (1979), describes the rise of an important social and economic group. On the Republicans' dismantling of the Federalist bureaucracy, see Leonard D. White, *The Jeffersonians: A Study in Administrative History, 1801–1829* (1951). See also Noble E. Cunningham, Jr., *The Process of Government Under Jefferson* (1979), and Robert M. Johnstone, Jr., *Jefferson and the Presidency* (1979). On Jefferson and Madison, see the monumental multivolumed biographies by Dumas Malone and Irving Brant.

Daniel Boorstin, *The Lost World of Thomas Jefferson* (1948), describes the rigidities of intellectual life in Republican circles, while Linda K. Kerber analyzes the Federalists' cultural problems in *Federalists in Dissent* (1970).

On the development of the West, see Reginald Horsman, *The Frontier in the Formative Years, 1783–1815* (1970). On the new cities of the West, see Richard C. Wade, *The Urban Frontier* (1959). Beverley W. Bond, *The Civilization of the Old Northwest: A Study of Political, Social and Economic Development, 1788–1812* (1934), is a good compilation. Land policy and land laws are covered in Malcom J. Rohrbough, *The Land Office Business . . . 1789–1837* (1968).

On the Louisiana Purchase, see Alexander De Conde, *The Affair of Louisiana* (1976), and the appropriate chapters of George Dangerfield, *Chancellor Robert R. Livingston of New York, 1746–1803* (1960). On Indian affairs, see Reginald Horsman, *Expansion and American Indian Policy, 1783–1812* (1967). For the tragic irony in the story of American relations with the Indians, see Bernard W. Sheehan, *Seeds of Extinction: Jeffersonian Philanthropy and the American Indian* (1973). A good, short, though unsympathetic, account of the Burr conspiracy can be found in Thomas Abernathy, *The South in the New Nation, 1789–1819* (1961).

On the politics of the judiciary, see Richard E. Ellis, *The Jeffersonian Crisis* (1971). The best biography of Marshall is still Albert J. Beveridge, *The Life of John Marshall* (4 vols., 1919). The origins of judicial review are treated in Edward S. Corwin, *The "Higher Law" Background of American Constitutional Law* (1955), and Charles G. Haines, *The American Doctrine of Judicial Supremacy* (1932). But despite all that has been written, the sources of judicial review remain perplexing. Understanding the problem requires less work on the Supreme Court and more on colonial jurisprudence. For a significant study of changes in law during the Revolution, and after, see William E. Nelson, *Americanization of the Common Law: The Impact of Legal Change on Massachusetts Society, 1760–1830* (1975), and Morton J. Horowitz, *The Transformation of American Law, 1780–1860* (1977).

On religion and the Revolution, see William W. Sweet, *Religion in the Development of American Culture, 1765–1840* (1952). On the varying definitions of the American Enlightenment and its relation to Protestantism, see the superb study by Henry F. May, *The Enlightenment in America* (1976). The opening chapters of Perry Miller, *The Life of the Mind in America* (1965), are very helpful for understanding the emergence of evangelicism. The essays collected in Elwyn A. Smith, ed., *The Religion of the Republic* (1971), are important in relating evangelical Protestantism and republicanism. Older studies that need updating are Catherine C. Cleveland, *The Great Revival in the West, 1797–1805* (1916), and Oliver W. Elsbree, *The Rise of the Missionary Spirit in America, 1790–1815* (1928). See also John Bole, *The Great Revival in the South, 1787–1805* (1972); Howard Miller, *The Revolutionary College: American Presbyterian Higher Education, 1707–1837* (1976); and especially Donald G. Mathews, *Religion in the Old South* (1977). For secular-minded approaches to evangelicism, see Charles I. Foster, *An Errand of Mercy: The Evangelical United Front, 1790–1837* (1960), and Clifford S. Griffin, *Their Brothers' Keepers: Moral Stewardship in the United States, 1800–1865* (1960). On the changing role of the ministry, see Donald M. Scott, *From Office to Profession: The New England Ministry, 1750–1850* (1978). On deism, see Gustav A. Koch, *Republican Religion* (1933), and Herbert M. Morais, *Deism in Eighteenth-Century America* (1934). On millennialism, see Ernest Lee Tuveson, *Redeemer Nation: The Idea of America's Millennial Role* (1968); James W. Davidson, *The Logic of Millennial Thought* (1977); and Nathan O. Hatch, *The Sacred Cause of Liberty* (1977).

The underlying eighteenth-century liberal assumptions about international politics are explored in Felix Gilbert, *To the Farewell Address: Ideas of Early American Foreign Policy* (1961). Lawrence S. Kaplan, *Jefferson and France: An Essay on Politics and Political Ideas* (1967), captures the idealism of Jefferson. The best discussion of the diplomatic steps into war is Bradford Perkins, *Prologue to War: England and the United States, 1805–1812* (1961). Burton Spivak, *Jefferson's English Crisis: Commerce, Embargo and the Republican Revolution* (1979), is the best study of the embargo. Julius W. Pratt, *Expansionists of 1812* (1925), stresses how the desire of Westerners and Southerners for land caused the war. However, A. L. Burt, *The United States, Great Britain and British North America* (1940), emphasizes the issues of impressment and neutral rights. Roger H. Brown, *The Republic in Peril: 1812* (1964), and Norman K. Risjord, *The Old Republicans* (1965), and J. C. A. Stagg, *Mr. Madison's War: Politics, Diplomacy, and Warfare in the Early American Republic, 1783–1830* (1983), offer the best perspective on the logic of the Republicans' foreign policy that led to war.

Harry L. Coles, *The War of 1812* (1965), and Reginald Horsman, *The War of 1812* (1969), are good brief surveys. Irving Brant, *James Madison: The Commander in Chief, 1812–1836* (1961), defends Madison's wartime leadership, but Ralph Ketcham, *James Madison* (1971), is better in recovering the peculiar character of Madison's republican aims. On the Treaty of Ghent, see Bradford Perkins, *Castlereagh and Adams: England and the United States, 1812–1823* (1964). James M. Banner, *To the Hartford Convention: The Federalist and the Origins of Party Politics in Massachusetts, 1789–1815* (1970), superbly describes the Federalists' attitudes and stresses their conservative purposes in calling the Convention.

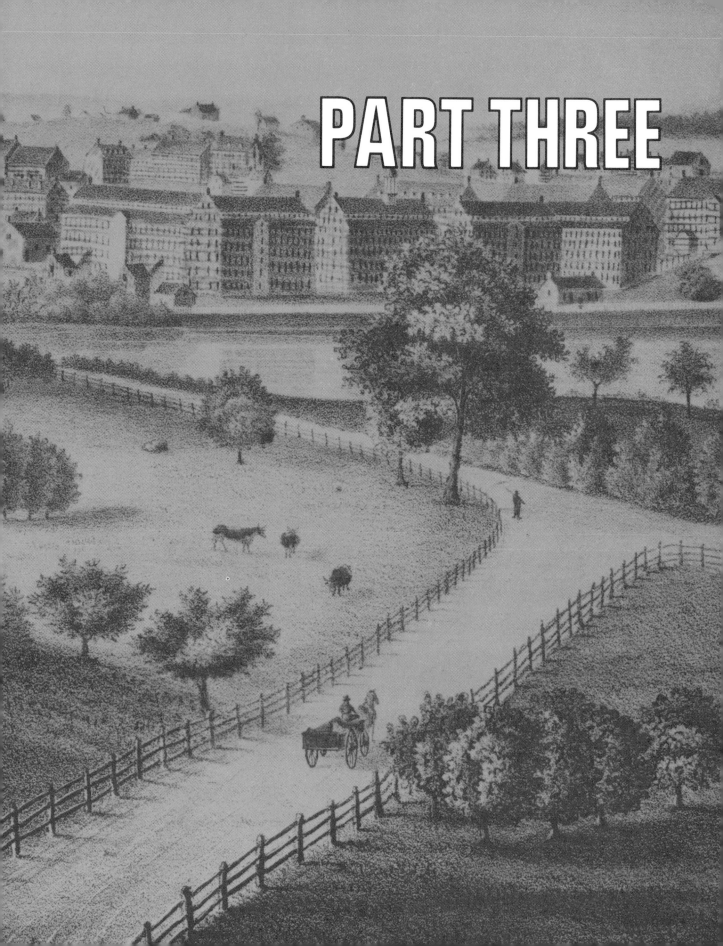

PART THREE

EXPANDING THE REPUBLIC, 1820–1860

David Brion Davis

*T*he end of the American Enlightenment and of the Revolutionary period also marked the end of attempts to model American society on European blueprints. By the 1820s it was becoming clear that the American people would quickly leap across restraints and limits of every kind. They were expansive, self-assertive, and extravagantly optimistic, and they believed that they had a God-given right to pursue happiness. In a nation of supposedly infinite promise, there could be no permanent barriers to the people's aspirations toward wealth and self-improvement.

This absence of barriers, of distinctions of rank, and of prescribed identities was what the famous French social critic Alexis de Tocqueville meant by "the general equality of condition among the people." When he visited the United States in 1831, nothing struck Tocqueville more forcibly than this leveling of ancient and inherited distinctions of rank. He took it to be "the fundamental fact" about American society; all other facts seemed "to be derived" from it. Tocqueville was aware of the economic and racial inequalities of American society. Indeed, he suggested that precisely the lack of traditional restraints, such as those associated with a landed aristocracy, opened the way for racial oppression and for a new kind of aristocracy created by business and manufacturing.

All societies require a system of rules, restraints, and limits. In a traditional, premodern society, such as the European feudal regime to which Tocqueville looked back with some nostalgia, there was a certain stability to the territorial boundaries of a kingdom, an estate, or a people. Similarly, few people in such a traditional society questioned the

Overleaf: Lowell, Massachusetts, in 1833. *Prints Division, The New York Public Library.*

customary rules that defined social rank, the rights and duties of lords and peasants, the inheritance of land, the limits of political power and economic enterprise, and the expectations appropriate for each individual. Men and women knew what they had been born to, what place they had been assigned by fate. There was a close relation between the narrow boundaries of the physical environment and the social boundaries that political, legal, and religious institutions imposed.

The United States, as Tocqueville repeatedly emphasized, had thus far managed to avoid anarchy while greatly expanding most people's possibilities of life. From the time of the first colonial settlements, Americans had evolved institutions that had ensured a degree of order and stability in social life, protecting the public good from the worst excesses of acquisitive self-interest. By the early nineteenth century, however, there was a growing faith that the public good would best be served by allowing maximum freedom to the individual pursuit of self-interest.

In the period 1820–60 this drive for individual self-betterment led to an unprecedented economic and territorial expansion, to the migration of millions of Europeans to America, and to the settlement of millions of Americans in the new states and territories of the West. Much of the nation's foreign policy was devoted to extending territorial boundaries and to preventing European attempts to impose future barriers to American influence and expansion in the Western Hemisphere. Federal land policy encouraged rapid settlement of the West. Both national and state governments committed a large share of public resources to the construction of roads, canals, and railroads to overcome the barriers of mountains and increasing distance. Government at all levels actively sought to stimulate growth and economic opportunity. Much of the political ideology of the period was directed against forces and institutions, such as the Second Bank of the United States, that could be portrayed as restricting individual opportunity.

But for many thoughtful Americans, reformers as well as conservatives, there was a danger that these expansive energies would erode all respect for order, balance, and community purpose. The fear arose that the competitive spirit would lead to a fragmented society ruled by the principle, "every man for himself and the devil take the hindmost." Some worried that the American people would become enslaved to money, success, and material gratification, and that the centrifugal forces of expansion would cause the nation to fly apart.

Most of the proposed remedies to social problems centered on the critical need to shape and reform individual character. Rather than looking to political institutions and governmental programs, most Americans sought social change through the moral reformation of individuals. They believed that if self-interest could be enlightened by a sense of social responsibility, the nation could be saved from the dehumanizing effects of commercialism and competitive strife. This improvement of the individual was the great goal of the public schools, the religious revivals, and most of the new reform movements. It was a mission that gave a new importance and an educational role to mothers and to the middle-class home. In one sense these efforts at shaping character embodied a nostalgic desire to restore a lost sense of community and united purpose. But the crusades for moral improvement also served to modernize society, for they encouraged predictable and responsible behavior and moreover aimed at giving moral legitimacy to a market-oriented society—that is, to a society governed by the standards of economic exchange, of supply and demand.

The issue of black slavery—the South's "peculiar institution"—finally dramatized the conflict between self-interest and the ideal of a righteous society, a society that could think of itself as "under God." And it was the westward expansion of black slavery that ultimately became the testing ground for defining and challenging limits—the territorial limits of slavery, the limits of federal power, and the limits of popular sovereignty and self-determination. For most of the period, all these matters remained ambiguous. This ambiguity allowed the North and South to expand together and to resolve periodic conflicts by compromise.

By the 1850s, however, southern leaders were insisting that the equal rights of slaveholders would be subverted unless the federal government guaranteed the protection of slave property in the common territories. Northern leaders, eventually including many moderates who had always favored compromise, drew a firm line against imposing slavery on a territory against the wishes of the majority of settlers. To paraphrase the twentieth-century poet Robert Frost, the territorial question came down to what Americans were willing to wall in or wall out. In one form or another, Americans had to face the question of whether, in a free society, any limits could be imposed on the total domination of one person over another.

12 Population Growth and Economic Expansion

To understand the American experience during the four decades preceding the Civil War, one must grasp the dimensions of demographic and economic change that occurred during this period. Other nations have undergone periods of rapid growth and industrialization, accompanied by painful cultural adjustment and social conflict. In general, however, this modernizing experience has occurred in long-settled communities with traditions, customs, and class interests that served simultaneously as barriers to change and as stabilizers of society. What distinguished American history in the period 1820–60 was that a modern market economy emerged in conjunction with the rapid settlement of virgin land and the unprecedented expansion of the western frontier.

There were few barriers to this double process, and the American people were determined to overcome what barriers there were. The American economy showed a remarkable freedom in the flow of goods, people, and capital in response to market forces. The ease with which resources were shifted from region to region and from agriculture to commerce or industry accounted for much of the economic growth in the early and mid-nineteenth century. No laws restricted the influx of European and Asian laborers. The Constitution ruled out any taxes on American exports. Thanks largely to southern pressure, the federal government gradually lowered protective tariffs on imports. The federal government's sale and donation of immense tracts of public land were intended to encourage individual enterprise in a free and unregulated market. Political stability, even in the rapidly created new states, helped to guarantee the security of private property and the legal enforcement of contracts. The states themselves actively promoted economic growth, but no other society had imposed so few fiscal, political, religious, and social restraints on the marketplace. No other society had been so confident that market forces constituted the "invisible hand" that kept the competitive economy in balance.

No other society had become so committed to the goals of maximizing individual profits by increasing productivity and lowering costs.

The result of this extraordinary freedom from limitations, along with the availability of land and the somewhat lagging availability of labor and capital, was extremely rapid economic growth. As perceived and experienced by living human beings, however, this growth was both liberating and extremely disruptive. It destroyed family self-sufficiency, pride in craftsmanship, and personal and family ties that unified residential communities with local economic markets. Although the growth of national markets broadened the range of individual choice for businessmen, there was little choice for native Americans, slaves, unskilled laborers, landless farmers, and domestic servants: in short, for all those who were excluded by force or circumstance from the benefits of the market. Despite a generally rising standard of living, Americans in the pre–Civil War decades witnessed growing economic inequalities. Moreover, the nation's triumphs in economic and territorial expansion depended on two forms of outright racial exploitation: the forcible removal of the Indian people from the rich lands east of the Great Plains; and the forced labor of black slaves who produced invaluable exports, mainly cotton, that helped finance America's economic growth.

Population Growth, Immigration, and Urbanization

From 1820 to 1860, America's population maintained the extraordinary rate of growth that had characterized the colonial and post-Revolutionary periods. The population increased by an average of 35 percent every decade, and the total population continued to double every twenty-five years. The United States sustained this high rate of growth until the 1860s. During

the nineteenth century no European nation achieved a growth rate one-half as high as America's for even two decades.

America's population growth cannot be attributed to any single, consistent cause. Before the mid-1840s most of the population growth resulted from the remarkable fertility—the rate of reproduction—of the American people, reinforced by a relatively low rate of infant mortality. Like many countries in modern Africa and South America, the United States literally swarmed with children. In 1830 nearly one-third of the total white population was under the age of ten. Yet in most parts of the country the birthrate had actually begun to decline before 1810, and it continued to fall throughout the century. By the 1840s it was only the influx of European immigrants, who accounted for one-quarter of the total population increase in that decade, that maintained the previous rate of national growth.

The Immigrants. Immigration was partly the result of economic distress in Europe. Few Europeans would have left for America if population growth in their homelands had not pressed hard on available supplies of land, food, and jobs, and if they had not been displaced and made expendable by technological change in a capitalist, industrializing economy. In 1845 the Irish potato crop—which provided most ordinary Irish with their basic food supply—failed disastrously. Five years of famine followed. Many Irish thus had little choice but to emigrate or starve. And the British landlords who controlled Ireland helped to subsidize emigration in the hope of reducing taxes that were being levied for the support of workhouses, which were spilling over with starving laborers who had been evicted from the land. In parts of Germany and Scandinavia, governments encouraged emigration as a way of draining off unemployed farmers and artisans, who had been displaced by the modernization of agriculture and by competition from imported machine-made goods.

But the most important stimulus to immigration was the promise of jobs in America. Immigration soared during America's years of greatest prosperity, and it lagged during America's years of economic recession. Mass emigration from Europe was a direct response to the sudden demand in America for labor in construction and manufacturing, and to the supposedly limitless opportunity for landownership in the West. American promoters, representing shipping firms, labor contractors, manufacturers, and even the governments of western states, enticed Europeans with glowing accounts of the United States. More persuasive were the reports of fellow villagers or family members who had already crossed the Atlantic. In the

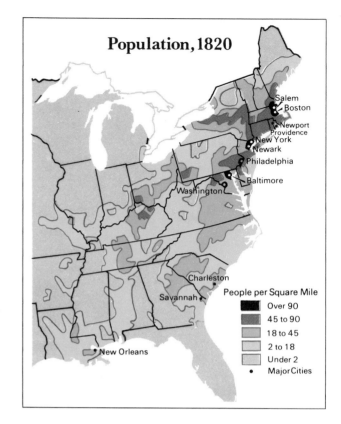

Population, 1820

People per Square Mile
- Over 90
- 45 to 90
- 18 to 45
- 2 to 18
- Under 2
- • Major Cities

1830s when northwestern Europe became aware of America's economic boom, of the North's shortage of labor, and of the opening of vast tracts of farmland in the West, the number of immigrants rose to nearly 600,000—approximately a fourfold increase over the previous decade. In the 1840s the number soared to about 1.5 million, and in the 1850s to about 2.8 million.

The swelling stream, although it originated almost entirely from northwestern Europe, was anything but homogeneous. It included illiterate peasants from Germany and Ireland, highly skilled artisans from England, Germany, Belgium, and Switzerland, political refugees escaping the repression that followed the abortive European revolutions of 1830 and 1848, and Jews and other victims of religious discrimination. The Germans amounted to about 1.3 million immigrants, and many had sufficient funds to purchase farms in the West or at least to make their way to thriving German communities in Cincinnati, St. Louis, and Milwaukee. The Irish, numbering some 1.7 million, had few skills and often arrived penniless, traveling in the holds of westbound ships that had carried American lumber, grain, cotton, and other bulk products to Europe. Cast off by Britain as an

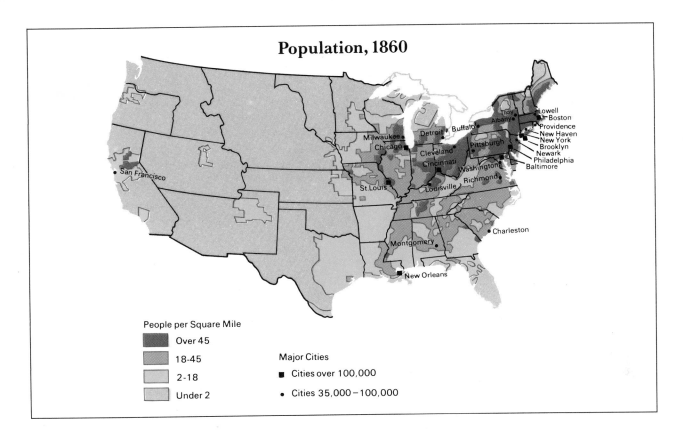

Population, 1860

People per Square Mile

- Over 45
- 18-45
- 2-18
- Under 2

Major Cities

- ■ Cities over 100,000
- • Cities 35,000–100,000

Cities labeled on map: San Francisco, Milwaukee, Chicago, St. Louis, Detroit, Cleveland, Cincinnati, Louisville, Buffalo, Pittsburgh, Washington, Richmond, Montgomery, New Orleans, Charleston, Troy, Albany, Lowell, Boston, Providence, New Haven, New York, Brooklyn, Newark, Philadelphia, Baltimore

---

unwanted population, the Irish peasants were in effect dumped in the northeastern port cities or sometimes in Canada, from which they migrated southward. Gradually they found employment in heavy construction work, in foundries and factories, and in domestic service. But for a while they enormously swelled the ranks of the recipients of public and private welfare.

Before the Civil War the proportion of foreign-born in the population as a whole never rose above 15 percent, but in Boston and New York City by the 1850s the figure had climbed to more than 50 percent. Over half the foreign-born lived in Ohio, Pennsylvania, and New York. This concentration of immigrants greatly accelerated the growth of cities in the Northeast and of the towns and villages along the Great Lakes and in the Ohio and Mississippi river valleys.

Urban Growth and Population Mobility.

In 1860 four out of five Americans still lived in rural environments—that is, on farms or in settlements of less than 2,500. Nevertheless, by 1850 more than half the populations of Massachusetts and Rhode Island lived in urban centers; the United States as a whole did not become so urbanized until the 1920s. By 1860 eight American cities (three of them west of the Appalachian Mountains) had more than 150,000 inhabitants, a population that was exceeded at the time by only seven cities in industrial England. Although America could boast no metropolis equivalent to London, in 1860 the combined populations of Manhattan and Brooklyn exceeded 1 million. New York City, endowed with a superior harbor and with the Hudson River, which provided deep-water navigation into the interior, had won a further competitive advantage over other East Coast cities when in 1818 its merchants established the first regular scheduled sailings to Europe. Seven years later the Erie Canal opened cheap access to the Great Lakes and to the markets of the West. Immigrants arrived and stayed in New York because it was America's great seaport and commercial center, a crucible of risk and opportunity.

Overall, the declining birthrate resulted in a slightly higher average age for the American population, but the influx of immigrants greatly enlarged the number of Northeasterners between the ages of twenty and thirty. In 1850 more than 70 percent of the American people were still under thirty, a figure that takes on greater meaning when compared with the 63 percent for England and the 52 percent for France. Before the Civil War the Americans remained an ex-

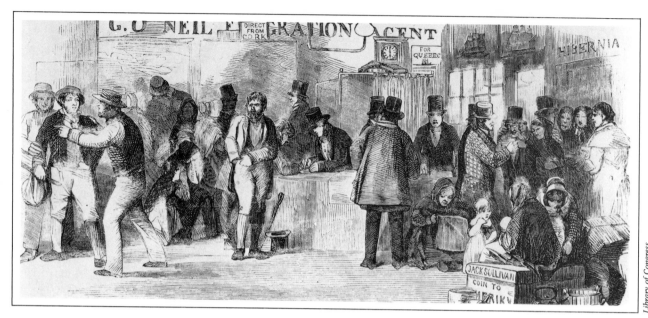

Library of Congress

EMIGRATION AGENT'S OFFICE
By the 1840s the expansion of transatlantic commerce had greatly reduced the westbound steerage fare from Europe to America. Nevertheless, many emigrants, such as the Irish portrayed here, had to depend on loans, charitable gifts, or funds sent from relatives in America.

traordinarily youthful people, a circumstance that helps to account for their restlessness, their venturesomeness, and their impatience with boundaries of any kind.

Alexis de Toqueville echoed the amazement of many Europeans at the "strange unrest" of a people who could be seen "continually to change their track for fear of missing the shortest cut to happiness":

In the United States a man builds a house in which to spend his old age, and he sells it before the roof is on . . . he brings a field into tillage and leaves other men to gather the crops; he embraces a profession and gives it up; he settles in a place, which he soon afterwards leaves to carry his changeable longings elsewhere . . . and if at the end of a year of unremitting labor he finds he has a few days' vacation, his eager curiosity whirls him over the vast extent of the United States, and he will travel fifteen hundred miles in a few days to shake off his happiness. Death at length overtakes him, but it is before he is weary of his bootless chase of that complete felicity which forever escapes him.

This sense of limitless possibility helps explain the feverish westward rush of population. By 1860 the settled area of the United States was five times what it had been in 1790, and nearly half the people lived beyond the 1790 boundaries of settlement. As late as 1820 many Americans had thought it would take at least a century to settle the vast territory west of the

Mississippi River. In 1860 the United States had firmly established its present continental boundaries, except for Alaska. No other nation had populated so much new territory in so short a time or had absorbed so many immigrants. No other had combined rapid urbanization with the dramatic expansion of an agricultural frontier and a transportation network.

Agriculture

Before the Civil War the majority of American families made their livings by supplying the primary human needs for food and clothing. Agriculture dominated the economy and provided the commodities for most of the nation's domestic and foreign trade. Even in towns and cities, families customarily kept a vegetable garden and perhaps a pig, a cow, and chickens. Many of the most seasoned urbanites could at least remember the smell of a barnyard from their childhoods.

Agricultural Expansion. The period 1820–60 was distinguished by two trends that might at first seem contradictory. On the one hand, the quickening pace of urbanization and industrialization brought a decisive shift toward nonagricultural employment. This shift had actually begun in the late eighteenth century, but it had started to slow before 1820, when approximately 79 percent of the labor force was gainfully em-

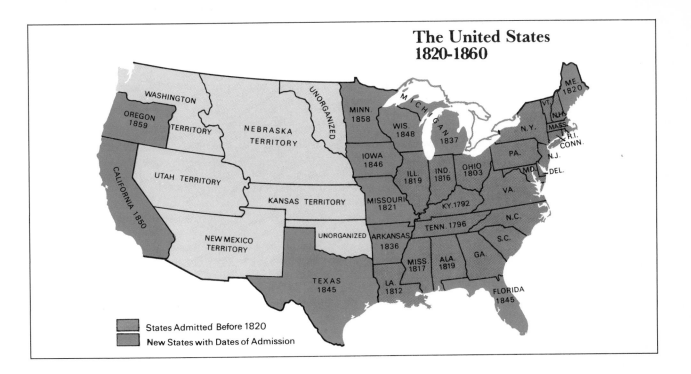

The United States 1820-1860

WASHINGTON TERRITORY

OREGON 1859

CALIFORNIA 1850

UTAH TERRITORY

NEBRASKA TERRITORY

UNORGANIZED

NEW MEXICO TERRITORY

KANSAS TERRITORY

TEXAS 1845

MINN. 1858

MICHIGAN 1837

WIS. 1848

IOWA 1846

MISSOURI 1821

UNORGANIZED

ARKANSAS 1836

MISS. 1817

LA. 1812

ALA. 1819

ILL. 1819

IND. 1816

OHIO 1803

KY. 1792

TENN. 1796

GA.

N.C.

S.C.

FLORIDA 1845

ME. 1820

VT.

N.H.

MASS.

R.I.

CONN.

N.Y.

PA.

N.J.

DEL.

MD.

VA.

States Admitted Before 1820

New States with Dates of Admission

ployed in agriculture. By 1850, however, the proportion of farmers had fallen to 55 percent. This was the most rapid structural change in the economy during the entire nineteenth century. On the other hand, the same period saw a phenomenal expansion of agriculture into the "virgin lands" of the West and the Old Southwest, accompanied by revolutionary changes in transportation and marketing.

But these two trends were actually intimately related. The urban East provided the capital and markets that made the agricultural expansion possible. The food and fiber of the West and Old Southwest were indispensable for the industries and urban growth of the East. Western farming, fur trapping, mining, and lumbering were the spearheads of an expansive capitalist economy that was increasingly integrated with the great markets of the world.

A nation of farmers is almost by definition a nation at an early stage of economic development. Yet in nineteenth-century America, agriculture did not suggest a conservative way of life limited by the entrenched customs of a feudalistic past. Farming increasingly took on the characteristics of a speculative business. The very isolation of individual farms, posted like sentries along lonely country roads, indicated that Americans placed efficiency above the community solidarity that was characteristic of tight-knit European peasant villages. The individual American farm family, practically imprisoned near the fields it

worked and usually owned, had proved to be the most effective unit of production.

Four central conditions shaped America's unprecedented expansion of cultivated land. First, public policy continued to favor rapid settlement of the immense public domain, amounting to a billion acres if one includes the territorial acquisitions of the 1840s. There was no opposing interest in conserving natural resources and future revenue. Second, despite population growth, agricultural labor remained scarce and expensive, especially in frontier regions. Most farm owners had to rely on an occasional hired hand to supplement the labor of their own families or of tenant families. In the South the price of slaves continued to rise. Third, the dispersion of settlement made farmers heavily dependent, for many decades, on navigable rivers and waterways for transportation. Fourth, the real-estate mentality of earlier periods burgeoned into a national mania as the westward movement and the mushrooming of towns brought spectacular rises in land values. Great land companies and private investors, representing eastern and European capital, purchased virtual empires of western land and then used every possible device to promote rapid settlement. Even the small farmers saw that it was more agreeable to make money by speculating in land than by removing stumps or plowing up the resistant bluestem grass of the prairies.

From one point of view the pioneering outlook

was progressive. There can be no doubt that Americans who moved were inventive, hardy, and willing to take risks. Often pushing forward ahead of roads and organized government, the frontier farmers engaged in a struggle by trial and error to succeed in the face of unfamiliar climate, insects, soil conditions, and drainage. In time they experimented with different crops, livestock, and transportation routes, searching for the commodity and market that would bring a predictable cash return. Although the federal government supplied little direct information to farmers, it continued Jefferson's tradition of promoting land surveys and sending expeditions into land west of the Mississippi River to collect information on flora and fauna, geology, watersheds, and Indians. This enterprising spirit, evident in both public and private endeavors, led to the discovery and exploitation of undreamed-of resources, confirming Tocqueville's judgment that "Nature herself favors the cause of the [American] people."

But the quest for immediate returns also led to a ruthless stripping of natural resources. In the absence of national legislation and national power, the timber, grasses, and minerals of the public domain invited a headlong scramble by the pioneers to cut trees, graze their cattle, and dig for ore. The government actually bought gold and silver that miners took from public property. European visitors were astonished at the American conviction that forests were a hostile element to be destroyed without regard for need. Trees, like the buffalo and beaver of the West, seemed so plentiful that few Americans could foresee a time of diminishing supply.

The soil itself, the most valuable of all resources, fared no better. Americans generally lacked the incentives and patience to conserve the soil by using fertilizers and by carefully rotating crops. They tended to look on land as a temporary and expendable resource that should be mined as rapidly as possible. This attitude, which was especially prevalent in the South and the West, reflected the common need to produce the most profitable single crop—wheat, corn, rice, tobacco, or cotton—in order to pay for land that had been purchased on credit.

The entrepreneurial character of American agriculture owed much to the way new lands were originally settled. It is difficult for Americans of the late twentieth century to grasp the significance of the fact that before the Civil War the chief business of the federal government was the management and disposal of public land. Seeking revenue as well as rapid settlement, the government hastily surveyed tracts of western land and sold them to the highest bidder at public auction; the remainder was offered at the minimum price of $1.25 per acre. Since there was no limit on how many acres an individual or company might buy, investors eagerly bought blocks of thousands of acres. The great peaks of speculation coincided with the expansion of bank credit in the early 1830s and the mid-1850s. The profitable resale of western land depended on promoting settlement.

Speculators and Squatters. Speculators had always helped to shape the character of American agriculture. The great theme of American settlement was the continuing contest of will between absentee owners and the squatters who first developed the land and who often had some partial claim to it. Although squatters frequently sold their own claims to the succeeding waves of migrants, they tended to picture wealthier speculators as greedy vampires. Yet the large speculators played a key role in financing the rapid settlement of the public lands. Pooling private capital, they lent money to squatters, often at illegally high interest rates, to finance the purchase of tools, livestock, and supplies. They extended credit for buying farms. They pressured local and national governments to subsidize canals and railroads. This speculation often involved considerable risk; the returns on investment depended on the speculators' ability to predict business conditions accurately and on how fast settlement took place.

Squatters for their part yearned for economic independence. They successfully agitated for state "occupancy laws" favoring the claims of actual settlers and guaranteeing them compensation, if evicted, for their cabins, fences, outbuildings, and other improvements. Squatters also pressed for a lowered minimum in the amount of public land that could be purchased—a restriction that by 1832 fell to 40 acres. Above all, squatters called on the federal government to sanction squatting, formally allowing settlers to clear and cultivate tracts of public land prior to purchase. This policy of "preemption," which was developed in limited acts in the 1830s and finally established in a general law of 1841, gave squatters the right to settle land and then purchase as much as 160 acres at the minimum price in advance of public sale.

In practice the federal land system was a compromise between the interests of farmers and those of speculators. Government measures did nothing to curb speculators, who were in fact favored by the requirement, beginning in 1820, of full cash payment for public land. Speculators were also favored by lavish government donations of public land to military veterans, railroad companies, and state governments, as well as by the eventual pricing, at as little as 12.5¢ an acre, of land that had long been unsold. Federal land policy allowed speculators to amass great private fortunes by acquiring valuable tracts of the public do-

THE JUNCTION OF THE ERIE AND NORTHERN CANALS, c. 1830–32
Although canals greatly reduced the cost of overland freight, it was a slow and arduous task to negotiate multiple locks and to pull barges by rope from the "tow path" alongside.

main. Yet the wide dispersion of freehold farms gave some substance to the myth that any American could become an owner of property and an independent producer for the capitalist market.

Demand for Better Transportation.

Access to growing markets was the overriding concern of the commercial farmer. Yet the craze during the early nineteenth century for building turnpikes, bridges, and plank roads failed to reduce significantly the cost of long-distance freight. The teams of horses that hauled wagons of freight over the nation's turnpikes averaged no better than two miles an hour. Not until canals began to link together other inland waterways could northern farmers think of concentrating on the production of corn and wheat for distant markets.

The Erie Canal, which was completed in 1825, united Northeast and West by providing a continuous waterway from Lake Erie to the Atlantic. It was by far the longest canal in the world, and it dramatically lowered shipping costs. In 1817 it had cost 19.2¢ per mile to ship a ton of freight overland from Buffalo to New York City. By the late 1850s the cost per mile, via the canal, had dropped to 0.81¢. New York State had directed and financed this enormous undertaking, and it soon reaped spectacular rewards. Foreign capital quickly flowed into the country to meet the demand of other state and municipal governments, setting off a canal-building mania that soon linked Pittsburgh with Philadelphia, and the Ohio River with the Great Lakes. The high cost of building this network of waterways, undertaken for the most part by the states themselves, severely strained the credit of Ohio, Pennsylvania, and Indiana. But by sharply lowering the costs of transport, the most successful canals had an enormous effect on northern agriculture and industry.

By the mid-1830s the basic pattern of internal transportation began to shift away from the traditional routes that had led from the Ohio and upper Mississippi valleys to New Orleans and ocean shipment via the Gulf of Mexico. Ohio Valley farmers would continue to ship grain and pork down the Mississippi by flatboat. The richest markets, however, lay east of the Great Lakes, and for a time the richest commercial agriculture developed in regions accessible by canal to Lake Erie. By 1840 Rochester, New York, had become the leading flour-milling center in the country. The marketing of grain became more efficient as brokers and other middlemen began to arrange for storage, transport, sale, and credit. This transformation preceded the East-West railroad connections of the early 1850s.

Harriet Martineau was a famous British writer and popularizer of laissez-faire economic theory. In 1837 she visited frontier Chicago, where she encountered wild speculation in building lots. Land values were expected to rise as a result of a proposed canal connecting the Great Lakes with the Mississippi waterways.

Harriet Martineau Describes Enterprise in Chicago (1837)

I NEVER saw a busier place than Chicago was at the time of our arrival. The streets were crowded with land speculators, hurrying from one sale to another. A negro, dressed up in scarlet, . . . announced the times of sale. At every street corner where he stopped, the crowd flocked round him; and it seemed as if some prevalent mania infected the whole people. The rage for speculation might fairly be so regarded. As the gentlemen of our party walked the streets, store-keepers hailed them from their doors, with offers of farms, and all manner of land-lots, advising them to speculate before the price of land rose higher. A young lawyer, of my acquaintance there, had realized five hundred dollars per day, the five preceding days, by merely making out titles to land. Another friend had realized, in two years, ten times as much money as he had before fixed upon as a competence for life. Of course, this rapid money-making is a merely temporary evil. . . . The absurdity of the speculation is so striking, that the wonder is that the fever should have attained such a height as I witnessed. The immediate occasion of the bustle which prevailed, . . . was the sale of lots, to the value of two millions of dollars, along the course of a projected canal; and of another set, immediately behind these. Persons not intending to game, and not infected with mania, would endeavor to form some reasonable conjecture as to the ultimate value of the lots, by calculating the cost of the canal, the risks from accident, from the possible competition from other places, etc., and, finally, the possible profits, under the most favorable circumstances, within so many years' purchase. Such a calculation would serve as some sort of guide as to the amount of purchase-money to be risked. Whereas, wild land on the banks of a canal, not yet even marked out, was selling at Chicago for more than rich land, well improved, in the finest part of the valley of the Mohawk [in New York State], on the banks of a canal which is already the medium of an almost inestimable amount of traffic. If sharpers and gamblers were to be the sufferers by the impending crash at Chicago, no one would feel much concerned; but they, unfortunately, are the people who encourage the delusion, in order to profit by it. Many a high-spirited, but inexperienced, young man; many a simple settler, will be ruined for the advantage of knaves.

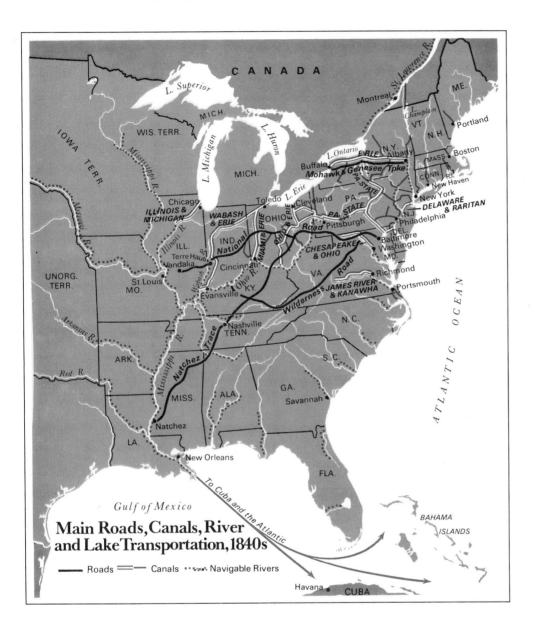

Main Roads, Canals, River and Lake Transportation, 1840s

—— Roads === Canals ····· Navigable Rivers

The Commercialization of Agriculture. In both North and South, the expansion and commercialization of agriculture provided the impetus for the economy's accelerated growth and modernization. During the 1840s the United States began to export an increasing proportion of its agricultural output, partly in response to poor harvests in Europe and to Britain's repeal of its Corn Laws, which had excluded American and other foreign grain, even during the worst of the Irish potato famine. This outflow helped pay for America's imports of manufactured products and the immense interest charges on foreign investment in American land, cotton, and railroads. Much of America's economic ex-

pansion depended on the country's ability to attract such investment from Europe. By preventing glutted domestic markets, agricultural exports also helped to raise the price of domestic farm products, thereby encouraging the further expansion of cash crops.

Continuing improvements in transportation enabled agricultural regions to specialize in the search for competitive advantages in response to the pressures of an increasingly national market. In the states of the Old Northwest, north of the Ohio River, farmers began to buy trademarked tools and machines from authorized distributors. Steel plows, invented in the 1830s but widely accepted only in the 1850s, made it

Agriculture 297

"GEESE IN FLIGHT"

This imaginative painting by Leila T. Bauman captures some of the mid-nineteenth-century excitement over movement and improved transport—the steam from the train and riverboat harmonizing with the movement of horses, geese and wind.

possible to break the tough sod and cultivate the rich but sticky soil of the prairies. Mechanical reapers had also been invented in the 1830s, but only in the 1850s did Cyrus McCormick's Chicago factory begin large-scale production and employ modern techniques of advertising and promotion. As the Old Northwest proved its superiority in producing wheat and other grains, along with wool, corn, pork, and beef, farmers in the East found it increasingly difficult to compete with their western counterparts. Instead, eastern farmers began to specialize in the production of hay for horses and perishable foodstuffs for urban markets.

Industrialization and Railroads

There is still much controversy over the stages of America's economic growth. Some economists have advanced the theory of a dramatic "takeoff" starting in the 1840s, in which the growth of the nation's output

shot far ahead of population growth. The best recent evidence suggests that a pattern of long-term accelerated growth preceded significant industrialization and probably originated in the 1820s or earlier from the interaction between urbanization and western agriculture. In those years manufacturing still mostly meant that goods were made by hand in households and in small shops or mills. Blacksmiths, coopers (barrel makers), cobblers, curriers (leather workers), hatters, tailors, weavers—these and other artisans and apprentices worked in central shops, mills, and stores, or traveled through the more sparsely settled countryside. Yet the independent artisans' world began to disintegrate in the 1820s as merchant capitalists expanded and reorganized markets and gradually gained control of the means of production.

Manufacturing. As had happened in England, cotton textiles became the leading industrial innovation. Aided

INDUSTRY IN NEW ENGLAND
Americans expressed an absorbing interest in diagrams of new machines, such as Christopher Tully's eighteenth-century spinning machine for wool. The woman tending a machine is weaving cloth on a power loom. The lithograph of the Pontoosuc Woolen Mills in Pittsfield, Massachusetts, dramatizes the rural setting of early American industry.

somewhat by protective tariffs, a group of wealthy Boston merchants pooled their capital and in the 1820s extended large-scale factory production to the new manufacturing centers like Lowell and Chicopee, in Massachusetts. This factory system was called the Waltham system and had been created by New England merchants when the War of 1812 had curtailed international trade. It exploited the latest British technology, such as the power loom, and it continued to draw upon the expertise of immigrant British artisans.

If their products were to compete successfully with imported British textiles, New England manufacturers had to lower the cost and increase the efficiency of labor. American manufacturers had traditionally cut costs by employing children or families including children, who increased the labor force without increasing wages. It soon became apparent, however, that children could not handle the frequent breakdowns of the new machinery or conform to the routine that was necessary for increased labor productivity.

By the late 1840s immigrants had begun to ease the general shortage of factory labor. But for a few decades the Boston merchants relied on the unique expedient of employing adult young women, who were attracted to the factories by the provision of chaperoned dormitories and various cultural amenities. The merchant-manufacturers desired, no doubt sincerely, to avoid the moral degradation that had been a black mark on the British factory system. As economy-minded entrepreneurs, they also hoped to influence their employees' leisure time, preventing the binges and self-proclaimed holidays that had always led to irregular work habits and absenteeism among preindustrial people. New England farm girls could also be hired for less than half the wages of male factory hands since they were secondary earners for their families and since the factory represented for them virtually the only possible liberation from the farm.

From 1815 to 1833 the cotton textile industry increased average annual output at the phenomenal rate of 16 percent. Slackening demand soon reduced the annual rate of growth to about 5 percent, but textile producers, including wool and carpet manufacturers, continued to pioneer in mechanization, in efficiency, and in the use of steam power.

New England also gave birth to the so-called American system of manufacturing. This innovation depended on the imaginative adaptation of a machine-tool technology that had first been developed in England. Unlike the British, however, American manufacturers could not draw on a plentiful supply of highly skilled craftsmen with many years of training in an established craft tradition. Therefore American manufacturers encouraged the perfection of light machine tools that not only eliminated many hand operations but also allowed ordinary mechanics to measure within one-thousandth of an inch and to mill or cut metal with great precision. At the British Crystal Palace exhibition of 1851—a great international show of industrial techniques and products—American machinery astonished European experts. In 1854 one of the British commissions that had been sent to study American achievements exclaimed over "the extraordinary ingenuity displayed in many of their labour-saving machines, where automatic action so completely supplies the place of the more abundant hand labour of older manufacturing countries."

The British investigators understood the significance for the future of such a seemingly ordinary device as a machine that produced 180 ladies' hairpins every minute. As early as 1853 an exuberant writer for the *United States Review* could predict that within a half-century machines would liberate Americans from the burdens of work: "Machinery will perform all work—automata will direct them. The only tasks of the human race will be to make love, study, and be happy."

In 1860 American industry was still at an early stage of transition. There were sharp contrasts in the degree of industrialization with respect to different products and different regions. For example, despite an impressive expansion of output, the American iron industry was not nearly as successful as the cotton industry in adopting and improving the latest British technology. The continued use of small blast furnaces that used charcoal to produce malleable iron has been explained by the cheapness and availability of wood for charcoal, by the absence of bituminous coal east of the Allegheny Mountains, by the belated discovery and use of anthracite coal, and by the particular needs of local blacksmiths. Whatever the reasons, American industry in the 1850s depended heavily on imported British wrought iron and railroad rails, and it lagged far behind Britain in exploiting coal, iron, and steam.

In the West manufacturing often reverted to pre-industrial methods that had almost disappeared in the East. But even in the Northeast many goods were produced not in factories but by merchants who still relied on the "putting-out" system—that is, distributing raw materials to laborers who often owned their own tools and worked at home. Other merchant capitalists hired laborers essentially as instruments of production, for the workers had no share in the ownership of tools and machines, in managerial decisions, in the risks of marketing, or in the industrial product.

In 1860 American manufacturing still depended largely on water power, not steam. The typical firm employed a handful of workers, was unincorporated, and engaged in the small-scale processing of raw materials. Few industries processed the products of other industries. The nation's largest industries included some that were thoroughly mechanized, such as the production of cotton goods, flour, and meal. Some, however, were only partly mechanized, such as the manufacture of boots and shoes. And some were characterized by premodern technology and low labor productivity, such as lumbering and the making of men's clothing.

Railroad Building. The great railroad boom of the late 1840s and 1850s dramatized the growing links between industry and agriculture. Although the nation's railroads equaled the canals in mileage as early as 1840, canal barges and river steamboats continued to carry a significant proportion of freight throughout the antebellum period, the years before the Civil War. But by providing speedy access to isolated farms and distant markets, railroads opened new horizons and extended the risks and promises of a commercial society.

The development of railway networks was long delayed by primitive technology, a high incidence of breakdowns and accidents, and construction costs that required unprecedented amounts of capital investment. As early as 1828, Baltimore promotors began building the first trans-Appalachian railroad to compete with New York's Erie Canal, which threatened to channel much of the western trade toward New York City. But not until 1853 did this Baltimore and Ohio Railroad reach the Ohio River. As late as 1860 there were still hundreds of small, independent lines with different widths of track. Nevertheless, by the early 1850s construction engineers were improving rails, roadbeds, bridges, and locomotives. Railroad corporations had amassed immense reserves of capital, and their managers were learning how to administer complex bureaucracies that employed

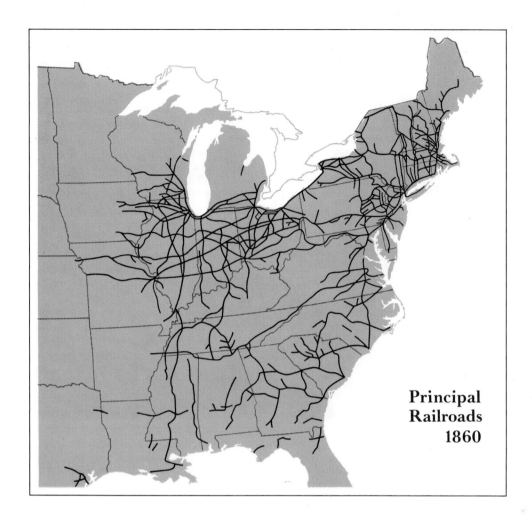

Principal
Railroads
1860

thousands of workers and required instant interstate communication by means of the recently perfected electric telegraph. By 1854 tracks extended from New York City to the Mississippi River, and by 1860 to the Missouri River at St. Joseph, Missouri. This burst of western railroad construction led to the beginning of consolidation into main lines that further cemented economic ties between the West and the Northeast. By 1860 railroads had become the nation's first billion-dollar industry, spawning the first giant corporations and linking cash-crop farming with the production of iron, coal, lumber, and machine tools.

Population Distribution and Opportunity

There can be no doubt that the nation's overall economic growth brought impressive gains in income and standard of living. By 1860 the United States was well ahead of western Europe in per capita income; even the South, which lagged behind the Northeast, was richer than most nations of Europe. But historians still have much to learn about the actual distribution of wealth in the pre–Civil War decades, to say nothing of the people's opportunity to acquire property or to rise in status and occupation.

Discussions of America's economic opportunities generally omit three groups: the Indians; the black slaves; and the free blacks in both North and South, whose small economic gains in various skilled trades and service industries were severely damaged by competition from white immigrants. Even excluding these oppressed minorities, one finds many indications that economic inequality increased substantially from 1820 to 1860.

The Rich Grow Richer, 1820–1860. According to the best recent estimates, by 1860 the upper 5 percent of families owned over half the nation's wealth. The disparity was far greater in parts of the South, where the wealth of the average slaveholder was growing far more rapidly than that of the average nonslaveholder. The typical slaveholder was not only more than five times as

FIVE POINTS, NEW YORK CITY, 1827
For many decades the region around "Five Points," the intersection of five streets in lower Manhattan, epitomized the worst of urban degradation: poverty, prostitution, crime, drunkenness, and mob violence. Fashionably dressed gentlemen and racially mixed crowds mingled with prostitutes and pigs.

wealthy as the average Northerner, but more than ten times as wealthy as the average nonslaveholding southern farmer. Even in the farming country of the eastern North Central states, where there was greater economic equality, the upper 10 percent of landholders owned nearly 40 percent of the taxable wealth. The national centers of inequality, however, were the growing urban regions from Boston to New Orleans. Although much statistical research remains to be done, it is clear that between 1820 and 1860 the big cities led the nation toward the increasing domination of the very rich. By 1860, according to one estimate, Philadelphia's richest 1 percent of population owned half the city's wealth; the lower 80 percent of the city's population had to be content with 3 percent of the wealth. A relatively modest estimate has concluded that the richest 5 percent of American families in 1860 received between 25 and 35 percent of the national income. Although these figures indicate an inequality far greater than that estimated for modern America, they are roughly comparable to the inequalities in northern Europe in the late nineteenth century.

This conclusion would not be startling if America's pre–Civil War decades had not once been described and almost universally accepted as "the age of the common man." American politicians and journalists of the era eagerly expanded on the theme of "equality of condition," supposedly confirmed by the observations of Alexis de Tocqueville and other European visitors. On closer inspection, however, it is clear that Tocqueville and others claimed only that American fortunes were "scanty" compared with fortunes in Europe; that in America "most of the rich men were formerly poor"; and that in America "any man's son may become the equal of any other man's son." In other words, American inequalities were thought to be temporary and to enhance the incentives of a race to success in which all were free to compete.

This belief in America's unique capacity for avoiding permanent inequalities was especially reassuring by 1850, when European industrialism had produced undeniable evidence of misery, class conflict, and seething revolution. By that date American leaders could not hide their alarm over similar contrasts of wealth and extreme poverty in their own country, particularly when the urban poor congregated in slums beyond the reach of traditional religious and social discipline. Yet affluent Americans persuaded themselves that the poor were free to climb the ladder of success. They also firmly believed that the wealthiest citizens were, in the words of the powerful Kentucky senator Henry Clay, "enterprising self-made men, who have whatever wealth they possess by patient and diligent labor."

In truth, however, the fortunes of the John Jacob Astor family and of other leading American families compared favorably with the fortunes of the richest Europeans. Notwithstanding a few astonishing examples of rags-to-riches achievement, the great majority of America's rich and successful men had benefited from inherited wealth, an affluent childhood, or a prestigious family tradition. Between 1820 and 1860 there was a marked persistence of family wealth. In effect, the rich grew richer. In the cities at least, they constituted an elite that became increasingly segregated by exclusive clubs, high social life, intermarriage, foreign travel, and business alliances.

At the other end of the spectrum was the mass of unskilled day laborers, who took what temporary jobs they could find and whose wages, even if regular, could not possibly support a family unless supplemented by the income of wives and children. No one knows the size of this unskilled, propertyless population, which drifted in and out of mill towns, flocked to the construction sites of canals and railroads, and gravitated to urban slums. In the 1840s and 1850s the largest cities attracted the chronic failures and castoffs who had no other place to turn. They jammed themselves into the attics and dank, windowless basements of Boston's Half Moon Place, where as many as one hundred people might share the same overflowing privy; or into New York's notorious Old Brewery, a foul tenement that supposedly housed over a thousand beggars, pickpockets, whores, robbers, alcoholics, and starving children. In contrast with the society of mid-nineteenth-century England, the relatively unstructured society of America provided very few public agencies that could enforce minimal standards of health, welfare, and safety.

Social Mobility.
The extremes of wealth and poverty tell little about the amount of upward movement from one class to another. Thus far, however, the available evidence indicates that the odds were heavily against an unskilled laborer's acquiring a higher occupational status. The ovewhelming majority of unskilled workers remained unskilled workers. It is true that in the 1850s many of the sons of unskilled workers were moving into semiskilled factory jobs. But this generational advance was almost always limited to the next rung on the ladder. It was extremely rare for the children of manual workers, even skilled manual workers, to rise to the level of clerical, managerial, or professional employment.

Despite growing signs of semipermanent boundaries between occupational groups in the pre–Civil War decades, there were remarkably few expressions of class conflict or class interest. Historians have sometimes been misled by the labor rhetoric of the Jacksonian period, a time when the rich felt it necessary to prove their humble origins and when everyone who could do so proudly claimed to be a workingman. The labor leaders of the era were typically artisan proprietors and small businessmen who were intent on fixing prices and reducing the hazards of interregional competition. This is not to deny the importance of British artisans who, displaced by the British factory system, had migrated to the United States. These men reinforced the preindustrial craft traditions in America, and they were schooled in the techniques of secret organization and industrial warfare. Nor can one deny the courage of union organizers who faced conspiracy trials in the 1820s and 1830s, who saw their gains wiped out by the depression of 1837–42, and who finally formed city federations of craft unions and national trade unions in the 1850s. Yet the great strikes for higher wages and for the ten-hour day were staged by skilled printers, typographers, hatters, tailors, and other artisans. Employers, who were mostly supported by the courts and who benefited from fresh supplies of cheap immigrant labor, had little difficulty in breaking strikes. Although the Massachusetts Supreme Court led the way, in the case *Commonwealth* v. *Hunt* (1842), in ruling that trade unions were not in themselves conspiracies in restraint of trade, in 1860 only 0.1 percent of the American labor force was organized.

Even by the 1840s America's relative freedom from class consciousness and class conflict evoked considerable comment. According to Karl Marx and other European observers, the explanation could be found in the fresh lands of the American frontier, which provided an outlet for surplus population. In America George Henry Evans's National Reform Association referred to the West as a "safety valve" that could and should provide an escape for workers whose opportunities were limited in the East. Evans contended in the 1840s that the nation owned enough land in the West to guarantee every family a farm. In the 1850s Horace Greeley, editor of the enormously influential New York *Tribune*, popularized the Republican party's slogan, "Vote yourself a farm." More than a generation later, the historian Frederick Jackson Turner and his followers developed a detailed theory

Courtesy of the Historical Society of Pennsylvania

VICTUALLERS IN PHILADELPHIA
Victuallers were licensed suppliers of food, drink, and provisions. This parade of Philadelphia victuallers was typical of the ceremonial processions of various trades and crafts, proud of their ancient emblems and symbols of public service, but concerned, even by the 1820s, over economic changes that threatened their distinctive identities.

that pictured the frontier as both a safety valve for the pressures of the industrializing East and a constant source of new opportunity.

The "safety-valve" theory, in its simplest and crudest form, has been thoroughly demolished. The eastern laborer, earning a dollar a day or less, could not afford to travel to the frontier and borrow funds for a farm and tools, even if he possessed the skills for western farming. The evidence shows that western land sales lagged in hard times, when a safety valve would be most needed, and increased when prosperity drove up the prices of wheat and cotton. Except for a few cooperative settlement associations and a few hundred wage earners sent by antislavery groups to settle Kansas in the 1850s, there are no records to show that industrial workers were transformed into frontier farmers.

On the other hand, the westward surge of millions of Americans intensified and dramatized the central fact of American life: physical mobility. Wages in the Northeast might well have been lower if the farmers, shopkeepers, artisans, and small businessmen who did go West had stayed put. Some of these aspiring adventurers might have been forced to seek factory employ-

ment. Some might have become America's counterparts of Europe's labor organizers. Ironically, since young males predominated in the migration away from industrial New England, an increasing number of women there had no prospect for marriage and thus became part of a permanent industrial labor force. These women found themselves living permanently on the low wages from jobs they had taken while awaiting marriage.

Intense geographical mobility reinforced the myth of America's boundlessness, of its infinite promise. By 1850 one-quarter of the entire population born in New England states had moved to other states. The South Atlantic states experienced a no less striking westward drain of whites and of black slaves. In each decade the northern cities, towns, and factories witnessed an extraordinary inflow and outflow of population. Although few of these mobile Americans had a chance to acquire farms, they moved because they had hopes of finding life better somewhere else. And the hope may have been more significant than the reality they found. The reality was often grim for unskilled laborers, but the factories and towns they left behind had no need to worry about their accumulating grievances. The more fortunate and competitive movers could not doubt that Illinois was preferable to Ohio, or that New York City offered more opportunities than the rocky hillsides of Vermont.

It was obvious that the condition of most white Americans, except for the floating population of impoverished laborers, was improving. Even the lowliest Irish laborers in a factory town like Newburyport, Massachusetts, found that they could accumulate more property if they stuck to their jobs for a decade or longer. To maintain a savings account or eventually to buy a house required discipline, frugality, and multiple incomes; for some, additional incomes came at the expense of family members' education and leisure time. The Irish put a greater premium on home ownership than on education or occupational achievement. The Jews, on the other hand, tended to make every sacrifice for their family's education. Particularly for the families of manual workers, the gains were extremely limited. But these gains engendered pride in achieving what others had not achieved, and they were sufficient to prevent even a permanent working class from becoming a permanent and propertyless proletariat.

The incessant turnover of population and the lack of physical roots also gave force to the ideology of an open and boundless society—an ideology that was repeatedly stressed in newspaper articles, sermons, and political speeches. Who could tell what had become of all one's former neighbors and fellow workers? No doubt, some had hit it rich. The mystery of everyone's past made it believable that most men's positions had been won according to talent and performance—that in America, where the only limits were individual will and ability, most men got what they were worth. If in time a manual worker could finally boast of a savings account of $300, of owning the roof over his head, or of a son who had moved up to the next rung on the ladder, why should he doubt the common claim, "This is a country of self-made men," where most of the rich had once been poor?

The Cost of Expansion: The Indians

The rapid expansion of agriculture, North and South, depended initially on the displacement of the native population. The white Americans, determined to go where they pleased and to seize any chance for quick profit, regarded the millions of acres of western land as a well-deserved inheritance that should be exploited as quickly as possible. But in 1820 the prairies and forests east of the Mississippi River still contained approximately 125,000 native Americans. Although millions of acres had been legally cleared of Indian occupancy rights, the physical presence of the Indians blocked the way to government sale of much public land that could lead to increased revenues, to profits from land speculation, and to the creation of private farms and plantations.

The Indians, hopelessly outnumbered by an invader with superior technology, had little room for maneuver. Although they had long sought trade and alliances with whites, native Americans had learned that advancing white settlements undermined tribal culture and destroyed the fish and game on which their economy depended. The Indians had little understanding of the whites' conceptions of private property and competitive individualism. But the whites were just as blind to the diversity and complexity of Indian cultures, to the native Americans' traditions of mutual obligation and communal ownership of land, and to the peculiarly advanced position of Indian women (Iroquois women, for example, played a crucial role in political and economic decisions). These cultural barriers made it easier for whites to think of Indians in terms of negative stereotypes—as deceitful and bloodthirsty savages or as a weak and "childlike" race doomed to extinction. In fact, the Indian response to white advances was complex, ranging from skillful warfare and stubborn negotiation to resigned submission in the face of treachery and superior force.

The native Americans had proved to be the major losers in the War of 1812. By ending the long conflict between Western settlers and European empires, this war had removed the Indians' last hope of finding white allies who could slow the advance of white Americans. The decisive victories of William Henry Harrison over the Shawnees in the Old Northwest, and of Andrew Jackson over the Creeks in the Old Southwest, had also shattered the hope of a union between northern and southern Indian confederations. These triumphs opened the way for the whites' exploitation of tribal divisions and for their abandonment of what Jackson termed "the farce of treating with Indian tribes" as units. Jackson thought that all Indians should be required as individuals to submit to the laws of the states, like everyone else, or to migrate beyond the Mississippi River, where they could progress toward civilization at their own pace.

Federal Indian Policy. The land-hungry frontiersmen faced controls on their actions in the form of a federal Indian policy that had evolved from imperial, colonial, and post-Revolutionary precedents. This makeshift policy rested on four premises that in time became increasingly contradictory.

First, in line with European legal concepts, the federal government continued to acknowledge that the Indian tribes were in some sense independent nations that had acquired rights of possession by prior occupancy of the land, even though they lacked many of the usual characteristics of sovereign countries. The federal government's continuing efforts to negotiate treaties, to purchase land, and to mark off territorial boundaries demonstrated that legitimate settlement by whites required at least symbolic consent from the native Americans. The same European model allowed the United States to punish "aggressor" tribes by demanding the cession of land as a legal compensation for the damages of war.

The second premise, a product of New World experience, was that Indian "occupancy" must inevitably give way to white settlement. White Americans, like the heirs of a dying relative, had an eventual right—an "expectancy," to use Jefferson's phrase—to the property that native Americans held. In theory this claim did not interfere with the existing property rights of Indians. It simply gave the American government an exclusive right to purchase Indian lands, thereby blocking any future imperial designs by European powers.

In practice, however, this doctrine led to the third premise—that of supreme federal authority over Indian affairs. Knowing the dangers of alliances between hostile Indians and foreign nations, the federal government had from the beginning assumed powers that would have been unthinkable in any other domestic sphere. It subjected all trade with the native Americans to federal licensing and regulation. It invalidated the sale or transfer of Indian lands, even to a state, unless made in accordance with a federal treaty. It guaranteed that the native Americans would be protected from white advances on lands that they had not ceded to the federal government. But unfortunately no federal administration had the will or military power to protect Indian rights while supervising the fair acquisition of land by whites. In a government that was increasingly inclined to listen to the voice of the people, the native Americans had no voice of their own.

The fourth premise, which Jefferson had stated and which gained momentum after the War of 1812, was that Indian culture, which whites called savagery, could not permanently coexist with American civilization. President James Monroe expressed the common conviction in a letter of 1817 to Andrew Jackson: "The hunter or savage state requires a greater extent of territory to sustain it, than is compatible with the progress and just claims of civilized life, and must yield to it." The government actively promoted schools, agriculture, and various "useful arts" among the native Americans, hoping to convert nomadic hunters into settled farmers. This hope was nourished by the progress of the more populous southern tribes, particularly the Cherokees, whose achievements in agriculture, in developing a written alphabet, and in adopting white technology seemed to meet the American tests of capability. But the government also pressured the Cherokees into ceding tracts of valuable eastern land in exchange for lands west of the Mississippi River. By 1824 it was becoming clear that the five southern confederations—Cherokees, Creeks, Choctaws, Chickasaws, and Seminoles—could not survive even as temporary enclaves without federal protection against white exploiters. The southern tribes occupied western Georgia and North Carolina, as well as major portions of Tennessee, Florida, Alabama, and Mississippi. Thus their lands covered the heart of the future Cotton Kingdom. In 1825 President Monroe officially proposed that these and all other remaining tribes be persuaded to move west of the Mississippi River, a plan that Jefferson and others had long regarded as the only way of saving America's original inhabitants from ultimate extinction.

Conflict of Federal and State Laws.

In Georgia white speculators, squatters, and gold miners had no desire to see civilized Indians living on choice land, and the fact that it was ancestral Indian land made little difference. In 1828, when the Cherokees adopted a constitution and claimed sovereign jurisdiction over their own territory, Georgia declared them to be mere tenants on state land, subject to the state's laws and authority. In 1832, in the case of *Worcester* v. *Georgia*, Chief Justice John Marshall ruled against the state. Georgia, he said, had no right to extend state laws to the Cherokees or their territory. "The several Indian nations," he maintained, were "distinct political communities, having territorial boundaries, within which their authority is exclusive, and having a right to all lands within those boundaries, which is not only acknowledged, but guaranteed by the United States." But President Jackson, who had already withdrawn the federal troops that had earlier been sent to protect Cherokee land from intrusion, had no intention of enforcing the Supreme Court's decision.

Jackson firmly believed that the native Americans should be subject to state law and to the forces of a free-market economy, in which individuals bought and sold commodities according to the laws of supply and demand. To deal with tribes as privileged corporate groups, he thought, was simply to reinforce the power of corrupt chiefs and cunning half-breeds, who prevented tribesmen from following their own best interest. Jackson had no doubt that the vast majority of Indians, when liberated from tribal tyranny, would willingly emigrate to the West. The civilized few would be free to cultivate modest tracts of land and would become responsible citizens of state and nation.

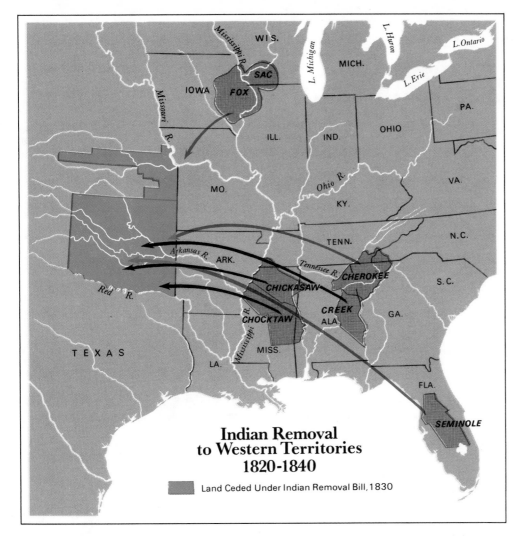

**Indian Removal
to Western Territories
1820-1840**

Land Ceded Under Indian Removal Bill, 1830

Jackson's denial of federal protection provided the needed incentives for a supposedly voluntary migration. Following Georgia's lead, other southern states harassed native Americans with laws that few tribesmen could comprehend. White traders and lawyers descended like locusts on Indian lands, destroying tribal unity and authority. In 1830 Congress supported Jackson's policy by voting funds that would enable the president to negotiate treaties for the removal of all the Indian tribes then living east of the Mississippi River. The government still considered it necessary to purchase title to Indian land and to grant allotments of land to individual tribal leaders who could prove a legitimate claim. Federal officials even sought to protect native Americans by supervising private contracts for the sale of land. The majority of Indians, however, had no concept of land as a measurable and salable commodity. A few of the more

experienced Chickasaws and other tribesmen secured good prices for rich cotton land, but white speculators, who swiftly cornered between 80 and 90 percent of southern allotments, reaped windfall profits.

The government thus furthered its goal of removal by dispossessing the native Americans of their land. Victims of wholesale fraud, trickery, and intimidation, the great mass of southern Indians had no choice but to follow the so-called Trail of Tears to the vacant territory of what is today Oklahoma. Subjected to disease, starvation, and winter cold, thousands died along the way. Military force gave a cutting edge to removal deadlines; in 1838 federal troops herded 15,000 Cherokees into detention camps. Meanwhile, Indians north of the Ohio River had earlier been demoralized as whites had cut down the supply of game, negotiated treaties with factions of certain tribes that had accepted more of white civilization, and ensnared

primitive societies with unfamiliar mechanisms of debt and credit. In 1832 the government crushed the resistance of Sac and Fox Indians in Illinois and Wisconsin, and in 1835 it launched a long and costly war against the Seminoles in Florida. By 1844, except for a few remaining pockets mainly in the backcountry of New York, Michigan, and Florida, removal had been accomplished.

In his Farewell Address of March 4, 1837, Jackson applauded this brutal policy of Indian removal as a great humanitarian achievement that had also happily removed the main block to America's economic growth.

While the safety and comfort of our own citizens have been greatly promoted by their removal, the philanthropist will rejoice that the remnant of that ill-fated race has been at length placed beyond the reach of injury or oppression, and that paternal care of the General Government will hereafter watch over them and protect them.

The Beginning of Indian Reservations.

Ten years later, however, the government had recognized the impossibility of a "permanent Indian barrier" west of the Mississippi River. Having defeated all Indian attempts to resist the pressure of westward white migration, the government now began moving toward a policy of fencing native Americans within specified "reservations" and opening the otherwise boundless territory of the great West to wagon trains, cavalry, miners, farmers, surveyors, and railroad builders. Even in the 1820s a few perceptive Indian chieftains had foreseen that western lands would be no more invulnerable than the lands in the East. This conclusion was soon confirmed by the destruction of tribal game reserves and by the purchase of remaining Indian lands in Missouri and Iowa. The Anglo-Saxon settlers in Texas, who won independence from Mexico in 1836, asserted the unprecedented claim that Indians had no right whatever to possession of the land. Texas reaffirmed this doctrine after being annexed as a state in 1845,

CATLIN'S AMERICAN INDIANS

Although Americans were continually reminded of the Indians' acts of cruelty, as in this scene of initiation rites in a Mandan tent, there was also a growing fascination with Indians as representatives of the exotic. Even by the early 1830s George Catlin had created a prototype for the commercial Wild West show. An accomplished painter of Plains tribesmen, Catlin also created the heroic image of Osceola, the Seminole chief who had been captured by American treachery and who posed for this portrait in prison, shortly before his death. For over two centuries Anglo-American settlers had magnified Indian violence in order to justify their own aggression against Indians. The Seminole War presented the opportunity for dramatizing the ultimate racial nightmare—the specter of supposedly docile blacks uniting with Indians to slaughter "defenseless" whites. Such images appealed to deep-seated racial fears and helped to justify the most extreme measures for removing "wild" Indians far beyond the geographic boundaries of a "civilized" slave society.

Far left, courtesy of the American Museum of Natural History; center, National Portrait Gallery, Smithsonian Institution; left, American Antiquarian Society

and even demanded that some 25,000 Apaches and other tribesmen be removed or face extermination. Years of border warfare finally led in 1854 to the Texans' acceptance of Indian reservations under federal jurisdiction. But the federal government found that it could not protect Texas tribes from being slaughtered by marauding whites and therefore authorized their removal to the territory north of the Red River, in what later became Oklahoma.

Meanwhile, between 1846 and 1860 government policy began to settle the fate of the strong western tribes that had previously been free to roam prairies and intermountain grasslands without concern for the conflicting claims of white nations. The American invasion and occupation of New Mexico in the Mexican War led to brutal punitive expeditions against the Navajo. In 1851 Congress passed the critically important Indian Appropriations Act, which was designed to consolidate western tribes on agricultural reservations, thereby lessening the danger to the tens of thousands of emigrants streaming toward California and Oregon and also to the proposed transcontinental railroad.

The degradation reached its climax in the 1850s in California, where federal restraints on white aggression disappeared. Whites molested the Diggers and other primitive native Americans, shooting the males for sport and enslaving the women and children. Farther east, the Apaches and powerful Plains tribes offered occasional and sometimes spectacular resistance. The famed encounters between Indians and the United States Cavalry came after the Civil War. But even by 1860 the western tribes had been demoralized, their economy had been fatally weakened when buffalo and other game became depleted, and increasing numbers of native Americans had been herded into compounds with boundaries that moved only inward.

SUGGESTED READINGS

For informative surveys and detailed bibliographies, see George Dangerfield, *The Awakening of American Nationalism, 1815–1828* (1965); Edward Pessen, *Jacksonian America: Society, Personality, and Politics* (1969); and Russel B. Nye, *Society and Culture in America, 1830–1860* (1974). Louis Hartz, *The Liberal Tradition in America* (1955), presents a brilliant and provocative interpretation of America's divergence from Old World norms. Lawrence A. Cremin, *American Education: The National Experience, 1783–1876* (1980), is a sweeping study not only of formal education, but of the transmission of knowledge in a democratic society. Cremin and Hartz, like most interpreters of the period, draw heavily on Alexis de Tocqueville's classic work, *Democracy in America*, of which there are many editions. Daniel J. Boorstin's *The Americans: The National Experience* (1965), also emphasizes America's uniqueness, although more recent work has reversed this trend. The period is illuminated in different ways by Yehoshua Arieli, *Individualism and Nationalism in American Ideology* (1964); Rowland Berthoff, *An Unsettled People: Social Order and Disorder in American History* (1971); and Fred Somkin, *Unquiet Eagle: Memory and Desire in the Idea of American Freedom, 1815–1860* (1967). An anthology of primary source material, accompanied by extensive commentary, is David B. Davis, ed., *Antebellum American Culture: An Interpretive Anthology* (1979).

Population growth is analyzed by J. Potter, "The Growth of Population in America, 1700–1860," in *Population and History . . .* , eds. D. V. Glass and D. E. C. Eversley (1965); and Richard A. Easterlin, *Population, Labor Force and Long Swings in Economic Growth: The American Experience* (1968). Maldwyn A. Jones, *American Immigration* (1960), is a useful introduction to the subject; it should be supplemented by Marcus L. Hansen, *The Atlantic Migration, 1607–1860* (1940); Oscar Handlin, *Boston's Immigrants* (1959); Robert Ernst, *Immigrant Life in New York City, 1825–1863* (1949); Kathleen N. Conzen, *Immigrant Milwaukee, 1836–1860* (1977); and Carl Wittke, *The Irish in America* (1956). For urbanization, see Sam Bass Warner, Jr., *The Urban Wilderness* (1972); Richard C. Wade, *The Urban Frontier* (1964); and Paul Boyer, *Urban Masses and Moral Order in America, 1820–1920* (1978). Anthony F. C. Wallace, *Rockdale: The Growth of an American Village in the Early Industrial Revolution* (1978), is an imaginative but controversial interpretation of the way industrialization affected the entire life and culture of an American community.

For overviews of antebellum economic growth, see W. Elliot Brownlee, *Dynamics of Ascent* (1974), and Stuart Bruchey, *Growth of the Modern American Economy* (1975). For a fascinating discussion of the economic thought of the pre–Civil War period, see Joseph Dorfman, *The Economic Mind in American Civilization*, Vol. 2 (3 vols., 1946–49). Douglass C. North, *The Economic Growth of the United States, 1790–1860* (1961), stresses the importance of international trade. Peter Temin, *The Jacksonian Economy* (1969), challenges many of the traditional beliefs of historians.

Ray A. Billington, *Westward Expansion* (1974), presents an excellent survey of the history of the American West as well as a comprehensive bibliography. The fullest histories of agriculture are Percy W. Bidwell and John I. Falconer, *History of Agriculture in the Northern United States,*

1620–1860 (1925), and Lewis C. Gray, *History of Agriculture in the Southern United States to 1860* (2 vols., 1933). A briefer and outstanding survey is Paul W. Gates, *The Farmer's Age: Agriculture, 1815–1860* (1960), which can be supplemented by Clarence H. Danhof, *Change in Agriculture in the Northern United States, 1820–1870* (1969).

The classic study of transportation is George R. Taylor, *The Transportation Revolution, 1815–1860* (1951). A monumental work, confined to New England, is Edward Kirkland, *Men, Cities, and Transportation* (2 vols., 1948). For canals, see Harry N. Scheiber, *Ohio Canal Era* (1969), and R. E. Shaw, *Erie Water West* (1966).

For railroads, see Albert Fishlow, *American Railroads and the Transformation of the Ante-Bellum Economy* (1965); Alfred D. Chandler, Jr., ed., *The Nation's First Big Business* (1965); and Thomas C. Cochran, *Railroad Leaders, 1845–1890* (1953). Christopher T. Baer, *Canals and Railroads of the Mid-Atlantic States, 1800–1860* (1981), is especially valuable for its detailed maps and tables. The organization and management of railroad corporations is masterfully analyzed in Alfred D. Chandler, Jr., *The Visible Hand: The Managerial Revolution in American Business* (1977). The role of government is treated in Carter Goodrich, *Government Promotion of American Canals and Railroads, 1800–1890* (1960); Louis Hartz, *Economic Policy and Democratic Thought* (1954); and Oscar Handlin and Mary F. Handlin, *Commonwealth: A Study of the Role of Government in the American Economy* (1969).

The best works on maritime trade are Robert G. Albion, *The Rise of New York Port* (1939), and Samuel E. Morison, *Maritime History of Massachusetts, 1789–1860* (1921). For the clipper ships, see C. C. Cutler, *Greyhounds of the Sea* (1930), and A. H. Clark, *The Clipper Ship Era* (1910). L. H. Battistini, *The Rise of American Influence in Asia and the Pacific* (1960), treats an important aspect of America's commercial expansion.

On manufacturing, Victor S. Clark, *History of Manufactures in the United States, 1607–1860* (3 vols., 1929), remains indispensable. Thomas C. Cochran, *Frontiers of Change: Early Industrialism in America* (1981), synthesizes the results of recent research and casts new light on the factors leading to rapid industrialization in Pennsylvania and New York. The best specialized studies are Peter Temin, *Iron and Steel in Nineteenth-Century America* (1964); Caroline F. Ware, *The Early New England Cotton Manufacture* (1931); Arthur H. Cole, *The American Wool Manufacture* (2 vols., 1926); and Otto Mayr and Robert C. Post, eds., *Yankee Enterprise: The Rise of the American System of Manufactures* (1981). Siegfried Giedion, *Mechanization Takes Command* (1948), contains a fascinating account of American technological innovation. A brilliant study of the significance of the new technology is Merritt R. Smith, *Harpers Ferry Armory and the New Technology: The Challenge of Change* (1977). H. J. Habakkuk, *American and British Technology in the Nineteenth Century* (1962), places American invention in a larger context, as does Carroll W. Pursell, Jr., *Early Stationary Steam Engines in America: A Study in the Migration of Technology* (1969). For a comprehensive reference work, see Melvin Kranzberg and Carroll W. Pursell, Jr., eds., *Technology in Western Civilization* (2 vols., 1967). The ideological impact of technology is imaginatively treated in John F. Kasson, *Civilizing the Machine:*

Technology and Republican Values in America, 1776–1900 (1976).

A pioneering study of social and economic mobility is Stephan Thernstrom, *Poverty and Progress* (1964). For disparities in the distribution of wealth and income, see Edward Pessen, *Riches, Class, and Power Before the Civil War* (1973), and Lee Soltow, "Economic Inequality in the United States in the Period from 1790 to 1860," *Journal of Economic History*, 31 (December 1971), 822–39. The discovery of poverty is analyzed in Robert H. Bremner, *From the Depths* (1956), and Raymond A. Mohl, *Poverty in New York, 1783–1825* (1971). On working-class culture and ideology, the best guides are Alan Dawley, *Class and Community: The Industrial Revolution in Lynn* (1977); Paul G. Faler, *Mechanics and Manufacturers in the Early Industrial Revolution: Lynn, Massachusetts, 1780–1860* (1981); Bruce Laurie, *Working People of Philadelphia, 1800–1850* (1980); Herbert G. Gutman, *Work, Culture, and Society in Industrializing America* (1976); Howard M. Gitelman, *Workingmen of Waltham* (1974); Peter R. Knights, *The Plain People of Boston* (1971); and Norman Ware, *The Industrial Worker, 1840–1860* (1959). For labor movements and protests, see David Montgomery, "Workers' Control of Machine Production in the Nineteenth Century," *Labor History*, 17 (1976); David Montgomery, "The Shuttle and the Cross: Weavers and Artisans in the Kensington Riots of 1844," *Journal of Social History* (Summer 1972); Joseph Rayback, *A History of American Labor* (1966); and Walter Hugins, *Jacksonian Democracy and the Working Class* (1960). For a richly informative analysis of women's experience in the most famous New England mill town, see Thomas Dublin, *Women at Work: The Transformation of Work and Community in Lowell, Massachusetts, 1826–1860* (1979). Two good studies of the ideology of the self-made man, Irvin G. Wyllie, *The Self-Made Man in America* (1954), and John G. Cawelti, *Apostles of the Self-Made Man* (1965), should be supplemented by Daniel T. Rodgers, *The Work Ethic in Industrial America, 1850–1920* (1978). Although dealing with a later period, Richard Weiss, *The American Myth of Success* (1969), also sheds light on the earlier history of the subject.

The best introduction to Indian removal is Wilcomb E. Washburn, *The Indian in America* (1975). Francis P. Prucha, *American Indian Policy in the Formative Years* (1962), is sympathetic to government policymakers. Ronald N. Satz, *American Indian Policy in the Jacksonian Era* (1975), provides an informative account of the subsequent period. The most comprehensive study of the so-called civilized tribes is Charles Hudson, *The Southeastern Indians* (1976); for the Far West, see Sherburne F. Cook, *The Conflict Between the California Indian and White Civilization* (1976). An outstanding work that corrects the mythology regarding the relation between the native Americans and western pioneers is John Unruh, *The Plains Across: The Overland Emigrants and the Trans-Mississippi West* (1979). There are three valuable related works in intellectual history: Roy H. Pearce, *The Savages of America* (1965); Richard Slotkin, *Regeneration Through Violence: The Mythology of the American Frontier, 1600–1860* (1973); and Roderick Nash, *Wilderness in the American Mind* (1967).

13 Shaping the American Character: Reform, Protest, Dissent, Artistic Creativity

The desire to transform character lay at the heart of American reform in the mid-nineteenth century. Like other Americans, reformers rejoiced that the nation was free from kings and nobles, from aristocratic institutions, and from status and roles defined at birth. They were cheered by the absence or removal of traditional barriers to human progress. But in pursuing the good life that had supposedly been made accessible by the sacrifices of the Founders, Americans had somehow created a society of astounding moral and physical contrasts—a society of luxury and of squalor, of spiritual uplift and of degradation, of freedom and of bondage. In the eyes of dissenters and reformers, it often seemed that America was ruled only by the principles of ruthless self-interest and power.

During the pre–Civil War decades, political and religious leaders repeatedly warned that the fate of free institutions depended on the moral and intellectual character of the American people. Religious beliefs continued to differ about humanity's sinfulness or inherent capacity for love and social harmony. But Americans of various outlooks agreed that human nature was much like clay that can be molded to any shape before it hardens.

This conviction could be inspiring. In 1823, for example, Charles Jared Ingersoll, a Philadelphia lawyer and former congressman, delivered the influential *Discourse Concerning the Influence of America on the Mind*. Ingersoll was confident that the average American, as a result of the free and republican environment, stood far above the average European in both intelligence and virtue. He promised that American achievements in the arts and sciences would soon show the world the full potentialities of human nature when it was not crippled by despotism and aristocratic privilege.

But a capacity for infinite improvement might also be a capacity for infinite corruption. Even the optimists tended to worry over the growing inadequacy of local religious and social institutions in the face of America's sensational expansion. The need to shape or change individual character gave a new social importance to educators, religious revivalists, popular essayists, phrenologists, and other promoters of self-improvement.

The spirit of reform and dissent was centered in the Northeast, and particularly in New England. During the years before the Civil War, this region spawned numerous crusades to regenerate the social order—to substitute love, harmony, and cooperation for what a leading religious reformer, William Ellery Channing, termed the "jarring interests and passions, invasions of rights, resistance of authority, violence, force" that were deforming the entire society. Whether these movements were religious or secular, most of them sought to bring American culture into harmony with a "higher law"—"the moral government of God"—as a means of preventing anarchy. Although reformers differed in their specific objectives, they shared a common desire to channel spiritual aspirations into the secular world of power.

The character of the reform movement of the pre–Civil War period was unique. Throughout history religious reformers had sent out missionaries to convert heathens and had sought to provide the world with models of saintly life, including dietary discipline and selfless commitment. But they had never created the kind of highly professional reform organizations that began to spring up in Britain and America in the early nineteenth century. These organizations were devoted to various goals—to building model penitentiaries, to persuading people to abstain from alcoholic drinks, and above all to abolishing slavery. The objectives were uncompromising, and the systematic techniques for mobilizing public opinion and exerting pressure on public officials were altogether novel.

Nevertheless, these reform movements usually embodied a nostalgia for a supposedly simpler and

312

more harmonious past. Members of the movements believed that the evils they combated had multiplied because of an alarming disintegration of family authority, of community cohesiveness, and of traditional morality. The various programs, therefore, had a dual objective for change and improvement. On the one hand, they attacked institutions, lifestyles, and traditional social roles that seemed to limit individual opportunity and to block the path of progress. On the other hand, they attempted to restore and revitalize the sense of purity, simplicity, and wholeness that had been lost in the headlong pursuit of modernity and material improvement.

"We Must Educate or Perish"

Shaping character, whether by school, church, prison, or asylum, seemed to be the only means of ensuring moral stability in an expansive and increasingly individualistic society. Lyman Beecher—best known today as the father of the novelist Harriet Beecher Stowe but in his own day the most prominent Protestant minister in the North—viewed the rapid settlement of the West with a mixture of exhilaration and alarm. By 1835 the states west of the Appalachian Mountains had grown so rapidly that he could predict a population of 100 million by 1900, "a day which some of our children may live to see." The West, Beecher believed, was a "young empire of mind, and power, and wealth, and free institutions." It contained the potential for nothing less than "the emancipation of the world." Beecher had no doubts about the West's material progress. The danger was "that our intelligence and virtue will falter and fall back into a dark minded, vicious populace—a poor, uneducated reckless mass of infuriated animalism." Beecher was aroused particularly by the supposed threat of Catholic immigrants, whom he pictured as the agents of foreign despots intent on subverting republican institutions. He therefore urged an immediate crusade to evangelize and educate the West: "For population will not wait, and commerce will not cast anchor, and manufacturers will not shut off the steam nor shut down the gate, and agriculture, pushed by millions of freemen on their fertile soil, will not withhold her corrupting abundance. We must educate! We must educate! or we must perish by our own prosperity."

The State of Education.
Educational reformers had some reason for alarm. Even Massachusetts, which in 1837 established the nation's first state board of education, suffered from broken-down school buildings, untrained and incompetent teachers, and dependence on unequal and unpredictable local funding. The one-room country schoolhouse, often idealized in later years, not only was dirty, drafty, and overheated, but was commonly packed with children of all ages—some old and rowdy enough to inflict beatings on male teachers and to prompt some women teachers to hide a pistol in a desk drawer. The soaring growth of eastern cities made middle-class citizens suddenly aware of begging street urchins, teen-age prostitutes, gangs of juvenile delinquents, and vagrant children, who, like Mark Twain's Huckleberry Finn, had little desire to be "civilized."

Until the second quarter of the nineteenth century, the education of Americans was informal, unsystematic, and dependent on parental initiative and ability to pay. Even so, compared with most Europeans, white American males had always enjoyed a high rate of literacy, especially in New England. During the 1790s a surprising number of artisans and skilled laborers had sent their children to the "common pay schools" in New York City, where children of rich and poor backgrounds mingled. By the early nineteenth century, illiteracy was rapidly disappearing among white females. Boys and girls frequently attended the same schools, despite prejudices against sexual integration. Some "free" schools expected parents to pay a small fee, and most tax-supported schools were intended only for the children of the very poor. Aside from school attendance, apprenticeship long served as a noteworthy means of education, providing the vocational skills that could not be learned in any school. Not until the mid-nineteenth century—and in the South not until after the Civil War—did education become increasingly confined to specialized institutions segregated from the mainstreams of adult social life.

Working-Class Demands.
Middle-class religious reformers were not alone in demanding educational reform. In 1828 the organized mechanics and journeymen of Philadelphia, most of whom were skilled artisans and craftsmen who had served their apprenticeship, began to protest. As in other northeastern cities, these workers were angered by low wages, by the substitution of temporary child "apprentices" for skilled adult laborers, and by the erosion of the traditional craft system that had allowed apprentices and journeymen to rise within a given trade. The Philadelphia Working Men's party pressed for a broad range of economic and social reforms. One of these was for better educational opportunities. "The original element of despotism," proclaimed a party committee in 1829, "is a monopoly of talent, which consigns the multitude to comparative ignorance, and secures the balance of knowledge on the side of the rich and the rulers."

The demand for free tax-supported schools became a rallying cry for the workingmen's parties and

"POPERY UNDERMINING FREE SCHOOLS"

A typical example of anti-Catholic iconography. While the American eagle hovers over the schoolhouse, this bulwark of democratic institutions is being literally undermined by sappers working under the directions of a priest, who in turn is executing the orders of the pope, pictured here as a foreign potentate.

associations that sprang up in New York, Boston, and dozens of small towns throughout the country. A group of New York workers expressed the typical rhetoric when they asked in 1830 "if many of the monopolists and aristocrats of our city would not consider it disgraceful to their noble children to have them placed in our public schools by the side of poor yet industrious mechanics." Although many of the leaders of these groups were not manual laborers, the short-lived workingmen's movement reflected an authentic desire for equal educational opportunity on the part of skilled laborers whose economic and social condition had begun to deteriorate.

For most workingmen economic grievances soon took precedence over education. The economic growth of the pre–Civil War decades called for more and more unskilled laborers, but not for a significant increase in the number of skilled and nonmanual workers who might benefit materially from an education beyond the "three Rs." In New York City, where the proportion of nonmanual and professional jobs changed very little from 1796 to 1855, many working-class parents questioned whether they should sacrifice family income in order to educate children for jobs that did not exist.

As early as 1832 the New York Public School Society pointed out: "The labouring classes of society will, to a great extent, withhold their children from school, the moment they arrive at an age that renders their services in the least available in contributing to the support of the family." Later evidence indicated that children under fifteen earned as much as 20 percent of the income of working-class families in Newburyport, Massachusetts. For such families compulsory attendance laws often threatened an unbearable drop in already subsistence-level income. Not surprisingly, 40 percent of Newburyport's laborers admitted to the census takers in 1850 that their school-age children had not been enrolled in any school during the previous year. And many children who were enrolled could not attend regularly.

Moreover, by the 1840s the working class in the Northeast was becoming increasingly Roman Catholic. Although the public schools were theoretically secular—in New York and elsewhere, denominational schools had been deprived of public funding—the values and teachings of the schools were unmistakably Protestant. Most Americans of the mid-nineteenth century still thought that Americanism meant Protestantism. Protestant clergymen played a critical role on school committees and in school reform. They saw nothing sectarian about public school teachers' reading aloud from the King James Bible or teaching that the sixteenth-century Protestant Reformation had represented a liberation from Catholic despotism. Bishop John Hughes and other Catholic leaders saw the matter differently. In 1840 New York Catholics launched a political offensive against the Protestant monopoly of public education. As a result of this conflict, the Catholic church decided to construct its own separate system of schools, a costly program that took many decades to complete.

For many immigrants, Catholics, and working-class parents, the Protestant school reformers threatened to impose a uniform set of values on all segments of American society. Resistance also arose from local authorities who feared any centralizing interference from a state board of education. Many conservatives insisted that parents should pay for education, if they could afford it, just as they would pay for any other service or commodity. Others, brought up on the tradition of church schools, feared that the teaching of moral values would be dangerously undermined if guided only by a vaguely Protestant and non-denominational spirit.

Educational Reformers.

These obstacles to the expansion of public education were finally overcome by reformers like Horace Mann, who as the chief officer of the Massachusetts Board of Education from 1837 to 1848 became the nation's leading champion of public schools. Mann was a severe, humorless puritan who denounced intemperance, profanity, and ballet dancing along with ignorance, violence, and black slavery. Having personally struggled with the terrors of his New England Calvinist heritage, he had finally concluded that children were capable of infinite improvement and goodness. As a kind of secular minister, still intent on saving souls, he insisted that there must have been a time in the childhood of the worst criminal when, "ere he was irrecoverably lost, ere he plunged into the abyss of infamy and guilt, he might have been recalled." Mann offended traditional Christians by winning the fight in Massachusetts against specific religious instruction in the public schools. He outraged conservatives by asserting that private property is not an absolute right but rather a trusteeship for society and future generations. Trained as a lawyer, he decided as a young man that "the next generation" should be his clients. In pleading the cause of generations to come, he held that school taxes were not a "confiscation" from the rich, but rather a collection of the debt the rich owed to society.

Reformers placed a stupendous moral burden on the public schools. Horace Mann proclaimed the common school to be "the greatest discovery ever made by man." "Other social organizations are curative and remedial," he said; "this is a preventive and antidote." This characteristic argument suggests that the schools were to be a defense against undesirable change, preserving the cherished values of a simpler, more homogeneous America. Educators spoke of the frenzied pace of American life, of the diminishing influence of church and home. They held that the school should thus serve as a substitute for both church and home, preventing American democracy from degenerating into what Mann called "the spectacle of gladiatorial contests." The school, representing the highest instincts of society, could alone be counted on for cultivating decency, cooperation, and a respect for others. Women, reformers believed, were best suited as teachers because they exemplified the noncombative and noncompetitive instincts. Because they could also be employed for lower wages then men, women teachers soon predominated in New England's elementary schools.

The character traits most esteemed by educational reformers were precisely those alleged to bring material success in a competitive and market-oriented society: punctuality, cheerful obedience, honesty, responsibility, perseverance, and foresightedness. Public schools seemed to promise opportunity by providing the means of acquiring these traits. In the words of one school committee, the children "entered the race, aware that the prize was equally before all, and attainable only by personal exertion." The famed McGuffey's "Eclectic" series of readers, which after 1836 became the basic reading textbooks in countless schoolrooms and of which well over 100 million copies were eventually sold, taught young students that no possession was more important for getting on in the world than reputation—"a good name." On the other hand, the readers held out little hope of rags-to-riches success. When the good little poor boy sees other children "riding on pretty horses, or in coaches, or walking with ladies and gentlemen, and having on very fine clothes, he does not envy them, nor wish to be like them." For he has been taught "that it is God who makes some poor, and others rich; that the rich have many troubles which we know nothing of; and that the poor, if they are but good, may be very happy."

From a present-day viewpoint the educational reformers were often insensitive to the needs of non-Protestants, non-Christians, nonwhites, and women. Throughout the North, except in a few scattered communities, the public schools excluded black children. Many localities made no provision for blacks to be educated. Other towns and cities, including New York and Boston, distributed a small portion of public funds to segregated and highly inferior schools for blacks. By 1850 blacks constituted no more than 1.5 percent of Boston's population, but it still required a prolonged struggle on the part of militant blacks and white abolitionists to achieve local desegregation. In 1855 Massachusetts became the single state in which no applicant to a public school could be excluded on account of "race, color or religious opinions." In marked contrast to the public schools, Oberlin, Har-

EDUCATING WOMEN
The pre–Civil War decades opened unprecedented opportunities for middle-class girls to advance beyond an elementary level of education. The price of this opportunity, however, was a system of strict discipline and of constant supervision of manners and morals.

vard, Bowdoin, Dartmouth, and some other private colleges opened their doors to a few black students. In 1837 Oberlin also became America's first co-educational college. In general, however, American women had no opportunities for higher education except in female seminaries and, by the 1850s, a few western state universities.

By the 1850s Massachusetts had acquired all the essentials of a modern educational system: special "normal schools" for the training of female teachers; the placement of pupils in grades according to age and ability; standarized procedures for advancement from one grade to another; uniform textbooks; and a bureaucracy extending from the board of education down to superintendents, principals, and teachers. Although Massachusetts led the nation, by the 1850s it was possible for a New York City male child to proceed from an "infant school" to a college degree without paying tuition. Educational reformers, many of them originally New Englanders, had helped to create state-

supported and state-supervised school systems from Pennsylvania to the new states of the Upper Mississippi Valley. In the 1850s the same cause made some headway in the South, particularly in Virginia and North Carolina.

Whatever prejudices and blind spots the public school movement may have had, it aroused the enthusiasm of hundreds of idealistic men and women who devoted time and energy to the cause. Northern legislators committed an impressive proportion of public spending to the education of succeeding generations. Particularly in the 1850s, the movement trained a young generation of teachers inspired with missionary zeal. After the Civil War they would descend on the devastated South, equipped with an ideology for "reconstruction." Above all, the movement reinforced the American faith that social problems could be solved by individual enterprise, a diffusion of knowledge, and a reconstruction of moral character.

The Evangelical Age

Americans continued to look on the church, no less than on the public school, as a decisive instrument for shaping the national character. As in the post-Revolutionary period, religion appeared to become more widespread the more it achieved independence from the government. (In 1833 Massachusetts became the last state to give up an established church.) Despite the officially secular stance of American governments, evangelical Protestantism became increasingly identified with patriotism, democracy, and America's mission in the world. And despite the continuing division and competition among religious denominations, Americans increasingly appealed to religion as the only force in American life that could preserve a sense of community and united purpose.

Religious Revivals. Between 1820 and 1860 religious revivalism became a powerful organizing and nationalizing force that reached into all parts of American life and all corners of the vast nation—the South as well as the North, the cities as well as the western frontier. Church membership figures can be misleading since many people who regularly attended church could not meet the religious or financial obligations that were required for formal membership. But it has been estimated that by 1835 as many as three out of four adult Americans maintained some nominal relationship to a church. Most foreign observers agreed with Tocqueville that by the 1830s there was no country in the world in which the Christian religion retained "a greater influence over the souls of men."

For the majority of adults, evangelical Protestantism provided a common language and a common frame of reference. It explained not only human nature and destiny, but also the meaning of democracy and of American nationality. In the words of a non-church member, a young self-made man and future president of the United States, Andrew Johnson, "Man can become more and more endowed with divinity; and as he does he becomes more godlike in his character and capable of governing himself." Like millions of other Americans, Johnson believed that Christianity and political democracy were together elevating and purifying the people, working toward the day when it could be proclaimed: "The millennial morning has dawned and the time has come when the lion and the lamb shall lie down together, when . . . the glad tidings shall be proclaimed . . . of man's political and religious redemption, and there is 'on earth, peace, good will toward men.'"

In some ways this evangelical vision transcended boundaries of class and section. Although it is possible to think of America as undergoing a single Great Revival during the six decades preceding the Civil War, the revival's social significance differed according to time and place. Some socioeconomic groups were more susceptible to religious enthusiasm than others. Some personality types were likely to view revivalists as self-righteous zealots who threatened to remove all fun from life. Others were likely to seize the chance to profess faith in Christ crucified, to announce repentance for their sins, to experience the liberation of rebirth, and as the popular hymn put it, to "stand up, stand up for Jesus!" For many Americans religion provided the key to social identity. It was not that people flocked to churches to meet the right kind of people, although some no doubt did. It was rather that the "right" kind of religion, as defined by employers, slaveholders, and other wielders of power, was often considered to bestow the "right" kind of character.

Religious revivalism depended on sensitivity to the community's norms and vital interests. In the South leaders of various denominations discovered that any open criticism of slavery could threaten the very survival of a church. The Baptist and Methodist churches thus gradually retreated from their cautious antislavery view of the late eighteenth century, which had supposedly bred discontent if not rebellion among black slaves. By the 1830s the most influential southern churches had begun to deny that there was any moral contradiction between slavery and Christianity. They also insisted that Christianity, rightly understood, posed no danger to "the peculiar institution."*

*For the impact of Christianity on the slaves' culture and on plantation life, as well as among the free blacks, see chapter 14, pp. 352–53.

Civilizing the West.

Revivalism also served as a socializing force in the nonslaveholding West, but the context and consequences were different. Easterners tended to think of the West as both lawless and sinful. From the lumber camps of Wisconsin to the mining camps of California, Easterners' image of Westerners was essentially the same: rough, dirty men who swore, gambled, got drunk, frequented houses of prostitution, and relished savage eye-gouging, knife-slashing fights. Although the stereotypes were exaggerated, there was no doubt that frontier communities strained nineteenth-century notions of decency and civilization.

The challenge of the West could not be met simply by building churches where none had existed before. When Theron Baldwin, a member of a Yale missionary group, arrived in Illinois in 1830, he was horrified by the ignorance of the settlers. Even in Vandalia, then the state's capital, Baldwin discovered that most of the pupils in his Sunday school class were illiterate. Nor could he find a literate adult in more than half the families he visited in the region. Religion, Baldwin concluded, could make no headway without education and an institutional rebuilding of society. Appealing for funds from the East, he expressed the New England ideal: "We wish to see the school house and church go up side by side and the land filled with Christian teachers as well as preachers." He added, significantly, that young men could come there "and in a short time get enough by teaching to purchase a farm that would ever after fill their barns with plenty and their hands with good things." Baldwin himself worked to secure from the legislature a charter for the first three colleges in the state. As a result of the labors of Baldwin and other young missionaries, the Old Northwest became dotted with academies, seminaries, and small denominational colleges.

Easterners who still thought of churches as fixed institutions within an ordered society did not understand that religious revivals were an effective instrument for shaping and controlling character. The frank emotionalism and homespun informality of the western and southern revivals disguised the fact that even the camp meetings were soon stabilized by rules, regulations, and the most careful advance planning. And camp meetings were by no means the most important tools of the revivals. The power of the movement flowed from the dynamic balance between popular participation and the control of leaders. According to the evangelical message, every man and woman, no matter how humble or trapped in sin, had the capacity to say "Yes!" to Christ's offer of salvation—to reject what was called "cannot-ism," and along with it an unsatisfying identity. Even for the poor and uneducated, consent opened the way for participation and decisionmaking.

Peter Cartwright, for example, grew up in one of

Courtesy of the New-York Historical Society, New York City

CAMP MEETING, c. 1835

The religious camp meeting, originally associated with the boisterous and unruly West, became an established and well-organized institution throughout rural America.

the most violent and lawless regions of Kentucky. His brother was hanged for murder, and his sister was said to have "led a life of debauchery." At the age of sixteen, Cartwright repented his sins at a Methodist camp meeting; at seventeen he became an "exhorter"; at eighteen, a traveling preacher; at twenty-one, a deacon; and at twenty-three, a presiding elder of the church. Each upward step required a trial period, followed by an examination of his conduct, ability, and purity of doctrine. The Methodists showed particular skill in devising a system that encouraged widespread participation and upward mobility in the church's organizational structure. But all the evangelical churches displayed the great American gift for organization. Revivals, they believed, could not take place by waiting for God to stir human hearts. Revivals required planning, efficient techniques, and coordinated effort. The need was not for educated theologians, but for professional promoters.

Christianity and the Social Order. Although revivalism was an organizing and socializing movement, it was also

by definition selective. The people most likely to be converted were those who had had some Christian upbringing or those who were already disturbed by excessive drinking, gambling, fighting, disorder, and irresponsibility. Conversion itself reinforced crucial social distinctions. For one part of the community, religion became more than a matter of going to church on Sunday. The obligations of a new religious life required sobriety and responsibility from friends, family, employees, and business associates. The weekly "class meetings" and "love feasts" provided fellowship and helped to prevent backsliding. No doubt the solidarity of the converted individuals brought order and discipline to the community at large. But if the evangelicals always insisted that every man and woman could say "Yes!," there were always those who said "No!" The congregations that loved to hear their preachers "pouring hot shot into Satan's ranks" knew that Satan's ranks were concentrated on the other side of the tracks.

Religious revivals could accentuate social distinctions by forging an alliance among the more ambi-

Frances Trollope, an Englishwoman who resided in the United States from 1827 to 1830, won fame in England by writing a popular and satirical critique of "democratic manners" in America. Americans deeply resented her unflattering descriptions and aristocratic prejudices. Although allowance must be made for Mrs. Trollope's distaste for religious emotionalism, much can be learned from her witty account of an Indiana camp meeting.

Frances Trollope Attends an Indiana Camp Meeting (1832)

*T*HE prospect of passing a night in the back-woods of Indiana was by no means agreeable, but I screwed my courage to the proper pitch, and set forth determined to see with my own eyes, and hear with my own ears, what a camp-meeting really was. I had heard it said that being at a camp-meeting was like standing at the gate of heaven, and seeing it opening before you; I had heard it said, that being at a camp-meeting was like finding yourself within the gates of hell; in either case there must be something to gratify curiosity, and compensate one for the fatigue of a long rumbling ride and a sleepless night.

We reached the ground about an hour before midnight, and the approach to it was highly picturesque. The spot chosen was the verge of an unbroken forest, where a space of about twenty acres appeared to have been partially cleared for the purpose. Tents of different sizes were pitched very near together in a circle round the cleared space. . . . We distinguished numerous fires burning brightly within it; and still more numerous lights flickering from the trees. . . .

Four high frames, constructed in the form of altars, were placed at the four corners. . . ; on these were supported layers of earth and sod, on which burned immense fires of blazing pine-wood. On one side a rude platform was erected to accommodate the preachers, fifteen of whom attended this meeting, and with very short intervals for . . . refreshment and private devotion, preached in rotation, day and night, from Tuesday to Saturday.

When we arrived, the preachers were silent; but we heard issuing from nearly every tent mingled sounds of praying, preaching, singing, and lamentation. The curtains in front of each tent were dropped, and the faint light that gleamed through the white drapery, backed as it was by the dark forest, had a beautiful and mysterious effect, that set the imagination at work; and had the sounds which vibrated around us been less discordant, harsh, and unnatural, I should have enjoyed it; but listening at the corner of a tent, which poured forth more than its proportion of clamor, in a few

moments chased every feeling derived from imagination, and furnished realities that could neither be mistaken nor forgotten. . . .

Great numbers of persons were walking about the ground, who appeared like ourselves to be present only as spectators; some of these very unceremoniously contrived to raise the drapery of this tent at one corner, so as to afford us a perfect view of the interior.

The floor was covered with straw, which round the sides was heaped in masses, that might serve as seats, but which at that moment were used to support the heads and the arms of the close-packed circle of men and women who kneeled on the floor.

Out of about thirty persons thus placed, perhaps half a dozen were men. One of these, a handsome-looking youth of eighteen or twenty, kneeled just below the opening through which I looked. His arm was encircling the neck of a young girl who knelt beside him, with her hair hanging dishevelled upon her shoulders, and her features working with the most violent agitation; soon after they both fell forward on the straw, as if unable to endure in any other attitude the burning eloquence of a tall grim figure in black, who, standing erect in the center, was uttering with incredible vehemence an oration that seemed to hover between praying and preaching; his arms hung stiff and immoveable by his side, and he looked like an ill-constructed machine, set in action by a movement so violent as to threaten its own destruction, so jerkingly, painfully, yet rapidly, did his words tumble out; the kneeling circle ceasing not to call, in every variety of tone, on the name of Jesus; accompanied with sobs, groans, and a sort of low howling inexpressibly painful to listen to.

CHARLES GRANDISON FINNEY (1792–1875)
Finney led highly publicized religious revivals in upstate New York, Philadelphia, and New York City before becoming president of Oberlin College. Tall, athletic, and highly musical, he had practiced law before his dramatic conversion to evangelical Christianity.

tious, self-disciplined, and future-oriented members of a community. In the fall of 1830, for example, the leaders of Rochester, New York, invited Charles Grandison Finney to save that booming town from sin. By far the most commanding and influential evangelist of the pre–Civil War period, Finney was a tall, athletic spellbinder, a former lawyer who had undergone a dramatic religious conversion in 1823. Although he lacked formal seminary training, Finney had been ordained as a Presbyterian minister and in 1825 had begun a series of highly unusual and spectacular revivals along the route of the newly constructed Erie Canal.

In 1831 Finney's triumphs in Rochester stunned Christian America. Communities from Ohio to Massachusetts appealed to him to save their collective souls. Finney's converts in Rochester were largely manufacturers, merchants, lawyers, shopkeepers, master artisans, and skilled journeymen. He appealed to people who had profited from the commercial revolution

initiated by the building of the Erie Canal but who had become deeply disturbed by the immense influx of young transient laborers looking for work. Rochester's leaders had no control over the behavior of these youths. Significantly, during Rochester's revival years church membership declined among the hotel proprietors and tavern keepers who catered to the floating population of young males traveling the Erie Canal. Rochester's Protestant churches, interpreting the revival as a sweeping popular mandate, launched a crusade to purge the city of its dens of vice and unholy amusement. They also offered a "free church"—free of pew rents and other financial obligations—to the workers on the canal. Increasingly Rochester became divided between a Christian minority dedicated to education and upward advancement and an essentially nonpolitical, free-floating majority of disoriented and unskilled young men.

Philadelphia differed from Rochester in important respects, but there too religious revivals eventually redefined the boundaries of respectable and "modern" behavior. Unlike Rochester, which grew by 512 percent in the 1820s, Philadelphia was not a new boom town. An old city by American standards, Philadelphia was relatively resistant to religious enthusiasm. Revivalism had little appeal to the wealthy Quakers and conservative Presbyterian clergymen who dominated the city's religious life. Evangelical morality was even less appealing to Philadelphia's workingmen, who preserved and cherished a traditional artisan, preindustrial culture. Largely because of irregular and undeveloped transportation to interior markets, Philadelphia workers suffered periodic layoffs. This forced leisure allowed them to enjoy traveling circuses, cockfights, drinking and gambling at the local taverns, and above all the boisterous comradeship of volunteer fire companies. Until 1837 neither the revival nor the closely related temperance movement made such headway among Philadelphia's manual workers. The people who reformed their drinking habits and who joined the reform-minded wing of the Presbyterian church were the professional and business groups who were ushering in the new industrial order. But in 1837 the financial panic and subsequent depression began to undermine the traditional habits and culture of the working class. Waves of religious revivalism, often Methodist in character, reached working-class neighborhoods. A new and more powerful temperance movement developed spontaneously from the ranks of master craftsmen, journeymen, shopkeepers, and the most ambitious unskilled laborers. In Philadelphia, as in Rochester, the decision to abstain from all alcohol was the key symbol of a new morality and of a new commitment to self-improvement. By the 1840s the evangelical workingmen could contrast their own sobriety and self-discipline with the moral laxity of mounting numbers of Irish immigrants. Not surprisingly, the revivalism that bolstered the self-respect of blue-collar native workers also contributed to passionate anti-Catholicism and to old-stock prejudice against a population that seemed to threaten the newly won dignity of manual labor.

Revivalism and Economic Prosperity.

Revivals appeared to be the only hopeful counterforce against rampant individualism, self-serving politics, and corrupting luxury. As Finney put it, "the great political and other worldly excitements" of the time distracted attention from the interests of the soul. He held, accordingly, that these excitements could "only be counteracted by *religious* excitements." Only revivals could prevent the United States from sliding into the decay and collapse of ancient Greece and Rome. Only revivals could prepare the nation "to lead the way," in Lyman Beecher's phrase, "in the moral and political emancipation of the world."

Revivalism was fed by the moral doubts that inevitably accompanied rapid economic growth, the disruption of older modes of work and responsibility, the sudden accumulation of wealth, and the appearance of new class differences. Revivalist preachers denounced atheism far less than "mammonism," the greedy pursuit of riches. They voiced repeated concern over the frantic pace of American life, the disintegration of family and community, and the worship of material success.

But revivalism seldom led to saintly withdrawal or to spiritualistic contemplation. Evangelical religion was above all activist, pragmatic, and oriented toward measurable results. The fame of Finney and the other great exhorters depended on the body count, or soul count, of converts. Finney proclaimed: "The results justify my methods"—a motto that could as well have come from John D. Rockefeller or other entrepreneurs in more worldly spheres. Finney confidently predicted: "If the church will do her duty, the millennium may come in this country in three years." He knew, however, that a millennium would require no revivals, and that as a revivalist, although dedicated to virtue, he needed sin as much as a soldier needs war.

There was a close relation between the revivals and America's expansive economy. The exuberant materialism of American life furnished revivalists with continuing targets for attack and with vivid signs of community strife and moral shortcoming. Without moral crises there would be no cause for national rededication, and calls for rededication have long been America's way of responding to social change. But on another level the revivalists had merged their cause with America's secular destiny. They had repeatedly warned that without religion, American democracy would speedily dissolve into "a common field of unbridled appetite and lust." Yet instead of dissolving, the nation continued to prosper, expand, and reveal new marvels. Sometimes clergymen hailed the achievements as signs of national virtue and divine favor. More important, as a reflection of their increasing respect for efficient methods and material results, they applauded technological improvements as the instruments that God had provided for saving the world.

The telegraph, railroad, and steamship all quickened the way for spreading the gospel around the world, and thus they could be interpreted as signs of the coming millennium. But America's technology and rapid westward expansion could be justified only if Americans took the burdens of a missionary nation seriously. Samuel Fisher, the president of Hamilton College in upstate New York, elaborated on this message in an address to the American Board of Commissioners for Foreign Missions:

Material activity, quickened and guided by moral principle, is absolutely essential to the development of a strong and manly character. . . . The product of this devotion to material interests is capital diffused through the masses; and capital is one of the means God uses to convert the world.

The diffusion of capital through the masses seemed to falter in 1857, when a financial crash brought a severe depression and unprecedented unemployment among factory workers. Economic insecurity formed the backdrop of what many took to be "the event of the century," the great urban revival of late 1857 and 1858. What distinguished this event from earlier religious revivals was the absence of revivalists. In Philadelphia and New York thousands of clerks and businessmen began to unite spontaneously for midday prayer. The New York *Herald* and the New York *Tribune* devoted special issues to the remarkable events—wealthy stockbrokers praying and singing next to messenger boys; revivals in the public high schools; joint services by Methodists, Episcopalians, Presbyterians, Baptists, and even the traditionally antirevivalist Unitarians. The spirit rapidly spread to manufacturing towns throughout the Northeast. Unscheduled and unconventional religious meetings sprang up in small towns and rural areas from Indiana to Quebec. "It would seem," wrote one enthusiast, "that the mighty crash was just what was wanted . . . to startle men from their golden dreams." Americans had become too overbearing, too self-confident, too complacent in their success. Yet if God had shown his displeasure, as countless interpreters maintained, he had also chosen means that underscored America's promise. He had punished Americans with economic loss, which even the hardest head among the business community could understand.

The great revival of 1858 gave a new sense of unity to Northerners, who had become increasingly divided by class and religious conflict, to say nothing of the issue of slavery. It also signified the maturity of an urban, industrial Protestantism that was committed to material progress and self-improvement. For good or for ill, the revivals reinvigorated America's official ideal of *Novus Ordo Seclorum*—a New Order for the World—the phrase today stamped on every dollar bill, conveying the message that a new social order is to exist, that Americans carry the high burden of helping to create a better world.

The Cult of Self-Improvement

What made public schools and religious revivals seem so indispensable by the 1830s was the relative absence of authoritative institutions that could define social roles, rules of conduct, and models of character. There was no standing army, for example, that could train a military class or enforce unpopular public policy. The abolition of public support for established churches gave semiliterate evangelists the same official status as college-trained theologians. Some states guaranteed any citizen, regardless of training, the right to practice law in any court. Americans showed less and less respect for any intellectual elite, religious or secular, or for any group of self-perpetuating masters who claimed to preserve and monopolize a body of knowledge that the public at large could not understand.

Not only had American law rejected European notions of privileged social orders, but as time went on the courts swept away most of the legal barriers that had restrained individuals from entering into certain kinds of risky or unfair agreements. In other words, the law assumed that all society was a marketplace of competitive exchange in which each individual calculated the probable risks of a given choice of action. As a result of this new burden of individual freedom and responsibility, Americans began to place enormous importance on acquiring effective skills and up-to-date knowledge. Continuous self-improvement became the great ideal of the age.

Lyceums and Learning. To Americans of the late twentieth century, there is nothing novel about fads, cults, and nostrums that promise the solution to life's problems. But in the 1830s and 1840s the cult of self-improvement was unprecedented in both the boldness and the variety of its appeals. Some conservatives expressed alarm over the credulity of public opinion, assuming that fads and quackery posed a threat to public order. But in general the people desired not the restructuring of society, but rather self-knowledge and self-advancement. In the 1820s numerous respectable societies and institutes for adult education and "mutual improvement" began to spread from England to the United States. Tens of thousands of adults, first in New England and then in the Old Northwest, grew accustomed to attending lectures, concerts, and various cultural events at lyceums (public halls). Lyceum lectures covered a vast range of subjects, but in the early years of the movement they tended to concentrate on "useful knowledge" associated with moral improvement and popular science.

Americans generally equated the advance of science with the advance of human liberty, a linkage that was part of the heritage of the European Enlightenment. They believed that everyone could benefit from the scientific method, that the marvels and secrets of nature were open to all. But what most impressed and fascinated American audiences were lectures and books on the applications of science, demonstrating the ingenious ways that human beings could master nature. As early as 1829, Jacob Bigelow's *Elements of Technology* not only helped to popularize a new word, but gave impetus to the general public's growing inclination to see invention as the key to national progress. Excitement over the uses of technology and steam power was matched by a new curiosity about the human mind, which had shown that it could unlock nature's secrets.

Mind Control.

The gap between public ignorance and the achievements of science could be bridged if someone invented the supreme technology, a technology for controlling the human mind. The quest for this power united many of the popular cults and fads. Mesmerists, for example, claimed to have discovered the laws of magnetic attraction and repulsion that governed relations between people. Spiritualists convinced hundreds of thousands that they had found techniques and apparatus for communicating with the dead and probing the laws of the occult. Even the manuals on self-improvement and character building, directed mainly at the young, presumed definitive knowledge of the mechanics of the brain. The Reverend John Todd's *Student's Manual* (1835), which sold by the hundreds of thousands, maintained that mental power depends on a strict conservation of bodily and especially sexual energies. Todd's thesis, repeated by countless physicians and other experts, was that masturbation and sexual excess posed the gravest threats to sanity, social order, and individual achievement. Self-

improvement thus required the rigorous avoidance of unwholesome thoughts and tempting situations.

Phrenology.

The most ambitious and institutionalized science of the mind, however, was phrenology, the invention of Franz Joseph Gall, a Viennese physician. Phrenology identified the supposed physical location in the brain of a large assortment of human "faculties," such as firmness, benevolence, acquisitiveness, destructiveness, and platonic love. Phrenologists claimed that they could precisely measure character from the form and shape of a head. Americans first responded to phrenology as a promising medical breakthrough. Gall's leading disciple, Johann Gaspar Spurzheim, became the first spreader of the cause. On a visit to America in 1832, he was ushered around as a celebrity by New England dignitaries, including Supreme Court Justice Joseph Story and the Yale chemist Benjamin Silliman. For a time phrenology enjoyed intellectual prestige through the support of Horace Mann, the famous Unitarian preacher William Ellery Channing, and a number of business leaders, among them Abbott Lawrence. As usual, however, the American public displayed far more interest in practical application than in theory. Two skillful promoters, Orson and Lorenzo Fowler, helped to convert phrenology into a major business enterprise. In the cities audiences of thousands paid fees for lengthy lectures expounding the new science. Thousands more flocked to

LYCEUM LECTURE
A caricature of the early
man-of-science, pontificating to
an audience of attentive women
and to a few apparently
inattentive men.

salons to have their characters analyzed. Traveling lecturers and mail-order courses enlightened the countryside. By the mid-1850s the *American Phrenological Journal* had a circulation of more than 50,000.

In many ways phrenology perfectly suited the needs of a population that was devoted to technique and uncertain of its own character. In an expansive and socially disruptive economy, phrenology provided a new set of guidelines that reduced the fear of risk. For example employers, who could no longer rely on long-term apprenticeships, on personal knowledge of an employee's family, or even on a worker's reputation in the community, could request a phrenological examination. Young men who dreamed of many careers but could decide on none welcomed a science that would measure their talents and capabilities. The great message of phrenology was individual adjustment. In a world of confusing and changing expectations, it furnished boundaries and specific identities. It told the individual which traits to cultivate and which to restrain. Criminologists not only found a physical explanation for deviant behavior, but also discovered a new hope for preventing crime by identifying potential criminals and by teaching convicts to control their overdeveloped antisocial faculties. Although Americans gradually came to realize that the results of phrenology could not substantiate its high promise, they had expressed an ardent desire—which would continue to our own time—for a popular science of human behavior.

Emerson. Ralph Waldo Emerson came closer than anyone else to being America's "official" philosopher of the nineteenth century. Like phrenology, Emerson's essays and lyceum lectures offered something for everyone and thus nourished hope for reducing friction and creating social harmony. There is no way of knowing how much influence Emerson actually had on American thought and culture, but he certainly helped to stimulate the great literary renaissance of the 1850s. For decades to come his writings were a source of inspiration for reformers, businessmen, and countless ordinary folk. It can be argued that Emerson's worship of power and of self-improvement provide the spiritual backdrop for the entire progressive era of the early twentieth century.

Yet Emerson's thought escapes all attempts at classification or categorization. His words awakened reformers, but he wrote the most penetrating critiques of reform of his generation. Although homespun and down-to-earth, at the same time he was among the most abstract American thinkers. An ardent champion of cultural independence, he defined the mission of native artists and writers, yet he exploited his knowledge of the newest currents of German and English thought. He was the leading figure in a group that

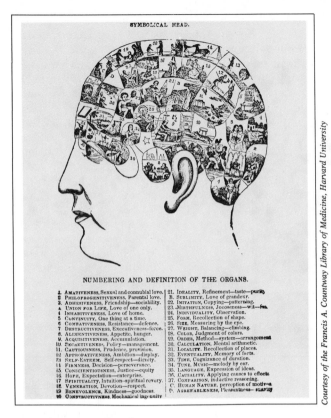

SYMBOLICAL HEAD.

NUMBERING AND DEFINITION OF THE ORGANS.

1. AMATIVENESS, Sexual and connubial love.
2. PHILOPROGENITIVENESS, Parental love.
3. ADHESIVENESS, Friendship—sociability.
4. UNION FOR LIFE, Love of one only.
5. INHABITIVENESS, Love of home.
6. CONTINUITY, One thing at a time.
7. COMBATIVENESS, Resistance—defence.
8. DESTRUCTIVENESS, Executiveness—force.
9. ALIMENTIVENESS, Appetite, hunger.
10. ACQUISITIVENESS, Accumulation.
11. SECRETIVENESS, Policy—management.
12. CAUTIOUSNESS, Prudence, provision.
13. APPROBATIVENESS, Ambition—display.
14. SELF-ESTEEM, Self-respect—dignity.
15. FIRMNESS, Decision—perseverance.
16. CONSCIENTIOUSNESS, Justice—equity.
17. HOPE, Expectation—enterprise.
18. SPIRITUALITY, Intuition–spiritual revery.
19. VENERATION, Devotion—respect.
20. BENEVOLENCE, Kindness—goodness.
21. CONSTRUCTIVENESS, Mechanical ingenuity.

21. IDEALITY, Refinement—taste—purity.
B. SUBLIMITY, Love of grandeur.
22. IMITATION, Copying—patterning.
23. MIRTHFULNESS, Jocoseness—wit—fun.
24. INDIVIDUALITY, Observation.
25. FORM, Recollection of shape.
26. SIZE, Measuring by the eye.
27. WEIGHT, Balancing—climbing.
28. COLOR, Judgment of colors.
29. ORDER, Method—system—arrangement.
30. CALCULATION, Mental arithmetic.
31. LOCALITY, Recollection of places.
32. EVENTUALITY, Memory of facts.
33. TIME, Cognizance of duration.
34. TUNE, Music—melody by ear.
35. LANGUAGE, Expression of ideas.
36. CAUSALITY, Applying cause to effects.
37. COMPARISON, inductive reasoning.
C. HUMAN NATURE, perception of motives.
D. AGREEABLENESS, Pleasantness—suavity.

"SYMBOLICAL HEAD"
This diagram illustrates the assortment of abilities, emotions, inclinations, and character traits that phrenologists claimed to identify as "organs" of the brain.

RALPH WALDO EMERSON (1803–82)

introduced to America German idealist philosophy, usually referred to by the awkward term *Transcendentalism*, taken from the work of the great German philosopher of the late-eighteenth century, Immanuel Kant. But Emerson advocated an extreme form of individualism and never felt comfortable as a member of any association. His brief, pointed sayings on self-reliance were later quoted by anarchists and yet were framed on the walls of the nation's business leaders.

Emerson's spongelike capacity to absorb ideas and the common attitudes of his time, as well as his empathy for all sides and commitment to none, had much in common with America's greatest weaknesses and strengths. To various audiences he proclaimed that "who so would be a man, must be a non-conformist." To the youth of America he delivered the reassuring thought: "We but half express ourselves, and are ashamed of the divine idea which each of us represents. . . . Trust thyself: every heart vibrates to that iron string." He criticized Americans for their single-minded pursuit of wealth and fame, for their obsession with material things. But the point of this protest against materialism and conformity—which became clearer as both Emerson and his audiences

grew older—was the need for a continuing reshaping and reinvigoration of the American character.

To Emerson the great peril that threatened the American people was not injustice, but a fragmentation of soul: "The reason why the world lacks unity and lies broken and in heaps, is because man is disunited with himself." The essential problem, then, was one of reconstituting character, of recovering a sense of the whole. By self-reliance Emerson really meant a detachment from society in order to achieve the sense of wholeness that flowed from unity with God—or, as Emerson put it, "the Oversoul." This notion that every "private man" possesses infinite and godlike capacities was an inspiring ideal, perfectly suited to the fantasies and aspirations of many Americans. At times, however, this doctrine meant that Emerson had no standard beyond power and success: "Power is, in nature, the essential measure of right."

Dissent: The Mormons as a Test Case

The history of the Mormons is seldom included in discussions of American dissent and reform. Yet Mormonism not only was America's first truly native religion; it began as a radical expression of dissent. This dissent was so extreme that Mormons found that they could survive only by building their own refuge in the remote deserts of the Far West. Because the early history of Mormonism exemplifies so many of the aspirations and difficulties of other dissenters—who also wished to live in their own ways in accordance with a higher moral law, free from the religious and political contaminations of their time—the Mormon experience can serve as an introduction, or a "test case." Essentially, the Mormons tested the outermost limits of permissible dissent, as well as the ability of any group or subculture to withstand the pressures of American secular society.

Joseph Smith, Founder. In 1830 Joseph Smith, Jr., published the Book of Mormon in Palmyra, New York. He said that the work was a translation of mysterious golden plates containing the history of an ancient Christian civilization in the New World. It portrayed the American Indians as the degenerate but saveable descendants of an ancient Hebrew tribe, and it foresaw a new American prophet who would discover the lost history and reestablish Christ's pure Kingdom in the New World. Smith in 1830 was an athletic, friendly, cheerful, intensely imaginative man of twenty-four, who was subject to visions and who claimed revelations. He was the son of one of America's many families of drifters, debtors, and habitual losers, whose poverty worsened as they drew closer to the belts of commercial prosperity. Smith had been born in the hills of Vermont, and his parents had migrated to that caldron of progress and poverty—of religious revivalism and new social movements—in upstate New York that was soon to be known as the Burned-Over District. Shortly after the publication of the Book of Mormon, Smith organized the Church of Christ, which in 1834 would be renamed the Church of Jesus Christ of Latter-day Saints.

Faced at the outset with religious persecution, Smith knew that the saints must ultimately move westward and build their city of God at some divinely appointed spot near the Indian tribes they were commissioned to convert. As he was told to do in his revelations, he dispatched missionaries to scout out the Missouri frontier. In 1831 a few Mormons established an outpost near Independence, Missouri, which Smith designated as the site of the New Jerusalem, and which was then the eastern end of the Santa Fe Trail. During the same year, Smith and his New York followers migrated to Kirtland, Ohio, where Mormon missionaries had converted an entire community.

Persecution of the Mormons. By 1839 the Mormons had met defeat in both Ohio and Missouri and were fleeing to a refuge of swampy Illinois farmland that Smith

had bought along the eastern shore of the Mississippi River. In Ohio the Mormons had experimented with communal ownership of property and with an illegal wildcat banking venture that had brought disaster during the Panic of 1837. In Missouri proslavery mobs, hostile to any group of nonslaveholding Yankees and inflamed by reports that Mormons intended to bring free blacks into the state, had destroyed the settlements around Independence. A series of armed encounters, beginning with an attempt to bar Mormons from voting, led to outright warfare and to Governor L. W. Boggs's proclamation that the Mormons had to be treated as enemies—that they "had to be exterminated, or driven from the state." At Haun's Mill a band of Missourians massacred nineteen Mormon men and boys. Smith himself was convicted of treason and sentenced to be shot. But he managed to escape, and in Illinois the Mormons finally built their model city of Nauvoo, which the legislature incorporated in 1840 as a virtually independent city-state. The Mormon's political power derived from the decisive weight they could throw in state elections that were fairly evenly balanced between Whigs and Democrats. Beginning in 1840 their numbers grew as the result not only of missionary work in the East, but also of the immigration of thousands who had been converted to Mormonism in the manufacturing districts of England. The English converts' route to the American Zion was eased by the church's highly efficient planning authority, which took care of the details of travel.

By the early 1840s visitors to Nauvoo marveled at the city's broad streets, carefully laid out in neat squares; at the steam sawmills and flour mill, the factories, hotel, and schools. Although the Nauvoo temple, supported by thirty gigantic pillars and walls of hewn stone, was not yet complete, it promised to be, in the words of the poet John Greenleaf Whittier, "the most splendid and imposing architectural monument in the new world." Dressed in the uniform of a lieutenant general, Smith commanded the Nauvoo legion of 2,000 troops. In 1843 he dictated the official revelation, which he never made public, justifying the practice of plural marriage, or polygamy. The next year he established the secret Council of Fifty, a secular authority independent of the church, and gave it the mission of building a world government that would prepare the way for Christ's Kingdom.

But Smith felt the American world closing in on him and his fellow Mormons. Sensing that the surrounding society would not long tolerate Mormon power, he unsuccessfully tried to persuade the new Republic of Texas to sponsor an independent Mormon colony along the contested border with Mexico. While also sending secret diplomatic missions to Russia and France, he tried to influence the established order

MORMONS EXPELLED FROM NAUVOO
Despite its inaccuracies, this romanticized view of the Mormons being expelled from Nauvoo conveys the reality of white American families being driven out of the city they built. The building on the horizon is the famous Nauvoo temple.

Church Archives, The Church of Jesus Christ of Latter-day Saints

through normal political channels. But neither the federal government nor the 1844 presidential candidates would defend the Mormons' claims against Missouri outlaws who had seized thousands of Mormon farms and buildings. As a gesture of protest, Smith finally announced his own candidacy for the highest office in the land. But long before the election, he ordered the destruction of a printing press that had been set up by Mormon dissidents, who had declared: "We will not acknowledge any man as king or lawgiver to the church." Illinois then charged Smith with treason and locked him and his brother in the Carthage jail. On June 27, 1844, a "mob" that included many prominent non-Mormon citizens stormed the jail and killed them both.

To the Mormons the Prophet's martyrdom brought shock, division, and a struggle for power. It also temporarily appeased the aggression of anti-Mormons and gave Smith's followers time to plan an exodus. Brigham Young, like Smith a man of humble Vermont origin, soon emerged as the leader of the church and as one of the nineteenth century's greatest organizers. Aided by the elite Quorum of the Twelve Apostles and the Council of Fifty, he preserved order and morale while considering and rejecting possible refuges in British and Mexican territory. Before the end of 1845, the Mormon leadership had decided to send an advance company of 1,500 men to the valley of

the Great Salt Lake, then still part of Mexico. As a result of mounting persecution and harassment, the Mormons soon concentrated their energies on evacuating Nauvoo, on selling property at tremendous sacrifice, and on setting up refugee camps stretching from eastern Iowa to Winter Quarters, a temporary destination in eastern Nebraska. The last refugees crossed the Mississippi River at gunpoint, leaving Nauvoo a ghost town. During the summer of 1846 some 12,000 Mormons were on the road; 3,700 wagon teams stretched out across the prairies of Iowa.

In the summer of 1847, Brigham Young led an advance party of picked men across the barren wastes of Nebraska and Wyoming to the Great Salt Lake Valley of Utah. In September a second band of 2,000 weary Mormons found a home in the new Zion. During the same year the American defeat of Mexico brought Utah within the boundaries of the United States. The Mormons had contributed a battalion of five hundred men who had marched with the American army across New Mexico to southern California, and whose pay had helped to finance the migration to Utah. Yet by 1848 the Mormons occupied an inland mountain fortress, a thousand miles beyond the Kansas frontier, and seemed at last to be the masters of their own destiny. When federal judges and other officials arrived in the territory, they found that the Mormons had held a census, adopted a constitution, elected

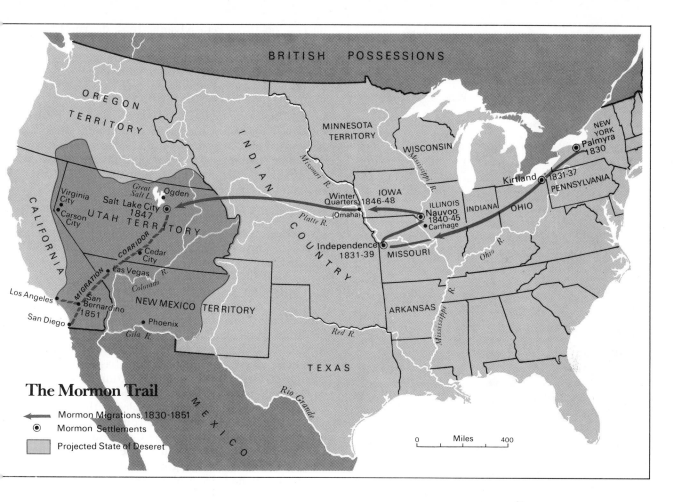

The Mormon Trail

← Mormon Migrations, 1830-1851
◉ Mormon Settlements
▨ Projected State of Deseret

Young governor, and established what they called the State of Deseret, complete with its own currency and army. The religiously run government was responsible for the remarkably rapid and orderly settlement of the valley, for the collective labor and central economic planning that brought irrigation to the dry but fertile land, and for the coordinated expansion that in ten years established ninety-six colonies, extending in a corridor from Salt Lake City to San Diego.

Ten years before the time when South Carolina defied federal authority by firing on Fort Sumter and thus beginning the Civil War, federal officials fled from Utah, denouncing Young's government as a church-state fundamentally disloyal to the United States. Although the Mormons claimed to be loyal to the Constitution and acknowledged their status as an American territory, they intended to pay little attention to the authorities who had been sent from Washington. When Young publicly proclaimed the sacred doctrine of polygamy, which Mormon leaders had privately practiced for more than a decade, he presented a ready-made issue to outraged reformers, ministers,

and politicians. President Buchanan felt the need for appeasing this popular clamor and of forcibly establishing federal authority in Utah. In 1857 he dispatched a regular army force of 2,500 men to impose federal law on the Mormons. In an irony of history, they were led by Albert Sidney Johnston, who would soon be a Confederate general resisting an invasion by the United States.

Fortunately for the Mormons, winter storms trapped the expedition in the Rocky Mountains, allowing time for behind-the-scenes negotiations. Governor Young proclaimed martial law and threatened to burn Salt Lake City to the ground and "to utterly lay waste" the land if Utah were invaded. States' rights Democrats had little enthusiasm for setting precedents that might be turned against southern slavery, and although Buchanan had sworn that he would "put down the Mormon rebellion," he decided early in 1858 to proclaim a "pardon" to the inhabitants of Utah if they would obey United States laws and cooperate with federal officials. To prove their strength, however, the Mormons evacuated Salt Lake City. Johnston's army

BRIGHAM YOUNG (1801–77)

parts of northern Pennsylvania; from the rural back-country of the Upper South and frontier Midwest; and eventually from both rural and manufacturing districts of Wales, Lancashire (in northern England), and Scandinavia. Few of these converts were well-to-do, well educated, or well established in settled communities. They were mainly small farmers who had been displaced by commercial agriculture, and footloose tradesmen and artisans who had been bypassed by expanding markets. All were people already uprooted and highly mobile, long engaged in a search for communal and religious security.

The Meaning of Mormon Dissent. Because the Mormon search for authority took religious form, it is easy to miss its radical challenge to American secular values and institutions. Against a pluralistic, permissive, and individualistic society, the Mormons pitted a higher authority that rested on a rock of unswerving certainty and conviction. Their institutions, based on divine authority, cast doubt on the legitimacy of popular sovereignty, secular law, and established government. The claim that divine revelation sanctioned such a practice as polygamy challenged the basic premises of secular law and morality. And according to their enemies, the Mormons' communal economy subverted private property, encouraged wholesale theft, and excluded non-Mormon enterprise from Utah. Far worse, the Mormons had shown little Christian patience in response to persecution. If like the earliest Christians they had looked for strength from the blood of their martyrs, they had also promised retaliation, or "blood atonement," to their enemies.

But the Mormons were not revolutionaries. Despite many points of dissent, Mormonism had much in common with the developing culture of pre–Civil War America. No other American denomination so fully incorporated the so-called Protestant ethic of work, or the rule of abstaining from tobacco and all alcoholic drinks as a symbol of their own self-discipline and modernizing values. In many respects the Mormons' ideal of a religious state was an extreme version of the ideal of Lyman Beecher, the New England revivalist reformer, and of countless other evangelists who insisted that rampant democracy must be guided by a higher moral force.

In sum, Mormonism was both a radical protest against the values of an individualistic, competitive, uprooting, and disinheriting world, and a way of achieving solidarity and authority that enabled its members to adjust to that world. During the pre–Civil War decades no other movement—with the exception of the movement among Southerners to defend black slavery—posed so serious a challenge to the ideology of the industrializing, urbanizing, and modernizing

entered a deserted city, greeted only by squads of tough police, "glowering from beneath their hat-brims, with clubs in their hands, and pistols ready slung at their belts." The later withdrawal of federal troops concluded the so-called Mormon War, which brought no change in the actual government of Utah. When Buchanan's successor, Abraham Lincoln, was asked what he proposed to do about the Mormons, he answered, "I propose to let them alone." Lincoln, of course, had other problems on his hands.

No story in American history is more incredible. From the outset Mormonism embodied the longings and hopes of people who had not shared in the growing prosperity and social modernization of the early nineteenth century. After listening to a Mormon service in Massachusetts, the poet Whittier observed that "they speak a language of hope and promise to weak, weary hearts, tossed and troubled, who have wandered from sect to sect, seeking in vain for the primal manifestation of the divine power." The new church recruited most of its members from the more remote and isolated parts of New England; from the sparsely populated southern districts of New York and the adjacent

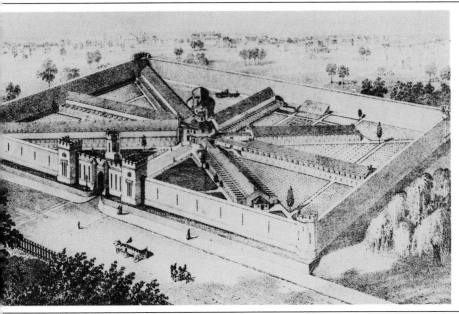

STATE PENITENTIARY, PENNSYLVANIA
The early nineteenth century witnessed the creation of asylums—totally planned and manipulated environments—which were intended to cure the insane, reform criminals, and liberate the handicapped from the effects of deafness and blindness. Whether liberating or repressive, these institutions exemplified the prevailing faith in the malleability of human nature.

Courtesy of the Pennsylvania Prison Society

North. The Mormons probed the outermost limits of tolerance, the violent limits where dissent verged on treason, and finally established their own fragile refuge beyond—but soon within—America's geographical frontiers. Unlike Southerners, they escaped the major confrontation of civil war. But their unique success required a prolonged accommodation with and ultimate surrender to the civilization against which the South finally waged civil war.

The Benevolent Empire

Like the founders of Mormonism, the reformers of the early nineteenth century were responding to the breakdown of social rules and moral authority associated with a traditional society. To restore "the moral government of God" was the supreme goal of the so-called Benevolent Empire—an informal coalition of home and foreign missionary societies, the American Tract Society, the American Sunday School Union, the American Society for the Promotion of Temperance, the American Colonization Society, the Prison Discipline Society, and the General Union for Promoting the Observance of the Christian Sabbath. Even William Lloyd Garrison, who later came to symbolize radical abolitionism and a defiance of both church and state, began his career in the 1820s as a lowly but ardent champion of these seemingly conservative reform organizations. Like many ministers and wealthy humanitarians, young Garrison deplored the rising "mobocracy," the "lawless multitude" who enjoyed liquor, violence, profanity, sexual vice, and vulgar en-

tertainment. American social reform originated in the crusade to purify public morals and to find new means, such as the asylum and penitentiary, for instilling habits of regularity, sobriety, obedience, and responsibility.

The Reform of Society. Ideals of purification and the exclusion of undesirables dominated the activities of the Benevolent Empire. Having already provided for the abolition of slavery in the northern states, many antislavery reformers wanted to send the free blacks back to Africa, an idea that gained increasing support during the early nineteenth century, especially among missionary groups who assumed that American blacks would help to Christianize the land of their ancestors. Drunkards were to be banished from the sight of respectable society. Criminals and deviants of various kinds were to be walled off in prisons and asylums, where "their stuborn spirits are subdued, and their depraved hearts softened, by mental suffering," as some New York reformers put it in 1822. When deviants were institutionalized, they could neither disturb nor contaminate a society that needed to concentrate on business and on moral virtue. Some enthusiastic prison reformers even argued that society itself should be modeled on "the regularity, and temperance, and sobriety of a good prison."

Unlike the Mormons, these reformers aspired to lead and transform the dominant secular society. Although they sought to gather together like-minded promoters of virtue, they originally gave no thought to withdrawing from a sinful society in order to practice virtue. Most of the leaders of the Benevolent Empire were men of economic and educational attainment. They could think of themselves, under "normal" circumstances, as the natural leaders of their communities. They tended to idealize the New England heritage of ordered and homogeneous communities governed by educated ministers and political leaders. Above all, they looked increasingly to Britain for models of "practical Christianity" and organized reform.

Organized humanitarianism had a long history in Britain, but during the Napoleonic wars (1798–1815) it grew dramatically. A vast campaign was undertaken in Britain to reform public morals, to Christianize the world, and to unite rich and poor by an affectionate bond of humanitarianism that would replace the traditional deference to the upper classes, which had begun to decay even in England. The British and Foreign Bible Society, founded in 1804, became the model for nonsectarian organizations committed to the ideal of "Christian unity." The Bible Society also became a pioneer in highly specialized organization as it acquired women's auxiliaries, skilled professional agents, and teams of "visitors" assigned to specific towns, districts, and streets to collect funds, interview poor families, and distribute Bibles. This kind of systematic division of labor was soon adopted by hundreds of British societies and was eventually copied by the Mormons to organize their community in Utah.

British societies were formed to promote Christianity among the Jews, observance of the Christian Sabbath, universal peace, and the abolition of slavery. There were societies to suppress immorality, antireligious publications, juvenile delinquency, and cruelty to animals; societies to aid the poverty-stricken blind, the industrious poor, orphans of soldiers and sailors, and "Poor, Infirm, Aged Widows, and Single Women, of Good Character, Who Have Seen Better Days." The English, who seem to have outdone the Americans as a nation of joiners, even launched the Society for Returning Young Women to Their Friends in the Country.

By the 1820s Britain appeared suddenly to have moved into the forefront of humanitarianism. The evangelical reformers won particular prestige by taking the lead in the successful campaign to abolish the African slave trade. Most Americans, however, remembered the British invasions of the United States during the War of 1812 and continued to think of England as a nation of tyranny and political corruption. Thus they remained suspicious of any alleged humanitarian change of heart in Britain. But the New England clergy welcomed news of England's moral transformation. Confronted by the collapse of Federalist political power, by the growing political force of public opinion, and by irresistible demands for the separation of church and state, many New England clergymen adopted the organizational apparatus of British benevolence as a means of securing control of American culture. With the aid of allies from the other parts of the Northeast, these New England ministers and reformers succeeded in capturing and Americanizing the British evangelical spirit and in institutionalizing it in New York City, Philadelphia, and regions stretching west to Illinois.

From about 1810 to 1830 the Benevolent Empire developed gradually as local societies for the reformation of morals enlarged their objectives through various interstate and interlocking personal networks. A remarkable number of the original promoters of benevolent societies were students or recent graduates of Andover Theological Seminary in Massachusetts, founded by Congregationalists in 1809 in opposition to Harvard's drift toward the liberal, rationalistic creed of Unitarianism. Andover was a seedbed for missionary work in Asia, Africa, and the American West. Many of the seminary's alumni took up such secular causes as black colonization, prison reform, and the suppression of intemperance. Louis Dwight, for example, who traveled the country as an agent for the American Bible Society, was so shocked by the squalor and disorder of jails that he became a leading crusader for the penitentiary system of total silence, close surveillance, and solitary confinement at night used in the Auburn, New York, prison. This Auburn system, Dwight maintained, "would greatly promote order, seriousness, and purity in large families, male and female boarding schools, and colleges."

These Andover reformers worked closely with serious-minded young ministers and laymen who had attended Yale or Princeton, as well as with rich and pious businessmen like Edward C. Delavan, Gerrit Smith, and the Tappan brothers. Delavan, a former wine merchant and Albany real estate magnate, contributed a fortune to the temperance cause. Gerrit Smith, a land baron in upstate New York, promoted innumerable reforms ranging from Sunday schools, penitentiaries, and temperance to radical abolitionism, women's rights, and world peace. Arthur and Lewis Tappan, who were wealthy importers and retail merchants in New York City, contributed money and leadership to a whole galaxy of local and national reform societies.

The Sabbatarian Movement.   The movement to enforce the Christian Sabbath reveals some of the basic concerns of the Benevolent Empire, as well as the obstacles that prevented the emergence of a much hoped-for "Christian party in politics." In 1810 Congress had passed a law requiring the mail to flow seven days a week, in order to meet the critical business demands for faster communication. Sunday mail service immediately drew fire from Lyman Beecher and other New Englanders, and subsequently it provoked national debate. For devout Christians the Sabbath evoked memories of a less hurried, agrarian past. Even merchants, although wrapped up in their own success and totally involved in worldly pursuits, found the silent Sabbath a reassuring symbol of spiritual goals that justified the previous six days of earthly cares and ambition.

It is significant that Sabbatarian reform originated in the boom town of Rochester, not in the long-settled urban areas along the coast. Rochester's established ministers had come from New England and New Jersey, where a quiet Sabbath had been enforced by custom and law. But the Erie Canal passed directly under the windows of Rochester's First Presbyterian Church, and the rowdy boatmen made no effort to lower their voices during the hours of Sunday prayer. In 1828 the town's leading ministers, real estate magnates, and entrepreneurs enlisted Lyman Beecher and Lewis Tappan in a national crusade to persuade Congress to enforce the laws of God. Although unsuccessful, the movement was historically important because it polarized "serious Christians" against the multitude; because it prepared the way for collaboration between wealthy New York humanitarians and social activists, inspired by the revivals of Charles Grandison Finney; and because it marked the transition between merely distributing Bibles and resorting to direct political and economic action. It should also be emphasized that Rochester lay at the heart of the Burned-Over District and that the Sabbatarian movement coincided with the Anti-Masonic crusade,* Finney's revivals, the perfection and extension of the Auburn penitentiary system, and the birth of Mormonism.

Although the various causes taken up by the Benevolent Empire appear conservative when compared with later abolitionism, feminism, and perfectionism, they too challenged vested interests and provoked immediate and furious resistance. The Sabbatarian movement, for example, threatened loss to owners of boat lines, ferries, taverns, theaters, and stores, much as the temperance movement threatened not only brewers, distillers, and distributors, but also thousands of grocers and storekeepers whose customers expected a free pick-me-up as a sign of hospitality. Like the more militant temperance reformers, the Sabbatarians urged true Christians to boycott offending proprietors. Between Buffalo and Albany they also established their own six-days-a-week Pioneer Stage

*For Anti-Masonry, see chapter 15, p. 382, 383–84.

Line, a counterpart of the special temperance hotels and of the abolitionist shops that sold only produce made by free labor. These "anti"-institutions, which were almost uniformly unsuccessful, were intended to be sanctuaries—virtuous, disciplined environments set off from a chaotic and corrupting society—and models for the world to imitate. But like other reformers, the Sabbatarians were also committed to an imperial mission. Setting a precedent for later abolitionists, they organized a great petition campaign to persuade Congress to stop the Sunday mails. Like the abolitionists, they warned that unless Congress acknowledged a "higher law," the nation had little chance for survival:

If this nation fails in her vast experiment, the world's last hope expires; and without the moral energies of the Sabbath it will fail. You might as well put out the sun, and think to enlighten the world with tapers . . . as to extinguish the moral illumination of the Sabbath, and break this glorious mainspring of the moral government of God.

But as the Mormons later discovered, many Americans were suspicious of people who claimed to stand for the moral government of God. By 1831 the Benevolent Empire had failed in its most daring and secular missionary efforts to regenerate society. Lyman Beecher had early defined the supreme goal of the missionary and benevolent societies: to produce "a sameness of views, and feelings, interests, which would lay the foundation of our empire upon a rock." But this purpose smashed against the rocklike resistance of people who refused to be homogenized, especially under Yankee direction. In response to the Sabbatarians' petitions, Congress agreed with a Kentucky senator who drafted a report stating that the national legislature was not "a proper tribunal to determine the laws of God." The colonization movement—the movement to send free blacks to Africa—did much to unite northern urban blacks in opposition to the idea. These blacks angrily affirmed that they would not accept a foreign refuge as a substitute for justice: "We will never separate ourselves voluntarily from the slave population of this country." "Let not a purpose be assisted which will stay the cause of the entire abolition of slavery." Ironically, resistance to the Benevolent Empire also appeared in the South and Southwest, where an antimission movement appealed to so-called Hard-Shell Baptists and rural Methodists. These groups found no biblical support for benevolent societies and bitterly resisted any attempts to bring religious instruction to the blacks. Further, as one Baptist declared, "our backwoods folks" simply could not understand the pretentious talk of the "young men come from the eastern schools."

The Benevolent Empire solved no social problems. It received no credit for legislative triumphs of the magnitude of Britain's abolition of the slave trade (1807) and gradual emancipation of West Indian slaves (1833). By 1837, moreover, internal conflicts had shattered all hope of a united front among evangelical reformers. Growing divisions over slavery simply intensified suspicions and grievances that had long been festering on every level. Rivalry between religious groups weakened the supposedly nondenominational societies that northern Presbyterians and Congregationalists had always controlled. In 1837, when the Presbyterian church separated into conservative Old School and liberal New School camps, the economic depression also sharply reduced humanitarian gifts and thus further weakened the various organizations of the Benevolent Empire. The major Protestant churches, however, continued much of the work under denominational auspices.

Waging the War. It can be argued that the true revolution in American reform began in the 1820s with the militancy, the dedication, the towering expectations, and the phenomenal organization of the nonsectarian, evangelical societies. It began, that is, when an agent of the Sunday School Union, addressing the well-to-do members of the Bible Society, repeated the British motto: "Not by exactions from the opulent but by the contributions from all"; it began when the organizer of foreign missions called for a "vast body like a host prepared for war"; it began when the benevolent societies developed the techniques of modern fund-raising campaigns. The real revolution began with the mass production of literally millions of moralistic tracts, priced cheaply enough to undersell all commercial publications and marketed by discounts and other techniques that were far ahead of commercial practice. By 1830, in short, the evangelicals had devised all the apparatus needed for a massive conquest of American culture.

Although the conquest had ethnic, class, and geographical boundaries, few invading armies or political revolutions have had such a far-reaching effect on an entire society as the Benevolent Empire did. In 1834 the Temperance Society estimated that it had more than 1.25 million members; in 1836 the American Tract Society alone sold more than 3 million publications. In 1843, in response to the depression that had filled New York City's streets with thousands of beggars and vagrants, the New York Association for Improving the Condition of the Poor imitated the earlier models and sent teams of agents to gather information district by district and to distribute food, fuel, and clothing. The needy recipients could not help but be influenced, one way or another, by the association's

links with the temperance movement, its conviction that poverty was a problem of individual morality, and its commitment to making the poor "respectable." If the reformers harbored little sympathy for sinners who refused to be saved, their ideology rested on a belief in human perfectibility, strongly laced with hopes for an American millennium.

The reformers' confidence in human perfectibility inspired a multitude of efforts, especially in the 1840s, to liberate individuals from all coercive forces and institutions. Perfectionism—the belief that people are capable of unlimited moral improvement—took both religious and secular forms. Suddenly, new things seemed possible, new ways of thinking and acting seemed worth trying. The nation had never before witnessed such frothy experimentation, such gusty defiance of traditional wisdom, or such faith in spontaneous love and harmony. Some reformers won fame for their success in emancipating individual victims of deafness, blindness, and insanity. Samuel Gridley Howe, best known for his pioneering work with the blind and deaf-blind, expressed the growing view that even criminals were "thrown upon society as a sacred charge." "Society," Howe said, "is false to its trust, if it neglects any means of reformation." Prison reformers tried, with little success, to transform penitentiaries into communities of rehabilitation and to persuade society of the need for parole, indeterminate sentences, and sympathetic care for discharged convicts. Nativists, who were alarmed by the increasing number of Catholic immigrants, publicized cases of Catholic women who had escaped from supposedly tyrannical and immoral nunneries, and demanded laws that would liberate Catholic laymen from the control of their priests.

Temperance. The temperance movement, a direct outgrowth of the Benevolent Empire, illustrates this mixture of humanitarianism, intolerance, progressivism, and self-righteousness. Although sometimes portrayed as religious cranks and killjoys, the temperance reformers were responding to a genuine social problem. During the early 1800s, per capita consumption of hard liquor far exceeded even the highest twentieth-century levels. Alcohol abuse undoubtedly contributed to family discord and child abuse, to public disorder, and to lowered productivity and rising social costs. By the mid-1830s various groups of urban artisans and northern free blacks endorsed temperance as a prerequisite for self-improvement. At the same time, middle-class champions of total abstinence became embroiled in bitter disputes over biblical approval or disapproval of drinking wine.

In 1840 the movement took a new direction when groups of reformed alcoholics began organizing

TEMPERANCE
The worst evil of alcohol, according to temperance reformers, was its destruction of family harmony and the sanctity of the home. Innumerable storybooks and illustrations pictured a husband and father inflamed by spiritous liquor, attacking his helpless wife and children.

"Washingtonian Societies," which appealed to working-class people and to members of subcultures that had not been reached by the traditional temperance organizations. At Society meetings former drunkards told rapt audiences what hell was really like, sometimes reenacting the agonies of the delirium tremens that their excessive drinking had induced. Old-guard temperance leaders tried to use and patronize the Washingtonians, much as some white abolitionists tried to use and patronize fugitive slaves. But the middle-class societies never felt comfortable with the former victims of intemperance or with the boisterous showmanship that induced thousands of disreputable-looking people to pledge themselves, at least temporarily, to total abstinence.

Faith in "moral suasion"—individual conversion to abstinence—disintegrated in the face of hundreds of thousands of German and Irish immigrants who had little taste for Yankee moralism. The celebrated "Maine law" of 1851, which outlawed the manufacture and sale of alcoholic beverages, marked the maturing of a new campaign for legal coercion in the form of statewide prohibition. On both local and state levels, bitter political conflicts erupted over the passage, repeal, and enforcement of prohibition laws. For temperance reformers of the 1850s, it was no longer safe to rely on the individual's mastery of temptation. The crucial act of will was now to be made by the state, which would attempt to remove the temptation. In less than thirty years, one of the supreme goals of the Benevolent Empire had been handed over to the realm of political power. Faith in moral influence and liberation had yielded to what the *American Temperance Magazine* hailed as the only force that drunkards could comprehend—"the instrumentality of the law."

Feminism and Perfectionism

By the second quarter of the nineteenth century, a broad protest movement, with strong religious undercurrents, was unfolding against forms of oppression and inequality that had long been accepted as inevitable. A major—and bitterly controversial—part of this protest movement attacked slavery.* But by the 1830s

*For abolitionism, see chapter 14, pp. 355–62.

abolitionism had become intertwined with attacks against the traditional subordination of women. The founders of the feminist movement, like the male abolitionists, had mostly served apprenticeships in the moral-reform and temperance societies of the Benevolent Empire. Hundreds of female benevolent societies provided women with invaluable experience in fund raising, organization, and public speaking. As women increasingly defied traditional restraints on engaging in public activities, they increasingly demanded equal educational and employment opportunities.

Women were not only deprived of higher education, barred from the professions, and denied the right to vote. Upon marriage, most women also surrendered any legal right to their own earnings and property. Harriet Robinson, who began working in a Massachusetts textile mill at age eleven and who in 1836 participated in one of the first women's strikes against wage cutting, recalled that many workers were "fugitives" from oppressive husbands and had thus assumed false names in order to prevent their husbands from legally seizing their wages. These conditions evoked a mounting protest from writers like Catharine Beecher, a daughter of Lyman Beecher and sister of Harriet Beecher Stowe. While conceding that women should not infringe upon the "male sphere" of business and politics, Catharine Beecher exposed the oppression of mill girls, fought for improved female education, and attempted to enlist thousands of American women as teachers in a great crusade "to secure a proper education to the vast multitude of neglected American children all over our land." This agitation focused attention on women's collective interests, problems, and responsibilities, and thus contributed to a new feminist consciousness.

Female Abolitionists.

Abolitionism provided female reformers with an egalitarian ethic and with a public forum for attacking entrenched injustice. From the outset, the radical abolitionist movement led by William Lloyd Garrison attracted a group of exceptionally talented writers such as Maria Weston Chapman, Lydia Maria Child, Abby Kelley, and Lucretia Mott. Among Garrison's most important converts were Sarah and Angelina Grimké, two outspoken sisters who had abandoned their father's South Carolina plantation and had then been converted to Quakerism and abolitionism in Philadelphia. Because they could speak of southern slavery from personal experience, the Grimkés had a striking effect on New England audiences. In 1837 they boldly lectured to mixed audiences of men and women, an offense that outraged ministers and conservative reformers who believed that women should move within a precisely limited "sphere." The Grimkés attacked the hypocrisy of con-

LUCY STONE (1818–93)
After rebelling as a girl against the subordination of her sex, Lucy Stone taught school and finally earned her way through Oberlin College. A radical abolitionist and lecturer on women's rights, she chose to keep her maiden name after she married Henry B. Blackwell, a businessman who fully supported her feminist views. Lucy Stone continued to fight for woman suffrage during and after the Civil War.

servative abolitionists who scoffed at the biblical justifications for slavery advanced in the South but who then invoked the Bible when defending female subservience. The Garrisonians convinced the Grimkés that the Christian "principles of peace" were at the root of all reform; the Grimkés helped to convince the Garrisonians that the same principles applied to the "domestic slavery" of women to men.

In 1840 the issue of women's participation in abolitionist conventions caused a final split in the national abolitionist organization, the American Anti-Slavery Society. The more conservative faction, led by Arthur and Lewis Tappan, abandoned the society to the Garrisonian radicals. Female abolitionists increasingly stressed the parallels between their own powerlessness and the legal status of slaves. At Seneca Falls, New York, in 1848, Elizabeth Cady Stanton and Lucretia Mott finally organized the first convention in history devoted to women's rights. The convention's Declaration of Sentiments, modeled on the Declaration of Independence, proclaimed that "the history of mankind is a history of repeated injuries and usurpations on the part of man toward woman, having in direct object the establishment of an absolute tyranny over her." Among the list of specific grievances, Stanton insisted on mentioning the exclusion of woman from "her inalienable right to the elective franchise."

Despite this demand for political rights, the National Women's Rights conventions of the 1850s devoted the greatest attention to legal and economic disabilities and to challenging ministers' insistence that the Bible placed the "weaker sex" in a subordinate "sphere." "Leave woman," Lucy Stone, a radical feminist leader, demanded, "to find her own sphere."

Although abolitionism provided the feminists with a sympathetic audience and with ready-made channels of communication, the relationship was also limiting in the sense that women's rights were always subordinate to the seemingly more urgent cause of slave emancipation. This dependence is evident even in the rhetoric of the radical feminists who compared the prevailing system of marriage to a private plantation in which every woman was a slave breeder and a slave in the eyes of her husband.

Communitarianism. The quest for social equality led some reformers, including abolitionists, to join experimental communities where they could escape from the coercions and frustrations of competitive labor and of the private, isolated family. Some of these communities were inspired by secular social theories. In the 1820s, for example, the socialist experiment at New Harmony, Indiana, was based on the doctrines of Robert Owen, a wealthy Scottish industrialist-turned-radical-humanitarian. In the 1840s a wide scattering of projects drew on the theories of Charles Fourier, a French social philosopher. The most successful communities, however, were those of religious sects like the Rappites and Shakers, or those disciplined by the authority of extraordinary leaders such as John Humphrey Noyes.

Noyes had studied theology at Andover and Yale. He was a perfectionist who believed that the millennium had already begun and that the time had arrived for "renouncing all allegiance to the government of the United States, and asserting the title of Jesus Christ to the throne of the world." Garrison's rejection of all coercive government owed much to the influence of Noyes, who had proclaimed that "as the doctrine of temperance is total abstinence from alcoholic drinks, and the doctrine of antislavery is immediate abolition of human bondage, so the doctrine of perfectionism is the immediate and total cessation from sin." For Noyes and his followers there was no point in attacking a single sin like slavery when all Americans were enslaved by the bonds of private property and monogamous marriage, both of which imprisoned the human spirit behind walls of sinful possessiveness. At

Putney, Vermont, and then at Oneida, New York, Noyes and his growing group of disciples developed a cohesive community based on a form of plural marriage, the collective ownership of property, and the discipline of "mutual criticism." The Oneida experiment, which flourished from 1847 to 1879, posed a radical alternative to the economic, sexual, and educational practices of the surrounding society.

The Tensions of Democratic Art

The continuing democratization of American culture produced a profound uneasiness about the artistic standards and precedents of European culture. On the one hand, American writers and artists felt the need to proclaim their independence from Europe and to create a genuinely native art, stripped of aristocratic associations. On the other hand, by the 1820s it was becoming clear that political independence did not guarantee cultural independence and that republican institutions would not automatically give birth to the Great American Masterwork. Improved transportation, coupled with a prolonged period of peace in Europe after the end of the Napoleonic wars in 1815, made it easier for Americans to cross the Atlantic in search of inspiration and training.

Even the more ardent cultural nationalists viewed Europe with awe and fascination. Often shocked by European contrasts between elegance and squalor, they were also dazzled by the great cathedrals, castles, spacious parks, monumental public buildings, museums, and villas. From Washington Irving's *Alhambra* (1832) to Nathaniel Hawthorne's *Marble Faun* (1860), American writers expressed their enchantment with castles and ruins, with places that had been steeped in centuries of history. Whatever its evils, Europe teemed with associations that fed the imagination. It was the continent of mystery, of beauty, of romance—in short, of culture. For many American artists it was also at least a temporary refuge from the materialism, vulgarity, and hurried pace of life they found in the United States. It is significant that Washington Irving was living in England when he created the classic American tales "Rip Van Winkle" and "The Legend of Sleepy Hollow" (1819–20). James Fenimore Cooper was living in Paris when he wrote *The Prairie* (1827). Horatio Greenough, America's first professional sculptor and a champion of democratic artistic theory, completed his gigantic, half-draped statue of George Washington—a statue that had been commissioned by the United States government—in his studio in Florence.

It would be a mistake, however, to think of American art of the period as slavishly imitative. Although Americans tended to express native subject matter in

Born into a wealthy slaveholding South Carolina family in 1792, Sarah Grimké as a young woman moved north to Philadelphia, where she became a Quaker and adopted the Quakers' strong antislavery beliefs. She and her sister, Angelina, became leaders of both the abolitionist and the feminist movements in the mid-1800s. In this passage from *Letters on the Equality of the Sexes and the Condition of Women*, the author draws a parallel between slavery and the subjugation of women.

Sarah Grimké on the Condition of Women in the United States (1837)

DURING the early part of my life, my lot was cast among the butterflies of the *fashionable* world; and of this class of women, I am constrained to say, both from experience and observation, that their education is miserably deficient; that they are taught to regard marriage as the one thing needful, the only avenue to distinction; hence to attract the notice and win the attentions of men, by their external charms, is the chief business of fashionable girls. They seldom think that men will be allured by intellectual acquirements, because they find, that where any mental superiority exists, a woman is generally shunned and regarded as stepping out of her "appropriate sphere," which, in their view, is to dress, to dance, and to set out to the best possible advantage her person. . . .

There is another and much more numerous class in this country, who are withdrawn by education or circumstances from the circle of fashionable amusements, but who are brought up with the dangerous and absurd idea, that *marriage* is a kind of preferment; and that to be able to keep their husband's house, and render his situation comfortable, is the end of her being. . . . For this purpose more than for any other, I verily believe the majority of girls are trained. . . .

Let no one think, from these remarks, that I regard a knowledge of housewifery as beneath the acquisition of women. Far from it: I believe that a complete knowledge of household affairs is an indispensable requisite in a woman's education. . . . All I complain of is, that our education consists so almost exclusively in culinary and other manual operations. I do long to see the time, when it will no longer be necessary for women to expend so many precious hours in furnishing "a well spread table," but that their husbands will forgo some of their accustomed indulgences in this way, and encourage their wives to devote some portion of their time to mental cultivation, even at the expense of having to dine sometimes on baked potatoes, or bread and butter. . . .

There is another way in which the general opinion, that women are inferior to men, is manifested, that bears with tremendous effect on the laboring class, and indeed on almost all who are obliged to earn a subsistence, whether it be by mental or physical exertion—I allude to the disproportionate value set on the time and labor of men and women. A man who is engaged in teaching, can always, I believe, command a higher price for tuition than a woman—even when he teaches the same branches, and is not in any respect superior to the woman. . . .

There is another class of women in this country, to whom I cannot refer, without feelings of the deepest shame and sorrow. I allude to our female slaves. Our southern cities are whelmed beneath a tide of pollution; the virtue of female slaves is wholly at the mercy of irresponsible tyrants, and women are bought and sold in our slave markets, to gratify the brutal lust of those who bear the name of Christians. In our slave States, if amid all her degradation, and ignorance, a woman desires to preserve her virtue unsullied, she is either bribed or whipped into compliance, or if she dares resist her seducer, her life by the laws of some of the slave States may be, and has actually been sacrificed to the fury of disappointed passion. . . .

Nor does the colored woman suffer alone: the moral purity of the white woman is deeply contaminated. In the daily habit of seeing the virtue of her enslaved sister sacrificed without hesitancy or remorse, she looks upon the crimes of seduction and illicit intercourse without horror, and although not personally involved in the guilt, she loses that value for innocence in her own, as well as the other sex, which is one of the strongest safeguards to virtue. She lives in habitual intercourse with men, whom she knows to be polluted by licentiousness, and often is she compelled to witness in her own domestic circle, those disgusting and heart-sickening jealousies and strifes which disgraced and distracted the family of Abraham. In addition to all this, the female slaves suffer every species of degradation and cruelty. . . ; they are indecently divested of their clothing, sometimes tied up and severely whipped, sometimes prostrated on the earth, while their naked bodies are torn by the scorpion lash.

> *"The whip on WOMAN's shrinking flesh!*
> *Our soil yet reddening with the stains*
> *Caught from her scourging warm and fresh."*

Can any American woman look at these scenes of shocking licentiousness and cruelty, and fold her hands in apathy, and say, "I have nothing to do with slavery"? *She cannot and be guiltless.*

conventional artistic forms, they became increasingly skilled and sophisticated in their mastery of the forms. The choice of native material also affected the total character of a work. For example, space, nature, and the wilderness took on new qualities as Thomas Cole, Asher B. Durand, and other painters of the Hudson River School sought to idealize the American landscape. Cooper's five "Leatherstocking Tales"—*The Pioneers* (1823), *The Last of the Mohicans* (1826), *The Prairie* (1827), *The Pathfinder* (1840), and *The Deerslayer* (1841)—were far more than American versions of Sir Walter Scott's "Waverley novels." Like William Gilmore Simms's tales of the southern frontier and backcountry, they gave imaginative expression to a distinctively American experience with Indians, violence, the law, and the meaning of social bonds in a wilderness setting. The popular New England poets and men-of-letters chose homey, everyday subjects that disguised both their literary skill and learnedness. Thus Henry Wadsworth Longfellow, a translator of Dante and a master of meter, celebrated the village blacksmith. John Greenleaf Whittier sang of the barefoot boy. And the highly cultivated James Russell Lowell delivered political satire in the homespun Yankee dialect of an imaginary Hosea Biglow.

Art as Product.
By the 1820s it was becoming clear that art in America would have to be marketed like any other commodity, and that the ideal of the dabbling gentleman amateur would have to give way to the reality of the professional who wrote, carved, or painted for a living. Federal, state, and local governments did award a few commissions for patriotic and historical subjects, but political squabbles over art (including the seminudity of Greenough's Washington) dampened artists' desire for government patronage. The need to compete for middle-class customers and audiences helps to explain the dominant patriotic, lesson-teaching, and sentimental themes of popular American culture.

Art as Character Shaper.
A self-consciously democratic art, as opposed to the remnants of folk art that it began to replace, had to justify itself by serving such an essentially nonartistic need as the shaping of character. Before the Civil War both literature and the so-called fine arts claimed to perform educational, quasi-religious functions. They provided models to imitate, they trained and refined the emotions, and they taught that sin is always punished and virtue rewarded. Art promoted patriotism by glorifying the American Revolution and deifying George Washington. It defined idealized sex roles by identifying the American male as the man of action and the conqueror of nature—hunter, trapper, scout, mountain man, seafaring

"THE GREEK SLAVE" AT THE DUSSELDORF GALLERY
The traveling exhibition of Hiram Powers's "The Greek Slave" created the greatest artistic sensation of the pre–Civil War decades. The daring—and to some, immoral—display of female nudity was justified by the "ideality" of the form and by the assumption that the enslaved girl had been immodestly stripped by her brutal Turkish captors.

adventurer—while at the same time associating the American female with confinement in a home and with refinement of emotions—physical frailty, periods of melancholy, and a sensitivity expressed by sudden blushing, paleness, tears, and fainting. Above all, art furnished models of speech, manners, courtship, friendship, and grief that helped establish standards of middle-class respectability.

A few writers achieved the imaginative independence to interpret character and sensibility in new ways. Edgar Allan Poe, who strove for commercial success while remaining committed to the ideal of art as an independent craft, gave a dark coloring to the stock themes of sentimental poetry and fiction. In a different way Nathaniel Hawthorne subtly went beyond the conventions of sentimental moralism in *The Scarlet Letter* (1850), *The House of the Seven Gables* (1851), and *The Blithedale Romance* (1852). This period of creativity, later termed the American Renaissance,

LOOKING NORTH TO KINGSTON
An example of the Hudson River School of landscape painting in which human settlement and transport are blended into a dreamy, spiritualized Nature.

included Walt Whitman's *Leaves of Grass* (1855), which not only celebrated the boundless potentialities of American experience but took joy in defying the conventional limits of poetic language. Herman Melville's *Moby-Dick* (1851), one of the world's great novels, also fused native subject matter with new and distinctively American artistic forms. Henry David Thoreau's *Walden* (1854) stated a goal that could be applied to many of the best works of the period. Thoreau had nothing but contempt for the conventional efforts to shape character in the interest of social conformity. But his decision to live by himself on Walden Pond was an experiment in self-improvement. The goal of his experiment, and of the art it produced, was to break free from the distractions and artificialities that disguised "the essential facts of life"—"to drive life into a corner, and reduce it to its lowest terms." "For most men, it appears to me," he said, "are in a strange uncertainty about it, whether it is of the devil or of God."

SUGGESTED READINGS

An excellent collection of source material on children can be found in the first volume of Robert H. Bremner, ed., *Children and Youth in America: A Documentary History* (1970–71). Two important studies of the history of juvenile delinquency are Joseph M. Hawes, *Children in Urban Society* (1971), and Robert M. Mennel, *Thorns and Thistles* (1973).

Lawrence A. Cremin, *American Education: The National Experience, 1783–1876* (1980), is the most comprehensive account of American education in antebellum America. Michael Katz, *The Irony of Early School Reform* (1968), sharply challenges the self-congratulatory tradition of educational history. Two important studies, also critical but more balanced, are Carl F. Kaestle, *The Evolution of an Urban School System: New York City, 1750–1850* (1973), and Stanley K. Schultz, *The Culture Factory: Boston Public Schools 1789–1860* (1973). Rush Welter, *Popular Education and Democratic Thought in America* (1962), presents a more traditional approach, and so does the excellent biography by Jonathan Messerli, *Horace Mann* (1972). Among the special studies of note are Bernard Wishy, *The Child and the Republic: The Dawn of Modern American Child Nurture* (1968); Marianna C. Brown, *The Sunday School Movement in America* (1961); Ruth Elson, *Guardians of Tradition: American Schoolbooks of the Nineteenth Century* (1964); Vincent P. Lannie, *Public Money and Parochial Education* (1968); and Merle Curti, *The Social Ideas of American Educators* (1935). The best introduction to higher education is Frederick Rudolph, *The American College and University* (1962), which can be supplemented by Theodore R. Crane, ed., *The Colleges and the Public, 1767–1862* (1963), and by Richard Hofstadter and Wilson Smith, *American Higher Education: A Documentary History* (2 vols., 1961).

The most imaginative treatment of revivalism is the first section of Perry Miller, *The Life of the Mind in America* (1965). William G. McLoughlin, Jr., *Modern Revivalism* (1959), gives a more detailed and systematic account of individual revivalists, and more recently McLoughlin has written a stimulating interpretive essay, *Revivals, Awakenings, and Reform: An Essay on Religion and Social Change in America, 1607–1977* (1978). Charles A. Johnson, *The Frontier Camp Meeting* (1955), is the standard history of the subject. The wider social impact of revivalism in New York State is brilliantly traced in Whitney R. Cross, *The Burned-Over District* (1950), but this must now be supplemented by Paul E. Johnson's *A Shopkeeper's Millennium: Society and Revivals in Rochester, New York, 1815–1837* (1978).

The fullest general history of American religion is Sydney E. Ahlstrom, *A Religious History of the American People* (1972). A provocative study analyzing the cultural alliance between Protestant ministers and middle-class women is Ann Douglas, *The Feminization of American Culture* (1977). Among the special studies of unusual interest are Henri Desroche, *The American Shakers from Neo-Christianity to Pre-Socialism* (1971); Nathan Glazer, *American Judaism* (1957); Daniel W. Howe, *The Unitarian Conscience* (1970); Martin Marty, *The Infidel: Freethought in American Religion* (1961); William G. McLoughlin, Jr., *The Meaning of Henry Ward Beecher* (1970); Theodore Maynard, *The Story of American Catholicism* (1960); Ernest L. Tuveson, *Redeemer Nation: The Idea of America's Millennial Role* (1968); D. H. Meyer, *The Instructed Conscience: The Shaping of the American National Ethic* (1972); T. D. Bozeman, *Protestants in an Age of Science: The Baconian Ideal and Antebellum American Religious Thought* (1977); and Winton U. Solberg, *Redeem the Time: The Puritan Sabbath in Early America* (1977).

Perry Miller, *Life of the Mind in America* (1965), contains a brilliant analysis of legal thought in America. A masterly interpretive work is James W. Hurst, *Law and Social Order in the United States* (1977), which should be contrasted with the challenging and highly innovative work by Morton J. Horwitz, *The Transformation of American Law, 1780–1860* (1977). An important aspect of constitutional development is traced in Bernard Schwartz, *From Confederation to Nation: The American Constitution, 1835–1877* (1973). Leonard W. Levy, *The Law of the Commonwealth and Chief Justice Shaw*

(1957), is an outstanding study of a leading jurist. The standard biographies of Marshall and Taney are Albert J. Beveridge, *The Life of John Marshall* (4 vols., 1916–19), and Carl B. Swisher, *Roger B. Taney* (1936).

On science, the last section of Perry Miller's *Life of the Mind* contains important insights. The best general work is George Daniels, *American Science in the Age of Jackson* (1968). For medicine, see Richard H. Shryock, *Medicine and Society in America* (1960), and Martin Kaufman, *Homeopathy in America: The Rise and Fall of a Medical Heresy* (1971). Among the best biographies of individual scientists are Edward Lurie, *Agassiz: A Life of Science in America* (1960), and Frances Williams, *Matthew Fontaine Maury* (1963).

John D. Davies, *Phrenology: Fad and Science* (1955), is highly informative. Carl Bode treats the popularization of knowledge in *The American Lyceum* (1956), and reveals popular taste and culture in *The Anatomy of American Popular Culture* (1959). Stephen Nissenbaum, *Sex, Diet, and Debility in Jacksonian America: Sylvester Graham and Health Reform* (1980), is a fascinating study of a popular but neglected aspect of self-improvement. Lewis O. Saum, *The Popular Mood of Pre-Civil War America* (1980), disputes the belief that most Americans were dedicated to progress and self-improvement.

The most illuminating studies of Emerson's thought are Joel Porte, *Representative Man: Ralph Waldo Emerson in His Time* (1979), and Stephen Whicher, *Freedom and Fate: An Inner Life of Ralph Waldo Emerson* (1953). Anne C. Rose, *Transcendentalism as a Social Movement, 1830–1850* (1981), succeeds in rooting Transcendentalism in the concrete needs and aspirations of New England society. Perry Miller, ed., *The Transcendentalists* (1950), is a difficult but magnificent anthology. Walter Harding's *Thoreau: Man of Concord* (1960), and Joseph W. Krutch, *Henry David Thoreau* (1948), can be supplemented with profit by Richard Lebeaux, *Young Man Thoreau* (1977). F. O. Matthiessen, *American Renaissance* (1941), is a brilliant and unsurpassed study of Emerson, Thoreau, Hawthorne, Melville, and Whitman.

Whitney R. Cross, *The Burned-Over District* (1950), analyzes the origins of secular reform as well as of Mormonism and other religious movements. Thomas F. O'Dea, *The Mormons* (1957), and Klaus J. Hansen, *Mormonism and the American Experience* (1981), are the best introductions to Mormonism. Fawn M. Brodie, *No Man Knows My History: The Life of Joseph Smith* (1945), is also indispensable. Klaus J. Hansen, *Quest for Empire* (1967), is a valuable account of the Mormons' efforts to prepare for a worldly Kingdom of God. Robert B. Flanders, *Nauvoo: Kingdom on the Mississippi* (1965), is a fascinating study of the Mormons' city-state in Illinois. A dramatic and authoritative narrative of the westward migration is Wallace Stegner, *The Gathering of Zion: The Story of the Mormon Trail* (1964). Leonard J. Arrington's two works, *Great Basin Kingdom* (1958), and *Building the City of God: Community and Cooperation Among the Mormons* (1976), are masterly accounts of the Mormon settlement of Utah. On polygamy, see Kimball Young, *Isn't One Wife Enough?* (1954). Norman F. Furniss, *The Mormon Conflict, 1850–1859* (1960), covers the so-called Mormon War.

There are no satisfactory general works on the relation between religion and secular reform. Important aspects of the subject are examined in Mary P. Ryan, *Cradle of the Middle Class: The Family in Oneida County, New York, 1790–1865* (1981); Carroll Smith-Rosenberg, *Religion and the Rise of the American City: The New York Mission Movement* (1971); Paul

E. Johnson, *A Shopkeeper's Millennium: Society and Revivals in Rochester, New York, 1815–1837* (1978); Charles I. Foster, *An Errand of Mercy: The Evangelical United Front* (1960); Clifford S. Griffin, *Their Brothers' Keepers: Moral Stewardship in the United States* (1960); and Timothy L. Smith, *Revivalism and Social Reform* (1957). The temperance movement, a critical link between evangelical religion and secular reform, is well described in Ian R. Tyrrell, *Sobering Up: From Temperance to Prohibition in Antebellum America* (1979). For American drinking habits, see W. J. Rorabaugh, *The Alcoholic Republic: An American Tradition* (1979).

An original work that is indispensable for understanding the changing status of women and the origins of feminism is Nancy F. Cott, *The Bonds of Womanhood: "Woman's Sphere" in New England, 1780–1835* (1977), which should be supplemented by Barbara J. Berg, *The Remembered Gate: Origins of American Feminism—The Woman and the City, 1800–1860* (1978), and Keith M. Melder, *Beginnings of Sisterhood: The American Woman's Rights Movement, 1800–1850* (1977). William Leach, *True Love and Perfect Union: The Feminist Reform of Sex and Society* (1980), is an original and provocative study of feminism and women's position in antebellum and postbellum society. The best overall survey of both family history and women's changing aspirations is Carl N. Degler, *At Odds: Women and the Family in America from the Revolution to the Present* (1980). Other useful works are Ellen C. DuBois, *Feminism and Suffrage: The Emergence of an Independent Women's Movement in America, 1848–1869* (1978); W. L. O'Neill, *Everyone Was Brave: The Rise and Fall of Feminism in America* (1970); and Page Smith, *Daughters of the Promised Land* (1970). For individual biographies, see Lois Banner, *Elizabeth Cady Stanton: A Radical for Woman's Rights* (1980); Alma Lutz, *Created Equal: A Biography of Elizabeth Cady Stanton* (1973); Otelia Cromwell, *Lucretia Mott* (1971); and Gerda Lerner, *The Grimké Sisters from South Carolina: Rebels Against Slavery* (1967). For the changes in state laws relating to women's ownership of property and other legal rights, see Peggy A. Rabkin, *The Legal Foundations of Female Emancipation* (1980).

David S. Rothman, *The Discovery of the Asylum* (1971), is a brilliant interpretation of reformatory institutions. The most imaginative study of early prisons is W. David Lewis, *From Newgate to Dannemora: The Rise of the Penitentiary in New York* (1965). Blake McKelvey, *American Prisons* (1936), is a more comprehensive reference. On the insane, the best guides are Helen E. Marshall, *Dorothea Dix: Forgotten Samaritan* (1937), and Gerald N. Grob, *Mental Institutions in America: Social Policy to 1875* (1973). For the reformer who did most for the deaf and blind, see Harold Schwartz, *Samuel Gridley Howe* (1956).

The classic work on the peace movement is Merle Curti, *The American Peace Crusade, 1815–1860* (1929), which should be supplemented by Peter Brock, *Pacifism in the United States: From the Colonial Era to the First World War* (1968).

On communitarian settlements, the best general works are Mark Holloway, *Heavens on Earth* (1951), and the relevant chapters in Donald D. Egbert and Stow Persons, *Socialism and American Life* (2 vols., 1952). The communitarian phase inspired by Robert Owen is masterfully covered by J. F. C. Harrison, *Quest for the New Moral World: Robert Owen and the Owenites in Britain and America* (1969). For the New Harmony experiment, see also William Wilson, *The Angel and the Serpent* (1964), and Arthur Bestor, *Backwoods Utopias*

(1950). The best introduction to the Oneida community is Maren L. Carden, *Oneida: Utopian Community to Modern Corporation* (1969). For Noyes himself, see Robert D. Thomas, *The Man Who Would Be Perfect: John Humphrey Noyes and the Utopian Impulse* (1977). Three other studies of unusual importance are Lawrence Veysey, ed., *The Perfectionists: Radical Social Thought in the North, 1815–1860* (1973); Michael Fellman, *The Unbounded Frame: Freedom and Community in Nineteenth-Century Utopianism* (1973); and William H. Pease, *Black Utopia: Negro Communal Experiments in America* (1963).

Of the numerous studies of important literary figures, the following have special value for the historian: Richard Chase, *The American Novel and Its Tradition* (1957); Joel Porte, *The Romance in America: Studies in Cooper, Poe, Hawthorne, Melville, and James* (1969); A. N. Kaul, *The American Vision: Actual and Ideal Society in Nineteenth-Century Fiction* (1963); R. W. B. Lewis, *The American Adam: Innocence, Tragedy and Tradition in the Nineteenth Century* (1955); and David Levin, *History as Romantic Art* (1959). For Whitman, see Gay Allen, *The Solitary Singer* (1967). The best introduction to Poe is Edward Wagenknecht, *Edgar Allan Poe: The Man Behind the Legend* (1963). Newton Arvin has written two fine literary biographies: *Herman Melville* (1950), and *Longfellow: His Life and Work* (1963). For Hawthorne, see Edward Wagenknecht, *Nathaniel Hawthorne: Man and Writer* (1961).

Van Wyck Brooks, *The Flowering of New England, 1815–1865* (1936), is still highly readable and informative. On the South, the best guide is Jay B. Hubbell, *The South in American Literature, 1607–1900* (1954). Henry Nash Smith, *Virgin Land: The American West as Symbol and Myth* (1950), is a brilliant study of the imaginative portrayal of the West. The early publishing industry is analyzed in William Charvat, *Literary Publishing in America, 1790–1850* (1959). For popular literature, see James Hart, *The Popular Book in America* (1950); Herbert R. Brown, *The Sentimental Novel in America, 1798–1860* (1940); and Frank L. Mott, *Golden Multitudes: The Story of Best Sellers in the United States* (1947). Mott, *American Journalism* (1962), is the standard source on newspapers. The first volume of Mott's monumental *A History of American Magazines* (5 vols., 1957) is a mine of information. For folk songs, see Alan Lomax, *The Folk Song in North America* (1969).

Oliver W. Larkin, *Art and Life in America* (1949), is the fullest study of the early history of art and architecture. On painting it should be supplemented by Barbara Novak's superb study, *Nature and Culture: American Landscape and Painting, 1825–1875* (1980), as well as by David C. Huntington, *Art and the Excited Spirit: America in the Romantic Period* (1972), and James T. Flexner, *That Wilder Image: The Painting of America's Native School from Thomas Cole to Winslow Homer* (1962). Neil Harris, *The Artists in American Society: The Formative Years, 1790–1860* (1966), is a sensitive study of art as a profession. Arthur H. Quinn, *American Drama* (2 vols., 1955), is a comprehensive introduction to the theater. A more imaginative work is David Grimstead, *Melodrama Unveiled* (1968). On architecture, see Talbot F. Hamlin, *Greek Revival Architecture in America* (1944), and Wayne Andrews, *Architecture in America* (1960). The best guides to early American music are Gilbert Chase, *America's Music* (1955); H. Wiley Hitchcock, *Music in the United States* (1969); and Dena J. Epstein, *Sinful Tunes and Spirituals: Black Folk Music Through the Civil War* (1977).

14 "The Peculiar Institution"

Historians still debate the importance of similarities and differences between the antebellum North and South. Was the South simply a variant form of American society and culture, or was it becoming a separate and indigestible nation within a nation? Clearly the two regions shared much in common: the American Revolutionary heritage; a commitment to constitutional government and to English laws and judicial procedure; a loyalty to national political parties and a growing acceptance of universal suffrage for white males; a widespread hunger for evangelical religion combined with an insistence on the separation of church and state. The typical Southerner, like the typical Northerner, was a small farmer who tried to achieve both relative self-sufficiency and a steady income from marketable cash crops. Nor was the South distinctive in its dedication to white supremacy. As slavery gradually disappeared in the North during the first decades of the nineteenth century, antiblack racism became more intense. Free blacks were barred from schools, colleges, churches, and public accommodations. Excluded from all but the most menial jobs, they were also deprived of the most elemental civil rights. But racism did not necessarily mean an approval of human slavery. As the North moved rapidly toward an urban and industrial economy, Northerners celebrated the virtues and benefits of free labor, which they hailed as the keystone of free institutions. Having earlier assumed that slavery was a "relic of barbarism" that would be gradually destroyed by the forces of social and economic progress, they looked on the South with dismay as black slavery became the basis for a vigorous, expanding economy and as Southerners took the lead in the rush for western land.

Rise of the Cotton Kingdom

From 1820 on, Southerners benefited from three advantages unavailable in the North. First, the climate and soil of large parts of the South were ideally suited to growing cotton, the indispensable raw material for the Industrial Revolution, which was well under way in Great Britain and was already beginning in New England. The perfection of the cotton gin and screw press, devices for extracting cotton from the plant and compressing it into bales, gave Southerners benefits of technological innovation that Northerners did not begin to approximate until the late 1850s. Second, the rapid improvement and wide use of steamboats opened the way to upriver navigation of the Mississippi and of the rich network of other southern rivers, thereby lowering transportation costs even more dramatically than the northern canals did. Third and most important, southern agriculture could exploit the labor of black slaves, whose numbers increased from 1.5 million in 1820 to nearly 4 million in 1860. A self-reproducing labor force had long distinguished the South from other slave societies in the New World. These included Brazil and Cuba, which until the mid-nineteenth century remained dependent on the continuing importation of slaves from Africa. The unprecedented natural increase of the slave population in the South enabled white Southerners to clear and settle the vast Cotton Kingdom, extending from Georgia to Louisiana, Arkansas, and eventually eastern Texas.

Scholars still dispute important questions relating to the economics of slavery. But one must begin by emphasizing the shortage of white labor as a crucial condition affecting both northern and southern agriculture. All American farmers wanted the independence and relative security of owning their own land. Since land was generally accessible, especially in the West, it was difficult for farmers to hire nonfamily labor in order to expand production and take advantage of a rising demand for cash crops, such as wheat, cotton, and corn.

In the North this labor shortage led to improved transportation, labor-saving machinery, and promotional schemes to attract immigrants. But in the South black slaves provided a highly mobile and flexible supply of labor. Large planters and specu-

The Illustrated London News, November 29, 1856

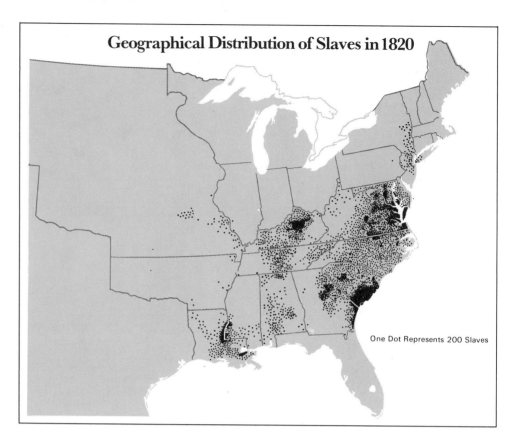

Geographical Distribution of Slaves in 1820

One Dot Represents 200 Slaves

lators could quickly transport an army of involuntary workers to clear rich western land or could sell slaves to meet the labor demands of expanding areas. Even prospering family farmers could buy or rent a few slaves to increase their output of cotton or other cash crops. The flexibility of the system also enabled planters to allocate needed labor to raising livestock and growing foodstuffs for domestic consumption. And when market conditions improved, slaveholders could increase the proportion of work time devoted to cotton or other cash crops.

These various advantages also meant that slaves became the major form of southern wealth, and slaveholding became the means to prosperity. Except for the bustling port of New Orleans, great urban centers failed to appear, and internal markets declined. European immigrants, having no wish to compete with slave labor, generally shunned the region. Investment flowed mainly into the purchase of slaves, whose soaring price reflected an apparently limitless demand. The large planters, who profited from the efficiency of mobilizing small armies of slave workers, soon ranked among America's richest men.

There can be no doubt that investment in slaves brought a considerable return, or that the slave economy grew rapidly throughout the pre–Civil War dec-

ades. Yet essentially, the system depended on the world's demand for cotton as it entered the age of industrialization, led by the British textile industry. At times the South's production of cotton exceeded international demand, and cotton prices fell sharply in the economic depressions known as the Panics of 1819 and 1837. But until the Civil War the world market for cotton textiles grew at such a phenomenal rate that both southern planters and British manufacturers thought only of infinite expansion. By 1840 the South grew more than 60 percent of the world's cotton; during the pre–Civil War boom more than three-fourths of the South's cotton was exported abroad. Much of it went to Britain, amounting to more than 70 percent of that country's cotton imports. In addition the South shipped cotton to the rising industries of continental Europe, including Russia. Throughout the antebellum period cotton accounted for over half the value of all American exports, and thus it paid for the major share of the nation's imports. A stimulant to northern industry, cotton also contributed to the growth of New York City as a distributing and exporting center that drew income from commissions, freight charges, interest, insurance, and other services connected with the marketing of America's number-one commodity.

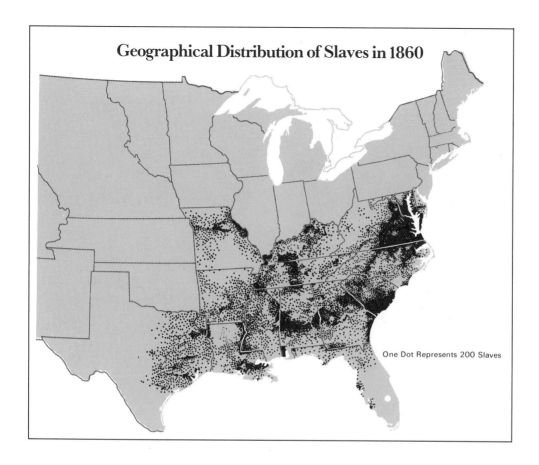

Geographical Distribution of Slaves in 1860

One Dot Represents 200 Slaves

Neither American sellers nor British buyers felt comfortable about their dependence on a single source of prosperity. British manufacturers searched unsuccessfully for alternative sources of high-grade cotton. Although the South continued to export large quantities of rice, tobacco, and other cash crops, southern business conventions unsuccessfully called for a more balanced economy. In Louisiana wealthy sugar growers expanded production by using new technology for the processing of cane. Plantation owners effectively applied slave labor to cultivating hemp, corn, and grain; to mining and lumbering; to building canals and railroads; and even to manufacturing textiles, iron, and other industrial products. Yet the South's economic growth and prosperity depended ultimately on foreign markets.

No other American region contained so many farmers who merely subsisted on their own produce; yet in no other region had agriculture become so speculative and commercial—for small cotton farmers who could not afford slaves, as well as for the planter elite. Like some of the later Third World regions where involuntary labor produced raw materials for industrial nations, the South was intimately connected with

industrial capitalism and yet cut off from its liberalizing and diversifying influences.

The Slave Masters. In theory the southern slaveholder possessed all the power of any owner of chattel property. This power was limited only by state laws (which were generally unenforceable) that protected slaves from murder and mutilation, that set minimal standards for food, clothing, and shelter; and that prohibited masters from teaching slaves to read or allowing them to carry firearms or roam about the countryside. These slave codes acknowledged that bondsmen were human beings who were capable of plotting, stealing, fleeing, or rebelling, and who were likely to be a less "troublesome property" if well cared for under a program of strict discipline. Yet the laws also insisted that the slave was a piece of property that could be sold, traded, rented, mortgaged, and inherited. They did not recognize the interests and institutions of the slave community, or the slave's right to marry, to hold property, or to testify in court.

In practice it proved impossible to treat human beings as no more than possessions or as the mere instruments of an owner's will. Most masters were

COTTON PLANTATION, BY C. GIROUX
Although southern slaves cultivated sugar, rice, hemp, tobacco, and other crops, it was the cotton plantation that gave a distinctive stamp to nineteenth-century American slavery.

primarily motivated by the desire for profit. They wanted to maximize their slaves' productivity while protecting the value of their capital investment, a value that kept rising with the generally escalating trend in slave prices. Accordingly, it made sense to provide a material standard of living that would promote good health and a natural increase in the size of slave families, and thus increase capital gains. It also made sense to keep the slaves' morale as high as possible and to encourage them to do willingly and even cheerfully the work they would be forced to do in the last resort. Convinced of the moral legitimacy of the system, most slaveowners sincerely believed that their own best interests were identical with their slaves' best interests. They therefore sought to convince the slaves of the essential justice of slavery, and they expected gratitude for their acts of kindness, indulgence, and generosity, and even for their restraint in inflicting physical punishment.

But slaves were not passive, agreeable puppets who could be manipulated at will. As human beings they had one overriding objective: self-preservation at a minimal cost of degradation and of loss of self-respect. To avoid punishment and win rewards, they carried out their owners' demands with varying degrees of thoroughness. But black slaves became cun-

ningly expert at testing their masters' will. They learned how to mock while seeming to flatter; how to lighten unending work with moments of spontaneity, song, intimacy, and relaxation; how to exploit the whites' dependence on black field drivers and household servants; and how to play on the conflicts between their masters and white overseers. In short, they learned through constant experiment and struggle how to preserve a core of dignity and self-respect.

Although slavery "worked" as an economic system, its fundamental conflict of interests created a highly unstable and violent society. The great sugar planters in Louisiana and cotton growers in the delta country of Mississippi, often employing more than one hundred slaves on a productive unit, tried to merge Christian paternalism with a kind of welfare capitalism. They provided professional medical care, offered monetary rewards for extra productivity, and granted a week or more of Christmas vacation. Yet these same plantations were essentially ruled by terror.

Even the most humane and kindly masters knew that only the threat of violence could force gangs of field hands to work from dawn to dusk "with the discipline," as one contemporary observer put it, "of a regular trained army." Frequent public floggings reminded every slave of the penalty for inefficient labor,

CAESAR, A SLAVE
Slaves included people of all types and ages, a full spectrum of humanity. This dignified elderly gentleman seems proud and well dressed. Yet all his life he carried a comic name assigned to him by a white master. This Caesar, unlike a Roman ruler, had always been dependent on a master for everything he wore or owned.

disorderly conduct, or refusal to accept the authority of a superior. Bennet H. Barrow, a particularly harsh Louisiana slaveowner, maintained discipline by ordering occasional mass whippings of all his field hands, by chaining offenders or ducking them under water, and even by shooting a black who was about to run away. Barrow also distributed generous monetary bonuses to his slaves and bought them Christmas presents in New Orleans. The South could point to far gentler masters who seldom inflicted physical punishment. Slaves understood, however, that even the mildest of whites could become cruel despots when faced with the deception or ingratitude of people who, regardless of pretenses to the contrary, were kept down by force.

Masters also uneasily sensed that circumstances might transform a loyal and devoted slave into a vengeful enemy. It is true that white Southerners could congratulate themselves on the infrequency of serious slave uprisings, especially when the South was compared with Brazil and most of the Caribbean. Yet in the French colony of Santo Domingo, which at one time had enjoyed an even more secure history than the

American South, the greatest of all slave revolts had begun in 1791 and had led to the creation of the black republic of Haiti. Toussaint L'Ouverture, the brilliant Haitian military commander who led the revolution, had been until age forty-five the trusted, docile, and privileged slave of an unusually kind and indulgent master. And indeed the South had no immunity from slave revolts. In 1822 South Carolinians hanged thirty-five blacks after uncovering Denmark Vesey's plot for a full-scale uprising, a plot that involved some of Charleston's most trusted household servants. Nine years later Nat Turner led some seventy slaves on a bloody rampage through Southampton County, Virginia. To the outside world Southerners presented a brave façade of self-confidence, and individual masters reassured themselves that their own slaves were happy and loyal. But rumors of arson, poisoning, and suppressed revolts continued to flourish. Alarmists frequently warned that outside agitators were secretly sowing discontent among the slaves. This widespread fantasy at least hinted at the truth: not only did slavery have little approval in the outside world, but the institution ultimately depended on the sheer weight of superior force.

The difficulties in generalizing about the slave's world are compounded by the geographic, climatic, and cultural diversities of the "South"—a region in which mountain highlands, pine forests, and swampy lowlands are all frequently encountered within a few hundred miles of one another.

Almost half of the southern slaveholders owned fewer than five slaves; 72 percent owned fewer than ten. The typical master could thus devote close personal attention to his human property. Many small farmers worked side by side with their slaves, an arrangement that might have been far more humiliating for the slaves than working in a field gang under black "drivers." From the slave's viewpoint, much depended on an owner's character, on the norms of a given locality, on the accidents of sale, and on the relative difficulty of harvesting cotton, rice, tobacco, or sugar.

Slave experiences covered a wide range—from remarkable physical comfort and a lack of restraint to the most savage and unrelieved exploitation. But to dwell on contrasting examples of physical treatment is to risk losing sight of the central horror of human bondage. As the Quaker John Woolman pointed out in the eighteenth century, no human is saintly enough to be entrusted with total power over another. The slave was an inviting target for the hidden anger, passion, frustration, and revenge from which no human is exempt. A slave's work, leisure, movement, and daily fate depended on the will of another person.

Moreover, despite the numerical predominance of small slaveholders, most southern slaves were concen-

White overseers faced the difficult task of trying to keep both their employers and slaves content. In this semiliterate letter, John L. Garner attempts to reassure his planter-employer about the forthcoming crop and labor discipline, but also reveals how slaves could resist, fight, and run away.

An Overseer Laments His Slaves' Flight

YOU wish to lern how the crop is turning out. I think from what I have gethered of boath cotton and corn, there wil bwe very little difference between this crop and last. I have gethered near half of my corn and have to weight until the ground dry some. my waggon mier down in the field so that I had to. stop. I have got sixty bales made and wil ship them in a few days if the river is high a nuf. we had the dryest sumer I ever experienced and for the last 5 or 6 weks hit has bin wraining a gradeel. wil make me more backward in getting the crop out. I have had the misfortune to loose the work of three of my negroes, cence yesterday three weks rhunawey from mee Henry, Gilbert, and Charls, the same boy that was out last fawl so long. I think they have taken another trip to Tennessee. there was no difference in the world between myself and two of them. Henry had become so indiferent about his duty I was compeld to corect him, [but] he resisted and fought mee. I awderd Charls to take hold of him, being the nearest, but [he] refused to dwo so. after Henry and myself [had been] combatting some time he got loose from mee and got into the swamp. wile I was pursuing him Gilbert, Charls, and Perry was running the other wey. the only reason was becaus they did not take holt of the other boy when awderd. I concluded that Henry wold try to get his cloths. while I was weying cotton at night, got a cople of men to watch for him. while watching for him Perry was slipping up and was awderd to stand, but he broke and he shot him in the legs with smawl shot; sow I got him, and he is at work. I have but very little doubt but what they have gone to Tennessee, likely trying for a free state. I lern that Charls told to the negroes that he cold of made his escape before if he had bin a mind to. the ballance of them are wel. Marier thinks Henry wil gow to his old master near Sumervill Ten.

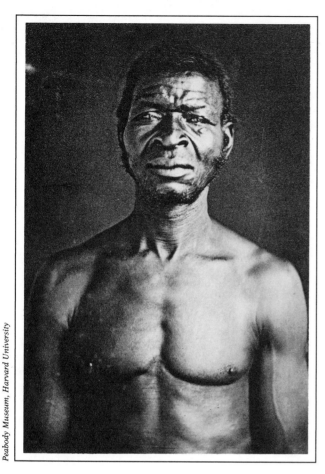

JACK, A SLAVE DRIVER

This remarkable photograph portrays "Jack," an African-born driver on B. F. Taylor's South Carolina plantation. It was recently discovered, along with other daguerreotypes of African-born slaves, at Harvard's Peabody Museum of Archaeology and Ethnology. The pictures were originally commissioned in 1850 by Louis Agassiz, a celebrated Swiss-born scientist eager to prove that God had created Africans as a distinct and separate species. It is ironic that Agassiz, who wanted to give scientific support to the enemies of abolitionism, could gather documents that were far more eloquent indictments of slavery than any of the literary evidence available to abolitionists.

trated on large farms and plantations. Over half belonged to owners who held twenty or more slaves; one-quarter belonged to productive units of more than fifty slaves. In the South slave ownership was the primary road to wealth, and the most successful masters cornered an increasing share of the growing but limited human capital. Therefore, most slaves experienced fairly standardized patterns of plantation life.

Life on the Plantation. By sunrise black drivers herded gangs of men and women into the fields. The older children served as water carriers or began to learn the lighter tasks of field work. Slaves too old for field work took care of small children and also worked in the stables, gardens, and kitchens. This full employment of all available hands was one of the economies of the system that increased the total output from a planter's capital investment. Nevertheless, slaves often succeeded in maintaining their own work rhythm and in helping to define the amount of labor a planter could reasonably expect. Bursts of intense effort required during cotton picking, corn shucking, or the eighteen-hour-a-day sugar harvest were followed by periods of festivity and relaxation. Even in relatively slack seasons, however, there were cattle to be tended, fences to be repaired, forests to be cleared, and food crops to be planted.

Black slaves were saved from becoming mere robots in the field by the strength of their own community and evolving culture. There has long been controversy over the survival in North America of African cultural patterns. In contrast to Brazil, where continuing slave importations sustained for blacks a living bond with African cultures, the South had a black population in which the vast majority were removed by several generations from an African-born ancestor. Yet recent research has uncovered striking examples of African influence in the southern slaves' oral traditions, folklore, songs, dances, language, sculpture, religion, and kinship patterns. The question at issue is not the purity or even the persistence of distinct African forms. In the New World all imported cultures have undergone blending, adaptation, and combination with other elements. The point is that slaves created their own Afro-American culture, which preserved the most crucial areas of life and thought from white domination. Within such a culture, sustained by strong community ties, slaves were able to maintain a sense of apartness, of pride, and of independent identity.

African kinship patterns seem to have been the main vehicle for the maintenance of cultural identity. As in West Africa, children were frequently named for grandparents, who were revered even in memory. Kinship patterns survived even the breakup of families. Strangers often took on the functions and responsibilities of grandparents, uncles, and aunts. Many younger slaves were cared for and protected by "aunts" and "uncles" who were not blood kin. These older teachers and guardians passed on knowledge of the time when their ancestors had not been slaves, before the fateful crossing of the sea. This historical awareness inspired hope in a future time of deliverance—a deliverance that slaves associated with the Jews' biblical flight from Egypt, with the sweet land of Canaan, and with the Day of Jubilee. In the words of one spiritual:

Courtesy of the Lightfoot Collection

MOSS PICKERS, SAVANNAH, GEORGIA

This remarkable photograph of American-born slaves depicts generational continuity from childhood to old age and also suggests the kind of household utensils and living quarters that could be seen in antebellum Georgia.

Dear Lord, dear Lord, when slavery'll cease
Then we poor souls will have our peace;—
There's a better day a-coming,
Will you go along with me?
There's a better day a-coming,
Go sound the jubilee!

Historians have recently recognized how important the slave family was as a refuge from the dehumanizing effects of being treated as chattel property. The strength of family bonds is suggested by the thousands of slaves who ran away from their owners in search of family members separated through sale. The myth of weak family attachments is also countered by the swarms of freedmen who roamed the South at the end of the Civil War in search of their spouses, parents, or children, and by the eager desire of freedmen to legalize their marriages.

Nevertheless, the slave family was a highly vulnerable institution. Although many slaveowners had moral scruples against separating husbands from wives or small children from their mothers, even the strongest scruples frequently gave way in times of eco-nomic need. The forced sale of individual slaves in order to pay a deceased owner's debts further increased the chances of family breakups. In some parts of the South, it was common for a slave to be married to another slave on a neighboring or even distant plantation, an arrangement that left visitation at the discretion of the two owners. At best, slave marriage was a precarious bond, unprotected by law and vulnerable to the will of whites.

In sexual relations there was a similar gap between moral scruples and actual practice. White planter society officially condemned miscegenation—interracial sexual unions—and tended to blame lower-class whites for fathering mulatto children. Yet there is abundant evidence that many slaveowners, sons of slaveowners, and overseers took black mistresses or sexually exploited the wives and daughters of slave families. This abuse of power was not as universal as northern abolitionists claimed, but it was common enough to humiliate black women, to instill rage in black men, and to arouse shame and bitterness in white women.

The larger slave communities provided some stability and continuity for the thousands of blacks who were sold and shipped to new environments. On the larger plantations one could find conjurers whose alleged magic powers were thought to ward off sickness, soften a master's heart, or hasten the success of a courtship. There were black preachers who mixed Christianity with elements of West African religion and folklore. In the slave quarters particular prestige was attached to those who excelled at the traditional memorizing of songs, riddles, folktales, superstitions, and herb cures—who were carriers, in short, of Afro-American culture. These forms of oral communication allowed free play to the imagination, enabling slaves to comment on the pathos, humor, absurdity, sorrow, and warmth of the scenes they experienced. Together with the ceremonial rituals, especially at weddings and funerals, the oral traditions preserved a sanctuary of human dignity that enabled slaves to survive the humiliations, debasement, and self-contempt that were inseparable from human bondage.

As a result of the evangelical revivals,* southern planters increasingly promoted the religious conversion of their slaves. Even by the first decades of the nineteenth century, a growing number of churchmen and planters had argued that religious instruction would make slaves more obedient, industrious, and faithful. The ideal Christian master would treat his slaves with charity and understanding. The ideal Christian slave would humbly accept his assigned po-

---

*On nineteenth-century revivalism in the South, see chapter 13, p. 318.

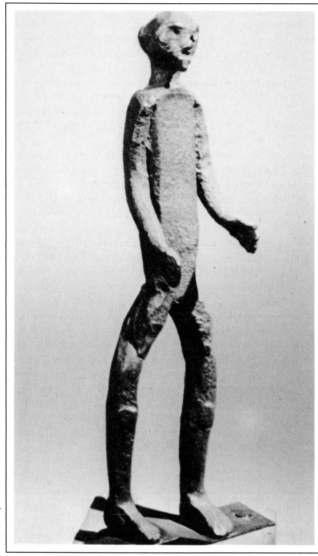

AFRO-CAROLINIAN FACE VESSEL
Recent research in art history has demonstrated a profound African influence on the folk sculpture of American slaves in such states as Georgia and South Carolina. This cultural continuity was always modified by the slaves' gift for improvisation and by their need to respond expressively to a new physical and social environment.

SCULPTURED FIGURE
Excavated at the site of a plantation forge in Virginia, this iron figure is an excellent example of eighteenth-century Afro-American sculpture.

sition in this world, knowing that his patience and faithfulness would be rewarded in heaven. Servitude, in short, could be softened, humanized, and perfected by Christianity. The reality of slavery fell short of the ideal. Religion may have induced many masters to take a sincere interest in their slaves' welfare, but it could not eliminate the cruelty and injustice inherent in the system.

No white preachers could entirely purge Christianity of overtones that tended to oppose slavery. Nor could whites prevent black preachers from converting Christianity into a source of self-respect, dignity, and faith in eventual deliverance—the longed-for Day of Jubilee. In both North and South free blacks responded to growing racial discrimination by forming what they called African churches, usually Baptist or Methodist. And despite the efforts by whites to control every aspect of their slaves' religion, the slaves created their own folk religion and shaped it to their needs and interests. As one ex-slave from Texas recalled, "The whites preached to the niggers and the niggers preached to theyselves."

The South as a "Slave Society"

By the 1830s black slavery had come to dominate all aspects of southern society. Old-fashioned defenses of slavery as an unfortunate although necessary evil were beginning to give way to aggressive self-justification. Ironically, as the South became increasingly isolated from the free-labor ideology of the Western world, the expansion of cotton cultivation helped assure southern leaders that slavery was indispensable to northern and British industry. Accordingly, slaveholders regarded their critics as ungrateful hypocrites who would bite the hand that fed them.

The meaning of the phrase *slave society* is best illustrated by the West Indian colonies of the eighteenth and early nineteenth centuries. There black slaves typically made up 90 percent or more of an island's population. Political and social life was wholly dominated by large plantation owners, their managers and agents, and the merchants who lived off the system. There was almost no dissent over the question of black slavery.

Parts of the South almost approximated this model: the swampy lowcountry of South Carolina and the adjoining Sea Islands; the fertile Black Belt, extending from Georgia to Mississippi; the delta counties of Mississippi and the sugar parishes (counties) of Louisiana. But unlike the small and isolated West Indian islands, the sprawling South was in no way a solid and uniform society. In 1860, out of a white population of some 8 million, roughly 10,000 families belonged to the planter "aristocracy." Fewer than 3,000 families owned over one hundred slaves. Barely one out of four white Southerners owned a slave or belonged to a family that did. There were extensive regions of eastern Tennessee and western Virginia where blacks, slave or free, were a rarity. Slavery had declined sharply in most of the Upper South—most dramatically of all in Delaware, where fewer than 2,000 slaves remained by 1860. Nor could most of the non-slaveholding majority be classed as hillbillies and poor whites. In addition to artisans, factory workers, and professionals, there were millions of small farmers in the South who worked their own land or who grazed herds of cattle, pigs, and horses in the forests and open range of the public domain.

Nevertheless, except for a few isolated pockets, the South did become a slave society dominated politically and ideologically by a plantation-owning elite. Throughout the pre–Civil War period, slaveholding remained the most widespread and obvious road to wealth and status. By 1860 millions of non-slaveholders believed that any serious threat to slavery was sufficient justification for southern independence; many of them, especially in the Southwest, had reasonable hopes of acquiring land and becoming planters. And small farmers often depended on a neighboring slaveowner's cotton gin or political patronage—and knew that in turn he depended for security on their services as armed patrols that searched the countryside for any unauthorized movement of blacks.

Dominance of the Planter Class. The planter class could also draw on a rich tradition of political leadership. In the South—but not in the North—the eighteenth-century connection between wealth and personal political power had endured. Political leadership sprang directly from the ownership of slaves, which was supposed to provide leisure, a concern for public order, and a certain paternalistic self-assurance in exercising authority. The southern planter elite demonstrated skill in commanding the loyalty of nonslaveholding whites and also in disciplining dissent within the white population. By the 1830s numerous southern abolitionists and Southerners with simply a strong distaste for slavery had emigrated to the North or West after abandoning hope of challenging the entrenched idea that black slavery was a necessary evil that should be discussed as little as possible. They left behind them a plantation-owning elite that was solidified in its defense of slavery and militantly intolerant of dissent.

Southern white unity centered on race. Southern society was dedicated to the ideal of equality of opportunity as long as the ideal applied only to whites. It was also a region that depended economically on a system of labor exploitation that was difficult to square with republican and liberty-loving principles. Racial doctrine—the supposed innate inferiority of blacks—became the primary instrument for justifying the persistence of slavery, for rallying the support of nonslaveholding whites, and for defining the limits of dissent.

Southern Free Blacks. The key to racial policy was the status of free blacks. Before the nineteenth century this status had been ambiguous, and the number of free blacks was insignificant. By 1810, however, as a result of the emancipations that had accompanied and followed the Revolution, there were 100,000 free blacks and mulattoes in the southern states. This group, the fastest-growing element in the southern population, was beginning to acquire property, to found "African" churches and schools, and to assert its independence, especially in the Upper South. In response, white legislators tightened restrictions on private acts of freeing slaves in an effort to curb the growth of an unwanted population. A rash of new laws, similar to the later Black Codes of Reconstruction,* reduced free blacks almost to the status of slaves without masters. The new laws regulated their freedom of movement, forbade them to associate with slaves, subjected them to surveillance and discipline by whites, denied them the legal right to testify in

---

*For the Black Codes, see chapter 20, p. 499, 506.

court against whites, required them to work at approved jobs, and threatened them with penal labor if not actual reenslavement. Ironically, in the Deep South free blacks continued to benefit from a more flexible status because there were fewer of them in the population than elsewhere in the South and they could serve as valued intermediaries between a white minority and a slave majority, as in the West Indies. Racial discrimination was worse in the Upper South, precisely because slavery was economically less secure in that region.

Decline of Antislavery in the South.

From the time of the Revolution, a cautious, genteel distaste for slavery had been fashionable among the planters of the Upper South. This Jeffersonian tradition persisted even after the more militant abolitionists had been driven from the region and after Methodist and Baptist leaders had backtracked on various resolutions encouraging gradual emancipation. The desire to find some way of ridding the South of its "burden" or "curse," as the Jeffersonian reformers called it, was kept alive by some of the sons of affluent plantation owners who went to the North or to Europe to study.

The hope of removing the South's burden also won support from a few broadminded plantation owners, mostly Whigs,* who were troubled by the economic decline of eastern Virginia and Maryland, and by the continuing loss of population to the Southwest. In 1832 the belief that slavery was "ruinous to the whites" received unexpected support in the Virginia legislature from nonslaveholders who lived west of the Blue Ridge Mountains and who had various motives for challenging the political control of tidewater planters. But in the end their arguments, advanced in a notable legislative debate of 1832 in response to Nat Turner's revolt,** demonstrated the power of racism. Even the nonslaveholding dissenters acknowledged that bondage had benefits for blacks and that its destructive effects on white society could be ended only by gradually freeing and deporting the entire black population. The antislavery delegates failed even to carry a resolution that would have branded slavery as an evil to be dealt with at some future time.

The Proslavery Argument.

By the early 1840s—less than a decade later—such a public debate would have been inconceivable in any southern state. By then regional loyalty, intensified by sectional conflict, required that Southerners believe slavery to be a "positive good." The proslavery argument ranged from appeals to ancient Greek and Roman precedents to elaborate bibli-

*For the southern Whigs, see chapter 15, pp. 379–84.

**For Nat Turner's revolt, see p. 349.

cal interpretations designed to prove that slavery had never been contrary to the laws of God. Drawing on the romantic and chivalric literary fashions of the time, southern writers represented the plantation as a feudal manor blessed with human warmth, mutual duties, knightly virtues, and loyalty to blood and soil.

The most striking part of the proslavery ideology was its indictment of liberalism and capitalism—its well-documented charge that the prevailing rule in so-called free societies, as George Fitzhugh put it, was "every man for himself, and the devil take the hindmost." In his *Sociology for the South* (1854) and *Cannibals All!* (1857), Fitzhugh sharply criticized the philosophic premises of an individualistic, egalitarian society. He also examined the destructive historical consequences of dissolving the social and psychological networks that had once given humanity a sense of place and purpose. Fitzhugh, the most rigorous and consistent proslavery theorist, presented the master-slave relation as the only alternative to a world in which unlimited self-interest had subjected propertyless workers to the impersonal exploitation of "wage-slavery." He was consistent enough to renounce *racial* justifications for actual slavery and to propose that the benefits of the institution he boasted of be extended to white workers. But these arguments, however interesting theoretically, only showed how far Fitzhugh had moved from social reality. Racism lay at the heart of the South's unity. The enslavement of whites was unthinkable, and in the 1850s the South even rejected extremist proposals for expelling or reenslaving a quarter of a million free blacks. Fitzhugh's theories did more to expose the moral dilemmas of free society than to illuminate the actual complexities and contradictions of the South.

It is true that moral doubts persisted, especially in the Upper South. But after the 1830s these doubts were more than counterbalanced by the conviction that emancipation in any form would be a disaster, for blacks as well as for whites. Southerners channeled their moral concern into dedicated efforts to reform, improve, and defend what they called the peculiar institution. It was almost universally accepted that to own slaves meant to have a sense of duty and a burden—a duty and a burden that defined the moral superiority of the South. This duty and burden was respected by nonslaveholding Southerners, who were prepared to defend it with their lives. That, perhaps, was the ultimate meaning of a "slave society."

Radical Abolitionism

Black slavery was the first issue to expose the limitations of the Benevolent Empire. Even by 1830 there was a striking gap between the public optimism of the

THE LIBERATOR

OUR COUNTRY IS THE WORLD---OUR COUNTRYMEN ARE ALL MANKIND.

evangelical humanitarians and their whispered despair concerning black slavery. Harsh realities made the gap increasingly noticeable. Despite the fact that federal law prohibited slave imports from Africa, the natural increase of the American slave population exceeded all earlier expectations. The number of slaves in the United States increased from approximately 1.5 million in 1820 to more than 2 million in 1830. This figure represented almost one-sixth of the total United States population and more than twice the number of slaves in the British and French West Indies. The number of free blacks grew during the 1820s from about 234,000 to 320,000.

The Failure of Black Colonization.

In 1830 the American Colonization Society transported a total of only 259 free blacks to Liberia, the West African colony that the society had established as a refuge for American blacks. Yet most reformers still regarded colonization as the only solution: "We must save the Negro," as one missionary put it, "or the Negro will ruin us." Racial prejudice was pervasive in the Benevolent Empire, and it was by no means unknown among later radical abolitionists. But the new and significant fact was the rising tide of virulent racism among the working classes of the North. Prejudiced as they may have been, many leaders of the colonization movement were sincere opponents of slavery who abhorred the growing racism of the northern masses and who saw black emigration as the only realistic means for preventing racial war in the North and for inducing southern masters to free their slaves.

A series of events reinforced the realization that white America could not solve its racial problem by shipping a few hundred free blacks each year to Liberia. In 1829 David Walker, a Boston black who belonged to the Massachusetts General Colored Association, published his revolutionary *Appeal to the Colored Citizens of the World*, which justified slave rebellion and warned white Americans that if justice were delayed blacks would win their liberty "by the crushing arm of power." The pamphlet created an uproar, and copies soon appeared among blacks in the Deep South. Then in 1831 Nat Turner, a trusted Virginia slave, led the bloodiest slave revolt the South had yet experienced. At the end of the same year a far larger uprising rocked the British colony of Jamaica. In Britain mass demonstrations continued to demand the immediate and unconditional emancipation of West Indian slaves. When Parliament responded in 1833 with monetary compensation to slaveowners to cover part of the financial loss of emancipation, and with an apprenticeship plan to prepare slaves for freedom, a few Americans concluded that effective political action of any kind required a mammoth mobilization of public opinion.

The Ethical Basis of Abolitionism.

To the young abolitionists who began to appear in the early 1830s, black slavery was the great national sin. The fusion of American religious revivalism with the influence of the British antislavery movement was symbolized by Theodore Dwight Weld, the son of a Connecticut minister. Weld was a convert and close associate of the famous evangelist Charles Grandison Finney in upstate New York. Weld's closest friend and religious model was Charles Stuart, a visiting British reformer who worked with Finney's disciples in the Burned-Over District and then in 1829 returned to England to throw himself into the battle for slave emancipation. After being urged by Stuart to take up the cause in America, Weld shifted from temperance and educational reforms to abolitionism, becoming one of the most fearless and power-

WILLIAM LLOYD GARRISON (1805–79)

ful lecturers in the area from Ohio to Vermont. Early in 1833 he wrote a letter to William Lloyd Garrison, whom he knew only by reputation. In it he illuminated the meaning of slavery as sin:

That no condition of birth, no shade of color, no mere misfortune of circumstances, can annul the birth-right charter, which God has bequeathed to every being upon whom he has stamped his own image, by making him a free *moral agent, and that he who robs his fellow man of this tramples upon right, subverts justice, outrages humanity, unsettles the foundations of human safety, and sacrilegiously assumes the prerogatives of God; and further, tho' he who retains by force, and refuses to surrender that which was originally obtained by violence or fraud, is joint partner in the original sin, becomes its apologist and makes it the business of every moment to perpetuate it afresh, however he may lull his conscience by the vain plea of expediency or necessity.*

Weld's statement sums up a moral command that sprang from three fundamental convictions. He believed that all men and women have the ability to do what is right and therefore are morally accountable for their actions; that the intolerable social evils are those that degrade the image of God in human beings, stunting or corrupting people's capacities for self-control and self-respect; and that the goal of all reform is to free individuals from being manipulated like physical objects. As one follower of William Lloyd Garrison put it, the goal of abolitionism was *"the redemption of man from the dominion of man."*

The fact that Weld and other abolitionists were almost wholly concerned with ideals was both their greatest strength and their greatest weakness. America was supposedly a nation of doers, of practical builders, framers, drafters, organizers, and technicians. The overriding question, in abolitionist eyes, was whether the nation would continue to accommodate itself to a social system that was based on sheer violence. To propose rational plans or to get embroiled in debates over the precise means and timing of emancipation would only give slavery's defenders an advantage. What the times required, therefore, was "an original motive power" that would shock and awaken public opinion, create a new moral perspective, and require legislators to work out the details, however imperfectly, of practical emancipation. In 1831 William Lloyd Garrison admitted: "Urge immediate abolition as earnestly as we may, it will alas! be gradual abolition in the end. We have never said that slavery would be overthrown by a single blow; that it ought to be we shall always contend."

The Abolitionists. On one level the abolitionists realistically saw that the nation had reached a dead end on slavery. Instead of gradually withering away, as earlier optimists had hoped, the evil had grown and had won increasing acceptance among the nation's political leaders and most powerful institutions. Therefore, the abolitionists took on the unpopular role of agitators, of courageous critics who stood outside the popular refuges of delusion, hypocrisy, and rationalization. In 1830 Garrison went to jail for writing libelous attacks against a New England merchant who was shipping slaves from Baltimore to New Orleans. After his fine was paid and his release was secured by the wealthy supporter of reform groups, Arthur Tappan, Garrison in 1831 founded his newspaper *The Liberator* in Boston. In the first issue he hurled out his famous pledge: *"I will be* as harsh as truth, and as uncompromising as justice. . . . I am in earnest—I will not equivocate—I will not excuse—I will not retreat a single inch—AND I WILL BE HEARD."

Although *The Liberator* had an extremely small circulation and derived most of its support from black subscribers in the Northeast, Garrison succeeded in being heard. In the South especially, newspaper editors seized the chance to reprint specimens of New England's radicalism, accompanied by their own furious rebuttals. Even before the end of 1831, mere months after *The Liberator* first appeared, the Georgia legislature proposed a reward of $5,000 for anyone who would kidnap Garrison and bring him south for trial. Garrison also championed the free blacks' grievances against the Colonization Society, which he had once supported, and mounted a blistering attack against the whole concept of colonization. He pointed out that the hope for colonization confirmed and reinforced white racial prejudice and that racial prejudice was the main barrier the abolitionists faced in the North. Largely as a result of Garrison's early and independent leadership, the American Anti-Slavery Society, founded in 1833, committed itself to at least a vague legal equality of whites and blacks, and totally rejected colonization.

Even though they had practically declared war against the values, institutions, and power structure of Jacksonian America, the abolitionists continued to think of their reform societies as simple extensions of the Benevolent Empire. They assumed that they could quickly win support from churches and ministers—that they could persuade the pious, influential, and respectable community leaders that racial prejudice was as harmful as intemperance. Then, after mobilizing righteous opinion in the North, they could shame the South into repentance. Abolitionists did not think of themselves as provokers of violence and disunion. Rather, it was slavery that had brought increasing violence and threats of disunion. A national commitment to emancipation, they believed, would ensure harmony and national union.

Like the wealthy British supporters of humanitarian causes (including antislavery), Arthur Tappan and his brother Lewis moved from various benevolent causes to that of immediate emancipation. By 1833 humanitarians in Great Britain had won the support of the established order, as well as of middle-class public opinion. But in America, precisely because the Tappans had wealth and prestige, they were viciously attacked for encouraging Garrison and other radicals and for betraying the common interests that had allowed leaders in different sections to do business with one another. Mass rallies in the South pledged as much as $50,000 for the delivery of Arthur Tappan's body, dead or alive. In New York City, business leaders vainly pleaded with the Tappan brothers, whose lives were being repeatedly threatened by 1834, to give up their radical activities. In that year prominent New Yorkers cheered on a mob of butcherboys and day laborers who smashed up Lewis Tappan's house and burned the furnishings. Only the unexpected arrival of troops prevented an armed assault on the Tappans' store.

Antiabolitionists played on popular suspicions of England, charging that men like George Thompson, an English friend of Garrison, had been sent "to foment discord among our people, array brother against brother . . . to excite treasonable opposition to our government . . . to excite our slave population to rise and butcher their masters; to render the South a desert, and the country at large the scene of fraternal war." Abolitionists continually invoked the ideals of the Declaration of Independence and portrayed themselves as fulfilling the Revolution's promise. But their enemies styled themselves as minutemen defending American liberties. The mob riots of the Revolutionary periods appeared to legitimize the antiabolitionist riots that spread across the North in the 1830s. For the most part this mob violence was carefully planned, organized, and directed toward specific goals, such as the destruction of abolitionist printing presses and the intimidation of free blacks. The leaders were "gentlemen of property and standing"—prominent lawyers, bankers, merchants, doctors, and local political leaders of both the Democratic and Whig parties. In most towns and cities the white abolitionists and free blacks received little protection from the forces of law and order. The colonizationists, already weakened by financial difficulties and internal division, took the lead in accusing the abolitionists of being "amalgamationists" who would not stop short of encouraging black men to woo the daughters of white America.

Abolitionism and Freedom of Speech.

This racist bugaboo brought the northern crowds into the streets and also lay behind the abolitionists' most dramatic break with the Benevolent Empire. Lane Theological Seminary in Cincinnati was meant to be one of the Empire's crowning achievements—a beachhead of benevolence on the Ohio River, a staging ground for the missionary conquest of the West. Arthur Tappan paid the salary of the president of the seminary, Lyman Beecher. He also paid the way for Theodore Weld, then thirty-one, to study there. Early in 1834 Weld conducted at Lane an eighteen-day soul-searching revival on the question of slavery. After converting many students and nonstudents to the doctrine of immediate emancipation, Weld led his band into the slums where the black residents of Cincinnati lived. There they set up libraries, conducted evening classes, and fraternized with the city's "untouchable" caste, the blacks. In Weld's view educational institutions had a duty to train minds for the new "era of disposable power and practical accomplishment."

But to the Tappans' dismay, Lane's board of trustees voted to get rid of Weld and the other antislavery leaders, and Lyman Beecher—who was still a supporter of colonization—went along with the decision.

Various leaders of American higher education agreed that antislavery agitation endangered the fundamental purposes of American colleges. In response, almost all the Lane students walked out of the seminary with Weld. Some ended up in Arthur Tappan's newly financed college, Oberlin. But many joined Weld as traveling agents for the American Anti-Slavery Society, of which Arthur Tappan was president, braving showers of rotten eggs and stones in order to address the American people.

As a product of the Benevolent Empire, abolitionism drew on and perfected techniques of mass communication that gave the nation its first taste of modern "public relations." By 1835 the new steam printing press and other technological improvements had reduced the cost and increased the volume of mass publication. In 1834 the Anti-Slavery Society distributed 122,000 pieces of literature; in 1835 the figure rose to 1.1 million. President Jackson and various national and local authorities expressed alarm over this attempt to apply the methods of the Bible Society and Tract Society to a revolutionary purpose—a purpose that threatened one of the nation's chief capital investments as well as a national system for racial control. But although the government encouraged the destruction of abolitionist mail, it could do nothing about the traveling abolitionist lecturers in the North, the "antislavery bazaars" held to raise funds and distribute literature, the auxiliary societies for ladies and children, or the flood of propaganda in the forms of medals, emblems, posters, bandannas, chocolate wrappers, songs, and children's readers.

The rapid growth of abolitionist societies, coupled with violent efforts to suppress them, led to sharp divisions of opinion over abolitionist principles and tactics. One turning point was the celebrated martyrdom in 1837 of Elijah P. Lovejoy, a New England abolitionist who, like the Mormons, had been driven out of Missouri and had established a refuge in Illinois. While trying to defend a new printing press from an antiabolitionist mob, Lovejoy was shot and killed. His violent death dramatized the issue of civil liberties and won new support for the abolitionists; and it also forced abolitionists to debate the proper response to violence, since Lovejoy and his men had used arms in self-defense.

Nonresistance.

Garrison, who had nearly been lynched in 1835 by a Boston mob, had become convinced that violence was a disease infecting the entire body of American society. He came to believe that whenever the nation faced any issue of fundamental morality, such as the treatment of Indians, blacks, or dissenters, it resorted to the principle that might makes right. The only Christian response, Garrison maintained, was to renounce all coercion and adhere to the perfectionist

ideal of absolute nonresistance. If abolitionists tried to oppose power with power, as Lovejoy had done, they were certain to be crushed. They would also dilute their moral argument, since the essence of slavery was the forcible dominion of man over man. In 1838 Garrison and his followers formed the New England Non-Resistance Society. This group condemned every kind of coercion—not only defensive war and capital punishment, but lawsuits, prisons, and insane asylums, unless designed solely for "cure and restoration."

Thus there began to emerge in New England abolitionism a radical repudiation of all limits imposed on the individual by the threat of force. Black slavery and racial oppression were merely extreme manifestations of an evil embodied in the male-dominated family, the criminal law, and the police power of the state. By 1843 Garrison concluded that the majority rule was simply the rule of superior power, with no protection for human rights. The Union, he asserted, had always been a compact for the preservation of slavery, and the Constitution was therefore "a covenant with death, and an agreement with Hell." The Garrisonians demanded withdrawal from corrupt churches and from all connection with the corrupt government. They refused to vote or engage in any political activities. Calling for disunion with the South, they also crossed the threshold of symbolic treason and declared themselves enemies of the Republic.

In interesting ways the Garrisonians' rhetoric paralleled the rhetoric of the Mormons. "The governments of the world," Garrison announced in 1837, "are all anti-Christ." Yet by 1845 he also cast off the Old Testament, arguing that God could never have approved of slavery and violence. Instead of moving beyond the geographic frontiers to establish the Kingdom of God, as the Mormons had done, Garrison defended his own fortress of moral independence within a hostile society.

Political Antislavery: From the Liberty Party to Free Soil.

By the 1840s, however, most abolitionists expressed new hopes for transforming the dominant society by means of the political process. There were various indications of this growing involvement in political action. During the late 1830s thousands of antislavery petitions poured into Congress as a popular challenge to the "gag rule," which prevented congressional discussions of slavery.* Former president John Quincy Adams, then a Whig congressman from Massachusetts, used every parliamentary trick to defend the petitioners' rights. Antislavery Whigs like congressmen Joshua Giddings and Salmon P. Chase, both of Ohio, capitalized on their constituencies' resentment of the "gag

*For the "gag rule," see chapter 15, p. 376.

rule" and other sectional compromises that sacrificed moral principle. Liberal Democrats, such as senators Thomas Morris of Ohio and John P. Hale of New Hampshire, voiced growing dissatisfaction with their party, which professed to attack economic privilege while serving the interests of wealthy slaveowners. And after 1842, when the Supreme Court ruled that the Fugitive Slave Law of 1793 applied solely to the federal government's responsibility in helping to recover fugitives, five northern states enacted "personal liberty laws" prohibiting state officials from assisting in the recapture of runaway slaves.

For the most part, political abolitionists hoped to pursue their goals by promoting antislavery candidates and by bringing well-organized public pressure on the two major parties to prohibit the interstate slave trade, to abolish slavery in the District of Columbia, and to prevent any further expansion of slavery in western states and territories. In 1839, however, Alvan Stewart, a lawyer and president of the New York State Anti-Slavery Society, drew most of the non-Garrisonian abolitionists into a temporary third party. It was hoped that this Liberty party, which ran James G. Birney for president in 1840, would win a balance of power in closely contested regions of the North and would thus free Whigs and Democrats from the stranglehold of what abolitionists called the Slave Power—an alleged conspiratorial alliance of southern slaveowners and their northern supporters.*

The Libertymen blamed the Slave Power for the economic depression that had begun in 1837, for the undermining of civil liberties, and for most of the other ills that the nation had suffered. Although Birney captured only a small fraction of the potential antislavery vote in the elections of 1840 and 1844, the Liberty party succeeded in popularizing the belief in a Slave Power conspiracy. By offering voters an abolitionist alternative to even moderately antislavery Whigs and Democrats, the Libertymen also stimulated figures like Giddings, Chase, and Hale to make a bolder appeal for antislavery votes.

By 1848 the more extreme political abolitionists had come to the conclusion that the Constitution gave Congress both the power and the duty to abolish slavery in the southern states. But in that year most abolitionists looked to the more moderate, broadly coalitionist Free Soil party, which promised only to remove all federal sanctions for slavery by abolishing the institution in the District of Columbia, by excluding it from the territories, and by employing all other constitutional means to deprive it of national support.

The Free Soil platform of 1848, unlike the platform of the Liberty party, ignored the legal discriminations that free blacks suffered. Many of the dissident northern Democrats who helped form the party had consistently opposed black suffrage and had exploited white racist prejudice. And indeed abolitionism in general became more acceptable in the North by accommodating itself to white racism. Many blacks increasingly resented the attention given to such other interests of white reformers as women's rights, nonresistance, and communitarian experiments, to say nothing of the hypocrisy of many reformers regarding racial equality in the North. They also resented the patronizing attitudes of white abolitionists who might defend abstract ideals of equality while in practice treating blacks as inferiors who had to be led.

Black Abolitionists.

From the outset black abolitionists had worked closely with the antislavery societies in

FREDERICK DOUGLASS (1817?–95)
The greatest black leader of the nineteenth century, Frederick Douglass was born into slavery in Maryland (he never knew his birth date), and as a house servant learned to read and write. In 1838 he escaped to the North, and in 1841 he began to lecture for the Massachusetts Anti-Slavery Society. After publishing his masterful *Narrative of the Life of Frederick Douglass*, he lectured widely in Britain. Returning to the United States in 1847, he edited his own newspaper, *The North Star*. An eloquent and prolific reformer, Douglass fought for women's rights as well as racial equality.

Library of Congress

*The politics of the 1840s, in which debate over the expansion of slavery played a central role, is discussed more fully in chapter 16.

CHARLES LENOX REMOND (1810–73)
A leading black abolitionist, Remond was born and educated in Salem, Massachusetts, where he worked for a time as a barber. As a representative of the American Anti-Slavery Society, he attended the 1840 World's Anti-Slavery Convention in London and then toured Britain as an extremely popular lecturer. Remond later helped lead the movement to desegregate Massachusetts schools.

New England and New York. Beginning with Frederick Douglass's celebrated escape from slavery in 1838 and his enlistment as a lecturer for Garrison's Massachusetts Anti-Slavery Society in 1841, fugitive slaves performed the indispensable task of translating the abolitionists' abstract images into concrete human experience. The lectures and printed narratives of Douglass, William Wells Brown, Ellen Craft, Henry Bibb, Solomon Northup, and other escaped slaves did much to undermine whatever belief there was in the North that slaves were kindly treated and contented with their lot. The wit and articulate militancy of black abolitionists like Henry Highland Garnet, James McCune Smith, Sarah Parker Remond, and Charles Lenox Remond, coupled with the towering dignity of Douglass, also helped to shake confidence in the popular stereotypes of black inferiority.

Yet black abolitionists faced barriers and physical dangers that made the difficulties of white abolitionists seem like child's play. When Douglass and Garrison traveled together on lecture tours, it was Douglass who experienced constant insult, humiliation, and harassment. Black vigilance committees could help a small number of fugitives find their way to relative security in Canada—and blacks were the main conductors on the so-called Underground Railroad—but except in Massachusetts black abolitionists had little leverage for loosening the rocklike discriminatory laws. Instead, white abolitionists kept pressuring blacks to keep a low profile, to act the part assigned to them by white directors (who presumably knew the tastes of an all-white audience), and to do nothing that might spoil the show.

In the 1840s black leaders gradually cast off the yoke that had bound them to a white man's cause, and tried to assert their own leadership. In 1843, at the Convention of the Free People of Color held at Buffalo, Garnet openly called for a slave rebellion, arguing that it was a sin to submit voluntarily to human bondage. Douglass adhered to his own version of nonresistance until 1847, when he broke with Garrison over the idea of founding a black abolitionist newspaper, *The North Star*. In the same year Garrison sadly reported that Charles Lenox Remond had proclaimed that "the slaves were bound, by their love of justice, to RISE AT ONCE, en masse, and THROW OFF THEIR FETTERS."

But speeches were one thing, action another. Black abolitionists had always looked to voting—a right few blacks possessed—as the most promising route to power. For the most part, therefore, they supported the Liberty party in 1840 and 1844, and the Free Soil party in 1848. The drift of antislavery politics, however, was away from black civil rights in the North and emancipation in the southern states. Rather, the drift was now toward walling off of the western territories—a walling off, in all probability, of free blacks as well as slaves. It is not surprising that by 1854 Martin Delaney and a few other black leaders were talking of a separate black nation, or that blacks who had proudly defended their American heritage and right to American citizenship were beginning to reconsider voluntary colonization.

By 1854, however, many northern whites had also concluded that the Slave Power had seized control of America's Manifest Destiny, thereby appropriating and nullifying the entire evangelical and millennial mission.* Moreover, the Fugitive Slave Law of 1850, requiring federal agents to recover fugitive slaves from their sanctuaries in the North, directly challenged the North's integrity and its new self-image as an asylum of liberty. The arrival of federal "kidnappers" and the spectacle of blacks being seized in the streets invited demonstrations of defiance and

---

*For Manifest Destiny, see chapter 16; for the contest over admitting Kansas as a slave state, chapter 17.

HARRIET TUBMAN

Born into slavery in Maryland, Harriet Tubman escaped to the North and then became the most celebrated leader of the Underground Railroad. Fearlessly returning to the South on many trips, she guided hundreds of slaves to freedom in the North or in Canada. She appears at the extreme left in this photograph with a group of blacks whom she rescued from slavery.

civil disobedience. Increasing numbers of former moderates echoed Garrison's rhetoric of disunion, and an increasing number of former nonresistants called for a slave uprising or predicted that the streets of Boston might "yet run with blood." Wendell Phillips, a Boston aristocrat and the most powerful of all abolitionist orators, rejoiced "that every five minutes gave birth to a black baby," for in its infant wail he recognized the voice that should "yet shout the war cry of insurrection; its baby hand would one day hold the dagger which should reach the master's heart."

In the 1850s northern abolitionists finally concluded that if the Slave Power were not crushed by rebellion or expelled from the Union, it would cross every legal and constitutional barrier and destroy the physical ability of Northerners to act in accordance with the moral ability that had been the main legacy of revivals. The western territories were thus the crucial testing ground that would determine whether America would stand for something more than selfish interest, exploitation, and rule by brutal power. All of the aspirations of the Benevolent Empire, of evangelical reformers, and of perfectionists of every kind could be channeled into a single and vast crusade to keep the territories free, to confine and seal off the Slave Power, and thus to open the way for an expansion of righteous liberty and opportunity that would surpass all worldly limits.

SUGGESTED READINGS

The best general guide to sectional conflict and the coming of the Civil War is David M. Potter, *The Impending Crisis, 1848–1861* (completed and edited by Don E. Fehrenbacher, 1976). Allan Nevins, *Ordeal of the Union* (2 vols., 1947), is a highly readable and informative survey of the same subject.

A comprehensive picture of the South as a slave society can be found in Clement Eaton, *A History of the Old South: The Emergence of a Reluctant Nation* (1975), and Eaton, *Freedom of Thought in the Old South* (1940). The growth of sectional feeling is outlined in more detail in Charles S.

Sydnor, *The Development of Southern Sectionalism, 1819– 1848* (1948), and Avery O. Craven, *The Growth of Southern Nationalism, 1848–1861* (1953). Carl N. Degler, *The Other South: Southern Dissenters in the Nineteenth Century* (1974), traces the decline of antislavery protest. H. Shelton Smith, *In His Image, But . . .* (1972), is a fine study of the growing racism in the southern churches. Frank Owsley, *Plain Folk of the Old South* (1949), contains valuable information on the nonslaveholding whites. A penetrating study of the mythology of the Old South, often northern in origin, is William R. Taylor, *Cavalier and Yankee* (1961). C. Vann

Woodward's essays in *The Burden of Southern History* (1960) and *American Counterpoint* (1971) are indispensable for understanding the South. The mind of the planter class is brilliantly illuminated by two accounts contemporary with the period: C. Vann Woodward, ed., *Mary Chesnut's Civil War* (1981), and Robert M. Myers, ed., *The Children of Pride: A True Story of Georgia and the Civil War* (1972). James Oakes, *The Ruling Race: A History of American Slaveholders* (1982), is a provocative interpretation of slaveholders as calculating capitalists. George M. Fredrickson, *White Supremacy: A Comparative Study in American and South African History* (1981), brilliantly compares the development of slavery and racism in the United States and South Africa.

Eugene D. Genovese, *Roll, Jordan, Roll* (1974), is a monumental study of black slavery in the South. Herbert G. Gutman, *The Black Family in Slavery and Freedom, 1750–1925* (1976), is no less impressive and innovative. For a briefer and illuminating discussion of the slaves' society, based mainly on slave narratives, see John W. Blassingame, *The Slave Community* (rev. ed., 1979). Two rich collections of source material are Willie Lee Rose, ed., *A Documentary History of Slavery in North America* (1976), and John W. Blassingame, ed., *Slave Testimony* (1977). As an overall survey of slavery as an institution, Kenneth Stampp's *The Peculiar Institution* (1956) has not been superseded. Willie Lee Rose, *Slavery and Freedom* (1982), is a collection of essays that combine wide-ranging interests with insightful wisdom. David B. Davis, *Slavery and Human Progress* (1984), places southern slavery and emancipation within a context of world history from antiquity to modern times.

A controversial work on the economics of black slavery is Robert W. Fogel and Stanley L. Engerman, *Time on the Cross: The Economics of American Negro Slavery* (1974). For important criticisms of this work, as well as for new information, see Paul A. David et al., *Reckoning with Slavery* (1976), and Herbert G. Gutman, *Slavery and the Numbers Game* (1975). Robert William Fogel, *Without Consent or Contract* (1984), revises and amplifies the thesis that southern slavery was profitable and contributed to a high rate of economic growth. An excellent survey of the more traditional literature is Harold D. Woodman, ed., *Slavery and the Southern Economy* (1966). For the use of slaves in nonagricultural employment, see Robert S. Starobin, *Industrial Slavery in the Old South* (1970). The synthesis of African and Christian religious forms is carefully studied in Albert J. Raboteau, *Slave Religion: The "Invisible Institution" in the Antebellum South* (1978). A rich and comprehensive study of black folklore and culture is Lawrence W. Levine, *Black Culture and Black Consciousness: Afro-American Folk Thought from Slavery to Freedom* (1977).

The standard work on proslavery thought is William S. Jenkins, *Pro-Slavery Thought in the Old South* (1935), which can be supplemented by Harvey Wish, *George Fitzhugh* (1943); Drew Gilpin Faust, *A Sacred Circle: The Dilemma of the Intellectual in the Old South, 1840–1860* (1977); and Drew Gilpin Faust, *James Henry Hammond and the Old South: A Design for Mastery* (1982). A fresh and highly original reinterpretation of southern society and culture is Bertram Wyatt-Brown, *Southern Honor: Ethics and Behavior in the Old South* (1982). For the evangelical revival in the South, see Anne C. Loveland, *Southern Evangelicals and the Social Order, 1800–1860* (1980). Ira Berlin, *Slaves Without Masters* (1975), is a superb analysis of free blacks in the South. John H. Franklin, *From Slavery to Freedom* (1974), is the best introduction to Afro-American history. George M. Fredrickson, *The Black Image in the White Mind: The Debate on Afro-American Character and Destiny, 1817–1914* (1971), is a brilliant study of racism in America. More specialized works of importance are Eugene H. Berwanger, *The Frontier Against Slavery: Western Anti-Negro Prejudice and the Slavery Extension Controversy* (1967), and William Stanton, *The Leopard's Spots: Scientific Attitudes Toward Race in America, 1815–1859* (1960).

The literature on abolitionism is voluminous. The historical precedents and background are covered in David B. Davis, *The Problem of Slavery in Western Culture* (1966), and *The Problem of Slavery in the Age of Revolution, 1770–1823* (1975). The best brief account of later abolitionism is James B. Stewart, *Holy Warriors: The Abolitionists and American Slavery* (1976). An innovative study of the motivations and inner dynamics of abolitionism is Lawrence J. Friedman, *Gregarious Saints: Self and Community in American Abolitionism, 1830–1870* (1982). Gilbert H. Barnes, *The Anti-Slavery Impulse* (1933), is a dramatic and readable study, emphasizing the role of Theodore Weld and the Lane Seminary rebels. For an opposing and brilliantly argued view, see Aileen S. Kraditor, *Means and Ends in American Abolitionism: Garrison and His Critics on Strategy and Tactics* (1967). A similarly powerful and creative work is Lewis Perry, *Radical Abolitionism: Anarchy and the Government of God in Antislavery Thought* (1973). Robert H. Abzug, *Passionate Liberator: Theodore Dwight Weld and the Dilemma of Reform* (1980), is a probing biography of one of the most fascinating abolitionists. Provocative new approaches can be found in Lewis Perry and Michael Fellman, eds., *Antislavery Reconsidered: New Perspectives on the Abolitionists* (1979). Leonard L. Richards, *"Gentlemen of Property and Standing": Anti-Abolition Mobs in Jacksonian America* (1970), keenly analyzes antiabolition violence. Concerning civil liberties, see Russel B. Nye, *Fettered Freedom: Civil Liberties and the Slavery Controversy* (1963), and Thomas O. Morris, *Free Men All: The Personal Liberty Laws of the North, 1780–1861* (1974).

For the politics of antislavery, see Richard H. Sewell, *Ballots for Freedom* (1976), as well as the following biographical studies: Bertram Wyatt-Brown, *Lewis Tappan and the Evangelical War Against Slavery* (1969); Betty Fladeland, *James Gillespie Birney: Slaveholder to Abolitionist* (1955); James B. Stewart, *Joshua R. Giddings and the Tactics of Radical Politics* (1970); Richard H. Sewell, *John P. Hale and the Politics of Abolition* (1965); Frank O. Gatell, *John Gorham Palfrey and the New England Conscience* (1963); Ralph V. Harlow, *Gerrit Smith* (1939); Edward Magdol, *Owen Lovejoy, Abolitionist in Congress* (1967); and David Donald, *Charles Sumner and the Coming of the Civil War* (1960). William Lloyd Garrison, who tried to abstain from political involvement, is the subject of two fine biographies: John L. Thomas, *The Liberator: William Lloyd Garrison* (1963), and Walter M. Merrill, *Against Wind and Tide: A Biography of William Lloyd Garrison* (1963).

Benjamin Quarles, *Black Abolitionists* (1969), is a pioneering study of a subject long neglected by historians. For the important role played by black American abolitionists who toured and lectured in Britain, see R. J. M. Blackett, *Building an Antislavery Wall: Black Americans in the Atlantic Abolitionist Movement, 1830–1860* (1983). The dilemma of black abolitionists is also illuminated by Jane H. Pease and William H. Pease, *They Who Would Be Free: Blacks' Search for Freedom, 1830–1861* (1974). For Frederick Douglass, see Arna Bontemps, *Free at Last: The Life of Frederick Douglass* (1971), and Douglass, *Life and Times of Frederick Douglass, Written by Himself* (1881).

15 Politics: Cohesion and Division, 1820–1840

The generation of Americans who came to maturity in the early nineteenth century carried a unique burden. As "children of the Founding Fathers," they could not achieve immortal fame by winning independence from British tyranny. Instead, their assigned mission was vigilant preservation—the preservation of what the famous lawyer Rufus Choate called the "beautiful house of our fathers" against divisive ambition, corruption, and arbitrary power.

For a time it seemed that Liberty and Union could be preserved by patriotic rhetoric honoring hallowed figures like Thomas Jefferson and John Adams (who both died on July 4, 1826, exactly fifty years after the adoption of the Declaration of Independence), and by the election of presidents from the so-called Virginia Dynasty. The last in that succession, James Monroe, still appeared in public dressed in his Revolutionary War uniform. After the War of 1812, the collapse of the Federalist party fostered the illusion of an Era of Good Feelings in which a single national party would guarantee republican simplicity, order, and self-restraint. In his second inaugural address in 1821, President Monroe invoked the image of harmony. The American people, he affirmed, constituted "one great family with a common interest." Four years later President John Quincy Adams, also a Republican, voiced similar sentiments and happily observed that "the baneful weed of party strife" had been uprooted. Most Americans still associated political parties with the self-serving, aristocratic factions that had dominated British politics. In a republican nation, as in a republican family, no room could be allowed for selfish alliances representing separate interests.

This ideal of family unity was, however, far removed from social and economic realities. Between 1819 and 1821 Congress faced the most dangerous crisis it had yet experienced when northern and southern representatives deadlocked over the admission of Missouri as a new slave state. Simultaneously, the financial panic of 1819, followed by a severe depression, aroused widespread hostility toward banking corporations and other groups that had used political influence to gain economic privilege. Economic recovery and expansion only intensified demands for equality of opportunity, as various competing classes, localities, and social groups became increasingly aware of the unequal effects of government policies concerning tariffs, banking and currency, and public land sales. By the mid-1820s it was becoming painfully clear that widening opportunities for some Americans meant narrowing opportunities for others. Ironically, the post-Revolutionary generation found a way of containing the many factions that had arisen by *institutionalizing* division in the form of political parties. From the early 1830s to the early 1850s, a two-party system helped preserve national cohesion. The Democrats and the National Republicans—succeeded later by the Whigs—were national coalitions of sectional, class, economic, ethnic, and religious interests, held together by compromise and cooperation. To maximize votes, politicians had to find ways of arousing apathetic citizens on more than immediate local issues. The basic political style that emerged in antebellum America—in the South and West as well as in the North—centered on the portrayal of some self-serving, privileged interest that had secretly consolidated power and had begun to shut off from others equal access to the rewards of national growth. In an era of relative security from foreign dangers, politicians continued to portray their opponents as heirs of the British and Tories who were seeking to undermine American liberties and betray the heritage of the Founding Fathers. The Democrats and Whigs survived as national coalitions as long as they drew significant

GEORGE CALEB BINGHAM'S "VERDICT OF THE PEOPLE"
Politics became the Americans' major public ritual. Like religious revivals, political events provided the occasion for sociability and emotional expression. But politics also evoked the excitement that springs from looking upon or touching the levers of power.

support from both the slaveholding and non-slaveholding states. But when black slavery, the institution that most flagrantly subverted liberty and opportunity, was seriously questioned in a national forum, the unifying force of the parties was destroyed.

"A Fire Bell in the Night": The Missouri Compromise

From the time of the Continental Congress, American leaders had recognized that a serious dispute over slavery could jeopardize their bold experiment in self-government. Beginning with the Constitutional Convention, the entire structure of national politics had been designed to prevent any faction from directly threatening southern slaveholders and thereby subverting common national interests. It is therefore not surprising that before 1819 slavery never became a central issue in national politics. But it was an issue that sat like an unactivated bomb in the minds of the foremost political leaders.

The agreement to keep the bomb unactivated rested on two unwritten understandings: that the North would recognize the property rights of southern slaveholders, and that the South would recognize slavery as an evil that should be discouraged and eventually abolished whenever it became safe and practicable to do so. Changing circumstances, including the shifting balance of sectional power, forced repeated challenges to these understandings. The challenges took the form of clashes in Congress, during which representatives from the Lower South threatened to dissolve the Union and even hinted at the possibility of civil war. On each occasion the resulting compromise strongly favored the South. This political process demonstrated the Americans' remarkable ability to make pragmatic adjustments in the interest of national stability. Yet these successful compromises depended on the dangerous assumption that southern threats of disunion would always be met by northern concessions.

The militancy of the Lower South's congressional

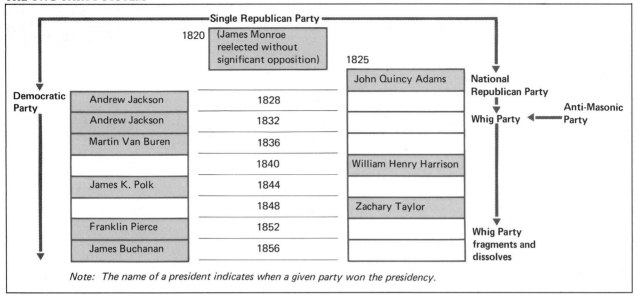

Note: The name of a president indicates when a given party won the presidency.

leaders was based on a realistic estimate of the future. For a time the North could afford to make concessions because slavery seemed to endanger no vital northern interests. But after 1815 humanitarian causes had increasing appeal in the North, and more and more Northerners expressed moral and patriotic misgivings over the westward expansion of slavery. Sooner or later, as Southerners like John Randolph predicted, these northern antislavery sentiments would become strong enough to create new sectional parties. Even by 1820, as a result of rapid population growth in the North, the major slaveholding states held only 42 percent of the seats in the House of Representatives. Only the Senate could provide a firm defense against potential northern encroachments, and the key to the Senate was new slave states. In the Senate, following the admission of Mississippi and Alabama (1817, 1819), eleven slave states balanced eleven free states.

Sectional Conflict. The Missouri crisis erupted in February 1819, when the House was considering a bill that would enable the people of Missouri to draft a constitution and be admitted as a slave state. Slaves constituted nearly one-sixth of the territory's population. James Tallmadge, Jr., a New York Jeffersonian Republican, offered an amendment that prohibited the further introduction of slaves into Missouri and provided for the emancipation, at age twenty-five, of all children of slaves born after Missouri's admission as a state. After a prolonged and often violent debate, the House approved Tallmadge's amendment by an ominously sectional vote. The Senate, after equally violent debates, passed a Missouri statehood bill without any restrictions on slavery. The issue seemed hopelessly deadlocked.

Virginia now took the lead in militancy, trying to arouse a generally apathetic South to a common peril. "This momentous question," Jefferson announced from Monticello, where he had retired, "like a fire bell in the night, awakened and filled me with terror." Along with Madison and other Virginia statesmen, Jefferson was convinced that the attempt to exclude slavery from Missouri was part of a Federalist conspiracy to create a sectional party and destroy the Union.

The Missouri crisis was aggravated by a sense that understandings had been broken, veils torn off, and true and threatening motives exposed. The congressional debates rekindled the most divisive issues that supposedly had been settled in the Constitutional Convention, and thus raised the hypothetical question of disunion. This reenactment of 1787 was underscored by the prominence in the congressional debates of two of the Constitutional Convention's surviving antagonists—Charles Pinckney of South Carolina, who now insisted that Congress had no power to exclude slavery from even the unsettled territories; and Rufus King of New York, the alleged leader of the Federalist conspiracy, who now announced that any laws upholding slavery were "absolutely void, because [they are] contrary to the law of nature, which is the law of God."

It was a new generation of Northerners, however, who had to reaffirm or reject the kind of compromises over slavery that had created the original Union. Like the Founders, the northern majority in Congress could

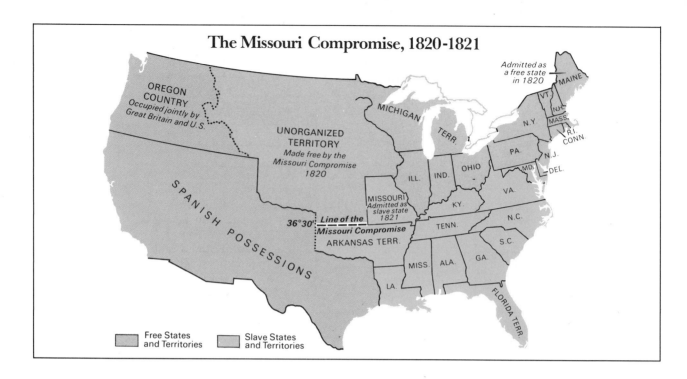

The Missouri Compromise, 1820-1821

OREGON COUNTRY
Occupied jointly by Great Britain and U.S.

SPANISH POSSESSIONS

UNORGANIZED TERRITORY
Made free by the Missouri Compromise 1820

36°30' — Line of the Missouri Compromise

ARKANSAS TERR.

MISSOURI
Admitted as slave state 1821

Admitted as a free state in 1820 — MAINE

MICHIGAN TERR.

VT. N.H. N.Y. MASS. R.I. CONN.

PA. N.J.

ILL. IND. OHIO MD. DEL.

VA.

KY.

TENN. N.C.

S.C.

MISS. ALA. GA.

LA.

FLORIDA TERR.

Free States and Territories   Slave States and Territories

do nothing about slavery in the existing states. But there had been an understood national policy, these Northerners believed, enshrined in the Northwest Ordinance, committing the government to restrict slavery in every feasible way. This understanding had seemingly been confirmed by southern statements that slavery was an evil inherited from the past. The North had accepted the original slave states' expectations that migrating slaveholders would not be barred from bringing their most valuable property— their slaves—into the territories south of the Ohio River and east of the Mississippi River. But Missouri occupied the same latitudes as Illinois, Indiana, and Ohio (as well as Kentucky and Virginia). To allow slavery to become legally entrenched in Missouri might thus encourage its spread throughout the entire West, harming free labor and industry. Southerners had long argued, however illogically, that if slavery were diffused over a large geographical area, it would weaken as an institution, and the likelihood of slave uprisings would diminish. In 1820 Daniel Raymond, a prominent northern political economist, gave the obvious reply: "Diffusion is about as effectual a remedy for slavery as it would be for the smallpox, or the plague."

Southerners were particularly alarmed by the argument of northern congressmen that the constitutional guarantee to every state of "a Republican Form of Government" meant that Missouri could not be admitted as a slave state. The argument implied that Virginia and other southern states fell short of having "a Republican Form of Government" and therefore would not be admissible to a new Union. If this argument prevailed, the southern states would be reduced to a second-class status. If they accepted the northern definition of a republican form of government, they had no choice but to take steps toward abolishing slavery or to face, like colonies, the punitive measures of an imperial authority.

The Terms of Compromise. Henry Clay, the Speaker of the House of Representatives, exerted all the powers of his office and of his magnetic personality in order finally to achieve a compromise. A small minority of northern congressmen agreed to drop the antislavery provision for Missouri, while a small minority of Southerners agreed that slavery should be excluded from the remaining and unsettled portions of the Louisiana Purchase north of latitude 36°30', the same latitude as the southern border of Missouri. In effect, this measure limited any further expansion of slavery within the Louisiana Purchase to Arkansas and what would later become Oklahoma. Given the sectional balance of power, the swing vote favoring these concessions was sufficient to carry the compromise. The way was now opened for admitting Maine as a free state, since the Senate had refused to accept Maine's statehood until the House had abandoned efforts to restrict slavery in Missouri.

The press and legislatures of the North generally

interpreted the Missouri Compromise as a victory for the South. A new hope arose that public pressure could force Missouri to adopt a constitution providing for gradual emancipation. But the defiant Missourians drafted a constitution that prohibited the state legislature from emancipating slaves without the consent of their owners and that barred free blacks and mulattoes from entering the state. Since free blacks had been recognized as citizens by some of the eastern states, this second provision violated the constitutional guarantee that "the Citizens of each State shall be entitled to all Privileges and Immunities of Citizens in the several States." Northern congressmen now stood firm in rejecting the Missouri constitution and in effect the entire compromise. Eventually, in 1821, Clay's skillful manipulation of committees produced a second compromise prohibiting Missouri from discriminating against the citizens of other states—an abstract resolution that still left citizenship undefined. The country applauded Clay for saving the Union.

But the Union would never be the same. In southern eyes the uninhibited debates on slavery had opened a Pandora's box of dangers. The free blacks of Washington had packed the galleries of the House and had listened intently to antislavery speeches. In 1822, during the trial of the conspirators associated with Denmark Vesey, a Charleston slave testified that Vesey had shown him an antislavery speech delivered by Rufus King, "the black man's friend." The link between the Missouri debates and a sizable slavery conspiracy stunned South Carolina, confirming its worst fears. The cumulative effect was twofold: to unite all whites in the suppression of dangerous discussion, and to strengthen the hand of states' rights extremists and of the defenders of slavery as a positive good.

The End of Republican Unity

The Missouri crisis alerted politicians to the perils of sectional division. The North's unexpected outrage over the admission of a new slave state convinced many Southerners that they needed to cultivate rising northern leaders. One such leader was Martin Van Buren, whose faction of young "Bucktails" had captured control of the New York Republican party by 1820. Van Buren, whose shrewdness, ambition, and personal charm made up for his lack of family prestige and connections, viewed the clamor over slavery as evidence of a dangerous breakdown in party loyalty. New national organizations were needed that could prevent sectional conflict. Party distinctions, he said, were infinitely safer than geographical ones. If party distinctions were suppressed, their place would inevitably be taken by "geographical differences founded

on local instincts or what is worse, prejudices between free and slaveholding states."

The Van Buren faction also stated a new conception of political parties as agencies of the people. When the Bucktails were attacked by their opponents as the Albany Regency, a label suggesting the oppressive British regency of the Prince of Wales (1811–20) that had governed in place of the insane George III, Van Buren's faction replied with a strong defense of political parties—a defense that later Democrats and Whigs would echo. In America, Van Buren's followers claimed, political parties drew their power from the people instead of from kings or aristocratic cliques; therefore, the American people could safely extend their loyalty to parties. American parties, far from being self-serving, required a selfless submission to the will of the organization. This respect for party discipline was later summed up by a prominent Whig who declared that he "would vote for a dog, if he was the candidate of my party." In theory, the excesses of one party would inevitably be exposed by the other party, and public opinion would decide between them. Responsiveness to the people would thus be ensured as each party strove to win the largest possible mandate from the people.

Van Buren's appeal for disciplined national parties came at the right moment. As early as 1821 it was evident that the Virginia Dynasty of presidents would end in 1825 with Monroe's second term. The Republicans, no longer confronted by Federalist opponents, were splitting into personal and sectional factions. One group responded to the vibrant nationalism of Henry Clay's so-called American System—a policy for economic expansion based on protective tariffs, a national bank, and federal aid for internal improvements. But other "Old Republicans," including Van Buren, viewed government intervention in the economy in terms of the old "country opposition" ideology—as a revival of the kinds of alliances between political power and special privilege that had corrupted Britain. By the early 1820s many Americans, especially in the South and West, had ample grounds for fearing that a northeastern elite would gain economic control of the nation's banks and system of credit.

Election of 1824. Monroe's second administration was dominated by political maneuvering to determine who would be his successor. Three of the leading contenders—William H. Crawford, John Quincy Adams, and John C. Calhoun—were nationally distinguished members of Monroe's cabinet. A Georgian born in Virginia, Crawford was secretary of the treasury during several administrations and had won prestige as America's minister to France during the

War of 1812. He was an advocate of states' rights and limited federal power, was supported by the aged Thomas Jefferson and other influential Virginians, and would be heavily favored in any congressional party caucus. Van Buren led the Crawford forces in Congress. But the skeleton congressional caucus that nominated Crawford carried little weight, and an incapacitating illness further diminished his chances.

The other leading candidates bypassed the established procedure of nomination by congressional party caucus and sought support from state legislatures. Three of the remaining aspirants were closely associated with the economic nationalism that had alienated the Old Republicans. John Quincy Adams, the secretary of state and the nation's most experienced diplomat, could easily expect solid support from his native New England but would always be aloof from the rough-and-tumble campaigning of the South and West. John C. Calhoun, the secretary of war, had little support outside his own state, South Carolina. A graduate of Yale and a product of America's first small law school, Calhoun was one of the few political leaders of his time who could be described as an intellectual. He withdrew from the presidential race before the election, assuming that his almost certain choice as vice-president would help him win the highest office in 1828. Henry Clay, the popular "Harry of the West," had won national prestige as a parliamentarian and engineer of compromise in the House of Representatives.

The fifth candidate, Andrew Jackson, entered the contest unexpectedly and at a later stage. Unlike the other candidates, he had taken no clear stand on the controversial issues of the day, and his brief terms in the House and Senate had been undistinguished. Jackson's national fame arose from his victory over the British at the Battle of New Orleans in the War of 1812, as well as from his unswerving efforts to clear the West of Indians, thus promising unlimited opportunities for white Americans. But "Old Hickory," as Jackson was widely known, was a good bit more than a military hero and an Indian fighter. Born on the Carolina frontier and orphaned at age fourteen, Jackson had studied law and had finally emigrated to Nashville, Tennessee, where he became attached by marriage and business connections to the local network of leading families. He prospered as an attorney, land speculator, and planter, and became the master of more than one hundred slaves. The Tennessee leaders who originally promoted Jackson for the presidency did not take his candidacy seriously, hoping only to use his popularity for their own local purposes. But in 1823 Jackson's backers were astonished when the movement caught fire in Pennsylvania and other states. The Old Hero, as he was called, turned out to be

HENRY CLAY

Henry Clay's campaign posters stressed national economic growth and public welfare, goals to be directly fostered by protective tariffs and a national bank.

an astute politician who perfectly gauged the national temper and who, once launched on the road to the presidency, skillfully managed his own campaign.

Jackson won a plurality of both the popular and the electoral votes in the election of 1824, and therefore he could legitimately claim to be the choice of the people. But because no candidate had won an electoral majority, the responsibility of electing a president fell to the House of Representatives. It had been expected that if no candidate should win the electoral majority,

J. Q. ADAMS, BY THOMAS GIMBREDE
John Quincy Adams personified the intellectual as statesman. A man of learning and of wide diplomatic experience, he was more at home in the courts and capitals of Europe than in the caucuses and public forums of American politics.

the House would elect Clay. But despite his appeal in Kentucky and other western states, Clay had run fourth in electoral votes and was therefore excluded by the Twelfth Amendment from further consideration. Clay threw his decisive support behind Adams, who was elected president and who soon appointed Clay secretary of state. This so-called corrupt bargain deeply embittered Calhoun, who was already beginning to defect from his former colleagues' economic nationalism. It also infuriated Jackson, who almost immediately launched a campaign to unseat Adams in 1828.

John Quincy Adams as President.

This final collapse of Republican unity proved to be a disaster for Adams's presidency. Adams inaugurated his administration by proposing a sweeping program of federal support for internal improvements, science, education, and the arts. For example, he hoped that Congress would subsidize western explorations and an astronomical observatory. He soon discovered, however, that he lacked the mandate and the power for even the simple tasks of government. One of the most intelligent and farseeing presidents, Adams was also one of the least successful. Unfairly accused of being a monarchist with an arrogant contempt for the people, he had the misfortune of inheriting the presidency when it had fallen into decay. His own inexperience with the realities of American political life helped to make him the unmourned victim, in 1828, of the first modern presidential contest.

Jackson's Rise to Power

Andrew Jackson, the leader of the rising Democratic coalition, precisely fitted the need for a popular national political leader. His stately bearing and natural dignity befitted one of "nature's noblemen," someone who had risen to greatness without benefit of family connections, formal education, or subservience to any faction. Jackson's promoters spread the romantic mythology by every conceivable means: ballads, placards, barbecues, liberty pole raisings, local committees, and militia companies. In contrast to the office-grubbing politicians and to the coldly dignified, highly cultivated John Quincy Adams, here was a frontiersman, a truly self-made man, a soldier of iron will who personified the will of the people, a man without disguises or pretension who moved decisively in the light of simple moral truths. The Jackson image, in short, was an image of reassuring stability in the face of bewildering social and economic change.

Jackson also fitted the need for a leader who understood the new meaning of party politics. Against the Adams-Clay alliance, he molded a coalition that included among other groups the followers of Calhoun (who became his running mate in 1828), Virginia's Old Republicans, influential Westerners who had become disillusioned with Clay, former Federalists who had lost office in New Jersey, and Van Buren's powerful Albany Regency. This new Democratic party appealed to many urban workers and immigrants, to frontier expansionists and Indian haters, to many southern planters, and to various northeastern editors, bankers, and manufacturers who built local Democratic machines as the means of gaining or preserving power.

The "Tariff of Abominations."

Looking ahead to the election of 1828, Jackson's state organizers bypassed the local ruling gentry and concentrated for the first time on mobilizing the necessary popular vote to capture the full electoral vote of critical states. Because the new coalition contained Pennsylvanians who clamored for higher tariffs and South Carolinians who detested tariffs, keeping unity required delicate manipu-

The Election of 1828

ELECTORAL POPULAR
Jackson (Dem.) 178 647,286
Adams (Nat.Rep.) 83 508,064

5 6 Divided

JACKSON POSTER, 1828

In the presidential campaign of 1828, Andrew Jackson appeared as a symbol of patriotism, military honor, and faithful preservation of the ideals of the Founding Fathers.

lation. In 1828 Jackson's leaders in Congress helped to pass the so-called Tariff of Abominations, an opportunistic bill that made arbitrary concessions to various groups that were demanding protection. These leaders assumed that southern support for Jackson was secure, that the new duties on raw materials would win votes from northern and western protectionists, and that the most objectionable provisions could be blamed on the Adams administration. The subsequent outrage in the South suggested that Jackson as president could no longer get by with vague statements favoring a "judicious" tariff. Yet Southerners knew that a Jackson-Calhoun alliance was far more promising than the economic nationalism of Adams and Clay, who were now known as National Republicans.

The Election of 1828. In a general sense the election of 1828 affirmed the people's rejection of policies that seemed to encourage special privilege, except for the privilege of owning slaves and counting three-fifths of the slave population for purposes of representation. In

the South, Jackson's 200,000 supporters, accounting for 73 percent of that section's vote, gave him 105 electoral votes; in the North, where he won only slightly more than half the popular vote, his 400,000 supporters gave him only 73 electoral votes. The election also proved the effectiveness of campaign organization and of the promotional techniques that Jackson's managers, particularly Van Buren, had perfected.

Once in power the Democrats soon adopted two instruments that solidified popular support for party rule. The first was a system of patronage, called the spoils system, that continued practices begun during previous administrations and tried to give them legitimacy. Jackson ardently defended the theory that most public offices required no special abilities or experience, that they should frequently rotate among loyal deserving party workers, and that party rule should prevent the establishment of a permanent and parasitic class of civil servants. In fact, however, Jackson actually removed no more than one-fifth of the surviving federal officeholders.

The second mechanism was the national party convention. This, like various other Jacksonian measures, had earlier been initiated by anti-Jackson forces. As an alternative to nomination by legislative caucus, the "convention" suggested by its very name a return to fundamental law—to the direct voice of the people assembled in a constitution-making body. Although party conventions could do no more than frame partisan platforms and nominate partisan candidates, they pretended to represent the true interests of the people. In theory, since they drew representatives from a broad spectrum of society, they were more democratic than legislative caucuses. In practice, they were more subject to manipulation by political machines. But like the partisan spoils system, the party convention symbolized the central appeal of Jackson's party. It promised to break the rigid crust of privilege and eliminate all institutional barriers to individual opportunity. It also provided the assurance of solidarity with a party headed by a man of the people, a man who magnified the idealized self-image of millions of Americans.

Certain principles and aspirations distinguished the Jacksonian Democrats from their National Republican (and later Whig) opponents. Jackson had long given voice to the West's demand for territorial expansion as a way to ensure economic opportunity. As the first Westerner elected to the presidency, he symbolized a geographical shift of political power. Of course, not all Westerners supported Jackson. Those who understood that western economic expansion depended on access to eastern markets and on investment capital from the East and Europe favored federal aid for internal improvements, a program that Henry Clay sponsored. But although Jackson vetoed the Maysville Road Bill (which would have authorized funds to build a road in Kentucky), suggesting that federal support for internal improvements was unconstitutional, he did not lose the majority of western voters. Many Westerners had come to view federally supported internal improvements as sources of waste and corruption. Others learned that, despite Jackson's pronouncements, federal support for roads and canals continued to pour in from a Congress that was less concerned with constitutional theory than with constituents' needs. On the whole, the West cheered for Jackson because it had come to see itself as the home of the values that Jackson fought for: a rural society of independent farmers, committed to individual enterprise and local self-determination.

To say that Jacksonian Democrats were advocates of laissez-faire policies is accurate but insufficient.*

Laissez-faire means the government's refusal to intervene in private economic matters.

Museum of the City of New York

ANDREW JACKSON

In this carving President Jackson appears as a stern, rough-hewn man of the people, a democratized Washington.

They knew that on the local and state levels, economic opportunity hinged on political power. And Jackson was the most forceful and aggressive president since Washington. During the preceding administrations the chief executive's powers had been siphoned off by cabinet rivals and a jealous Congress. With the aid of party discipline, Jackson soon exerted his dominance over Congress by an unprecedented use of vetoes and pocket vetoes (the refusal to sign a bill during the last ten days of a congressional session). Except for Van Buren, whom he chose as secretary of state, Jackson treated his cabinet in the manner of the army's commander in chief. Unlike his predecessors, Jackson escaped the coercion of disloyal and powerful cabinet members by relying on a group of informal advisers, the so-called Kitchen Cabinet, who could be trusted or dismissed at will.

The Threat of National Division: Tariffs, Nullification, and the Gag Rule

Protective Tariffs. Tariffs and fiscal policy were obvious testing grounds for defining the federal government's role in national economic life. The economy was still more regional than national, and the national government had few functions. The critical issues of the day therefore grew out of the commitment to protective tariffs and a national bank that had resulted from the War of 1812. The Middle Atlantic states, which were the most vulnerable to competition from European manufactured goods, had long been the political stronghold of protectionism. During the 1820s, as New England's economy became increasingly dependent on the production of wool and on textile manufacturing, Daniel Webster and other New England leaders abandoned their traditional defense of free trade and portrayed protective tariffs as the key to economic growth and individual opportunity. Simultaneously, however, the Lower South became increasingly hostile to tariffs that threatened to raise the price of manufactured goods and to curtail foreign markets for rice and cotton exports. For a time the Democrats successfully arranged compromises among the various interests and regions that were represented in the party. But in 1832 Congress passed a tariff bill that was unresponsive to the demands of the Lower South. South Carolina thereupon defied federal authority and sought to arouse the rest of the slaveholding South to the dangers of being victimized economically by the federal government. South Carolinians believed that acceptance of this dependence would reduce their state to the status of a colony and deprive it of any effective protection against antislavery ideas.

South Carolina's sudden threat of disunion severely tested the American political system, and it involved issues that went far beyond the protective tariff. In no other state had a planter elite succeeded so well in commanding the allegiance of small farmers, both slaveholding and nonslaveholding, and in preventing the development of an effective two-party system. Despite continuing conflicts between the coastal and upcountry regions, there were few checks on states' rights extremists who were able to exploit fears of a slave uprising and anger over persisting agricultural depression, high consumer prices, and sagging prices for rice and cotton in foreign markets.

Moreover, of all the southern states South Carolina had the closest historical, geographical, and cultural ties with the British West Indies. Like those British colonies, South Carolina had a dense concentration of slaves, and its merchants and plantation owners had continued to import African slaves until 1808, when the Atlantic slave trade was forbidden by federal law. South Carolinians were acutely aware that in Britain a seemingly harmless movement to end the slave trade had been transformed, by 1823, into a crusade for slave emancipation. And they knew that the West Indians, although still a powerful faction in Parliament, had found no way of countering commercial policies that had hastened their economic decline. The lesson was clear. The West Indian colonies had once been far richer and more valued than Canada or New England. But in 1832 they faced possible devastation—a massive slave revolt had broken out in Jamaica after Christmas 1831—and certain economic ruin.

Theory of Nullification. South Carolina's leaders believed that their state could escape a similar fate only by reasserting state sovereignty and insisting on the strict limitation of national power. The tariff issue made an ideal testing ground for the defense of slavery without risking the explosive effects of debating the morality of slaveholding. Because the power to tax and regulate trade could also be used to undermine slavery, the two questions had been linked in the Constitutional Convention of 1787 and in the Missouri debates. Conversely, a state's power to nullify a tariff would be a guarantee not only against economic exploitation but also against direct or indirect interference with slavery. Calhoun anonymously wrote the South Carolina *Exposition* on behalf of that state, refining the theoretical arguments that were being put forward by South Carolina's most militant leaders. According to Calhoun, in any dispute between federal and state interests the ultimate appeal must be directed to a state convention—the same body that had originally enabled the state to ratify the Constitution. Otherwise, a national majority, controlling the federal courts as well as Congress, would have unlimited power. The tyranny of the majority could be curbed only if each state retained the right to either accept or nullify, within its own jurisdiction, the national

JOHN C. CALHOUN (1782–1850)

majority's decisions. Calhoun carefully distinguished nullification from secession. He looked for means by which states might exercise an authentic, although limited, sovereignty while remaining within the Union.

The nullification controversy was complicated by the shifting pressures of state, sectional, and national politics. Calhoun, the vice-president, hoped to succeed Jackson as president, and many South Carolinians still believed they could achieve their goals through the Democratic party. Calhoun did not disclose his authorship of the *Exposition* until 1831, when he had split with Jackson over various personal and political issues. When Jackson purged Calhoun's followers from his cabinet and administration, Van Buren became in effect the president's chosen successor. Nevertheless, Calhoun continued to aspire to the presidency. He believed that nullification would be a means of satisfying South Carolina's "fire-eater" extremists and of establishing the Union on a more secure basis, while still preserving his own national following.

By 1832, however, South Carolina had become increasingly isolated from the rest of the South and had also failed to unite the West against an alleged northeastern conspiracy to discourage western settlement. Although many Southerners detested protective tariffs and maintained that states had a right to secede from the Union, southern legislatures turned a stony face to nullification. As a result, there was no regional convention of southern delegates that might have moderated South Carolina's suicidal course by reinforcing the hand of the South Carolina unionists who risked their lives and reputations in a violent and losing struggle with the extremists. In the fall of 1832, South Carolina held a state convention that directly challenged federal authority by making it unlawful after February 1, 1833, to collect tariff duties within the state.

South Carolina chose the wrong president to test. Andrew Jackson was a wealthy slaveholder, but he was also a shrewd politician. Although his maturing views on tariffs and internal improvements were close to those of the South Carolina elite, he had fought for the military supremacy of the United States, crushing British and Indian armies; he had hanged English meddlers in Spanish Florida; and he had ordered the execution of an unruly teen-age soldier. He was probably the toughest of America's presidents. When South Carolina nullified the tariff of 1832, the old general privately threatened to lead an invasion of the state and have Calhoun hanged. He sent reinforcements to the federal forts in Charleston harbor but publicly sought to avoid armed conflict by relying on civilian revenue agents to enforce the law and by warning that armed resistance would be punished as treason.

As in 1820, the crisis ended in a compromise that failed to resolve fundamental conflicts of interest and ideology. In an attempt to head off civil war, Henry Clay, assisted by Calhoun, secured the passage of a compromise bill that would gradually reduce tariff duties over a period of nine years. But this measure was accompanied by a "force bill," reaffirming the president's authority to use the army and navy, when necessary, to enforce federal laws. South Carolina's fire-eaters continued to call for armed resistance; the governor himself recruited a volunteer army. Early in 1833, however, the state convention repealed its earlier nullification of the tariff and, to save face, nullified the force bill. Jackson ignored this defiant gesture. He had already branded as unlawful and unconstitutional the claim that any state could annul the laws of the United States. In effect he had told rebellious states that secession was their only escape, and that secession would be met with armed force.

"Gag Rules." The compromise did not relieve South Carolina's suspicions and anxieties. The nullification controversy had failed to provide the assurance of constitutional safeguards against a hostile national ma-

"THE DOWNFALL OF MOTHER BANK"
In this popular cartoon Jackson's removal of federal deposits from the Bank of the United States carries overtones of Christ's chasing the moneylenders from the ancient temple. Biddle, in the form of the devil, flees along with Webster, Clay, and the various minions of the Money Power.

jority. Southern extremists demanded ironclad guarantees that would permanently bar the abolitionists' "incendiary publications" from the mails and prevent Congress from receiving petitions calling for the abolition of slavery in the District of Columbia. In actuality, the Democratic party fulfilled these objectives in a less formal way. The Jackson and Van Buren administrations, dependent on the large Democratic vote in the South, encouraged federal postmasters to stop abolitionist literature at its point of origin. Despite continuing protest from northern Whigs, northern Democrats also provided southern congressmen of both parties with enough votes to maintain "gag rules" from 1836 to 1844, a procedure that automatically tabled abolitionist petitions in Congress and helped prevent explosive debates on the subject of slavery. Many Northerners were outraged by these infringements on civil and political liberties. But South Carolinians were also dissatisfied with pragmatic mechanisms for security that depended on the continuing support of the national Democratic party.

Without further constitutional protections, they feared that a shift in northern opinion might induce Congress to withdraw all federal sanction and protection of slavery.

The Bank War, the Panic of 1837, and Political Realignments

The Bank War. Meanwhile, President Jackson had extended his national popularity by declaring "war" on the Second Bank of the United States (BUS). Jackson had long harbored a mistrust of banks in general, especially of the BUS. Van Buren, Senator Thomas Hart Benton of Missouri, Amos Kendall of the Kitchen Cabinet, and other key presidential advisers shared these sentiments. To understand their "hard-money" position, it is important to realize that the national government issued no "paper money" like that in circulation today. Payment for goods and services might be in gold or silver coin (specie) or, more likely, in paper notes issued by private commercial banks. The value of this paper currency fluctuated greatly. The hard-money Democrats realized that large commercial transactions could not be carried on with specie. But they believed that the common people, including small businessmen as well as farmers and wage earners, should not be saddled with the risk of being cheated by a speculative currency. They also knew that a policy favoring the greater circulation of gold and silver coin, which seemed magically endowed with some fixed and "natural" value, would win votes for the party.

To a large degree, however, the reserves and transfers of specie were controlled by the BUS. The BUS performed many of the functions of a truly national bank. Its own notes could be exchanged for specie, and they were accepted by the government as legal payment for all debts to the United States. The BUS had large capital reserves and it limited the issue of its own highly stable notes. It was therefore a creditor to the hundreds of state-chartered banks throughout the country. It also served as a clearinghouse and regulatory agency for their money, refusing to accept notes that were not backed by sufficient reserves of specie. By promoting monetary stability, the BUS helped to improve the public reputation of banks in general and eased the difficulties of long-distance transfers of goods and credit. Moreover, it mobilized a national reserve of capital on which other banks could draw. Consequently most state banks favored congressional renewal of the BUS charter, which was scheduled to expire in 1836.

Opponents of the bank feared the concentration of so much economic power in a few hands and worried that the federal government had practically no control over the bank, although it provided one-fifth of the bank's capital. The bank's critics complained that, even under the expert management of the bank's president, Nicholas Biddle, this partly public institution was far more oriented to the interests of its private investors than to the interests of the general public. Senator Daniel Webster, the main lobbyist for rechartering the BUS, not only was the director of the Boston branch but also relied heavily on Biddle for private loans and fees for legal and political services. To Jackson the BUS had become a "monster institution," unconstitutionally diverting public funds for private profit.

The famous "Bank War" erupted into open conflict in 1832, when Webster and Clay launched a legislative offensive, partly to prevent Jackson's reelection. They knew that they could win support from many Democrats for the passage of a bill rechartering the BUS. Therefore, they were confident that the president could not veto the measure without fatally damaging his chances for reelection in the fall. But Jackson took up their challenge. In a masterful veto message he spelled out the principles that would be the basis for "Jacksonian democracy" and for populist politics in the decades to come. Jackson denounced the BUS as a privileged monopoly, and he vowed to take a stand "against all new grants of monopolies and exclusive privileges, against any prostitution of our Government to the advancement of the few at the expense of the many." Jackson in no way favored equalizing wealth or otherwise removing distinctions derived from "natural and just advantages." He insisted that "equality of talents, of education, or of wealth cannot be produced by human institutions." But he believed that government should provide "equal protection, and, as heaven does its rains, shower its favors alike on the high and the low, the rich and the poor." The BUS, he declared, represented a flagrant example of government subsidy to the privileged—of laws that made "the rich richer and the potent more powerful." Jackson also warned of the dangerous provisions that allowed foreigners to buy BUS stock and thus to acquire influence over American policy. In defiance of the Supreme Court's decision in *McCulloch* v. *Maryland* (1819), the president argued that the BUS was unconstitutional.

Webster and other conservative leaders immediately cried that the president was trying "to stir up the poor against the rich." But the election of 1832 decisively vindicated Jackson's bold leadership and political shrewdness. Old Hickory would have won a sweeping victory even if the opposition votes had not been divided between Henry Clay, the National Republican candidate, and William Wirt, the reluctant leader of the Anti-Masons, a party based on the widespread fear that free institutions were endangered by the secret society of Freemasons. Having been reelected, Jackson was confident that the supporters of the BUS could never override his veto. He vowed to pull out the fangs of the "monster institution" by removing all of the deposits placed in the bank by the federal government.

Many of the president's advisers opposed this aggressive policy, since the BUS already seemed doomed. The removal policy also raised new problems. According to Jackson's plan, which his secretary of the treasury, Roger B. Taney, soon put into operation, federal funds would be dispersed among chosen state-chartered banks that were soon dubbed "pet" banks. For the policy to succeed, Jackson had to persuade the banking community that decentralization would not bring economic disaster. On the other hand, the BUS's president, Nicholas Biddle, needed to produce a minor financial panic to underscore the powerful role of the BUS in maintaining financial stability.

"THE TIMES"

This complex cartoon portrays the allegedly disastrous results of the Democratic rule: the government's hard money policy leads to a run on the bank, which has suspended specie payments; the custom house is deserted; debtors are herded into the sheriff's office; beggars and unemployed artisans crowd the streets; scenes of drunkenness are linked with the unruliness of immigrants and Locofoco radicals.

Biddle could not exert his full financial powers, however, without adding to popular hostility to the bank. In the winter of 1832–33 Biddle instituted a tight-money policy, but the limitation on credit was not serious enough to shake Jackson's resolution. Jackson also gained political leverage through his careful choice of pet banks to which federal funds were to be transferred. Many bankers who had earlier hoped to keep clear of the political struggle were eager to receive interest-free federal funds that would enable them to expand their loans and other commercial operations. Jackson's victory was fairly complete by the spring of 1834.

Jackson's Hard-Money Policy.

Like many triumphs, the destruction of the BUS caught the victors in a web of problems. The Democrats claimed that by slaying the "monster," they had purged the nation of a moral evil. Yet the deposit of federal funds in pet banks encouraged the expansion of credit, and in the mid-1830s the nation reeled from the intoxication of a speculative boom. The federal surplus grew—an unimaginable phenomenon for twentieth-century generations, who have known only federal deficits and mounting public debts. Some of the more obstinate Jacksonian advisers even bemoaned this surplus because there seemed to be no place to put the funds that would not corrupt the Republic. Whatever the administration did invited trouble. On the one hand, if it distributed funds to the states, it would feed the speculative boom by encouraging further construction of roads and canals and other kinds of "improvements." On the other hand, if it kept the funds in the pet banks, these banks clearly had to be regulated by the federal government: otherwise they too might feed inflation by issuing vast quantities of paper money based on the new reserves of federal funds they had received.

Slowly Jackson and his successor, Van Buren, who was elected in 1836, moved toward a policy of hard money. They tried to reduce or eliminate the circulation of small-denomination bank notes and to set a minimal requirement for the pet banks' specie reserves. In 1836 Jackson also issued an executive order, the so-called specie circular, requiring payment in specie for purchase of public land. The specie circular represented a direct federal effort to curb speculation and thus to control economic fluctuations. This controversial measure was a sign of the growing dominance of the antibank and hard-money factions in the Democratic party. The subsequent nomination and election of Van Buren strengthened the hand of those Democrats who found hostility to all banks politically effective.

The Panic of 1837.

In 1837 a banking panic brought an abrupt end to the speculative boom. By 1839 a severe depression had developed that persisted to the mid-1840s. This painful downturn in investment, prices, and employment was primarily the product of a business cycle still tied to agriculture (mainly cotton) and related to British demand, British investment, and the international flow of silver. In many respects the American economy still resembled the economy of a colony or underdeveloped nation dependent on foreign investment and on raw material exports. Hence the American economy was vulnerable to sudden contractions of British credit coupled with temporary drops in the British demand for cotton.

As bankruptcies multiplied, the business community blamed the widespread suffering on Jacksonian fiscal policies. These policies, they charged, had first fueled reckless expansion by destroying the BUS and then had suddenly limited credit by requiring specie for the purchase of public land. But as bankers and businessmen deserted the Democratic party, the dominant hard-money, laissez-faire faction argued that the economic collapse proved the folly of government partnership with even pet banks.

After three years of bitter Democratic-Whig struggle, President Van Buren finally achieved a "divorce of bank and state" with the passage of the Independent Treasury Act (1840). But this measure probably prolonged the depression. It locked federal funds into "independent" subtreasuries of the United States government that were insulated from the banking community, thereby depriving the banking system of reserves that might have encouraged loans and aided economic recovery.

Laissez-Faire Capitalism.

The Democrats' program can be illuminated by pointing to two inconsistencies. First, their economic policies did little to aid the groups of farmers and artisans whom the Democrats claimed to represent. Although the political attacks on privilege may have revitalized democratic ideology, the ultimate beneficiaries were southern planters who were aided by Indian removal, lowered tariffs, and the suppression of antislavery literature and petitions. Moreover, the policy of economic laissez-faire seemed to offer the South assurances that the federal government would not interfere with the interstate movement of slave labor. By 1838 Calhoun and his followers returned to the Democratic party, which they had earlier left. As it turned out, Calhoun's return paved the way for southern domination of the Democratic party in the two decades to come.

Second, the nation's banking system continued to grow into an integrated system, and the nation's economy continued to grow with serene disregard for the fluctuation of power between the Democrats and Whigs. Jackson's and Van Buren's attempts to withdraw the government from what they saw as a corrupting economy had little effect on the general trends of economic development.

Whigs and the Two-Party System

The Democrats controlled the White House for most of the thirty years following Jackson's 1828 victory. Between 1828 and 1856 their presidential nominees defeated every opposition candidate except William Henry Harrison in 1840 and Zachary Taylor in 1848, both of whom died in office. John Tyler, the vice-president who succeeded Harrison only a month after the latter's inauguration, soon returned to his original Virginia Democratic loyalties and principles. Millard Fillmore, Zachary Taylor's successor, was a genial but colorless Whig party hack who had begun his political career as an Anti-Mason and ended it by running for president in 1856 on the nativist and anti-Catholic "Know-Nothing" (or American) party ticket.

But the Democrats' dominance of the presidency is deceptive. By the late 1830s Whigs could match Democratic strength in most parts of the country. Although the South has commonly been pictured as a preserve for states' rights Democrats, Whigs predominated as the South's representatives in three out of five Congresses elected between 1832 and 1842. Whig strength was particularly evident on local, county, and state levels. The viability of the two-party system depended essentially on vigorous local conflict—on the ability of a second party to challenge incumbents by convincing voters that a genuine alternative was available. To maintain party loyalties, leaders tried to exploit or manufacture conflicts, to dramatize party differences, and to be responsive enough to public demands to convince voters that their grievances could be resolved through the ballot. The Whigs, like the Democrats, claimed to represent the interests of the *excluded* people against a privileged and self-serving "power." Since no incumbent party could possibly avoid patronage, the game of two-party politics con-

DANIEL WEBSTER (1782–1852)

sisted of proving that the incumbents were partial to their friends and thus insincere in claiming to serve the common good. In effect, both parties were torn between a desire to battle for the special interests of their permanent followers and a need to advocate bland, lofty goals that would attract the widest possible national following.

Webster, Clay, and Calhoun.

Like the Democrats, the Whigs were a wholly new coalition. They were not, as the Democrats charged, simply Federalists in disguise— the Democrats themselves recruited an impressive number of ex-Federalist leaders. In Congress the Whigs first began to emerge in a legislative rebellion against Jackson's so-called Executive Usurpation. During the summer of 1832, Jackson's veto of the bill rechartering the BUS led to the temporary coalition of three of the most formidable senators in American

history. All longed for the presidency. By 1832 they had won fame as godlike deliverers of majestic oratory that dazzled aspiring young men.

Daniel Webster struck the keynote when he attacked "King Andrew" as a reincarnation of the French monarch Louis XIV, who had declared, "I am the State." A man of humble New Hampshire origins and aristocratic Boston tastes, Webster had risen in the legal profession by emulating and paying deference to New England's commercial elite. He was a heavy drinker, given to extravagant living and continual debt. His rich, booming voice and commanding physical presence could never quite convey the moral sincerity that most northeastern Whigs expected of their leaders. Yet Webster upheld their traditional mistrust of divisive parties and their traditional ideal of government by "disinterested gentlemen." He succeeded in blending this conservative tradition with a celebration of material and moral progress. As the agent of commercial and manufacturing interests in Massachusetts, he was flexible enough to shift his style of argument from the forums of the Supreme Court and the Senate to the stump of popular politics. Always, however, he pleaded for the natural harmony of interests that, he claimed, the Democratic party threatened to undermine.

Henry Clay joined Webster's assaults on Jackson's alleged despotism. He considered himself a Jeffersonian Republican and the leader of the National Republicans, the label originally applied to Jackson's opponents. Clay's program, which he called the American System, was designed to maximize federal support for industry, economic growth, and national self-sufficiency. He was a Kentuckian born in Virginia, and he had also risen from humble origin. Like Webster, he was notorious for extravagant living, although Clay's self-indulgence took the typically southern forms of gambling, dueling, and horse racing. A slaveowner and brilliant courtroom lawyer, Clay assumed two contradictory political roles. He competed with Jackson as a western man of the people, a coonskin man of nature. But Clay had also helped to negotiate the Treaty of Ghent, which had ended the War of 1812; he had been John Quincy Adams's secretary of state; and he had represented the western business and commercial interests that demanded federal aid for internal improvements. One of the greatest political manipulators in nineteenth-century America, Clay had unequaled talents in caucuses, committee rooms, and all-night boardinghouse negotiations.

John C. Calhoun was the most unpredictable of the three anti-Jackson leaders. Calhoun had originally been a militant nationalist, but in the 1820s he had become a militant defender of slavery and states' rights. He had been Jackson's nominal ally until personal conflicts had provoked a fatal split. Despite Calhoun's dramatic turnabouts, contemporaries admired the clarity and logical force of his arguments and respected his earlier distinguished service as secretary of war. But Calhoun's role in the nullification controversy made him a dangerous ally in the developing Whig coalition. Most southern Whig leaders shared the economic and nationalist views of the northern Whigs; Calhoun did not.

Whig Philosophy. The Whig outlook on the world was almost too diffuse to be termed an ideology. Like the Democrats, Whigs dreamed of a glorious future for America as the greatest nation the world had ever seen, and they found confirmation of that dream in the measurable growth of the country's population, wealth, and power. Far more than the Democrats, they associated the "spirit of improvement" with concrete technological and social inventions. They assumed that steam power, the telegraph, railroads, banks, corporations, prisons, factories, asylums, and public schools all contributed to an advancing civilization and to an increasing equality of opportunity. For individuals and the nation alike, they advocated saving from income, capital accumulation, budgetary planning, and fiscal responsibility. Whigs opposed aggressive territorial expansion as a cure-all for economic problems. They insisted that America's expansion and power should be harnessed to social objectives and stabilized by publicly acknowledged moral boundaries. Alarmed by the excesses of uncontrolled individualism, they expressed continuing and sometimes hysterical concern over the loss of community—over what they saw as demagogues who won support by inciting the poor against the rich, children against parents, wives against husbands, and geographic section against geographic section.

Whigs thought of themselves as conservatives, and they often invoked European theories that stressed the organic unity of society and the necessity of balancing human rights with social duties. Yet the Whig ideal of government was essentially optimistic and progressive. In 1825, long before the Whig party began to take shape, John Quincy Adams advanced the central Whig idea that the Constitution had given the central government both the duty and the necessary powers to promote "the progressive improvement of the condition of the governed."

The Whig party began to appear on a popular level by 1834. At that time it was essentially a loose coalition of state and local groups opposed to Jacksonian Democrats. Because they were reluctant to allow the Jacksonians a monopoly of the popular label "democrat," the anti-Jacksonians sometimes called themselves Democratic Whigs. The final acceptance of

Library of Congress

"KING ANDREW THE FIRST"

The Whig image of Jackson as an autocratic king, brandishing the veto and trampling the Constitution under foot.

the term *Whig* was significant. Superficially the label suggested an identity with the British "country-opposition" that had allegedly defended the British constitution against the despotism of the pro-Catholic Stuart kings in the late seventeenth century and against the encroachments of George III in the eighteenth century. This imagery linked "King Andrew" with the various arbitrary and despotic European monarchs. These parallels may seem far-fetched, but the very act of drawing parallels with Europe contained a deeper significance. Unlike the Democrats, the Whigs tended to deny the uniqueness of the American experience and to place less faith in political institutions than in economic and cultural progress. They also tended to look on Britain, despite its monarchical and aristocratic institutions, as a model of economic and cultural progress. The most thoughtful Whig spokesmen considered America less a revolutionary departure from the rest of the world than a testing ground for progressive forces that were universal and that depended essentially on moral character.

The Whig Constituency.

In all parts of the country, Whigs attracted a broad cross section of the electorate. This cross section was often weighted in favor of the wealthy, the privileged, and the aspiring. But it also included the victims of overt discrimination. In the North this constituency included most of the free blacks; British and German Protestant immigrants; manual laborers sympathetic with their employers' interests; business-oriented farmers; educators, reformers, and professional people; well-to-do merchants, bankers, and manufacturers; and active members of the Presbyterian, Unitarian, and Congregationalist churches. In the South the party had particular appeal to urban merchants, editors, bankers, and to those farmers and planters who associated progress with expanding commerce, capital accumulation, railroads, and economic partnership with the North.

During their initial stages of organization the Whigs faced three formidable problems. First, in the populous northern states like New York, Pennsylvania, and Massachusetts they had to find strategies for uniting the economic interests of the National Republicans with the moral and cultural aspirations of various groups alienated by the incumbent Democrats. Second, they had to get rid of the elitist stigma that had been fastened first on John Quincy Adams and then on the defenders of the BUS. Thus they had to prove somehow that they were better democrats than the Democrats. Finally, they had to find delicate maneuvers for bypassing senatorial prima donnas like Webster and Clay and selecting less controversial presidential candidates who could appeal to the nation without arousing dissension and jealousy among the various state party organizations.

The way these problems were met is well illustrated by the career of Thurlow Weed of New York, who became the model of the nineteenth-century political boss and manipulator. A self-made man, Weed first acquired a voice in New York politics as editor of the Rochester *Telegraph* and a bitter foe of Van Buren's Albany Regency. In 1827 Weed and his young protégé William H. Seward took up the cause of Anti-Masonry as a means of embarrassing the ruling Van Buren machine. In western New York Anti-Masonry had suddenly become a kind of religious crusade after the abduction and probable murder of a former Freemason who was thought to have disclosed the secrets of the fraternal society. The crusade expressed widespread popular resentment against the Masonic fraternity, which knit many of the wealthier and more powerful urban leaders of the state into a secret brotherhood that was pledged to mutual aid and support. Weed and Seward succeeded in portraying the Van Buren regime as the agent of Freemasonry—a "monster institution"—intent on suppressing legal investigation and prosecution of the alleged murder and on disguising statewide links between Masonic political influence and economic privilege. This antielitist rhetoric helped to counteract the Democrats' claims of being the true champions of the people against the unpopular Adams administration in Washington. By 1830 Anti-Masons had captured approximately one-half the popular vote in New York State. When the movement showed increasing signs of strength in other northern states, Weed and other strategists worked to absorb the National Republicans into a new anti-Jackson coalition.

But although the Anti-Masons organized the first national political convention in American history, Weed began to sense that the movement could be no more than a springboard for a successful national party. Weed launched his powerful Albany *Evening Journal* as an Anti-Masonic newspaper, but he increasingly downplayed Masonry and combined blistering attacks on the Albany Regency with the advocacy of various social reforms. To his political cronies and businessmen backers, Weed kept insisting that the Jacksonians could never be beaten so long as they continued to convince the people that they alone represented "the principle of democracy . . . the poor against the rich." By 1834 Weed had abandoned Anti-Masonry and had succeeded in organizing a New York Whig coalition.

In 1836 the Whigs tried to broaden their appeal by nominating various regional candidates for president, including Daniel Webster of Massachusetts and Hugh White of Tennessee. But it was Weed's candidate, William Henry Harrison of Ohio, who won the most electoral votes. "Old Tippecanoe," famous for his military defeat of the Shawnee Indians in 1811, appealed to many former Anti-Masons and won strong support in the South as well as in New York, Ohio, and Pennsylvania. After years of patient organizing, wirepulling, and passing out cigars, Weed finally came into his own in 1838 when he succeeded in getting Seward elected governor of New York. As the master of patronage, the official state printer, and the "dictator" of the New York machine, Weed was now in a position to challenge his old archrival Van Buren, who claimed to be the president of the common people.

The Election of 1840.

In 1840 Weed played a key role in blocking the Whigs' nomination of Clay and in opening the way for Harrison. Weed's young follower, Hor-

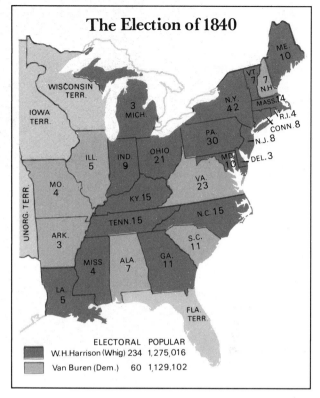

TIPPECANOE CLUB POSTER

By 1840 the Whigs could match the Democrats as a popular people's party with their own distinctive songs, clubs, and political symbols. Here William Henry Harrison is presented as a simple farmer standing with a plow in front of his log cabin and barrel of cider.

ace Greeley, edited the Whigs' most influential newspaper, *The Log Cabin*, which set the pace for the campaign by attacking President Van Buren as an affected dandy who had transformed the White House into a palace of effeminate luxury. Greeley and others portrayed Harrison as a frontiersman of simple tastes. His symbols were a barrel of cider (whether hard or soft depended on the locality) and a log cabin with a welcoming coonskin at the door. Harrison's victory seemed to show that Weed and fellow strategists had overcome the Whigs' political liabilities. They could rival the Democrats in populistic appeals, in carnival-style hucksterism, and, above all, in grassroots organization.

Nevertheless, the Whigs never found a magnetic national leader who, like Jackson for the Democrats, could become a unifying symbol for their party. John Tyler, the vice-president who succeeded Harrison, soon betrayed the economic principles of the party. In 1844 the Whigs nominated Clay, but he went down to defeat for the third time. Thereafter the Whigs re-

turned to the tested expedient of nominating apolitical military heroes—Zachary Taylor in 1848 and Winfield Scott in 1852.

The Whigs' difficulties went beyond the weaknesses of their presidential candidates. Despite their political pragmatism and impressive party discipline, the Whigs contained a militant, reform-minded element that resented the compromises necessary for a national party. Anti-Masonry had been one of the early expressions of such reformist and issue-oriented politics, and many of the Anti-Masons who had joined the Whigs had never been comfortable with the opportunism of the Weed school of leaders, who placed victory above principle. In addition to the Anti-Masons, the Whig party became the uneasy home for people who wanted laws enforcing a stricter Sabbath, laws prohibiting the sale of alcohol, laws barring slavery from the territories and abolishing slavery in the District of Columbia, and laws prolonging the time before an immigrant could be naturalized or allowed to vote. These causes were nourished by the spread of Protestant religious revivals in the North. They had little appeal among southern Whigs and hard-headed supporters of Clay's American System.

Limitations of the Two-Party System.

Nevertheless, although a national party's strength depended on a continuing sensitivity to the needs of its constituent groups, it also served as a disciplining and educational force, imposing definite limits to individual, local, and regional self-assertion. The political issues of the 1840s tended to reinforce such party loyalty. The majority of state legislators voted a strict Whig or Democratic line even when a different position might have harmonized better with local or personal interests. Whig or Democratic nerve centers were established at the grassroots level through the appointment of loyal party men to positions in local land offices, post offices, and customhouses. Until the early 1850s, when voters became disillusioned with traditional alternatives and when the Whig party began to fall apart, the two-party system worked as a powerful cohesive force in American society. Unfortunately, this political stability depended on the illusion of constant and sharply defined differences between two parties—parties that were intended to represent the interests of white Americans alone. The existence of national parties succeeded in moderating sectional conflict, but it did so at the cost of suppressing alternatives to the expansion of slavery and of stifling national debate over America's most dangerous conflict of interest.

CHRONOLOGY

1820	Missouri Compromise.
	Maine admitted as twenty-third state.
	Reelection of James Monroe without opposition symbolizes "Era of Good Feelings."
1821	Henry Clay effects "Second Missouri Compromise."
	Missouri admitted as twenty-fourth state.
1822	Denmark Vesey's conspiracy to lead massive slave uprising in South Carolina exposed.
1824	John Quincy Adams elected president by House of Representatives after failure of any candidate to win electoral majority.
1827	Thurlow Weed takes up cause of Anti-Masonry.
1828	John C. Calhoun's anonymous *South Carolina Exposition and Protest*.
	Congress passes "Tariff of Abominations."
	Election of Andrew Jackson as president brings triumphant victory to new Democratic party.
1830	Jackson vetoes Maysville Road Bill.
	Anti-Masonic party holds first national party convention.

1832	Beginning of Jackson's "war" against Second Bank of the United States (BUS).
	Special convention in South Carolina nullifies new protective tariff.
	Jackson reelected president.
1833	Congress provides for a gradual lowering of tariffs but passes Force Bill authorizing Jackson to enforce federal law in South Carolina.
1836	Jackson's "specie circular."
	Martin Van Buren elected president.
1837	Financial panic brings many bank failures and suspension of specie payment.
1839	A major depression begins, leading to widespread bankruptcies and default of several states.
1840	Congress passes Van Buren's Independent Treasury Act.
	William H. Harrison elected president; Whigs in power.
1841	John Tyler becomes president upon Harrison's death.
1844	James K. Polk elected president.

Arthur M. Schlesinger, Jr., *The Age of Jackson* (1945), should be used with caution but is still an indispensable introduction to political democratization. Other studies that illuminate the same subject are Shaw Livermore, Jr., *The Twilight of Federalism* (1962); Chilton Williamson, *American Suffrage: From Property to Democracy* (1960); Henry Christman, *Tin Horns and Calico: A Decisive Episode in the Emergence of Democracy* (1945); David M. Ludlum, *Social Ferment in Vermont* (1939); and Marvin E. Gettleman, *The Dorr Rebellion* (1973).

Lee Benson, *The Concept of Jacksonian Democracy: New York as a Test Case* (1961), challenges the traditional historical categories of liberalism and conservatism. Richard P. McCormick, *The Second American Party System: Party Formation in the Jacksonian Era* (1966), also deemphasizes political issues and ideology. These pioneering works should be supplemented by Richard Hofstadter, *The Idea of a Party System* (1969); Ronald P. Formisano, *The Birth of Mass Political Parties: Michigan, 1827–1861* (1971); Formisano, *The Transformation of Political Culture: Massachusetts Parties, 1790s–1840s* (1983); Joel Silbey, ed., *Transformation of American Politics, 1840–1860* (1967); Douglas T. Miller, *Jacksonian Aristocracy: Class and Democracy in New York, 1830–1860* (1967); and Michael F. Holt, "The Antimasonic and Know-Nothing Parties," and Holt, "The Democratic Party," in *History of U.S. Political Parties,* ed. Arthur M. Schlesinger, Jr., Vol. 1 (1789–1860: *From Factions to Parties*), (4 vols., 1973). For a fascinating study of the Anti-Masonic party, see William Preston Vaughn, *The Antimasonic Party in the United States, 1826–1843* (1983). Michael F. Holt, *The Political Crisis of the 1850s* (1978), points to connections between political ideology and the working of the party system.

For the election of 1828, see R. V. Remini, *The Election of Andrew Jackson* (1963). Two imaginative studies of Jacksonian ideology are Marvin Meyers, *The Jacksonian Persuasion* (1957), and John W. Ward, *Andrew Jackson: Symbol for an Age* (1955). For a comprehensive portrait of Jackson's early years, see R. V. Remini, *Andrew Jackson and the Course of American Empire* (1977); for his presidency, see Richard B. Latner, *The Presidency of Andrew Jackson: White House Politics* (1979). John Niven, *Martin Van Buren and the Romantic Age* (1983), brings out the central importance of a much underrated political leader. Informative essays on all of the presidential elections can be found in Arthur M. Schlesinger, Jr., ed., *History of American Presidential Elections, 1789–1968,* Vol. 1 (4 vols., 1971). See also Richard P. McCormick, *The Presidential Game: The Origins of American Presidential Politics* (1982).

The standard work on the tariff issue is Frank W. Taussig, *The Tariff History of the United States* (1931). The best introduction to the banking controversy is R. V. Remini, *Andrew Jackson and the Bank War* (1967). The main authorities on the history of banking are Bray Hammond, *Banks and Politics in America from the Revolution to the Civil War* (1957); J. Van Fenstermaker, *The Development of American Commercial Banking 1782–1837* (1965); and Fritz Redlich, *The Molding of American Banking* (2 vols., 1947–51). Thomas P. Govan, *Nicholas Biddle* (1959), presents a strong defense of the pres-

ident of the Bank of the United States. The wider political ramifications of the controversy are examined in William G. Shade, *Banks or No Banks: The Money Question in Western Politics* (1972), and John M. McFaul, *The Politics of Jacksonian Finance* (1972).

On the Missouri crisis of 1820, Glover Moore, *The Missouri Controversy* (1953), is still the most thorough and convincing account. William W. Freehling, *Prelude to Civil War* (1966), presents a masterful interpretation of South Carolina's growing militancy and of the nullification and gag-rule controversies. For the general question of sectionalism, see William J. Cooper, *The South and the Politics of Slavery, 1828–1856* (1978). The most penetrating and informative study of politics in a southern state is J. Mills Thornton III, *Politics and Power in a Slave Society: Alabama, 1800–1860* (1978).

There is still no adequate history of the Whig party and its antecedents, but Daniel W. Howe, *The Political Culture of the American Whigs* (1980), brilliantly illuminates the Whig ideology. See also Lynn L. Marshall, "The Strange Stillbirth of the Whig Party," *American Historical Review,* 62 (January 1967), 445–68; Charles G. Sellers, Jr., "Who Were the Southern Whigs?" *American Historical Review,* 59 (January 1954), 335–46; Glyndon G. Van Deusen, "Some Aspects of Whig Thought and Theory in the Jacksonian Period," *American Historical Review,* 63 (January 1958), 305–32; and Thomas H. O'Connor, *Lords of the Loom: The Cotton Whigs and the Coming of the Civil War* (1968).

Political history is always illuminated by the biographies of influential figures. Richard Hofstadter, *The American Political Tradition* (1948), provides brilliant sketches of a number of pre–Civil War leaders. Among the best biographies are Martin Duberman, *Charles Francis Adams, 1807–1886* (1961); Samuel F. Bemis, *John Quincy Adams and the Foundations of American Foreign Policy* (1949), and *John Quincy Adams and the Union* (1956); W. N. Chambers, *Old Bullion Benton: Senator from the New West* (1956); William E. Smith, *The Francis Preston Blair Family in Politics* (2 vols., 1933); Richard N. Current, *John C. Calhoun* (1966); C. M. Wiltse, *John C. Calhoun: Nationalist, 1782–1828* (1944), *Nullifier, 1829–1839* (1949), *Sectionalist, 1840–1850* (1951); Clement Eaton, *Henry Clay and the Art of American Politics* (1957); Marquis James, *Life of Andrew Jackson* (1938); Harry Ammon, *James Monroe: The Quest for National Identity* (1971); Charles G. Sellers, Jr., *James K. Polk: Jacksonian, 1795–1843* (1957), *Continentalist, 1843–1846* (1966); Robert Dawidoff, *The Education of John Randolph* (1979); Glyndon G. Van Deusen, *William Henry Seward* (1967); David H. Donald, *Charles Sumner and the Coming of the Civil War* (1960); Carl B. Swisher, *Roger B. Taney* (1935); Holman Hamilton, *Zachary Taylor* (1951); William Y. Thompson, *Robert Toombs of Georgia* (1966); James P. Shenton, *Robert John Walker: A Politician from Jackson to Lincoln* (1961); Robert F. Dalzell, Jr., *Daniel Webster and the Trial of American Nationalism, 1843–1852* (1973); Sydney Nathans, *Daniel Webster and Jacksonian Democracy* (1973); Glyndon G. Van Deusen, *Thurlow Weed: Wizard of the Lobby* (1947); and John W. DuBose, *The Life and Times of William Lowndes Yancey* (2 vols., 1892).

16 Expansion and New Boundaries

The 1840s marked the beginning of a new era. In the North recovery from a long depression was accompanied by rapid urban growth, the extension of machine production and of the factory system, the influx of hundreds of thousands of immigrants, and the construction of vast railway networks linking western farms with eastern markets. In the South the remarkable profitability of cotton and sugar plantations confirmed a whole region's unapologetic commitment to slave labor. The moral discomforts that had troubled Jefferson's generation of Southerners had finally given way to a proud and self-conscious identity as a "progressive slave society." This sectional confidence was bolstered not only by the world's demand for cotton but also by the American annexation of Texas. The resulting Mexican War, which extended America's boundaries to the Pacific, led some southern leaders to dream of a vast tropical empire based on the slave labor of an "inferior race." These spectacular fulfillments of trends and aspirations that had been developing since the War of 1812 posed grave challenges to governmental policy and to the nation's sense of its own character.

There were other dark shadows in this overall picture of growth and economic integration. In the mid-1850s investment and industrial production both underwent a slowdown, which culminated in the financial panic of 1857. For the first time, the business cycle seemed to be primarily geared to the fluctuations of nonagricultural forces in the domestic economy, among them speculative investment in railroads. Significantly, the South suffered little from the essentially industrial depression of the late 1850s. Southern leaders could not refrain from gloating over the economic vulnerability of northern industry and the insecurities of "wage slavery." Northern leaders angrily accused the South of contributing to the depression by defeating northern moves for protective tariffs and free homesteading in the West. Slave-grown cotton remained an important contributor to the North's industrial growth. But many Northerners perceived the South as a holdover of colonial dependency—a dependecy on British markets that blocked the way to national self-sufficiency.

Foreign Dangers, American Expansion, and the Monroe Doctrine

America's foreign policy had always presupposed the national government's commitment to protect and support the South's "peculiar institution." However, the nation's foreign policy reflected many other interests and motives, and protecting slavery was not explicitly acknowledged as a vital objective until 1844. The overriding objective in the early nineteenth century, as in the post-Revolutionary period, was to prevent Britain or France from acquiring a foothold in the increasingly vulnerable Spanish territories of North America. But those territories, including Cuba, East and West Florida, and Texas, were a threat mainly to the slaveholding South. The War of 1812 made clear that possession of the Floridas was essential for the security of the entire Lower South. From bases in supposedly neutral Spanish Florida, the British had incited Indian raids, had encouraged slave desertions, and had originally planned to launch an invasion to cut off New Orleans from the rest of the United States. The revolution of 1791–1804 in the French colony of Santo Domingo (which became the Republic of Haiti) had also shown that war could ignite a massive slave uprising and totally destroy a slaveholding society.

Decline of New World Slavery. One of the consequences of the Napoleonic wars at the beginning of the nineteenth century was the fatal weakening of slaveholding regimes in most parts of the New World. Not only did France lose Haiti, the most valuable sugar colony in the world, but Napoleon's seizure of Spain

opened the way for independence movements in the immense Spanish territories from Mexico to Chile. The prolonged wars of liberation undermined the institution of slavery and committed the future Spanish American republics to programs of gradual emancipation. After the British abolished the slave trade in their own colonies at the beginning of the nineteenth century, they embarked on a long-term policy of suppressing the slave trade of other nations. By 1823, when little remained of the former Spanish, Portuguese, and French New World empires, slavery was a declining institution except in Brazil, Cuba (still a Spanish colony), and the United States.

This wider context of New World slavery dramatizes a momentous irony of American foreign policy from the time of Jefferson's presidency to the Civil War. The extension of what Jefferson called an "empire for liberty" was also the extension of an empire for slavery and thus a counterweight to the forces that threatened to erode slavery throughout the hemisphere. Jefferson himself initiated the policy of trying to isolate Haiti economically and diplomatically in order to end the spread of black revolution. In 1820, in the midst of the Missouri crisis and in response to Spain's delay in ratifying the Transcontinental Treaty of 1819, ceding East Florida, Jefferson privately assured President Monroe that the United States could soon acquire not only East Florida but also Cuba and Texas. Cuba was at the time becoming the world's greatest producer of slave-grown sugar, and Jefferson confidently predicted that Texas would be the richest state in the Union, partly because it would produce more sugar than the country could consume.

There is no reason to think that American statesmen consciously plotted to create a vast empire for slavery—at least until the 1840s. From the annexation of Florida in 1821 to the annexation of Texas in 1845, the United States acquired no new territory that could upset the balance between free states and slave states achieved by the Missouri Compromise. The Old Southwest contained immense tracts of uncleared and uncultivated land, and many Southerners feared that reckless expansion would lead to excessive production, which would lower the price of cotton and other cash crops.

Slavery and Territorial Expansion. The connections between slavery and national expansion were more indirect. They involved two basic and continuing assumptions that governed foreign policy. The first assumption was that territorial expansion was the only means of protecting and extending the principles of the American Revolution in a generally hostile world. "The larger our association," Jefferson had predicted, "the less will it be shaken by local passions." According to this nationalist view, Americans could deal with domestic

imperfections once the nation had achieved sufficient power to be secure. Thus ardent nationalists like John Quincy Adams felt that personal misgivings over slavery had to give way to the need for a united front against the monarchical despots of Europe. During the Missouri crisis the antislavery forces could never overcome the unfair charge that they were serving Britain's interests by fomenting sectional discord and blocking the westward expansion of the United States.

The second assumption, held with passionate conviction by every president from Jefferson to Polk, was that Great Britain was America's "natural enemy." These presidents saw Britain as a kingdom ruled by selfish interest, filled with a deep-rooted hatred for everything America represented, and committed to the humiliation and subjugation of its former colonies. Anglophobia had much to do with the swift death of the Federalist party. This hatred of England was nourished by contemptuous anti-American essays in British periodicals and by unflattering descriptions by English travelers that were widely reprinted in the United States. Many Americans blamed Britain for the economic depressions of 1819 and 1837. Irish immigrants regarded the English as their hereditary enemies. No American politician could risk even the suspicion of being an unintentional agent of British interests. It was thus an unhappy coincidence that British interests veered increasingly toward antislavery—which some American leaders interpreted, not without some reason, as a cloak for new forms of economic and ideological imperialism.

The American takeover of Florida established precedents for the future and also coincided with the dramatic southwestward expansion of cotton and slavery. As early as 1786 Jefferson had warned against pressing "too soon on the Spaniards." For the time being, he believed, it was best that East and West Florida be in Spanish hands. He feared, however, that the Spanish were "too feeble to hold them [the Floridas] till our population can be sufficiently advanced to gain it [the Floridas] from them piece by piece." By 1810 there were enough American settlers in the Baton Rouge district of West Florida to stage an armed rebellion against Spanish rule. President Madison, claiming that West Florida was part of the Louisiana Purchase, promptly annexed the section of the Gulf coast extending eastward to the Perdido River. To prevent any possible transfer of West Florida to Great Britain, Congress sanctioned Madison's annexation. But it balked at plans to seize East Florida during the War of 1812.

The Transcontinental Treaty of 1819. Negotiations with Spain after the War of 1812 involved not only Florida but also the entire western boundary of the United

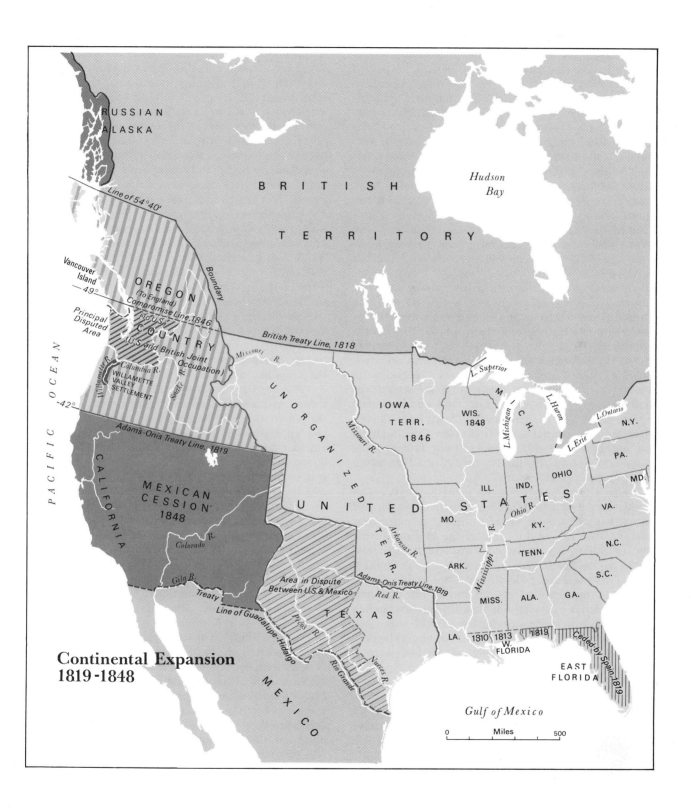

RUSSIAN
ALASKA

Line of 54°40'

B R I T I S H

T E R R I T O R Y

*Hudson
Bay*

PACIFIC OCEAN

Vancouver
Island
— 49°

Principal
Disputed
Area

Boundary

OREGON
(To England)
Compromise Line, 1846
(To U.S)

COUNTRY
(US and British Joint
Occupation)

Willamette R.

Columbia R.

WILLAMETTE
VALLEY
SETTLEMENT

Snake R.

Missouri R.

British Treaty Line, 1818

L. Superior

L. Michigan

M I C H

L. Huron

L. Ontario

L. Erie

N.Y.

WIS.
1848

IOWA
TERR.
1846

U N O R G A N I Z E D

Missouri R.

PA.

—42°

Adams-Onis Treaty Line, 1819

CALIFORNIA

MEXICAN
CESSION
1848

Colorado R.

Gila R.

Treaty

Line of Guadalupe-Hidalgo

U N I T E D   T E R R.

Arkansas R.

Area in Dispute
Between U.S. & Mexico

Red R.

T E X A S

Pecos R.

Adams-Onis Treaty Line, 1819

Rio Grande

Nueces R.

M E X I C O

U N I T E D   S T A T E S

ILL.

IND.

OHIO

Ohio R.

MO.

KY.

VA.

MD.

N.C.

Mississippi R.

ARK.

TENN.

S.C.

MISS.

ALA.

GA.

LA.

1810   1813   1819
W.
FLORIDA

Ceded by Spain 1819

EAST
FLORIDA

Gulf of Mexico

**Continental Expansion
1819-1848**

0   Miles   500

States. Spain had never recognized the validity of Napoleon's sale of Louisiana, a sale prohibited by the treaty that had earlier transferred the territory from Spain to France. Luis de Onís, the Spanish minister to the United States, tried to limit American claims to the narrowest strip possible west of the Mississippi River. But as the negotiations dragged on, the South American wars of independence increasingly undermined Spain's position. Secretary of State John Quincy Adams proved to be a tough and skillful bargainer, and in 1818 Andrew Jackson, then the American military commander in the South, immensely strengthened Adams's hand. Without official authorization Jackson invaded East Florida, captured the main Spanish ports, deposed the governor, and hanged two English troublemakers. The excuse was that Florida had become a refuge for fugitive slaves and a base for Seminole Indian raids on American settlements.

Thus Onís was faced with the temporary seizure of his main bargaining card, and he feared that the United States would begin aiding the rebellious Spanish colonies. He therefore agreed to the Transcontinental Treaty of 1819, which ceded the Floridas to the United States in return for American acknowledgment that Texas was not part of the Louisiana Purchase—a questionable claim that the Americans had already put forward. In fact, Onís had been desperate enough to give up most of Texas. But as President Monroe assured General Jackson, "We ought to be content with Florida, for the present, and until the public opinion . . . [in the Northeast] shall be reconciled to any further change."

For Adams the Transcontinental Treaty (also known as the Adams-Onís Treaty), which was ratified in 1821, was "a great epoch [turning point] in our history." Not only did it transfer the Floridas to the United States, but it extended American territorial claims to the Pacific Ocean. The rather weak Spanish claims to the Pacific Northwest were ceded to the United States. Spain also agreed to an international boundary that extended northward from the Sabine River (which divided Louisiana from Texas) to the Red River, westward along the Red and Arkansas rivers to the Rocky Mountains, and then along the forty-second parallel to the Pacific.

At the time the Transcontinental Treaty was being negotiated, Spain was reasserting its control in Mexico, which had revolted for the first time in 1808–15. But the revival of Spanish rule proved temporary. In 1820 a revolution in Spain itself permitted the Mexicans to declare their independence once again. By 1822 the burden of defending the boundaries that had been established by the Transcontinental Treaty had fallen upon an independent but weak and war-torn Mexico.

Events Leading to the Monroe Doctrine. The collapse of the Spanish Empire led directly to the Monroe Doctrine. By 1823 it was clear that Spain could never force its rebellious colonies to return to their former status. Moreover, Britain and the United States had a common interest in preventing the autocratic monarchies of continental Europe from intervening in Latin America in Spain's behalf. Under pressure from the Russian czar, France was about to invade Spain to put down its revolution, which aimed at establishing a constitutional monarchy. It was known that the French foreign minister had grandiose schemes for imposing on Latin America the kind of reactionary monarchical government that predominated in continental Europe. Although Great Britain was not willing to risk war, it was strongly opposed to French intervention in Spain. And while not a promoter of independent republics, the British government had no intention of allowing the continental powers' antirevolutionary zeal to interfere with Britain's growing commercial dominance in the former Spanish Empire. George Canning, the British foreign minister, therefore proposed a joint Anglo-American declaration that would assert that neither Britain nor the United States had designs on former Spanish territory, and would warn other nations against intervention.

The British offer presented the Monroe administration with a serious dilemma. The United States was the only nation that had begun to recognize the independent republics of Spanish America, but only Britain had the power to deter France and Spain from trying to reconquer them. Moreover, Russia—which was leading the reactionary crusades in Europe and which already occupied Alaska—in 1821 claimed a monopoly over the North Pacific. Russian traders were becoming more active in the Oregon country, a region that Britain and the United States had agreed to occupy jointly at least until 1828. Accepting the British offer of a joint declaration would have the drawback of temporarily preventing the American annexation of Cuba. Despite this disadvantage, the idea appealed to the elder statesmen Jefferson and Madison, as well as to Monroe and most of his cabinet.

But the question of accepting the British offer was complicated by the forthcoming presidential election of 1824. The nationalist, anti-English vote was much on the minds of the leading candidates. Secretary of State John Quincy Adams was already being portrayed by his rivals as a former Federalist and as secretly pro-British. Despite his proved nationalism and loyal service to Republican administrations, Adams was vulnerable to these charges because of his New England and Federalist background. He was also the only candidate who was not a slaveowner. He knew that as secretary of state he would bear the largest share of political liability resulting from any Anglo-

American alliance. He had long gone out of his way to publicize his resistance to British pressure for an anti-slave-trade treaty. Therefore Adams now insisted on a unilateral American declaration against European intervention in the New World, much as he insisted on a unilateral policy against the slave trade. It would be more candid and dignified, Adams pointed out, to declare the United States' principles directly to Russia and France than "to come in as a cock-boat in the wake of the British man-of-war."

Adams's arguments prevailed, and thus the famous Monroe Doctrine was proclaimed, reaffirming America's diplomatic independence from Europe. By stating that America would not intervene in the "internal concerns" of European states, Monroe in effect repudiated the popular clamor in the United States for aiding the various revolutionary struggles against despotism in Europe, including the Greek war for independence from Turkey. But America's warning to Europe against its future colonization of the New World extended to Britain as well as to Russia and France. And the Monroe Doctrine in no way prevented America's own expansion in the New World.

For some time the Monroe Doctrine had little practical consequence, except perhaps in proving Adams to be a nationalist and thus in helping him to win the presidency. Regardless of American pronouncements, it was British naval power that ensured the independence of Spanish America. Yet by rejecting an Anglo-American alliance, the Monroe administration also set a precedent for opposing any foreign attempts to limit the expansion of slavery. No doubt Monroe was thinking only of monarchical institutions when he warned that the United States would consider as dangerous to America's peace and safety any attempt by Europeans to extend "their system" to the Western Hemisphere. By the 1830s, however, antislavery was an integral part of the British "system," and many Southerners regarded the expansion of slavery as vital to America's "peace and safety."

Annexation of Texas.
The Texas issue eventually tested this point and led to a proslavery reformulation of the Monroe Doctrine. For abolitionists in both Britain and the United States, it was not inevitable that Texas should become a slave state. In 1829 Mexico had abolished slavery in all its provinces (including California), and it provided loopholes only for the stubborn Anglo-American settlers in Texas. By 1830 the Mexican government had become alarmed by the growing autonomy of the Anglo-American settlements in Texas, by the intrigue accompanying the United States government's secret efforts to purchase Texas, and by the Jacksonian press's agitation for annexation. Consequently in 1830 the Mexican govern-

SAM HOUSTON (1793–1863)
Leader of the badly outnumbered Texans whose spectacular victory at San Jacinto in 1836 secured Texas's independence from Mexico, Houston went on to become president of the new republic, then senator from the new state. In 1861 as governor, Houston's stand against Texas's secession from the Union forced him out of office.

ment tried to prohibit the further immigration of Anglo-Americans and the further importation of slaves. It also sought to promote European settlements in Texas, which would be a buffer against encroachments from the United States. Since black slavery had only begun to take root in Texas, British reformers were beginning to look on the province as a promising site for cultivating cotton with free labor. Benjamin Lundy, an American Quaker abolitionist, even tried in the early 1830s to establish a refuge in Texas for free blacks from the United States.

But during his travels in Texas, Lundy found evidence of growing proslavery sentiment and of various plots to throw off Mexican rule and annex Texas to the United States. The Mexican government was in fact capable of neither governing the Anglo-Texans nor satisfying their needs. In 1836, after President Antonio López de Santa Anna had abolished Mexico's federal constitution and had imposed centralized rule, the

McKAY'S SHIPYARD

Donald McKay's shipyard in East Boston, established in 1845, constructed some of the fastest, most graceful, and most beautiful sailing ships ever made. McKay's clipper the *Flying Cloud* made San Francisco in less than ninety days from New York. The *James Baines* set a world record of twelve days six hours from Boston to Liverpool. McKay's best clippers could average more than four hundred nautical miles in a day.

Texans proclaimed their independence. Their new constitution, modeled on the United States Constitution, specifically legalized black slavery. Meanwhile, Santa Anna's army had wiped out a small band of Texas rebels at San Antonio's Alamo Mission, and cries for revenge resounded in the American press. A great influx of volunteers from the officially neutral United States went to the aid of the Texans. Led by General Sam Houston, Texan forces crushed the Mexican army at San Jacinto and captured Santa Anna. Soon thereafter the Texans voted overwhelmingly to join the United States.

As late as 1835 President Jackson had tried to buy not only Texas but all the Mexican territory stretching northwestward to the Pacific. His main object was to secure "within our limits the whole bay of St. Francisco." By then Americans had long been engaged in trade along the Santa Fe trail, and settlers were beginning to arrive by sea in sparsely populated California. After the Texan revolution, however, Jackson knew that a premature attempt at annexation would in all

likelihood bring on a war with Mexico, which refused to acknowledge Texan independence. It would also arouse the fury of the Northeast and lead to a sectional division within the Democratic party in the election year of 1836. But Jackson knew that California was important to the whaling and maritime interests of the Northeast. New England whalers and cargo ships had begun to make portions of the Pacific an American preserve. Jackson therefore secretly advised the Texans to bide their time and to establish a claim to California, "to paralyze the opposition of the North and East to Annexation." He assumed that this opposition would fade as soon as Northerners concluded that annexing Texas would lead to the acquisition of California.

The passage of time, however, encouraged the hopes of American and British opponents of slavery. Jackson's Democratic successor, Martin Van Buren, was too dependent on northeastern support to risk agitating the public with the question of annexation. John Quincy Adams's eloquent speeches in the House

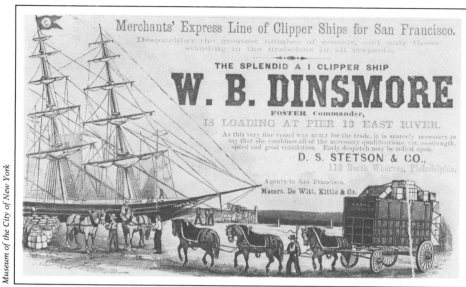

"THE SPLENDID, A1 CLIPPER SHIP"
An advertisement for the highly competitive clipper ship travel to San Francisco.

of Representatives, in which he served for seventeen years after he retired as president, popularized the view that the southern Slave Power had engineered the Texas Revolution and the drive for annexation. In 1838 Adams carried on a three-week filibuster, presented hundreds of antislavery petitions, and finally defeated a move to annex Texas by joint resolution. The rebuffed Texan leaders withdrew their formal proposal for annexation and began to think seriously of building an independent empire. As time went on, they looked to Britain and France for financial support and for diplomatic aid in ending the dangerous state of war with Mexico.

The spring and summer of 1843 marked a decisive turn of events. John Tyler, who had been elected as Harrison's vice-president in 1840 and had then become president after Harrison's death, had been disowned by the Whig party. He was therefore courting southern Democrats and searching for an issue that would win him reelection. Daniel Webster, the last of his Whig cabinet members, finally resigned as secretary of state after negotiating with Britain the Webster-Ashburton Treaty, which settled disputed borders with Canada and provided for cooperative measures in suppressing the Atlantic slave trade. The treaty was immediately attacked by Democrats for betraying American interests. Through Calhoun's influence, Webster was replaced by Abel P. Upshur, a Virginian who had defended slavery as a "positive good." For the first time, an entire administration was in the hands of ardent proslavery Southerners who saw territorial expansion as the key to southern security.

Britain and Texas. Although British leaders did not want to antagonize the South, on which Britain depended for cotton, they were sensitive to one abolitionist argument. An independent Texas might begin importing slaves from Africa, thereby adding to Britain's difficulties in suppressing the Atlantic slave trade. The British had evidence that American officials in Cuba were conniving with slave smugglers and that American ships participated in the illegal slave trade to Cuba. Texas might open another rich market for the same interests. Therefore, when Britain offered Texas a treaty of recognition and trade, it included a secret agreement to outlaw the slave trade. Otherwise, under close questioning from a delegation of abolitionists, Foreign Secretary Lord Aberdeen conceded only two points: first, that in serving as mediator between Texas and Mexico, Britain hoped that any peace agreement would include a commitment to slave emancipation; and second, that as everyone knew, the British public and government hoped for the abolition of slavery throughout the world.

These words caused anger and alarm in Washington. The Tyler adminstration was convinced that West Indian emancipation had proved to be an economic and social disaster. According to the prevailing southern theory, the British were now determined to undermine slavery in other nations in order to improve the competitive advantage of their own colonies, including India. But Southerners never comprehended the depth of antislavery sentiment among the British middle class. Having subsidized West Indian emancipation by paying £20 million in compensation to former slaveowners, British taxpayers wanted assurance that

Chicago Historical Society

JOHN TYLER (1790–1862)

A Jeffersonian Republican from Virginia, Tyler was a strong supporter of states' rights and became a maverick Whig largely because he opposed some of Andrew Jackson's policies. In 1841 Tyler became the first vice-president to succeed a president, and he soon broke with the Whigs over the bank issue and other questions. He proved to be an able administrator, even without party backing, and succeeded in preparing the way for the annexation of Texas.

Britain's short-term sacrifices would not lead to the expansion of plantation slavery in neighboring regions of the Caribbean and the Gulf of Mexico.

Regardless of the truth, however, Southerners had long been inclined to believe that British antislavery was part of a long-term diplomatic plot to seal off and contain the United States within an arc of British influence extending from Cuba and Texas to California, Oregon, and Canada. In 1843 this conviction was seemingly confirmed by the exaggerated reports of Duff Green, President Tyler's secret agent in Britain and France and a friend of Calhoun. According to Green, the British government was about to guarantee interest on a loan to Texas on the condition that Texans abolish slavery. The plan would make Texas a British satellite and a place of refuge, like Canada, for fugitive slaves from the United States. Green claimed that, by erecting a barrier of freedom across the southwestern flank of the slaveholding states, the British

could effectively join northern abolitionists in destroying both slavery and the federal Union.

Like many myths, this elaborate fantasy rested on a thin foundation of truth. It interpreted every event as part of a master plan, and it justified national desires that were otherwise difficult to justify. It furnished the pretext for the grand strategy that would govern American expansionist policy for the next five years. In response to an appeal for advice from Secretary of State Upshur, Calhoun in 1843 secretly spelled out the steps for implementing this policy. He called for private assurances to Texas that as soon as a propaganda campaign had been launched to soften northern opposition, the administration would secure annexation. In order to win support from the land-hungry farmers of the Old Northwest, Calhoun also suggested linking Texas annexation with the assertion of American claims to Oregon. As a preliminary step in carrying out this plan, he wanted to demand a formal explanation from Britain for policies that threatened "the safety of the Union and the very existence of the South."

Calhoun himself soon had the power to begin implementing this grand design. Early in 1844 Upshur was killed in an accident, and Calhoun succeeded him as secretary of state. Soon afterwards a Whig newspaper revealed that the administration had been engaged for months in secret negotiations with Texas and that Tyler was about to sign an annexation treaty. In response to a growing northern uproar, Calhoun seized on and made public the British government's private statement that Britain "desires, and is constantly exerting herself to procure, the general abolition of slavery throughout the world." By skillfully distorting and publicizing the British diplomatic notes, Calhoun tried to identify the anti-annexation cause with a British plot to destroy the Union. He lectured the British on the blessings of black slavery, employing faulty statistics from the census of 1840 to argue that emancipation in the North had produced black insanity, crime, suicide, and degeneracy. He also informed Mexico that because of the British conspiracy to subvert southern slavery, the United States was forced to annex Texas in self-defense.

The Expansionist Issue and the Election of 1844. This open defense of slavery by an American secretary of state marked the beginning of a sectional conflict over slavery and expansionism that severely tested the party system. President Tyler's defection from the Whigs, in addition to Calhoun's presidential ambitions and independence from party discipline, complicated the political maneuvering that set the stage for the 1844 campaign. With an eye to northern votes, both Henry Clay and Martin Van Buren, the leading Whig and

The Metropolitan Museum of Art, Morris K. Jesup Fund, 1933

"Fur Traders Descending the Missouri" by George Caleb Bingham.

The Perils of Civilization

By the second quarter of the nineteenth century, a growing number of artists were giving imaginative expression to the changing American experience. Some of these artists drew on the rich resources of primitive painting and popular folklore; an increasing number had received formal training in Europe and in the new artistic academies of the East. Apart from training and talent, American artists were becoming more sensitive to the opportunities and coercions of a market economy in which art competed with other luxuries. They were becoming more responsive to the exotic and romantic fashions of the time, largely derived from Europe, and, above all, to America's dramatic expansion, which seemed at once exhilarating and dangerous. For the central legacy of Old World culture, running like a blinking danger light from the ancient Greeks to Shakespeare and Milton, was the message that destruction inevitably follows excessive human pride,

"Death Struggle" by Charles Deas.

arrogance, or a defiance of the boundaries that God and nature had imposed on humankind.

Nature became the central theme of American art in the pre–Civil War era. It was still a nature that stood above and apart from humankind—a source of inspiration, a force to be conquered, but not a *resource* to be preserved in parks or commemorated in museums. George Caleb Bingham, who grew up on the frontier, could portray the penetration and exploitation of nature as an idyllic moment of harmony. He depicts fur traders descending the great Missouri River, not fishermen or hunters in a protected game preserve. The boat is laden with pelts, and a live fox is chained to the bow. The young trapper lounges over his gun and

a dead waterfowl. The colorful detail and sharp, angular lines of the men and boat stand out against the feathery trees in the background. Yet Bingham has skillfully blended the human forms with the watery reflections and mist of the wild landscape. His trappers are less intruders upon nature than converts to its serenity.

Even when conflict became explicit, nature retained a sense of transcendence or "otherness." Civilization had not yet won supremacy. In Charles Deas's melodramatic painting *Death Struggle,* a white trapper, still clutching a mink he has caught in a trap, is locked in combat with an Indian. In contrast to Bingham's peaceful mist and mirrorlike river, nature now assumes the beautiful

"The Interior of Fort Laramie" by Alfred Jacob Miller.

awe and terror that romantics termed the "sublime"—a boiling conflict between light and darkness that recalls nineteenth-century illustrations of Dante's *Divine Comedy* and Milton's *Paradise Lost*. Deas's painting also echoes the themes of the contemporary *Leatherstocking Tales* of James Fenimore Cooper. Deas's trapper, like Cooper's heroes, is in dire peril, but the white audience can confidently assume that his Indian foe will plunge into the dark abyss below.

Yet there was open space in the West that remained unconquered. The first pictorial images of conquest focused on trading posts that enclosed small fortified spaces in the midst of boundless plains and barren mountains. Alfred Jacob Miller's views of Fort Laramie represented a compromise between the harmonious blending of Bingham and the stark combat of Deas. Miller, enlisted in 1837 as the official artist for an expedition led by a Brit-

ish explorer and army officer, made the first on-the-spot paintings of the Rocky Mountains fur-trapping region. Fort Laramie had been built on the North Platte River, northeast of the later town of Laramie, Wyoming, at the crossroads of Indian trading routes and in the direct path of the future Oregon Trail. Miller depicted it as an outpost of white civilization, a protected space filled with rectangular lines and jutting towers reminiscent of medieval European castles. A secure oasis for tens of thousands of future overland emigrants, it was also surrounded by the tepees of nomadic Oglala Sioux. As portrayed here in *The Interior of Fort Laramie* by Miller, the fort stakes off a physical space for controlled intercourse between whites and Indians—the Indians who were sometimes allowed to enter the gate, trade, stare at the cannon, and be exploited, sexually and otherwise, by a superior power.

For pre–Civil War Americans, the Far West represented only one aspect of nature, a raw nature that sometimes seemed to threaten the moral and psychological foundations of civilization. East of the Mississippi, where civilization faced no more than a mopping-up operation, the victors could afford a certain nostalgia for the wilderness landscape that was being transformed and enclosed. Most of the East was still woodland, swamp, and pasture, but "nature," in the sense of an environment that affects humans more than it is affected by humans, seemed increasingly vulnerable. It could therefore be enshrined and for a time preserved in its precarious autonomy by landscape painting, a form of art that enjoyed increasing popularity. The reverent imagery of the so-called Hudson River School suggested a divine spirit within hills, brooks, forests, rocks, clouds, and illuminated skies. Building on this tradition, Martin Heade evolved an eerie realism that captured fleeting moments of changing light and atmosphere, often set off by wide horizons where civilized land gives way to a wild and ominous sea. In his *Coming Storm*, the luminous sailboat and human figures seem almost frozen in place, yet threatened by the distant flash of lightning and heavy rain clouds. In the works of Heade and other landscape painters, nature could startle viewers, bringing a delight of recognition as well as a moment of humility. As the symbol of something beyond human reach, nature could thus serve as an aesthetic counterweight to civilization's demands for predictability, mastery, and control.

"The Coming Storm" by Martin J. Heade.

"The Lackawanna Valley" by George Innes.

In a way, however, American culture demanded that nature somehow assimilate and give legitimacy to the machine. This demand was most imaginatively met by George Innes, who in 1854 accepted a commission from the Lackawanna Railroad Company to paint such unorthodox subjects as a railroad roundhouse and steam locomotive. In Innes's *Lackawanna Valley*, a pastoral landscape seems to embrace and merge with civilization's smoke and iron. A lone spectator, similar to the contemplative figure in Heade's *Coming Storm*, looks out upon a peaceful valley. The train's plume of smoke is echoed by a distant wisp beyond the church steeple. The curving track links the background hills with the tall tree in the foreground. Despite the stumps, despite the signs of encroaching industry, the human intrusion on nature appears to be in harmony with nature's rhythms.

But antebellum artists evolved no similar formula for romanticizing the city, a subject they generally shunned. A few anonymous painters did succeed in documenting the squalor, moral degra-

"The Consummation of Empire" by Thomas Cole.

dation, and jostling confusion of New York's growing slums. It was Thomas Cole, however, the original leader of the Hudson River School and the painter who did the most to popularize the American landscape, who expressed the era's most striking vision of the consequences of "over-civilization."

Cole painted his five canvases on *The Course of Empire* after returning from a residence in Europe, where he had contemplated the ruins of antiquity. His choice of classical imagery had special mean-ing for a modern republic that had taken so many of its moral and aesthetic models from classical Rome. Cole's first two canvases show the evolution from primitive origins of a pastoral, creative, classical society. In *The Consummation of Empire*, however, chasteness and innocence have given way to luxurious decadence. The scene represents a total subjugation and defiance of nature. Except for a jutting cliff in the background, the landscape has become wholly encrusted with marble temples and monuments. An imperial procession of the

"The Destruction of Empire" by Thomas Cole.

bridge suggests the arrogance of unlimited power. The sinuous fountain and voluptuous setting at the lower right suggest moral decay.

In *The Destruction of Empire* the viewer's perspective has shifted to the right and rear. The jutting cliff is still visible in the distance, and is the only landmark certain to survive the catastrophic destruction. Civilization is engulfed in a storm of flame and swirling smoke. People spill like ants from the bridge, while in the foreground the statue of a gigantic headless warrior holds his helpless shield above the scene of pillage and rape. On the base of the statue Cole inscribed the large numbers "1836," which was not only the date of the painting but a year when financial panic caused many

Americans to ponder the future course of their own empire.

Cole's final canvas presents lifeless ruins and rubble covered by creeping vegetation—a view of nature unperturbed by the extinction of civilization. A similar theme of catastrophism, qualifying the exuberant optimism of antebellum society, was not uncommon in American literature and art. It drew on traditions of religious millennarianism as well as on the fear that any republic, no matter how virtuous its origins, might share the fate of Rome. Both models suggested the spasmodic anxieties of a people who continued to defy the limits and boundaries of their Old World heritage.

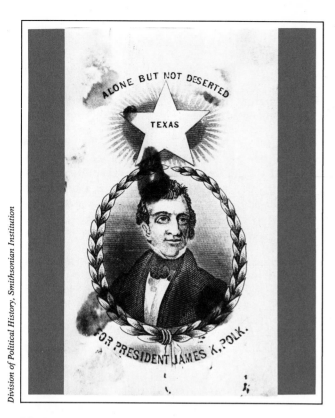

POLK CAMPAIGN RIBBON

As Speaker of the House of Representatives, Polk served President Andrew Jackson as a loyal lieutenant. In 1844 Jackson, as the retired elder statesman of the Democratic party, supported Polk's candidacy for president after Martin Van Buren had taken a public stand against annexing Texas. As a young "dark horse" in the race, Polk defeated the veteran Van Buren for the Democratic nomination. Polk's election as president helped the outgoing Tyler administration to secure Texas's annexation.

Democratic contenders, felt compelled by April 1844 to express their opposition to the immediate annexation of Texas.

In the Senate the Missouri Democrat Thomas Hart Benton led the attack against the trickery of Tyler and Calhoun. Seven other Democratic senators, all Northerners, joined the Whigs in decisively rejecting the annexation treaty. Yet the Whig opposition to expansion encouraged the Democratic party to close ranks and rally behind patriotic demands for the "reannexation of Texas" and the "reoccupation of Oregon." (These demands assumed that Texas had been part of the Louisiana Purchase and that Britain had never had legitimate claims to the region south of 54°40', the border of Russian Alaska.) The issue of expansion diverted attention from the Democrats' internal disputes over banking and fiscal policy, and it also enabled a southern-dominated coalition to defeat Van Buren and nominate James K. Polk, a Jacksonian ex-

pansionist from Tennessee, as the Democratic candidate.

As Calhoun had predicted, the Oregon question became an ideal means for exploiting national Anglophobia and winning northern support for national expansion. For decades the British Hudson's Bay Company had ruled the region north of the Columbia River, although the United States had strong claims to the Columbia itself and to the territory extending southward to latitude 42°. New England ships had long frequented the entire Pacific Northwest in search of sea otter furs for the China trade, and since the 1820s American trappers had developed a thriving trade in beaver and other furs within the region west of the Rockies. As American traders challenged the political and judicial authority of the powerful Hudson's Bay Company, it became more difficult to resolve conflicting Anglo-American claims. Moreover, in 1827, when the two nations had renewed a "joint occupation" agreement that simply deferred any settlement of national boundaries, no one could foresee the future appeal of the fertile Willamette Valley to farmers in the Old Northwest. American missionaries working with the Indians sent back glowing reports of the rich farmland in the Willamette Valley, and these helped spread the "Oregon fever" of the 1840s. Thousands of families risked the perils of overland travel to the Pacific. In 1843 the first of the great overland wagon migrations along the Oregon Trail took place, and the resulting claims to "All Oregon" acted as a political balance wheel for the annexation of Texas.

In the 1844 election, as in other elections of the time, voter preference depended less on issues than on ethnic, religious, and party loyalty. And so, concerned about the crucial swing vote, Clay, the Whig candidate, retreated from his earlier stand against Texas annexation. His last-minute gestures for southern support persuaded thousands of northern Whigs to vote for James G. Birney, the Liberty party candidate, who stood firm against annexation. More popular votes were actually cast against Polk than for him. Although Polk won the election, he would certainly have lost it if Birney's votes in New York and Michigan had gone to Clay.

Nevertheless, the incumbent President Tyler and the triumphant Democrats interpreted the election as a mandate for immediate annexation. The Democrats in Congress united in championing the new expansionism, allowing the outgoing Tyler administration to secure annexation by joint resolution of both houses of Congress. After a tense period of international intrigue, the Republic of Texas rejected offers of peace from Mexico and mediation from Britain. In December 1845, having bypassed territorial status, Texas entered the Union as a new slave state.

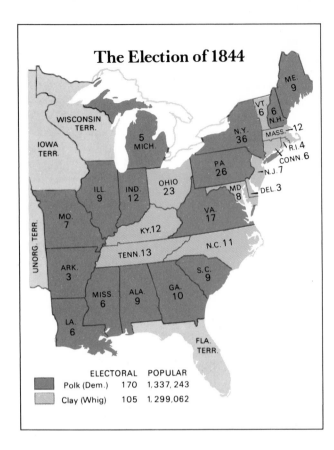

The Election of 1844

	ELECTORAL	POPULAR
Polk (Dem.)	170	1,337,243
Clay (Whig)	105	1,299,062

The Mexican War and Manifest Destiny

The admission of Texas coincided with President Polk's aggressive reformulation of the Monroe Doctrine. In his annual message of December 2, 1845, Polk warned that henceforth the United States would not tolerate any kind of European interferences designed to limit the spread of the American form of government or the right of any peoples of North America "to decide their own destiny." By this Polk meant the right to be annexed to the United States. In the case of Texas, whose boundaries were still extremely controversial, annexation meant a federal commitment to the restoration of slavery in a region in which it had earlier been outlawed by Mexico. Only the future could determine the fate of Cuba, California, and Oregon—provinces that Polk very much had in mind. And the future too would determine precisely how the people would "decide their own destiny," an ideal soon to be known as "popular sovereignty."

Oregon and California. President Polk's warnings about European interference were directed mainly at Britain. He emphasized that the danger of British economic or political interference, even apart from phys-

ical colonization, justified an indefinite expansion of America's boundaries. He also rejected further negotiation with Britain over the Oregon question and asked Congress to give notice of the termination of the 1827 joint occupation agreement. The dismayed British government ignored the belligerent rhetoric, but it commissioned new steam warships and ordered a naval force to the northeast Pacific.

Although Polk hoped to force British concessions regarding Oregon, his primary objective was California. In 1845 a British consul correctly observed that California, which contained no more than 10,000 white inhabitants, was at the mercy of whoever might choose to take possession of it. Polk feared that the British might seize the province as compensation for money owed by Mexico. Months before Polk's December message, the government had ordered the commodore of the American Pacific Squadron to take San Francisco and other ports if he could "ascertain with certainty" that Mexico had declared war against the United States.

Polk's secretary of state, James Buchanan, also sent secret instructions to Thomas Larkin, the American consul at Monterey, California, telling him to foil British plots and to foment, as cautiously as possible, a spirit of rebellion among the Spanish Californians. Finally, only days after Polk's belligerent message, America's dashing "Pathfinder," Captain John C. Frémont, arrived in California at the head of a "scientific expedition" of heavily armed engineers. Frémont had been exploring the Mexican West without permission from Mexico, and he would soon defy the Mexican authorities in California and encourage the Anglo-American settlers in an uprising, supposedly in their own self-defense.

Slidell's Mission. December 1845 also marked the arrival in Mexico City of Polk's secret minister, John Slidell, who had orders to win Mexican acceptance of the Rio Grande River as the new border with the United States, as well as to purchase as much of New Mexico and California as possible. His instructions emphasized the determination of the United States to prevent California from becoming a British or French colony, and authorized Slidell to extend to Mexico as much as $25 million for the territories desired. The Americans also offered to assume the debts owed by Mexico to American citizens.

The Mexican government had previously been willing to settle the Texas dispute. But one of Mexico's numerous revolutions was about to erupt, and the unstable government could not dare recognize an American envoy who made such sweeping demands— demands that had already been leaked to the American press. Mexican nationalists considered

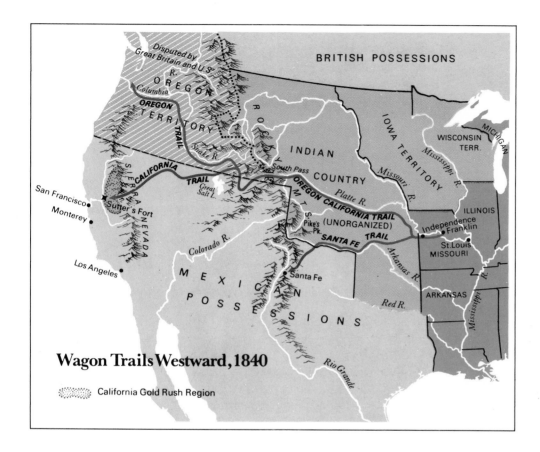

Wagon Trails Westward, 1840

California Gold Rush Region

Texas a "stolen province," and they especially resented the wholly unfounded claim that Texas extended to the Rio Grande. In 1816 Spain had designated the Nueces River, 130 miles north and east of the Rio Grande, as the boundary between the provinces of Tamaulipas and Texas; this was the boundary that appeared on American and European maps. In 1836, however, when the Texans had captured the Mexican president, Santa Anna, he had been forced to agree to the Rio Grande boundary as a condition for his release. The Mexican government had promptly rejected this extortionary agreement. By the end of 1845, Mexican nationalists hoped for European support and were eager for a war of revenge against American imperialists.

War with Mexico.   On learning of Slidell's failure, the Polk administration was also eager for war but wanted a pretext that would justify seizing California. In January 1846 the president ordered General Zachary Taylor, who had been poised for the move, to march to the Rio Grande. Without opposition, American ships blockaded the river and Taylor took up a position across the Rio Grande from the Mexican town of Mat-

amoros, toward which he aimed his cannons. By early May, however, Washington had heard no news of hostilities, and the impatient president and cabinet decided that Mexico's unpaid debts and the rebuff to Slidell were sufficient grounds for war. Then, just as Polk had drafted a war message to Congress, news arrived of a minor skirmish between Mexican and American patrols. Polk could now indignantly inform Congress that war already existed. He said, "Notwithstanding all our efforts to avoid it [war] exists by the act of Mexico herself. [Mexico] has passed the boundary of the United States, has invaded our territory and shed American blood upon the American soil."

By any objective interpretation, Americans had crossed the Mexican boundary and had shed Mexican blood on Mexican soil. American expansionists, however, believed that the protests from Europe simply confirmed that the growth of the United States was a blow to political and religious tyranny. It was America's mission, expansionists assumed, to liberate the peoples of California, Mexico, Cuba, Central America, and even Canada, allowing them to share in the blessings of republican government, religious freedom, and modern technology. In 1845 an influential

AMERICAN SOLDIERS HEADING SOUTH
General Thomas John Wood, a member of Zachary Taylor's staff, leads American troops through the streets of Saltillo, the capital of Coalhuila province in northern Mexico.

Democratic editor had coined the electric phrase "Manifest Destiny," at the same time denouncing the policy of other nations of

hampering our power, limiting our greatness and checking the fulfillment of our manifest destiny to overspread the continent allotted by Providence for the free development of our yearly multiplying millions.

But the crusade to prevent Europe from imposing a "balance of power" in North America strained the fragile balance on which the Union had always depended—the balance of power between North and South. In the Northeast and particularly in New England, the Mexican War provoked thunderous outrage. It was denounced from press and pulpit as a war of brutal aggression, plotted by the Slave Power to extend slavery and secure permanent control over the free states. The Massachusetts legislature went so far as to proclaim the war unconstitutional.

The war remained unpopular with the great majority of Whig leaders, even in the South, who objected to Polk's devious tactics and to the way in which Congress had been stampeded into a declaration of war in order to rescue Zachary Taylor's army, which had falsely been said to be endangered.

Settlement of the Oregon Controversy. By June 1846, a month after the war had begun, even the prowar western Democrats were angered when Polk allowed the Senate to assume full responsibility for approving a treaty that gave to Britain Vancouver Island and all of the

**Major Campaigns
of the Mexican War**

Oregon country north of the forty-ninth parallel. As the western expansionists rightly suspected, Southerners had never been enthusiastic about adding probable free states in the Pacific Northwest, and Polk had no wish to risk war with Britain when he was intent on dismembering Mexico.

Yet the nation as a whole supported the war. Remembering that opposition to the War of 1812 had split and destroyed the Federalist party, Whigs in Congress dutifully voted for military appropriations and congratulated themselves on the fact that the army's two leading generals, Zachary Taylor and Winfield Scott, were also Whigs. Taylor was the first to win glory. Within a few months, and with few American casualties, he defeated Mexican armies much larger than his own, crossed the Rio Grande, and captured the strategic town of Monterrey, thereby commanding northeastern Mexico. According to Democratic critics, he then settled down to prepare for the presidential campaign of 1848, which he won. In February 1847, however, Taylor crushed another Mexican army more than three times the size of his own in the battle of

Buena Vista. The Mexican army was led by Santa Anna, who had earlier been exiled from Mexico. Polk had allowed Santa Anna to enter Mexico from Cuba because he believed that this self-styled Napoleon of the West would persuade Mexico to sue for peace.

By early 1847 Polk's professed objectives had been achieved. Mexico's defense of California collapsed so suddenly that the only serious conflict stemmed from the rival and uncoordinated American onslaughts: Consul Larkin's efforts to mobilize the dissatisfied Spanish Californians; Frémont's leadership of the Anglo-American settlers; the American navy's capture of the port towns; and the arrival of an overland force, led by Stephen W. Kearny, which conquered New Mexico on the way to San Diego.

But the war was far from over. What the Mexicans lacked in leadership and modern armament, they made up for in national pride and determination. The United States could hardly claim an efficient military machine, but the army sparkled with talent. The roster of young officers read like a gallery of later Union and Confederate heroes: Lee, Grant, Sherman, Meade,

LIEUTENANT B. W. ARMSTRONG
Many young officers did not live to fight in the later Civil War. Second Lieutenant B. W. Armstrong, a West Point graduate, contracted a fatal disease while serving in Mexico.

McClellan, Beauregard, Stonewall Jackson, and even Jefferson Davis. For Europeans, whose memories of Napoleonic battles had receded into more than thirty years of romantic haze, the American triumphs were stupendous. The Manchester *Guardian* wrote that the American victories were without parallel, "except in that of Alexander the Great through Persia, Hannibal from Spain to the gates of Rome, or Napoleon over the Alps into Italy." Instead of one Napoleon, America had them "by the dozen."

Treaty of Guadalupe Hidalgo.

The events that astonished even hostile Europeans began with General Scott's invasion of central Mexico in March 1847. By September, after winning a series of hotly contested battles, American troops had captured Mexico City and were resting in the halls of the Montezumas. The Mexicans still refused to surrender. In the United States Americans were becoming increasingly divided over the meaning of Manifest Destiny. As the American army pushed toward Mexico City, "our Destiny higher an' higher kep' mountin'," in the caustic words of the

New England poet James Russell Lowell. Some Southerners believed that slavery could be extended at least into the northern states of Mexico; some anti-slavery Northerners believed that Mexico would be a force for freedom, and therefore they favored annexing the whole country. In general, however, the Democratic leaders—Polk, Buchanan, Lewis Cass, Stephen Douglas, Sam Houston, Jefferson Davis—demanded and expected to get no less than a third of the country south and west of the Rio Grande. They were therefore outraged when Nicholas Trist, whom Polk had angrily recalled as America's negotiator, proceeded to conclude the unauthorized Treaty of Guadalupe Hidalgo. Instead of capitalizing on America's conquests, Trist settled for the same terms that Slidell had been prepared to offer before the war: the United States was to pay Mexico $15 million and assume up to $3.25 million in Mexican debts to American citizens. In return, the United States obtained California, New Mexico, and the Rio Grande boundary. Polk would have liked to reject the treaty, but he feared that further war and prolonged negotiations would split the Democratic party in an election year. Alarmed by the growing antiwar and Free Soil movement among northern Democrats, he reluctantly submitted the treaty to the Senate, which approved it in March 1848.

Attempts to Acquire Cuba.

But Polk had other cards up his sleeve. In 1848 the Democratic expansionists launched an intensive propaganda campaign to annex the Yucatán Peninsula, a rebellious province that had seceded from Mexico and whose white inhabitants were in danger of being exterminated by hostile Indians. Polk feared British intervention and realized that the American army in Mexico was virtually unemployed, and thus he invited Congress to act. But enthusiasm waned when news arrived that the Yucatán racial crisis had subsided.

Polk was actually far more interested in acquiring Cuba. Like the Yucatán Peninsula, Cuba guarded access to the Gulf of Mexico. Its traditional strategic importance would be increased by any future canal connecting the Gulf of Mexico with the Pacific—something that was already much discussed. Britain was on the verge of war with Spain in 1848, and thus it might at any time gain control of Cuba. Many of Cuba's sugar growers, resenting Britain's increasing interference with their slave-labor system and fearing the continuing spread of emancipation in the West Indies, believed that annexation to the United States was their only guarantee of remaining a prosperous slave society.

The Polk administration knew, however, that the North would not approve the use of military force to acquire more than one-third of a million additional

"THE OCCUPATION OF THE CAPITAL OF MEXICO BY THE AMERICAN ARMY" BY P.S. DAVAL
Americans enter the historic square, or Zocalo, of Mexico City, March 1847.

black slaves. Polk's only alternative was to try, with the utmost caution and secrecy, to persuade Spain that $100 million was a good price for a colony that was about to rebel or to be lost to Britain. But Spain greatly prized the only rich remnant of its once-great empire and contemptuously rejected the bungled overtures of Polk's minister. The prospects for annexing Cuba were further dashed when Lewis Cass, the Democratic presidential candidate who favored the purchase of Cuba and the annexation of Yucatán, was defeated in the fall of 1848 by the nonexpansionist Zachary Taylor.

Southern hopes for acquiring Cuba now turned to encouraging a Cuban revolution against Spain. Groups of Cuban emigrés, aided by American expansionists, planned a series of "filibustering" invasions to liberate the Cuban people. By 1850, however, the anxieties of Cuban planters had subsided and their desire to be taken over by the United States had faded. In 1851, in an episode that strangely anticipated the Bay of Pigs disaster of 1961, Cubans captured the entire expedition of Narciso López, a southern hero, and executed him and fifty of his American followers.

Schemes for further expansion revived under the Democratic administration of Franklin Pierce (1853–57). Members of Pierce's cabinet gave encouragement to John A. Quitman, a filibuster from Mississippi who spent years waiting for the opportune moment to lead a gigantic invasion of Cuba. The invasion never took place, and in 1854 President Pierce warned that the government would prosecute Americans who violated the laws ensuring the nation's neutrality in foreign conflicts. Yet in 1856 Pierce's administration accorded diplomatic recognition to a regime established in Nicaragua by another American filibuster, William Walker. Walker, a native of Tennessee, had earlier led an invasion of Lower California (part of Mexico), where he had unsuccessfully proclaimed an independent republic. Having won acquittal for this violation of America's neutrality laws, Walker became involved in a revolution in Nicaragua. In 1856, aided by a small army of American volunteers, he emerged as president of the Central American nation.

Because Nicaragua occupied a strategic location as a transit point between the Atlantic and Pacific oceans, it became the site of intense Anglo-American rivalry. In the Clayton-Bulwer Treaty of 1850, both nations agreed not to take over any territory in Central America and to ensure that any future interoceanic canal would be unfortified and open to vessels of all countries. But the Clayton-Bulwer Treaty was extremely unpopular, especially in the South, and Walker appealed to American Anglophobia to win support for his dream of a Caribbean empire. He also reestablished slavery in Nicaragua but was soon driven out of the country by the armed forces of neighboring Central American nations that were supported by powerful American shipping interests.

Except for some ardent expansionists in the South, Americans were cooling toward proposals for further territorial acquisitions. In 1854 the Senate almost defeated a treaty that provided for the purchase from Mexico of a parcel of land south of the Gila River in what is now southern New Mexico and Arizona. The land was considered essential for building a railroad that would connect the southeastern states with southern California. But although James Gadsden, Pierce's negotiator with Mexico, had originally sought to obtain the northern part of five Mexican provinces and all of Lower California, the Senate insisted on cutting 9,000 square miles from the modest segment of desert that Mexico had been willing to sell.

In 1854 the expansionist intrigues of Pierce's administration culminated in the secret meetings of America's ministers to Spain, France, and Great Britain, who drafted a long memorandum to the State Department justifying the forcible seizure of Cuba if the island could not be purchased from Spain. Labeled the Ostend Manifesto, the secret memorandum was leaked to the American public at a moment of explosive sectional conflict. It confirmed many Northerners' belief that the Slave Power would continue to expand unless checked by political might. One of the authors of the manifesto was James Buchanan, the minister to Britain. In 1856 Buchanan became the Democratic presidential candidate, and his platform openly called for annexing Cuba. By this time, however, the heated controversy over legalizing slavery in Kansas had diverted attention from further national expansion.

CHRONOLOGY

1819	Transcontinental (Adams-Onís) Treaty. Spain renounces claims to the Floridas and Pacific Northwest; United States renounces claims to Texas.
1823	President issues Monroe Doctrine.
1829	Mexico abolishes slavery.
1836	Texas proclaims its independence from Mexico.
	Martin Van Buren elected president.
1838	John Quincy Adams's filibuster defeats move to annex Texas.
1841	John Tyler becomes president on death of Harrison.
1842	Webster-Ashburton Treaty settles disputed U.S.-Canada boundary; provides for extradition of fugitives.
1843	"Oregon Fever"; first overland caravans to Oregon.
	Duff Green, Calhoun, and others begin planning imperial expansion to thwart British plots to undermine American slavery.
1844	Senate rejects Calhoun's Texas annexation treaty.
	James K. Polk elected President.
1845	Texas enters Union as slave state.
	Polk gives aggressive reformulation to Monroe Doctrine.
	John Slidell's unsuccessful mission to Mexico to negotiate purchase of New Mexico and California.
1846	Beginning of Mexican War. General Zachary Taylor invades Mexico from the north.
	Treaty with Britain divides Oregon Territory along forty-ninth parallel.
1847	General Winfield Scott captures Vera Cruz and Mexico City.
1848	Treaty of Guadalupe Hidalgo ends Mexican War and establishes Rio Grande as border.
	Secret attempts to purchase Cuba from Spain.
	Zachary Taylor elected president.
1854	Ostend Manifesto favors U.S. purchase or annexation of Cuba.
	Railroads link New York City with the Mississippi River.
1857	Financial panic and depression.

Ray A. Billington, *Westward Expansion* (1974), covers every aspect of America's westward expansion and contains an encyclopedic bibliography. Albert K. Weinberg, *Manifest Destiny* (1935), is a fascinating study in intellectual history, but it should be supplemented by Edward M. Burns, *The American Idea of Mission: Concepts of National Purpose and Destiny* (1957). In three outstanding revisionist studies, Frederick W. Merk reemphasizes the importance of slavery and the fear of British encroachments on the West: *Manifest Destiny and Mission in American History: A Reinterpretation* (1963); *The Monroe Doctrine and American Expansionism 1843–1849* (1966); and *Slavery and the Annexation of Texas* (1972). For a detailed treatment of western diplomatic history, see D. M. Pletcher, *The Diplomacy of Annexation: Texas, Oregon and the Mexican War* (1973).

The fullest history of the origins of the Monroe Doctrine is Dexter Perkins, *The Monroe Doctrine, 1823–1826* (1927). Ernest R. May, *The Making of the Monroe Doctrine* (1975), stresses the importance of domestic politics preceding the presidential election of 1824. For the European background, see E. H. Tatum, Jr., *The United States and Europe, 1815–1823* (1936), and C. C. Griffin, *The United States and the Disruption of the Spanish Empire* (1937). For a general introduction to American foreign policy, see Lloyd C. Gardner et al., *Creation of the American Empire* (1973); and, for a more traditional view, Samuel F. Bemis, *A Diplomatic History of the United States* (1965). The standard work on Asia is A. Whitney Griswold, *The Far Eastern Policy of the United States* (1938).

On Texas two of the standard works are by William C. Binkley: *The Texas Revolution* (1952), and *The Expansionist Movement in Texas, 1836–1850* (1925). Much can still be learned from the older, nationalistic studies: J. H. Smith, *The Annexation of Texas* (1911), and E. C. Barker, *Mexico and Texas, 1821–1835* (1928). For a meticulous portrayal of the Mexican point of view, see Gene M. Brack, *Mexico Views Manifest Destiny, 1821–1846* (1976).

Frederick W. Merk has written several superb essays on the Anglo-American diplomacy regarding Oregon: *Albert Gallatin and the Oregon Problem* (1950), and *The Oregon Question: Essays in Anglo-American Diplomacy and Politics* (1967). For general histories of the Northwest, see Norman A. Graebner, *Empire on the Pacific* (1955); Oscar O. Winther, *The Great Northwest* (1947); and Earl Pomeroy, *The Pacific Slope: A History* (1965).

Ray A. Billington, *The Far Western Frontier, 1830–1860* (1956), is a lively and scholarly survey of the exploration and settlement of the Great West. By far the best account of the overland emigration to the Far West is John D. Unruh, Jr., *The Plains Across: The Overland Emigrants and the Trans-Mississippi West, 1840–1860* (1979). For the experience of women and the division of sex roles, see John Mack Faragher, *Women and Men on the Overland Trail* (1979). The fascinating story of government exploration is described with admirable care in William H. Goetzmann, *Army Exploration in the American West, 1803–1863* (1959). Gloria G. Cline, *Exploring the Great Basin* (1963), in an invaluable study. H. M. Chittenden, *The American Fur Trade of the Far West* (3 vols., 1935), is still the most comprehensive story of the fur trade, although important new work has long been in progress. Although sometimes scorned by professional historians, Bernard DeVoto's *Across the Wide Missouri* (1947), which deals with the Mountain Men and the fur trade, and DeVoto's *The Year of Decision, 1846* (1943), which considers the political, social, and cultural events surrounding America's war with Mexico, are exciting, readable, and basically accurate accounts of the early West.

J. H. Smith, *The War with Mexico* (2 vols., 1919), remains the fullest account of the Mexican War. Gene M. Brack, *Mexico Views Manifest Destiny* (1976), deserves special mention for its insight into the Mexican motives for war. The best recent account of the military campaigns is K. Jack Bauer, *The Mexican War, 1846–1848* (1974). For Mexican-American relations, see G. L. Rives, *The United States and Mexico: 1821–1848* (2 vols., 1913). John H. Schroeder, *Mr. Polk's War: American Opposition and Dissent, 1846–1848* (1973), is an excellent study of antiwar sentiment. For American involvement in Cuba and Central America, see William O. Scroggs, *Filibusters and Financiers: The Story of William Walker and His Associates* (1916), and Robert E. May, *The Southern Dream of a Caribbean Empire, 1854–1861* (1973).

17 Compromise and Conflict

On the surface the two-party system resolved the dangerous sectional conflicts that had been unleashed by the annexation of Texas, the Mexican War, and the acquisition of a new continental empire. By the early 1850s cohesion and compromise seemed to have triumphed over division. Americans were more prosperous than they ever had been before, and for the most part they were able to ignore or rationalize evidence of continuing injustice and exploitation. Public interest in further empire building faded, despite attempts by Democratic leaders to revive the people's enthusiasm. There was sufficient challenge, it seemed, in building railroads, settling a continent, and extending American commerce. In 1854, for example, Commodore Matthew Perry used diplomatic tact and a display of naval power to help break down the Japanese government's already crumbling resistance to Western trade and influence. Political realists believed that the North did not desire to interfere with slavery in South. In the eyes of moderates, there was no reason for the North to fear that slavery would expand beyond its "natural limits" in Missouri, Arkansas, and Texas.

There were hazards, however, in this triumph of moderation. The stormy passions that culminated in the Compromise of 1850 gave way to political apathy and disenchantment. Voters complained that Whigs and Democrats had the same self-serving lust for office, mouthed the same stale rhetoric on stale issues, and were equally unresponsive to public needs and fears. For reasons that varied in each state and locality, significant numbers of voters abandoned their former party allegiance. One consequence of this broad realignment was the rapid disintegration of the Whigs, especially in the South. By 1855 the anti-Catholic Know-Nothing party had replaced the Whigs as the dominant alternative to the Democrats in the Northeast. In all sections of the country, the weakening of balanced national parties opened the way for new and more extreme appeals to resist the encroachments of some supposedly antirepublican "power."

The American fear of unchecked power was deeply rooted in the colonial and Revolutionary past. The fear acquired new dimensions, however, as the restraints of local customs and traditions gave way to individual enterprise and unrestrained capitalism. For a time the party system had succeeded in channeling and moderating public alarm over the rise of various "powers," such as the Freemasons, the "Monster Bank," the "Money Power," Jackson's "monarchical" presidency, and the alleged British conspiracy to block American expansion. By the mid-1850s, however, the controversy over slavery in the territories began to distract attention from anti-Catholic nativism, and the Americans' fear of unchecked power became grounded in the concrete conflict of interests between free and slave societies.

Like a magnetic field, black slavery polarized opposing clusters of values, interests, and aspirations. Southerners believed that any withdrawal of federal sanction and protection for slavery would expose private property to the tyranny of a national majority, undermine the equal sovereignty of the states, and lead America in the direction of European "wage-slavery" and class warfare—to say nothing of race mixing and black revolt.

By the mid 1850s a growing number of Northerners had become convinced that black slavery, by supporting "idle planters" and by associating work with servility, undermined the dignity of labor. As an alternative to the whips and chains of the South, the North offered an idealized vision of prosperity and progress without exploitation—a vision of industrious farmers and proud artisans, of schoolhouses, churches, town meetings, and self-made men. The vast territories of the West, unfenced and held in common by the American people, would thus become the critical testing ground for two competing versions of the American dream.

Free Soil and the Challenge of California

Once the United States had acquired the vast Mexican territories from Texas to California, national decisions had to be made. All the constitutional issues and the political and moral arguments of the Missouri crisis of 1819–21 were revived. Would the South be able to maintain its balance of power in the Senate? What was the precise nature of congressional power over territories and the creation of new states? Would the government limit the future expansion of slavery? Would it adopt a policy of non-interference? Or would it perhaps openly sanction slavery by recognizing black slaves as a form of property entitled to federal protection in the western territories?

The Wilmot Proviso. It was predictable that a move would be made in Congress to prohibit slavery in the territories acquired during the Mexican War; similar moves had been made since 1784 concerning the trans-Appalachian West, Mississippi, Louisiana, Arkansas, and Missouri. In 1846 the motion came from David Wilmot, a Pennsylvania Democrat, in the form of a proposed amendment to an appropriation bill. The Wilmot Proviso was extraordinarily significant because it was used to challenge what was called Mr. Polk's War and all that it meant. The legislatures of fourteen free states eventually endorsed the proviso's principle. Although many northern senators ignored the instructions of their states, the House of Representatives several times approved the measure, which antislavery members continued to offer.

From 1847 to 1850 this sectional insistence that the territories ceded by Mexico remain "free soil" challenged Whig and Democratic party unity. Many southern Whigs denounced any proposal for excluding slavery from the territories as a direct violation of southern rights and of state equality. The more extreme Calhounites tried to erode national party loyalty by uniting all Southerners in defense of sectional rights and in opposition to any candidate who failed to oppose the Wilmot Proviso. In the North in the election of 1848, both Whigs and Democrats suffered losses to the new Free Soil party, which nominated Martin Van Buren for president. So-called Conscience Whigs, centered in Massachusetts, refused to vote for Zachary Taylor, the former general and Louisiana slaveholder nominated by the Whigs. The Conscience Whigs claimed that moral protest against the further expansion of slavery should take precedence over the material and political advantages of a united Whig party. Free Soil Democrats were led by the so-called New York Barnburners, politicians who had been angered when the Democrats rejected Van Buren in favor of Polk in 1844 and who then had been further alien-

POSTER FOR A FREE SOIL RALLY

ated when Polk's administration had favored rival Democratic factions in distributing patronage.

But this upsurge of sectional politics proved to be quite unsuccessful in undermining the two-party system. Both the Whig and the Democratic parties evaded official commitment on the territorial issue and unashamedly made contradictory appeals to northern and southern voters. In the election of 1848, Van Buren received only 14 percent of the popular vote in the North and won no electoral votes for his Free Soil party. Taylor carried even Massachusetts, where the Whig defections seemed most threatening; Whigs actually gained strength in the South. As a result of this defeat, Van Buren and most of his Democratic followers returned to the national party that now shared common interests in opposing a new Whig administration. The Conscience Whigs mostly returned to their uneasy alliance with the so-called Cotton Whigs, led by such powerful New England textile manufacturers as Abbott Lawrence and Nathan Appleton, who looked to a continuation of their profitable trade relations with the cotton-producing South. And early in 1849 it became clear that the Calhounites had little hope of winning support for a new southern rights coalition.

The survival of national parties did nothing, however, to resolve the territorial issue or to break the congressional deadlock over the Wilmot Proviso. Northern Democrats had favored either extending the

Missouri Compromise line of 36°30′ to the Pacific, or leaving the question of slavery to territorial legislatures without congressional interference. The latter alternative was known as popular sovereignty. President Taylor, on the other hand, tried to prevent further sectional confrontations by urging California and New Mexico to draft constitutions and to apply for immediate statehood. This strategy would have avoided congressional action either sanctioning or banning slavery. Both Taylor and his southern opponents recognized that the inhabitants of the Far West, if allowed to organize state governments, would almost certainly vote to exclude black slavery. These settlers, most of whom had lived in the intensely racist states of the Old Northwest, cared little about the fate of the slaves in the South, but they feared the competition of slave labor in a "land of promise" that was supposedly reserved for aspiring whites.

Suddenly antiblack feeling became acute in California. Gold was discovered in the American River in 1848, and the great gold rush of 1849 brought tens of thousands of settlers who resented the prolongation of ineffective military government and who clamored for instant statehood. It also brought a small number of southern masters and slaves—and of free black prospectors who, according to hostile whites, were "proverbially lucky." White miners considered it unfair to compete with slave labor, and they also considered it degrading "to swing a pick side by side with the Negro," whether free or slave. Fear and hatred of blacks, particularly in the mining regions, led the California constitutional convention of 1849 to copy the sections of the newly written Iowa constitution that prohibited slavery.

In Oregon, which was organized as a separate territory south of the Columbia River, the fusion of racism with antislavery was even more clear-cut. Although few blacks had arrived in the region by 1844, the provisional government followed the models of the Old Northwest and ordered the removal of both slaves and free blacks. The South succeeded in delaying Oregon's elevation to territorial status until 1848, and as late as 1857 there was a strong drive to legalize slavery in the Oregon Territory. After heated public debate, a referendum decisively rejected slavery but approved even more decisively the constitutional exclusion of free black settlers—a measure that Congress accepted as part of the state's constitution.

By 1849, however, Southerners tended to interpret even these dubious forms of antislavery as abolitionism in disguise. Most southern leaders, whether Whig or Democrat, had moved from a defensive policy of censorship and gag rules to an aggressive hostility to any barrier, however theoretical, to the expansion of slavery. They feared that enactment of the Wilmot

California State Library, Sacramento

BLACK AND WHITE PROSPECTORS
Black and white miners sometimes worked together, as at this sluice in Spanish Flat, California, in 1852.

Proviso would swing the full weight of the federal government against the institution of slavery, which it had always protected. By 1849 Free Soil and antislavery congressmen had already linked the proviso with demands for abolishing slavery in the District of Columbia, which, like the territories, was subject to federal legislation. The new personal liberty laws of the northern states raised the prospect that the North would become as secure a refuge for runaway slaves as British Canada, to which a small number of blacks had successfully escaped.

Indeed, for a growing number of southern diehards, the Northeast was by the late 1840s becoming a perfect replica of the British enemy. Britain, these Southerners believed, had first exploited its own slave colonies, then ruined them under the influence of misguided humanitarianism, and finally used antislavery as a mask of righteousness in assuming commercial and ideological domination of the world. The Northeast, like England, was attracting millions of immigrant wage earners, was developing vast urban centers, and was gaining mastery over the mysterious sources of credit and investment capital. Unless Dixie made its stand, it would therefore share the fate of the

ZACHARY TAYLOR (1784–1850)
A professional soldier, "Old Rough and Ready" served in a long series of Indian wars before becoming a Mexican War hero. He opposed extremism of all kinds and sought to head off what he considered to be needless sectional conflict.

The preceding administration, that of the Democrat Polk, had reestablished the Independent Treasury, reaffirming the Democrats' opposition to any alliance between government and banks.* It had also enacted the Walker Tariff, which had drastically reduced the duties the Whigs had established in 1842. To the dismay of Old Whigs, Taylor balked at proposals to repeal both these Democratic measures, and he advocated compromises that would avoid unnecessary conflict. Simultaneously southern Whigs, who had thought they could trust a Louisiana planter, were shocked to discover that Taylor had no objection to admitting California as a free state. In fact, Taylor even dumbfounded his powerful Georgia backer Robert Toombs by saying that if Congress saw fit to pass the Wilmot Proviso, "I will not veto it."

When the Thirty-First Congress convened in December 1849, there was a prolonged and ominous conflict over electing the Speaker of the House. It soon became clear that Taylor's program for admitting California and New Mexico as states would receive no support from southern Whigs or even from such party chieftains as Clay, Webster, and Seward. Tensions were heightened by the knowledge that all northern legislatures, with one exception, had instructed their senators to insist on the Wilmot Proviso in any agreement concerning the territories. Also, a growing number of southern legislatures were appointing delegates to a convention at Nashville in June 1850 to consider potentially revolutionary measures for the defense of southern rights.

Clay's Resolutions. In January 1850 the aging Henry Clay temporarily recovered leadership of the Whig party by offering the Senate a series of compromise resolutions. As an alternative to the Wilmot Proviso and to the popular southern plan that would extend the Missouri Compromise line to the Pacific, Clay favored admitting California as a free state. He proposed that no restrictions on slavery be imposed in the rest of the territory that had been acquired from Mexico. Clay also attempted to resolve the critical Texas issue. Texas claimed a western boundary that included more than half of the present state of New Mexico. As a result there was an imminent danger of border conflict between the armed forces of Texas and the United States, a conflict that could easily escalate into civil war. Further, when Texas had become an American state it had lost its former customs revenue, which was a matter of considerable concern to the influential holders of Texas bonds. To resolve these problems, Clay proposed that the United States government assume the Texas debt—which promised windfall

*For the Independent Treasury, see chapter 15, p. 379.

exploited, debt-ridden, and ravaged West Indies. If the South were deprived of land and labor for expansion, its boundaries pushed back from the west and the Gulf of Mexico as well as from the north, it would then be subjected by a tyrannical government to slave emancipation and race mixing.

The Crisis of 1850

The Taylor administration faced a succession of problems that exposed irreconcilable divisions within the Whig party. Zachary Taylor was a recent convert to the Whig party (previously, he had never even voted); he had run for president as a military hero and as a man "above party." As president he aggravated the mistrust of the so-called Old Whigs when, seeking to broaden the administration's national support, he bypassed party faithfuls in distributing patronage. Taylor also seemed to betray traditional Whig principles when he tried to build a broad coalition that could compete with the Democrats, who were gaining enormous strength from the votes of recent immigrants.

profits to Texas bondholders—as compensation for Texas's acceptance of New Mexico's territorial claims.

In a gesture to northern feelings, Clay recommended that Congress prohibit professional slave trading in the District of Columbia, to rid the national capital of the moral eyesore of slave pens and public auctions. But he also urged that Congress ease southern fears of abolitionists' intentions by formally denying that it had authority to interfere with the interstate slave trade and by promising that slavery would never be abolished in the District of Columbia without the consent of its citizens, as well as the consent of neighboring Maryland. Finally, Clay proposed that Congress adopt a fugitive slave law that would severely punish anyone who obstructed slaveholders' efforts to recover runaway slaves in any part of the United States.

The Compromise of 1850.

The ensuing congressional struggle to achieve the so-called Compromise of 1850 took place on two distinct levels. On the loftier level the Senate became a public forum for some of the most famous and eloquent speeches in American history—speeches that clarified conflicting principles, conflicting political philosophies, and conflicting visions of America's heritage, mission, and destiny. Calhoun, so ill and so near death that he could not personally deliver his farewell address to the nation, argued that a tyrannical northern majority had gradually excluded Southerners from 1.25 million square miles of territory. No further compromises could save the South from a continuing loss of power or prevent the day when a hostile and increasingly centralized government would carry out the demands of the abolitionists. The Union, he declared, might be saved if the North agreed to open all the territories to slaveholders and to restore, by constitutional amendment, an equal and permanent balance of sectional power. Otherwise, self-preservation would require the South to separate—and to fight if the North refused to accept secession in peace.

Daniel Webster, in his famous reply on March 7, 1850, insisted: "There can be no such thing as a peaceable secession." Recoiling in horror from the prospect of disunion and civil war, he pleaded for compromise and for a charitable spirit toward the South. He agreed with southern complaints against the abolitionists and supported Clay's demand for an effective fugitive slave law. The territorial issue, he claimed, should be no cause for further discord. Convinced that slave labor could never be profitable in the western territories, Webster saw no need for a further legal exclusion that could only antagonize the South.

On March 11 the growing antislavery audience in the Senate found a spokesman in William H. Seward, the New York Whig leader who had helped engineer Taylor's candidacy but who now failed to support the president's plan. Seward, whom Webster described as "subtle and unscrupulous" and dedicated "to the one idea of making himself president," gave political force to the traditional abolitionist doctrine concerning the territories: "There is a higher law than the Constitution, which regulates our authority over the domain . . . the common heritage of mankind."

These and other great speeches raised momentous issues, but it is unlikely that they changed many votes. The second level of struggle involved political infighting that ranged from bribes and lobbying by speculators in Texas bonds to patient and tireless work by committees of experts faithful to American political procedures and to the technicalities of constitutional law. Apart from the moderating influence of powerful banking and business interests, which stood to gain by national unity, four circumstances contributed to the final congressional approval of the Compromise of 1850.

First, despite signs of an ominous sectional division of parties, Stephen Douglas rallied a core of Democrats, particularly from the Old Northwest and border states, who could counteract the combined pressures of southern and northern extremists. Second, Douglas's drive to win southern support for a railroad connecting Chicago with the Gulf of Mexico (soon known as the Illinois Central Railroad) demonstrated the rewards that could be gained through sectional cooperation. Third, under Douglas's leadership the Senate wisely abandoned a so-called Omnibus Bill that combined most of the compromise in one package. This move allowed both houses of Congress to form sectional alliances that were just barely strong enough to carry each measure—the North overcoming southern resistance to the admission of California and the abolition of the slave trade in the District of Columbia; the South, thanks to many northern abstentions, having its way in enacting the new Fugitive Slave Law. Finally, President Taylor, who had shown no sympathy for the compromise, died suddenly in July. Millard Fillmore, his successor, was close to Webster and Clay and threw the full weight of his administration behind the compromise. Fillmore also skillfully defused the explosive crisis over the Texas–New Mexico boundary. In September 1850 much of the nation sank back in relief, assuming that the adoption of Clay's and Douglas's proposals marked the end of serious sectional conflict.

Thus the Compromise of 1850 was made up of the following points: (1) the admission of California as a free state; (2) the organization of the rest of the Mexican cession into two territories, New Mexico and Utah, without a federal restriction on slavery; (3) the

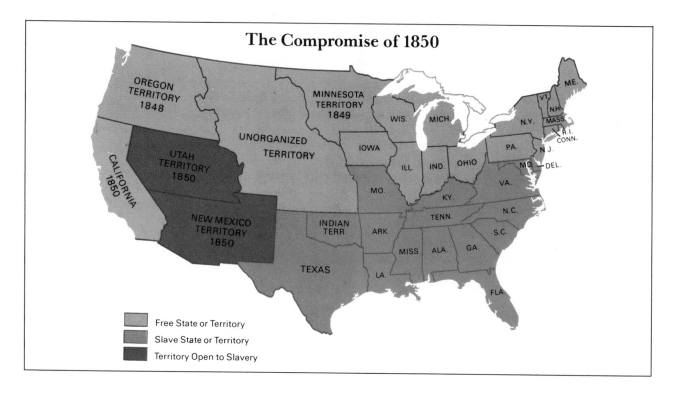

The Compromise of 1850

Legend:
- Free State or Territory
- Slave State or Territory
- Territory Open to Slavery

adjustment of the Texas–New Mexico boundary; (4) the award of $10 million to Texas as compensation for the land yielded to New Mexico; (5) the prohibition of the slave trade but not of slavery itself in the District of Columbia; and (6) a stringent fugitive slave law. This complex congressional agreement created an illusion of peace, but there was no real consensus on any of the critical issues. In the District of Columbia, trading and selling of slaves continued, although not as openly as before. Blacks, and particularly Indians, continued to be held as slaves on the supposedly free soil of California. The Fugitive Slave Law, which deprived accused blacks of a jury trial and of the right to testify in their own defense, dramatized the agonizing consequences of enforcing a national compromise for which the North had little taste.*

One of the northern responses to this law was the serial publication in 1851 of Harriet Beecher Stowe's *Uncle Tom's Cabin,* a novel that soon reached millions in book form and in stage presentations. Mrs. Stowe's popular classic, today often underrated as a literary work, interpreted the moral and psychological evils of slavery in terms that were perfectly attuned to the culture of northern evangelical Protestantism, especially to its belief in the sanctity of the family. *Uncle Tom's Cabin* vividly demonstrated the ability of slav-

---

*For northern reactions to the Fugitive Slave Law, see chapter 14, pp. 361–62.

ery to destroy or corrupt the family unit. And it encouraged every reader who sympathized with the fictional fugitives, in their terrible ordeal of escape, to share the guilt of a compromise that gave national sanction to slave catchers.

Popular Sovereignty. It was on the territorial issue that the Compromise of 1850 seeded the worst storm clouds of the future. The compromise was deliberately ambiguous concerning the territories. Congress appeared to reaffirm its authority to prohibit slavery in the territories, for it delegated this authority to the legislatures of Utah and New Mexico, subject to the possible veto of a federally appointed governor or of Congress itself. To appease the South, however, Congress publicly expressed doubts about the constitutionality of this authority, which could be determined only by the Supreme Court. In effect, Congress invited slaveholders to challenge the constitutionality of any restrictions that territorial governments might make on their property rights before the state governments had been established. Most Southerners reluctantly accepted "popular sovereignty" because it at least left the doors open to slavery. Northern moderates—called "doughfaces" by their antislavery enemies—were convinced that popular sovereignty would ultimately guarantee free states but would avoid a congressional showdown that would lead to the South's secession.

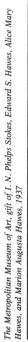

HARRIET BEECHER STOWE (1811–96)
The daughter of Lyman Beecher, Harriet Beecher Stowe suddenly became not only the most famous member of an illustrious family, but also the world's most admired and hated woman. Bitterly attacked in the South, she was lionized in England and soon became an international literary celebrity.

To pragmatists like Daniel Webster and Stephen Douglas, it seemed inconceivable that national policy of any kind could reverse the dominant western pattern of free-labor settlement. Cultivating cotton was too profitable and the value of slaves too great to encourage risky experiments in the semiarid West. It is true that in 1852 Utah legally recognized slavery and that in 1857 New Mexico adopted a slave code. Yet neither territory acquired more than a handful of black slaves. Southerners, long accustomed to the security of slave patrols and local law enforcement agencies, were fearful of taking valuable human property into a region where courts might invoke the old Mexican law prohibiting slavery and where legislatures might at any time be swayed by the convictions of the free-soil and antiblack majority. Moderates like Douglas claimed that the Compromise of 1850 was a "final settlement," but in fact it narrowed the area of future acceptable compromise. The belief grew in the South that disunion would be the inevitable—and the only honorable—response to any further northern threats.

The Know-Nothing Upsurge and the Collapse of the Whigs

Between 1853 and 1856 the two-party system rapidly disintegrated. The Whigs literally disappeared, and the Democrats suffered disastrous losses in the North while acquiring unquestionable dominance in the South. The reasons for this dramatic political transformation are still controversial. Even in 1852 the Whigs were seriously divided over the Compromise of 1850. In deference to southern demands, the party's 1852 platform endorsed this essentially Democratic "final settlement" of the slavery issue. Southern Whigs, however, were infuriated by the party's refusal to renominate Fillmore, whom many Northerners saw as a puppet of the Slave Power. Winfield Scott, the military hero who was finally nominated, showed signs of becoming a Seward protégé, like Zachary Taylor.

The Election of 1852. Because Southerners no longer trusted northern Whigs as reliable allies in the defense of slavery, the party suffered a devastating defection of southern voters in the election of 1852. In the North, simultaneously, a distinctive Whig identity was blurred. The Whig platform was very similar to the Democratic platform, and Whigs made clumsy and unsuccessful attempts to compete with the Democrats for the votes of immigrant Catholics. This strategy alienated the growing number of Whig nativists—as well as many native-born Democrats of Protestant background—who believed that the professional politicians' hunger for votes had betrayed America's heritage of republicanism, Protestantism, and independence from foreign influence, including that of the Catholic pope.

The remarkable upsurge of political nativism, manifested in 1854 by the Know-Nothing party, indicated a widespread popular hostility toward the traditional parties.* On the one hand, the decisive victory in 1852 of Franklin Pierce, a bland northern Democrat from New Hampshire, could be interpreted as confirmation of a national desire for compromise and mediocrity. On the other hand, the results of state and local elections showed that voters felt that the existing parties were unresponsive to the people's needs. Anti-Catholic nativism suddenly became the way of asserting previously vague grievances.

Know-Nothing Victories. Although anti-Catholicism had been deeply embedded in colonial America, until 1854 this prejudice had lacked national political focus. The

*The name Know-Nothing came from the fact that party members, when asked by outsiders about the party's organization, were supposed to say they "knew nothing."

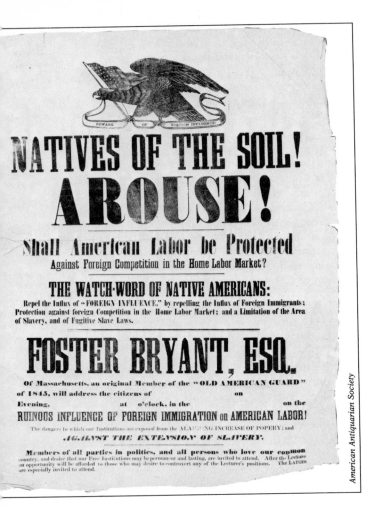

NATIVES OF THE SOIL!
AROUSE!

Shall American Labor be Protected

Against Foreign Competition in the Home Labor Market?

THE WATCH-WORD OF NATIVE AMERICANS:

Repel the Influx of "FOREIGN INFLUENCE," by repelling the Influx of Foreign Immigrants; Protection against foreign Competition in the Home Labor Market; and a Limitation of the Area of Slavery, and of Fugitive Slave Laws.

FOSTER BRYANT, ESQ.

Of Massachusetts, an original Member of the "OLD AMERICAN GUARD" of 1845, will address the citizens of   on

Evening,   at   o'clock, in the   on the

RUINOUS INFLUENCE OF FOREIGN IMMIGRATION on AMERICAN LABOR!

The dangers to which our Institutions are exposed from the ALARMING INCREASE OF POPERY; and

AGAINST THE EXTENSION OF SLAVERY.

Members of all parties in politics, and all persons who love our common country, and desire that our Free Institutions may be permanent and lasting, are invited to attend. After the Lecture an opportunity will be afforded to those who may desire to controvert any of the Lecturer's positions.   The LADIES are especially invited to attend.

BROADSIDE FOR A KNOW-NOTHING LECTURE

Order of the Star-Spangled Banner, which was the nucleus of the Know-Nothing party, remained an obscure secret society until the local spring elections of 1854, when entire tickets of secret Know-Nothing candidates were swept into office by write-in votes. Local dignitaries of the traditional parties, often confident that they were unopposed, found themselves thrown out of office by men they had never heard of. In Massachusetts the Know-Nothings won 63 percent of the popular vote. By 1855 the Know-Nothings, officially called the American party, had captured control of most of New England. They had become the dominant party opposing the Democrats in New York, Pennsylvania, California, and the border states. They had also made striking inroads in Virginia, North Carolina, Georgia, and other southern states, and for a time they held the balance of power in Congress. In much of the Northeast the Know-Nothings had defeated or prevented the spread of the new Republican party, which had been founded in 1854 to prevent the extension of slavery into the western territories. In effect, in two years the Know-Nothings had replaced the Whigs as a national political force.

The causes of this far-reaching realignment are difficult to assess. The religious revivals of the 1820s and 1830s had cultivated the belief that the survival of republican government depended on the liberating and unifying force of Protestantism. Protestant revivalists had repeatedly attacked any cohesive group, such as the Freemasons or the Mormon or Catholic churches, that supposedly put institutional loyalty above individual moral choice. Prominent northern clergymen, mostly Whigs, had saturated the country with lurid and often hysterical anti-Catholic propaganda. Their actions had contributed to mob violence and church burning, which culminated in a bloody Philadelphia riot in 1844.

Between 1845 and 1854 this traditional prejudice was greatly intensified by the arrival of nearly 3 million immigrants, the majority of whom were Catholics. These newcomers, with their divergent values and lifestyles, threatened the Whig dream of an ordered, morally progressive, and homogeneous society—what one Know-Nothing congressman referred to as a "unity of character and custom." And Catholic leaders, among them Archbishop John Hughes of New York, made no apologies for their own mobilization of political power or for their own vision of a Catholic America. As Hughes launched a counteroffensive against Protestant indoctrination in the public schools, nativists warned that immigrant voters slavishly obeyed the orders of their priests who, as agents of European despotism, sought to undermine America's republican institutions. The fact that the Catholic church had opposed the European revolutionary movements of 1848—and supported the subsequent restoration of repressive government in Germany, Austria, Hungary, Italy, and France— reinforced many Americans' fear of antirepublican subversion.

Disintegration of the National Party System. The Know-Nothing movement also reflected more immediate ethnic and economic conflicts, especially as native-born workers began blaming immigrants for low wages and unemployment. Although there was little foundation for this belief, nativism had special appeal for artisans and manual workers who associated immigrants with a new and threatening America—an America of increasing urban poverty, of factories and railroads, and of rising prices and abruptly changing markets. In the South and in the border states, people also hoped that the Know-Nothing movement would finally end the "needless" sectional disputes over slavery.

In 1856 Millard Fillmore ran as the candidate of the combined American (Know-Nothing) and Whig parties and received nearly 44 percent of the popular vote in the slaveholding states. Nativism was weaker in the Old Northwest, where there was a greater tolerance of immigrants. Yet there the Republican party capitalized on a similar disenchantment with the old parties, often at the expense of the Democrats. Moreover, in 1854 the Democrats had suffered irretrievable losses throughout the North; in that section their representation in Congress had fallen from ninety-one seats to twenty-five. These sudden defections to the Know-Nothing and Republican parties meant that, henceforth, northern Democrats would have little leverage within their restructured national party, which became increasingly southern-dominated.

The Know-Nothing movement is significant because it helped to destroy the existing party system. Once in power, the Know-Nothings failed to restrict immigration or to lengthen the traditional five years' residence required for naturalized citizenship. Like other parties, the short-lived American party proved to be vulnerable to political ambition and compromise. But before being absorbed by the Republicans, the Know-Nothings brought about a massive shift in voter alignments, undermined national party discipline, and hastened the total disappearance of the Whigs. The importance of this ominous development cannot be exaggerated. When the discipline of the party system was swept away, sectional conflict could no longer be suppressed or safely contained.

The Confrontation over Kansas

Stephen Douglas had long been interested in the organization and settlement of the Nebraska Territory—the vaguely defined region west and northwest of Missouri and Iowa. This immense portion of the Louisiana Purchase had been reserved for Indians, and there were few white settlers. As a senator from Illinois, Douglas had a frank interest in the transcontinental railroad routes, which, he expected, would make Chicago the hub of mid-America. He was also an ardent patriot and expansionist, convinced that America should free the world from despotism. He thought the only serious obstacle to this mission was England, which had instigated the subversive activities of the American abolitionists, who in turn had provoked the militancy of the southern extremists. These Southerners had then blocked the organization of the territories north of the Missouri Compromise line of 36° 30'.

By 1854, when Douglas was chairman of the Senate Committee on Territories, he had concluded that the Missouri Compromise must be modified to overcome southern fears. This course of action, he thought, was the only way to open the Nebraska country to settlement, to bind the nation together with transcontinental railroads and telegraph, to fulfill the American mission of driving Great Britain from the continent, and to reunite the fractured Democratic party under his own leadership. He therefore drafted a bill that applied to Nebraska the popular sovereignty provision that Congress had already applied to Utah and New Mexico under the terms of the Compromise of 1850. This unexpected move destroyed nearly four years of relative sectional peace.

The Kansas-Nebraska Act. At first Douglas tried to play down the contradiction between popular sovereignty and the slavery prohibition of 1820, which applied to all the Louisiana Purchase territory north of the present state of Oklahoma. In 1850 Congress had left it to the courts to resolve any conflicts between popular sovereignty and the unrepealed Mexican law prohibiting slavery in Utah and New Mexico. Douglas hoped to bypass the Missouri Compromise in the same way. But William Seward and other antislavery Whigs plotted to make the Nebraska bill as objectionable as possible. At the same time, a powerful group of southern senators, the disciples of Calhoun, conspired to make repeal of the Missouri Compromise a test of Democratic party loyalty.

After a series of caucuses Douglas recognized that the Nebraska bill would not pass unless Southerners were assured that all territories would be legally open to slaveholders. Aided by his Southerner allies, Douglas helped to persuade President Pierce to throw administration support behind a new proposal that would declare the Missouri Compromise "inoperative and void" because it was "inconsistent with the principles of nonintervention by Congress with slavery in the States and Territories, as recognized by the legislation of 1850." This new bill would also provide for the organization of two separate territories, Kansas and Nebraska. By simply affirming that the rights of territorial governments were "subject only to the Constitution of the United States," Douglas's new bill evaded the critical question of whether popular sovereignty included the right to exclude slavery. In this form the Kansas-Nebraska bill of 1854 won almost unanimous support from southern Whigs and Democrats and from enough northern Democrats to pass both houses of Congress.

Southern leaders, no less than Stephen Douglas, were astonished by the outrage that exploded across the North. Opponents interpreted the bill as the violation of a "sacred compact," the Missouri Compromise, and as a shameless surrender to the Slave Power. The legislatures of five northern states passed resolutions condemning the Kansas-Nebraska Act. When

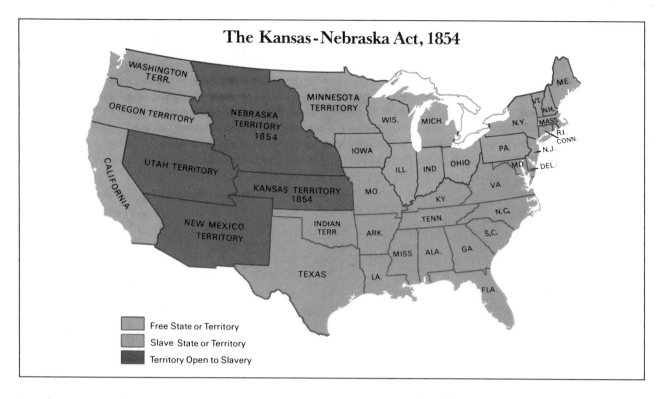

The Kansas-Nebraska Act, 1854

Free State or Territory

Slave State or Territory

Territory Open to Slavery

Douglas was traveling by train, he saw so many figures of himself hanging from trees and burned in effigy that he joked, "I could travel from Boston to Chicago by the light of my own effigy." According to the law's defenders, the cries of betrayal were sheer hypocrisy, for antislavery Northerners themselves had rejected the principle of the Missouri Compromise by refusing to extend the compromise line to the Pacific coast. Yet the breach of faith, however interpreted, led to a rapid dissolution of other shared understandings and political restraints. For the first time, antislavery and proslavery moderates began to perceive each other as more dangerous than the extremists.

Rise of the Republican Party.

What most alarmed proslavery moderates was the sudden appearance of a new and wholly sectional party, which they scornfully termed the "Black Republicans." In the eyes of its enemies, this party professed moderation but tried to use the goal of excluding slavery from the territories as a means of capturing control of the federal government. Even moderate Southerners believed that, instead of being satisfied that California was free and that the number of free states was bound to increase, the self-styled Republicans (who had resurrected Jefferson's old party label) were intent on humiliating the South and on reducing the slaveholding states to colonial status.

By the mid-1850s Southerners were keenly aware of the growing contrast between their own rural economy and the economy of the urbanizing Northeast. The great cotton boom of the 1850s seemed to prove that even unparalleled southern prosperity could not narrow the gap in wealth. Picturing themselves as the nation's true producers of wealth, slaveholders blamed northern middlemen—epitomized by Wall Street bankers and merchants—for siphoning off their just rewards. The new Republican party represented the final and fatal spearhead of a conspiracy that allied Free-Soilers, antislavery Democrats, and the remnants of powerful Whig combines, such as the Seward and Weed machine of New York. The earlier Liberty and Free Soil parties had never had a chance of success. But in 1856 the Republicans, hardly two years after their appearance, carried eleven of the sixteen free states. Colonel John C. Frémont, the Republican presidential candidate, amassed an astonishing popular vote and would have defeated James Buchanan, the Democratic candidate, if he had carried Pennsylvania and Illinois.

The Crisis over Kansas.

Even for antislavery moderates, however, the events in Kansas following passage of the Kansas-Nebraska Act showed that compromise had only encouraged proslavery conspirators to take over the western territories. The Republicans believed that unless drastic countermeasures were taken, America's

Theodore Parker's famous speech of 1855 on the "Nebraska Question" typified the militant protest against what many Northerners saw as a betrayal of America's Revolutionary heritage and glorious destiny. A popular Unitarian minister and reformer, Parker celebrated the new power of the industrial North and linked the abolition of slavery with a grandiose vision of America's progress and world leadership.

Theodore Parker on Slavery as a Barrier to Progress (1855)

HALF a million immigrants annually find a shelter on our shores. "Westward the course of empire takes its way." Aye, it will come eastward—and Asia already begins to send us her children. What a noble destination is before us if we are but faithful. Shall politicians come between the people and the eternal Right—between America and her history! When you remember what our fathers have done; what we have done—substituted a new industrial for a military state, the self-rule of this day for the vicarious government of the middle ages; when you remember what a momentum the human race has got during its long run—it is plain that slavery is on the way to end.

As soon as the North awakes to its ideas, and uses its vast strength of money, its vast strength of numbers, and its still more gigantic strength of educated intellect, we shall tread this monster underneath our feet. See how Spain has fallen—how poor and miserable is Spanish America. She stands there a perpetual warning to us. One day the North will rise in her majesty, and put slavery under our feet, and then we shall extend the area of freedom. The blessing of Almighty God will come down upon the noblest people the world ever saw—who have triumphed over Theocracy, Monarchy, Aristocracy, Despotocracy, and have got a Democracy—a government of all, for all, and by all—a Church without a Bishop, a State without a King, a Community without a Lord, and a Family without a Slave.

SILK BANNER FOR FRÉMONT
Although he was born and reared in the South, John C. Frémont, a daring explorer and a conqueror of California, was an attractive candidate for the Republicans in 1856. Frémont was untainted by political commitments and associations until he joined the crusade for free soil in Kansas and other territories.

free white workers would be deprived of the land and opportunity that was their birthright. By failing to provide definite legal measures for excluding slavery from the territories, Congress had guaranteed that the issue would be decided by numerical and physical force.

The crisis over Kansas was actually the result of complex rivalries and aspirations. The government opened the territory to settlement before Indian treaties had been ratified and before Indian tribes—many of them recently moved to Kansas from the East—had been dispossessed and pushed onto reservations. In 1854 thousands of white settlers began the scramble for Kansas land, searching for the best town sites and the most likely railroad routes of the future. Even without the slavery issue Kansas would have been the scene of a speculative mania and a shameless defrauding of the Indians.

But the passions that were generated by slavery swept aside the last fragile restraints, including the frontier's customary rules against "jumping" (disregarding) prior land claims. According to Missouri's fiery senator David R. Atchison, a free Kansas would inevitably lead to the end of slavery in Missouri: "We are playing for a mighty stake; if we win we carry slavery to the Pacific Ocean; if we fail we lose Missouri, Arkansas, and Texas and all the territories; the game must be played boldly." Atchison thus helped to organize bands of so-called Border Ruffians to harass settlers from the free states. On the opposite side, New Englanders organized an emigrant aid crusade with the purpose of colonizing Kansas with free-state settlers. Although Stephen Douglas referred to the Emigrant Aid Society as "that vast moneyed corporation," the movement was in fact poorly financed, and it succeeded in transporting barely 1,000 settlers to Kansas. But the movement's sensational promotion fed the fantasies of Missourians and Southerners that eastern capitalists were recruiting armies of abolitionists and equipping them with Sharps rifles.

The acts of terrorism reached a climax in 1856 and became, in effect, a civil war. Antislavery newspapers declared that war had actually begun when a large proslavery force, supposedly acting under the authority of law enforcement officials, sacked the free-state town of Lawrence. The revenge for such proslavery outrages was even more savage. Even fervid southern alarmists had not imagined anything as brutal as John Brown's retaliatory massacre at Pottawatomie Creek. Brown, a fanatical ne'er-do-well with an abolitionist background and abolitionist connections, thought of himself as an agent of God's vengeance. He led four of his sons and two followers in a night attack on an unprotected settlement, brutally executing five men and boys who were vaguely associated with the proslavery party.

All pretense of civility collapsed in the Senate. In 1856 speakers became inflamed, personal, malicious. Senator Charles Sumner of Massachusetts, after denouncing "the crime against Kansas" and "the rape of a virgin territory, compelling it to the hateful embrace of slavery," delivered studied insults to the elderly Andrew Butler, a senator from South Carolina. On the Senate floor Butler's cousin, Preston Brooks, a young congressman from South Carolina, later savagely attacked the seated Sumner with a cane, leaving him unconscious and seriously injured. This triumph of "Bully" Brooks won applause from much of the South. For many Northerners, Sumner's Senate seat, which remained empty for more than three years during his prolonged recovery, was a silent warning that Southerners could not be trusted to respect any codes, agreements, or sets of rules.

The same warning on a larger scale seemed to come out of the chaos of Kansas politics. By 1857 there could be no doubt that the overwhelming majority of Kansas settlers opposed admitting the territory as a slave state. Like the white settlers in California and Oregon, they wanted to exclude free blacks along with slaves. For most Kansans these were minor matters compared to other issues, among them squatter rights, rival railroad routes, the disposal of Indian lands, and the desirability of free homesteads. What made slavery an explosive question in Kansas—and what made Kansas a detonating fuse for the nation—was the federal government's effort to bypass the people's will.

The Pierce and Buchanan administrations made a series of miscalculations. In the first tumultuous stage of settlement, the Pierce adminstration had legally recognized a proslavery territorial legislature established by wholesale fraud: some 1,700 Missourians had crossed the border to cast illegal votes. Many moderates hoped that the flagrant acts of this provisional legislature—such as making it a felony to question the right to hold slaves in Kansas—would soon be repealed by a more representative body. But the free-state settlers chose to boycott the elections that the "legal" proslavery government authorized and to establish their own extralegal government and constitution.

The Lecompton Constitution.

In 1857 the Buchanan administration was thus committed to support the outcome of an official election of delegates to a constitutional convention in Lecompton, Kansas, in preparation for Kansas statehood, even though only one eligible voter in twelve went to the polls. By then Southerners had become convinced that the security of the slave system hinged on making Kansas a slave state. Buchanan had become equally convinced that the survival of the Democratic party hinged on appeasing the South—in 1856, 119 of his 174 electoral votes had come from slave states. In Kansas there were no moderating influences on the proslavery convention that drafted the so-called Lecompton constitution. In Washington the declining power of the northern Democrats gave a similarly unrestrained hand to the southern Democrats who dominated Buchanan's administration.

Stephen Douglas considered the vote in Kansas on the proslavery Lecompton constitution a total subversion of popular sovereignty. Instead of being allowed to accept or reject the constitution as a whole, voters were asked only to approve the article guaranteeing for the future the right of slave property. If the article were rejected, the Lecompton constitution would still protect the legal status of the slaves already in the territory. Although the free-state majority again protested by abstaining from voting, Buchanan used the powers of his office to pressure Congress into admitting Kansas as a slave state. This policy caused a bitter break with Douglas, who denounced Buchanan's attempt to "force this constitution down the throats of the people of Kansas, in opposition to their wishes." In 1858 as in 1854, Congress became the scene of a violent sectional struggle. But this time Douglas led the antiadministration forces. Buchanan stood firm, sacrificing much of his remaining Democratic support in the North. In the end, in 1858, the Buchanan administration suffered a crushing defeat when advocates of Kansas's admission as a free state forced a popular vote in Kansas on the whole of the Lecompton constitution. The territory's electorate rejected the constitution by a vote of nearly ten to one, although at the cost of indefinitely postponing statehood. (Kansas ultimately became a free state in 1861.)

Dred Scott and the Lincoln-Douglas Debates

By the stormy 1850s the largest Protestant churches had divided along sectional lines; the Whig party had collapsed. The Democratic party had survived, but the Lecompton struggle helped to split it fatally. Although the Democratic party had given the South disproportionate access to national power, this access depended on winning the support of northern allies. As the number of such allies began to dwindle, they were partly replaced by southern Whigs. Thus as the Democratic party became more southern in character, there were fewer restraints on attempts to test the party loyalty of northern Democrats and to adopt an openly proslavery program. The Lecompton constitution was actually the second such critical test imposed on northern Democrats. The first test was the *Dred Scott* decision.

The *Dred Scott* Decision.

The Southerners who dominated the Supreme Court decided to use the *Dred Scott* case as a way to resolve critical issues that Congress had long evaded. From the time that the Court had received the case, late in 1854, to the Court's long-delayed decision in 1857, the primary issue was whether Congress had the constitutional right to prohibit slavery in any territory or to delegate such a right to territorial governments, as implied by Stephen Douglas's formula of "popular sovereignty." In the recently disputed territories of New Mexico, Utah, and Kansas, no judicial cases involving the exclusion of slavery had yet arisen.

There had been many previous suits for freedom by slaves who had lived with their masters as temporary residents of free states. Even southern courts had sometimes granted freedom to such slaves, but the decisions had depended on complex technical issues that mostly involved state law. What distinguished Dred Scott, a Missouri slave who sued the state for his freedom, was that he and his master, an army surgeon, had lived together for several years not only in the free state of Illinois, but also in a part of the Wisconsin Territory where slavery had been federally prohibited by the Missouri Compromise. Despite this clear violation of federal law, Scott's initial trials in Missouri courts were confined to narrower issues.

In 1854 technical complications allowed Scott's lawyers to transfer his suit for freedom to the United States Circuit Court for the District of Missouri. This first federal trial raised a preliminary question that courts had never resolved and that affected the enforcement of the Fugitive Slave Law of 1850. Were any black persons citizens to the extent of being qualified by the Constitution to bring suit in a federal court? After years of debate and postponement in the United States Supreme Court, this jurisdictional question enabled Chief Justice Roger Taney to link Scott's individual claim with momentous constitutional issues. For if blacks were not citizens entitled to constitutional rights and privileges, Dred Scott would be subject only to the laws of Missouri, and blacks seized under the Fugitive Slave Law of 1850 would have no recourse to federal courts. Moreover, the *Dred Scott* case involved a second question of enormous significance. The Court had to decide whether Congress had exceeded its powers in 1820 when it had outlawed slavery in the Louisiana Purchase north of 36°30'. If so, Dred Scott was still a slave and therefore could not bring suit in federal court.

By the end of 1856 the *Dred Scott* case had received widespread national publicity, with newspapers summarizing the opposing arguments that were delivered before the Court. Although informed observers anxiously awaited a verdict that might have explosive political consequences, they generally expected the Court to deny its jurisdiction on narrow technical grounds, thus confirming the judgment of lower courts that Scott was still a slave. When the decision was finally announced, in 1857, seven of the justices rejected Scott's claim to freedom, but all nine wrote separate opinions. There is still controversy over what parts of the "Opinion of the Court," written by Chief Justice Taney, represented the opinion of a majority of the justices.

Taney's opinion stated three sweeping conclusions. First, Taney held that at the time the Constitution of the United States had been adopted, blacks had "for more than a century been regarded as beings of an inferior order . . . so far inferior that they had no rights which the white man was bound to respect; and that the negro might justly and lawfully be reduced to slavery for his benefit." Taney further contended that neither the Declaration of Independence nor the Constitution had been intended to apply to blacks— whether slave or free. Even if free blacks in certain states had later been granted citizenship, Taney said, they were not citizens "within the meaning of the Constitution of the United States." They were not entitled to the rights and privileges of a citizen in any other state, nor could they sue in a federal court.

After thus denying the Supreme Court's jurisdiction over Dred Scott, the second major conclusion of Taney's decision dealt with the substantive issues. As for Scott's residence in Illinois, the Court had already recognized the principle that the status of a slave taken to a free state should be determined by the laws of the slave state to which he had returned. On Scott's residence in the federal territory north of 36°30', Taney ruled that the Missouri Compromise had been unconstitutional. Congress, he declared, had no more power to take away a citizen's property in a federal territory than it did in a state.

Finally, having argued that slaves could not be differentiated from other forms of property protected by the Fifth Amendment, Taney stated his third major conclusion. Congress, he ruled, could not give a territorial government powers that exceeded those of the federal government: "It could confer no power on any local Government, established by its authority, to violate the provisions of the Constitution." This judgment struck directly at Douglas's interpretation of popular sovereignty, and it upheld the extreme southern view that the people of a territory could not legally discriminate against slave property until they acquired the sovereignty of statehood.

Reaction to the Decision. Both the South and President Buchanan were jubilant. Despite vigorous dissenting opinions from justices John McLean and Benjamin R. Curtis, the highest court in the land had ruled that excluding slavery from the territories—the goal that had brought the Republican party into existence— was unconstitutional. Republican newspapers, among them the New York *Tribune*, scornfully replied that the decision was "entitled to just as much moral weight as would be the judgment of a majority of those congregated in any Washington bar-room." Stephen Douglas, the leading contender for the Democratic presidential nomination in 1860, remained silent for many weeks. He wholly agreed with the denial of black citizenship and took credit for the congressional repeal of the Missouri Compromise. Yet his relations with Buchanan and the South were already strained, and he knew that his future career hinged on finding a way to reconcile the southern version of limited popular sovereignty, embodied in the *Dred Scott* decision, with his own constituents' demand for genuine self-determination.

Douglas finally presented his response to the *Dred Scott* decision in an important speech at the Illinois statehouse in May 1857. He argued that the constitutional right to take slaves into a territory was a worthless right unless it was sustained, protected, and enforced by "police regulations and local legislation." By contrasting an empty legal right with the necessary public support to enforce such a right, Douglas denied any meaningful contradiction between the *Dred Scott* decision and his own principle of popular sovereignty.

Two weeks later Abraham Lincoln gave his reply to Douglas from the same forum. Terming the *Dred Scott* decision erroneous, Lincoln reminded his audience that the Supreme Court had frequently reversed its own decisions, and he promised that "we shall do what we can to have it to over-rule this."

Elected to Congress as a Whig in 1846, Lincoln had suffered politically from his opposition to the Mexican War. But since 1854, when he had attacked the Kansas-Nebraska Act, he had been making a new career by pursuing Douglas. Lincoln was a self-educated Kentuckian, shaped by the Indiana and Illinois frontier. In moral and cultural outlook, however, he was not far from the stereotyped New Englander. He abstained from alcohol, revered the idea of self-improvement, dreamed of America's technological and moral progress, and condemned slavery as a moral and political evil. He told a Chicago audience in 1858, "I have always hated slavery I think as much as any Abolitionist. . . . I have always hated it, but I have always been quiet about it until this new era of the introduction of the Nebraska Bill began. I always believed that everybody was against it, and that it was in course of ultimate extinction."

The Kansas-Nebraska Act taught Lincoln that men like Douglas did not care whether slavery was "voted *down* or voted *up*." It also allowed him to exercise his magnificent talents as a debator and stump speaker—talents that had already distinguished him as a frontier lawyer, a state legislator, and an attorney and lobbyist for the Illinois Central Railroad and other corporations. Lincoln's humor, his homespun sayings, and his unaffected self-assurance all diverted attention from his extraordinary ability to grasp the central point of a controversy and to compress an argument into its clearest and most striking form. In 1856, after a period of watchful waiting, Lincoln played an important part in the belated organization of the Illinois Republican party. Two years later the Republican state convention unanimously nominated him to run for Douglas's Senate seat.

The Lincoln-Douglas contest was unprecedented in both form and substance. At the time senators were elected by state legislatures,* and no party convention had ever nominated a candidate. In an acceptance speech on June 16, 1858, Lincoln concisely and eloquently stated the arguments he would present directly to the people, appealing for a Republican legislature that would then be committed to elect him to the Senate. Since Douglas had unexpectedly rejected the proslavery Lecompton constitution and had joined the Republicans in fighting it, Lincoln needed to persuade the electorate that Douglas's own crusade for popular sovereignty had rekindled the agitation over slavery and led directly to the *Dred Scott* decision and the Lecompton constitution. According to Lincoln, Douglas's moral indifference to slavery disqualified him as a leader who could stand firm against the Slave Power. For Lincoln was wholly convinced that the conflict over slavery would continue until a crisis had been reached and passed. As he said in his famous "House divided" speech:

> "A house divided against itself cannot stand."
> I believe this government cannot endure, permanently half slave and half free.
> I do not expect the Union to be dissolved—I do not expect the house to fall—but I do expect it will cease to be divided.
> It will become all one thing, or all the other.
> Either the opponents of slavery, will arrest the further spread of it, and place it where the public mind shall rest in the belief that it is in course of ultimate extinction; or its advocates will push it forward, till it shall become alike lawful in all the States, old as well as new—North as well as South.
> Have we no tendency to the latter condition?

The "House Divided" speech signified a turning point in American political history. Lincoln stated that expediency and a moral neutrality toward slavery had undermined the Founders' expectation that slav-

---

*Only after 1913, with the adoption of the Seventeenth Amendment, did the direct popular election of senators begin.

DOUGLAS AND LINCOLN
These anonymous wooden folk sculptures portray Stephen A. Douglas and Abraham Lincoln, who opposed each other both in the 1858 Illinois senatorial campaign and in the presidential election of 1860.

ery was "in course of ultimate extinction." If the North continued to make compromises and failed to defend a boundary of clear principle, the South was certain to dictate "a second Dred Scott decision," depriving every state of the power to discriminate against slave property. In Lincoln's view, Douglas's Kansas-Nebraska Act had been part of a master plan or conspiracy, which Lincoln compared to "a piece of *machinery*" that had been designed to legalize slavery, step by step, throughout the United States. In asserting that "the people were to be left 'perfectly free' 'subject only to the Constitution,'" Douglas had provided "an exactly fitted *niche*, for the Dred Scott deci-

sion to afterwards come in, and declare the perfect freedom of the people, to be just no freedom at all."

Lincoln was not an abolitionist. He was convinced that prohibiting the further spread of slavery would be sufficient to condemn it to "ultimate extinction," a belief shared by many southern leaders. Yet he insisted on a public policy aimed at that goal—a public policy similar to that of Great Britain in the 1820s or, in Lincoln's eyes, to that of the Founders. For Lincoln, rejecting popular sovereignty was the same as rejecting the moral indifference exemplified by Douglas; and this was the first step toward national redemption.

The Lincoln-Douglas Debates.

Douglas seemed to be the nation's most likely choice for president in 1860. His struggle with Lincoln for reelection to the Senate in 1858 therefore commanded national attention. Making full use of newly constructed railroads, the two candidates traveled nearly 10,000 miles in four months. They crisscrossed Illinois, their tireless voices intermingling with the sound of bands, parades, fireworks, cannon, and cheering crowds. Each community tried to outdo its rivals in pageantry and in winning the greatest turnout from the countryside. Lincoln and Douglas agreed to participate in seven face-to-face debates, which are rightly regarded as classics in the history of campaign oratory. Douglas tried to make the most of his experience as a seasoned national leader (at forty-five he was four years younger than Lincoln), and to portray his opponent as a dangerous radical. According to Douglas, Lincoln's "House Divided" speech showed a determination to impose the moral judgments of one section on the other. Lincoln's doctrines threatened to destroy the Union and to extinguish the world's last hope for freedom. Douglas also exploited his listeners' racial prejudice, drawing laughter from his sarcastic refusal to question "Mr. Lincoln's conscientious belief that the negro was made his equal, and hence his brother."

Lincoln searched for ways to counteract the image of a revolutionary. Always insisting on the moral and political wrong of slavery, he repeatedly acknowledged that the federal government could not interfere with slavery in the existing states. He opposed repeal of the Fugitive Slave Law. He wholly rejected the idea of "perfect social and political equality with the negro." He did maintain, however, that blacks were as much entitled as whites to "all the natural rights enumerated in the Declaration of Independence, the right to life, liberty, and the pursuit of happiness." If the black was "perhaps" not equal in moral or intellectual qualities, "in the right to eat the bread, without leave of anybody else, which his own hand earns, *he is my equal and the equal of judge Douglas, and the equal of every living man.* [Great applause.]"

The election in Illinois was extremely close. The Republicans did not win enough seats in the legislature to send Lincoln to the Senate, but the campaign immediately elevated him to national prominence. Lincoln had expressed and defended a Republican antislavery ideology that combined fixed purpose with a respect for constitutional restraints. Lincoln had also magnified the gap that separated the Republicans from Douglas and other anti-Lecompton Democrats. He had further isolated Douglas from proslavery southern Democrats who were already embittered by Douglas's "treachery" with regard to the Lecompton constitution. They were then outraged by Douglas's response to Lincoln in the debate at Freeport, Illinois, where Douglas had maintained that regardless of what the Supreme Court might decide about the constitutionality of slavery in a territory, the people had the "lawful means to introduce it or exclude it" as they pleased. Repeating his familiar point that slavery could not exist "a day or an hour anywhere" unless it was supported by local police regulations, Douglas emphasized that the "unfriendly legislation" of a territorial government could effectively prevent slavery from being introduced. As Lincoln quipped, this was to say, "A thing may be lawfully driven from a place where it has a lawful right to stay."

In 1859 the breach between Douglas and the South could no longer be contained. The people of Kansas ratified a new constitution prohibiting slavery, thereby giving bite to Douglas's so-called Freeport Doctrine. In the Senate, where Douglas had been ousted from his chairmanship of the Committee on Territories, he led the fight against the southern demand for a federal slave code protecting slave property in all the territories. During a tour of the South, Douglas became alarmed by the growing movement, led by young proslavery "fire-eaters," to revive and legalize the African slave trade. Looking ahead to the Democratic convention of 1860, Douglas issued what amounted to an ultimatum about the party platform. Northern Democrats, he insisted, would not allow the party to be used as a means for reviving the African slave trade, securing a federal slave code, or pursuing any of the other new objectives of southern extremists. Douglas warned the South that Northerners would not retreat from defending genuine popular sovereignty, even though popular sovereignty was clearly running against the interests of the South.

The Ultimate Failure of Compromise

By 1860 a multitude of previously separate fears, aspirations, and factional interests had become polarized into opposing visions of America's heritage and destiny. Traditional systems of trust and reciprocity had collapsed.

John Brown's Raid.

John Brown, who had warred against slavery in Kansas, was a key symbol in this polarization. Since 1857 Brown had been held in high esteem by the most eminent New England reformers and literary figures. Backed financially by a secret group of abolitionists, Brown also cultivated close ties with free black communities in the North. On the night of October 16, 1859, he and some twenty heavily armed white and black followers seized part of the federal arsenal at Harpers Ferry, Virginia (now West Virginia). Brown hoped to begin the destruction of slavery by igniting a slave revolt and creating in the South a free-soil refuge for fugitives. After resisting federal troops for two days, Brown surrendered; he was tried for conspiracy, treason, and murder, and was hanged.

During his trial Brown claimed to have acted under the "higher law" of the New Testament. He insisted that "if I had done what I have for the white men, or the rich, no man would have blamed me." For Brown the higher law was not a philosophical abstraction but a moral command to shed blood and die in the cause of freedom. In the eyes of armchair reformers and intellectuals, Brown's courage to act on his principles made him not only a revered martyr but also a symbol of all that America lacked. Democratic editors and politicians, however, saw Brown's criminal violence as the direct result of the irresponsible preaching of William H. Seward and other so-called Black Republicans. The Democratic New York *Herald* reprinted Seward's speech on the "irrepressible conflict between slave and free states" alongside news accounts from Harpers Ferry. Many Southerners came to the stunned realization that Brown's raid could not be dismissed as the folly of a madman, since it had revealed the secret will of much of the North. A Virginia senator concluded that Brown's "invasion" had been condemned in the North "only because it failed." In the words of Jefferson Davis, a Mississippi senator who had been Pierce's secretary of war, the Republican party had been "organized on the basis of making war" against the South.

Ironically, both the Republicans and the southern extremists agreed that slavery must expand under national sanction if it were to survive. They also agreed that if the *Dred Scott* decision was valid, the government had an obligation to protect slave property in all the territories. This denial of any middle ground made it logical for southern fire-eaters to argue that a revived African slave trade would allow more whites to own slaves and would thus help to "democratize" the institution. Above all, both the Republicans and the southern extremists rejected popular sovereignty as Douglas had defined it. For Southerners the Constitution prohibited either Congress or a territorial legislature from depriving a settler of his slave property. For the Republicans the Constitution gave Congress both the duty and the power to prevent the spread of an institution that deprived human beings of their inalienable right to freedom.

Because these positions were irreconcilable, the northern Democrats held the only keys to possible compromise in the presidential election of 1860. But like the Republicans, the Douglas Democrats had drawn their own firm limits against further concessions to southern extremists. Early in 1860 Jefferson Davis challenged those limits by persuading the Sen-

ate Democratic caucus to adopt a set of resolutions committing the federal government to protect slavery in the territories. For Davis and other southern leaders, a federal slave code was the logical extension of the *Dred Scott* decision. They also agreed that the forthcoming Democratic platform must uphold the principle of federal protection of slave property. The Douglas Democrats knew that such a principle of guaranteed protection would completely undercut their reliance on legislation "unfriendly" to slavery in a territory—and that such a plank would guarantee their defeat in the North.

Division of the Democratic Party.

In April 1860 the fateful Democratic national convention met at Charleston. When a majority of the convention refused to adopt a platform similar in principle to Davis's Senate resolutions, the delegates from eight southern states withdrew, many of them assuming that this disunionist gesture would force the Douglas faction to compromise. Douglas held firm to his principle of popular sovereignty, and as a result he could not muster the two-thirds majority that was needed for nomination. In a surprise move the northern Democrats then agreed to adjourn the convention and to reconvene six weeks later in Baltimore.

At Baltimore the Democratic party finally destroyed itself as a national force. Delegates from the Lower South again seceded, and this time they adopted an extreme proslavery platform and nominated Vice-President John C. Breckinridge of Kentucky for the presidency. The northern remnants of the party remained loyal to popular sovereignty, however it might be modified in practice by the *Dred Scott* decision, and nominated Douglas.

Meanwhile, the division of the Democrats at Charleston had given the Republicans greater flexibility in nominating a candidate. In 1858 Douglas had portrayed Lincoln as a flaming abolitionist, and the South had accepted the image. To the North, however, Lincoln appeared more moderate and less controversial than the better-known Senator Seward of New York. Unlike Seward, Lincoln was not popularly associated with the higher-law doctrines that had led to Harpers Ferry. Although Lincoln disapproved of Know-Nothing nativism, he was more discreet than Seward and thus stood less chance of losing the nativist vote in Pennsylvania and other critical states. If some Northerners regarded him as a crude buffoon from the prairies, he appealed to many other Northerners as the tall rail-splitter of humble origins, a man of the people, an egalitarian. Except for his general endorsement of the proposed Homestead Act, protective tariffs, and a transcontinental railroad—all programs that were popular in the North and West and that had been blocked in Congress by the South—

CAMPAIGN POSTER
The Republican candidates for president and vice-president in 1860.

Lincoln was associated with few issues and had made few enemies. In May, at the Republicans' boisterous convention in Chicago, Lincoln finally overcame Seward's early lead and received the nomination.

The presidential campaign of 1860 was filled with the noisy hucksterism and carnival atmosphere that had been standard since 1840. The Republicans tended to discount the warnings of serious crisis, and they contemptuously dismissed southern threats of secession as empty bluff. The Breckinridge Democrats tried to play down these threats and to profess their loyalty to the Constitution and the Union. Yet various groups of moderates realized that both the Constitution and the Union were in jeopardy. This was the message of the new Constitutional Union party, which was led largely by former Whigs and which won many supporters in the Upper South. And this was the message that Stephen Douglas repeated bravely and incessantly—in the South as well as in the North—in the first nationwide speaking campaign by a presidential candidate.

The Election of 1860.

In November the national popular vote was divided among four candidates, and Lincoln received only 40 percent of the national total. Yet he received 180 electoral votes—57 more than the combined total of his three opponents. He carried every free state except New Jersey, and he won 4 of New Jersey's 7 electoral votes. In ten of the slave states, however, he failed to get a single popular vote. Breckinridge, the southern Democrat, captured all the states of the Lower South as well as Delaware, Maryland, Arkansas, and North Carolina. John Bell, the leader of the once powerful Whig party in Tennessee and the candidate of the Constitutional Union party, carried Tennessee, Kentucky, and Virginia. Although Douglas received approximately 525,000 more popular votes than Breckinridge, and trailed Lincoln by only 491,000, he won a mere 12 electoral votes (9 from Missouri and 3 from New Jersey). In many respects it was not really a national election. In the North it was essentially a contest between Lincoln and Douglas; in the South, between Breckinridge and Bell.

For the South the worst fears and predictions of forty years had come true. The United States had never had an administration that was openly hostile to black slavery. Lincoln's reassurances regarding the constitutional protection of slavery in the existing states could not mitigate the crucial facts. The election had proved that the North was populous enough to bestow national power on a minority party that had no support in the South. The Republican party was committed to free-labor ideology and to the proposition that slavery was morally wrong. Slaveholders

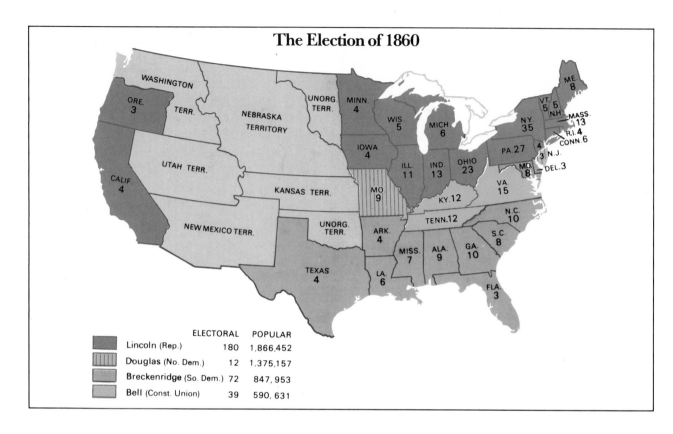

The Election of 1860

	ELECTORAL	POPULAR
Lincoln (Rep.)	180	1,866,452
Douglas (No. Dem.)	12	1,375,157
Breckenridge (So. Dem.)	72	847,953
Bell (Const. Union)	39	590,631

would have to take Lincoln's professions of restraint on good faith. If he or his successors should become more militant, they could not be checked by a balance of political power. A dominant sectional party would control federal patronage, the postal service and military posts, and the appointment of federal judges and other officeholders. Considerations of this kind strengthened the hand of secessionists. On December 20, 1860, South Carolina crossed the threshold that had been so closely approached during the nullification crisis. A special convention repealed the state's ratification of the Constitution and withdrew South Carolina from the Union. Unlike Jackson when faced with similar defiance, President Buchanan maintained that the federal government could do nothing to prevent the move.

Unionists mounted stiffer resistance to secession in other states of the Lower South. The chief controversies, however, involved timing—whether to follow the stampede of the fire-eating militants or to wait until Lincoln had shown his true colors. By February 1, 1861, the militants had triumphed in Mississippi, Florida, Alabama, Georgia, Louisiana, and Texas. Inevitably the shock produced reflex actions toward the traditional saving compromise. Senator John Crittenden of Kentucky initiated the first of such moves two days before South Carolina officially seceded. Al-

though Crittenden's proposed amendments to the Constitution were defined as moderate, they matched the most extravagant southern demands of a few years before. Even so, the leaders of the Lower South knew that no "compromise" would be secure unless the Republican party miraculously cast off its antislavery principles. Most Republicans could not publicly approve Crittenden's "unamendable" amendment that would have guaranteed the permanent security of slavery. Nor could they return to the old Democratic proposal for extending the Missouri Compromise line to the Pacific. The 1850s had shown that federal commitment to establishing and protecting slavery south of that line would only encourage southern ambitions in the Caribbean and Latin America. As Lincoln confidentially warned William Kellogg, his spokesman in Congress: "Entertain no proposition for a compromise in regard to the *extension* of slavery. The instant you do, they have us under again; all our labor is lost, and sooner or later must be done over. . . . The tug has to come and better now than later."

By 1860 the North and South had moved beyond the reach of compromise. The United States had originally emerged from an act of secession—from a final rejection of compromise with Britain. Even after independence had been won, Americans continued to perceive Britain as a conspiratorial power that threat-

William Henry Holcombe was a prominent physician who moved to Mississippi in 1852 and only then became an ardent southern nationalist. In the crisis of 1860 he advocated secession and a separate southern nationality as the only alternative to "the Africanization of the South."

William Henry Holcombe Argues for Secession (1860)

A SECTIONAL party [the Republicans], inimical to our institutions, and odious to our people, is about taking possession of the federal government. The seed sown by the early abolitionists has yielded a luxurious harvest. When Lincoln is in place, Garrison will be in power. The Constitution, either openly violated or emasculated of its true meaning and spirit by the subtleties of New England logic, is powerless for protection. We are no longer partners to a federal compact, but the victims of a consolidated despotism. Opposition to slavery, to its existence, its extension and its perpetuation, is the sole cohesive element of the triumphant faction. It did not receive the countenance of a single vote in any one of the ten great cotton states of the South! The question is at length plainly presented: submission or secession. The only alternative left us is this: *a separate nationality or the Africanization of the South.*

He has not analyzed this subject aright nor probed it to the bottom, who supposes that the real quarrel between the North and the South is about the territories, or the decision of the Supreme Court, or even the Constitution itself; and that, consequently, the issues may be stayed and the dangers arrested by the drawing of new lines and the signing of new compacts. The division is broader and deeper and more incurable than this. The antagonism is fundamental and ineradicable. The true secret of it lies in the total reversion of public opinion which has occurred in both sections . . . in the last quarter of a century on the subject of slavery. . . .

We anticipate no terminus to the institution of slavery. It is the means whereby the white man is to subdue the tropics all around the globe to order and beauty, and to the wants and interests of an ever-expanding civilization. . . .

The southern view of the matter, destined to revolutionize opinion throughout the civilized world, is briefly this: African slavery is no retrograde movement, no discord in the harmony of nature, no violation of elemental justice, no infraction of immutable laws, human or divine—but an integral link in the grand progressive evolution of human society as an indissoluble whole.

ened to hold back the nation's expansive energies. But despite this threat, America had continued to prosper and expand. The period from 1820 to 1860 witnessed a continuing extension of limits, an overleaping of boundaries of every kind. History seemed to confirm the people's wish for total self-determination. The American people, like the American individual, seemed to be free from the burdens of their past and free to shape their own character. The one problem that their ingenuity could not resolve was black slavery, which the Founding Fathers had seen as an unwanted legacy of British greed. Ironically, the South increasingly came to regard black slavery as the necessary base on which freedom must rest. For the North a commitment to slavery's ultimate extinction was the test of freedom. Each section detected a fatal change in the other—a betrayal of the principles and mission of the Founding Fathers. Each section feared that the other had become transformed into a despotic and conspiratorial "power" very similar to the original British enemy. And both sections shared a heritage of standing firm against despotism.

It was not accidental that the greatest American novel of the period, Herman Melville's *Moby-Dick* (1851), tells of the destruction that inevitably flows from denying all limits, rules, and boundaries. The novel concerns Captain Ahab's relentless and stubborn pursuit of a great white whale, a "nameless, inscrutable, unearthly thing" that becomes a symbol for all the opposing, unknown forces of life. Ahab, who commands a crew containing most of the races and types of humanity, thinks that he can become the master of his own fate. Ignoring a series of warnings and portents, he is incapable of admitting that he might be wrong or that there might be forces beyond his control.

Melville's novel is full of rich and universal meaning concerning the heroic yet impossible quest to know the the unknowable. Since Americans of the 1850s believed that God would ensure the triumph of democracy in the world, they could not accept Melville's brooding skepticism. Nevertheless, there was a lesson for pre-Civil War America in this tale of a highly rational but half-crazed captain—a captain who becomes so obsessed with his mission that he finally throws his navigation instruments overboard so that he can steer only toward the visible spout of the whale. Captain Ahab seeks liberation in an unswerving pursuit and conquest of limits. In the end he dooms himself and his ship to destruction.

CHRONOLOGY

1846	Wilmot Proviso fuses question of slavery's expansion with consequences of Mexican War.
	Walker tariff, adopted for revenue only, eliminates principle of protection.
1848	Gold discovered on American River in California.
	Van Buren, running for president on Free-Soil ticket, receives 10 percent of popular vote.
	Zachary Taylor elected president.
1850	In Congress, violent sectional debate culminates in Compromise of 1850.
	Fugitive Slave Law requires federal agents to recover escaped slaves from sanctuaries in the North.
	Taylor's death makes Millard Fillmore president.
1851	Herman Melville's *Moby-Dick*.
1852	Franklin Pierce elected president.
	Harriet Beecher Stowe's *Uncle Tom's Cabin*.
1853	Upsurge of political nativism, the Know-Nothings.
1854	Spectacular Know-Nothing election victories.
	Collapse of Whigs.
	New Republican party emerges.
	Commodore Perry opens Japan to American trade.
	Kansas-Nebraska Act rekindles sectional controversy over slavery.
1856	John Brown's murderous raid at Pottawatomie Creek.
	James Buchanan elected president.
1857	*Dred Scott* decision.
	In Kansas, proslavery Lecompton constitution ratified as free-state men refuse to vote.
1858	Lincoln-Douglas debates.
1859	John Brown's raid on Harpers Ferry.
1860	Democratic party, deadlocked at Charleston convention, finally divides along sectional lines at Baltimore.
	Abraham Lincoln elected president.
	South Carolina secedes from the Union.
1861	Mississippi, Florida, Alabama, Georgia, Louisiana, and Texas secede.

David M. Potter, *The Impending Crisis, 1848–1861* (1976), continues to be the best guide to the topics discussed in the present chapter. See also William J. Cooper, *The South and the Politics of Slavery 1828–1865* (1978). The titles on the causes of the Civil War, listed at the end of chapter 18, are also highly relevant.

On California, the best general guide is Andrew F. Rolle, *California: A History* (1969). For the California gold rush and western mining in general, see Rodman W. Paul, *California Gold: The Beginnings of Mining in the Far West* (1947), and Paul, *Mining Frontiers of the Far West, 1848–1880* (1963). Kevin Starr, *Americans and the California Dream, 1850–1915* (1973), presents brilliant vignettes of early California history. For the experiences of blacks in California, see Rudolph M. Lapp, *Blacks in Gold Rush California* (1977). Chinese immigration and anti-Chinese sentiment is admirably treated in Alexander Saxton, *The Indispensable Enemy: Labor and the Anti-Chinese Movement in California* (1975).

Holman Hamilton, *Prologue to Conflict* (1964), is the most detailed and accurate account of the Compromise of 1850. For the preceding presidential election, see Joseph G. Rayback, *Free Soil: The Election of 1848* (1970). Stanley W. Campbell, *The Slave Catchers: Enforcement of the Fugitive Slave Law, 1840–1860* (1968), traces the consequences of the most unpopular provision of the Compromise of 1850. Stephen Douglas's motives for introducing the Kansas-Nebraska Act are judiciously weighed in Robert W. Johannsen, *Stephen A. Douglas* (1973). This definitive biography is also an excellent source on the later Kansas controversy and the Lincoln-Douglas debates. Roy F. Nichols, "The Kansas-Nebraska Act: A Century of Historiography," *Mississippi Valley Historical Review*, 43 (September 1956), 187–212, is an invaluable guide to the controversial issues. The tangled local conflicts over land and railroad sites are illuminated in Paul W. Gates, *Fifty Million Acres: Conflicts over Kansas Land Policy, 1854–1890* (1954), and James C. Malin, *The Nebraska Question, 1852–1854* (1953). For Harriet Beecher Stowe's world-famous response to the Kansas controversy, see Philip van Doren Stern, *Uncle Tom's Cabin, an Annotated Edition* (1964), and Charles H. Foster, *The Rungless Ladder: Harriet Beecher Stowe and New England Puritanism* (1956).

The political realignment of the 1850s has been reinterpreted in Michael F. Holt, *The Political Crisis of the 1850s* (1978). Ray Billington, *The Protestant Crusade, 1800–1860* (1938), provides an outstanding overview of anti-Catholic nativism. The best studies of political nativism are Michael F. Holt, "The Politics of Impatience: The Origins of Know-Nothingism," *Journal of American History*, 60 (September 1973), and Holt, *Forging a Majority: The Formation of the Republican Party in Pittsburgh* (1969).

The best brief account of the origins and early history of the Republican party is Hans L. Trefousse, "The Republican Party, 1854–1864," in *History of U.S. Political Parties*, ed. Arthur M. Schlesinger, Jr., Vol. 2, 1141–72 (4 vols., 1973). See also Trefousse, *The Radical Republicans* (1969). Eric Foner, *Free Soil, Free Labor, Free Men: The Ideology of the Republican Party Before the Civil War* (1970), is a penetrating study of the Republicans' thought and values. The definitive study of the *Dred Scott* decision is Don E. Fehrenbacher, *The Dred Scott Case: Its Significance in American Law and Politics* (1978). Paul Finkelman, *An Imperfect Union: Slavery, Federalism and Comity* (1981), examines the problem of slaveholders who took their slaves into free states and shows that Lincoln had grounds for fearing a "second Dred Scott decision."

John Brown, a man of violence, has been the subject of violently conflicting interpretations. For traditional and hostile views, see James C. Malin, *John Brown and the Legend of Fifty-Six* (1942), and the brilliant essay by C. Vann Woodward in *The Burden of Southern History* (1960). More sympathetic evaluations can be found in Stephen B. Oates, *To Purge the Land with Blood: A Biography of John Brown* (1970); Benjamin Quarles, *Allies for Freedom: Blacks and John Brown* (1974); and Louis Ruchames, ed., *John Brown: The Making of a Revolutionary* (1969).

Robert W. Johannsen's biography of Douglas, listed above, treats the Lincoln-Douglas debates, and a penetrating analysis can be found in Don E. Fehrenbacher, *Prelude to Greatness: Lincoln in the 1850s* (1962). The debates themselves are presented in an authoritative edition by Paul M. Angle, ed., *Created Equal? The Complete Lincoln-Douglas Debates of 1858* (1958). Harry V. Jaffa, *Crisis of the House Divided: An Interpretation of the Issues in the Lincoln-Douglas Debates* (1959), gives the brilliant, far-reaching, and somewhat eccentric interpretation of a conservative political philosopher.

Most of the biographical studies of Lincoln listed at the end of chapter 18 are relevant here. Fehrenbacher's *Prelude to Greatness* is important, and mention should be made of James G. Randall, *Lincoln, the Liberal Statesman* (1947); Benjamin Quarles, *Lincoln and the Negro* (1962); and, above all, Allan Nevins, *The Emergence of Lincoln* (2 vols., 1950).

The climactic impasse between North and South is imaginatively presented in two major studies: Roy F. Nichols, *The Disruption of American Democracy* (1948), and David M. Potter, *Lincoln and His Party in the Secession Crisis* (1942). Avery O. Craven, *The Coming of the Civil War* (1942), stresses the importance of propaganda and irrationality. For the hopes and fears of contemporaries, see J. Jeffrey Auer, ed., *Antislavery and Disunion, 1858–1861: Studies in the Rhetoric of Compromise and Conflict* (1963). No one has yet written a wholly satisfactory account of the secessionist movements in the South. For conflicting interpretations, see William L. Barney, *The Secessionist Impulse: Alabama and Mississippi* (1974); Steven A. Channing, *Crisis in Fear: Secession in South Carolina* (1970); Charles B. Dew, "Who Won the Secession Election in Louisiana?" *Journal of Southern History*, 36 (February 1970), 18–32; Dwight L. Dumond, *The Secession Movement, 1860–1861* (1931); William J. Evitts, *A Matter of Allegiances: Maryland from 1850 to 1861* (1974); and R. A. Wooster, *The Secession Conventions of the South* (1962).

Two works that give a fascinating picture of the northern response to secession are Kenneth M. Stampp, *And the War Came: The North and the Secession Crisis, 1860–61* (1950), and Howard C. Perkins, ed., *Northern Editorials on Secession* (2 vols., 1942). For the election of 1860, see Elting Morison, "Election of 1860," in *History of American Presidential Elections, 1789–1968*, ed. Arthur M. Schlesinger, Jr., Vol. 2, 1097–1122 (4 vols., 1971). On the futile gestures for compromise, see Albert J. Kirwan, *John J. Crittenden: The Struggle for the Union* (1962), and Robert G. Gunderson, *Old Gentlemen's Convention: The Washington Peace Conference of 1861* (1961).

PART FOUR

UNITING THE REPUBLIC, 1860–1877

David Herbert Donald

*T*hese [Northern] people hate us, annoy us, and would have us assassinated by our slaves if they dared," a Southern leader wrote
when he learned that a "Black Republican," Abraham Lincoln,
would certainly be elected president in 1860. "They are a *different*
people from us, whether better or worse and *there is no love* between
us. Why then continue together?" The sectional contests of the previous
decades suggested that Americans had become members of two distinct—and conflicting—nationalities. By 1860 Northerners and Southerners appeared not to speak the same language, not to share the same
moral code, and not to obey the same law. Compromise could no longer
patch together a union between two peoples so fundamentally different.
"I do not see how a barbarous and a civilized community can constitute
one state," Ralph Waldo Emerson gravely concluded, and many Northerners concurred with him. "The North and the South are heterogeneous and are better apart," asserted the New Orleans *Bee*. "We [South-
erners] are doomed if we proclaim not our political independence."

On first thought, the four-year civil war that broke out in 1861
seems powerfully to confirm this idea that the Union and the Confederacy were two distinct nations. Yet the conduct of the war suggested
that Northerners and Southerners were not so different as their political
and intellectual leaders had maintained. At the beginning of the
conflict, both governments tried in much the same ways to mobilize
their poorly organized societies for battle. As the war progressed, both
Union and Confederacy adopted similar diplomatic, military, and economic policies. By the end of the war, both governments were committed to abolishing slavery, the one institution that had most clearly divided the sections in 1860.

Overleaf: "The Grand
Review, 1865." *Library
of Congress.*

430

Postwar events gave further evidence that the inhabitants of the North and the South were—as they had always been—part of the same nationality. To be sure, some Republicans wanted a radical revolution in the social and economic system of the conquered Confederacy. But in fact there were relatively few, and only limited, social experiments or political innovations during Reconstruction. In both the North and the South, shared beliefs in limited government, in economic laissez-faire, and in the superiority of the white race blocked drastic change. Meanwhile shared economic interests and national political parties pulled the sections back into a common pattern of cooperation.

During the decade after the Civil War, other tensions in American society, largely ignored during the long period of sectional controversy, began to be evident. Opponents of expansionism clashed with expansionists. Native Americans tried to defend their tribal lands from white encroachments. Small businesses fought to keep from being swallowed up by monopolies. Farmers struggled to break the power of the railroads and the grain elevators that controlled their access to markets. Seeking fairer wages, hours, and conditions of work, labor came into conflict with capital.

These issues did not merely divert attention from the old controversies between North and South, between white and black. They helped place those controversies in perspective. They made it evident that the Civil War had not been so much a conflict between two separate nations as one contest in a series of continuing struggles within the American nation to define a boundary between the centralizing, nationalizing tendencies of American life and the opposing tendencies toward localism, parochialism, and fragmentation.

18 Stalemate, 1861–1862

During the first two years of the Civil War, as the Union and the Confederacy grappled with each other inconclusively, it seemed that two distinct and incompatible nations had emerged from the American soil. Certainly the aims announced by their leaders were totally inconsistent. President Abraham Lincoln announced that the United States would "constitutionally defend, and maintain itself"; the territorial integrity of the nation must not be violated. For the Confederate States, President Jefferson Davis proclaimed that his country's "career of independence" must be "inflexibly pursued." As the rival governments raised and equipped armies, attempted to finance a huge war, and sought diplomatic recognition and economic assistance abroad, the people of the two sides increasingly thought of each other as enemy nations: Yankees and Rebels. It is easy to understand why Lord John Russell, the British foreign minister, concluded: "I do not see how the United States can be cobbled together again by any compromise. . . . I suppose the break-up of the Union is now inevitable."

A shrewder observer might have reached the opposite conclusion. Perhaps the most striking thing about the war in America was the fact that both sides carried it on using virtually identical methods. The Union and the Confederate governments faced the same wartime problems and arrived at the same wartime solutions. Northerners and Southerners on the battlefields found each other to be not two alien peoples, but kindred peoples. That identity made the conflict truly a brothers' war.

The Rival Governments

The government of the Confederate States was in most respects a duplicate of the United States government from which the Southern states had just withdrawn. Delegates of the six states of the Lower South (South Carolina, Georgia, Alabama, Mississippi, Florida, and Louisiana) met in Montgomery, Alabama, in early February 1861 and promptly drafted a Confederate Constitution; delegates from Texas, which had seceded on February 1, arrived late. The new charter largely followed the wording of the one drawn up in Philadelphia in 1787. To be sure, the Confederate Constitution recognized the "sovereign and independent character" of the constituent states, but it also announced that these states were forming "a permanent federal government," and it listed most of the same restrictions on state action that had been included in the United States Constitution. Unlike that document the Confederate charter used no euphemism about persons "held to Service or Labour" but instead recognized explicitly "the right of property in negro slaves." Otherwise, the two documents were substantially and intentionally identical. As the secessionist Benjamin H. Hill of Georgia explained, "We hugged that [United States] Constitution to our bosom and carried it with us."

Inaugurating the Presidents. For president of the new republic, the Montgomery convention chose Jefferson Davis of Mississippi, who had ardently defended Southern rights in the United States Senate but who had only reluctantly come to advocate secession.* If the crowds that thronged the streets of Montgomery on February 18, 1861, hoped to hear a stirring inaugural from the new Southern head of state, they were disappointed. Stepping forward on the portico of the Alabama statehouse, Davis gave a long, legalistic re-

*The Montgomery convention drew up a provisional constitution of the Confederacy, established itself as the new republic's provisional legislature, and named Jefferson Davis the provisional president. It also drew up a permanent constitution, which was submitted to the states for ratification. Regular elections were held in the fall of 1861 both for members of the Confederate Congress and for president. Reelected without opposition, Davis was formally inaugurated as the first and only regular president of the Confederate States on February 22, 1862.

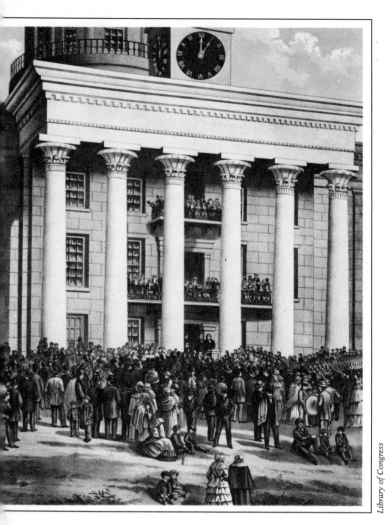

INAUGURATION OF JEFFERSON DAVIS

On February 18, 1861, Jefferson Davis, standing in front of the state capitol at Montgomery, Alabama, took the oath of office as the first—and, as it proved, only—president of the Confederate States of America. Davis is the thin, tall figure behind the lectern. To his right is William L. Yancey, a leading secessionist; to his right, Howell Cobb, president of the Confederate Senate, who administered the oath.

view of the acts of Northern aggression that had led to the formation of the new government. He pledged to use force, if necessary, to "maintain . . . the position which we have assumed among the nations of the earth." But he spoke in a tone more melancholy than martial. He saw himself as the leader of a conservative movement. "We have labored to preserve the Government of our fathers in its spirit," he insisted.

Just two weeks later, from the portico of the yet unfinished Capitol in Washington, another conservative took his inaugural oath. The capital city was thronged, as Nathaniel Hawthorne wrote, with "office-seekers, wire-pullers, inventors, artists, poets, prosers (including editors, army correspondents, attachés of foreign journals, and long-winded talkers), clerks, diplomatists, mail contractors, [and] railway directors." On public buildings along the route of the inaugural procession, sharpshooters were strategically placed, to prevent any pro-Southern interruption of the proceedings. Abraham Lincoln's inaugural address was similar in tone to Davis's. Lincoln vowed that the Union would be preserved and gave a low-keyed version of the previous sectional quarrels. He explained his personal view on slavery, but he also pledged that he contemplated "no invasion—no using of force" against the seceded states. In a warning softened by sadness, he reminded his listeners of the oath he had just taken to preserve, protect, and defend the government of the United States, and he entreated his Southern fellow citizens to pause before they assailed it. "In *your* hands, my dissatisfied fellow-countrymen," he concluded, "and not in *mine*, is the momentous issue of civil war."

Organizing the Two Administrations.

In the weeks immediately following the two inaugurations, the central problem confronting both Davis and Lincoln was not so much whether either should start a civil war as whether they could form viable governments. In Davis's Confederacy everything had to be started afresh. Even the most routine legal and governmental matters could not be taken for granted. For example, until the Confederate Congress passed an act that addressed the matter, it was not certain whether the laws of the United States enacted before 1861, and the decisions of the United States courts, were binding in the seceded states. The new nation had to choose a flag—although some purists objected, claiming that the Confederacy, which represented the true American spirit, ought to retain the Stars and Stripes and let the Union look for a new banner.

In selecting his cabinet advisers, President Davis theoretically had a free hand, but in fact his range of choice was severely limited. No man of doubtful loyalty to the new government could be permitted a place in the cabinet. Thus no Southern Unionist in the tradition of Henry Clay, John J. Crittenden, and John Bell was invited. On the other hand, because Davis wanted the world to see that the Confederacy was governed by sober, responsible men, he excluded all the most conspicuous Southern fire-eaters. Then, too, he had to achieve some balance between former Whigs and former Democrats, and he felt obliged to secure a wide geographical spread by appointing one member of his original cabinet from each of the seven Confederate states except Mississippi, which he himself represented. Davis's cabinet thus consisted neither of his

ABRAHAM LINCOLN
"Probably," wrote Walt Whitman, "the reader has seen physiognomies . . . that, behind their homeliness or even ugliness, held superior points so subtle, yet so palpable, making the real life of their faces almost as impossible to depict as a wild perfume or fruit taste . . . such was Lincoln's face—the peculiar color, the lines of it, the eyes, mouth, expression. Of technical beauty it had nothing—but to the eye of a great artist it furnished a rare study, a feast, and fascination."

personal friends nor of the outstanding political leaders of the South, except for Secretary of State Robert Toombs, a Georgian who served only briefly.

Such a cabinet might have sufficed in a country where administrative procedures and routines were firmly rooted. Instead in the Confederacy there was everywhere a lack of preparation, a lack of resources for running a government. Typical was the Confederate Treasury Department, which initially consisted of one unswept room in a Montgomery bank, "without furniture of any kind; empty . . . of desks, tables, chairs or other appliances for the conduct of business." The secretary of the treasury had to pay for the first rickety furniture out of his own pocket.

Disorganization and improvisation also characterized Lincoln's government in Washington. The Union had the advantage of owning the Capitol, the White House, and the permanent records of the United States government, and it had a recognized flag and a postal system. But in other respects it was thoroughly demoralized. Lincoln's government had no clear mandate from the people, for the president had received less than 40 percent of the popular vote in the 1860 election. The Union had an army of only 14,657 men, and every day army and navy officers announced that they were defecting to the South. Its treasury was empty. Some of the most experienced clerks in the Washington offices were leaving to join the Confederacy, and some who remained were of suspect loyalty. Adding to the confusion was the fact that Lincoln's was the first Republican administration, and under the spoils system party workers who had helped elect the Republican candidate now flocked to Washington, expecting to oust Democratic officeholders. Accompanied by their representatives or senators and bearing huge rolls of recommending letters, the office seekers besieged Lincoln in the White House. Wryly the president compared himself to an innkeeper whose clients demanded that he rent rooms in one wing of his hotel while he was trying to put out a fire in the other.

To add to the confusion, not one member of the Lincoln administration had previously held a responsible position in the executive branch of the national government. Many, including the president himself, had no administrative experience of any sort. Like Davis, Lincoln made no attempt to form a coalition government. His cabinet included no leaders of the Douglas wing of the Democratic party or of the Constitutional Union party. Nor, after a few unsuccessful efforts, did he name Unionists from the South. Instead, all members of his cabinet were Republicans. That fact, however, scarcely gave his government unity, for several of Lincoln's cabinet appointees had themselves been candidates for the Republican nomination in 1860 and hence were rivals of Lincoln and of each other. The most conspicuous member was the wily and devious secretary of state, William H. Seward, a man who spoke extravagantly but acted cautiously. Seward felt that he had a duty to save the nation through compromise and conciliation despite its bumbling, inexperienced president. Seward's principal rival in the cabinet was Secretary of the Treasury Salmon P. Chase, pompous and self-righteous, who had an equally condescending view of Lincoln's talents and who lusted to become the next president. The other members, with whom Lincoln had only the slightest personal acquaintance, were appointed because they were supposed to have political influence or to represent key states.

Winning the Border States

Desperately needing time to get organized, these two shaky rival administrations immediately confronted a problem and a crisis, which were intimately interrelated. The problem concerned the future of the eight remaining slave states, which had not yet seceded. These states had refused to rush out of the Union, although they were tied to the Deep South by blood and sentiment and feared abolitionist attacks upon their "peculiar institution" of slavery. In January 1861 Virginia had elected a convention to consider secession, but it dillydallied and did nothing. In February North Carolinians and Tennesseans voted against holding secession conventions. When the Arkansas and Missouri conventions met in March, they voted not to secede. Up to April 1861 Kentucky, Maryland, and Delaware held neither elections nor conventions. But the loyalty of all these states to the Union clearly depended on the policy Lincoln's government adopted toward the Confederacy.

Crisis over Fort Sumter.

The Fort Sumter crisis was the first test of that policy. It concerned the fate of the United States installations in the seceded states that still remained under the control of Washington. At Fort Pickens in Pensacola Bay, an uneasy truce held between the Union troops in the garrison and the Confederate forces on the Florida mainland. The real trouble spot was Fort Sumter, in the harbor of Charleston, South Carolina. Its garrison, which consisted of about seventy Union soldiers and nine officers under the command of Major Robert Anderson, was no serious military threat to the Confederacy. But its presence at Charleston, the very center of secession, was intolerable to Southern pride. Confederates insisted that President Davis demonstrate his devotion to the Southern cause by forcing Anderson and his men out immediately. Many Northerners, who had despairingly watched as fort after fort was turned over to the Confederates during the final months of the Buchanan administration, also saw Sumter as a test of the strength and will of the Lincoln administration.

Despite these pressures powerful voices in both governments urged compromise or at least delay. All but two members of Lincoln's cabinet initially thought that Sumter should be evacuated. Davis's secretary of state was equally opposed to hasty action. When the Confederate cabinet discussed attacking Fort Sumter, Toombs solemnly warned: "The firing upon that fort will inaugurate a civil war greater than any the world has yet seen."

But Anderson's situation made some action necessary. When Charleston authorities prohibited further sale of food to the troops in the fort, the garrison faced starvation. On March 5, the day after he was inaugurated, Lincoln learned that Anderson and his men could hold out no longer than April 15 unless they were resupplied. Since Lincoln had just pledged that he would "hold, occupy, and possess" all places and property belonging to the government, he promptly directed his secretary of the navy to begin outfitting an expedition to bring provisions to Fort Sumter. At the same time, recognizing how dangerously explosive the Charleston situation was, he explored alternatives. One possibility was to reinforce Fort Pickens, in the relatively calm area of Florida. Doing so would allow Lincoln to demonstrate his firmness of purpose, even if he had to withdraw Anderson from the Charleston harbor. But the naval expedition sent to Florida miscarried, the Union commander at Pickens misunderstood his orders, and the planned reinforcement could not be completed in time for Lincoln to know about it before Anderson's deadline for surrender. Another possibility was to consent to a peaceable withdrawal from Fort Sumter in return for assurances that the still undecided border states would remain in the Union. "If you will guarantee to me the State of Virginia, I shall remove the troops," Lincoln confidentially promised a prominent Virginia Unionist. "A State for a fort is no bad business." But the Virginians delayed, and a rainstorm kept a delegation of Unionists from reaching Washington; Lincoln received no firm pledge. Seeing no other possible course, he let the expedition bearing food and supplies sail for Sumter.

President Davis understood that Lincoln was not committing an act of aggression in merely supplying Fort Sumter. Indeed, he predicted that for political reasons the United States government would avoid making an attack so long as the hope remained of retaining the border states. But the Confederate president's hand was forced, too. Hot-headed Governor Francis Pickens and other South Carolina extremists were impatient with Davis's caution and prepared to attack the fort. Rather than let Confederate policy be set by a state governor, Davis ordered General P. G. T. Beauregard, in command of the Confederate forces at Charleston, to demand the surrender of Fort Sumter. Anderson responded that he would soon be starved out, but he failed to promise to withdraw by a definite date. Beauregard's officers felt they had no alternative but to take the fort by force. At 4:30 A.M. on April 12, firing began. Outside the harbor the relief expedition Lincoln had sent watched impotently while Confederates bombarded the fort. After thirty-four hours, with his ammunition nearly exhausted, Anderson had to surrender.

Promptly Lincoln called for 75,000 volunteer soldiers to put down the "insurrection" in the South. On

Sarah Morgan Dawson, a Louisiana girl, shared the sentiments of her elders toward the North and toward secession. Despite her high-flying rhetoric, which was characteristic of Southerners at the time, she cared less for the Confederacy than for vindicating Southern "honor."

A Confederate Girl Writes on Secession and the War

I HAVE a brother-in-law in the Federal army whom I love and respect as much as any one in the world, and shall not readily agree that his being a Northerner would give him an irresistible desire to pick my pockets, and take from him all power of telling the truth. No! There are few men I admire more than Major Drum, and I honor him for his independence in doing what he believes right. Let us have liberty of speech and action in our land, I say, but not gross abuse and calumny. Shall I acknowledge that the people we so recently called our brothers are unworthy of consideration, and are liars, cowards, dogs? Not I! *If* they conquer us, I acknowledge them as a superior race. . . .

I was never a Secessionist, for I quietly adopted father's views on political subjects without meddling with them. But even father went over with his State, and when so many outrages were committed by the fanatical leaders of the North, though he regretted the Union, said, "Fight to the death for our liberty." I say so, too. I want to fight until we win the cause so many have died for. I don't believe in Secession, but I do in Liberty. I want the South to conquer, dictate its own terms, and go back to the Union, for I believe that, apart, inevitable ruin awaits both. It is a rope of sand, this Confederacy, founded on the doctrine of Secession, and will not last many years—not five. The North Cannot subdue us. We are too determined to be free. They have no right to confiscate our property to pay debts they themselves have incurred. Death as a nation, rather than Union on such terms. We will have our rights secured on so firm a basis that it can never be shaken. If by power of overwhelming numbers they conquer us, it will be a barren victory over a desolate land. We, the natives of this loved soil, will be beggars in a foreign land; we will not submit to despotism under the garb of Liberty. The North will find herself burdened with an unparalleled debt, with nothing to show for it except deserted towns, burning homes, a standing army which will govern with no small caprice, and an impoverished land.

If that be treason, make the best of it!

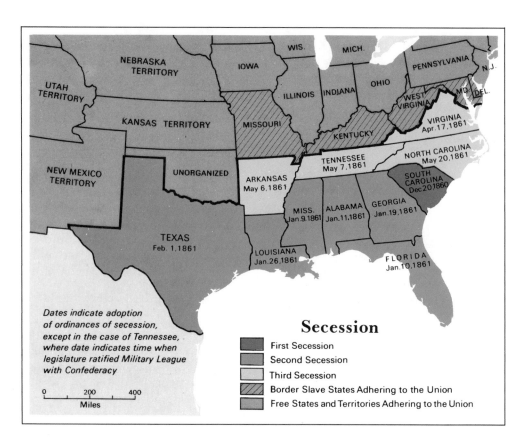

Dates indicate adoption of ordinances of secession, except in the case of Tennessee, where date indicates time when legislature ratified Military League with Confederacy

Secession

- First Secession
- Second Secession
- Third Secession
- Border Slave States Adhering to the Union
- Free States and Territories Adhering to the Union

May 6 the Confederate Congress countered by formally declaring that a state of war existed. The American Civil War had begun.

Both at the time and later there was controversy about the responsibility for beginning the conflict. Critics claimed that, by sending the expedition to resupply Fort Sumter, Lincoln deliberately tricked the Confederates into firing the first shot. Indeed, some months after the event, Lincoln himself told a friend that his plan for sending supplies to Major Anderson had "succeeded." "They attacked Sumter," he explained; "it fell, and thus, did more service than it otherwise could." That statement clearly reveals Lincoln's wish that if hostilities began, the Confederacy should bear the blame for initiating them, but it does little to prove that Lincoln wanted war. It is well to remember that throughout the agonizing crisis, the Confederates took the initiative at Sumter. It was Charleston authorities who cut off Anderson's food supply; it was Confederate authorities who decided that, although the fort offered no military threat, Anderson must surrender; and it was the Southerners who fired the first shot. Writing privately to the Confederate commander at Fort Pickens, President Davis had acknowledged that there would be a psychological advantage if the Southerners waited for the Union government to make the initial attack. But, he

added, "When we are ready to relieve our territory and jurisdiction of the presence of a foreign garrison that advantage is overbalanced by other considerations." These other considerations impelled Davis to demand Fort Sumter's surrender.

Decisions in the Border States. If intent can be tested by the consequences, it is evident that, initially at least, the Confederacy, not the Union, benefited from the attack on Fort Sumter. The slave states still in the Union now had to make a choice of allegiances, and for a time it seemed that all would join the Confederacy. Virginia governor John Letcher spurned Lincoln's call for troops as a bid "to inaugurate civil war," and on April 17 the state convention hastily passed a secession ordinance. Technically secession was subject to popular ratification. But in fact the convention's action immediately linked to the Confederacy the most populous and influential state of the Upper South, with its long tradition of leadership, its vast natural resources, and its large Tredegar Iron Works.

Other border states acted only a little less quickly. On May 6 the Arkansas convention voted, with only five members dissenting, to withdraw from the Union. When Lincoln's call for troops reached Governor Isham Harris of Tennessee, he replied haughtily, "In such an unholy crusade no gallant son of Tennessee

STAND WATIE

Small in stature but with great strength and endurance, Stand Watie raised the first Cherokee regiment of volunteers for the Confederate army. An effective raider, he also took part in the major battles of Wilson's Creek and Pea Ridge. Appointed brigadier-general in 1864, he was one of the last Confederate officers to surrender, not yielding up his sword until June 23, 1865.

 *National Archives*

will ever draw his sword," and he began private negotiations with Confederate officials. On May 7 the Tennessee state legislature ratified the arrangements Harris had already made and voted to secede. On May 20 the North Carolina convention, under pressure from pro-Confederate newspapers to withdraw from the "vile, rotten, infidelic, puritanic, negro-worshipping, negro-stealing, negro-equality . . . Yankee-Union," unanimously adopted a secession ordinance.

Far to the west, the Confederacy scored another victory in the Indian Territory (later to become the state of Oklahoma). Confederate Commissioner Albert Pike had little success with the Plains Indians there, but he won over most of the Five Civilized Nations, many of whom were slaveowners. The Confederacy agreed to pay all annuities that the United States government had previously provided, and it allowed these tribes—the Choctaws, Chickasaws, Creeks, Seminoles, and Cherokees—to send delegates to the Confederate Congress. In return these tribes promised to supply troops for the Confederate army. Most of them loyally supported the Southern effort throughout the war, and the Cherokee chief, Brigadier General Stand Watie, did not formally surrender until a month after the war was over. A rival faction among the Cherokees, headed by Chief John Ross, and most of the Plains Indians favored the Union cause.

Elsewhere along the border, the Confederacy fared less well. Although it was a slave state with sentimental ties to the South, Delaware never really contemplated secession. In Maryland, a bitterly divided state, the decision was much more painful. On April 19 a pro-Confederate mob in Baltimore fired upon a Massachusetts regiment en route to Washington, and communications were then cut between the Union capital and the rest of the country. For a time it seemed highly probable that Maryland would secede. But Lincoln arranged for further shipments of Union troops to bypass Baltimore until passions could cool. By May Baltimore was back under Northern control, and the mayor, along with nineteen members of the state legislature, was unceremoniously arrested and jailed without trial. In the 1861 fall elections, Maryland chose an uncompromising Unionist as governor, and thereafter there was no further question of secession.

In Missouri the Union cause was managed with less skill. Although the pro-Southern governor denounced Lincoln's call for troops as "illegal, unconstitutional, revolutionary, inhuman, [and] diabolical," public opinion was so evenly divided that secession probably would not have occurred except for the Union commander Nathaniel Lyon, who started hostilities by overrunning an encampment of pro-secessionist militia near St. Louis. Confederate sympathizers rallied to protect them, and for two days there was bloody street fighting in the city. Open warfare followed. Union forces controlled the area around St. Louis; secessionists commanded by Sterling Price dominated most of the rest of the state. After General John C. Frémont became commander of the department of the West, with his headquarters in St. Louis, the territory under Union control was gradually extended. During the next three years, guerrilla warfare devastated the Missouri countryside as neighbor fought neighbor. The bitterness was further aggravated when free-soil men from Kansas, remembering how Missouri "border ruffians" had once tried to extend slavery into their territory, crossed the border to take revenge upon secessionist sympathizers. In turn, Confederate gangs (the most notorious led by the horse thief and murderer William C. Quantrill) preyed upon Missouri Unionists.

Far more skillful was Lincoln's handling of Kentucky—his native state, as well as Jefferson Davis's. As in Missouri, the governor was an outright secessionist, but strong Unionist sentiment prevented the calling of a state convention. Thus there was a stalemate, and Kentucky declared itself neutral in any conflict between the United States and the Confederacy. Between May and September 1861, both the Lincoln and the Davis governments claimed to accept this neutrality; but at the same time, each tried to strengthen the hands of its supporters in Kentucky. Finally, suspecting that Union forces were about to seize a position in Kentucky, the Confederates moved first and took Columbus. Federal troops then entered Paducah, and neutrality was dead. But these months of wavering had given Kentucky Unionists a chance to plan and organize, so that the state did not join the Confederacy like Tennessee or become a fierce battleground like Missouri. Lincoln himself played a large role in bringing about this outcome. He gave Kentucky affairs close attention and was careful to assure prominent Kentuckians privately that he "intended to make no attack, direct or indirect, upon the institution or property [meaning slavery] of any State."

Although most Virginians favored the Confederacy, the Union had loyal supporters in the western counties of the state. The people of these counties had long resented the domination of the state by the planters of the tidewater region and had little interest in slavery. When the Virginia convention voted for secession, a sizable minority of the delegates, mostly from these western counties, were opposed, and they went home vowing to keep their state in the Union. A series of exceedingly complex maneuvers followed, including the summoning of several more or less extralegal conventions and the creating of a new government for what was termed "reorganized" Virginia, rivaling the secessionist government at Richmond. This "reorganized" government then gave its permission—as required by the United States Constitution—for the counties west of the mountains to form a new and overwhelmingly Unionist state of West Virginia. Not until 1863, when all these steps were completed, was the new state admitted to the Union. Thus by that date there were no fewer than three state governments on Virginia soil: the pro-Confederate government at Richmond; the "reorganized" pro-Union government, which had few supporters and huddled under the protection of Northern guns at Alexandria; and the new Union government of West Virginia.

In summary then, after Fort Sumter was fired upon, the border states divided. Virginia, Arkansas, Tennessee, and North Carolina went with the Confederacy; Delaware, Maryland, Missouri, Kentucky, and, presently, West Virginia remained in the Union.

Importance of the Border States. It is impossible to exaggerate the importance that these decisions, made early in the conflict, had upon the conduct of the Civil War. For the Confederacy it was essential that states from the Upper South join the secession. For all the brave talk at Montgomery, the Confederacy was not a viable nation so long as it consisted only of the seven states in the Deep South. The population of these seven states was only one-sixth that of the remaining states of the Union. In all the Gulf States in 1861, there was not a single foundry to roll heavy iron plate or to cast cannon, nor a large powder works, nor indeed a single important factory. But when Virginia, North Carolina, Arkansas, and Tennessee joined the Confederacy, they almost doubled its population. What is more, they brought to the new nation the natural resources, the foundries and factories, and the skilled artisans that made it possible to rival the Union. To recognize the economic and psychological strength added by these states of the Upper South—and also to escape the sweltering summer heat of Montgomery—the Confederacy in May 1861 moved its capital from Montgomery to Richmond.

But if the states of the Upper South brought the Confederacy strength, they also limited its freedom of action. Richmond and Virginia became so important to the South that the Confederate government became obsessed with defending them—at the expense of neglecting the vital western theaters of military operations.

For Lincoln's government, too, the border states were vital. If Maryland had seceded, the capital at Washington would have been surrounded by enemy territory—cut off from the Union states of the North and the West. Confederate control of Kentucky would have imperiled river transportation along the Ohio, and the secession of Missouri would have endangered traffic on the Mississippi and cut off communication with Kansas and the Pacific coast. Although Lincoln grieved over the secession of the states that joined the Confederacy, he could take comfort in the fact that by keeping four slave states in the Union he was preventing the Southern armies from recruiting from an additional population that was three-fifths as large as that of the original Confederacy.

So important were the border states for the Union that special pains had to be taken not to disturb their loyalty. In particular, Lincoln saw that there must be no premature action against slavery. European nations might fail to understand the nature of the American Civil War, and Northern abolitionists might denounce their president as "the slave-hound from Illinois," but Lincoln knew that to tamper with slavery would result in the loss of the border states, particularly Kentucky. "I think to lose Kentucky is nearly the same as to lose the whole game," he wrote to a friend. "Kentucky gone, we cannot hold Missouri, nor, as I think, Maryland. These all against us, and the job on

PRIVATE JOHN WERTH, RICHMOND HOWITZER BATTALION, C.S.A., AND AN ILLINOIS VOLUNTEER OF 1861
As soon as volunteers were sworn in and received their uniforms and equipment, most rushed to photographers' studios to have pictures made for their loved ones.

our hands is too large for us. We would as well consent to separation at once, including the surrender of this capitol."

Raising the Armies

While Lincoln and Davis were moving in parallel fashion to win the support of the border states, ordinary folk in the North and South were rallying around their flags. On both sides the firing on Fort Sumter triggered a rush to enlist. "War! and volunteers are the only topics of conversation or thought," an Oberlin College student reported when the news reached Ohio. "The lessons today have been a mere form. I cannot study. I cannot sleep, I cannot work, and I don't know as I can write." An Arkansas youth recorded identical emotions: "So impatient did I become for starting that I felt like a thousand pins were pricking me in every part of the body and [I] started off a week in advance of my brothers."

The Rush to Volunteer.   Ordinarily a volunteer offered to enlist in one of the regiments that was being raised in his community. Wealthy citizens and prominent politicians usually took the lead in recruiting these companies. Inevitably these regiments displayed a wide variety of arms, ranging from rusty flintlocks to the latest sharpshooting rifles. Often their uniforms bore distinctive insignia. (For example, a Louisiana battalion recruited from the daredevil New Orleans roustabouts called themselves the Tigers, and their scarlet skullcaps bore mottoes like "Tiger on the Leap" and "Tiger in Search of a Black Republican." Perhaps the most colorful—and impractical—uniforms were those of the Northern Zouave regiments, dressed in imitation of the French troops in North Africa. These soldiers, wearing their red fezzes, scarlet baggy trousers, and blue sashes, were magnificent in military reviews, but when they had to wade across a stream, their baggy garments ballooned around them and they floated down the current like so many exotic water-

**RECRUITING POSTER FOR
ZOUAVE REGIMENT**

**PRESENTATION OF COLORS, 1ST MICHIGAN
INFANTRY, MAY 1861**
Regiments were raised under state, not national, auspices. Before a regiment left home to join the Union or Confederate army, there was usually a formal ceremony at which the governor or some other high-ranking state official made a patriotic speech and presented the fighting men with their regimental flag.

lilies.) When a regiment's ranks were filled, there was invariably a farewell ceremony, featuring rousing addresses, lengthy prayers, and the presentation of the regimental flag, often hand-sewn by patriotic wives and sweethearts of the enlisted men. Then, loaded with hams, cakes, and sweetmeats provided by fond mothers and wives, the men went off to war.

Wartime Maladministration. Neither the Union nor the Confederate War Department knew what to do with the flood of volunteers. Leroy P. Walker, the first Confederate secretary of war, had had no military training and no administrative experience. An amiable Southern gentleman, fond of prolonged conversations with visitors, of writing rambling three-page business letters, and of filing his correspondence by piling it on a chair after he had read it, Walker was wholly unable to cope with the situation. Complaining that he lacked

arms and equipment, he refused the services of regiment after regiment. Perhaps 200,000 Confederate volunteers were thus rejected in the first year of the war.

The Northern war office was equally chaotic. Simon Cameron, the secretary of war, had been forced upon Lincoln as part of a political bargain. Cameron's main objective was to become the undisputed boss of Pennsylvania politics. There is no evidence that he used his cabinet position to line his own pockets, but he did employ his huge patronage to strengthen his faction of Pennsylvania Republicans. Lacking administrative talents, Cameron, like Walker, simply could not deal with the flood of volunteers, nor could he supervise the hundreds of contracts his office had to make for arms, ammunition, uniforms, horses, and dozens of other articles for the army. Haste, inefficiency, and corruption inevitably resulted. For example, in October 1861 General Frémont, desper-

"CAVALRY OFFICER" BY WINSLOW HOMER
Even after a year of combat, Americans, North and South, could not reconcile themselves to the fact that modern war requires regimentation. They continued to think of themselves as individualists, like this dashing Union cavalry officer, sketched by Winslow Homer.

Courtesy of the Cooper-Hewitt Museum, the Smithsonian Institution's National Museum of Design

ately needing horses for his cavalry in Missouri, contracted to purchase 411 animals. Subsequent investigation proved that 350 of the horses supplied him were undersized, under- or overaged, ringboned, blind, spavined, and incurably unfit for service; 5 were dead. Unable to equip the Union volunteers as they rushed to defend the flag, Cameron thought it was his principal duty "to avoid receiving troops faster than the government can provide for them."

As the war wore on, the initial zeal for volunteering abated. Many of the men rejected by Walker and Cameron in the early months of the conflict were never available again. Soon even those whose services had been accepted began to exhibit less enthusiasm for the war. Most had expected the army to be like the peacetime militia, to which all able-bodied white men belonged; the monthly militia rallies had been the occasion for fun and frolic, punctuated by a little uneven military drill, a considerable amount of political oratory, and a great deal of drinking. Now they discovered that war was not a lark. Belonging to the army meant discipline, spit-and-polish cleaning of equipment, and hours of close-order drill. A soldier's life was one of endless monotony, interrupted occasionally by danger from enemy bullets and more frequently by diseases resulting from inadequate food and clothing, lack of vaccination, filthy drinking water, and open latrines. By the end of 1861, many Union volunteers were beginning to count the weeks until the end of their three-year term of enlistment. Confederate regiments, which had been enrolled for a year, were about ready to disband in the spring of 1862.

Reorganization and Conscription.
Of necessity Lincoln and Davis moved almost simultaneously to strengthen their war departments in order to give more central

Private Alfred Bellard, of the Fifth New Jersey Infantry, enjoyed serving in the army but did not like the fighting because, he said candidly, "There is a little too much risk for me." His personal recollections of the war, written apparently only for himself and his family, tell less about strategy and battles than they do about the everyday life of a soldier. His spelling was eccentric (he never could get that word *dessicated*, meaning "dried" or "dehydrated," quite right), but his memory of army routine was accurate.

A Union Private Describes Army Rations

OUR rations were for the most part good and plenty of it. Consisting of hard tac (that is square biscuit) that sometimes had to be broken with your heel or musket. Soft bread when in a permanent camp. Fresh beef. Salt junk (pork). Salt horse (beef). Peas. Beans. Potatoes. Desecated vegetables. Rice etc.

The following bill of fare taken at random for 9 days while we lay in Washington will answer for the rest of the time, as it was about the same, only that we sometimes had vegetable soup and occasionally tea instead of coffee. Our breakfast and supper always consisted of bread and coffee unles we were saving enough to reserve some meat. Here it is.

Nov. 19, 1861 "Dinner." Salt Beef and Potatoes.
20th Fresh Beef and Rice Soup.
21st Salt Pork and Bean soup.
22nd Fresh Beef and Pea Soup.
23rd Salt Beef.
24th Fresh Beef and Rice with raisons.
25th Salt Pork and Pea Soup.
26th Salt Pork and Bean Soup.
and 27th Salt Beef and Pea Soup.

The raisons mentioned, were bought out of the company funds and had nothing to do with Uncle Sam. The desacated vegetables were all kinds of green stuf pressed into a square cake, and when we wanted any soup a piece of it was broken off and put in the pot, when it would swell out and make a very nice soup. The bean soup was good, but with some cooks it was made so thin that the boys used to say that there was one bean to a quart of water. Our coffee when we first went out was issued to us green, so that

we had to roast and grind it, which was not always a success, some of it being burnt, while some would be almost green. In roasting it we put a quantity of it in a mess pan, and placing the pan over the fire would have to keep stirring it round with a stick in order to have it roasted as evenly as possible.

These mess pans were used to fry our pork in and also as a wash bason. Our soup, coffee and meat were boiled in camp kettles suspended over the fire . . . which were also used for boiling our dirty clothes. Not a very nice thing for a soup pot, especially when they were full of vermin, as they were most of the time when on active service. Our stomachs were strong enough however to stand it, and our appetites did not suffer on that account.

Fresh beef was taken along with us on the march, the cattle following in the rear of the army to be killed when wanted. . . . On one of the hot days at Fair Oaks, the meat when issued to us was fly blown, and the maggots had to be scraped off before it was put into the pot, although the beef was just killed and was yet warm when I carried some of it to the cooks. The salt junk as we called our pork was sometimes alive with worms, as was also an occasional box of crackers, but that did not happen very often. Instead of having our pork boiled, we sometimes had it fried and in order to do it up quick, we had a large square frying pan made in Washington that would fry enough at once to furnish the entire company.

When on the march we had to do our own cooking as the rations were issued out to last 3 days. The pork we fried on a pan of our own construction consisting of half a canteen and a stick, or else broiled it on our home made toasting fork. Coffee and sugar we kept in a bag mixed together, and when we wanted a cup of coffee we put two tablespoons full of the mixture in a pint cup of water and placing the cup on two sticks with some hot coals beneath let it boil. And it often happened that just as the coffee was about boiled enough some one in lighting his pipe at the fire would touch one of the sticks with his foot and over went the coffee, when we had to do without or else use up more of our supply of coffee. Our crackers we used to fry, to make them more palatible soaking them an hour or two to make them soft. . . .

As forraging was strictly forbidden in general orders, we could not do much of that but still managed to get a little on the sly. I know one day we passed a corn field, when some of the men went after some. As they were busy filling their haversacks the old farmer came across his farm with a gun and big dog, to frighten us off I suppose, but when he saw we were armed and not disposed to go, he took the hint and went himself.

direction to their armies. In January 1862, having persuaded Cameron to become American minister to Russia, Lincoln named a former Democrat, the brusque and imperious Edwin M. Stanton, to the War Department. Stanton quickly reorganized the department, regularized procedures for giving out war contracts, and investigated frauds. Standing behind an old-fashioned writing desk, looking like an irritable schoolmaster before a willful class, Stanton heard all War Department business in public. He curtly dismissed patronage seekers, even when a congressman accompanied them; contractors had to state their prices in loud, clear voices; and even a petitioner bearing a letter of introduction from the president might be abruptly shown to the door. Working incessantly, Stanton saw to it that the Union army became the best-supplied military force the world had ever seen.

It took a bit longer for Davis to find a war secretary to his liking. When Walker, to everyone's relief, resigned in September 1861, Davis replaced him briefly with Judah P. Benjamin and then, after Benjamin became the Confederate secretary of state, with George Wythe Randolph. Randolph did much to see that Robert E. Lee and Thomas J. ("Stonewall") Jackson had the necessary arms and supplies for their 1862 campaigns. But when Randolph and Davis disagreed over strategy, the secretary had to go, and in November 1862 the sallow and cadaverous James A. Seddon succeeded Randolph. As one of his clerks remarked, Seddon looked like "an exhumed corpse after a month's interment." Nevertheless, he was diligent and efficient. He also had the good sense to give solid support to subordinates of great ability. Perhaps the most competent of these was General Josiah Gorgas, head of the Confederate ordnance bureau. Thanks to Gorgas's efforts, the Confederacy, which in May 1861 had only about 20 cartridges for each musket or rifle, by 1862 had built powder plants capable of producing 20 million cartridges. This was enough ammunition to supply an army of 400,000 men for twelve months.

While both presidents were strengthening their war departments, they also moved, in 1862, to take a more active role in recruiting troops. Because the twelve-month period of enlistment of Confederate troops expired in the spring of 1862, Davis warned that the Southern army would be decimated just as Union forces were approaching Richmond. The Southern Congress felt uncomfortable in ignoring the principle of state sovereignty proclaimed in the Confederate Constitution. But on April 16, 1862, it passed a national conscription act, which made every able-bodied white male between the ages of eighteen and thirty-five subject to military service. This first conscription law in American history, however, exempted numerous groups from military service, ranging from druggists to Confederate government officials; and a subsequent law excused planters or overseers supervising twenty or more slaves. The Confederate conscription act was meant less to raise new troops than to encourage veterans to reenlist. The law provided that if the men stayed in the army, they could remain in their present regiments and elect new officers; but if they left, it threatened, they could be drafted and assigned to any unit that needed them.

Lincoln's government moved toward conscription a little more slowly. Volunteering all but stopped after the bloody campaigns in the summer of 1862,* and the army needed 300,000 new men. Union governors suggested to the president that a draft would stimulate volunteering, and on July 17 the United States Congress passed a loosely worded measure authorizing the president to set quotas of troops to be raised by each state and empowering him to use national force to draft them if state officials failed to meet their quotas. This first Union conscription law was intentionally a bogeyman that the governors used to encourage enlistments, and it brought in only a handful of men.

Financing the War

If it became hard for the Union and Confederate governments to raise troops, it was even harder to supply and pay for them. Although the United States in 1860 was potentially one of the great industrial nations of the world, it was still primarily an agricultural country, with five out of six of its inhabitants living on farms. The factories that would be called upon to supply vast armies were mostly small in scale. Some 239 companies manufactured firearms in 1860; their average invested capital was less than $11,000. Textile mills, especially for the manufacture of woolens, were larger, but ready-made clothing was still sewn in small shops. The country produced an abundance of foodstuffs, but there was no effective wholesale marketing system for meat and grain. Maps showed that by 1860 30,000 miles of railroads crisscrossed the country, but most of these were in fact short spans, each under its own corporate management. Often they were not connected to other lines at common terminals and had different rail gauges. Sending a boxcar from, say, Baltimore to St. Louis required diplomacy, improvisation, frequent transshipment, long delays, and a great deal of luck. Commercial transactions were impeded because the United States did not have a national bank; indeed, the country did not even have a national currency, for most of the circulating money

*For these military operations, see below, pp. 454–55.

consisted of bills issued by the numerous state banks, depreciating at various rates.

Problems of the Treasury Departments.

Yet Union and Confederate leaders had somehow to mobilize this disorganized economy to support an enormous war effort. Both governments relied primarily upon privately owned rather than government-operated factories to supply their armies. Necessity more than a theoretical preference for free enterprise lay behind this choice. If individual businessmen and corporations had little experience in the large-scale production of goods, the civil servants in Washington and Richmond had even less. Where it seemed useful, both governments supplemented the output of private industry with production from government-owned plants. While the Lincoln administration was purchasing firearms from Colt, Remington, and dozens of other manufacturers, it continued to rely upon its own armories, especially the one at Springfield, Massachusetts, for some of its best weapons. The South was even more largely rural and agricultural than the North, and thus it had to be more active in establishing government-owned plants, the most successful of which was the huge powder factory at Augusta, Georgia. But both governments contracted with private individuals and corporations for most of the arms, clothing, and other equipment needed for the armies.

It was easier to contract for supplies than to pay for them. Both Union and Confederacy began the war with empty treasuries. When Secretary of the Treasury Chase took up his duties in Washington, he was horrified to discover that between April and June 1861 the expenses of the Union government would exceed its income by $17 million. Chase, who had built his reputation on his work as an antislavery lawyer and politician, was inexperienced in financial matters. Thus he had to cast about desperately for solutions.

But Chase's difficulties were nothing compared with those of his Confederate counterpart, Christopher G. Memminger, who had to make bricks without clay as well as without straw. Like Chase, Memminger had no extensive experience in financial matters, and his neat, systematic mind was troubled by the free and easy ways of government wartime expenses. He did what he could to make order—by requiring Confederate Treasury employees to keep regular nine-to-five hours, by outlawing drinking on the job, and by insisting that his visitors curb their customary long-windedness and promptly state their business. These measures, however, did little to solve Confederate financial difficulties.

Sources of Revenue.

Neither secretary seriously thought of financing the war through levying taxes. For either the Union or the Confederacy to impose heavy taxation in 1861 might well have killed the citizens' ardor for war. Americans simply were not used to paying taxes to their national government. For thirty-five years before the war, there had been no federal excise duties. In 1860 the United States Treasury had no internal revenue division, no assessors, no inspectors, and no agents. Since tariffs were a more familiar method of raising revenues, both secretaries hoped for large customs receipts. But when the Republicans in the Union Congress passed the high protective Morrill Tariff in 1861 and raised rates even higher in 1862, they effectively killed that source of revenue. Similarly, the Union blockade of the South reduced the amount and value of goods brought into Confederate ports and cut the Southern income from tariffs. In desperation the Union government in August 1861 resorted to a direct tax, levied upon each state in proportion to population, of $20 million; much of it was never collected. That same month, the Confederates imposed a "war tax" of 0.5 percent on taxable wealth. Davis's government, like Lincoln's, had to rely upon the states to collect this tax, and most of them preferred issuing bonds or notes rather than levying duties upon their people.

In neither country was borrowing a realistic possibility for financing the war. Americans of the 1860s were products of the Jacksonian era, with its suspicion of paper certificates of indebtedness. Thus Americans preferred to hoard rather than to invest their surplus funds. The rival Union and Confederate governments themselves shared this same suspicion of paper and this trust in hard money, or specie. In the North Secretary Chase insisted that the banks of New York, Philadelphia, and Boston lend money under a $150 million federal bond issue, but he was unwilling to take anything but gold or silver in payment. In December 1861 the resulting drain on bank reserves of precious metals, coupled with uncertainty over the course of the war, forced Northern banks to suspend payments in specie for the notes they had issued to the public in past years. Nor was Chase more successful in his early attempts to sell Union bonds directly to small investors. The Confederacy followed much the same course in its borrowing. An initial loan of $15 million was quickly subscribed to, with the result that Southern banks, including the strong institutions of New Orleans, were obliged to give up virtually all their precious metals to the new government. Consequently they could no longer redeem their notes in gold or silver. Memminger's attempt to sell subsequent Confederate bonds directly to the Southern people ran into the difficulty that nobody had any precious metals. Urged by Vice-President Alexander H. Stephens and other Confederate orators, plantation owners in

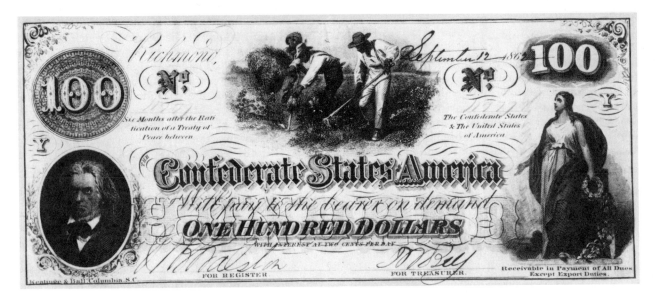

CONFEDERATE PAPER MONEY
Both the Confederacy and the Union were obliged to resort to paper money in order to finance the war. In the South engravers were few and incompetent. As a result the likenesses they produced—like this portrait of John C. Calhoun—were so unprepossessing as to raise doubts about the artists' loyalty to the Southern cause.

the fall of 1861 subscribed tobacco, rice, cotton, and other commodities to purchase bonds. But since the Union blockade cut off the market for these products, the Confederate government realized little from the loan.

Recourse to Paper Money.   In consequence, by early 1862 both governments began to issue paper money, backed only by the promise that someday they would redeem the paper money in specie. Both treasury secretaries agreed to this policy reluctantly. Memminger, a prominent hard-money advocate before the war, had to resort to the printing presses in 1861. The Confederacy issued $100 million in paper money in August 1861, and the next year it printed millions of dollars more. Having denounced "an irredeemable paper currency, than which no more certainly fatal expedient for impoverishing the masses and discrediting the government of any country, can well be devised," Chase found it even more embarrassing than Memminger to resort to treasury notes. But in January 1862 he had no alternative. Declaring that an issue of paper money was now "indispensably necessary," he persuaded Congress to authorize the printing of $150 million in non-interest-bearing United States treasury notes (which were promptly dubbed "greenbacks" because of their color). Rarely does history provide such a tidy illustration of how huge impersonal forces overrule the preferences and will of individual statesmen.

Wartime Diplomacy

In diplomacy as in economic policy, the Union and the Confederacy moved along parallel paths during the first two years of the war. Neither Lincoln nor Davis had much knowledge of diplomacy or took an active role in the conduct of foreign policy. Both, however, had difficulties with their secretaries of state.

Seward, Lincoln's principal adviser, would ultimately rank as one of the greatest secretaries of state, but in the early stages of the Civil War he gave evidence of wild eccentricity, coupled with deep personal ambition. At the height of the Sumter crisis, he submitted to Lincoln a private memorandum complaining that the government as yet had no policy for dealing with secession, announcing his readiness to take over the president's function and shape a suitable policy, and suggesting that the administration's proper course was to "change the question before the public from one upon slavery . . . for a question upon union or disunion." This redefinition of the critical issue was to be accomplished by provoking a confrontation with foreign powers. If allowed, Seward would "seek explanations from Great Britain and Russia"—for what offenses he did not specify; he "would demand explanations from Spain and France, categorically, at once," presumably over their threatened intervention in the affairs of Santo Domingo and Mexico; and if Spain and France did not respond forthwith, he would urge a declaration of war against these powers. Lincoln, to his enduring credit, quietly filed away this memorandum, refrained from dismissing a secretary who planned to bring on a world war, and allowed Seward time to come to his senses.

Despite Lincoln's efforts to keep the matter quiet, word of Seward's aggressive inclinations leaked out in conversations at Washington dinner tables, and diplomats at the capital soon had a pretty good idea of what was in the secretary's mind. During the first two years of the war, European governments learned from diplomatic dispatches to be skeptical of all Seward's policies, even after the secretary had become more moderate. Perhaps, however, the awareness of Seward's hair-trigger temper did something to make those governments more cautious in their relations with the United States and less willing to recognize the Confederacy.

Davis, too, had trouble with his state department. Robert Toombs, the first Confederate secretary of state, was as ambitious and overbearing as he was able. It was a relief when, having decided that the path to glory lay on the battlefield rather than in the cabinet, Toombs resigned to take a commission in the Southern army. His successor, R. M. T. Hunter, was equally ambitious, and—perhaps with an eye on the 1868 Confederate presidential election—he too promptly resigned, to become senator from Virginia. In March 1862 Davis finally found his man in Judah P. Benjamin, who had already been Confederate attorney general and secretary of war. Serving until the end of the war, Benjamin cleverly reflected the changing moods of his chief, but he was not an innovator in foreign policy. In the words of a critical Northerner who visited Richmond during the war, Benjamin had a "keen, shrewd, ready intellect, but not the stamina to originate, or even to execute, any great good, or great wickedness."

Union and Confederate diplomatic appointments abroad were a rather mixed lot. Lincoln perhaps, lacked tact in appointing the German-born Carl Schurz as minister to conservative, monarchical Spain, for Schurz was considered a "red republican" for his participation in the German revolution in 1848. But Davis showed a total failure to understand British antislavery sentiment by sending William L. Yancey, the most notorious Southern fire-eater, as first Confederate commissioner to Great Britain. On the positive side, the Union minister to Great Britain, Charles Francis Adams, exhibited the patience and restraint that were required in his difficult assignment. The dignity of this son of President John Quincy Adams and grandson of President John Adams made him a match even for the aristocratic British foreign minister, Lord John Russell. Of the Confederate emissaries abroad,

John Slidell of Louisiana probably proved the ablest. The wily, adroit, and unscrupulous Slidell was perfectly at home in the court of Napoleon III, Napoleon Bonaparte's nephew, who had reestablished the imperial regime in France and was eager to spread French influence in the world.

European Neutrality. Much to the disappointment of Americans on both sides, the European powers' attitudes toward the Civil War were not primarily shaped by the actions of American ministers, secretaries of state, or even presidents. Nor, during 1861 and 1862, were they shaped by appeals to economic self-interest. Southerners firmly believed that cotton was king and expected that pressure from British and French textile manufacturers would compel Great Britain and France to recognize the Confederacy and to break the Union blockade. But European manufacturers had an ample stockpile of cotton, purchased before the outbreak of hostilities, and therefore they were not much affected by the cut-off of Southern cotton in 1861. By 1862 cotton mills in both Britain and France were suffering, but Union and Confederate orders for European arms, ammunition, and other equipment counterbalanced these losses. There was great hardship among the workers in the cotton mills, especially in the Lancashire district of England, where unemployment was high. But these workers' complaints were relatively ineffectual because Britain still did not allow the workers to vote.

Northerners were equally disappointed by the attitudes of the European governments. Knowing the strength of the antislavery movement abroad, particularly in Great Britain and France, they expected the European powers to condemn the slaveholding Confederacy. Their hope was unrealistic because, during the early years of the war, the Union government took no decisive steps toward emancipation. Indeed, Lincoln pledged that he would not interfere with slavery where it existed, Seward branded the abolitionists and "the most extreme advocates of African slavery" as equally dangerous to the Union, and Union generals helped Southern masters reclaim their runaway slaves. It was scarcely surprising that European opponents of slavery were confused and could do little to influence the attitudes of their governments toward the war in America.

Northerners and Southerners alike failed to understand that the policy of European states toward the Civil War would be determined largely by considerations of national self-interest. An uneasy balance of power prevailed in Europe, and no nation was eager to upset it by unilateral intervention in the American conflict. But joint action by the European powers was always difficult because of mutual suspicion, and in

COTTON IN THE STOCKS.

M. Mercier:—"HOW MUCH LONGER IS THIS TO LAST? OR ARE YOU WAITING
UNTIL WE INTERFERE?"

"COTTON IN THE STOCKS"
The Union blockade sealed off Southern exports of cotton and helped produce severe hardships in the textile-producing regions of Great Britain and France. This 1862 cartoon shows the French minister to Washington, Henri Mercier, threatening Uncle Sam with European intervention if the blockade is not lifted.

the 1860s it was virtually impossible because of the nature of the British government. The British prime minister, Lord Palmerston, who was nearly eighty years old, headed a shaky coalition government that was certain to fall if it undertook any decisive action. With the British government thus immobilized, Russia favoring the Union cause, and Prussia and Austria mostly indifferent to the conflict, the ambitious Napoleon III found his inclinations to meddle in favor of the Confederacy effectively curbed.

As a result, European nations announced their neutrality early in the war. Queen Victoria's proclamation of May 13, 1861, was typical in recognizing that a state of war existed between the United States and "the states styling themselves the Confederate States of America" and in declaring neutrality. None of the European proclamations recognized the Confederacy as a nation—that is, no one declared that it was

a legitimate, independent power, entitled to send ambassadors and ministers abroad and to receive those from other nations, to enter into treaties with other powers, or, in general, to be treated just like any other sovereign state. But the proclamations did recognize the Confederates as belligerents. That acknowledgment meant that the Southerners were to be considered not simply as a group of riotous or rebellious individuals, but as participants in a systematic, organized effort to set up their own independent government. Under international law, recognition as a belligerent entitled the Confederacy to send out privateers without their being considered pirate ships. Acknowledgment that a state of war existed in America also meant that the Union government could not simply declare Southern ports closed to foreign ships. To exclude foreign shipping, the North would have to maintain an effective blockade of the Confederacy. Initially, therefore, these European proclamations of neutrality and recognition of Southern belligerency seemed a great Confederate success. In fact, however, they were both necessary and warranted by international law—and, despite Seward's rantings, they were truly impartial.

The Trent Affair. In November 1861 the rash action of a Union naval officer threatened to upset this neutrality. Union Captain Charles Wilkes learned that President Davis was replacing the temporary commissioners whom he had sent to France and Britain with permanent envoys, John Slidell and James M. Mason. Wilkes decided to capture these diplomats en route. Off the shore of Cuba on November 8, 1861, his warship stopped the British merchant ship *Trent*, Union officers boarded and searched the vessel, and Mason and Slidell were unceremoniously removed, to be transferred to Boston for imprisonment. Wilkes's action was a clear violation of international law. When news of the incident reached Europe, hostility toward the Union government flared up. "You may stand for this," Prime Minister Palmerston told his cabinet, "but damned if I will!" The British foreign minister, Russell, drafted a stiff letter demanding the immediate release of the envoys. It was clear that the Lincoln government faced a major crisis if it held its prisoners. After conferring with cabinet members and senators, Lincoln decided on Christmas Day to release the Southern envoys. He would fight only one war at a time.

Even with the firm intention of remaining neutral, European powers found their patience tested as the American war stretched on without apparent chance of ending. International relations were disturbed, commerce was disrupted, textile manufacturing was suffering, and neither North nor South seemed able to achieve its goal. Increasingly, support built up in both France and Britain for offering mediation to the combatants, and such an offer inevitably involved recognition of the Confederacy as an independent nation. In September 1862 Palmerston and Russell agreed to explore a mediation plan involving France and Russia as well as Great Britain, but pro-Union members of the British cabinet, among them the Duke of Argyll and George Cornewall Lewis, replied with strong arguments against mediation. Faced with dissension within his unstable coalition and given no encouragement by Russia, Palmerston by October 1862 had changed his mind and concluded that the European states must continue to be lookers-on until the war took a more decided turn.

Battles and Leaders

But on the battlefields in 1861 and 1862, there were no decided turns. Engagement followed engagement, campaign followed campaign, and neither side could achieve a decisive victory. The stalemate was baffling to both Northern and Southern armchair strategists, who had been sure that the war would be short and decisive and would end in an overwhelming victory for their own side.

Confederate war planners counted among their assets the fact that some of the best graduates of West Point led their armies and that President Davis himself had military training and experience. They believed that Southern men had more fighting spirit than Northerners, and they were probably correct in thinking that Southerners had more experience in handling firearms and were better horsemen. They knew that the Confederacy would generally act on the defensive and assumed that the offensive Union army would have to be at least three times as large as the Southern army. Since Southern forces could operate on interior lines, they could move more quickly and easily than Union forces, which would have to travel longer distances. While recognizing the superiority of the Northern navy, Southerners knew that the Confederacy had 3,500 miles of coastline, with innumerable hidden harbors and waterways through which shipping could escape. When Confederate strategists added to all these assets the fact that Southern soldiers were fighting on their home ground, where they knew every road and byway, they saw no reason to doubt ultimate victory.

But an equally good case could be made for the inevitability of a Union victory. The population of the Union in 1860 was about 20.7 million; that of the Confederacy, only 9.1 million. Moreover, 3.5 million of the inhabitants of the South were blacks—mostly slaves, who, it was presumed, would not be used in the Confederate armies. Along with this superiority in manpower, the North had vastly more economic strength than the Confederacy. The total value of all manufactured products in all eleven Confederate states was less than one-fourth that of New York alone. The iron furnaces, forges, and rolling mills in the United States were heavily concentrated in the North. The North in 1860 built fourteen out of every fifteen railroad locomotives manufactured in the United States. Northern superiority in transportation would more than compensate for Southern interior lines, as only 30 percent of the total rail mileage of the United States ran through the states forming the Confederacy. The Union navy, which experienced few defections to the South, was incomparably superior. And the blockade that President Lincoln announced at the outbreak of hostilities would cut off, or at least drastically reduce, Southern imports from Europe. When Northern planners added to the advantages of their side the possession of an established government, the recognition of foreign powers, and the enormous enthusiasm of the people for maintaining the Union, they could not doubt that victory would be sure and swift.

Jomini's Game Plan. In fact, these assets substantially canceled each other during the first two years of the war and produced not victory, but deadlock. As the armies engaged in complex maneuvers and in indecisive battles, Union and Confederate commanders largely employed the same strategic plans, for most had learned the art of war from the same teachers. In fifty-five of the sixty biggest battles of the war, the generals on both sides had been educated at West Point, and in the remaining five, a West Pointer led one of the opposing armies. At the military academy they had studied the theories of the French historian and strategist Baron Henri Jomini. Some had read Jomini's works in the original French or in translation; more, doubtless, had absorbed his ideas from the abridgment and interpretation of his work, *Elementary Treatise on Advance-Guard, Outpost, and Detachment of Service of Troops* (1847), written by Dennis Hart Mahan, who for a generation taught at the academy and greatly influenced his students.

Jomini's military theories constituted a complex body of doctrine, subject to many differing interpretations. But as his theories were understood by American commanders, they stressed the importance of the conquest of territory and emphasized that the seizure of the enemy's capital was "ordinarily, the objective point" of an invading army. Jomini had pictured a battle situation in which two armies were drawn up in opposing lines, one offensive and the other defensive, and he had even prepared a set of twelve diagrams showing the possible orders of battle.

In all twelve, a major determinant of victory was the concentration of force—the bringing to bear of a powerful, united force upon the enemy's weakest point. Warfare was thus something like an elaborate game of chess, an art that only professional soldiers could fully master.

Most of the military operations during the first two years of the Civil War can best be understood as a kind of elaborate illustration of Jomini's theories, slightly modified to fit the American terrain. The first big battle of the war occurred on July 21, 1861, when the Union General Irwin McDowell, under much pressure from Northern newspapers and much badgered by exuberant politicians in Congress, reluctantly pushed his poorly organized army into Virginia. He expected to encounter the Confederates, under General Beauregard, near Centreville. Numerous sightseers from Washington followed the Union forces, expecting to witness a spectacular victory. In the ensuing battle of Bull Run (or Manassas), both armies tried to apply the same battle plan from Jomini's treatise: each attempted a main attack upon the enemy's left flank, to be followed by a secondary thrust at his center and right wings. If completely executed, the two plans would have had the amusing result of leaving each army in the opponent's original place. But the Confederates also followed another of Jomini's principles, that of concentration of force. By using the railroad, they rushed General Joseph E. Johnston's troops from the Shenandoah Valley to join Beauregard's main force. The Union troops fought bravely and initially seemed to be carrying the day, but after Johnston's men were in position, the Union army was thrown back and then routed. Weary and disorganized, Northern troops limped back to the Potomac and safety. Panic among the onlookers heightened the confusion. The Confederates were almost equally demoralized by their victory and were unable to pursue. The South thus lost its easiest opportunity to follow Jomini's maxim and seize the enemy's capital.

After this initial engagement it was clear that both armies needed reorganization and training before either could attempt further campaigns. Thus, despite growing impatience for action, there was little significant military engagement during the rest of 1861 except for minor encounters in Kentucky and Missouri. During this period General George Brinton McClellan, who was credited with some overrated small successes in western Virginia, was summoned to Washington to bring order to the Union army. With enormous dash and enthusiasm, the young commander began to whip the Northern regiments into fighting shape. He insisted on careful drill and inspection; he demanded the best of food and equipment for his men; and he refused to move forward until his army was thoroughly prepared.

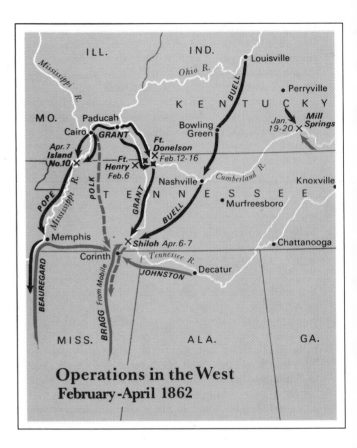

**Operations in the West
February–April 1862**

The War in the West, 1862.

By early 1862 Union armies were ready to advance, not only in the East, but in all the theaters of war. Taking advantage of numerical superiority, Union commanders concentrated on a series of weak spots in the Confederate defenses, just as Jomini had directed. In January General George H. Thomas defeated a Confederate force at Mill Springs, Kentucky, and made a significant break in the Southern defense line west of the Appalachian Mountains. The next month General Ulysses S. Grant made an even more important breach in that line. In collaboration with the Union gunboats on the Tennessee and Cumberland rivers, Grant captured Fort Henry and Fort Donelson, requiring the Confederate army in the latter fort to accept his terms of unconditional surrender.

The Southerners now had to abandon Tennessee. Union armies under Grant and Don Carlos Buell pushed rapidly after them until stopped at the battle of Shiloh (April 6–7). General Henry Wager Halleck, the Union commander for the entire western theater, was dissatisfied with Grant's generalship and took personal charge of the army after Shiloh. Halleck was a dedicated disciple of Jomini (whose works he had translated) and concentrated his force for a push on Corinth, Mississippi, in order to break the important

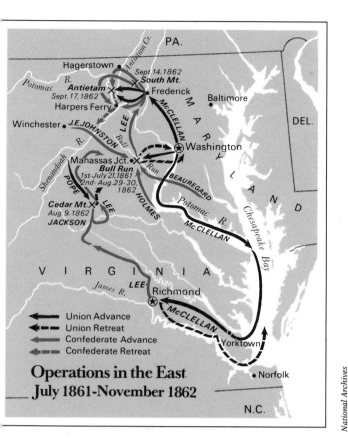

Operations in the East
July 1861–November 1862

Legend:
- → Union Advance
- ⇢ Union Retreat
- → Confederate Advance
- ⇢ Confederate Retreat

UNION ORDNANCE READY FOR TRANSPORTATION FROM YORKTOWN
For McClellan's push up the peninsula in the hope of capturing Richmond, the Union war department assembled the largest collection of men and materiel ever collected on the American continent. But, as events proved, Union generalship did not equal Union resources.

rail connection that linked Memphis and the western portion of the Confederacy with the East.

The Peninsula Campaign.

A Union advance in the eastern theater promised to be equally successful. After long delays McClellan began his offensive against Richmond. Instead of attacking overland from the north, he transported his troops to Fort Monroe, on the peninsula between the York and James rivers. McClellan complained bitterly because Lincoln violated the principle of concentration and held back 40,000 troops to defend Washington. Nevertheless, McClellan prepared to follow Jomini's advice and seize the Confederate capital.

At this point in the gigantic, synchronized Union offensive, designed to crush the Confederacy, everything began to go wrong. The difficulties stemmed in part from human inadequacies. Although good theoreticians and able administrators, Halleck and McClellan were indecisive fighters. Halleck took nearly two months to creep from Shiloh to Corinth, stopping to fortify his position every night. By the time he reached his destination, the Southern army had moved south with all its provisions. Equally cautious was McClellan's advance on the peninsula, where he allowed 16,000 Confederate soldiers under General

John B. Magruder to hold up his magnificent army of 112,000 until the Confederates could bring reinforcements to Richmond. The trouble was partly that these Union campaigns required the coordinated movement of forces larger than any seen before on the American continent, although few of the commanding officers had ever led anything larger than a regiment. But the Union failed chiefly because able Confederate generals had read the same books on strategy as the Union commanders and knew how to fight the same kind of battles.

While McClellan slowly edged his way up the peninsula, the Confederate commander, Joseph E. Johnston, who had rushed in with reinforcements, kept close watch until the Union general unwisely allowed his forces to be divided by the flooded Chickahominy River. Applying Jomini's principle of concentration on the enemy's weakest spot, Johnston on May 31–June 1 fell upon the exposed Union wing in battles at Fair

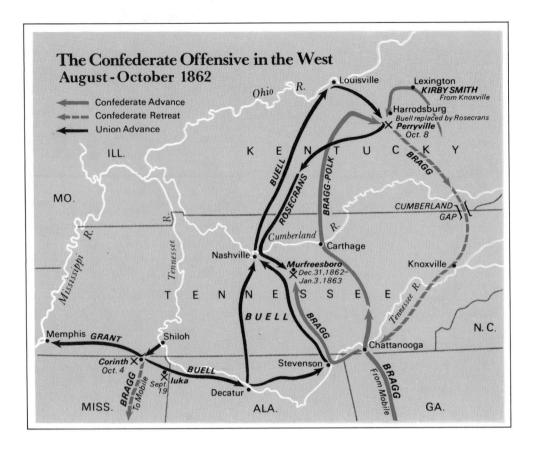

**The Confederate Offensive in the West
August – October 1862**

→ Confederate Advance
⇢ Confederate Retreat
→ Union Advance

Oaks (or Seven Pines), which narrowly failed of being a Confederate triumph. When Johnston was wounded in this engagement, President Davis chose Robert E. Lee to replace him.

Lee quickly revealed his military genius by showing that he knew when to follow Jomini's principles and when to ignore them. Remembering from his days at West Point how slow McClellan was, Lee allowed "Stonewall" Jackson to take 18,000 men from the main army for a daring campaign through the Shenandoah Valley. Jackson defeated and demoralized the Union forces in the Shenandoah and so threatened Washington that Lincoln withheld reinforcements that he had promised McClellan. When Jackson had accomplished this objective, Lee reverted to the principle of concentration and ordered Jackson promptly to rejoin the main army before Richmond. The combined Confederate force fell upon McClellan's exposed right flank at Mechanicsville. Lee failed to crush McClellan; but in a series of engagements known as the Seven Days (June 25–July 1), he forced the Union armies to beat a slow, hard-fought retreat to the banks of the James River, where it lay under the protection of Northern gunboats. Lee had saved Richmond.

The Confederate Counteroffensive. As the Union advances ground to a halt by midsummer 1862, the Confederates planned a grand offensive of their own. In the West two Southern armies under generals Braxton Bragg and Edmund Kirby-Smith swept through eastern Tennessee in August; by September they were operating in Kentucky, where they were in a position to cut the supply line for Buell's army in Tennessee. The early phases of their offensive were brilliantly successful, but the campaign as a whole was fruitless because of a lack of coordination between the two Southern armies and because of Bragg's indecisiveness. After a bloody battle at Perryville (October 8), the Confederate forces withdrew toward Chattanooga, followed by the Union army at a respectful distance.

The more daring part of the Confederate offensive was in the East. While McClellan's army was slowly being withdrawn from the peninsula, Lee turned quickly upon the Union forces in central Virginia under the braggart general John Pope. Concentrating his entire strength upon this segment of the Union army, Lee scored a brilliant Confederate victory in the second battle of Bull Run (August 29–30) and was now free to push into the North. He crossed the Potomac

PRESIDENT LINCOLN AND GENERAL McCLELLAN AT ANTIETAM, OCTOBER 3, 1862
After the battle of Antietam, McClellan remained inactive while Lee slipped back across the Potomac into Virginia. Troubled by the general's complaints that he needed more troops and more supplies, Lincoln observed that the Union army seemed to dwindle "like a shovelfull of fleas tossed from one place to another." On October 3 he himself went to Antietam in a vain effort to prod McClellan into advancing. "I say 'try,'" he told the general; "if we never try we shall never succeed."

into Maryland, where he hoped to supply his ragged army and to rally the inhabitants of that state to the Confederate cause.

Lee's invasion of Maryland ended with the battle of Antietam (September 17), an indecisive engagement whose very inconclusiveness clearly demonstrated the impossibility of ever ending the war as long as it was fought by the conventional rules. McClellan, once again the Union commander, moved slowly to catch up with Lee's army because he wanted to concentrate all his forces for an attack. Lee in turn waited in a defensive position behind Antietam Creek at Sharpsburg, Maryland, because he too needed to concentrate his troops, a portion of whom had been sent on a successful expedition to capture Harpers Ferry. When McClellan was finally ready to take the offensive, he followed one of Jomini's battle plans precisely, and Lee defended his position by the same rules. The result was the bloodiest day of the Civil War. In areas of the battlefield like the cornfield, the Dunker church, the Bloody Lane, and Burnside's bridge, men fell as in a slaughterhouse. By the end of the day, there were more than 25,000 casualties, with at least 5,000 dead. The next day an eyewitness noted "the most appalling sights upon the battle-field . . . the ground strewn with the bodies of the dead and the dying . . . the cries and groans of the wounded . . . the piles of dead men, in attitudes which show the writhing agony in which they died—faces distorted . . . begrimed and covered with clotted blood, arms and legs torn from the body or the body itself torn asunder."

Quietly Lee slipped back into Virginia, and McClellan did not pursue him. The Confederate offensive was over, and with it ended an era. If Jomini's strategy could only lead to stalemate, it was time for both Union and Confederacy to experiment with new ways of waging war.

CHRONOLOGY

1861 Secession of remaining states of Deep South (Texas, Louisiana, Mississippi, Alabama, Georgia, and Florida).

Jefferson Davis begins term as president of the Confederate States of America.

Abraham Lincoln inaugurated as president of the United States of America.

Firing on Fort Sumter precipitates war.

Secession of border slave states (Virginia, North Carolina, Tennessee, and Arkansas).

Union army routed at first battle of Bull Run (Manassas).

McClellan heads Union forces.

Trent affair threatens to change European neutrality.

1862 Both Union and Confederacy adopt paper money.

Union general U.S. Grant captures Fort Henry and Fort Donelson.

Grant defeated at Shiloh.

Battle of the ironclads: *Virginia (Merrimack)* vs. *Monitor*.

McClellan's peninsula campaign brings Union army to outskirts of Richmond, the Confederate capital.

Robert E. Lee becomes commander of Army of Northern Virginia.

Confederate victory at second battle of Bull Run.

Bloody battle between Lee and McClellan at Antietam.

Confederate invasion of Kentucky.

Lincoln issues preliminary Emancipation Proclamation.

Confederate victory at Fredericksburg.

SUGGESTED READINGS

The best guide to the extensive literature on the causes of Civil War is Thomas J. Pressly, *Americans Interpret Their Civil War* (1954).

Peter J. Parish, *The American Civil War* (1975), is the best one-volume history. *The Civil War and Reconstruction* (1969), by J. G. Randall and David Donald, is more comprehensive and has a fuller bibliography. James M. McPherson, *Ordeal by Fire: The Civil War and Reconstruction* (1982), is accurate and up-to-date. Of the older large-scale studies, James Ford Rhodes, *History of the United States from the Compromise of 1850 . . .* , Vols. 3–5 (1895–1904), remains valuable. The most complete modern account is Allan Nevins, *The War for the Union* (4 vols., 1959–71).

On the Sumter crisis, see David M. Potter, *Lincoln and His Party in the Secession Crisis* (1942), Kenneth M. Stampp, *And the War Came* (1950), and Richard N. Current, *Lincoln and the First Shot* (1963).

The best history of the Confederacy is Emory M. Thomas, *The Confederate Nation, 1861–1865* (1979). The fullest life of the Confederate president is Hudson Strode, *Jefferson Davis* (3 vols., 1955–64); the most recent is Clement Eaton, *Jefferson Davis* (1977). Rembert W. Patrick, *Jefferson Davis and His Cabinet* (1944), is revealing on Confederate administration. Three Confederate diaries are invaluable: *Mary Chestnut's Civil War*, ed. by C. Vann Woodward (1981); John B. Jones, *A Rebel War Clerk's Diary* (2 vols., 1866); and Robert G. H. Kean, *Inside the Confederate Government*, ed. by Edward Younger (1955).

The most recent biography of Abraham Lincoln is Stephen B. Oates, *With Malice Toward None* (1977). Benjamin P. Thomas, *Abraham Lincoln* (1952), has long remained standard. The fullest and most flavorful of the biographies is Carl Sandburg, *Abraham Lincoln: The War Years* (4 vols., 1939). The most scholarly and critical is *Lincoln the President* (4 vols., 1945–55), by J. G. Randall and Richard N. Current. A brilliant psychoanalytical interpretation is Charles B. Strozier, *Lincoln's Quest for Union* (1982). *The Abraham Lincoln Encyclopedia*, by Mark E. Neely, Jr. (1982), is exceptionally useful. The diaries of three of Lincoln's cabinet officers are indispensable: Howard K. Beale, ed., *The Diary of Edward Bates* (1933); David Donald, ed., *Inside Lincoln's Cabinet* [Salmon P. Chase] (1954); Howard K. Beale and Alan W. Brownsword, eds., *Diary of Gideon Welles* (3 vols., 1960).

The standard work on Anglo-American relations remains Ephraim D. Adams, *Great Britain and the American Civil War* (2 vol., 1925). Frank L. Owsley, *King Cotton Diplomacy* (1959), David P. Crook, *The North, the South, and the Powers* (1974), and Brian Jenkins, *Britain & the War for the Union* (2 vols., 1974–80), are valuable. See also Glyndon G. Van Deusen, *William Henry Seward* (1967), Martin B. Duberman, *Charles Francis Adams* (1961), and David Donald, *Charles Sumner and the Rights of Man* (1970). Franco-American relations are admirably covered in Lynn M. Chase and Warren F. Spencer, *The United States and France: Civil War Diplomacy* (1970), and Daniel B. Carroll, *Henri Mercier and the American Civil War* (1971).

On social and economic conditions, see Paul W. Gates, *Agriculture and the Civil War* (1965), and Mary E. Massey, *Bonnet Brigades: American Women and the Civil War* (1966). Developments on the Southern home front are sketched in Charles W. Ramsdell, *Behind the Lines in the Southern Confederacy* (1944), and Bell I. Wiley, *The Plain People of the Confederacy* (1943). Emerson D. Fite, *Social and Industrial Conditions in the North During the Civil War* (1910), remains the best survey. For the continuing debate on the effect of the war on American economic growth, see Ralph Andreano, ed., *The Economic Impact of the American Civil War* (1961), and David T. Gilchrist and W. David Lewis, eds., *Economic Change in the Civil War Era* (1965).

Studies dealing with other aspects of the war years are listed at the end of the following chapter.

19 Experimentation, 1862–1865

At the outset of the Civil War, both President Lincoln and President Davis assumed that the conflict would be a limited and relatively brief one, waged in conventional fashion by armies in the field and having little impact on the economic, social, and intellectual life of their sections. The events of 1861–62 proved these expectations utterly wrong. It slowly became clear that to carry on the war, Americans in both North and South had to break with tradition and experiment broadly. They had to try new forms of government action, new modes of social and economic cooperation, and new patterns of thought.

Since the Union was ultimately victorious, it would be easy to conclude that Northerners were more willing to experiment, and better able to mobilize all their resources, for what has been called the first modern war. But such a judgment makes the historian the camp follower of the victorious army. The record shows, instead, that both the Confederacy and the Union attempted innovations that were daringly original for the time. It also shows that both sides resorted to much the same kinds of experimentation during the final years of the war.

Evolution of a Command System

The bloody and indecisive campaigns of 1861 and 1862 made innovators out of both Union and Confederate soldiers. Experience under fire convinced them not to follow Jomini's tactics. The French writer had conceived of a tactical situation in which infantrymen, drawn up in close, parallel lines, blazed away at each other with muskets that could be loaded perhaps twice a minute and that had an effective range of one hundred yards. But Civil War soldiers were equipped with rifles that not only were more quickly loaded, but had an effective range of about eight hundred yards. In Jomini's day the offensive force had the great advantage: rushing forward with bayonets fixed, charging troops could break the defenders' line before they had

time to reload. But in the Civil War the advancing force was exposed to accurate fire during the last half-mile of its approach. In consequence, nine out of ten infantry assaults failed, and the Civil War soldier had little use for his bayonet—except perhaps as a spit on which to cook meat.

Soldiers on both sides rapidly learned how to make defensive positions even stronger. At the beginning of the war, most military men were scornful of breastworks and entrenchments, arguing that they simply pinned down a defending force and made it more vulnerable to a charge. When Lee, upon assuming command of the Army of Northern Virginia in 1862, ordered his men to construct earthworks facing McClellan's advancing troops, Confederate troops bitterly complained and called their new general the King of Spades. But when they saw how entrenchments saved lives, they changed their tune. Lee became to the Confederate common soldier "Marse Robert," the general who looked after his men's welfare. What Confederate generals started, Union commanders imitated. By the end of 1862, both armies dug in wherever they halted. Using spades and canteens, forks and sticks, soldiers pushed up improvised earthworks and strengthened them with fence rails and fallen logs.

Experience also quietly killed off Jomini's view that warfare was restricted to professionals. In the early days of the conflict, commanders believed that warfare should not do harm to civilians or their property. When McClellan's army pushed up the peninsula, the general posted guards to keep his soldiers from raiding Confederate farmers' cornfields. Similarly Halleck permitted slaveowners to search his camp in order to reclaim their runaway slaves. By the end of 1862, such practices had vanished. Soldiers joyfully foraged through civilians' watermelon patches, cornfields, and chicken roosts while their officers ostentatiously turned their backs. Northern generals exhibited a growing reluctance to permit the recapture

"CONTRABANDS APPROACHING THE UNION LINES NEAR CULPEPER COURT HOUSE" BY EDWIN FORBES
Wherever Union armies advanced into the South, slaves deserted the plantations and flocked after them. "I ran away," one woman declared, " 'cause master too bad; couldn't stay no longer."

Library of Congress

of fugitive slaves who had fled to the Union lines. As early as May 1861 General Benjamin F. Butler at Fort Monroe, Virginia, refused to return three such fugitives on the grounds that they were contraband of war. "Contrabands" became a code name for escaped slaves, and in 1862 the United States Congress showed what it thought of Jomini's notion of limited warfare by prohibiting military officers from returning runaways.

Lincoln Takes Command.

The deadlock of 1861–62 also brought about a transformation of the command systems of both the Union and the Confederate armies. Because the Union lost so many battles during the first two years of the conflict, Lincoln was forced to experiment. His initial venture came in mid-1862. Since he distrusted McClellan's capacity to keep an eye on the overall progress of the war while also leading a campaign to capture Richmond, Lincoln brought in Halleck from the West to serve as his military adviser, and gave him the grand title of general in chief. The position was not a viable one, for it placed Halleck in conflict with the other generals, especially McClellan.

It also often put him at odds with Secretary of War Stanton and exposed him to what he called the "political Hell" of pressure from congressmen. In addition, Halleck's slowness, his indecisiveness, and his rigid adherence to Jomini's principles made him hostile to all innovation, and Lincoln soon concluded that he was of little more use than a clerk.

Seeing no alternative, Lincoln then tried to direct military operations himself. In the eastern theater he replaced McClellan, after his failure to follow up his partial success at Antietam, with that bumbling incompetent, Ambrose E. Burnside. Burnside led the Army of the Potomac into the battle of Fredericksburg on December 13, 1862, one of the most disastrous—and surely the least necessary—Union defeats of the war. "Fighting Joe" Hooker then replaced Burnside. But the appointment of this boastful egotist, who was fond of the bottle, brought no better luck to the Union cause. The battle of Chancellorsville (May 1–4, 1863) was still another Confederate triumph—but a victory won at a great price, for "Stonewall" Jackson was accidentally fired upon by his own Southern soldiers and was mortally wounded.

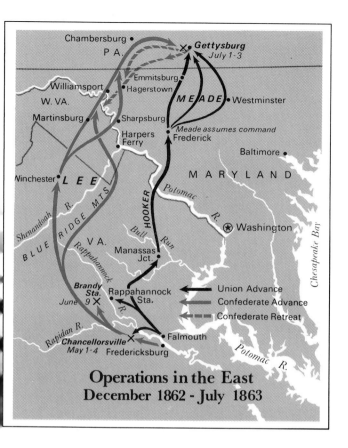

**Operations in the East
December 1862 - July 1863**

Map legend:
← Union Advance
← Confederate Advance
- - → Confederate Retreat

eracy, but en route Rosecrans encountered Bragg's army in the bloody and indecisive battle of Murfreesboro (December 30, 1862–January 2, 1863). Although Rosecrans claimed victory, his army was so badly mauled that he could not advance for another six months. Finally, in June 1863 he maneuvered the Confederates out of Chattanooga, but in pursuing Bragg's army he received a smashing defeat at Chickamauga (September 19–20). Only the rocklike determination of General George H. Thomas prevented the reverse from becoming a rout, and Rosecrans's army limped back into Chattanooga. Disoriented by defeat, Rosecrans, as Lincoln said, behaved "like a duck hit on the head," and allowed Bragg to besiege the city.

Farther west, Lincoln's personal direction of the Union armies proved equally ineffectual. Here the major objective was Vicksburg, the last major city on the Mississippi River still in Confederate hands; when it fell, the eastern part of the Confederacy would be severed from the trans-Mississippi region.

Grant's Success at Vicksburg. Grant commanded the Union forces in this area after Halleck went to Washington, and William Tecumseh Sherman was his ablest lieutenant. After a frontal assault on the almost impregnable bluffs of Vicksburg failed to drive out the Confederates, commanded by General John C. Pemberton, Grant devised a bold new strategy without aid from Washington. Using the navy's gunboats and transports to run his ammunition and supplies past the Vicksburg batteries, Grant marched his army to a point on the west bank south of the city, staged a rapid amphibious crossing, and—before the Confederates could recover from their surprise—pushed rapidly inland. To Lincoln's dismay he thus abandoned his base of supplies, announcing that he planned to live on the countryside. First he struck at Jackson, the capital of Mississippi, to drive back the small Confederate force that General Joseph E. Johnston had collected there. Then he turned on Pemberton's army and forced it into Vicksburg. After two ill-advised assaults, the Union army settled down to besiege the city, while from the river the Union gunboats kept up a constant bombardment. As civilians in the city took to caves for safety, and as starvation made mule meat a delicacy, Pemberton fought back as well as he could, but on July 4, 1863—the day after Gettysburg—he had to surrender his army and the city.

When the news reached Washington, Lincoln, who had distrusted Grant's strategy, wrote the general a handsome apology: "I now wish to make the personal acknowledgment that you were right, and I was wrong." The president was happy to be proved wrong, for Grant's success meant that he finally had a general

Still trying to direct military operations himself, Lincoln watched anxiously as Lee in the midsummer of 1863 began his second invasion of the North, this time pushing into Pennsylvania. When Hooker appeared unable or unwilling to pursue the Confederates, Lincoln replaced him with the shy, scholarly George Gordon Meade, who assumed command of the army only three days before the climactic battle of Gettysburg (July 1–3, 1863). Rushing all available forces to that Pennsylvania town, Meade succeeded in turning back the invaders. At last the Army of the Potomac had won a victory—but Meade failed to pursue, and Lee's army recrossed the Potomac to safety. "We had them within our grasp," Lincoln lamented. "We had only to stretch forth our hands and they were ours. And nothing I could say or do could make the Army move."

Lincoln was no more successful in trying to plan strategy for the trans-Appalachian theater of war. After the battle of Perryville in October 1862, it was clear that Don Carlos Buell must be replaced, and the president chose W. S. Rosecrans. Lincoln urged him to push on to Chattanooga, the rail hub of the Confed-

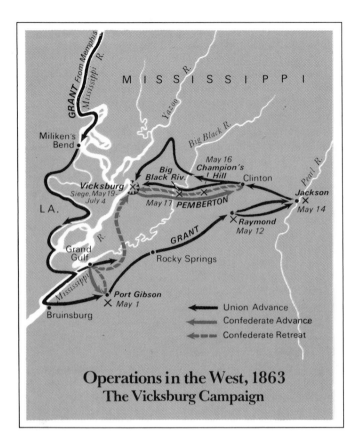

Operations in the West, 1863
The Vicksburg Campaign

MAJOR GENERAL ULYSSES SIMPSON GRANT, U.S.A.,
IN THE FALL OF 1863
Grant lacked the polish of McClellan, the brilliance of Sherman, and the flamboyance of Sheridan. But he had one quality more important than any of these. As Lincoln concisely put it: "I can't spare this man—he fights."

who knew how to plan a campaign and fight it. Putting Grant in command of all the troops in the West, Lincoln directed him to relieve the army cooped up in Chattanooga. Quickly Grant and Sherman came to the rescue. They opened up a line of communication to the starving Union troops in Chattanooga, now commanded by Thomas instead of the inept Rosecrans, and brought in reinforcements. On November 23–25 the combined forces routed Bragg's encircling army and drove it back into Georgia.

Two New Systems of Command. This further victory gave Lincoln a solution to the problem of command, which had so long troubled him. Early the next year he brought Grant to Washington. Grant became a lieutenant general and was assigned to command all the armies of the United States. Initially Washington observers thought the burden might be too much for this "short, round-shouldered man," whom they now saw for the first time. One observer reported that the new

lieutenant general "had no gait, no *station*, no manner, rough, light-brown whiskers, a blue eye, and rather a scrubby look withal . . . rather the look of a man who did, or once did, take a little too much to drink." But appearances were deceiving, for in the next few days Grant set forth a broad strategy for winning the war. Taking advantage of Northern superiority in manpower, he planned a simultaneous advance of all Union armies, so that the Confederates must divide their forces or else leave their territory open to invasion. The idea of involving all the Northern forces at once made sense to Lincoln. "Oh, yes! I can see that," he exclaimed. "As we say out West, if a man can't skin he must hold a leg while somebody else does." Accepting Grant's plan, Lincoln created a modern command system for the United States army, with the president as commander in chief, Grant as general in chief, and Halleck as essentially a chief of staff, while Stanton as secretary of war ably supported all the others.

Meanwhile the Confederate command system was

also evolving through experimentation. The tremendous victories won by Lee and the Army of Northern Virginia made it unnecessary constantly to change commanders in the East, but by 1863 it was evident that there must be a reorganization of Confederate commanders in the West. Davis instituted what was, in effect, a theater command system. Lee led the forces in Virginia, Joseph E. Johnston (now recovered from his wound) commanded the troops between the mountains and the Mississippi River, and Edmund Kirby-Smith was in charge of all troops in the vast trans-Mississippi region.

The new system was only partially successful. Kirby-Smith became a kind of super-commander of the trans-Mississippi theater (which was becoming increasingly isolated as Union forces captured point after point on the Mississippi) and did an effective job of recruiting and organizing the troops in his region. He stepped up trade with Mexico, so that impressive amounts of European munitions and supplies came in by way of Matamoros, Mexico. So strengthened, "Kirby-Smithdom," as it was popularly called, fared better than most of the rest of the South. But Kirby-Smith did little to make the vast resources of his command available to the government at Richmond.

In the central theater a strong Confederate command system failed to emerge. Johnston claimed that he did not know the extent and nature of his duties. Repeatedly he asked whether he was supposed to take field command of the widely scattered armies of Bragg (near Chattanooga) and of Pemberton (at Vicksburg), or was merely to serve as adviser to those generals. Knowing that both were protégés of President Davis, Johnston did not dare give a positive order to either. In consequence, he made only a feeble effort to replace the unpopular Bragg and diverted a few of his troops to support Pemberton. Johnston could not persuade Pemberton to leave Vicksburg while there was still time, and thus he watched in impotent impatience as the Confederate army there was cornered and starved into surrender.

In the eastern theater the brilliant successes of Lee and his lieutenants allowed the Army of Northern Virginia to operate essentially as it wished, without much regard for the needs of the Confederacy elsewhere. Lee, who had direct access to President Davis, resisted any attempt to weaken his force. In mid-1863, rather than attempt to relieve Vicksburg, Lee deliberately chose to invade the North again, in the vain hope that this course would relieve pressure on Confederate armies elsewhere. The result was the defeat at Gettysburg and the capture of Vicksburg.

Even so, by 1864 Lee was the only Confederate commander who retained the confidence of the country and of his troops. As Southern defeats became more numerous than victories, a strong demand welled up in the Confederate Congress for coordinated direction of all Southern armies, and men naturally looked to Lee. The general was, however, opposed to accepting these broader responsibilities and did all that he could to discourage the plan. When the Confederate Congress in January 1865 passed an act requiring the appointment of a commander in chief of all the armies, it had Lee in mind, and Davis named him. But Lee made it clear that he would continue to be essentially a theater commander, responsible only to Davis. Thus the Confederacy never developed a truly unified command system like the Union's.

The Naval War

Necessity compelled the Confederacy to take the lead in experimentation in naval warfare. Southerners were not a seagoing people and had no tradition of shipbuilding. Initially Secretary of the Navy Stephen R. Mallory had not a single ship at his command. He had to improvise, and he did so with imagination and remarkable success.

In the early months of the war, the long Southern coastline seemed to be at the mercy of the Union fleet, which could pick the most vulnerable points for attack. In November 1861 a Union naval force commanded by Flag Officer Samuel F. DuPont routed the weak Confederate defenders of Port Royal Sound, on the South Carolina coast, and Northern troops occupied Beaufort and the adjoining South Carolina Sea Islands. The victory gave the vessels in the Atlantic blockading fleet a much-needed fueling station and also brought freedom to the numerous slaves of the area. In February and March 1862 another Union expedition easily reduced Confederate positions on Roanoke Island and at New Bern, North Carolina, and enabled the Northern blockaders to keep a closer watch on Hatteras Sound. David G. Farragut's fleet in April 1862 helped capture New Orleans, the Confederacy's largest city.

By this time the Confederacy had greatly strengthened its coastal defenses, and further Union successes came slowly and at great cost. In April 1863 the Confederates repelled a vast Union armada, commanded by DuPont, that tried to capture Charleston. That stronghold of secession remained in Confederate hands until nearly the end of the war. Equally effective were the Confederate defenses of Wilmington, North Carolina, which became the main Southern port on the Atlantic through which supplies from Europe were imported. Not until January 1865 could Union troops capture Fort Fisher, the principal defense of Wilmington. The powerfully protected harbor of Mobile remained in Southern hands until August 1864, when

THE U.S.S. GALENA

Confederate ironclads were mostly converted steam frigates, overlaid with armor above the water line. The Union navy relied more upon newly constructed iron or wooden vessels designed to carry a metal sheath. Some of these had the unique form of the *Monitor*—"a tin can on a raft"—but more looked like the *Galena*, which helped drive the Confederates up the peninsula toward Richmond in 1862.

Library of Congress

the sixty-three-year-old Admiral Farragut, lashed in the rigging of his flagship so that he would not fall to his death if wounded, led his fleet past the defending Confederate forts to seize the last remaining major Southern port on the Gulf of Mexico.

Innovations in Naval Warfare.

To supplement the coastal batteries that protected these and other harbors, the Confederate navy experimented with new weapons. They used torpedoes extensively for the first time in warfare. These "infernal machines," constructed of kegs, barrels, and cans filled with explosives, were sometimes anchored at the entrance of Southern harbors. At other times they were turned loose to float with the tide toward attacking Union vessels, and on still other occasions they were propelled at the end of a long pole by a small boat whose crew was willing to undertake the suicidal risk. Even more risky were the several Confederate experiments with submarines. The most successful of these novel vessels was the *H. L. Hunley*, propelled under water by a crank turned by its eight-man crew. After four unsuccessful trials,

in which all members of the crews were killed, the *Hunley* in February 1864 sank the Union warship *Housatonic* in Charleston harbor, but the submarine itself was lost in the resulting explosion.

Mallory quickly concluded that the Confederacy could never build as large a fleet as the Union. But early in the war he urged the construction of iron-armored ships, against which the wooden vessels of the North would stand no chance. Despite shortages of iron and a lack of rolling mills, the Confederacy developed a surprising number of these vessels. The most famous of the Confederate ironclads was the *Virginia*, originally the United States warship *Merrimack*, which had been sunk when Union forces abandoned the Norfolk navy yard at the beginning of the war. Raised and repaired, the *Virginia* had its superstructure covered with four-inch iron plate and carried a cast-iron ram on its prow. On March 8, 1862, just as McClellan began his campaign on the peninsula, the *Virginia* emerged and began attacking the wooden vessels of the Union fleet at Hampton Roads. In the first day's action the ship destroyed two of the largest ships in the squadron and ran a third aground. Reappearing on the second day, the *Virginia* found its way barred by a curious Union vessel, the *Monitor*, which looked like a tin can on a raft. Belatedly contracted for by the slow-moving Union navy department, the *Monitor*, designed by John Ericsson, was a low-lying ironclad with a revolving gun turret. The battle between the *Virginia* and the *Monitor* proved to be a draw, but the Confederate ship had to return to Norfolk to repair its defective engines. Two days later, when forced to abandon Norfolk, the Southerners ran the *Virginia* ashore and burned the vessel to prevent its capture. The South's most promising hope for breaking the blockade was lost.

Mallory was equally prompt in purchasing or commissioning conventional vessels for the Confederate navy. These ships were designed not to combat Union warships, but rather to harass the United States merchant marine. The most successful of these vessels was the C.S.S. *Alabama*, built to Southern specifications at the Laird shipyards in Liverpool, England, and commanded by Raphael Semmes. Ranging over the Atlantic, Indian, and Pacific oceans, the *Alabama* between 1862 and 1864 hunted down and destroyed sixty-nine Union merchantmen, valued at more than $6 million. Not until nearly the end of the war could the Union navy corner and sink the raider. By this time, however, the *Alabama*, along with other Confederate cruisers, had virtually exterminated the United States carrying trade.

But however imaginative and innovative, Confederate navy officials could not keep pace with the growth of the Union navy under the slow but honest direction of Navy Secretary Gideon Welles. Drawing upon the vast industrial resources of the North and upon the experience of its seagoing population, Welles was able to build up the United States navy from its 42 active vessels in 1861, only 26 of which had steam power, to 671 ships in December 1864, of which 71 were ironclad. Navy personnel rose from 7,400 at the start of the war to 68,000 at its end. Superbly equipped and managed, the Union fleet maintained an ever-tightening blockade of the Southern coast. According to the best—but not wholly reliable—statistics, the Union fleet captured not more than one in ten blockade runners in 1861, and not more than one in eight in 1862. But by 1864 it caught one in three, and by 1865, every other one.

The Wartime Economy

Inevitably these huge military and naval operations put a heavy strain upon the economic resources of the combatants. In the Confederacy one result was a sharp shift in the nature of Southern agriculture. When the outbreak of war cut off Northern markets and the blockade increasingly sealed off European outlets for cotton and tobacco, farmers—at the urging of the Confederate and state governments—turned to producing grain and other foodstuffs. Cotton production in the South dropped from 4 million bales in 1861 to 300,000 bales in 1864.

In the North, too, farmers began producing more grain. Partly because of inflation, the price of wheat rose from 65¢ a bushel in December 1860 to $2.26 a bushel in July 1864. Farmers, especially in the Middle West, saw a chance to make money. At first the labor shortage kept them from expanding their acreage, for many farmhands enlisted in the Union army at the outbreak of the war. But machines soon made up for the absent men. One of Cyrus Hall McCormick's reapers could replace from four to six farmhands, and McCormick sold 165,000 of his machines during the war.

Industry also grew in both the Union and the Confederacy. As the Union blockade cut off imports, Southern factories gained a virtual monopoly in that region, and military and civilian needs provided an insatiable market. It is hard to measure Southern industrial growth, both because there was no Confederate census and because inflation affected all prices, yet there are some indications that manufacturing could be very profitable. For example, the 1862 conscription acts exempted the owners of certain basic industries provided that their annual profits were no more than 75 percent. Under the astute management of Joseph Anderson, the Tredegar Iron Works at Richmond, the largest privately owned factory in the South and the primary source of Confederate cannon, made profits of 100 percent in 1861 and of 70 percent in 1862.

Northern manufacturing was equally profitable, especially when it produced items needed for the army. The demand for uniforms enabled woolen mills to pay 25 percent dividends by 1865, compared to the 9 percent dividends they had paid before the war. Moreover, the number of woolen mills more than doubled during the war. Investors were willing to pour money into industry more confidently than before because Congress raised tariffs to levels that virtually excluded competing European products. War demands made the mass production of ready-made clothing profitable, and the army's need for shoes speeded the introduction of Gordon McKay's machine for sewing soles to uppers. Simultaneously, in an unrelated development, the discovery of oil at Titusville, Pennsylvania, in 1859 led to a wartime boom in the new petroleum industry.

Structural Changes in the Two Economies. These changes had an important impact on the structure of the American economy. The increase in the number of factories, particularly in the Confederacy, encouraged entrepreneurship. In the North men like John D. Rockefeller and Andrew Carnegie, who started their fortunes during the war, continued to dominate the industrial scene after 1865. When the South began rebuilding its industry in the 1870s and 1880s, it looked for leadership to its wartime entrepreneurs and to the Confederate commanders who likewise had experience in directing the labor of large numbers of men. The war also encouraged the growth of large, rather than small, factories. Obliged to contract for huge shipments, both the Union and the Confederate governments naturally turned to those manufacturing companies that were financially and physically able to handle them. The selective process was accelerated because larger firms could pay an agent in Washington or Richmond who understood the requirements of the army and navy—as well as those of influential congressmen and bureaucrats.

Most important of all, the wartime experience changed attitudes toward the role of the national government in the economy. Since the destruction of the Second Bank of the United States in the Jacksonian era, the national government had done little to regulate or control the economy. But during the war both the Union and the Confederate governments took steps that affected every branch of economic life. In passing the Homestead Act of May 20, 1862, which offered any citizen 160 acres of the public domain after five years of continuous residence on the land, the Union Congress signaled its intention henceforth to give more attention to the nation's farmers—as it did in creating the federal Department of Agriculture that same year. The Morrill Act of 1862, designating vast tracts of the public domain to support agricultural (land-grant) colleges, was further evidence of the same purpose. Both governments found it necessary to regulate transportation, especially railroads, during the war. Davis, despite his strict interpretation of the Confederate Constitution, urged his Congress to finance the construction of some missing links in the Southern rail system. Lincoln in July 1862 signed the Pacific Railroad Act, giving enormous tracts of the public land to support the construction of a transcontinental rail route.

In both the United States and the Confederate States, private citizens became aware, often for the first time, of the economic impact of their national governments. In the Confederacy, the Impressment Act of March 1863 authorized government agents to seize civilians' food, horses, wagons, or other supplies if required for the army, and to set an arbitrary price for the confiscated goods. In the Union the creation of a new national banking system in 1863 (amended and strengthened in 1864) meant, among other things, that

a uniform national currency began to replace the dozens of issues by local banks.* Citizens, paying national taxes in national currency, grew accustomed to the idea that their national government would henceforth play a positive role in the economic life of the country.

Inflation and Its Consequences

During the desperate final years of the Civil War, the Union and Confederate treasury departments had to experiment with new ways to finance the war. Both imposed broad excise duties. The Internal Revenue Act, enacted by the Union Congress on July 1, 1862, has been fairly characterized as an attempt to tax everything. The act imposed duties upon all sorts of manufactures, with a fresh duty levied each time the raw material underwent a new process. In a carriage, for example, the leather, the cloth, the wood, and the metal were each taxed; then the manufacturer was taxed for the process of putting them together; the dealer was taxed for selling the carriage; and the purchaser, having paid a sufficient price to cover all these duties, was taxed in addition for ownership. Heavy duties fell upon luxuries like billiard tables and yachts, and taxes upon professions and occupations covered, as Representative James G. Blaine said, "bankers and pawn brokers, lawyers and horse-dealers, physicians and confectioners, commercial brokers and peddlers." Ultimately these taxes brought in about 21 percent of the total wartime expenditures of the Union government.

The Confederacy moved more slowly, but on April 24, 1863, it too adopted a comprehensive tax measure. This included an income tax, occupational and license taxes ranging from $40 for bowling alleys to $500 for bankers, and what later generations would call an excess profits tax. A unique feature of the Confederate legislation was the tax-in-kind, which compelled producers of wheat, corn, oats, potatoes, sugar, cotton, tobacco, and other farm products to pay one-tenth of their crop each year to the government. A last, desperate attempt in March 1865 to tax all coin, bullion, and foreign exchange was made too late to have any effect. All told, the Confederacy raised only about 1 percent of its income from taxes.

The sale of bonds contributed little more to the Confederate treasury. Values were so uncertain in the wartime South that investors were afraid to tie up their money in such fixed investments, and doubts spread as to when and whether the Confederate government would even pay the interest on its obligations. In the Union, on the other hand, bonds be-

*For the long-range impact of the National Banking Act of 1864, see chapter 21, p. 525.

came a major source of revenue. Treasury Secretary Chase at first could not sell bonds, even at a discount, until he appointed his friend Jay Cooke, the Philadelphia banker who also had an office in Washington, as special agent of the Treasury Department. Using high-pressure advertising, Cooke launched an extensive propaganda campaign that extolled the merits of the "five-twenties"—bonds bearing 6 percent interest, which could be paid off after five years and must be redeemed in twenty years. Cooke was so successful that between 600,000 and a million citizens were persuaded to invest in the public debt, and the entire loan of half a billion dollars was oversubscribed. But in 1864, as the war stretched on endlessly and victory appeared nowhere in sight, the market for bonds collapsed. Resigning for political reasons, Chase left office at an opportune moment to preserve his reputation as a financier, and Cooke went with him. Chase's successor, William Pitt Fessenden, could only raise money through short-term loans at an exorbitant rate of interest. Not until the very end of the war, when victory was obviously near, did the sale of Union bonds pick up, and Cooke, reappointed special agent, attracted many additional investors.

The Resort to Paper Money.

Thus through necessity both governments continued to depend on paper money. The Union treasury, which had cautiously issued its first greenbacks in 1862, printed more and more during the rest of that year and during 1863 as well, until most of the $450 million authorized by Congress was in circulation. The value of the greenbacks gradually declined. A Union treasury note with a face value of one dollar was worth 99.86¢ in gold in 1862, but by 1864 it was worth only 62.66¢ and by early 1865, 50.3¢. In the Confederacy, where the printing presses never stopped, paper money had even less value. Perhaps $2 billion in unredeemable paper was issued in

all. A Confederate treasury note for one dollar, worth 82.7¢ in gold in 1862, dropped to 29¢ in 1863 and to 1.7¢ in early 1865. In a desperate attempt to halt the slide, the Confederate Congress in February 1864 undertook a partial repudiation of these notes, but the confusing and complex legislation was badly administered and served further to undermine trust in the government and its money. Having lost the confidence of the country, Treasury Secretary Memminger resigned in the summer of 1864—at about the same time that Chase left the Union Treasury Department. Memminger's successor, the South Carolina banker and businessman George A. Trenholm, could devise no better solution for the Confederacy's financial woes than to urge citizens to donate to the government their money, jewels, gold and silver plate, and public securities.

The excessive amount of paper money was only one of many factors that produced runaway inflation in both the North and the South. With importations largely cut off (in the North by the high protective tariff, and in the South by the Union blockade), with the productive labor force sharply reduced because of the number of men in military service, and with a huge portion of all goods required to supply the armies and navies, civilians had to expect shortages and high prices.

Profits and Deprivation.

In both sections some people profited from the wartime economy. War contracts helped pull the Union economy out of a sharp depression, and higher prices spurred on manufacturers, who could now look for higher profits. The demand for grain, along with the Homestead Act, encouraged new settlers to begin farming, and the development of petroleum and other new industries made for quick fortunes. The wartime boom in the North had a hectic quality about it, and men spent their easily earned money quickly lest it be worth less in the future. Many of the new rich were extravagant and hedonistic. Angrily the New York *Independent* asked in June 1864:

Who at the North would ever think of war, if he had not a friend in the army, or did not read the newspapers? Go into Broadway, and we will show you what is meant by the word "extravagance." Ask [A. T.] Stewart [the department-store owner] about the demand for camel's-hair shawls, and he will say "monstrous." Ask Tiffany what kinds of diamonds and pearls are called for. He will answer "the prodigious," "as near hen's-egg size as possible," "price no object." What kinds of carpetings are now wanted? None but "extra." . . . And as for horses the medium-priced five-hundred-dollar kind are all out of the market. A good pair of "fast ones" . . . will go for a thousand dollars sooner than a basket of strawberries will sell for four cents.

But not everyone in the North shared in this wartime prosperity. Wages lagged sadly behind prices, so that in real income a worker between 1861 and 1865 lost 35 percent of his wages. Women, who composed one-fourth of the nation's manufacturing force in 1860, were especially hard hit. Soldiers could send their wives and mothers only a pittance for support, and as more and more women found it necessary to work, employers actually cut their wages. Even the United States government participated in this practice. At the Philadelphia armory, the government in 1861 paid a seamstress 17¢ for making a shirt; three years later, when prices were at their highest, it cut the wage to 15¢. Meanwhile private contractors paid only 8¢.

Suffering in the North was, however, relatively minor when compared to that in the South. To be sure, residents of some parts of the agricultural South who were never disturbed by Union troops had only minor shortages to complain of. As imported goods disappeared from the grocers' shelves, they resorted to sassafras tea and to "coffee" made of parched rye, okra seeds, corn, and even sweet potatoes, the grounds of which were said to be a remarkable cleaning agent for curtains and carpets. Since salt was in short supply, meat could not be preserved, and Southerners ate more chicken and fish. As clothing wore out, they increasingly turned to homespun, and velvet draperies and brocaded rugs found new uses as gowns and overcoats.

But the thousands of Southerners in the path of the armies had to think not just of shortages, but of survival. Hundreds of families fled before the invading Union armies, often attempting to take their slaves with them, but nowhere could these refugees find assurance of safety. Their lives took on a desperate, nightmarish quality, and merely existing from one day to the next was a struggle. There was never enough of anything, including food. Recalling those unhappy days, one writer declared that "the Confederacy was always hungry."

The greatest destitution appeared in towns and cities, where supplies had to be brought in over the rickety Southern railroad system. White-collar workers, especially those on fixed government salaries, were particularly hard hit. The famous diary of J. B. Jones, a clerk in the Confederate War Department at Richmond, is a melancholy record of shortages and high prices. In May 1864 he reported that beans in Richmond were selling for $3 a quart, meal for $125 a bushel, and flour for $400 a barrel. Richmond, he observed, was an astonishingly clean city since "no garbage or filth can accumulate." The citizens of the Confederate capital were obliged to be "such good scavengers" that there was "no need of buzzards."

Deprivation was the more painful because, as in the North, some made enormous profits from the war. The blockade runners, who preferred to bring in compact, expensive items like silks and jewels rather than bulky supplies for the army, often reaped fantastic profits. Speculators flourished. As early as the winter of 1862, the governor of Mississippi learned that the families of volunteers in his state were seriously suffering because of the lack of corn and salt, while rich planters held back their ample supply of both commodities, waiting for the inevitable rise in prices. Trading with the enemy was even more profitable. The practice was completely illegal but tacitly permitted by both Confederate and Union officials. Southern women and men who were initiated into the mysteries of the trade bought up as much cotton as they could find in their neighborhoods and took it to convenient exchange points like Memphis and Natchez to sell to the Yankees for coffee, clothing, and luxuries. Late in the war they accepted payment in United States greenbacks, which Southerners valued more than their own depreciated currency.

Conscription and Conflict

Along with economic grievances, the unfairness of conscription was the source of bitter complaints by Northerners and Southerners alike during the Civil War.

The Confederate conscription act of 1862 theoretically made all able-bodied white males between the ages of eighteen and thirty-five equally eligible for military service, but the Southern Congress promptly began exempting large categories of men. As men rushed to enter "bombproof" occupations and claim exemptions, the outcry against the Confederate conscription system grew louder. One of the strongest critics was Governor Joseph E. Brown of Georgia, who protested, "The conscription Act, at one fell swoop, strikes down the sovereignty of the States, tramples upon the constitutional rights and personal liberty of the citizens, and arms the President with imperial power." After attempting unsuccessfully to induce the Georgia supreme court to declare conscription unconstitutional, Brown proceeded to undermine the policy by naming his supporters to state jobs exempt from military service. According to some estimates he put 15,000 able-bodied Georgians into this exempt category; certainly he created 2,000 justices of the peace and 1,000 constables, none of whom had to serve in the army. Less prominent than Brown but equally potent were the critics who complained that conscription was class legislation that benefited the educated and the wealthy. They objected especially to the so-called twenty-nigger provision, which clearly favored plantation owners at the expense of farmers. "Never did a law meet with more universal odium than the exemption of slave owners," wrote Senator James Phelan of Mississippi to President Davis. "It has aroused a spirit of rebellion . . . and bodies of men have banded together to desert."

Despite intense criticism and dubious results, the Davis administration continued conscription, for it saw no other way to raise the needed number of men. Indeed, as the war progressed, the Confederacy was obliged to experiment with even more stringent legislation. In a new conscription act of February 17, 1864, the Confederate Congress declared that all white males between the ages of seventeen and fifty were subject to the draft, with the seventeen-year-old boys and the men above forty-five to serve as a reserve for local defense. As a concession to small planters, the act exempted one farmer or overseer for every plantation with fifteen slaves; but it abolished most other exemptions, on the theory that once skilled laborers were in the army, the government could detail them to the forges and factories where they were most needed. Total mobilization of manpower was, however, far beyond the competence of the shaky Confederate government, and in practice the industrial-detail system never worked. As the Confederacy scraped the bottom of the barrel, more and more white Southerners began thinking about the one group of able-bodied males who did not serve in the armies, the blacks.

In the North, too, conscription evoked bitter criticism. The first effective Northern draft act, passed by the Union Congress on March 3, 1863, was obviously unfair. The act declared that all able-bodied males between the ages of twenty and forty-five (except for certain high governmental officials and the only sons of widows and of infirm parents) were liable to mil-

AN 1862 NEW YORK CITY BOUNTY POSTER
Even the very inadequate 1862 Union conscription legislation stimulated a profusion of bounty offers. If a locality could fill its quota of soldiers with volunteers—even with those induced to volunteer by what was then a very considerable amount of money—its citizens could avoid what was considered the humiliation of conscription.

itary service. But it promptly contradicted itself by permitting those who could afford to do so to hire substitutes. In an effort to keep the price of substitutes down, it also permitted a man to purchase outright exemption from military service for $300.

As in the South, there was immediate and widespread hostility toward conscription. The system favored the wealthiest citizens and the most prosperous sections of the country. A well-to-do man like George Templeton Strong of New York, for example, did not dream of serving in the army; he paid $1,100 for a substitute, "a big 'Dutch' boy of twenty or thereabouts," who, as Strong remarked complacently, "looked as if he could do good service." Rich towns and counties raised bounty funds to encourage volunteering, so that none of their citizens would have to be drafted; and as the war went on, they offered higher and higher bounties. The volunteers they sought were by no means all local residents who needed a little financial inducement; many of them were professional bounty hunters, who went from place to place en-

THE NEW YORK DRAFT RIOTS: BATTLE IN SECOND AVENUE AND 22ND STREET AT THE UNION STEAM WORKS, JULY 14, 1863
Conscription triggered resistance in the North. The largest riot was in New York City, where Union troops, fresh from the Gettysburg campaign, had to be called in to restore order.

listing, receiving bounties, and promptly deserting. Perhaps the record for bounty jumping was held by one John O'Connor, who when arrested in March 1865 confessed to thirty-two such desertions.

Part of the outcry against conscription in the North stemmed from the unfairness of the quotas the president was authorized to announce for each state, presumably giving credit for the number of volunteers it had previously supplied. The Democratic governor of New York, Horatio Seymour, engaged in angry correspondence with Lincoln and finally forced the president to admit that the quota assigned to New York was excessive. This and similar concessions, however, came too late to placate those who were threatened by the draft. In Wisconsin, Kentucky, and Pennsylvania, in Troy, Newark, and Albany, there was outright resistance to the enrolling officers, and in several instances federal troops had to be brought in to quell the uprisings. But none of these outbreaks was as large or ferocious as that in New York City, where the drawing of the first draftees' names triggered a three-day riot (July 13–15, 1863) by a mob of predominantly Irish workingmen. Turning first against the enrollment officers and the police, the rioters then exhibited their hostility toward the rich by plundering fine houses and rifling jewelry stores. The mob acted with hideous brutality toward blacks, whom the rioters feared as economic competitors and blamed for the war and hence for conscription. After sacking and looting a black orphan asylum, the rioters chased down any blacks unwary enough to appear on the streets and left those they could catch hanging from lampposts. The Union government had to rush in troops from the Gettysburg campaign to stop the rioting and disperse the mob.

Despite all resistance, Lincoln's government continued conscription because, as in the Confederacy, there seemed to be no other source of soldiers. Even so, the draft remained cumbersome and often ineffectual. In 1864, for example, 800,000 names were drawn, but so many were exempted because of health or occupation, and so many others hired substitutes or paid the commutation fee, that only 33,000 were actually inducted into the army. As conscription proved both unfair and ineffective, citizens in the North, like those in the South, began to think of the value of black soldiers.

Steps Toward Emancipation

Just as the black man played a central role in causing the Civil War, so he was to play a major role in determining its outcome. At the beginning there was an unspoken agreement that the Civil War was to be a white man's fight, and both the Union and the Confederate governments in 1861 refused to accept black regiments. In the Confederacy during the first two years of the war, virtually nobody questioned the correctness of this decision. After all, as Vice-President Alexander H. Stephens announced, slavery was "the real 'cornerstone'" upon which the Confederate States had been erected, and few Southern whites could even

BLACK TEAMSTERS NEAR THE SIGNAL TOWER AT BERMUDA HUNDRED, VIRGINIA, 1864
Although there was opposition in both the Confederacy and the Union to the emancipation of slaves, neither side was reluctant to employ blacks in nonmilitary service. For both armies blacks served as teamsters, butchers, drovers, boatmen, bakers, shoemakers, and nurses. Nearly 200,000 blacks performed labor for the Union armies.

contemplate the possibility of arming slaves or of freeing blacks who became soldiers.

In the Union, on the other hand, powerful voices from the beginning urged the emancipation of slaves and the enlistment of blacks. Frederick Douglass, the leading spokesman of blacks in the North, repeatedly insisted: "Teach the rebels and traitors that the price they are to pay for the attempt to abolish this Government must be the abolition of slavery." Abolitionists, white and black, again and again instructed Lincoln that he could win the war only if he emancipated the slaves. Senator Charles Sumner of Massachusetts visited the White House almost daily in his efforts to persuade Lincoln that emancipation was the "*one way to safety*, clear as sunlight—pleasant as the paths of Peace."

This antislavery sentiment was so influential that several of the president's subordinates who fell into disfavor with the administration tried to appeal to it. But President Lincoln, aware of the dangerous complexity of the issue, patiently overruled each of these subordinates, declaring that emancipation was a question "which, under my responsibility, I reserve to myself."

Nonmilitary Employment of Blacks.

Unwillingness to arm or emancipate the slaves did not signify any reluctance to employ blacks in nonmilitary service. Slaves were the backbone of the Confederate labor force. If blacks had not continued to cultivate and harvest the grain, the Confederacy could never have fielded so large an army. Equally important was the role played by blacks, slave and free, in the industrial production of the Confederacy. In the Tredegar Iron Works, for example, half the 2,400 employees were blacks; they included not merely unskilled workers, but puddlers, rollers, and machinists. Blacks also performed indispensable service for the quartermaster and commissary departments of the Confederacy, laboring as teamsters, butchers, drovers, boatmen, bakers, shoemakers, and blacksmiths; and they were nurses in many Confederate hospitals.

So essential was black labor to the existence of the Confederacy that President Davis had to ensure that

"PRESIDENT LINCOLN WRITING THE PROCLAMATION OF FREEDOM," BY DAVID GILMOUR BLYTHE: A NORTHERN VIEW
A Northern artist shows Lincoln consulting the history of the United States, United States court decisions, Daniel Webster's views of the Constitution, and other documents in preparing his Emancipation Proclamation. A bust of the ineffectual President Buchanan hangs by a noose from the book case.

enough blacks were available for this service. From the beginning of the war, Confederate authorities from time to time compelled slaves to work on fortifications. Some states, notably Virginia, moved promptly to require owners to lease their slaves to the government when needed. But the Confederate government itself did not act until March 1863. At that time the Confederate Congress, despite much opposition from slaveowners, authorized the impressment of slaves, whose owners were to receive $30 a month. In February 1864 the Southern Congress permitted military authorities to impress more slaves, whether or not these officials had obtained the consent of the slaveowners.

Meanwhile the Union was also making full use of black labor. As slaves fled from their masters to the Union army, they were put to use as teamsters, cooks, nurses, carpenters, scouts, and day laborers. Perhaps half a million blacks crossed over to the Union lines, and nearly 200,000 of these performed labor for the army. Many of these "contrabands" brought with them valuable information about the location of Confederate troops and supplies. Occasionally some brought even more valuable assets. Robert Smalls and his brother, who were slaves in Charleston, South Carolina, in May 1862 daringly seized the Confederate sidewheel steamer *Planter*, navigated it out of the harbor ringed with Confederate guns, and delivered it to the blockading Union fleet.

Debate over Emancipation in the North. When the war seemed to have reached a stalemate, Northern sentiment grew more favorable to freeing and arming the slaves. Republican congressmen were ahead of the president on these questions. As early as August 1861, they had passed an act declaring that slaves who had supported the Confederate military were free. In March 1862 Congress forbade the Union army to return fugitive slaves. And on July 17, 1862, in a far-reaching confiscation act, Congress declared that slaves of all persons supporting the rebellion should be "forever free of their servitude, and not again [to be] held as slaves." These measures were, however, poorly drafted and not readily enforced, so that they had little practical consequence. But Congress's abolition of slavery in the District of Columbia on April 16, 1862, was more effective.

Powerful forces in the North, however, opposed emancipation. The loyalty of the border states, where slavery still prevailed, was so uncertain that they might try to break away from the Union if emancipation became a Northern war aim. Antiblack prejudice was rampant in the free states, and many feared that emancipation would produce a massive migration of blacks to the North, where they would compete with white laborers for jobs. Belief in black inferiority was general, and the experience of Union soldiers in the South often strengthened this stereotype, for the fugitive slaves who fled to their camps were for the

"LINCOLN WRITING THE EMANCIPATION PROCLAMATION," BY ADALBERT VOLCK: A SOUTHERN VIEW

A Confederate caricaturist depicts Lincoln with his foot on the Constitution, sitting beneath a painting of slave insurrection in Santo Domingo, as he dips his pen into an inkwell held by Satan to draft the proclamation of freedom.

most part illiterate, ragged, and dirty.

Lincoln hated slavery, but during the initial stages of the war he could move toward emancipation only in a roundabout way. In early 1862 he made an earnest, although ultimately unsuccessful, plea to the border states to devise plans of gradual, compensated emancipation, for which he promised federal financial assistance. At the same time, he took antiblack sentiment into account by favoring plans to settle freedmen (ex-slaves) in Central America and Haiti.

By the fall of 1862, however, Lincoln felt able to act decisively against slavery. In failing to adopt his program of gradual emancipation, the border states had lost their chance. Blacks showed little interest in his plans for colonizaton, which in any case were poorly thought out and could only lead to disaster. As casualties mounted, Northern soldiers came to think that it was time to enroll blacks in the army, although they did not necessarily shed their prejudices against blacks. But most influential in changing Lincoln's mind was his grim recognition that after eighteen months of combat, the war could not be ended by traditional means. "We . . . must change our tactics or lose the war," he concluded.

Waiting only for McClellan to end Lee's invasion at Antietam, Lincoln on September 22, 1862, issued a preliminary emancipation proclamation. This announced that unless the rebellious states returned to their allegiance, he would on January 1, 1863, declare that "all persons held as slaves" in the territory controlled by the Confederates were "then, thenceforward, and forever free." Since the president justified his action on the ground of military necessity, it was appropriate that the definitive Emancipation Proclamation, which was issued at the beginning of the new year, officially authorized the enrollment of black troops in the Union army.

The War Department promptly began to accept black recruits. These were not, to be sure, the first black soldiers to serve in the war, for without permission from Washington a few blacks had been enrolled in the Union forces on the Sea Islands of South Carolina, in Louisiana, and in Kansas. But large numbers of blacks now joined the army. They were enrolled in segregated regiments, nearly always with white officers, and they received less pay than did white soldiers. By the end of the war, there were 178,895 black soldiers in the Union army—more than twice the number of soldiers in the Confederate army at Gettysburg.

At first most Union officials thought that black regiments would be useful only for garrison duty, but in such bitterly contested engagements as Fort Wagner and Port Hudson, Miliken's Bend and Nashville, they demonstrated how well they could and would fight. The battle record of these black troops did much to change popular Northern stereotypes of the black man. In the early stages of the war, cartoonists and caricaturists portrayed blacks as invisible men; their

FERROTYPE OF SERGEANT J. L. BALLDWIN OF COMPANY G, 56TH U.S. COLORED INFANTRY
Early in the war even President Lincoln thought "that the organization, equipment and arming of negroes, like other soldiers, would be productive of more evil than good." But after the Emancipation Proclamation the Union government began systematically to recruit for black military units. By the end of the war, 178,895 black soldiers were serving in the Union armies, and they saw action in Virginia, South Carolina, Florida, Mississippi and elsewhere. "The emancipation policy and the use of colored troops," Lincoln declared, were "the heaviest blow yet dealt to the rebellion."

faces were vague and featureless blobs of black, hardly human. But with emancipation and the enrollment of blacks in the army, war artists began to take a closer look, to depict blacks with distinctive, recognizably human features, and finally, in a kind of perverse tribute to their merit, to sketch them with profiles resembling those of whites.

The South Moves Toward Emancipation.
Meanwhile, and much more slowly, sentiment was growing in the Confederacy for the military employment of blacks. Support for arming the slaves emerged first in those areas devastated by Northern armies. After Grant's successful Vicksburg campaign, the Jackson *Mississippian* boldly called for enrolling slaves in the Confederate army. Although other Mississippi and Alabama newspapers echoed the appeal for black recruits, the most powerful voice for arming the slaves was that of General Patrick R. Cleburne, who witnessed how easily the powerful Union army broke the thin Confederate line at Chattanooga. Seeing no other source of manpower, Cleburne and his aides addressed a long letter to General Joseph E. Johnston, who had succeeded Bragg as commander of the army of Tennessee, urging "that we immediately commence training a large reserve of the most courageous of our slaves, and further that we guarantee freedom within a reasonable time to every slave in the South who shall remain true to the Confederacy in this war."

So drastic a proposal was bound to rouse strong opposition. Upon learning of Cleburne's letter, President Davis ordered it suppressed. But the subject would not die. As Union armies moved closer to the Confederate heartland, Virginia editors also began to urge arming the blacks, and in October 1864 a meeting of Southern governors proposed "a change of policy on our part" as to the slaves. Finally, on November 7, 1864, President Davis put himself at the head of the movement in a deliberately obscure message to Congress. Urging further impressment of blacks for service with the army, Davis argued that the Confederate government should purchase the impressed slaves.

However obscurely it was phrased, Davis's proposal clearly looked toward the end of slavery, and it at once encountered powerful resistance. Davis, said his enemies, proposed the confiscation of private property; he was subverting the Constitution. His plan would be a confession to the world of the South's weakness. It would deplete the labor force needed to feed the army. And most frightening of all, it would arm black men, who at best might desert to the Union armies and at worst might take up arms against their masters.

Despite all opposition, the Confederate government pushed ahead with the plan, for it had no other reservoir of manpower. In February 1865 the scheme received the backing of General Lee, who wrote that employing blacks as soldiers was "not only expedient but necessary" and announced plainly that "it would be neither just nor wise . . . to require them to serve as slaves." The next month, by a very close vote, the Confederate Congress passed an act calling for 300,000 more soldiers, irrespective of color. No provision was made to free blacks who enrolled, but the Confederate War Department in effect smuggled emancipation into the measure through the orders it issued for its enforcement. Promptly the recruiting of black troops began, and some black companies were raised in Richmond and other towns. By this time, however, it was too late even for such a revolutionary experiment, and none of the black Confederate soldiers ever saw military service.

Europe and the War

Although the Union and Confederate governments moved toward emancipating and arming the blacks because of military necessity, both recognized how profoundly their actions affected the continuing struggle for European recognition and support. Well-informed Americans were aware of the intensity of European antislavery sentiment. But so long as neither government took a bold stand against the South's peculiar institution, European antislavery leaders were puzzled and divided by the war. Lincoln's Emancipation Proclamation ended the confusion. European antislavery spokesmen soon recognized that the proclamation marked a new era. Within three months after the final Emancipation Proclamation was issued, fifty-six large public meetings were held in Great Britain to uphold the Northern cause.

Union diplomacy needed such popular support, for there was still a possibility of European intervention in the war. Although the gravest threat had passed in the fall of 1862, before the full effect of the Emancipation Proclamation could be sensed abroad, Emperor Napoleon III of France continued to contemplate the advantages that might come of meddling in American affairs. Napoleon hoped that the division of the United States would help him establish a puppet empire in Mexico under Archduke Maximilian of Austria. When Northern military fortunes were at their low point in February 1863, after the battle of Fredericksburg, Napoleon offered to mediate between the two belligerents. Shrewdly judging that Great Britain and Russia were not behind the French move, Secretary of State Seward spurned the offer.

The warships being built for the Confederacy in British shipyards were more dangerous to the Union cause than was Napoleon's clumsy diplomacy. Supplying either belligerent in war with armed ships was contrary both to international law and to British statutes, but a loophole in the law made it possible to sell unarmed vessels separately from the armaments that would convert them into men of war. In March 1862 the ship that became the C.S.S. *Florida* sailed from a British shipyard, and in July of that year the more powerful *Alabama* set forth to begin its raids. Even as these raiders swept the Union merchant marine from the high seas, a more formidable Confederate naval threat—this time to the blockade itself—was being forged in the form of two enormous ironclad steam rams under construction at the Laird yards in Liverpool.

The British government wished to observe its neutrality laws, but the legal machinery was slow and cumbersome. When Union minister Charles Francis Adams called the attention of the foreign office to the rams, Lord Russell replied that he could not act to detain them unless there was convincing evidence of Confederate ownership. Adams and his aides rushed to secure proof that the vessels were intended for the Confederacy, but British law officers were unconvinced. Finally, in utter exasperation, Adams on September 5, 1863, sent Russell a final warning against permitting the ships to sail, adding "It would be superfluous in me to point out to your Lordship that this is war." Fortunately, two days before receiving Adams's ultimatum, Russell had already decided to detain the rams, and the Confederates' final hope of breaking the blockade was lost.

With that crisis, the last serious threat of European involvement in the American war disappeared. So indifferent, or even hostile, to the Southern cause was the British cabinet that late in 1863 Confederate Secretary of State Judah P. Benjamin ordered James M. Mason, his envoy, to leave London on the grounds that "the Government of Her Majesty [Queen Victoria] . . . entertains no intention of receiving you as the accredited minister of this government."

President Davis was keenly aware of the influence that emancipation had exerted in uniting European opinion against the South, and he sought similarly to capitalize on the actions against slavery that the Confederate States took during the final months of the war. In January 1865 he sent Duncan F. Kenner, one of Louisiana's largest slaveholders, on a secret mission to Europe. Kenner was authorized to promise the emancipation of slaves in return for European recognition and aid to the Confederacy. The experiment came too late, for now it was evident that Northern victory was inevitable. Neither the French nor the British government expressed interest in Kenner's proposal.

Wartime Politics in the Confederacy

The military and diplomatic advantages resulting from emancipation were to a certain extent counterbalanced by its political disadvantages. In the Confederacy there had been from the beginning of the war a sizable disloyal element. Unionism was strong in the Upper South, in the mountain regions, and in some of the poorer hill counties. As the war went on, some of the Southern malcontents joined secret peace societies such as the Order of the Heroes, which had its following in the Carolinas and Virginia. Disloyalty extended into the ranks of the Confederate army, especially after conscription was initiated, and desertion was widespread. Some men left because their families needed them at home; some felt a greater loyalty to their states than to the Confederacy as a whole; but many were disillusioned with the whole idea of Southern independence. About one out of every nine soldiers who enlisted in the Confederate army deserted. Sometimes deserters formed guerrilla bands that preyed equally upon Confederate and Union sympathizers. When halted by an enrollment officer and asked to show his pass to leave the army, a deserter would pat his gun defiantly and say, "This is my furlough."

Probably no action of the Davis administration could have won over these actively disloyal citizens, but the policies of the Confederate government alienated also a large number of entirely loyal Southerners. Some of these critics complained that President Davis was timid and tardy. He was sickly, neurasthenic, and indecisive, they said; he could not tolerate strong men around him and relied for advice upon yes men; he did not know how to rouse the loyalty and passions of the Southern people; he lacked courage to put himself at the head of the Southern armies and lead the Confederacy to victory.

A much larger group of Confederates were bitterly critical of their president for exactly the opposite reasons. Davis's plan to arm and free the slaves reinforced their conviction that he intended to undermine the principles upon which the Confederacy had been founded. Conscription, they argued, had begun the subversion of state sovereignty, guaranteed by the Constitution. They found evidence of Davis's dictatorial ambitions in his requests that Congress suspend the writ of habeas corpus, so that disloyal persons could be arrested and imprisoned without trial. Congress grudgingly agreed to the suspension for three limited periods, but late in 1864 it rejected Davis's appeals for a further extension on the ground that it would be a dangerous assault upon the Constitution. Although infringements on civil liberties were infrequent in the Confederacy, and no Southern newspaper was suppressed for publishing subversive editorials, the critics warned that Davis was reaching after imperial powers. Leading this group of Davis's critics was none other than the vice-president of the Confederate States, Alexander H. Stephens, who spent most of the final years of the war not in Richmond but in Georgia, stirring up agitation against the president's allegedly unconstitutional usurpation of power, and simultaneously complaining of Davis's "weakness and imbecility."

The congressional elections of 1863, held after Southerners had begun to realize the gravity of their defeats at Gettysburg and at Vicksburg, greatly strengthened the anti-Davis bloc. During the following year the president often could muster a majority in Congress only because of the consistent support of representatives from districts overrun or threatened by advancing Northern armies. In some instances these districts were unable to hold regular elections in 1863, and their incumbent congressmen, chosen in the early days of complete commitment to the Confederate cause, remained in office; in any case, representatives

from the occupied regions had little to lose from measures that taxed and bled the rest of the Confederacy. But by the desperate winter of 1864–65, not even this support could give Davis control of Congress. Now in a majority, the president's critics refused his request for control over the state militias and rejected his plea to end all exemptions from conscription. Even as Sherman's army advanced through the Carolinas,* Congress endlessly debated Davis's plan for arming the slaves. Over presidential opposition, it passed an act creating the position of general in chief, advising Davis to name Lee. Fearful of attacking the president directly, congressional critics began investigations of several of his cabinet officers, and they introduced resolutions declaring that the resignation of Secretary of State Benjamin, Davis's closest friend and most trusted adviser, would be "subservient of the public interest." Secretary of War James A. Seddon also came under fire, and when the Virginia delegation in Congress called for his resignation, he felt obliged to leave the cabinet. In January 1865, for the first and only time, the Confederate Congress overrode a presidential veto.

Wartime Politics in the North

Meanwhile in the North, Abraham Lincoln and his government were subjected to the same kinds of criticism. Pro-Confederate sympathy was strongest in the states of the Upper South that remained in the Union, in those parts of the Old Northwest originally settled by Southerners, and in cities like New York, where the Irish immigrant population was bitterly hostile to blacks. Northerners joined secret societies, such as the Knights of the Golden Circle and the Order of American Knights, devoted to bringing about a negotiated peace, which inevitably would entail recognizing Confederate independence. Although most members of these secret "Copperhead" organizations intended nothing more subversive than replacing a Republican administration with a Democratic one, certain of the leaders were ready to accept the dissolution of the Union. Some idea of the extent of unrest in the North can be gained from the figures on desertion: one out of every seven who enlisted in the Union armies deserted.

Much of the criticism of the Lincoln administration came from those who were entirely loyal to the Union but who deplored the measures the president took to save it. They complained bitterly when Lincoln, without waiting for congressional approval, suspended the right of habeas corpus so that suspected subversives could be arrested without warning and

*For Sherman's advance in 1864–65, see below, pp. 479–80.

imprisoned indefinitely. Although Chief Justice Roger B. Taney protested against the unconstitutionality of these arrests, Lincoln refused to heed his objections. More than 13,000 persons were thus arbitrarily imprisoned. Critics also complained when the Lincoln administration curbed the freedom of the press. Because of the publication of allegedly disloyal and inflammatory statements, the Chicago *Times,* the New York *World*, the Philadelphia *Evening Journal*, and many other newspapers were required to suspend publication for varying periods of time.

Lincoln's Emancipation Proclamation, followed by the arming of black soldiers, gave his critics further evidence of his ambition to become dictator and of his diabolical plan to change the purpose of the war. So unpopular was the policy of emancipation that Lincoln's preliminary proclamation, together with the inability of Union generals to win victories, seriously hurt his party in the congressional elections of 1862. In virtually every Northern state there was an increase in Democratic votes. The Republican majority in Congress was now paper-thin, and the administration kept that lead only because the army interfered in the Maryland, Kentucky, and Missouri elections. Just as Jefferson Davis's control of the Confederate Congress after 1863 depended upon the votes of border state representatives, so Abraham Lincoln's majority in the Union Congress rested on the support of representatives from the same region.

Republican Criticism of Lincoln.

If Democrats complained that Lincoln acted arbitrarily and too swiftly, critics within his own party held that he was too slow, too cautious, and too indecisive. His own attorney general, Edward Bates, felt that the president could cope with "neither great *principles* nor great *facts.*" Lincoln lacked "practical talent for his important place," concluded Senator Sumner, who thought that in his slowness to act and his indecisiveness the president resembled the bumbling French king Louis XVI more than any other ruler in history.

Dissatisfaction with Lincoln was so widespread that when Congress reassembled in December 1862, after the fiasco at Fredericksburg, the Senate Republican caucus tried to force the president to change his cabinet. Just as Davis's critics made Benjamin their target, so Republican senators blamed Secretary of State Seward for the weakness of the Lincoln administration and the poor handling of the war. By forcing Seward's resignation, these critics hoped to make Chase (who had fed them stories of Lincoln's incompetence) in effect premier. This maneuver distressed Lincoln deeply, and he thwarted it with great skill. He secured Seward's resignation and forced Chase also to offer his; then he declined both resignations by announcing that either one would leave the cabinet unbalanced. His cabinet remained intact, and the president remained responsible for Union policy.

Such sleight of hand was not enough to make dissent within Lincoln's own party disappear. Gradually two rival Republican factions emerged, the Conservatives, or Moderates, and the Radicals—whom their enemies called Jacobins, comparing them to the extremists of the French Revolution. The Conservatives were represented by Seward in the cabinet and by Senator James R. Doolittle of Wisconsin in Congress. They continued to think that the war could be won by conventional means and opposed such experiments as emancipation, the arming of slaves, and the confiscation of rebel property. The Radicals, on the other hand, represented by Chase in the cabinet and by Sumner and Thaddeus Stevens in Congress, were eager to try more drastic experiments. They demanded that the entire Southern social system be revolutionized, that Southern slaveholders be punished, and, increasingly, that blacks be given not merely freedom, but civil and political equality as well.

Lincoln refused to align himself with either faction and tried to be even-handed in distributing federal patronage to both. He shared the Conservatives' desire for a speedy peace and a prompt reconciliation between the sections; but he recognized that in casting about for votes to carry through their plans, they would be "tempted to affiliate with those whose record is not clear," even persons infected "by the virus of secession." As for the Radicals, he conceded that "after all their faces are set Zionwards," but he objected to their "petulant and vicious fretfulness" and thought they were sometimes "almost *fiendish*" in attacking Republicans who disagreed with them. Because of his neutrality, the president gained the distrust and abuse of both factions.

The Election of 1864.

The split within the Republican party was the more serious because the presidential election of 1864 was approaching. The Democrats had a handsome, glamorous candidate in General George B. McClellan, and they had a powerful set of issues. They could capitalize upon war weariness. They made much of Lincoln's arbitrary use of executive power and the infringement of civil liberties. They objected to the unfairness of the draft. They showed how the Republican Congress had benefited the Northeast by enacting protective tariffs, handing out railroad subsidies, and creating a national banking system. The Democrats endlessly harped on the antiblack theme, charging that the Lincoln administration had changed the war for Union into a war for emancipation. If Lincoln was reelected, they charged, Republicans were planning to amalgamate the black and white races. The word *miscegenation* (race mixing) made its first appearance in an 1864 campaign document.

Even in the face of such powerful opposition, the Republicans in the winter of 1863–64 divided sharply when Lincoln in December 1863 announced a plan for reconstructing the Southern states. The president promised amnesty to all Confederates except for a few high government officials. He also proposed to reestablish civilian government in the conquered areas of the South. In any state where 10 percent or more of those who had voted in 1860 would take an oath swearing future loyalty to the United States and pledging acceptance of emancipation, he offered to recognize the legality of the government these voters set up. Fearing that his program would put the prewar leadership back in control of the South and would leave freedmen in peonage, the Radicals pushed the Wade-Davis bill through Congress. This bill required that more than half the number of 1860 voters in each Southern state swear allegiance and participate in drafting a new constitution before their state could be readmitted to the Union. This measure was passed at the end of the 1864 congressional session, and Lincoln killed it by refusing to sign it after Congress had adjourned. The Radicals were furious. Senator Benjamin F. Wade and Representative Henry Winter Davis, the sponsors of the vetoed bill, issued a public statement accusing the president of "usurpations" and claiming that he had committed a "studied outrage upon the legislative authority of the people."

Lincoln had control of the federal patronage and of the party machinery, and so he was readily renominated in June 1864 by the Republican national convention, which selected Andrew Johnson of Tennessee as his running mate. But the unanimity of the vote was only a façade. After an unsuccessful attempt to run Chase as a rival to Lincoln, some ultra-Radicals had already thrown their support to a third-party ticket headed by General Frémont, who had been hostile to the president since his removal from command in Missouri. Even after Lincoln had been renominated, other Radicals tried to persuade the party to pick a new candidate. As late as September 1864, a questionnaire sent to Republican governors, leading editors, and prominent congressmen drew a virtually unanimous response that if Lincoln could be persuaded to withdraw from the race, Republicans should name another standard-bearer. As Massachusetts Governor John A. Andrew expressed the general sentiment, Lincoln was "essentially lacking in the quality of leadership." So bleak was the outlook that a few weeks before the elections, the president himself conceded that McClellan was likely to win.

Northern Victory

Until the fall of 1864, then, the wartime history of the United States and of the Confederate States moved in parallel lines as each government improvised experiments that might lead to victory. But in the final months of the struggle, the course of the two rivals dramatically diverged. Increasing dissension and unrest marked Jefferson Davis's last winter in office, while Abraham Lincoln won triumphant reelection in November 1864. By April 1865 the Confederacy was dead, and a month later Davis was in irons, like a common criminal, at Fort Monroe, Virginia. The Union was victorious, and Lincoln, killed by the bullet of the mad assassin John Wilkes Booth, lived in memory as the nation's martyred president who had freed the slaves and saved the Union.

Campaigns in the East, 1864–1865. The very different fates of the Lincoln and Davis administrations were decided, in large part, on the battlefield. When Grant became general in chief of the Union armies in 1864, he decided to make his headquarters not in Washington, but with the often defeated Army of the Potomac. Working closely with Meade, the actual commander of that army, Grant developed a plan for pushing Lee back upon the defenses of Richmond. Stopped in the bloody battle of the Wilderness (May 5–7), Grant did not retreat, as other Union commanders had done. Instead, he pushed around Lee's right flank, attempting to get between him and the Confederate capital. Stopped again at Spotsylvania (May 8–12), Grant again did not retreat but sent word to Washington: "I propose to fight it out along this line if it takes all summer."

After a disastrous direct assault on the Confederate lines at Cold Harbor (June 3), Grant again skillfully maneuvered around Lee's right flank, crossed the James River, and joined Union troops already there under General Butler. He then began what became known as the "siege" of Petersburg and Richmond—incorrectly so, since the two cities were not fully surrounded and since supplies continued to come in from the South and West. But as Grant's lines constantly lengthened, he cut these access routes one by one. Pinned down before Richmond, Lee remembered "Stonewall" Jackson's brilliant diversionary campaign of 1862 and sent what men he could spare under Jubal A. Early into the Shenandoah Valley. Although Early achieved initial success and even pushed on to the outskirts of Washington, Grant did not loosen his grip on Richmond. Instead, he sent brash, aggressive Philip H. Sheridan to the Shenandoah Valley, ordering him not merely to drive out the Confederates, but to devastate the countryside so that thereafter a crow

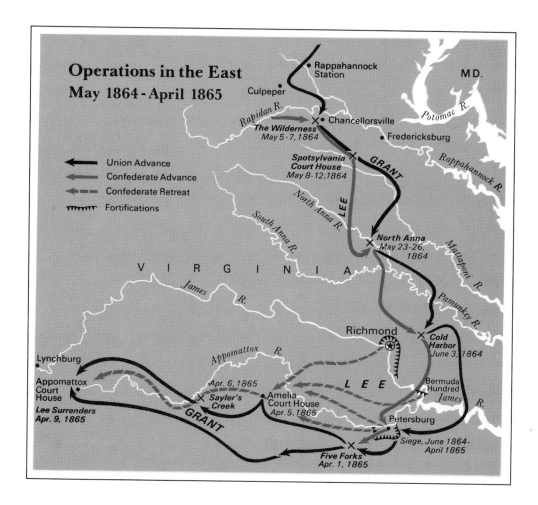

Operations in the East May 1864-April 1865

Union Advance
Confederate Advance
Confederate Retreat
Fortifications

MD.

Rappahannock Station
Culpeper
Rapidan R.
Potomac R.
Chancellorsville
Fredericksburg
The Wilderness May 5-7, 1864
GRANT
Rappahannock R.
Spotsylvania Court House May 8-12, 1864
North Anna R.
LEE
North Anna May 23-26, 1864
South Anna R.
Mattaponi R.
V I R G I N I A
Pamunkey R.
James R.
Richmond
Cold Harbor June 3, 1864
Lynchburg
Appomattox R.
L E E
Bermuda Hundred
James R.
Appomattox Court House
Lee Surrenders Apr. 9, 1865
Apr. 6, 1865
Sayler's Creek
Amelia Court House Apr. 5, 1865
Petersburg
GRANT
Five Forks Apr. 1, 1865
Siege, June 1864-April 1865

flying over it would have to carry its own rations. Sheridan followed his orders explicitly, and Early's army was smashed. More than ever before, the fate of the Confederacy was tied to Richmond and to Lee's army.

Campaigns in the West, 1864–1865.

Meanwhile, on May 7, 1864, Sherman had begun his slow march through northwestern Georgia, opposed by the wily Joseph E. Johnston, who made the Union troops pay for every foot they advanced. But as Sherman neared the railroad hub of Atlanta, President Davis—who had never trusted Johnston—removed the general and put John B. Hood in command. In a series of attacks upon the overwhelmingly superior Union forces (exactly the sort of engagement Johnston had so skillfully avoided), Hood was defeated. On September 2 Sherman occupied Atlanta. News of the victory reached the North just before the presidential election and made a farce of the Democratic platform's assertion that the war was a "failure."

Next, casually dispatching Thomas to fend off Hood and to hold Tennessee, Sherman turned his back on the smoking ruins of Atlanta and set out on a march toward Savannah and the sea, where he knew that a Union fleet was waiting with supplies.* Meeting only light resistance, Sherman's men cut a swath through central Georgia, destroying railroads, military supplies, and even many private houses. Sherman's objective was as much psychological as military. "I can make the march," he had promised Grant, "and make Georgia howl!"

Offering captured Savannah to Lincoln as a Christmas present, Sherman turned his army north, pushing aside the depleted Confederate forces that again were under the command of Johnston. His men took Columbia, South Carolina, which was burned ei-

---

*Attempting to force Sherman back, Hood invaded Tennessee but was stopped in the battle of Franklin (November 30, 1864) and routed in the battle of Nashville (December 15–16).

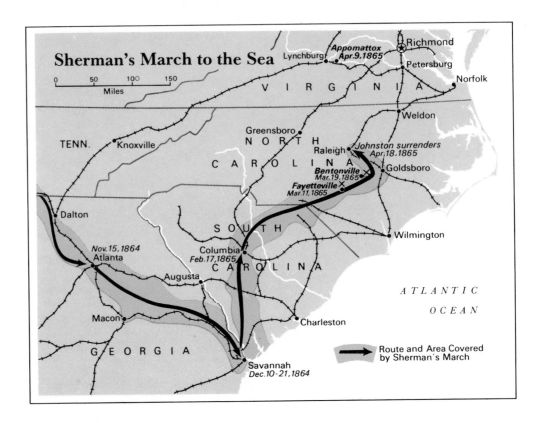

Sherman's March to the Sea

ther by intention or by accident, and drove on into North Carolina. Grant meanwhile clamped down ever tighter on Richmond. At last, on April 2, 1865, Lee found his position untenable. Warning President Davis and his government to flee, he tried to lead his ragged troops to join Johnston's dwindling force. Cut off by Grant, Lee had no alternative but to surrender, and on April 9 at Appomattox Court House he told his weary, hungry men to lay down their arms. On April 18 Johnston followed by surrendering to Sherman (although the final terms were not agreed on until April 26). When the news reached the trans-Mississippi region, Kirby-Smith surrendered in June. The war had lasted almost precisely four years.

The Union cause and the Lincoln adminstration were the beneficiaries of these victories. The critics of the government had been most vocal, their opposition most powerful, in the heartbreaking summer months of 1864, when Grant seemed to be getting nowhere in Virginia and Sherman appeared unable to bag his enemy in Georgia. Northern morale and support for the president mounted perceptibly at the news of Sherman's success at Atlanta and of Farragut's victory at Mobile Bay. Conversely, support for Davis's administration dwindled and critical voices became louder as Confederate reverse followed reverse. In a certain sense, then, victory begot victory, and defeat begot defeat.

Why the North Won the War. Yet this is circular reasoning and does not explain the final Union triumph after so many earlier Confederate successes. For a fuller understanding one must turn to the slow but steady mobilization of the North's infinitely superior economic resources and to the gradual erosion of those in the South. The effect of Northern economic and industrial superiority was not fully felt until after more than two years of war; it took time to award contracts, to expand factories, to recruit skilled laborers, and to deliver the products. But observers noted that by 1863 Lee's veterans invading Pennsylvania looked like a gaggle of "barefooted, ragged, lousy, [but] disciplined, desperate ruffians." These troops were so badly supplied and so poorly fed that their line of march was "traceable by the deposit of dysenteric stool the army leaves behind it." By 1863 the Union armies, on the other hand, were so completely equipped that their paraphernalia became a hindrance. When Northern soldiers advanced, they shucked off layers of greatcoats, blankets, and other unnecessary supplies. By the end of the war, Union economic superiority was most evident in the Northern transportation system. Southern railroads by that time had simply worn out. In the Union, on the other hand, some 5,000 more miles of railroad were in operation in 1865 than at the start of the war—a figure that does not include the numerous military railroads operated in the South.

In December 1864 Eliza F. Andrews, the daughter of a Georgia judge and an intelligent, high-spirited, but partisan diarist, crossed the path of desolation left by Sherman's army in central Georgia. The gin houses and packing screws to which she referred were used to remove the seed from the cotton and to compress it into bales. Sherman's soldiers regularly destroyed them, since cotton was the mainstay of the Southern economy.

A Georgia Girl Deplores the Ruin of the South

ABOUT three miles from Sparta [Georgia] we struck the "Burnt Country, " as it is well named by the natives, and then I could better understand the wrath and desperation of these poor people. I almost felt as if I should like to hang a Yankee myself. There was hardly a fence left standing all the way from Sparta to Gordon. The fields were trampled down and the road was lined with carcasses of horses, hogs, and cattle that the invaders, unable either to consume or to carry away with them, had wantonly shot down, to starve out the people and prevent them from making their crops. The stench in some places was unbearable; every few hundred yards we had to hold our noses or stop them with the cologne Mrs. Elzey had given us, and it proved a great boon.

The dwellings that were standing all showed signs of pillage, and on every plantation we saw the charred remains of the gin-house and packing-screw, while here and there lone chimney-stacks, "Sherman's sentinels," told of homes laid in ashes. The infamous wretches! I couldn't wonder now that these poor people should want to put a rope around the neck of every red-handed "devil of them" they could lay their hands on.

Hay ricks and fodder stacks were demolished, corn-cribs were empty, and every bale of cotton that could be found was burnt by the savages. I saw no grain of any sort, except little patches they had spilled when feeding their horses and which there was not even a chicken left in the country to eat. A bag of oats might have lain anywhere along the road without danger from the beasts of the fields, though I cannot say it would have been safe from the assaults of hungry man.

Crowds of [Confederate] soldiers were tramping over the road. . . . They were mostly on foot, and I saw numbers seated on the roadside greedily eating raw turnips, meat skins, parched corn—anything they could find, even picking up the loose grains that Sherman's horses had left. I felt tempted to stop and empty the contents of our provision baskets into their laps, but the dreadful accounts that were given of the state of the country before us made prudence get the better of our generosity.

A DEAD CONFEDERATE SOLDIER AT FORT MAHONE, NEAR PETERSBURG, VIRGINIA, APRIL 2, 1865

In the final bloody battles of the war, the Confederacy lost men who could not be replaced. "Where is this to end?" asked General Josiah Gorgas. "No money in the Treasury—no food to feed Gen. Lee's army—no troops to oppose Gen. Sherman— what does it all mean . . . ? Is the cause really hopeless?"

Moreover, because they had to link up with the newly authorized Union Pacific Railroad, Northern lines had all converted to a standard rail gauge.

Supplies, however, do not fight wars, nor do trains; men do. From the start the North's overwhelming population advantage counted heavily against the Confederacy. That advantage increased during the conflict. In the course of the four years of war, more than 180,000 male immigrants of military age settled in the North, whereas there was virtually no immigration to the Confederacy. In addition, the black population became another vast source of Union manpower. Confederates dared not tap this source until their cause was already lost.

But men, no matter how numerous, fight well only if ably led by their military commanders and inspired by their political leaders. It would be hard to argue that Northern generalship was superior to that of the South. While Grant has his admirers, most students of Civil War military history consider Robert E. Lee the greatest commander. Nor is it easy to maintain that the political leadership of the North was markedly superior. Later generations, recalling the eloquence of the Gettysburg Address and the mystical beauty of the second inaugural address, have found it difficult to

remember that for most of his administration Lincoln was considered uninspiring and ineffectual. Had Lincoln been defeated for reelection in 1864, he would doubtless be rated as an honest but unsuccessful president. On the other hand, had the Southern states been able to win their independence, Jefferson Davis would undoubtedly rank as the George Washington of the Confederacy.

There were, of course, important differences between the two wartime presidents, but these were of less significance than the differences in the political systems in which they had to work. Like many more recently emerging nations, the Confederacy tried to present a façade of unity to the world. It was a one-party—or, more properly, a no-party—state. Southerners feared that party divisions would suggest that they were less than unanimous in seeking independence. The most careful analysis of the voting records of Confederate congressmen has been able to show, at most, only the beginnings of party lines. Small temporary factions rather than permanent political parties dominated the Confederate Congress. President Davis had many enemies, and they were constantly attacking him from all directions, like a swarm of bees. His friends were divided, and he could never rally

"GENERAL ROBERT E. LEE LEAVING THE McLEAN HOUSE AFTER THE SURRENDER AT APPOMATTOX, 1865" BY A. W. WAUD

After accepting Grant's terms of surrender, Lee stepped out to the porch of the McLean House and signaled his orderly to bring up his horse. While the animal was being bridled, one of Grant's aides remembered, Lee "gazed sadly in the direction . . . where his army lay—now an army of prisoners. He thrice smote the palm of his left hand slowly with his right fist in an absent sort of way." Then he mounted, and Grant saluted him by raising his hat. "Lee raised his hat respectfully, and rode off at a slow trot to break the sad news to the brave fellows whom he had so long commanded."

them into a unified group. As with the Congress, so with the people. It is safe to guess that if at any point the voters of the Confederacy had been asked to endorse their president or to topple him, Davis would have received overwhelming support. But lacking political parties, Southerners had no way of making this sentiment felt.

In the Union, on the other hand, the two-party system remained active. The Democrats continued as a formidable, if not always united, force throughout the war. They came close to winning a majority in Congress in the 1862 elections; and even in 1864 McClellan received 45 percent of the popular vote—at a time when the strongest opponents of the Republican party were still out of the Union and, of course, not

voting. Such a powerful opposition party compelled the Republican factions, however bitterly at odds with each other, to work together. Conservatives and Radicals might disagree over slavery, emancipation, and reconstruction, but they all agreed that any Republican administration was preferable to a Democratic one.

It was, then, the absence of political machinery in the South that weakened Davis's regime and rendered him unable fully to mobilize the material and spiritual resources of the Confederacy. And it was the much-maligned two-party system that allowed Lincoln, despite quarrelsome and impassioned attacks from fellow Republicans, to experiment boldly and to grow into an effective wartime leader.

CHRONOLOGY

1863 Lincoln issues final Emancipation Proclamation.

Confederates defeat Union army under Hooker at Chancellorsville.

Lee's invasion of the North checked by Union army under Meade at Gettysburg.

Grant captures Vicksburg.

Draft riots in the North.

Confederate army under Bragg defeats Union forces at Chickamauga.

Union victory at Chattanooga (Lookout Mountain and Missionary Ridge).

Lincoln offers lenient reconstruction program.

1864 Grant named Union general in chief.

Grant's direct advance on Richmond checked at the Wilderness, Spotsylvania, and Cold Harbor.

Grant moves south of James River to begin "siege" of Petersburg.

Sherman pushes back Confederates under Joseph E. Johnston and captures Atlanta.

Farragut captures Mobile.

Lincoln reelected president over Democrat McClellan.

Sherman marches from Atlanta to the sea.

1865 Sherman pushes northward through South Carolina and North Carolina.

Lee gives up Petersburg and Richmond, and Confederate government flees.

Lee surrenders at Appomattox. Johnston surrenders to Sherman. Kirby-Smith surrenders Confederate forces west of the Mississippi.

Lincoln assassinated; Andrew Johnson becomes president.

SUGGESTED READINGS

Most of the studies listed at the end of the previous chapter also relate to the topics discussed in this chapter.

The best general analysis of military operations is Herman Hattaway and Archer Jones, *How the North Won* (1983). On the Northern armies the most comprehensive work is Kenneth P. Williams's *Lincoln Finds a General* (5 vols., 1949–59). The most readable is Bruce Catton's trilogy on the Army of the Potomac: *Mr. Lincoln's Army* (1951), *Glory Road* (1952), and *A Stillness at Appomattox* (1953). Michael C. C. Adams, *Our Masters the Rebels* (1978), is a provocative interpretation. Among the best biographies of Union generals are Warren W. Hassler, Jr., *General George B. McClellan* (1957); Bruce Catton, *Grant Moves South* (1960), and *Grant Takes Command* (1969); and Lloyd Lewis, *Sherman* (1932).

The fullest account of military operations from a Southern point of view is Shelby Foote, *The Civil War* (3 vols., 1958–74). More interpretive is Grady McWhiney and Perry D. Jamison, *Attack and Die* (1982). Douglas S. Freeman, *Lee's Lieutenants* (3 vols., 1942–44), examines Confederate commanders in the eastern theater, while Thomas Connelly, *Army of the Heartland* (2 vols., 1967–71), is an excellent account of those in the west. Among the most significant biographies of Confederate generals are Douglas S. Freeman, *R. E. Lee* (4 vols., 1934–35); Frank E. Vandiver, *Mighty Stonewall* (1957); Grady McWhiney, *Braxton Bragg and Confederate Defeat* (1969); and Richard M. McMurry, *John Bell Hood and the War for Southern Independence* (1982).

Two books by Bell I. Wiley provide a fascinating social history of the common soldiers of the Civil War: *The Life of Johnny Reb* (1943), and *The Life of Billy Yank* (1952).

The best accounts of Civil War naval operations are Virgil C. Jones, *The Civil War at Sea* (3 vols., 1960–62), and Bern Anderson, *By Sea and by River* (1962). Rowena Reed, *Combined Operations in the Civil War* (1978), is an important study. See also John Niven's fine biography, *Gideon Welles: Lincoln's Secretary of the Navy* (1973).

The story of Confederate politics has to be pieced together from Wilfred B. Yearns, *The Confederate Congress* (1960); Thomas B. Alexander and Richard E. Beringer, *The Anatomy of the Confederate Congress* (1972); and Frank L. Owsley, *State Rights in the Confederacy* (1925). See also Paul D. Escott, *After Secession: Jefferson Davis and the Failure of Confederate Nationalism* (1978).

James A. Rawley, *The Politics of Union* (1974), is the best general study. There are several analyses of Republican factions and leadership: T. Harry Williams, *Lincoln and the Radicals* (1941); William B. Hesseltine, *Lincoln and the War Governors* (1948); Hans L. Trefousse, *The Radical Republicans* (1969); and Allan G. Bogue, *The Earnest Men: Republicans of the Civil War Senate* (1981). On the Democrats see Joel H. Silbey, *A Respectable Minority* (1977), and Jean H. Baker, *Affairs of Party* (1983).

Benjamin Quarles, *The Negro in the Civil War* (1953), is comprehensive. James M. McPherson, ed., *The Negro's Civil*

War (1965), is a valuable set of documents, skillfully interwoven. *Freedom: A Documentary History of Emancipation*, ed. by Ira Berlin and others (1982), is richly rewarding. Bell I. Wiley, *Southern Negroes, 1861–1865* (1938), is a standard account. The early chapters of Leon F. Litwack, *Been in the Storm So Long* (1979), superbly recapture slave life during the war. The authoritative account of Negro troops in the Union army is Dudley T. Cornish, *The Sable Arm* (1956).

For explanations of the collapse of the Confederacy, see Henry S. Commager, ed., *The Defeat of the Confederacy* (1964); David Donald, ed., *Why the North Won the Civil War* (1960); and Bell I. Wiley, *The Road to Appomattox* (1956).

20 Reconstruction, 1865–1877

"A house divided against itself cannot stand," Abraham Lincoln prophesied in 1858. The Civil War proved that the United States would stand, not as a loose confederation of sovereign states but as one nation, indivisible. Never again would there be talk of secession. The war also ended slavery, the most divisive institution in antebellum America. Weakened by the advances of the Union armies and undermined by Lincoln's Emancipation Proclamation, slavery received its death blow in February 1865, when Congress adopted the Thirteenth Amendment, outlawing slavery and involuntary servitude. After three-fourths of the states had ratified it, the amendment became part of the Constitution in December 1865.

But the Civil War did not settle the terms and conditions on which the states, sections, races, and classes would live in the firmly united "house." Those problems formed the agenda of the Reconstruction era, one of the most complex and controversial periods in American history. During these postwar years some basic questions had to be answered. What, if any, punishment should be imposed on Southern whites who had supported the Confederate attempt to break up the Union? How were the recently emancipated slaves to be guaranteed their freedom, and what civil and political rights did freedmen have? When and on what conditions were the Southern states, so recently in rebellion, to be readmitted to the Union—that is, entitled to vote in national elections, to have senators and representatives seated in the United States Congress, and, in general, to become once more full-fledged, equal members of the United States?

The initial moves to answer these questions came from the president, whose powers had grown significantly during the war years. In December 1863 President Lincoln announced a generous program of amnesty to repentant rebels and inaugurated a plan for reorganizing loyal governments in the South when as few as 10 percent of the voters in 1860 were willing to support them. After Lincoln's assassination in April 1865, President Andrew Johnson, his successor, continued the process of Reconstruction under a similar plan. Johnson, like Lincoln, expected Southern whites to take the lead in establishing new state governments loyal to the Union. To begin the process, the president appointed a provisional governor for each of the former Confederate states (except those in which Lincoln had already initiated Reconstruction). Johnson directed these provisional governors to convene constitutional conventions, which were expected to adopt the Thirteenth Amendment ending slavery, to nullify or repeal the ordinances of secession, and to cancel state debts incurred for the prosecution of the war. By early 1866 each of the states that had once formed the Confederacy had completed most of these required steps, and the president viewed the process of Reconstruction as concluded. He recommended that the senators and representatives chosen by these reorganized governments promptly be given their rightful seats in Congress.

Presidential Reconstruction was criticized from the outset. Having jealously watched executive power grow during the war, Congress was ready to reestablish its political equality with the presidency, and even to reassert its superior influence. Unlike President Lincoln, Andrew Johnson had no popular mandate. Johnson, a Tennessee Democrat and former slaveholder, was a quiet, inflexible, and aggressive man who did not understand that politics is the art of compromise.

After an initial attempt to cooperate with the new president, Republican leaders in 1866 began to draw up their own plans for Reconstruction. The first congressional plan was embodied in the Fourteenth Amendment to the Constitution, which made it clear that blacks were citizens of the United States and tried to define the rights and privileges of American citizens. When the Southern states refused to ratify this amendment, congressional republicans moved in 1867 to a tougher program of reorganizing the South by insisting that blacks be allowed to vote. Under this

RUINS OF RICHMOND
When the Confederate government evacuated Richmond on April 3, 1865, orders were given to burn supplies that might fall into the enemy's hands. There were heavy explosions as ironclads, armories, and arsenals were blown up. The next morning, as the fires spread, a mob of men and women, whites and blacks, began to plunder the city.

second plan of congressional Reconstruction, every Southern state (except for Tennessee, which had been readmitted to the Union in 1866) received a new constitution that guaranteed to men of all races equal protection of the laws. Between 1868 and 1871, all these states were readmitted to the Union. Republican governments, which depended heavily on black votes, controlled these states for a period ranging from a few months in the case of Virginia to nine years in the case of Louisiana.

Paths Not Taken

Contemporaries called this the period of Radical Reconstruction—or, very often, Black Reconstruction. It is easy to understand why many Americans of the 1860s and 1870s viewed these changes as little short of revolutionary. No amendments had been added to the Constitution since 1804; but within the five years after the Civil War, three new and far-reaching amendments were adopted. The Thirteenth Amendment ended slavery, the Fourteenth Amendment defined the

rights of citizens, and the Fifteenth Amendment (1870) prohibited discrimination in voting on account of race or color. The national government, which so recently had tottered on the edge of defeat, was now more powerful than at any previous point in American history. The Southern ruling class of whites, lately in charge of their own independent government, now had to ask for pardon. More than 3 million blacks, slaves only a few months earlier, were now free and entitled to the same privileges as all other citizens. Americans fairly gasped at the extent and the speed of the changes that had occurred in their society, and it is hardly surprising that most subsequent historians accepted this contemporary view of the Reconstruction era as one of turbulent disorder.

Without denying that real and important changes did occur during the Reconstruction period, it might help to put these changes into perspective by inventing a little counterfactual, or imaginary, history—conceivable historical scenarios that never in fact occurred. For example, it would be easy to imagine how the victorious North might have turned angrily on the defeated South. In 1865 Northerners had just finished four years of war that had cost the Union army more than 360,000 casualties. Americans of the Civil War era and subsequent generations had to pay at least $10 billion in taxes to destroy the Confederacy. Northerners had reason to believe, moreover, that their Confederate opponents had conducted the war with fiendish barbarity. Sober Union congressmen informed their constituents that the Confederates had employed "Indian savages" to scalp and mutilate the Union dead. Reliable Northern newspapers told how in April 1864 General Nathan Bedford Forrest and his Confederates overran the defenses of Fort Pillow, Tennessee, manned by a black regiment, and, refusing to accept surrender, deliberately beat, shot, and burned their prisoners. The influential *Harper's Weekly Magazine* carried apparently authentic drawings of a goblet that a Southerner had made from a Yankee soldier's skull and of necklaces fashioned of Yankee teeth that Southern ladies wore. When Union armies liberated Northern prisoners from such hell-holes as Andersonville, Georgia, pictures of these half-starved skeletons of men, clad in grimy tatters of their Union uniforms, convinced Northerners that Jefferson Davis's policy had been "to starve and freeze and kill off by inches the prisoners he dares not butcher outright."

After the murder of President Lincoln by the Southern sympathizer John Wilkes Booth, an outraged North could easily have turned on the conquered Confederacy in vengeance. The victorious Northerners might have executed Jefferson Davis, Alexander H. Stephens, and a score of other leading Confederates and might have sent thousands more into permanent exile. The triumphant Union might have erased the boundaries of the Southern states and divided the whole region into new, conquered territories. Northerners might have enforced the confiscation acts already on the statute books and have seized the plantations of rebels, for distribution to the freedmen.

But nothing so drastic happened. No Confederate was executed for "war crimes" except Major Henry Wirtz, commandant of the infamous Andersonville prison, who was hanged. A few Southern political leaders were imprisoned for their part in the "rebellion," but in most cases they were promptly released. To be sure, Jefferson Davis remained in prison for two years at Fort Monroe, and he was under indictment for treason until 1869, when all charges were dropped. His case was, however, as unusual as it was extreme. One reason for the long delay in bringing him to trial was the certainty that no jury, Northern or Southern, would render an impartial verdict. There was no general confiscation of the property of Confederates, and no dividing up of plantations.

Another scenario—this time featuring the Southern whites—is equally conceivable, but it too did not happen. For four years Confederate citizens had been subjected to a barrage of propaganda designed to prove that the enemy was little less than infernal in his purposes. Many believed the Southern editor who claimed that Lincoln's program was "Emancipation, Confiscation, Conflagration, and Extermination." According to the North Carolina educator Calvin H. Wiley, the North had "summoned to its aid every fierce and cruel and licentious passion of the human heart"; to defeat the Confederacy it was ready to use "the assassin's dagger, the midnight torch, . . . poison, famine and pestilence." Charges of this kind were easy to credit in the many Southern families that had relatives in Northern prison camps, such as the one at Elmira, New York, where 775 of 8,347 Confederate prisoners died within three months for lack of food, water, and medicine. The behavior of Union troops in the South, especially of Sherman's "bummers," members of raiding forces who plundered indiscriminately in Georgia and the Carolinas, gave Southerners every reason to fear the worst if the Confederate government failed.

It would therefore have been reasonable for Confederate armies in 1865, overwhelmed by Union numbers, to disband quietly, disappear into the countryside, and carry on guerrilla operations against the Northern invaders. Indeed, on the morning of the day when Lee surrendered at Appomattox, Confederate General E. P. Alexander advocated just such a plan. He argued that if Lee's soldiers took to the woods with their rifles, perhaps two-thirds of the Army of Northern Virginia could escape capture. "We would be like rabbits and partridges in the bushes," he claimed, "and they could not scatter to follow us." The history of more recent wars of national liberation suggests that Alexander's judgment was correct. At least his strategy would have given time for thousands of leading Southern politicians and planters, together with their families, to go safely into exile, as the loyalists did during the American Revolution.

But again, no such events occurred. A few Confederate leaders did go into exile. For example, General Jubal A. Early fled to Mexico and from there to Canada, where he tried to organize a migration of Southerners to New Zealand. But when he found that nobody wanted to follow him, Early returned to his home and his law practice in Virginia. A few hundred Confederates did migrate to Mexico and to Brazil. But most followed the advice of General Lee and General Wade Hampton of South Carolina, who urged their fellow Southerners to "devote their whole energies to the restoration of law and order, the reestablishment of agriculture and commerce, the promotion of education and the rebuilding of our cities and dwellings which have been laid in ashes."

Still another counterfactual historical scenario comes readily to mind. Southern blacks, who for generations had been oppressed in slavery, now for the first time had disciplined leaders in the thousands of black soldiers who had served in the Union army. They also had weapons. The blacks could very easily have turned in revenge on their former masters. Seizing the plantations and other property of the whites, the freedmen might have made the former Confederacy a black nation. If the whites had dared to resist, the South might have been the scene of massacres as bloody as those in Haiti at the beginning of the nineteenth century, when Toussaint L'Ouverture drove the French from that island.

Many Southern whites feared, or even expected, that the Confederacy would become another Haiti. They were frightened by reports that blacks were joining the Union League, an organization that had originated in the North during the war to stimulate patriotism but during the Reconstruction era became the stronghold of the Republican party in the South. The secrecy imposed by the league on its members and its frequent nighttime meetings alarmed whites, and they readily believed reports that the blacks were collecting arms and ammunition for a general uprising. Fearfully, Southern whites read newspaper accounts of minor racial clashes. Indeed, whites were told, racial tension was so great that blacks "might break into open insurrection at any time."

But no such uprising occurred. Although the freedmen unquestionably hoped to obtain the lands of their former masters, they did not seize them. Indeed, black leaders consistently discouraged talk of extralegal confiscation of plantations. Nor did freedmen threaten the lives or the rights of whites. One of the earliest black political conventions held in Alabama urged a policy of "peace, friendship, and good will toward all men—especially toward our white fellow-citizens among whom our lot is cast." That tone was the dominant one throughout the Reconstruction period, and in many states blacks took the lead in repealing laws that disfranchised former Confederates or disqualified them from holding office.

The point of these three exercises in counterfactual history is, of course, not to argue that the Civil War brought no changes in American life. The preservation of the Union and the emancipation of the slaves were two consequences of tremendous importance. Instead, these exercises suggest that conventional accounts of the Reconstruction period as a second American Revolution are inadequate. During these postwar years there were swift and significant changes in Southern society, but the shared beliefs and institutions of the American people—North and South, black and white—set limits to these changes.

Constitutionalism as a Limit to Change

One set of ideas that sharply curbed experimentation and political innovation during the Reconstruction period can be labeled constitutionalism. It is hard for twentieth-century Americans to understand the reverence with which their nineteenth-century ancestors viewed the Constitution. Next to the flag, the Constitution was the most powerful symbol of American nationhood. Tested in the trial of civil war, the Constitution continued to command respect—almost veneration—during the Reconstruction era.

States' Rights. Among the most unchallenged provisions of the Constitution were those that separated the powers of state and national government. Although the national government greatly expanded its role during the war years, Americans still tended to think of it as performing only the specific functions listed in the Constitution. These functions allowed the national government virtually no authority to act directly on individual citizens. For example, the national government could neither prevent nor punish crime; it had no control over public education; it could not outlaw discrimination against racial minorities; and it could not even intervene to maintain public order unless requested to do so by the state government. Virtually everybody agreed, therefore, that if any laws regulating social and economic life were required, they must be the work of state and local, not of national, government.

Consequently, nobody even contemplated the possibility that some federal agency might be needed to supervise the demobilization after Appomattox. Everybody simply assumed that after some 200,000 of the Union army volunteers bravely paraded down Pennsylvania Avenue on May 23–24, 1865, and received applause from President Johnson, the cabinet, the generals, and members of the diplomatic corps, the soldiers would disband and go back to their peaceful homes. This is precisely what they did. Of the more than one million volunteers in the Union army on May 1, 1865, two-thirds were mustered out by August, four-fifths by November. The United States government offered the demobilized soldiers no assistance in finding jobs, purchasing housing, or securing further education. It paid pensions to those injured in the war and to the families of those who had been killed, but assumed no further responsibility. Nor did anyone think of asking the national government to oversee the transition from a wartime economy to an era of peace. By the end of April 1865, without notice the various bureaus of the army and navy departments simply suspended requisitions and purchases, government arsenals slowed down their production, and surplus supplies were sold off.

Hardly anybody thought that the national govern-

"Westward the Course of Empire Takes its Way" (Mural Study, U.S. Capitol), by Emanuel Leutze.

From Eden to Babylon

Just as the Civil War required Americans to reconsider the meaning of national loyalty, so it compelled them to rethink the bases of a good society. Before the war their vision of America was primarily agrarian. Most of the inhabitants of the United States lived on farms, plantations, and ranches. Of course there were bustling cities, but most city dwellers had been born in the countryside, whether in the United States, Ireland, Germany, or England. It was natural, then, that when midcentury Americans portrayed themselves, it was as farmers, herdsmen, trappers, and explorers—not as businessmen, factory laborers, or clerks.

Just before the outbreak of the war, Emanuel Leutze accurately recaptured the Americans' definition of themselves in *Westward the Course of Empire Takes Its Way*, which filled a six-hundred-square-foot panel in the rotunda of the national

"The Garden of Eden" by Erastus Salisbury Field.

Capitol. It was not a great painting, not even a good painting; in it, as one contemporary remarked, "confusion reigns paramount." But it did serve to perpetuate the myth that Americans were a people close to the land, who drew their strength from nature.

Nature had a special place in the thought of antebellum Americans. The most influential American philosophical work published in the first half of the nineteenth century was Ralph Waldo Emerson's essay on that topic. "Nature," to Emerson and the thousands who read his essays and heard him lecture, included those "essences unchanged by man: space, the air, the river, the leaf." It was to be distinguished from "art," the imposition of man's will upon nature that resulted in "a house, a canal, a statue, a picture." "Nature," then, had emotional and moral primacy over "art," and most Americans believed, with Emerson himself, that by shedding all artifice man could again become part and parcel of nature itself.

A self-taught Massachusetts painter, Erastus Salisbury Field, perfectly recaptured the spirit behind Emerson's ideas. With only three months of informal training as an artist, Field personified the spirit of spontaneity and improvisation that Emerson extolled. More important, his early paintings showed an attachment to, and a meticulous interest in, nature. The land he portrayed was a tidied-up, New England version of Leutze's sprawling continent. Field's *Garden of Eden* did not have a specifically American setting, although his neatly paired animals of peculiar anatomy and his trees with their improbable fruit might have flourished in America, if anywhere. There is, however, a distinctively American note in Field's treatment of nudity in the Garden of Eden: a clump of strategically placed lilies preserves Adam's modesty, and Eve lurks behind some unlikely blossoms. Clearly for Field, as for Emerson, man is at his best when most closely linked to nature, in a scene unmarred by human artifice or ingenuity.

"Proposed Arcade Railroad"
by Ferdinand Mayer and Sons.

During the Civil War years Americans' perception of the good society dramatically changed. The war may not have stimulated economic growth, but it did promote mechanization. Steam power largely replaced horse power and water power. Machines of ever increasing complexity, with fascinating gears and gauges, replaced men. The vast foundries and rolling mills that had turned out cannons during the war were diverted to the production of structural iron girders and, later, steel beams, which made possible a new American architecture. No longer was it necessary to erect buildings out of huge piles of masonry, and no longer was it dangerous to build them too high. Using steel beams, innovative architects like Louis Sullivan invented the skyscraper, a triumphant fusing of form and function. Imaginative engineers like Samuel B. B. Nowlan of New York foresaw the day when whole cities would be made of steel, and Nowlan's sketch, *Proposed Arcade Railroad*, looked ahead to a new era in urban design.

"Historical Monument of the American Republic" by Erastus Salisbury Field.

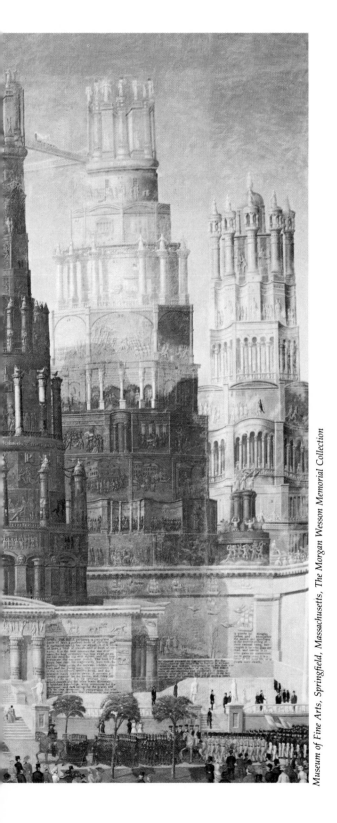

Postwar Americans found the new technology exhilarating to the point of intoxication. Gone now was the day when Erastus Field portrayed man in the bosom of nature. Instead, looking forward to the Centennial Exposition in Philadelphia, the aging Field painted his *Historical Monument of the American Republic*. Field's picture showed America as wholly urban, entirely built over with huge towers, with round or octagonal sides, rising in diminishing stages. The central and tallest tower commemorated Abraham Lincoln and the Constitution. Near the top, several of these towers were joined together with vaulting steel bridges, along which steam railroad trains puffed. As a significant reminder of Civil War days, soldiers paraded the avenue in front of Field's monumental vision of America as Babylon.

By 1876, then, Field's ideas, like those of most Americans, had completely shifted. Rural peace paled beside the attractions of mechanized urban life. The machine was now the magnet of the American mind. When the novelist William Dean Howells visited the Centennial Exposition, he, like thousands of other Americans, was most impressed by the gigantic Corliss engine, which gave power to the 8,000 other machines, large and small, that sewed cloth, printed newspapers, made shoes, and pumped water on the thirteen-acre Exposition grounds. After comparing the displays of painting and sculpture with the Corliss engine, Howells concluded: ''It is in these things of iron and steel that the national genius most freely speaks.''

Metropolitan Museum of Art, Purchase, 1940, Alfred N. Punnett Fund and Gift of George D. Pratt

"Max Schmitt in a Single Scull" by Thomas Eakins.

The greatest painter of the postwar period, Thomas Eakins of Philadelphia, shared Howells's admiration of the machine and his respect for the scientific knowledge that it represented. Just as the Corliss engine was "an athlete of steel and iron, without a superfluous ounce of metal on it," so a painting, thought Eakins, should be lean and objective. In order to portray the human figure scientifically, he studied anatomy at Jefferson Medical College. Eakins also linked painting with mathematics, because both were disciplines in which "the complicated things are reduced to simple things." Eakins's portrait *Max Schmitt in a Single Scull* shows how perfectly he fused art, anatomy, and the mathematics of perspective. More subtly it also speaks of the changed values of postwar American society. In decisive contrast to the absence of all manmade artifacts in Leutze's painting and in Field's *Garden of Eden*, a superb steel bridge is a vital part of Eakins's portrait. More emphatically than any number of words, the presence of that bridge shows that, by the end of the Civil War era, Americans had come to think of nature as something to be spanned, conquered, and controlled.

A GROUP OF FREEDMEN IN RICHMOND, VIRGINIA, 1865
A central problem of Reconstruction years was the future of the freedmen. Nobody had made any plans for a smooth transition from slavery to freedom. Consequently, when emancipation came, as one former slave recalled, "We didn't know where to go. Momma and them didn't know where to go, you see, after freedom broke. Just like you turned something out, you know. They didn't know where to go."

ment might play a role in rebuilding the warworn South. The devastation in the South was immense and ominous. The Confederate dead totaled more than a quarter of a million. In Mississippi, for example, one-third of the white men of military age had been disabled for life or killed. Most Southern cities were in ruins. Two-thirds of the Southern railroads were totally destroyed; the rest barely creaked along on worn-out rails with broken-down engines. But none of these problems was thought to be the concern of the United States government.

The national government's failure to come to the rescue was not caused by vindictiveness. To the contrary, Union officials often behaved with marked generosity toward Confederates. After Lee's hungry battalions surrendered at Appomattox, Grant's soldiers freely shared their rations with them. All over the South, federal military officials drew upon the full Union army storehouses to feed the hungry. But the federal government did not go beyond these attempts to prevent starvation, and very few thought that it should. Not until the twentieth century did the United States make it a policy to pour vast sums of money into the rehabilitation of enemies it had defeated in war.

Rebuilding therefore had to be the work of the Southern state and local authorities, and this task imposed a heavy burden on their meager resources. In Mississippi one-fifth of the entire state revenue in 1866 was needed to provide artificial limbs for soldiers maimed in the war. The resources of the South were obviously inadequate for the larger tasks of physical restoration. Drawing upon antebellum experience, Southern governments did the only thing they knew how to—namely, they lent the credit of the state to back up the bonds of private companies that promised to rebuild railroads and other necessary facilities. These companies were underfinanced, and the credit of the Southern states after Appomattox was questionable, to say the least. Therefore these bonds had to be sold at disadvantageous prices and at exorbitant rates of interest. In later years, when many of these companies defaulted on their obligations and Southern state governments had to make good on their guarantees, these expenditures would be condemned as excessive and extravagant. Democrats blamed them on the Republican regimes established in the South after 1868. In fact, however, immediately after the war the need for physical restoration was so obvious and so pressing that nearly every government—whether controlled by

Democrats or Republicans—underwrote corporations that promised to rebuild the region.

The Freedmen's Bureau.

Even in dealing with the freedmen—the some 3 million slaves emancipated as a result of the war—the United States government tried to pursue a hands-off policy. In North and South alike, few influential leaders thought that it was the function of the national government to supervise the blacks' transition from slavery to freedom. Even abolitionists, genuinely devoted to the welfare of blacks, were so accustomed to thinking of the black man as "God's image in ebony"—in other words, a white man in a black skin—that they had no plans for assisting him after emancipation. In 1865 William Lloyd Garrison urged the American Anti-Slavery Society to disband because it had fulfilled its function, and he suspended the publication of *The Liberator*. Sharing the same point of view, the American Freedmen's Inquiry Commission, set up by the Union War Department in 1863, unanimously opposed further governmental actions to protect the blacks. "The negro does best when let alone," argued one member of the commission, Samuel Gridley Howe, noted both for his work with the deaf, dumb, and blind and for his hostility to slavery. "We must beware of all attempts to prolong his servitude, under pretext of taking care of him. The white man has tried taking care of the negro, by slavery, by apprenticeship, by colonization, and has failed disastrously in all; now let the negro try to take care of himself."

But the problem of caring for the freedmen could not be dismissed so easily. Wherever Union armies advanced into the South, they were "greeted by an irruption of negroes of all ages, complexions and sizes, men, women, boys and girls . . . waving hats and bonnets with the most ludicrous caperings and ejaculations of joy." "The poor delighted creatures thronged upon us," a Yankee soldier reported, and they insisted: "We'se gwin wid you all." "What shall be done with them?" commanders in the field plaintively wired Washington.

The administration in Washington had no comprehensive answer. Initially it looked to private humanitarian organizations to rush food, clothing, and medicine to the thousands of blacks who thronged in unsanitary camps around the headquarters of each Union army. The New England Freedmen's Aid Society, the American Missionary Association, and the Philadelphia Society of Friends [Quakers] promptly responded, but it was soon clear that the problem was too great for private charity.

Gradually sentiment grew in the North for the creation of a general Emancipation Bureau in the federal government—only to conflict directly with the even stronger sentiment that the national government had limited powers. Out of this conflict emerged the Freedmen's Bureau Act of March 3, 1865. Congress established the Bureau of Refugees, Freedmen, and Abandoned Lands under the jurisdiction of the War Department. It entrusted to the new agency, for one year after the end of the war, "control of all subjects relating to refugees and freedmen." To head the new organization, Lincoln named Oliver O. Howard, a Union general with paternalistic views toward blacks.

At first glance, the Freedmen's Bureau seems to have been a notable exception to the rule that the national government should take only a minor, passive role in the restoration of the South. Howard had a vision of a compassionate network of "teachers, ministers, farmers, superintendents" working together to aid and elevate the freedmen; and, under his enthusiastic impetus, the bureau appointed agents in each of the former Confederate states. The bureau's most urgent task was issuing food and clothing, mostly from surplus army stores, to destitute freedmen and other Southern refugees. This action unquestionably prevented mass starvation in the South. The bureau also took the initiative in getting work for freedmen. The bureau agents feared on the one hand that Southern landlords would attempt to exploit and underpay the freedmen, but they were also troubled by the widespread belief that blacks, once emancipated, would not work. The agents therefore brought laborers and landlords together and insisted that the workers sign labor contracts.

The bureau's most successful work was in the field of education. The slow work of educating the illiterate Southern blacks had already begun under the auspices of army chaplains and Northern benevolent societies before the creation of the bureau. Howard's bureau continued to cooperate with these agencies, providing housing for black schools, paying teachers, and helping to establish normal (teachers') schools and colleges for the training of black teachers. The freedmen enthusiastically welcomed all these educational efforts. During the day, black children learning the rudiments of language and arithmetic crowded into the classrooms; in the evenings adults "fighting with their letters" flocked to the schools, learning to read so that they would not be "made ashamed" by their children. "The progress of the scholars is in all cases creditable and in some remarkable," reported one of the teachers. "How richly God has endowed them, and how beautifully their natures would have expanded under a tender and gentle culture."

Even more innovative was the work of the bureau in allocating lands to the freedmen. During the war many plantations in the path of Union armies had been deserted by their owners, and army commanders

THE FREEDMEN'S UNION INDUSTRIAL SCHOOL, RICHMOND, VIRGINIA
Freedmen were eager to learn, and both the old and the young flocked to schools sponsored by the Freedmen's Bureau. Most of these schools taught only reading, writing, and arithmetic, but this one, in Richmond, gave instruction in sewing, cooking, and other domestic skills.

like Grant arranged to have these lands cultivated by the blacks who flocked to their camps. The largest tract of such abandoned land was in the Sea Islands of South Carolina, which Union troops had overrun in the fall of 1861. Although speculators bought up large amounts of this land during the war, many black residents were able to secure small holdings. When General W. T. Sherman marched through South Carolina, he ordered that the Sea Islands and the abandoned plantations along the riverbanks for thirty miles from the coast be reserved for black settlement and directed that the black settlers be given "possessory titles" to tracts of this land not larger than forty acres. The act creating the Freedmen's Bureau clearly contemplated the continuation of these policies, for it authorized the new bureau to lease confiscated lands to freedmen and to "loyal refugees." The bureau could also sell the land to these tenants and give them "such title thereto as the United States can convey."

But if the Freedmen's Bureau was an exception to the policy of limited federal involvement in the reconstruction process, it was at best a partial exception. Although the agency did extremely valuable work, it

was a feeble protector of the freedmen. Authorized to recruit only a minimal staff, Howard had to rely heavily on Union army officers stationed in the South—at just the time when the Union army was being demobilized. Consequently the bureau never had enough manpower to look after the rights of the freedmen; toward the end of its first year of operation, it employed only 799 men, 424 of whom were soldiers on temporary assigned duty. Important as the work of the bureau was in black education, its chief function was to stimulate private humanitarian aid in this field. In providing land for the freedmen, the bureau was handicapped because it controlled only about 800,000 acres of arable land in the South, at best enough for perhaps one black family in forty. Moreover, its efforts to distribute land to the blacks were repeatedly undercut by Congress and the president. The very wording of the act creating the bureau suggested congressional uncertainty about who actually owned deserted and confiscated lands in the South. President Johnson issued pardons to Southerners that explicitly included "restoration of all rights of property." In October 1865 the president directed Howard to go in person to the

This letter from a Northern teacher in the freedmen's school at Staunton, Virginia, reveals a good deal about the attitudes of both the teachers and the students in such schools. The desperate eagerness of blacks, young and old, to learn is evident. The teacher's insistence that students pay a small tuition reflected not merely financial need, but the conviction that freedmen who were compelled to pay for their education would acquire general habits of thrift and industry.

A Northerner Educates Virginia Freedmen (1869)

SIX or eight left school a few days ago because they could not pay their tuition, and although I called and informed them that while I desired them to pay if they could I should not send any away who were actually unable to, they had too much pride to accept my offer and still refused to come until they could pay.

One little boy about eight years old, who had not paid for a month, and who began to think I was going to send him home, after hearing me urge the children to bring their ten cents, came next morning with forty cents, which he handed to me with more pride than a Wall St. broker has with his millions. "Well," said I, "how did you get this money?" "I made it dis mornin' down town holdin horses for ge'm'an." And sure enough I found he had been out on the street ever since sun-rise to watch for jobs, lest he should lose his place in the schoolroom. Indeed the interest manifested on the part of those who still attend school is greater than at any time previous. Neither rain, darkness, or anything else, prevents them from coming, though many are compelled to come late, being hired out to those who care more for their labor than their education.

The old minister who commenced his alphabet last December is still poring over the Primers, but now begins to read short words quite readily. Last Monday night, when I called to hear him recite, I found him studying with the greatest enthusiasm. "O," said he, "if I could only read a chapter in the Bible, or give out a hymn to be sung, I would give all that I am worth," and that is perhaps $2000, which he has saved since his freedom. The day before he had been out to a neighboring town to preach, and such is his memory of Scripture that several of the white people who were present declared that he must have been able to read; yet his only means of getting information from the Bible as yet is by having his little boy read to him. He declares he will succeed.

Sea Islands to notify blacks there that they did not hold legal title to the land and to advise them "to make the best terms they could" with the white owners. When blacks bitterly resisted what they considered the bureau's betrayal, Union soldiers descended on the islands and forced blacks who would not sign labor contracts with the restored white owners to leave. Elsewhere in the South the record of the bureau was equally dismal.

In short, belief in the limited role to be played by the national government affected the rehabilitation of the freedmen, just as it did the physical restoration of the South and the demobilization in the North. The United States government was supposed to play the smallest possible part in all these matters, and its minimal activities were to be of the briefest duration.

It is certain that most whites in the North and in the South fully approved of these strict limitations on the activities of the national government. It is harder to determine what the masses of freedmen thought. On the one hand stands the protest of the Sea Island blacks when they learned they were about to be dispossessed: "Why, General Howard, why do you take away our lands? You take them from us who have always been true, always true to the Government! You give them to our all-time enemies! That is not right!" On the other is Frederick Douglass's reply to the question, "What shall we do with the Negroes?" The greatest black spokesman of the era answered: "Do nothing with them; mind your business, and let them mind theirs. Your *doing* with them is their greatest misfortune. They have been undone by your doings, and all they now ask and really have need of at your hands, is just to let them alone."

Laissez-Faire as a Limit to Change

Along with the idea of limited government went the doctrine of laissez-faire ("let things alone"), which sharply limited what the government could do to solve the economic problems that arose after the Civil War. Except for a handful of Radical Republicans, such as Charles Sumner and Thaddeus Stevens, most congressmen, like most academic economists, were unquestioning believers in an American version of laissez-faire. Although they were willing to promote economic growth through protective tariffs and land grants to railroads, they abhorred government inspection, regulation, and control of economic activities. These matters, they thought, were ruled by the unchanging laws of economics. "You need not think it necessary to have Washington exercise a political providence over the country," William Graham Sumner, the brilliant professor of political and social science, told his students at Yale. "God has done that a great deal better by the laws of political economy."

Reverence for Private Property.

No violation of economic laws was considered worse than interference with the right of private property—the right of an individual or group to purchase, own, use, and dispose of property without any interference from governmental authorities. There was consequently never a chance that congressmen would support Thaddeus Stevens's radical program to confiscate all Southern farms larger than two hundred acres and to divide the seized land into forty-acre tracts among the freedmen. "An attempt to justify the confiscation of Southern land under the pretense of doing justice to the freedmen," declared the *New York Times*, which spoke for educated Republicans, "strikes at the root of all property rights in both sections. It concerns Massachusetts quite as much as Mississippi."

Experts in the North held that the best program of Reconstruction was to allow the laws of economics to rule in the South with the least possible interference by the government. Obsessed by laissez-faire, Northern theorists failed to consider the physical devastation in the South caused by the war, and they did not recognize how feeble were the South's resources to rebuild its economy. Even excluding the loss of slave property, the total assessed property evaluation of the Southern states shrank by 43 percent between 1860 and 1865.

Southern Economic Adjustments.

Northern experts also failed to take into account the psychological dimensions of economic readjustment in the South. For generations Southern whites had persuaded themselves that slavery was the natural condition of the black race, and they truly believed that their slaves were devoted to them. But as Union armies approached and slaves defected, these Southerners were compelled to recognize that they had been living in a world of misconceptions and deceits. So shattering was the idea that slaves were free that some Southern whites simply refused to accept it. Even after the Confederate surrender, some owners would not inform their slaves of their new status. A few plantation owners angrily announced that they were so disillusioned that they would never again have anything to do with blacks, and they sought, vainly, to persuade European immigrants and Chinese coolies to work their fields.

Even those whites who on the surface accepted emancipation betrayed the fact that, on a deeper emotional level, they still could only think of blacks as performing forced labor. "The general interest both of the white man and of the negroes requires that he should be kept as near to the condition of slavery as possible, and as far from the condition of the white man as is practicable," announced one prominent South Carolinian. "Negroes must be made to work, or else cotton and rice must cease to be raised for export."

The contracts that in 1865 planters signed with their former slaves under pressure from the Freedmen's Bureau were further indications of the same attitude. Even the most generous of these contracts provided that blacks were "not to leave the premises during work hours without the consent of the Proprietor," that they would conduct "themselves faithfully, honestly and civilly," and that they would behave with "perfect obedience" toward the landowner.

Nor did the advocates of laissez-faire take into account the blacks' difficulties in adjusting to their new status. *Freedom*—that word so often whispered in the slave quarters—went to the heads of some blacks. A few took quite literally the coming of what they called Jubilee, thinking that it would put the bottom rail on top. Nearly all blacks had an initial impulse to test their freedom, to make sure that it was real. Thus during the first months after the war there was much movement among Southern blacks. "They are just like a swarm of bees," one observer noted, "all buzzing about and not knowing where to settle."

Much of this black mobility was, however, purposeful. Thousands of former slaves flocked to the Southern towns and cities where the Freedmen's Bureau was issuing rations, for they knew that food was unavailable on the plantations. Many blacks set out to find husbands, wives, or children, from whom they had been forcibly separated during the slave days. A good many freedmen joined the general movement of the Southern population away from the coastal states, which had been devastated by war, and migrated to the Southwestern frontier in Texas. Most blacks, however, did not move so far but remained in the immediate vicinity of the plantations where they had labored as slaves.

The freedmen's reluctance in 1865 to enter into labor contracts, either with their former masters or with other white landowners, was also generally misunderstood. Most blacks wanted to work—but they wanted to work on their own land. Freedmen knew that the United States government had divided up some abandoned plantations among former slaves, and many believed that on January 1, 1866—the anniversary of their freedom under Lincoln's Emancipation Proclamation—all would receive forty acres and a mule. With this prospect of having their own farms, they were unwilling to sign contracts to work on plantations owned by others.

Even when the hope of free land disappeared, freedmen resisted signing labor contracts because, as has been noted, so many white landowners expected to continue to treat them like slaves. The blacks were especially opposed to the idea of being again herded together in the plantation slave quarters, with their communal facilities for cooking and washing and in-fant care, and their lack of privacy. Emancipation did much to strengthen the black family. Families divided by slave sales could now be reunited. Marital arrangements between blacks, which had not been legally valid during slavery, could be regularized. Freedmen's Bureau officials performed thousands of marriage ceremonies, and some states passed general ordinances declaring that blacks who had been living together were legally man and wife and that their children were legitimate. This precious new security of family life was not something blacks were willing to jeopardize by returning to slave quarters. Before contracting to work on the plantations, they insisted on having separate cabins, scattered across the farm, each usually having its own patch for vegetables and perhaps a pen for hogs or a cow.

When these conditions were met, freedmen in the early months of 1866 entered into labor contracts, most of which followed the same general pattern. Rarely did these arrangements call for the payment of wages, for landowners were desperately short of cash and freedmen felt that a wage system gave landowners too much control over their labor. The most common system was sharecropping. Although there were many regional and individual variations, the system usually called for the dividing of the crop into three equal shares. One of these went to the landowner; another went to the laborer—usually black, although there were also many white sharecroppers in the South; and the third went to whichever party provided the seeds, fertilizer, mules, and farming equipment.

This system had several advantages for the landowner. At a time when money was scarce, he was not obliged to pay out cash to his employees until the crop was harvested. He retained general supervision over what was planted and how the crop was cultivated, and he felt he was more likely to secure a good harvest because the freedmen themselves stood to gain by a large yield. Blacks, too, found the sharecropping system suited to their needs. They had control over how their crops were planted and when they were cultivated and harvested. They could earn more money by working harder in the fields.

The "Breakup" of the Plantation System.

To some observers the disappearance of the slave quarters and the resettling of families in individual, scattered cabins seemed to mark a revolution in the character of Southern agriculture. According to the United States census, the number of Southern landholdings doubled between 1860 and 1880, and their average size dropped from 365 acres to 157 acres. In fact, the census figures are misleading, because the census takers failed to ask farmers whether they owned their land or were sharecroppers. An examination of tax records, which show

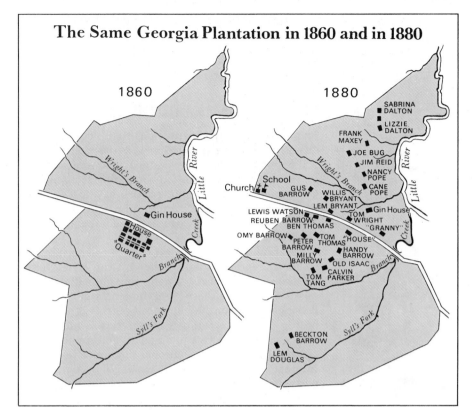

The Same Georgia Plantation in 1860 and in 1880

1860

1880

SABRINA DALTON
LIZZIE DALTON
FRANK MAXEY
JOE BUG
JIM REID
NANCY POPE
CANE POPE
School
Church
GUS BARROW
WILLIS BRYANT
LEM BRYANT
LEWIS WATSON
REUBEN BARROW
BEN THOMAS
TOM WRIGHT
Gin House
"GRANNY"
OMY BARROW
TOM THOMAS
"HOUSE"
PETER BARROW
HANDY BARROW
MILLY BARROW
OLD ISAAC
CALVIN PARKER
TOM TANG
BECKTON BARROW
LEM DOUGLAS

Wright's Branch
Little River
Creek
Branch
Syll's Fork

Gin House
House
"Quarter"
Wright's Branch
Little River
Creek
Branch
Syll's Fork

THE SAME GEORGIA PLANTATION IN 1860 AND 1880
Before the Civil War, slave quarters were located close together, all near the white master's house, so that he could impose order and prevent secret meetings of the blacks. After emancipation, freedmen insisted upon scattering out over the plantation, so that each family could have its own house and some privacy.

landownership, in the representative state of Louisiana helps correct the census distortion. Between 1860 and 1880 in Louisiana, the number of independently owned farms of less than one hundred acres actually dropped by 14 percent, while during the same period the number of plantations increased by 287 percent. By 1900 plantations of one hundred acres or more encompassed half the cultivated land in the state, and more than half the farmers were not proprietors.

If the postwar period did not see the breakup of large plantations, it did bring some significant changes in ownership and control of the land. Hard hit by debt, by rising taxes, and by increasing labor costs, many Southern planters had to sell their holdings, and Northern capital flowed into the region after the war. More tried to cling to their acres by going heavily into debt. Since the postwar Southern banking system was inadequate, the principal source of credit was the local merchant, who could supply both the landowner and his sharecroppers with clothing, shoes, some food, and other necessities to tide them over the lean months between the planting of the tobacco or cotton crop and its harvest. On each sale the merchant charged interest, to be paid when the crop was sold, and he also charged prices ranging from 40 percent to 110 percent

higher for all goods sold on credit. It is hardly surprising that those landowners who could afford to do so set up their own stores and extended credit to their own sharecroppers—and quite soon they discovered they were making more profits from mercantile enterprises than from farming. Planters who could not make such arrangements frequently had to sell their lands to the neighborhood merchant. It is not accidental that in William Faulkner's twentieth-century fictional saga of Southern history, the power of landowning families like the Compsons and the Sutpens diminished during the postwar years, while the Snopes family of storekeepers—hard-trading, pennypinching, and utterly unscrupulous—emerged prosperous and successful.

It would be a mistake, however, to accept without reservation the novelist's hostile characterization of the Southern merchant. The storekeeper insisted on the crop-lien system, which required the farmer legally to pledge that the proceeds from his crop must go first to pay off his obligations to the merchant, because he knew that crops could fail throughout the South, as they did in both 1866 and 1867. And if the merchant urged farmers to forget about soil conservation, diversification, and experimentation with new crops,

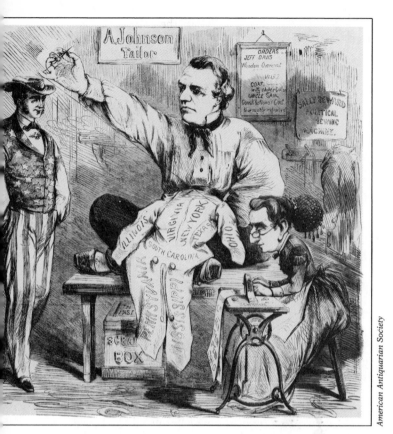

RECONSTRUCTION: UNCLE SAM VISITS THE SHOP OF A. JOHNSON, TAILOR
Taking off from Andrew Johnson's frequent bragging about his humble origins as a tailor, this cartoon shows the president and Secretary of State Seward busily mending Uncle Sam's coat, badly torn by the recently ended Civil War.

he did so because he realized that the only way to pay his own debts was to insist that his debtors raise cotton and tobacco, for which there was a ready cash market.

Thus merchants, landowners, and sharecroppers—white Southerners and black Southerners—became locked into an economic system that, at best, promised them little more than survival. At worst, it offered bankruptcy, sale of lands, and hurried nighttime migrations in an attempt to escape from a set of debts in one state but with little more than the hope of starting a new set in another.

By the 1880s, then, the South had become what it remained for the next half-century—the nation's economic backwater. In 1880 the per capita wealth of the South was $376, compared with per capita wealth outside the South of $1,086. Yet this impoverished region had to deal with some of the most difficult political and racial problems that have ever confronted Americans. In attacking these problems, Southerners, black and white, could expect no assistance from the government, since such intervention would violate the unchanging laws of laissez-faire economics.

Political Parties as a Limit to Change

The most influential institutions that blocked radical change during Reconstruction were the national political parties. The fact that both parties were conglomerates of different and often competing sectional and class interests meant that parties had to decide on their policies through compromise and concession. That process nearly always screened out extreme and drastic measures.

Nationally the Democratic party was torn by two conflicting interests during the postwar years. On the one hand, Democrats sought the immediate readmission of the Southern states under the governments President Johnson had set up. Controlled by whites hostile to the Republican party, these states would surely send Democrats to Congress and support Democratic candidates in a national election. Even during the 1850s, the South had increasingly become a one-party region; now the goal of a solidly Democratic South appeared within reach. On the other hand, too-enthusiastic advocacy of the Southern cause could hurt Democrats in the North by reviving talk of disloyalty and the Copperhead movement during the war. To blunt such attacks, Democrats had no choice but to urge restraint on their colleagues in the former Confederacy.

Among Republicans, similar constraints dampened any ideas of taking vengeance on the South or of encouraging blacks to seize control of that region. From its beginnings the Republican party had been an uneasy alliance of antislavery men, former Whigs, dissatisfied Democrats, and Know-Nothings. The factional disputes that racked Lincoln's administration showed the weakness of the ties that bound these groups together. It was a bad omen for the party that Republicans disagreed most sharply over Lincoln's plan to reorganize the Southern state governments.

Presidential Reconstruction. During the first year after Lincoln's death, quarrels among Republicans were somewhat muted because practically all members of the party joined in opposing President Johnson's program of Reconstruction. Followed by only a handful of Conservative Republicans, including Secretary of State Seward and Navy Secretary Gideon Welles, Johnson began to work closely with the Democrats of the North and South. He announced that the Southern states had never been out of the Union, and he insisted

Library of Congress

PRESIDENT ANDREW JOHNSON
Before the war Andrew Johnson dared to attack the slave-holding oligarchs of the South, and in the secession crisis he fought to keep Tennessee in the Union. He continued to demonstrate such boldness during his presidency—but it was boldness unrelieved by humor, tact, or personal warmth. Charles Dickens thought his face indicated "courage, watchfulness, and certainly strength of purpose," but he found "no genial sunlight in it."

that, under the provisional governments he had set up, they were entitled to be represented in Congress.

It is easy to understand why almost all Republicans—whether they belonged to the Radical or Moderate faction—rejected the president's argument. Members of both these wings of the party were outraged when the Southern elections of 1865, held at the president's direction, resulted in the choice of a Confederate brigadier-general as governor of Mississippi, and they were furious when the new Georgia legislature named Alexander H. Stephens, the vice-president of the Confederacy, to represent that state in the United States Senate.

Republicans had even more reason to fear these newly elected Southern officials because, although many of the Southerners had been Whigs before the war, they clearly contemplated allying themselves with the Democratic party. However much Republi-

cans disagreed among themselves, they all agreed that their party had saved the Union. They believed, with Thaddeus Stevens, "that upon the continued ascendancy of that party depends the safety of this great nation." Now this ascendancy was threatened. What made the threat so grave, and so ironic, was the fact that when the Southern states were readmitted to the Union they would receive increased representation in Congress. Before the Civil War, only three-fifths of the slave population of the South had been counted in apportioning representation in the House of Representatives; but now that the slaves were free men, all would be counted. In short, the Southern states, after having been defeated in the most costly war in the nation's history, would have about fifteen more representatives in Congress than they had before the war. And under the president's plan all Southern Congressmen unquestionably would be Democrats.

Republicans of all factions were equally troubled by the fear of what white Southerners, once restored to authority, would do to the freedmen. The laws that the Southern provisional legislatures adopted during the winter of 1865–66 gave reason for anxiety on this score. Not one of these governments considered treating black citizens just as they treated white citizens. Instead, the legislatures adopted special laws, known as the Black Codes, to regulate the conduct of the freedmen. On the positive side, these laws recognized the freedmen's right to make civil contracts, to sue and be sued, and to acquire and hold most kinds of property. But with these rights went restrictions. The laws varied from state to state, but in general they specified that blacks might not purchase or carry firearms, that they might not assemble after sunset, and that those who were idle or unemployed should "be liable to imprisonment, and to hard labor, one or both, . . . not exceeding twelve months." The Mississippi code prevented blacks from renting or leasing "any lands or tenements except in incorporated cities or towns." That of South Carolina forbade blacks from practicing "the art, trade or business of an artisan, mechanic or shopkeeper, or any other trade, employment or business (besides that of husbandry, or that of a servant)." So clearly did these measures seem designed to keep the freedmen in quasi-slavery that the Chicago *Tribune* spoke for a united, outraged Republican party in denouncing the first of these Black Codes, that adopted by the Mississippi legislature: "We tell the white men of Mississippi that the men of the North will convert the state of Mississippi into a frog-pond before they will allow any such laws to disgrace one foot of soil over which the flag of freedom waves."

The Fourteenth Amendment. For these reasons, all Republicans were unwilling to recognize the regimes Johnson had set up in the South; and when Congress reassembled in December 1865, they easily rallied to block seating of the Southern senators and representatives. All agreed to the creation of a special joint committee on Reconstruction to handle questions concerning the readmission of the Southern states and their further reorganization. In setting up this committee, congressional Republicans carefully balanced its membership with Radicals and Moderates. Its most conspicuous member was the Radical Stevens, but its powerful chairman was Senator William Pitt Fessenden, a Moderate.

Congressional Republicans found it easier to unite in opposing Johnson's plan of Reconstruction than to unite in devising one of their own. Congressional leaders recognized that it would take time to draft and adopt a constitutional amendment and then to have it ratified by the required number of states. Therefore, early in 1866 they agreed on interim legislation that would protect the freedmen. One bill extended and expanded the functions of the Freedmen's Bureau, and a second guaranteed minimal civil rights to all citizens. Contrary to expectations, Johnson vetoed both these measures. Refusing to recognize that these measures represented the wishes of both Moderate and Radical Republicans, the president claimed that they were the work of the Radicals, who wanted "to destroy our institutions and change the character of the Government." He vowed to fight these Northern enemies of the Union just as he had once fought Southern secessionists and traitors. The Republican majority in Congress was not able to override Johnson's veto of the Freedmen's Bureau bill (a later, less sweeping measure extended the life of that agency for two years), but it passed the Civil Rights Act of 1866 over his disapproval.

While relations between the president and the Republicans in Congress were deteriorating, the joint committee on Reconstruction continued to meet and consider various plans for reorganizing the South. With its evenly balanced membership, the committee dismissed the president's theory that the Southern states were already reconstructed and back in the Union, as well as Thaddeus Stevens's view that the Confederacy was conquered territory over which Congress could rule at its own discretion. It also rejected Charles Sumner's more elaborate argument that the Southern states had committed suicide when they seceded, so that their land and inhabitants now fell "under the exclusive jurisdiction of Congress." More acceptable to the majority of Republicans was the "grasp of war" theory advanced by Richard Henry Dana, Jr., the noted Massachusetts constitutional lawyer who was also the author of *Two Years Before the Mast*. Dana argued that the federal government should hold the defeated Confederacy in the grasp of war only for a brief and limited time, during which it must act swiftly to revive state governments in the region and promptly to restore the constitutional balance between national and state authority. Dana's theory was an essentially conservative one: it called for only a short period of federal domination and looked toward the speedy restoration of the Southern states on terms of absolute equality with the loyal states.

Finding in Dana's theory a constitutional source of power, the joint committee after much hard work produced the first comprehensive congressional plan of Reconstruction—the proposed Fourteenth Amendment to the Constitution, which Congress endorsed in June 1866 and submitted to the states for ratification. Some parts of the amendment were noncontroversial. All Republicans accepted its opening statement: "All persons born or naturalized in the United States, and subject to the jurisdiction thereof, are citizens of the United States and of the State wherein they reside." There was also no disagreement about the provision declaring the Confederate debt invalid.

All the other provisions of the amendment, however, represented a compromise between Radical and Moderate Republicans. For example, Radicals wanted to keep all Southerners who had voluntarily supported the Confederacy from voting until 1870. Indeed, the arch-Radical Stevens urged: "Not only to 1870 but 18,070, every rebel who shed the blood of loyal men should be prevented from exercising any power in this Government." Moderates favored a speedy restoration of all political rights to former Confederates. As a compromise, the Fourteenth Amendment excluded high-ranking Confederates from office, but it did not deny them the vote.

Similarly, the Fourteenth Amendment's provisions protecting the freedmen represented a compromise. Radicals like Sumner (who was considered too radical to be given a seat on the joint committee) wanted an outright declaration of the national government's right and duty to protect the civil liberties of the former slaves. But Moderates drew back in alarm from entrusting additional authority to Washington. The joint committee came up with a provision that granted no power to the national government but restricted that of the states: "No State shall make or enforce any law which shall abridge the privileges and immunities of citizens of the United States; nor shall any State deprive any person of life, liberty, or property, without due process of law; nor deny to any person within its jurisdiction the equal protection of the laws."

Finally, another compromise between Radicals and Moderates resulted in the amendment's provision concerning voting. Although Sumner and other Radicals called black suffrage "the essence, the great essential," of a proper Reconstruction policy, Conservatives refused to give the national government power to interfere with the state requirements for voting. The joint committee thereupon devised a complex and, as it proved, unworkable plan to persuade the Southern states voluntarily to enfranchise blacks, under threat of having their representation in Congress reduced if they refused.

The Fourteenth Amendment's feasibility as a program of Reconstruction was never tested because of the outbreak of political warfare between President Johnson and the Republican party, which had elected him vice-president in 1864. During the summer of 1866, Johnson and his friends tried to create a new political party, which would rally behind the president's policies the few Conservative Republicans, the Northern Democrats, and the Southern whites. With the president's hearty approval, a National Union Convention held in Philadelphia in August stressed the theme of harmony among the sections. The entry into the convention hall of delegates from Massachusetts and South Carolina, arm in arm, seemed to symbolize the end of sectional strife. The president himself went on a "swing around the circle" of leading Northern cities, ostensibly on his way to dedicate a monument to the memory of another Democrat, Stephen A. Douglas. In his frequent public speeches he defended the constitutionality of his own Reconstruction program and attacked Congress—and particularly the Radical Republicans—for attempting to subvert the Constitution. In a final effort to consolidate sentiment against Congress, he urged the Southern states not to ratify the proposed Fourteenth Amendment. With the exception of Tennessee, which was controlled by one of Johnson's bitterest personal and political enemies, all the former Confederate states rejected the congressional plan.

The Second Congressional Program of Reconstruction.
When Congress reassembled in December 1866, the Republican majority therefore had to devise a second program of Reconstruction. Cheered by overwhelming victories in the fall congressional elections, Republicans were even less inclined than previously to cooperate with the president, who had gone into political opposition, or to encourage the provisional regimes in the South, which had rejected their first program. Republican suspicion that Southern whites were fundamentally hostile toward the freedmen was strengthened by reports of a race riot in Memphis during May 1866, when a mob of whites joined in a two-day indiscriminate attack on blacks in that city. An even more serious affair occurred four months later in New Orleans, when a white mob, aided by the local police, attacked a black political gathering with what was described as "a cowardly ferocity unsurpassed in the annals of crime." In New Orleans, 45 or 50 blacks were killed, and 150 more were wounded.

Once again, however, the Republican majority in Congress found it easier to agree on what to oppose than on what to favor in the way of Reconstruction legislation. Stevens urged that the South be placed under military rule for a generation and that Southern plantations be sold to pay the national debt. Sumner wanted to deny the vote to large numbers of Southern whites, to require that blacks be given the right to vote, and to create racially integrated schools in the South. Moderate Republicans, on the other hand, were willing to retain the Fourteenth Amendment as the basic framework of congressional Reconstruction and to insist on little else except the ratification of the amendment by the Southern states.

The second congressional program of Reconstruction, embodied in the Military Reconstruction Act of March 2, 1867, represented a compromise between the demands of Radical and Moderate Republican factions. It divided the ten former Confederate states that had not ratified the Fourteenth Amendment into five military districts. In each of these states, there were to be new constitutional conventions, for which black men were allowed to vote. The task of these conventions was to draft new state constitutions that provided for black suffrage, and they were required to ratify the Fourteenth Amendment. When thus reorganized, the Southern states could apply to Congress for readmission to the Union.

It was easy to recognize the radical aspects of this measure, which were pointed out by Democrats during the congressional debates and denounced by President Johnson in his unsuccessful veto of the act. In particular, the requirement of black suffrage, which Sumner sponsored, seemed to Radicals "a prodigious triumph."

In fact, however, most provisions of the Military Reconstruction Act were more acceptable to Moderate than to Radical Republicans. The measure did nothing to give land to the freedmen, to provide education at national expense, or to end racial segregation in the South. It did not erase the boundaries of the Southern states. It did not even sweep away the provisional governments Johnson had established there, although it did make them responsible to the commanders of the new military districts. So conservative was the act in all these respects that Sumner branded it as "horribly defective."

Intent on striking some kind of balance between the Radical and Conservative wings of the Republican party, the framers of the Military Reconstruction Act drafted the measure carelessly. As Sumner had pre-

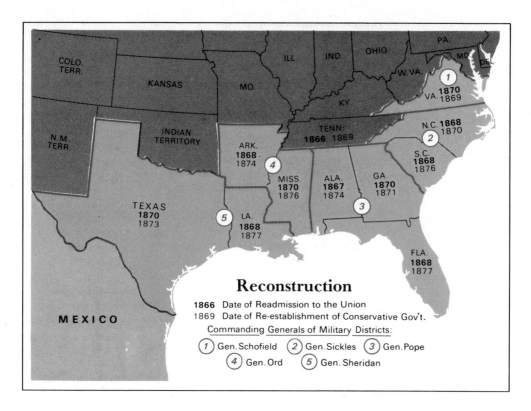

Reconstruction

1866 Date of Readmission to the Union
1869 Date of Re-establishment of Conservative Gov't.
<u>Commanding Generals of Military Districts:</u>

(1) Gen. Schofield (2) Gen. Sickles (3) Gen. Pope

(4) Gen. Ord (5) Gen. Sheridan

dicted, the act promptly proved to furnish "Reconstruction without machinery or motive power." Having to choose between military rule and black suffrage, the Southern provisional governments chose the former, correctly believing that army officers generally sympathized with white supremacy. To get the Reconstruction process under way, Congress therefore had to enact a supplementary law (March 23, 1867), requiring the federal commanders in the South to take the initiative, when the local governments did not, in announcing elections, registering voters, and convening constitutional conventions. During the summer of 1867, as the president, the attorney general, and Southern state officials tried by legalistic interpretations to delay the Reconstruction program, Congress had to pass two further supplementary acts, explaining the "true intent and meaning" of the previous legislation.

With these measures, the congressional Reconstruction legislation affecting the South was substantially completed. Both the first and the second congressional plans of Reconstruction were compromises between the Radical and the Moderate factions in the Republican party. The Radicals' insistence on change was essential in securing the adoption of this legislation, but the Moderates blocked all measures that would have revolutionary social or economic consequences in the South.

Impeachment. The same need to compromise between the factions of the Republican party dictated Congress's policy toward the president during the Reconstruction years. Almost all Republicans were suspicious of the president and feared that he intended to turn the South over to Confederate rule. Johnson's repeated veto messages, assailing carefully balanced compromise legislation as the work of Radicals and attacking Congress as an unconstitutional body since it refused to seat congressmen from all the states, angered Republicans of both factions. Therefore, most Republicans wanted to keep a close eye on the president and sought to curb executive powers that had grown during the war. In 1867, fearing that Johnson would use his power as commander in chief to subvert their Reconstruction legislation, Republican factions joined to pass an army appropriations bill that required all military orders to the army—including those of the president himself—to go through the hands of General Grant. Suspecting that Johnson wanted to use the federal patronage to build up a political machine of his own, they adopted at the same time the Tenure of Office Act, which required the president to secure the Senate's consent not merely when he appointed officials, but also when he removed them.

The Republicans in Congress were prepared to go this far in impressive unanimity—but no farther. When Radical Republican James M. Ashley in January

"AWKWARD COLLISION ON THE GRAND TRUNK COLUMBIA RAILROAD"

This cartoon depicts presidential and congressional Reconstruction as two engines going in opposite directions on the same rails. Andrew Johnson, driver of the locomotive "President," says: "Look here! One of us has got to back." But Thaddeus Stevens, driver of the locomotive "Congress," replies: "Well, it ain't going to be me that's going to do it, you bet!"

1867 moved to impeach the president, he was permitted to conduct a half-serious, half-comic investigation of Johnson's alleged involvement in Lincoln's assassination, his purported sale of pardons, and other trumped-up charges. But when Ashley's motion reached the House floor, Moderate Republicans saw that it was soundly defeated.

A subsequent attempt at impeachment fared better, but it also revealed how the Radical and Moderate factions blocked each other. In August 1867, President Johnson suspended from office Secretary of War Edwin M. Stanton, whom he correctly suspected of having collaborated closely with the Radicals in Congress. As required by the Tenure of Office Act, he asked the Senate to consent to the removal. When the Senate refused, the president removed Stanton and ordered him to surrender his office. News of this seemingly open defiance of the law caused Republicans in the House of Representatives to rush through a resolution

impeaching the president, without waiting for specific charges against him to be drawn up.

The trial of President Johnson (who was not present in court but was represented by his lawyers) was a test of strength not merely between Congress and the chief executive, but also between the Radical and the Moderate Republicans. Impeachment managers from the House of Representatives presented eleven charges against the president, mostly accusing him of violating the Tenure of Office Act but also censuring his repeated attacks upon Congress. With fierce joy Radical Thaddeus Stevens, who was one of the managers, denounced the president: "Unfortunate man! thus surrounded, hampered, tangled in the meshes of his own wickedness—unfortunate, unhappy man, behold your doom!"

But Radical oratory could not persuade Moderate Republicans and Democrats to vote for conviction. They listened as Johnson's lawyers challenged the constitutionality of the Tenure of Office Act, showed that it had not been intended to apply to cabinet members, and proved that, in any case, it did not cover Stanton, who had been appointed by Lincoln, not Johnson. When the critical vote came, Moderate Republicans like Fessenden voted to acquit the president, and Johnson's Radical foes lacked one vote of the two-thirds majority required to convict him. Several other Republican Senators who for political expedience voted against the president were prepared to change their votes and favor acquittal if their ballots were needed.

Nothing more clearly shows how the institutional needs of a political party prevented drastic change than did this decision not to remove a president whom a majority in Congress hated and feared. The desire to maintain the unity of the national Republican party, despite frequent quarrels and endless bickering, overrode the wishes of individual congressmen. Throughout the Reconstruction period Moderate Republicans felt that they were constantly being rushed from one advanced position to another in order to placate the Radicals, who were never satisfied. More accurately, Radical Republicans perceived that the need to retain Moderate support prevented the adoption of any really revolutionary Reconstruction program.

Racism as a Limit to Change

A final set of beliefs that limited the nature of the changes imposed upon, and accepted by, the South during the Reconstruction period can be labeled racism. In all parts of the country, white Americans looked with suspicion and fear upon those whose skin was of a different color. For example, in California white hatred built up against the Chinese, who had

ANTI-CHINESE AGITATION IN SAN FRANCISCO: A MEETING OF THE WORKINGMEN'S PARTY ON THE SAND LOTS
Racism in postwar America took many forms. In California its strongest manifestation was in the hostility toward the Chinese immigrants stirred up by Dennis Kearney's Workingman's party.

begun coming to that state in great numbers after the discovery of gold and who were later imported by the thousands to help construct the Central Pacific Railroad. White workers resented the willingness of the Chinese to work long hours for "coolies'" wages; they distrusted the unfamiliar dress, diet, and habits of the Chinese; and they disliked all these things more because the Chinese were a yellow-skinned people. Under the leadership of a newly arrived Irish immigrant, Dennis Kearney, white laborers organized a workingman's party with the slogan, "The Chinese must go."

The depression that gripped the nation in 1873* gave impetus to the anti-Chinese movement. Day after day thousands of the unemployed gathered in the San Francisco sand lots to hear Kearney's slashing attacks on the Chinese and on the wealthy corporations that employed them. In the summer of 1877, San Francisco hoodlums, inspired by Kearney, burned twenty-five

*For the Panic of 1873, see chapter 21, pp. 535–36.

Chinese laundries and destroyed dozens of Chinese homes. The movement had enough political strength to force both major parties in California to adopt anti-Chinese platforms, and California congressmen succeeded in persuading their colleagues to pass a bill limiting the number of Chinese who could be brought into the United States each year. Since the measure clearly conflicted with treaty arrangements with China, President Rutherford B. Hayes vetoed it, but he had his secretary of state initiate negotiations leading to a new treaty that permitted the restriction of immigration. Congress in 1882 passed the Chinese Exclusion Act, which suspended all Chinese immigration for ten years and forbade the naturalization of Chinese already in the country.

Northern Views of the Black Race.

If white Americans became so agitated over a small number of Chinese, who were unquestionably hard-working and thrifty and who belonged to one of the most ancient of civilizations, it is easy to see how whites could consider blacks an even greater danger. There were more than 3 million blacks in the United States, most of them recently emancipated from slavery. The exploits of black soldiers during the war—their very discipline and courage—proved that blacks could be formidable opponents. The fact that blacks were no longer portrayed as invisible men but now, in photographs and caricatures, had sharply etched identities worsened, rather than relieved, white fears. More than ever before, blacks seemed distinctive, alien, and menacing.

Most American intellectuals of the Civil War generation accepted black inferiority unquestioningly. Although a few reformers like Charles Sumner vigorously attacked this notion, a majority of philanthropic Northerners accepted the judgment of the distinguished Harvard scientist Louis Agassiz concerning blacks. He held that while whites during antiquity were developing high civilizations, "the negro race groped in barbarism and never originated a regular organization among themselves." Many adopted Agassiz's belief that blacks, once free, would inevitably die out in the United States. Others reached the same conclusion by studying Charles Darwin's recently published *Origin of Species* (1859), and they accepted the argument put forward by Darwin's admirers that in the inevitable struggle for survival "higher civilized races" must inevitably eliminate "an endless number of lower races." Consequently the influential and tenderhearted Congregational minister Horace Bushnell could prophesy the approaching end of the black race in the United States with something approaching smugness. "Since we must all die," he asked rhetorically, "why should it grieve us, that a stock thousands of years behind, in the scale of culture, should die with few and still fewer children to succeed, till finally the whole succession remains in the more cultivated race?"

When even the leaders of Northern society held such views, it is hardly surprising that most whites in the region were openly antiblack. In state after state whites fiercely resisted efforts to extend the political and civil rights of blacks, partly because they feared that any improvement in the condition of blacks in the North would lead to a huge influx of blacks from the South. At the end of the Civil War only Maine, New Hampshire, Vermont, Massachusetts, and Rhode Island allowed blacks to have full voting rights; in New York only blacks who met certain property-holding qualifications could have the ballot. During the next three years in referenda held in Connecticut, Wisconsin, Kansas, Ohio, Michigan, and Missouri, constitutional amendments authorizing black suffrage were defeated, and in New York voters rejected a proposal to eliminate the property-holding qualifications for black voters. Only in Iowa, a state where there were very few blacks, did a black suffrage amendment carry in 1868, and that same year Minnesota adopted an ambiguously worded amendment. Thus at the end of the 1860s, most Northern states refused to give black men the ballot.

In words as well as in votes, the majority of Northerners made their deeply racist feelings evident. The Democratic press constantly cultivated the racial fears of its readers and regularly portrayed the Republicans as planning a "new era of miscegenation, amalgamation, and promiscuous intercourse between the races." From the White House, denouncing Republican attempts "to Africanize the [Southern] half of our country," President Andrew Johnson announced: "In the progress of nations negroes have shown less capacity for self-government than any other race of people. . . . Whenever they have been left to their own devices they have shown an instant tendency to relapse into barbarism." Even Northern Republicans opposed to Johnson shared many of his racist views. Radical Senator Timothy O. Howe of Wisconsin declared that he regarded "the freedmen, in the main . . . as so much animal life," and Senator Benjamin F. Wade of Ohio, whom the Radical Republicans would have elevated to the presidency had they removed Johnson, had both a genuine devotion to the principle of equal rights and an incurable dislike of blacks. Representative George W. Julian of Indiana, one of the few Northern congressmen who had no racial prejudice, bluntly told his colleagues in 1866: "The real trouble is that *we hate the negro*. It is not his ignorance that offends us, but his color. . . . Of this fact I entertain no doubt whatsoever."

Both personal preferences and the wishes of their constituents inhibited Northern Republicans from supporting measures that might have altered race relations. When Sumner sought to remove from the books federal laws that recognized slavery or to prohibit racial discrimination on public transportation in the District of Columbia, his colleagues replied: "God has made the negro inferior, and . . . laws cannot make him equal." Such congressmen were hardly in a position to scold the South for racial discrimination or to insist on drastic social change in that region.

Southern Views of the Black Race. If racism limited the innovation that Northerners were willing to propose during the Reconstruction period, it even more drastically reduced the amount of change that white Southerners were prepared to accept. Racial bigotry runs through both the private correspondence and the public pronouncements of Southern whites during the

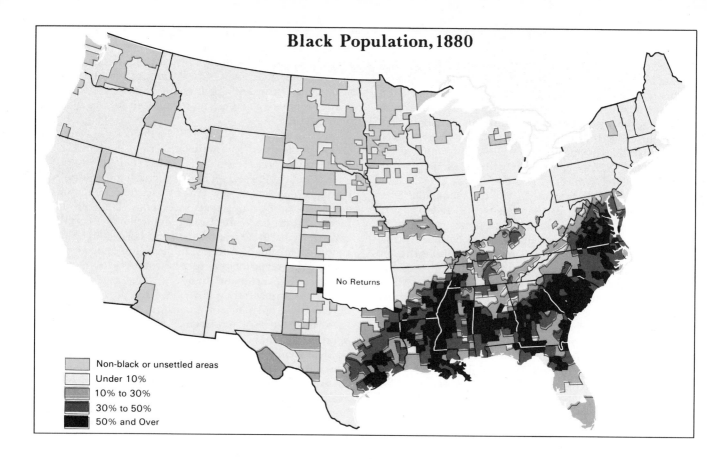

Black Population, 1880

Legend:
- Non-black or unsettled areas
- Under 10%
- 10% to 30%
- 30% to 50%
- 50% and Over

No Returns

postwar era. "Equality does not exist between blacks and whites," announced Alexander H. Stephens. "The one race is by nature inferior in many respects, physically and mentally, to the other. This should be received as a fixed invincible fact in all dealings with the subject." A North Carolina diarist agreed: "The Anglo-Saxon and the African can never be equal . . . one or the other must fall." Or, as the Democratic party of Louisiana resolved in its 1865 platform: "We hold this to be a Government of white people, made and to be perpetuated for the exclusive benefit of the white race; and . . . that people of African descent cannot be considered as citizens of the United States, and that there can, in no event, nor under any circumstances, be any equality between the white and other races." The Black Codes were the legal embodiment of these attitudes.

These racist views shaped the attitudes of most Southern whites toward the whole process of Reconstruction. White Southerners approved of President Johnson's plan of Reconstruction because it placed government in the Southern states entirely in the hands of whites. They rejected the Fourteenth Amendment primarily because it made blacks legally equal to whites. They watched with utter disbelief as Con-

gress passed the 1867 Military Reconstruction Act, for they simply could not imagine that the freedmen were to vote. Stunned, they saw army officers supervise voter registration—a process that excluded many prominent whites who had participated in the Confederate government but included more than 700,000 blacks, who formed a majority of the eligible voters in South Carolina, Florida, Alabama, Mississippi, and Louisiana. Knowing that these black voters were well organized by the Union League, often with the assistance of agents of the Freedmen's Bureau, whites were more apathetic than surprised when the fall elections showed heavy majorities in favor of convening new constitutional conventions.*

With hostile and unbelieving eyes, most Southern whites observed the work of these conventions, which between November 1867 and May 1868 drafted new constitutions for the former Confederate states. To Southern whites unaccustomed to seeing blacks in any positions of public prominence, the presence of freedmen in these conventions meant that they were black-

---

*The Texas election was not held until February 1868. Tennessee had no election, because it had already been readmitted to the Union.

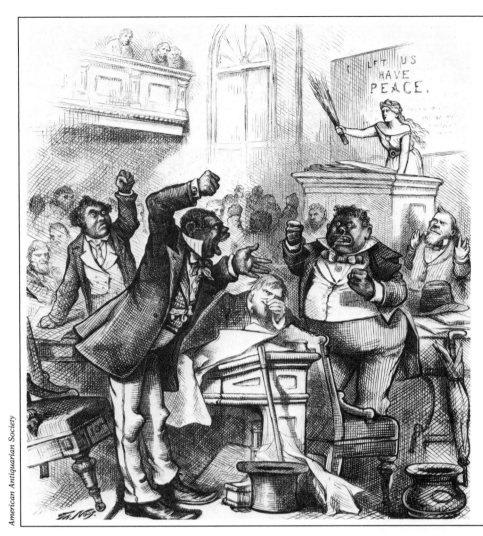

LET US
HAVE
PEACE.

"COLORED RULE IN A RECONSTRUCTED (?) STATE," BY THOMAS NAST

As postwar racism mounted, cartoonists no longer depicted Negroes as handsome, intelligent fighters for freedom but painted them as grotesque and animal-like. In addition to perpetuating racial stereotypes, this drawing exaggerates the number and influence of blacks in the Southern legislatures.

dominated. In fact, except in the South Carolina convention, in which blacks did form a majority, only between one-fourth and one-ninth of the delegates were blacks. Whites ridiculed the black members' ignorance of parliamentary procedures, and they laughed sarcastically when they read about how the "coal black" temporary chairman of the Louisiana convention put a question by asking those who favored a motion "to rise an stan on der feet" and then directing "all you contrairy men to rise."

Racial prejudice also determined Southern whites' reactions to the constitutions produced by these conventions. Generally the whites denounced these new charters as "totally incompatible with the prosperity and liberty of the people." In fact the constitutions, often copied from Northern models, were generally improvements over the ones they replaced. In addition to giving blacks the right to vote (as Congress

had directed), they promised all citizens of the state equality before the law. They reformed financial and revenue systems, reorganized the judiciary, improved the organization of local government, and, most important of all, instituted a state-supported system of public education, hitherto notably lacking in most Southern states.

The Reconstruction Governments in the South. Because these constitutions guaranteed racial equality, Southern whites tried, without great success, to block their ratification. In Alabama whites boycotted the ratification election; in Mississippi they cast a majority of votes against the new constitution. In Virginia ratification was delayed because the conservative army commander of that district discovered that there was no money to hold an election, and in Texas all moves toward the creation of a new government lagged several months behind those in the Eastern states. But despite all the foot dragging, new governments were set up, and in June 1868 Congress readmitted representatives and senators from Alabama, Arkansas, Florida, Georgia, Louisiana, North Carolina, and South Carolina. Two years later the Reconstruction of Virginia, Mississippi, and Texas was completed, and in early 1870 these states were also readmitted. Meanwhile Georgia experienced one further reorganization after its state legislature attempted to exclude blacks who had been elected to it. But by 1871, when the Georgia senators and representatives again took their seats in Congress, all the states of the former Confederacy had undergone Reconstruction and had been readmitted to the Union.

Most Southern whites were bitterly hostile to this reorganization of their state governments. The name "Black Reconstruction," as they called the ensuing period of Republican domination in the South, reveals the racial bias behind their opposition. In fact, these Southern state governments were not dominated by blacks, and blacks held a smaller proportion of offices than their percentage of the population. Blacks dominated the state legislature only in South Carolina. No black was elected governor, although there were black lieutenant governors in South Carolina, Louisiana, and Mississippi. Only in South Carolina was there a black supreme court justice. During the entire Reconstruction period only two blacks served in the United States Senate—Hiram R. Revels and Blanche K. Bruce, both from Mississippi and both men of exceptional ability and integrity. Only fifteen blacks were elected to the House of Representatives.

Even to the most racist Southern whites, it was obvious that most of the leaders of the Republican party in the South, and a large part of the Republican following as well, were white. Racists called the Northern-born white Republicans carpetbaggers because they allegedly came South with no more worldly possessions than could be packed into a carpetbag (a small suitcase), ready to live on and exploit the conquered region. The term, with its implication of corruption, was applied indiscriminately to men of Northern birth who had lived in the South long before the war, as well as to newly arrived fortune hunters, many of them recently discharged Union army officers.

Southern-born white Republicans were called scalawags, a term that cattle drivers applied to "the mean, lousy and filthy kine [cattle] that are not fit for butchers or dogs." Again the term was used indiscriminately. Southern racists applied it to poor hill-country whites, who had long been at odds with the plantation owners in states like North Carolina and Alabama and now joined the Republican party as a way of getting back at their old enemies. But other scalawags were members of the plantation-owning, mercantile, and industrial classes of the South. Many were former Whigs who distrusted the Democrats, and they felt at home in a Republican party that favored protective tariffs, subsidies for railroads, and appropriations for rebuilding the levees along the Mississippi River. A surprising number of Southern-born white Republicans were former high-ranking officers in the Confederate army, like General P. G. T. Beauregard and General James Longstreet, who knew at first hand the extent of the damage caused by the war and were willing to accept the victors' terms promptly.

Bitterly as they attacked these white Republicans, Southern Democrats reserved their worst abuse for blacks. They saw in every measure adopted by the new state governments evidence of black incompetence, extravagance, or even barbarism. In truth, much that these state governments did supplied the Democrats with ammunition. The postwar period was one of low political morality, and there was no reason to expect that newly enfranchised blacks would prove any less attracted by the profits of politics than anybody else. Petty corruption prevailed in all the Southern state governments. Louisiana legislators voted themselves an allowance for stationery—which covered purchases of hams and bottles of champagne. The South Carolina legislature ran up a bill of more than $50,000 in refurbishing the statehouse with such costly items as a $750 mirror, $480 clocks, and two hundred porcelain spittoons at $8 apiece. The same legislature voted $1,000 to the Speaker of the House of Representatives to repay his losses on a horse race.

Bad as these excesses were, Southern Democrats were angered less by them than by the legitimate work performed by the new state governments. Unwilling to recognize that blacks were now equal citizens, they objected to expenditures for hospitals, jails, orphanages, and asylums to care for blacks. Most of all they objected to the creation of a public school system. There was considerable hostility throughout the South to the idea of educating any children at the cost of the taxpayer, and the thought of paying taxes in order to teach black children seemed a wild and foolish extravagance. The fact that black schools were mostly conducted by Northern whites, usually women, who came South with a reforming mission, did nothing to increase popular support. Too many of the teachers stated plainly and publicly their intention to use "every endeavor to throw a ray of light here and there, among this benighted race of ruffians, rebels by nature." Adding to all these hostilities was a fear that a system of public education might someday lead to a racially integrated system of education.

These apprehensions had little basis in fact, for during the entire period of Reconstruction in the whole South there were significant numbers of children in racially mixed schools only in New Orleans between 1870 and 1874.

The Ku Klux Klan. Not content with criticizing Republican rule, Southern Democrats organized to put an end to it. They made a two-pronged attack. On the one hand, they sought to intimidate or to drive from the South whites who cooperated politically with the Republican regimes. On the other hand, they tried to terrorize and silence blacks, especially those active in politics. Much of this pressure was informal and occasional, but much was the work of racist organizations that sprang up all over the South during the postwar years. The most famous of these was the Ku Klux Klan, which originated in 1866 as a social club for young white men in Pulaski, Tennessee. As the Military Reconstruction Act went into effect and the possibility of black participation in Southern political life became increasingly real, racists saw new potential in this secret organization with its mysterious name and its bizarre uniforms of long flowing robes, high conical hats that made the wearers seem unnaturally tall, and white face masks.

In 1867 the Klan was reorganized under a new constitution that provided for local dens, each headed by a Grand Cyclops. The dens were linked together into provinces (counties), each under a Grand Titan, and in turn into realms (states), each under a Grand Dragon. At the head of the whole organization was the Grand Wizard—who, according to most reports, was former Confederate General Nathan Bedford Forrest. Probably this elaborate organizational structure was never completely filled out, and certainly there was an almost total lack of central control of the Klan's activities. Indeed, at some point in early 1869 the Klan was officially disbanded. But even without central direction its members, like those of the Order of the White Camellia and other racist vigilante groups, continued in their plan of disrupting the new Republican regimes in the South and terrorizing the blacks who supported these administrations.

Along with other vigilante organizations, the Klan expressed traditional Southern white racism. White Southerners were willing to accept the defeat of the Confederacy and were prepared to admit that slavery was dead. But they could not bring themselves to contemplate a society that would treat blacks and whites as equals. As a group of South Carolina whites protested to Congress in 1868: "The white people of our State will never quietly submit to negro rule. . . . We will keep up this contest until we have regained the heritage of political control handed down to us by

honored ancestry. That is a duty we owe to the land that is ours, to the graves that it contains, and to the race of which you and we alike are members—the proud Caucasian race, whose sovereignty on earth God has ordained."

The appeal was shrewdly pitched, for the Southern racist knew how to reach his Northern counterpart. Joined together, their fears of men with darker skins helped to undercut the Reconstruction regimes in the South and to halt any congressional efforts at further innovative Reconstruction legislation.

The Restoration of "Home Rule"

The effectiveness of these limitations on social and political experimentation in the South became evident as early as the fall elections of 1867, to elect governors and state legislators and to fill vacancies in the House of Representatives. The Democrats won by a landslide. Responding to the popular mood of conservatism, the Republican party in 1868 passed over Radical presidential candidates like Benjamin F. Wade and nominated Ulysses S. Grant, who had only recently affiliated with the Republicans but whose broad popular appeal as a military hero was unrivaled. Elected by a surprisingly narrow margin over the Democratic candidate, former Governor Horatio Seymour of New York, Grant shrewdly sized up the country's attitude toward Reconstruction. In his inaugural address Grant announced his policy: "Let us have peace."

Just what he meant was not immediately clear. Some thought the new president was appealing to the white Ku Kluxers who were trying to overthrow the Reconstruction governments in the South; others believed that he was speaking to Northern Radicals who wanted to bring about further changes in Southern society. As it proved, Grant had both extremes in mind. On the one hand, the president warmly supported the immediate and unconditional readmission of Virginia to the Union, even though Radicals like Sumner warned that the Virginia legislature was "composed of recent Rebels still filled and seething with that old Rebel fire." On the other hand, Grant was outraged by the terrorism rampant in the South, and he insisted that Congress pass a series of Enforcement Acts (1870–71) enabling him to crush the Ku Klux Klan. Under this legislation the president proclaimed martial law in nine South Carolina counties in which white terrorists were most active, and federal marshals arrested many suspected Klansmen in North Carolina, Mississippi, and other Southern states. In brief, then, Grant's policy was to warn Southern whites that the national government would not tolerate open violence and organized military activity—

1868 REPUBLICAN CAMPAIGN POSTER
Because of Democratic victories in the 1867 elections, the Republicans passed over the leaders of the party—Wade, Sumner, Stevens—and nominated the politically inexperienced but widely popular General Grant. His running mate was Schuyler ("Smiler") Colfax, an Indiana congressman who had made an agreeable Speaker of the House of Representatives. In 1868 the party still retained "National Union"—the label under which Lincoln had run in 1864—as part of its official title, in the hope of attracting Democratic and independent voters.

but to let them understand that at the same time they would not be harassed if they regained control of their state governments through less revolutionary tactics.

The "Redemption" of the South.

Southern whites quickly accepted the hint. They promptly undertook the restoration of what they called home rule—the rule of native white Democrats. Aware of Northern sensitivities, they now downplayed, when possible, the more brutal forms of terrorism and outright violence. White Republicans had to face social pressure and economic boycott; many fled the South, and others joined the Redeemers (as the advocates of home rule and white supremacy liked to call themselves). Redeemers exerted economic pressure on blacks by threatening not to hire or extend credit to those who were politically active.

In several states whites organized rifle clubs, which practiced marksmanship on the outskirts of Republican political rallies. Usually blacks were cowed by these tactics. In a few cases, however, they organized and tried to defend themselves. On such occasions there occurred what Southern newspapers called race riots—a better term would have been "massacres," for the more numerous and better-armed whites overpowered the blacks and slaughtered their leaders. In state after state, Republican governors appealed to Washington for additional federal troops, but Grant refused, convinced that the public was tired of "these annual autumnal outbreaks" in the South.

In consequence of Grant's policy, the Redeemers quickly seized power in Virginia, North Carolina, Tennessee, and Georgia. In 1875 they won control of Alabama, Mississippi, Arkansas, and Texas, and early in 1877 they ended Republican rule in Florida. By the end of Grant's second administration, South Carolina and Louisiana were the only Southern states with Republican governments.

The Election of 1876.

The fate of these two remaining Republican regimes in the South became intricately connected with the outcome of the 1876 presidential election. The Democratic nominee, Samuel J. Tilden, undoubtedly received a majority of the popular votes cast—although, equally undoubtedly, thousands of blacks who would have voted for his Republican rival, Rutherford B. Hayes, were kept from the polls. But Tilden lacked one vote of having a majority in the electoral college unless he received some of the votes from South Carolina, Florida, and Louisiana, all of which submitted to Congress competing sets of Democratic and Republican ballots. (There was also a technical question of the eligibility of one Republican elector from Oregon.)

Congress therefore confronted a crisis when it assembled in December 1876. If it decided to accept the disputed Democratic electoral votes, Republican control of the White House would be broken for the first time in a quarter of a century and the Reconstruction of the South would be ended. If Congress accepted the Republican electoral votes, that decision would run contrary to the will of a majority of the voters in the country.

Thus to resolve the impasse a compromise was needed—and not just a single compromise, but a complicated, interlocking set of bargains. After elaborate and secret negotiations, several agreements were reached. First, Congress decided that the disputed electoral votes should be referred to a special electoral commission, which should consist of five members from the House of Representatives, five members from the Senate, and five associate justices of the Supreme

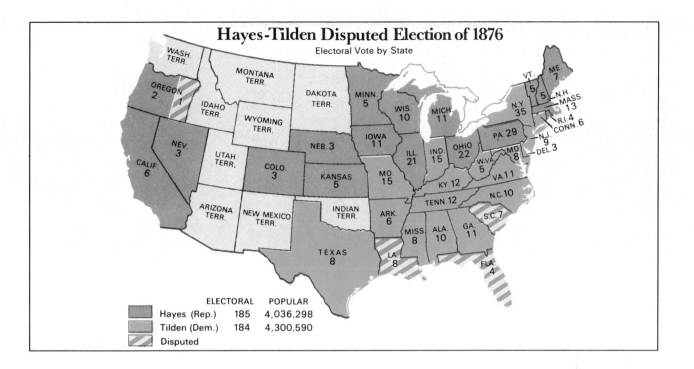

Hayes-Tilden Disputed Election of 1876

Electoral Vote by State

	ELECTORAL	POPULAR
Hayes (Rep.)	185	4,036,298
Tilden (Dem.)	184	4,300,590
Disputed		

Court. This body was composed of eight Republicans and seven Democrats, and on every disputed ballot the commission ruled in favor of Hayes by the same eight-to-seven vote. In consequence of these decisions, Tilden's electoral vote remained at 184, while Hayes's slowly mounted to 185. In March 1877, for the fifth time in succession, a Republican president was inaugurated.

Democrats reluctantly accepted Hayes's election because of some other bargaining that took place while the electoral votes were being counted. One set of compromises came to be known as the Wormley agreement because it was negotiated in the luxurious Washington hotel owned by the black restaurateur James Wormley. Representing Hayes at these sessions were Senator John Sherman, Representative James A. Garfield, and other prominent Republicans. Across the table sat Southern Democratic leaders, including Senator John B. Gordon, the former Confederate general who now represented Georgia in Congress, and L. Q. C. Lamar, once the Confederate envoy to Russia and now a senator from Mississippi. The Republicans promised the Southerners that, if allowed to be inaugurated, Hayes "would deal justly and generously with the South." Translated, this statement meant that Hayes would withdraw the remaining federal troops from the South and allow the overthrow of the Republican regimes in South Carolina and Louisiana. The Southerners found the terms acceptable, and they promptly leaked the news of the agreement, so as to protect themselves from charges that they had betrayed their section.

Behind the Wormley agreement lay other, less formal, compromises. Hayes's backers promised that the new president would not use federal patronage in the South to defeat the Democrats. They further pledged that he would support congressional appropriations for rebuilding levees along the flood-ridden Mississippi River and for construction of a transcontinental railroad along a Southern route. In return, Southerners agreed to allow the Republicans to elect Garfield Speaker of the new House of Representatives—a position that gave him the power to determine the membership of congressional committees. More important, the Southerners promised to protect the basic rights of blacks, as guaranteed in the Thirteenth, Fourteenth, and Fifteenth amendments to the Constitution.

Virtually all these informal agreements were ignored by both sides once Hayes was inaugurated. For his part, Hayes ordered the removal of federal troops from the South and did appoint a Southerner, former Confederate David M. Key, to his cabinet as postmaster general. But two-thirds of the federal officeholders in the South remained Republicans. Hayes changed his mind about supporting a Southern transcontinental railroad, alleging that federal funding would lead to corruption.

Southern Democrats likewise went back on their promise to support Garfield for Speaker. They eagerly

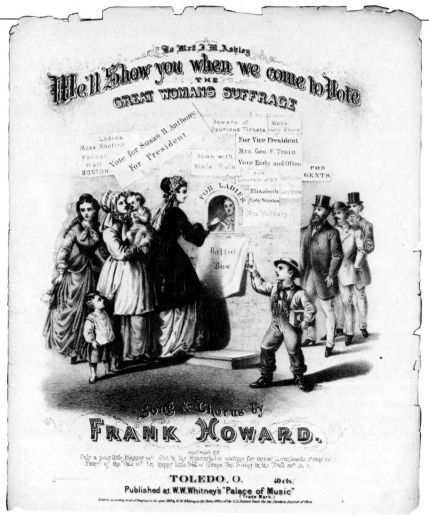

"WE'LL SHOW YOU WHEN WE COME TO VOTE"
The attitude of Northern women contributed to the declining interest in the problems of the South. Many women who had loyally supported the war and emancipation felt that they, as well as the freedmen, should have been enfranchised under the Reconstruction amendments to the Constitution. In 1869 Elizabeth Cady Stanton, Susan B. Anthony, and others organized the National Woman Suffrage Association to promote a sixteenth amendment to the Constitution, enfranchising women.

joined in an investigation of alleged fraud in Hayes's election once the House was organized under Democratic leadership. Only a very few Southern Democratic politicians, among them Governor Wade Hampton of South Carolina, remembered their promise to respect the rights of blacks. Instead, almost all took the final withdrawal of federal troops from the South as a signal that blacks, already put in a position of economic inferiority, could also be excluded from Southern political life.

Disfranchisement of Blacks.
Southern whites moved steadily and successfully to reduce black voting, although they had to act cautiously, so as not to offend public opinion in the North or to invite renewed federal intervention. One of the simplest devices was the poll tax, adopted in Georgia in 1877 and quickly copied by other Southern states. To Northerners the require-

ment that a voter pay $1 or $2 a year did not seem unreasonable. Yet since three-fourths of the entire Southern population had an average income of only $55.16 in 1880, the poll tax was a considerable financial drain, especially to poverty-stricken blacks. More imaginative was the "eight box" law adopted by South Carolina in 1882 and imitated by North Carolina and Florida. Under this system ballots for each contested race had to be deposited in separate boxes—one for governor, one for sheriff, and so forth. The system frustrated the illiterate black voter, who could no longer bring to the polls a single ballot, marked for him in advance by a Republican friend. To make the task of semiliterate voters more difficult, election officials periodically rearranged the order of the boxes. Still another device, which did not become popular until the late 1880s, was the secret ballot, also called the Australian ballot. The secret ballot was supposedly introduced in the South, as in the North, to prevent fraud. But actually it discriminated heavily against blacks, for as late as 1900 the number of illiterate black males ranged from 39 percent in Florida to 61 percent in Louisiana.

Despite all these obstacles, Southern blacks continued to vote in surprising numbers. In the 1880 presidential election, for example, more than 70 percent of the eligible blacks voted in Arkansas, Florida, North Carolina, Tennessee, and Virginia, and between 50 percent and 70 percent voted in Alabama, Louisiana, South Carolina, and Texas. These black voters posed a double threat to the Redeemers. Black voters were numerous enough that ambitious Northern Republicans, hoping to break the now solidly Democratic South, might be tempted again to try federal intervention in state elections. Even more dangerous was the possibility that Southern poor whites, whose needs for public education and welfare were consistently neglected by the business-oriented Redeemers, might find common cause with the poor blacks.

The Redeemers saw both these dangers materialize after 1890. Shortly after the Republicans gained control of the House of Representatives in 1889, Representative Henry Cabot Lodge of Massachusetts introduced a strong bill for federal control of elections, which promptly became known as the Force Bill. Although Democrats in the Senate defeated Lodge's bill in January 1891, Redeemers saw in it a threat to renew "all the horrors of reconstruction days." Their fear was doubtless greater because the almost simultaneous rise of the Populist movement threatened, as never before, to split the white voters of the region.* The Populist party appealed to farmers and to small planters and was the enemy of lawyers, bankers, and the rising commercial and industrial spokesmen of the so-called New South. Some of the Populist leaders, like Thomas Watson of Georgia, openly criticized the

*For the rise of the Populist movement, see chapter 23.

Redeemers' policy of repressing the blacks and seemed to be flirting with the black voters.

Faced with this double threat, Southern states moved swiftly to exclude the blacks completely and permanently from politics. Mississippi led the way with a constitutional convention in 1890 that required voters to be able to read and interpret the Constitution to the satisfaction of white registration officials. It is not hard to imagine how difficult even a graduate of the Howard University Law School would have found this task. In 1898 a Louisiana constitutional convention improved on the Mississippi example by requiring that a literacy test be passed by all voters except the sons and grandsons of persons who had voted in state elections before 1867. Since no Louisiana blacks had been permitted to vote before that date, this provision allowed illiterate whites to vote, while the literacy test excluded most black voters.

State after state across the South followed, or elaborated on, these requirements. South Carolina held a disfranchising convention in 1895. North Carolina amended its constitution to limit voting in 1900. Alabama and Virginia acted in 1901–02, and Georgia adopted a restrictive constitutional amendment in 1908. The remaining Southern states continued to rely on the poll tax and other varieties of legislative disfranchisement. When opponents of these measures accused their advocates of discriminating against blacks, Senator Carter Glass of Virginia replied for his entire generation: "Discrimination! Why that is precisely what we propose; that exactly is what this convention was elected for."

It took time, then, for the complete working out of the political compromises of the Reconstruction era. Not until the end of the nineteenth century did white Southerners receive the full price they had demanded in permitting the election of Rutherford B. Hayes. But by 1900 that payment had been made in full. The black man was no longer a political force in the South, and the Republican party was no longer the defender of black rights.

1865 Lincoln assassinated; Andrew Johnson becomes president.

Johnson moves for speedy, lenient restoration of Southern states to Union.

Congress creates Joint Committee of Fifteen to supervise Reconstruction process.

Thirteenth Amendment ratified.

1866 Johnson breaks with Republican majority in Congress by vetoing Freedmen's Bureau bill and Civil Rights bill. Latter is passed over his veto.

Congress approves Fourteenth Amendment and submits it to states for ratification.

Johnson and Republicans quarrel. Republicans win fall congressional elections.

Ku Klux Klan formed.

1867 Congress passes Military Reconstruction Act over Johnson's veto. (Two supplementary acts in 1867 and a third in 1868 passed to put this measure into effect.)

Congress passes Tenure of Office Act and Command of Army Act to reduce Johnson's power.

1868 Former Confederate states hold constitutional conventions, in which freedmen are allowed to vote, and adopt new constitutions guaranteeing universal male suffrage.

Arkansas, Alabama, Florida, Georgia, Louisiana, North Carolina, and South Carolina readmitted to representation in Congress. Because of discrimination against black officeholders, Georgia representatives are expelled. (State is again admitted in 1870.)

President Johnson impeached. Escapes conviction by one vote.

Republicans nominate Ulysses S. Grant for president; Democrats select Governor Horatio Seymour of New York. Grant elected president.

1869 Congress passes Fifteenth Amendment and submits it to states for ratification.

1870 First Ku Klux Klan (or Enforcement) Act gives Grant power to move against white terrorists in South. A second act in 1871 further strengthens president's hand.

1872 Grant reelected president.

1876 Republicans nominate Rutherford B. Hayes for president; Democrats nominate Samuel J. Tilden. Tilden secures majority of popular vote but electoral vote is in doubt because of disputed returns from three Southern states.

1877 After elaborate political and economic bargaining, Congress creates an electoral commission, which rules that all disputed ballots belong to Hayes, who is inaugurated president.

SUGGESTED READINGS

The Civil War and Reconstruction (1969), by J. G. Randall and David Donald, and *Ordeal by Fire* (1982), by James M. McPherson, are useful extensive treatments. Three modern interpretations are John H. Franklin, *Reconstruction After the Civil War* (1961); Kenneth M. Stampp, *The Era of Reconstruction* (1965); and Rembert W. Patrick, *The Reconstruction of the Nation* (1967).

The best account of steps taken during the Civil War to reorganize the Southern states is Herman Belz, *Reconstructing the Union* (1969). William B. Hesseltine, *Lincoln's Plan of Reconstruction* (1960), argues that Lincoln had not one but many approaches to Reconstruction, all of them unsuccessful. LaWanda Cox, *Lincoln and Black Freedom* (1981), is an important study. Peyton McCrary, *Abraham Lincoln and Reconstruction* (1978), is the authoritative account of developments in Louisiana, where Lincoln's approach to Reconstruction was most fully tested.

The Presidency of Andrew Johnson (1979), by Albert Castel, is a balanced account. Favorable versions of Johnson's Reconstruction program include George F. Milton, *The Age of Hate* (1930), and Howard K. Beale, *The Critical Year* (1930). The following accounts are critical: Eric L. McKitrick, *Andrew Johnson and Reconstruction* (1960); LaWanda Cox and John H. Cox, *Politics, Principle, and Prejudice* (1963); and W. R. Brock, *An American Crisis* (1963).

On constitutional changes in the postwar period, see Harold M. Hyman, *A More Perfect Union* (1973); Hyman and William M. Wiecek, *Equal Justice Under Law* (1982); Stanley I. Kutler, *Judicial Power and Reconstruction Politics* (1968); and Charles Fairman, *Reconstruction and the Union* (1971).

George R. Bentley, *A History of the Freedmen's Bureau* (1955), is a standard work, but it should be supplemented by William S. McFeely, *Yankee Stepfather: General O. O. Howard and the Freedmen* (1968). Claude F. Oubre, *Forty Acres and a Mule* (1978), discusses the abortive efforts of the bureau in land distribution.

Leon Litwack, *Been in the Storm So Long* (1979), is a masterful account of the transition from slavery to freedom. See also Peter Kolchin, *After Freedom* (1972), on Alabama; Willie Lee Rose, *Rehearsal for Reconstruction* (1964), and Joel Williamson, *After Slavery* (1965), on South Carolina; and Vernon L. Wharton, *The Negro in Mississippi* (1947).

Fred A. Shannon, *The Farmer's Last Frontier* (1945), and E. Merton Coulter, *The South During Reconstruction* (1972), give good general accounts of economic changes in the postwar South. Recently historians and economists using sophisticated quantitative methods have reexamined these changes: Stephen J. DeCanio, *Agriculture in the Postbellum South* (1974); Robert Higgs, *Competition and Coercion: Blacks in the American Economy* (1977); and Roger Ransom and Richard L. Sutch, *One Kind of Freedom: The Economic Consequences of Emancipation* (1977). On the alleged breakup of the plantation system, see Roger W. Shugg, *Origins of Class Struggle in Louisiana* (1939), and on the continuing dominance of the planter class, see Jonathan M. Wiener, *Social Origins of the New South* (1978).

On Radical Reconstruction see Michael L. Benedict, *A Compromise of Principle* (1974); David Donald, *The Politics of Reconstruction* (1965); and Hans L. Trefousse, *The Radical Republicans* (1969). The best account of Grant's Southern policy is William Gillette, *Retreat from Reconstruction* (1980). Among the fullest biographies of Reconstruction politicians are Fawn M. Brodie, *Thaddeus Stevens* (1959); David Donald, *Charles Sumner and the Rights of Man* (1970); William S. McFeely, *Grant* (1981); and Benjamin P. Thomas and Harold M. Hyman, *Stanton* (1962).

David M. DeWitt, *Impeachment and Trial of Andrew Johnson* (1903), remains the standard account, but it should be supplemented with Michael L. Benedict's book of the same name (1973) and with Hans L. Trefousse, *Impeachment of a President* (1975).

On American racial attitudes, George M. Fredrickson, *The Black Image in the White Mind* (1971), is excellent. On Northern racism, see V. Jacque Voegeli, *Free But Not Equal* (1967), and Forrest G. Wood, *Black Scare* (1967).

For a favorable view of the Reconstruction governments in the South, see W. E. B. DuBois, *Black Reconstruction* (1935). Some excellent accounts of Reconstruction in individual states are Francis B. Simkins and Robert H. Woody, *South Carolina During Reconstruction* (1932); Jerrell H. Shofner, *Nor Is It Over Yet: Florida in the Era of Reconstruction* (1974); James W. Garner, *Reconstruction in Mississippi* (1901); and Joe G. Taylor, *Louisiana Reconstructed* (1974).

On the education of blacks after the war, see Henry A. Bullock, *A History of Negro Education in the South* (1967); William P. Vaughn, *Schools for All* (1974); and Roger A. Fischer, *The Segregation Struggle in Louisiana* (1974). Two useful accounts of the educational work of the Freedmen's Bureau are Ronald E. Butchart, *Northern Schools, Southern Blacks, and Reconstruction* (1980), and Robert C. Morris, *Reading, 'Riting, and Reconstruction* (1981).

Southern white resistance to the Reconstruction process is the theme of Michael Perman, *Reunion Without Compromise* (1973). Allen W. Trelease, *White Terror* (1971), is a harrowing recital of white vigilantism.

C. Vann Woodward, *Reunion and Reaction* (1951), is an original reexamination of the compromise of 1876–77. For an analysis of the Redeemer regimes, see Woodward's *Origins of the New South* (1951). The best study of the disfranchisement of blacks is J. Morgan Kousser, *The Shaping of Southern Politics* (1974).

21 National Problems, 1865–1877

The Civil War strongly encouraged nationalist sentiments among Northerners. The primary Northern war aim was not to guarantee equal rights to all men nor even to end slavery; it was to preserve the Union. By that often repeated phrase, men and women of the war years meant something more than merely maintaining the country as a territorial unit. The idea of union implied an almost mystical sense of the wholeness of the American people. Americans viewed themselves as a chosen people, selected to conduct an experiment in self-government, to be a test case of the viability of democratic institutions. As Lincoln declared, the United States was nothing less than "the last, best hope of earth."

That faith in the special destiny of the United States gave courage and hope to Northerners during the darkest hours of the war. Defeats on the battlefield, properly understood, seemed to them the fire that burned away the impurities in American life. As the Reverend Marvin R. Vincent of Troy, New York, announced: "God has been striking, and trying to make us strike at elements unfavorable to the growth of a pure democracy; and . . . he is at work, preparing in this broad land a fit stage for a last act of the mighty drama, the consummation of human civilization." A similar inspiration moved Julia Ward Howe to draw on the imagery of the Book of Revelation in composing the most powerful and popular battle hymn ever written:

Mine eyes have seen the glory of the coming of the Lord:
He is trampling out the vintage where the grapes of wrath are stored;
He has loosed the fateful lightning of his terrible swift sword:
His truth is marching on.

Northerners believed that the Union would emerge from the war more powerful, more firmly united than ever before. They expected that the United States would no longer be a confederation, or union of states, but rather a nation in the fullest sense. A small shift in grammar tells the whole story. Before the Civil War many politicians and writers referred to the United States in the plural—"the United States *are*"—but after 1865 only a pedant or the most unreconstructed Southerner would have dreamed of saying anything but "the United States *is*."

The word *nation* now came easily to American lips. Unlike his predecessors, who generally avoided the term, Lincoln regularly referred to the United States as a nation. For example, he used the word no fewer than five times in his brief Gettysburg Address, most eloquently in the concluding pledge: ". . . that this nation, under God, shall have a new birth of freedom." In 1865, when Republicans agreed to establish a weekly journal that would reflect their views, they called it, as a matter of course, *The Nation*, and it became, as it has remained, one of the most influential periodicals in the country. When Charles Sumner in 1867 took to the lecture circuit to supplement his senatorial salary, he chose for his topic, "Are We a Nation?" The answer, he believed, was obvious. Americans were "one people, throbbing with a common life, occupying a common territory, rejoicing in a common history, sharing in common trials." Never again should any "local claim of self-government" be permitted "for a moment [to] interfere with the supremacy of the Nation." He concluded: "Such centralization is the highest civilization, for it approaches the nearest to the heavenly example."

Political theorists as well as public men in the postwar generation exalted American nationalism. In 1865 Orestes Brownson, once a spokesman for Jacksonian ideals, published the first book-length contribution to the bibliography of American nationalism, *The American Republic: Its Constitution, Tendencies, and Destiny.* "Nations are only individuals on a larger scale," Brownson argued. His book was designed to resolve the identity crisis of the Civil War by persuad-

516

THE LAST ACT OF THE MONROE DOCTRINE
Reflecting exuberant postwar American nationalism, this artist in 1866 predicts the simultaneous expulsion of the French (personified by an effete Emperor Maximilian) from Mexico and of the British (represented by a corpulent John Bull) from Canada.

ing the American nation to "reflect on its own constitution, its own separate existence, individuality, tendencies, and end." Even more soaring were the claims of the Reverend Elisha Mulford's *The Nation: The Foundations of Civil Order and Political Life in the United States* (1870). Mulford's argument derived from the views of the early-nineteenth-century German philosopher Hegel: the nation was a mystic body, endowed with a spirit and a majesty of its own. "The Nation," he concluded, "is a work of God in history. . . . Its vocation is from God, and its obligation is only to God."

American Diplomacy

This mood of high nationalism helps explain American expansionism in the decade after the Civil War. Hardly a year passed without some significant American diplomatic move, either to assert the dominance of the United States in the Western Hemisphere or to annex new territory.

These foreign policy initiatives received considerable popular support. After Appomattox there was a general feeling that the United States, with a million seasoned veterans under arms, was in a position to humiliate the French emperor Napoleon III, to have a showdown with Great Britain, and to pick up any adjacent territory that it pleased. The expansionist spirit

of Manifest Destiny, which had flourished in the 1840s but had languished during the war, sprang to life again. Even those who feared expansionism expected its triumph. The more optimistic rejoiced in the prospect. Advocating the annexation of both Haiti and the Dominican Republic, and hoping for the future acquisition of the Kingdom of Hawaii, President Johnson concluded in his 1868 annual message to Congress: "The conviction is rapidly gaining ground in the American mind that with the increased facilities for intercommunication between all portions of the earth the principles of free government, as embraced in our Constitution, if faithfully maintained and carried out, would prove of sufficient strength and breadth to comprehend within their sphere and influence the civilized nations of the world."

Even if the accomplishments of American foreign policy did not live up to Johnson's predictions, they were, nevertheless, considerable. From the point of view of national security, the most important feat was Seward's success in getting French troops removed from Mexico. Introduced into Mexico during the Civil War, ostensibly to compel the bankrupt Mexican government of President Benito Juarez to pay its debts, French troops in 1864 provided the support for installing Archduke Maximilian of Austria as emperor of Mexico. While the war was going on, Seward could do no more than protest against this violation of the Monroe Doctrine's principle that European powers not extend their "system" to the New World. But he adopted a more vigorous tone after Appomattox. Yet, knowing that the French emperor was a proud and volatile man, Seward refrained from direct threats and allowed Napoleon to discover for himself how expensive, unpopular, and unsuccessful his Mexican adventure was proving. By 1867 Napoleon finally decided to cut off further financial support for Maximilian's shaky regime and, under steady American pressure, withdrew his troops. Captured by Juarez's forces, Maximilian was shot by a firing squad on June 19, 1867.

A second diplomatic achievement of the Reconstruction years was the settlement of the *Alabama* claims—claims of American shippers against the British government for damages that British-built Confederate raiders had inflicted during the war. Immediately after the war it probably would have been possible to clear up this controversy speedily and inexpensively, had not the British government haughtily denied that it had violated international law by permitting Confederate raiders to be built in its shipyards. American grievances deepened with delay. Sumner, the powerful chairman of the Senate Committee on Foreign Relations, began to argue that the British not only owed repayment for actual damages done by the *Alabama* and other vessels; they also were responsible, he said, for prolonging the war—for the "immense and infinite" cost of the entire last two years of the conflict. Americans were further embittered by the failure of Reverdy Johnson, Seward's special envoy to Great Britain, to secure an apology or an expression of regret from the stubborn British government. A settlement was worked out only when Grant put Hamilton Fish in charge of the American State Department and there was a change of government in Great Britain.

In the Treaty of Washington of 1871, Great Britain admitted negligence in permitting the Confederate cruisers to escape and expressed regret for the damages they had caused; and the United States quietly abandoned the extravagant claims put forward by Sumner and agreed that the amount of damages should be assessed by an arbitration commission representing five nations. Ultimately, damages to American shipping were estimated at $15.5 million, and the British government paid this amount. However, the precedent of settling international disputes by arbitration was more important than any monetary settlement, and the Treaty of Washington paved the way for an improvement in relations between the two greatest English-speaking nations. Not until the two world wars of the twentieth century would the full consequences of this development emerge.

Apart from the almost unnoticed American occupation of the Midway Islands in August 1867, the United States' sole territorial acquisition during the Reconstruction era was the purchase of Alaska. Seward's 1867 treaty to purchase Russian America for $7.2 million brought under the American flag new territory one-fifth as large as the entire continental United States, a land of vast natural and mineral resources and of obvious strategic importance for the future of the United States in the Pacific. Nevertheless there was little popular enthusiasm for the purchase. Newspapers called Alaska "a national icehouse" consisting of nothing but "walrus-covered icebergs." Congressmen were equally unenthusiastic. Yet after much grumbling the Senate finally ratified the treaty and the House reluctantly appropriated the money for the purchase. Seward's success in part reflected his ability to convince senators that Alaska had vast hidden natural resources. It was also in part the result of the judicious payment of money to American congressmen by the Russian minister in Washington. The most important factor, however, was the general feeling that rejecting the treaty would alienate Czar Alexander II, who alone of the leading European rulers had been sympathetic to the Union cause during the Civil War.*

Nothing came of other postwar plans for expansion. Each of them ran into snags that made American diplomats draw back. For example, the desire of many United States politicians, including Grant, Fish, and Sumner, to annex Canada had to be abandoned when it became clear that the British would not withdraw without a fight. Grant's plan to acquire the Dominican Republic aroused the opposition of Sumner, who considered himself the blacks' senatorial voice and wanted the island to become not an American possession, but the center of "a free confederacy [of the West Indies], in which the black race should predominate." Seward's proposal for the purchase of the Danish West Indies (now the Virgin Islands) was pigeonholed by the Senate when those unfortunate islands were visited by a hurricane, a tidal wave, and a series of earthquake shocks.

It would, however, be a mistake to put too much stress on these special factors that stopped American expansionism. Broader forces were also at work. The

---

*The czar's pro-Union policy resulted in part from unrest in the Russian-ruled Polish territories, which revolted in 1863 and were reconquered by military force. Like the Union, Russia feared European intervention in what both regarded as internal matters. After the Civil War, the czar concluded that Alaska was vulnerable to seizure by the British in the event of a future conflict and that it would be better to sell the territory to the United States.

American people were exhausted by four years of fighting, and they were not prepared to support a vigorously nationalistic foreign policy if it threatened another war. Northern businessmen felt that it was more important to reduce taxes and to return to a sound monetary policy than to engage in foreign adventures. The difficulties of racial adjustment in the South made increasing numbers of politicians hesitate before agreeing to annex additional populations of dark-skinned inhabitants. During Johnson's administration many Republicans opposed all Seward's expansion plans because they might bring credit to the unpopular president. During Grant's tenure alienated Republicans had similar motives for blocking the president's diplomatic schemes; by 1872, these dissidents had joined the Liberal Republican party and were opposing Grant's reelection. Most important of all, the American people were generally aware that they had plenty of room for expansion closer to home, in the lands still occupied by the Indians.

Indian Wars

At the end of the Civil War, most of the Great Plains and the Rocky Mountains belonged to native Americans, whom whites labeled "Indians." The term *Indian* itself revealed white misperceptions. Of course everyone had known for centuries that native Americans were not related to the inhabitants of India, which Columbus and the other Spanish explorers thought they had reached. But even in the last half of the nineteenth century, most whites still did not understand that "Indians" consisted of numerous culture groups at least as different as the inhabitants of the nations of Europe. Native American peoples ranged from the peaceable Pueblos of the Southwest to the fierce and devious Crows, who ranged over Wyoming and Montana. The Utes of Utah, who barely subsisted by grubbing roots from the arid soil, were "Indians," as were the members of the Five Civilized Nations—the Cherokees, Choctaws, Chickasaws, Creeks, and Seminoles, transplanted from the Southeast in Andrew Jackson's day—who had developed a sophisticated agricultural economy in the Indian Territory (later to become the state of Oklahoma).

Whites called all these diverse peoples Indians—meaning really "Wild Indians." President Lincoln voiced the general paleface view of the redskin. To leaders of several western native American nations who visited the White House in March 1863, just after the bloody battle of Fredericksburg, the president announced, with no intentional irony: "We are not, as a race, so much disposed to fight and kill one another as our red brethren."

Native Americans During the Civil War. Union leaders took advantage of the opportunities presented during the Civil War to limit the rights of native Americans and to restrict their territories. The loyalties of the Five Civilized Nations were divided between the Union and the Confederacy, and after the Union victory the treaties governing the Indian Territory were renegotiated. As a result, the native Americans were forced to give up huge tracts of land and to grant a right of way to railroads crossing the territory.

Far to the north, wartime inefficiency and delay, along with the endemic corruption of the federal Indian Bureau, which regulated white-Indian relations, kept promised supplies from reaching the Santee Sioux. In desperation, the Indians took to the warpath and threatened white settlements in Minnesota. Lincoln appointed John Pope, fresh from his defeat at the second battle of Bull Run, to command the armed forces in the Northwest, and the general announced that he would deal with the Sioux "as maniacs or wild beasts, and by no means as people with whom treaties or compromises can be made." When the Sioux surrendered in September 1862, about 1,800 were taken prisoner and 303 were condemned to death. Against the strong objections of local authorities, Lincoln commuted the sentences of most, but he authorized the hanging of 38—the largest mass execution in American history.

In 1864 warfare spread to the Central Plains after the discovery of gold in Colorado and the opening of the Pike's Peak trail led to an influx of whites. Since the regular army was fighting the Confederacy, maintaining the peace was the job of the poorly trained Colorado territorial militia. On November 29, 1864, a group of Colorado volunteers, under the command of a former minister, Colonel John M. Chivington, fell on Chief Black Kettle's unsuspecting band of Cheyennes at Sand Creek in eastern Colorado, where they had gathered under the protection of the governor. "As an act of duty to ourselves and civilization," the militia slaughtered about 150 native Americans, mostly women and children.

Indians' Struggle for Survival, 1865–1877. Soon the entire Plains became a battlefield. For nearly two decades after the Civil War, hardly a year passed without significant encounters between United States soldiers, now released from the battlefields of the South, and Indian warriors. Often the native Americans were the victors, for the United States army, loaded with heavy supply trains, was unable to fight a guerrilla war. In 1866, for instance, when army officers attempted to establish a series of forts along the Bozeman Trail, which linked the North Platte River with the newly opened mines of Montana, the Sioux opposed them every step of the way. On December 21 the Sioux, led by Chief Crazy Horse, exterminated a band of eighty soldiers commanded by the boastful Captain William J. Fetterman.

The 1862 Sioux war in Minnesota originated in the treaties of 1851 and 1858 that forced the tribe to give up most of its land in return for an annuity from the United States government. Payments were slow to arrive, and the Sioux had to buy goods on credit from the Indian traders, who had a government monopoly. In August 1862 some hungry young warriors raided a farm near Acton, demanding food, and in the ensuing struggle five white settlers were killed. Soon there was a full-scale Sioux insurrection along the whole frontier.

A Minnesota Indian Chief's Views on Whites' Treatment of His People

OF the causes that led to the outbreak of August, 1862, much has been said. . . . There was great dissatisfaction among the Indians over many things the whites did. The whites would not let them go to war against their enemies. This was right, but the Indians did not then know it. Then the whites were always trying to make the Indians give up their life and live like white men—go to farming, work hard and do as they did—and the Indians did not know how to do that, and did not want to. . . . If the Indians had tried to make the whites live like them, the whites would have resisted, and it was the same way with many Indians. The Indians wanted to . . . go where they pleased and when they pleased; hunt game wherever they could find it, sell their furs to the traders, and live as they could.

Then the Indians did not think the traders had done right. The Indians bought goods of them on credit, and when the government payments came the traders were on hand with their books, which showed that the Indians owed so much and so much, and as the Indians kept no books they could not deny their accounts, but had to pay them, and sometimes the traders got all their money. I do not say that the traders always cheated and lied about these accounts. I know many of them were honest men and kind and accommodating, but . . . I know that many white men, when they go to pay their accounts, often think them too large and refuse to pay them, and they go to law about them and there is much bad feeling. The Indians could not go to law, but there was always trouble over their credits. . . .

Then many of the white men often abused the Indians and treated them unkindly. Perhaps they had excuse, but the Indians did not think so. Many of the whites always seemed to say by their manner when they saw an Indian, "I am much better than you," and the Indians did not like this. There was excuse for this, but the Dakota did not believe there were better men in the world than they. Then some of the white men abused the Indian women in a certain way, . . . and surely there was no excuse for that.

All these things made many Indians dislike the whites.

CHIEF BLACK KETTLE (SEATED, THIRD FROM LEFT, IN THE MIDDLE ROW) AND OTHER NATIVE AMERICANS CONFER WITH U.S. ARMY OFFICERS IN DENVER, SEPTEMBER 1864
The discovery of gold brought large numbers of white settlers into the Colorado Territory. The Cheyenne, Arapaho, Comanche, and Kiowa tribes resented this intrusion on their tribal lands. Fearing a general outbreak of violence, Governor John Evans held a series of unsuccessful council meetings with tribal chiefs during the last half of 1864. Shortly afterward Colonel John M. Chivington and the Colorado militia attacked an encampment of the Cheyenne at Sand Creek. Although Chief Black Kettle raised both a white flag and an American flag, Chivington's soldiers overran the camp, slaughtering children, scalping women, butchering pregnant women, and castrating men.

Colorado State Historical Society

More familiar is the fate, ten years later, of George Armstrong Custer, the golden-haired boy-general of the Civil War who had won several victories over the Southern Plains Indians. The survey of the route of the newly chartered Northern Pacific Railroad and the discovery of gold in the Black Hills brought whites into the lands of the Cheyenne and the Sioux. Since the Black Hills were the sacred dwelling place of the Sioux gods, Sitting Bull and Crazy Horse resisted the white encroachments with all their power. General Philip H. Sheridan, who now commanded the United States army in the West, planned to force concessions by capturing the large Indian encampment on the Little Bighorn River (which the native Americans called Greasy Grass). A three-prong attack was mounted. But Custer, leading one of the columns, reached the encampment first and ordered his men to advance. As the white soldiers charged, Chief Low Dog called to his men: "This is a good day to die; follow me." They did, and within an hour on June 25, 1876, not merely "Long Hair" (as the Indians called Custer) but all of his men were killed.

The Defeat of the Native Americans. But such victories were short-lived, and the native Americans were finally overcome. In part, their defeat was the consequence of superior white force and resources. The prolonged wars cost, according to the Commissioner of Indian Affairs, $1 million and the lives of twenty-five white soldiers for each native American warrior killed. But the wars bled the Indian nations of their best leaders. Ultimately, however, the building of two transcontinental railroads—the Union Pacific and the Northern Pacific—did more to defeat the native Americans than the campaigns of the soldiers. The rail lines, and the permanent settlements built along them, disrupted the traditional migrating patterns of the Plains Indians. The slaughter along these railroads of hundreds of thousands of bison, the chief food supply for the nomadic Indians, ended the restless hunting life that had characterized the native Americans of the Plains.

As the proud and brave nations that once had dominated the American continent were defeated by the white man's arms, deprived of their lands by the

MAJOR GENERAL GEORGE ARMSTRONG CUSTER, U.S.A.

Made a brigadier general in the Union army at the age of only twenty-four, Custer was the personification of youthful impetuosity. Tall, slender, and lithe, with piercing blue eyes and long golden hair (which, however, he cut after the war), he dashed ahead of Grant's army in April 1865 and, by blocking Lee's further retreat, helped bring about the Confederate surrender at Appomattox. The same tactics served him far less well in the subsequent Indian wars in the West. On June 26, 1876, instead of waiting for reinforcements, he precipitated a battle with a well-armed force of between 2,500 and 4,000 Indians on the Little Big Horn River. Custer and all of the 215 men he led were killed.

white man's settlements, and debauched by the white man's alcohol, humanitarians across the United States became aware that they were witnessing what Helen Hunt Jackson called *A Century of Dishonor*. This was the title of her 1881 book, which reviewed the shabby record of government dealings with the native Americans. But it was by no means clear how this record could be reversed. Probably a majority of white Americans favored confining the Indians to eversmaller reservations in the most arid western lands, where they would surely and swiftly become extinct.

The only alternative reformers could suggest was to transform native Americans into homogenized citizens of the Republic. One means to this end, embodied in the Dawes Severalty Act of 1887, was to divide Indian lands into small holdings, giving the head of each native American family title to 160 acres. (That process incidentally freed vast areas hitherto under Indian control for white settlement.) Along with this plan went one proposed by President Merrill E. Gates of Amherst College, who told the Lake Mohonk Conference of the Friends of the Indians:

To bring him out of savagery into citizenship we must make the Indian more intelligently selfish before we can make him unselfishly intelligent. We need to awaken in him wants. . . . Discontent with the teepee and the starving rations of the Indian camp in winter is needed to get the Indian out of the blanket and into trousers—and trousers with a pocket in them, and with a pocket that aches to be filled with dollars.

Thus even the friends of the native Americans saw assimilation or extermination as the only solution to the "Indian problem."

Toward a National Economy

As the native Americans were pushed back, white settlers rushed in to occupy their lands. In 1860 the western frontier of settlement lay near the Missouri River, and between eastern Kansas and California there were hardly any white inhabitants except the Mormon settlement in Utah and in the Spanish-speaking community at Sante Fe. Thirty years later, immigrants pushing west into the Great Plains and Rocky Mountain region and pushing east from California formed a virtually uninterrupted pattern of settlement across the continent. In 1890 the superintendent of the United States census announced—a bit prematurely—that the frontier was gone. "Up to and including 1880 the country had a frontier settlement," he said, "but at present the unsettled area has been so broken into by isolated bodies of settlement that there can hardly be said to be a frontier line."

Westward Expansion. To some extent the peopling of the West was triggered by the passage in 1862 of the Homestead Act, which offered 160 acres of public lands free of charge to any citizen who was over twenty-one or the head of a family, provided he resided on the land for five continuous years. Alternatively, a homesteader could purchase his land from the government for $1.25 an acre after six months' residence. Between 1862 and 1900 about 400,000 families received free homesteads under this program, but the dream that free public land would siphon off industrial workers from the overcrowded eastern cities was not realized. Very few urban artisans could afford to transport themselves and their families to the frontier, to pay the required fees at the land office, to construct a cabin, to purchase the necessary tools and seeds, and to buy food during the long growing season before the

Westward Expansion and Indian Wars 1864-1876

The first date indicates the establishment of the territory with the boundaries shown. In several instances earlier territories were formed with the same names but with different boundaries.

wheat or corn was harvested. Even fewer knew how to farm. Consequently the great majority of homesteaders were men and women who had spent all their earlier years on the land. Even experience was no guarantee of success, for fully two-thirds of all homestead claimants before 1890 failed at the venture.

Most settlers in the West did not stake claims under the Homestead Act but continued, as they had always done, to purchase land directly from the government. Thousands more bought land from the railroad companies, which received from state and national governments enormous tracts of land, equal to more than twice the acreage made available to homesteaders. For instance, Congress gave the Union Pacific and the Central Pacific lines ten square miles of public land for every mile of track completed in the states, and twenty square miles for every mile built in the territories.

The growth of western settlements was part of the general increase in the national population. During the decade from the end of the Civil War to 1876, when the Republic celebrated its centennial year, the population of the United States jumped by 30 percent, from 35.7 million to 46.1 million. During these same years more than 3 million immigrants, mostly from Europe, poured into the country.

Economic Growth. Along with the increase in population came fantastic economic growth. Between 1866 and 1876 the number of bushels of corn produced in the United States increased by 100 percent. Railroad mileage increased by 111 percent. The production of bituminous coal increased by 163 percent. Almost no steel was manufactured in the United States at the end of the Civil War; 390,000 tons were made ten years later.

Growth strengthened the tendency to consolidate the American economy into one huge functional unit. This had been the dream of some businessmen long before the war, but after 1865 the necessary preconditions for economic integration existed for the first time. Never before had the United States had a na-

WAGON TRAIN CROSSING THE PLAINS DURING THE 1870s
For able-bodied single men, a pack train was the most efficient way of moving west. But for families that were undertaking a trip that might last from three to five months, a wagon train was more practicable. The covered wagon, or prairie schooner, usually pulled by oxen, had iron tires four inches wide and held up to 7,000 pounds. Such a wagon allowed a family to bring along its cherished possessions, and it also offered a place where the pregnant mother could rest, the children could sleep, or a sick member of the family could recuperate.

tional currency, and earlier businessmen had been obliged to settle their obligations with an assortment of state bank notes, local scrip, and coin. Passage of the National Banking Act of 1864, however, created a uniform circulating medium. In return for purchasing government bonds, banks chartered by the national government were allowed to issue the new national bank notes supplied by the federal comptroller of the currency. A tax placed on state bank notes in 1865 ensured that these national bank notes would have no competition in the future.

For the first time, too, the United States after 1865 was bound together by a modern communications network. Before the Civil War a number of rival telegraph companies had been constructing lines, and as early as 1861 it was possible to send a wire from San Francisco to Washington, D.C. But early construction was haphazard and service was poor and sporadic. Thanks in part to the extensive military use of the telegraph during the war, the Western Union Telegraph Company grew strong enough to absorb smaller rivals. After 1866 it secured a virtual monopoly in the field. Western Union made it possible for a person in almost any part of the country to communicate almost instantaneously with his fellows in any other part of the reunited nation. After Alexander Graham Bell invented

the telephone in the 1870s, and particularly after he demonstrated the miraculous ability to transmit the human voice by electrical current at the great Centennial Exhibition at Philadelphia in 1876, a second communications network appeared. By the 1880s most city physicians had telephones, and during President Hayes's administration an instrument was installed in the White House. The telephone was still such a novelty that, when it rang, the president himself was likely to pick up the receiver.

An improved transportation network also cemented the nation together. A transcontinental railroad—which had long been advocated but repeatedly postponed because of sectional controversies—received congressional support in 1862, when Congress incorporated the Union Pacific Railroad Company. Financed by the grant of vast tracts of public lands, the Union Pacific began constructing a line from western Iowa to join the Central Pacific Railroad, which was pushing eastward from San Francisco. In 1869 the two roads met at Promontory Point, Utah, and it became possible to move passengers and freight by rail from the Atlantic Ocean to the Pacific. Less dramatic but more economically significant was the simultaneous coordination and consolidation of rail lines in more settled areas. Before the Civil War, there

THE OFFICIAL CATALOGUE OF THE UNITED STATES INTERNATIONAL EXHIBITION, 1876

Held during the worst year of the great postwar depression, at a time when the conquered South was still in turmoil and the United States government was wracked by scandals, the International Exhibition at Philadelphia was an affirmation of the basic vitality of American life. In nearly 450 acres in Philadelphia's Fairmount Park, 10 million visitors could gawk at exhibits, both from the United States and foreign countries, that included everything from Yale locks to fine china. This demonstration of power, of abundance, of technological skill, and of industriousness heartened American patriots.

had been eleven different rail gauges in use on northern roads. President Lincoln's choice of the 4-foot 8 1/2-inch gauge for the Union Pacific led to the standardization of all roads at this width. Before the war travel from New York to Chicago had been barely possible by using eight or ten independent lines, with repeated transfers. In 1869 Commodore Vanderbilt consolidated the New York Central and Hudson River railroads to give continuous service from New York to Buffalo, and five years later he completed arrangements with western railroads to offer through service to Chicago. At about the same time, the Pennsylvania Railroad, the Erie Railroad, and the Baltimore and Ohio Railroad also completed connections with Chicago.

Economic Consolidation.

A national communications and transportation network encouraged businessmen to seek national markets for their products. Business consolidation, already under way before the war, proceeded rapidly. A striking number of new entrepreneurs—"robber barons," as later critics called them—were men whose wartime experience had taught them the advantages of technological innovation and large-scale management. For instance, Andrew Carnegie, who came to the United States as a poor Scottish immigrant and trained himself to become a skilled telegraph operator, served during the war as aide to Thomas A. Scott, the assistant secretary of war in charge of all government railroads and transportation lines. From this vantage point Carnegie shrewdly foresaw the postwar expansion and reorganization of the railway system, and he invested his early savings in the company that owned the patents for Pullman sleeping cars. When these cars became standard equipment on railroads, Carnegie was on his way to acquiring a huge fortune, with which he subsequently helped build the steel industry in the United States.

John D. Rockefeller, a pious young Baptist from Cleveland, Ohio, got his start through handling wartime government contracts for hay, grain, meat, and other commodities. Quickly he learned how a company that was managed with order and enterprise could drive inefficient competitors out of business, and he decided to apply this lesson to the new petroleum industry. Astutely recognizing that the way to dominate the industry was to control the refining process, Rockefeller in 1863 constructed the largest refinery in Cleveland, and two years later he built a second one. His brother, William, developed the eastern and the export markets for their products. Enlisting Harry M. Flagler as a partner in 1867, Rockefeller worked systematically to cut costs and to nationalize an industry hitherto unstandardized and intensely competitive. By 1870 Rockefeller's company, Standard Oil of Ohio, made its own barrels, built its own warehouses, and owned its own fleet of tankers. Because of the volume of his business, Rockefeller was able to force the railroads to give his firm lower rates, or rebates, on all his shipments. Then, as his power grew, he compelled the railroads to turn over to Standard Oil "draw-backs," or a portion of what other oil companies had to pay for freight. As a consequence of these shrewd and unscrupulous business practices, Standard Oil by 1880 controlled 95 percent of the refining business in the country and practically all the transportation of oil, whether by pipeline or railroad.

While industry was expanding to reach a national market, other segments of the economy were be-

PIONEER RUN, 1865
The discovery of petroleum in western Pennsylvania led to its rapid and wasteful exploitation. Not more than one well out of twenty was properly sunk and carefully managed.

Courtesy of the American Petroleum Institute

coming integrated into the national system. In the post–Civil War years a huge western range-cattle industry became the prime supplier of beef for the East and also for Europe. Even before the Civil War, cattle raising had become a major occupation in the Great Plains area, stretching from Texas to Canada. There hardy cattle, descendants of Mexican longhorns, fed on open ranges. At yearly roundups calves were branded so that their owners could identify them, and cowboys selected the strongest steers for the long drive east. The war cut off markets for Texas cattle, so that herds became uncomfortably large. As soon as peace was restored, Texas cattlemen renewed their annual drive of cattle on an unprecedented scale. Initially these vast herds headed for Sedalia, Missouri, where they could be transported by rail to Chicago, St. Louis, and other eastern markets. But when the Kansas Pacific Railroad reached Abilene, Kansas, in 1867, cattlemen found a shorter, safer route to market. From Texas alone, 35,000 head of cattle came to the new railhead in its first year of operation; 350,000 in 1869; and 700,000 in 1871. Thereafter, as the national rail network extended farther west, Wichita and Dodge City came to rival, if not to replace, Abilene. These were rowdy frontier towns, where the cowboys, black as well as white, lonely after long months on the range, could let off steam in the dance halls, the saloons, and the red-light districts. But these cattle towns also served a basic economic function by tying the range cattle industry into the national economy.

Farmers, too, became part of that national network in the postwar era. The first few years after the war were boom times for northern and western farmers. The domestic demand for grain constantly increased with the growth of American cities, and at the same time Great Britain was becoming more dependent on American harvests. By 1880, for the first time, the value of American wheat and flour exports nearly equaled that of exported cotton.

Heartened by rising prices, northern and western farmers expanded their operations. Using new and improved farm machinery, such as Cyrus Hall McCormick's reaping machine, they were able to cultivate and harvest large crops with fewer workers. Since this machinery was expensive and operated best on large, level tracts of land, small, self-sufficient farmers, who were chronically short of cash, were at a disadvantage. The future seemed to belong to large producers, and confident western farmers went heavily into debt to buy more land and better machines. More than in any previous era, they were now tied to the national market economy. Their fortunes depended not only on the land, the weather, and their efforts, but also on the grain elevators, the railroads, and the national and international markets.

Inevitably the movement toward a national economy in the post–Civil War decades encountered opposition. It rapidly became evident that complete integration could be achieved only at enormous economic, social, and psychological costs. Not even the business interests of the Northeast, which were the primary beneficiaries of a national economic system, unanimously favored such integration. If New York City grew because of the increasingly centralized financial and transportation networks, that growth was at the expense of such former rivals as Boston and Philadelphia. If Standard Oil profited from Rockefeller's nationalization of the refining industry, hundreds of less efficient oil companies were forced into bankruptcy. If mass production of nails at Andrew Carnegie's J. Edgar Thompson steel mill made building construction cheaper and safer, it also cost local blacksmiths and ironmongers their markets.

Politics in the Gilded Age

These economic and social tensions rarely surfaced as political issues during the Gilded Age—so-called from the novel by Mark Twain and Charles Dudley Warner, which depicted the boom-and-bust mentality of businessmen of the post–Civil War era and the willingness of politicians to serve the needs of these speculators. This was a period of low public morality in the United States, and few citizens were willing to entrust serious decisions to public officials—whether national, state, or local—tainted by favoritism, fraud, and bribery.

Scandals and Corruption. Disrespect for the government mounted during the 1870s, when reformers and crusading newspaper editors started to expose shocking scandals. The earliest revelations concerned New York City, which had fallen under the control of "Boss" William Marcy Tweed, who proceeded joyfully to loot the taxpayers. Tweed's ring began construction of a new county courthouse, on which $11 million was spent. Nearly $3 million went to a man named Garvey for plastering; after the amount of his fees leaked out, he became known as the "Prince of Plasterers." Tweed approved the purchase of so many chairs, at $5 each, that if placed in a line they would have extended seventeen miles. In 1871, when the New York *Times* began to expose the ring's padded bills, faked leases, false vouchers, and other frauds, the entire nation's attention was attracted, and when *Harper's Weekly* started carrying Thomas Nast's devastating caricatures of the Boss, Tweed's face became more familiar to Americans that that of any other man except Grant.

Soon revelations about the national government began to make equally fascinating reading. Shortly before the 1872 election, the New York *Sun*, a Democratic paper, exposed the workings of the Crédit Mobilier, the construction company that the Union Pacific Railroad Company paid to build its transcontinental route. Investigation proved that members of the Crédit Mobilier were also members of the board of

"BOSS TWEED," BY THOMAS NAST
Thomas Nast's caricatures of the corrupt William M. Tweed of New York were devastatingly effective. When the "Boss" fled the United States to escape prosecution, a Spanish immigration official identified him on the basis of Nast's drawings, and he was sent back to New York to serve his prison sentence.

American Antiquarian Society

directors of the Union Pacific, who were thus paying themselves huge profits. Even more damaging was the revelation that, in order to prevent public inquiry, the Crédit Mobilier offered stock to Vice-President Schuyler Colfax, Representative (and future President) James A. Garfield, and other prominent politicians. They were allowed to "purchase" the stock on credit, the down payment being "earned" by the high dividends that the stock began to pay.

Although Republicans found it advisable to drop Colfax from their ticket in 1872, scandal did not seriously touch the Grant administration until after the election. Then, in short order, stories of fraud began to appear about practically every branch of the executive offices. In the Treasury Department unscrupulous customhouse officers, especially in New York, preyed on importers. Merchants who failed to pay off the thieves had their shipments delayed, their imported goods subjected to minute, time-consuming inspection, and their crates and boxes that were not immediately removed from the docks stored at exorbitant rates. Corruption was rampant in the Navy Department, where political favoritism dictated everything from the employment of workers in the shipyards to the contracts for the construction of new vessels. Secretary of War William W. Belknap was proved to have accepted bribes from Indian traders, who had the exclusive and well-paying franchise to sell goods to Indians and soldiers at frontier posts. He resigned to avoid impeachment.

Of all these scandals, the closest to the White House was the Whiskey Ring. In order to avoid heavy excise taxes, first levied during the war, whiskey distillers, especially those at St. Louis, had for years been conspiring with officials of the Internal Revenue Service. During Grant's administration the dealers secured the cooperation of none other than Orville E. Babcock, the president's private secretary, who warned the swindlers whenever an inspection team was sent out from Washington. In return for his assistance, Babcock received such favors as a $2,400 diamond shirt stud—which he found defective and asked to have replaced with another, more expensive one—and from time to time the services of a prostitute. When Grant first learned of the scandal, he urged, "Let no guilty man escape." But as it became clear that his close friends and his personal staff were involved, he did everything he could to block further investigation. When Babcock went on trial, the president of the United States offered a deposition expressing "great confidence in his integrity and efficiency." Babcock was acquitted, and Grant retained him on the White House staff.

Civil Service Reform.

The desire to reduce political corruption led to the emergence of the civil service reform movement during the Gilded Age. Although the spoils system had been criticized long before the Civil War, an organized reform drive did not appear until after Appomattox. Knowledge of widespread corruption among government officials, fear that President Johnson might convert the government bureaucracy into a tool to promote his renomination, and the example of the British system of appointing civil servants after competitive examinations gave strength to the movement. Early efforts to require federal appointees to pass competitive examinations failed in Congress, but the reformers, led by the politically ambitious George William Curtis, editor of *Harper's Weekly*, and by E. L. Godkin of *The Nation*, hoped for success under Grant's administration.

The reformers were doomed to disappointment, for on this, as on all other controversial topics, Grant perfectly understood that compromise was the mood

Harper's Weekly, April 28, 1877

IN MEMORIAM—OUR CIVIL SERVICE AS IT WAS
Thomas Nast proposes a substitute for Clark Mills's famous equestrian statue of Andrew Jackson, in Lafayette Square across from the White House. Nast incorrectly attributes to Jackson the phrase, "To the Victors belong the Spoils," which was a remark of William L. Marcy, a New York Democrat.

of the age, and he straddled. He made no mention of civil service reform in his first message to Congress. The future historian Henry Adams—the son of Lincoln's minister to Great Britain and the grandson and great-grandson of presidents—remarked in his snobbish way that Grant was inaugurating "a reign of western mediocrity." But when angry civil service reformers began to talk loudly about joining the Liberal Republican movement, Grant moved swiftly to head them off. In 1871 he pressured Congress into creating the Civil Service Reform Commission, and he neatly co-opted his chief critic by naming Curtis chairman. Although the commission had little power and achieved less success, the move kept Curtis and a sizable number of reformers as supporters of Grant's re-election. Once the election was over, Grant lost interest in the commission and so blatantly violated its rules that Curtis had to resign.*

Strengthened by news of the scandals that rocked Grant's second administration, civil service reformers claimed some of the credit for the nomination of Rutherford B. Hayes in 1876. But they found him as difficult to manage as Grant had been. On the one hand, the new president did take on the powerful political machine of New York's Senator Roscoe Conkling, and he succeeded in ousting some of Conkling's supporters—called Stalwarts and including the future president Chester A. Arthur—from the New York customhouse. On the other hand, at election time the president wanted his own appointees to contribute to Republican campaign funds and to help organize Republican state conventions, much as their predecessors had done. "I have little or no patience with Mr. Hayes," exclaimed the reforming editor of the New York *Times*. "He is a victim of . . . good intentions and his contributions to the pavement of the road to the infernal regions are vast and various."

Hayes's successor, James A. Garfield, gave civil service reformers little more satisfaction. With cruel accuracy one Massachusetts reformer characterized the new president as a "grand, noble fellow, but fickle, unstable, . . . timid and hesitating." Civil service reform advocates noted suspiciously that Garfield's vice-president was Arthur, named by the Republican national convention in a vain attempt to placate Conkling. Consequently reformers felt no special sense of victory when Garfield began to remove more of Conkling's Stalwarts from the New York customhouse. Conceited and arrogant, Conkling resigned from the Senate in a huff and rushed to Albany seeking vindication through reelection. To his surprise, the removal of his friends from federal office undercut his support, and the New York legislature failed to send him back to the Senate. Shortly afterward, a crazed office seeker named Charles Guiteau assassinated Garfield, shouting that he was a Stalwart and rejoicing that Arthur was now president. Shocked by Garfield's assassination, Congress in 1883 passed the Pendleton Act, which required competitive examinations of applicants for many federal jobs. Although the measure covered only a fraction of all government employees, it was a genuine measure of civil service reform and permitted the emergence of a professional government bureaucracy.

---

*The Liberal Republicans were a reform-minded element within the Republican party that broke with Grant and nominated Horace Greeley for president in 1872. Although the Democrats also endorsed Greeley and ran no candidate of their own, Grant easily won reelection.

Tariff and Currency Controversies

In addition to distrust of fraud and favoritism, there was a deeper reason why government, and in particular the national government, had so little to do with the basic economic problems of the Gilded Age. In dealing with economic issues, just as in dealing with those relating to the South and the freedmen, Americans were constrained by the doctrines of constitutionalism—by the belief that the government had only the fixed powers set forth in the Constitution. In the area of economics, only the tariff and the currency seemed to be clearly under the control of the national government. Therefore during the postwar years disagreements over economic issues were usually voiced in connection with these two endlessly troublesome, highly technical questions, so complex that only a handful of congressmen fully understood them.

The Tariff Problem. Debates on the tariff rested on basic questions of whether the industrial sector of the economy should be favored at the expense of the exporting agricultural sector, and of whether the factories of the Northeast should benefit at the expense of the farmers of the South and West. These questions did not surface clearly, however, and during the debates the issue was rarely put in terms of free trade versus protection. Almost everybody during the Gilded Age recognized that some tariff barrier was needed to protect American industries from cheap foreign imports. The debates in Congress revolved around which industries and how much protection.

By 1865 almost everybody agreed on the need to modify the high tariffs that had been enacted during the Civil War to protect heavily taxed American industry from untaxed foreign competition. A bill intended to make a reasonable adjustment was drafted by the New England economist David A. Wells, who was appointed Special Commissioner of the Revenue in 1866. Wells's bill proposed to reduce duties on imported materials such as scrap iron, coal, and lumber, eliminated arbitrary and unnecessary duties on items like chemicals and spices, and made slight reductions in duties on most manufactured articles. Most lawmakers admitted the theoretical excellence of Wells's bill—and most opposed the provisions that lessened or removed protection from their own constituents' businesses. Consequently Wells's bill was rejected, and during the next fifteen years there was no general revision of the tariff legislation.

The absence of general tariff acts did not mean that discussion of tariff rates had ended. To the contrary, throughout the period there was constant pulling and hauling between economic interests that stood to gain or lose from changes in duties on specific imported items. For example, during the war Boston and

Baltimore had developed a considerable copper industry that smelted and refined Chilean ore, which paid a very low tariff duty. But in the late 1860s, the great copper mines around Lake Superior began to be worked on a large scale, and their owners asked Congress to protect their product by raising duties on imported ore. After sharp disagreement, in which President Johnson supported the refiners and most congressional Republicans sided with the ore producers, the tariff on copper ore was increased in 1869 to a point at which most of the eastern smelting firms had to go out of business.

Other tariff changes were the consequence of combined efforts by the producers and processors of raw materials. An 1867 act revising the duties on raw wool and on woolen cloth was drafted at a convention of wool producers and manufacturers at Syracuse, and it was lobbied through Congress by the tireless and effective secretary of the Wool Manufacturers' Association, John L. Hayes.

Some of the minor adjustments made in the tariff during the postwar years reflected political pressures. In a general way Republicans, with some notable exceptions, tended to favor high protective tariffs, and Democrats, especially those in the South who needed foreign markets for their cotton, wanted to reduce duties. But the issue was rarely clear-cut, for Democrats in manufacturing states like Pennsylvania were high-tariff men. Moreover, both parties tinkered with the tariff issue at election time. In 1872, for instance, the Republican party faced a split. Many tariff reformers in the Liberal Republican movement were preparing to join the Democrats. Attempting to check the bolt, the Republican-dominated Congress rushed through a bill reducing all duties by 10 percent. Once Grant was triumphantly reelected, Congress promptly repealed the reduction. Again in 1883, when it seemed likely that in the next election the Democrats would elect Grover Cleveland president and would win majorities in both Houses of Congress, Republicans hurriedly enacted the first general tariff act since the Civil War. They claimed that it reduced duties by an average of 5 percent, but in fact the measure was so complex and so contradictory that nobody could predict its impact. John L. Hayes, now president of the United States Tariff Commission, gave the secret away when he explained, shortly after the passage of the 1883 act: "In a word, the object was *protection through reduction.* . . . We wanted the tariff to be made by our friends."

Debates over Currency.

The controversies over currency during the post–Civil War generation were more complex, but in general they illustrate the same tension between the needs of a national economy and the desires of local and special economic interests.

Unless a historian is prepared to write a book about these monetary issues, perhaps he ought to confine his account to two sentences: During the generation after the Civil War there was constant controversy between those who wished to continue, or even to expand, the inflated wartime money supply and those who wanted to contract the currency. Most debtors favored inflation since it would allow them to pay debts in money that was less valuable than when they had borrowed it; and creditors favored contraction, so that the money they received in payment of debts would be more valuable than it had been when they lent it.

But these two sentences, accurate enough in a general way, fail to convey the full dimensions of the controversy. They make the whole issue seem a purely economic question of profit and loss. In fact, for many people the resumption of specie payment—that is, the redemption in gold, at face value, of the paper money that had been issued by the United States government—involved the sanctity of contracts, the reliability of the government's pledges, and the rights of private property. Indeed, the return to the gold standard seemed to have almost a religious significance. Probably most economists of the period shared the conviction of Hugh McCulloch, Johnson's secretary of the treasury, that "gold and silver are the only true measures of value. . . . I have myself no more doubt that these metals were prepared by the Almighty for this very purpose, than I have that iron and coal were prepared for the purposes for which they are being used." On the other hand, the advocates of so-called soft—or paper—money argued that it was downright un-American to drive greenbacks out of circulation and return to the gold standard. "Why," asked the promotor Jay Cooke, "should this Grand and Glorious Country be stunted and dwarfed—its activities chilled and its very life blood curdled—by these miserable 'hard coin' theories, the musty theories of a bygone age?"

That two-sentence summary also ignores the fact that the currency controversy involved economic interests falling into categories more sophisticated than debtors and creditors. Merchants in foreign trade were ardent supporters of resumption because fluctuations in the gold value of United States paper money made the business of these importers and exporters a game of chance. On the other hand, many American manufacturers, especially iron makers, were staunch foes of resumption because they needed an inflated currency to keep their national markets expanding.

Finally, that two-sentence summary does not indicate that attitudes toward these monetary policies changed over time. Throughout the postwar period farmers were mostly debtors, but they were primarily concerned with such issues as railroad regulation and until 1870 showed little interest in the currency. Creditor interests of the Northeast were indeed mostly supporters of resumption, but when a depression began in 1873 they unsuccessfully urged President Grant to sign the so-called Inflation Bill of 1874, which would have slightly increased the amount of paper money in circulation. In other words, they preferred mild inflation to economic collapse. Moreover, by the late 1870s, inflationists were no longer calling for additional greenbacks; instead, they joined forces with western mining interests to demand that the government expand the currency by coining silver dollars. When they discovered that, partly by oversight and partly by plan, the Coinage Act of 1873 had discontinued the minting of silver, they were outraged. Protesting the "Crime of '73," they demanded a return to bimetallism (both gold and silver being accepted in lawful payment of all debts) and the free and unlimited coinage of silver dollars.

With so many opposing forces at work, it is scarcely surprising that the history of currency policy and financial legislation in the postwar years is one of sudden fits and starts. Right after the war, Secretary McCulloch assumed that everybody wanted to return to specie payments promptly, and, in order to raise the value of the paper currency, he quietly held back greenbacks paid into the United States treasury for taxes and for public lands. His mild contraction of the currency restricted business expansion, and Congress forced him to stop. Subsequently the greenbacks that had been taken out of circulation were reissued, and they remained in circulation for the next decade in the total amount of $382 million.

Indirectly the currency became an issue in the presidential election of 1868. During the previous year, what became known as the Ohio Idea gained popularity in the Middle West. Critics of hard money objected to the government's practice of paying interest on the national debt in gold—which was, of course, much more valuable than greenbacks. The critics argued that since the bonds had been purchased with greenbacks, it would be entirely legal and proper to pay their interest in the same depreciated currency. In this way the crushing burden of the national debt on the taxpayer would be reduced. This argument was so attractive that the Democratic national convention incorporated a version of the Ohio Idea in its 1868 platform. However, the party negated the move by nominating Governor Horatio Seymour of New York, an earnest hard-money man, for president. The Republican national convention sternly rejected the Ohio Idea—against the wishes of many western delegates—and nominated Grant with a pledge to reject "all forms of repudiation as a national crime."

Despite this commitment, Grant's administration witnessed the completion of a series of compromises on currency. The new president announced that he favored a return to the gold standard; but at the same time he warned: "Immediate resumption, if practicable, would not be desirable. It would compel the debtor class to pay, beyond their contracts, the premium on gold . . . and would bring bankruptcy and ruin to thousands." But lest anyone think that this last statement meant that he desired further issues of paper money, Grant vetoed the Inflation Bill of 1874, against the wishes of many of his advisers.

It was within this broad policy of affirmation checked by negation that John Sherman, the Senate expert on finance, persuaded Congress in 1875 to pass the Resumption Act. This law announced the United States government's intention to redeem its paper money at face value in gold on or after January 1, 1879. On the surface this legislation was a victory for hard-money interests, but in fact it was a brilliant compromise. It did commit the United States to resumption—but only after four years' delay. Sherman sweetened this pill for the silver-mining interests by providing that "as rapidly as practicable" silver coins would be minted to replace the "fractional currency"—notes of postage-stamp size in 3-, 5-, 10-, 15-, 25-, and 50-cent denominations—issued during the war. To placate the greenback interests in the South and West, Sherman's measure made it easier to incorporate national banks, which had the right to issue treasury notes, in those regions.

Although efforts were made after 1875 to repeal the Resumption Act, it was such a carefully constructed compromise that all these attempts failed. Sherman, who became secretary of the treasury in President Hayes's cabinet, skillfully managed the transition in 1879 so that resumption took place without fanfare and without economic disturbance. The whole controversy over currency during the Gilded Age thus illustrates the tension between the needs of a national economy and the desires of local and special economic interests. The national policy of resumption, desired by most businessmen and needed if the United States was to play a part in world trade, was sustained; but local business interests were able to delay and modify implementation of the policy so that it did not impose too sudden or heavy a burden on groups adversely affected by hard money.

Discontent Among Farmers and Laborers

If the emergence of a national economy produced strains within the business community, it created severe problems for farmers and laborers, who felt that they were not fairly sharing its rewards. Discontent first erupted among farmers. Even in the buoyant

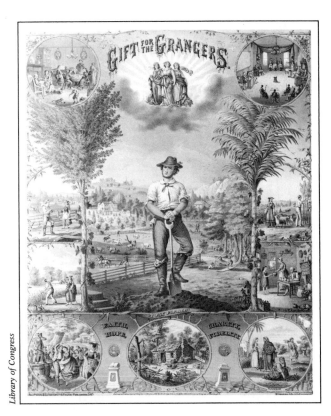

GIFT FOR THE GRANGERS

The Patrons of Husbandry (the Grange) stressed the prime importance of agriculture. "I Pay for All" reads the caption below this romanticized drawing of a remarkably clean and tidy farmer. The ruined cabin in the circle immediately below him bears the signposts "Ignorance" and "Sloth," while the vignettes in the upper corners give idealized pictures of the "Farmer's Fireside" and the "Grange in Session."

years immediately after the Civil War, the life of the northern and western farmer was often lonely and dull. On the western plains, where farmers lived miles from stores, schools, and churches, where there were often no near neighbors, and where there was no regular mail service, even the prosperous farmers lived stunted lives.

Perhaps farm women felt the isolation even more deeply than the men. At least occasionally men had to go into the nearest town, to purchase supplies, to negotiate with the bank, or to sell the farm produce, and here they could meet friends, exchange news about crops and economic conditions, and discuss politics. But wives rarely accompanied their husbands into town, because women were not supposed to be involved in business or politics. Instead they were virtually confined to the farm, where their long days were a lonely litany of cooking, cleaning, scrubbing, and caring for the children.

The Granger Movement. In an effort to remedy these problems, Oliver Hudson Kelley, a clerk in the United States Department of Agriculture, in 1867 founded a secret society called the Patrons of Husbandry. Kelley had lived in Massachusetts, Iowa, and Minnesota, and he had traveled extensively in the South after the war. Thus he knew at first hand the bleakness and the deprivation of rural living, and he wanted to give farmers all over the country a broader vision and a livelier social and intellectual life. The Patrons of Husbandry was intended to stimulate farmers' thinking through lectures, debates, and discussions, and it was designed to promote a sense of social solidarity through group singing, picnics, and other family entertainment. Each local unit of Kelley's society was called a Grange, and women as well as men belonged as equal members. American farmers found the whole idea so new that the organization got off to a slow start, and at the end of 1868 only ten Granges and been established.

But in the following year, when the price of farm commodities dropped sharply, agrarian discontent mounted. By the mid-1870s about 800,000 farmers, mostly in the Middle West and the South, joined the Granger movement. Although the Granges never abandoned their social and intellectual objectives, the meetings came increasingly to focus on economic issues important to farmers, such as the declining price of wheat and the mounting costs of railroad transportation. The constitution of the Patrons of Husbandry forbade the Grangers to engage in politics. Therefore, typically after the Grange ceremonies were completed and the standard literary or musical program concluded, the Grangers moved to adjourn the meeting; and, technically no longer Grangers but simply farmers gathered together, they discussed politics and endorsed candidates who favored the farmers' cause.

The agrarian cause embraced a variety of discontents with the way the national economy was operating. Farmers in Iowa, Nebraska, and Kansas complained that it took the value of one bushel of corn to pay the freight charges for shipping another bushel to eastern markets; farmers in Minnesota and Dakota said the same of wheat. Middle Western farmers protested the policy of the grain elevators that were used to store their wheat and corn until it could be picked up for rail shipment. Elevator operators frequently misgraded grain, offering the farmer with superior produce only the price for a lower grade; and the farmer usually had to accept, for he could not dump his grain on the ground. Southern and western farmers also objected to the limited bank credit available in their regions. When the national banking system was set up, the war was still going on, and no provision was made for establishing national banks in the

South. In the West there were few national banks because Congress required a minimum capital of $50,000, which few western towns could raise. Consequently the circulation of national bank notes, and hence the availability of loans, were grossly inequitable. Connecticut alone had more national bank notes in circulation than Michigan, Wisconsin, Iowa, Minnesota, Kansas, Missouri, Kentucky, and Tennessee.

Farmers' dissatisfaction with the national economy blended into a more general pattern of Middle Western discontent. It was not farmers alone who objected to high and discriminatory railroad rates; businessmen in Middle Western cities and towns, especially those served by only one rail line, also protested. Because the railroads set rates that favored large grain terminals, wheat produced twenty miles from Milwaukee might be diverted to Chicago. Because railroads gave special preference to long-distance shippers, lumber merchants in, for example, Clinton, Iowa, found that Chicago lumber dealers could undersell them; trainloads of lumber rumbled in from Chicago on the way to central and western Iowa without even slowing down at Clinton. The inequities of the national banking system affected western businessmen at least as much as they did the farmers, for the absence of credit crippled business expansion in the South and West.

Out of these general western grievances emerged what came to be known, somewhat inaccurately, as the Granger laws. Between 1869 and 1874 legislatures in Illinois, Iowa, Wisconsin, and Minnesota set maximum charges for grain elevators and railroads, and some of these states established regulatory commissions with broad powers. Although farmers supported this legislation, it was actually drawn up by lawyers and pushed by western businessmen; only in Wisconsin were the Grangers the principal advocates of regulation. The railroad and grain elevator companies promptly challenged the constitutionality of these acts. But the United States Supreme Court in *Munn* v. *Illinois* (1877) upheld the right of states to regulate railroads, even to the point of setting maximum rates. In the long run, state regulation of railroads and grain elevators proved ineffectual, and the Granger laws were repealed or modified. Nevertheless, their temporary success marked a victory for agrarian—and, in general, Middle Western—interests injured by the operation of the national economy.

Organization of Labor.

Industrial laborers were slower than farmers to find spokesmen for their discontent with the national economy. Factory workers came from many national backgrounds and spoke many languages. In the decade after the Civil War, more than 3.25 million immigrants, mostly from northern Eu-

SPECIMEN DIAL FOR MECHANICSVILLE TOWN HALL—HANDS EMPLOYED TO WORK EIGHT HOURS ONLY
The eight-hour movement was the most popular of the early postwar labor reform drives. Its slogan was: "Eight hours work a day leaves eight for sleep and eight for play."

rope, poured into the United States, and from these the labor force was largely recruited. By 1880 87 percent of the inhabitants of Chicago, 84 percent of those in Detroit and Milwaukee, and 80 percent of those in New York and Cleveland were immigrants or the children of immigrants. Divided along ethnic and religious lines, they had little sense of workers' solidarity. Many members of the work force, moreover, regarded their status as transient. They hoped, unrealistically, to move west as homesteaders or, having made their fortunes, to return to their European homelands.

It was almost impossible for a meaningful national labor movement to emerge from such a fractured work force. One of the earliest efforts was the eight-hour movement, led by Ira Stewart, a Boston machinist who sought legislation to limit the work day to eight hours without reduction of wages. Under this pressure the United States established an eight-hour day for its employees in 1868, and legislatures in six states passed acts to make eight hours a legal day's work. In private industry these laws proved ineffectual because they instituted the eight-hour restriction only "where there is no special contract or agreement to the contrary." Consequently most businessmen required employees to agree to work longer hours as a condition of employment.

The National Labor Union, created in 1866 at a Baltimore conference of delegates from various unions, proved little more effective. It was headed by William H. Sylvis, a dedicated propagandist and a superb speaker, whose interests, however, were not in conventional labor issues like hours and wages, but rather in cooperatives and currency reform. Sylvis recruited many members for the National Labor Union—it claimed 640,000 in 1868—but whether these were actual workingmen is questionable. A scornful observer remarked that the National Labor Union was made up of "labor leaders without organizations, politicians without parties, women without husbands, and cranks, visionaries, and agitators without jobs." After Sylvis's death in 1869, the organization began to decline, and it disappeared during the depression of 1873.

A more successful labor movement was the Knights of Labor, founded in 1869 by Uriah Stephens and other garment workers of Philadelphia. It grew slowly at first and, like the National Labor Union, received a serious setback in the depression. By the 1880s, however, its membership increased spectacularly as it attempted to create a broad union of all workingmen, skilled and unskilled. But its leadership, like that of the National Labor Union, disliked discussing hours, wages, and working conditions and was reluctant to call strikes. After 1879, the General Master Workman of the Knights of Labor was the idealistic, eloquent, and neurasthenic Irishman Terence V. Powderly, who preferred to think of himself as the head of a national educational institution rather than of a labor union.

Only a small fraction of the industrial labor force belonged to either the National Labor Union or the Knights of Labor. And the tactics of both organizations did little to relieve the day-to-day problems of working men and women. Hours were long, wages were miserably low, regular employment was uncertain, health or accident insurance was absent, and there were no pension or retirement programs. Child labor was exploited, and employees who dared to speak out against such abuses found themselves blacklisted by employers.

The Panic of 1873. These labor organizations were even less able to help in the severe depression that followed the Panic of 1873, precipitated by the failure of the financial firm of the Civil War financier Jay Cooke, who had subsequently become deeply involved in speculative ventures. Between 1873 and 1879 business activity in the United States declined by about one-third, and bankruptcies doubled. Thousands of workers lost their jobs. During the winter of 1873–74, about one-fourth of all laborers in New York City were unemployed, and during the following winter the number increased to one-third. In this time of crisis, the National Labor Union virtually collapsed, and many local unions disappeared as well. In New York City, for example, membership in all unions dropped from 45,000 in 1873 to 5,000 in 1877.

Private charities did what they could to relieve distress. But nobody seemed to know how to end the depression. Experts tended to view the panic and the subsequent unemployment and suffering as part of the natural workings of the national economic order, necessary to purge unsound businesses and speculative practices. Economists warned that "coddling" laborers would only retard this inevitable and necessary process. Blaming the depression on the wartime habit of looking to the federal government for leadership, Democratic Governor Samuel J. Tilden of New York called for a return to "government institutions, simple, frugal, meddling little with the private concerns of individuals . . . and trusting to the people to work out their own prosperity and happiness."

Those labor leaders who remained active were little more helpful. Many sought panaceas for the economic crisis. A writer in the *Radical Review* found the cause of the depression in private landownership, which, in his words, "begets . . . ground rent, an inexorable, perpetual claim for the use of land, which, like air and light, is the gift of Nature." Later, in 1879, Henry George made that idea the basis for the economic system proposed in his book *Progress and Poverty*. Other labor voices supported the Socialist Labor movement, founded in 1874, which foresaw the ultimate overthrow of the capitalist system through a socialist revolution. As interim measures to combat the depression, the movement advocated federal aid for education, industrial accident compensation, and women's suffrage. It attracted only a tiny following.

Some labor spokesmen sought the way out of the depression by supporting independent political parties pledged to protect labor's position in the national economy. There was considerable labor support for the Greenback, or National Independent, party, which was organized in 1874 at Indianapolis. The party's national program opposed the resumption of specie payments and advocated further issues of paper money to relieve the country's depressed industries. But the Greenback party was not exclusively a labor movement: its presidential candidate in 1876 was the eighty-five-year-old New York iron manufacturer Peter Cooper. The 80,000 votes Cooper received came mostly from Middle Western farm states. In the congressional elections two years later, however, more

THE BALTIMORE AND OHIO RAILROAD STRIKE—THE MARYLAND STATE MILITIA FIRING ON THE MOB IN BALTIMORE, JULY 20, 1877
An outbreak of labor violence in 1877 sent shudders through the business community. When Governor Carroll of Maryland called out the state militia on July 20 to break a strike on the Baltimore and Ohio Railroad, rowdy townsmen pelted the soldiers with stones, and the rattled militia fired into the crowd, killing and wounding several men. During the following night the troops were practically held prisoners in the Baltimore and Ohio station while a mob ravaged the city. Not until President Hayes sent regular U.S. army troops was the disorder quelled.

laborers supported the National Independent party because it campaigned for governmental regulation of the hours of labor and for the exclusion of Chinese immigrants. Like other advocates of inflation, the party by this time had moved beyond favoring greenbacks and urged expansion of the currency through silver coinage. Candidates endorsed by the National Independent party received more than a million votes in the 1878 congressional elections.

Labor Unrest and Federal Intervention.

Other laborers during the depression rejected politics in favor of direct action. With the collapse of the trade union movement, the so-called Molly Maguires, a secret ring that controlled the popular Irish fraternal society, the Ancient Order of Hibernians, gained power in the anthracite coal region of Pennsylvania. Soon mine owners re-

ported a "crime wave" in collieries, as the Mollies allegedly intimidated and even murdered bosses and superintendents they considered unfair. Eventually, on the dubious testimony of a paid infiltrator, some of the ringleaders were arrested; and when twenty-four of them were convicted in late 1876, the disturbances ended.

Labor unrest reached its peak in 1877, the worst year of the long depression. Railroad managers precipitated a crisis when, without warning, they cut wages on most railroads east of the Mississippi River by 10 percent. On July 17, the day after the cut became effective, workers on the Baltimore and Ohio Railroad went on strike. They seized the railyards at various points and refused to let any freight trains depart. Promptly employees of other eastern railroads also went on strike, and traffic on the four main lines connecting the Atlantic coast and the Middle West was paralyzed. Shortly afterward, the strike spread to some of the roads beyond the Mississippi and into Canada.

Local and state governments proved unable or unwilling to cope with the crisis. The governor of Maryland called out the state militia, but these civilian soldiers fraternized with their friends and relatives among the strikers. In Pittsburgh the strikers had the sympathy of the local government, for the city fathers had long felt that the Pennsylvania Railroad was discriminating against their city. Employees of nearby ironworks joined the railroad men in blocking all traffic on the Pennsylvania. When the governor sent in state militia companies from Philadelphia to clear the tracks, the troops succeeded in dispersing a large mob by killing twenty-six persons. But this action aroused so much additional hostility that the soldiers had to retreat into the roundhouse, which the mob promptly surrounded and set on fire. The next morning the Philadelphia soldiers fought their way out of the roundhouse and retreated from the city, leaving it in control of a mob of strikers, sympathizers, and looters, who proceeded to destroy rail property worth some $5 million.

To protect the national system of transportation so essential to the United States economy, President Hayes sent in regular army troops. This action marked the first time in American history that the army had been used on any extensive scale to crush a labor disturbance. The army promptly restored order, and the strike collapsed. Deeply disturbed members of the business community took steps to prevent any recurrence of such labor violence. State legislatures began passing conspiracy laws directed against labor organizations, and the courts began to invoke the doctrine of malicious conspiracy to break strikes and boycotts. Throughout the North the state militia, which had so often proved untrustworthy during the 1877 crisis, was reorganized and given stricter training. The inventor and manufacturer Cyrus Hall McCormick personally purchased equipment for the Second Regiment of Illinois militia because it had, he said, "won great credit for its action during . . . [labor] disturbances and can be equally relied on in the future."

Thus labor protests failed at just the time when farmer protest movements won at least some tempo-rary successes. The difference in outcome resulted in part from the fact that there was a long history of agrarian discontent in the United States, and that the Granger movement seemed as American as apple pie. Urban labor, labor unions, and massive strikes, however, were something novel to most Americans, and no doubt all three seemed the more dangerous since so many industrial laborers were immigrants with strange-sounding names and alien ways of behavior. In part, too, the differences stemmed from the fact that farmers and their allies lived in a distinct region of the United States, where they were strong enough to control local and state governments in the South and Middle West, while industrial laborers were scattered geographically, and nowhere did the labor movement have political power to equal its numbers.

More important than either of these differences was the fact that agrarian discontent did not pose a basic threat to the structure of the national economy. Many businessmen agreed with the farmers that limits should be imposed on the power of railroads and a few other monopolies. Labor unrest, however, appeared to strike at the heart of the national economic system. A popular Boston minister declared that the rioting of "the lawless classes at the bottom of our cities" had been instigated by "secret socialistic societies." The prominent financial editor W. M. Grosvenor spoke for much of the business community when he announced that "the light of the flames at Pittsburgh" foreshadowed "a terrible trial for free institutions in this country." He warned: "The Communist is here."

The Gilded Age faced many problems: overseas expansion and Indian wars, governmental corruption and controversies over the tariff and the currency, farmer movements and labor unrest. The cumulative result of all these problems was to distract most Northerners' attention from problems of the South. Increasing numbers of Americans came to understand that the basic tension between majority rule and minority rights was not something confined to relations between whites and blacks, or between Northerners and Southerners. The end of the era left Americans facing the unresolved problem of reconciling the centralizing, nationalizing tendencies in American life with the opposing tendencies toward localism, parochialism, and fragmentation.

CHRONOLOGY

1866 National Labor Union formed.
  Sioux Indians massacre Fetterman and troops.
1867 Maximilian's empire in Mexico falls.
  Purchase of Alaska.
  Patrons of Husbandry (the Grange) founded.
1868 Ulysses S. Grant elected president in contest with Democrat Horatio Seymour.
1869 Knights of Labor organized.
  Union Pacific and Central Pacific link at Promontory Point to form first transcontinental railroad.
1870 Standard Oil Company of Ohio organized.
1871 Treaty of Washington, settling differences between United States and Great Britain, signed.
  Tweed Ring scandals in New York City exposed.
1872 Crédit Mobilier scandals revealed.
  Grant names G. W. Curtis to head Civil Service Commission.
  Grant reelected over Horace Greeley, candidate of Liberal Republicans and Democrats.
1873 Coinage Act demonetizes silver in so-called Crime of '73.
  Panic of 1873 begins long depression.

1874 Grant vetoes Inflation Bill.
1875 Specie Resumption Act provides for return to gold standard by 1879.
1876 Exposure of Whiskey Ring reveals further corruption in Republican administration.
  Custer and his men slaughtered at battle of the Little Big Horn.
  Centennial Exhibition opens in Philadelphia.
  Republicans nominate Rutherford B. Hayes for president; Democrats nominate Samuel J. Tilden. Disputed returns leave outcome in doubt.
1877 Congress creates electoral commission, which rules that all disputed ballots belong to Hayes, who is inaugurated president.
  In *Munn* v. *Illinois* Supreme Court upholds Granger legislation.
  Nationwide railroad strike and ensuing violence lead to first significant use of federal troops to suppress labor disorders.

SUGGESTED READINGS

The best general treatment of social and economic change during the post–Civil War period is Allan Nevins, *The Emergence of Modern America, 1865–1878* (1927). Ellis P. Oberholtzer, *History of the United States Since the Civil War*, Vols. 1–4 (1929–31), contains an enormous amount of unassimilated data.

Foreign affairs during the Reconstruction era are treated in Glyndon G. Van Deusen, *William Henry Seward* (1967); Allan Nevins, *Hamilton Fish* (1936); and David Donald, *Charles Sumner and the Coming of the Civil War* (1970). Adrian Cook, *The Alabama Claims* (1975), is authoritative. Thomas D. Schoonover, *Dollars over Dominion* (1978), examines Mexican-American relations. On expansionism the standard work is A. K. Weinberg, *Manifest Destiny* (1935).

Wilcomb E. Washburn, *The Indian in America* (1975), and Robert F. Berkhofer, Jr., *The White Man's Indian* (1978), are superior works. On governmental policy toward the native Americans see David A. Nichols, *Lincoln and the Indians* (1978); Francis P. Prucha, *American Indian Policy in Crisis*

(1975); and Loring B. Priest, *Uncle Sam's Stepchildren* (1942). *The American Heritage History of the Indian Wars* (1977) is a spirited illustrated account. See also Eugene H. Berwanger's important study, *The West and Reconstruction* (1981).

Edward C. Kirkland, *Industry Comes of Age* (1961), traces the growth of a national economy. *The Visible Hand* (1977), by Alfred D. Chandler, Jr., analyzes the managerial revolution that took place in American business. Two richly detailed biographies of American business leaders are Allan Nevins, *Study in Power: John D. Rockefeller* (2 vols., 1953), and Joseph F. Wall, *Andrew Carnegie* (1970).

On the agricultural sector, see Fred A. Shannon, *The Farmer's Last Frontier* (1945). Walter P. Webb, *The Great Plains* (1931), gives a brilliant account of the settling of the trans-Mississippi West, and Robert F. Dykstra, *The Cattle Towns* (1968), is a fascinating study.

For a spirited, irreverent, and not entirely accurate account of the politics of the Gilded Age, read Matthew Josephson, *The Politicos, 1865–1896* (1938). Morton Keller, *Af-*

fairs of State: Public Life in Late Nineteenth Century America (1977), is much more judicious and analytical. For balanced studies of three Republican presidents, see William S. McFeely, *Grant* (1981), Harry Barnard, *Rutherford B. Hayes and His America* (1954), and Allan Peskin, *Garfield* (1978). Two full studies of corruption in New York City are Alexander B. Callow, *The Tweed Ring* (1966), and Seymour Mandelbaum, *Boss Tweed's New York* (1965). Ari A. Hoogenboom, *Outlawing the Spoils* (1961), is a model history of the civil service reform movement.

Three modern, sophisticated analyses of the currency controversy are Robert P. Sharkey, *Money, Class, and Party* (1959); Irwin Unger, *The Greenback Era* (1964); and Walter T. K. Nugent, *The Money Question During Reconstruction* (1967).

Solon J. Buck, *The Granger Movement* (1913), remains a standard work, but George H. Miller, *Railroads and the Granger Laws* (1971), shows the influence of western businessmen on the so-called Granger legislation. Labor organization and unrest are treated in depth in John R. Commons et al., *History of Labor in the United States*, Vol. 2 (1918).

PART FIVE

NATIONALIZING THE REPUBLIC, 1877–1920

John L. Thomas

As the American people completed their industrial revolution in the half-century following the Civil War, they continued to celebrate unprecedented growth even as they were driven to experiment with new ways of regulating it. In 1900 as in 1850, most Americans saw a reason for national self-congratulation in the numerous signs of prosperity all around them. The standard of living was improving, the population was growing rapidly, great cities were rising, and the stock of consumer goods was steadily increasing. More thoughtful observers, however, noted that a high social price had been paid for all these achievements. A rural people had been suddenly uprooted and their communities disrupted, new masses of underprivileged persons had been forced into mobility, too many Americans worked under deplorable conditions, and a conspicuously unequal distribution of wealth persisted. Still, for most people caught up in America's industrial transformation, the benefits of rapid material growth clearly outweighed its costs.

Economic growth continued to verify earlier predictions of unlimited betterment, and most Americans continued to believe in the cherished ideal of progress. Freedom from external restraints on individual ambitions was the key concept in the doctrine of progress, and this concept had survived the Civil War—if not unscathed, at least largely intact. In 1900 a majority of Americans continued to maintain a simple faith in the individual, just as it had a generation earlier.

Yet despite the country's optimistic mood, by 1880 reform-minded citizens in all walks of life were beginning to note the signs of mounting social disorder. Industrialization, modernization, and urbanization forced a growing number of leaders in all parts of the national community to recognize the need for controls and systems in order to make American society efficient and stable. To improve their operations and increase their profits, businessmen sought consolidated power within their firms. Farmers quickly discovered an urgent need for better credit facilities and marketing mechanisms. Social theorists and urban reformers began to adjust their vision to the requirements of systematic planning. By 1890 the American way of life, which had once seemed a

Overleaf: The first train over the last spike en route to Portland, Oregon, from St. Paul, Minnesota, 1883. *Haynes Foundation Collection, Montana Historical Society, Helena, Montana.*

self-regulating device for producing happiness automatically, had come to be seen as a machine badly in need of repair, if not of a complete overhaul.

These would-be reformers of American society after 1890 did not always agree on priorities and means. But the thrust of their ideas and programs pointed unmistakably toward the construction of a new national order. In historical terms this new vision seemed to reject the libertarian philosophy of Thomas Jefferson and to revive the nationalist model of Alexander Hamilton. In the fields of law and constitutional theory, formal definitions of rights and duties were replaced by more flexible concepts of social utility, requiring new roles for lawyers and legislators alike. In social reform there was a new emphasis on training, expertise, and the predictive functions of science. In politics an organizational revolution brought new styles of leadership and new approaches to the workings of government.

The distance the nation had traveled by 1920 could be measured in two widely different assessments of American politics and society. The first assessment was that of the individualist prophet Ralph Waldo Emerson at the height of moral reform before the Civil War. Emerson located the essence of the American spirit in the "wise man" with whose appearance "the state expires." "The tendencies of the times," Emerson predicted, "favor the idea of self-government, and leave the individual . . . to the rewards and penalties of his own constitution which works with more energy than we believe whilst we depend on artificial restraints." But three-quarters of a century later, the progressive sociologist Charles Horton Cooley dismissed Emerson's self-enclosed individual as a moral abstraction unknown to history. "In a truly organic life the individual is self-conscious and devoted to his work, but feels himself and that work as part of a large joyous whole. He is self-assertive, just because he is conscious of being a thread in the great web of events." The story of the years separating Emerson, the sage of Concord, from the progressive social scientist Cooley is the account of the American discovery of the great social web and the multitude of connecting threads that composed it.

22 Stabilizing the American Economy

In the first years of the Republic, Alexander Hamilton predicted that industry and agriculture would advance together in the American march toward abundance. Hamilton's promise was echoed a few years later by Henry Clay in his prophecy of the eventual triumph of his American System, and it was repeated again and again in the years before the Civil War by businessmen and promoters eager to exploit the country's resources. While in power, Hamilton, and later Clay and John Quincy Adams, had tried to provide the framework for industrial growth. But not until the last decades of the nineteenth century did the American people finally make good on Hamilton's initial promise. At the end of the Civil War, the United States still stood on the threshold of the modern industrial world—as did France, Germany, Japan, and Russia. Thus in 1865 the United States continued to be a hungry importer of capital, labor, and most of its technology. Thirty years later the nation had transformed itself into a major exporter of foodstuffs and the producer of a mammoth stockpile of industrial and consumer goods. Within a generation it had joined Great Britain and Germany as one of the world's leading industrial powers.

Statistics, which Americans were just beginning to collect and interpret, told a story of unprecedented economic growth. The value of American manufactured products soared from $3 billion in 1869 to more than $13 billion at the turn of the century. In the 1890s alone the national wealth climbed from $65 billion to $90 billion while national income rose from $12 billion to $18 billion. In the same years, production soared. The figures were startling.

Between the Civil War and 1900 the output of manufactured goods tripled; the product of the key, all-important steel industry jumped from 68,000 tons of finished steel in 1870 to 4.2 million tons in 1890. The national labor force rose sharply too, from 13 million to 19 million, and the percentage of the national income that went to pay wages increased from 37 percent to 47 percent.

Figures like these led Charles E. Perkins, president of the Chicago, Burlington, and Quincy Railroad, to ask his fellow citizens, "Have not great merchants, great manufacturers, great inventors, done more for the world than preachers and philanthropists?... Can there be any doubts that cheapening the cost of necessities and conveniences of life is the most powerful agent of civilization and progress?" Some Americans had little love for great merchants and great manufacturers, whom they tended to blame for the period's economic disruptions. But most of them probably also agreed that material progress came first because the intellectual and cultural achievements of their civilization depended on such progress. In turn, material progress resulted from an industrial revolution that had changed the face of American society in less than a generation. What was this revolution? How did it happen? What forces accounted for it?

The Foundations of the American Industrial Revolution

Growth of Cities. A principal factor in the United States' dramatic transformation in the last quarter of the nineteenth century was the unprecedented growth of American cities. An enormous demographic shift that had begun before the Civil War continued for the rest of the century. Native-born citizens and recently arrived immigrants crowded into metropolitan areas, where they furnished huge new markets for consumer goods of all kinds—basic necessities like food and clothing; as well as such new products as sewing machines, typewriters, and cigarettes. By 1880 over a quarter of the nation's people lived in urban areas. In the remaining years of the century, the urban population grew at the phenomenal rate of 6 percent per decade, until by 1900 a full 40 percent of the American people lived in cities. Even more important, they tended to concentrate in giant centers, like New York, Chicago, Philadelphia, and Detroit, where they

544

CITY TRAFFIC IN THE NINETIES
Trolleys, horse-drawn cabs, delivery wagons, and wary pedestrians compete for space on Chicago's Clark Street.

quickly became dependent on a steady supply of consumer goods provided by manufacturers, processors, and distributors. "We cannot all live in cities," Horace Greeley, the aging editor of the New York *Tribune*, complained to a younger generation headed toward the metropolis, "yet nearly all seem determined to do so. . . . 'Hot and cold water,' baker's bread, the theatre, and the streetcars . . . indicate the tendency of modern taste."

American cities expanded at a pell-mell pace, pushing the boundaries of old commercial centers into surrounding suburbs along elevated railroad and trolley lines. The cities thus became giant consumers of heavy industrial goods—electrical dynamos, telephone wire, lead pipe and copper tubing, streetcars and the motors to run them. Whether they subsidized a huge public construction like John and Washington Roebling's magnificent Brooklyn Bridge, or encouraged a massive private venture like architect Louis Sullivan's steel-framed Wainwright Building in St. Louis, American cities provided an insatiable appetite for the products of the industrial machine. And with both labor and electric power available, major cities

attracted new factories and quickly became producers as well as consumers of industrial abundance.

Railroads. Railroads also played a crucial role in developing a powerful national economy. They fed heavy industry with ever-larger orders for steel rails, machines, and equipment. In their search for the necessary capital, railroad leaders probed new investment markets in every sector of the economy, private and public. Soon the railroads linked the nation's cities, first in a loose network and then in a tighter web that composed a national market system. Here again statistics tell the story: 35,000 miles of track in 1865 had become 242,000 by 1897. At the end of the Civil War, railroads stopped just across the Mississippi River, in Iowa and Missouri. By the century's end there were no less than five transcontinental railroads. Even more important was the rapid consolidation of the railroad empire east of the Mississippi River, where trackage doubled in the 1870s and doubled again in the 1880s. By 1890 railroad transportation was dominated by a small group of integrated lines like the New York Cen-

BUILDING BROOKLYN BRIDGE
Dignitaries pose on the catwalk leading to the pier.

tral and the Pennsylvania roads in the Northeast, the Burlington system in the Midwest, and the Union Pacific, Northern Pacific, and Great Northern routes to the West Coast.

The railroads quickly acquired unsavory reputations—usually well deserved. In the last quarter of the century, they were accused (frequently with ample proof) of disregarding the safety and comfort of their passengers, jerrybuilding their roads, rigging rates that discriminated against small shippers, lobbying Congress for special legislation, and in general both preaching and practicing a public-be-damned philosophy. "They exact success, and do not cultivate political morality," complained Charles Francis Adams, Jr., a severe but fair critic of the railroads.

Nevertheless the railroads compiled an impressive record in establishing new national traffic patterns. In 1865 the railroads were a collection of local systems without standard gauge and equipment and lacking even a common timetable. Twenty-five years

later, without ever having given serious thought to public policy, railroad magnates had provided for the country an immense system of rail lines. Across these tracks moved wheat, corn, and hogs from the Great Plains, cotton from the Mississippi Delta, lumber from Wisconsin and the Northwest, oil products from Pennsylvania, and coal from West Virginia and Kentucky—all in increasing quantity and with predictable regularity. With the development of the refrigerated car at the end of the century came meat from Chicago, Omaha, and Kansas City, and fruit and vegetables from California and Florida. Once this efficient distributing system had been equipped with instantaneous communication by the telegraph and the telephone, American businessmen could envision for the first time a national complex of business firms that would practice economies made possible by huge volume—economies of scale—and that would pass these savings along to consumers nationwide in the form of lower prices. Both as economic fact and

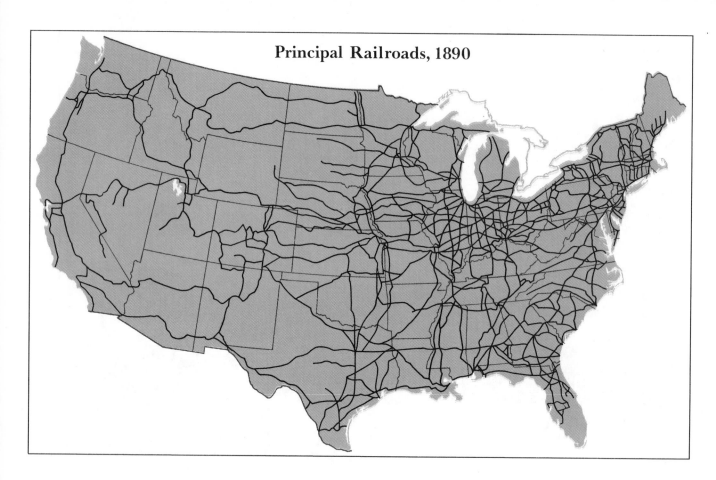

Principal Railroads, 1890

organizational idea, the railroads dominated the development of the American economy.

Technology. Another powerful stimulant to economic growth was the swiftly developing technology. The number of inventions mounted steadily after the Civil War, and the annual total of patent applications reached 25,000 in 1890. In 1871 the Hoe press and the Ingersoll air drill were invented, and three years later came the third rail for subways and elevated lines. Then in 1879 came the first railroad signal system; in 1883 in Chicago, the first elevated electric railway, which formed the Loop; in 1886, alternating current. In every branch of industry and manufacturing—machine tools, steel, mining, flour milling, lumbering—new inventions expanded productivity and reduced man-hours of labor.

Unlike twentieth-century technology, most of which is based on a "knowledge revolution" and is produced by highly trained experts, nineteenth-century inventions were developed by trial and error. The discovery and development of the Bessemer converter—the original key to making large quantities of steel—is an example. Only after some clever guesswork and haphazard experimenting did Sir Henry Bessemer in England and William Kelly in the United States learn to force blasts of air into molten pig iron to burn out the carbon. With this discovery the modern science of metallurgy began. Important as the Bessemer process was in producing high-grade steel in large amounts, it was soon supplemented by the "open hearth" method, powered by gas furnaces that eliminated the need for the air blast. Like many industrial improvements in the United States in the nineteenth century, steel technology originated in Europe but was quickly adapted to American conditions. Thus by the mid-1870s Bessemer mills in this country were producing 50 percent more steel than their British counterparts, a margin that widened every year as homegrown technological geniuses, among them Carnegie Steel's Captain "Bill" Jones, designed more efficient layouts for mills and found better ways of moving hot steel through them.

In every field American technology proved remarkably flexible in borrowing and improving foreign

WRECK ON THE NEW YORK CENTRAL AT BATAVIA, NEW YORK, 1885
Passenger safety was not always a top priority for the nation's railroads.

designs. Sometimes it provided lighter and faster machinery, as in the textile industry; at other times it developed bigger and stronger equipment, like the mammoth steam shovels needed for heavy construction. In the oil industry the "cracking" process, which was developed in the 1870s, allowed refiners to control various yields by altering the molecular structure of the petroleum. Often an invention broke a technological bottleneck that had blocked an entire process, as in the case of George Westinghouse's system for transmitting alternating current over long distances.

Technology and a new science of management worked together to train the labor force in the new skills and work patterns that were needed for industrialization. A huge pool of unskilled labor was still considered essential to American economic expansion, but the long-term trend pointed toward mechanization and, in the end, automation. Despite the willingness of native-born boys fresh from the farm, and young immigrants just off the boat, to feed the furnaces and work the lathes, it was machinery that sent American productivity soaring, and consumption with it.

Capital Investment. Technology bred great expectations and a mounting hunger for capital. In the early years of the oil business, just after the Civil War, John D. Rockefeller was able to acquire a small refinery for $10,000 and a large one for $50,000. By 1910 the market value of Rockefeller's Standard Oil was $600 million. Technology promised greater efficiency but also required increased investment. Such investment was readily forthcoming. In 1860 a total of $1 billion was invested in the nation's manufacturing plants, which turned out a collective product worth $1.8 billion and employed 4.3 million workers. By 1900 the size of the work force had grown fivefold, and the total value of products nearly tenfold; at the same time, the amount of invested capital had multiplied twelvefold.

The sudden availability of massive amounts of capital was one of the most striking features of the American Industrial Revolution. For the first seventy-five years of the nineteenth century, most of the capital for industrial investment had come out of the savings of the firms that used it. But the last half of the nineteenth century was a period of what economists call "capital deepening": people reserved a much larger share of the gross national product for savings and investment. To put this new money to work, a host of new financial institutions appeared—commercial banks, savings banks, life insurance companies, and investment houses. These new institutions served as intermediaries between the eager investor and the needy business firm. By 1900 the stock market had established itself as the main mechanism for exchanging securities and mobilizing the vast funds that were needed by new industrial firms. By the time the United States entered the First World War, Wall Street had succeeded in creating a genuine national market for capital.

The pace of the American Industrial Revolution was unregulated and hence uneven. For the first time a combination of potent economic forces was at work—a huge urban market, an efficient distribution system, a highly motivated work force, and vast amounts of capital. All that was lacking was a public policy that recognized the need for regulation and direction. Without such a program the transformation of the American economy was destined to be disorganized and at times chaotic.

Economic Instability. The instability of the American economy in the last quarter of the nineteenth century was a hard-edged reality. The American economy swung like a pendulum between good times and hard times, and back again. The Panic of 1873 plunged the country into six years of depression, with massive unemployment, wage cuts, and price declines. Following a short season of recovery, a second recession buffeted the economy in 1884 and again sent prices skidding and workers into the ranks of the unemployed. Once more, after a brief respite, the Panic of 1893 brought four more years of economic paralysis, from which the country recovered only at the end of the century.

All three depressions were triggered by financial panics—the collapse of the investment house of Jay Cooke in 1873, of Grant and Ward in 1884, and of nearly the entire railroad empire in 1893. But satisfactory explanations of the causes of depressions were hard to come by. American observers compared depressions to a swing of the pendulum, the breaking of a wave, or the onset of a fever. But the experts despaired of controlling the business cycle or of easing the effects of periodic slumps. Despite the lessons in the need for economic planning that the Civil War had taught, the great majority of Americans still believed in the self-regulating market. And conventional wisdom declared that government should not interfere with this market. "Money-getters," the great showman P. T. Barnum warned the politicians, "are the benefactors of our race." Stand aside and let them do their work!

The result of this popular belief in unlimited business opportunity was a national government that frequently subsidized business but seldom regulated it. Politicians and businessmen alike predicted marvelous achievements for a new industrial statesmanship left to its own devices. Corporations, the wealthy ironmaster Abram S. Hewitt told the Chicago Board of Trade in 1885, were the "best friends" the American people had. Farseeing industrialists were now "doing the work which was done by Jefferson and Madison in the early years of the Republic." Sociologist William Graham Sumner, the great defender of American rugged individualism, amended this judgment only slightly. "The great leaders in the development of the industrial organization need those talents of executive and administrative skill, and fortitude, which were formerly called for in military affairs and scarcely anywhere else."

As Gilded Age politicians deferred to business leadership and praised business values, the directive force of government tended to disappear in misty hopes for automatic prosperity. The great steel manufacturer and self-made man Andrew Carnegie explained the terms of the new social contract in a language that a business civilization instinctively understood. It would be a mistake, Carnegie insisted, for the American community to shoot its millionaires since, after all, they were the "bees" that made the most honey. "Under our present conditions the millionaire who toils on is the cheapest article which the community secures at the price it pays for him, namely, his shelter, clothing, and food." Carnegie need not have worried: there would never be an open season on American millionaires.

Business Fills a Vacuum

Because the federal government was reluctant to assert its control over the economy, and state governments responded only gradually with piecemeal legislation, the job of providing a measure of economic stability fell to American businessmen. Blessed with organizational talent and energy, American businessmen were the first to respond to the challenge of disorder, even though they tended to concentrate on the specific problems confronting their own businesses. In most businessmen's view, their needs did not require public policy; rather, they could be met by a series of limited private strategies to protect their own firms. Slowly a general pattern of self-regulation emerged in response to threats to continued prosperity.

The most obvious threat was a long-term drop in prices in the last decades of the nineteenth century.

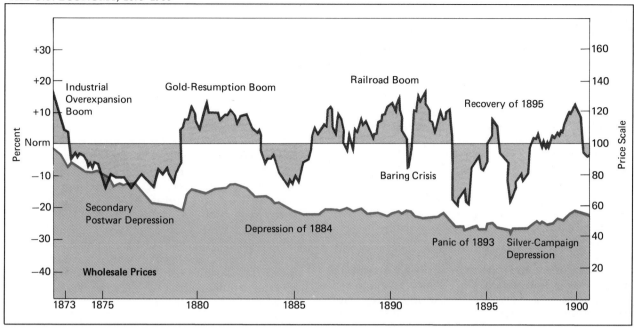

The wholesale price index sank from 100 in 1880 to 82 in 1890. Faced with recurrent panics and slumps, and threatened by growing competition and the prospects of shrinking profits, the boldest of the nation's businessmen began to experiment with various ways of gaining greater control over their enterprises. Their experiments were improvised attempts at stability made by a business community that was suddenly confronted with severe problems but left to its own devices to find solutions. In deciding to demolish a small-business economy with its free-market system and to replace it with new combinations, American business leaders played—often without realizing it—a genuinely revolutionary role.

Cartels and Trusts.

The earliest and simplest forms of consolidation—those requiring the least amount of change—were *cartels*. These were loose trade associations, or *pools*, of independent business firms joined together to dominate an industry. The organizer of the Wire Nail Association explained his case for a pool with disarming candor:

There is nail machinery enough in this country to produce four times as many nails as can be sold. When there is no pool the makers simply cut each other's throats. Some people think there is something wicked about pools. When we were trying to get up the nail pool, I talked with directors of companies who held up their hands against going into any sort of combination. I said to them, "How much did you make last year?" "Not a cent." "Are you making anything now?" "No." "Well, what do you propose to do? Sit here and lose what capital you have got in the business . . . ?" There is only one way to make any money in a business like the nail business, and that is to have a pool.

Pools attempted to meet the problem of overproduction and falling prices through gentlemen's agreements: competitors, while maintaining their independence, agreed among themselves to accept quotas and refrain from price cutting. For example, in organizing their pool in 1881, the whiskey distillers agreed that "only 28 percent of the full capacity shall be operated, and no stocking up beyond this amount under any circumstances." To tighten sagging steel prices, the steel rail manufacturers in 1887 formed the Steel Rail Association, which established a strict quota system and provided for a series of stiff fines for uncooperative members. Although the Steel Rail Association continually denied charges of price fixing, it nevertheless enjoyed a period of remarkable price stability thereafter.

Yet cartels had their drawbacks. They flourished in good times but fell apart under the pressure of recessions. Their agreements could not be enforced in the courts, and American consumers regarded them as an undue restraint of trade. Recognizing these limitations and sensitive to an aroused public opposition to secret agreements, pioneer organizers, among them John D. Rockefeller, turned to "horizontal" combinations, or *trusts*. The trust was the brainchild of a member of Standard Oil's legal staff, the affable and shrewd Samuel C. T. Dodd, who patiently explained its advantages to hesitant colleagues. Because state laws prohibited a company's outright ownership of another company's stock, there was no foolproof way of consolidating, holding, and managing a string of separate companies, Dodd admitted.

But you could have a common name, a common office, and a common management by means of a common executive committee. . . . If the Directors of one of the companies and their successors shall be made Trustees of all such stock, you thus procure a practical unification of all the companies.

The idea worked. In 1882 forty-one stockholders in the Standard Oil Company of Ohio signed an agreement creating a board of nine trustees to whom they transferred all the properties and assets of their companies in exchange for trust certificates. The visible signs of this financial feat were 700,000 hundred-dollar certificates, the price of consolidated control over the American oil industry. The corporate spirit had worked its first miracle.

Once they acquired formal control over production and prices, many trusts and *holding companies* (similarly integrated firms that were allowed to hold stock in other corporations) were content to operate as loose cartels, simply parceling out shares of the market without trying to impose a centralized management or authority. The hoped-for efficiency and economies were not always forthcoming in such cases of partial consolidation. But soon the largest and most powerful businesses began to follow the examples of the Carnegie Steel Company and of Gustavus Swift in meatpacking, by achieving "vertical" integration of their industries. They sought to combine under single management all the processes of production and distribution—from the sources of raw material to new marketing systems. More and more frequently after 1890, big business tried to secure control that extended "backward" to resources and transportation, as well as "forward" to control of the market through research departments and central business offices.

The Merger Movement. In the last years of the nineteenth century, the American economy entered a second phase of "horizontal" consolidation with the sudden growth of industrial and financial mergers that demolished the old order of Gilded Age capitalism and cleared the ground for new twentieth-century corporate giants. From one angle the great merger movement at the turn of the century appeared to be a towering peak of corporate consolidations. The annual number of mergers traced a sharp trajectory: 69 in 1897, 303 in 1898, and 1,208 in 1899, leveling off in the next three years at between 350 and 425. By 1900 there were 73 so-called trusts, each with a total capital investment of more than $10 million. Two-thirds of them had been established the previous three years.

Viewed negatively, the merger movement simply looked like a gigantic hole into which some 300 businesses tumbled each year, swallowed by huge new combinations like United States Steel and General Electric. United States Steel absorbed more than 200 manufacturing and transportation companies, and it swiftly gained control over two-thirds of the steel market. American Tobacco combined 162 independent companies and ruled all but 10 percent of the tobacco market. By 1904 the approximately 2,000 largest firms in the United States composed less than 1 percent of the total number of the nation's businesses yet produced 40 percent of the annual value of the nation's industrial goods. By 1910 *monopoly* (entire control of an industry by a single firm) and *oligopoly* (rule by a few large firms) had secured the commanding positions from which to dominate twentieth-century American life.

The merger movement, which climaxed a half-century's search for economic order, was both a logical outgrowth of rapid industrial development and an unsettling departure from remembered ways. It was natural for a new generation of promoters and industrial bankers to see in industrial combination, if not the hand of God, at least an unchanging law of nature at work ordering the business affairs of the world. Samuel C. T. Dodd, Rockefeller's counsel, warned of the futility of tinkering with the celestial machinery. "You might as well endeavor to stay the formation of the clouds, the falling of the rains, or the flowing of the streams as to attempt by any means or in any manner to prevent organization of industry, association of persons, and the aggregation of capital to any extent that the ever growing trade of the world may demand." And indeed, the success of mergers was hard to deny.

By 1895 the remarkable growth and sizable profits of Standard Oil, American Sugar Refining, and American Tobacco marked what appeared to be a sure route to salvation through combination. Simply to ponder the scale of these new enterprises was exhilarating! The Federal Steel Corporation, Judge Elbert Gary boasted, "takes the ore from the ground, transports it, manufactures it into pig iron, manufactures pig iron into steel, and steel into finished products, and delivers those products." Even more impressive was the formation in 1901 of United States Steel, into which went not only some 200 manufacturing plants

Department of the Interior, National Park Service, Edison National Historic Sight; Museum of Modern Art, New York

TWO AMERICAN HEROES
The portrait of Thomas A. Edison in his laboratory in the legendary pose of the native American genius (left) contrasts sharply with Edward Steichen's portrait of J. Pierpont Morgan as the awesome financial wizard (right).

and transportation companies, but also 1,000 miles of railroad, 112 blast furnaces, and 78 ore boats. Soon U.S. Steel was employing 170,000 workers as it gathered control over 60 percent of the country's steel. Its initial capital investment at $1.4 billion was three times the annual expenditure of the federal government.

Increased efficiency, elimination of waste, bigger shares of the market, and anticipated but often elusive economies of scale—all these convinced adventurous businessmen of the need to pursue mergers. By 1910 mergers had spread to all the principal sectors of the economy. When the great wave of mergers receded in 1903, it left in its wake a new corporate capitalism—a system of mammoth integrated enterprises with interlocking structures, managed by professionals with newly acquired expertise, selling their increasing variety of products in shared markets at administered prices. The great merger movement declared the bankruptcy of old-fashioned, small-scale competition

and announced the arrival of a modern corporate society that needed new definitions and values to replace the outworn Horatio Alger pieties of pluck and luck. In place of a host of small- and medium-sized businesses scrambling for a share of the market, there now stood huge unified structures. The corporate revolution was by no means over by 1914, and the nation throughout this period—known as the Progressive era—continued to support a dual economy of big and little businesses. But the central message of the merger movement was clear to most Americans: bigger was better.

Organizing the mergers and raising the capital to launch them became the specialty of investment bankers like J. P. Morgan and Jacob Schiff. Their role was critical, and they dominated the American economy at the turn of the twentieth century as they never would again. While taking a handsome slice of stock in the consolidations they created, these bankers became powerful middlemen between a public eager to invest and an expansive business community. The investment bankers arranged mergers and floated (sold) stock, established the workings of their new creations, and manufactured favorable publicity. Their success could be read in the achievements of the House of Morgan, which by 1912, together with the Morgan-controlled First National Bank of New York and the Rockefeller-managed National City Bank, held 341 directorships in 112 corporations worth $22.2 billion.

To the public the investment banker personified the whole merger movement. He was part savior of a threatened economy, part devil in disguise. As though to conceal embarrassing questions of right and wrong, an air of conspiracy characterized even the fictional portraits of the American businessmen of the day—Van Harrington in Robert Herrick's *The Memoirs of an American Citizen*, Magnus Derrick in Frank Norris's *The Octopus*, and Frank Cowperwood in Theodore Dreiser's trilogy of desire. For their everyday heroes Americans might have preferred the inventor and the engineer—Thomas Edison, Alexander Graham Bell, George Westinghouse—but they also admired, feared, envied, and puzzled over the new captains of industry and the financial wizards who presumably ran the country: the awesome J. P. Morgan, the cautious Jacob Schiff, and their clients and lesser breeds of big businessmen.

The leaders of the new corporate age, like their many admirers, were never entirely clear about their ultimate aims. Heavy investment capital, rapid plant expansion, increased production and reduced overhead, economies of scale, market control—all to what greater good? For profit, surely, and for rising quantities of consumer goods for more and more people. But beyond that? What did the manufacture and constant manipulation of consumer demand mean for individual freedom of choice? Was standardization of products and prices really so desirable? How were Americans to balance rising standards of living with loss of control over production? How could big business be called to account and made to deliver on its promise of economic security for all citizens? Were huge industrial and financial combinations compatible with political democracy and social responsibility? Neither the corporate revolutionaries nor their uneasy admirers could quite answer these questions, which posed a continuing twentieth-century dilemma.

The Counterrevolution Fails

These same questions troubled the opponents of big business, whose numbers and influence also grew rapidly in the late nineteenth century. If the antimonopolists ultimately failed to stop economic concentration, it was not for lack of numbers. The antimonopoly

The Metropolitan Museum of Art, gift of J. B. Neumann, 1958

army in the last quarter of the nineteenth century included at one time or another farmers and workingmen with their strong beliefs in equal opportunity; small businessmen with their individualist creed; and liberal publicists, country lawyers, clergymen, and educators. Antimonopoly found a congenial home in the major protest parties of the period, from the Grangers and the Greenbackers of the 1870s to the Populists of the 1890s.

The antimonopolists voiced many different complaints. Monopolies, it was widely held, misallocated and underused resources and thus kept the nation's total output lower than it should have been. Trusts, it was said, tied the people's hands while picking their pockets. They were thought to be inefficient and to shelter incompetent producers within huge integrated structures where their inefficiencies went undetected. If pools, trusts, and all other instruments of business collusion did not inevitably raise prices, at least they had the power to do so at will. And that power had been acquired by driving out honest competitors.

Clarence Davies Collection, Museum of the City of New York

NEW YORK: WINTER AND SUMMER
Alfred Steiglitz's famous photograph of Fifth Avenue in a snowstorm (1892) contrasts with one of a Madison Square Park cab stand in summer (1900).

The Case Against Monopoly. The heart of the case against trusts and monopolies was the belief in a "natural development" that presumably had been violated. The chief spokesmen against business consolidation were three social prophets, Henry George, Edward Bellamy, and Henry Demarest Lloyd, whose best sellers *Progress and Poverty* (1879), *Looking Backward* (1888), and *Wealth Against Commonwealth* (1894) commanded national attention. For this trio of social reformers, as for countless other publicists and popularizers of the case against monopoly, "natural" economic growth meant a steady rate of development accompanied by full employment and widespread consumption. According to this reasoning, although healthy societies like the United States enjoyed a "normal" pace of steady growth, the monopolies played havoc with it by accelerating the growth rate abnormally and by stimulating a feverish speculation. If trusts, pools, holding companies, and all the other artificial contrivances could simply be dismantled and their special privileges annulled, the American economy would return to a steadier rate of "real growth" that would spread the benefits of industrialism evenly through society.

The antimonopolists' case against economic concentration rested on a set of moral assumptions that defined the good society and called upon Americans to recapture it. First came the distinction between the world's true producers and the parasites who fed on them. The second assumption included both a faith in natural cooperation and a sense of community inherent in a society of small producers. Finally, the antimonopolists believed in a moral economy derived from an eighteenth-century tradition of artisanship that established a just price and a fair wage with ethical precision. As Henry George explained in the opening of *Progress and Poverty*:

So long as all the increased wealth which modern progress brings goes but to build up great fortunes, to increase luxury and make sharper the contrast between the House of Have and the House of Want, progress is not real and cannot be permanent. The reaction must come.

Public opposition to monopoly accomplished little before 1890. In the 1870s the Patrons of Husbandry, or the Grange, as the national farmers' organization was called, turned to politics in states like Illinois and Wisconsin. Together with shippers, the Grange passed laws regulating the rates that the railroads charged for hauling freight and storing grain. Although the Supreme Court originally upheld these so-called Granger laws in *Munn* v. *Illinois* (1877), nine years later in *Wabash, St. Louis & Pacific Railway Co.* v. *Illinois* a more conservative-minded majority declared that individual states could not regulate rates for interstate carriers.*

On the federal level the Interstate Commerce Act (1887) was not much more successful in bringing the railroads to heel. The act prohibited pools, rebates, and rate discriminations, and it set up a commission to investigate violations. But the commission's findings could be enforced only by the courts, a costly and cumbersome procedure. The Interstate Commerce Act marked the beginning of the American public's acceptance of the principle of government intervention, but it did not provide effective regulation. For that the country had to await Theodore Roosevelt's Square Deal.

By the time Congress responded to the public clamor to "do something about the trusts" by passing the Sherman Antitrust Act in 1890, more than a dozen states had already attempted some kind of antitrust legislation aimed at making restraint of trade "illegal, actionable, and indictable." Big business, however, countered these attempts at control by moving into more permissive states like New Jersey, where they secured favorable laws. Henry Demarest Lloyd, perhaps the severest critic of monopoly, complained that Standard Oil, in its bid for favors, had done everything to the legislature of Pennsylvania except refine it.

The Sherman Antitrust Act.

The Sherman Antitrust Act did not destroy the monopolies. The bill that Ohio senator John Sherman introduced in the Senate was quickly rewritten by the Judiciary Committee before the Senate passed it by a vote of 52 to 1. The House in turn passed the measure unanimously. The Sherman Act was an honest although confused attempt to regulate the trusts. But the long list of unanswered questions

*For the so-called Granger laws, see chapter 21, p. 534.

involving enforcement of the act showed that big business still had ample leeway. The act declared "unreasonable restraint" illegal—but what did "unreasonable" mean? What constituted a monopoly? How much power over an industry spelled "control"? How, in short, was the government to proceed with the job of breaking up trusts?

The Sherman Act left these questions to government attorneys and judges, who, at least during the administrations of Grover Cleveland and William McKinley in the 1890s, were not disposed to stop the merger movement. Richard Olney, President Cleveland's waspish attorney general, spoke for big businessmen everywhere when he approved the Supreme Court's refusal to break up the sugar trust in the *E. C. Knight* case (1895). "You will observe that the government has been defeated in the Supreme Court on the trust question. I always supposed it would be, and have taken responsibility of not prosecuting under a law I believed to be no good." Labor unions, on the other hand, seemed to Olney and the capitalists he served thoroughly objectionable conspiracies against trade. When Eugene Debs's American Railway Union, in its momentous battle with the Pullman Company in Chicago in 1894, refused to move the mails, Olney drew up an injunction declaring the union to be in restraint of trade and successfully prosecuted Debs for contempt of court in violating the injunction. On appeal the Supreme Court upheld the application of the Sherman Act to labor unions.

The Sherman Act was successfully applied in two railroad cases in 1897 and in 1898. It was applied again—and more notably—in the *Northern Securities* case of 1904, which ended J. P. Morgan's dream of merging the Northern Pacific, Union Pacific, and Burlington railroads. Still, only eighteen cases were initiated in the first ten years following the passage of the act. And in the crucial *E. C. Knight* case, a poorly drafted government brief allowed a conservative majority on the Supreme Court to declare the American Sugar Refining Company—a trust controlling 98 percent of the sugar industry—not technically in restraint of trade.

When Theodore Roosevelt took office in 1901, the fortunes of the antimonopolists appeared to improve. Moreover, Roosevelt's successor, William Howard Taft, continued to initiate suits against the trusts. The Sherman Act, besides breaking up the Northern Securities Company, was applied successfully in 1911 against the Standard Oil and American Tobacco companies. Yet by then it was clear that the act, far from achieving the results its framers had intended, was strengthening rather than stopping the forces behind the merger movement. By admitting that not every restraint of trade was unreasonable, and by ruling cartel behavior unacceptable but full-blown mergers legitimate, the courts invited big business to abandon looser forms of organization for tighter and more controlled ones.

The spirit of antimonopoly survived down to the First World War. Trustbusting gathered new coherence from the economic analysis and social ideas of several of President Woodrow Wilson's advisers, and it supplied the impetus for the passage in 1914 of the Clayton Antitrust Act. Yet although the Clayton Act also defined certain unfair practices, like interlocking directorates and price discrimination, and although a supplementary Federal Trade Commission Act provided for publicity and the prosecution of violators, the momentum of business combination was scarcely broken. The advantages of bigness now seemed unarguable, a fact that was attested to by the incorporation of the giant General Motors soon after the Clayton Act was passed. With few accomplishments to show for forty years of continual agitation, the opponents of monopoly quit the field to await another call to battle in the last years of Franklin D. Roosevelt's New Deal. The counterattack against big business had failed.

The Farmers' Fight Against Disorder

Although American farmers refused to admit it, their problems in the last quarter of the nineteenth century were not very different from those confronting businessmen—enormously increased production, glutted markets, and falling prices. Just as technology was revolutionizing industrial production, so mechanical reapers, harrowers, spreaders, and harvesters were expanding the farmers' productivity. A wheat farmer could cut two acres a day with a traditional cradle scythe; with a self-raking reaper he could cut twelve. By 1880, 80 percent of American wheat was being harvested by machine. The nation's farm machinery, valued at $42 million in 1870, exceeded $100 million thirty years later.

The Last Frontier.
The key to agricultural surplus was the new land across the Mississippi River—the Great Plains stretching westward from the tier of states along the river, across the hundredth meridian to the foothills of the Rockies. Only a generation earlier this huge area had been marked the "Great American Desert" on the most up-to-date map, but now it was being billed by promoters and boosters as the "Great Bread Basket of the World."

In the 1880s the Great Plains furnished a gigantic stage for the clash of four very different civilizations, each with its own receding frontier. The Indian wars of the late 1860s and 1870s, together with the destruction of the buffalo, had already begun the work of confining the High Plains Indians. The Apache, Hopi, and Comanche were forced into reservations in the Southwest; in the North the same fate befell the Sioux, Blackfeet, Nez Percé, and Cheyenne. The misnamed "battle" of Wounded Knee (South Dakota, 1890), in which federal troops butchered two hundred Indian men, women, and children, climaxed twenty years of repression and extermination. The miner's frontier was also closing, after a thirty-year scramble up the California side of the mountains and down the other side into Nevada, Colorado, Idaho, and Montana. By 1880 the lone "placer" miner, with his pick, shovel, and sluice box, was already retreating into myth as the heavy rockcrushers and trained engineers of the mining syndicates advanced. Five years later, the big cattle barons who had driven their herds up the Texas Panhandle to the railroad heads at Abilene, Dodge City, and Cheyenne were enjoying one last year of magnificent open range before being defeated by the farmers with their barbed wire and by the blizzard of 1886, which wiped out the cattle barons' herds.

The future lay with the farmers and their last frontier. The opening-up of the Great Plains reached its peak in the 1880s and 1890s, when the total amount of improved land in the United States doubled from 189 million to 414 million acres. Railroad agents, boasting of bonanza farms and of the richness of the soil, and local chambers of commerce, promising everything from a cure-all environment for the sickly to husbands for young women, seized control of the Great Plains through a land policy tailored to mythical yeoman-farmers and a homestead law written for an earlier generation.

Settlers who were enticed across the ninety-eighth meridian found an environment different from any they had ever experienced. John Wesley Powell, the geologist and explorer of the High Plains, spent much of his career trying to tell Americans what it was like to farm land where less than twenty inches of rain fell annually. The choice, he explained, was between organizing what he called "this new industry of agriculture by irrigation" on the High Plains as a voluntary community of small holders, and a forced monopoly of "a few great capitalists, employing labor on a large scale, as is done in the great mines and manufactories of the United States." Few of Powell's contemporaries, least of all the individualistic farmer, heeded his predictions of an emerging agribusiness. Yet by 1900 the outlines of the new system were already clear.

One of the causes of a growing agricultural surplus was increasing crop specialization—wheat, hogs, and beef in the trans-Mississippi West; dairy products in the Old Northwest; and cotton in the South. This

INDIAN CHIEFS MEETING WITH THE U.S. ARMY
Native Americans, overrun by white settlers, defeated by the Army, their lands seized by the federal government, were forced to sign peace treaties relinquishing their rights. Here Chief Has the Big White Horse (seated, center) poses with his comrades during negotiations with General Nelson Miles.

specialization was encouraged by the railroads and by new machinery. Even more important was a rising world demand for staples, which acted much like the growing American urban demand in providing markets for industrial goods. In fact, the two developments were related. As American staples flooded Europe, prices for foodstuffs fell sharply there and land prices collapsed. The agricultural depression in Europe, beginning in the 1870s, drove millions of peasants and small farmers out of the countryside and into seaports, the first stopping point en route to American cities. In both Europe and America, cheaper food hastened industrial transformation. In the United States, however, the farmers paid a large part of the price for this transformation by ensuring a favorable balance of trade with massive exports of staple crops at declining prices.

On the one hand the American farmer could consider the move from subsistence farming to specialized commercial farming as progress toward a higher standard of living. But this advantage was soon offset by the staple-crop farmer's suspicions that he had become the prisoner of the market, locked into a price structure from which there was no ready means of escape. With the onset of the world agricultural depression in the 1870s, the price curve for staple crops plummeted, and the farmer's income slid with it. Wheat fell from $1.19 a bushel in 1881 to a low of 49¢ in 1894. Corn fell in these same depression years from 63¢ a bushel to 18¢. Buying in a market that was protected by tariffs, and selling in an unprotected market, the staple-crop farmer saw himself the victim of an absurd situation; he was forced to grow more and more in order to earn less and less. Why, he asked, as the producer of the largest share of the nation's abundance, should he sink deeper into the mire each year? A Kansas farmer in 1891 summed up these feelings of betrayal:

At the age of 52 years, after a long life of toil, economy, and self-denial, I find myself and family virtually paupers. With hundreds of hogs, scores of good horses, and

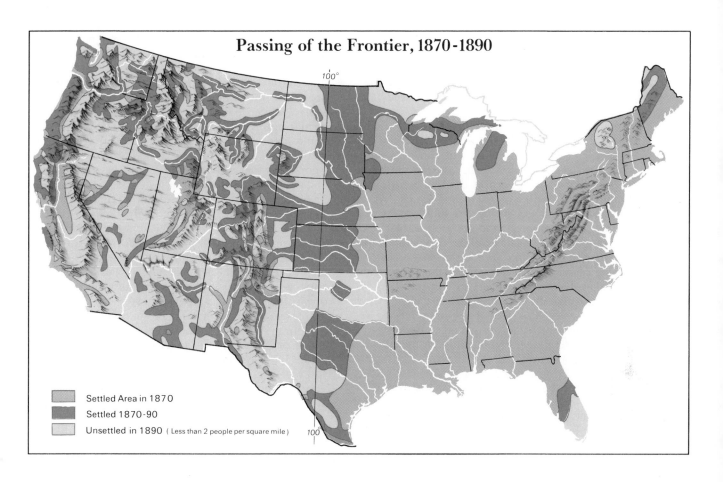

Passing of the Frontier, 1870-1890

Settled Area in 1870
Settled 1870-90
Unsettled in 1890 (Less than 2 people per square mile)

a farm that rewarded the toil of our hands with 16,000 bushels of golden corn we are poorer by many dollars than we were years ago. What once seemed like a neat little fortune and a house of refuge for our declining years, by a few turns of the monopolistic crank has been rendered valueless.

Farmers as Businessmen. To put it another way, most American farmers were now businessmen in a business that was always unstable and at times hazardous. To increase output and cut costs, many staple-crop farmers, like their small-businessmen counterparts, borrowed heavily to buy machinery, only to find themselves saddled with high interest rates. The farmers reasoned that tight money lay at the root of their troubles: as consumption fell, so too did prices. Bankers and eastern creditors might try to blame overproduction, but farmers in the West and South knew that the problem was "underconsumption" and cursed both the "gold-bugs" and Wall Street.

Tight money and sharp price drops combined to drive the farmers into protest politics and third parties. Reform politics came first to the farmers of the Old Northwest in the aftermath of the Panic of 1873, as the Grangers began to experiment with cooperative storage and marketing schemes. At the same time, these midwestern farmers, together with businessmen and shippers of the region, forced state legislatures to pass measures regulating the railroads. Yet significant rate regulation came slowly to the farmers. When it did come, it was more a result than a cause of their improved bargaining power.

The 1880s saw the rapid growth of regional farm organizations like the Agricultural Wheel and the National Farmers Alliance, which joined in 1880 to form the powerful Southern Alliance with more than a million members. In the Great Plains states the Northern Alliance became the collective voice of staple-crop producers. The West and the South agreed in their diagnosis and prescriptions: opposition to the trusts, marketing cooperatives, and cheap money. But only reluctantly could they agree to enter the political arena as a third party. Out of their agreement in Omaha in 1891 came the Populist crusade, which rallied the discontented with symbols of conspiracy and prophecies of decline, while making specific interest-group demands. Populism stirred profound convictions of betrayal.

American farmers' basic insight throughout the nineteenth century was the moral primacy of agriculture over all other aspects of life. This view was stated most eloquently by William Jennings Bryan in his famous "Cross of Gold" speech at the Democratic convention in 1896.* "You come to us and tell us that the great cities are in favor of the gold standard," Bryan thundered. "We reply that the great cities rest upon our broad and fertile prairies. Burn down your cities and leave our farms and your cities will spring up again as if by magic; but destroy our farms and grass will grow in the streets of every city in the country." Bryan confirmed the average farmer's own belief, borne out by the record, that the yeoman-farmer had indeed built America—clearing and cultivating the land, raising the foodstuffs, feeding his own people and other people throughout the world, and laying the material base on which a modern industrial society now rested. Despite the damage methodically done to it, the land remained foremost in the American moral imagination. "On the land we are born, from it we live, to it we return again—children of the soil as truly as is the blade of grass or the flower of the field," Henry George wrote. And his message reached millions of already converted farmers who sought only an endorsement of their faith.

The Farmer as Populist: A Holy War.

Farmers knew that the land had produced the foodstuffs with which the United States purchased the European goods and capital needed for modernization. They lashed out with mounting frustration as an ungrateful urban society denied their achievements, ridiculed their proposals for reform, and mocked their provincial ways and narrow lives. Out of this massive loss of confidence came the politics of Populism. When the Populists put forward their presidential candidate for the election of 1892, they were determined to rescue the nation from moral as well as material ruin. "A vast conspiracy against mankind has been organized on two continents and is taking possession of the world," their platform declared. "If not met and overthrown at once it forebodes terrible social convulsions, the destruction of civilization, or the establishment of an absolute despotism." With the coming of Populism, American farmers' twenty-year crusade became a holy war.

*For Bryan and the election of 1896, see chapter 23, pp. 590, 591, 592.

By 1900, however, the predicted end of the world had failed to materialize. The twentieth century opened with a sharp economic upturn, and in this upturn the American farmers abandoned their earlier hopes for monumental change. In return they accepted the more immediate gains furnished by rising farm incomes as domestic consumption and world demand suddenly mounted. The advantages of organization, consolidation, and integration, which were the same lessons being taught by big business, had now become too obvious for the farmers to ignore. They too could learn to read the statistics that told them what to do. The encouraging figures on production and price that the farmers began to consult were being compiled by the Division of Statistics of the Department of Agriculture, whose other departmental divisions—soils, chemistry, and animal husbandry—were proof of the continuing bureaucratic revolution in American agriculture.

These figures, whether for soaring staple prices, declining shipping costs, or estimates of increasing staple production, continued to assure farmers down to the First World War that their sudden prosperity was real. Between 1900 and 1910 the price of corn shot up from 35¢ to 52¢ a bushel, wheat from 62¢ to 91¢. The wholesale farm price index jumped 50 percent, and the average price of farmland doubled from $20 to $40 an acre. As staple-crop farmers recalled with chagrin, their frantic third-party politics had done nothing to accomplish this; nevertheless, the economy was at last responding to their needs and demands. Just as American businessmen by 1900 were applying the lessons of consolidation, so American farmers were learning to follow seemingly simple rules for finding safety in system and security in new organization.

Cooperatives.

The most efficient of the early-twentieth-century farm organizations were producers' cooperatives, which concentrated on solving the problems of pricing and marketing. Except for their official nonprofitmaking status and their democratic voting procedures, cooperatives were really modern corporations—as streamlined and efficient as their counterparts in business. Like corporations, cooperatives came to rely on experts and specialists, trained managers and accountants, legal advisers, lobbyists, and public relations men. And like integrated industrial firms, they achieved forward integration by building their own facilities at railroad terminals and by writing ironclad contracts with their members, compelling them to hold their crops off the market until the price was right. By 1910 the antimonopoly scruples of big farmers were fast disappearing.

Prosperous farmers, like the big businessmen they were becoming, designed and built cooperatives as

POPULIST COUNTRY
Beyond the 100th meridian rain was scarce, trees nonexistent, neighbors few, and life bleak.

simple interest-group devices for solving particular problems. The Grangers, Knights of Labor, and Populists, who pioneered with commodity cooperatives, had hoped to preserve conditions of independence and equality. The new farm cooperatives advertised no such grandiose social aims. Rather, they were content, with the return of prosperous times, to perfect the means that the organizational revolution had assigned them. Their members were essentially agricultural trade-unionists who thought and behaved like cotton planters, corn-hog producers, and dairy farmers. Why, they asked themselves, replace an economic system capable of producing the abundance that, however belatedly, was now being showered upon them?

The chief advocates of the bureaucratic revolution in American agriculture were not the staple-crop farmers in the trans-Mississippi West, but the dairy, poultry, and fruit and vegetable farmers of the older sections of the East and Northwest, and their competitors on the Pacific Coast, all of whose fortunes had risen steadily with the growth of railroads and metropolitan markets. With the return of prosperity, these groups put aside their interest in protest politics in favor of scientific methods and interest-group associations.

Soon the cooperative marketing movement was in full swing, and dozens of livestock unions, dairymen's leagues, grain exchanges, cotton cooperatives, and tobacco pools were being founded each year. Cooperatives in turn spawned hundreds of new pressure groups—the Farmers' Equity Union, the Farmers' Mutual Benefit Association, the Farmers' Social and Economic Union, the Farmers' Relief Association. All these groups proclaimed as their own the slogan of the American Society of Equity: "What the farmer wants to produce is not crops, but money." In 1912 cooperatives secured the blessing of the Department of Agriculture, which provided them with their own fact-finding agency, the Bureau of Markets. Eight years later the formation of the American Farm Bureau Federation announced the arrival of modern agriculture as a national force. Although the chief gains in numbers and influence were not to come until the 1920s, the commercialization of American farmers, and their conversion to agribusiness, had already been accomplished.

The dramatic shift in farmers' thinking that came with the return of prosperity after 1900 was expressed in the changed outlook of one of the farmers' most impassioned spokesmen. Returning home to the Mid-

Photo by Smith Brothers, October 1910, Library of Congress

APPLE PICKING IN WEST VIRGINIA
Not all farming was mechanized by 1910.

dle Border in 1889 at the height of the agrarian distress, Hamlin Garland, still an unknown but an aspiring young writer, found his old neighbors caught up in a social crisis and engaged "in a sullen rebellion against government and against God."

Every house I visited had its individual message of sordid struggle and half-hidden despair. . . . All the gilding of farm life melted away. The hard and bitter realities came back upon me in a flood. Nature was as bountiful as ever . . . but no splendor of cloud, no grace of sunset, could conceal the poverty of these people; on the contrary, they brought out, with a more intolerable poignancy, the gracelessness of these homes, and the sordid quality of the mechanical routine of these lives. I perceived beautiful youth becoming bowed and bent.

Convinced that "men's laws" rather than God's were responsible for both "industrial slavery" and the degradation of farmers, Garland brought to the Populists an enthusiasm for far-reaching reform and an aesthetic theory to match. Yet fifteen years later, with the Populist years a memory, Garland left the "main travelled thoroughfares" of agrarian protest for nostalgic excursions into the romantic highcountry of the Far Northwest, abandoning reform to settle for the prom-

ises of Theodore Roosevelt's Country Life Commission.

The Country Life Commission itself was proof of the revival of the farmers' influence. Appointed in 1908, it was charged with the task of improving rural life in the United States. After taking the pulse of rural America and listening to a recital of its ailments, the commissioners concluded that farmers simply needed to catch up with their city cousins, to "even-up" the distribution of amenities between city and country. This recovery, according to the commissioners' diagnosis, involved agricultural credits, a highway program, rural free delivery, better schools, a country church movement to rescue lost souls, and very little else. Prosperity had soothed old discontents. By 1910 Hamlin Garland's outraged cry for justice "for the toiling poor wherever found" had become a faint echo. American farmers moved into their golden age, which statistics, government recognition, and their own pockets told them had come at last.

Workers and the Challenge of Organization

Of all the groups caught up in the late-nineteenth-century American economic revolution, industrial workers depended least on statistics to confirm what they already knew: that their rewards for tending the national industrial machine hardly matched their services. Real wages rose 25 percent in the 1880s, but in 1882 Massachusetts's commissioner of labor, Carroll Wright, reported that male Fall River textile workers could not support their families unless their wives also worked. Data that were gathered in the last years of the century show that the work week for the "average" worker in industry was a little less than 60 hours, and that the average wage for skilled workers was 20¢ an hour—and only half that amount for unskilled workers. Annual wages for most factory workers in 1900 came to an average of $400 to $500, from which a working family saved an average of $30 per year. Nearly half the remainder was spent on food, another quarter on rent, and the balance on fuel, light, and clothing.

Earnings for workers in manufacturing continued to go up 37 percent between 1890 and 1914, but the cost of living between 1897 and 1914 climbed 39 percent. Despite growing national wealth, American workers and their families managed on very narrow margins. Their share of the pie, although larger than it had been a half-century earlier, was still comparatively small. A statistical breakdown of national income, had they consulted it, would have strengthened workers' convictions that they, too, had to organize for bargaining power. The richest tenth of the population received 33.9 percent of the nation's income; the poorest tenth received 3.4 percent. The wealthier half of the population accounted for more than 70 percent of all the country's income. The rich were certainly getting richer, while the American workers, if not absolutely poorer, were still not enjoying much of the wealth they were creating. Nor had they yet found the organizational power with which to counter the growing strength of American business. The growth of labor unions lagged behind the rapid expansion of the work force. In 1870 one worker in ten was a union member; in 1900, one in twelve.

Strikes and Work Stoppages.

With or without union help, workers turned to the strike as their chief defensive weapon. There were 477 work stoppages in 1881, nearly 2,000 a decade later, and more than 1,800 a year at the turn of the century. Strikes were usually responses to wage cuts. The Great Railroad Strike of 1877,* the so-called Great Upheaval on Jay Gould's Southwestern system in 1886, and the rash of railroad strikes culminating in the Pullman Strike of 1894 were all triggered by management's determination to slash wages. The pattern was the same in nearly every in-

*For this strike, see chapter 21, pp. 536–37.

dustry: strikes followed employers' attempts to increase hours by "grinding" or "driving" workers beyond agreed-upon limits or, more frequently, to cut wages during recessions.

Many businessmen's attitude toward the "labor supply" before 1900 was likely to be that of the steelmaker who admitted to a congressional committee that "if I wanted boiler iron I would go out on the market and buy where I could get it the cheapest, and if I wanted to employ men I would do the same thing." The views of independent shop owners were often more pronounced. "While you are in my workshop," one manufacturer told his workers, "you must conform to my rules. . . . You must not attempt to take the control of the workshop out of my hands." As for American workers' well-known preference for "lager and leisure," Joseph Medill, publisher of the Chicago *Tribune*, warned his readers that the indulgences of the workers must be stopped by teaching them that their "impecunious condition" was a direct result of their "improvidence and misdirected efforts. . . . The wageclasses cannot support in idleness a quarter of a million saloonkeepers . . . and at the same time hope to prosper themselves."

To correct such attitudes, the Knights of Labor president, Terence V. Powderly, proposed educating employers in the advantages of arbitration. Powderly also tried to persuade his some 700,000 members (1886) of the "folly of strikes." But education converted neither businessmen (who until the late nineteenth century were inclined to consider union leaders as bad as Civil War secessionists) nor the leadership of union locals. A series of strikes culminated in the Knights' disastrous contest with Jay Gould's Texas Pacific Railroad in 1886, and soon the Knights entered a period of sharp decline—victims of business antagonism, craftunion fears, and their own delusions of grandeur.

Labor Consolidation.

The American Federation of Labor (AFL), a flexible organization of craft unions formed in 1886, represented a new generation's coming to terms with the corporate revolution. Workers too could learn the lessons of consolidation. Samuel Gompers, the founder and longtime president of the AFL, and his lieutenant, Adolph Strasser, readily confessed that their sole concern was for the skilled trades that they represented and for the immediate welfare of their members. When Strasser was asked to define the "ultimate ends" of "pure and simple unionism," he replied at once that the two terms were contradictory. "We have no ultimate ends. We are going on from day to day. We are fighting for immediate objects—objects that can be realized in a few years."

The new union leaders reminded businessmen that they too were "practical men"—not closet

One of the presumed benefits of rapid industrialization in the United States during the Gilded Age was the invention of "labor-saving" machines that would make the American worker's task easier. In testifying before a congressional investigating committee in 1883, a New York City tailor explains that the real effect of introducing the sewing machine in the garment industry was precisely the opposite. Although willing to point out the exploitative practices of the bosses, he is understandably reluctant to provide the committee with names.

A Tailor Testifies on Working Conditions (1883)

BEFORE we had sewing machines we worked piecework with our wives, and very often our children. We had no trouble then with our neighbors, nor with the landlord, because it was a very still business, very quiet; but in 1854 or 1855, and later, the sewing machine was invented and introduced, and it stitched very nicely, nicer than the tailor could do; and the bosses said: "We want you to use the sewing machine; you have to buy one." Many of the tailors had a few dollars in the bank, and they took the money and bought machines. Many others had no money, but must help themselves; so they brought their stitching, the coat or vest, to the other tailors who had sewing machines, and paid them a few cents for the stitching. Later, when the money was given out for the work, we found out that we could earn no more than we could without the machine; but the money for the machine was gone now, and we found that the machine was only for the profit of the bosses; that they got their work quicker, and it was done nicer. . . . The machine makes too much noise in the place, and the neighbors want to sleep, and we have to stop sewing earlier; so we have to work faster. We work now in excitement — in a hurry. It is hunting; it is not work at all; it is a hunt.

Q. You turn out two or three times as much work per day now as you did in prior times before the war? — A. Yes, sir; two or three times as much; and we have to do it, because the wages are two-thirds lower than they were five or ten years back. . . .

Sen. Blair: What proportion of them are women and what proportion men, according to your best judgment? — A. I guess there are many more women than men.

Q. The pay of the women is the same as the pay of the men for the same quantity of work, I suppose? — A. Yes; in cases where a manufacturer — that is, a middleman — gets work from the shop and brings it into his store and employs hands to make it, women get paid by the piece also.

Q. What is your knowledge as to the amount that workers of that class are able to save from their wages? — A. I don't know any one that does save except those manufacturers.

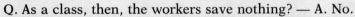

Q. As a class, then, the workers save nothing? — A. No.

Q. What sort of house-room do they have? What is the character, in general, of the food and clothing which they are able to purchase with what they can make by their labor? — A. They live in tenement houses four or five stories high, and have two or three rooms.

Q. What is the character of their clothing? — A. They buy the clothing that they make — the cheapest of it.

Q. What about the character of food that they are able to provide for themselves? — A. Food? They have no time to eat dinner. They have a sandwich in the middle of the day, and in the evening when they go away from work it is the same, and they drink lager or anything they can get.

Q. They are kept busy all the time and have but little opportunity for rest? — A. Yes.

Q. What is the state of feeling between the employers and their employees in that business? How do you workingmen feel towards the people who employ you and pay you? — A. Well, I must say the workingmen are discouraged. If I speak with them they go back and don't like to speak much about the business and the pay. They fear that if they say how it is they will get sent out of the shop. They hate the bosses and the foremen more than the bosses, and that feeling is deep.

Q. Why do they feel so towards the foremen? — A. They know that they do a wrong onto them; they know that.

Q. Do not the foremen act under the instruction of the bosses? — A. Well, it seems so. . . .

Sen. Blair: Have you any objection to giving us the names of some of the bosses and foremen that you know, who control a large number of laborers of the class to which you belong? This committee desires to obtain such information as you can give in regard to the condition of those engaged in your trade, and if there is any attempt to punish you for giving such information I think you can find protection from the country, or from some source. . . . — A. Now, sir, if I lose my work who can give me another work? I am an old man now, you know, and the young ones, they get the work and they say, "He is an old man; what can he do?"

TWO DOCUMENTARY VIEWS OF URBAN POVERTY

Both artists and photographers aimed their message at the American social conscience. The lithograph is John Sloan's "Roofs, Summer Night"; the photograph of the web of washlines crisscrossing a courtyard on the Lower East Side's Thompson Street is by Jacob Riis, who illustrated his own exposé of urban poverty, *How the Other Half Lives.*

theorists or reformers, but pragmatists and opportunists. Like their employers, the union leaders were organizers with their eyes on the main chance. The distance the AFL had come from the cooperative industrial unionism of the Knights of Labor could be measured in Gompers's reply to Socialist Morris Hillquit. Bent on discrediting his rival, Hillquit demanded to know whether Gompers really believed that American workers received the "full product" of their labor. Gompers brushed aside the question as meaningless. "I will say," he replied, "that it is impossible for anyone to definitely say what proportion the workers receive as a result of their labor, but it is the fact that due to the organized labor movement they have received and are receiving a larger share of the product of their

labor than they ever did in the history of modern society." Irate socialists and labor radicals accused Gompers of having sold out the movement by refusing to develop a genuine social philosophy. Gompers and his craft unionists cheerfully admitted to a belief in half a loaf and a willingness to follow "the lines of least resistance."

"Least resistance" for organized labor as the twentieth century began meant accepting the merger movement and bargaining with big business. The trusts, Gompers announced, "are our employers, and the employer who is fair to us, whether an individual, or a collection of individuals in the form of a corporation or a trust, matters little to us so long as we obtain fair wages." Little, he felt, could be gained by

Photograph by Jacob A. Riis, Jacob A. Riis Collection, Museum of the City of New York

quarreling with the wage system on which capitalism rested or by dreaming up substitutes. "The hope for a perfect millennium," Gompers told the U.S. Industrial Commission, "well, it don't come every night."

Enlightened Business.

The American Federation of Labor, modest in its aims, overcame employers' resistance only with difficulty and at some cost. Although membership grew from 140,000 at its founding in 1886 to more than 2 million in 1914, less than a third of the country's skilled workers could be found in its ranks in 1900. When the First World War broke out in Europe in 1914, only 15 percent of the nonagricultural workers in the United States were members of any union. They still faced such obstacles as the injunction and the yellow-dog contract (in which an employee promised not to join a union), and small businessmen tried to stop them from unionizing. In 1903 the National Association of Manufacturers (NAM) was formed, and

it founded the Citizens Industrial Association to spread the gospel of the non-union "open shop" under the name "The American Plan." The success of the American Plan, conservative businessmen promised, would spell the doom of labor unions.

More enlightened business leaders hoped to control labor through the concept of guided democracy. They stressed a paternal concern for the American worker, along with arbitration schemes and appeals for "responsible leadership." "A man who won't meet his men half-way is a God-damn fool!" Mark Hanna, one of the new business leaders, announced in deriding the obstinacy of George Pullman and similarly old-fashioned businessmen. The new business leaders recognized that labor's grievances were real and that many of its demands were legitimate—an acknowledgment that workers' needs for security and stability were not so very different from the needs of management. In 1900 progressive industrialists like George E.

Perkins and financiers like J. P. Morgan struck a bargain with Gompers and founded the National Civic Federation. The federation's basic principle was that labor, like business, must be encouraged to organize its interests and rally its forces for full participation in the new corporate society.

Any strategy for enlightened business interests required, first of all, vastly improved working conditions. Factory work was still alarmingly dangerous. A survey of industrial accidents for the year 1913 showed that some 25,000 workers had been killed on the job and another 750,000 seriously injured. Then there were the problems of incentive, alienation, and the loss of community resulting from increased scale and the impersonality of the factory. These conditions were eloquently described to the Industrial Commission in 1899 by a veteran shoe worker, who recalled the days of what might be termed rough shop-floor socialism before the coming of the giant mechanized factory. "In these old shops, years ago," he told the commissioners, "one man owned the shop; and he and three, four, five or six others, neighbors, came in there and sat down and made shoes right in their laps, and there was no machinery. Everybody was at liberty to talk."

But could this vanished past be recovered or recreated? "We do not want to go back to the time when we could do without the sewing machine or the machinery for manufacturing purposes, or the large aggregations of capital," the shoemaker replied, "but we want capital controlled in such a way that it will not result in the displacement of three-fourths of the population for the increased wealth of one-fourth of the population." In grudging admissions like this lay the secret of big business's success.

Working-Class Life.
Workers, packed in slums and ghettos of center cities, knew precisely how far they stood from the margins of plenty. The quality of life in the working-class districts of most American cities was appalling. In 1915 President Wilson's Industrial Commission, still another investigatory body that was appointed to examine the causes of industrial unrest, concluded: "A large part of our industrial population are . . . living in actual poverty." The commissioners did not care to estimate exactly what proportion of the nation's working class lived below the subsistence level. They added, however, "It is certain at least one-third and possibly one-half of the families of wage earners employed in manufacturing and mining earn in the course of the year less than enough to support them in anything like a comfortable and decent condition." For new arrivals from Europe and the American countryside, urban housing—whether three-story wooden firetraps in South Boston or dumbbell tenements on New York's Lower East Side or dilapidated single-family shanties in Cincinnati, St. Louis, or Chicago—was generally deplorable and, worse still, expensive. Gas, water, electricity, sanitation, and transportation—all the services that were needed to make the life of city workers tolerable—were in short supply and of poor quality as late as 1900.

The main surge in urban improvement began with the new century, and within a decade municipal services improved, giving cities a public face-lift and new vitality. But housing and personal standards of living improved much more slowly. The public life of American cities responded to the work of urban reformers, with their vision of a revived democratic purpose; yet blighted neighborhoods, fractured communities, crumbling apartments, and stunted lives continued as a stark reality for too many American workers.

Recently arrived immigrants who endured these conditions and made up the major portion of the industrial labor force by 1900 faced still another and more subtle kind of exploitation: the cultural drive to "Americanize" them as quickly as possible. All the ethnic groups arriving in such great numbers after 1880—Italians, Greeks, Poles, Russian Jews—were viewed at one time or another as potential bomb throwers who needed the saving word from "100 Percent" Americans. Earlier generations had singled out the political party as the chief agent of cultural adjustment; reformers after the 1880s emphasized the school. As one observer explained to the readers of *World's Work* in 1903, "There are many things in which, as a rule, the public consider that the public schools fail, but one thing that cannot be denied—and it is the greatest—is that these boys and girls of foreign parentage catch readily the simple American ideas of independence and individual work and, with them, social progress." "Social progress" in the half-century after 1880 meant vigorous Americanization: widespread literacy, technological education, elimination of child labor, cultural conformity, and, last but not least, stimulating an aspiring working class's appetite for all the consumer goods produced by the huge American industrial machine.

Just as American businessmen after 1900 continued to form monopolies and oligopolies, and farmers launched their own organizational revolution, so the nation's industrial workers began to adjust their roles to the demands of corporate capitalism. American workers largely ignored the alternative of socialism and seemingly accepted their assignments—and thus they added to the impression of inevitability that the production statistics had created.

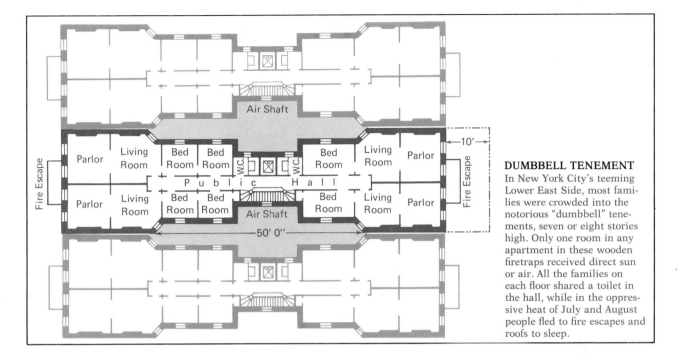

DUMBBELL TENEMENT
In New York City's teeming Lower East Side, most families were crowded into the notorious "dumbbell" tenements, seven or eight stories high. Only one room in any apartment in these wooden firetraps received direct sun or air. All the families on each floor shared a toilet in the hall, while in the oppressive heat of July and August people fled to fire escapes and roofs to sleep.

The Fruits of the Industrial Revolution

The economic transformation of the United States, like all revolutions, had unintended consequences. Used as an index of national prosperity, the statistics of growth seemed a simple instrument for measuring the accomplishments of a whole people. In 1860 the national wealth was $16 billion according to government statisticians' estimates. By 1900 it had grown to $88 billion, a per capita increase from $500 to $1,100. But these figures effectively masked differences of class, region, and occupation, as well as the persistence of a grossly uneven distribution of income. Americans were being affected by the organizational revolution in drastically different ways.

Yet the American dream of 1900 remained what it had been a half-century earlier: a vision of a people uniquely equipped to create and enjoy abundance. Economic integration itself seemed convincing proof of the near approach of what the journalist Herbert Croly called "the promise of American life." A national market had been built and the nation's shelves stocked with an incredible variety of goods. In this sense the economic well-being of the United States appeared to be exactly what a new generation of American businessmen pronounced it—a single economic system binding citizen and nation together in a network of mutual benefits.

But beneath the surface, as the new century began, lay not unity, but multiplicity; not a single national purpose, but competing and even warring interests; not pressures unifying American society, but forces threatening to fling it apart; not the conservation of national energies, but their diffusion in politically volatile forms. Americans in 1900 thus confronted a paradox capping a half-century of growth: the economic integration that had seemingly saved them from the waste of competition had set in motion cultural and political counterforces that threatened fragmentation, dispersion, diffusion, and isolation. To cope with these threats to national order, the American people would need new and more sophisticated concepts of social and political organization, and the capacity somehow to use them.

CHRONOLOGY

1873 Panic of 1873 begins six years of depression.

1876 Alexander Graham Bell invents the telephone.

1877 Great Railroad Strike.

1879 Henry George's *Progress and Poverty* published.

Thomas Alva Edison perfects the electric light bulb.

1880 Farmers' Agricultural Wheel and National Farmers' Alliance join together to form Southern Alliance.

1882 John D. Rockefeller's Standard Oil of Ohio consolidates American oil industry under Standard Oil Trust.

1883 Chicago builds first elevated electric railway.

Brooklyn Bridge completed.

1884 Recession and unemployment jar the economy.

1886 AFL (American Federation of Labor) founded.

The "Great Upheaval" stops work on Jay Gould's Texas Pacific Railroad.

George Westinghouse founds Westinghouse Electric Co. and subsequently perfects use of alternating current.

1887 Interstate Commerce Act passed to control railroads.

1888 Edward Bellamy's *Looking Backward* published.

1890 Sherman Antitrust Act passed in attempt to regulate monopolies in restraint of trade.

Sherman Silver Purchase Act passed, resulting in depleted gold reserves.

At "Battle" of Wounded Knee, South Dakota, federal troops massacre 200 Indians.

1891 Hamlin Garland's *Main-Travelled Roads* describes hardships of midwestern farmers' lives.

Louis Sullivan's Wainwright Building completed in St. Louis.

1892 Populists organize; nominate General James B. Weaver for president at a national convention in Omaha.

Grover Cleveland elected president.

Homestead Strike in Carnegie steel mills.

1893 Financial panic sends U.S. economy into four years of depression.

Repeal of Sherman Silver Purchase Act.

Historian Frederick Jackson Turner, in "The Significance of the American Frontier," announces closing of the frontier.

1894 Pullman Strike broken by federal troops; Eugene V. Debs jailed.

Henry Demarest Lloyd's *Wealth Against Commonwealth*, exposé of Standard Oil Company, published.

1895 In *U.S. v. E. C. Knight Co.*, government defeated in antitrust suit against sugar monopoly.

1896 William McKinley elected president, defeating William Jennings Bryan and "Free Silver."

1900 McKinley reelected president, defeating Bryan once again.

National Civic Federation established by labor leaders and industrialists.

Theodore Dreiser's *Sister Carrie*, naturalistic novel, causes literary stir.

1901 Theodore Roosevelt becomes president after McKinley assassinated.

United States Steel Corporation formed.

1903 Wright brothers make their first flight.

National Association of Manufacturers (NAM) formed.

Citizens Industrial Association formed to secure open shop in American industry.

1904 Case of *Northern Securities Co.* v. *U.S.* upholds government's case against railroad mergers.

1911 Triangle Shirtwaist Factory fire in New York City's East Side kills 146 women; investigation and revision of state factory codes follow.

SUGGESTED READINGS

There are two outstanding general interpretations of the organizational revolution in American society in the half-century following 1870. A succinct account that remains the model for more recent interpretations is Samuel P. Hays, *The Response to Industrialism* (1957). Robert Wiebe, *The Search for Order* (1968), traces the shift from small-town America to modern mass society in terms of changing political outlooks and social values. Ray Ginger, *The Age of Excess* (1965), is a lively and impressionistic survey, and Howard Mumford Jones, *The Age of Energy: Varieties of American Experience, 1865–1915* (1970), explores Gilded Age manners and morals with sympathy and gusto.

The best recent overview of the American economy in these years is Stuart Bruchey's brief but perceptive essay, *Growth of the Modern Economy* (1975). The early chapters in Alfred D. Chandler, Jr., *Strategy and Structure: Chapters in the History of American Industrial Enterprise* (1966), provide a compact summary of the first phase of business concentration. Ralph L. Nelson, *Merger Movements in American Industry* (1959), gives a good account of the great merger movement at the end of the nineteenth century, and Hans B. Thorelli, *Federal Antitrust Policy: The Origination of an American Tradition* (1955), traces the course of the countermovement against monopoly. The industrial transformation of the United States is described as a success story in Edward C. Kirkland's survey, *Industry Comes of Age: Business, Labor, and Public Policy, 1860–1897* (1961), which can be read along with Thomas Cochran, *The Inner Revolution* (1965).

The connections between economic theory and public policy are explored in Sidney Fine, *Laissez-Faire and the General Welfare State* (1956). Richard Hofstadter, *Social Darwinism in American Thought* (1945), and Robert McCloskey, *Conservatism in the Age of Enterprise* (1951), are highly readable accounts of conservative thinking in the Gilded Age. Irvin G. Wyllie, *The Self-Made Man in America* (1954), scrutinizes a venerable American myth, and Edward C. Kirkland's lively essays in *Dream and Thought in the Business Community, 1860–1900* (1956) describe the musings of businessmen on the American social order. For an account of the careers of three notable critics of Gilded Age business practices, see John L. Thomas, *Alternative America: Henry George,* *Edward Bellamy, Henry Demarest Lloyd and the Adversary Tradition* (1983).

Urban growth and its accompanying problems are admirably summarized in Howard Chudacoff, *Evolution of American Urban Society* (1975), and Zane Miller, *Urbanization of America* (1973). The story of the mounting difficulties of the American farmer is well told in Fred Shannon, *The Farmer's Last Frontier* (1963). For an illuminating study of agrarian politics in the South in this period, see Theodore Saloutos, *Farmer Movements of the South, 1865–1933.* Grant McConnell, *The Decline of Agrarian Democracy* (1953), describes the rise of commercial farming. The elimination of the Indian in the trans-Mississippi West is chronicled in two highly readable accounts: Ralph K. Andrist, *The Long Death: The Last Days of the Plains Indians* (1964), and Dee A. Brown, *Bury My Heart at Wounded Knee* (1971). On American labor there are two useful surveys: Joseph G. Rayback, *A History of American Labor* (1959), and Henry Pelling, *American Labor* (1959). Herbert G. Gutman, *Work, Culture and Society in Industrializing America* (1976), points toward a new synthesis of cultural and labor history, and Daniel T. Rogers, *The Work Ethic in Industrial America, 1850–1920* (1975), examines shifting attitudes toward work that accompanied the industrial transformation of the United States. Daniel Walkowitz, *Worker City, Company Town: Iron and Cotton Worker Protest in Troy and Cohoes, New York, 1855–1884* (1978), compares two different social and cultural settings as they determine the responses of industrial workers.

Biographies of leaders in the American industrial revolution are many. Among the best are three monumental works: Joseph Wall, *Andrew Carnegie* (1970); Alan Nevins, *Study in Power: John D. Rockefeller, Industrialist and Philanthropist* (2 vols., 1953); Matthew Josephson, *Edison* (1940).

23 The Politics of Reform

In the quarter-century after the Civil War, politics gave Americans the sense of stability that their economic system lacked. The Jacksonian generation had first discovered in the political party the means of containing the disruptive forces of modern democracy. Now the Jacksonian generation's sons, the professionals who ruled the Republican and Democratic parties after 1870, perfected this political machinery, which they proceeded to run with skill and zest until the end of the century.

They created a new political equilibrium. It depended, first of all, upon restoring a regional balance of power within both parties. Throughout the so-called Gilded Age the Republicans sought to include both northeastern urban workers and midwestern farmers in their plans for economic development, and until the 1890s they continued to dream of competing with the Democrats in the South. The Democrats were busy repairing the broad Jacksonian coalition of southern planters and northern city bosses that had been smashed by the war. The basic unit in this postwar party system was the state machine; both parties functioned as loose coalitions of independent state organizations. But states also composed regions, each with its own cultural identity and economic interests that required careful tending. After 1880 national tickets were increasingly arranged—and party slates balanced—with regional as well as state and city claims in mind.

The smooth operation of American politics in the Gilded Age also depended upon the mastery of a few basic rules. Chief among them was the principle, accepted by politicians in both parties, that their organizations did not differ in class or economic interests, which were often quite similar, or even in general policies, which were frequently fuzzy. Both parties were now financed by wealthy citizens whose opinions party leaders carefully acknowledged while maintaining an egalitarian posture before the rest of the country. Party managers realized that the voters seldom approached political questions like the tariff and the currency as clear issues. Instead, party leaders considered these questions symbols that could be used to mobilize support for the party and its candidates. The skilled practitioners of Gilded Age politics had learned from the stormy debates of the Civil War years that most American voters' electoral behavior was ultimately determined by images and impressions, prejudices and preferences. Voters might consider themselves both rational and informed, but no office seeker could ignore these vague but deeper forces at work in the political population. Both parties, in fact, were broad-based nonideological coalitions that appealed to businessmen, farmers, professionals, and workers. Wealth, political principles, and social status did not separate Republicans and Democrats as much as did differing clusters of religious, ethnic, and cultural values.

One way of describing this difference between Republicans and Democrats is to use religious terms—*pietistic* and *ritualistic*—which denote two opposite tendencies in American thinking about religion and politics. *Pietism*, with its stress on conscience, duty, and personal purity, points toward a political outlook emphasizing morality. *Ritualism*, which pays less attention to personal purity and places greater importance on adherence to outward ceremony, looks toward a politics emphasizing toleration of personal behavior and conformity to tradition. Pietistic thinking had dominated the original Whig party and its stepchild, the Republican party, before the Civil War. Whig and Republican party members were primarily Protestant, predominantly of native stock or Anglo-Saxon descent, aggressively reform-minded, and eager to use government at all levels to force their behavioral standards on the rest of the community. George F. Hoar, a Republican senator from Massachusetts, drew on these pietistic sources when he described his party as filled with "the men who do the work of piety and charity in our churches, the men who administer

572

UNVEILING A STATUE
Patriotism and purity combined readily in the Gilded Age imagination.

our school systems, the men who own and till their own farms, the men who perform the skilled labor in the shops."

Given this image of Republicanism, it was easy for party faithfuls to dismiss their Democratic opponents as "the old slave owner and slave driver, the saloon keeper, the ballot box stuffer, the Ku Klux Klan, the criminal class of the great cities, the men who cannot read and write." Business interests steadily infiltrated the Republican party after 1880, but the party continued to attract a broad range of social moralists—prohibitionists, sabbatarians, blue law advocates, and moral reformers of every sort. Only at the very end of the century had these evangelical types become marginal enough in the party as a whole for the managers to cast them aside as political liabilities.

With its "ritualistic" outlook the Democratic party seemed very different from the Republican party. It embraced Catholics as well as Protestants, and it claimed a tolerance of immigrants who lacked the compulsive morality of the native-born. Democrats preached a "personal liberty" that was thought safest when government was kept local and minimal. The New York party organization expressed this viewpoint when in 1881, drawing on the tradition of Andrew Jackson, it declared itself "unalterably opposed to centralization of power in either state or federal governments." While Republicans expected all government to be generous and active, Democrats hoped to keep it grudging and stingy, if only to end the Anglo-Saxon Republicans' "cultural imperialism" toward immigrants (who tended to vote Democratic), as well as to curb the Republicans' appetite for patronage. Thus the differences between the two parties in 1880 were real, but they derived more from ethnic origins, religious backgrounds, and cultural outlook than from economic interest.

This pattern of politics survived until the last decade of the century, when suddenly the very idea of party rule came under attack by a younger generation of political reformers. By 1890 rural Populists and urban progressives were challenging the code of the old professionals and forcing them to respond to new pressures. Out of their revolt came a transformation of politics that paralleled the revolution in the national economy and created new forms in the American political process, along with new ways of ordering it.

The Politics of Equilibrium

The Civil War shaped the thinking and molded the political behavior of Americans for a generation. Gilded Age politicians succeeded in tapping the emotions that had been aroused by the war. They were able, first of all, to inspire remarkably high levels of voting. In the six presidential elections between 1876 and 1896, an average of 78.5 percent of the country's eligible voters actually voted, and an equally impressive 62.8 percent turned out for off-year elections. (In the late twentieth century, even presidential elections bring slightly less than half the eligible voters to the polls.) If political democracy is measured by a high rate of voter participation, then the Gilded Age remained flamboyantly, defiantly democratic despite its glaring social and economic inequalities.

The voting patterns remained consistent. Whether they marched to the polls behind candidates waving the "bloody shirt"—the radical Republicans' vengeful rhetoric aimed at preserving northern hostilities toward the South—or stirred to the memories of the Confederacy's Lost Cause, voters across the nation kept alive the Civil War even after the ideological struggles of Reconstruction had ended. Joining enthusiastically in campaigns that came complete with mounted military troopers and fancy drill teams, they made national elections extremely close. Sixteen states could always be counted on to go Republican; fourteen just as regularly voted Democratic. Presidential elections were usually decided by the voters in five key states—Connecticut, New York, Indiana, Nevada, and California. Between 1872 and 1912 the Republicans had a grip on the presidency that was broken only by Grover Cleveland's two victories in 1884 and 1892. They appeared to be a well-established majority party. But in fact the Democrats controlled the House of Representatives with sizable majorities in seven out of ten congressional elections. In key states the margins of victory were perilously thin, particularly in New York and Indiana. With such intense competition and close elections, winners were not only lucky, but often surprised. In the three presidential contests in the 1880s, the victor edged out his closest opponent by less than 1 percent. In the election of James A. Garfield in 1880 and of Cleveland in 1884, fewer than 25,000 votes separated the candidates. In 1888 the winner in electoral votes, the Republican Benjamin Harrison, received fewer popular votes than did Cleveland, the loser.

Party Lines Drawn. Throughout the 1880s the two parties remained drawn up against each other like two equally matched armies, their skirmishes resembling the engagements of the still familiar Civil War. Famous military figures were featured in political rhetoric until well into the 1880s—in songs, war whoops, and speeches by bewhiskered colonels "late of the Confederate Army" or by beribboned commissary generals of the Grand Army of the Republic. The median age of voters in the Gilded Age was thirty-seven, and so generally they had arrived at political maturity under the guidance of fathers who had fought to preserve the "glorious Union" or to rescue a "prostrate nation." Ticket splitting suggested a lack of patriotism, and the voter who switched parties was regarded as little better than a bounty jumper. Novelist Brand Whitlock remembered that in his youth, being a Republican was "a fundamental and self-evident thing. . . . It was merely a synonym for patriotism, another name for the nation. . . . It was inconceivable that any self-respecting person should be a Democrat." Nor was it likely that in the South, increasingly solid for the Democratic party, a true gentleman would require any greater political comfort than the security that was provided by what was called Bourbon conservatism.

Yet, for all its apparent stability, politics in this era was in the process of transformation—the same stage of transformation that small-scale entrepreneurial capitalism was undergoing. Newly arrived immigrants were urban consumers in need of jobs, favors, and services. Here was a vast human market in which a wise investment of political capital could pay off handsomely. The new business of politics, unlike more established concerns, was open to fresh talent and offered unlimited opportunity for making good. As a go-getter, the professional politician—ward heeler, precinct captain, county chairman, state assemblyman, or senatorial aspirant—was a salesman who had to know the buying habits of every prospective customer in his territory.

George Washington Plunkitt, one of the leaders of New York City's Democratic organization Tammany Hall, described the political district in terms familiar to every salesman out of New York or Chicago with a territory to cover, concluding: "If he holds his district and Tammany is in power, he is amply rewarded by a good office and the opportunities that go with it." The Gilded Age boss was the Horatio Alger rags-to-riches hero, in ward heeler's attire, sporting a campaign button. "Yes, many of our men have grown rich in politics," Plunkitt confided. "I have myself. I've made a big fortune out of the game, and I'm gettin' richer every day." The shortest route to success in the business of politics lay through the upstairs room at party head-

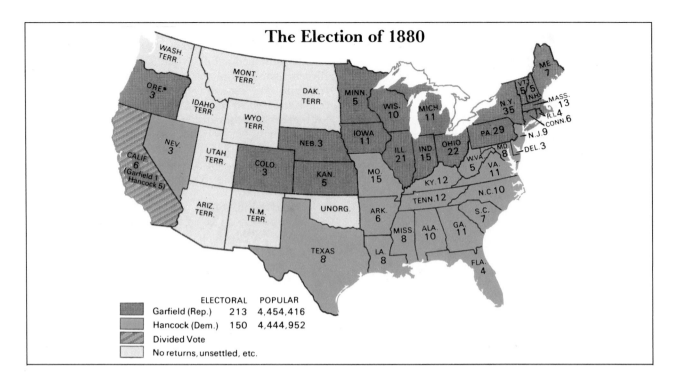

The Election of 1880

ELECTORAL	POPULAR	
Garfield (Rep.)	213	4,454,416
Hancock (Dem.)	150	4,444,952
Divided Vote		
No returns, unsettled, etc.		

quarters where the sign over the door read "Never Closed."

The Urban Political Boss.

From the city to the Senate, politics in the Gilded Age constituted a revitalized patronage society that in some ways resembled its eighteenth-century ancestor.* Under the guiding hand and sharp eye of the boss, political power was organized vertically within the machine in a hierarchical system of patrons and clients. The style of the Gilded Age boss was new and coarse, more personalized and direct than that of his gentleman predecessor. To reform critics, among them Moisei Ostrogorski, whose *Democracy and the Organization of Political Parties* summed up the reformers' indictment of machine politics, the political boss was an all-powerful leader, unsleeping, devious, and ruthless, who commanded through his "strength of will, his cleverness, his audacity and his luck." In short he was the Renaissance political theorist Niccolò Machiavelli's prince come to life. As Ostrogorski described the political boss:

To this one he lends a dollar; for another he obtains a railroad ticket without payment; he has coal distributed in the depth of winter; he makes gifts of other kinds; he sometimes sends poultry at Christmas time; he buys medicine for a sick person; he helps bury the dead by

*For eighteenth-century political patronage, see chapter 5, p. 130 ff.

procuring a coffin on credit or half-price. He has a kind heart in virtue of his position and his position gives him the means of satisfying his need for kindness: the money which he distributes comes from the chest of the Machine; the latter has obtained it by the most reprehensible methods . . . but no matter. With this money he can also dispense an ample hospitality in the drinking-saloons. As soon as he comes in, friends known and unknown gather round him, and he treats everybody, he orders one drink after another for the company; he is the only one who does not drink; he is on duty.

The urban political machine's stock in trade was jobs and appointments, transit franchises, paving contracts, public construction bids, licenses, permits, and a hundred other salable items needed to conduct the business of the nation's cities.

The impulse motivating the city boss was essentially conservative: the need to bring a semblance of order to his district. "Politics ain't bean bag," observed the Chicago Irish saloonkeeper Mr. Dooley, the fictional creation of the humorist Finley Peter Dunne. "'Tis a man's game; an' women, childher an' prohybitionists do well to keep out iv it." The reformer, bosses knew, always suffered from innocence and amateurism. "He hasn't been brought up in the difficult business of politics," Plunkitt of Tammany Hall complained, "and he makes a mess of it every time." From at least midcentury, bosses like New York City's William Marcy Tweed and Philadelphia's James McManes had watched the aimless spreading of their

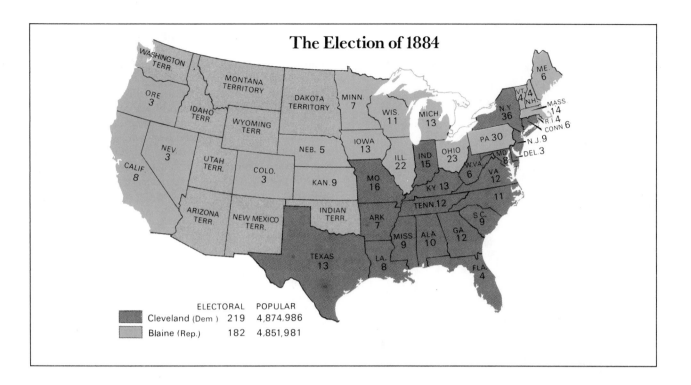

The Election of 1884

	ELECTORAL	POPULAR
Cleveland (Dem.)	219	4,874,986
Blaine (Rep.)	182	4,851,981

cities and understood the problem of managing them. Tweed frankly admitted that New York's population was "too hopelessly split into races and factions to govern it under universal suffrage, except by bribery of patronage and corruption." Their domains, the bosses realized, were fragmented like giant jigsaw puzzles. Only a professional could provide the liberal application of patronage to glue them together, even though his workmanship might be both slipshod and expensive. In New York City immediately after the Civil War, Boss Tweed secured a grip on the city government, built a mammoth new county courthouse, completed plans for Central Park, and began work on a city-wide transit system. All these achievements came at the cost of widespread corruption and an astronomical increase in the city's bonded debt.

Bosses seldom achieved the efficiency they sought. At best they surrounded themselves with oligarchies that presided over loose federations of wards and precincts. In the 1890s the bosses' failings in efficiency and accountability would give progressive reformers much ammunition in attacking the urban machines. But in the absence of a genuine science of administration and of a corps of professional managers to apply it, the bosses at least provided a minimum of order and services—however lavishly and corruptly they improvised with the materials at hand.

Patronage Politics in the States.

In the 1870s such state bosses as Roscoe Conkling in New York and James G.

Blaine, the "Plumed Knight" from Maine, were highly visible and colorful figures who cultivated the arts of demagoguery and personal leadership. By the 1880s, however, a new generation was taking over, achieving political control in many states, and building loyal organizations. The powerful new bosses of the 1880s were quieter and more efficient than their predecessors, clever, cautious, and determined to avoid the feuds that had marred their forerunners' rule. Matt Quay in Pennsylvania, Tom Platt in New York, Nelson Aldrich in Rhode Island, William Vilas in Wisconsin, and George Hearst in California were typical of a new breed of party chieftains who conducted national business in Washington while keeping a close eye on their cronies back home, mediating patronage quarrels, settling factional disputes, and smoothing discontent.

The key device for harmonizing party interests at the state level was the caucus, where local bosses, county chairmen, and state legislators gathered to stamp approval on the state boss's choice of candidates. But the real work was often done in advance and on the sly. Michigan boss James McMillan explained to his supporters how his rise to the Senate only proved "what quiet work and an active continuance of party organization can accomplish. . . . When party organization is perfect, campaigns are more easily conducted and victory more certain."

Democratic party bosses won control over their states more slowly than Republicans, and, particu-

IMMIGRANTS ARRIVING AT ELLIS ISLAND, NEW YORK CITY
New recruits for the American political army.

dle and their hopes for holding the South dim and then disappear. In 1880 the party was still torn by contending factions—"Stalwarts" taking their orders from New York's arrogant Roscoe Conkling, and "Half-Breeds" following paths blazed by James G. Blaine. These factional squabbles concerned patronage rather than matters of policy, but they were serious enough to deadlock the Republican convention in 1880 and send delegates scurrying for a compromise candidate, James A. Garfield of Ohio. Having gone down to defeat with three civilian contenders since the war, the Democrats decided to try their luck with the military and thus nominated General Winfield Scott Hancock, the hero of the battle of Gettysburg.

For the professional politicians in both parties, politics could not be cut and trimmed by moral shears or patched together with the principles of reform. Dismissing reform as contrary to human nature, and ridiculing its champions as long-haired men and short-haired women, the bosses snarled their defiance in crude and unambiguous language. Let the civil service reformers remain in their well-furnished parlors, exchanging rumors of political misbehavior while sipping their lemonade, declared Senator John J. Ingalls of Kansas. The real world, the Ingallses and Blaines and Conklings insisted, was their own world of cigar smoke and fifteen-dollar votes, rolling logs and brimming pork barrels.

As the presidential election of 1880 approached, however, and neither party appeared to have an edge with the voters, the professionals' confidence in a robust style suddenly evaporated. Throughout the decade a new cautionary political style was unmistakable, and nowhere was it more evident than among a new breed of presidential contenders.

The Lost Decade

The twentieth-century novelist Thomas Wolfe once observed that for most Americans the Gilded Age presidents from Hayes to Harrison have become irretrievably lost;

their gravely vacant and bewhiskered faces mixed, melted . . . together in the sea-depths of a past, intangible, immeasurable, and unknowable. . . . For who was Garfield, martyred man, and who had seen him in the streets of life? . . . Who had heard the casual and familiar tones of Chester Arthur? And where was Harrison? Where was Hayes? Which had the whiskers, which the burnsides: which was which?

The oblivion to which these shadowy figures have been consigned is a result of the limited concept of the presidential office in the Gilded Age and the equally limited political imaginations of the men who filled it.

larly in the one-party South, kept a looser grip on the party reins. Yet southern Democratic, or "Bourbon," conservatism soon became the model for long-time Democrats who continued to invoke the name of Jefferson in deploring the "spirit of centralization" while quietly employing just that principle in staffing and strengthening their organizations. In both parties, as in the business world after 1880, concentration was the order of the day.

A New Breed of Politicians. As late as 1880, however, much remained to be done. Democrats in that election year were entering the third decade of their prolonged period as the opposition party, and they still suffered from unimaginative leadership, a negative program, and a philosophy of "go slow." The Republican party had also fallen on evil days. Republicans had spent the 1870s watching their share of the popular vote dwin-

The Shadow Presidents. The principal task given to these presidents by party managers in Congress was to get themselves elected without compromising their reputations by saying anything provocative, and then to dispense patronage to the party worthies. Winning the presidency was not easy, especially when no clear-cut issues of public policy divided the two parties. James Bryce, the British minister in Washington who observed his first presidential election in 1884 in the contest between Blaine and Cleveland, was amazed to find that neither party had a distinctive platform. "Neither party has any principles, any distinctive tenets. Both have traditions. Both claim to have tendencies. . . . All has been lost, except office or the hope of it."

Once elected, the new president found that the first order of business was handing out jobs, a process that was both complicated and time-consuming. In his brief time in office, Garfield was exhausted by job hunters, although he had been chosen by Republican leaders precisely for his sensitivity to the patronage demands of the party's warring factions. Soon after his inauguration in March 1881, Garfield's mutterings about party office seekers swelled to a sustained wail: "My God! What is there in this place that a man should ever want to get into it?" He was not to remain in it long. In July 1881, as he was boarding a train in Washington for a well-earned vacation, he was shot in the back by a crazed government clerk who had recently been dismissed. Garfield lingered through the summer and died in September. "I am a Stalwart," Charles Guiteau had shouted as he fired at Garfield, "and Arthur is President now."

"My God! Chet Arthur!" was the response of liberal Republicans and Democrats alike at the prospect of four years of boss rule by a veteran spoilsman. Chester A. Arthur, former head of the corrupt New York Custom House and follower of Roscoe Conkling, had been given second place on the ticket chiefly to placate New York's Stalwart faction, since Garfield was widely recognized as a protégé of Blaine and his Half-Breeds. Arthur was suave, accommodating, and thoroughly hardened to the work of dispensing patronage. The new president genially oversaw the staffing of the federal bureaucracy with party hacks even as he signed the Pendleton Act (1883), which established the independent Civil Service Commission charged with classifying federal jobs and with administering examinations. In two notable respects Arthur surprised his critics: he urged the prosecution of those involved in the fraudulent Star Route postal contracts, and he vetoed an unprecedented $18 million Rivers and Harbors bill. The fact that the Star Route prosecutions failed and that Congress passed the pork barrel appropriation over his veto in no way lessened

THE WOMAN'S SPHERE
For the Gilded Age politician the woman's proper occupations were domesticity and motherhood.

the appreciation of liberals and reformers in both parties who agreed, upon his retirement, that Chet Arthur "had done well . . . by not doing anything bad."

In 1885 it was Grover Cleveland's turn to suffer the demands both of Democratic bosses clamoring for jobs and of civil service hopefuls bent on cleaning up the spoils system. Cleveland, like Garfield before him, endured a "nightmare" and complained constantly about "this dreadful, damnable office seeking." Cleveland's discomfort was the sharper because he had made his political fortune out of reform, first as the so-called Veto Mayor of Buffalo, New York, where he got rid of corrupt street-cleaning and sewer contracts, and then in the governorship of New York, where he quickly became known as the "Great Obstructionist" of the special interests. The "Big One," as the young assemblyman Theodore Roosevelt called him, looked the part of the reform-minded man of integrity—a

Culver Pictures, Inc.

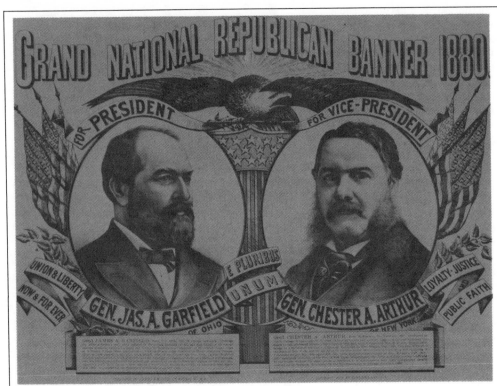

Smithsonian Institution, Division of Political History

CAMPAIGN PROPAGANDA FOR THE CUSTODIAL PRESIDENCY
The "Grand National Republican Banner" provides the answer to Thomas Wolfe's question: "Which had the whiskers, which the burnsides: which was which?"

massive three hundred pounds of jut-jawed, rocklike imperturbability—who called for "the application of business principles to public affairs" and perfected the veto as his chief weapon.

The Republicans had chosen as their 1884 standard-bearer the perennial favorite James G. Blaine. This move had made Cleveland the obvious "reform" preference of the Democrats along with those disaffected Republicans (called the Mugwumps) who bolted their party in the hope of destroying the spoils system. Still, even in this election, genuine issues were difficult to discern. Blaine concentrated on the tariff issue, and Cleveland stressed his leadership of a "far-reaching moral movement," which left the two candidates much like Tweedledee and Tweedledum. Both men, Bryce noted, openly declared their hatred of monopolies, their love of the flag, and their determination to defend the rights of Americans around the globe. Neither was willing to venture beyond these pronouncements, and it was only a question of time before the issues became personalized and cheapened.

The Republicans announced their discovery that Cleveland, that "libertine" and "moral leper," had fathered an illegitimate child in Buffalo. The Democrats produced the so-called Mulligan Letters with their own disclosures of Blaine's corruption as Speaker of

the House. Blaine's chances were further damaged by a fund-raising dinner at New York's fashionable Delmonico's Restaurant attended by such business luminaries as Jay Gould, John Jacob Astor, and sugar king Henry Havemeyer—an affair that was promptly denounced in the Democratic press as *The Royal Feast of Belshazzar Blaine and the Money Kings.* Then in the final days of the campaign, a misguided Protestant clergyman, speaking at a Blaine rally in New York City, referred to the Democratic party as the party of "rum, Romanism, and rebellion," a remark hardly designed to appeal to the city's working-class majority. Largely on the strength of these two mistakes, Cleveland carried New York by 1,200 votes out of more than a million cast, and the country by the very slim margin of 25,000.

As president, Cleveland attempted to play the role of the realistic reformer. He admitted, however, that the "boss system" survived in American politics, and, since it did, it was a necessity—"a disagreeable necessity, I assure you"—for him to recognize it. Thus he doubled the number of jobs covered under civil service from 14,000 to 28,000, at the same time appointing his own people to all the jobs left untouched by the Pendleton Act. He had not been elected "merely for the purpose of civil service," he reminded his critics, and

National Portrait Gallery, Smithsonian Institution, Washington, D.C.

1888 WOODCARVING OF BENJAMIN HARRISON
Folk artist and medium combine to catch the essential man.

asked to be saved from "the misguided zeal of impracticable friends." No one could accuse Grover Cleveland of pandering to reform!

Benjamin Harrison, a prosperous railroad lawyer from Indiana and grandson of "Old Tippecanoe," President William Henry Harrison, narrowly defeated Cleveland in his bid for reelection in 1888 in what was probably the most corrupt presidential election in American history. He then announced that "Providence" had awarded his party a great victory. "He ought to know," snorted Matt Quay, the Republican boss of Pennsylvania, "that Providence hadn't a damn thing to do with it." Harrison, he added, would never know "how close a number of men were compelled to approach the gates of the penitentiary to make him President." The new president—whose personality, one observer noted, had all the warmth of a "dripping cave"—was scarcely the man to meddle in patronage matters. Harrison preferred to leave patronage to congressional bosses, who quickly replaced some 30,000 Democratic postmasters with Republicans.

Yet by 1890 the civil service principle had taken root in the federal bureaucracy, and it continued to grow until by 1900 there were 100,000 positions subject to the rules enforced by the Civil Service Commission. The gradual triumph of civil service affected the president's work quite directly. With fewer and fewer officeholders who could be dunned for contributions to party coffers, it fell to the president as party leader to seek out wealthy donors—for Republicans the Rockefellers and the Jay Goulds, for Democrats the Levi Mortons and Henry B. Paynes—who now contributed the lion's share to the party's treasury. In this sense civil service reform strengthened the president's role as party leader.

The Custodial Presidency. In other respects, however, the Gilded Age presidents were content with their custodial role. The real power—to make budgets, authorize expenditures, and design legislation—remained with Congress, which in the 1880s was just beginning to modernize itself with an effective system of chairmanships and committees. With the great political questions of Reconstruction now dead letters, there seemed no compelling demand for presidential leadership. To congressional Republicans and Democrats alike, their president seemed simply a first-among-equals in constant need of advice and direction.

Grover Cleveland defined the custodial presidency by insisting on the "entire independence" of the executive from the legislative branch. Cleveland's power lay in the veto with which he sought to make Congress accountable and the federal government honest, impartial, frugal, and not very energetic. He used the veto sweepingly: in his first term (1885–89) he vetoed three times as many bills as all his predecessors combined. His veto messages embodied a social as well as a legal conservatism. In the aftermath of a series of devastating crop failures in the Texas Panhandle, Congress in 1887 passed the Texas Seed Bill, appropriating the modest sum of $10,000 for seed grain for needy farmers. But the assumption that in times of distress the federal government could lend a helping hand aroused Cleveland's ire:

> *I do not believe that the power and duty of the General Government ought to be extended to the relief of individual suffering which is in no manner properly related to the public service or benefit. A prevalent tendency to disregard the limited mission of this power and duty should, I think, be steadfastly resisted, to the end that the lesson should constantly be enforced that though the people support the Government, the Government should not support the people.*

Republican presidents were less inflexible, but they agreed that fashioning policies and programs was no part of their duties. None of the major pieces of Republican legislation passed during Harrison's administration (1889–93)—the Sherman Silver Purchase Act, the Sherman Antitrust Act, and the McKinley Tariff—bore the stamp of his design or the mark of his favor. Presidents of both parties were generally content with the narrow functions that had been assigned them by antebellum tradition.

Thus Congress was the most visibly active branch of the federal government, even though its pace, accelerating slightly, was still leisurely, and its sense of itself as a national lawmaking body limited. The volume of congressional business had doubled from an average of 37,000 public and private bills* per session in the 1870s to 74,000 by the mid-1880s. Gradually both houses of Congress were organizing themselves, modifying an older deliberative style and adapting it to the routine of new and stronger committees like the House's powerful Ways and Means Committee. By 1890 a Republican-dominated Senate was being managed by an informal but highly organized clique of a half-dozen senators who controlled all committee appointments. In the House both parties reluctantly were beginning to agree on the need for tightening rules and procedures. Slowly Congress was shedding its reputation for amateurism. The average length of congressional tenure increased. In the 1870s more than half the membership in each session was new. During the 1880s only one member in three was newly elected, and a decade later only one in four. By the end of the century Congress was filled with seasoned professionals.

Still, Congress was slow to break with its past. Senators and representatives still used Congress as the forum for debate among politicians whose connections with their local constituencies were all-important. Lawmaking under these circumstances tended to become an involved exercise in horse trading by representatives of competing interests. Nowhere was this process more clearly shown than in the making of the tariff.

Tariff Making. The difficult and seemingly insoluble problem for Congress after the Civil War was not raising revenue, but spending it. There was a surplus of federal revenue every year between 1866 and 1893, and the average annual surplus in the 1880s was $100 million, with more than half this amount coming from customs duties. To spend this enormous sum, legislators had only pork barrel legislation and the patronage system that sluiced off some of the reserve into federal jobs (although for the latter the passage of the

*A private bill was one introduced on behalf of a private citizen, usually to facilitate collecting a Civil War pension.

Pendleton Act restricted the use of federal funds). The tariff had become an embarrassment, and complaints multiplied against the principle of protection that took from the poor consumer and gave to the already rich corporations. Republicans, suddenly in need of a strong defense of the tariff, took up on James G. Blaine's cry that all the "wonders" of the previous twenty years were the result of high tariff schedules. Democrats gradually came to agree with Grover Cleveland that tariffs were "vicious, inequitable and illogical" and needed amendment.

By the mid-1880s the tariff question had come to serve as a distinguishing symbol for Republicans and Democrats in much the same way that the race issue had functioned during Reconstruction and the free-silver cause would operate in the 1890s. The tariff question had a political rather than an economic significance. Combined imports and exports accounted for less than 10 percent of the gross national product. What kept the economy going, it was clear, was a burgeoning domestic market. The tariff, to be sure, was important for particular economic interests—wool growers, steel manufacturers, sugar refiners—who stood to gain directly from high import barriers. It was also true that as the decade opened, none of these interest groups had irrevocably tied itself to either the Republican or the Democratic party. Yet five years later "protection" had become the watchword of the Republican party, which increasingly catered to business and industry, and "a tariff for revenue only" was the war cry of the Democratic party, identified with farmers and urban consumers.

Tariff making defied science, reason, and all but the most tireless lobbyists. Enacting a new tariff—raising rates with Republicans or lowering them with Democrats—was an elaborate three-act drama. The opening act was filled with speeches concerning the dangers to civilization lurking behind higher or lower schedules—the babble of the innocents. Act Two was set in the legendary smoke-filled room where the lobbyists held court and the amendments were drafted. The final act contrasted the embarrassment of the bill's original sponsors with the quiet satisfaction of the special interest groups who had rewritten it. This ritual began in 1882 when President Arthur appointed a blue-ribbon Tariff Commission and charged it with finding ways to lower the schedules for those American industries long past infancy and no longer in need of the paternal care provided by the tariff. The commission promptly obliged by drawing up a model bill that lowered the rates by an average of 20 percent. When it was submitted to Congress, however, the carefully drafted bill lost whatever symmetry and harmony its drafters had originally claimed for it. The hammerings of the lobbyists and their representatives quickly reduced it to rubble. Still dissatisfied with their demolition work, both House and Senate wrote separate bills and then joined forces to pass a "compromise" that raised the schedules on almost every product.

In all the tariff contests between 1880 and 1900, the Republicans consistently frustrated the Democrats' attempts to lower schedules. Both the McKinley Tariff (1890) and the Dingley Tariff (1897) legislated sizable increases in protection, and the Democrats could not prevent their enactment. From 1880 until Woodrow Wilson's first administration more than thirty years later, Democrats failed to achieve a meaningful downward revision of the tariff schedules.

The real significance of the tariff debate lay in the experience in national policy planning it provided. In invoking Hamilton in support of an active government prepared to intervene in the economy, or in citing Jefferson in defense of limited government action, congressional debates brought the outlines of national policy into focus across the country.

Toward a National Policy. The same recognition of the need for new national controls lay behind the Interstate Commerce Act (1887). In 1886 the Supreme Court in the *Wabash* case invalidated a state attempt to regulate rates for interstate railroads. In response the Senate appointed the Cullom Committee to investigate complaints against the railroads and to report on the feasibility of establishing a federal regulatory commission. Conservatives from both parties dominated the Cullom Committee, and the Interstate Commerce Act was a conservative law, even though anguished reactionaries like Senator Nelson W. Aldrich cried out that any regulation amounted to revolution. The Interstate Commerce Commission, which the law established, was empowered to forbid collusive manipulation by the railroads in the form of rebates, rate discrimination, and railroad pools. But its supervisory powers were narrowly defined, and its decisions were subject to review by the courts. The Interstate Commerce Act was intended as a means of establishing national railroad policy, but the commission itself never achieved that goal.

The politics of this era produced only the semblance, not the substance, of national policy. Neither the president nor Congress had a clear understanding of the powers needed by government to function effectively in national affairs. The concepts of a comprehensive national policy and executive leadership capable of effecting it did not emerge until the twentieth century. Meanwhile rapid industrialization was producing severe economic and social disruption. Farmers were caught in a downward spiral of prices and credit. Industrial workers were locked in combat with management over wages, hours, and the right to organize. And small-town America, uneasy with the new political order, felt the stirrings of still another crusade for a Christian society. Ever since the Civil War, farmers, laborers, and moral reformers had been involved in third-party politics, but with scant success. Their main efforts—the Greenback Labor party and the Prohibition party—had never won more than 3.5 percent of the vote in a national election. Watching the repeated failures of these would-be reformers, the Republican and Democratic party bosses felt sure that the political stability they had achieved was permanent.

But there were deeper stirrings by 1890. In both agrarian revolts in the countryside and civic campaigns in the cities, reformers were beginning to draw on the resources of two deep-lying traditions in American politics. The Populist movement in the trans-Mississippi West and in the South revived a spirit of social reform with strongly religious overtones—a millennial spirit—which had erupted repeatedly in the past in moments of crisis. And by 1895, in the nation's cities, progressive reformers were challenging boss politics by drawing on the fears of the established elite groups, on business notions of efficiency and economy, and on the scientific ideas of a new generation of professionals and academics. Together in the midst of industrial strife and rural discontent, these two groups of reformers—Populists and urban progressives—shattered the professional politicians' confidence by confronting them with new interpretations of American life.

Conditions Without Precedent: The Populist Revolt

The first reform effort to challenge the late-nineteenth-century political establishment was the Populist movement. The Populists' hopes stemmed from a millennial outlook that had long flourished in the Protestant frontier democracy, helping to inspire the "country-opposition" ideals of Revolutionary-era republicans and the visions of Jacksonian-era reformers and abolitionists. This idea of reform was based on utopian blueprints for a world beyond politics, in which power and strife would finally give way to the rule of "good men." Those who envisioned this utopia thought of politics pietistically—in terms of personal good and evil—and they defined their task as one of religious regeneration. Their language was openly evangelical. A new, divinely inspired reordering of the world, they declared, would bring a new heaven on earth; social salvation required men of Old Testament

THE SOD-HOUSE FRONTIER
Picnicking in the front yard, Custer County, Nebraska, 1886.

vision who would lead true believers out of the political wilderness and into the promised land, where they would need only the Lord to rule over them. Politics as practiced by the ungodly was an abomination, and political professionals were the willing instruments of the devil. Good politics was as simple and direct as the Golden Rule.

These political pietists demanded a complete change in the rule of conventional political behavior. In place of the easy tolerance of broker politics, they advocated cultural and political uniformity. Instead of competing interest groups, they proposed a national congregation of the right-minded. They wanted no more minor skirmishes between equally corrupt contestants, but one last mighty battle for the Lord. Pietism invited total participation at the grassroots level, chiefly in the form of camp meetings of the faithful. The Populists sought to restore a lost sense of community, to recover a preindustrial solidarity, and to return to old values. In its purest form Populist pietism promised counterrevolution—the overthrow of the modern, secular, boss-run, or bureaucratic state, and a return to the Golden Age.

The Populists' rejection of modernity, moreover,

was matched by their economic program. This program bore all the marks of small-scale entrepreneurial capitalism, with its hopes for the independent producer, steady growth rate, and voluntary cooperation. These hopes had once sustained the North and the Republican party in the war against slavery. But instead of the millennium of small producers, the Civil War had brought business consolidation and the rule of the spoilsmen; the original vision had dimmed until it guided only such marginal groups as the prohibitionists and the Greenbackers. Thus the first calls for a "new politics" in the 1880s came from the political margins—from Henry George's legion of "single-taxers," from the recruits to Edward Bellamy's "industrial army," and from the advocates of what was called the Social Gospel (an attempt to translate New Testament ethics into modern political and social reform), preaching Christian cooperation. All these marginal groups' pietistic grievances centered on issues with social and cultural as well as economic meaning—cheap money (that is, lower interest rates and more credit), the power of monopolies, and Wall Street conspiracies. These grivances underscored the isolation and insignificance of the little man in an increasingly impersonal society. The deepest seedbed of Populism lay in these attitudes of the economically and socially dispossessed, and particularly in the fears and frustrations of staple-crop farmers, who were certain that they were being victimized by urban forces.

Regional Populism.

The Populist grievances were real enough. In the trans-Mississippi West they were the result of the hectic pace of unregulated economic development; in the South they were the product of a new feudal order complete with tenancy, a crop-lien system,* and a large submerged class of dirt-poor farmers, both black and white. In the South and the Midwest alike, Populist leaders strove to overcome the sectional hatreds that survived from the Civil War era and to unite the farmers of both sections in defense of their common interests. In both regions after 1887, exorbitant shipping charges, greedy middlemen, and extortionate mortgage rates were compounded by a series of crop failures that sent land prices and farm income skidding. Years of retrenchment and retreat followed, and destitute farmers trekked back eastward from the sod-house frontier, leaving behind ghost towns with gilded opera houses and empty stores.

In the trans-Mississippi West, western Kansas lost half its population between 1882 and 1892, and South Dakota's population shrank by some 30,000. In 1891 an estimated 18,000 prairie wagons lumbered back to Iowa from the Nebraska frontier. A sign on an abandoned farmhouse in Blanco County, Texas, in the drought year 1886 read: "200 miles to the nearest post office; 100 miles to wood; 20 miles to water; 6 inches to hell. God bless our home! Gone to live with the wife's folks." Populist Mary E. Lease put it this way:

We were told two years ago to go to work and raise a big crop, that was all we needed. We went to work and plowed and planted; the rains fell, the sun shone, nature smiled, and we raised the big crop they told us to; and what came of it? Eight-cent corn, ten-cent oats, two-cent beef, and no price at all for butter and eggs—that's what came of it. Then the politicians said that we suffered from overproduction.

Populism in the South, while plagued by many of the same problems, showed distinctive features. Tenancy and crop liens exploited an underclass of black and white farmers, whose keen sense of their plight was limited by their fears of challenging an elite based on white supremacy. Western farmers risked little more than failure in organizing a third party. But in attacking the political establishment, southern farmers put their personal security and sometimes their lives on the line. In some parts on the South, Populists made genuine attempts to appeal to both black and white farmers.

In both regions Populism emerged rapidly from a nonpartisan background in 1890 and drew into politics groups that previously had been incapable of or uninterested in expressing their grievances. Some of the new recruits were women: Mary Lease, who gave impassioned speeches on the power of monopolies; Annie L. Diggs, a strict prohibitionist who was bent on saving the West from alcohol as well as from Wall Street; Sarah Emery, whose tract, *Seven Financial Conspiracies*, traced the national decline along a descending curve of democratic participation. For every seasoned veteran of third-party politics such as Ignatius Donnelly, "the Sage of Nininger," there were three new converts, including Georgia's Tom Watson, fired by Populist speeches for campaigns "hot as Nebuchadnezzar's furnace."

The atmosphere at Populist meetings was heavy with the spirit of revivalism—"a pentecost of politics," according to one observer, "in which a tongue of flame sat upon every man." Recruits, like converts, came from everywhere: farmers, hard-pressed local merchants, cattlemen, miners, small-town editors; men with chin whiskers, broad-brimmed hats, and muddy boots, accompanied by wives "with skin tanned to parchment by the hot winds, with bony hands of toil, and clad in faded calico." Quickly they became stereotypes to the rest of the world—comic hayseeds to the political opposition, heroic figures in the folklore of Populism with nicknames to match: "The Kansas Pythoness," "Bloody Bridles," "Sockless Socrates." Behind the mask appeared the original type, frequently a biblical figure like William A. Peffer, a Topeka editor elected to the United States Senate, who, with his full beard, steel-rimmed glasses, frock coat, and "habitual expression" of gravity on an otherwise inscrutable face, reminded Hamlin Garland of the Old Testament prophet Isaiah. "He made a peculiar impression on me, something Hebraic," Garland recalled, "something intense, fanatical."

The Populist, or People's, party drew a great variety of contrasting types into the reform movement. Southern Populists listened for the saving word not only from "Stump" Ashby, the Texas cowpuncher, and "Cyclone" Davis, toting his volumes of Jefferson, but also from the shrewd and hard-hitting country editor C. W. Macune, the professional North Carolina organizer Leonidas L. Polk, and Virginia patricians bearing the names of Page, Beverly, and Harrison. In the Midwest Ignatius Donnelly's fiery campaign in Minnesota was offset by the sober advice of Charles H. Van Wyck, the party's candidate for governor in Nebraska, who singled out solid issues like railroad regulation for his campaign. For the most part, however, Populists were political innocents, and among them

---

*For southern tenancy and the crop-lien system, see chapter 20, pp. 496–98.

Farming was an unprofitable and often hazardous undertaking in the arid regions of the western Great Plains, where the natural elements themselves—droughts, dust storms, blizzards, and plagues of grasshoppers—were the farmers' worst enemy. In this selection a newspaperman in Emporia, Kansas, describes the dilapidated outfit and forlorn appearance of one of the defeated army of homesteaders in retreat "out of the wilderness" to "God's own country" back in eastern Kansas.

A Journalist Describes Going Broke in Kansas (1895)

*T*HERE came through Emporia yesterday two old-fashioned "mover wagons," headed east. The stock in the caravan would invoice four horses, very poor and very tired; one mule, more disheartened than the horses; and one sad-eyed dog, that had probably been compelled to rustle his own precarious living for many a long and weary day.

A few farm implements of the simpler sort were in the wagon, but nothing that had wheels was moving except the two wagons. All the rest of the impedimenta had been left upon the battlefield, and these poor stragglers, defeated but not conquered, were fleeing to another field, to try the fight again.

These movers were from western Kansas—from Gray County, a county which holds a charter from the state to officiate as the very worst, most desolate, God-forsaken, man-deserted spot on the sad old earth. They had come from that wilderness only after a ten years' hard, vicious fight, a fight which had left its scars on their faces, had beat their bodies, had taken the elasticity from their steps, and left them crippled to enter the battle anew.

For ten years they had been fighting the elements. They had seen it stop raining for months at a time. They had heard the fury of the winter wind as it came whining across the short burned grass, and their children huddling in the corner. They have strained their eyes watching through the long summer days for the rain that never came. They have seen that big cloud roll up from the southwest about one o'clock in the afternoon, hover over the land, and stumble away with a few thumps of thunder as the sun went down. They have tossed through hot nights wild with worry, and have arisen only to find their worst nightmares grazing in reality on the brown stubble in front of their sun-warped doors.

innocence was widely considered a virtue. To eastern professionals in the two major parties, the Populists, gathered under banners urging the steadfast to vote as they prayed, presented the strange spectacle of an embittered interest group talking in tongues much like the early Christians.

Building a National Party.

The Populists were inexperienced in organizing a national party and therefore encountered formidable obstacles in building a platform that would advance farmers' interests and at the same time attract urban workers. They discovered that appeals for votes could be made in two distinct ways. First, they could explain their problems as staple-crop farmers and call on the federal government for help. Second, they could avoid interest-group appeals altogether and call on all those who lived by the sweat of their brow to join the crusade of "true producers" against the Money Power. Populism undertook both of these assignments at the same time.

The interest-group program of the Populists grew out of the reasoning of political leaders who urged the federal government to respond to the needs of all its citizens—in effect, to come to the rescue. They demanded a graduated income tax to lift the financial burden from farmers and workers. They called for postal savings banks and a flexible currency to replace the rigidly limited money supply that had been created by the gold standard—thereby ensuring continued high interest rates and declining prices. And they advocated a subtreasury plan for storing surplus crops and issuing loans that would circulate like money. The Populists could justify all these demands as protective measures for producers who lacked the security and the privileges that had been made available to the more favored industrial interests. Some of the Populist leaders who formulated these demands had a sophisticated grasp of what should be done to relieve the farmers' economic plight. And many of these demands would eventually be enacted in the twentieth century—an income tax, a paper currency freed from the gold standard and pegged to the strength of the national economy, and government price-support programs. But the late-nineteenth-century Populists would have no role in carrying out these reforms.

Another set of Populist demands represented an attempt to reach out to urban workers. It called for immigration restriction, punitive legislation against the Money Power, and farmer-labor cooperation, suggesting eternal brotherhood for the nation's real producers. Party delegates to the Populist convention in Omaha in 1892 cheered lustily as their leaders denounced the "governmental injustice" that was dividing the country into two great classes, "tramps and millionaires." To postpone the day of wrath, the Omaha party platform called for the people to seize power as they had in founding the nation:

Assembled on the anniversary of the birthday of the nation, and filled with the spirit of the grand general and chieftain who established our independence, we seek to restore the government of the Republic to the hands of the plain people with whose class it originated. . . . We declare we must be in fact, as we are in name, one united brotherhood of freemen.

In the ideal society that the Populists envisioned, righteousness would infuse God's chosen people with high purpose. In the depths of the Populist imagination lay hopes for a realm of harmony beyond politics, a haven where peace and virtue reigned supreme over a vast empire of rejuvenated yeomen. The triumph of American justice would come only when the people had purified national life at the source. Only part of such a gigantic task involved the passage of "wise and reasonable legislation." A larger part involved a moral upheaval "to bring the power of the social mass to bear upon the rebellious individuals who thus menace the peace and safety of the state."

Populism went beyond conventional politics in declaring itself "not a passing cloud on the political sky" nor a "transient gust of political discontent," but rather "the hope of realizing and incarnating in the lives of common people the fullness of the divinity of humanity." And with this shift in political perception came glimpses of catastrophe should the people's courage fail—the swift approach of the "last days" before the end of the world, nightmare visions of "men made beastlike by want, and women shorn of the nobility of their sex" pouring through city streets past plutocrats who stand "grabbing and grinning" as the mob rushes to its destruction.

The ordinary political rules no longer applied in this apocalyptic realm. If the crisis facing the nation could be reduced to a simple choice between justice and injustice, liberty and slavery, what was the need for complicated debates and sophisticated analysis? "The very fact of widespread suffering," a Nebraska Populist insisted, "is sufficient evidence that the whole system under which they have lived is a lie and an imposture." Once the people destroyed the Money Power, politics as a selfish pursuit of wealth and power would disappear. Like the abolitionists before the Civil War, the Populists concentrated on issues that had symbolic as well as practical meaning—above all the Money Question and, later, Free Silver.

For western Populists particularly, "fusion" with the Democrats appeared increasingly attractive. The Populists' presidential candidate in 1892, Civil War General James Weaver, won more than a million popular votes and twenty-two electoral votes, and the

THE LABOR QUESTION
Middle-class readers of American newspapers and magazines preferred a vantage point on the labor problem similar to that of the New York dignitaries shown looking down on an orderly night parade of workingmen, June 4, 1887.

Historical Pictures Service, Chicago

Populist party sent a dozen congressmen to Washington while securing governors' chairs in Kansas, North Dakota, and Colorado. As the Panic of 1893 tipped the country into the deepest depression it had ever known, the Populists tried to reach into the industrial cities for support. But the party was underfinanced, lacked a roster of appealing candidates, and was beset with severe organizational and financial problems. It therefore made few electoral gains in 1894, even though it increased its total vote by nearly 50 percent. Two years later, many Populist leaders decided that fusion with the Democrats on the Free Silver platform was the only alternative to continued failure.

The issue of fusion with the Democrats split the Populists into two camps. Resistance to fusion was headed by diehard reformers who agreed with Ignatius Donnelly that while the Democratic party had learned a few of its lessons, Populists ought not to "abandon the post of teacher and turn it over to [a] slow and stupid scholar." The diehards realized that the Democrats were not interested in any reforms except the free coinage of silver in addition to gold—and that the free-silver movement largely reflected the in-

terests of a powerful lobby backed by western mine owners.* For southern Populists, moreover, fusion seemed suicidal, because it meant joining the Bourbon conservatives, whose ranks they had so recently deserted—and whose response to the Populist challenge had often been intimidation, ballot-box stuffing, and racist appeals to white supremacy. But for a majority of the delegates to the Populist convention in St. Louis in 1896, a "Demopop" ticket headed by William Jennings Bryan seemed to offer the only sure way out of the political wilderness. Following an angry debate in which it was charged that the People's party had become "more boss-ridden, gang-ruled, gang-gangrened than the two old parties of monopoly," the delegates agreed to unite with their former enemies under the banner of Free Silver.

The Great Reversal: The Election of 1896

By 1896 the Democratic party was bitterly divided between agrarians and eastern business interests, and it needed all the help it could get. Grover Cleveland's return to office four years earlier had been marked by a depression and a series of industrial strikes that seemed to many Americans the opening shots in a class war. In 1892 the first of these labor upheavals came outside of Pittsburgh, at Homestead, Pennsylvania, when Andrew Carnegie sailed for Scotland and left Henry Clay Frick, his hard-driving manager and an implacable enemy of labor unions, in charge of his steel company.

Frick took advantage of his chief's absence by attempting to break the Amalgamated Association of Iron and Steel Workers, which two years earlier had won a favorable wage settlement from the company. Frick decided on a wage cut to destroy the union. When Amalgamated refused his terms, he cut off negotiations and hired a private police force to take over the plant at Homestead. The union retaliated by calling a strike, and prepared to repel the private Pinkerton guards who had been sent by barge up the Monongahela River with orders to seize the plant. The invaders, some three hundred, were met with a hail of bullets from the workers lining the shore. In the pitched battle that followed, the Pinkertons were routed and their barges burned to the water line. But final victory, as Frick had foreseen, lay with the company, which prevailed on the governor of Pennsylvania to send the militia to open the plant. Frick's union busting nearly cost him his life: in the course of the strike, a young anarchist, Alexander Berkman, attempted to assassinate him but bungled the job. Frick's principle of the open shop emerged triumphant. After five months out on strike, the Home-

*For the silver coinage issue, see below, p. 590.

stead workers were forced to accept the harsh new terms of the settlement, suffering a defeat that ended effective organizing in the steel industry for nearly half a century. Carnegie, who had kept in close touch with Frick throughout the strike, congratulated his manager for a job well done when the union was finally broken.

The Pullman Strike.

Cleveland threw his weight on the side of management against the forces of organized labor in the Pullman strike of 1894. The Pullman strike, like the Homestead strike, was a response to the antiquated ideas of a businessman whose sense of duty to his employees involved building them a model company town but did not extend to allowing them the right to negotiate their wages. When workers in the railroad-car shops went on strike, George Pullman, president of the Pullman Palace Car Company and chief planner of the company town named after him, ordered his managers to refuse to bargain and to evict the strikers from their homes. Then in the late spring of 1894, Eugene V. Debs and his recently organized American Railway Union, fresh from a victory over the Great Northern Railroad, came to the rescue of the Pullman strikers with funds and an offer to help settle their grievances. When the company again declined to bargain, the ARU voted to boycott all Pullman cars by refusing to couple them to any trains, even those carrying the mail. With the support of the railroads' General Managers Association, the Pullman Company, turning this issue to its own advantage, sought an injunction and the dispatch of federal troops to Chicago. Over the angry protests of Illinois Governor John P. Altgeld, President Cleveland obliged and sent in federal troops. Faced with a choice between the rights of labor and the rights of property, Cleveland sided with the men of property.

The Depression of 1893.

The American economy hit bottom in 1894. Five hundred banks closed their doors, sixteen thousand business firms collapsed, and unemployment reached nearly 20 percent. New issues on the New York Stock Exchange plummeted from $100 million to $37 million, and 2.5 million jobless workers tramped winter streets looking for work. Municipal governments and private charity organizations could not cope with the large numbers of destitute men who wandered aimlessly from city to city, finding factory gates closed everywhere and long lines at the soup kitchens. Not since the dark days of the Civil War had the country seemed so threatened.

Workers met the depression and the accompanying wage cuts with the only weapon they had— the strike. In 1894 alone there were more than 1,300 strikes. The mining industry was hit by a wave of strikes that rolled across the country from the coal

Chicago Historical Society

"STRIKE!"

As in this illustration of the riot at the McCormick factory in Chicago in May 1886, strikes and violence were frequently depicted as clashes between the "forces of law and order" and maddened mobs.

fields of the East to Coeur d'Alene in Idaho, where besieged miners fought with sticks and dynamite, and Cripple Creek, Colorado, where armed deputies broke up demonstrations. For such acute economic distress President Cleveland proposed the heroic remedies of self-denial and sacrifice.

The specter of masses of starving men marching on the nation's cities to plunder and pillage in an uprising of the dispossessed turned into a farce in the spring of 1894 with the arrival in Washington of Coxey's Army, a "petition in boots" that had come to the capital to ask for work. The leader of the few hundred jobless men who finally straggled into the city was the self-appointed "General" Jacob Coxey, a small-town businessman from Massillon, Ohio. Coxey simply wanted to present his plan for solving unemployment with a "good roads bill," which would finance public improvement with $500 million worth of government bonds. The Cleveland administration's reaction to this living petition was a measure of its fear of mass upheaval: Coxey's followers were dispersed and their leader was jailed on a technicality, while rumors of revolution swept through the city.

Cleveland blamed the free-silver forces for the depression. In 1890 Congress had responded to the clamor of the silver interests and had passed the Sherman Silver Purchase Act, which required the government to buy 4.5 million ounces of silver each month and to pay for it with treasury notes redeemable in gold or silver. The Sherman Silver Purchase Act brought a sudden rush on the gold reserves of the United States by investors frightened by high imports and falling crop prices. The gold reserves plunged from $190 million to $100 million in just three years. As the depression deepened, Cleveland persuaded Congress to repeal the Silver Purchase Act. After a bitter struggle Congress complied in 1893, but the repeal seriously weakened Cleveland's control over his own party. He had succeeded in limiting the flow of silver from the mines in the West, but in so doing he had also lost the support of the agrarian half of the Democratic party, as well as of the senators representing western silver-mining interests. By 1895 the president was complaining that there was "not a man in the Senate with whom I can be on terms of absolute confidence."

The Gold Standard: "A Crown of Thorns"?

To stop the drain on American gold, Cleveland issued government bonds at a generous interest rate to attract European investors. In calling on the banking syndicates of J. P. Morgan and August Belmont to market the bonds, Cleveland only added to his political difficulties. Working together, the administration and the bankers arranged the sale of government bonds for gold on terms that allowed the banking houses to manipulate exchange rates in their own favor. To the Populists and to irate Democrats in the South and West, Cleveland's deal with the bankers was powerful proof of a Wall Street conspiracy to rig the economy against them.

The silverites proceeded to make the presidential election of 1896 a one-issue campaign. Silver and gold quickly became organizing symbols for diametrically opposed (and to modern economists, equally misguided) strategies for economic recovery. Financial policy was treated as sacred truth, and the opposing view was denounced as utterly wrong. According to its defenders silver was the "people's" money—abundant, cheap, and flexible. To businessmen and bankers gold was the only "honest" currency—solid and time-tested. Cleveland chose "sound money," the gold standard, and currency restriction as the only ethical course, while William Jennings Bryan described gold as "a crown of thorns" for bankrupt farmers and western debtors, pressed on the brow of the honest laborer who was being crucified by the moneylenders. In fact Cleveland's monetary policy did worsen the effects of the depression. But more important, it gave farmers a highly visible target for their grievances. Addressing his backcountry constituents, South Carolina demagogue Ben Tillman denounced the president as a Judas who three times had betrayed the democracy. "He is an old bag of beef, and I am going to Washington with a pitchfork and prod him in his fat ribs."

With similar intentions Democrats gathered in Chicago for the convention of 1896. Southern and western Democrats quickly realized that by rejecting Cleveland's policies and advocating the free and unlimited coinage of silver they had an opportunity to upstage the Populist party. The thirty-six-year-old Bryan immediately emerged as the choice of the agrarian wing of the party, which rode roughshod over the "sound money" advocates and drove them out of the convention to form their own splinter organization. Bryan spoke the mood of his followers in sounding a new note of resistance:

We have petitioned, and our petitions have been scorned; we have entreated, and our entreaties have been disregarded; we have begged and they have mocked when our calamity came. We beg no longer; we entreat no more; we petition no more. We defy them!

The eastern press, both Republican and Democratic, replied with charges of anarchy and treason. "The Jacobins are in full control at Chicago," one editor announced, comparing Bryan and his followers to the radicals of the French Revolution. "No large political movement in America has ever before spawned such hideous and repulsive vipers." Both the promise and the danger of a Democratic victory seemed greater after the Populists' convention in St. Louis also endorsed Bryan for president. Not since 1860 had the fate of the nation appeared to hang in the balance of a single election. In 1896 as in 1860, the differences were sectional and economic, but they were also social and cultural, as two fundamentally opposed views of politics competed for the American voter's allegiance.

Bryan and his Republican opponent, William McKinley, between them gave more than nine hundred speeches in the campaign of 1896; the Republican from his front porch in Canton, Ohio, to throngs of admiring visitors shipped in by party managers, and the "Boy Orator of the Platte" at every whistlestop in the West where local leaders could collect a crowd. Their speeches riveted national attention on the money question, which quickly brought into focus cultural and social disagreements between urban and rural America. Bryan soon expanded his economic indictment of the Money Power to a plea for a national moral revival. Republicans, capitalizing on the gradual upturn in the economy late in the summer, continued to denounce the Democratic platform as "revolutionary and anarchistic . . . subversive of na-

CAMPAIGN STYLES: OLD AND NEW
Bryan (left) barnstormed the country in the time-honored political fashion, while Republicans advertised McKinley (right) with an icon of prosperity.

tional honor and threatening to the very life of the Republic."

Bryan: A Crusading Prophet.

A powerful orator and an appealing political figure, Bryan was new to the business of presidential campaigning. In casting his party adrift from its eastern financial moorings, he was forced to improvise. The professional politicians of the Democratic party withheld their support, sensitive to the sound-money opinions of their business backers, and appalled by the prospect of an inflationary free silver. Bryan rejected the limited offers of the few party leaders who remained loyal. Sensing the need for new rules and definitions, he cast himself in the role of a crusading prophet who could purify his party and country—by eliminating corruption, paring the campaign budget, purging the party of hacks, and preaching principles rather than praising men.

As the new leader, Bryan appeared an avenging angel of outraged American yeomanry, the people's savior stopping his campaign train for just one more sermon to his flock. He invariably apologized to his listeners, confessing that "a large portion of my voice has been left along the line of travel, where it is still calling sinners to repentance." His speeches drew on a fund of stock pietist images as he mixed indictments of the Money Power, the tariff, and the gold standard with allusions to the Old Testament. His message was always the same: the people must arise in their majesty to smite the moneylenders and destroy their temple. Audiences came to know his arguments by heart and gathered to hear confirmation of their beliefs in the Protestant ethic of hard work and a just reward. When their leader assured them that "every great economic question is in reality a great moral question," they understood instinctively and they cheered. As Bryan preached the saving word of free silver, his audiences saw the stone suddenly rolled away and "the door . . . opened for a progress which would carry civilization up to higher ground."

"Live and Let Live" with McKinley.

Republicans, following the orders of their new managers, among them Mark Hanna of Ohio, willingly exchanged places with their

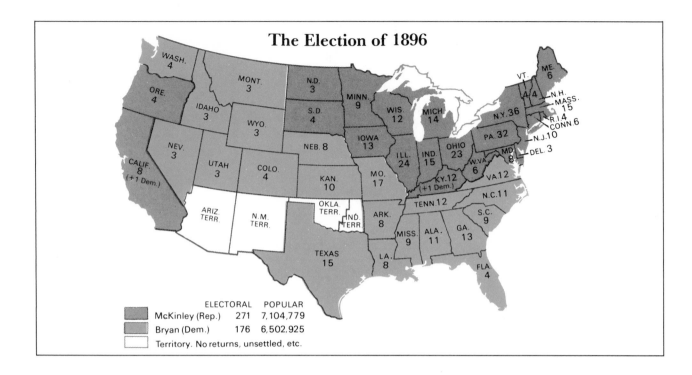

The Election of 1896

	ELECTORAL	POPULAR
McKinley (Rep.)	271	7,104,779
Bryan (Dem.)	176	6,502,925
Territory. No returns, unsettled, etc.		

Democratic rivals. Tossing aside their pietistic heritage as a burden, they embarked on a pragmatic course toward a coalition of business and labor in the cities where most of the votes lay. Their chosen candidate, McKinley, was a born compromiser, bland and amiable, with no strikingly original ideas but presumably with plenty of common sense. To McKinley's front porch in Canton, Ohio, came some three-quarters of a million people, carried there on 9,000 railroad cars paid for by the party, to stand behind a white picket fence and listen to sermons on the honest dollar and the full dinner pail.

McKinley's image was a clever contrivance of Republican managers who recognized both the liabilities of pietism in an age of secular industrial organization, and the need for full-time professional organizers, effective propaganda, and a full treasury. During the campaign Republicans released an unprecedented flood of pamphlets, posters, speeches, and editorials that reached every corner of the country. All their efforts were carefully orchestrated to new themes of cultural and ethnic toleration and were arranged to appeal to farmers and workers, small businessmen and big bankers, shippers and consumers, Catholics as well as Protestants, and a variety of ethnic groups to whom the gold standard was offered as the last best hope of democracy. McKinley himself summed up the new Republican message: "We have always practiced the Golden Rule. The best policy is to 'live and let live.'" With the blessings of their candidate, the Re-

publicans turned their backs on their pietist past and squared to the task of engineering a broad social consensus.

The Republicans won a decisive victory in the election. With 7 million popular and 271 electoral votes, McKinley swept the entire East and Midwest, carried California and Oregon, and held on to Minnesota, North Dakota, and Iowa. Bryan, with 6.5 million popular votes and 176 electoral votes, won the Solid South together with the plains and the mountain states. Beneath the regional features of the election of 1896 lay the deeper meaning of the political turnabout. With their votes, a majority of Americans declared their preference for toleration and accommodation.

The meaning of the Democrats' defeat was clear. The American electorate had rejected the pietist countercrusade against modernism and secularism. There would undoubtedly be reforms as the twentieth century opened, but they would not be carried out by millennial dreamers of purity and perfection. From now on, political parties would have to consider and cater to the wishes of a multitude of social interests, welcoming newcomers from a wide variety of ethnic, cultural, and religious groups, meeting their demands, listening to their complaints, and serving their needs.

The election of 1896 also made it clear that the organizational revolution that was transforming business and finance had now invaded politics. Just as both houses of Congress were beginning to modernize their procedures for doing the nation's business, so the two principal political parties had learned the importance of efficient organization, continuing communications, flexible and sophisticated candidates, and, above all, money with which to run their political machinery.

The Party System Realigned.

Finally, and most significant for the immediate future, the election of 1896 broke the grip of party discipline and loyalty that had long been considered a permanent feature of American politics. The election freed the American party system for a long-term realignment of voting patterns that would reveal the average voter as considerably more independent than the professionals had once assumed.

Bryan had uncovered a latent American suspicion of politics, a set of misgivings that had been buried in the rubble of the Civil War. In his unsuccessful campaign he had located this skepticism in the agrarian mind, had attempted to exploit it, and had failed. But by 1896 new urban reformers were already experiencing a similar distrust of entrenched power and were beginning to experiment with still another form of politics. The political program of these emerging reformers, while it promised to end machine politics and return power to the people, envisioned not the rule of righteousness, but the triumph of the middle-class professionals. The vision of social reformers organizing American cities after 1890 centered on an efficient, economically run "organic city" that was man-made rather than God-given. With the stirring of these reform hopes came a second and more potent challenge to the old politics—the challenge of progressivism.

CHRONOLOGY

1880	James A. Garfield elected president.
1881	Garfield assassinated; Chester A. Arthur becomes president.
1883	Pendleton Act establishes independent Civil Service Commission.
1884	Grover Cleveland elected president, defeating Republican James G. Blaine.
1887	Interstate Commerce Act attempts to control railroads.
1888	Benjamin Harrison narrowly defeats Cleveland and is elected president.
1890	Sherman Silver Purchase Act passed, resulting in depleted gold reserves.
	Sherman Antitrust Act passed in attempt to regulate monopolies in restraint of trade.
	McKinley Tariff raises duties to average 49.5 percent.
1892	Populists organize, nominate General James B. Weaver for president.
	Grover Cleveland elected president.
	Homestead Strike in Carnegie steel mills.
1893	Financial panic sends U.S. economy into four years of depression.
	Congress repeals Silver Purchase Act.
1894	Pullman Strike broken by federal troops; Eugene V. Debs jailed.
	"Coxey's Army" of unemployed marches on Washington.
1896	William McKinley elected president, defeating William Jennings Bryan and "Free Silver."
1897	Dingley Tariff raises duties to a new high of 57 percent.

SUGGESTED READINGS

An invaluable introduction to American politics and society from the end of the Civil War to 1900 is Morton Keller, *Affairs of State: Public Life in Nineteenth Century America* (1977). There are several useful guides to politics in the Gilded Age. David Rothman, *Politics and Power: The United States Senate, 1869–1901* (1966), traces the emergence of the modern Senate as it is organized in the 1890s by new wealthy representatives of big business. H. Wayne Morgan, *From Hayes to McKinley: National Party Politics, 1877–1896* (1969), concentrates on the organizational problems of the two major parties. Robert D. Marcus, *Grand Old Party: Political Structure in the Gilded Age, 1880–1896* (1971), analyzes the workings of the Republican party, and Samuel Merrill, *Bourbon Democracy of the Middle West, 1865–1896*, gives a good regional account of the Democrats for the same period. Southern politics is perceptively treated in four important works: C. Vann Woodward, *The Origins of the New South, 1877–1913* (1951); Dewey Grantham, Jr., *The Democratic South* (1963); Albert D. Kirwan, *Revolt of the Rednecks: Mississippi Politics: 1876–1925* (1951); and Morgan Kousser, *The Shaping of Southern Politics: Suffrage Restriction and the Establishment of the One-Party South, 1880–1910* (1974). Lawrence Goodwyn, *Democratic Promise: The Populist Movement in America* (1976), rehabilitates the image of southern Populists. Stanley P. Hirshon, *Farewell to the Bloody Shirt: Northern Republicans and the Southern Negro, 1877–1893*, considers the race issue as it affected party politics. Mary R. Dearing, *Veterans in Politics* (1952), covers the activities of Civil War veterans, and Marc Karson, *American Labor Unions and Politics, 1900–1918* (1958),

discusses unions and politics in the opening years of the twentieth century.

There are a number of good studies of crucial elections in the 1880s and 1890s. Among the best are Paul W. Glad, *McKinley, Bryan, and the People* (1964); Stanley Jones, *The Presidential Election of 1896* (1964); and J. Rogers Hollingsworth, *The Whirligig of Politics: The Democracy of Cleveland and Bryan* (1963). Two challenging studies, Paul Kleppner, *The Cross of Culture: A Social Analysis of Midwestern Politics, 1840–1900* (1970), and Richard J. Jensen, *The Winning of the Midwest* (1971), explore cultural factors as determinants of voting behavior in the Midwest during the Gilded Age.

There are several excellent biographies of major political figures. Three of the best studies of Bryan are Paolo E. Coletta, *William Jennings Bryan: Political Evangelist, 1860–1908* (1964); Paul W. Glad, *The Trumpet Soundeth: William Jennings Bryan and His Democracy, 1896–1912* (1964); and Louis W. Koenig, *Bryan: A Political Biography of William Jennings Bryan* (1971). For McKinley see H. Wayne Morgan, *William McKinley and His America* (1963), and the very readable study of McKinley's life and times, Margaret Leech, *In the Days of McKinley* (1959). Biographies of other major figures include Horace Samuel Merrill, *Bourbon Leader: Grover Cleveland and the Democratic Party* (1957); Kenton J. Clymer, *John Hay: The Gentleman as Diplomat* (1975); and a brilliant recent biography of Eugene V. Debs by Nick Salvatore, *Eugene V. Debs: Citizen and Socialist* (1982).

On the troubled 1890s a good overview is Harold U. Faulkner, *Politics, Reform and Expansion, 1890–1900* (1959).

The cultural and intellectual climate of the decade is analyzed in Larzar Ziff, *The American 1890s: Life and Times of a Lost Generation* (1966), and in the idiosyncratic and amusing Thomas Beer, *The Mauve Decade* (1952 ed.).

The origins and growth of urban progressivism are chronicled in Melvin Holli, *Reform in Detroit: Hazen Pingree and Urban Politics* (1969); James B. Crooks, *Politics and Progress: The Rise of Urban Progressivism in Baltimore,* *1895–1911* (1968); William D. Miller, *Memphis During the Progressive Era, 1900–1917* (1957); and Jack Tager, *The Intellectual as Urban Reformer: Brand Whitlock and the Progressive Movement* (1968). Nancy Weiss, *Charles Francis Murphy, 1858–1924: Respectability and Responsibility in Tammany Politics* (1968), paints a colorful portrait of the boss of New York City's redoubtable Democratic machine at the end of the nineteenth century.

24 The Progressive Impulse

I n 1915, as the progressive movement neared its peak, a young professor of government at New York University, Benjamin Parke DeWitt, published a book entitled *The Progressive Movement*, in which he catalogued the political and social reforms in the United States in the previous two decades. DeWitt, an active progressive and ardent admirer of Theodore Roosevelt, looked behind the campaigns and the elections and discovered three interlocking reform tendencies:

The first of these tendencies is found in the insistence by the best men in all political parties that special, minority, and corrupt influence in government—national, state, and city—be removed; the second tendency is found in the demand that the structure or machinery of government . . . be so changed and modified that it will be more difficult for the few, and easier for the many, to control; and finally, the third tendency is found in the rapidly growing conviction that the functions of government are too restricted and that they must be increased and extended to relieve social and economic distress.

DeWitt's analysis was accurate. The progressives believed that government at all levels was both inefficient and corrupt. Because it was corrupt, it ignored the needs of the people. Therefore, the people themselves had to seize the initiative in repairing the whole system. According to progressive logic, the first job was to remove unworthy and inept politicians and to replace them with reliable public servants drawn from the popular ranks and equipped with the needed expertise. These new leaders would then see to it that government—city, state, and national—performed an expanding range of tasks efficiently and responsibly. Progressives, in short, found in the idea of scientific government the materials for building a national reform movement.

A variety of forces shaped the progressive movement. There was no single progressive type among the

leaders or the rank and file; there was no typical age, status, background, religion, or education. The progressives were drawn from the mainstream of the native-born middle class that dominated American politics in the first two decades of the twentieth century. Educated, articulate, and eager to apply their ideas for reforming society and politics, they held no monopoly on political gentility and could be found in equal numbers in the reform wings of both the Republican and the Democratic parties.

The progressives had no uniform platform. They offered a wide array of reform proposals: initiative, referendum, recall, corporate regulation, child labor laws, tariff reform, city-manager plans, zoning regulations, immigration restriction—even prohibition. Their priorities differed according to region and immediate interest. Farmers fought hard for regulation of railroad rates but ignored the problem of industrial accidents. Southern progressives pushed hard for tariff and banking reform but disfranchised the blacks. Settlement-house workers grappled with the bosses for control of their cities but neglected the problems of the small-town businessman.

With this great variety in progressivism from 1890 to 1914, it seems useful to analyze it not as a movement at all, but rather as a patchwork of the efforts of different interest groups that occasionally agreed on specific measures but were unable to combine behind a unified and coherent program. The progressives thought otherwise. They realized that the United States was entering a new era of economic and political consolidation, one that required new techniques for managing what all of them agreed was a flourishing national enterprise. Even though they admitted that there was much wrong with America, they saw little that could not be mended by using governmental authority and scientific efficiency. In the spirit of the Founding Fathers whose nationalism they so admired, progressive reformers, despite their differences, thought of themselves as the architects of a

stable social order based on many of the principles that had guided their Federalist ancestors.

With their experiments in new political techniques, the progressives were innovators, but at a deeper level they were conservatives and restorationists. They picked up the promise of American life where their eighteenth-century forebears had dropped it—with the creation of a strong national government capable of harnessing and directing the energies of all its citizens. Part of the progressives' call for the people to take power back from their corrupt rulers seemed to invoke the spirit of Jefferson. But the heart of their program was the Hamiltonian demand for a new national leadership using the power of government to set priorities and provide direction. The ghosts of Hamilton and Jefferson fought over the progressive terrain just as the two statesmen had bitterly contested each other's principles a century earlier. To the delight of his many progressive admirers, Hamilton won the victory that had been denied him during his lifetime. For in effect, if not in intent, progressivism marked the rebirth of original Federalist hopes for a managed republic in which men of talent and training guided the affairs of a prosperous people.

Cities in Revolt: The Rise of Urban Progressivism

The progressive search for order in a disordered world began in the city. Wherever urban reformers looked in the closing years of the nineteenth century, they saw disorganization and fragmentation. Wealthy neighborhoods with million-dollar mansions were set apart by parks and boulevards from teeming ghettos with dilapidated tenements and filthy streets. These conditions presented all too visible proof of the immense distances—social and psychological as well as economic and geographical—that separated the rich from the poor.

It was to close the distance between urban affluence and sprawling poverty that in 1889 Jane Addams, the pioneer settlement-house worker, moved into Hull House, a battered mansion on the corner of Polk and South Halstead streets in the heart of Chicago's Nineteenth Ward.

The streets are inexpressibly dirty [she reported], *the number of schools inadequate, factory legislation unenforced, the street-lighting bad, the paving miserable and altogether lacking in alleys and smaller streets, and the stables defy all laws of sanitation. . . . Hundreds of houses are unconnected with the street sewer. . . . Back tenements flourish; many houses have no water supply save the faucet in the back yard; there are no fire escapes; the garbage and ashes are placed in wooden boxes which*

are fastened to the street pavements. . . . Our ward contains two hundred and fifty-five saloons; our own precinct boasts of eight. . . . There are seven churches and two missions in the ward.

In listing the Nineteenth Ward's needs, Jane Addams summarized the main points in the urban progressive indictment of boss politics. Progressivism began as a spontaneous revolt of city dwellers who were convinced that they had been short-changed in their share of the American social fund.

A pragmatic assessment of urban blight was the first phase in the drive to clean up the nation's cities. Broad coalitions of voters demanded immediate solutions to a wide range of problems: they sought tax reforms, more effective health regulations, lower streetcar fares, better utility services, and efficient city governments free of corrupt bosses and greedy special interests. The depression of the 1890s, by placing new burdens on consumers, created a sense of urgency and focused public attention on the shortcomings of rule by the political machines.

The progressive attack centered on "invisible government," the alliance between municipal authorities and business interests. The connection between "corrupt government" and "corporate arrogance," which the progressives fought to destroy, was a simple one of mutual need. In attempting to modernize their cities, machine politicians had discovered that secret agreements with transit, utility, and construction interests were a handy device for providing minimal service while lining their own pockets. At the same time, the new and unstable industries that were involved with urban development were undergoing rapid reorganization and were always short of funds. These industries saw in monopoly franchises, wholesale bribery, and kickbacks a measure of certainty in an otherwise unpredictable world. By 1890 such bargains had been sealed in most of the country's major cities. The only real loser in this arrangement was the public.

Thus progressivism began as a "people's movement" aimed at eliminating corruption and inefficiency. Cutting across class lines and focusing on specific issues like dangerous railway crossings, poor sanitation, and high streetcar fares, the progressive movement in its early years developed a style that was both democratic and moralistic. The twin devils in the reformers' morality plays were the businessman and the boss. Lincoln Steffens, the dean of reform journalists, pronounced the American businessman "a self-righteous fraud." "I found him buying boodlers in St. Louis, defending grafters in Minneapolis, originating corruption in Pittsburgh, sharing with the bosses in Philadelphia, deploring reform in Chicago, and beat-

TENEMENTS, WASHINGTON, D.C.
Lewis W. Hine's famous photograph of the capital's black slums documents the urban progressive challenge.

ing good government with corruption funds in New York." From the beginning the progressives developed an antibusiness rhetoric that continued to obscure the real contributions of businessmen to urban reform.

Progressive Mayors.

The bosses offered even more enticing targets. Urban reformer Frederick C. Howe reported that Boss Cox of Cincinnati ruled his city "as a medieval baron did his serfs." The only remedy for boss rule lay in building citizens' coalitions to unite a fragmented community. "The very nature of city life," one progressive commentator pointed out, "compels manifold cooperation. The individual cannot 'go it alone'; he cannot do as he pleases; he must conform his acts in an ever increasing degree to the will and welfare of [his] community. . . ." This concept of the organic city fitted neatly with the interests and ambitions of a new group of reform mayors in the 1890s who launched individual campaigns to overhaul their cities.

The first of these progressive mayors was Hazen

Pingree, mayor of Detroit from 1889 to 1896, when he was elected governor of Michigan. Pingree, a shoe manufacturer turned "reform boss," campaigned vigorously in all the wards of the city. He steered clear of controversial moral and religious questions like prohibition and parochial schools, concentrating instead on the hard economic issues that would win him the broadest support. Pingree exposed bribery in a local electric company's dealings with his predecessors and embarked on an extensive program of school and park construction. After a long battle with the transit and utility interests, he succeeded in reducing streetcar fares and gas rates while building the city's municipal lighting plant. During the depression of the 1890s, he started work-relief programs for Detroit's unemployed and extended a variety of social service programs. Pingree set a pattern for his successors by attacking Detroit's "invisible government" and replacing it with an efficient, responsive administration.

It remained for Tom Johnson, the mercurial mayor of Cleveland from 1901 to 1909, to exploit most

In her classic account of settlement-house life, *Twenty Years at Hull-House*, Jane Addams graphically describes the working conditions that she and her staff discovered in Chicago's factories and sweatshops. A subsequent investigation directed by Florence Kelley and culminating in a report studded with case histories and statistics resulted in the passage of Illinois' first factory law.

Jane Addams Urges Factory Legislation in Illinois

*T*HREE boys from a Hull-House club were injured at one machine in a neighboring factory for lack of a guard which would have cost but a few dollars. When the injury of one of these boys resulted in his death, we felt quite sure that the owners of the factory would share our horror and remorse, and that they would do everything possible to prevent the recurrence of such a tragedy. To our surprise they did nothing whatever, and I made my first acquaintance then with those pathetic documents signed by the parents of working children, that they will make no claim for damages resulting from "carelessness."

The visits we made in the neighborhood constantly discovered women sewing upon sweatshop work, and often they were assisted by incredibly small children. I remember a little girl of four who pulled out basting threads hour after hour, sitting on a stool at the feet of her Bohemian mother, a little bunch of human misery. But even for that there was no legal redress, for the only child labor law in Illinois, with any provision for enforcement, had been secured by the coal miners' unions, and was confined to children employed in mines.

We learned to know many families in which the working children contributed to the support of their parents, not only because they spoke English better than the older immigrants and were willing to take lower wages, but because their parents gradually found it easy to live upon their earnings. . . . An Italian father came to us in great grief over the death of his eldest child, a little girl of twelve, who had brought the largest wages into the family fund. In the midst of his genuine sorrow he said: "She was the oldest kid I had. Now I shall have to go back to work again until the next one is able to take care of me." The man was only thirty-three and had hoped to retire from work at least during the winters. No foreman cared to have him in a factory, untrained and unintelligent as he was. It was much easier for his bright, English-speaking little girl to get a chance to paste labels on a box than for him to secure an opportunity to carry pig iron. . . .

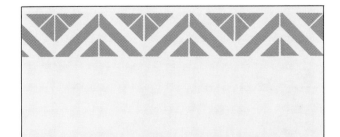

There was at that time no statistical information on Chicago industrial conditions, and Mrs. Florence Kelley, an early resident of Hull-House, suggested to the Illinois State Bureau of Labor that they investigate the sweating system in Chicago with its attendant child labor. The head of the Bureau adopted this suggestion and engaged Mrs. Kelley to make the investigation. When the report was presented to the Illinois Legislature, a special committee was appointed to look into the Chicago conditions. I well recall that on the Sunday the members of this commission came to dine at Hull-House, our hopes ran high, and we believed that at last some of the worst ills under which our neighbors were suffering would be brought to an end.

As a result of its investigations, this committee recommended to the Legislature the provisions which afterwards became those of the first factory law of Illinois, regulating the sanitary conditions of the sweatshop and fixing fourteen as the age at which a child might be employed.

fully a whole new range of possibilities for leadership. Johnson had made his fortune by reorganizing transit systems, and he had been converted to reform after reading Henry George's *Social Problems*. After two successful terms in Congress as a reform Democrat, he returned to Cleveland to build a political coalition to fight Republican boss Mark Hanna and the transit interests. Energetic, tough-minded, and the ultimate politician, down to the unlit cigar he waved while speaking from the nearest soapbox, Johnson borrowed the techniques of the machine politicians and improved on them. He inaugurated his reform program by arranging for a regulated system of prostitution free from police graft. Like Hazen Pingree, he threatened the transit interests with regulation; his most widely acclaimed achievement was the 3¢ fare. Johnson provided his city with free public bathhouses, recreational facilities, and effective sanitary inspection, and he continued to agitate for municipal ownership of utilities.

Progressive mayors who launched their careers from a platform of pragmatic opposition to the "interests" were frequently driven to face broader questions of social welfare. Some mayors—like Pingree, Johnson, and later Brand Whitlock in Toledo, Ohio, and Mark Fagan in Jersey City, New Jersey— were forced to adjust to shifting economic interests within their reform coalitions and to support welfare measures that went far beyond the political and structural reforms they originally had called for. The "social justice" mayors, as they have been called, also came to question the value of strict party identification. Increasingly they relied on the advice and services of new nonpartisan experts in municipal management who were concerned with finding more efficient ways of running American cities.

Social Experimentation. "Streetcar politics" was only the most visible sign of the urban revival in the 1890s. City churches were keenly aware of their declining membership among the working class and responded to the crisis by developing the "institutional church" in lower-class neighborhoods. By providing services like lodging houses, reading rooms, recreational halls, and day nurseries, church progressives hoped to spread the "social gospel" of Christianity. Then too, by 1890 groups of earnest young college graduates, many of them women, were moving into slums to live in settlement houses modeled on London's famed Toynbee Hall. By 1895 there were more than fifty such settlements in major cities around the country, each with a staff of idealistic college graduates and seminarians.

Settlement-house workers were invariably young (most were under thirty), religious (predominantly Congregationalists and Presbyterians), college-

Photograph by Jessie Tarbox Beals, Museum of the City of New York

Library of Congress

HENRY STREET SETTLEMENT HOUSE VISITING
NURSE, NEW YORK, 1908
A short cut leads over the roofs of the tenements.

educated, and single, and overwhelmingly they came
from middle-class families. For these young intellectuals and professionals, some of them with advanced training in the new social sciences taught in
German universities, the city settlement offered an
escape from gentility and from feelings of uselessness,
and provided the chance to practice new skills. Settlements freed them from what Jane Addams called
"the snare of preparation" for unknown careers. More
important, they developed a new and deeper understanding of the complex social and cultural relations
that made up the modern city. Teachers, housing reformers, charity organizers, child labor opponents,
health inspectors, and visiting nurses found a congenial home in the reform settlements, which seemed
to them miniature models of the good society.

The progressive movement was not only a major
effort in social engineering. It involved also a profound
intellectual revolution. The reformers came to understand the complexity and the interconnectedness of
modern life. They experienced at first hand the
difficulty of isolating the underlying causes of the
problems they dealt with, and the futility of proposing
simple solutions. Whether they were lawyers, engineers, clinicians, historians, sociologists, or economists, the progressives found themselves working
with a new approach to knowledge that the philosopher John Dewey, one of their teachers, called
"creative intelligence," and another powerful intellectual, William James, called "pragmatism." James
taught these young reformers to seek truth not in abstractions, but in action. "How will truth be realized?
What, in short, is truth's cash-value in experiential
terms?" Truth was not a "stagnant property" inherent
in an idea, as Emerson and the Transcendentalists had
believed. Truth *worked*, James insisted. "*True ideas are*

THE PROGRESSIVE SOCIAL WORKER'S CLIENTS
Life inside city tenements and outside on slum streets, like Thomas Hobbes's state of nature, was nasty, brutish, and frequently short. Lewis Hine took these photographs of the victims of social callousness and entitled them simply "New York Tenement" and "Italian Children in Chicago."

those we can assimilate, validate, corroborate, and verify. False ideas are those we cannot."

John Dewey, whose interest in social reform was as strong as James's, saw the origins of this so-called instrumentalist logic in Charles Darwin's evolutionary biology and in the scientific thinking that did away with the old search for "absolutes and finalities." This new logic, Dewey told his progressive students, brought new intellectual responsibilities. Philosophy would hereafter have to deal with "the more serious of the conflicts that occur in life" and develop a method of "moral and political diagnosis and prognosis." Oliver Wendell Holmes, Jr., judge and legal instrumentalist, was even more specific. He taught the progressives that the true function of law was the expression not of abstract principles, but of "accurately measured social desires."

By 1900 the settlement house had become an in-dispensable laboratory of social experimentation. In devising urban programs and services, the progressives relied heavily on new methods of research and fact gathering as essential to the work of reordering urban society. One of Jane Addams's first assignments was to collect and collate the raw data on the surrounding neighborhood; in 1895 *Hull House Maps and Papers* appeared as the first detailed account of an immigrant community published in the United States. In 1903 Lawrence Veiller and Robert W. DeForest published their two-volume *Tenement House Problems,* an attempt to relate housing to the larger setting through statistics and first-hand observation. Perhaps the most ambitious project for studying the city in its entirety was the six-volume *Pittsburgh Survey* (1909–14), which treated politics, crime, prostitution, the family, housing, and working conditions as aspects of a functioning social organism.

Social surveys underscored the need for trained personnel and scientific management. The independent commission, staffed by trained professionals and given the power to revamp tax structures, regulate transit and utility rates, and provide efficient city services, quickly became an essential agency of effective urban reform. The multiplication of commissions increased the demand for trained personnel. University education in key fields spread throughout the nation, and a new range of professions, each with its own organization, arose. By 1910 economists, political scientists, sociologists, tax reformers, charity organizers, settlement-house workers, and dozens of other specialized professionals had formed national societies, each with its own publications and communications network. These national organizations both strengthened the sense of professional community among progressives and cemented an alliance with newly founded universities that provided the training and facilities for investigating urban problems. In Chicago the residents of Hull House soon established close connections with the new University of Chicago through reform-minded academics like John Dewey, sociologists Albion Small and William I. Thomas, and political scientist Charles Merriam. In New York economists and sociologists from Columbia University joined freelance writers and publicists in analyzing city problems and working out solutions. Settlement houses proved vital for young professors by providing laboratories for testing their new concepts of behavior and by drawing them into the exciting world of business and politics beyond university walls.

Businessmen and professors often disagreed, however, on the question of how to apply the new critical spirit of reform. University scholars—historians, economists, and social theorists—now had sharp analytical tools for dissecting old conservative myths and challenging entrenched institutions. Historian Charles A. Beard was the best known of the young professors who were beginning to question the narrow interpretations of American law and the Constitution as well as the ancestor worship they encouraged. Beard's own Columbia University typified the new tradition-breaking spirit. There, economist Edwin Seligman, James Harvey Robinson, an earnest advocate of the "New History" as a reform tool, and pioneer students of administrative law such as Frank Goodnow were busy probing the economic roots of political behavior. At the same time, political scientist Arthur F. Bentley, in the *The Process of Government* (1908), approached political decisionmaking as a complex process that was subject to the shifting forces of interest groups. At the University of Washington radical historian J. Allen Smith, in a book entitled *The Spirit of American Government* (1907), dismissed the Constitution as a "reactionary document" designed to restrict the forces of democracy. After 1900 the alliance between highly critical academics and their corporate financial supporters grew increasingly strained as the professors began to question the very business civilization on which their universities had come to depend.

Scientific Reform. The universities also supplied a more conservative product. With the appearance of concepts of "social control" and "scientific efficiency," progressive reformers made contact with another reform tradition. This tradition was alien to the open tolerance of reform politicians and to the democratic and humanitarian hopes of social workers, and concentrated instead on efforts to impose strict efficiency and economy. For many progressives the modern corporation embodied these business values and procedures. The picture of the efficient, impersonal corporation was not drawn by businessmen alone. It was a widely accepted model of organization that appealed to intellectuals and professionals as well as to industrialists and financiers who recognized its uses in rebuilding American politics. The progressives criticized the trust largely because unscrupulous promoters had misused it, not because of its seemingly rational structure. "The trust is the educator of us all," Jane Addams announced in explaining the need for new kinds of collective action. Seen in this light, the corporation appeared as a corrective of the waste and inefficiencies of an earlier age, an actual model of social and political reform that, like the utopian communities before the Civil War, could be extended to American society as a whole.

The "scientific" urban reformers believed, however, that they could manage the city simply by tightening expenditures, consolidating power in the hands of experts, and revising the political system without particular regard to human needs. Good government, they reasoned, would be rigorously honest, determinedly efficient, unfailingly frugal, and strictly accountable. But such scientific reform restricted democratic participation. It limited the influence of "uninformed" voters—workers and immigrants—whose numbers it sought to reduce through literacy tests and tighter political registration laws. Such restrictions were comparable in spirit to the disfranchisement of blacks then under way in the South.

These scientific reformers considered the city a challenge that was not very different from the challenges met by industrialists and financiers. Efficiency and economy came to be equated with business practices of budget paring, cost cutting, tax trimming, and service chopping according to the ledger-book ethics of corporation accountants. "Municipal government is business, not politics," was the slogan of the scientific reformers. The modern corporation's shaping power in determining these reformers' outlook was reflected in their vocabulary, which developed a set of useful analogies. The mayor served as *chairman of the board* of an urban *corporation* composed of big and little *stockholders*, who were expected to vote their *proxies* at *annual meetings* and to accept their *dividends* without constantly interfering with the *managers* of the *enterprise*.

It was hardly a coincidence that the last years of the century, which saw the triumph of the corporation and the advent of scientific municipal reform, also witnessed the opening assault on the concept of a rational "public opinion," once considered the cornerstone of democratic politics. In dismissing ordinary public opinion as frivolous or perverse, scientific reformers demonstrated a distrust of democracy. The first order of reform business, insisted Frank Goodnow, an expert in administrative law and spokesman for the scientific reformers, was to recruit loyal and politically unambitious civil servants whose efficiencies would allow "the business and professional class of the community to assume care of the public business without making too great personal sacrifice." For the good-government advocates and business-dominated mayors who tried to clean up the cities after 1900, urban reform meant a chance for middle- and upper-class Americans, armed with new technical skills, to regain control of urban politics that an earlier generation had abandoned to the bosses.

The progressive businessmen and professionals shared a new set of values that reshaped their aims into concepts of system, control, stability, and predictability. Charity organizers now realized the need for accurate data in drafting workable solutions to social disorganization. A giant lumber company like Weyerhaeuser came to appreciate the importance of planning and cooperation with the new experts in the United States Forestry Service. College professors and high school teachers recognized the need for professional solidarity to protect their rights. Public-service lawyers, among them Louis Brandeis, acknowledged the complexities of new legal relations and began to play the role of "counsel to the situation" in experimenting with new techniques of arbitration.

The social perceptions of these middle-class leaders in the bureaucratic revolution stemmed from their sense of American society as a national collectivity in need of a new set of operating procedures. To implement their bureaucratic values, progressive reformers centralized authority in a hierarchical order, concentrated decisionmaking power in an energetic executive, established impersonal relations in restructuring their organizations, and above all planned for maximum efficiency.

The urban reform movement was therefore split between those who sought to extend popular influences in government and those whose programs limited popular participation. Reformers faced a choice between two widely different estimates of democracy and human nature. Some of them, like sociologist Edward A. Ross, frankly rejected the idea of democratic participation in favor of open elitism. Politically, Ross argued, democracy meant not the sovereignty of the average citizen, "who is a rather narrow, shortsighted, muddleheaded creature," but the "mature public opinion" of an educated elite. The case for democracy was most forcefully explained by Brand Whitlock, novelist, social welfare reformer, and mayor of Toledo from 1905 to 1913, who defined the "city sense" as democracy and as "the spirit of goodwill in humanity." Whitlock predicted that cities would arise that would "express the ideals of the people and work wonderful ameliorations in the human soul."

The conservative bias of many progressive reformers could be clearly seen in their attacks on the boss and the machine, but their real intentions were often obscured, even to themselves, by their seemingly democratic enthusiasm. "The people are finding a way," exclaimed progressive publicist William Allen White, who pointed in astonishment to the rapid growth of "fundamental democracy" throughout the country. A whole roster of progressive proposals for open government was billed as a democratic device for ensuring popular control at the grassroots. Thus the direct primary and direct election of senators would release the bosses' stranglehold on the electoral process. Referendum would send important questions of policy to the people, over the heads of unresponsive legislators. Recall would return the power to remove officeholders to the voters, with whom it belonged.

Urban progressives were not hypocrites in advertising their reforms as democratic, but they did not always make it clear that by "the people" they meant not the huddled masses in center cities, but solid citizens with sensible views and sober habits. Below the blaring trumpets of democracy could be heard, subdued but distinct, the progressive call for the politically vanquished middle class to return to the struggle armed with new weapons.

By 1900 a dual tradition had emerged, polarized around conflicting values of social efficiency and democratic liberation. These contrasting principles, which had combined briefly in the 1890s to challenge the politics of the bosses, would continue to diverge in the twentieth century, creating tensions within progressivism that would make it a confused yet creative movement.

The nerve center for urban progressivism after 1900 consisted of municipal leagues, civic federations,

TWO PORT CITIES IN THE PROGRESSIVE AGE
Right, New Orleans docks in 1895. Opposite, San Francisco wharves in 1900.

Historic New Orleans Collection

citizens' lobbies, commercial clubs, and bureaus of municipal research. These civic groups provided forums for the lively exchange of ideas between academics and businessmen eager to try out new concepts of efficiency and economy. From organizations like the National Municipal League and the National Civic Federation poured a flood of proposals and plans for repairing city government: home rule and charter revision; ballot reform and literacy tests; city-wide election schemes and city-manager plans, all of them aimed at the bosses' power base.

At first the reformers concentrated on improving procedures. They proposed segregated budgets for economy. They introduced time clocks, work sheets, job descriptions, and standardized salaries. They developed systematic ways of giving out contracts to replace the old patronage system. But the heart of their reform program was the commission and city-manager plans, modeled on the corporation. Combining executive and legislative functions in a single board, the commission plan spread rapidly until by 1913 more than three hundred cities in the United States had adopted it. The city-manager plan, a refinement of the original commission idea, further consolidated decisionmaking in municipal government, and by the 1920s it too had been widely adopted.

Urban progressives never succeeded in putting the political boss out of business. Nevertheless, progressivism successfully challenged boss politics by confronting it with another way of doing the business of the city. The machine's power lay in the center city, with its immigrants and working classes. Middle-class reformers generally operated from power bases along the suburban periphery. Boss politics, for all its sins, was marked by a high degree of accountability and popular participation in the wards and precincts. Progressives tried to reduce direct popular involvement at both the voting and the officeholding level. Bosses were wasteful but democratic; progressives were economical and bureaucratic.

Progressive success was limited. All too often, procedures changed but official policy did not. Still, if the boss and his clients proved adept at smashing the electoral hopes of reform candidates, they could no longer ignore the cries for more effective city government.

The progressives' dream of a shiny, streamlined administrative model never materialized. Yet the modernizing of American cities proceeded with or without the politicians' approval. In their partial overhaul of the nation's cities, the progressives scored important gains for the new bureaucratic order.

The Man with the Muckrake

Many of these contradictions could be seen in the work of the muckrakers who supplied progressivism with an agenda. The name *Muckrakers* was given to a new brand of reform journalists by President Theodore Roosevelt, who complained that their relentless exposure of corruption in high places hindered rather than helped him in his work of improving American society. Roosevelt compared this group of headstrong publicists to the gloomy figure who, in the seventeenth-century English Puritan John Bunyan's *Pilgrim's Progress*, refused a celestial crown and kept a muckrake. The president denounced these muckrakers' "crude and sweeping generalizations" and their delight in pointing the finger of civic shame. For

their part the muckrakers—Lincoln Steffens, Ida Tarbell, Ray Stannard Baker, David Graham Phillips, and many less famous colleagues—accepted the label and wore it defiantly as proof of their devotion to the Jeffersonian principle of a free and vigilant press.

Muckraking was the product of two forces that had combined by the end of the nineteenth century: major advances in the technology of printing, which made it possible to produce inexpensive, illustrated popular magazines; and the simultaneous arrival on the metropolitan scene of reform reporters sensitive to the new social concerns of the middle-class reader and eager to exploit them. S. S. McClure, founder of *McClure's*, was one of the pioneer explorers of the lucrative field of reform journalism, and he was quickly joined by dozens of competitors who were drawn to social criticism by their keen sense of the market and the prospect of sizable profits. From the outset muckraking proved that reform could be a paying proposition. Gathering a staff of trained, well-paid newspapermen, McClure and other editors launched an attack on the underside of American life with articles on sweatshops, tainted meat, the white slave traffic, insurance company scandals, labor racketeering, city bosses, and high finance. Muckrakers happily compiled a list of all the social wrongs that their enlightened readers would presumably set right.

Muckraking offered both a new kind of factual reporting and an old form of moral publicity. Always extravagant and frequently sensational, the muckrakers perfected the uses of contrast and contradiction in pointing to the gap between venerable American ideals and startling social facts. In an article for *Cosmopolitan* on child labor in southern cotton mills, for example, poet Edwin Markham depicted "The Hoe Man in the Making" in the faces of "ill-fed, unkempt, unwashed, half-dressed" children penned in the narrow lanes of the mills, little victims whose dreary lives mocked the "bright courtesy of the cultured classes." Social gospelist Ernest Crosby contrasted the appearance of a majestic United States Senate with the reality of a "House of Dollars," a political monopoly modeled on an industrial trust. Samuel Hopkins Adams explained the national failure to regulate the food and drug industries as the result of "private interests in public murder" when "everybody's health is nobody's business."

Muckraking thus presented a publicity technique rather than a philosophy, a popular journalistic style rather than a searching analysis. As social critics, journalists like Lincoln Steffens and David Graham Phillips were tough-minded and factual but also romantic, moralistic, and sentimental. Like their millions of readers, they were the beneficiaries of a fundamental change in the idea of publicity, which they conceived of as an open-ended process of fact gathering that reflected the shifting nature of social reality. Read in this subdued light, their articles could be considered wholesome remedies and useful correctives. Their work, the muckrakers insisted, was never done, since an unfolding social process required constant adaptation of old theories to new facts—of accepted values to changing conditions.

Muckraking also tapped traditional morality while exploiting the time-honored role of the disinterested observer—the clear-eyed, hard-nosed investigator with a fierce desire to get all the facts and expose them to the sanitizing rays of publicity. Muckrakers liked to think of themselves as brave detectives, dashing from one hidden clue to another, looking for the fragments of information that, once collected and arranged, would tell reformers what to do next. There was a strong bias against party government in the muckrakers' view of American politics, as well as a weakness for conspiratorial interpretations. They believed that the masses of American voters, once given the facts, would demand reform. Tell the people the truth, they said, and they would correct injustice

forthwith. Conscience, duty, character, virtue—these were the muckrakers' watchwords, and also a measure of their limited understanding of the problems confronting progressive America. Muckrakers identified the symptoms of disorder, but they could not isolate its causes or prescribe effective remedies. For these tasks a clearer understanding of the workings of modern industrial society was needed.

Progressivism Invades the States

After 1900 the progressives, building on urban achievements, set out to reform state politics. Beginning in 1900 with the first administration of Wisconsin governor Robert M. La Follette, reform swept across the nation in the next decade and transformed the conduct of state politics.

Although progressivism varied widely in the different sections of the country, there were enough similarities to give political reform at the state level the appearance of a national movement. In the South progressives who had inherited a number of Populist grievances often wore the trappings of a redneck revolt against the business-minded Bourbons. By the opening years of the twentieth century, one governorship after another was falling to economy-minded agrarians from upcountry or downstate. The southern rebellion against the alliance of big business and Democratic politicians drew on popular sympathies and produced railroad and corporate regulation, antimonopoly laws, insurance company controls, and improved public education and child labor laws—but all with mounting racist demagoguery and the continuing disfranchisement of the black population.

Progressivism in the Midwest and on the Pacific Coast also grew out of a revolt, usually within the Republican party, which was perceived to be too generous to railroads and corporations. Midwestern progressives drew more heavily from the arsenal of democratic political reforms—the initiative and referendum, for example—than did their counterparts in the East, who tended to rely more on administrative reforms. But everywhere big business's control of state legislatures made an inviting target. Corporate dominance of New Jersey state politics, for example, was all but complete by 1900. "We've got everything in the state worth having," a spokesman for corporate interests boasted. The legislature regularly elected two senators who represented the utility interests and the insurance companies; and the executive branch of the state government was staffed by former employees of the Pennsylvania Railroad.

The governors who organized the revolts against these statehouse rings headed the cast of new progressive folk heroes. The most popular of the reform governors cast themselves as western heroes, riding into office with a mandate to clean up the state, setting about their task with grim determination, and moving on to bigger things when the job was done. Typically the reform governor, denied office by state party leaders, collected his small band of rebels and tried, unsuccessfully at first, to take over the party. To help in subsequent efforts, he enlisted other mavericks and began to explore such electoral reforms as the primary system of party nomination and the direct election of senators. Fixing his sights on the "interests," he eventually defeated the party regulars.

Once elected, the progressive governor moved quickly to neutralize his opposition by absorbing some of its members into his reform coalition. He learned to wield patronage with a surprising ruthlessness, and with secure majorities in the legislature he went to work on his reform program. This generally included strict regulation of railroads and public service corporations, a revamped tax structure, and major pieces of social legislation to improve working and living conditions in the state. After a hectic term or two in which he managed to complete at least part of this reform program, the progressive governor moved on to the United States Senate, where he was joined by other like-minded rebels from similar backgrounds who had the same hopes of imposing their reform designs on national politics. The career of one such progressive hero, Robert M. La Follette, illustrates the main features of this legend of progressive reform.

"Battling Bob" La Follette.

La Follette, an intense, unsmiling, self-made man, was a small-town lawyer who struggled to the top of the political heap in Wisconsin. In his three terms as governor after 1900, he enacted a reform program that became the envy of progressives across the country. Young La Follette was a walking example of the Protestant ethic. Born in Primrose, Wisconsin, in meager circumstances, he put himself through the state university at Madison by teaching school, and he prepared himself for a career in politics by studying for the bar. At the University of Wisconsin he came under the reform influence of its president, John Bascom, who was just beginning to build a public service institution, a task that La Follette himself would complete a quarter of a century later.

Short and wiry, with a shock of bristly iron-gray hair, La Follette combined a rock-hard moralism with a fanatical combativeness. He won his first office as district attorney without the endorsement of the Republican machine by barnstorming the county and haranguing rural voters on the need for integrity and independence. In 1884, again without the support of party regulars, he was elected to the first of three terms in Congress, where he was the youngest member

"BATTLING BOB" LA FOLLETTE CAMPAIGNING
La Follette was famous for his style of political barnstorming.

of the House. He was defeated for reelection in the Democratic landslide of 1890 and came home to a lucrative law practice.

In Wisconsin as in a number of other states, the Republican party had been the effective instrument of the railroad and lumber companies. Faced with a lawsuit against their corrupt state treasurers, the party bosses tried to bribe La Follette to secure his influence with a judge, who happened to be his brother-in-law. La Follette promptly cried havoc and later reckoned the attempted bribe as the turning point of his career. "Nothing else ever came into my life that exerted such a powerful influence upon me as that affair." In exposing the machine's crime to the voters, he effectively isolated himself from the party leaders and spent nearly a decade trying to collect enough votes from Scandinavian farmers and industrial workers in Milwaukee to overthrow the machine. By 1900 he had succeeded.

La Follette's victory won him instant national acclaim. After destroying the power of the old machine by winning over some of its leaders to his own cause, he set out to modernize Wisconsin. The "Wisconsin

Idea," as it came to be known, depended on a progressive majority in the state legislature, which the new governor secured by campaigning personally for his supporters and then holding them strictly accountable. Soon his enemies were complaining that he had made himself the boss of a ruthlessly efficient machine of his own. The substance of the Wisconsin Idea was a set of related reforms: a direct primary law, an improved civil service, a railroad rate commission, a fair tax program, state banking controls, conservation measures, a water power franchise act, and protective labor legislation. At the center of La Follette's reform movement stood the independent regulatory commission, staffed by experts from the state university and given wide administrative latitude.

To his many admirers across the country, La Follette seemed a political anomaly, a popular leader with his feet firmly planted in the grassroots but at the same time an enthusiastic convert to scientific government. Exacting, fiercely partisan, and a powerful hater, he often viewed the world as a gigantic conspiracy against "Battling Bob." He kept ready for display at a moment's notice the image of the sea-green incorruptible who preached the virtues of direct democracy and constantly urged his followers to "go back to the people." "Selfish interests," he declared, "may resist every inch of ground, may threaten, malign and corrupt, [but] they cannot escape the final issues. That which is so plain, so simple, and so just will surely triumph."

The other half of La Follette's reform equation, however, was filled with the facts and figures that his investigatory commissions collected. His own interminable speeches came loaded with statistics and percentages provided by a corps of tax experts, labor consultants, industrial commissioners, and social workers. He hammered these facts at the voters of Wisconsin in the belief that the people, once they learned their meaning, would hardly fail him. The conflicting principles of popular democracy and government by an expert elite hardly bothered La Follette. The expert commission, secure above the battle of parties and interests—the key agency of the Wisconsin Idea—seemingly embodied the detachment and patriotism it was designed to foster in the people. La Follette's growing national reputation, in fact, rested on the belief he inspired that direct democracy and scientific government were not simply compatible, but complementary.

State Progressive Reform.

An important feature of progressive reform programs in the states was a package of new laws, drawn up by civic groups, women's organizations, and consumer interests, that humanized working conditions. As late as 1900, more than half the states had no laws that established a minimum age for workers. By 1914 every state but one had an age limit on the employment of children. In most states new laws for the protection of women in industry paralleled the drive to abolish child labor. Illinois led the way in 1892 by limiting hours for women. New York and Massachusetts followed, and then the movement spread rapidly westward. When the Supreme Court upheld the principle of state regulation of hours for women in the celebrated case of *Muller* v. *Oregon* in 1908, barriers collapsed. By the time America entered the First World War in 1917, thirty-nine states had written new laws protecting women or had significantly strengthened old laws, while eight states had gone even further by passing minimum wage laws for women. Another feature of the progressive social reform program was the campaign for employers' liability laws and industrial accident insurance, which did away with the worst abuses of the older legal rules that governed workplace safety and contributory negligence. By 1916 nearly two-thirds of the states, reacting to mounting pressures from a progressive public, had established insurance programs.

Progressivism, taking different forms in different states, marked a shift in power within the American political system. Cumbersome, interest-dominated legislatures gave way to a new public authority lodged in the executive branch and in its supporting administrative agencies that were charged with discovering and then serving the public interest. To justify their roles as custodians of the public interest, progressives unearthed a national-interest theory of politics as old as the Founding Fathers. "I would not be a dredger congressman, or a farm congressman, or a fresh-egg congressman," a typical progressive told his constituents in summoning up the spirit of Edmund Burke and virtual representation.* "I would like to be an American congressman, recognizing the union and the nation." If warring economic and class interests were chiefly responsible for the lack of direction and the low tone of American politics, progressives reasoned, then it was wise to ignore them and appeal instead to a potential public virtue in the concept of citizenship. "Progressivism," another reformer added, "believes in nationalism . . . opposes class government by either business, the laboring class, or any other class." This tendency to reject interest-group government (government as a bargaining process between blocs of big business, big labor, and big agriculture) drove progressives to embrace the idea of leadership from above—from those "good men" in whom idealism presumably ran deeper than selfishness. "While the inspi-

---

* For Burke and virtual representation in the eighteenth century, see chapter 7, pp. 179–80.

ration has always come from below in the advance of human rights," the California progressive William Kent insisted, the real accomplishments in improving American society must always be "the disinterested work of men who, having abundant means, have ranged themselves on the side of those most needing help." In the progressive interpretation of American politics, underdogs announced their needs, but topdogs filled them.

Draped with the mantle of disinterested benevolence, state progressivism resembled, more than anything else, a rebuilt model of Federalism, suitably modernized to fit an industrial society. Like their Federalist ancestors progressives feared the idea of party government and class division, and they sought to take the politics out of American life in the name of scientific management. In place of eighteenth-century rule by republican notables, they substituted leadership by experts whose skills were to command the instant allegiance of all enlightened citizens. Most progressive political reforms aimed at securing stability and control. And in the same fashion, the progressive social justice programs initiated by the states were designed to strengthen corporate capitalism by empowering the government to reassign responsibilities and lessen the harshness of the American industrial environment. To carry out their policies at the national level, the progressives looked to the figure of the new statesman, and in Theodore Roosevelt they found their hero.

Theodore Roosevelt: The Progressive as Hero

In September 1901 President William McKinley died in Buffalo of an assassin's bullet, and Theodore Roosevelt—"this crazy man," as Republican managers thought him—was catapulted from the vicepresidency into the post of national leader. Blueblood, historian, student of the classics, amateur naturalist, cowpuncher, and Rough Rider, Roosevelt at forty-two appeared to millions of admirers as the last of the universal men, but to uneasy Republican bosses like Mark Hanna as "that damned cowboy."

With an audible sigh of relief, Old Guard Republicans heard the new president announce his intentions "to continue, absolutely unbroken, the policy of President McKinley." McKinley had stood for high tariffs, the gold standard, a not-too-vigorous prosecution of the trusts, and just the right amount of imperial ambition.* The prospect of a continuing custodial presidency reassured those congressional conservatives who feared above all a rambunctious executive. Yet

* For American expansionism under McKinley, see chapter 26, pp. 651–57.

within the year, Roosevelt had begun to challenge congressional authority, and, by the time he retired from his second term in March 1909, he had succeeded in creating a national progressive movement, reinvigorating American foreign policy, and laying the foundations of the twentieth-century welfare state.

A Patrician Cowboy. Roosevelt was the product of New York society, the son of a banker-philanthropist who had dabbled in genteel reforms and organized the city's upper-class contribution to the Union cause during the Civil War. A graduate of Harvard, where he had amused his classmates with his odd earnestness and vibrancy, young Roosevelt immediately settled on a life of politics among the "kittle-kattle" of spoilsmen and mugwumps. He held the comfortable classes chiefly to blame for the moral chaos of Gilded Age politics, and with a highly developed sense of the upper class's social responsibility he entered the New York State Assembly as a representative from one of the city's wealthy Republican districts.

In the assembly, where he served a single term from 1882 to 1884, he displayed the unique mixture of social conservatism, pugnacity, and political shrewdness that was to become his distinguishing mark. In 1886 he accepted the Republican nomination in the three-way mayoralty race in New York City and ran a respectable third behind Democratic winner Abram S. Hewitt and single-taxer Henry George. The 1880s also saw the growth of a sizable body of Roosevelt's historical writing—*The Winning of the West*, a biography of Gouverneur Morris, and another of Thomas Hart Benton—in which Roosevelt proclaimed his unqualified approval of the nationalist designs of the Federalists, denounced Jefferson as a humbug and a hypocrite, and hymned the glories of westward expansion and the fulfillment of America's continental destiny.

When his first wife died in 1884, Roosevelt retired to the frontier he had described so eloquently, finding solace in Dakota ranch life filled with cowboys, frontier justice, and manly virtues. As a steadfast but unpredictable young Republican, he was appointed to the United States Civil Service Commission by President Benjamin Harrison in 1889 and served in Washington in a blaze of publicity until 1895, when he returned to New York to head the Board of Police Commissioners. Here he made another name for himself as a result of late-night prowls with his friend, journalist Jacob Riis, in futile efforts to enforce the city's blue laws. McKinley rewarded such energy by appointing him assistant secretary of the navy, despite Roosevelt's outspoken views on behalf of American military power.

The Spanish-American War in 1898 drew Roosevelt out of the shadows of appointive office and into the limelight of electoral politics. As self-appointed leader of the Rough Riders, the First Regiment of the United States Cavalry Volunteers, he caught the fancy of a jingoistic public that followed with keen interest his dramatic, if somewhat excessive, exploits in charging up San Juan Hill, pausing now and then to exult over all "those damned Spanish dead" as he rallied his own disorderly troops.

Disembarking to the tune of "There'll Be a Hot Time in the Old Town Tonight," Roosevelt was promptly elected governor of New York and just as quickly upset party bosses by taking a firm progressive stand on a state factory inspection law and on another law regulating the hours of state employees. "If there is going to be any solution of the big social problems of the day," he warned his supporters, "it will come, not through a sentimental parlor socialism, but through actually taking hold of what is to be done, working right in the mire." Republican leaders in New York responded by lifting their governor out of the mire of reform politics and into the clean and safe office of the vice-presidency. Their hopes for squelching the exuberant progressive were curtailed when McKinley's assassination put Roosevelt in the White House.

Roosevelt as President.

Americans soon learned what kind of president they had acquired, for Roosevelt had strong opinions on every conceivable subject and delighted in publishing them in pungent and readable phrases. The objects of his interest ranged from the novels of the French writer Emile Zola (which he generally disliked) to the "full baby carriage" (which he heartily endorsed); and his advice ranged from conduct becoming football players and would-be reformers ("Don't flinch, don't foul, hit the line hard!") to what one observer called an "unflagging approval of the Ten Commandments." A vigorous intellectual, interested in birds and political bosses, trusts and big game, divorce and "practical idealism," Roosevelt collected facts and ideas that he regularly assembled in print—not writing with a pen, as one reader put it, so much as charging with it.

Roosevelt's forceful and sometimes contradictory opinions revealed two distinct personalities. The first was described by a New York politician as "the most indiscreet guy I ever met," the keeper of the national conscience always ready to speak his mind. This public Roosevelt served as the confident spokesman of an aggressive American nationalism—prophet of a coming Anglo-Saxon supremacy, celebrant of military valor, unblushing advocate of power politics, and a true believer in the American mission to order the affairs of the rest of the world. The national hero, "Teddy"—a name he disliked—looked the part. With pince-nez adorning a bulbous nose, toothy grin stretched in a near grimace, a full square face with its several chins resting on heavyset shoulders, a reedy voice, and pump-handle gestures, he was a cartoonist's dream.

In the role of the mad American of his generation, as he has been called, Roosevelt could and frequently did talk great nonsense. He lashed out with equal contempt at "radical fanatics" and the "lunatic fringe" of soft-headed reformers. "Sentimental humanitarians" he denounced as "a most pernicious body, with an influence for bad hardly surpassed by that of the professional criminal classes." He stressed the importance of "good blood" flowing through the veins of well-bred, self-denying gentlemen. He predicted race suicide for any of the world's people who preferred "effeminacy of character" to the "rougher and manlier virtues." For handling mobs he recommended "taking ten or a dozen of their leaders out, standing . . . them against a wall, and shooting them dead." For anarchists and socialist agitators he had a similar prescription—troops supplied with real bullets and "the most wholesome desire to do them harm." Americans, whether delighted or appalled by such balderdash, recognized in Roosevelt the authentic American hero, the compulsive man of action who shot from the hip and whose motto read: "Get action; do things; be sane."

The other Roosevelt, unlike the trigger-happy dispenser of justice, was a thoughtful if highly partisan student of American history with a keen appreciation of the original work of the Founding Fathers. Young progressives entering the political arena after 1900 with credentials from the new universities brought with them training in such new disciplines as economics and sociology. But for the slightly older progressive leaders, the study of history was still the primary tool for examining American society. Despite the rapid growth of the "scientific" monograph, much of the popular history written after 1880 continued to be the work of gentlemen amateurs like Roosevelt and his friends Henry Adams and retired industrialist James Ford Rhodes, who measured the achievements and noted the shortcomings of nineteenth-century American democracy. The thrust of much of this popular history was toward political nationalism and social conservatism, whether in John Fiske's admiring account of the Founding Fathers, in Henry Adams's search for the principles of scientific government in his magnificent nine-volume history of the administrations of Jefferson and Madison, or in Roosevelt's own hymns to national valor in *The Naval War of 1812* and *The Winning of the West*.

Roosevelt's Political Philosophy.

This reflective, history-minded Roosevelt was the first president after Lincoln and the last of the moderns with an understanding of

THE TWO SIDES OF THEODORE ROOSEVELT
A reflective Roosevelt appears in the doorway of his Dakota ranch house (left). Surrounded by the paraphernalia of patriotism, Roosevelt campaigns in New Castle, Wyoming, in 1903 (right).

the eighteenth century. Beneath his dramatic account of America's rise to greatness lay a clear grasp of the original Federalist design and the men who fashioned it. National greatness, it seemed to Roosevelt, was based, just as it had been in the past, on the "power to attain a high degree of social efficiency." By this he meant "love of order" and the "capacity to subordinate the interests of the individual to the interests of the community." The Federalists, he believed, led by such farseeing nationalists as Hamilton and Gouverneur Morris, had tried to teach the first Americans the same lesson that his own generation had just learned—that "the sphere of the State's action may be vastly increased without in any way diminishing the happiness of either the many or the few."

Roosevelt was convinced that the American people had been given the wrong directions by a demagogic Jefferson and had drifted steadily toward the Civil War even as they had expanded and enriched

their domain. From Jefferson and his Jacksonian heirs they had acquired the illusions that little government was needed and that the moral order was self-regulating. Despite their magnificent material accomplishments in filling out a continent and building an industrial empire, the American people had failed to devise the political means of managing it. Only briefly during Lincoln's wartime administration had Americans caught a glimpse of true national unity. With the onset of the Gilded Age, the original stateman's question "Will it work?" had been replaced by the huckster's demand "Does it pay?" and the national energy had been squandered in money grubbing. One fact was clear at last—Americans had to "abandon definitely the *laissez-faire* theory of political economy, and fearlessly champion a system of increased Governmental control."

The opening years of the twentieth century, Roosevelt believed, represented "an era of federation and combination" that had been foreshadowed by the age of the Founding Fathers. The president, like his Federalist teachers, deplored class politics and called for the rule of enlightened men of integrity, whom he always identified with the better half of the Republican party. But wherever found, the disinterested patriot, Roosevelt was convinced, held the key to the future. By the time Roosevelt took over the presidency in 1901, he had acquired a clear definition of his role as general manager of the United States, even though the details of his plan for its "orderly development" emerged only gradually from the recesses of his conservative mind.

"Wise Radicalism and Wise Conservatism": The Square Deal

As president, Roosevelt firmly established the regulatory principle as the foundation of administrative government. What he and the country came to call the Square Deal as he campaigned for reelection in 1904 began as a loose collection of proposals for directing national economic development. Roosevelt had inherited from Gilded Age Republicanism an Old Guard of conservatives. They had built their stronghold in the Senate, where they kept firm control over the lawmaking process and saw to it that presidents followed their dictates. Roosevelt was immediately forced to bargain with their leader, Senator Nelson W. Aldrich of Rhode Island, and to agree to keep his hands off the tariff question in exchange for a limited freedom to pursue his plans for intervention elsewhere. These concerns, like those of his progressive followers, first centered on the trusts.

Trustbusting. Roosevelt shared the progressives' ambivalence toward big business. "Nothing of importance is gained," he admitted, "by breaking up a huge interstate and international organization which has not offended otherwise than by its size. . . . Those who would seek to restore the days of unlimited and uncontrolled competition . . . are attempting not only the impossible, but what, if possible, would be undesirable." He believed that the trusts' behavior, not their size, constituted the test of their utility, and he declared it the government's duty to operate "in the interest of the general public." To prevent the trusts from fixing prices and manipulating the market, he proposed a watchdog agency modeled on the Interstate Commerce Commission, a body appointed by him and staffed with "trained administrators, well known to hold the scales exactly even in all matters." After a sharp skirmish with big business and its defenders in Congress, he succeeded in 1903 in establish-

ing the Bureau of Corporations within the new Department of Labor and Commerce to police business practices and report its findings to the public.

Publicity formed the keystone of Roosevelt's regulatory program, and he quickly perfected the art of disclosure in launching a series of actions under the Sherman Antitrust Act. He advised the beef trust of his strictly honorable intentions to "Destroy the Evils in Trusts, But Not the Prosperity," and he insisted publicly on settling "the absolutely vital question" of federal power to regulate the trusts with the Northern Securities Company, the United States Steel Company, and the American Tobacco Company. It was essential, he announced, for the president and his administrators to maintain "strict supervision" of big business and see that it did not go wrong.

To make good his promise, in 1902 Roosevelt gave the signal to the Department of Justice to move against J. P. Morgan's railroad combine, the Northern Securities Company. Morgan, he recalled with relish, "could not help regarding me as a big rival operator who intended to ruin all his interests." But it was power that interested the president, who considered the clash with Morgan a dynastic one of rival sovereignties. In upholding the government's case against the railroad merger in *Northern Securities Co.* v. *United States* in 1904, the Supreme Court gave Roosevelt his precedent. In the *E. C. Knight* case (1895), he announced with obvious satisfaction, the Court had erroneously decided that the federal government lacked the power to break up dangerous combinations. "This decision I caused to be annulled." He did not add what soon became obvious—that he had not at the same time suppressed the merger movement.

Roosevelt's views on organized labor mirrored his convictions on big business: the ultimate test for both sides was a willingness to provide order and stability of their own volition. If trusts threatened the balance of economic power with irresponsible behavior, Roosevelt reasoned, labor could prove disruptive and greedy. If there were "good" and "bad" trusts, there were also dependable labor leaders like Samuel Gompers, and dangerous visionaries like Eugene Debs. In either case it was the president who had to distinguish legitimate demands from crackpot notions. The only standard he could finally invoke was conduct. "Where in either one or the other, there develops corruption or mere brutal indifference to the rights of others, and short-sighted refusal to look beyond the moment's gain, then the offender, whether union or corporation, must be fought."

The test of Roosevelt's opinion of unions, strikes, and injunctions came early in the first administration, when the United Mine Workers struck against the anthracite coal operators. The confrontation alarmed the whole country and gave Roosevelt welcome public support. Led by the canny John Mitchell, the miners demanded a pay increase and an eight-hour day along with acknowledgment of their right to organize the coal industry. George Baer, president of the Reading Railroad, bungled the case for the coal operators from the outset. Baer proclaimed it his "religious duty" to defeat the strikers, insisting that "the rights and interests of the laboring men will be protected and cared for—not by labor agitators, but by Christian men to whom God in his infinite wisdom has given control of the property interests of the country."

Roosevelt, his hand strengthened by the operators' obstinacy, quickly called for an investigation by his labor commissioner and used the findings to try to force the coal companies to compromise. When they refused, he ordered both parties to a conference in Washington, where the operators, under a presidential threat to send in troops, finally agreed to an arbitration panel. The Anthracite Coal Strike Commission awarded a 10 percent pay increase and a reduction of hours to the miners, while refusing their demand for a closed shop. Once again, as in regulating the trusts, it was principle and procedure—the orderly disposition of grievances by disinterested men—that most concerned the president.

New Consumer Legislation.

Roosevelt's theory of expanded executive power developed from his belief that only "a great exertion of federal authority" could meet the needs of all the people. The most vulnerable members of a largely unregulated commercial society were American consumers. In consumer legislation, as in his dealings with big business and labor, Roosevelt assumed the leadership of forces that had already begun to organize by 1900. The Pure Food and Drug Law, passed in 1906, was the result of a carefully orchestrated public outcry and shrewd presidential direction. Although limited, the law capped a strenuous campaign for effective legislation by Harvey Wiley, chief chemist of the Department of Agriculture, who twice had seen his recommendations accepted in the House only to languish in the Senate, where the food and drug interests dominated. Aided by a series of lurid exposés furnished by the muckrakers, Roosevelt finally collected the votes he needed to prohibit the manufacture and sale of misbranded or adulterated foods and drugs, a limited power that has been wielded cautiously ever since.

Support for the Meat Packing Act (1906) also came from consumers, many of whom learned of the appalling conditions in the industry from Upton Sinclair's sensational novel *The Jungle*. In attacking the packers, Sinclair traced the shipment, from prairie to slaughterhouse, of cows "that developed lumpy jaw, or fell sick, or dried up of old age," carcasses "covered with boils that were full of matter." Although Roosevelt was annoyed by Sinclair's fictionalized account, the president promised him action. An investigation verified most of Sinclair's charges in a fact-studded report that Roosevelt, in a calculated piece of blackmail, threatened to release unless the packers accepted minimum regulation. Like most of the Square Deal legislation, the final bill represented a series of compromises—increased appropriations for inspection in exchange for the removal of inconvenient requirements for enforcement. The legislation left the matter of appeal to the courts in what Roosevelt called "purposeful ambiguity." Once the industry had accepted the principle of federal regulation, the big packers welcomed those requirements that could be expected to drive out their smaller competitors. For his part the president was perfectly willing to compromise on details in order to gain the principle of federal control.

In his willingness to sacrifice specifics for the precedent, Roosevelt frequently disappointed his more determined progressive supporters, who complained that he gave in too easily on points that might have been won. His critics appear to have won their case in the tug of war over the Hepburn Act (1906), which regulated railroad rates. In 1903 the Elkins Act, a piece of legislation supposedly prohibiting discriminatory rebates to favored shippers, had been drafted by the railroad senators who refused to grant the government effective control over rate making. But Roosevelt was determined to acquire this authority. An administration measure passed by the House was designed to strengthen the Interstate Commerce Act by giving it genuine power to fix rates and make them stick. In the Senate, however, Roosevelt's plan met the stubborn opposition of Nelson Aldrich and the railroad senators, who had decided to teach the president a lesson. Aldrich and his conservatives quickly bottled up the bill in committee, where they conducted interminable hearings for the benefit of its enemies.

Roosevelt tried a second time with another bill, this one sponsored by Representative William P. Hepburn of Ohio. This even more moderate measure would empower the ICC to set reasonable rates after hearing complaints from shippers. Once again Aldrich stepped in, sent the bill to the Senate floor without endorsement, and looked on with detachment as one amendment after another stripped the bill of its original intent. In the end Roosevelt failed to rally a successful coalition of faithful Republicans and disgruntled Democrats, but he did manage to win over enough moderate Republicans to force Aldrich to compromise. The final version of the Hepburn bill increased the powers of the ICC but left intact the provision against enforcing new rates in cases that were

CHICAGO STOCKYARDS STRIKE
Police guard the load from an overturned meatwagon.

under court appeal. At best, Roosevelt had won a very limited victory.

A Formula for Conservation.

In the case of conservation, the last main item on the Square Deal agenda, compromise again weakened principle. Although Roosevelt himself was a nature lover and preservationist by inclination, he abandoned the tradition of the naturalists Henry David Thoreau and John Muir for a developmentalist strategy designed for multiple use of the nation's natural resources. He called on citizens to look ahead to "the days of our children" and warned against the waste and destruction that would "result in undermining . . . the very prosperity" that ought to be passed on to them "amplified and developed." Yet his formula for conservation remained the same as that for other national needs: expert advice from scientists committed to development rather than preservation, much publicity, and permissive governmental oversight of private interests.

These long-term limitations were obscured for the moment in the flurry of executive actions during Roosevelt's second term as he added 43 million acres to the national forests, withdrew from entry more than 2,500 water power sites and 65 million acres of coal lands, and established 16 national monuments and 53 wildlife refuges. The issue of conservation assumed a crucial symbolic significance in Roosevelt's mind as he found himself blocked by Congress from pursuing other social justice goals. He turned to the management of natural resources as "the fundamental problem which underlies almost every other problem in national life," the acid test of federal power. He flouted the congressional will with a "midnight proclamation" that set aside twenty-three new forest reserves and then threw down his challenge: "If Congress differs from me . . . it will have full opportunity in the future to take such positions as it may desire anent the discontinuance of the reserves." While Congress fumed, he moved rapidly ahead with plans for building a conservation empire consisting of bureaus and commissions filled with geologists, hydrologists, foresters, and engineers taking their orders from Gifford Pinchot, his volatile but capable chief forester. In 1908, sensing widespread public interest, Roosevelt called a National Conservation Congress, which was attended by forty-four governors and over five hundred conservation experts.

Yet despite its appearance as a popular crusade, Roosevelt's conservation program was less a grassroots movement to save the environment than an executive scheme for national resource management imposed from above. The president envisioned a grand design in which irrigation, flood control, forestry, and reclamation would be "interdependent parts of the same problem" of regional development. He had to settle for much less. Government experts and lumber company executives shared a strong distaste for the preservationists' ideas. The new federal agencies were understaffed and underfinanced, and they soon found themselves dependent on the goodwill of the same private interests they were supposed to police. Small operators, whose reputation for gouging the landscape was well earned, were sometimes driven out, but the large companies continued their policies of exploiting national resources under a government seal of approval. From the perspective of three-quarters of a century, Roosevelt's national conservation program, like the original Federalist partnership between wealth and government, appears to have identified with the welfare of powerful private interests.

The Limits of Neofederalism

Having retired from the presidency after two terms in office, Roosevelt embarked for Africa on a hunting trip in the spring of 1909, leaving in the White House his hand-picked successor, the ponderous William Howard Taft, to "carry on the work substantially as I have carried it on." In many ways the conservation issue symbolized both the partial success and the ultimate limitations of Roosevelt's attempt to forge a new national purpose. The key to his plan was teaching the American electorate the meaning of national unity and strong government, an educational task he performed admirably for seven years.

The conservation campaign, which slowly moved to the center of the progressive consciousness, meant a fight against sectionalism, states' rights, business interests, and a Congress that gave them all voice. To halt these divisive forces and hold the allegiance of his reform followers, Roosevelt had revitalized the presidential office and buttressed it with new concepts of civic duty and loyalty. "I believe in a strong executive; I believe in power," he announced, and he proceeded to use his power in ways that no president since Lincoln had contemplated. To aid him in his work of executive renovation, he drew heavily from the ranks of progressive experts and professionals, whose cause of scientific government he championed enthusiastically. His reform program, for all its timid approach to the regulatory principle and its deference to vested interests, marked at least a step toward the orderly republic he envisioned.

If Roosevelt's utopia lay well over the horizon in 1909, it was because he intentionally set conservative limits to the application of governmental power and in the last analysis believed firmly in a guided democratic process. Although he chafed under the restraints placed on him by his party and a laggard Congress, he managed both of them with consummate skill, alternately bullying and cajoling both, but breaking with neither. In negotiating for his limited reforms, he was willing more often than not to take the shell and leave the kernel, concerned as he was with winning a principle. Yet his presidency was no mere exercise in educational politics. Roosevelt wanted results that the country would accept, and to get them he willingly used traditional and even conservative political methods. When he left office, the results were clear. He had raised the presidency to its twentieth-century position of dominance. He had laid the foundation for a governmental bureaucracy and had collected the presumably disinterested professionals to run it. And finally, he had preached with unflagging zeal the virtues of high-mindedness, integrity, and service as indispensable to the new citizenship.

Further than this neither Roosevelt nor the nationalist-minded progressives could go. Roosevelt spoke for progressives across the country in demanding the return to service of "the man of business and the man of science, the doctor of divinity and the doctor of law, the architect, the engineer, and the writer," all of whom owed a "positive duty to the community, the neglect of which they cannot excuse on any plea of their private affairs." The ordinary citizen, "to whom participation in politics is a disagreeable duty," had long since been defeated by an organized army of political hacks. Now, Roosevelt and the progressives believed, it was time to try the extraordinary citizen wherever he could be found. Neither Roosevelt nor the progressives would have been surprised to learn that the average citizen was taking less rather than greater interest in politics. Voter turnout, which in the Gilded Age had averaged nearly 80 percent in presidential years and 60 percent in off-years, fell a full 15 percent after 1900. Possibly because they were disenchanted with the prospects of a managed republic that the progressives promised them, or perhaps simply because they were discovering more pressing concerns outside the political arena, fewer

Americans were troubling themselves with the duty of taking what Roosevelt called "their full part in our life."

Here indeed lay the outermost reaches of Roosevelt's political domain. If Jefferson's political formula had long since proved hopelessly inadequate for managing an industrial republic, his original estimate of the diverse sources of American energy had not. Jefferson had counted the advantages as well as the dangers of sectional division, religious variety, ethnic diversity, and even class disagreement. With Roosevelt's retirement in 1909, these forces of social and political pluralism began to take revenge on his promise of national unity, first shaking the party structure and then disrupting the national social consensus that Roosevelt and his followers had attempted to construct. In a suddenly revived Democratic party the American people would find a different variety of progressive reform, and in Woodrow Wilson a very different kind of leader.

CHRONOLOGY

1889 Jane Addams founds Hull House; beginning of settlement-house movement.
Hazen Pingree elected mayor of Detroit; first progressive mayor.

1890 Muckraking photo-journalist Jacob Riis publishes *How the Other Half Lives*, depicting life in New York's slums.

1893 First issue of *McClure's* magazine.
Conference for Good City Government inaugurates urban progressive reform movement.

1899 John Dewey's *School and Society*, pioneer progressive education tract.

1900 Robert La Follette elected to his first of three terms as progressive governor of Wisconsin.
William McKinley reelected president, defeating William Jennings Bryan.

1901 Theodore Roosevelt becomes president after McKinley assassinated.
Tom Johnson elected mayor of Cleveland.

1902 Roosevelt launches antitrust action against Northern Securities Company.
Roosevelt settles anthracite coal strike through arbitration.

1903 Bureau of Corporations established within new Department of Labor and Commerce.

1904 Roosevelt elected president, defeating Democrat Alton B. Parker and Socialist Eugene V. Debs.
Case of *Northern Securities Co.* v. *U.S.* upholds government's case against railroad mergers.
Lincoln Steffens's *The Shame of the Cities* published.

1906 Upton Sinclair's novel *The Jungle* published.
Meat Packing Act passed.
Pure Food and Drug Act passed.
Hepburn Act passed, strengthening powers of Interstate Commerce Commission.
John Spargo's *The Bitter Cry of Children*, exposé of child labor, published.

1907 Financial panic; Roosevelt turns to J. P. Morgan and the bankers for help.
William James's *Pragmatism* published.

1908 Supreme Court upholds state regulation of working hours for women in *Muller* v. *Oregon*.
Roosevelt convenes National Conservation Congress.
William Howard Taft elected president, defeating Bryan and Debs.

1911 Frederick Winslow Taylor's *Principles of Scientific Management*, pioneer work in industrial efficiency.
"Dissolution" of Standard Oil and American Tobacco trusts.

SUGGESTED READINGS

George E. Mowry, *The Era of Theodore Roosevelt, 1900–1912* (1958), and Arthur S. Link, *Woodrow Wilson and the Progressive Era, 1900–1917* (1954), provide an excellent survey of the politics of the progressive period. Recent interpretive essays include William L. O'Neill, *The Progressive Years: America Comes of Age* (1975); David M.

Kennedy, ed., *Progressivism: The Critical Issues* (1971); Lewis L. Gould, *The Progressive Era* (1973); and John D. Buenker, *Urban Liberalism and Progressive Reform* (1973).

The literature on bosses and machines in the progressive period is impressive. Among the best accounts are Lloyd Wendt and Herman Kogan, *Bosses in Lusty Chicago: The Story of Bathhouse John and Hinky Dink* (1943); Zane L. Miller, *Boss Cox's Cincinnati* (1968); Lyle Dorsett, *The Pendergast Machine* (1968); and Walton E. Bean, *Boss Ruef's San Francisco* (1952).

Two autobiographical accounts provide the best introduction to muckraking: Lincoln Steffens, *The Autobiography of Lincoln Steffens* (1931), and Ida M. Tarbell, *All in the Day's Work* (1939). Harold S. Williamson, *McClure's Magazine and the Muckrakers* (1970), is a good account of the career of the pioneer muckraking editor. Arthur Weinberg and Lila Weinberg, eds., *The Muckrakers* (1961), and Harvey Swados, ed., *Years of Conscience: The Muckrakers* (1962), offer a wide range of muckraking reporting.

Robert La Follette's career in Wisconsin and in the United States Senate is chronicled in David Thelen, *Robert La Follette and the Insurgent Spirit* (1976); Robert S. Maxwell, *La Follette and the Rise of Progressivism in Wisconsin* (1956); and Herbert Margulies, *The Decline of the Progressive Movement in Wisconsin, 1890–1920* (1968). For a portrait of another progressive political leader who was the temperamental opposite of La Follette, see Robert F. Wesser, *Charles Evans Hughes: Politics and Reform in New York State, 1905–1910* (1967).

There are many good biographies of major political figures on the national scene during the progressive era. For Roosevelt they include William H. Harbaugh, *The Life and Times of Theodore Roosevelt* (1961); the brief but perceptive John Morton Blum, *The Republican Roosevelt* (1954); G. Wallace Chessman, *Theodore Roosevelt and the Politics of Power* (1969); and Edmund Morris, *The Rise of Theodore Roosevelt* (1979), a highly readable account of Roosevelt's prepresidential years. A useful study of Taft is Donald E. Anderson, *William Howard Taft* (1973). Biographies of other important progressives include Alpheus T. Mason, *Brandeis: A Free Man's Life* (1946); Dexter Perkins, *Charles Evans Hughes and American Democratic Statesmanship* (1956); Richard Lowitt, *George W. Norris: The Making of a Progressive* (1963); John A. Garraty, *Right-Hand Man: The Life of George W. Perkins* (1960); Richard Leopold, *Elihu Root and the Conservative Tradition* (1954); and M. Nelson McGeary, *Gifford Pinchot: Forester-Politician* (1960).

Progressive social issues have been discussed in several important works. James H. Timberlake, *Prohibition and the Progressive Crusade* (1963), examines the connections between progressive politics and moral reform. Jack Holl, *Juvenile Reform in the Progressive Era* (1971), explores another important aspect of progressive reform. The progressive concern with eugenics and birth control is described in Donald K. Pickens, *Eugenics and the Progressive Era* (1971), and David Kennedy, *Birth Control in America: The Career of Margaret Sanger* (1970). Changing patterns of morality emerge clearly from William L. O'Neill, *Divorce in the Progressive Era* (1967), and crucial developments in progressive education from Lawrence Cremin, *The Transformation of the School: Progressivism in American Education, 1876–1956* (1961). Samuel P. Hays, *Conservation and the Gospel of Efficiency* (1959), provides a close look at the less democratic features of that reform movement.

The intellectual climate of progressivism has been discussed in several excellent studies. Charles Forcey, *The Crossroads of Liberalism: Croly, Weyl, Lippmann and the Progressive Era, 1900–1925* (1961), gives a lively account of three leading progressive publicists. Robert W. Schneider, *Five Novelists of the Progressive Era* (1965), traces reform ideas through popular fiction. Roy Lubov, *The Progressives and the Slums* (1962), shows the concerns of leading reformers with cleaning up the cities. The best introduction to the writing of progressive history is Richard Hofstadter, *The Progressive Historians* (1968). Samuel J. Konefsky, *The Legacy of Holmes and Brandeis* (1956), explains the legacy of the two great progressive jurists. Samuel Haber, *Efficiency and Uplift: Scientific Management in the Progressive Era, 1890–1920* (1964), shows the effect of the ideas of Frederick Winslow Taylor in shaping progressive values. For sharply etched portraits of three key intellectuals in the progressive era, see David Riesman, *Thorstein Veblen: A Critical Introduction* (1963); Ralph Barton Perry, *The Thought and Character of William James* (2 vols., 1935); and Sidney Hook, *John Dewey: An Intellectual Portrait* (1939).

Personal reflections—sometimes illuminating, always entertaining—on the meaning of progressivism by two active progressives are collected in William Allen White, *The Autobiography of William Allen White* (1946), and Frederic C. Howe, *The Confessions of a Reformer* (1925).

25 Progressives and the Challenge of Pluralism

In 1910 Theodore Roosevelt, after a year's trek through Africa and the capitals of Europe, returned home to a rebellion in his own party. Once he learned of the widening rift between President William Howard Taft's supporters and his own leaderless progressive followers, Roosevelt moved quickly to return the Republican party to his original vision of a unified national purpose. In an incisive speech in 1910 dedicating a state park in Osawatomie, Kansas, where John Brown had fought with Missouri ruffians a half-century earlier, Roosevelt gave his program a name—the "New Nationalism." In part, Roosevelt's speech owed its clarity to his recent reading of Herbert Croly's *The Promise of American Life*, a progressive's indictment of American political drift with which the former president fully agreed. But in a broader sense both Croly's lengthy analysis and Roosevelt's call to action at Osawatomie summed up the arguments for an organized national society that Roosevelt had formulated years earlier.

Roosevelt was not calling for "overcentralization," he assured his Kansas audience, but for "a spirit of broad and far-reaching nationalism" to guide the American people as a whole. His New Nationalism, which put national needs ahead of sectional interests and private advantage, would bring an end to "the utter confusion that results from local legislatures attempting to treat national issues as local issues." After listing the many unfinished tasks awaiting federal action, Roosevelt drove home his point with a comparison that he hoped would have meaning for the few aging veterans of the Civil War in the crowd. "You could not have won simply as a disorderly mob," the Rough Rider reminded them. "You needed generals; you needed careful administration of the most advanced type. . . . You had to have the administration in Washington good, just as you had to have the administration in the field. . . . So it is in our civil life."

Unfortunately for Roosevelt, administration of the most advanced type was not yet a fact, as the man who was to be his chief rival in the election of 1912 already sensed. Woodrow Wilson, a Southerner and a Democrat, drew on both these traditions in sounding the principal countertheme of progressivism. As a former professor of political science and president of Princeton, currently the reform governor of New Jersey, Wilson was fully Roosevelt's match as a historian and intellectual. In examining the American political and social system in 1910, he came closer to understanding the complex play of social forces at work in the country than both of his Republican rivals, Taft and Roosevelt.

Roosevelt's New Nationalism called for the reordering of American priorities and the acquiring of new habits and duties. The "New Freedom"—as Wilson came to call his vision—offered another view of progressivism as a liberation movement. Wilson pictured an open, complex society, composed of immigrants and women as well as native-born white males, Catholics and Jews as well as Protestants, reformers as well as professional politicians, and visionaries of all sorts as well as political realists. In the election year of 1912, these broader strokes of Wilson's New Freedom seemed to present a truer picture of the complexity of early-twentieth-century American life than did the views of Roosevelt and the New Nationalists. But it remained to be seen whether the Democratic party, emerging from sixteen years of enforced retirement, could succeed in turning these various energies into a political program.

Changing the Progressive Guard

By 1910 it seemed that reform had slowed. Congress, with a bipartisan faction of conservatives in both houses, was in no mood to finish the work of building a national banking system or designing a program of business regulation. And a watchful conservative Supreme Court stood ready to stop any further advances toward the social service state.

620

THE NEW YORK STOCK
EXCHANGE AT THE TURN OF THE
CENTURY

Of all the branches of the federal government, the Supreme Court was the least responsive to the problems confronting industrial society and the most alert to the dangers of curtailing corporate privilege. Although it had agreed to Roosevelt's breaking up of the Northern Securities trust and the oil and tobacco monopolies, the Court was much less enthusiastic about the new progressive forms of administrative regulation and the use of commissions to make and enforce rulings. The struggle for administrative effectiveness after 1890 often seemed to be waged between a handful of conservative justices clinging tenaciously to the right of judicial review and a circle of frustrated congressional reformers hoping to strengthen the administrative arm of the federal government. To these reformers the Supreme Court's stubborn defense of its prerogatives seemed a usurpation—taking away from the Interstate Commerce Commission and other federal agencies the power to do their job. Progressives remembered, too, that the Supreme Court had recently declared a federal income tax unconstitutional and had set severe limits on the powers of the states to enact social legislation.

Justice Holmes and the Court.

The spirit of progressivism invaded the Supreme Court with the appointment of Oliver Wendell Holmes, Jr. He was chosen by Roosevelt in the hope that he would reeducate his senior colleagues in the uses of judicial restraint and bring a more enlightened view of regulatory power to the Court. Holmes considered the Constitution not a yardstick for measuring the shortcomings of imperfect laws, but rather a flexible instrument for providing for the "felt necessities" of the modern age. The life of the law, he was convinced, was inherent in its utility and function. Holmes dismissed those of his colleagues on the Court who still claimed to believe in higher law as willing captives of "that naïve state of mind that accepts what has been familiar and accepted by them and their neighbors as something that must be accepted everywhere." As for himself, the outspoken newcomer admitted, "I . . . define truth as the system of my limitations and leave absolute truth for those who are better equipped."

Holmes explained his belief in the necessity of social experimentation in the famous *Lochner* case of 1905, a decision overturning a New York law that reduced the work week for bakers to sixty hours. In a five-to-four decision the majority of the Court declared that the law was another "meddlesome interference with the rights of individuals" and thus unconstitutional. In his dissent Holmes lectured his fellow justices on the danger of intruding their laissez-faire views into the law. The Constitution, he declared, had not been intended "to embody a particular economic theory, whether of paternalism and the organic relation of the citizen to the state or of laissez-faire." Instead it was made for people who frankly differed, and "the accident of our finding certain opinions natural and familiar, or novel and even shocking, ought not to conclude our judgment upon the question whether statutes embodying them conflict with the Constitution of the United States." In a series of similar dissents during the next two decades, Holmes—together with Justice Louis Brandeis, who joined the liberal side of the Court in 1916—argued for restraint on the judicial activism of a conservative majority that was concerned with slowing the progressive drift toward a managed society.

Political Conflicts Under Taft.
Congress was frequently divided within itself after 1909 and could make little headway against the Supreme Court's certainty of conservative purpose. Both the House and the Senate witnessed a series of sharp clashes between aggressively reform-minded Insurgents and stubborn conservatives over tariffs, conservation, and governmental reorganization. With no leadership from President Taft, who backed the majority of conservative Republican regulars, reformers lost heart.

Meanwhile Taft's political lethargy and his ineptitude made an inviting target for the barbs of Republican reformers, including La Follette. Although Roosevelt had recommended Taft as a thorough-going reformer, the new president lacked Roosevelt's concern with strengthening the federal government, as well as the former president's skill in managing his party. Taft was graceless, stubborn, unschooled in the arts of political persuasion, and wholly lacking in Roosevelt's popular appeal—and he quickly made it clear that he was no crusader.

WILLIAM HOWARD TAFT
Taft preferred conservative Republicans to crusading Insurgents.

Taft's administration accordingly was punctuated by a series of political explosions. The first was touched off by a struggle over conservation policy. Gifford Pinchot, chief of the U.S. Forest Service, "Sir Galahad of the Woods," as his numerous enemies called him, accused Taft's secretary of the interior, Richard Ballinger, of neglecting his duties. More specifically, Pinchot accused Ballinger of unsavory conduct in validating the Bering River coal claims that had mysteriously come into possession of the Morgan-Guggenheim syndicate. Although a congressional investigation cleared Ballinger of any hint of fraud, and although the feisty and self-righteous Pinchot overplayed his hand by appealing to the American public at large, Ballinger felt obliged to resign. Taft, who had supported Ballinger, lost face and with it the loyalty of a sizable group of Roosevelt progressives.

Taft only increased his problems in his handling of the tariff question. After promising downward revision of the schedules, he backed away from the ensuing congressional struggle and looked on as the protectionist forces of Nelson Aldrich and the Old Guard loaded the original bill with higher schedules. Then, to the amazement of the progressive Insurgents, the president hurried to their midwestern stronghold, where he proclaimed the now unrecognizable Payne-Aldrich Act the "best tariff ever passed by the Republican party."

Roosevelt: The Bull Moose Candidate.

Roosevelt watched Taft's mismanagement of his party with growing disdain. "A lawyer's administration," he snorted, was proving itself "totally unfit" to lead the country. For like-minded progressives who had recently formed the Progressive Republican League, there were two choices. The first was to appeal to Roosevelt to intervene in party councils in their behalf and help them replace Taft with a candidate of their choosing; the second, and more desperate, strategy was to bolt the Republican party altogether and set up an independent reform party. By 1912 Republican progressives remained sharply divided on this question.

As the election year approached, Roosevelt himself was undecided about the best course. On the one hand, he was convinced that the Taft regime had paid little attention to the "needs of the country." On the other hand, he was dubious of the success of any movement on his own behalf, and he confessed to little enthusiasm for "staggering under a load on my shoulders through no fault of my own."

Whether he knew it or not, Roosevelt had practically declared his availability with his "New Nationalism" speech at Osawatomie. The New Nationalism, composed of schemes for the improved regulation of corporations, physical evaluation of railroads, a graduated income tax, a reformed banking system, labor legislation, a direct primary, and a corrupt practices act, seemed exhilarating to his progressive followers but nothing less than revolutionary to the Old Guard Republicans. Far from closing the breach between the two wings of the Republican party, the New Nationalism speech in effect was Roosevelt's challenge to Taft and his conservatives.

When Taft refused to step out of Roosevelt's way and Senator Robert La Follette entered a rival bid for the nomination, Roosevelt, who distrusted Taft and heartily disliked La Follette, decided to run. But Taft regulars put to good use the southern Republican delegates, whom they held securely. Roosevelt's hopes at the convention rested on some 252 contested seats, at least 100 of which he needed in order to win the nomination. With the credentials committee and the whole party apparatus in the hands of the regulars, he succeeded in winning only 14 of these contested seats. After hurried consultations with his financial backers, George W. Perkins and Frank Munsey, who promised to see him through, Roosevelt agreed to bolt and call his own convention to launch an independent Progressive party.

The loyal 10,000 who gathered in the Chicago Auditorium in August 1912 to hear their leader pronounce himself as fit as a "bull moose" and to sing with them the "Battle Hymn of the Republic" constituted a motley collection of mavericks and reformers, nationalists and big businessmen, social workers and intellectuals, all determined to stand with the "Colonel" at Armageddon and to "battle for the Lord." Conspicuously absent were most of the original liberal Insurgents, who declined to make a risky investment in third-party politics. Although the vibrant spirit of the old progressivism was evident at Chicago, Roosevelt and his advisers realized that winning the election would prove difficult. As Roosevelt intoned the Eighth Commandment and called down divine judgment on his Republican betrayers, he must have known that a Democratic victory was all but inevitable.

Wilson: The Shining Knight of Progressivism.

Yet if fortune was about to shine its face on the Democrats in the election of 1912, it gave no sign. Democrats had their own liabilities, chief among them their titular head and perennial candidate, William Jennings Bryan, who had labored sixteen years to undo the damages of his ill-fated experiment in pietistic politics. In the center ring at the 1912 Democratic convention stood "Champ" Clark, Speaker of the House and veteran southern leader of the party, who had the support of the rural wing; William Randolph Hearst, the demagogic newspaper publisher and pseudo-reformer; and Woodrow Wilson, the shining knight of New Jersey progressivism. Fresh from a series of legislative encounters that had seen the passage of a direct primary law, railroad legislation, workmen's compensation, and a corrupt practices act, Wilson represented the hopes of urban progressives in the East.

The Democratic convention in Baltimore was every bit as uproarious as the Republican convention. Clark, armed with preconvention pledges, jumped out

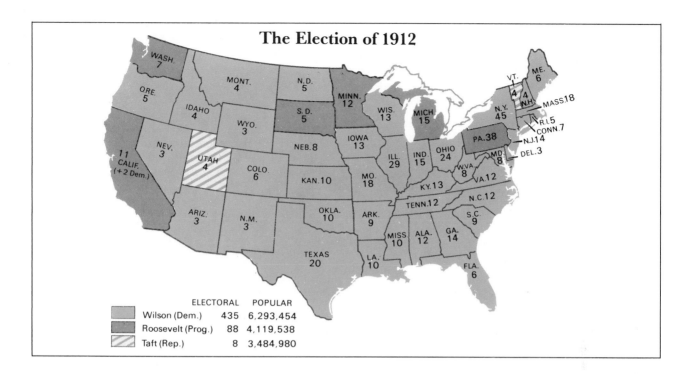

The Election of 1912

	ELECTORAL	POPULAR
Wilson (Dem.)	435	6,293,454
Roosevelt (Prog.)	88	4,119,538
Taft (Rep.)	8	3,484,980

to an early lead, which he maintained until the Wilson forces finally caught up. On the forty-sixth ballot, after endless maneuvering and a final agreement between southern agrarians and northern city bosses, the deadlock was broken and Wilson received the two-thirds vote necessary for nomination. Before they adjourned, the Democrats patched up their differences in a platform that roundly condemned Republican centralization—as Democratic platforms had unfailingly done since Reconstruction—and advertised its own brand of progressivism guaranteed to lower the tariff and break up the trusts, give the banks back to the people, and destroy all special privilege.

But the heart of the Democratic promise in 1912 lay in Wilson's call for liberation from the rule of big business and big government. Taft's official Republicanism, Wilson predicted, would spell continuing business domination, while Roosevelt's plan for monitoring the trusts simply added the powers of the government to those of the monopolists. Wilson pictured Democratic deliverance as "coming out of the stifling cellar into the open," where people could "breathe again and see the free spaces of the heavens." Remove the restrictions on private enterprise, Wilson urged, so that the younger generation would never become "the protégé of benevolent trusts" but rather would be free to go about making of their lives whatever they wished.

Wilson won the presidency with 6,286,214 popular votes—42 percent—and 435 electoral votes. Even

with the split among the Republicans, who gave Taft some 3.5 million votes and Roosevelt's Progressive party more than 4 million, Wilson's victory was impressive. It remained to be seen whether the new president represented a new kind of leadership.

President Wilson: Schoolmaster to the Nation. If the intellectual sources of Roosevelt's New Nationalism lay in the eighteenth-century world of the Founders, the roots of Woodrow Wilson's New Freedom were firmly planted in nineteenth-century morality. Wilson, who was born in 1856 in Staunton, Virginia, grew up in the heart of the Confederacy, briefly attended Davidson College, and graduated from Princeton in 1879. After a year spent studying the law, for which he had no particular liking, he turned to his real interests, political science and history. He studied with the great historian of institutions, Herbert Baxter Adams, at the Johns Hopkins University and earned a doctorate there in 1886. Then came several years of climbing the academic ladder, with appointments at Bryn Mawr, Wesleyan, and Princeton, where he taught for twelve years before becoming its president in 1902. Wilson's books, polished although not sparkling works of political science and history, made a varied collection: *Congressional Government* (1885); an extended essay, *The State* (1889); a history of the Civil War Years, *Division and Reunion* (1893); the five-volume *History of the American People* (1902); and *Constitutional Government in the United States* (1908).

**WOODROW WILSON
CAMPAIGNING, 1912**
Although his style differed
markedly from Theodore
Roosevelt's, Wilson was an effec-
tive and persuasive speaker.

By temperament as well as training, Wilson was an academic, an educator-scholar who felt a calling to instruct a progressive generation in the science of good government. As schoolmaster to the nation, he looked the part—with a lean, angular face, a long nose adorned by a pince-nez, full pursed lips, and eyes that seemed to look through his visitors rather than at them. Distant, formal, somewhat severe in his relations with the public, he appeared correct but cold. He recognized this deep reserve in himself and thought it a weakness. "I have a sense of power in dealing with men collectively," he once confessed, "which I do not feel always in dealing with them singly." There was little familiarity in the man and no feeling of camaraderie. As president of Princeton, governor of New Jersey, and chief executive, Wilson was a man one worked *for* but not *with*. Both as a teacher and an administrator, he had a problem not so much in disciplining his followers, at which he excelled with a frosty politeness, as in controlling his own high-voltage temper and his tendency to bristle when challenged. When opposition to his plans mounted, as it did in a serious struggle over the graduate school at Princeton, Wilson would cling to his position, personalize the conflict, and accuse his opponents of malice while avowing the purity of his own motives.

At his best, however, Wilson was a superb leader, directing the work of his subordinates with cool precision, holding their loyalty with ideals, and winning the American public over with his moral authority. On the few occasions when his self-confidence flagged in the face of enemy attack, he could be petty and vindictive. But at all times, he lived the role of the statesman as educator, standing before and slightly above the American people, to whom he sought to teach effective government.

Some of the lessons Wilson taught were curiously old-fashioned and abstract—moral precepts rather than practical proposals. For him words like *liberty*, *justice*, and *progress* still retained their mid-nineteenth-century clarity. In his mind these words were connected with the Christian principles of "obligation," "service," and "righteousness" that his father, a Presbyterian minister, had preached. These moral abstractions were the skeletal truths around which Wilson packed such flesh-and-blood meaning as fitted his southern Democratic heritage. His intellectual origins led him to view American politics in terms of both individual rights and pluralistic values. In his vision of America, Wilson agreed with the English liberal philosopher John Stuart Mill's definition of liberty as the absence of external restraint. On the other hand, Wilson's southern upbringing had given him a generally unenlightened view of race and a quiet respect for the South's reasoning in discriminating against blacks.

Wilson sensed clearly that American life in the opening years of the twentieth century remained too disorganized, its forms too complex to be encased in a formula like the New Nationalism. "The life of the nation has grown infinitely varied," he reminded his fellow Democrats in pointing to a flourishing cultural and ethnic diversity. In his view the most urgent American reform task was releasing the creative impulses of a free people. Nations, he argued with strict Jeffersonian logic, are renewed from the bottom up, from "the great struggling unknown masses of men" at the base of society. These Jeffersonian values must be preserved even as the nation industrialized and urbanized. Ultimately, Wilson hoped to reconcile modernization with the traditional values of small-town and rural America.

If America discourages the locality, the community, the self-contained town, she will kill the nation. A nation is as rich as her free communities. . . . The welfare, the very existence of the nation rests at last upon the spirit in which they go about their work in the several communities throughout the broad land.

What the nation needed most, Wilson firmly believed, was to listen to the counsel of the working men and women of the country—and indeed Wilson sought and received labor backing in his campaigns, although he did not always give the labor movement what it asked.

Americans—New and Old

Many of the men and women who did the nation's daily work were recent arrivals from Europe. The decade after 1900 saw the climax of a century-long European exodus in the cresting of a wave of new immigrants from new sources. Until roughly 1890 the great majority of immigrants had come from northern and western Europe. Although these early newcomers were the source of fears and of problems of cultural identity for native-born Americans, these anxieties paled beside those accompanying the arrival of the so-called new immigration. In the first place, the very number of new immigrants overwhelmed the nativists, who stood for the values and interests of old-stock Americans. The nativists' worst fears were

confirmed in statistics. In the quarter-century before the First World War, 18 million new arrivals walked down the gangplanks, 80 percent of them from southern and eastern Europe. In the first decade of the twentieth century alone, some 5.8 million people arrived from Austria-Hungary, Spain, Italy, and Russia.

Another set of figures reinforced the nativists' fears. In the peak year, 1882, when more than three-quarters of a million immigrants had disembarked at Atlantic ports, a third of their numbers had come from Germany, while Italy sent only 32,000 people and Russia not quite 17,000. The peak year in the progressive era, 1907, reversed this balance: Germany sent only 37,000, while Italy dispatched 285,000 citizens; the Austro-Hungarian empire, another 338,000; and Russia (including Russia's Baltic provinces) still another 250,000 people. For the entire period the Italians headed the list of European immigrants with 3 million. Next came the Jews, most of them from Russia, numbering about 2 million, followed by a million Poles by 1914. These three main groups, together with Hungarians, Greeks, Armenians, Syrians, and Turks, attested to the results of leaving the gates open.

A Bewildering Ethnic Variety. Four out of five of the new arrivals settled in industrial cities in the Northeast and the Midwest in areas where jobs could be found. Their collective impact on these cities became clear to progressives when they suddenly realized that 75 percent of the populations of New York, Chicago, Cleveland, and Boston were immigrants or children of immigrants. Like it or not, progressives faced a bewildering ethnic and religious variety in the unmistakable presence of many new people eager to get ahead in their new home.

The new immigrants, like the earlier ones, were attracted by economic opportunity, which drew them off worn-out lands and out of the ghettos of European port cities into an American setting of deprivation that at first seemed all too familiar. Once arrived, they started at the bottom of the occupational ladder doing the nation's dirty work—construction, mining, smelting, factory work, and domestic service. They usually settled in tight ethnic communities near their work, finding security in an enforced segregation. This pattern of inner-city concentration fed old-stock American fears even as it made the "foreigners" invisible to suburbanites. Frequently, too, the newcomers elbowed their predecessors out of the neighborhoods, sending them further out along the city's extremities.

Old-stock Americans tended to assign the new arrivals a national identity that most of them did not possess. For example, nativists were inclined to stereotype these new immigrants as Poles, Italians, or Russians, but in fact the vast majority did not conform to

Most of the new immigrants from eastern and southern Europe at the turn of the century had left their native countries because the land could no longer support them. In the following selections two young Polish peasants explain both their reasons for leaving home and their fervent hopes for a better life in America.

Polish Peasants Look to the Promise of America

PRAISED be Jesus Christus. . . . I inform you that I intend to emigrate to America where I have many friends, for the most part relatives, who write that I can come to them and they will find work for me. . . . I know only one handicraft, carpenter's. I practiced with a country carpenter, but at the present time it is very difficult to find material, and therefore difficult to earn.

We have little land, and I have a sister and two brothers. I am 18 years old; so if I can go to America and get work, as I have the intention of doing, before the call to the army I could earn still more money. . . . I know how to read and I read many books and papers. . . . I also know something about writing, as you can see from this letter. I have been to some monthly agricultural courses in Lublin, where I learned a little about the science of agriculture and model farming. . . . I hope if I live to try with all my strength to organize a model farm but now, because of lack of money and because my father has still a debt, it is difficult to make practical improvements . . . or to buy agricultural machines, which are very dear.

*   *   *   *   *

I have served as farm-steward 4 years in a single place. Formerly I served as farm-clerk in other places. I am a bachelor 32 years old. I am very economical and I have put aside nearly 150 roubles, which ought to suffice for my journey. I shall be obliged to leave my parents, who are already old, without any means to live. My father served for more than 30 years in a single place and during this time was never noticed for bad behavior. Even now he is sometimes employed, if his health allows him to make a levy on a debtor, or as overseer of workmen. Nevertheless, he lives in a poor cabin rented from a peasant and if his children did not sustain him he would probably die from cold and hunger. . . .

I am not afraid of any physical work. I understand builder's and carpenter's work perfectly. . . . It is true that agriculture is the most pleasant occupation to one who has grown up in it, but considering the slavery which binds one when serving and the solitude within four walls, as in a prison, which I have here, it is impossible to hold out any longer. And about marriage one does not even dare to think!

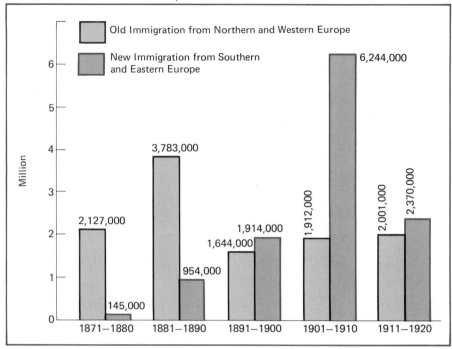

Old Immigration from Northern and Western Europe

New Immigration from Southern and Eastern Europe

the stereotypes. Most had come from provincial cultures whose outlook had long been restricted to the locale, the region, or the village. Although the immigrant enclaves in American cities appeared compact and uniform to outsiders, in fact they were splintered ethnic and religious clusters: each neighborhood boasted its own churches and patron saints, feast days, and civic associations.

Packed into slums, exploited by native-born employers and their own contractors alike, harassed by nativist groups and earlier arrivals, fighting among themselves for a foot on the economic ladder, millions of the new immigrants at first lived marginal lives close to the edges of defeat. The going rate for piecework in New York's garment industry was 8¢ an hour. Steelworkers in Pittsburgh sweated a sixty-hour week for $12.50. A husband-and-wife team on Tenth Street in New York's Lower East Side in 1900 could expect $3.75 for every thousand cigars they wrapped. By working fifteen hours a day, the two of them could turn out 3,000 cigars. Leisure for educational and cultural pursuits was a scarce commodity in America's Little Italys and Little Warsaws.

Slowly these immigrant communities gained a measure of stability. Neighborhoods built lively subcultures through their churches, foreign-language newspapers, service organizations like the Sons of Italy and the Pan-Hellenic Union, and a variety of so-cial agencies and immigrant-aid societies. Edward Corsi, who later became President Herbert Hoover's commissioner of immigration and naturalization, recalled the congested tenement-house life of New York's East Harlem, with "five thousand human beings in one city street, as many as fifteen to a four-room flat; two, three, and even four hundred to a tenement intended for fifty"—twenty-seven nationalities all told, including Chinese laundrymen, Syrian shopkeepers, and gypsy phrenologists. On the East River there were Italians; along Pleasant Avenue, Poles, Austrians, and Hungarians; over in West Harlem, Jewish shopkeepers besieged by Turks and Spaniards. And driving all before them, the blacks. Old-stock Americans lived in lonely social islands in this sea of immigrants, "like refugees in exile."

Corsi's East Harlem boasted a lusty popular culture—not the imposing façades of opera houses, theaters, and hotels, but Old World pageants in cafés, rathskellers, spaghetti houses, cabarets, and dance halls. "We have Yiddish theaters and Italian marionette shows," Corsi boasted, "not to mention movie and vaudeville houses. Our secondhand book shops are as good as those of Paris. So are our music stores."

The "New Immigration": Unassimilable?

Mystified and a little frightened by the variety of immigrant life, most progressive Americans took refuge in increasingly ir-

The Lower East Side

The Jewish Immigrant District of New York City

1910

The Metropolitan Museum of Art, gift of Clarence McK. Lewis, 1954

relevant schemes for "Americanizing" the new arrivals. At dockside civic-aid societies handed out pamphlets, printed in English, warning the newcomers to be "honest and honorable, clean in your person, and decent in your talk"; but these instructions scattered in the swirl of numbers like so many pious hopes. Advocates of immigration restriction agreed with Theodore Roosevelt in deploring the "tangle of squabbling nationalities" as "the one certain way of bringing the nation to ruin," yet the fact remained that hy-

phenated Americanism—Italian-Americanism, Greek-Americanism, Polish-Americanism—was the only avenue to full citizenship. Even the hopeful immigrant Israel Zangwill, looking ahead to the day of total assimilation, described a dream rather than a reality. The composer-hero of Zangwill's popular play *The Melting Pot* hears the melodies for his "American symphony" in the "seething crucible—God's crucible," where a new amalgam, "the coming superman," is being forged over divine fires. Yet Zangwill told pro-

Photograph by Byron, the Byron Collection, Museum of the City of New York

PASSENGERS WHO MISSED THE MAYFLOWER
Immigrants on the steerage deck; Lewis Hine's
"Madonna of Ellis Island."

gressive audiences what they wanted to hear, not what they saw around them.

A clearer view of the forces of cultural pluralism came from the more reflective immigrants themselves, who exposed the progressive idea of complete Americanization as the myth it really was. "There is no such thing as an American," a Polish priest told the genteel social worker Emily Greene Balch. Poland, he explained, was a nation, but the United States was simply a country—in the beginning an empty land open to all comers in turn. Immigrants, according to the recently arrived Mary Antin, who later published a vivid account of the immigrants' hardships, were just people who had missed the *Mayflower* and taken the next available boat.

A growing number of young progressive intellectuals responded enthusiastically to this concept of cultural diversity and ethnic pluralism. In the excitement of cultural variety they found escape from stifling middle-class gentility. Randolph Bourne, a radical young student of John Dewey at Columbia University, found a title for this diversity—"Trans-National America"—and hailed the United States as

the "intellectual battleground of the world . . . a cosmopolitan federation of national colonies, of foreign cultures, from whom the sting of devastating competition has been removed."

Bourne's concept of America as a world federation in miniature ran headlong into the barrier of national fears. The concept of the "new immigrants" took on a variety of ugly shapes. Immigrants, some said, were dangerously illiterate and culturally deprived; they brought with them either an unenlightened Catholicism or private visions of the destruction of free society; they were doomed to a permanently inferior place on the Darwinian scale of races and could never master the skills that democracy demanded. Amateur and professional sociologists consulted the numbers and predicted "race suicide." Sociologist Franklin Giddings announced hopefully, if somewhat ambiguously, that the traits of Americans—who were "preeminently an energetic, practical people"—would undergo "softening" as Mediterranean instincts crept into the national character. Eventually, he claimed, old-stock Americans with their original Baltic and Alpine ethnic heritage would be transformed into "a more versatile,

RURAL VIRGINIAN FAMILY
In 1900 most black American families, like this one, still lived in the rural South.

a more plastic people," both gentler and more poetic. But Giddings's prophecy raised the inevitable question that a progressive reformer asked in an article in the magazine *Charities:* "Are we not, most of us, fairly well satisfied with the characteristics, mental and physical, of the old American stock? Do we not love American traits as they are?"

The Dillingham Commission, a joint House-Senate investigatory panel appointed by Theodore Roosevelt in 1907, underscored these progressive anxieties by making an official distinction between the already assimilated "old immigration" and the presumably unassimilable "new immigration." The commission took four years to complete its report, which filled forty-two volumes. Although it collected much useful information on the work patterns and living conditions of immigrants, the Dillingham Commission assumed from the beginning the need to limit the flow of new arrivals—if not through a literacy test, then through a quota system. When Congress obliged by passing a literacy test bill in 1913, the outgoing president Taft vetoed it in deference to Republican employers who still sought cheap labor. But the idea of a quota system survived, and it was made into law in the 1920s. The Dillingham Report marked a reversal in American attitudes toward cultural minorities:

by 1910 the hopes of the immigration restrictionists soared as the more tolerant aims of the pluralists flickered and died.

Wholesale Discrimination Against Blacks.

In the case of black Americans, white fears produced an even harsher reaction. The progressive generation had inherited from the late nineteenth century most of the ingredients of a racist myth, and progressives improved the formula of exclusion with new "scientific" evidence of the black race's biological inferiority. Not surprisingly, the opening years of the twentieth century saw the nearly total disfranchisement of black voters in the South.

This disfranchisement was hastened by the defeat of Populism everywhere in the South. Populism had pitted the poor white farmers against the region's white establishment and had sometimes appealed to black farmers as well. Thus the rise of the Populist movement had offered blacks an opportunity to gain political leverage by supporting the side that offered them the most. In some areas blacks quickly became politically active. After Populism went down to defeat, the white political establishment decided that such a danger would not recur and set about systematically denying blacks the right to vote. The techniques varied from state to state—poll taxes, grandfather clauses,

THE LYNCHING OF JESSE WASHINGTON
In the progressive years as in the Reconstruction era, the ultimate sanction in the South in maintaining white supremacy was lynching. Here a crowd of white citizens in Waco, Texas, in 1918 pose for the camera beneath their victim.

literacy tests, white primaries—but all served effectively to bar the great majority of blacks from the polls throughout the South. Politically, the Solid South was now firmly in the grip of the Democratic party, which vowed to keep the blacks "in their place." Some former Populists, among them Georgia's Tom Watson, who had once courted the black vote, turned to bitter racist appeals in order to keep their political careers alive. While deploring such crude demagoguery, southern liberals and progressives often justified discrimination against the black man with a variant of the argument that northern reformers used to exclude the immigrant—that good government required the political removal of the untrained, the inferior, and the unfit.*

Most northern liberals continued to regard blacks as a uniquely southern problem, despite mounting evidence to the contrary. But it was South Carolina's racist demagogue Ben Tillman who probed the softest spot in the progressives' plan for political improvement—the lack of moral certainty. "Your slogans of the past—brotherhood of man and fatherhood of God—have gone glimmering down the ages," he

---

* For the disfranchisement of the southern blacks, see also chapters 20 and 24.

chortled. A progressive age, lacking the moral absolutes that once guided the abolitionists, readily accepted the racist conclusions presumably proved by up-to-date science.

In the opening decade of the twentieth century, however, statistics obscured the long-term effects of the Industrial Revolution on southern blacks, most of whom were tied to the land by tenancy and sharecropping. In 1900 there were fewer than 1 million blacks north of the Mason-Dixon line, and thirty years later a full 80 percent of the black community still lived in the South. Nevertheless, the intervening years saw a net gain to northern cities of 1.4 million black migrants from the South, drawn northward by the often illusory lure of economic opportunity and personal freedom. Herded into big-city ghettos—New York's black community numbered 70,000 by the turn of the century—they encountered wholesale discrimination. As lynchings in the South slowly declined, their northern counterpart, race riots, increased—in the small Indiana town of Greensburg in 1906; in Springfield, Illinois, two years later; and in explosive racial tensions in New York, Chicago, Philadelphia, and most of the major industrial cities of the North. Blacks paid a high price for their escape from sharecropping and the Jim Crow laws.

Booker T. Washington and W. E. B. Du Bois. Black American leaders attempted to counter discrimination and economic exploitation with two strategies, neither of them very successful in overturning white progressive prejudices. The official black spokesman, the "office broker for the race," as admiring white officials called him, was Booker T. Washington. The son of a slave, Washington learned the gospel of self-help at Hampton Institute in Virginia and put it into practice at Tuskegee, Alabama, where he founded the Normal and Industrial Institute for Negroes. There he trained thousands of young men and women in the industrial and domestic arts. Washington explained his philosophy in a famous address at the Atlanta Exposition in 1895: he urged his black listeners to strike their roots in southern soil by "making friends in every manly way of the people of all races by whom we are surrounded." To whites he offered the same suggestion, urging them to cast down their buckets among a race "whose habits you know, whose fidelity and love you have tested." Publicly, Washington continued to disclaim the vote for southern blacks, explaining in his autobiography *Up from Slavery* (1901) that "the opportunity to freely exercise such political rights will not come in any large degree through outside or artificial forcing, but will be accorded to the Negro by the Southern white people themselves." Privately and often secretly, however, Washington supported many of those blacks calling for stronger measures.

Most white liberals took Booker T. Washington to their hearts as a "credit to his race," although not all of them approved of Theodore Roosevelt's inviting him to lunch at the White House. Washington became the symbol of the "good Negro" who knew his place and aspired only to keep it—the man of sorrows who accepted the fact of racial prejudice while rejecting all its assumptions and who labored patiently to lift his people the few notches that a dominant white society allowed. The question Washington's program did not address, however, was the one that muckraker Ray Stannard Baker asked in his pessimistic commentary on American race relations, *Following the Color Line* (1908): "Does democracy really include Negroes as well as white men?"

By 1900 the black progressive William E. B. Du Bois, together with several northern liberals of both races, had concluded that until blacks gained full political rights, democracy would never be theirs. The northern black leadership in the big cities appealed to a constituency different from Booker T. Washington's, and it presented another approach to black advancement. Du Bois, a New Englander and a graduate of Harvard, had followed the typical progressive route to professionalism by studying in Berlin before returning to an academic career at Atlanta University in 1897.

Like his counterparts among white liberals, he recognized the pressing need for accurate data on the actual living conditions of blacks, particularly in urban America. To provide some of the evidence, Du Bois pioneered with a sociological study of the Philadelphia blacks, in which he gave a clear picture of life in the ghetto. In *The Souls of Black Folk* (1903), he appealed to potential black solidarity by criticizing Booker T. Washington's "gospel of work and money." Washington's doctrine, complained Du Bois, "has tended to make the whites, North and South, shift the burden of the Negro problem to the Negro's shoulders and stand aside as critical and rather pessimistic spectators; when in fact the burden belongs to the nation." In place of accommodation and outmoded programs for industrial arts, Du Bois suggested the cultivation of a black intellectual and cultural elite—the "Talented Tenth"—and called for immediate plans to mobilize a black political vanguard. In this early and optimistic phase of his career before the First World War, Du Bois developed an unmistakably progressive program aimed at substituting "man-training" for moneymaking, and at fostering "intelligence, broad sympathy, knowledge of the world" in a new elite.

Although Washington's accommodationist tactics and Du Bois's elitist strategies complemented each other in theory, a bitter rivalry for the limited support available developed between the Tuskegee machine and the Niagara Movement of northern radicals agitating for full political and social equality for blacks. By the time the National Association for the Advancement of Colored People was founded in 1909 through the joint efforts of white neo-abolitionists Mary Ovington and Oswald Garrison Villard and the black followers of Du Bois, neither a moderate nor a militant approach to the "race problem" had succeeded in denting the prejudices of most white Americans. Actively or passively, whites continued to support strict segregation and the fiction of "separate but equal"—a formula endorsed by the United States Supreme Court in its 1896 decision in *Plessy* v. *Ferguson*, which upheld the practice of racial segregation.

The Jeffersonian tradition of decentralization and localism worked to the distinct disadvantage of black Americans throughout the progressive period. It perpetuated sectional patterns of discrimination and fostered a national disregard for what was quickly becoming the fundamental challenge of the twentieth century. The progressive compromise with bigotry and prejudice blocked any real hopes for a federal program to give blacks their political rights or to open the door of economic opportunity. For all its liberating idealism, progressivism rested on unspoken racist assumptions and condoned discrimination that had changed little since the Civil War.

The Rise of Social Feminism

The arrival of large numbers of American women on the social and industrial scene after 1900 also disrupted nationalist-progressive plans for completing the ordered society. The percentage of working women rose most spectacularly in the first decade of the twentieth century. Gainfully employed women between the ages of sixteen and forty-four composed 21 percent of the country's work force in 1910. Their rapid recruitment into industry effectively dismissed the question of their suitability for factory and office work, and it raised a series of new issues. Were there certain "natural" occupations for women? Did they have the right to organize? to strike? For a raw industrial society that had yet to fashion *any* labor policy, these questions became increasingly urgent and were raised after 1910 in a militant fashion by a small group of women workers.

An even more difficult question for American men in the progressive age was that of the proper role and acceptable behavior of the so-called New Woman—the young, educated, unmarried woman in revolt against a smothering gentility and the prospects of perpetual domesticity. Some of the more vocal new feminists echoed progressive demands for greater efficiency in managing American society. Radical feminist Charlotte Perkins Gilman, for example, indicted the American home for its shocking waste of human energies. The home, she scoffed, was a case of arrested development. "Among the splendid activities of our age it lingers on, inert and blind, like a clam at a horse race." By reducing the wife to a "social idiot" and subjecting the child to the constant care of an ignorant "primeval mother," the home was the chief deterrent to progress.

Equally subversive of the progressive program for social order was the feminist theme of liberation that Jane Addams and the legions of settlement-house women sounded in announcing the need for new socially creative outlets. Addams cited not simply the inefficiencies of family arrangements, but also the waste of individual lives in enforced domesticity. In her widely read account of social settlements, *Twenty Years at Hull-House*, she acknowledged that the conditions in urban slums needed correction, but she stressed the "subjective necessity" for useful work to fill the empty lives of educated women languishing in the family circle. While admitting the need to expand all aspects of social democracy, Addams worried that the feminine personality, if denied a full range of experience, would wither and die. Where Gilman and other efficiency-minded reformers urged better organization of public resources, Addams and her colleagues emphasized the release of vital creative energies.

Yet viewed as either an efficiency or a liberation movement, the new feminism collected little ideological power. Even in its attempts to improve the lot of working women, the feminist movement did not challenge corporate capitalism or even the profit motive. Its capacity to unsettle the American male order stemmed from a different source. Nineteenth-century American women had concentrated for the most part on removing legal barriers to full citizenship—on winning the vote and acquiring the right to hold and bequeath property, and otherwise to stand equal before the law. The new social feminists read the challenging —and, to many Americans, shocking—writings of Ibsen, Nietzsche, Bergson, and Freud. From these European thinkers feminists absorbed a set of entirely new intellectual arguments for their self-realization. The emphasis on the unconscious and the irrational that swept across the Atlantic at the turn of the twentieth century gave women as well as men new standards of social and sexual behavior not yet legitimized in the moral politics of progressivism. It was precisely here that the challenge of feminism was so troubling.

The revolt began inauspiciously as an uprising of educated young women against the male-imposed definition of female duty as limited by hearth and home. One of the leaders in this feminine revolt, appropriately named Lydia Commander, pointed to the decline of the Victorian ideals of humility, obedience, and self-sacrifice, which were once "assiduously cultivated as the highest womanly virtues." Now, she declared, these qualities had fallen from grace, and the "principle of self-development" reigned supreme. Gone too, feminists agreed, was the old-fashioned notion of female innocence. "What good does it do her?" snapped Charlotte Gilman.

Women's Organizations. One of the outlets for women's growing social concerns was the Women's Club movement, which provided a useful, if somewhat limited, perspective on the problems of industrial society. The General Federation of Women's Clubs grew rapidly from an initial membership of 20,000 in 1890 to nearly a million twenty years later. The clubs were thoroughly genteel organizations, devoted (at least in the beginning) chiefly to self-culture. At no time did the federation encourage a high degree of political consciousness. Nevertheless, individual branches took up issues like factory inspection and child labor, lobbied for criminal justice reforms, and even experimented with tenement-house improvements. In a variety of "study groups," middle-class women discovered an expanding range of problems: the poor quality of municipal services, urban political graft, the need for pure food and drug laws, conservation, and, belatedly, the importance of the vote for women.

[both] *George Eastman House, Inc.*

LEWIS HINE'S CHILDREN
The pioneer documentary photographer Lewis W. Hine (1874–1940) had acquired a degree in sociology from Columbia when in 1908 he joined the staff of the National Child Labor Committee as investigator-photographer. Hine's primary subjects throughout the progressive years remained children and immigrants whose drab lives and harsh routines he caught with unforgettable clarity.

Women's clubs popularized rather than initiated reforms. Ultimately their most important contribution lay in their support, however tardy, for women's suffrage. Neither innovative nor consistently liberal, the General Federation of Women's Clubs did, however, succeed in shifting the interests of well-to-do women from the home to national social concerns.

A second and more sharply focused women's organization, which gave a practical point to the humanitarian concerns of the women's clubs, was the National Consumers' League. Modeled on English precedents, the NCL grew out of the early work of the upper-class charity organizer Josephine Shaw Lowell, who had taken up the cause of New York City's working girls late in her career. Out of her efforts in the 1890s came a small group of well-to-do women who decided to use their buying power to enforce an enlightened labor policy on the city's employers. As the consumer movement spread to other cities, a national league arose in 1899, headed by a remarkable administrator, Florence Kelley. An abolitionist congressman's daughter, trained at Cornell University and later in Zurich, a socialist, a superb lobbyist, and Illinois's first factory inspector, Florence Kelley brought impressive credentials and skills to her job. Under her firm guidance the National Consumers' League grew rapidly until it numbered sixty local branches in twenty states, all applying the league's White Label to approved products.

The league specialized in protective legislation for women and children, lobbying successfully for the Ten-Hour Law in Oregon and retaining Louis Brandeis to argue this law's constitutionality before the United States Supreme Court. The league also joined the campaign for establishing the Children's Bureau within the Department of Labor; and it helped its sister organization, the National Child Labor Committee, to press Congress for a child-labor law. Working together in a new spirit of professionalism, the social feminists recruited such dedicated administrators as Frances Perkins (later to be Franklin D. Roosevelt's secretary of labor) and Pauline and Josephine Goldmark, who would carry their crusade against child labor and social abuse into the 1920s. These women reformers, skilled in bureaucratic methods but free from the profit motive, were experimenting with an alternative to what feminist Rheta Childe Dorr called the "commercial ideal" of American business.

Settlements. The same distaste for the business world also characterized the settlement-house movement. In contrast to its British counterpart, in which young men from Oxford and Cambridge universities took the lead in founding settlements in the slums of London's East End, the American wing of the movement was dominated by women from the outset. The settlements themselves stood in the middle of sprawling slums and quickly became focal points for the public activities of their inhabitants. To the busy complex at Hull House, for example, or to New York's Henry Street Settlement or Boston's South End House came neighborhood children to nurseries and playgrounds, their mothers for classes in hygiene and domestic economy, and, in the evenings, men for lessons in English and discussions of politics.

The impulse behind settlements was religious, although not sectarian, and the atmosphere of all of them—Graham Taylor's Chicago Commons, New York's University Settlement, Kingsley House in Pittsburgh—was dominated by Christian ethics. Inevitably the earnestness of young college women, bent on lifting the tone of immigrant neighborhoods with lectures on the English art critic John Ruskin and with displays of reproductions of pre-Raphaelite paintings, drew sneers. Economist and social critic Thorstein Veblen dismissed the settlements as "consistently directed to the incubation, by precept and example, of certain punctilios of upper-class propriety." But it was not long before the settlement-house workers learned to estimate the needs of their neighbors more accurately, and cultural uplift gave way to hard practicality.

The restless energies of residents, combined with their vagueness about political means, gave the settlement houses all the features of a full-fledged alternative to progressive bureaucracy. Turnover remained high in the settlement houses, which were often mere collecting points for members whose jobs as teachers, social workers, visiting nurses, architects, and planners kept them out in city streets. For both men and women reformers, settlements provided halfway houses between the closed intellectual communities of the college or university and the specialization of a professional career. Settlement houses made possible flexible arrangements of work and leisure based on shared commitments to solving social problems.

Education formed the core of settlement-house work. Initially settlement workers conceived of the educational process as a one-way street of instruction and learning that would lead immigrants toward citizenship. But education was quickly redefined as a mutual learning experience, one that involved genuine exchange and not simply the bestowal of education. As Jane Addams explained to an increasingly receptive public, "A settlement is a protest against a restricted view of education." The settlement-house workers' guide was the educational theory of John Dewey, which defined learning as a social experience and sug-

gested ways of unifying settlements and the life of the community.

When women first founded their settlements, they carefully avoided clashes with the city bosses on the theory that urban politics was hopelessly corrupt. Soon, however, they came to agree with Jane Addams that "to keep aloof from it [politics] must be to lose one opportunity of sharing the life of the community." Still, they found it difficult and often impossible to work with the unsympathetic ward bosses, who distrusted them as do-gooders and rivals for the affections of their clients. Cooperation turned to confrontation over matters of garbage removal, street lighting, police protection, and the location of a neighborhood park. The boldest of the settlement-house workers opposed the bosses, but the contest was unequal, as Jane Addams learned in trying to unseat Alderman Johnny Powers in Chicago's Nineteenth Ward. She attacked Powers with every argument she could muster and capped her indictment with the charge that, although he dispensed free turkeys at Christmastime, he gave poor service on the other 364 days of the year. But turkeys continued to turn the political trick, and the likes of Johnny Powers generally succeeded in maintaining political control in their districts.

Struggling to resist the politicians' counterattacks, the settlement-house women deliberately turned their institutions into public forums where social and political opinions of every kind could be aired. Chicago Commons, for example, featured a weekly "Free Floor Discussion" billed as "self-conscious democracy," in which a labor leader, a college professor, an anarchist, and a businessman discussed the future of capitalist society. From these discussions the women themselves learned valuable political lessons as the logical thread connecting reform to the vote became too obvious to ignore: women needed the vote to make good their promise to improve American life. Without the franchise they could do little more than advance moral arguments, while their enemies—the crooked contractors and sweatshop owners—used their votes to intimidate the politicians. By 1910 mounting frustrations were beginning to lead many settlement-house women to join the drive for women's suffrage.

The Suffragists Divided. The two main groups in the suffrage movement after 1912 were the staid and cautious National American Woman Suffrage Association, headed by Carrie Chapman Catt, and its more militant offshoot, the National Women's Party, organized by the formidable Quaker agitator Alice Paul. Suffragists presented two basically different and even contradictory arguments. The first was well suited to the progressive political temper and was summed up by

EAST SIDE SETTLEMENT
CLASS, c. 1910
A settlement teacher and her
pupils.

Brown Brothers

Mary Putnam Jacobi, a veteran suffragist and leading woman doctor:

No matter how well born, how intelligent, how highly educated, how virtuous, how refined, the women of today constitute a political class below that of every man, no matter how base born, how stupid, how ignorant, how vicious, how poverty-stricken, how brutal.

The second suffragist argument singled out women's special interests and capabilities that were in need of recognition. According to this reasoning, women were uniquely endowed with humanizing qualities and, given the vote, could soften the rigors of industrial society and nurse the United States back to health. Such was Jane Addams's explanation for the feminine political role: "If women have in any sense been responsible for the gentler side of life which softens and blurs some of its harsher conditions, may not they have a duty to perform in our American cities?" In justifying their claim to the vote, middle-class women could take their choice between a demand for simple justice and the promises of a healing creed.

Idealistic or purely practical, the case for women's suffrage was strengthened by the more glaring absurdities of its male opponents. One of them, a worried military officer, warned against the "dilution with the qualities of the cow, of the qualities of the bull upon which the herd's safety must depend."

The suffrage movement gathered momentum at the state level. In 1910 the state of Washington gave the vote to women, and the next year California succumbed to a high-pressure campaign and also awarded women the vote. In 1912 Arizona, Kansas, and Oregon followed suit as Theodore Roosevelt's Bull Moose party, despite its leader's initial reservation, adopted a plank calling for national women's suffrage.

In the presidential election campaign of 1912, a more militant strategy emerged, which concentrated on congressional and presidential candidates—few of whom were particularly sympathetic to the suffragist cause. Alice Paul, the leader of a small band of radical suffragists working at the national level, began to take direct action. She was a grimly determined feminist who had earned a doctorate at the University of Pennsylvania and had spent five years in England studying

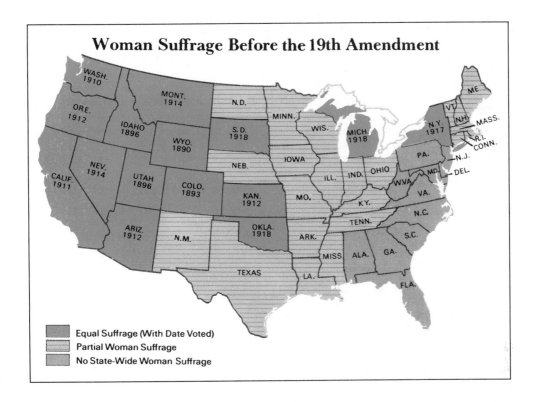

Woman Suffrage Before the 19th Amendment

Equal Suffrage (With Date Voted)
Partial Woman Suffrage
No State-Wide Woman Suffrage

suffragist Emmeline Pankhurst's disruptive tactics before returning home to try them out for herself. Intense, untiring, a stickler for principle, and an able tactician, Alice Paul promptly singled out Woodrow Wilson and the occasion of his inauguration for a giant protest parade, involving 5,000 women, which ended in a near riot. Then, applying the idea of the English suffragists, she organized an aggressive and highly verbal lobby, which soon became the National Women's Party, dedicated to direct action. The National American Woman Suffrage Association, stung by the success of its more militant rival, began to revive under Mrs. Catt's leadership, and a reorganized board of directors redoubled its efforts to reach women at the state and local levels.

By 1917, as the country prepared to enter the First World War, Wilson's administration faced two groups of political feminists with distinctly different views of the world conflict: a small organization of militants who bitterly protested American participation in the war and demonstrated against "Kaiser Wilson" with marches and hunger strikes; and a much larger group of moderates who supported the war in the belief that peace would bring victory to women as well as to the cause of democracy. In June 1919 Congress rewarded the moderates' patience by passing the Nineteenth Amendment, which gave the vote to all adult Americans regardless of sex. Yet the cause of democracy and

reform, American women would learn, was not to be advanced by their sudden invasion of the polls. Notwithstanding their arguments to the contrary, women did not compose an interest group with special needs and talents, nor did their demands for their share of political responsibility alter the course of progressivism. Proposals for a comprehensive recasting of industrial society and for the complete reordering of American priorities were put forward only by the socialists.

Paradise Lost: Socialism in America

American socialism in the years before the First World War was a lively and varied critique of the capitalist system presented by an inventive but faction-ridden party, drifting steadily away from its nineteenth-century revolutionary moorings. Despite its official collectivist ideology, American socialism in action kept alive a Jeffersonian tradition that defied the wishes of progressive nationalists.

In its best days between 1900 and 1914, the socialist movement was a volatile combination of regional groups. Party members included industrial workers in the cities of the Northeast, members of older ethnic groups in the urban enclaves of the upper Midwest, agrarians with memories of Populism in the Plains states, hard-bitten miners and lumber stiffs from the Rocky Mountains and the Pacific Northwest, and a core of college-trained intellectuals preaching everything from Christian Socialism and gradualist doctrines derived from the British Fabians to revolution-for-the-hell-of-it. If socialists never quite lived up to their reputation as the chief American menace to law and order, they nevertheless presented a case against corporate capitalism that progressives found deeply disturbing.

Socialism as a political force dated from the turn of the twentieth century. In 1901 disgruntled members of the tiny Socialist Labor party, fed up with the dictatorial ways of their hard-lining Marxist leaders, bolted. Collecting other splinter groups, including Eugene V. Debs's Social Democratic party, they formed the Socialist Party of America. The 94,000 votes Debs won in the presidential election of 1900 marked the beginning of a shift among the majority of American socialists toward the moderate center. They also drifted toward a theory of nonviolent parliamentary socialism, a move that was not always clear to the embattled participants themselves.

The Two Faces of Socialism.

American socialism showed two faces. To progressive outsiders it was a menace to their capitalist system. According to the socialists, capitalism was traveling a historically determined road to oblivion, destroying small-scale enterprise, saturating international markets, and establishing spheres of influence and imperialist outposts along the way. Most progressives took comfort in the conviction that class war did not in fact appear likely. Yet to most Americans the very vehemence of socialist prophesying suggested a conspiracy of chronic grumblers and political madmen. The progressives prepared to deal with the enemy in the best way they knew—by intimidation and suppression.

To socialists themselves, American development seemed a baffling exception to the doctrines of economic determinism. Their list of unanswered questions lengthened as American capitalism continued to display surprising powers of accommodation. Did the immediate goals of shorter hours and improved working conditions strengthen class solidarity, or did they simply adjust workers to a wage system in which they had no power? Could socialists accomplish more through political action—by running candidates of their own—or did such politicking amount to betraying the interests of the working class? Was the overthrow of the capitalist system imminent, or would the socialist takeover come only gradually, following the education of the workers? The socialists' failure to reach agreement on these matters was seen by most progressives as proof of the absurdity of their ideas—but also as a warning to a society willing to tolerate them.

Gradually the center of the Socialist party was occupied by solid and sensible moderates—men like Milwaukee's shrewd tactician, Victor Berger; New York's scarred veteran of innumerable ideological campaigns, Morris Hillquit; and the "Pennsylvania Dutchman," James Hudson Maurer, who hoped for an alliance with the major trade unions. This moderate center hoped to educate the country away from its capitalistic habits with the lessons of evolutionary socialism. The moderates were bitterly attacked by the diehard members of the militant Socialist Labor party, and also by their own left wing, which had come to believe in industrial unionism and direct action. In the years after 1900, the Socialist party, far from solving its theoretical and organizational problems, kept on dividing into camps of pragmatists and hard-lining idealists, opportunists and "impossibilists."

The "Wobblies."

Of all the dissident left-wing socialist groups, the most alarming to progressives was the Industrial Workers of the World (IWW), a faction of militant industrial unionists led by the charismatic "Big Bill" Haywood. The "Wobblies," as they were called by a derisive but apprehensive American public, rejected all forms of political action and recommended strikes and sabotage as the only way to make the world over. The IWW aroused fear and resentment far out of proportion to its membership, which was mostly made up of unskilled and migratory workers. The Wobblies saw their mission as the total destruction of capitalist exploitation and the forming of a new society "within the shell of the old." Progressives shuddered at the prospect.

The Wobblies waged a desperate struggle for survival during their brief and stormy existence. Although they scored short-lived victories in strikes in the Pennsylvania steel town of McKees Rocks in 1907 and again in the Lawrence, Massachusetts, mills in 1912, they lacked the funds and the organization for sustained membership drives and strikes. Their myth of the "general strike" and the vision of "one big union" served chiefly to rally the spirits of marginal men who dreamed of participatory democracy among the downtrodden. At no time did the Wobblies threaten the American capitalist order.

Seen in perspective, the Wobblies represented another attempt of a nineteenth-century producerist mentality to recover an imaginary world without politics, where abundance automatically rewarded the natural cooperation of free men. "Big Bill" Haywood could have been speaking for progressives when he confessed his hopes for the elimination of politics:

DO WOMEN HAVE THE RIGHT TO STRIKE?
Striking garment workers in Chicago in 1911 give their answer.

I have had a dream that I have in the morning and at night and during the day, that there will be a new society sometime in which there will be no battle between capitalist and wage-earner . . . there will be no political government . . . but . . . experts will come together for the purpose of discussing the means by which machinery can be made the slave of the people instead of part of the people being made the slave of machinery.

Ironically, it was a progressive majority bent on finding another way of going beyond politics with the rule of experts that clubbed the Wobblies' dream to death.

Moderate socialists were burdened with many of the same liabilities that the radicals faced—a tradition of local self-government within the movement, fierce rivalries for leadership, and a host of competing views on the meaning of history. Somehow Eugene Debs retained the leadership of this splintered party. Tall, angular, with a shambling gait and an easygoing manner, Debs served the party faithfully as a national walking-delegate, captivating hundreds of thousands with homely speeches filled with allusions to America's past. His talents were the home-grown ones of the moral agitator; his heroes were the abolitionists

Wendell Phillips and William Lloyd Garrison. A spellbinder with no large fund of useful ideas, Debs was nevertheless an able conciliator and a durable campaigner. In 1904 he won some 400,000 votes for his party, and four years later he duplicated the feat with a whirlwind rail tour across the country in his "Red Special," giving as many as twenty speeches a day. The big leap in Socialist party totals, however, came in 1912, when voters gave Debs nearly a million votes in his fourth try for the presidency.

Socialism as a Dissenting Party. The chief socialist contribution to the American pluralist tradition was the example it set of the open society it sought to create. The Socialist party remained a model of pluralism in action—a loosely organized, tactically divided community that was in general agreement on condemning capitalism but unable to unite on the question of how to replace it. These disagreements crystallized in the lives of young academics, artists, and intellectuals who were drawn to socialism as much by its promise of cultural revolution as by its economic platform. Socialist intellectuals made it clear that they opposed both the moral pieties of progressivism and the bureaucratic collectivism of Socialist party centrists. They made their spiritual home in the Intercollegiate Socialist Society (ISS), the brainchild of the novelist Upton Sinclair, which was composed primarily of students and their teachers, artists, and intellectuals. The membership rolls of the ISS listed some of the most impressive and varied talent in the country and offered a range of criticism extending from the moderate Fabianism of John Spargo to the protocommunism of Louis Budenz; from the civil libertarianism of Roger Baldwin and Alexander Meiklejohn to the protest fiction of Ernest Poole and Zona Gale; from the progressivism of Walter Lippmann to the pacifism of A. J. Muste and Jessie Wallace Hughan. Connecting these diverse personalities were a strong distaste for the commercial spirit, an abiding fear of privilege, and not much more.

The striking variety of American socialism, its shifting assessment of ends and means, and its inventiveness in tapping the rich reserves of American dissent made it a lively, if not ultimately powerful, opponent of progressivism. Despite occasional successes at the local level, the Socialist party was never a major political force, even before the First World War. Perhaps its greatest days were spent in vocal but isolated opposition to that war and to the destructive mindlessness of superpatriots.* Its most effective role, like the role of the Populist party before it, was largely

---

* For the home-front excesses of the First World War and its aftermath, see chapter 27, pp. 677–81.

educational. It taught, more by example than by design, the uses of a secular, imaginative, permissive society. In doing so it supplied useful correctives for a compulsive progressive order, from which Americans might have profited. Its disruption and decline with the coming of the war dealt a major setback to the Jeffersonian tradition that Woodrow Wilson was pledged to preserve.

The New Freedom

Woodrow Wilson, like Theodore Roosevelt before him, believed in a strong presidency. In the course of his scholarly career, Wilson had made an extensive examination of American institutions and political leadership. His training at Johns Hopkins had come at a time when political scientists were beginning to turn away from their preoccupation with constitutional questions and definitions of sovereignty, but before they had acquired the economic and sociological skills to examine the ways institutions actually function. "My purpose," Wilson announced in one of his books, "is to show . . . our constitutional system as it looks in operation." Yet the workaday reality of American politics was precisely what Wilson's analysis always lacked—the linking of larger social forces with political action. Despite repeated promises to "look below the surface" of American institutions, Wilson was at his best in expounding a philosophy of politics that his rival Theodore Roosevelt would have endorsed: "All the country needs is a new and sincere body of thought in politics, coherently, distinctly, and boldly uttered by men who are sure of their ground." Like Roosevelt, Wilson believed that the key to effective democratic government rested in the hands of a powerful and energetic president who offered "the best chance for leadership and mastery."

Wilson's Program. Wilson, then, favored strong executive leadership yet felt a contradictory urge to dismantle federal power and liberate the energies of a free people. These seeming contradictions—strong presidential authority and the reduction of regulatory power—were linked in his mind by the figure of the national leader, such as the great nineteenth-century British prime minister William Gladstone, who could sense the aspirations of the common people and give them voice as commands to the legislature. But more would be required than sensing the "generous energies" of citizens. The federal government, in particular the presidency, had its uses, as Wilson understood. The real question was whether it could be used to eliminate business coercion, break up clusters of privilege, restore competition, and rescue the little man from the grip of impersonal economic forces. For this work Wilson needed a man with a better understanding of social and economic forces than he himself possessed.

The chief architect of the New Freedom was Louis Brandeis, the nation's leading progressive lawyer, who had made a career of challenging big business. In the course of this combat, Brandeis had worked out a complete alternative to Roosevelt's New Nationalism. His program rested on the conviction—reached after watching corporate capitalists play loosely with other people's money—that the country was drifting toward oligarchy. Financial power, he warned, would soon become political despotism through the same process that had made Julius Caesar master of the ancient Roman Republic. In referring to the fate of Rome, Brandeis touched a sensitive Democratic nerve in Wilson, who also feared monopoly but had not yet devised an effective method of controlling it.

Brandeis supplied the guiding concepts for Wilson's first administration. The core of Brandeis's program was a dismantling operation that would ensure the survival of regulated business competition by shoring up small businesses, breaking up new conglomerates, returning the market to free enterprise, dispersing wealth more widely, and reaching out a helping hand to the workingman.

Out of the collaborative thinking of Wilson and Brandeis came the New Freedom's attack on monopoly and a distinction between acceptable and antisocial business behavior, which recalled Roosevelt's program. Big business, Wilson agreed, was natural and thus inevitable, but trusts were artificial and wholly undesirable. "A trust is an arrangement to get rid of competition, and a big business is a business that has survived competition by conquering in the field of intelligence and economy," the president announced in explaining how it was that he could support big business yet oppose monopoly. Wilson was also sure that Roosevelt's scheme of a regulatory commission to oversee the operations of big business was impractical. "As to the monopolies, which Mr. Roosevelt proposes to legalize and welcome, I know that they are so many cars of juggernaut, and I do not look forward with pleasure to the time when juggernauts are licensed and driven by commissioners of the United States." But could the New Freedom offer a better solution? Was the destruction of monopoly really feasible?

Before Wilson tackled the trusts, he decided to make good on the perennial Democratic party promise to lower the tariff. Calling Congress into special session and breaking precedent by appearing in person, he called for immediate tariff reduction. The Underwood Tariff rode through the House quickly, but in the Senate it ran into a barrier erected by Republicans and Democrats representing the sugar and wool interests. Wielding patronage skillfully, Wilson turned aside the protectionists' attacks. The Underwood Tariff lowered duties an average of 10 percent, placed the manufactured goods of the trusts on the free list, and added a small income tax to compensate for the loss of revenue.

Tariff reform tested Wilson's skills as an "honest broker," but banking reform strained them to the limit. Most Americans were primarily interested in obtaining more credit than the eastern banking establishment was currently providing. But there were also traces of Andrew Jackson's Bank War in the struggle between big bankers in the East, with their plans for a central banking system under their direct control, and smaller regional bankers, who sought freedom from Wall Street in a decentralized system. Ranged somewhere between these contenders was a third group of progressives in both parties who wanted a genuinely national system under government management that would ensure stability.

Federal Control of Currency.

The Federal Reserve Act (1913) was another compromise between conflicting interest groups with diametrically opposed notions of what the country needed. Establishing twelve districts, each with a Federal Reserve branch bank owned and directed by the member banks, the act provided for a certain degree of decentralization and regional control. But the creation of a new national currency—Federal Reserve notes—and a supervisory seven-member board in Washington gave the federal government an effective instrument of monetary control.

Big bankers need not have fretted, however. Much depended on the willingness of the Federal Reserve Board to interpret its powers generously. Not for another two decades would the board feel a vigorous urge to regulate the nation's financial machinery. The immediate effect of the Federal Reserve Act was to strengthen rather than weaken the control of New York banks by consolidating their partnership with the government. As a stabilizing device for corporate capitalism involving a minimum amount of government interference and direction, the Federal Reserve System worked with reasonable efficiency. As a "democratic" reform designed to parcel out financial power to the people, it was an illusion. The gain for monetary efficiency was immediate, but the democratic social goals would be postponed for a later generation to achieve.

Wilson's experience with the trusts also ended in compromise. The confusions of a quarter-century's attempted enforcement of the Sherman Act had made clarification essential. The question was how to proceed. What degree of monopolistic control of an industry was permissible, and what degree constituted un-

due restraint of trade? The Clayton Act, as originally drafted in 1914, had tried to answer this question with a long list of "thou shalt nots." The bill listed unfair trade practices in tedious and confusing detail. Continuing debate, however, and anguished cries from big business made it increasingly obvious that a complete list of forbidden practices was an impossibility. Yet if it was impossible to specify each and every example of wrong conduct, the only alternative lay in vesting a regulatory commission with the discretionary power to make concrete applications of a very general rule. Here was the course Roosevelt and the New Nationalists had advised all along—regulating rather than forbidding and dismantling.

In reluctantly agreeing to the commission proposal, Wilson endorsed administrative government, which he had earlier rejected. His intentions in securing passage of the supplemental Federal Trade Commission Act in 1914 closely paralleled Roosevelt's aim of creating an objective body of experts whose judgments would rest on scientifically assembled evidence.

As a regulatory agency with power to mediate conflicts between public needs and private economic opportunity, the Federal Trade Commission disappointed its progressive champions. During the First World War its functions in preventing business concentration were drastically curtailed, and after the war even its fact-finding powers brought down the wrath of big business and of Congress itself. Congressional conservatives demanded an investigation of its methods. In a series of adverse decisions, the courts stripped the FTC of its power to define unfair practices. Business simply defied the FTC by denying it access to company records and ignoring its rulings. Government by commission in the 1920s provided no cure for a new rash of financial consolidations.

In other areas of national life as well, Wilson's dream of liberating the energies of "the great struggling unknown masses of men" ended in perplexity and defeat. Not the "people" of his earlier progressive imaginings, but highly organized interest groups—exacting, clamorous, selfish—descended on Washington, seeking protection and advancement of their concerns. In some cases Wilson's administration proved generous: for newly organized farmers there were rural credit facilities; for labor, a federal employees' compensation act; for consumer groups, the National Child Labor Act (promptly declared unconstitutional). But there were limits to Wilson's receptivity to interest-group politics. He disapproved of women's suffrage, and he refused to lift the burden of antitrust suits from the backs of labor organizations. He also tacitly supported the secretary of the interior and the postmaster general in maintaining racial segregation in their departments and only reluctantly reversed himself when liberals objected. Not all interests, it was clear, could command the attention of a broker president.

Wilson's Program: More, Not Less, Government.

By 1916, as Americans watched the war in Europe settle into a protracted and bloody stalemate, the Wilson administration had largely completed its progressive program. The president's initial promise of reversal and restoration had not been fulfilled. In each of his major attempts at reform—lowering the tariff, building the Federal Reserve System, controlling the trusts—the president had preferred to disperse power; but instead he had been driven in exactly the opposite direction. He had created the Tariff Commission to systematize the nation's trade policies, the Federal Reserve Board to manage the monetary affairs of the country, and the Federal Trade Commission to police big business.

The meaning of these reforms was unmistakable. *More*, not *less*, government; an increase rather than a decrease in governmental agencies; a greater rather than a lesser reliance on experts and bureaucratic procedures; and a supportive relationship rather than a supervisory one between government and the large organized interest groups it presumably sought to regulate in the name of the people. And presiding over this expanded system of government agencies and bureaus was a president who was fully as powerful as the most ambitious New Nationalist could ever have wished.

CHRONOLOGY

1896	Supreme Court in *Plessy* v. *Ferguson* establishes "separate but equal" doctrine, whereby separate facilities for blacks and whites are declared constitutional.
1899	National Consumers' League founded.
1901	Socialist Party of America organized.
	Booker T. Washington's autobiography *Up from Slavery* published.
1902	Oliver Wendell Holmes appointed to Supreme Court by Roosevelt.
1903	W. E. B. Du Bois's *The Souls of Black Folk* published.
1904	Theodore Roosevelt elected president.
	Anna Howard Shaw becomes head of National American Woman Suffrage Association.
1905	*Lochner* v. *New York;* Supreme Court declares unconstitutional a state law regulating work hours for bakers.
	Niagara Movement formed to agitate for integration and civil rights for blacks.
	Industrial Workers of the World (IWW) formed.
1907	Dillingham Commission investigates "new" immigration problem.
1908	William Howard Taft elected president, defeating William Jennings Bryan and Eugene Debs.
1909	Payne-Aldrich Tariff raising rates to protect eastern manufacturers provokes opposition of South and Midwest.
	National Association for the Advancement of Colored People (NAACP) founded.
1910	Woodrow Wilson elected New Jersey governor.
	Roosevelt's "New Nationalism" speech at Osawatomie, Kansas.
	Women enfranchised in state of Washington.
1911	Triangle Shirtwaist Factory fire in New York City's East Side kills 146 women; investigation and revision of state factory codes follow.
1912	Woodrow Wilson elected president, defeating Republican regular Taft, Progressive "Bull Moose" Theodore Roosevelt, and Socialist Eugene Debs.
	Lawrence (Massachusetts) strike against American Woolen Company led by IWW.
	Radical National Women's Party under Alice Paul formed.
1913	Federal Reserve System created.
	Underwood Tariff lowers duties.
1914	Clayton Antitrust Act passed.
	First World War begins in Europe.
	Federal Trade Commission created to regulate business practices.
1916	Louis Brandeis appointed to Supreme Court.
1919	Congress passes Nineteenth Amendment, giving vote to women; ratified in following year.

SUGGESTED READINGS

A good introduction to the study of immigration and assimilation is Leonard Dinnerstein and David Reimers, *Ethnic Americans: A History of Immigration and Assimilation* (1975). Oscar Handlin, *The Uprooted* (2nd ed., 1973), although challenged on many points by more recent studies, is nevertheless a classic, as is John Higham, *Strangers in the Land: Patterns of American Nativism* (1955), on the hostile reactions of native Americans. Philip Taylor, *The Distant Magnet* (1971), is particularly good on the European setting. Milton Gordon, *Assimilation in American Life: The Role of Race, Religion and National Origins* (1964), corrects old American myths of the melting pot and easy assimilation.

The literature on specific minorities is extensive. Among the best collective portraits are Moses Rischin, *The Promised City: New York's Jews, 1870–1914* (1970); Irving Howe, *World of Our Fathers: The Journey of the East European Jews to America and the Life They Found and Made* (1976); Humbert Nelli, *The Italians of Chicago, 1880–1920* (1970); Stanford M. Lyman, *Chinese Americans* (1974); and Stephan Thernstrom, *The Other Bostonians: Poverty and Progress in the American Metropolis, 1880–1970* (1973).

August Meier, *Negro Thought in America, 1880–1915* (1963), is the best assessment of black aspirations and programs during these years. Jack Temple Kirby, *Darkness at the Dawning: Race and Reform in the Progressive South* (1972), gives an accurate estimate of the social price of progressive reform in the region, while the story of Harlem is well told in Gilbert Osofsky, *Harlem, The Making of a Ghetto, 1890–1930* (1966). Louis R. Harlan, *Booker T. Washington* (1972), is a definitive account of that leader, and Elliot M. Rudwick, *W. E. B. DuBois: Propagandist of the Negro Protest* (1969), analyzes the contributions of a mercurial black progressive.

Two readable surveys of women's rights and social feminism are Eleanor Flexner, *Century of Struggle: The Woman's Rights Movement in the United States* (1959), and Lois Banner, *Women in Modern America* (1974). Aileen Kraditor, *The Ideas of the Women's Suffrage Movement, 1890–1900* (1965), is an account of the ideology of suffragism, and Robert Smuts, *Women and Work in America* (1959), discusses the problem of work.

On socialism Howard Quint, *The Forging of American Socialism* (1953), and David Shannon, *The Socialist Party of America: A History* (1955), present helpful overviews. For more critical treatments of the subject see James Weinstein, *The Decline of Socialism in America* (1967), and Daniel Bell, *Marxian Socialism in the United States* (1967). An excellent survey of the rest of the radical spectrum in the early twentieth century is contained in John P. Diggins, *The American Left in the Twentieth Century* (1973). Melvyn Dubofsky, *We Shall Be All: A History of the Industrial Workers of the World* (1969), is a full account of the Wobblies, and Christopher Lasch, *The New Radicalism in America, 1889–1963* (1965), presents an indictment of cultural radicalism in the progressive era.

On the intellectual and cultural transformation of American society in the opening years of the century, Henry F. May, *The End of American Innocence* (1959), is still standard. Literary histories of the new Age of Realism abound. Among the best are Alfred Kazin, *On Native Grounds* (1942), and two volumes by Maxwell Geismar: *Rebels and Ancestors: The American Novel, 1890–1915* (1953), and *The Last of the Provincials: The American Novel, 1915–1925*. Kenneth S. Lynn, *William Dean Howells: An American Life* (1970), is a sensitive portrait of a fractured artistic sensibility in a rapidly modernizing age.

Indispensable for an understanding of Woodrow Wilson and the New Freedom is the magisterial Arthur S. Link, *Wilson* (5 vols., 1947–65), although the hostile John Blum, *Woodrow Wilson and the Politics of Morality* (1956), and the skeptical John Garraty, *Woodrow Wilson* (1956), offer critical insights unavailable to the sympathetic Link. Biographies of other important figures during the New Freedom years include Dorothy Rose Blumberg, *Florence Kelley: The Making of a Social Pioneer* (1966); Charles Larsen, *The Good Fight: The Life and Times of Ben Lindsey* (1972); Julius Weinberg, *Edward Alsworth Ross and the Sociology of Progressivism* (1972); Robert C. Bannister, *Ray Stannard Baker: The Mind and Thought of a Progressive* (1966); and H. C. Bailey, *Edgar Gardner Murphy* (1968).

26 The Path to Power: American Foreign Policy, 1890-1917

For most of the nineteenth century, Americans managed their affairs with no general foreign policy except that of George Washington's determination to avoid entangling alliances. The defeat of Napoleon in Europe, coupled with the brilliant success of the American peace commissioners in 1815 following the near disaster of the War of 1812, brought a strong conclusion to an era of diplomatic failure for the new nation, perched so precariously on the rim of the Atlantic world and subject to the buffetings of the two major European powers, Britain and France. After 1815 geographical isolation and ideological separation gave the American people an open continent to explore and exploit without interference. By the mid-nineteenth century, George Washington's prediction of a separate American destiny had seemingly come true. Secure on its own continent, its dominance of the Western Hemisphere guaranteed by British sea power, the United States turned inward to explore its interior and develop its resources.

A favorable international climate, together with unlimited opportunity at home, fostered extravagant versions of an American "Manifest Destiny," which at one time or another pointed to the annexation of Canada, the acquisition of Cuba, and the taking of "all Mexico." Expansionists such as the naval officer and oceanographer Matthew Fontaine Maury, who plotted to colonize Mexico with ex-Confederates, dreamed of the Caribbean as an American lake, or of the Mississippi Valley as the center of a vast heartland empire reaching eastward across the Atlantic and westward to China shores. But these flickering dreams of empire, like the extravagant reckonings of farmers, businessmen, and shippers who visualized huge profits to be found in untapped foreign markets, were hopeful predictions rather than policy directives. Despite occasional American interest in the fate of republican movements in Europe, Manifest Destiny remained primarily an article for home consumption—exuberant,

aggressive, but not really intended for export. The slavery problem also curbed the American expansionist appetite after the Mexican War; the debate over the future of slavery in the newly opened territories monopolized national attention and absorbed the nation's political energies.

By the last quarter of the nineteenth century, however, a chain of circumstances abroad began to draw the United States into international power politics. The most important development was the sudden imperialist scramble by the major European powers—first Britain, then France, Germany, and Russia—to carve out generous colonies for themselves in Asia and Africa. American diplomats abroad and politicians in Washington watched with growing apprehension as the European powers, following the lead of business investments, rushed for possessions and spheres of influence in the undeveloped regions of the world.

Still, in his inaugural address in 1885, President Grover Cleveland offered only the briefest word on American foreign policy. The unique nature of American democratic institutions and the real needs of the people, Cleveland explained, required a "scrupulous avoidance of any departure from that foreign policy commended by the history, the traditions, and the prosperity of our Republic." In case his audience might have forgottten that traditional policy, he restated it clearly. "It is the policy of independence, favored by our position. . . . It is the policy of peace suitable to our interests. It is.the policy of neutrality, rejecting any share in foreign broils and ambitions upon other continents and repelling their intrusion here."

This traditional passivity was reflected in the dilapidated foreign-policy establishment over which the president presided. A casual and still largely amateur operation, the diplomatic service had no effective fact-gathering apparatus; although it boasted a handful of able diplomats, it was saddled with a great many no-

Culver Pictures, Inc.

bodies and friends of influential politicians. Most of the useful information trickling back to Washington from European capitals came from cosmopolitan private citizens personally concerned with the shifting scenes of international politics. Until 1890 Europe appeared willing to take this American claim of disinterest at face value and considered the United States a second-class power. The diplomatic corps residing in Washington was not on the whole a distinguished one, and more than once a European state simply neglected to fill a vacant post in this country that had come to seem unnecessary.

Yet at the very moment when Cleveland spoke the platitudes that had passed for foreign policy throughout the nineteenth century, new forces were beginning to collect around a different set of propositions, which were drawn directly from the study of European imperialist adventures. Lord Bryce, whose perceptive analysis of American government and society, *The American Commonwealth*, appeared in 1888, noted the difference between those who shaped foreign policy in England and their counterparts in the United States. In America, Bryce explained, "there are individual men corresponding to individuals in that English set, and probably quite as numerous." There were a sizable number of journalists of real ability, a handful of literary men, and not a few politicians who understood the mechanisms of international power politics. But these Americans remained isolated and disorganized for the most part, vulnerable constantly to public pressures and mass opinions, while the "first set" in England clearly was not. "In England the profession of opinion-making and leading is the work of specialists; in America . . . of amateurs." By the time Bryce published this observation, however, a small group of like-minded amateurs concerned with foreign affairs was already at work in Washington, building the intellectual foundations for a foreign-policy establishment and calling for a more vigorous pursuit of world power.

The Origins of American Expansionism

By the 1890s it began to dawn on the small number of Americans concerned with the conduct of foreign affairs that the United States was in danger of being left far behind in the race for territory and markets. Looking back on the last decade of the nineteenth century, the rabid expansionist Senator Albert J. Beveridge summed up the lessons taught the American people as trustees "under God" of world civilization: "He has made us the master organizers of the world to establish system where chaos reigns." Not all Americans in 1900 agreed with Beveridge that destiny had mapped an imperial course for the nation, but it had become clear that they could no longer view the international scene indifferently. Somehow the United States would have to catch up with its European rivals.

A second force pushing the United States into the imperialist competition—a concern with world markets—was not so easy to analyze. After 1875 American businessmen, bankers, industrialists, and shippers began to call for readier access to global markets. Their demands took on dramatic point with the erratic development of the domestic market—the repeated depressions and gluts—and growing doubts as to its capacity to absorb American manufactured and staple goods. But the American market in the undeveloped areas of the globe remained quite small as late as 1900, despite increasingly noisy demands for enlarging it. The state of overseas markets furnished a focus for popular debate around which both expansionists and antiexpansionists, interventionists and isolationists argued over the proper role for the United States. No one denied the importance of foreign markets in the American economy and their importance too in spreading the blessings of democracy. But did the search for markets necessarily mean intervention in the domestic affairs of undeveloped and politically unstable countries? Did it require outright annexation? Were markets for the investment of capital fundamentally different from markets for manufactured or staple goods? And, most troublesome of all, how could the spokesmen for new and bigger markets catch and hold the attention of an unresponsive federal government?

Conditions in the United States also helped focus attention on possibilities abroad. The 1890s were years of severe economic disorder, rising class conflict, political instability, and intellectual discord. The combined effect of these tensions and struggles was a growing popular belief that the United States had reached maturity as a fully developed modern nation. Whether or not they read the historian Frederick Jackson Turner's famous warning in 1893 of the consequences of the closing of the frontier, many Americans were well aware of the passing of an era in which free land and geographical mobility had been all-important. Viewed as a fact or a symbol of America's vast, seemingly limitless possibilities, the frontier had dominated the American imagination for two centuries. The announcement of its closing reinforced a widely shared sense of irreversible change. For the generation of the 1890s, the extension of the frontier concept into territories overseas quickened the old sense of mission and enterprise, and it released pent-up feelings of humanitarianism as though the answer to a loss of certainty at home was the vigorous pursuit of democratic purpose abroad.

Pacifism or Power? In these shifting circumstances abroad and at home, a struggle developed for control

SENATOR BEVERIDGE'S "TRUSTEES" PACIFYING THE PHILIPPINES

of an emerging American foreign policy. The contestants played a variety of roles in the quarter-century before American entry into the First World War. Some upheld international law or preached pacifism. Others advocated national power or defended American honor. Yet beneath the diversity lay two conflicting ideas about American power and responsibility.

The first view of the nature of power and of America's future was forcefully summarized by Captain Alfred Thayer Mahan, naval strategist and geopolitical theorist, in his *Interest of America in Sea Power, Present and Future* (1897). Mahan argued that since governments could not be expected to act on any ground except national interest, patriotism and the will to fight were indispensable human qualities.

Not in universal harmony, nor in any fond dream of unbroken peace, rest now the best hopes of the world. . . . Rather in the competition of interests, in that reviving sense of nationality . . . in the jealous determination of each people to provide first for its own . . . are to be heard the assurance that decay has not touched yet the majestic fabric erected by so many centuries of courageous battling.

The second and opposing view of the American mission was most effectively expressed by William Jennings Bryan, who limited the nation's role to that of providing a moral example. Nations, Bryan insisted, redeem only by force of example. "Example may be likened to the sun, whose genial rays constantly coax the buried seed into life, and clothe the earth, first with verdure, and afterward with ripened grain; while violence is the occasional tempest, which can ruin, but cannot give life."

Until 1900 Mahan's invitation to national greatness took precedence over Bryan's warnings of its eventual costs. Mahan had spent most of his career wandering about the world observing the patterns of European imperial politics. Now his notice to Americans was direct and unmistakable. The United States, he announced, must pursue an aggressive expansionist foreign policy based on naval supremacy and undisputed control of the world's sea lanes, a vigorous development of foreign markets, and an energetic cultivation of all the domestic spiritual resources needed to promote the national mission overseas. In a Darwinian world of warring nations, he argued, the United States must organize itself into a spiritual and military garrison ready to defend its interests with

THE GREAT WHITE FLEET
In 1907 President Roosevelt dispatched the new American navy on a world cruise as a display of American strength.

Brown Brothers

power. Mahan did not deny the existence of a universal law of conscience, but he anchored it in the concept of the national state fully aware of its duty and prepared to perform it. In his view, the "evils of war" paled before the dangers of "moral compliance with wrong." In the last analysis all depended on Americans' willingness to take up their appointed tasks as the democratic saviors of civilization. "Whether they will or no, Americans must now begin to look outward."

Architects of Empire. Mahan's arguments, which won him enthusiastic support in Britain and Germany, were also warmly received by a small circle of influential Americans whose own examination of the international situation in the 1890s led them to conclude that the United States should take its place among the imperialist powers. "You are head and shoulders above us all," wrote Theodore Roosevelt in promising Mahan that he would do all he could "toward pressing your ideas into effect." Other important converts to the captain's expansionist doctrines joined in: John Hay, soon to become McKinley's secretary of state; the freewheeling romantic reactionaries Brooks and Henry Adams, and their protégé, Senator Henry Cabot Lodge; young, aggressive cosmopolitans like the diplomat Richard Olney, and staid conservatives like lawyer Joseph Choate; academic popularizer John Fiske, with his own version of Manifest Destiny; and social-gospeler Josiah Strong, whose best-selling *Our Country* (1885) argued the

Christian evangelist's case for spiritual renewal through expansion. The views of these would-be architects of American empire were expressed with increasing frequency in metropolitan newspapers and liberal journals, which called for a higher appraisal of American capabilities. And when the test of strength came between imperialists and anti-imperialists over a "large policy" for the United States, these spokesmen for expansion would prove to be particularly effective.

In the meantime, American diplomacy continued to heat up. A series of minor crises early in the 1890s signaled America's intention to take a firmer hand in managing foreign policy by asserting national interest and defending national honor whenever the opportunity arose. In the South Pacific a German threat to impose a protectorate over the entire group of Samoan islands brought United States naval forces steaming into the Samoan harbor of Apia—in time to be destroyed by a typhoon. In Chile a barroom brawl involving American sailors ended in an American ultimatum to that country. And in 1895 a dispute between the unstable and financially irresponsible Venezuela and Great Britain over the boundary of British Guiana called forth a declaration of American power in the Western Hemisphere. "Today," Richard Olney, Cleveland's secretary of state, boasted to the startled British, "the United States is practically sovereign on this continent, and its fiat is law upon the subjects to which it confines its interposition . . . its infinite resources combined with its isolated position renders it master of the situation and practically invulnerable against any or all other powers." By 1896 events like

Detail from "Stag at Sharkey's" by George W. Bellows.

Art as Urban Experience

The great Chicago architect Louis Sullivan summed up the meaning of the twentieth-century city for a progressive generation of Americans when he defined it as a scene of "strife"—both an "arena" for contending social energies and the center of a new democratic culture. For Sullivan a "culture of democracy" meant a "culture of action." His tall office buildings, as he called them, embodied the "mobile equilibrium" that symbolized for him the fusion of individual genius and the massed energies of a whole people. The architect, he explained, "causes the building by acting on the body social" following a design "struck out at a single blow." As for the building, "the force and power of altitude must be in it, the glory and pride of exaltation must be in it. It must be every inch a proud and soaring thing, rising in sheer exaltation that from bottom to top it is a unit without a single dissenting line." Sullivan's own

"The Spielers"
by George B. Luks.

buildings, with their sharp verticality, contrasting piers and planes, hard-edged mouldings, and exuberant ornamentation, represented the encased energy and power of "becoming" that their creator identified with the democratic spirit and the city.

American artists in the opening years of the century shared Sullivan's vision of the city as the focus of national life and the center of a new culture. For Robert Henri and his "black gang" of realists who gloried in the name of the Ashcan School, New York City served as a backdrop for an exciting procession of urban scenes and types that they recorded in the documentary style they had perfected as newspaper illustrators—swirling crowds on gusty street corners, slum kids swimming in the East River, working girls drying their hair on a sunny tenement roof, ragamuffins gaily dancing the two-step on a crowded pavement—all the "drab, happy, sad, and human" moments in the life of the metropolis. Henri's student, John Sloan, took West Fourteenth Street for his reporter's beat and painted the energy he discovered in ordinary people and familiar neighborhood scenes. George Bellows extended the idea of energy from subject to slashing technique in his famous *Stag at Sharkey's* with its two faceless fighters

"Cliff Dwellers," by
George W. Bellows.

Los Angeles County Museum of Art: Los Angeles County Funds

"Election Night
in Herald Square"
by John Sloan.

Memorial Art Gallery of the University of Rochester,
Marion Stratton Gould Fund

"Steaming Streets" by George W. Bellows.

Whitney Museum of American Art

straining against each other. "Who cares what a prize fighter looks like," Bellows exclaimed. "It's his muscles that count."

The New York Eight were boisterously democratic and proletarian in sympathy. "A child of the slums will make a better painting than a drawing room lady gone over by a beauty shop," insisted George Luks, the most colorful and obstreperous of the Eight. In the city's "incredible panorama" of clattering els and gigantic excavations, towering skyscrapers and shabby tenements, vaudeville houses and open-air markets, the Eight discovered an infinitely renewable America. "What a mistake we have made in life seeking for the finished product," Henri scoffed. "A thing that is finished is dead." To the Ashcan School, as to Louis Sullivan, the city promised a democratic immortality.

Another group of younger and more adventurous American artists fresh from encounters with European postimpressionism, who exhibited at Alfred Stieglitz's Photo-Secession Gallery at 291 Fifth

"Hammerstein's Roof Garden" by William J. Glackens.

The Brooklyn Museum, Dick S. Ramsay Fund

"Hester Street" by George Luks.

"Rush Hour, New York" by Max Weber.

Avenue, also responded to the clashing energies of the city, which they caught and fixed in abstract patterns and bold colors. Like the Ashcan School, the new abstract painters sought vitality in their work in the conviction, as Stieglitz put it, that "it is the spirit of the thing that is important. If the spirit is alive, that is enough for me." But John Marin, Georgia O'Keeffe, Marsden Hartley, Max Weber, Arthur Dove and the other modernists gathered at 291 to celebrate not the Eight's triumph of life over art, but the liberating forces of the aesthetic experience itself. The modernists, unlike the Ashcan School, were defiantly *avant garde*, and the freedom they sought was freedom from the conventions of pictorial art and the chance to experiment with new forms with which to record a kaleidoscopic urban world. "I see great forces at work, great movements," John Marin declared, "the large buildings and the small buildings, the warring of the great and the small. . . . While these

"Lower Manhattan (Composing Derived from Top of Woolworth)," 1922, by John Marin.

powers are at work . . . I can hear the sound of their strife, and there is a great music being played."

The modernists, in the spirit of the progressives who often failed to understand them, approached their art as a process of experimentation and research, one demanding innovative technique and bold improvisation. "There was life in all these new things," Marsden Hartley explained in recalling the years before the First World War. "There was excitement, there was healthy revolt, investigation, discovery, and an utterly new world out of it all." Art, as the modernists conceived it, was what the instrumentalist John Dewey called "a process of doing or making," a confrontation with partially disorganized nature with its "breaks and reunions" that plunged the viewer into "the ongoing world around him." The young abstract painters were struck with the action, clash, and tension of city life, which they captured in new

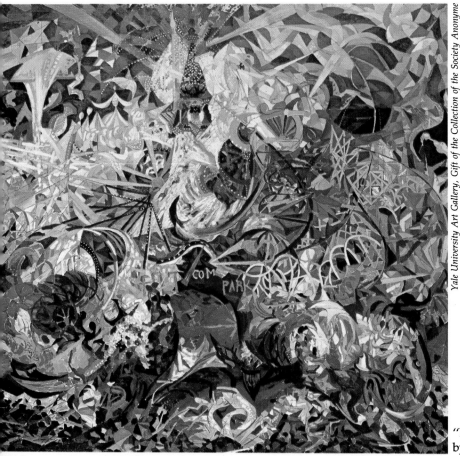

"Battle of Lights, Coney Island" by Joseph Stella.

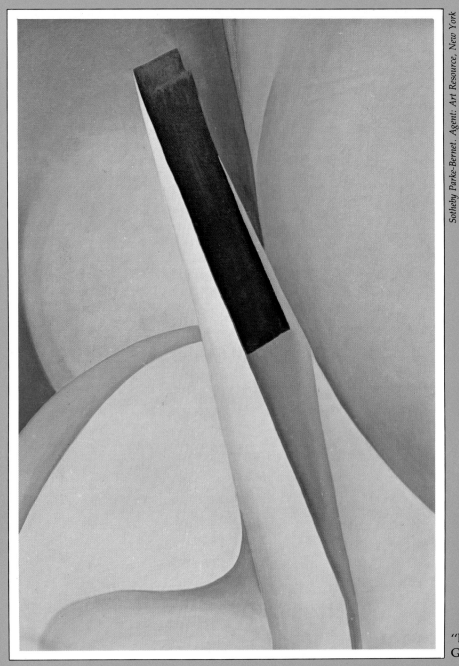

Sotheby Parke-Bernet. Agent: Art Resource, New York

"Black Spot No. 2" by Georgia O'Keeffe.

dynamic patterns quite unlike the static forms of such European cubists as Georges Braque and Juan Gris. The futurist Joseph Stella found the most powerful image of conflicting urban forms in the Brooklyn Bridge, with its "massive dark towers dominating the surrounding tumult of surging skyscrapers . . . the eloquent meeting point of all the forces arising in a superb assertion of their powers, an apotheosis." His *Coney Island*, an ar-rangement of splinters of light, Stella entitled *Battle of Lights*. Georgia O'Keeffe confessed to a fascina-tion with New York's skyscrapers and determined to make her flowers "big like the huge buildings going up. People will be startled and look."

With the arrival of the twentieth century, the city came to dominate the imaginations of artists and architects, who continued to seek in it the source of a vital American art.

these, minor irritations evoking a disproportionate American belligerence, paved the way for a popular crusade on behalf of Cuban independence.

President McKinley's "Wonderful Experience"

In 1895 the Cuban revolution against Spain, which had been smoldering for nearly a quarter of a century, flared up once again, and Spain sent 50,000 soldiers to extinguish it. American sympathies, a mixture of genuine outrage and "jingo" bluster, instinctively went to the underdogs, who were widely credited with wanting to establish a Yankee-style republic. The Cuban rebels responded to this encouragement by dispatching a high-powered lobby to New York City with orders to raise money and goodwill while supplying a steady stream of atrocity stories to the reporters of the sensationalist newspapers owned by William Randolph Hearst and Joseph Pulitzer. Soon the Cuban revolutionaries in New York began to receive help from unexpected quarters—from Latin American trading interests, promoters of a canal across Central America, a variety of patriotic groups, and even trade unions. Carefully orchestrated "spontaneous" rallies across the country whipped up enthusiasm for American intervention. Democrats and Populists vied with their Republican rivals in denouncing Spain and demanding a declaration in support of the Cuban rebels. It was obvious to the incoming McKinley administration that the president would have to move quickly to avoid being captured by a warlike public mood.

Annexation or "Cuba Libre." As late as 1896, however, the exact meaning of this public clamor over Cuba's fate was not altogether clear. To the small group advocating the "large policy," intervention on the island seemed a foregone conclusion. Roosevelt, who admitted to being "a quietly rampant 'Cuba Libre' [Free Cuba] man," told Mahan that intervention was inevitable if the United States was to retain its self-respect. Many expansionists agreed: the Cuban affair would be a heaven-sent opportunity to annex Hawaii. As for Cuba's fate, no one could predict. Even Roosevelt, although he angrily dismissed "the craven fear and brutal selfishness of the mere money-getters" who opposed American intervention, doubted the wisdom of annexing Cuba "unless the Cubans wished it." "I don't want it to seem that we are engaged merely in a land-grabbing war," he explained. Until war was actually declared, there was little support for the idea of permanent United States involvement on the island, even among the most vocal interventionists.

In the fiercely contested presidential election of 1896, the issue of Cuba had given way to domestic problems of free silver and the tariff. It took the re-

newed campaigns of the Cuban revolutionaries in December 1896 and the murder of their leader, Maceo, to anger the American public once more. This time the response was different. Instead of planned demonstrations and organized rallies, there were loud outbursts of protest all over the country—genuinely spontaneous meetings in which businessmen joined patriots and humanitarians in demanding an end to Spanish rule. McKinley's administration now had to contend with a powerful popular indignation.

At this point Spain added fuel to the interventionist fire when its troops on the island began brutally herding Cubans into makeshift camps, where they died by the thousands. Meanwhile, a wavering government in Madrid continued to agonize over the dwindling options left to it. The decaying Spanish monarchy, torn by rival factions of liberals and conservatives, unable to pacify the island but unwilling to give it up, temporized hopelessly. Confusion was nearly as great within the McKinley administration as the president found himself in an intense crossfire between Republican expansionists crying for justice at the point of an American sword, and his conservative business backers fearful of the effects of a war on business recovery from the depression of the 1890s. As popular pressure for intervention rose alarmingly, McKinley was also driven to play for time. Publicly the president demanded promises of instant reform from Madrid, while privately he reined in the most radical members of his party with promises of his own.

War with Spain. By 1897 the horrors of Spain's reconcentration program in Cuba had forced the president to press for even firmer Spanish concessions. Then a series of incidents brought relations between the two countries to the breaking point. First came the release of an indiscreet letter from Depuy de Lôme, the Spanish minister in Washington, to his government, in which he ungenerously—but not inaccurately—described McKinley as "weak" and "a bidder for the admiration of the crowd." Then came the explosion in Havana harbor that destroyed the American battleship *Maine*. There were rumors everywhere that Spain had engineered the explosion—this "gigantic murder" of innocent American sailors, as Senator Lodge put it. At last the expansionist jingoes had an aroused American public crying for retaliation in the name of justice and democracy.

McKinley's dilemma grew more painful as conflicting reports of Spanish intentions came flooding into Washington. On the one hand there were accounts of the Spanish government's total unwillingness to compromise; on the other there were assurances that it was ready to comply with demands for full self-

"THE SPANISH BRUTE ADDS MUTILATION TO MURDER"
The jingoistic tone of the American press during the Spanish-American War is revealed in this cartoon.

government for Cuba. Given the choice between waiting and taking immediate action, McKinley finally decided to act. Two days after Spain had agreed to his demands for an immediate armistice and an end to reconcentration—while still declining to grant Cuban independence—the president sent a message to Congress requesting authority to intervene and restore peace on the island. By the time word of Spain's partial compliance reached Washington, it was too late. Intervention, McKinley knew, meant war, and Congress made the decision official on April 19, 1898, by declaring that a state of war existed. McKinley had lacked a clearly defined set of goals and the means of achieving them, and he had been caught in a domestic political crossfire. He accepted the prospect of what Secretary of State John Hay called "a splendid little war" for no particularly compelling reasons of national interest.

In the brief war that followed, the United States made short work of Spain's broken-down navy and demoralized army. Commodore George Dewey's Asiatic Squadron quickly demolished the monarchy's Pacific fleet in the battle of Manila Bay, and the United States' Atlantic Squadron as easily penned up Admiral Cervera's ships in Santiago, Cuba, and systematically destroyed them. Spanish troops scarcely did any better when they fought the American land forces, although the Americans were poorly trained, badly equipped, and disorganized. After endless confusion General William R. Shafter finally succeeded in assembling some 18,000 troops for an invasion of Cuba and managed to land his army, complete with press corps, foreign dignitaries, and well-wishers, near Santiago. There Colonel Roosevelt and his Rough Riders, a flamboyant cavalry regiment recruited from the cattle ranges and mining camps of the West, seized the lion's share of the glory of what the colonel called a "bully fight," the capture of San Juan Hill. The battle of Santiago capped the successes of the navy, and American soldiers settled in on the jungle heights

BEFORE AND AFTER TAKING: UNCLE SAM TELLS HIS PHYSICIAN THAT HIS TREATMENT HAS BEEN A SUCCESS
Borrowing the popular advertising gimmick for selling patent medicines, an "anti-imperialist" cartoonist spoofs the expansionist argument for acquiring new American territory overseas.

above San Juan, where more of them died from yellow fever than in actual combat. A small expeditionary force that was dispatched to nearby Puerto Rico encountered no real resistance. In August 1898, Spain's meager military resources were entirely spent, and its morale shattered. The Spanish had no choice but to give up and sign the peace protocol.

The Philippines: "Those Darned Islands."

The problem of disposing of the remnants of Spain's empire caught McKinley by surprise. In the case of Cuba, Congress in an unaccountable burst of self-denial had rushed through the Teller Amendment, declaring the island free and independent and disavowing any American intentions of annexing it. Not for conquest nor for empire had American soldiers fought so bravely, but, as one Republican senator put it, "for humanity's sake . . . to aid a people who have suffered every form of tyranny and who have made a desperate struggle to be free." But within a year these expressions of high-mindedness had been cast to the winds.

The new question of the Philippines, together with the old problem of Hawaii, added to McKinley's worries. "If old Dewey had just sailed away when he smashed the Spanish fleet, what a lot of trouble he would have saved us," the president grumbled, confessing that he "could not have told where those darned islands were within 2,000 miles." But with Spain's collapse the barriers to American empire also began to fall, both within the administration and in the nation at large, as groups once hostile to the idea of acquiring new territory began to have second thoughts. Business leaders, banking and mercantile interests, church organizations, and even social reformers joined in calling for the retention of the Philippines, if not as a permanent possession, at least as a temporary way station on the route to Asian markets.

When the Senate came to debate the question of annexation, the opponents of the new imperialism argued strenuously that "political dominion" was not commercially necessary and that, in any case, both the Constitution and the Declaration of Independence forbade it. Under the Declaration, Senator George F. Hoar told his colleagues, "you can not govern a foreign territory, a foreign people, another people than your own . . . you can not subjugate them and govern them against their will, because you think it is for their good. . . ." But the logic of expansion worked against the anti-imperialists. Annexationists argued that if, in order to secure commercial opportunity, the United States needed political stability in Hawaii and the Philippines, then why not go the whole way and at the same time lift untutored peoples to the level of democratic self-government? McKinley spoke the public mood in presenting a narrow range of choices. It would be "cowardly and pusillanimous," he insisted, for the United States "to turn the islands back to Spain, giving them power again to misrule the natives." Equally "despicable" was the notion of handing them over to Britain or allowing Japan to take them by default. "There is only one logical course to pursue," McKinley announced:

Spain has shown herself unfit to rule her colonies, and those [that] have come into our possession as a result of war, must be held, if we are to fulfill our destinies as a nation . . . giving them the benefits of a christian civilization which has reached its highest development under our republican institutions.

The problem of ruling the Philippines admitted of no such simple solution as McKinley proposed. Before

National Archives

war with the United States broke out, Spain had finally suppressed an uprising of Filipino independence fighters by bribing their leader, General Emilio Aguinaldo, to leave the islands. Following his smashing naval victory, Admiral Dewey brought Aguinaldo back to Manila to help fight the Spanish in exchange for a vague promise of eventual independence. But when it became clear that the United States had no intention of giving up control of the Philippines, Aguinaldo and his followers took up arms again, this time against their former allies. In the course of a savage four-year guerrilla war, the Filipino patriots, suffering heavy military and civilian casualties at the hands of American "pacifiers," killed more than 4,000 American soldiers before surrendering and swearing allegiance to the American flag.

As the debate over the peace terms intensified, there emerged a small vocal group of "anti-imperialists," as they called themselves, hastily assembled and ranged along a broad spectrum of opinion. The nucleus of this anti-imperialist opposition consisted of venerable mid-nineteenth-century liberals whose distinguishing mark and chief liability was their advanced age and distrust of mass democratic politics. Veteran antislavery campaigner Carl Schurz was seventy-one; free trader Edward Atkinson, seventy-three; Republican maverick George F. Hoar, seventy-four; steelmaker Andrew Carnegie, sixty-five. Most of

the anti-imperialists stood on the margins of their parties and the government, respected but minor figures who held long and honorable records in the cause of dissent against the Gilded Age. As imperial ambition swept up the majority of their countrymen, they found themselves severely handicapped by their caution and self-denial. "Who will embarrass the government by sowing seeds of dissatisfaction among the brave men who stand ready to serve and die, if need be, for their country?" McKinley demanded of a cheering crowd in Omaha in the heartland of America. "Who will darken the counsels of the republic in this hour, requiring the united wisdom of all?" The anti-imperialists could not prevail against such expansionist ardor. Unskilled in the new arts of mass propaganda, advocating a negative program, often distrustful of the democratic forces supporting the president, the anti-imperialists were quickly outmanned and outmaneuvered by the expansionists.

Some anti-imperialist arguments expressed racist doubts about the wisdom of incorporating dark-skinned, unschooled peoples. Others appealed to the Constitution and the spirit of the Founding Fathers in denying Congress the power to govern other people against their wills. With social scientist William Graham Sumner, a loyal few railed against the prostitution of statesmanship to mere party interest. But the core of the anti-imperialists' case against expan-

THE CAUSE AND THE CURE
The battleship *Maine* on the morning after the explosion (opposite page), and Theodore Roosevelt surrounded by his Rough Riders (left).

sionism was the charge that in betraying the cherished principles of the Declaration of Independence, their country had abandoned the moral law. Charles Eliot Norton, professor of the arts at Harvard, spoke to this point most eloquently:

We believe that America had something better to offer to mankind than those aims she is now pursuing, and we mourn her desertion of her ideals which were not selfish nor limited in their application, but which are of universal worth and validity. She has lost her unique position as a potential leader in the program of civilization, and has taken up her place simply as one of the grasping and selfish nations of the present day.

A few of the older anti-imperialists looked back to a less complex world of a half-century earlier, when the United States, as one traditionalist put it, was "provincial, dominated by the New England idea." These venerable men, however, were joined by younger pragmatic critics of imperialism, among them William James, who skillfully probed the false "realism" of the expansionists and dissected their empty arguments. As the bloody and inconclusive pacification program in the Philippines dragged on and the freedom fighter Emilio Aguinaldo gave American troops a lesson in jungle warfare, James centered

his own attack on the American inclination to substitute "bald and hollow abstractions" for the "intensely living and concrete situation." An unrestrained appetite for power, he scoffed, had caused the country to "puke up its ancient soul . . . in five minutes without a wink of squeamishness."

Could there be a more damning indictment of that whole bloated idol termed "modern civilization" than this amounts to? Civilization is, then, the big, hollow, resounding, corrupting, sophisticating, confusing torrent of mere brutal momentum and irrationality that brings forth fruits like this?

Until the Philippine uprising revealed the shallowness of American expressions of benevolence, the opponents of expansion made very little headway against the winds of imperial destiny. McKinley, after wrestling with his conscience, announced that "without any desire or design on our part," the war had brought new duties to "a great nation." Accordingly, he instructed his peace commissioners to stand firm against any and all Spanish protests over the dismantling of Spain's empire. By the terms of the peace treaty signed late in 1898, Spain agreed to dismemberment, giving up Cuba, the Philippines, Puerto Rico, and Guam. In 1898 the United States also an-

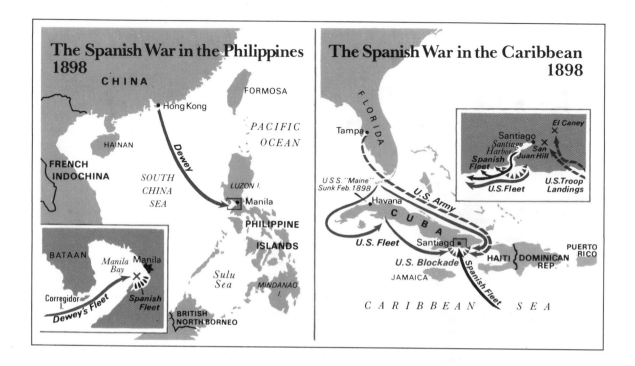

The Spanish War in the Philippines 1898

The Spanish War in the Caribbean 1898

nexed Hawaii, which was dominated by American sugar planters who five years earlier had overthrown the native queen, Liliuokalani, and established a nominal republic.

Colonial Fruits of War. In the Senate the treaty was taken in hand by the Republican faithfuls, including Lodge and Beveridge, who were aided in their work by Bryan's odd notion that the course of empire could only be determined in the presidential election of 1900. The majority of senators agreed with Beveridge in striking a balance between the immediate material rewards of expansion and long-term spiritual gains. "It is God's great purpose," Beveridge declared, "made manifest in the instincts of the race whose present phase is our personal profit, but whose far-off end is the redemption of the world and the Christianization of mankind." Despite the anti-imperialists' warnings that the nation was descending from the "ancient path" of republican righteousness into the "cesspool" of imperialism, the Senate voted fifty-seven to twenty-seven to accept the treaty. Hawaii became an incorporated territory under the Organic Act of 1900. Guam was acquired as a naval station administered by the Navy Department. And Puerto Rico, under the Foraker Act (1900), was attached as unincorporated territory with an elective legislature and a governor appointed by the president.

With the gathering of the colonial fruits of war with Spain and the arrival of Theodore Roosevelt in the White House, the initiative in formulating foreign policy fell to the activists who agreed with the new president that the aggressive pursuit of national interest provided the only sound base for a democratic foreign policy. "If we stand idly by," Roosevelt warned as the century opened, "if we seek merely swollen, slothful ease and ignoble peace, if we shrink from the hard contests where men must win at hazard of their lives and the risk of all they hold dear, then the bolder and stronger people will pass us by. . . . Let us therefore boldly face the life of strife." Strife marked and often marred Roosevelt's conduct of foreign policy from first to last—in Cuba and Panama and throughout Latin America, and in American dealings with China and Japan. In the Roosevelt years national interest came to mean national egotism.

In Cuba the occupation by American forces continued as the United States launched a program of administrative and public health reforms that culminated in a successful campaign against yellow fever. The Platt Amendment of 1901 drew even tighter the "ties of singular intimacy" between the United States and the island by providing for American intervention in case an unstable new government failed to protect life, liberty, and property. With the help of some heavy pressure on the Cuban leadership, this provision was written into the new republic's constitution in 1901 and was incorporated in the treaty between Cuba and the United States two years later. By 1903 the United States, despite earlier disavowals, had established a virtual protectorate on the island and reserved to itself the right to intervene in the internal affairs of its

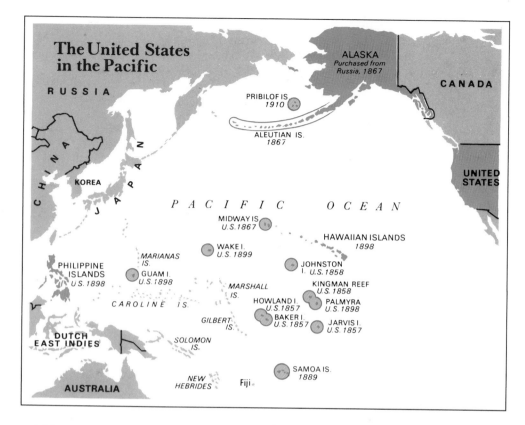

The United States in the Pacific

neighbor, a privilege it would regularly invoke in the next half-century.

In the Philippines the establishment of American control awaited the outcome of Aguinaldo's uprising, which dragged on until March 1901, when the Filipino leader was captured and his scattered forces surrendered. Under the terms of the Philippine Organic Act of 1902, the United States provided for a bicameral legislature and a governor with broad executive powers appointed by the president. Although there would be a gradual loosening of the governmental reins in the Philippines for the next three decades, full independence would not be achieved until 1946.

The turn of the century marked the final achievements of American expansion. Within a decade the dreams of a handful of "large policy" advocates had become a reality. The United States, without actually willing it, had acquired an imperial base for commercial and ideological expansion throughout the world.

Open and Closed Doors: Progressive Foreign Policy Under Roosevelt and Taft

If a "splendid little war" had suddenly thrust the United States into the ranks of the world's big powers, the war's aftermath taught corrective lessons on the limits of American influence. The United States proved a slow and often stubborn pupil in the school of international power politics, and as late as 1914, when war broke out in Europe, it still had much to learn about world affairs and a democracy's proper role in managing them.

An "Open Door" in China.
American education in the limits of power began in China at the turn of the century. The dream of a rich and limitless China market was older than the nation itself; it had been a prime motive in original explorations and in the search for the fabled Northwest Passage. After the American Revolution the dream became a reality as the new nation began to open markets in the Far East to compensate for the loss of old ones. Success in these distant markets in the age of the clipper ships, the 1840s and 1850s, continued to feed American hopes for gaining untold riches in the Orient. Still, by the end of the nineteenth century, less than 2 percent of United States foreign trade involved China, and it was with expectations of increasing this slim total that commercial and banking interests, concession hunters, and investment seekers nervously watched European influence mount in the Far East. The fatal weakness of the Manchu dynasty, which ruled China, had become apparent in China's disastrous war with Japan in 1894–95. By 1900 Germany, France, Russia, and Japan had secured

generous "spheres of influence" in China, together with exclusive economic "concessions" to develop these areas through long-term leases and special trading privileges. If the United States intended to establish its own foothold on the Chinese mainland, it would have to move quickly.

Once again, as in the case of the Monroe Doctrine seventy-five years earlier, American and British interests coincided on the point of equal trading rights and market opportunity for all nations. And once again the British Foreign Office proposed a joint statement, only to be told by the McKinley administration that the United States preferred to make its own unilateral pronouncement. The result of this decision was a series of notes dispatched to the European capitals and Tokyo by Secretary of State John Hay, announcing America's Open Door policy. This policy embodied three principles. Nations with spheres of influence in China (1) would promise to respect the "vested interests" of other nations within their own spheres; (2) would agree to allow Chinese customs officials to continue to collect duties in every sphere of interest "no matter to what nationality it may belong"; and (3) would pledge not to discriminate against competitor nations in levying port dues and railroad rates within their respective spheres of interest. At best Secretary Hay received ambiguous replies from all the governments to which he had sent the notes setting forth American policy. Nevertheless, he boldly announced the "final and definitive" acceptance of the principles of the Open Door.

Hay's optimism was soon severely tested by the Boxer Rebellion, a series of militant antiforeign riots in China that cut off the international community in Peking from the outside world. The European powers, Japan, and the United States retaliated by sending a rescue expedition (including 2,500 American soldiers fresh from the Philippines) to lift the siege and punish the Chinese nationalists. Once again the road lay open to further Chinese concessions that might lead to the dismantlement of the Chinese empire. Now Hay was forced to write a second note to the other powers, this one announcing simply that the United States intended to maintain the territorial integrity of the empire. Here was a sharp departure in American diplomacy—not simply a commitment to preserving equal economic opportunity on the mainland, but a pledge to uphold the sovereignty of China.

The Open Door, it was clear, would control imperialistic ambitions exactly to the extent that Britain and the United States wanted it to. Events soon disillusioned American policymakers. The Chinese empire lay in shambles, its days numbered before revolution toppled the dynasty in 1911. In the decade between the Boxer Rebellion and the outbreak of the Chinese Revolution, Britain accepted the inevitable by hastening to make overtures to Japan, acknowledging that country's predominant interests on the Chinese mainland. Meanwhile the rivalry between Russia and Japan over mining and railroad concessions in Manchuria led to the outbreak of war in 1904. In a series of smashing victories over the Russians, Japan played to perfection the part of "underdog" so appealing to Americans, and forced Russia to accept the mediation of President Roosevelt, who suddenly appeared in the unfamiliar role of peacemaker.

The Portsmouth Treaty. The Portsmouth (New Hampshire) Treaty of 1905, which Roosevelt forced on an unhappy but thoroughly beaten Russia, established Japan as the dominant power in the Far East. But the treaty did not advance the principles of the Open Door. In a secret agreement in 1907, Russia and Japan agreed to divide Manchuria, Mongolia, and Korea into spheres of influence with "special interests." Roosevelt reluctantly recognized Japan's special interests in Manchuria in the Root-Takahira Agreement (1908), thus presiding over the ceremonial closing of the Open Door. Although the president admitted that the Open Door principle was "an excellent thing" so far as it could be upheld by general diplomatic agreement, he nevertheless confessed that the policy simply disappeared once a nation like Japan chose to disregard it. In this sense the Open Door ended in failure.

Intervention in North Africa. In the Moroccan crisis of 1905–06, Roosevelt managed to salvage at least some aspects of an Open Door policy while improving on his record as a peacemaker. The crisis grew out of conflicting French and German interests in North Africa, and a clash resulted in which the United States, according to Roosevelt's secretary of state, Elihu Root, was not justified in taking "a leading part." Nevertheless, Roosevelt broke a tradition of nonintervention by actively directing the Algeciras Conference (1906). As he intended, the settlement halted German penetration of North Africa momentarily, united France and Great Britain in solid opposition to Kaiser Wilhelm II, and reaffirmed for the United States the principles of the Open Door. Roosevelt, who already distrusted German military power, boasted of having stood the Kaiser on his head "with great decision." Yet imperial Germany soon righted itself, and it was clear that Roosevelt's departure from a century-long tradition of nonentanglement in European affairs would not soon be repeated.

Intervention in the Caribbean. No such doubts about the American role of policeman inhibited progressive foreign policy in the Caribbean. Here economic interests

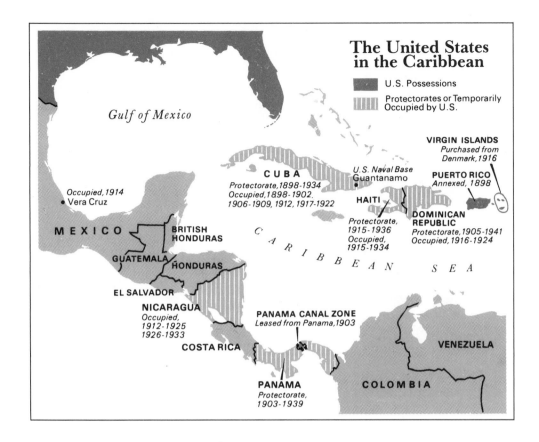

The United States in the Caribbean

▨ U.S. Possessions

▥ Protectorates or Temporarily Occupied by U.S.

Gulf of Mexico

VIRGIN ISLANDS
Purchased from Denmark, 1916

CUBA
Protectorate, 1898-1934
Occupied, 1898-1902,
1906-1909, 1912, 1917-1922

U.S. Naval Base
Guantanamo

PUERTO RICO
Annexed, 1898

HAITI

DOMINICAN REPUBLIC
Protectorate, 1905-1941
Occupied, 1916-1924

HAITI
Protectorate,
1915-1936
Occupied,
1915-1934

Occupied, 1914
• Vera Cruz

MEXICO

BRITISH HONDURAS

GUATEMALA

HONDURAS

EL SALVADOR

NICARAGUA
Occupied,
1912-1925
1926-1933

COSTA RICA

PANAMA CANAL ZONE
Leased from Panama, 1903

VENEZUELA

CARIBBEAN SEA

COLOMBIA

PANAMA
Protectorate,
1903-1939

and dominant American power combined in a short-sighted policy of constant intervention that would leave a legacy of ill will and distrust. American interference in the internal affairs of unstable Latin American governments quickly became a pattern. Behind this pattern lay rapidly expanding American economic interests—not just in trade, but in banking, investments, and the development of natural resources, all of which seemingly required a favorable political climate and the willingness of Caribbean governments to grant generous concessions to the United States.

Trouble began in that "infernal little Cuban republic," as Roosevelt called it, in admitting to a recurrent urge to "wipe its people off the face of the earth." Four years after the removal of American forces in 1902, the troops were back again for another attempt at restoring order. A policeman's lot, the president agreed, was not a happy one. "All that we wanted from them was that they would behave themselves and be prosperous and happy so that we would not have to interfere." Instead, the Cubans persisted in playing at revolution and "may get things into such a snarl that we have no alternative save to intervene—which will at once convince the suspicious idiots in South America that we do wish to interfere after all, and perhaps

have some land hunger." The president neglected to add that it was not land hunger but the drive to establish economic dominance in Latin America that dictated his interventionist strategy.

A habit of constantly intervening in the domestic affairs of neighbors to the south required an explanation, and Roosevelt provided this in the famous "corollary" to the Monroe Doctrine in his annual message to Congress in 1905. Once again, as in Cleveland's administration ten years earlier, the occasion was a fiscal crisis in Venezuela, where a chronically unstable and corrupt dictatorship refused to honor its debts. In 1903 Germany tried to nudge the Venezuelan government toward a more conciliatory stance by bombarding Fort San Carlos, and the Germans were dissuaded from taking further measures only by prompt American condemnation of the "outrage." To forestall similar European moves to protect their investments, Roosevelt offered his corollary. "Chronic wrongdoing," he admitted, would inevitably invite retaliation from the "civilized" nations determined to protect their investments in Latin America. Since the Monroe Doctrine effectively prevented the European powers from intervening directly, the United States, "however reluctantly," might be forced to step in "in

DIGGING THE PANAMA CANAL
Roosevelt poses at the controls of a giant steam shovel in Panama.

Bettmann Archive, Inc.

triqued Americans for more than a century. A combination of French adventurers and American entrepreneurs succeeded in convincing Roosevelt, Mark Hanna, and other Republican leaders of the distinct advantages of the route through Panama, which was then a province of Colombia. With the help of a few carefully placed investments in the future of their party, they managed to win congressional support for their lucrative deal. By 1902 all that remained was to convince the inept Colombian government of the benefits that civilization was about to confer.

For a while negotiations proceeded smoothly. The Hay-Herran Treaty of 1903 gave the United States rights to a canal zone six miles wide for the price of $10 million plus an annual rental of $250,000. Then suddenly Colombian patriots, preparing to overthrow a corrupt dictator and realizing that they were being swindled, forced the Colombian senate to withdraw the treaty.

Roosevelt duly denounced his new opponents as "inefficient bandits" and "contemptible little creatures" who were willfully blocking the march of progress across the hemisphere. With his initial scheme now frustrated, the president agreed to an alternative plan for a pocket revolution in Panama, engineered by canal promoters and by a handful of native *insurrectos*, who proceeded to establish Panamanian independence from Colombia with the blessing of the United States and the help of its navy. After hasty recognition by the United States, the new state of Panama obliged its benefactor by granting the terms for the canal that Colombia had just refused. Roosevelt had his canal project, the Panamanian patriots had their revolution, and the promoters had their profits. Roosevelt never ceased defending his part in the affair. "If I had followed traditional conservative methods, I would have submitted a dignified state paper of probably two hundred pages to Congress and the debates on it would have been going on yet; but I took the Canal Zone and let Congress debate; and while the debate goes on the Canal does also."

Roosevelt's Style of Diplomacy.

With this bald assertion of presidential and national power, Roosevelt drew together the strands of his diplomacy. In the first place, his diplomatic style was a highly personal one that assumed that most of the issues in foreign affairs were best handled, as he said, "by one man alone." Although on occasion he made effective use of his secretaries of state, John Hay and Elihu Root, just as often he bypassed them completely, and he seldom gave them credit for decisions that he rightly or wrongly considered his own. Roosevelt was determined to play the lone hand, and he fumed at the Senate's constant interference and its tampering with what he considered an executive prerogative. Deliberative bodies, he insisted, were virtually useless when there was "any

flagrant cases of such wrongdoing or impotence." In short, Latin America properly belonged within the sphere of influence of the United States, which would undertake the work of an "international police power."

The meaning of the Roosevelt Corollary became clear in the Dominican Republic in 1905 when, after considerable urging from the United States, the Dominican government agreed to request American assistance in straightening out its finances. Despite congressional reservations, President Roosevelt was more than happy to provide such advice. With the control of the Dominican customhouse firmly in American hands, the United States succeeded in preventing German intervention once again, but at the cost of a policy that would continue to breed hemispheric ill will throughout the twentieth century.

The Panama Canal Affair.

The problem of Panama and of securing American rights to a canal across the Central American isthmus offered the clearest example of a foreign policy based on narrow and shortsighted national interest. High-powered lobbying by the new Panama Canal Company, the successor of a defunct French company that had tried and failed to build a Panamanian canal, caused the American government to abandon the Nicaraguan route, which had inefficient work" to be done. It was for the president alone to take charge of foreign policy in the same way that he took the lead in formulating domestic priorities of reform and reorganization. His aim in intervening in Latin American affairs, he later wrote, was to wake up the American people "so that they would back a reasonable and intelligent foreign policy which would have put a stop to the crying disorders at our very doors."

"Crying disorders"—here was the link between domestic progressive reform and foreign policy. Order and stability in Asia, Roosevelt was to learn, lay beyond the reach of American policy. In Europe, where his leverage was greater, he could mix balance-of-power diplomacy with hopes for a perpetual Anglo-American supremacy throughout the world. But it was in the Western Hemisphere that the benefits of order and system seemed to him the greatest, and he did not hesitate to seek these benefits for American business.

Although Roosevelt presided over the transformation of territorial imperialism into a policy of economic penetration, his language revealed his ignorance of his historical role. He spoke constantly of "honor, territorial integrity and vital interests" as the only basis for an American foreign policy. There were higher things in life, he kept insisting, than the enjoyment of material comforts or the pursuit of wealth. "It is through strife, or the readiness for strife, that a nation must win greatness." And greatness for Roosevelt was primarily spiritual. His speeches rang with the clichés of "righteousness" and "duty" as he combined moralism and nationalism in a blend of power politics that glossed over the hard economic motives he never clearly acknowledged.

The central theme running through Roosevelt's foreign policy pronouncements was the danger that American preoccupation with domestic prosperity would turn right-minded citizens into a mere "assemblage of well-to-do hucksters" who cared for nothing beyond their own borders. But to argue the case for an aggressive foreign policy purely in terms of high-mindedness was to ignore the economic forces that increasingly controlled the making of American foreign policy. These forces included investment opportunities, concessions, corporate resource development, and other forms of economic penetration—all requiring political and economic stability, which was essential to the effective exploitation of colonial economies. Roosevelt's rhetoric concealed the fact that as president he became, if not the captive, at least the ally of exactly the economic forces he presumably distrusted.

Taft's "Dollar Diplomacy."

The Taft administration substituted dollars for bullets and displayed no such squeamishness in acknowledging the reality of economic imperialism. Taft's choice of secretary of state,

corporation lawyer Philander C. Knox, was itself proof of the growing intimacy between the Wall Street investment community and the State Department. Knox, who was given a much freer hand in formulating policy than Roosevelt had allowed his secretaries of state, was the chief architect of Taft's program of "dollar diplomacy." Dollar diplomacy, a form of democratic state capitalism, used American export capital, together with dominant political and military power, to give force, as Taft himself put it, "alike to idealistic humanitarian sentiments, to the dictates of sound policy and strategy, and to legitimate commercial aims."

Dollar diplomacy extended the principles of domestic progressivism to the conduct of foreign policy. Investment capitalists were encouraged to proceed with the economic penetration of undeveloped areas under conditions of stability and profitability provided by the government. "In China," Taft told Congress in citing his favorite example, "the policy of encouraging financial investment to enable that country to help itself has had the result of giving new life and practical application to the open-door policy." Taft's administration was committed to encouraging the use of American capital in China to promote "those essential reforms" that China had pledged to the United States and to the other major powers. Taft offered for congressional approval a "new diplomacy," practiced by a foreign service "alert and equipped to cooperate with the businessmen of America" and dedicated to "improved governmental methods of protecting and stimulating it."

Taft's open avowal of the economic motive did not alter the pattern of American success and failure—conspicuous success in attracting investment to nearby Latin America, where the bankers were more than willing to go, and nearly total failure in the Far East, where the bankers were not willing to go. In attempting to open China once more to American capital, Taft met the determined resistance of British, French, and German bankers, who excluded the Americans from an international business group to finance and build the Hukuang Railway in China, an ill-considered project that was never completed. By placing heavy diplomatic pressure on the Chinese emperor, Knox succeeded in gaining admission to the railway consortium. But he needlessly made trouble for himself by another poorly conceived experiment in state capitalism in Manchuria. Like Hay's original plan, the Taft administration's attempt to pry open the door for American capital ended in failure.

No such difficulties were encountered in Latin America, where American capital continued to pour in. Here a combination of supersalesmanship and regular government intervention to protect American investments—in Nicaragua, Guatemala, Honduras, and Haiti—kept the gates open.

Taft's foreign policy concentrated on Latin America and the Far East and virtually neglected Europe. In warning against an exclusive concern with the Far East, progressive writer Herbert Croly (who had also presumed to advise Roosevelt in *The Promise of American Life*) predicted the early arrival of an international confrontation of major powers that might force the United States to interfere "in what may at first appear to be a purely European complication." When that time came, Croly hastened to add, American policymakers ought to meet it with "a sound, well-informed, and positive conception of American national interest rather than a negative and ignorant conception." Taft, however, preferred to keep his distance. The legal framework for dollar diplomacy was provided by a deep faith in arbitration: with arbitration Taft hoped to defuse international crises in much the same way that boards of mediators in domestic affairs depoliticized economic conflict. Twenty-five arbitration treaties had been signed in the last days of the outgoing Roosevelt administration, and Taft sought to apply the same principle to all "justiciable" issues. The Senate, however, eliminated the procedures for discussion and consultation in every case in which the United States might be presumed to have an interest. Nevertheless, the arbitration scheme lived on as a progressive panacea, drawing the attention of Woodrow Wilson and his secretary of state, the "Prince of Peace," William Jennings Bryan. There would be continuities as well as new departures in Wilson's missionary diplomacy.

"The Organized Force of Mankind": Wilsonian Diplomacy and World War

At first Woodrow Wilson appeared to represent a new constituency in American foreign policy. The years after 1900 saw peace groups, proponents of arbitration, and other idealists combine in a broad coalition behind the principles of missionary diplomacy, moral publicity, and open rather than secret international agreements. In rejecting both Roosevelt's role of big brother to the oppressed and Taft's dollar diplomacy, Wilson entered office with an appeal to national high-mindedness that warmed the hearts of moralists everywhere. "My dream is that as the years go on and the world knows more and more of America," the president told a Fourth of July audience in 1914, "it . . . will turn to America for those moral inspirations which lie at the basis of all freedoms . . . and that America will come into the full light of day when all shall know that she puts human rights above all other rights and that her flag is the flag not only of America but of humanity." Yet three months earlier Wilson had ordered the occupation of the Mexican port of Vera Cruz to vindicate American honor.

One of the ironies of American foreign relations in the early twentieth century was that both of the widely divergent formulations of policy—national egotism and national high-mindedness—led directly to similar involvements of the United States throughout the world and almost constantly to forcible intervention in the affairs of neighboring countries. Both the demands of national interest and the less precise requirements of moral mission ended in the application of raw power. By 1917 the United States had clearly arrived as a world power, but it remained to be seen how American power would be used in reordering a world at war. Americans entered the First World War still seeking an answer to this question.

Like most Americans before 1914, Woodrow Wilson had given little serious attention to the specifics of American foreign policy. Diplomatic questions had not figured prominently in the campaign of 1912, and to solve such questions Wilson could offer only the conventional wisdom of an active peace movement in the United States concerning the exportability of the American democratic way. During his two terms Wilson often served as the mouthpiece of this movement and adopted many of its principles, fashioning them into an alternative to balance-of-power politics.

By 1914 there was a well-established faith among progressive intellectuals in the imminent arrival of an age of international harmony. Progressive reformers and professionals believed that improved worldwide communications, international technology, and arbitration would soon create a new moral order. The peace movement in the United States was made up of a variety of groups and interests: church-affiliated peace societies and new secular foundations (including Andrew Carnegie's Endowment for International Peace); students of international law intent on constructing new legal frameworks; preachers of disarmament; and prophets of a vast people-to-people crusade. Many of these peace advocates shared a uniquely American set of assumptions that defined peace as an adjunct to domestic progressive reform.

Arbitration: The Key to World Order.
The first of these assumptions was the belief that the path to world order had been discovered by the United States as it progressed from a loose federation of sovereign states to a genuine union of all the people. From similar beginnings, the promoters of peace reasoned, one world of harmony and democratic striving might take shape. A second assumption that was associated with this golden vision of an Americanized world order was a stubborn faith in arbitration itself. Arbitration, many assumed, was a key mechanism for resolving

tensions and potential conflicts. This mechanism could take various forms: the International Court at the Hague, the Netherlands, which had been created by international agreement in 1899; a body of international law; or bilateral "cooling off" treaties.

These progressive beliefs led Wilson to accept the views of the peace advocates. His language, like Roosevelt's, was consistently abstract. But whereas Roosevelt, a self-declared "realist," spoke of national duty, honor, and integrity, Wilson translated these terms into the language of idealism. He denounced narrowly understood national interest as "selfishness" and the rule of unbridled materialism. "Balance of power" to him meant unstable coalitions of aggressive interests. The outlook of "average" people the world over, on the other hand, was becoming "more and more unclouded" as national purposes fell more and more into the background and the "common purpose of enlightened mankind" took their place. Wilson spoke of the time, not far distant, when these "counsels of plain men" would come to replace the "counsels of sophisticated men of affairs" as the best means of securing peace. Then the statesmen of the world would be forced to heed the "common clarified thought," or they would be broken.

These views constituted a preliminary version of Wilson's plan for an alternative system of world politics, which had begun to take shape in his mind even before war broke out in Europe. Wilson's schoolmasterish language was equal to his vision as he took on what his critics called his "papal role" in dispensing a humanitarian theology. "I do not know that there will ever be a declaration of independence or grievances for mankind," he told an audience at Independence Hall in Philadelphia in 1914, scarcely a week before the outbreak of war, "but I believe that if any such document is ever drawn it will be drawn in the spirit of the American Declaration of Independence, and that America has lifted high the light which will shine unto all generations and guide the feet of mankind to the goal of justice and liberty and peace." The president, noted the acid-tongued editors of *The New Republic* magazine, uttered nothing that might sound trivial at the Last Judgment.

The first fruits of this Wilsonian "missionary" spirit were bitter ones for the promoters of dollar diplomacy. Wilson quickly dashed the hopes of the outgoing Taft administration for continued investment in China by rejecting a scheme for railroad financing as a violation of Chinese sovereignty. In the delicate negotiations over the Panama Canal tolls, he argued that American exemption from payment showed a "dishonorable attitude," and at the risk of dividing his own party he secured a repeal. Then in October 1913, in an address in Mobile, Alabama, that became famous, he completed the reversal of dollar diplomacy by promising to emancipate Latin America from its "subordination" to "foreign enterprise."

Intervention in Mexico.

Yet in Latin America, where U.S. business interests were real and compelling, Wilson found it impossible to reverse his predecessors' policy of intervention. His formal disavowal of American interference ended in bitter irony. In fact, under Wilson the United States intervened in the affairs of its neighbors more often than ever before. There was a military occupation of Haiti in 1915; financial supervision in the Dominican Republic in 1916; renewed controls in Cuba in 1917; and minor meddling in behalf of American investors throughout the Caribbean. Moralistic though he frequently was, Wilson was not blind to the operation of economic motives nor deaf to the appeals of American entrepreneurs. His difficulties in Latin America resulted in large part from his tendency to identify the beneficent workings of American capital with the welfare of "the submerged eighty-five per cent" of native populations, to whom he wanted to bring the blessings of parliamentary democracy.

Wilson's theories of moral diplomacy were tested by events in Mexico and were found inadequate. In 1911, following a long period of oppressive rule, Mexican dictator Porfirio Díaz was overthrown by moderate constitutionalists led by Francisco Madero. The new government received prompt recognition from the Taft administration. Then, less than two years later, Madero himself fell victim to a counterrevolutionary coup directed by one of his lieutenants, Victoriano Huerta, who murdered his former chief and seized the presidency. This was the situation confronting Wilson as he took office.

Outraged by Huerta's brutality, Wilson lost no time in denouncing him as a thug and a butcher, and refused to recognize his government. Wilson's refusal to grant recognition rested partly on genuine moral revulsion but also on the knowledge that Britain had recognized Huerta's dictatorship in the hope of gaining further economic concessions. Wilson meant to put an end to Britain's pretensions by toppling Huerta. Although economic and strategic concerns usually appeared on the fringes of Wilson's moral vision, they were never quite out of sight. He continued to insist that the United States must never abandon morality for expediency. But in Mexico, profits for American investors and parliamentary democracy for the Mexican people seemed to him wholly compatible.

Wilson was determined to replace Huerta with the moderate rule of Venustiano Carranza, another constitutionalist who had succeeded in rallying popular opposition to the dictator. Wilson seized the occa-

[both] *Library of Congress*

MEXICAN-AMERICAN RELATIONS, 1916–17
Pancho Villa's raid on a New Mexico town and his murder of American citizens called for a U.S. punitive expedition led by General John J. Pershing.

sion for overthrowing Huerta when a boatload of American sailors was arrested and unlawfully detained in Tampico. The president demanded an immediate apology. When Huerta predictably refused to concede to a government that had refused to recognize him, Wilson ordered the occupation of Vera Cruz, an exercise that cost the lives of nineteen Americans and a great many more Mexicans. Under heavy pressure from the United States, and besieged by the forces of Carranza's constitutionalists, Huerta resigned and fled to Spain in 1914. Yet Carranza's liberal regime was no more willing to tolerate American intervention than the deposed dictator had been. Only a timely offer by the so-called ABC Powers (Argentina, Brazil, and Chile) to mediate the dispute allowed Wilson to withdraw American forces and save face.

The second act of the Mexican crisis opened with the attempt of Pancho Villa, a bandit leader and an unsavory associate of Carranza, to overthrow his chief and take power for himself by provoking war with the United States. Wilson very nearly obliged him. On January 10, 1916, Villa and his band stopped a train at Santa Ysabel in the northern provinces, took seventeen Americans off, and shot sixteen of them. Then in March Villa raided the tiny New Mexico town of Columbus, burned it to the ground, and killed nineteen more American citizens. Wilson responded, as Villa had hoped he would, by dispatching General John J. Pershing and his troops on a punitive expedition. Pershing chased the bandit chief some three hundred miles back into Mexico without managing to catch him. Carranza demanded the immediate withdrawal of Pershing's expeditionary force. Faced with the near certainty of war with Germany, Wilson could only comply. In 1917, as Villa roamed the Mexican countryside and an unstable Carranza government lurched toward still another constitutional crisis, Wilson had nothing to show for his five-year labors. Now, however, his attention was fixed on Europe.

War in Europe. In the summer of 1914 the First World War broke out in Europe. When Serbian nationalists assassinated the heir of the multinational Austro-Hungarian empire in June 1914, Austria-Hungary decided to crush its troublesome small neighbor, Serbia. Russia, as Serbia's protector, warned Austria-Hungary not to attack and began to mobilize its vast armies. Germany, which regarded Austria-Hungary as its sole dependable ally, demanded that Russia halt its mobilization; when the Russian czar refused, Germany declared war on August 1. Germany then demanded that Russia's ally, France, give assurances that it would not come to Russia's aid; and when these assurances were not offered, Germany declared war on France on August 3. Germany promptly set its military plan in motion by striking a heavy blow in the west to knock out France before the slow-moving Russian armies could do serious harm in the east. The German plan involved an invasion of France through neutral Belgium. On August 4, when Germany attacked Belgium, Britain declared war on Germany. The German armies in the west drove deeply into northern France, but Paris was saved, and by the late fall of 1914 the war had settled down to a bloody stalemate on the Western Front. After a Russian offensive against Germany and Austria-Hungary failed, a similar stalemate developed in eastern Europe. Meanwhile Japan entered the war in order to seize Germany's Pacific islands and holdings in China. By 1915 Italy had joined the anti-German coalition, and Bulgaria and Turkey had taken Germany's side.

The outbreak of war caught the Wilson administration and the entire United States by surprise. At first the news that Austria was threatening tiny Serbia evoked little more than the traditional American sympathy for the underdog. Because neither European nor American diplomats yet realized the scope of the coming catastrophe, it was not difficult for Wilson to declare American neutrality and to call on all citizens to remain "impartial in thought as well as in action." Behind the proclamation of neutrality lay the president's conviction that the war would be a short one that would end in a settlement that the United States, from its Olympian station above the battle, could help arrange. And behind this unwarranted assumption lay still another belief—that America could play an effective role in creating a new moral order.

As the war dragged into its second year, all of Wilson's hopes for remodeling the world of power politics came to hinge on a doctrine of neutrality that itself rested on two misconceptions. First, developments quickly showed that the United States was not and could not be unconcerned with the outcome of the war. As shrewd observers had noted before the war broke out, Britain had directly contributed to American growth and well-being by upholding the European balance of power throughout the entire nineteenth century. And Germany, at least since 1890, had consistently threatened American security with a belligerent new diplomacy, an arms buildup, and a frightening doctrine of militarism. An Anglo-German conflict was thus bound to affect the United States in crucial ways.

The first year of the war drove this lesson home.

Britain increasingly monopolized direct access to information about the war and supplied the American press with a constant stream of accounts (most of them greatly exaggerated) of German "atrocities." Except for many German Americans and Irish Americans, ordinary people in the United States came to view the war in pro-Allied, anti-German terms, even if they did not favor actual American entry. The British skillfully manipulated their propaganda advantage until the president and his advisers came to argue, as one of them put it, that "Germany must not be permitted to win this war." By 1915 the administration began, not always consciously, to act on that assumption. The American economy was placed at the disposal of the Allies, who, despite the embarrassing presence on their side of Imperial Russia, were presumed to be fighting autocracy and militarism in the name of democracy and freedom. The government proclaimed trade with the Allies "legal and welcome." When Allied credit soon evaporated, American bankers rushed to the rescue with credits and loans that totaled $2.5 billion by the time the United States entered the war in 1917. On the other hand, there were virtually no American wartime investments in Germany. Wilson continued to press both Britain and Germany for a settlement of the war, but when neither side agreed he tended to excuse the former and blame the latter for the disastrous military stalemate.

The *Lusitania* Incident.

The second misconception underlying Wilson's doctrine of neutrality stemmed from his failure to understand the logic of total war or to acknowledge the effect of modern technology. The submarine had made the traditional rights of neutrals obsolete. As they grappled for an economic stranglehold on each other, both combatants had to resort to novel practices that were clear violations of the established rules of war. Britain extended the right of naval search to new lengths and established a blockade that virtually extinguished the rights of neutrals. Yet American diplomatic exchange with Britain settled into a predictable pattern of violation, protest, discussion, and eventual resumption of the objectionable practice.

With Germany, on the other hand, the exchange grew brittle, and Wilson's language became increasingly blunt. The Germans' use of submarines, which struck without warning and made no provision for the safety of passengers and crew, touched a raw nerve in the American people. When in May 1915 a German U-boat torpedoed without warning the British liner *Lusitania* with the loss of 128 American lives, Wilson initiated an angry dialogue that grew more and more strident in the next year and a half. Germany quite correctly pointed out that the ship was carrying

PRESIDENT WILSON CONSIDERS HIS DWINDLING OPTIONS

the president. Submarine warfare, he informed Germany, "of necessity, because of the very character of the vessels employed," was "incompatible" with the "sacred immunities of noncombatants." Unless the Kaiser's government agreed to abandon its methods forthwith, the United States would have no choice but to sever relations. Germany agreed to discontinue the practice, but only if the United States could force Britain to lift the blockade. Until then the German government reserved the right to take back its pledge. The president's options were dwindling fast.

Wilson's growing indignation reflected another, more personal, anxiety. For three years he had continued to pile a heavy load of moral principles onto the conventional concept of neutral rights. Now he was forced to admit that the United States might not be able to impose its will on warring Europe without joining the Allies. A nation that, as he had said, had been "too proud to fight" and that had reelected him on the slogan "He kept us out of war" now faced the prospect of securing a "peace without victory" only by becoming a participant. As he became aware of this, Wilson began to redefine America's mission as nothing less than the building of a system of collective security to replace the collapsed system of balance of power. If compelled to fight, the United States would fight for utopia.

A New World Order. In January 1917, a week before Germany announced its decision to resume unrestricted submarine warfare, Wilson described his vision of a new world order to the Senate. The United States, prepared by "the very principles and purposes" of its humanitarian policy, must rebuild the machinery of diplomacy. Its terms for peace must "win the approval of mankind" and not merely "serve the several interests and immediate aims of the nations engaged." As an integral part of the peace settlement, Wilson proposed the establishment of a perpetual league of peaceful nations. This league should be a collective instrument that would be "so much greater than the force of any nation now engaged or any alliance hitherto projected," that governments and their leaders would instinctively bend to its dictates. The future of the world would thus come to depend not on a balance of power, but on a community of opinion; not on "organized rivalries," but on "organized peace." Wilson proposed, in short, to concentrate the moral force of peoples themselves who, with open convenants openly arrived at, would enforce their collective will for national self-determination, democratic government, and lasting peace. To skeptical senators, particularly those in the Republican ranks, Wilson explained that his were at once "American principles" and "the principles of all mankind."

munitions, but that fact hardly weakened Wilson's determination to apply the old rules. For the president, the sinking of the *Lusitania* was proof of the practical impossibility of using submarines "without disregarding those rules of fairness, reason, justice, and humanity, which all modern opinion regards as imperative." In deciding to hold Germany "strictly accountable," Wilson put the United States on a collision course. Secretary of State Bryan, realizing that Wilson's policy was no longer truly neutral, resigned in protest.

In the meantime, following the *Lusitania* incident, Germany said it would comply with Wilson's terms. Then in 1916 the German attack on the unarmed French passenger ship *Sussex* in the English Channel resulted in injury to American citizens, and the meaning of "strict accountability" suddenly became clear to

LIBERTY LOAN DRIVE
The American people prepare
for war.

A week later the German imperial government renewed its submarine attacks in a desperate gamble to win the war before the United States could enter. In March German submarines without warning sank four unarmed American merchantmen, and on April 2, 1917, Wilson appeared before a joint session of Congress to request that it accept the war that had been "thrust" upon the United States. By a vote of 82 to 6 in the Senate and 373 to 50 in the House, Congress agreed to the presidential request.

United States citizens would learn from a year and a half of war and another year of peacemaking that their country had arrived at a position of world power that very few of them could have envisioned thirty years earlier. The nation had gone to war with Spain on the flimsiest of pretexts and had built an empire on its victory. But in the intervening years most Americans, far from embracing imperial responsibilities, had neglected the chores of maintaining an empire. Except in their own hemisphere, they had forgotten their regenerative mission. Now as their president called on them to fight another and infinitely greater war, they turned to him for a sense of direction and for a definition of their moral commitment.

For his part the president, having determined that war was the only option left open to him, made a prophecy to the nation and a private confession in considering his course. "We are at the beginning of an age," he told the country, "in which it will be insisted that the same standards of conduct and responsibility for wrong done shall be observed among nations and their governments that are observed among individual citizens of civilized states." But privately, in the solitude of the White House on the eve of his appearance before Congress, he admitted to fears about the unintended and uncontrollable effects of going to war. "Once lead this people into war," he told Frank Cobb, the editor of the New York *World*, "and they'll forget there ever was such a thing as tolerance. To fight you must be brutal and ruthless, and the spirit of ruthless brutality will enter into the very fibre of our national life, infecting Congress, the courts, the policeman on the beat, the man in the streets." The meaning of Wilson's prophecy of a new international morality awaited the outcome of the war, but his prediction of the domestic dangers involved in fighting it soon proved all too accurate.

1895 United States intervenes in boundary dispute between Britain and Venezuela as Secretary of State Richard Olney declares nation "practically sovereign on this continent."

Spain sends troops to quell Cuban revolution.

1896 Cuban rebel leader Maceo murdered, resulting in American popular support for Cuba.

William McKinley elected president.

1897 A letter from Spanish minister to Washington, Depuy de Lôme, in which he calls McKinley "weak" and "a would-be politician," is intercepted, worsening American and Spanish relations.

U.S. battleship *Maine* explodes in Havana harbor.

1898 Spanish-American War; United States acquires Philippines, Puerto Rico, and Guam, and annexes Hawaii.

1899 Hay's "Open Door" notes to world powers, calling for "equal and impartial trade" in China and preservation of "Chinese territorial and administrative" integrity.

Senate ratifies peace treaty with Spain.

United States, Germany, and Great Britain partition Samoa.

1900 Foraker Act establishes civil government in Puerto Rico.

Organic Act incorporates Hawaii as a territory of the United States.

McKinley reelected president, defeating Bryan once again.

Boxer Rebellion in China.

1901 Platt Amendment authorizes U.S. intervention in Cuba.

Theodore Roosevelt becomes president after McKinley assassinated.

Hay-Pauncefote Treaty with Great Britain gives United States sole right to build, control, and maintain neutrality of an isthmian canal in Central America.

Philippine Organic Act passed, making Philippine islands an unorganized territory of the U.S.

1902 United States returns civil government to Republic of Cuba.

1903 Hay-Herran Treaty with Republic of Colombia, giving United States ninety-nine-year lease on Canal Zone, is rejected by Colombia.

Roosevelt aids revolt in Panama.

Hay-Bunau-Varilla Treaty gives United States full sovereignty in Canal Zone.

United States–Cuba reciprocity treaty forms close economic ties between both countries.

1904 Roosevelt Corollary to Monroe Doctrine.

Roosevelt elected, defeating Democrat Alton B. Parker and Socialist Eugene V. Debs.

1905 Roosevelt mediates in Russo-Japanese War.

1906 American troops intervene in Cuba to restore order.

Algeciras Conference with Roosevelt's help settles French-German conflict in Morocco.

1908 William Howard Taft elected president, defeating Bryan and Debs.

Root-Takahira Agreement; United States recognizes Japan's interests in Manchuria.

1909 Taft inaugurates "Dollar Diplomacy" in China and Latin America.

United States intervenes in Haitian and Nicaraguan finances.

1911 Marines sent to Nicaragua.

1912 Woodrow Wilson elected president, defeating Republican regular William Howard Taft, progressive "Bull Moose" Theodore Roosevelt, and Socialist Eugene V. Debs.

1914 First World War begins; Wilson declares American neutrality.

Wilson orders occupation of Vera Cruz, Mexico.

Panama Canal opened.

1915 United States troops occupy Haiti.

United States recognizes Carranza government in Mexico.

Germans declare unrestricted submarine warfare and sink *Lusitania* with loss of American lives.

Preparedness movement.

1916 Wilson reelected, narrowly defeating Charles Evans Hughes.

House-Grey Memorandum on United States' efforts for negotiated peace.

American troops occupy Dominican Republic.

General John J. Pershing's expedition into Mexico.

1917 Germans resume unrestricted submarine warfare and United States enters war.

Purchase of Danish Virgin Islands.

The boundaries of post-1890 American foreign policy are established in two critical surveys. George F. Kennan, *American Diplomacy, 1900–1950* (1951), points to consistently unprofessional and uninformed leaders as the chief difficulty, while William Appleman Williams, *The Tragedy of American Diplomacy* (1959), cites economic expansion as the source of a peculiar kind of American imperialism. Robert E. Osgood, *Ideals and Self-Interest in America's Foreign Relations* (1953), evaluates the positions of both parties to the great debate over ends and means in the conduct of American diplomacy. Richard W. Leopold, *The Growth of American Foreign Policy* (1962), provides an excellent survey of the development of American interests in the rest of the world, as does Foster R. Dulles, *America's Rise to World Power, 1898–1954* (1955).

The origins of American expansionism are critically but carefully examined in Walter LaFeber, *The New Empire: An Interpretation of American Expansion, 1860–1898* (1963). The best account of the diplomatic crisis leading to the Spanish-American War is Ernest R. May, *Imperial Democracy: The Emergence of America as a Great Power* (1961). Robert L. Beisner, *The Anti-Imperialists, 1898–1900* (1968), and E. Berkeley Tompkins, *Anti-Imperialism in the United States: The Great Debate, 1890–1920* (1970), assess the arguments and the futile activities of the opponents of expansionism. Leon Wolff, *Little Brown Brother* (1961), gives an outraged account of the Philippine insurrection and the American pacification program.

Areas of growing American interest and control in international affairs have been covered in a number of excellent monographs: Merze Tate, *The United States and the Hawaiian Kingdom* (1965); Charles Vevier, *The United States and China, 1906–1913* (1955); Paul A. Varg, *The Making of a Myth: The United States and China, 1899–1912*; Warren Cohen, *America's Response to China* (1971); Charles E. Neu, *The Troubled Encounter: The United States and Japan* (1975); Howard F. Cline, *The United States and Mexico* (1953);

Samuel F. Bemis, *The Latin American Policy of the United States* (1967).

On Theodore Roosevelt's foreign policy see Howard K. Beale, *Theodore Roosevelt and the Rise of America to World Power* (1956), and the more recent Raymond A. Esthus, *Theodore Roosevelt and the International Rivalries* (1970). Dwight C. Miner, *Fight for the Panama Route* (1966), tells a complicated story well, and Robert A. Hart, *The Great White Fleet: Its Voyage Around the World* (1965), is a highly readable account of Roosevelt's colorful gesture. Walter V. Scholes and Marie V. Scholes, *The Foreign Policies of the Taft Administration* (1970), analyzes the workings of dollar diplomacy, and Dana G. Munroe, *Intervention and Dollar Diplomacy in the Caribbean, 1900–1921* (1964), examines its consequences in Latin America.

The fullest discussion of Woodrow Wilson's diplomacy from a presidential point of view is to be found in the volumes of Link's *Wilson*. P. Edward Haley, *Revolution and Intervention: The Diplomacy of Taft and Wilson with Mexico, 1910–1917* (1970), is an even-handed assessment of Mexican policy, as is Robert Freeman Smith, *The U.S. and Revolutionary Nationalism in Mexico* (1972), for the later period. Robert E, Quirk, *An Affair of Honor: Woodrow Wilson and the Occupation of Veracruz* (1962), criticizes the president for his misguided actions in that unfortunate affair.

Neutrality and American intervention in the First World War fascinated a depression generation reluctantly preparing for another war and produced a number of highly critical accounts of American intervention, the best of which is Walter Millis, *The Road to War* (1935). Among the best of more recent accounts are Ernest R. May, *The World War and American Isolation, 1914–1917* (1959); John M. Cooper, Jr., *The Vanity of Power: American Isolation and the First World War, 1914–1917* (1969); Ross Gregory, *The Origins of American Intervention in the First World War* (1971); and Daniel M. Smith, *The Great Departure: The United States in World War I, 1914–1920* (1965).

27 Progressivism and the Great War

By the time the United States entered the war in April 1917, the European powers were rapidly approaching exhaustion. After three years of stalemate, Germany was suffering from starvation as a result of Britain's naval blockade, as well as a collapse of civilian morale. Austria-Hungary managed to continue the war only by imposing martial law. Russia was crippled by astronomical losses that had led to the overthrow of the czarist regime in March 1917, and now it stood on the brink of a second revolution that would bring Lenin's Bolsheviks to power by the end of the year. France, its national will shattered, faced widespread mutiny in its armies. Britain, having sacrificed an entire generation of young men to German machine guns since 1914, was beset with severe manpower shortages both at home and in the field.

Slaughter on the Western Front

The original prediction of both sides—Germany's hopes for a six-week war and the Allies' plans for rolling back the enemy on the vast Western and Eastern fronts—had long since been buried under mounds of casualties. Shared strategic obsessions with artillery barrages and with massed infantry assaults on entrenched positions had created a war of appalling senselessness and butchery. Two million casualties on the Western Front in 1916 had failed to move the line of advance for either side, and the war had descended once again into the trenches, which stretched in an unbroken line from the sea to the mountains. A week after President Wilson asked for a declaration of war in April 1917, the British launched still another frontal assault in Belgium on the Ypres sector of the front; in five days they gained only 7,000 yards, at the terrible cost of 160,000 dead and wounded.

Although the United States entered the war late and suffered proportionately fewer losses, the meaning of the slaughter lingered in the American imag-

ination for a generation. In a scene in F. Scott Fitzgerald's *Tender Is the Night*, one of the characters leads a party of sightseers across the Somme Valley after the war. "See that little stream," he says. "We could walk to it in two minutes. It took the British a whole month to walk to it—a whole empire walking very slowly, dying in front and pushing forward behind. And another empire walked very slowly backward a few inches a day, leaving the dead like a million bloody rugs." American soldiers in the last year of the war followed the footsteps of their British and French predecessors. In joining the Allies the United States committed its forces to a war in which the ultimate loser was the side that won the most battles. Woodrow Wilson's hopes for a just peace died along with more than 100,000 American soldiers on the Western Front.

It took eight months for American troops to join the fighting on the Western Front in effective numbers, and it was nearly a year before they were decisively engaged in helping to turn back the final German offensive. In the meantime the Allied cause hung in the balance. In November 1917 Lenin and the Bolsheviks overthrew the provisional revolutionary government of Russia, established a party dictatorship, and took Russia out of the war. Russia's withdrawal released badly needed German divisions for a last offensive on the Western Front. In the spring drive along the Somme beginning in March 1918, the Germans routed the British and penned up the French, but without making a decisive breakthrough.

In May and June the American Second Division was dispatched to the Marne River, where it bolstered sagging French defenses. In the first big American engagements of the war, United States forces halted a German advance at Chateau-Thierry and slowly drove the enemy out of Belleau Wood. These American actions were only preliminaries to the great Allied counteroffensive, which in late summer began to push the German army relentlessly back toward its frontier. By

670

UPI/Bettmann Archive

SAYING GOOD-BYE . . .
War Department photograph, 1917.

National Archives

abdicate, and a coalition of socialists and liberals proclaimed a republic. Forty-eight hours later the new German republic accepted as the basis for an armistice the peace proposals that Wilson had put forward in January 1918, the Fourteen Points.* The Great War was over.

It was immediately clear that the American entry had brought desperately needed troops and supplies to the Allies at a critical moment. American troops provided the decisive advantage of power needed to win the war. Equally important was the role of the United States in replenishing stockpiles of food and materiel with its "bridge of ships," replacing the merchantmen sunk by German submarines, and experimenting successfully with the convoy system of protecting Allied shipping, which in the last analysis saved the Allies. The American contribution was essential, and it came at a crucial time. Yet despite the provisional German acceptance of the Fourteen Points as the agenda for peacemaking, the American war effort had not wiped out national fears and hatreds embodied in wartime secret agreements and arrangements among the Allies, nor had it established the moral climate, either at home or in Europe, that Wilson knew was essential to lasting peace.

With the American entrance, a conflict that had already grown fiercely ideological became a crusade for democracy and national rebirth. All the powers had secured control over the actions and opinions of their civilian populations as they accepted the logic of total war. But the United States entry completed an ideological shift for the Allies by defining the war in moral as well as political terms, as a struggle of the forces of peace and democracy against the dark powers of militarism. In announcing his Fourteen Points, and by explaining American war aims as "the right of those who submit to authority to have a voice in their own government" and "a universal dominion of right by . . . a concert of free peoples," Wilson unconsciously hardened the resolve of his allies to seek an unconditional surrender and a punishing peace. Perhaps the greatest irony of the First World War lay in the president's determination to inject into it a democratic ideology that in the end would make his own role as the evenhanded peacemaker impossible.

Total war also imposed an organizational logic on the participants, all of whom were forced to adjust to the national need for centralization and control. Early in the war Germany recruited civilian administrators for its War Raw Materials Department, which established efficient mechanisms for allocating manpower, arms, and equipment. Britain organized its dwindling resources under the Defense of the Realm Act, which

September the American commander, General John J. Pershing, who had stubbornly held out for an independent command, had over half a million men at his disposal, a number that would double by the end of the war two months later. In October Pershing, in conjunction with British and French offensives elsewhere along the line, opened a massive American drive out of the Argonne Forest aimed at the railhead at Sedan—the last sustained American action of the war.

On November 3 Austria-Hungary collapsed, and on the same day the German navy mutinied at its main base, Kiel, raising the specter of another communist revolution. Six days later a general strike in Germany, led by the Independent Socialists, forced the Kaiser to

*For the Fourteen Points, see below, p. 688 ff.

AMERICAN SOLDIERS IN FRANCE
Elderly French couple welcomes American doughboys.

provided for full mobilization of all available manpower. France, which had lost its northern industrial provinces for the duration, used the powers of government to relocate factories and regulate food production. Once in the war the United States followed the same pattern in building a war machine, enlisting civilians in the war effort, and improvising the bureaucratic controls demanded by the emergency. By the time the war ended in November 1918, Wilson's administration had completed an organizational revolution and had brought the power of government into nearly every phase of American life.

War and the Health of the State

For some progressives the coming of the war seemed a heaven-sent opportunity to realize the American promise. The war, they confidently predicted, would bring genuine national unity and an end to class and ethnic division. It would discredit dangerous radicalism by giving the nation's citizens a new spirit of patriotism. The demands of war would also destroy all selfish materialism and preoccupation with profits and replace both with the higher goals of service and sacrifice. National preparedness and mobilization,

central features of the New Nationalism, would foster moral virtue and civic purity in soldiers and civilians alike. Those progressives who continued to define their basic purpose as creating a new American morality and citizenship saw in the impending war effort the outlines of what one of them called a "true national collectivism" based on efficiency, social control, high-mindedness, and revived moral purpose.

On a more practical plane many more progressives responded enthusiastically to the organizational and reform challenges that were furnished by the war. Those reformers who saw their work as a form of moral cleansing—of vice, alcoholism, and prostitution—viewed the war as a chance to purify democracy at home while saving it abroad.

The war advanced the progressives' hopes in a number of important ways. The preparedness campaign furthered the ideal of universal military service as a school for citizenship. Americanization programs aimed at controlling the immigrant took on new life. Prohibitionist hopes soared, and women's suffrage suddenly seemed possible. City planners, social-justice workers, child-labor reformers, and other progressive humanitarians warmed to the prospects of a domestic reformation in the midst of a foreign war.

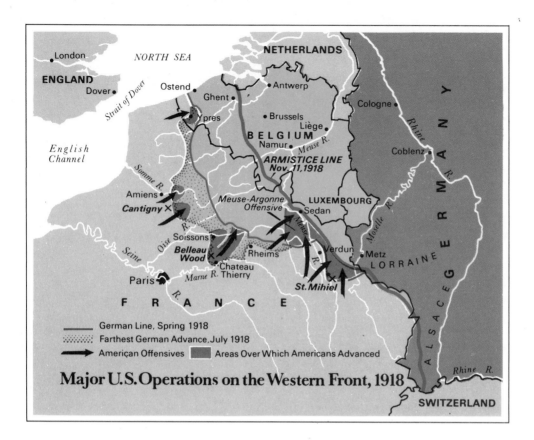

Major U.S. Operations on the Western Front, 1918

German Line, Spring 1918
Farthest German Advance, July 1918
American Offensives
Areas Over Which Americans Advanced

The war seemed to hold the greatest promise for progressives in administration and public service—those reformers who sought to join Roosevelt's New Nationalist emphasis on efficiency, administrative centralization, and executive power with Wilson's New Freedom faith in fact finding, voluntary cooperation, and democratic participation. "We must speak, act, and serve together," Wilson reminded the nation. Efficiency quickly became the watchword for a new managerial elite that descended on Washington with proposals for a planned war effort. Wesley C. Mitchell, a professor-turned-bureaucrat who joined the Division of Planning and Statistics of the War Industries Board, explained why government service appealed to professionals and businessmen, many of whom signed up for the duration. "Indeed I am in a mood to demand excitement and make it up when it doesn't offer of itself. I am ready to concoct a new plan for running the universe at any minute." Efficiency as the dominant progressive ideal fixed itself to the image of the war machine turning out men and materiel automatically without the interference of politics and partisanship.

Regulations and Controls. American performance fell far short of the progressive ideal. The most urgent task for Wilson's war state was mobilizing industry. Even be-

fore war was declared, Congress established the Council of National Defense, an advisory body composed of cabinet members and industrial and labor leaders, which was charged with taking an inventory of national resources. Out of the council's preliminary survey came the War Industries Board, which attempted—at first unsuccessfully—to control production, arrange purchases, allocate scarce resources, and regulate labor relations. The War Industries Board failed to function effectively until Congress overhauled it, conferring near-dictatorial powers on the president. In turn Wilson brought Wall Street banker Bernard Baruch to Washington early in 1918 to head the agency and gave him sweeping powers to establish priorities and increase production. Baruch's agency, however, was hampered in its work by inadequate information. By the end of the war, the War Industries Board was just beginning to unsnarl the problems of production.

In addition to regulating industry, Wilson moved quickly to bring food, fuel, and transportation under control. To head the Food Administration he appointed Herbert Hoover, who used his powers under the Lever Act to extend government control over staples. Poor harvests complicated Hoover's problems, and he was forced to experiment with price fixing and

FIFTEENTH REGIMENT ON
FIFTH AVENUE

a massive consumer-education campaign to limit consumption. His strategy succeeded, first doubling and then tripling the amount of food that could be exported to starving Europe. Hoover's efficient management of food production represented the chief accomplishment of wartime progressivism. The Fuel Administration, headed by progressive Harry A. Garfield, followed Hoover's lead in the Food Administration by seeking to increase coal production with price supports fixed to guarantee profits, and, less successfully, with schemes for systematizing production and distribution on a national scale.

Managing the nation's railroads proved even more difficult than increasing food production. At first Wilson experimented unsuccessfully with a voluntary system under the Railroads War Board. Attempts to increase the number of railroad cars and to equalize traffic broke down completely in December 1917. Congress demanded an investigation, out of which came a revised United States Railroad Administration with effective power. Gradually the Railroad Administration extricated itself from confusion, and by the end of the war it too, like the War Industries Board, was beginning to function effectively. Shipping presented Wilson's administration with its most severe problem. Here the challenge was deceptively simple—to build

or commandeer ships faster than the German U-boats could sink them. The solution, the Emergency Fleet Corporation—originally an offshoot of the United States Shipping Board—failed. Divided leadership impeded effective planning, and the heads of the competing agencies spent half the war quarreling over priorities and programs. Wilson finally removed them and put the competing interests under a single director. By September 1918 the Emergency Fleet Corporation had built only 500,000 tons of new shipping, less than German submarines had sunk in an average month early in 1917.

The Wilson administration's labor policy was aimed at including the workingman in the wartime partnership with business and government—as a junior partner, but one entitled to a fair share of war prosperity. Yet here too success came slowly. Not until April 1918 did Wilson move to establish the National War Labor Board, with power to hear and settle disputes between labor and management. Under the direction of former President Taft and progressive lawyer Frank P. Walsh, the National War Labor Board heard over a thousand cases during the war involving three-quarters of a million workers. In general, Wilson's labor policy was a generous one that was designed to tolerate, if not encourage, unions; to estab-

"OVER THERE"

U.S. Air Force

American aviators prepare to take off in French-built Caudron in France (1918).

lish an eight-hour workday; to avert strikes through the use of arbitration; and to sanction limited increases in wages.

Overall, the wartime effort in planning was hardly an unqualified success. Lacking an effectual bureaucracy at the outset, Wilson's administration necessarily fumbled and improvised, dispersing rather than centralizing power through a host of overlapping and competing agencies. Not surprisingly, confusion and inefficiency resulted as bureaucrats painfully groped their way toward centralization, learning slowly from their many mistakes. When the armistice came, the American war machine was just beginning to produce at a level approaching full capacity.

The most important consequence of the national war effort was the completion of the alliance between big business and the government. This collaboration was inevitable, because it was only from within the consolidated national industries that the government could recruit needed managerial talent. To Washington, accordingly, came the leaders of business and industry, primed with patriotism but also determined to advance the interests of their sector—which they

quickly identified with the national good. Wilson's appointment of Bernard Baruch was only the most visible symbol of this new alliance. From the ranks of railroad management and from big steel, the machine tool industry, finance, and banking came the self-appointed leaders of national mobilization. Along with expertise all of them brought demands for stability and predictability in their industries, which could be furnished only by the government.

Corporate War Profits. Big business profited from the war directly and indirectly—directly, in the form of arrangements like the cost-plus contract, which guaranteed high levels of profit; indirectly, in the education that business leaders received in the uses of government power. Labor fared less well. The cost of living, soaring on the crest of wartime inflation, more than doubled between 1913 and 1920 and cut deeply into wage increases. Farmers benefited from a substantial rise in real income during the war, a gain that would quickly disappear with the return of peace. But corporate profits skyrocketed in the years between 1914 and 1919, increasing threefold by the time the United States entered the war and leveling off in the following

Library of Congress

National Archives

WOMEN ON THE HOME FRONT
Women contributed significantly to the war effort with various kinds of work.

years at an annual increase of 30 percent. Gains in the steel industry ranged from 30 percent to 300 percent. In the lumber industry they averaged 17 percent; in oil, 21 percent; in copper, 34 percent. Even with the moderate excess-profits tax and steeper levies on higher incomes, the war made an estimated 42,000 millionaires. If the progressive programs of Theodore Roosevelt and Woodrow Wilson had sought, at least in part, a fairer distribution of American wealth, the war tended to reverse the effects of their efforts by piling up profits in the upper reaches of the economy.

The progressive plans for constructing an effective system of bureaucratic management also came to little. American governmental bureaucracy in 1917 was still in its infancy. The handful of federal agencies at the policymaking level—the Federal Reserve Board, the Federal Trade Commission, and other fledgling agencies—had not yet fully asserted their powers. Inevitably, the wartime administrative apparatus creaked and strained under the pressures of mobilization. Ambitious reorganizational schemes were never carried out. Programs broke down. Authority almost always overlapped, and agencies collided over matters of precedence and priority. By a method

marked by more trial and error than most progressives expected, the United States moved hesitantly from administrative chaos to at least some bureaucratic order at war's end.

Repression and Hysteria. If the gains for the federal bureaucracy brought by the war proved partial and in some cases temporary, the same was not true of the wartime campaign for loyalty and uniformity. Here the original progressive dream of an aroused and patriotic citizenry turned into a chauvinist nightmare, and the country experienced a crisis of civil liberties.

The American people responded to war with a spontaneous burst of nationalist fervor, which triggered a chain reaction of repression and hysteria. In the first few months of the war, hundreds of thousands of self-styled patriots banded together in vigilantelike groups bearing impressive titles—the American Defense Society, the National Security League, the American Anti-Anarchy Association, even the Boy Spies of America—and dedicated to rooting out heresy wherever they found it. The directors of these grassroots purges were usually leaders in local communities—businessmen, professionals, and merchants—who

For American radicals and dissenters of all kinds, the First World War brought a reign of terror. In the following excerpt a member of the IWW in Oklahoma tells of his experiences at the hands of a local mob of businessmen given a free hand by the police.

A Vigilante Group Assaults the IWW

ON the night of November 5, 1917, five men entered the hall, to whom I at first paid no attention, as I was busy putting a monthly stamp in a member's union card book. After I had finished with the member, I walked back to where these five men had congregated at the baggage-room at the back of the hall, and spoke to them, asking if there was anything I could do for them.

One, who appeared to be the leader, answered "No, we're just looking the place over." . . . I told him we were paying rent for the hall, and I did not think anyone had a right to search this place without a warrant. He replied that he did not give a damn if we were paying rent for four places, they would search them whenever they felt like it. . . .

Shortly after, the patrol-wagon came and all the members in the hall—10 men—were ordered into the wagon. . . . We were taken to the police station. . . .

Trial on a charge of vagrancy was set for November 7th. . . . After some argument . . . the case against Gunnard Johnson, one of our men, was called. After four and a half hours' session the case was again adjourned until November 9th at 5 P.M., when we agreed to let the decision in Johnson's case stand for all of us. . . .

Johnson . . . was reprimanded by the judge for not having a Liberty Bond, and as near as anyone could judge from the closing remarks of Judge Evans, he was found guilty and fined $100 for not having a Liberty Bond.

Our lawyer made a motion to appeal the case and the bonds were then fixed at $200 each. I was immediately arrested, *as were also five spectators in the open court-room*, for being I.W.W.'s. . . .

In about forty minutes, as near as we could judge about 11 P.M., the turnkey came and called "Get ready to go out you I.W.W. men." We dressed as rapidly as possible, were taken out of the cells, and the officer gave us back our possessions. . . . We were immediately ordered into automobiles waiting in the alley. Then we proceeded one block north . . . and stopped.

Then the masked mob came up and ordered everybody to throw up their hands. . . . We were then bound, . . . [and] the police were ordered to "beat it," which they did, running, and we started for the place of execution.

When we arrived there, a company of gowned and masked gunmen were there to meet us standing at "present arms." We were ordered out of the autos, told to get in line in front of these gunmen, and another bunch of men with automatics and pistols lined up between us. Our hands were still held up, and those who were bound, in front. Then a masked man walked down the line and slashed the ropes that bound us, and we were ordered to strip to the waist, which we did, threw our clothes in front of us, in individual piles—coats, vests, hats, shirts, and undershirts. The boys not having had time to distribute their possessions that were given back to them at the police station, everything was in the coats, everything we owned in the world.

Then the whipping began. A double piece of new rope, $\frac{5}{8}$ or $\frac{3}{4}$ hemp, being used. A man, "the chief" of detectives, stopped the whipping of each man when he thought the victim had had enough. After each one was whipped another man applied the tar with a large brush, from the head to the seat. Then a brute smeared feathers over and rubbed them in.

After they had satisfied themselves that our bodies were well abused, our clothing was thrown into a pile, gasoline poured on it and a match applied. By the light of our earthly possessions, we were ordered to leave Tulsa, and leave running and never come back. The night was dark, the road very rough, and as I was one of the last two that was whipped, tarred and feathered, and in the rear when ordered to run, I decided to be shot rather than stumble over the rough road. After going forty or fifty feet I stopped and went into the weeds. I told the man with me to get in the weeds also, as the shots were coming very close over us, and ordered him to lie down flat. We expected to be killed, but after 150 or 200 shots were fired they got in their autos.

After the last one had left, we went through a barbed-wire fence, across a field, called to the boys, collected them, counted up, and had all the 16 safe, though sore and nasty with tar. . . . I built a fire to keep us from freezing.

We stood around the fire expecting to be shot, as we did not know but what some tool of the commercial club had followed us. After a long time . . . we . . . found an I. W. W. friend . . . and 5 gallons of coal oil or kerosene, with which we cleaned the filthy stuff off of each other, and our troubles were over, as friends sent clothing and money to us that day, it being about 3 or 3:30 A.M. when we reached the cabin.

JOIN THE NAVY
America's new prestige in world affairs will mean a greater Navy
BE A PART OF IT

AMERICA ADVANCES

Apply at Navy Recruiting Station:

U. S. NAVY RECRUITING S
LAW BUILDING

WORLD WAR I RECRUITMENT POSTER

combined more useful service for the Red Cross and Y.M.C.A. with the witch-hunting escapades common to superpatriots in any age. Wilson's administration, unable or unwilling to stop these popular excesses, joined in purging dissent. The result was a fevered public uprising against nonconformity of all kinds, and the ruthless suppression of American liberties.

The war hysteria fed a progressive appetite for national unity that had not been offset by a tradition of civil liberties. The central weakness of the progressive program had been the absence of a libertarian concern with protecting basic freedoms, and this absence made a domestic war on liberalism wholly predictable. Patriots and vigilantes, equipped with ropes, whips, and tar and feathers, enjoyed a ritualistic field day complete with flag-kissing ceremonies and forced declarations of loyalty. German Americans, including some prominent persons, were often the targets of this

reign of terror. But the victims were mainly marginal people, uneducated or alienated, isolated and without power. In Bisbee, Arizona, the "best" people rounded up some 1,200 striking miners led by the Industrial Workers of the World ("Wobblies"), piled them into freight cars, and hauled them across the state line into the desert, where they were left stranded. In Montana a mob dragged the IWW organizer Frank Little out of his boardinghouse and hanged him from a railroad trestle. Soon the federal government itself joined in the campaign to crush radical dissent: in September 1917 Justice Department agents rounded up 113 officers and organizers of the IWW and impounded five tons of books and pamphlets with which to arraign and convict them.

Out of these acts of suppression came loose national organizations and federations, perversions of the original progressive consumer and reform leagues, dedicated to rooting out subversion and punishing disloyalty. With support from local and state law enforcement agencies, the National Security League and the Council of Defense fixed on new targets—the Non-Partisan League in North Dakota, which aimed at nothing more seditious than interest-group politics, and the People's Council of America for Peace and Democracy, a group of pacifists widely condemned as "traitors and fools." Within six months of Wilson's declaration of war, a rigid censorship, combined with political repression, had reached into the American press, schools and universities, the churches, and even the new movie industry.

A Pyramid of Repression. This mass popular reaction formed the base of a pyramid of repression supporting a middle range of official and semiofficial bodies, from citizens' councils to state administrative agencies such as the Minnesota Commission on Public Safety, which became a model for the rest of the country. Other states passed criminal syndicalism laws that were aimed primarily at left-wing dissenters but were also designed as dragnets for a variety of nonconformists. Soon the traditional American distinction between public and private had dissolved in a welter of competing patriotic agencies.

The federal government itself completed the apex of this national system of extralegalism through a number of agencies and activities. The chief agency was the Committee on Public Information, headed by progressive journalist George Creel and charged with mobilizing public opinion behind the war. Creel perfected the progressive technique of moral publicity and encouraged a voluntary censorship program. And he turned to the new public relations industry for a national core of opinion shapers, who launched a propaganda campaign of frightening proportions.

Another weapon in the government's domestic arsenal was an administrative technique inherited from prewar progressivism—deportation of undesirable aliens and radicals. The deportation procedure was a simple administrative process. Not courts but magistrates made the decision to deport undesirable aliens. As a result, maximum freedom was provided for administrators and minimum safeguards for the rights of the accused. This original procedure for the swift removal of undesirables had been created by the Immigration Act of 1903, and the war simply gave widened scope for these summary actions.

The federal government's main contributions to the repression of basic liberties were the Espionage Act of 1917 and the Sedition Act of 1918. Like the Federalists' Alien and Sedition Acts of the 1790s,* these laws were twin declarations of bankruptcy by a society that had reached the limits of toleration. The Espionage Act dictated fines of up to $10,000 and twenty years in prison for anyone convicted of causing insubordination, mutiny, or disloyalty in the armed forces by "false reports or false statements." The law also empowered the postmaster general to withhold mailing privileges to newspapers and periodicals that were considered subversive. Wilson's postmaster general, Albert S. Burleson, turned this authority into a formidable weapon against dissent. With Wilson's knowledge, if not always with his approval, Burleson wielded discretionary power with a vengeance in banning socialist periodicals such as *The Masses* and Victor Berger's *Milwaukee Leader*; he even banned a single-tax journal for suggesting that more revenue be raised through taxation.

The Sedition Act of 1918 was designed to close the few loopholes in the Espionage Act through which thousands of "spies" and "traitors" were presumed to have escaped. The new law provided punishment for anyone who should "utter, print, write or publish any disloyal, profane, scurrilous, or abusive language about the form of government in the United States, or the uniform of the Army or Navy" or any sentiments intended to bring the government or the military "into contempt, scorn, contumely, or disrepute."

More than 1,500 Americans were tried and more than 1,000 convicted under these laws. Senator Hiram Johnson pointed out that the government was simply warning, "You shall not criticize anything or anybody in the Government any longer or you shall go to jail." For example, Eugene Debs was convicted and sentenced to ten years in prison under the Sedition Act for telling a socialist audience that the master class causes wars while the subject class fights them. But most of the victims of this heresy hunting were ordinary people guilty of nothing worse than saying that

*For the Alien and Sedition Acts, see chapter 10, p. 251.

John D. Rockefeller was a son of a bitch who helped start a capitalist war.

Administrative Agencies. In part, the war hysteria of the years 1917–19 was simply a deviation, a brief departure from good sense, and a betrayal of progressive ideals. But at a deeper level the excesses were growths—malignant, to be sure—of progressivism itself. Discretionary power vested in administrative agencies—a progressive innovation—provided flexibility and promptness but at the expense of more deliberate regular processes amenable to judicial oversight. The progressive device of administrative government, whose aim was to free policymakers and administrators from constant interference by the legislature, had its merits. But when it was applied to citizens' ideas and opinions rather than to administrative procedures, the new process revealed the evils of government action cut adrift from accountability and control.

At times the war crisis lowered the principle of administrative autonomy to the level of license. In the case of Postmaster General Burleson, for example, even the president was unable to limit misguided enthusiasm and the personal conviction that no American should ever be allowed "to say that this Government got into the war wrong. . . . It is a false statement," Burleson fumed, "a lie, and it will not be permitted." Such arbitrary power lodged either in the federal bureaucracy or in the lower levels of state and local administrations inevitably fostered an alarming national irresponsibility by subjecting opinion and expression to the whims and caprices of petty officials who were freed entirely, as one of them boasted, from "exaggerated sentimentalism [or] a misapplied reverence for legal axioms."

It would have been difficult in any case for Wilson's administration to have curbed the patriotic passions of an American generation preoccupied with rescuing national unity from a vigorous cultural pluralism. But the wartime policy of the federal government amounted to issuing hunting licenses to superpatriots to track down and destroy dissent—in pacifists, liberal reformers, socialists, anarchists, and also in many cultural as well as political radicals opposed to the war. These dissenters were not simply outside the mainstream of the war effort. They were part of a more general movement, growing quickly after 1900, of what might be called cultural radicalism—a movement running counter to progressivism with deep roots in America's prewar experience. By 1917 a major shift in the artistic and intellectual life of the country had long been evident in a series of clashes, some symbolic and others real, between an inherited system of truth and the powerful, diverse forces of cultural modernism.

The Little Rebellion: Progressivism and the Challenge of Culture

On February 17, 1913, the International Exhibition of Modern Painting opened in the cavernous Sixty-Ninth Regiment Armory in New York City. To the music of a military band, beneath rafters festooned with huge banners and pine boughs, visitors strolled through a maze of 1,600 paintings, drawings, prints, and pieces of sculpture. The Armory Show, two years in the planning, took for its motto "The New Spirit," which was emblazoned on a mammoth replica of the Revolutionary-era Massachusetts Pine Tree flag—a message that many American viewers translated as "the harbinger of universal anarchy."

The exhibition had originally been conceived as a strictly American affair, and it was actually dominated numerically by American work, which made up three-quarters of the show. The initial plans, however, had been scrapped for the more ambitious idea of a vast international retrospective tracing the rise of modernism from its nineteenth-century sources in Goya, Ingres, and Delacroix, through the French realist Courbet, to impressionism and the bewildering canvases of post-impressionists, expressionists, and cubists. It was not the dark, looming shapes of the American painter Albert Pinkham Ryder that outraged patrons, or the realistic cityscapes of the "New York Eight," with their conventional images and brushwork, but rather what one critic called "the imported ideology" of the new European artists—Picasso, Matisse, Brancusi, Picabia, Léger, Rouault, Kandinsky, Duchamp, and Lehmbruck. Their collective impact carried the force of revolution. Staid art critic Kenyon Cox admitted to spending "an appalling morning" at the show, where he had witnessed the "total destruction of the art of painting. . . . To have looked at it is to have passed through a pathological museum where the layman has no right to go. One feels that one has seen not an exhibition, but an exposure."

The Armory Show collected into a single public image the disparate meaning of European modernism. In the bold thin colors of Matisse's *The Red Studio* or the splashes of one of Kandinsky's *Improvisations* or the frozen motion of Duchamp's *Nude Descending a Staircase*, Americans viewed the results of a perceptual revolution that had transformed the European intellectual and artistic world and had now arrived in the United States. Here were the visible effects of a general revolt—embodied in the work of such controversial European cultural figures as Nietzsche, Bergson, Sorel, Freud, Ibsen, and Strindberg—against nineteenth-century positivism, with its faith in scientific objectivity. The new art was the all-too-apparent result of recent explorations into the unseen, the unknown, the irrational, and the relative, yielding new definitions of time, space, energy, force, and will. For those progressives who chose to examine the work of the modernists, the Armory Show took on the dimensions of a social crisis.

An Artistic Revolution. The crisis rose directly out of the challenge to the comfortable realism and moralism of the average educated American, who firmly believed in the solidity of the objective social world and in the power of "good art," whether in print or on canvas, to represent that world. Socially useful art, most progressives believed, was the art of representation. Progressivism was nourished by a strong sense of social reality— the belief that the world, after all, consisted of commonplace and everyday occurrences strung in orderly and predictable sequences. Progressivism had been born in the country and had moved to the city, and it relied upon the moral code of an earlier rural society to make otherwise bewildering problems manageable. There was also a lingering idealism in the progressive outlook—Theodore Roosevelt called it "practical idealism"—that combined easily with newly discovered techniques of social analysis. These two halves of the progressive outlook were held together by the belief that science and the scientific method, baffling as they might seem to the layman, would ultimately establish the unity of truth and the fact of progress.

These social opinions supported a set of aesthetic preferences. The progressives' favorite novelist was the reliable William Dean Howells, who once (like so many progressives) had been a young man from the provinces who had come to the metropolis to make his way. Howells built a career and a considerable fortune as a novelist and an editor with his cautious, sensitive probings of modern issues: divorce and the disintegration of the family; economic inequality and the insecurities of a commercial existence; the decline of an older business ethic in a new world of bigness. Howells weighed all these complexities in terms of the loss of certainty among small-town Americans and the hope that it might somehow be restored. In his portraits of the puzzled editor Basil March in *A Hazard of New Fortunes* and of the confused businessman in *The Rise of Silas Lapham*, Howells offered recognizable modern types, and progressive readers could find their own problems stated and finally solved in his fiction. And when realism paled, there was always fantasy and that favorite fictional hero, Owen Wister's "Virginian," the unassuming yet self-assured cowboy untainted by corrupting commercialism.

Tolerance of the excessive, the outsized, and the grotesque was strictly limited by a psychology that insisted on the rational, the measurable, the predicta-

THE ARMORY SHOW MAKES NEWS

Marcel Duchamp's cubistic "Nude Descending a Staircase" was one of the European paintings in the 1913 exhibit that outraged critics and viewers and inspired this *Chicago Record-Herald* cartoon "The Rude Descending a Staircase—Rush Hour on the Subway."

SEEING NEW YORK WITH A CUBIST

The Rude Descending a Staircase
(Rush Hour at the Subway)

ble. Whatever lay beyond these borders was ignored or rejected as unhealthy or unclean—Frank Norris's examination of regression and bestialism in *McTeague*, Henry James's subtle studies of corruption, Mark Twain's experiment in determinism in *The Mysterious Stranger*, Theodore Dreiser's frank exploration of sexuality in *Sister Carrie*.

In the visual arts informed opinion had reluctantly come to terms with the so-called Ashcan School of New York painters, among them John Sloan, George Luks, and George Bellows, whose realistic paintings of street scenes and city types (see color insert) drew from the same sources as those of progressive reformers and writers. The New York Eight, as members of this group were also called, sought to encompass the whole city scene with their illustrators' techniques and documentary style. Most progressives understood and accepted the social realism of the Eight, for it was directly involved with the pictorial aspects of twentieth-century urban life. "The tramp sits on the ege of the curb," the Eight's spokesman, Robert Henri, explained. "He is huddled up. His body is thick. His underlip hangs. His eyes look fierce. . . . He is not beautiful, but he could well be the motive for a great and beautiful work of art." Progressives who were engaged in similar explorations of city life agreed with Henri, for they shared his insistence on "fundamental law" and those axioms "controlling all existence." By 1910 realism had broken the Genteel Tradition's grip on the American imagination without, however, dissolving its view of objective reality.

It was just this sense of the manageability of their world that gave progressives the confidence to reform and improve it. Experimenting with the new tools of social analysis helped sharpen the progressive method, but it also strengthened the belief that the world was plastic after all and could be molded into a controlled environment. The recent knowledge explosion in American universities had shaken but not destroyed the progressive idea that the great facts in life were simple.

This conviction that art and politics amounted to the same thing made the Armory Show a troubling spectacle for most American viewers. It threatened not simply their aesthetic preferences, but also their belief in the possibilities of planning and social control. The "detestable things" created by Picasso, Matisse, and Duchamp—"degraded, indecent, and insane," they were called— disclosed the lurking presence of the unpredictable and the ungovernable, of flux and formlessness. A Matisse painting reminded humorist Gelett Burgess of the havoc a "sanguinary" girl of eight, "half-crazed with gin," might wreak on a blank wall with a box of crayons. In choosing a revolutionary

theme for their exhibition, the organizers of the Armory Show were only following the path their European counterparts had taken for more than a century. But American viewers took the show's political challenge literally. As one hostile critic announced: "The exploitation of a theory of discords, puzzles, ugliness, and clinical details is to art what anarchy is to society and the practitioners need not so much a critic as an alienist [psychiatrist]." Artistic madness would certainly lead to barbarism.

Criticism flowed naturally from aesthetic into political channels. "The United States is invaded by aliens," warned the archconservative critic Royal Cortissoz, "thousands of whom constitute so many acute perils to the health of the body politic. Modernism is of precisely the same heterogeneous alien origin and is imperiling the republic of art in the same way." The Armory Show, Cortissoz warned, was dominated "by types not yet fitted for their first papers in aesthetic naturalization—the makers of true Ellis Island art."

Proletarian Art: The Paterson Pageant.

Modernism in the Armory Show presented most viewers with a symbolic dilemma: how to ensure the improvement of American society without underwriting revolution. Once again, as in all other matters concerning America, Theodore Roosevelt had the last word. "It is vitally necessary," the retired president reminded his followers, "to move forward to shake off the dead hand of the reactionaries; and yet we have to face the fact that there is apt to be a lunatic fringe among votaries of any forward movement." Still, the problem remained— how to give support to the sane and deny it to the dangerous. The political evidence was obvious. In New York City on a June evening in 1913, less than four months after the Armory Show, 1,000 silk workers from Paterson, New Jersey, stepped off the ferry and marched in a solid phalanx up Broadway and into Madison Square Garden. There, before a crowd of 15,000, they proceeded to reenact the events of their prolonged strike against mill owners. Spectators witnessed a new form of proletarian art—social drama as participatory ritual.

The Paterson Pageant was the brainchild of young radical journalist John Reed and a handful of socialist intellectuals and artists who dreamed of fashioning a new mass art out of working-class grievances and the formal protest of the intellectuals. The Paterson strike had been triggered by the mill owners' decision to increase the workload for unskilled silk weavers and dyers already living on the edge of destitution. Most of the workers in the Paterson dye houses and mills, some 25,000 in all, were new immigrants from Italy, Russia, and eastern Europe, a large number of them young girls earning an average wage of $6 or $7 a

PATERSON STRIKERS AND THEIR ART
Strikers march up Broadway to Madison Square Garden to produce the pageant advertised in the poster.

United Press International Inc.

week. The IWW entered the town in the winter of 1913 to help organize this unpromising material around the immediate issues of shorter hours and higher wages. "Big Bill" Haywood, fresh from his triumph in the Lawrence, Massachusetts, textile workers' strike, joined the young Wobbly agitator Elizabeth Gurley Flynn and the romantic syndicalist Carlo Tresca in teaching the Paterson workers that it was "far better to starve fighting than to starve working." By February 1913 they had succeeded in uniting the unskilled workers and shutting down the town.

In trying to break the strike with its skilled workers, the AFL fed the progressive tendency to identify the immigrant with radicalism. Yet throughout the spring the strikers' ranks held firm. The mill owners fought back, stirring up hatred of "outside agitators" and enlisting the police in their efforts to break the strike. "There's a war in Paterson," John Reed told his fellow artists and intellectuals in Greenwich Village. "But it's a curious kind of war. All the violence is the work of one side—the Mill Owners."

Reed had reason to know. Like many of the Village

socialists and radicals, he had made the Sunday excursion to Paterson to see for himself the clash between the workers and the bosses. He had been jailed, and he later returned to New York to compose his indictment of the owners for Max Eastman's *The Masses*. A cultural radical as yet without any clear sense of ideological direction, Reed dreamed of rallying artists and intellectuals to the strikers' side as the beginning of a permanent alliance for the radical reconstruction of American life. This was the idea he brought back to socialite Mabel Dodge's salon, the gathering place of New York's radical writers and intellectuals. Out of the sessions at Dodge's came the plans for a gigantic pageant to raise money for the strike fund and to educate liberals on working-class solidarity. Reed threw himself headlong into the project, spending eighteen hours a day on the script, drilling a thousand amateur performers into a theatrical company, designing the massive sets with the artist John Sloan and stage designer Robert Edmond Jones. By June he was ready, Sloan's huge factory scenes and red curtains were in place, and the cast was primed for performance.

The pageant caught the spirit of solidarity that Reed had sensed in Paterson. As it opened, throngs of workers moved down the center aisle to linger in front of the huge gray mills before entering to the sound of whirring machinery. Suddenly the chant began—"Strike! Strike!"—growing louder and more insistent until the workers came pouring out of the factory doors, and life moved outside the empty, dark mills. In front of these dead industrial husks, the workers reenacted the scenes of the strike—mass picketing, police harassment, the clash between strikers and the scabs in which a worker was killed, and finally the climactic funeral procession.

The audience, many of them workers admitted at 25¢ a seat, joined in booing the police, chanting strike slogans, and lustily singing the socialist anthem, the "Internationale." For a brief moment it seemed that Reed and the radical cultural critics had succeeded in forging new weapons for social justice out of the materials of mass art.

But life did not imitate art, and the pageant brought a cresting of radical hopes that quickly receded. The spectacle had originally been intended to replenish the strike fund, but actually it yielded a check for only $150. The 24,000 strikers who had not participated began to question the dubious honors bestowed on them by the intellectuals. "Bread was the need of the hour," Elizabeth Gurley Flynn complained, "and bread was not forthcoming." The gulf between art and politics could not be bridged by mere ceremony. The skilled workers broke ranks during the summer and returned to the mills. Then the mill owners, in a series of shop-by-shop settlements that conceded nothing to the unskilled workers, shattered their morale and routed the IWW leadership. By summer's end the Paterson workers were back on the job on their employers' terms. John Reed's script for the oppressed laborers of America acting out "the wretchedness of their lives and the glory of their revolt" had failed to close the distance between the intellectual radicals and the workers.

Artists and Scientists: Critics of Progressivism

Other critics of progressivism before the First World War perceived different divisions in American society and suggested other ways of closing them. In 1914 Walter Lippmann published his *Drift and Mastery*, and a year later Van Wyck Brooks brought out his bitter essay, *America's Coming of Age*. Both authors demanded a reassessment of progressives' aims and aspirations. Lippmann and Brooks represented a new intellectual type, the liberal publicist directing criticism toward the progressive elite. They were neither journalists in a traditional sense nor philosophers, but rather saw themselves as cultural and social commentators whose task it was to direct the flow of American life through channels of publicity and informed criticism toward new national goals. They sought to lift their roles as critics to the realm of public power through their analysis of American society.

Brooks's Critique. Van Wyck Brooks, a recent graduate of Harvard where he had studied under philosophers William James and George Santayana, was the chief spokesman for the "little renaissance" in American art and culture that swept across the country after 1912. By the time Brooks issued his challenge to progressivism, the signs of cultural rebellion were everywhere. Brooks joined the expanding circle of artists and intellectuals in Greenwich Village after a brief teaching career at Stanford University and at the Worker's Educational Association in Cambridge, England. In the Village he met Walter Lippmann, who urged him to contribute to the literary renaissance by closely examining the "noble dream" of American democratic culture in the light of the "actual limitations of experience." Brooks promptly obliged with what he called an address to his own "homeless generation" of intellectuals and would-be critics.

Brooks perceived a basic American duality in the cultural split between "highbrow" and "lowbrow"—a fatal division, he said, that had paralyzed the creative will of the nation for more than a century. He argued that the American impasse stemmed from the conflict between high-flown theory and the "catchpenny realities" of a business civilization. Between these poles lay a cultural wasteland in which no true community could thrive. Brooks traced the roots of this American schizophrenia to the original sin of Puritanism, "the all-influential fact in the history of the American mind." He attributed to Puritanism both the "fastidious refinement" of current tastes and the "opportunism" of American moneymakers.

Like the progressive historian Vernon L. Parrington, who was already at work compiling the materials for his *Main Currents of American Thought* that would document this view, Brooks presented his authors in sets of paired opposites: Jonathan Edwards and Benjamin Franklin; Henry Wadsworth Longfellow and Mark Twain; James Russell Lowell and Walt Whitman—figures on opposite sides of a chasm between literate and illiterate America. Brooks argued that throughout the nineteenth century the divorce of the real from the ideal had resulted in an "orgy of lofty examples, moralized poems, national anthems and baccalaureate sermons" until the average citizen was now "charged with all manner of ideal purities, ideal honorabilities, ideal femininities, flagwavings and skyscrapings of every sort." In the meantime the

American landscape had become a stamping ground for every greedy commercial impulse of every last businessman who held that "society is fair prey for what he can get out of it."

Brooks pointed to the shortcomings of the progressive approach to reform. Progressivism, for all its moral certainties and good-government ideals, had failed to solve the fundamental problem of modern industrial society—the "invisible government" of business and the profit motive. So far, well-meaning progressive reformers' efforts to change American priorities had added up to nothing. Progressivism simply consolidated the rule of "commercialized men." Of what use was it, Brooks demanded, to tinker with political mechanisms or "do any of the other easy popular contemporary things" unless the quality of American life could also be improved?

Here Brooks reached the core of his critique. Meaningful betterment of American society would require more than rationalizing a business system, more than the cheerful cooperation of business and government, whether in the name of the New Nationalism or the New Freedom. All that would suffice now would be the massive shift of American energies from business and politics to psychology and art. Otherwise progressivism would fail in its mission to give America new life. When the First World War broke out, Brooks still hoped for the cultural rebellion for which he spoke. Three years later, American entrance into the war broke these hopes on the rocks of the war state.

Lippmann's Analysis.

Walter Lippmann also saw a split in twentieth-century American life that progressivism had failed to repair. But his definition centered on the conflict between Victorian silences—what he called the "sterile tyranny of taboo"—inherited from the nineteenth century, and his own generation's desire "to be awake during their own lifetime." "Drift" was the result of the rule of old bogeys. "Mastery" meant applying the scientific method to politics. Like Brooks, although for different reasons, Lippmann faulted the progressives for their lack of rigorous thought. Although the New Nationalism had examined some of the worst abuses of industrialism, it still spoke the language of the old moralists. The New Freedom continued to make false promises of a return to free competition. "You would think that competitive commercialism was really a generous, chivalrous, high-minded stage of human culture," Lippmann scoffed, instead of "an antiquated, feeble, mean, and unimaginative way of dealing with the possibilities of modern industry." Lippmann agreed with Brooks on the need for relocating American energies outside politics, but he differed dramatically on the means. Unlike Brooks and the cultural radicals, he championed the cause of business consolidation and the rule of industrial statesmen who would go beyond politics by lifting decisionmaking out of the marketplace to the level of scientific management. Whereas the cultural radicals hoped to destroy the rule of big business, Lippmann sought to rationalize and reform it. His aim was to create a truly cooperative society, neither strictly capitalistic nor wholly collectivist, but a new commonwealth composed of managers, workers, and consumers, each applying the instruments of measurement and control provided by modern science.

The Seven Arts and The New Republic.

American entry into the First World War threatened Van Wyck Brooks's plans for reconstructing American culture. But it brought a welcome test for Lippmann's pragmatic liberalism and his design for a businessmen's government. Brooks deplored the war as a betrayal of his dreams; Lippmann embraced it as a challenge. By 1917 these two critiques of progressivism had been institutionalized in two very different magazines: *The Seven Arts*, which Brooks and his cultural radical friends Randolph Bourne and James Oppenheim founded in 1916 and nursed through a year of shaky existence; and *The New Republic*, which Lippmann together with liberal nationalists Herbert Croly and Walter Weyl had launched in 1914. The war records of these two magazines testified to the divergent fates of cultural radicalism and liberal nationalism under emergency conditions.

The Seven Arts lasted just a year before being killed by the fervor of the patriots. Brooks's mantle fell on the diminutive frame of Randolph Bourne, who more clearly than any of the other opponents of the war saw the coming defeat of "that America of youth and aspiration" standing below the battle. In "War and the Intellectuals," the most scathing of his attacks on Lippmann and the prowar liberals, Bourne ridiculed the "war technique" of liberal reform that had led the intellectuals to the illusion that they had willed the war "through sheer force of ideas." Bourne charged that in welcoming the war *The New Republic* editors had allied themselves with the least democratic forces in American society, those primitive interests that still were trumpeting notions of the national state and the doctrines of economic privilege. The war, Bourne concluded, provided an escape for progressives who had become prisoners of their own fantasies of the ordered society. The collapse of *The Seven Arts* after a year of lonely opposition to the war, along with Bourne's untimely death, marked the end of the cultural radical attempt to reconstruct progressivism by supplying it with higher values.

Lippmann and the other editors of *The New Republic* continued to cling to the belief that they could help direct a democratic war and write a liberal peace. The American entrance, Lippmann explained soon after Wilson's declaration of war, would prove "decisive in the history of the world": the United States could now proceed to "crystallize and make real the whole league of peace propaganda." Nor did he fear the effects of a war psychology on the prospects of liberalism. In October 1917 he offered his services to the administration and was appointed secretary of The Inquiry, Wilson's hand-picked body of experts charged with preparing the American agenda for the peace table. Herbert Croly, who remained in his editorial post at *The New Republic*, quickly grew disillusioned as he realized the nature of the liberal impasse both at home and abroad. Lippmann's hopes for a liberal peace remained high. But eighteen months later, discouraged by the president's failure at the Paris Peace Conference and dubious now about the uses of war as a means of social reconstruction, Lippmann joined those "tired radicals" seeking to defeat the treaty.

The Ordeal of Woodrow Wilson

In his address to Congress on January 8, 1918—at the low point in the American war effort— Woodrow Wilson outlined the steps the United States and the Allies would have to take to ensure a postwar world "made fit to live in." Wilson presented his Fourteen Points as a blueprint for peacemaking drawn to his own progressive specifications. The central element in his thinking was the principle of "open covenants openly arrived at"—the extension of the New Freedom idea of moral publicity to international politics. A counterweight to this first point in Wilson's moral scales was the fourteenth, calling for "a general association of nations . . . formed under specific covenants for the purpose of affording mutual guarantees of political independence and territorial integrity to great and small states alike." The main substantive points in Wilson's utopian scheme included a general disarmament, complete freedom of the seas, fair adjustment of colonial claims in the interests of the peoples involved, and a series of specific provisions for drawing national boundaries in Europe on the basis of the language spoken in each region ("linguistic nationalism"). These were the lofty terms that Wilson, in the face of mounting opposition from his war partners, intended to impose at the peace table.

Problems with the Fourteen Points. In attempting to achieve his aims, Wilson was driven by circumstance, as well as by his own intensely moral nature, to make several costly miscalculations. Part of his trouble lay in the Fourteen Points themselves. What, for example, did

his principle of national self-determination mean, and by what general formula could it be applied? What adjustments might be needed when linguistic nationalism failed to coincide with economic viability or military aims? Then, how could the new Soviet regime with an exportable totalitarian ideology, which had been established two months before, be given "an unhampered and unembarrassed opportunity" for political development? How, in short, could Wilson, as the representative of the only impartial power at the peace table, establish in each and every instance his claim to be the enlightened conscience of mankind?

A related set of problems concerned Wilson's political position at home. Who but himself—the president—he asked, could convert the Allies to his program and ensure the triumph of collective security? Determined to play the dominant role at the Paris conference, he insisted on making his peace program a partisan issue in the fall elections of 1918 by warning that a Republican victory would be a rejection of his leadership and vision. Republicans, who had already grown restive under the nonpartisan war policy, now retaliated by accusing Wilson himself of partisan dealings. In 1918 the Republicans regained control of both houses of Congress. If their victory did not quite mean a vote of no confidence, it did serve to warn Wilson that the spirit of party politics had been revived and would be decisive in settling the fate of his peace program.

Even more serious was Wilson's refusal to include Republican leaders among his advisers at the peace conference. Former President Taft, the 1916 Republican presidential nominee Charles Evans Hughes, and a number of other leading Republicans had expressed cautious interest in the idea of a League of Nations. But Wilson's calculated exclusion of these men from the American delegation to Paris isolated him from the moderate Republican internationalism he so desperately needed. On the eve of his departure for Europe in December 1918, there were already ominous signs of a growing presidential detachment from the realities of domestic politics, as Wilson began to retreat into the recesses of his moralistic nature. "Tell me what is right," he urged his advisers as he prepared for the conference, "and I'll fight for it." Wilson fought tenaciously, even heroically, for his Fourteen Points against overwhelming odds. But in forgetting the first rule of politics and ignoring the domestic disarray he had left behind, he fatally compromised his position.

Problems in Paris. In Paris the president confronted other national leaders who, as he came to realize with chagrin, spoke for their countrymen as he could not: David Lloyd George of Great Britain, Georges Clemenceau of France, and Vittorio Orlando of Italy. The Al-

THE COUNCIL OF FOUR
From left to right: Vittorio Orlando of Italy, David Lloyd George of England, Georges Clemenceau of France, Woodrow Wilson.

lies had suffered grievously during the war, and their leaders could count on unwavering support at home for a peace that would punish Germany—one that would assign all the war guilt to Germany, completely strip it of its colonial possessions, extract enormous reparations, and provide all the necessary safeguards against future aggression. To counter these narrow nationalistic aims, Wilson brought with him to Paris only the Fourteen Points and his vision of a new concert of power. Despite his initial popularity with the peoples of Europe, his lone voice became lost in the clamor of competing nationalisms. The American story of the peace deliberations was one of mounting frustration and a forced retreat from idealism.

The first of the Fourteen Points to be abandoned was the utopian concept of "open covenants." Soon after the conference began, the plenary sessions (open meetings of all delegations) gave way first to a Council of Ten, dominated by the heads of state and their for-

eign ministers, and then to a Council of Four, composed of Wilson, Lloyd George, Clemenceau, and Orlando, meeting behind closed doors. The press was barred from working sessions and became almost wholly dependent on news releases that were handed out after each plenary session. Wilson added to his problems of communication by withdrawing coldly from his colleagues on the council and ignoring most of his advisers, who complained of his aloofness. Removed from presidential oversight, the American staff floundered in confusion. Wilson announced that he had no desire "to have lawyers drafting the treaty of peace" and played a lone hand at Paris. He quickly exhausted his reserves of moral capital.

On a few of the specific issues of the peace settlement, Wilson was partially successful in moderating the extortionate demands of his partners. After an epic battle of wills with the cynical Clemenceau, who likened his adversary to Jesus Christ and Moses bearing the Ten Commandments, Wilson forced France to agree to a multinational defense pact. But he gained this victory at the cost of the immediate return to France of Alsace-Lorraine,* French occupation of Germany's Rhineland, and huge reparations to be paid by Germany. On the question of the former German colonies, he abandoned the principle of "impartial adjustment" but salvaged his plan for a mandate system under League auspices. For Poland he secured a corridor to the sea at the expense of linguistic nationalism.** In constructing a new Austria out of the Austro-Hungarian empire, which had disintegrated at the end of the war, he presided over the transfer of some 200,000 German-speaking people to Italy in order to assure the latter of a militarily defensible frontier. When he refused to agree to a similar transfer to Italy of a strip of the Dalmatian coast—territory inhabited overwhelmingly by Yugoslavs—he brought on a major crisis by appealing for self-restraint directly to the Italian people over the heads of their representatives. This blunder only hardened Italian resolves and further discredited Wilson with his colleagues at the peace table. Self-determination of peoples speaking the same language—a legacy of nineteenth-century romantic nationalism—was violated at Paris as often as it was successfully applied.

But the president suffered his sharpest defeat on the question of reparations. France originally suggested the preposterous figure of $200 billion, and Britain seemed unwilling to settle for much less. Clemenceau and Lloyd George, bowing to heavy pressure from their respective publics, overrode Wilson's objections to their crippling demands and forced him to accept the inclusion of civililan damages and military pensions in the final assessment on Germany. The president, pushed beyond the limits of endurance, had become ill and confused. He agreed to the principle of massive repayments and allowed the fixing of specific amounts to be postponed. The Council of Four provided for a reparations commission, which in 1921 set

the indemnity at $56 billion without regard for Germany's ability to pay or for the political consequences for the struggling new German republic.

The League of Nations.

Throughout the agony of daily defeat, Wilson was sustained by his hopes for the League of Nations and the work of drafting the League Covenant. The League, he told himself, would correct the mistakes and make good the deficiencies of the peace settlement, to which it must be firmly tied. By tying the League closely to the treaty,* the president hoped to get around his congressional opponents by presenting them with a complete package that they would have to accept or reject as a whole. He never seriously considered that they might succeed in destroying his great work.

Article X of the League Covenant became the great symbolic issue that eventually wrecked his dream. Article X provided that

the members of the League undertake to respect and preserve as against external aggression the territorial integrity and existing political independence of all the Members of the League. In case of any such aggression or in case of any threat or danger of such aggression the Council shall advise upon the means by which this obligation shall be fulfilled.

For Wilson Article X represented the triumph of moral force. The details of applying sanctions against future aggressors concerned him less than did the simple recognition by the nations of the world of his principle of collective security. This principle, at least, he had managed to rescue from the ruins of the treaty, and he meant to defend it at all costs.

The League of Nations, on which Wilson ultimately pinned all his hopes, in part represented the progressive idea of commission government applied to international politics. Like a federal commission designed to free policymaking from the whims of politicians, the League, together with its various branches and agencies, would provide the means of defusing international crises and resolving conflicts through arbitration. But in another and more profound sense, Wilson's League was simply the application of inherited nineteenth-century liberal principles and a doctrine of progress.

In the president's mind the League embodied old truths and moral principles. The most important of these was the belief that as American institutions and

---

*Alsace-Lorraine was a largely German-speaking region in eastern France that Germany had annexed in 1871, against the wishes of most of its inhabitants. The recovery of Alsace-Lorraine had been a primary French aim in the First World War. Wilson would have preferred settling the issue by a plebiscite.

**The so-called Polish Corridor, a strip of territory assuring Poland access to the Baltic Sea, contained a large German minority unwilling to come under Polish rule. The corridor also cut the province of East Prussia off from the rest of Germany. The German-speaking port of Danzig (Gdańsk) was transformed into a free city under League of Nations auspices. In 1939 Hitler's demand for the return of Danzig and the Polish Corridor led to the outbreak of the Second World War.

*Actually, not one peace treaty was drawn up, but five. The Treaty of Versailles, which included the League Covenant, applied only to Germany; separate treaties were imposed on each of Germany's allies: Austria, Hungary, Bulgaria, and Turkey.

ideas reformed the rest of the world, and as the beneficent workings of trade and commerce gathered peoples together in harmony and abundance, the old selfish national interests would die out. Ultimately a worldwide legal community would arise in place of the discredited system of balance of power. Wilson had witnessed four years of international slaughter and had seen embittered nationalists at Versailles impose a savage, punishing peace on Germany, and he was convinced that the time had finally come for building such an international moral order. Although he was willing to concede much—and in fact had conspicuously failed to control the peace conference—he was not prepared to compromise on the League of Nations or on the role his country would have to play in its creation.

Wilson's utopian commitment led him to overlook two fundamental problems. The first resulted from attaching the League to the peace treaty. A second problem was that of intent. Was the League intended simply to enforce a victor's peace, or would it work to adjust shifting balances of national power, incorporate new members including the defeated nations, and underwrite orderly change and development? No amount of Wilsonian rhetoric about "the general moral judgment of mankind" could obscure the basic uncertainty of purpose in the president's attempt to replace power relations with moral force.

The Red Scare.

Wilson returned to the United States in the summer of 1919 and found a nation already in the throes of reaction. The shadow of the Russian Revolution, which had fallen over the peace table, now lengthened across the Atlantic. The threat of revolution strengthened the forces of reaction everywhere in Europe as conservatives rushed to defend their states from the Bolshevik menace. The Soviet challenge seemed particularly frightening to Americans because it threatened their own revolutionary tradition. Russia was undergoing no mere political rebellion and rearrangement, sensibly completed and solicitous of property rights and personal liberties, but instead a vast social upheaval with a collectivist ideology that was the antithesis of Western capitalist democracy.

The American response to the new Soviet regime was twofold. First, the Wilson administration undertook an abortive attempt to strengthen the counterrevolutionary forces in Russia by landing American troops (soon withdrawn) at Murmansk in North Russia and Vladivostok in the Far East. These operations were undertaken in conjunction with larger (but equally unsuccessful) British, French, and Japanese interventions. Second, there was a tendency at home to see "Reds" everywhere. By the summer of 1919, the so-called Red Scare had taken full possession of the

national imagination as a wartime fear of subversion was suddenly turned into a dread of imminent revolution. In fact, two rival American Communist parties were established in September 1919. (They united only in 1921 under pressure from Lenin.) One was led by left-wing defectors from the Socialist party and the other by John Reed, recently returned from witnessing the Russian Revolution, which he described dramatically in his book *Ten Days That Shook the World*. Neither group attracted an important following, and Reed soon returned to Russia, where he died in an epidemic and was buried in Red Square. Much more significant was the widespread fear of radicalism. This fear branded as subversive not only the tiny communist and IWW movements and the larger, moderate Socialist party, but also liberal ideas in general, whether in art or politics. All were met with strident protests against nonconformity and demands for unconditional loyalty.

Republicans Oppose Wilson.

Wilson also felt the force of a congressional reaction that had been building since the armistice. Mobilization for war had concentrated power in the executive branch of the government, thus completing the political cycle that had begun with Theodore Roosevelt's presidency. But now, with reconversion and demobilization, the political pendulum began to swing the other way, as Congress moved firmly to reassert its control over foreign affairs as well as domestic policy.

Congressional resurgence had already become a highly partisan matter with the revival in the 1918 elections of the Republican party, which with fortynine seats in the Senate now enjoyed a two-vote margin over the Democrats. Republicans could scarcely resist an opportunity to limit Wilson's power by modifying the terms of American participation in the new League of Nations. Republican leaders were also prepared to roll back wartime controls and curb the regulatory power of federal agencies, whose activities they now tended to equate with socialism. The League was only the most obvious issue with which the Republican party aimed to establish itself in the majority once again.

Yet the Republican members of the Senate remained divided on the question of accepting Wilson's treaty and American participation in the League. On the right of the party stood some dozen or fifteen "irreconcilables"—isolationists opposed to nearly any continued international involvement. At the other end of the spectrum were the "mild reservationists," who supported the League in principle but were concerned with the extent of Wilson's commitment to collective security and were anxious to limit it. Ranged between these two ideological poles were the "strong reservationists," making up the majority faction and led by Senator Henry Cabot Lodge. Lodge combined a cordial hatred of the president with a narrow nationalism that had not changed since the Spanish-American War. The "strong reservationists" were willing to consider United States participation in the League only on their own terms, and they were fully prepared to force on Wilson significant reservations limiting American commitments and making Congress rather than the president the final judge of their applicability.

Within his own party Wilson could count on solid internationalist support, but it was clear at the outset of the struggle that he would have to win a sizable majority of moderates away from Lodge in order to gain acceptance of his League of Nations. By July 1919 Wilson faced a formidable but not an impossible task, one that would require great patience and even greater flexibility.

For his part Lodge followed a clever strategy contrived to exploit every advantage over his opponent. He packed the Senate Foreign Relations Committee with his followers; he conducted lengthy hearings that gave voice to every conceivable opponent of the League; he courted right-wing businessmen like Henry Clay Frick and Andrew Mellon; and he loaded the treaty down with amendments. By fall his original forty-five amendments had been reduced to fourteen reservations—one for each of Wilson's initial Fourteen Points. The first reserved to the United States the sole right to decide whether it had fulfilled its obligations under the covenant, and it gave Congress the power to withdraw the United States from the League. The second, directed at the controversial Article X, was also aimed at Wilson's greatest weakness. It provided that the United States would accept no obligation to enforce the collective-security provisions of the covenant without the consent of Congress in each and every case. Other reservations rejected any mandates assignable to the United States, reserved the right to determine which questions involving American interests might be submitted to the League, and stipulated that the Monroe Doctrine was not to be subjected to international debate. Taken together, Lodge's reservations were significant but not crippling modifications, as the subsequent history of the League would show.

Yet, as Lodge hoped, Wilson believed otherwise. He consistently refused to make a realistic assessment of the situation. He was unwilling to discuss the specific circumstances under which the United States might be called on to apply sanctions—either economic or military—against other nations because he was convinced that full discussion in the forum of the League would make sanctions unnecessary. For him the real questions were simple: Was the United States

WARRIOR'S RETREAT

To win public suport for his League of Nations, Woodrow Wilson, tired and ailing, embarked on an 8,000-mile speaking tour across the country. In Pueblo, Colorado, he suffered a stroke and was ordered home by his doctor. Although he was able to walk through Washington's Union Station and to manage a grim smile for photographers, a second stroke soon left him totally incapacitated.

prepared to make the significant moral gesture toward peace and international security? Would the American people see to it that the Senate carried out its obligation? Although the actual fight in the Senate grew complicated with proposals and counterproposals, amendments, reservations, and interpretations, the president's position remained essentially the one he had taken in presenting the treaty to the Senate: "The stage is set, the destiny disclosed. . . . We cannot turn back. We can only go forward, with lifted eyes and freshened spirit, to follow the vision."

Wilson's own vision led him away from Washington on an 8,000-mile tour of the nation, during which he gave forty speeches explaining to the American people the League's importance to their future security and welfare. In taking his case to the country, Wilson was violating one of his own rules. "The Senate," he once wrote, "is not . . . immediately sensitive to [public] opinion and is apt to grow, if anything, more stiff if pressure of that kind is brought to bear upon it." Now President Wilson ignored Professor Wilson's advice. His tour of the nation carried him farther and farther away from political reality and the problem of securing the Senate's consent. Although he referred frequently to specific issues and explained the limited nature of the American commitment, he returned to the theme of moral principle:

You have no choice, my fellow citizens. . . . You cannot give a false gift. . . . Men are not going to stand it. There is nothing for any nation to lose whose purposes are right and whose cause is just. . . . The whole freedom of the world not only, but the whole peace of mind of the world, depends upon the choice of America. . . . I can testify to that. . . . The world will be absolutely in despair if America deserts it.

Worn out and distraught, collapsing under the weight of his moral mission, Wilson suffered a stroke in Pueblo, Colorado, on September 26, 1919, and was rushed back to Washington. A week later a second stroke left him paralyzed. Wilson in effect had spoken his last word on the treaty. Desperately ill, physically isolated from his followers and advisers, he was locked in a private moral world. Loyal Democrats received their presidential orders: vote to reject the treaty with the Lodge reservations. On November 19, 1919, by a vote of thirty-nine for and fifty-five against, the Senate rejected the Treaty of Versailles with the reservations; the Democrats had dutifully joined with the irreconcilables to defeat it. Wilson still hoped to make the presidential election of 1920 the occasion of a giant referendum on the League. But his advisers, along with more objective observers, knew the fight was over. The president's dream was dead.

Domestic discord in the year 1919 mirrored the collapse of Wilson's moral world. A calendar of vio-lence marked the decline of original progressive hopes:

In January shipyard workers in Seattle struck for higher wages, organized a general strike, and paralyzed the city. At the mayor's request the federal government sent in the Marines.

In May four hundred soldiers and sailors sacked the offices of a socialist newspaper, the New York Call, *and beat up the staff.*

In the summer race riots erupted in twenty-five cities across the country; the most serious outbreak was in Chicago, where thirty-eight were killed and more than five hundred injured.

In September the Boston police force struck for the right to unionize, and the city experienced a wave of looting and theft until leading businessmen and Harvard students restored order.

In September 350,000 steelworkers struck for the right to unionize and for an eight-hour day.

In November a mob in Centralia, Washington, dragged IWW agitator Wesley Everett from jail and castrated him before hanging him.

In December agents of the Labor Department rounded up 249 Russian-born American communists and deported them to Finland.

There were Americans in 1919 who recalled Wilson's definition of the progressive task six years earlier as "the high enterprise of the new day. . . . Our duty is to cleanse, to reconsider, to correct the evil without impairing the good, to purify and humanize every process of our common life without weakening or sentimentalizing it." For those who remembered, there could be little doubt that the new day had ended.

CHRONOLOGY

1913 Armory Show in New York City.
Paterson strike.

1914 First World War begins; Wilson declares American neutrality.
"Ludlow Massacre"; National Guard attacks tent colony of strikes in Ludlow, Colorado, killing eleven women and two children.

1915 Germans declare unrestricted submarine warfare and sink *Lusitania* with loss of American lives.

1916 Wilson reelected, narrowly defeating Charles Evans Hughes.
House-Grey Memorandum on United States efforts for negotiated peace.

1917 Germans resume unrestricted submarine warfare and United States enters war.
Russian Revolution; "February Revolution," establishing provisional government; "October Revolution," engineered by Bolsheviks.
Draft Act.
Espionage Act.
Purchase of Danish Virgin Islands.
Creation of War Industries Board.
First Pulitzer prizes awarded.

1918 Wilson's Fourteen Points, outlining administration's peace aims.
United States troops at Belleau Wood.
Saint Mihiel salient, first United States offensive.
Meuse-Argonne offensive.
Sedition Act, providing severe penalties for expressing "disloyal" opinions.
Armistice; Germany defeated.

1919 *Schenck* v. *U.S.*, upholding Espionage Act and government curtailment of free speech during wartime.
Abrams v. *U.S.*, upholding Sedition Act.
Eighteenth Amendment (Volstead Act), prohibiting sale or manufacture of alcoholic beverages.
Steel strike.
Race riots in Chicago, East Saint Louis, and Washington.

1920 Great Red Scare.
Defeat of Versailles Treaty by Senate.
Nineteenth Amendment gives vote to women.
Warren G. Harding elected president, defeating James M. Cox and Eugene Debs.

SUGGESTED READINGS

There are two good surveys of American military conduct of the war: Edward M. Coffman, *The War to End Wars: The American Military Experience in World War I* (1968), and Russell F. Weigley, *The American Way of War* (1973).

The years since World War II have seen a growing number of studies of American civil liberties during and after the First World War. Beginning with Zechariah Chafee, *Free Speech in the United States* (1941), the list includes Harry N. Scheiber, *The Wilson Administration and Civil Liberties, 1917–1921* (1960); Donald M. Johnson, *The Challenge to American Freedoms* (1963); H. C. Peterson and Gilbert Fite, *Opponents of the War, 1917–1918* (1957); William Preston, Jr., *Aliens and Dissenters: Federal Suppression of Radicals, 1903–1933* (1963); and Paul L. Murphy, *Red Scare: A Study of National Hysteria, 1919–1920* (1955).

The immediate shock of war as experienced by artists and intellectuals is described in Stanley Cooperman, *World War I and the American Novel* (1967), and its lingering effects in Malcolm Cowley, *Exiles Return: A Literary Odyssey of the 1920's* (1951). Sam Hunter, *American Painting and Sculpture* (1959), and Barbara Rose, *American Art Since 1900: A Critical History* (1967), are good accounts of American art in the early twentieth century. For the Armory Show see Milton Brown, *The Story of the Armory Show* (1963); the best brief discussion of its revolutionary impact is Meyer Schapiro, "Rebellion in Art," in Daniel Aaron, ed., *America in Crisis* (1952).

The best approach to the intellectual history of the progressive years is through the writers themselves. Major works of social and political analysis, now considered classics, include Jane Addams, *Twenty Years at Hull House* (1910); Randolph Bourne, *Youth and Life* (1913), and a collection of Bourne's war pieces, *War and the Intellectuals* (1964), edited by Carl Resek; Louis Brandeis, *Other People's Money* (1914); Van Wyck Brooks, *America's Coming of Age* (1915); Charles H. Cooley, *Human Nature and the Social Order* (1922); Herbert Croly, *The Promise of American Life* (1909); John Dewey, *School and Society* (1899); W. E. B. DuBois, *Souls of the Black Folk* (1903); Charlotte Perkins Gilman, *Women and Economics* (1898); Walter Lippmann, *Drift and Mastery* (1914); John Reed, *Insurgent Mexico* (1914), and *Ten Days That Shook the World* (1919); and Walter Weyl, *The New Democracy* (1912).

On the diplomacy of war and peacemaking, Arno J. Mayer, *Political Origins of the New Diplomacy, 1917–1918*

(1959), and *Politics and Diplomacy of Peacemaking: Containment and Counterrevolution at Versailles, 1918–1919* (1967), are both ponderous and provocative. N. Gordon Levin, *Woodrow Wilson and World Politics: America's Response to War and Revolution* (1968), focuses on the presidential strategies, as does Warren Kuehl, *Seeking World Order: The United States and World Organization to 1920* (1969). Two older works by Thomas A. Bailey, *Woodrow Wilson and the Lost Peace* (1944) and *Woodrow Wilson and the Great Betrayal* (1945), detail Wilson's tragic postwar course. On the opposition to the League of Nations, Ralph A. Stone, *The Irreconcilables: The Fight Against the League of Nations* (1970), is admirable. John Garraty, *Henry Cabot Lodge* (1953), offers a sympathetic but not uncritical appraisal of Wilson's

arch-enemy. On Soviet-American relations, see George F. Kennan, *Russia Leaves the War* (1956), and *The Decision to Intervene: Prelude to Allied Intervention in the Bolshevik Revolution* (1958). Peter G. Filene, *Americans and the Soviet Experiment* (1967), and Christopher Lasch, *The American Liberals and the Russian Revolution* (1962), consider the varied American reactions to the Revolution. Betty M. Unterberger, *America's Siberian Expedition* (1956), explains the failure of that misguided action. Lawrence E. Gelfand, *The Inquiry: American Preparations for Peace, 1917–1919* (1963), is an account of the role of the president's advisers at Versailles. Paul Birdsall, *Versailles: Twenty Years After* (1973), assesses the peacemaking from the perspective of a later crisis.

PART SIX

MODERNIZING THE REPUBLIC,

1920 TO THE PRESENT
Robert Dallek

The years in American history since 1920 constitute an era in which the nation has struggled to accommodate itself to new principles governing its economic, political, social, and diplomatic affairs.

At the core of America's modern state is a national political economy that acquired its basic form in the 1920s. Beginning with the industrial consolidations of the late nineteenth century, the main subdivisions of the economy—the production and distribution of goods; finance; skilled labor; and commercial agriculture—had become increasingly organized, increasingly committed to nationwide cooperation, and increasingly alert to the usefulness of the government in Washington. The First World War had accelerated these trends. By the middle of the 1920s, the national government adopted a consistent policy of support for these organized groups, and the components of America's modern political economy fell into place. Although the operations of the political economy grew vastly more complex during the next five decades, its essential character did not change. But alternations between prosperity, depression, recession, inflation, and stagflation have raised fundamental questions about the modern political economy and have led to an ongoing search for more effective means of maintaining the nation's prosperity.

American politics since 1920 has undergone a major transformation. Authority has largely shifted from local centers of power—cities, counties, and states—to the federal government in Washington. In response to the Great Depression, the Second World War, the Cold War, and enduring economic and social injustices, the national government acquired unprecedented powers to manage the economy, reduce poverty and inequality, and defend the national security. But abuses by federal officials, and bureaucratic red tape—especially in the executive branch, where the nation witnessed the rise of the "imperial presidency"—have troubled many Americans. They have become increasingly ambivalent about a powerful central government that has conferred desirable benefits on numerous citizens and defended the national interest overseas, but has created a federal establishment that has seemed to intrude excessively into people's daily lives and has mismanaged many of its responsibilities.

Overleaf: Contemporary View of Manhattan. *George W. Gardner, Stock, Boston.*

698

Twentieth-century Americans have also fretted over what values should govern the individual in society. The growth of large business organizations employing the bulk of Americans, as well as the rise of a consumer culture emphasizing leisure and self-indulgence, has sharply challenged traditional assumptions about rugged individualism and hard work. If Americans have found much to attract them to the new cultural values of the post-1920 period, they have also worried about the loss of old habits, and have given at least rhetorical allegiance to traditional ideas. By the mid-1980s, although firmly committed to an organized, centralized society, and devoted more to consumption and personal absorptions than to frugality and public concerns, the American people have also clung to the conventional, locally oriented mores enunciated by Ronald Reagan, one of the most popular presidents of the twentieth century.

In its foreign relations as well, the nation has swung between two poles. In the twenties and thirties the United States tried to limit its involvement in world affairs as much as possible, relying principally on moral injunctions against aggression and war. To protect itself against the Axis challenge in the forties, however, the nation entered the Second World War. When a postwar threat from international communism deterred Washington from returning to old-style isolationism, the United States developed a long-range, systematic pattern of foreign commitments that extended American power around the globe. But the unsuccessful war in Vietnam eroded popular support for the global containment of communism and revived the habit of national soul searching about what America's proper role in world affairs should be.

These various tensions over America's domestic and international problems and actions triggered an open revolt in the sixties against the nation's leaders, first among well-to-do youths and then among millions of middle-class people and minority groups. In the seventies and eighties, while Washington's leaders tried to fashion answers to economic, political, social, and international difficulties, the economy fell on its hardest times since the Great Depression. Uncertainties about generally accepted answers to the problems of the modern era have grown over time. As the Republic looks ahead to its third century, it struggles to find new solutions to yet unresolved questions.

28 The Emergence of the Modern Republic: The Twenties

Popular images of the 1920s have obscured the importance of the decade. The Roaring Twenties of a new technology, a new prosperity, a new emphasis on personal self-indulgence, and a new faith in the future has been one way of looking at the decade; a cramped, mean-spirited time of repression and conformity at home and old-fashioned isolationism abroad has been another. In fact, however, the 1920s era was all these things, and more: a period in which the foundations of the modern nation were laid. The economic structure, government responsibilities, social divisions, and overseas commitments that evolved during these years marked the emergence of modern America and shaped its development in later decades.

Vicious Years, 1920–1924

Political events at the start of the twenties gave no indication of the major changes about to occur in the nation. In a reaction against the crusading fervor and the growth of presidential power during the eight preceding years of the Wilson administration, both major parties nominated for president conventional mediocrities who reflected a nostalgia for an earlier way of life. For the Democrats, Governor James M. Cox of Ohio offered the best alternative to the stricken but still ambitious President Wilson. Adding a dash of color to Cox's candidacy, the Democrats nominated jaunty young Franklin D. Roosevelt as his running mate. The Republicans, in order to break a convention deadlock, selected weak, affable Senator Warren G. Harding, also from Ohio, and for vice-president the inconsequential governor of Massachusetts, Calvin Coolidge. As the candidates traded platitudes, the tide that had been flowing against the Democrats since 1918 swept the Republicans to power. Soured by the disruptions of the war and the disillusionment of the peace, 61 percent of the American voters, a larger popular majority than any previously given to a presidential candidate, chose the amiable Harding. It was the first national election in which, as a consequence of the Nineteenth Amendment (1920), women throughout the United States voted. With Harding's election, conservative Republicans reestablished their control over the White House.

Antiradicalism. Harding, a decent man, came to office with vague impulses toward creating a quiet national harmony. "America's present need," he had declared during the campaign, "is not heroics, but healing; not nostrums, but normalcy." For many Americans, however, there could be no healing without major surgery first. Movements against disruptive radicals, labor unions, and immigrants, which had originated early in the century and swelled during the war, were cresting. Neither Harding nor his successor, Coolidge, had the will or the strength to check this repressive nativism.

Fears of a Bolshevik revolution in America, touched off by the Russian upheaval of 1917, created the so-called Red Scare of 1919–20 in the United States. During these years a host of private vigilantes and public officials moved with devastating effect against organized radicalism. They completed the destruction of the Industrial Workers of the World (IWW),* ransacked offices of the Socialist party, and even stopped legally elected Socialists from taking their seats in the House of Representatives and the New York Assembly. Wilson's attorney general, A. Mitchell Palmer, twice ordered extensive raids on America's fledgling Communist party and came very close to annihilating it. Eventually the absence of real revolutionaries overcame the public's nightmares of a Bolshevik under every bed. When Palmer predicted that there would be massive bombings on May Day of 1920 and nothing happened, the scare rapidly subsided, and with it ended one phase of antiradicalism.

*For background on the IWW, see chapter 25, pp. 640–41.

Sears, Roebuck
and Co., Chicago

Nevertheless, a more general antiradicalism remained during the early twenties. Such groups as the American Legion imposed provincial, patriotic textbooks on the public schools and forced the firing of liberal teachers. Officials in the Navy Department campaigned against an imaginary "spider web" of women's organizations that were said to be subverting the nation's fighting spirit. "America," evangelist Billy Sunday declared, "is not a country for a dissenter to live in." One victim of this antiradical attitude was the Non-Partisan League, an alliance of respectable farmers, lawyers, and merchants in the Northwest that won control of the North Dakota government and tried to use state funds to aid local farmers. In 1921 and 1922 a group of bankers boycotted the League and succeeded in undermining its "socialist" program.

Antiradicalism also merged with the drives against organized labor. Immediately after the war, businessmen and their allies created "open shop" committees throughout the nation to smash the unions. Although Samuel Gompers, the president of the American Federation of Labor (AFL), and most other labor leaders were vigorous antiradicals, they still could not protect their own unions from sweeping charges of socialism and un-Americanism. The steel companies crushed an ambitious drive to organize workers in their industry in 1919. Two years later the biggest meatpackers cleared the unions from their plants. Conservative judges prohibited a variety of strikes, including ones by the coal miners in 1919 and the railway shopmen in 1922. Under these blows union membership fell from a peak of more than 5 million in 1920 to about 3.6 million in 1923, and union morale suffered even more than statistics could reveal.

The antiradicalism of the time also expressed itself in the famous Sacco-Vanzetti case. In 1921 two immigrant anarchists, Nicola Sacco and Bartolomeo Vanzetti, were tried, convicted, and sentenced to death for the murder of a paymaster in South Braintree, Massachusetts. For years legal appeals delayed their execution. The bias of the trial, and the dignity and eloquence of the prisoners during their long ordeal, attracted a wide range of sympathizers, who fought fervently for their pardon. But in August 1927, as large crowds here and abroad mourned in public, Sacco and Vanzetti died in the electric chair. The burden of protest had shifted. Now the conservatives were on the defensive. Prominent citizens who had once screamed "Bolshevik!" remained remarkably quiet while an embarrassing legacy from the recent past ran its course.

Bigotry of the Twenties.
The early twenties was generally an oppressive time for immigrants, who faced not only social and economic problems, but also widespread charges that their alien influences were permanently corrupting American society. Even before the war a growing number of "native Americans"—white Protestants with northern and western European ancestors—became convinced that they needed special protection against the deluge of Catholics and Jews from southern and eastern Europe. Some accused the immigrants of flooding the labor market and lowering the American standard of living. Others, citing the newcomers' support of political bosses, declared them unfit to vote. Advocates of Prohibition condemned their saloons, and urban reformers condemned their living habits. By 1920 innumerable Americans were justifying these prejudices with racial theories that categorized the "dirty little dark people" of southern and eastern Europe as a genetically inferior breed that was mongrelizing the American population. Unrestricted immigration, the popular writer Kenneth Roberts declared, would create "a hybrid race of people as worthless and futile as the good-for-nothing mongrels of Central America and southeastern Europe."

Despite the efforts of a minority of Americans who defended the immigrants and the American tradition of open gates, public debate in the early twenties focused on the best techniques for restricting the immigrant flow. The government's first attempt, the Literacy Test of 1917, had failed because, contrary to common prejudice, most immigrants could read and write. Consequently, the opponents of immigration shifted to a more effective device: the setting of annual immigration quotas by nationality. In 1921 Congress used 3 percent of the number of foreign-born in the 1910 census as the basis for each European country's quota. Then in the comprehensive National Origins Act of 1924, Congress substituted even lower quotas as an interim measure until experts could prepare the long-range solution, an annual limit of 150,000 immigrants divided according to the presumed percentage of each European nation's historical contribution to the white population in the United States.*

The justification of these laws was explicitly racial and defensive. They were passed at a time when there was a considerable amount of anti-Semitism throughout American society. At each stage in the legislative sequence, Congress discriminated more harshly against southern and eastern Europe, where by far the largest number of potential immigrants

---

*The complicated calculations on national origins were not completed until 1929. The system then went into effect and remained the fundamental law on immigration until 1965, when Congress in a new law used the nation's need for skills as the basis for deciding who should be admitted.

THE KKK ON THE MARCH

At its height in the early 1920s, the Klan used this kind of pomp and mystery to attract new members, focus attention on its activities, and intimidate its enemies.

lived. Not only did the act of 1924 place a ceiling on immigration that was less than one-fifth of the normal prewar flow, but it assigned the English, Germans, and Scandinavians higher quotas than they were able to fill and almost closed the door on the Italians, Poles, and Russians. In a direct slap at the Japanese, the law totally excluded Asians. Seldom had Congress managed to embitter so many people here and abroad with a single law.

The Ku Klux Klan.   The Ku Klux Klan came to embody all the bigotry of the early twenties. In 1920 two talented promoters, Edward Clarke and Elizabeth Tyler, took charge of a small southern organization with a name made famous in the days of Reconstruction.* By capitalizing on the attractions of its fraternal secrecy,

*For the nineteenth-century origins of the Ku Klux Klan, see chapter 20, pp. 509–10.

white-hooded ritual, and elaborate titles, they built the Ku Klux Klan into a nationwide organization of about 4 million members by 1924. The Klan viewed blacks, aliens, and "moral degenerates" as its primary enemies, and in fighting them it often resorted to intimidation and violence. The fiery cross and the midnight whipping became its symbols of justice.

Basically the Klan was a collection of local organizations that fought particular enemies in each community. In the Oklahoma oil fields a local "klavern" boasted of transforming "'no counts' of men and females . . . almost [into] a 'Sunday-School class.'" Its counterpart in Calypso, North Carolina, announced, "All the Catholic gold in the universe can't buy our manhood and our liberty." In Denver the Klan opposed labor unions and welfare programs. But it also extended its influence into state and national politics. Early in the 1920s its leaders claimed political control of states as varied as Oklahoma, Oregon, and Indiana.

The Klan's national spokesmen supported every campaign against radicals and immigrants, and Klansmen paraded in the streets of the nation's capital. At the Democratic convention of 1924, a resolution condemning the Klan, which narrowly lost, almost tore the party apart.

The Klan remained a formidable presence in American politics until 1925. It represented only an exaggerated, somewhat disreputable, version of a common impulse. Its members longed openly for a mythical America of hard-working, church-going, small-town citizens, all white, Anglo-Saxon, and Protestant. The same themes of a lost virtue and a lost unity were woven throughout the movements against radicals, unions, and immigrants. Klansmen, like other Americans in all walks of life, expected public policy to reflect their cultural and moral visions, and to a striking degree by 1924 these expectations were fulfilled.

Yet these grim assaults dwindled rapidly at mid-decade. The battle against radicals, unions, and immigrants had largely been won. In 1924 the national government abandoned the cause of antiradicalism, and by 1928 thirty-four states allowed the feeble Communist party a place on their ballots. Pressure on the public schools lifted. At the annual meeting of the American Legion in 1925, one officer complained that "Americans have become apathetic to the monotonous appeal of the patriotic exhorter." Vigilante activities also declined dramatically. Between 1922 and 1926 the American Civil Liberties Union reported, the number of disrupted public meetings dropped from 225 to 21. By 1925 the Klan was demoralized by exposés of corruption and by the conviction of Indiana's leading Klansman, David Stephenson, in the sex murder of his secretary, and its membership fell from 4 million in 1924 to 200,000 in 1928. By the mid-twenties traditional consensus politics and individual economic advance were once again at the center of American life.

Traditional Politics, 1923–1929

If antiradicalism and nativism were central features of the twenties, so were conventional politics. The presidential candidates of both parties, the cabinet officers, and congressional leaders were generally familiar political figures. They were also representatives of the business interests and political machines that had become mainstays of the nation. The chief executives during the decade—Warren G. Harding, Calvin Coolidge, and Herbert Hoover—stood for the traditional values of rugged individualism, free enterprise, and limited government powers. In a time of significant economic innovations, their administrations provided a strong sense of continuity with the past.

Scandals. The bigotry and repression of the twenties occurred against a backdrop of ineffective national political leadership. Harding, essentially a small-town American, was hopelessly beyond his depth as president. "I knew that this job would be too much for me," he confided to one White House visitor. Although Harding made some excellent appointments, he surrounded himself with old friends—his system has been described as "government by crony"—and brought a number of people to Washington who embarrassed and undermined his administration. A close friend of Harding's attorney general, Harry Daugherty, was caught accepting bribes to protect his clients from federal prosecution, and he committed suicide. Then Charles Forbes, a chance acquaintance whom Harding had appointed director of the Veterans' Bureau, and Thomas Miller, the alien property custodian, were indicted and jailed for extensive frauds. Most sensational of all, a long congressional inquiry in 1923 and 1924 exposed a crude string of bribes and back-room deals behind the leasing to private concerns of government oil lands on Teapot Dome in Wyoming and Elk Hill in California. Two oil men, Harry Sinclair and Edward Doheny, had bought the leases from Secretary of Interior Albert Fall for almost half a million dollars in cash, bonds, and cattle. As a consequence of the "Teapot Dome Scandal," Fall, who looked for all the world like a Hollywood sheriff, was convicted of bribery and became the first cabinet officer in history to serve a prison sentence. Harding's close associate Daugherty barely escaped being the second.

The ineffectual Harding had sensed disaster. "My God, this is a hell of job," he told a journalist. "I have no trouble with my enemies . . . , but my God-damn friends . . . keep me walking the floor nights!" In August 1923, while touring the western states, a despondent Harding died of a heart attack.

Vice-President Calvin Coolidge inherited the mess. A taciturn, morose New Englander of no apparent talents—he impressed Theodore Roosevelt's daughter as having been weaned on a pickle—Coolidge nevertheless appealed to the country as a symbol of old American virtues: frugality, honesty, hard work, and religious faith. Coolidge turned this image to his advantage in the 1924 election. His identification with old Puritan virtues was the perfect antidote to the corruption of the Harding administration. It also gave the Republicans a satisfactory answer to a collection of dissident farm spokesmen, union officials, socialists, and reformers who revived the Progressive party under the leadership of Robert La Follette.* Too divided among themselves to form a workable coalition,

*For the earlier political career of Robert La Follette, see chapters 24 and 25.

CALVIN COOLIDGE
A thoroughly conventional American, Coolidge symbolized traditional values in an unsettling era.

the Progressives carried only Wisconsin. Likewise, a splintered Democratic party could not effectively challenge Coolidge. Torn between an eastern urban bloc and a southern and western rural bloc, the Democratic convention had gone through 103 ballots before nominating John W. Davis, a drab Wall Street lawyer. In November "Silent Cal" swamped Davis by 382 electoral votes to 136.

Coolidge and Congress. Coolidge's triumph coincided with a new calm in national affairs. Indeed, few presidents have encountered as meek a Congress as Coolidge faced after 1924. Liberal opponents such as Senator William Borah of Idaho and Senator George Norris of Nebraska won occasional skirmishes but no important campaigns. The president's Bureau of the Budget, relying on the advice of the United States Chamber of Commerce, set the level of government spending, and congressional appropriations were an almost perfect carbon of the bureau's recommendations. In 1926 even the controversial tax program of Secretary of the Treasury Andrew Mellon was enacted.

To release more money for private investment, Congress lowered the rate of income tax for the very wealthy from 46 percent to 26 percent and cut inheritance taxes in half. As Coolidge neatly explained to the nation, "The business of America is business."

The only significant signs of a congressional rebellion came over farm policy. Commodity prices, which had fallen sharply in 1921, revived sluggishly during the 1920s. In 1929 net farm income was still $3 billion lower than it had been in 1919. During the early twenties the farm lobby had won an array of laws from Congress, including higher tariffs, tighter regulation of the grain exchanges and the stockyards, and easier credit for commercial farmers. When none of these helped very much, sentiment shifted toward the proposals of the persistent George Peek, a manufacturer of agricultural equipment who crusaded for agricultural reforms throughout the twenties. Seal off the domestic market with high tariffs, Peek told the farmers, and sell what you can in this protected market. Then have the government buy the surplus, dump it abroad at the best price, and tax the farmers a small amount to cover any losses.

In Washington, Peek's plan became the McNary-Haugen bill. First in the West and then in the South, Peek gathered enough support to push a McNary-Haugen bill through Congress twice, in 1927 and again in 1928. Coolidge vetoed it both times. Yet by 1928 the actual difference between the farm lobby and the Coolidge administration was not very great. The administration's solution, which was enacted into law in 1929, also sought to regulate the marketing of agricultural products. When prices fell, commodity cooperatives would receive temporary government payments while they stored their products. As prices improved, the cooperatives would gradually sell their surplus and repay the government. In fact, the second McNary-Haugen bill included this scheme. Therefore, considerable optimism prevailed in 1929 when Congress created the Federal Farm Board with an unprecedented $500 million in government credit to help the cooperatives market their products at the best prices.

Old-Fashioned Politics. In the twenties Americans had a strong sense of neighborhood and community. They cared very much about jobs and income, but they tried to manage these problems locally. Their networks were personal ones, woven through families, friends, and local business contacts. They reinforced these strands with a high degree of cultural consciousness. Outside the cities, this usually meant pride in being white, Anglo-Saxon, and Protestant. These same qualities were also important in the cities, but there many groups were trying to preserve their ethnic differences. Black, brown, yellow, or white skin; Italian,

Polish, German, or Irish ancestors; Catholic, Protestant, or Jewish religion—all drew critical social lines.

In the cities, small towns, and countryside alike, these tight local attachments made it extremely difficult to create any kind of broad political organization. Local politics remained the one natural center for this mixture of economic, cultural, and moral concerns. Traditional local politics dominated innumerable county organizations in which friendship and family ties, not efficiency and expertise, determined who would receive most of the jobs and favors. In the big-city political wards, similar private bargains tied individuals, families, and cultural groups into little political alliances. On a large scale, these many personal arrangements were linked together to form the political machines that thrived during the 1920s. Although these machines were known by the names of their bosses—Tom Pendergast in Kansas City, Big Bill Thompson in Chicago, Ed Crump in Memphis, Frank Hague in Jersey City, and James Michael Curley in Boston—their roots were decentralized and popular.

Prohibition as a Rallying Point.

During the twenties it took an exceptionally powerful force to excite national interest. The strongest magnet was the Eighteenth, or "Prohibition," Amendment, which banned the production and sale of liquor. Put into effect in January 1920 and enforced by the strict Volstead Act, the Eighteenth Amendment began its career in an atmosphere of high optimism. Drinking, declared William Jennings Bryan, was as dead an issue as slavery. But countless Americans decided otherwise. Continuing demand in the big cities and a considerable market elsewhere in the nation created a massive business out of illicit production and distribution. As one investigating commission ruefully noted, "Few things are more easily made than alcohol." A little machinery and a bathtub transformed any thirsty citizen into a distiller. Moreover, the long boundary of the United States provided many unpatrolled areas where illegal importers could smuggle liquor into the country. Rumrunners trucked it in from Canada and Mexico, and ferried it in small boats to isolated coves along both coasts. To police these many violations, the Treasury Department employed about 2,000 officials. Herbert Hoover later estimated that effective enforcement would have required at least 250,000. Indeed, Prohibition's most serious long-term consequence was to expand and strengthen the organized crime syndicates that quickly established control over the illegal liquor traffic.

In 1920 most prominent citizens dutifully endorsed the Eighteenth Amendment. But in the course of the decade, successful Americans increasingly

AL SMITH ON THE COVER OF "LIFE" MAGAZINE, 1928
Loyal to Tammany and hostile to Prohibition, Smith could never escape the image of the New York ward boss who had made good.

turned against Prohibition. Millions of citizens came to consider Prohibition an insufferable violation of their rights. Prohibition, they said, artificially created a new class of criminals—those who drank and those who supplied the liquor—spread disrespect for the law, and then increased taxes to pay for the enforcement of the law. Those who favored repeal assumed that the use of alcohol did not matter very much: drinking should be a question of individual choice.

The "wets" not only made a joke of the law in their neighborhoods and communities; they increasingly demanded action from national and state governments. In 1923 New York repealed the state law that enforced Prohibition. By 1930 six other states had followed New York's lead. But with equal fervor millions of locally oriented "drys" regarded Prohibition as the keystone of American morality. Beyond pressing for Prohibition in their localities, they sponsored stern laws to uphold what Herbert Hoover called "the noble experiment." In Michigan a fourth offense under the

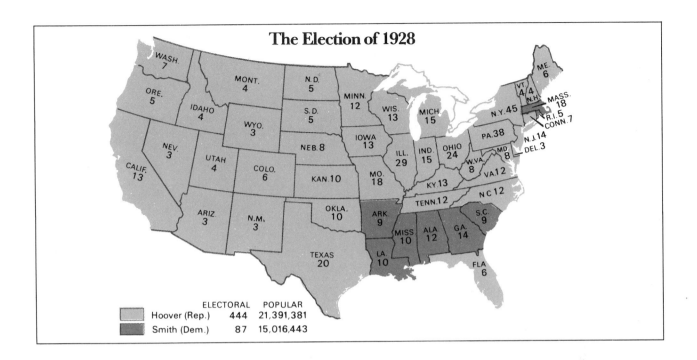

The Election of 1928

	ELECTORAL	POPULAR
Hoover (Rep.)	444	21,391,381
Smith (Dem.)	87	15,016,443

Prohibition law meant life imprisonment. Basically the story of Prohibition was this stream of local passions pouring through the nation and battling in the name of irreconcilable truths.

Modern Versus Traditional Politics. From these same sources came the emotions that made Alfred E. Smith the most controversial politician of the 1920s. A capable governor of New York who very much wanted to be president, Al Smith touched the nerve centers of traditional, local politics. He was a Catholic, an anti-prohibitionist, and a self-taught politician who wore Tammany Hall's traditional brown derby askew and spoke in the accents of Manhattan's East Side streets. The thought of Al Smith in the White House roused feelings of wonder and horror across the nation. Self-conscious ethnic groups in the northern cities who were Catholic and wet gave him their fanatical devotion. White Protestant Democrats in the rural South who were dry looked on Smith as the Antichrist. At the Democratic convention of 1924, Smith's friends and enemies had fought over his nomination to the point of exhaustion before turning to John W. Davis. But in 1928, in the absence of a serious competitor, southern delegates finally allowed Smith's nomination for president, although with the most profound misgivings.

The election of 1928 provided a unique meeting ground for the conflicting spirits of modern and traditional politics. To oppose Smith, the Republicans chose Herbert Hoover, by all odds the outstanding leader of the modern political economy, but, like Coolidge, also a symbol of old America. After an impressive early success in business as a mining engineer, Hoover had won renown during the First World War as an administrator, first of international relief, then of agriculture. There had been talk of Hoover as president in 1920. Instead, he had served in the cabinets of Harding and Coolidge and made himself the unofficial center of the executive branch: "Secretary of Commerce and assistant secretary of everything else." He was serious and shy, extremely proud and highly ambitious. Too formidable for Coolidge, who disliked him, and too independent for many professional politicians, who preferred a weaker man, Hoover still went after the nomination with absolute confidence in his ability to be president. Successful Americans overwhelmingly supported him. Of those listed in *Who's Who*, for example, 87 percent endorsed his candidacy.

Al Smith sought to pitch his campaign to all Americans. An essentially conservative man, the Democratic candidate thought of himself as an eminently qualified leader for the American system, not as a product of New York City's Lower East Side. To oversee his campaign, Smith selected a prominent General Motors executive, John J. Raskob, rather than a professional politician. The partisans of traditional politics, however, would not let Smith rise above his origins. In November 1928 Smith's name on the ballot drew large, jubilant majorities in the industrial cities, but it also sent millions of Protestant townspeople to the polls with a religious commitment to Hoover and put seven formerly Democratic southern states in the Republican column. Hoover, the shining symbol of both modern prosperity and old American values, swept to victory with 444 electoral votes against Smith's 87.

The Modern Political Economy, 1920–1929

Opposing the reactionary political trends of the early twenties were fundamental changes in social and economic organization that prepared the way for America's future. None of the changes individually made the headlines; in combination they completed an organizational revolution that had been under way for more than a generation. Since the turn of the century, national groups in business, labor, agriculture, finance, and the professions had been forming— associations of lumber companies, retail druggists, railroad workers, investment bankers, civil engineers, and the like. Each group was organized according to the special economic function it performed, and each wanted to stabilize its own sphere with its own rules. Each expected long-range planning to increase its efficiency and its income. Each recognized the importance of linking its activities with the activities of other groups around it. Taken together, they created a new national system of specialized organizations that were integrated by a common national outlook, a common concern for the vigor of the whole economy, and a common belief in the value of cooperation and coordination.

Business in the Twenties.

The most successful means of business stabilization was oligopoly, the domination of an industry by a few large firms. By 1920 oligopolies controlled almost every basic industry that needed a heavy investment of capital. In railroading, for example, a handful of corporations, approximately equal in strength, divided the nation's territory among themselves. In the automobile industry Ford and General Motors set the standard for a competitive expanding market. In steel one huge firm, United States Steel, rose above the other corporations—called Little Steel—to become the industry's leader. Oligopoly simplified the problems of industrial coordination by limiting the number of companies that had to agree on a common business policy. Buccaneers of business like Jay Gould no longer ran these industrial giants. Now management teams, working through elaborate corporate structures, coordinated the nation's big business.

In such industries as clothing manufacture, building construction, and most branches of retailing, where capital demands were less and many small

firms competed, trade associations were an alternative way of minimizing competition. About 2,000 trade associations already existed in 1920, and they continued to multiply. With activities ranging from secret price-fixing pacts to occasional lunch meetings, the trade associations shared a belief that pooling information would stabilize their industries and increase their profits. Although they seldom coordinated business affairs as effectively as the oligopolies did, the trade associations still moved in the same general direction of cooperation and planning.

Most businessmen expected wage earners to play their part in these coordinating programs. Unlike the captains of industry of the late nineteenth century, who had usually treated wage earners much as they did hunks of ore or gears in the machinery, the modern business managers considered laborers as key individuals whose efficiency would increase as their morale and incentive improved. Specialists in personnel policy organized company recreational programs, prepared chatty company bulletins, and invited workers to suggest improvements in the firms' procedures. Large corporations in particular sponsored shop committees, company unions, and employee representation plans—"the world's greatest democracy," boasted the president of Standard Oil of Indiana. More and more of the unions in the AFL and the Railroad Brotherhoods adapted to such company policies. Under an accommodating new president, William Green, the AFL in 1925 listed the improvement of industrial productivity among its primary objectives. "[The] new, suave, discreet unionism," one commentator noted late in the 1920s, "talks the language of the efficiency engineer and busies itself about ways and means of increasing output." But despite their leaders' willingness to cooperate with business, workers shared only part of the economic benefits of the period. In the best years of the twenties, the annual income of about two-thirds of the nation's families fell below $2,500, which experts considered adequate to maintain a decent standard of living. These families had only an indirect stake in the economic system that was forming on the national level.

For good reason, successful commercial farmers regarded themselves as businessmen. As chemical fertilizers and the gasoline engine were revolutionizing agriculture, only the wealthy investor, using the latest improvements on a large scale, could expect to profit from modern farming. These "agribusinessmen," like their industrial counterparts, wanted to coordinate their affairs, and they too organized. Local farm bureaus distributed information about scientific farming techniques, and through the national organization, the American Farm Bureau Federation, lobbied for favorable government policies. Dairy farmers formed cooperative marketing associations. Groups of commercial farmers behaved so much like conventional business organizations that the same men who had staffed Bernard Baruch's War Industries Board in 1918 became the most prominent agricultural advisers of the twenties.

Bankers acted as auxiliaries to these various business groups. The wizards of Wall Street no longer dominated American business as they had twenty years earlier. Not only did the regional structure of the new Federal Reserve System encourage financial decentralization, but an increasing number of important corporations also gained control over their own banking. During the 1920s, companies as diverse as Eastman Kodak, Aluminum Corporation of America, Ford, and Sears, Roebuck routinely financed business expansion from their own vast profits. Banks too, as agencies of service, organized themselves in subdivisions that matched the needs of their business clients. The professions formed a second band of auxiliaries to business. Legal specialties in such areas as contracts, taxation, and labor policy were growing alongside modern industry. A variety of engineers, economists, statisticians, psychologists, sociologists, and educators also became willing helpers to the nation's business. Where an important profession, such as research chemistry, was not adequately developed, powerful industries encouraged its growth.

Most wage earners during the 1920s were not union members, and most farmers never joined the agricultural organizations. Everywhere, very small businesses remained outside the economic leagues and trade associations; the United States Chamber of Commerce discouraged membership in towns under 5,000, and businessmen in these small communities kept largely to themselves. But although so many Americans did not belong to them, the emerging national economic organizations were the principal force in shaping the nation's economic life.

The New National Economy.

Because the new network of economic groups was national in scope and outlook, only the government in Washington could meet its needs. In the broadest sense, the national government was expected to facilitate the work of private groups, to promote cooperation among them, and to surround them with a favorable legal framework. During the early twenties, one after another of the government's offices shaped its policies to serve the new national economy. Herbert Hoover, as secretary of commerce (1921-29), the most important cabinet official of the decade, led his department in its efforts to help manufacturers standardize production; to distribute business statistics for the trade associations; to enable the major broadcasting companies to stabilize the new radio industry; and, at every opportunity, to publicize the virtues of business cooperation.

Less dramatically, other departments expanded their services to commercial farmers, hydroelectric power companies, and private industries in food, mining, and lumber. Each of the independent regulatory commissions, so vital to progressive reform, found a way to assist business coordination. Through the Transportation Act of 1920, the Interstate Commerce Commission secured extensive authority over almost all areas of the railroad industry, and it used these broad powers to encourage oligopoly and cooperative agreements. By 1925 the Federal Trade Commission was specializing in conferences for trade associations. Because the Federal Reserve Board in Washington proved to be ineffective, the New York Regional Board coordinated national banking policy. By 1925, as a consequence of the federal government's expanded activities, the nation's budget had increased by 250 percent over its 1915 level.

The Supreme Court endorsed all these developments. First, it sanctioned oligopolies. In *United States* v. *United States Steel Co.* (1920), the Court allowed the nation's largest corporation to dominate its industry as long as some competitors survived. Then, after considerable hesitation, the Court in the *Maple Flooring Manufacturers' Association* case of 1925 declared that trade associations, like oligopolies, were legal if they did not eliminate competition in their areas of business. The Justice Department advised the trade associations on how best to stay inside the law. Meanwhile, the court limited the constraints that the labor unions might impose on business. Led by its new chief justice, William Howard Taft, whom Harding had appointed in 1921, the Court sharply restricted organized labor's right to picket and boycott, and it watched approvingly as the lower courts expanded the use of injunctions against striking workers. In addition, the Supreme Court overturned a national child labor law in *Bailey* v. *Drexel Furniture Co.* (1922) and a state minimum wage law in *Adkins* v. *Children's Hospital* (1923).

The national economic system could not function without the government's assistance. At the center of the national system were production and distribution, with agriculture connected at the side and labor linked below, and bankers and professionals contributing specialized services; the government's part was to wrap the system in protective rules, expert counsel, and helpful mediation. The leading proponent of this national political economy, Herbert Hoover, envisaged the system as a "third alternative" to laissez-faire capitalism and state socialism—a voluntary, cooperative commonwealth that followed the scientific principles of coordination and efficiency.

THE PROUD CONSUMERS
In the 1920s the radio revolutionized mass communication in America as countless citizens gathered around their radio sets every evening to "tune in" to their favorite programs.

Brown Brothers

A Consumer Paradise. By the mid-1920s the new national system was in place and performing miracles. After a sharp recession in 1921–22, the gross national product (GNP) climbed 5 percent a year, and during the decade manufacturing output rose 64 percent. The leaders of the boom were the automobile and construction industries. Both the number of automobile sales and the value of construction more than tripled between 1915 and 1925, and these economic leaders created benefits widely for such related industries as steel, petroleum, rubber, and cement. By the end of the twenties, the number of registered cars almost equaled the number of families. America's passionate love affair with the automobile had begun.

Cars, roads, and houses were nationally visible benefits. So was a second category of consumer products that relied on the spread of electricity. Midwestern utilities magnate Samuel Insull pioneered in selling metered electrical service to households, and other companies soon recognized the genius of his scheme. By the end of the twenties, two out of three households had electricity, in contrast to one out of five before the First World War. Into their new electrical outlets Americans plugged lamps, refrigerators, washing machines, and toasters, each a marvel in the twenties. Above all, electricity brought the radio. In November 1920 the crackling sounds of America's first radio station, KDKA of East Pittsburgh, opened a modern era of personal mass communication. By 1923 over five hundred broadcasting stations with much-improved equipment were in operation. Electrical technology also created a new lord of the entertainment world, motion pictures, which grew from a scattering of nickelodeon shows and occasional full-length features to a systematized $2 billion industry with a steady flow of films. By the end of the twenties, more than 80 million people were going to the movies each week.

To countless white, middle-class Americans, all this created a consumer paradise. Abandoning the time-honored rules to buy cautiously, fear debt, and save each small surplus, they made consumer credit a national necessity, and it soon became available through a great variety of convenient outlets. How the economy worked impressed some people even more than how much it produced. A broad range of manufacturing plants, following the lead of Henry Ford, introduced the moving assembly line, a revolution in factory procedure. Through electricity in industry and the gasoline engine in agriculture, the amount of horsepower per worker rose well over 50 percent during the twenties. As a consequence of these changes, output per working hour increased an astonishing 35 percent, almost twice the gains of the previous decade. America, it seemed, had answered all the riddles of economic growth. Throughout the decade a stream of delegations came from abroad in hopes of discovering the secret of American productivity.

Contemporaries declared the arrival of a "New Era." "The first responsibility of an American to his country," announced one newspaper, "is no longer that of a citizen, but of a consumer." Former critics of American society now became its ardent champions. Socialism was "reactionary," said John Spargo, once a leader of the Socialist party, and American capitalism offered "the greatest hope for mankind." As the number of strikes declined drastically, praise for the nationwide spirit of cooperation filled the air. "I can find no historic parallel, outside of the great religious revivals, with which [the present] has much in common," marveled a veteran of the social gospel. "Thru business . . . ," another publicist promised even more grandly, "the human race is to be redeemed." From the vantage point of the Great Depression, it would be easy to ridicule the grandiose claims: poverty on the verge of extinction, a chicken in every pot and two cars in every garage, anyone with self-discipline and common sense a millionaire. Yet during the late twenties innumerable Americans were believers.

America's Response to the World, 1920–1930

At the close of the First World War, the great majority of Americans wished to insulate themselves from further contact with the outside world. Disillusioned with the outcome of the fighting, fearful of Bolshevism, and antagonistic toward immigrants bringing alien habits to the nation's shores, the country rejected participation in the League of Nations in 1920. It reduced its army and navy to fewer than 250,000 men in 1921, raised barriers to trade in the Fordney-McCumber Tariff Act of 1922, and refused to recognize the Soviet Union throughout the decade. Americans, it seemed, wanted walls to protect themselves against everything foreign—people, goods, ideas, and responsibilities.

Yet disengagement after the war was not a simple process. American soldiers who had entered Siberia in a muddled attempt to counter the Bolsheviks lingered there until 1920 in an equally muddled attempt to counter Japanese influence. Until 1923 the United States also kept a token force in Germany's occupied Rhineland provinces, more to temper French belligerence than to punish Germany. Despite cries of outrage from America's former allies, the United States insisted on the repayment of large loans that had been made during the war. Because the European debtors tried to link their payments to the United States to the amount of reparations they were collecting from Germany, the United States once more found itself entangled in the issues that had defeated Wilson at Versailles.

Perhaps most important in the country's continuing involvement in world affairs after 1920 were its enduring sense of responsibility for international peace and its extensive ties to the world economy. Eager to support political and economic stability abroad without commitments that could force it into another war, the country settled on a policy of what has been called "moral cooperation": paper agreements to control arms, and unofficial backing for private financial arrangements, to prevent international economic collapse.

The first step in this process was the Washington Conference of 1921–22. This international meeting occurred in response to postwar demands for disarmament and for economy in government, and to fears of Japan's imperial ambitions on the mainland of Asia and toward Western-controlled colonies in the Pacific, especially the Philippine Islands. With the Far East in mind, Secretary of State Charles Evans Hughes, an astute diplomat, used the growing concerns over a worldwide naval armaments race as the justification for calling the conference. During the winter of 1921–22, representatives from industrial nations with interests in East Asia (except Russia) met in Washington. To everyone's surprise, Hughes insisted that the delegates act as well as talk. Consequently the Washington Conference produced three important agreements. All of them sought in some way to freeze the existing balance of power and privileges in East Asia. One, the critical Four-Power Treaty of nonaggression among the United States, Japan, Great Britain, and France, superseded the prewar Anglo-Japanese alliance and committed the signatories to respect each other's rights in the Pacific. A second agreement, the Five-Power Treaty, added Italy to the big four and established tonnage limitations on major warships according to a ratio approximating the current strength of these nations. Finally, the Nine-Power Treaty committed all imperial nations to the principle of equal opportunity inside an independent China—the American doctrine of the "Open Door."

On the one hand, these treaties reflected America's inward-turning, defensive impulses. They pulled the United States away from a naval confrontation with Japan, and they included no provisions for enforcement. On the other hand, they acknowledged a crucial interconnection among the world's industrial nations, a mutual dependence that required negotiation, coordination, and a broad structure of rules.

In the same spirit of coordination and stabilization, Americans responded to the European crisis of 1923–1924. When Germany defaulted on its reparations and French troops occupied the industrial nerve center of the Ruhr, the German economy experienced runaway inflation. The French economy also staggered. Through the Dawes Plan of 1924, the United States unofficially took the lead in negotiating large private loans to revive Germany. Simultaneously, J. P. Morgan and Company arranged a loan to France on the understanding that it would not disrupt the fragile German recovery. As Germany resumed paying reparations, the former Allied Powers then made some payments on their war debts, and the United States did not press them very hard for more. Without a formal government commitment, the United States presided over a complex process of international stabilization.

These initial efforts to create international order remained basic to American policy. The Young Plan of 1929 reformulated the Dawes Plan in hopes of managing war debts and reparations far into the future. A year later the London Naval Conference expanded the scope of the Washington Conference naval agreement to cover a full range of warships. In addition, the United States diverted France's proposal in 1927 for a bilateral treaty into a general, multilateral declaration against war. More than sixty nations eventually ratified the Kellogg-Briand Peace Pact of 1928, which took its name from the principal negotiators, Coolidge's Secretary of State Frank B. Kellogg and France's Foreign Minister Aristide Briand. "An international kiss," snorted Missouri's flinty Senator James Reed. Nevertheless, the pulls of a popular isolationism would allow no greater American involvement in global enforcement. When the Coolidge administration recommended that the United States join the World Court, the League of Nations' weak judicial arm, the Senate attached so many special conditions to America's participation that the other members of the World Court refused the terms.

As the financial plans for Europe demonstrated, American policymakers saw an intimate connection between international stability and economic expansion. Each, they thought, could be made to serve the other. At home or abroad, of course, the modern political economy was a profit system. Herbert Hoover's Department of Commerce gathered and distributed to American business extensive data on foreign markets. When American diplomats failed to break the European petroleum monopoly in the Middle East, the government allowed American oil companies to conduct their own diplomacy, with Washington's approval. At the same time, in Latin America the United States tried to preserve the near monopoly of American companies against their European competitors. Yet foreign trade remained only about 5 percent of the national income during the twenties, and foreign investments never reached 3 percent of the nation's total assets. It was difficult to argue that the health of the American economy required drastic diplomatic measures abroad. Hence, within the limits of the voluntary cooperative system, Washington's leaders tried to assimilate business expansion into what they thought was a healthy international order.

This aversion to aggressive action extended to Latin America as well. During the twenties the three Republican administrations gradually rejected the "Roosevelt Corollary" to the Monroe Doctrine, which had made the United States a policeman over Latin America's unstable, defaulting governments. The best evidence of a changing approach came from the long, difficult negotiations with Mexico over the rights of American corporations in its oil industry. President Coolidge dispatched the adroit banker Dwight Morrow as ambassador and won a settlement of the oil controversy in 1928.

In all, American foreign policy in the twenties endorsed an international rule of law by which nations were to settle their differences without resorting to war. From the perspective of the Second World War and the Cold War, the international system that the United States helped to construct in the twenties looks particularly naïve. But the peace-loving, isolationist temper of the time would not allow policymakers to do more. Not until the Great Depression and the rise of aggressive regimes in Germany and Japan did Americans become persuaded that international affairs required more than paper promises to ensure economic and political stability around the globe. Only then would more "realistic" assumptions about the world shape Washington's handling of overseas affairs.

Modern Culture

American dreams of a peaceful, cooperative world partly reflected a desire to ignore foreign affairs and concentrate on exciting developments at home. The new technology revolutionized the personal experiences of a great many Americans in the 1920s and created a stronger sense of national identity. The average middle-class person could now afford an automobile, so that people who had never traveled fifty miles from their home towns were discovering a wider world and coming home with different points of view. Through extended and improved telephone services, they wove wider networks of family, friendship, and community ties. Radio and motion pictures brought still another dimension to their lives. The voices from the radio and faces on the screen generated a new, synthetic world of familiarity and trust in which no personal participation was necessary, or even possible. In a distinctively modern way, millions now felt more intimately involved with people they would never meet than with the people next door.

Rapid standardization in production in the automobile, radio broadcasting, and film industries created an illusion of American homogeneity. By 1930 three automobile manufacturers—General Motors, Ford, and Chrysler—made 83 percent of the nation's automobiles. Soon they would be synchronizing

Collection of Business Americana, Smithsonian Institution

Features of the Ford car

Sturdy body construction ~ ~ Ease of control ~ ~ Four Houdaille hydraulic double-acting shock absorbers ~ ~ Triplex shatter-proof glass windshield ~ ~ Fully enclosed, silent six-brake system ~ ~ Quick acceleration ~ ~ 55 to 65 miles an hour ~ ~ Smoothness and security at all speeds ~ ~ Vibration-absorbing engine support ~ ~ Choice of colors ~ ~ Tilting beam headlamps ~ ~ Theft-proof ignition lock ~ ~ Reliability ~ ~ Economy ~ ~ Long life

THE 1929 FORD
In the twenties the automobile, which came within the reach of most American families, helped to promote a national economic boom and to give Americans a greater sense of freedom.

industry-wide changes in car styles. The formation of the National Broadcasting Company in 1926 and of the Columbia Broadcasting System in 1927 superimposed national network programming over the previously decentralized radio industry, and after 1927 the total number of stations declined. In the fall of 1931, one-third of the population listened weekly to the comedy "Amos 'n' Andy." A flourishing industry of advertising had Americans everywhere humming the jingles for Campbell's soup and Rinso soap. Hollywood films issued from a handful of gigantic studios such as Warner Brothers and Metro-Goldwyn-Mayer. Standardization was a hallmark of the decade.

Modern Values. Among the messages coming from America's modern centers of communication was a new model of the good life. The era of frugality, when Americans made work and economic gain the focus of their lives, now gave way to an emphasis on leisure and play, conformity and personal charm. Where scientists, businessmen, and statesmen, the "idols of production," had been the most prominent Americans at the turn of the century, now the most admired public figures were the professional athletes and entertainers,—the "idols of consumption." The newspapers of the era began to describe American life less as a political and economic struggle than as "a hilarious merry-go-round of sport, crime, and sex."

In the twenties Americans began to live with an exhilarating sense of their freedom to enter the consumer market and simply enjoy themselves. Clothes worn during leisure hours became a matter of personal taste rather than an expression of solid character. The styles of the 1920s emphasized the modern freedom: new colors and patterns for men's clothing, the departure of corsets and hobbling long skirts for women. Both men and women now smoked casually in public, and cigarette sales climbed 250 percent during the decade. The symbol of the exciting new freedom was the "flapper." With hair bobbed, face painted, and cigarette in hand, she airily waved good-bye to yesterday's rules. Her flattened breasts, loose-fitting clothes, and short skirt gave her the appearance of a modern Peter Pan, seizing the pleasure of the moment in the spirit of eternal youth.

As the areas of private discretion expanded, leisure came to have a new meaning. Leisure activities no longer had to be justified as morally beneficial but were simply considered good ways for people to release their tensions and return refreshed to their jobs. Between 1919 and 1929 American expenditures on recreation more than doubled. The best expression of the new meaning of leisure was the annual vacation, a period of time set aside specifically for relaxation. Once the prerogative of a very small, prosperous minority, the annual vacation became widely accepted during the twenties. Early in the decade, according to a study by the sociologists Robert and Helen Lynd, most white-collar employees in Muncie, Indiana, assumed for the first time in their lives that they had a right to an annual vacation, and many received one with pay. Increasing numbers flocked to the parks maintained by the expanding National Park Service for those vacations. Parks were recognized as a valuable public facility where the nation's city dwellers could turn once a year for their recreation.

Changing Morals. A higher premium on personal freedom meant a lower premium on traditional morals. Although church membership increased a striking 31 percent between 1916 and 1926, so did the emphasis in white-collar congregations on a soothing, largely undemanding religion that stressed good human relations rather than sin and salvation. Not every liberal Protestant welcomed Bruce Barton's bestselling *The Man Nobody Knows* (1925), which transformed Jesus into a vigorous executive who had taken "twelve men from the bottom ranks of business and forged them into an organization that conquered the world."

The description by the sociologists Robert and Helen Lynd of the impact of the automobile on Muncie, Indiana, a typical small midwestern city, illustrates the transformation of American values in the twenties.

Middletown Takes to the Road

THE first real automobile appeared in Middletown in 1900. About 1906 it was estimated that "there are probably 200 in the city and county." At the close of 1923 there were 6,221 passenger cars in the city, one for every 6.1 persons, or roughly two for every three families. . . . As, at the turn of the century, business class people began to feel apologetic if they did not have a telephone, so ownership of an automobile has now reached the point of being an accepted essential of normal living. . . .

Many families feel that an automobile is justified as an agency holding the family group together. "I never feel as close to my family as when we are all together in the car," said one business class mother, and one or two spoke of giving up Country Club membership or other recreations to get a car for this reason. "We don't spend anything on recreation except for the car. We save every place we can and put the money into the car. It keeps the family together." . . .

But this centralizing tendency of the automobile may be only a passing phase; sets in the other direction are almost equally prominent. "Our daughters [eighteen and fifteen] don't use our car much because they are always with somebody else in their car when we go out motoring," lamented one business class mother. And another said, "The two older children [eighteen and sixteen] never go out when the family motors. They always have something else on." "In the nineties we were all much more together," said another wife. "People brought chairs and cushions out of the house and sat on the lawn evenings. We rolled out a strip of carpet and put cushions on the porch step to take care of the unlimited overflow of neighbors that dropped by. We'd sit out so all evening. The younger couples perhaps would wander off for half an hour to get a soda but come back to join in the informal singing or listen while somebody strummed a mandolin or guitar." "What on earth *do* you want me to do? Just sit around home all evening!" retorted a popular high school girl of today when her father discouraged her going out motoring for the evening with a young blade in a rakish car waiting at the curb. . . .

Sharp, also, is the resentment aroused by this elbowing new device when it interferes with old-established religious habits. The minister trying to change people's behavior in desired directions through the spoken word must compete against the strong pull of the open road strengthened by endless printed "copy" inciting to travel. Preaching to 200 people on a hot, sunny Sunday in midsummer on "The Supreme Need of Today," a leading Middletown minister denounced "automobilitis—the thing those people have who go off motoring on Sunday instead of going to church. . . ."

But if the automobile touches the rest of Middletown's living at many points, it has revolutionized its leisure; more, perhaps than the movies or any other intrusion new to Middletown since the nineties, it is making leisure-time enjoyment a regularly expected part of every day and week rather than an occasional event. The readily available leisure-time options of even the working class have been multiplied many-fold. As one working class housewife remarked, "We just go to lots of things we couldn't go to if we didn't have a car." Beefsteak and watermelon picnics in a park or a near-by wood can be a matter of a moment's decision on a hot afternoon.

Not only has walking for pleasure become practically extinct, but the occasional event such as a parade on a holiday attracts far less attention now. . . . Today the week before the Fourth [of July] brings a pale edition of the earlier din, continuing until the night before. But the Fourth dawns quietly on an empty city; Middletown has taken to the road.

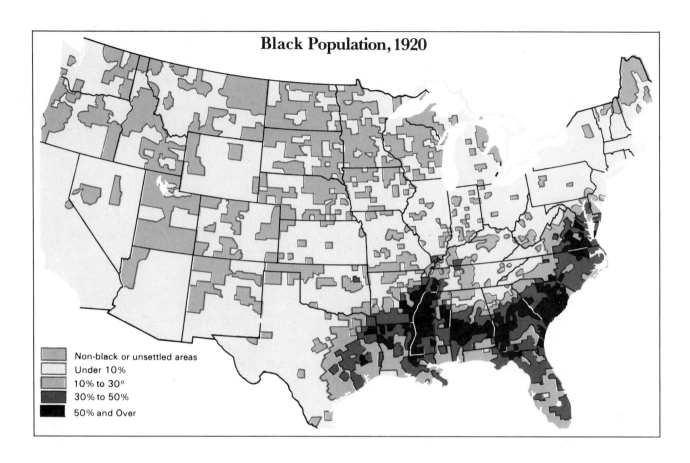

Black Population, 1920

Non-black or unsettled areas
Under 10%
10% to 30°
30% to 50%
50% and Over

Nevertheless, few liberal Protestants during the twenties expressed much concern of any kind for theological details or even denominational distinctions. To many of them, Catholicism now seemed less an evil religion than an odd but purely private choice. The anti-Catholic furor surrounding Al Smith's presidential campaign in 1928 simply made no sense from the new, liberal Protestant perspective.

Nor did the long-standing association between sex and sin. During the twenties a variety of psychologists, including the American disciples of Sigmund Freud, told Americans to consider sex a human need to satisfy; the more complete the satisfaction, the healthier the individual. Repression and guilt only warped the personality. Public displays of affection did not, as in the past, imply loose morals. Even premarital sex became a legitimate subject for discussion. Margaret Sanger, America's pioneer advocate of birth control, who had once been scorned in respected circles, now won the approval and even the financial support of many well-to-do Americans. Although too much "petting" remained a parental worry and any hint of "free love" was sharply condemned, sex emerged in the twenties as a subject for rational examination instead of moral taboo.

The New Urban Standard. The new values concerning recreation, religion, and sex found their strongest support in metropolitan areas. During the 1920s cities of 100,000 or over grew more than twice as fast as the population as a whole. White-collar workers, whose numbers were increasing at about the same rate, congregated in and around these cities and reinforced one another's values. An urban way of life became the ideal, and they used it to judge the rest of the nation. Instead of praising the education given at the little red schoolhouses in the countryside, urban educators recommended that these schools be consolidated to lower costs and modernize instruction. At the University of Chicago, sociologists declared the urban family emotionally healthier than the rural family. The farther that life was removed from the styles of the big city, the less attractive it appeared. The descriptions of the small town as a prison in Sherwood Anderson's *Winesburg, Ohio* (1919) and Sinclair Lewis's *Main Street* (1920) were enthusiastically received by urban readers.

The new urban standard was particularly hard in its judgment of the South. In 1925 Henry L. Mencken, critic, essayist, and high priest of the new urban culture, visited Dayton, Tennessee, to report on the trial

"MARCUS GARVEY IN REGALIA, 1924"
Black nationalism found a spectacular leader in the fiery Garvey.

of a high school biology instructor, John Scopes, who had broken a state law by teaching Darwin's theory of evolution. Because the trial pitted the famous criminal lawyer Clarence Darrow, speaking for modern values, against William Jennings Bryan, the aging champion of traditional evangelical Protestantism, it became a national spectacle.

An urban audience, unable to comprehend why anyone would legislate against science, treated the Scopes trial like a carnival of freaks. As H. L. Mencken described the "anthropoid rabble" of Tennesseans protecting themselves "from whatever knowledge violated their superstitions," the modern caricature of the South was taking shape. Sharecropping, soil leaching, and unmechanized farming retarded southern agriculture. A crude racism seemed to dominate its society, and a narrow Protestant theology seemed to tyrannize its spirit. Support for Prohibition and opposition to Al Smith thrived there. When Erskine Caldwell's *Tobacco Road* appeared in 1932, many Americans were already prepared to accept this account of a stunted life on Georgia's barren soil as a picture of the true South.

Black Americans in the Cities.

During the 1920s close to a million blacks left the South in search of jobs in northern cities, almost double the number that had migrated in the previous decade. The northern urban experience altered black attitudes. First, it encouraged their assertiveness. During the same years that whites argued over what percentage of which race should be allowed to immigrate, urban blacks were also showing a stronger racial consciousness. Claude McKay, Langston Hughes, Countee Cullen, and other contributors to the "Harlem Renaissance" of the 1920s wrote eloquently about the black spirit. Early in the twenties, millions of blacks found inspiration in the African nationalism of Marcus Garvey, an immigrant from Jamaica whose Universal Negro Improvement Association promised racial glory in the Empire of Africa.* Second, the northern urban experience stimulated a national movement for black rights. Its primary organization was the National Association for the Advancement of Colored People (NAACP), and the primary spokesman was Walter White, a talented writer and persistent lobbyist who in 1931 began his twenty-four-year tenure as national secretary for the NAACP. When it became clear that only the national government could significantly improve the position of blacks in America, the NAACP pressed two kinds of arguments on the government's leaders. One, appealing to their conscience, demanded racial equality. The other, appealing to their political interests, offered to trade black votes for black rights. Unlike the southern

---

*Garvey's conviction in 1923 for mail fraud disorganized his movement, and nothing comparable arose to take its place.

VARIETIES IN BLACK LEADERSHIP
A. Philip Randolph (left), who organized the black railroad workers in the 1920s, won a striking victory for fair employment practices from President Roosevelt in 1941. Marching in suit and tie, he continued the drive for black rights at the Democratic convention of 1948. The poet Langston Hughes (above) was one of the prominent voices in the Harlem Renaissance.

cotton fields, the northern cities lay in competitive, two-party states with large electoral votes, and the NAACP tried to convince the Democratic party in particular that urban blacks could tip the balance in these states.

Modern Families and Careers.

Modern values also reshaped the role of the family in American life. In the white-collar world around the cities, occupations were the primary source of men's prestige; their reputations were created in their offices. Extramarital sex, especially in the large cities, became increasingly acceptable. So in Sinclair Lewis's *Babbitt* (1922), the hero could have a brief affair without damaging his career, even in the small fictional city of Zenith. Wives were expected to restrain their husbands' drift away from the family. Advertisements promised housewives who made efforts to serve better dinners and to maintain cleaner houses miraculous results in keeping husbands close to home. Newspaper advice columns revealed how to soothe a tense, weary man at the end of the workday. Accompanying the new explicitness about sex, a thriving cosmetics industry encouraged wives to enhance their physical charms as a means of holding husbands within the home.

Unlike the nineteenth-century wife who had been

HOLLYWOOD DREAMS
Behind the fantasy of this movieland poster lay important changes in public behavior that sharpened the conflict between modern and traditional values and institutionalized the "adolescent rebellion."

solemnly charged with preserving society's morals, her modern counterpart had no such high responsibilities. In a system of values that honored expertise, her talents as a homemaker could never compete with the claims of business and the professions despite the national promotion of a "science" of home economics. As women's traditional sphere shrank, however, other opportunities beckoned. "Bedroom towns"—the residential areas from which men commuted daily to their downtown offices—became uniquely female domains where women moved and talked and acted much as they chose during the daytime hours. Under radically less surveillance than their grandmothers had experienced, they purchased most of the food and clothing for their families, and consequently their preferences had a powerful influence on the local consumer market.

Few of these women, however, had their own occupations. The great majority of white married women did not work outside the home. In 1920 only some 6.5 percent of these women were in the work force, and by 1940 this number had grown only to about 12 percent.

Modern mothers and fathers reared their children to enter the same kind of occupationally oriented world in which they lived. The home, it was assumed, could provide very little of the knowledge that children would later need to make their way in twentieth-century society. Because parents had a relatively small part in equipping their children for successful adult careers, they had to prepare their sons and daughters to accept directions from outside the home. Experts on child rearing warned parents of the dangers of an excessive emotional attachment or a domineering authority over them. Mothers heard about the perils of the Oedipus complex, in which sons competed with fathers for mothers' affections. Manuals on child care gave specific instructions on cuddling and comforting that would prevent the development of psychological "invalidism." Further, a well-developed and widely publicized youth culture provided adolescents with the means of rebelling against their parents and declaring themselves ready for the occupational world. Modern parents not only subsidized the youth culture; they were told to worry if their children did not fully participate.

Expanding Influence of the Schools. The erosion of the family coincided with greater and greater influence for the schools. During the twenties and thirties the public school system underwent considerable expansion and adaptation. The elementary grades, which changed the least, increasingly served as feeders into the high schools. Enrollment in high schools doubled during the 1920s and then rose another 50 percent during the 1930s. In 1920 one-sixth of America's adult population had high school diplomas; in 1940 one-half held them. Indeed, secondary education became so significant to white-collar families that some of them chose places to live on the basis of the local high school's reputation. The Winnetka System under Carleton Washburne, for example, made that Illinois community nationally famous.

What modern families sought in a school system was a combination of instruction in the basic skills and socialization for modern America. The prevailing trends in "progressive" education favored precisely this combination. The modern high school tried to prepare young minds, as one committee of educational experts stated in 1929, "to be suited to the changing situations" of modern society. Therefore, the more progressive high schools taught general methods of thinking and a general open-mindedness rather than a specific body of information and moral absolutes.

If young people could make a successful adjustment in high school, it was assumed, they would be prepared for a happy, rewarding life in modern America. Aptitude tests and counseling centers, both suddenly prominent in the high schools of the 1920s, guided students into the proper occupational areas or, for increasing numbers, to college for further specialization. Those college graduates who entered the best white-collar occupations were supposed to have superior mental powers. According to a variety of publicists during the twenties, individuals who mastered a specialty in business or the professions developed a general capacity for rational thought that placed them in a select minority. By implication, the majority of Americans, in Mencken's blunt but revealing term, were "boobs," a highly suggestible public that could be manipulated by an intellectually superior few.

Behaviorism as a Manipulative Force.

Along with this belief came a popular psychology called "behaviorism," which contained a simple, persuasive formula for mass manipulation. As psychologist John B. Watson explained the human personality, a clear stimulus produced a predictable response in the individual, and, when such a stimulus was regularly repeated, a habit was established. With occasional reinforcement, this reaction became automatic. During the 1920s behaviorism became an article of faith among many Americans and gave them extraordinary confidence in their powers of social control. By using the right techniques, an expert in mass communication boasted, the rational minority could "regiment the masses according to our will without their knowing it."

A number of otherwise routine white-collar jobs, particularly selling, now took on a new significance. The insights into mass manipulation even offered a fresh view of history. "Galileo failed because he was an investigator and not a salesman," one psychologist revealed in 1925. "Consequently, he could not get his goods marketed. . . . His competitors, Aristotle, Moses, and the church fathers, had monopolized the market, and their stockholders would not let him do business." Advertising developed into an especially honored field. A new group of experts in personnel management also used the same basic formula of mass manipulation to guarantee employers a loyal and productive work force.

Americans of many different persuasions accepted this assumption of a two-tiered society: a minority of manipulators and a mass to be manipulated. Neither liberal nor conservative, the notion simply came with America's modern values. What Republican businessmen in the 1920s applied to the sale of their goods, New Dealers in the 1930s applied to the sale of their reforms. By the Second World War these habits of modern leadership were so ingrained that businessmen and reformers alike automatically went about the tasks of "selling" the war, "conditioning" the public for bad news from the battlefront, and experimenting with better ways to improve American "morale."

The American Dream.

Perhaps the most important need of the mass of Americans was some evidence that they could still succeed without abandoning their values. During the 1920s an abundance of publicity assured them that the avenue upward was not only broad but especially well traveled by people of solid character and good habits. Salesmanship offered a particularly enticing route because it held out the prospect of success without a highly specialized training. Throughout the twenties a popular passion for the salesman's skills was fed by numerous manuals, lectures, and correspondence courses that promised to reveal the secret of the selling art to any ambitious American. The example of certain businessmen encouraged hopes of an even more dramatic rise to riches. If immigrants such as utilities magnate Samuel Insull, banking king A. P. Giannini, and movie mogul Samuel Goldwyn could make it to the top, American society must still be rewarding the traditional virtues of hard work and high ambition.

No one's reputation benefited more grandly from such reasoning than Henry Ford's. Here was a country boy who had turned mechanical genius and dogged persistence into a fabulous fortune and international fame. He had mastered the modern economy so thoroughly that everyone came to him to learn the best techniques of mass production and distribution. Yet he gave the appearance of a man who never capitulated to the slick ways around him. He attacked the evils of Wall Street, belittled the significance of higher education, and demanded strict moral standards from his workers. He could even give new values the sound of old truths: "One day some one brought to us a slogan which read: 'Buy a Ford and Save the Difference.' I crossed out the 'save' and inserted 'spend'—'Buy a Ford and Spend the Difference.' It is the wiser thing to do. Society lives by circulation and not by congestion."

Traditional Local Values in a Modern Society.

A great many Americans responded to these modern trends with mixed feelings. Most people's jobs—in shops, on farms, in factories—did not belong in the specialized upper ranks of the economy and therefore brought very little national prestige. Moreover, mass communication made it impossible to ignore the disparity between their own lives and the lives of the most successful Americans. Millions of Americans with unskilled or routine jobs hoped that they, or their children, would eventually rise on the occupational ladder. Yet almost all of them found the modern values unacceptable to some degree. They lived by local values. In rural communities and city neighborhoods, people judged one another by family reputations, church preferences, work habits, and a variety of other personal characteristics—standards that applied specifically to their own localities.

During the twenties and thirties the churches, particularly in the countryside, attempted to reject the new values. Condemning the new liberalism in dressing, drinking, dancing, smoking, and sex, they refused to consider such behavior a matter of private choice and set firm rules against the modern "self-indulgence." A large majority of Protestant church members belonged to the evangelical denominations. Many Baptist and Methodist congregations, which had always shown serious concern with their members' public behavior, denounced the new ways as sinful. Smaller bodies of Lutherans and Seventh-Day Adventists were even stricter about such practices as dancing and smoking.

As the modern system subdivided knowledge into a bewildering array of specialties, the churches continued to guide tradition-minded Americans in understanding the basics of life. Evangelical Protestantism produced the political pressure behind Tennessee's anti-evolutionary law of 1925, which led to the Scopes trial. In other southern states as well, officials cooperated in keeping the theory of evolution out of the classroom. In the northern cities, the Catholic church often set its considerable weight against the new values, especially those on sex. As in the public schools in areas where evangelical Protestantism predominated, in the Catholic parochial system pupils were carefully instructed in religious morality. According to nation-

Nebraska Art Association, Lincoln

"WOMAN WITH UMBRELLA," BY KENNETH HAYES MILLER
This 1928 painting of a sophisticated modern woman suggests her greater concern with current fashion than with traditional family values.

wide studies in the 1920s and 1930s, a majority of American schoolchildren were still receiving this kind of traditional, moral education.

Some of the mass media also catered to traditional values. In magazines and newspapers, countless stories told of how the time-honored virtues of honesty, thrift, and perseverance had enabled ordinary people to weather their troubles and win in the end. To vast daytime audiences, such radio soap operas as "Ma Perkins' Family" and "Just Plain Bill" recounted the trials and tribulations of ordinary, small-town people who preserved their simple goodness under the most extraordinary hardships. Norman Rockwell's famous covers for the *Saturday Evening Post*, depicting the comforts of life in the family and the small town, ennobled many of the same traditional values. The success ethic also remained intact. In the late 1930s the black heavyweight boxing champion Joe Louis was almost worshiped in the black ghettos as a model of how a poor man could rise to fame and fortune.

Only a minority of Americans in a few localities totally rejected the new ways. A compromise between new and traditional values was much more common. Almost all Americans wanted some share in the new culture, and a great many of them hoped to participate without feeling that it would corrupt them. At the beginning of the twenties, for example, sex was exploited so rampantly in motion pictures that a majority of state legislatures threatened to censor them. In 1922 the movie industry responded by creating the Hays Office, Hollywood's center for self-censorship, which designated what parts of the female anatomy had to be covered, decided what language was taboo, and determined what values must triumph in the end. These moral formulas created just the right aura of respectability. Without basically altering the movies, they appeased the critics and assured a mass audience.

Dangers to the Individual.

The alterations of the twenties jeopardized the freedom of the individual. Signs of a new concern for the individual were already appearing before 1920. The American Civil Liberties Union, which had originated as an emergency committee to defend dissenters during the First World War, remained after the war as a permanent center to protect the individual's freedom of speech, religion, assembly, and press under the First Amendment. Even before the war, America's most creative poets, Ezra Pound and T. S. Eliot, had moved to Europe, starting an exodus of young writers and artists who felt stifled by American culture. "A Lost Generation" was the way Gertrude Stein described these intellectual exiles. In 1920 America's greatest playwright, Eugene O'Neill, won the first of four Pulitzer prizes for *Beyond the Horizon*, launching his long, agonizing exploration into the power of irrational forces over the individual's fate. From such scattered beginnings developed a broader and broader survey of the perils faced by the individual in modern society.

The first danger to receive serious attention was the dehumanizing quality of modern society's organization. During the 1920s the best of the so-called antiwar novels—John Dos Passos's *The Three Soldiers* (1921), e e cummings's *The Enormous Room* (1922), and Ernest Hemingway's *A Farewell to Arms* (1929)—said relatively little about war itself. Instead, they used the war as a means of portraying the individual's jeopardy inside an impersonally mobilized society. In 1923 theater critics gave a warm reception to the American version of Karel Capek's play *R.U.R.*, introducing the robots as modern society's citizen, and to *The Adding Machine*, Elmer Rice's biting comedy on the effects of dull, repetitive work.

Of all the routine tasks in modern America, intellectuals considered work on the assembly line the most threatening to the individual. In fact, it was less wearing than harvesting fruit, less demanding than working in a sweatshop, and less dangerous than mining coal. But factory labor combined monotony and mechanization in a way that seemed especially dangerous to people who were already worried about modern society's depersonalization. Henry Ford's plant produced cars at the price of humanity, the young pastor Reinhold Niebuhr bitterly recorded in his journal, and a company spokesman validated Niebuhr's fears: "[Ford] prefers machine-tool operators who . . . will simply do what they are told to do, over and over again from bell-time to bell-time. The Ford help need not even be able bodied." One of the most acclaimed scenes in an American movie was Charlie Chaplin's rebellion in *Modern Times* (1936) against the intolerable discipline of the assembly line, and his glorious escape through a maze of giant gears and monstrous machinery. America's great challenge, the cultural critic Lewis Mumford wrote in 1934, was to make "the machine . . . our servant, not our tyrant." By the 1930s it had become commonplace for intellectuals to condemn everything about the factory as ugly and alien.

Critics were also disturbed by the all-consuming passion for goods and money. The modern era, one observer acidly concluded, was testing the proposition "that human beings can live a generally satisfactory life . . . so long as they are kept powerfully under the spell of a great number of mechanical devices." During the 1920s old progressives as dissimilar as the moralistic westerner George Norris and the patrician easterner Gifford Pinchot warned of the corrosive influence that the pursuit of money was having on American values. John Dos Passos made this corrupting passion a central theme in his powerful, rambling trilogy *USA* (1930–36).

No part of the nation's heritage suffered more severely at the hands of American writers than the success ethic, which such important novels as F. Scott Fitzgerald's *The Great Gatsby* (1925) and Theodore Dreiser's *An American Tragedy* (1925) attacked for its destructive effects on the individual. In *I'll Take My Stand* (1930) twelve southern intellectual writers, attacking the worship of money along with "the tempo of industrial life" and the cult of machinery, declared that their region's agrarian tradition offered the sole "defense of the individual" in modern America. To the surprise of both authors and publisher, the book won an enthusiastic national following.

As urgent as many of these critics sounded, they were rarely either desperate or radical. They located danger spots in America's industrial order. They usually cautioned the individual to keep a safe distance from modern society's most threatening centers. The individual's protection, in other words, was a calculated detachment. The clearest summary of this view

CHARLIE CHAPLIN IN THE 1936 MOVIE "MODERN TIMES"
Charlie Chaplin, a Pied Piper for the working stiffs, romps through the dehumanizing machinery of a modern factory.

appeared in Hemingway's *A Farewell to Arms*, in which Lieutenant Frederic Henry, an American who had volunteered for the Italian ambulance corps early in the First World War, watched the impersonal forces of the war devour more and more people around him. When they threatened to swallow him too, he deserted—a sane and courageous act, as Hemingway described it. Escaping to Switzerland, he found fulfillment briefly in a love affair with a nurse, Catherine Barkley. When her death left Frederic Henry absolutely alone, his core of inner strength enabled him to survive in an insensitive universe.

One threat to the individual, the emptiness of old age, required a separate set of compensations. For two reasons, the problem of the aged was growing more severe in modern times. First, as the average life expectancy for an American rose from forty-seven years

in 1900 to fifty-eight years in 1950, the proportion of old people increased dramatically. Second, as the numbers increased, the sources of self-respect for the aged were shrinking. Wherever America's modern values prevailed, old people felt useless. Knowledge in a specialized society was supposed to be advancing too rapidly for an older generation to master. Only the young could keep pace with America's highly technical and increasingly complex progress. As adults reached middle age, therefore, they had good reason to feel that their best years were behind them and that the future, which belonged to the young, opened a huge void before them.

Star Quality. The new American society of the twenties gave birth to a new kind of hero for the traditional rags-to-riches tale—a hero endowed with an all-

"SHIPWRECK" KELLY
Flagpole sitting in the twenties represented a triumph of individual will over modern conformist pressures.

STAR QUALITY
Americans could almost feel the power of the bat as Babe Ruth walloped one of his towering homers.

conquering power. In the nineteenth-century form of this tale, the hero had won the rich man's daughter through his sterling character and her father's approval. In the modern variation, however, physical charm alone catapulted the hero to the top. The rich man's daughter, finding the poor but virile man irresistible, convinced an angry father that she could not live without him. In the mirror image of this tale, a sexually charged Cinderella story, the poor but beautiful woman finally fell into the arms of a rich, adoring husband.

The "star" system that came to dominate the entertainment industry during the 1920s reflected a growing popular demand for heroes who possessed an all-conquering power. The stars themselves seemed to have such powers: the irresistible lover, Rudolph Valentino, thrilling millions of moviegoers; the "Galloping Ghost," Red Grange, scoring five touchdowns in one game; the courageous young Gertrude Ederle,

swimming the English Channel; even the publicized flagpole sitters who, perched high in the air, stayed awake for days on end.

Whether accentuating the personal qualities of success or endowing modern heroes with traditional attributes of initiative and individualism, Americans showed a strong preference for the idiosyncratic star who ignored many of the usual rules of the game. Among fans there was more enthusiasm for the erratic fighter Jack Dempsey than for the steadier "boxing machine" Gene Tunney, and more feeling for the high-living, casual "Sultan of Swat," Babe Ruth, than for the intense, consistent batting champion Ty Cobb. In a crowded arena of eager competitors, success depended on a star's ability to attract public attention through a carefully staged, dramatic "event." J. Edgar Hoover, the popular director of the Justice Department's Federal Bureau of Investigation, mastered the technique in a series of orchestrated manhunts for criminals, each of whom he spotlighted as "Public Enemy Number One." An enthralled audience followed the real-life Hoover crime show, chapter by chapter.

Against this background Charles Lindbergh, the star of stars, rose to fame in the most dramatic event

Brown Brothers

Charles Lindbergh soared to fame as a transatlantic pilot in his "Spirit of St. Louis."

of the twenties. In May 1927, as liberally financed and elaborately organized competitors were stalled on the ground, this unknown pilot became the first person to complete a solo airplane flight from New York to Paris. Americans instantly made the quiet, handsome midwesterner a national idol. Lindbergh's triumph, as millions interpreted it, was the accomplishment of an indomitable individual. Both literally and figuratively, the "Lone Eagle" had soared beyond the ordinary individual's limitations to purely personal success. Moreover, Lindbergh's sudden fame did not appear to affect his traditional virtues of modesty, simplicity, and self-reliance. Of all the stars, Lindbergh had the greatest popularity.*

But however strong the impulse to preserve traditional individualism in the twenties, and however great the desire to cling to familiar American customs and truths, the attraction to old, local ways was not powerful enough to hold back the economic and social trends that began the modern period of American life.

*The tragic kidnaping and death of Lindbergh's son produced a new surge of public interest in 1932. But Lindbergh's advocacy in 1941 of a negotiated settlement with Hitler's Germany sharply diminished his popularity.

CHRONOLOGY

1920 Warren G. Harding elected president.
Transportation Act gives ICC extensive authority over railroads and other means of transportation.

1921 First bill restricting immigration by national quotas passed.

1922 Fordney-McCumber Act reestablishes high tariff.
Washington Conference treaty limits naval tonnage among major powers.

1923 President Harding dies; Calvin Coolidge becomes president.

1924 Dawes Plan negotiates loans to revive Germany.

National Origins Act further limits immigration by quotas.
Teapot Dome and other Harding administration scandals exposed.
Coolidge elected president.

1927 Sacco and Vanzetti executed.

1928 Kellogg-Briand Pact outlaws war.
Second McNary-Haugen bill to regulate the marketing of agricultural products passed but vetoed.
Herbert Hoover elected president.

1929 Congress creates Federal Farm Board.
Young Plan reformulates Dawes Plan to manage war debts.

SUGGESTED READINGS

John D. Hicks, *Republican Ascendancy, 1921–1933* (1960), is a good general guide to national politics. Robert K. Murray, *The Harding Era* (1969), and Donald R. McCoy, *Calvin Coolidge* (1967), generously assess these presidents and their policies, and Burl Noggle, *Teapot Dome* (1962), covers the major scandal of their administrations. David Burner's perceptive study, *The Politics of Provincialism* (1967), recounts the pulling and hauling in the Democratic party during the twenties. An interesting picture of the politics of natural resources emerges from Donald C. Swain, *Federal Conservation Policy, 1921–1933* (1963), and from Norris Hundley, Jr., *Water and the West* (1975). Gilbert C. Fite's *George W. Peek and the Fight for Farm Parity* (1954) analyzes the politics of commercial agriculture.

For the limitations of liberal reform, see LeRoy Ashby, *The Spearless Leader: Senator Borah and the Progressive Movement in the 1920s* (1972), Richard Lowitt, *George W. Norris: The Persistence of a Progressive, 1913–1933* (1971), and Arthur Mann, *LaGuardia: A Fighter Against His Times, 1882–1933* (1959). In *Seedtime of Reform* (1963), on the other hand, Clarke A. Chambers discovers a maturing process during the twenties. For Supreme Court decisions, see Paul L. Murphy, *The Constitution in Crisis Times, 1918–1969* (1972). George B. Tindall's *The Emergence of the New South, 1913–1945* (1967) sets that region in a national context.

The most provocative interpretation of "The Age of Corporate Capitalism" appears in William Appleman Williams, *The Contours of American History* (1961), which may be supplemented with James Gilbert, *Designing the Industrial State* (1972). Thomas C. Cochran, *American Business in the Twentieth Century* (1972), gives a clear overview of its subject. The final section in Alfred D. Chandler, *The Visible Hand* (1977), analyzes the managerial structure of the giant corporations, while Louis Galambos, *Competition and Cooperation: The Emergence of a National Trade Association* (1966), traces the pattern of organization among the scattered firms in cotton textiles. Allan Nevins and Frank Ernest Hill, *Ford: Expansion and Challenge, 1915–1933* (1957), covers the peak years of the flivver king's career. On labor, the best study is Irving L. Bernstein's *A History of the American Worker, 1920–1933: The Lean Years*

(1960). Grant McConnell's *The Decline of Agrarian Democracy* (1953) centers on the American Farm Bureau Federation.

The best introduction to the ethnic and cultural issues of the twenties is John Higham's excellent *Strangers in the Land* (1955), which deals with American nativism to 1925. Paul A. Carter, *Another Part of the Twenties* (1977), also comments generally on these issues. David M. Chalmers, *Hooded Americanism* (1965), is a lively history of the Ku Klux Klan, and Kenneth T. Jackson, *The Ku Klux Klan in the City, 1915–1930* (1967), is an important supplement to the story. G. Louis Joughlin and Edmund M. Morgan, *The Legacy of Sacco and Vanzetti* (1948), remains the richest account of events surrounding the trial of these men. The rise and fall of the "noble experiment" is traced skeptically in Andrew Sinclair, *Prohibition: The Era of Excess* (1962), and sympathetically in Norman H. Clark, *Deliver Us from Evil* (1976). Joseph R. Gusfield, *Symbolic Crusade* (1963), explores the emotional force behind Prohibition, and Norman F. Furniss, *The Fundamentalist Controversy, 1918–1931* (1954), reviews the antimodernist legislative campaigns. How cultural issues have translated into politics is described generally in Oscar Handlin, *Al Smith and His America* (1958), and more specifically in J. Joseph Huthmacher, *Massachusetts People and Politics, 1919–1933* (1959). See in addition Humbert S. Nelli, *The Business of Crime* (1976).

There is a growing literature on the impact of blacks during the twenties. Nathan Irvin Huggins, *Harlem Renaissance* (1971), minimizes the cultural significance of its subject. On the very different aspirations of Marcus Garvey and his followers, see E. David Cronon, *Black Moses* (1955), and Thomas G. Vincent, *Black Power and the Garvey Movement* (1971). St. Clair Drake and Horace R. Cayton, *Black Metropolis* (2 vols., rev. ed., 1962), remains a valuable study of the Chicago ghetto. The most important organizations serving blacks are discussed in Langston Hughes, *Fight for Freedom: The Story of the NAACP* (1962), and Nancy J. Weiss, *The National Urban League, 1910–1940* (1974). Also see Walter White's autobiography, *A Man Called White* (1948).

L. Ethan Ellis, *Republican Foreign Policy, 1921–1933* (1968), is a sound introduction to the postwar years. However, the most influential work on America's international affairs is William Appleman Williams, *The Tragedy of American Diplomacy* (rev. ed., 1962), an essay on the dominance of economic expansion in the nation's foreign policy. Two excellent books, Joan Hoff Wilson's *American Business and Foreign Policy, 1920–1933* (1971), and Michael J. Hogan's *Informal Entente: The Private Structure of Cooperation in Anglo-American Economic Diplomacy, 1918–1928* (1977), further explore the process of economic expansion, and so, in a particular case, does Gerald D. Nash, *United States Oil Policy 1890–1964* (1968). Stephen A. Schuker, *The End of French Predominance in Europe* (1976), is a complicated but rewarding account of the issues surrounding the Dawes Plan. Melvyn Leffler, *The Elusive Quest: America's Pursuit of French Security and European Stability, 1919–1933* (1979), is first-rate.

A clear, reliable survey of United States policy in East Asia is presented in Warren I. Cohen, *America's Response to China* (1971). Akira Iriye's *After Imperialism: The Search for a New Order in the Far East, 1921–1933* (1965) locates American policy in an international setting. The postwar treaties on Asia and arms limitation are studied in Roger Dingman, *Power in the Pacific: The Origins of Naval Arms Limitation* (1976), and Raymond G. O'Connor, *Perilous Equilibrium: The United States and the London Naval Conference of 1930* (1962). Keith L. Nelson, *Victors Divided: America and the Allies in Germany, 1918–1923* (1975), is a careful study. Peter G. Filene's *Americans and the Soviet Experience, 1917–1933* (1967) traces responses from the Bolshevik Revolution to America's recognition of the Soviet Union. In *Herbert Hoover's Latin American Policy* (1951), Alexander DeConde finds a liberalizing trend.

Modern culture is explored broadly in Daniel J. Boorstin, *The Americans: The Democratic Experience* (1973). William E. Leuchtenburg, *The Perils of Prosperity, 1914–32* (1958), has particularly revealing chapters on the consumer culture of the twenties and the changes in values accompanying it, subjects that are also covered in Frederick Lewis Allen's *Only Yesterday* (1931). Isabel Leighton, ed., *The Aspirin Age* (1949), contains a lively set of essays on the twenties. There are perceptive analyses of the new sexual morality in Christopher Lasch's *The New Radicalism in America 1889–1963* (1965) and in Paul Robinson's *The Modernization of Sex* (1976). Robert H. Elias, *Entangling Alliances with None* (1973), probes the meaning of individualism in the twenties. The city's dominance in twentieth-century society is discussed generally in Zane L. Miller, *The Urbanization of Modern America* (1973), and more interpretively in Sam Bass Warner, Jr., *The Urban Wilderness* (1972). Some effects of urbanization on suburban values appear in Peter J. Schmitt, *Back to Nature* (1969). Carl Bode, *Mencken* (1969), assesses the leading spokesman for the new urban culture. An intriguing section in Gilman M. Ostrander, *American Civilization in the First Machine Age: 1890–1940* (1970), defines the place of youth in modern society, and John R. Seeley et al., *Crestwood Heights* (1956), examines the importance of the schools in modern suburban life. Three books evaluate women's part in the new culture. William L. O'Neill, *Everyone Was Brave: The Rise and Fall of Feminism in America* (1969), and William Henry Chafe, *The American Woman* (1972), trace the decline of earlier trends toward emancipation, while J. Stanley Lemons, *The Woman Citizen: Social Feminism in the 1920s* (1973), concentrates on women's continuing action after the First World War. In *Birth Control in America* (1970), David M. Kennedy adds a critical analysis of Margaret Sanger's career.

Several books illuminate the values of important institutions and occupations. James W. Prothro, *Dollar Decade* (1954), summarizes the attitudes of businessmen during the twenties. Otis Pease, *The Responsibilities of American Advertising* (1958), and Stuart Ewen, *Captains of Consciousness* (1976), provide contrasting interpretations of a particularly thriving field. The engineer's dedication to business values is the subject of Edwin T. Layton, Jr., *The Revolt of the Engineers* (1971), and the social scientists' dedication to the same values is the subject of Loren Baritz, *The Servants of Power* (1960). Roy Lubove, *Professional Altruists* (1965), describes the businesslike efficiency of social workers. The section on the United States in Reinhard Bendix's *Work and Authority in Industry* (1956) investigates the strategy of the new specialists in personnel management. Also see Milton Derber, *The American Idea of Industrial Democracy, 1865–1965* (1970). The effects of the new culture on education are analyzed in Patricia Albjerg Graham, *Progressive Education from Arcady to Academe: A History of the Progressive Education Association, 1919–1955* (1967), August Hollingshead, *Elmtown's Youth* (1949), and Solon Kimball and James E. McClellan, Jr., *Education and the New America* (1962). Christopher Jencks and David Riesman, *The Academic Revolution* (1968), explores the modern university. Barry D. Karl, *Charles E. Merriam and the Study of Politics* (1974), and Fred H. Matthews, *Quest for an American Sociology: Robert E. Park and the Chicago School* (1977), discuss a new breed of academic entrepreneurs.

Traditional values in modern America have attracted less scholarly attention. Two interesting books analyze these values under challenge: Ray Ginger's *Six Days or Forever? Tennessee v. John Thomas Scopes* (1958), and Don S. Kirschner's *City and Country: Rural Responses to Urbanization in the 1920s* (1970). *Middletown* (1929) and *Middletown in Transition* (1937), classic studies of Muncie, Indiana, by Robert S. and Helen Merrell Lynd, reveal a mixture of traditional and modern values. Donald B. Meyer, *The Positive Thinkers* (1965), examines modern variations on the traditional doctrine of self-help. Other books cast light on traditional values through the study of popular heroes. In *The Hero* (1959), Kenneth S. Davis discusses the fame of Charles Lindbergh. Reynold M. Wik, *Henry Ford and Grass-Roots America* (1972), explains the automobile magnate's powerful appeal, and Keith T. Sward, *The Legend of Henry Ford* (1948), contrasts the public image with the actual record. Robert Sklar, *Movie-Made America* (1975), interprets the development of a new mass medium, and John G. Cawelti, *Adventure, Mystery, and Romance* (1976), anatomizes the most popular forms of fiction.

The best account of modern relativism is Morton G. White, *Social Thought in America: The Revolt Against Formalism* (rev. ed., 1957). Three excellent books discuss early discontents with relativism and various quests for certainty: Donald B. Meyer, *The Protestant Search for Political Realism, 1919–1941* (1960), Edward A. Purcell, Jr., *The Crisis of Democratic Theory: Scientific Naturalism and the Problem of Values* (1973), and David A. Hollinger, *Morris R. Cohen and the Scientific Ideal* (1975).

Other studies trace ideas in creative writing. Alfred Kazin, *On Native Grounds: An Interpretation of Modern American Prose Literature* (1942), is a stimulating essay. Frederick J. Hoffman, *The Twenties* (rev. ed., 1966), discusses American fiction in an artistically critical decade. The strains of modern society are revealed in Maxwell Geismar's *Writers in Crisis: The American Novel, 1925–1940* (1942). Thomas R. West, *Flesh of Steel* (1967), deals with the effects of the machine on the literary imagination. Of course, the creative writers themselves remain our indispensable sources.

29 The Modern Republic in Crisis, 1929–1941

The soaring hopes of the 1920s suddenly vanished in the great stock market crash of October 1929. The 1930s decade was one of the most difficult and critically important periods in American history. Confronted by the worst economic collapse in history at home and by a challenge from totalitarianism abroad, the Republic met these crises with unprecedented actions in domestic and foreign affairs. Herbert Hoover, the symbol of the 1920s business ethos, was humiliatingly rejected by the voters in 1932. Under the leadership of his successor, Franklin D. Roosevelt, the national government took innovative steps to revive the economy and to ensure that all Americans would have a minimum standard of well-being during their lives. Overseas, the United States moved from a limited policy of moral cooperation with the major world powers to all-out military resistance to antidemocratic forces around the globe.

Depression, 1929–1932

By 1929 countless Americans were convinced that they were riding on an escalator of unlimited progress, and they anticipated, along with Herbert Hoover, "the day when poverty will be banished from this nation." A wealthy minority expressed this happy faith by investing in the stock market. Excited by stories about a millionaire who multiplied his fortune thirtyfold in eight months and a peddler who turned $4,000 into $250,000, investors pushed up prices on the New York Stock Exchange by 40 percent in 1927, then another 35 percent in 1928, to heights that bore no relation to the actual growth of the nation's production. Yet the Great Bull Market charged heedlessly onward. With scarcely a pause, stock prices continued to climb week after week until by September 1929 they stood at a dizzying 400 percent above their level of only five years earlier.

Spasms of doubt shook the stock market in September and early October. Then on October 23, 1929,

confidence died. For almost a week the stock exchange was a mad scene of frantic sellers, elusive buyers, and exhausted clerks struggling to sort out the wreckage. By October 29 all the paper profits of 1929 had been lost. Early in November the gains of 1928 disappeared, and during the summer of 1930 those of 1927 dissolved. Finally, on June 8, 1932, the stock market hit bottom, 50 percent below its modest level at the time of Coolidge's inauguration.

The Great Depression. The collapse of the Great Bull Market triggered the Great Depression. Consumption dropped. Business retrenched. Marginal enterprises in farming, banking, and business went bankrupt. During the first three years after the crash, the economy, like a tin can in a vise, was relentlessly squeezed to half its size. Some indicators—such as labor income, salaries, and national income—fell somewhat less than 50 percent; others, such as industrial production, manufacturing wages, dividends, and farm income, somewhat more. For people living through these years, there seemed to be no bottom at all.

The human costs were incalculable. Dramatic headlines told about the fall of the mighty—among them, the utilities king Samuel Insull and the New York banking baron Charles Mitchell—whose empires of speculation crumbled. Later studies argued that the most severe anxieties struck white-collar males, whose sense of personal worth depended entirely on their jobs and earnings. But the most crushing burdens of depression fell on the poor. Millions already living on the edge of poverty could afford no decline in farm income, no shorter hours of work. And the unemployed, about one-third of the labor force by early 1933, soon had nothing. "Folks that ain't never been poor," said one struggling housewife, "don't know nothin' a-tall about doing on nothing." The chicken once promised for every pot had gone into charity's soup kettle, and each year longer and longer lines of hungry, bewildered people formed in front of it with their empty bowls.

HELP UNWANTED

The depression forced as many as 13 million Americans onto the unemployment rolls. In 1939 there were still 9 million Americans who could not find work.

Why the depression was so deep and the fall so prolonged is not easily explained. But an inventory of economic weaknesses in 1929 provides a significant part of the answer. By that year a maldistribution of income, with workers and farmers sharing substantially less in the prosperity of the twenties than did industry, reduced consumer purchasing power and the demand for manufactured goods. Major industries like construction and auto making were forced to reduce production; that reduction in turn caused cutbacks in other industries and led to a general downturn in the economy. All these factors combined with monetary, tariff, and federal tax policies favoring special business interests over national ones, a faulty banking system, and excesses in consumer credit to send the economy into a tailspin.

Yet by 1931 the economy was improving, and the crisis looked similar to many other sharp downturns. Because farm prices had fallen much farther than wages, most urban consumers actually benefited. An intelligent person with money to invest in business or the stock market could find a variety of attractive prospects at home and abroad. Yet the consumers and the investors refused to spend. By summer the Great Depression was sweeping Europe, and the American economy was sliding toward new depths. Hoover sensed the profound importance of this paralyzing irrationality. How else could one explain a drop of 95 percent in private investment while most indicators were declining about 50 percent?

President Hoover's initial responses to the depression were clear and firm. If the cooperative principles behind the modern economy were correct, as everyone seemed to believe, Americans should use them to recover prosperity. "Progress is born of cooperation," the president reminded the nation. "The Government should assist and encourage these movements of collective self-help by itself cooperating with them." For business, Hoover sponsored meetings at the White House to establish common industrial policies. For

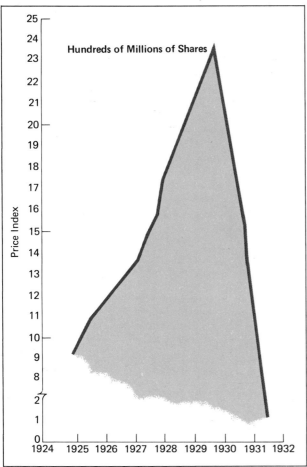

Hundreds of Millions of Shares

Price Index

1924 1925 1926 1927 1928 1929 1930 1931 1932

THE GREAT ENGINEER

A man of extensive ability and little charm, President Hoover gave an impression of cold detachment during the agonies of depression.

The Bettman Archive, Inc.

labor, he won a promise from business leaders to spread the work in their firms rather than simply fire some percentage of their employees. For agriculture, the new Federal Farm Board issued large amounts of credit so that the commodity cooperatives could keep their products off the market and halt the decline in farm prices. For hard-pressed Americans everywhere, Hoover made the president's office the coordinator of private relief. Between 1929 and 1932 donations for relief increased about eightfold, a remarkable accomplishment by any previous standard. Viewing the economy as a national system, Hoover was the first president in history to attack depression systematically.

The Deepening Depression. But Hoover, like the economy, took a grim turn downward in the middle of 1931. As his sense of control over affairs began to slip, he grew more rigid, more persecuted by the specter of vast, oppressive forces. The White House became a funeral parlor. The president, never a charmer, looked, as one visitor remarked, as if a rose would wilt at his touch. In that mood, Hoover called together the villains of Wall Street who, in the president's view, had fed the Great Bull Market instead of facilitating legitimate business. When he demanded that they make massive new investments, they stalled. Finally Hoover accepted the necessity of an emergency government credit agency, the Reconstruction Finance Corporation (RFC), which in 1932 invested $1.5 billion in private enterprise. Meanwhile, to ease the pressures on international finances, he issued a moratorium on the payment of war debts owed to the United States by its former allies against Germany.

By 1932 the president's policies lay in shambles. The exceptionally high Hawley-Smoot Tariff, which Hoover had signed in 1930, was intensifying worldwide depression by cutting off the flow of international trade. Employers discarded their programs for spreading the work, and unemployment shot above 12

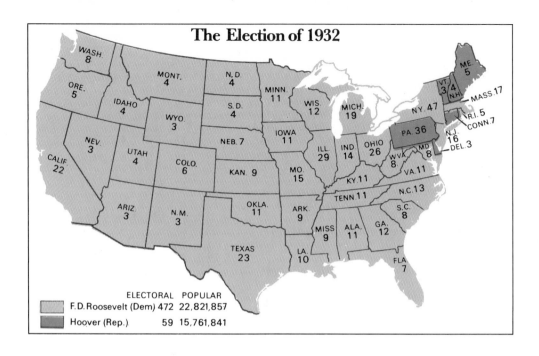

The Election of 1932

	ELECTORAL	POPULAR
F.D.Roosevelt (Dem)	472	22,821,857
Hoover (Rep.)	59	15,761,841

million. Local relief funds, both public and private, evaporated. Abhorring the thought of federal relief, Hoover fought with Congress, which the Democrats now controlled, and eventually approved an inadequate law that authorized some new public works and modest loans to the states for relief.

As commodity prices continued to fall, the Federal Farm Board simply ran out of credit. Farmers burned their corn and left their cotton unpicked because it no longer paid them to market the crop. In some midwestern county seats, silent men with hunting rifles closed the courts so that their mortgages could not be foreclosed. When thousands of jobless veterans marched to Washington asking for early payment of bonuses for their services in the First World War, President Hoover thought he heard revolution in their cries for a little cash, and in July 1932 he allowed the army to drive them away. By the end of the year 20 percent of the banks that had been operating in 1929 were closed. As tremors shook the entire banking system, Hoover hardened the conviction he had held in October 1929: "We have been fighting for four years to preserve the system of production and distribution from . . . [the] failure of the financial and credit system."

During the the years 1921–29 relatively little was expected of the president as an individual. The modern political economy was, after all, a complex impersonal system, not the product of a particular administration, and it appeared to operate on its own momentum. But when the thoroughly national system broke down, only the national government had the scope and authority to repair it. Because the executive branch dominated the national government, people naturally looked there for help. Atop the executive branch stood the president, and the longer the depression lasted, the more he alone seemed the one person who could lead them out of the wilderness. Hoover was judged by new, demanding standards, and the popular verdict condemned him. By 1932 millions who had no other place to turn were blaming Hoover in a bitter, personal way for their troubles. A humane man with great administrative talents, Hoover lacked the flexibility, political instincts, and inspirational leadership required by the crisis. "I have no Wilsonian qualities," he freely admitted to friends. Millions of Americans wanted desperately to believe that a brave new leader with a magic touch might still transform the toad of depression into a dazzling prince of prosperity.

The New Deal Arrives, 1933–1934

The hope for a dynamic, masterly executive focused on Franklin D. Roosevelt, whose name associated him with his distant cousin Theodore, a strong leader and exceptional president. FDR had been assistant secretary of the navy in the Wilson administration, then the vice-presidential candidate in the futile Cox campaign of 1920. A year later an attack of poliomyelitis paralyzed him from the waist down. With dedicated assis-

From Stefan Lorant's The Glorious Burden

A GRAND SMILE AND A BUSTLE OF ACTIVITY
Opening the presidency to a flow of visitors and newsmen, Roosevelt demonstrated how effectively a dynamic style of leadership could raise public confidence.

tance from his wife, Eleanor, and his aide Louis Howe, Roosevelt returned to politics, resisted the Republican tide in 1928 to become governor of New York, and began gathering delegates for the 1932 national convention. A bargain with John Nance Garner of Texas, which made "Cactus Jack" his running mate, sealed Roosevelt's nomination. Demonstrating the dramatic flair that marked his entire career, Roosevelt flew to the convention, stood erect at the podium, the weight of his body supported by his powerful arms, and thrilled the hall with a ringing acceptance speech, promising a "new deal for the American people." The rest was easy. On the waves of public sentiment that swamped his predecessor, Roosevelt received 472 electoral votes to the hapless Hoover's 59.

Roosevelt's Administration. Roosevelt's margin of 17 percent in popular votes, duplicating Hoover's margin of victory in 1928, represented the greatest party reversal in presidential history. The reversal in presidential character was just as striking. Hoover, one associate remarked, "didn't like the human element." Roosevelt reveled in it. Not only did he mix easily with all kinds of people, but he also made them feel that intuitively he sympathized with them. Hoover, taking no one's counsel, thought he knew what the nation wanted. Unlike Hoover, Roosevelt welcomed the challenge of selling his programs to a demoralized nation. A master of popular phrasing and simple analogies, Roosevelt had a strong, warm voice that reached into millions of American homes through radio "fireside chats" that

were bits of genius in the use of a mass medium. Where Hoover cast somber eyes downward, the tilt of Roosevelt's chin and the cocky angle of his cigarette holder invariably gave the sense of a man looking upward. Always he radiated confidence.

Urging "bold experimentation" for a devastated land, Roosevelt attracted a swarm of newcomers to Washington, a curiously mixed but effective group of advisers. For secretary of the treasury, Roosevelt selected his close friend and neighbor from Hyde Park, Henry Morgenthau, whose conscientiousness and loyalty made him indispensable to the president. For secretary of agriculture, Roosevelt appointed Henry A. Wallace, the son of Harding's secretary of agriculture, whose broad liberal vision compensated for his occasional inattention to practical matters. Another liberal Republican, Harold Ickes, became secretary of the interior and watched over his domain with a fierce jealousy and a scrupulous honesty. From his New York administration, Roosevelt brought both the first woman to hold a cabinet post, Frances Perkins, to become secretary of labor, and the tough, dedicated administrator of relief, Harry Hopkins. All of them served to the end of Roosevelt's presidency.

The new administration also drew people who had never before influenced government policy: an obscure Montana professor named M. L. Wilson with a proposal for limiting agricultural production; Raymond Moley, Rexford Tugwell, and Adolf Berle of Columbia University, the "brains trust" of Roosevelt's 1932 campaign, with ambitions to improve the econo-

CLOSED
Once the pillars of economic stability, the banks became a symbol of national catastrophe as the entire financial structure collapsed in 1933.

my's organization; social workers with plans to aid the unemployed, the disabled, and the aged; and many more. Together, this patchwork of people composed the "New Dealers." During Roosevelt's long tenure this term became part of America's everyday language—used with affection by some and with hatred by others to express their strong feelings about Roosevelt and his administration.

Beneath Roosevelt's easy public style and gracious private manner lay a keen, calculating mind that always sought to direct people and events. The din of demands around his powerful office never ruffled him. Moreover, Roosevelt brought to office a firm faith in the basic principles of the new national system. He wanted business to organize, industry by industry; and agriculture, commodity by commodity. He believed that an efficient labor force and private financial institutions working with industry and agriculture could restore prosperity. The government had only to assist them in regaining their strength and finding their proper places in the system. Roosevelt would experiment—but within these boundaries. Not surprisingly, the new president selected equally orthodox men for the crucial administrative posts of the early New Deal: Hugh Johnson and Donald Richberg in business affairs, George Peek and Chester Davis in

agriculture, Jesse Jones for the Reconstruction Finance Corporation (RFC), and Lewis Douglas for the Bureau of the Budget. In fact, these appointments gave a slightly conservative cast to Roosevelt's initial list of lieutenants, but they were more than balanced by the imaginative, liberal appointees, among them Ben Cohen and Tom Corcoran, who set the long-term tone and direction of the New Deal.

The "Hundred Days." Roosevelt's very first problem—the collapse of the banking structure—fell upon him as he entered the White House. He responded with a fine sense of style and an instinctive moderation. During the worst winter of depression, 1932–1933, accumulating panic spread from banks in the agrarian regions toward America's financial centers. State after state closed its banks until on March 4, 1933—inauguration day itself—the pressure finally overwhelmed the main citadels of national finance, New York and Chicago. As those doors closed, the entire system stopped. Borrowing an adman's phrase, Roosevelt immediately declared a nationwide "Bank Holiday," dispatched expert teams to classify all banks as either strong, wavering, or hopeless, and started a transfusion of over a billion dollars from the RFC into the banking system. The president spoke soothing words to the nation; in less than two weeks 90 percent of the frozen deposits were again available to customers, and all over the country money came out of the mattresses to fill the banks. It was an exemplary performance in the service of a free-enterprise financial system, and Wall Street joined Main Street in cheering the president. "In one week," the journalist Walter Lippmann declared, "the nation, which had lost confidence in everything and everybody, has regained confidence in the government and itself."

Roosevelt's treatment for the banking emergency revealed the broad strategy of the New Deal's first months. Among the many popular prescriptions for halting an apparently endless economic decline, none appealed more to the Roosevelt spirit than a nationwide surge of activity that headed upward instead of downward. Mobilize confidence, synchronize energy, and prosperity would return because throughout the land people would suddenly behave as if it *were* returning. To a president who told Americans "that the only thing we have to fear is fear itself," that kind of grandiose bootstraps operation made perfect sense. As Roosevelt took office, he called Congress into special session, plied it with proposals, and during a whirlwind "Hundred Days" guided through fifteen major laws, the greatest outburst of far-reaching legislative activity in American history. They seemed to cover everything: unemployment relief, agricultural aid, mortgage supports, industrial cooperation, banking reforms, conservation of natural resources, and more.

The NRA and the AAA. From this array of legislation, two measures formed the heart of the early New Deal. One was the National Industrial Recovery Act of June 1933, which represented a continuation of government-sponsored business cooperation. Its most important provisions authorized each specialized segment of business to prepare a code of self-governance, and established the National Recovery Administration (NRA) to supervise the process. To serve as chief of the NRA, the president chose General Hugh Johnson, a brash, noisy veteran in public affairs, who immediately launched a circus of a campaign to rally all Americans behind his program. Through parades, speeches, and assorted hoopla, Johnson made the Blue Eagle, the NRA's emblem of cooperation, almost synonymous with the New Deal itself, and he counted on public opinion to make it almost synonymous with Americanism.

In the NRA's first four months, business groups wrote over seven hundred constitutions to govern their affairs. Where one or more large firms dominated an industry, the NRA relied on them to prepare the codes; where no firm dominated an industry, the NRA turned to a trade association. Although the codes var-

ied from industry to industry, they usually included some agreement on prices, wages, and the acceptable limits of competition. The only integration among them was a common commitment to stabilization, a common freedom from antitrust prosecution, and a common dependence on the industrial groups themselves to regulate their own members. Johnson exalted the spirit of cooperation and swore at the "slackers," but never coerced the businessmen.

Section 7a of the National Industrial Recovery Act authorized workers to organize and bargain in their own behalf, and some labor leaders, notably John L. Lewis of the United Mine Workers, acted as though the government was now their sponsor: "THE PRESIDENT WANTS YOU TO JOIN THE UNION!" Although the NRA did not actually encourage an independent labor movement, it provided labor with other important benefits: it fostered a national pattern of maximum hours and minimum wages, and it eliminated child labor and the sweatshop.

Critics rightly complained that the NRA did not bring sustained recovery; nevertheless, it achieved significant accomplishments. It stopped the downward economic spiral, gave jobs to nearly 2 million workers, and reduced some of the cutthroat business competition that hurt the economy.

The second basic law of the early New Deal was the Agricultural Adjustment Act of May 1933. A grab bag of alternatives, it included provisions for almost every farm program that had been proposed in this century: marketing agreements, commodity loans, export subsidies, government purchases, and—reminiscent of William Jennings Bryan—even currency inflation. To these familiar devices the government added a favorite in New Deal circles, production restrictions, aimed at reducing agricultural surpluses at their source. During its first months the Agricultural Adjustment Administration (AAA) used production cutbacks as a way of getting emergency cash relief to the countryside. In midseason farmers were paid to plow under their crops and slaughter their livestock, a bitter expedient with so much hunger in the nation. After 1933 the AAA expected each farmer growing a particular crop to reduce production by a nationally fixed percentage.

The goal of the new law was to increase farm income to a level of "parity," or equality, with the farmers' purchasing power just before the First World War. Although the AAA gave farmers little immediate relief from the depression, it had a solid impact in the longer run. By the close of FDR's first term, gross farm income had risen 50 percent and rural debt had dropped sharply. The rise in farm prices and improved conditions for farmers in part has to be attributed to a drought in 1934; but the AAA, by curtailing pro-

FDR'S NEW DEAL REMEDIES
The New Deal experimented with a variety of measures to overcome the depression and permanently improve living conditions for the mass of Americans.

duction, subsidizing farmers, and eliminating abuses suffered by sharecroppers, also did its share.

Financial Regulation.

Roosevelt and many of his advisers considered financial institutions particularly guilty of causing the depression. "The money changers have fled from their high seats in the temple of our civilization," the president bitingly said of the bankers in his inaugural address. While congressional investigations were revealing how bankers had speculated with bank deposits, new laws sought to hold finance within proper bounds. Through the Glass-Steagall Act of 1933, Congress required banks to separate their investments in securities from normal commercial banking. The next year it placed the stock exchange under the regulation of the Securities and Exchange Commission (SEC). In 1935 Congress outlawed holding companies that had been formed in the 1920s for no other purpose than the sale of stock, and it gave the SEC authority to dissolve other questionable holding companies.

Between 1933 and 1935 the federal government also acted to ensure the future stability of the banking industry and to protect the savings, farms, and homes of the mass of Americans. The Reconstruction Finance Corporation pumped loans into the nation's solvent banks. In 1933 Congress created the Federal Deposit Insurance Corporation so that ordinary citizens would no longer lose their savings if a bank failed. New executive agencies, especially the Farm Credit Administration and the Home Owners Loan Corporation, underwrote farm and housing mortgages. In 1935, when Congress consolidated the regulatory powers of the Federal Reserve System in a centralized board of governors, the government had completed the construction of a national framework of supports around American finance that protected the country from the kind of financial instability that had plagued it in 1932–33. The effect of these laws was to make the federal government the watchdog and the guarantor of America's banks and stock exchanges.

Public Relief.

The New Deal responded to the problem of unemployment and relief with an innovative use of government power. To generate new jobs, Congress appropriated $3.3 billion for the Public Works Administration (PWA) as part of the National Industrial Recovery Act of 1933. Secretary Harold Ickes, the PWA's director, vowed that no corruption would tarnish his bureau and spent the funds with a miser's caution. The Civilian Conservation Corps (CCC), one of the most popular measures of the "Hundred Days," functioned like an army summer camp for unemployed young

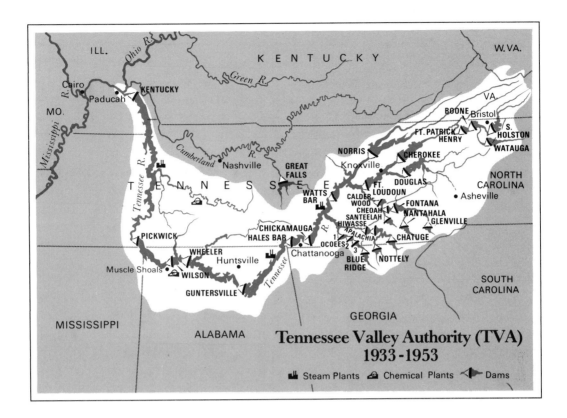

Tennessee Valley Authority (TVA) 1933-1953

Steam Plants ⚒ Chemical Plants ⚒ Dams

men. The 2.5 million Americans employed by the Corps during its existence labored on flood control and soil conservation projects and helped restore America's forests. Their planting of new growth exceeded all that had previously been done in the nation's history.

Although Roosevelt opposed a permanent use of federal funds for relief, he understood how essential it was for the government to come to the aid of the destitute. To meet this challenge, the New Deal established the Federal Emergency Relief Administration (FERA) in 1933. When an initial appropriation of $500 million for FERA proved inadequate, Roosevelt drew an additional $400 million from Ickes's PWA for a hastily devised program, the Civil Works Administration (CWA). In February 1934 Congress finally authorized more funds for FERA. Harry Hopkins, Roosevelt's administrator of relief, employing a small staff, relied on private groups and local governments to distribute most of the money. "Nothing in the new federal act was meant to change that local responsibility, nor did the federal administration have any intention of doing so," an expert on public relief concluded. To the starving, all that mattered was that a humane administration was providing desperately needed help.

The Tennessee Valley Authority. The most daring government venture of the early New Deal was the Tennessee

Valley Authority (TVA). Its origins lay in a long, inconclusive debate during the 1920s over the disposition of a dam at Muscle Shoals, Alabama, that the government had started to build in wartime but never completed. When Henry Ford, widely regarded in the 1920s as a great public benefactor, offered to lease and develop it, the tenacious old progressive senator George Norris of Nebraska skillfully blocked the proposal. In time, Norris convinced a majority of his colleagues that the government itself should develop the dam. During the 1920s, however, no one anticipated the vast undertaking ahead. Beginning in 1933, Muscle Shoals became merely the point of departure for a new concept in regional rehabilitation, which soon gained international fame. The Tennessee Valley Authority, with sweeping administrative powers over a domain that wound through seven southern states, embarked on two decades of activity that created a network of dams and canals, rejuvenated the soil and protected it against floods, and harnessed electric resources to service millions of homes and thousands of new businesses.

From the outset the TVA challenged the customary rights of private enterprise by selling the electric power it generated. Consequently, conservatives probably hated it as much as any New Deal program. Nevertheless, the TVA had not completely abandoned the traditional principle of local control. The regional concept itself was a way of avoiding distant direction from Washington. At every step the TVA's directors worked through the existing organized groups in their region. Chambers of commerce, leagues of bankers, commercial farming associations, and the farmers' local associates from the Department of Agriculture and the state agricultural colleges channeled the TVA's information, chose its demonstration farms, and distributed many of its political benefits. The same local groups were the TVA's primary allies in the long legal battle with the private utility companies over the issue of publicly controlled electric power, a battle that the TVA did not fully win until 1939. None of this, however, held back the TVA from bold actions that significantly altered the life of the region it served.

In 1934, shortly before Raymond Moley left the New Deal to become its conservative critic, he commented, "This administration is as far from socialism or communism as any group ever assembled in a national government." The sheer quantity of government activities during 1933 and 1934 had misled some people into believing that the country was abandoning its free-enterprise system for a state-controlled economy. But they were wrong. Despite the broadened range of government services and innovations that made America a more humane society, the nation's leaders had no radical intentions. With fresh faces and tactics, through experiments and expedients, the New Deal fought to preserve a particular political economy that had formed during the 1920s—but also to alter it, so that such an awful depression could not occur again.

The New Deal at the Crossroads, 1935–1936

The New Deal did not bring full recovery. By late 1934 the NRA was faltering, the victim of the businessmen's self-serving codes, widespread violations of these same rules, and criticism from almost every segment of American society. Now it was the National Run Around. The administration's own review board condemned the NRA, and Roosevelt himself lost interest in the grand experiment. The depression refused to lift. Although unemployment declined from the darkest months of early 1933, it was about as bad as it had been the day Roosevelt was elected. Net farm income was a dismal 50 percent of its level in 1929, and food shortages—caused by a cruel drought on the Great Plains, choking the farmers in vast clouds of topsoil that swept across the region—accounted for most of the price increases since 1933. Only corporate profits were making strong gains in 1934.

Formulas for Prosperity.
As confidence in the New Deal weakened, millions of angry, suffering Americans ap-

SENATOR HUEY LONG OF LOUISIANA
Long, Roosevelt's most powerful critic, expressed the anger and frustration of poor people who had not benefited from the early New Deal.

peared to be finding new leaders and new causes. From Louisiana came the shrewd, flamboyant Huey Long, who promised to make "every man a king." By appealing to the forgotten poor whites of his state, Long became governor in 1929 and quickly established an almost dictatorial control of Louisiana, ruling through an extensive, ruthless political machine. After his election to the Senate in 1930, the Louisiana "Kingfish" used it as a forum to spread the gospel of Share Our Wealth, a simple, sweeping program that would expropriate the wealth of the very rich in order to provide all families with a $5,000 homestead and an annual income of about $2,500, a glorious vision at depression prices.

From a Detroit suburb came the rich radio voice of a Catholic priest, Father Charles Coughlin, who blasted Wall Street, called for the nationalization of the banks, and demanded an immediate, massive monetary inflation. From Long Beach, California, came Dr. Francis E. Townsend, who envisioned prosperity for everybody through monthly government payments of $200 for each unemployed person over sixty years of age. By requiring the pensioners to spend their $200 within the month, the Townsend Plan promised to revitalize the entire economy. All three campaigns were rapidly accelerating in late 1934 and early 1935.

No one ever knew how many Americans accepted these formulas for prosperity, which recalled the spirit of 1890s Populism. Although Long, Coughlin, and Townsend each claimed millions of adherents, none formed an effective organization. The imposing facades of Long's Share Our Wealth clubs, Coughlin's National Union for Social Justice, and Townsend's Old Age Revolving Pensions club covered a thoroughly scattered, locally oriented following that defied a head count. Nor could the New Dealers calculate the number of workers who had given up on the system and were ready for a revolution. During 1934 an upheaval of strikes, involving more than 7 percent of the labor force, shook the nation. Longshoremen in San Francisco, teamsters in Minneapolis, and textile workers along the East Coast were embroiled in particularly bloody conflicts that had radical overtones.

Relief and Old-Age Insurance.

Partly because no one could estimate the strength of these rumbling movements, they sent tremors of anxiety through the Roosevelt administration. With the New Deal also stalled late in 1934 and a more liberal Congress sent to Washington by the 1934 elections, the president felt compelled to push a new package of recovery and reform legislation in 1935. Wasting no time, in January he called for a huge work relief program and a comprehensive social security measure.

Three months later, Congress established the Works Progress Administration (WPA). The very size of the appropriation indicated how central the New Deal considered relief. With almost $5 billion—the greatest single appropriation by any nation in history to date, and ten times the amount originally given to FERA—the WPA absorbed close to half the government's total expenditures. Like its predecessors, the act claimed to be a temporary measure. By 1935, however, very few people thought that local or private contributions could ever again carry the burdens of relief in a depression. Harry Hopkins, who administered the WPA, now emerged as Roosevelt's most powerful lieutenant. Through Hopkins's large staff the WPA supervised an extraordinary variety of projects, ranging from theatrical productions to road repairs, and on the average employed over 2 million people who would otherwise have been jobless. The WPA was testimony to the administration's determination to create, in Roosevelt's words, "a government that lives in a spirit of charity."

The Social Security Act of August 1935, more cautious in approach, was an equally striking innovation with a more lasting influence. It established a national system of old-age insurance that was funded by a tax on workers' wages and an equivalent tax on their employers. The act also taxed employers to finance state programs for unemployment compensation, and it offered the states matching grants to aid dependent mothers and children and the disabled. If the Social Security Act was a conservative version of the schemes for social insurance that had been discussed since the early 1900s, and if the act did not equal the generosity of the Townsend Plan, it nevertheless coped with the same ills. Moreover, Social Security was an expandable formula, and later Congresses gradually extended its range until by the 1970s it covered almost all employees and many more of life's hazards.

Liberal congressmen produced the third basic law, which the president after months of hesitation finally endorsed. Passage of the National Labor Relations Act—the Wagner Act—in July 1935 marked another startling shift in New Deal policy. Before 1935 the government had considered labor primarily as a dependent part of industry. With the Wagner Act, however, the New Deal committed itself unequivocally to supporting unions that were independent of management. The Wagner Act outlawed company unions and any form of company discrimination that might inhibit workers from joining an independent union. The National Labor Relations Board (NLRB), which was created to administer the law, could conduct an election among a company's employees to ensure their free choice of a bargaining agent, and it could compel employers to comply with the new rules.

Passionate Reactions.

The first important consequence of these three unprecedented acts was a powerful release of emotions. During 1935 and 1936 the New Deal, and above all Roosevelt himself, generated both hope and hatred that would run like a high-voltage charge through the next generation of American politics. If the New Deal neither cured the depression nor saved the nation from suffering, it communicated a humane concern when no one else seemed to care. "I do think that Roosevelt is the biggest-hearted man we ever had in the White House," declared one typical citizen. The legislation of 1935, which offered millions of hard-pressed Americans a bit of help, simultaneously held out the promise of much more to come. Moreover, it offered a promise of dignity. The WPA gave people real jobs, not charity. Social Security raised miraculous visions of a decent life in old age. The Wagner Act told countless wage earners that through their own organization they could command respect as full-fledged citizens. In one worker's words, "Roosevelt is the only president we ever had that thought the Constitution belonged to the poor man too."

What gave hope at the bottom of society spread horror at the top. Among many people with a strong stake in the existing system—bankers, lawyers, cor-

The recollections of educator Elsa Ponselle demonstrate the extent to which the depression shaped the lives of everyone during the thirties, middle-class professionals as well as laborers and farmers, and sensitized Americans to the need for greater economic and social justice.

A Teacher Reminisces on the Depression

I BEGAN to teach in December, 1930, and I was paid until June, 1931. When we came back, the city had gone broke. We kept on teaching, of course. I didn't go hungry and had a place to live. My father provided me with enough money to get by. But it was another thing for the men who were married and had children.

They began to pay us with warrants, which carried six percent interest. A marvelous investment. But not for the teachers who had to take them for pay. They had to peddle those warrants for what they could get. It was a promise to pay when the city got some money. We didn't think we'd ever get paid, but the businessmen knew better. . . .

Finally, with F.D.R. in the White House, somebody went to Washington and we got a federal loan. And that didn't happen without a shove. At the time, the chairman of the Board of Education said we should be happy with what we were getting. We asked him if his wife could live on what we were making. A group got together and organized us. Everybody was heart and soul in the unions those days. Somebody said, "Why not a teachers' union?" And why not?

There were objections, of course: We're not tradespeople, we're not laboring class. We're professionals. As professionals, we're entitled to starve to death quietly and with refinement. Some of us weren't that much interested in being refined and professional. We were much more interested in improving our conditions.

We didn't have sit-ins, of course. That would hurt the children. We determined on one thing: We were not going to hurt the children. We went on teaching, whether we were being paid or not. We kept them apart from it.

We marched down LaSalle Street, we marched down Dearborn, we marched down Michigan Avenue. We marched everywhere. People were appalled. Teachers were supposed to be meek and mild. We were supposed to be the bulwark of the status quo and here we were, joining the revolution. . . .

The Depression was a way of life for me, from the time I was twenty to the time I was thirty. I thought it was going to be forever and ever and ever. That people would always live in fear of losing their jobs. You know, *fear*. And, yet, we had, in a way, a wonderful time. We were young.

Remember? The one great thing was the end of Prohibition. The liquor we drank before was awful. Whoever thought about enjoying a drink? I'm talking about the bootleg. To this day, I can't drink gin, because every time I get a very fine Beefeater martini, all I can remember is that white stuff I drank during Prohibition.

How can you talk about the Depression without talking about F.D.R.? I remember when he was at the Chicago Stadium and all of us ran from school to get there. He came in on his son's arm. We didn't realize that he was really and truly crippled until we saw the braces. He got up there and the place just absolutely went up in smoke. What was tremendous about him was—with all the adoration—his sense of humor. He acted as though he didn't take himself seriously.

And Eleanor. Eleanor. I think she's the greatest thing that ever happened to anybody. I think of the way they talked about her, about her looks, about her voice. I used to get so rabid. Why I didn't have high blood pressure, I don't know.

poration executives, and doctors—the new laws created images of a chaotic society where government was pitting the masses against everyone else's privileges. Year after year, their inability to explain what had gone wrong with the economy or predict what the government would do next had been deepening their frustration. Conservative doubts about the New Deal in 1933 turned into charges of incompetence in 1934, then outright hatred in 1935. Much more powerful than the millions who loved Roosevelt, the wealthy foes of the New Deal had the means of making their feelings heard. They spoke from chambers of commerce and from bar, medical, and banking associations. They formed new organizations such as the American Liberty League, which spent millions to discredit the New Deal. Through newspapers, radio, and venomous little rumors ("Polio? Syphilis!"), they mounted a furious assault on "that man in the White House" even more than on his administration.

The New Deal Coalition.

After 1929 opponents of Prohibition had argued persuasively that liquor production would generate more jobs. The national Democratic party had led the campaign for the Twenty-First Amendment, which in December 1933 had repealed the Eighteenth and left the rules governing alcohol to local choice. Overjoyed to have Prohibition behind them, the New Dealers had expected to concentrate exclusively on the problems of depression. It had never dawned on them, for example, to revive the old progressive wars against immigrant radicals or prostitution. Although Roosevelt had selected the first woman to hold a cabinet post, neither Frances Perkins nor Roosevelt's active wife, Eleanor, nor anyone else in the New Deal had wanted to revive the pre–World War I movement for women's rights. By 1935 these crusades were over, and no one in the Roosevelt administration was recommending a new one.

Yet on matters of race and religion, the New Dealers were in many ways impressively liberal. As the battles over Al Smith had demonstrated, the Democrats had been collecting a mixture of ethnic groups during the twenties. The elections of 1932 and 1934 had added even more urban cultural segments to the party's new majority. Prominent members of the administration were closely identified with the nation's minorities. Secretary of Interior Harold Ickes was a veteran member of the National Association for the Advancement of Colored People (NAACP). Eleanor Roosevelt spoke eloquently for racial and religious equality. In the 1940s Henry Wallace became one of the most prominent white champions of black rights. The president himself appointed a Jew as secretary of the treasury, an ironic reply to the anti-Semitic hallucination about a Jewish plot to control world finance.

Catholics were also prominent in a government that reached out to America's minorities more than any administration had in the past. Perhaps most impressive of all, the New Deal tried to reverse the long, cruel trend of native American impoverishment and tribal disintegration. In the late 1920s government reports began to reveal the rampant white greed and injustice that under the terms of the old Dawes Act of 1887 had transformed tribal lands into the private property of individual members. In 1934, spurred on by John Collier, the New Deal's director of Indian affairs, Congress passed the Indian Reorganization Act, which enabled nations of native Americans to recreate communal control over their lands, and offered some assistance toward tribal self-sufficiency. Throughout the thirties, the zealous Collier scrambled for money to implement this program.

If Roosevelt and other New Deal leaders were demonstrably broad-minded on racial matters, they also knew that their liberality was good politics. The New Deal primarily worked through local Democratic leaders and machines that were spokesmen for minorities who had begun to vote in great numbers in the 1920s and 1930s. These Democratic "bosses" and machines had little genuine interest in racial justice or equality, but they recognized that their power rested on their ability to speak effectively to the concerns of local minorities. National Democratic leaders gave local politicians the financial means to attend to such needs by allowing them to distribute public funds in their own areas by their own standards. In the large cities government funds passed through urban politicians to the interested families and cultural groups. In only five of the forty-eight states did the WPA bypass the established local powers. Moreover, when Congress rejected an amendment to the Wagner Act that would have required racial equality on the job, the New Deal left the issue of bias in the unions to the labor leaders themselves. The immediate responses to these policies were politically heartening. Enthusiasm for the New Deal ran very high in the South, where the dominant Democratic party remained "lily white" and segregation was unchallenged. In such cities as Pittsburgh and Kansas City, the New Deal's relief laws shored up the existing political machines, and in Chicago, WPA funds actually saved the budding Democratic organization of Mayor Edward Kelley. These beneficiaries ranked among the Roosevelt administration's most dedicated supporters. Across the country organized labor declared Roosevelt its champion.

Blacks and the New Deal.

Black Americans did not fare as well under the New Deal as other minority groups. The NRA and the AAA provided blacks with few eco-

ELEANOR ROOSEVELT GREETING EDUCATOR MARY McLEOD BETHUNE
Although black Americans were not a favored minority in the New Deal years, the Roosevelt administration was impressively liberal on matters of race and religion and extended enough of a helping hand to blacks to break their traditional affiliation with the Republican party.

nomic benefits, and by 1935 the NAACP complained "that the powers-that-be in the Roosevelt administration have [done] nothing for" the black American. Moreover, later black leaders pointed out that not a single civil rights law was passed during FDR's twelve years in office. Nor did he ever give more than guarded support to legislation aimed against lynchings in the South; no antilynching law was passed during his term. Yet black Americans were increasingly drawn to the New Deal coalition because under Roosevelt more blacks were appointed to high government jobs than ever before in the country's history and, more important, because New Deal agencies like the WPA and the National Youth Administration (NYA) provided blacks with a measure of economic relief. Moreover, in matters of personal discrimination, Roosevelt's circle responded with sensitivity and imagination. In 1939, for example, when the world-famous black contralto Marian Anderson was denied the use of Constitution Hall in Washington, Harold Ickes arranged for a dramatic concert at the steps of the Lincoln Memorial. Although blacks were last in line under the New Deal, they did receive enough to break their identification with the Republican party and to make them solid backers of Roosevelt and the Democrats.

The Election of 1936.

The primary political test of the New Deal's methods came in the elections of 1936. Roosevelt's Republican opponent was the honest, uninspired governor of Kansas, Alfred Landon. The Union party, formed by Coughlin, Townsend, and the remnants of Long's supporters (left in disarray by Long's assassination in 1935), nominated Representative William Lemke of North Dakota for president. Although Coughlin personally promised 9 million votes for Lemke and the *Literary Digest* predicted Landon's victory, most people expected Roosevelt to win. The margin of victory, however, would serve as the critical index to the New Deal's success. And Roosevelt won by a tremendous landslide, carrying every state except Vermont and Maine. Along with huge Democratic majorities in Congress—75 senators and 333 representatives—the election gave Roosevelt a breathtaking 523 electoral votes to a mere 8 for Landon. The Socialist and Communist parties did very poorly. The woebegone Union party did not even collect a million popular votes, and Coughlin announced his retirement from politics.

The Democratic conquest of 1936 ratified the New Deal's policies in two crucial and interrelated areas. First, it placed responsibility for the national economy squarely in the lap of the government. After 1936 Washington became the guarantor of the nation's economic welfare, and the populist economics of people like Long, Coughlin, and Townsend never again won a mass following. The business leadership of the twenties was trounced. Wealthy haters of Roosevelt had to bide their time and fight another day. Second, the landslide of 1936 solidified the core of the new and enduring Democratic majority that had been forming since 1924. To the solid South were added the nation's industrial centers, where the party's greatest strength came from the relatively poor, the Catholics, the Jews, and the blacks. Other voters would slip away from the Democrats after 1936, but the heart of their support was to hold quite firm for decades to come.

The New Deal Loses Its Way, 1937–1939

Although Roosevelt swept into his second term on a high tide of popularity, his next four years produced far less domestic change than his first. The president's first objective in 1937 was to reform the Supreme Court. In the tense climate of 1935 and 1936, as the New Deal was expanding its scope, the Court grew increasingly rigid. A bare majority of five justices attacked the national government's primary source of power over the economy—the regulation of interstate commerce. Mining and farming, in the Court's view, were local, not interstate, activities. By implication, these interpretations jeopardized a full range of the New Deal's policies in industry and agriculture. Moreover, a narrow construction of interstate commerce automatically cast doubts on the government's authority to regulate labor-management relations through the Wagner Act, and to tax employers and employees through the Social Security Act.

FDR Versus the Supreme Court. The most publicized of the court's many decisions during 1935 and 1936 were the *Schechter* case (1935), which struck down the National Recovery Administration (NRA), and *United States* v. *Butler* (1936), which invalidated the tax on food processing in the Agricultural Adjustment Act. Neither decision crippled the New Deal. The NRA, a loosely worded delegation of powers to the executive that all nine justices condemned, was practically dead by 1935; the Court's judgment in the *Schechter* case merely gave it a decent burial. Following the *Butler* decision Congress continued the New Deal's farm program of restricted production under the guise of soil

conservation. But the Court's willingness to strike down two such important laws, along with so many other threatening precedents in 1935 and 1936, forced a confrontation between the Roosevelt administration and the Supreme Court. As the president stated, the New Deal could not function with a "horse and buggy" conception of interstate commerce.

Reading his victory in 1936 as a mandate to storm this conservative outpost, the Supreme Court, Roosevelt submitted a judiciary reorganization bill to Congress in February 1937. The president requested the right to enlarge the Court from nine to a maximum of fifteen members if those justices over seventy years old did not voluntarily resign. If, as Chief Justice Charles Evans Hughes stated, the Constitution was what the Court made it, Roosevelt would remake the Court. But the president pretended that the issue was judicial efficiency rather than judicial interpretation. The existing Court, he claimed, could not manage its heavy load of work, a charge that Hughes easily refuted. In this political battle Roosevelt was uncharacteristically inept. When Congress rebelled at his plan, Roosevelt refused to negotiate. Although liberal congressmen were prepared to impose extensive restrictions on the Court through constitutional amendment, the president held stubbornly to his own scheme. Meanwhile, the Court defused the central issue through an abrupt change in constitutional law. By a vote of five to four, the Court in *NLRB* v. *Jones and Laughlin Steel* (1937) upheld the Wagner Act with a broad interpretation of interstate commerce. Then, by a larger margin, the Court validated the Social Security Act. "A switch in time saved nine," the wags declared. The president's campaign looked more and more like a personal war against the Court, and a reach for unprecedented power. Defensively, he gave the public "solemn assurance" that he did not seek "the destruction of any branch of government or any part of our heritage of freedom." It did no good. After 168 days of exhausting, bitter battle, Roosevelt's bill was defeated.

In the end the conservatives did lose their judicial stronghold. A rapid sequence of retirements and deaths between 1937 and 1941 enabled the president to select seven associate justices and a chief justice. By the time of *United States* v. *Darby* (1941), the New Deal Court had authorized sweeping powers over interstate commerce and approved all the principal legislation that still mattered. But the price of victory was high. Roosevelt's attempt to pack the Court with pro–New Dealers tarnished his reputation as a leader. Instead of pitting the New Deal against the Court, his course set Congress against the president. In the future even Democratic congressmen would feel much freer to vote against the president.

VIOLENCE IN THE FACTORIES
The drives to organize America's mass production industries exposed the raw nerve of class conflict, as they pitted workers against both employers and their allies in local government.

United Press International, Inc.

The Strengthening Labor Movement. Nevertheless, the court battle was only one part of a complex process leading to the New Deal's decline. At least as much strain in the New Deal coalition came from the labor movement. As the Wagner Act passed in 1935, the labor movement split into warring camps. John L. Lewis, president of the powerful United Mine Workers, led a group of dissident unions out of the craft-oriented AFL in order to organize the semiskilled and unskilled workers in the major mass-production industries. The rebels eventually formed the Congress of Industrial Organizations (CIO), while the skilled trades remained in the AFL. Looking at the leaders of the two organizations, one saw little contest. Lewis's dramatic flair and imaginative leadership made him a national attraction in the mid-1930s, second only to Roosevelt, and the baggy giant of the CIO appeared capable of demolishing the AFL's mild little William Green with words alone. "Explore the mind of Bill Green," the advocates of labor compromise had suggested to Lewis. "I have done a lot of exploring in Bill's mind," Lewis declared, "and I give you my word there is nothing there." But the AFL proved to be a resourceful enemy that mobilized local opposition to the CIO, collaborated with employers who were fighting the new unions, and helped antiunion congressmen brand the CIO a communist organization.

In addition, the CIO faced a formidable challenge from the unorganized industries themselves. From the docks of San Francisco to the textile mills of North Carolina, employers murdered, gassed, beat, and intimidated their workers in order to demoralize them and to block the CIO's unionizing efforts. The first crisis in this rough, uncertain struggle began in December 1936, when workers at a number of General Motors affiliates sat inside the company plants to gain recognition for their new organization, the United Auto Workers (UAW). Ignoring court orders to evacuate the buildings, receiving supplies from their friends outside, and turning back the police in "The Battle of the Running Bulls," the auto workers, with the help of cooperative state and national politicians, including Roosevelt, achieved the CIO's first great victory. In February 1937 General Motors and the UAW signed a peace pact. Illegal sit-down strikes quickly spread nationwide.

Meanwhile, a CIO drive in the steel industry won a second stunning success. In March 1937 U.S. Steel, the very symbol of anti-unionism in America's mass production industries, ended a bitter strike by recognizing the steelworkers' union. Almost all the corporations in "Little Steel," however, adamantly refused to follow suit, and bloody counterattacks stalled the organizing campaign there. In the "Memorial Day Massacre" outside Republic Steel's plant in Chicago, for example, police shot into a fleeing crowd, killing or wounding dozens of strike sympathizers. In fact, there was an epidemic of industrial violence in 1937.

The turmoil of sit-down strikes and local warfare broke an uneasy truce over labor policy within the Democratic party. While an exasperated Roosevelt condemned management and labor alike by declaring "a plague on both your houses," Democratic factions in Congress angrily debated the sins of employers and unions. Fortunately for the CIO, a partisan National Labor Relations Board continued to fight vigorously in behalf of the new unions. By 1941, with almost 10 million members divided between the AFL and the CIO, the union movement had safely passed the first round of crisis. In the process, however, it had made a host of enemies, Democrats as well as Republicans.

Growing hostility to the labor movement decreased the likelihood that the government would assist other Americans to organize in their own behalf. Tenant farmers, for example, were particularly in need of the government's help. Always the poor relations in an era of commercial agriculture, they had suffered cruelly from depression and drought in the 1930s. In 1935, when some of them formed the Southern Tenant Farmers' Union, landlords and sheriffs crushed their organization. When reformers in the Department of Agriculture argued the tenants' cause, they were fired.

PRINCIPAL NEW DEAL MEASURES, 1935–1938

Works Progress Administration (WPA)	May 1935
Wagner Act, creating the National Labor Relations Board (NLRB)	July 1935
Social Security Act	August 1935
Bankhead-Jones Farm Tenancy Act, creating the Farm Security Administration (FSA)	July 1937
Fair Labor Standards Act	June 1938

The first serious attempt to reverse this tide was the Bankhead-Jones Farm Tenancy Act of 1937. Through a new agency, the Farm Security Administration (FSA), the law provided credit with which tenants could purchase the farms they were working. In addition, the FSA explored ways to develop a diversified, cooperative community life for small farmers and to protect the interests of the forgotten farm laborers. The FSA was one logical extension of the New Deal's innovations in 1935, a rural counterpart of the program for organized labor. But in 1937 the opposition of the established agricultural organizations and the flagging reform spirit in Congress kept the FSA budget small and the agency's future precarious.

The only solid expansion of the New Deal came in the Fair Labor Standards Act of 1938. After much wrangling, Congress established a minimum wage level and an official rate of time-and-a-half for overtime work, and it abolished child labor. With wholesale exemptions in agriculture, special dispensations for southern employers, and meager minimum wage scales, this law represented only a first step toward fair labor practices. Yet in combination with Social Security and WPA, the Fair Labor Standards Act reinforced a fundamental new assumption: the national government should protect the economic welfare of its poorer citizens.

The New Deal in Retrospect.

By 1938 the New Deal was drifting. Its limited accomplishments in the two years after 1936 reflected the decline in Roosevelt's authority. On Capitol Hill an informal coalition of Republicans and conservative, largely southern Democrats moved into the vacuum of leadership. A defensive league, it concentrated primarily on opposing "socialist" measures that would enlarge the national government's responsibilities, or "giveaway" programs that would expand its services. In the spirit of the 1920s, many of the opposition still equated pros-

perity with a self-regulating economy. In 1938, when the president proposed a bill for executive reorganization to manage the government's broadening obligations, the conservative coalition—with cries of dictatorship—defeated the measure. And when Roosevelt tried to "purge" a few prominent opponents in his own party during the off-year elections of 1938, his failure only emphasized before the public the president's diminishing power.

Most fundamental of all its problems, the New Deal lacked a clear purpose. When the New Deal changed course in 1935, it abandoned the vision of the economy that had dominated public policy since the First World War. During the 1920s and early 1930s, policymakers sought harmony among the nation's big economic units: business, labor, agriculture, and finance. It was assumed that business, with encouragement from Washington, would lead the other units in a coordinated march to prosperity. By 1935 it was no longer possible to picture the economy as a complex of big interdependent blocs. More and more little economic units came to Washington, demanding their own programs to serve their own interests.

There were no more NRAs for all of American business. Instead, Congress in 1935 created "little NRAs" for coal, for trucking, and, through an interstate oil compact, for petroleum. Two new laws strengthened the rights of small businessmen. The Robinson-Patman Act of 1936 sought to protect independent retailers against such huge chains as A & P and Woolworth, and the Miller-Tydings Act of 1937 legalized "fair trade" agreements, or fixed retail pricing, in behalf of similar small firms. Between 1934 and 1937 special legislation responded to particular agricultural interests such as cattle grazers, cotton and tobacco growers, and dairy farmers. The labor movement not only sharpened the distinction between the unorganized and the organized, but also highlighted the very different grievances separating carpenters from steelworkers from longshoremen from hatmakers—a decentralization of interests far greater than just a division between the AFL and the CIO.

Only the hub in Washington connected these many spokes of special interest. Economic policy was now government policy. But no one in the New Deal had a clear strategy for integrating these economic fragments. Since the beginning of the New Deal, some voices had advocated national planning. Yet their statements were studies in vagueness. Reach "a reasonable meeting of minds," the historian Charles Beard proposed; "coordinate private industry" with public enterprises like TVA, the philosopher John Dewey suggested. The president had authorized the Justice Department to bring more antitrust suits against big business. Yet Roosevelt never longed for the old days of small-unit competition, and the administration's new antitrust policy did little to destroy giant corporations.

Some advisers recommended a closer alliance between the New Deal and the unions, but Roosevelt was reluctant to entangle himself in organized labor's raw battles, and he distrusted John L. Lewis, its strongest leader. Marriner Eccles, the chairman of the Federal Reserve Board, wanted to regain prosperity through government spending. But Roosevelt retained a traditional faith in balanced budgets. He even contributed to a new economic crisis in 1937 by sharply reducing the government budget when, in fact, only a radical increase in government spending would have worked. The budgets of the thirties were simply too small a fraction of the economy's total activities, and the New Deal was attempting to move a boulder with a stick. Although Roosevelt was profoundly disturbed by the vision of "one-third of a nation ill-nourished, ill-clad, ill-housed," even by the late thirties he had no clear strategy for overcoming these problems. By 1939 the weight among the president's domestic advisers had shifted well to the left of the balance in 1933, but liberals no more than conservatives knew how to manage America's fragmenting economy.

Still, the New Deal accomplished more in five years than any other administration in American history. Taking office in 1933, Roosevelt set out to save a crumbling American system, and he succeeded. Through new departures in 1933–38, the New Deal generated popular hopes where despair had prevailed, and it set the political economy in a fresh, more promising direction. Most important, through a series of bold reforms, it made America a more humane industrial society.

Yet if events between the onset of the Great Depression and America's entry into the Second World War worked fundamental changes in American life, they by no means cut the country off from its old habits. Although the Roosevelt presidency did much to bring the country more fully into the modern era, in part building on what had occurred in the twenties, it maintained an attachment to traditional ways, refusing to be too innovative; and by so doing, it left many questions unanswered. By 1941 prosperity had returned, but the government had no program for sustaining it; war had come, but the Roosevelt administration had no goal beyond winning it. There were still years of groping ahead.

The Republic in Crisis and the American Dream

The Great Depression irreparably damaged the American dream of the poor man rising to wealth and power, which in the 1920s Henry Ford had symbol-

ized. After 1929 Ford's popularity declined drastically, and no businessman ever replaced him. Not even the prosperous 1940s revived the vision of a simple man's rise from humble origins to the pinnacle of the corporate system. The avenues to fame and fortune grew increasingly obscure. Dale Carnegie's phenomenally popular *How to Win Friends and Influence People* (1936), the counterpart for the 1930s of the salesman's manuals of the 1920s, promised wonders for its readers if only they would master an elementary set of rules for tapping their inner resources. Yet unlike the literature of salesmanship, Carnegie's book was quite vague about where in modern society the ambitious but poor person should look for his success. A critical element of hope was dwindling in the lives of millions of Americans.

The Roosevelts were the idols of the Depression years—not only because New Deal policies rekindled hope, but also because both Franklin and Eleanor Roosevelt possessed warm, friendly personalities that they communicated to a traditionalist public. The president's battle with polio, his hobbies, and his anecdotes, all gave indispensably human qualities to the nation's leader. Far more than had any other president's wife, Eleanor Roosevelt traveled throughout America to express her personal concern for the needs of its citizens. Her syndicated newspaper column, "My Day," significantly lessened the distance between the nation's First Lady and a large, attentive body of readers.

Conservative Responses to Depression. In the short run, the Great Depression contributed to the most powerful general force in behalf of traditional values. Immediately after the crash of 1929, Americans rejected the twenties as frivolous, wasteful, and amoral. It was widely believed that the economy could be revived through a reassertion of solid, old-fashioned common sense in everyday life. Skirt lengths dropped well below the knees, and women were lectured on their primary obligations inside the home. Public tolerance for innovative architecture, design, and music declined, and a simple realism in painting and sculpture became the vogue. After a burst of creativity in literature during the 1920s, the experimental novels of a major writer such as William Faulkner were largely ignored in the thirties, and Margaret Mitchell's nostalgic *Gone with the Wind* (1936) was the hit of the decade.

As Americans rejected the recent past, they looked back to earlier traditions that they could reaffirm. Thomas Jefferson and Walt Whitman, who were interpreted as simple, homespun democrats, enjoyed a surge of popularity. In *The Flowering of New England* (1936), Van Wyck Brooks glorified the same antebellum literary heritage that he had dismissed so dis-

MIGRANT FIELD WORKER, IMPERIAL VALLEY, CALIFORNIA, 1937
Migrant farmers, depicted movingly in John Steinbeck's *The Grapes of Wrath*, were some of the depression's worst victims.

dainfully twenty years before. A deepening sense of democracy at bay in a totalitarian world strengthened the conservative cast of this search for cultural roots. In direct contrast to the Wilsonian dream of democracy's global expansion, the nightmare of the thirties pictured America fighting firmly to preserve its traditions against the swelling currents of fascism and communism that were sweeping across Europe. Now was a time for bedrock values, not for trivial novelties. Then, as the Second World War revived the economy, the temporary constraints on cultural innovation disappeared, and traditionalists once again found themselves living in an atmosphere resonant with modern values.

The Yearning for Unity. During the twenties and thirties, the individual had received a good deal of general advice and a variety of palliatives. But a clear statement of the individual's situation and future prospects in modern society failed to appear. A new round in search of an answer to this problem began rather vaguely in the depression, when a number of prominent figures conceived of the individual as part of a broad social enterprise. New Deal enthusiasts attacked the evils of "rugged individualism" and foresaw a new age of social responsibility. The reputation of philosopher John Dewey, America's leading advocate of a social ethic, rose impressively during the 1930s. Moreover, as depression crippled America, one group of intellectuals looked abroad to the Soviet Union as a model of the healthy society. A few of them also took the next logical step and applied Karl Marx's theories of class conflict to American society. But in most cases, the affair between American intellectuals and the Soviet Union was a brief infatuation. Never willing to relinquish the individual in favor of the class, they were revolted by the bloody Soviet "purge" of the late thirties. Increasingly they became convinced that Americans would have to develop their own kind of social consciousness.

At best, the search in the thirties offered a hope for the future, but not a solution for the times. John Steinbeck, who had once been attracted by Marxism and who continued to have a strong social conscience, captured this hope for the future at the end of his finest novel, *The Grapes of Wrath* (1939). Steinbeck told the grim story of an impoverished Oklahoma farm family, the Joads, tracing them from their uprooting early in the depression through their futile quest for a fresh start in California. Then on the last page of his otherwise tragic novel, Steinbeck suddenly shifted moods and in a few sentences sketched a vision of a new fellow feeling just beginning to surface in America.

For a great many Americans, that spirit of a collective endeavor finally arrived with the Second World War. In 1940 Hemingway's hero from the 1920s reappeared in *For Whom the Bell Tolls* as Robert Jordan, who was no longer alone because he found a social commitment. This time Hemingway's hero was fighting in the Spanish Civil War. Instead of deserting, as Frederic Henry had done in *A Farewell to Arms*, Jordan chose to die for human values in the battle against fascism. A year later, the former pacifist Robert E. Sherwood, winner of four Pulitzer prizes, announced his conversion to the same crusade in his play *There Shall Be No Night*. The Second World War found Americans, intellectuals and ordinary people alike, even more genuinely united in a sense of common, uplifting purpose than had the First World War—and far more united than they would be in America's subsequent wars in Korea and Vietnam.

International Disintegration, 1931–1939

The system of moral cooperation sponsored by the United States in the twenties fell apart in the thirties. By 1931 the pall of depression had spread worldwide. The German economy was virtually bankrupt, the British credit system was tottering, and the foundation beneath every other industrial nation was badly shaken. Economic nationalism thrived, as government after government moved to protect its weakened domestic economy from outside competition. Some powers—notably Japan, Germany, and Italy—also tried to renew their economic strength through military imperialism. Where they conquered, they assimilated, absorbing governments and integrating dependent economies into their own.

The first of the military imperialists to strike was Japan. When depression pinched its lifelines of commerce, Japan looked more avidly than ever to its most natural area for economic expansion, the Asian mainland. But Japan could expect little profit in China as long as the latter was plagued by civil wars and carved into many spheres of foreign influence. In September 1931 Japan's Kwantung Army, which was stationed in Manchuria, took the initiative by seizing all of this rich province in northern China. Twelve months later, Manchuria became the Japanese puppet state of Manchukuo.

Only a year before the Manchurian assault, President Hoover's Secretary of State, Henry L. Stimson,

had thought of Japan as a stabilizing force in East Asia, a "buffer state" between the United States and a chaotic China. Outraged, Stimson now hastened to find some way of thwarting Japan through collective international action. As an outsider, however, the United States could not collaborate effectively with the League of Nations. And the Nine-Power Treaty on the Open Door in China, a vague document at best, contained no sanctions against a violator.* Wanting at least to threaten Japan with a stronger American policy, Stimson was blocked by Hoover, who publicly renounced either economic or military sanctions against Japan. What emerged was a purely American statement of principle. The Hoover-Stimson Doctrine of 1932, relying on the Kellogg-Briand Peace Pact's repudiation of war, stated that the United States would refuse to recognize any treaty that impaired the sovereignty of China or infringed on the Open Door policy.

An even more formidable imperialism emerged in Germany. Against a background of economic collapse, the National Socialist party worked its way into the German government early in 1933, established its leader, Adolf Hitler, as dictator, and proceeded to eliminate its opponents. For a time, outsiders refused to take seriously the Nazis' militaristic pomp, crude racism, and ranting speeches. But the new government proved ingenious in attracting German loyalties and mobilizing the country's resources. As the Nazis consolidated their power at home, they also asserted it abroad. Hitler, repudiating the Versailles Treaty as an unfair settlement needlessly accepted by Germany's democratic politicians, left the League in 1933 and two years later announced that Germany would rearm. Italy also joined the new imperialists. Benito Mussolini, a fascist who had risen as Italy's dictator in 1922, longed to dominate the Mediterranean but lacked the power. In October 1935, hoping to distract Italians from their economic woes at home, the opportunistic Mussolini settled for an invasion of the independent African state of Ethiopia.

America's Mixed Response. Franklin Roosevelt entered office eager to sustain the commitments to peace and arms control reached in the twenties, and to expand America's role in world affairs. During his first two years in office, he supported international economic agreements, additional arms limitations, and a continuing role for the League of Nations in keeping the peace. More substantively, he recognized the Soviet Union in November 1933, signed a reciprocal trade bill in June 1934, and proposed American participation in the World Court in January 1935.

*For the Nine-Power Treaty, see chapter 28, p. 711.

PEACE IN OUR TIME
As British Prime Minister Neville Chamberlain waved a copy of the Munich agreement with Adolf Hitler, he fanned the last spark of hope that another world war could be avoided.

Yet he quickly found himself hamstrung by economic and political conditions at home and abroad. Recognizing that national economic recovery had to take precedence over international agreements, which in any case world tensions had put beyond reach, Roosevelt felt compelled to make overseas cooperation a secondary goal. Consequently, at the London Economic Conference in 1933, the last faint hope for a collective approach to the world's financial crisis, the president disrupted proceedings by rejecting European proposals contrary to American interests. At the same time, he took the United States off the gold standard, tinkered for a while with the international value of the dollar, and generally let it be known that America would solve its depression alone.

Unable to do much about European or Asian affairs, Roosevelt concentrated on the Western Hemisphere. The administration's policy toward Latin America completed a process that had begun in the twenties: the United States formally abandoned any authority to intervene in a Latin American state. With his uncanny talent for the right phrase and gesture, Roosevelt declared a "Good Neighbor Policy" and in

1936 made an unprecedented, highly successful tour of Latin America. Beneath the new surface, however, the old substance held quite firm. The United States still sought to consolidate its hemispheric authority. In 1933, when a revolutionary government arose in Cuba, for example, the Roosevelt administration undermined it through nonrecognition, then supported the military regime of Fulgencio Batista.* The Cuban economy fell even further under American control, and the State Department pursued reciprocal trade agreements with special zeal in Latin America. Still, the administration demonstrated genuine regard for the autonomy of the Latin republics, and, as a consequence, greatly improved its relations with America's southern neighbors.

Military Actions.   In 1936 the pace of military imperialism abroad quickened. In May, Italy annexed Ethiopia as a colony. Two months later, civil war in Spain offered Mussolini another chance to extend Italy's

---

*Batista would remain in power until 1959, when he was ousted by Fidel Castro.

influence in the Mediterranean. That same year, the Italian and German dictatorships forged an alliance. Between 1936 and 1938, Italian military intervention on behalf of General Francisco Franco's army, more than matching the assistance that France and the Soviet Union gave to the Spanish Republicans, made a critical difference in the war. By 1939 Franco's reactionary Falange ruled Spain. In another sphere of activity, German troops in 1936 occupied the Rhineland provinces, which the Versailles Treaty had demilitarized. Then in March 1938, demanding the political unification of all German-speaking people, Hitler sent his soldiers into Austria, and Germany annexed it. Across the Pacific, Japan in 1936 discarded the international agreements that limited the size of its navy. A year later, after a vain attempt to make a vassal of China's most successful warlord, Chiang Kai-shek, Tokyo released its impatient army to conquer all of China. By October 1938, Japan occupied China's most important cities.

In response to these waves of violence, each threatened nation set its own course. The League of Nations' futile attempt to impose economic sanctions against Italy for attacking Ethiopia merely exposed the League's helplessness. No European power had the energy to confront Japan. Britain and France, though fretful about their own imperial interests in Asia, neither condoned nor seriously challenged Japan's conquests. The Soviet Union and France were particularly vehement in condemning Hitler's advances, yet neither trusted the other sufficiently to take an effective joint stand. Moreover, both Hitler and Mussolini, by keeping the hopes for compromise alive with hints of moderation, discouraged a collective retaliation. It was British Prime Minister Neville Chamberlain who most earnestly explored these prospects of a peaceful settlement. When Hitler demanded Czechoslovakia's German-speaking borderlands, the Sudetenland, Chamberlain carried the primary burden of diplomacy that culminated in the Munich Conference of September 1938. At Munich, England and France averted war by agreeing that Germany and its Central European allies could divide about one-third of Czechoslovakia among themselves. Chamberlain returned to London promising "peace in our time."

American Isolationism.
America reacted to the deteriorating conditions abroad by withdrawing more than ever from world affairs. The more violent the world became, the more intensely most Americans felt a chasm between their lives and the bloody struggles overseas. "Europe's quarrels are not ours," one isolationist declared. "To hell with Europe and the rest of those nations!" exclaimed Minnesota's Senator Thomas D. Schall. Reinforcing the urge toward sepa-

Wide World Photos, Inc.

A PRELUDE TO MODERN AIR WAR
To horrified Americans in 1937, this scene in Shanghai symbolized the savagery of Japanese imperialism.

ration, a committed band of liberals branded war the "enemy of democracy," and that viewpoint found a wide audience through the investigations of Senator Gerald Nye's subcommittee, which blamed bankers and munition makers for America's entry into the First World War. Where ethnic loyalties did give some Americans attachments abroad, they usually strengthened the case against a confrontation with fascism and for isolationism. Catholics could identify much more readily with Franco than with his anticlerical Republican enemies asking help from the United States. Italian Americans rarely demanded war with Mussolini, and Irish Americans rarely sided with the British against any opponent.

As these sentiments deepened, Congress translated them into law. The Tydings-McDuffie Act of 1934, which set a schedule for attaining independence for America's Philippine colony, promised to remove a particularly dangerous outpost of responsibility. The Johnson Debt-Default Act of 1934, establishing the narrowest possible definition of America's friends and enemies abroad, denied credit to any foreign government that had not honored its war debt. Then between 1935 and 1937 Congress enacted major neutrality laws to prevent a repetition of action that had led into the previous war. It embargoed arms and munitions to belligerents, banned the use of American vessels to ship them, prohibited the arming of American merchant ships, and proscribed the extension of credit to belligerents. Later, the neutrality laws would be ridiculed as a scheme to "Keep America Out of the First World War." But Americans, determined not to repeat the experience of 1914–18, praised these laws as their protection against the madness of a world in arms. A final step in this sequence barely failed. In 1938, when Congress debated the "Ludlow amendment," requiring a national referendum to declare war, only heavy pressure from the White House kept it from passing.

Most Americans concentrated their feelings of horror on Japan and Germany. The full-scale Japanese invasion of China in 1937 gave Americans their first appalling revelations of what a modern air force could do to an urban population. On the eve of the Second World War, Japan's bombing of China's cities produced the same kind of humanitarian outcry in America that talk of bayoneted babies had roused during the First World War. *Kristallnacht*, a nationwide attack by the Germans in November 1938 on German Jews and their property, horrified Americans. FDR recalled his ambassador from Berlin, but resistance in America to relaxing immigration quotas barred most German Jews from escaping to the United States. Although most Americans would not realize until the mid-1940s how literally the Nazis sought to exterminate the Jews, news about mass arrests and concentration camps increasingly identified Hitler's anti-Semitism as a threat to all civilized values. Japan and Germany, a majority of Americans concluded, were the centers of an insane barbarism.

Between 1933 and 1939 Roosevelt moved with the dominant currents of opinion. Although in private he despised the Axis* dictators, Hitler and Mussolini, and wished to block their aggressive moves, he seldom said anything in public on foreign affairs. Convinced that any sustained attempt to reverse the country's isolationist course would undermine his ability to ensure the success of the New Deal at home, Roosevelt accepted the neutrality laws without significant opposition. He also congratulated the British and French leaders for their efforts at the Munich Conference to keep the peace.

Yet at the same time, Roosevelt made subtle gestures toward stopping the fascist advance. In 1936 and 1938 he sponsored agreements among all the American republics declaring that an external threat to one

of them would be the common concern of all. Moreover, in October 1937 he warned Americans of international dangers by publicly calling for a "quarantine" of aggressors. Speaking in Chicago, the heartland of isolationist sentiment, the president directly challenged the opponents of a more active foreign policy. When isolationists warned that a "quarantine" would mean America's political and military involvement abroad, however, Roosevelt denied having any such aim in mind.

World War, 1939–1941

In March 1939 Hitler devoured the rest of Czechoslovakia and hungrily eyed the former German territories placed under Polish rule after the First World War.* As Chamberlain's illusion of peace dissolved, Britain and France committed themselves to Poland's defense and frantically prepared for war. Then in August 1939 Germany and the Soviet Union, the most relentless European foes, shocked the world by signing a nonaggression pact. With the Nazi army prepared to strike at Poland, all eyes fixed on Berlin.

The invasion came on September 1, 1939, and Britain and France immediately declared war on Germany. After the quick conquest and division of Poland by Berlin and Moscow, the fighting slowed until the spring of 1940. Then in April Germany began a lightning sweep through western Europe, taking Norway, Denmark, the Netherlands, and Belgium. By June, France itself had fallen. Only Britain remained. German bombers devastated its cities, and German submarines squeezed its lifeline of supplies, apparently in preparation for an invasion of the British Isles.

While Germany was swallowing Europe, Japan extended its rule southward into French Indochina—ostensibly to tighten the blockade of China but actually to control a new area rich in natural resources. Beyond lay Southeast Asia's precious oil and rubber. In September 1940, Japan joined the Axis powers in a defensive pact. It was a tentative connection: many Japanese leaders never trusted Hitler. Yet from the outside, Tokyo's link with Berlin and Rome verified the impression of a unified fascist force rolling toward global domination.

At the outbreak of war, America had hugged its shore. In 1939 the United States had induced the Latin American nations to join it in declaring a huge neutrality zone between Europe and the Western Hemisphere. A revision of the neutrality law had allowed Britain and France to purchase war materials in the United States, but the terms had been "cash and

*In October 1936 Hitler and Mussolini signed an agreement creating what they called the Berlin-Rome Axis, which Japan later joined. Before and during the Second World War, the members of this alliance were generally known as the Axis Powers.

*For the transfer of German-speaking populations to Poland under the Treaty of Versailles, see chapter 27, p. 690.

The Bettmann Archive, Inc.

THE NAZI MENACE
Through public demonstrations of Germany's mobilized martial spirit, Hitler tried to awe his opponents into submission even before he struck.

country could close itself off from the war began to shrink. A majority held tight to their desire for peace, but a growing minority believed that the United States should support Britain's resistance. The rough guideline became "all aid short of war."

Roosevelt's Unprecedented Third Term. As the war raged, the nuances in Roosevelt's thinking grew ever more critical, for in an emergency the president had immense power over foreign policy. Early in his career, Roosevelt came to believe that a great power such as the United States should play an important role in world affairs. His background and training equated Anglo-American culture with civilization, and his instincts told him that Germany was the nation's enemy. Unlike many of his contemporaries, Roosevelt had never questioned either the wisdom or the justice of America's entry into the First World War. But Wilson's political difficulties over the League of Nations convinced FDR that effective action abroad required a stable foreign policy consensus at home, and he was determined to ensure that his handling of the current crisis would rest on majority support. These attitudes were central to all Roosevelt did in the period between 1939 and 1941, including his decision to run for an unprecedented third term.

If Roosevelt had doubts about running for reelection, world crisis resolved them. By 1939 the nation's parlor game was guessing whom the president might designate as his successor. But by keeping a serene silence, Roosevelt held the spotlight on himself and at the last minute allowed the Democratic convention of 1940 to nominate him. That event stirred the latent emotions about Roosevelt the aspiring dictator and Roosevelt the indispensable man. As the president knew very well, he himself would be the issue of the 1940 campaign.

This time, the Republicans selected a candidate able to challenge Roosevelt. Wendell Willkie, a former utilities executive who had once led the fight against the TVA, was an inspired amateur in national politics. Liberal enough to attract independent voters yet conservative enough to satisfy most opponents of the New Deal, Willkie eagerly took on "the Champ" in a vigorous presidential campaign. With flailing arms and sparkling eyes he became the first Republican candidate in twenty years to elicit a warm popular response. Moreover, some former allies of the president, including John L. Lewis and Vice-President Garner, deserted him, while many conservative Democrats talked as if they might bolt the party when Roosevelt selected the liberal Henry Wallace to replace Garner as his running mate.

Nevertheless, the New Deal's coalition of diverse ethnic and regional groups continued to be a powerful

carry": Americans could provide neither credit nor shipping for a belligerent. They had hoped that the arms reaching Hitler's democratic opponents would be enough to defeat him and keep the United States out of the fighting.

With Germany astride western Europe and threatening Britain with invasion, Americans no longer felt so distant or safe. In the summer and fall of 1940, the number of Americans who believed that the

political force, especially as defense spending buoyed up the economy. Willkie's chances lay in foreign affairs. Here, however, the Republican's enthusiasm for resisting fascism at least matched the president's. When fierce debates surrounded a bill to create America's first peacetime draft, Willkie supported it. In September 1940, when the president announced an exchange of fifty old American destroyers for the lease of British bases in the Western Hemisphere, Willkie also approved this clear commitment to the British cause. Then at the last moment, Roosevelt gave the guarantee most Americans wanted desperately to believe: "Your president says this country is not going to war." By 449 electoral votes to Willkie's 82, "the Champ" won four more years.

U.S. Aid to Britain.

After the election the politician who had promised peace became the president who, in defense of the national interest, prepared for war. By the winter of 1940–41, Britain's dwindling assets in the United States could not begin to pay for the war materials it needed. Describing the United States as the "arsenal of democracy," Roosevelt proposed that Britain have an almost unlimited access to American production and credit. An "America First" movement, which had opposed his reelection, fought frantically against lend-lease legislation. Lend-lease, its enemies cried, was a Grim Reaper's AAA that would "plow under every fourth American boy." Publicly, Roosevelt tried to calm these fears of war. But in private he knew that passage of lend-lease legislation would wipe out the last traces of American neutrality and bring the country closer to war. In March 1941 Congress, despite these dangers, passed the open-ended Lend-Lease Act.

By the summer of 1941, Roosevelt and other administration leaders were convinced that the United States would eventually have to join the fighting. Although the Royal Air Force was winning the battle of Britain, the danger did not diminish. Hitler turned eastward, and the Nazis, with feeble assistance from their Italian ally, conquered the Balkans. Then in June 1941 Hitler launched the fateful thrust of the war, an attack into Russia. The Nazi-Soviet Pact of 1939 had been a calculated expedient between enemies, enabling Hitler to dominate the heart of Europe, and the Russians to seize a portion of Poland, the Baltic states of Latvia, Lithuania, and Estonia, and a slice of Finland. Now the Nazis were ready to smash their last great opponent on the Continent, and the German war machine rumbled across a broad eastern front against Russia's primary cities.

As determined as ever to supply their English ally, American convoys carried their lend-lease cargoes closer and closer to the British Isles. In April 1941 the United States extended its patrols to the mid-Atlantic. Then in July, following Germany's invasion of Russia, American convoys moved a big step closer to the British ports by escorting the supplies as far as Iceland, and FDR committed himself to sending Moscow material support. A month later, Roosevelt astonished the nation by meeting with British Prime Minister Winston Churchill on an American cruiser off Newfoundland, where the two leaders announced an "Atlantic Charter" of postwar principles. Meanwhile, the American navy expanded its protection to cover British merchant ships, as well as American, and along the Atlantic sea lanes the two nations collaborated in locating and attacking German submarines. In September one German submarine, as it fled from the U.S.S. *Greer*, fired at the American destroyer. Roosevelt, pretending that the submarine had been the aggressor and likening German power to a "rattlesnake" that was coiled to strike at the Western Hemisphere, authorized American ships to "shoot on sight." By October Congress allowed convoys to land in Britain. "All aid" to Britain could not stop "short of war."

Pearl Harbor.

During these crucial months of 1940 and 1941, Asian affairs appeared to be far less important. Most Americans agreed that Japanese imperialism in China and Indochina during the previous decade had posed some kind of threat, but few could define it. Fewer still in 1940 believed that Japan would dare to fight the United States. Roosevelt largely left the negotiations with Japan to his crusty secretary of state, Cordell Hull, who in turn relied on the rigid, moralistic Stanley Hornbeck, a state department expert on Asian matters. Hull demanded that Japan honor the Nine-Power Treaty on the Open Door, which, in effect, required a withdrawal from the mainland of Asia. As leverage, the United States imposed an increasingly tight embargo on trade wth Japan. During most of 1941, conciliatory forces in the Japanese government under Prince Fuminaro Konoye, the prime minister, sought some way of mollifying the United States short of a Japanese capitulation. Although Konoye would not reopen the question of Manchuria, he proposed a Japanese military withdrawal elsewhere on the Asian mainland in exchange for a friendly Chinese government and American economic cooperation. But Hull was unrelenting. Before serious negotiations could begin, he insisted, Japan must accept the Open Door throughout the area of Japanese expansion. In the midst of American efforts to counter Nazi aggression, it was inconceivable to Hull and most Americans that they should recognize Tokyo's conquest of Manchuria or any other foreign territory.

PEARL HARBOR

By the summer of 1941, the two nations were drifting toward a war neither one wanted. In July, Japan completed its occupation of French Indochina, and Roosevelt retaliated by freezing Japanese assets in the United States. Washington was now in the curious position of battling Japanese imperialism to defend European imperialism in Southeast Asia. Appraising their limited resources, Japan's leaders realized that if they had to fight the United States for their empire, the time had come. Although Prince Konoye continued to explore various formulas of compromise, his authority at home was waning. In October 1941, the militant Hideki Tojo replaced him as prime minister, and Japan prepared for war. Washington, beginning to sense much deeper trouble than it had expected, finally gave hints of flexibility. It was too late.

Because American intelligence had broken Japan's secret code, Washington knew that a Japanese attack of some kind was pending. Roosevelt's inner circle guessed that Japan would strike in Southeast Asia. For two reasons, no one seriously considered Hawaii. First, American policymakers to the very end underrated Japan as a second-class power with more bluff than nerve. Second, American intelligence intercepted so many clues leading in so many directions that it made no sense from any of them. At dawn on December 7, as waves of Japanese planes roared across the naval base at Pearl Harbor, Hawaii, and crippled America's Pacific force, no one was ready. A stunned nation officially went to war.

Within days, the attack on Pearl Harbor clarified issues around the world. Congress declared war on Japan after Roosevelt, in a memorable speech, called December 7 "a date that will live in infamy." Britain immediately joined the United States against Japan. The unpredictable Hitler had no obligation to act, but he decided to declare war on the United States, and Italy followed suit. Hence, a surprise attack precipitating an unwanted war became the event that dissolved America's doubts and propelled it into global conflict. The vast long-range consequences of the plunge—the destruction of isolationism as a controlling policy—would take years to unfold.

1929	Stock market crash begins the Great Depression.			rights, sets up NLRB.

1929 Stock market crash begins the Great Depression.

1930 Hawley-Smoot Tariff raises protective barriers.

1931 Japan occupies Manchuria.

1932 Hoover-Stimson Doctrine refuses recognition of Japanese conquests.

Franklin D. Roosevelt elected president.

Reconstruction Finance Corporation invests $1.5 billion in private enterprise.

1933 Nationwide "Bank Holiday."

Federal Deposit Insurance Corporation guarantees depositors' savings.

Agricultural Adjustment Act passed.

Civilian Conservation Corps formed.

National Industrial Recovery Act creates National Recovery Administration and Public Works Administration.

Tennessee Valley Authority established.

Prohibition repealed.

1934 Reciprocal Trade Agreement Act passed.

1935 Supreme Court broadens attacks on New Deal legislation.

Social Security establishes old-age, other social insurance programs.

Wagner Act affirms collective bargaining rights, sets up NLRB.

Works Progress Administration increases funds for relief of unemployed.

Hitler announces Germany's intent to rearm.

Italy invades Ethiopia.

1936 Roosevelt reelected president.

Spanish Civil War erupts.

Wave of sit-down strikes begins.

1937 U.S. Steel recognizes CIO.

Law to reorganize Supreme Court fails.

Japan invades China.

1938 Fair Employment Practices Act establishes a minimum wage and outlaws child labor.

Munich Conference attempts to appease Hitler by surrendering Czechoslovakia.

1939 Germany invades Poland, starting Second World War.

1940 Germany conquers western Europe.

Japan joins Axis Powers.

Roosevelt elected to a third term.

1941 Congress approves Lend-Lease, American supplies to Allies.

Japan attacks Pearl Harbor; United States enters war.

SUGGESTED READINGS

John Kenneth Galbraith's *The Great Crash, 1929* (rev. ed., 1972) is an interesting essay, but Lester V. Chandler, *America's Greatest Depression* (1970), and Peter Temin, *Did Monetary Forces Cause the Great Depression?* (1976), are more authoritative. Arthur M. Schlesinger, Jr., *The Crisis of the Old Order* (1957), the first volume of his *The Age of Roosevelt*, evokes the desperate confusion of depression. More on its human meaning can be found in Federal Writers' Project, *These Are Our Lives* (1939), and Studs Terkel, *Hard Times: An Oral History of the Great Depression* (1970). David Burner, *Herbert Hoover: A Public Life* (1979), is the standard account of his career to 1933; Joan Hoff Wilson's *Herbert Hoover: Forgotten Progressive* (1975) provides another interesting evaluation of that controversial president. J. Joseph Huthmacher and Warren I. Susman, eds., *Herbert Hoover and the Crisis of American Capitalism* (1973), adds the spice of debate. Fuller accounts of government policy during Hoover's administration appear in Albert U. Romasco, *The Poverty of Abundance* (1965), and Jordan A. Schwarz, *The Interregnum of Despair* (1970).

William E. Leuchtenburg, *Franklin D. Roosevelt and the New Deal, 1932–1940* (1963), is an outstanding survey. For a more critical appraisal, see Paul K. Conkin, *The New Deal* (rev. ed., 1975). Volumes 2 and 3 of Arthur M. Schlesinger, Jr.,

The Age of Roosevelt—The Coming of the New Deal (1958) and *The Politics of Upheaval* (1960)—provide a thorough and readable account of Roosevelt's first administration. The initial problem that he encountered is considered in detail in Susan Estabrook Kennedy's *The Banking Crisis of 1933* (1973). Robert F. Himmelberg, *The Origins of the National Recovery Administration* (1976), analyzes the complex background to NRA.

For the history of NRA and its aftermath, the most valuable work is Ellis W. Hawley's *The New Deal and the Problem of Monopoly* (1966). Van L. Perkins, *Crisis in Agriculture* (1969), covers the beginning of the Agricultural Adjustment Administration. On the most innovative New Deal policy, C. Herman Pritchett, *The Tennessee Valley Authority* (1943), supplies basic information; Phillip Selznick, *TVA and the Grass Roots* (1949), discusses the Authority's social orientation; and Thomas K. McCraw, *TVA and the Power Fight, 1933–1939* (1971), traces the principal challenge to its program. Grace Abbott, *From Relief to Social Security* (1966), records the story of public assistance; and Roy Lubove, *The Struggle for Social Security, 1900–1935* (1968), explains the origins of the Social Security Act. Michael E. Parrish, *Securities Regulation and the New Deal* (1970), is an illuminating monograph on that area of public policy; and Kenneth R. Philp, *John Collier's Crusade for Indian Reform, 1920–1954* (1977), is the basic study of another area.

The battle over the Supreme Court that opened Roosevelt's second administration is reported in Joseph Alsop and Turner Catledge, *The 168 Days* (1938). On the struggles of organized labor, the best survey is Irving Bernstein's *A History of the American Worker, 1933–1941: Turbulent Years* (1970). Sidney Fine, *Sit-Down* (1969), captures the drama of a crucial strike in the automobile industry; and Jerold S. Auerbach, *Labor and Liberty: The La Follette Committee and the New Deal* (1966), examines one form of government assistance to the new unions. For the curious story of labor's outstanding leader, see Melvyn Dubofsky and Warren Van Tine, *John L. Lewis* (1977). Raymond Wolters, *Negroes and the Great Depression* (1970), tells a grim story of the early thirties, and Dan T. Carter's smoothly written *Scottsboro* (1969) recounts the most notorious abuse of justice in the South during that decade. The bottom of the rural economy is explored in David E. Conrad, *The Forgotten Farmers: The Story of Sharecroppers in the New Deal* (1965), in Pete Daniel, *The Shadow of Slavery: Peonage in the South, 1901–1969* (1972), and most feelingly in James Agee and Walker Evans, *Let Us Now Praise Famous Men* (1941). Sidney Baldwin's *FSA* (1968) is an appealing history of the New Deal's major effort to help the rural poor. Two interesting studies—Paul Conkin, *Tomorrow a New World: The New Deal Community Program* (1959), and Jane DeHart Mathews, *The Federal Theater, 1935–1939* (1967)—suggest the breadth of interests affected by the New Deal. Barry Dean Karl, *Executive Reorganization and Reform in the New Deal* (1963), and Richard Polenberg, *Reorganizing Roosevelt's Government: The Controversy over Executive Reorganization, 1936–1939* (1966), discuss an important political contest in the late thirties. These studies, along with two other fine books—Richard S. Kirkendall's *Social Scientists and Farm Politics in the Age of Roosevelt* (1966) and James T. Patterson's *Congressional Conservatism and the New Deal* (1967)—help to explain the decline of reform.

On Roosevelt himself, the best study for the New Deal years is James MacGregor Burns, *Roosevelt: The Lion and the Fox* (1956). Frank Freidel's massive biography, *Franklin D. Roosevelt* (4 vols. to date, 1952–73), has carried FDR through his first critical months in the White House. Additional insights into the Roosevelt household appear in Alfred B. Rollins, Jr., *Roosevelt and Howe* (1962), and Joseph P. Lash, *Eleanor and Franklin* (1971). Among the many published journals and memoirs by participants in the New Deal, Raymond Moley's critical *After Seven Years* (1939) and Rexford G. Tugwell's appreciative *The Democratic Roosevelt* (1957) are especially useful. J. Joseph Huthmacher, *Senator Robert F. Wagner and the Rise of Urban Liberalism* (1968), Paul A. Kurzman, *Harry Hopkins and the New Deal* (1974), and George Martin, *Madam Secretary: Frances Perkins* (1976), are complimentary accounts of these important officials. Otis L. Graham, Jr., *An Encore for Reform* (1967), explores the generally unfavorable responses of the old progressives to the New Deal, and George Wolfskill, *The Revolt of the Conservatives* (1962), decribes the outrage of the American Liberty League.

Local politics is an elusive subject. James Patterson, *The New Deal and the States* (1969), analyzes one source of resistance to national power. John M. Allswang's *A House for All People: Ethnic Politics in Chicago, 1890–1936* (1971) sketches an interesting picture for one big city, and Arthur Mann's *La Guardia Comes to Power: 1933* (1965) explores the roots of an important election in New York City. The relation between the New Deal and the local bosses is considered in Bruce M.

Stave, *The New Deal and the Last Hurrah: Pittsburgh Machine Politics* (1970), Lyle W. Dorsett, *The Pendergast Machine* (1968), and Charles H. Trout, *Boston, the Great Depression, and the New Deal* (1977). Charles J. Tull, *Father Coughlin and the New Deal* (1965), and T. Harry Williams, *Huey Long* (1969), examine the New Deal's leading competitors in local politics, and Alan Brinkley, *Voices of Protest: Huey Long, Father Coughlin and the Great Depression* (1982), analyzes the roots of their appeal. The cultural values of the New Dealers themselves are summarized in E. Digby Baltzell, *The Protestant Establishment* (1964).

America's reaction to the early imperialist crisis in Asia is explored in Sara R. Smith, *The Manchurian Crisis, 1931–1932* (1948), Richard N. Current, *Secretary Stimson* (1954), and Robert H. Ferrell, *American Diplomacy in the Great Depression: Hoover-Stimson Foreign Policy, 1929–1933* (1957). Dorothy Borg's *The United States and the Far Eastern Crisis of 1933–1938* (1964) continues the story into the full-scale Sino-Japanese War. The best discussion of the London Economic Conference appears in Frank Freidel's *Franklin D. Roosevelt: Launching the New Deal* (1973). The title of Arnold A. Offner's *American Appeasement: United States Foreign Policy and Germany, 1933–1938* (1969) indicates the author's approach to the years when Hitler was consolidating power. Alton Frye, *Nazi Germany and the American Hemisphere, 1933–1941* (1967), minimizes Hitler's transatlantic ambitions. Lloyd C. Gardner's *Economic Aspects of New Deal Diplomacy* (1964) emphasizes an insatiable urge for profits. David H. Culbert, *News for Everyman: Radio and Foreign Affairs in Thirties America* (1976), brings a new perspective to the decade's developments.

The most thorough account of diplomatic events leading to the Second World War is the two-volume study by William L. Langer and S. Everett Gleason, *The Challenge to Isolation, 1937–1940* (1952) and *The Undeclared War, 1940–1941* (1953), a detailed justification of American policy. Robert A. Divine's two volumes, *The Illusion of Neutrality* (1962) and *The Reluctant Belligerent* (1966), are only slightly more critical. On the other hand, Charles A. Beard's *President Roosevelt and the Coming of the War, 1941* (1948) indicts FDR for maneuvering the nation into war, and Bruce M. Russett's thin but thoughtful essay, *No Clear and Present Danger* (1972), dismisses the claims of a fascist threat to the United States. Manfred Jonas, *Isolation in America, 1935–1941* (1966), presents the basic facts about the domestic opposition to the government's policies, and Warren F. Kimball, *The Most Unsordid Act: Lend-Lease, 1939–1941* (1969), discusses the issue that aroused the fiercest resistance. James R. Leutze, *Bargaining for Supremacy: Anglo-American Naval Collaboration, 1937–1941* (1977), traces secret adjustments of power preceding the war. The narrow American vision is revealed in Paul W. Schroeder's *The Axis Alliance and Japanese-American Relations, 1941* (1958) and Charles E. Neu's *The Troubled Encounter: The United States and Japan* (1975). The official in Tokyo who tried to broaden Washington's view is the subject of Waldo H. Heinrichs, Jr., *American Ambassador: Joseph C. Grew and the Development of the United States Diplomatic Tradition* (1966). Roberta Wohlstetter, *Pearl Harbor: Warning and Decision* (1962), analyzes the controversy surrounding the Japanese strike at Hawaii. The debate is continued in Gordon W. Prange, *At Dawn We Slept: The Untold Story of Pearl Harbor* (1981), and John Toland, *Infamy: Pearl Harbor and Its Aftermath* (1982). All these issues in the Roosevelt foreign policy are reviewed in Robert Dallek, *Franklin D. Roosevelt and American Foreign Policy, 1932–1945* (1979).

30 A Global Setting for the Modern Republic, 1941–1952

The Second World War produced lasting changes in American life. In the short run, involvement in the fighting both led to an expansion of the economy that ended the Great Depression, and pushed the United States into a military and political alliance with Britain, China, and Russia that did not outlive the war. But there were also more enduring effects. The war permanently expanded the power of the national government at home, and it raised the country's responsibilities abroad to unprecedented levels. The question for American leaders immediately after 1945 was no longer whether they should broaden the authority of the government, but how they should translate their power into systematic national and international policies.

The Second World War, 1941–1945

Between December 1941 and May 1945, the United States, unlike its allies, was continuously engaged in two very different wars. In the Pacific theater of war, where victory hinged on control of the seas, the United States fought almost alone. In the European theater, where victory could be won only on the Continent, the Republic contributed to a complex collective effort.

Initial Defeats. During the early months of the war, both theaters offered a dismal picture of retreat and jeopardy. Japanese units swept away the remnants of resistance in Southeast Asia, occupying the Netherlands East Indies (Indonesia), capturing the British base at Singapore, and penetrating to the frontiers of India. Japan's naval victory in the Java Sea assured its control of the western Pacific. In May 1942 the remnants of America's small, isolated force in the Philippines surrendered to the Japanese. Across a vast expanse from the tip of the Aleutian Islands near Alaska through the central Pacific to the mountain passes of Burma, imperial Japan dominated. From beleaguered China, General "Vinegar Joe" Stillwell, America's ad-

viser to Chiang Kai-shek, summarized the first round of the Asian war: "We got a hell of a beating." The only bright spot was General Douglas MacArthur's escape from the Philippines to Australia, where he rallied Allied spirits by declaring, "I came through, and I shall return."

In Europe, Germany's successes were even more ominous. Its fleet of submarines, which had been held in check before December 1941, unleashed a devastating attack on the Allies' Atlantic supply lines. In the early months of the war, they roamed along the American coast and into the Caribbean, as the United States had not yet developed an effective counterattack to the elusive submarine. Nor could American shipyards yet replace the tonnage lost at sea. Meanwhile, Nazi mechanized divisions under General Erwin Rommel drove across North Africa into Egypt, threatening the Suez Canal. Above all, a renewed offensive in Russia spread German troops from the outskirts of Leningrad in the north to the strategic industrial city of Stalingrad in the south. Into the late fall of 1942, the greatest disaster, a Soviet collapse, loomed as a strong possibility.

Establishing War Strategy. How could the United States best use its massive resources to alter the balance of the war? In broad strategic matters, the answers came quickly and clearly. The European theater had priority over the Pacific. Anglo-American leaders agreed that the defeat of Germany before Japan was the most direct path to total victory. The first objective, therefore, was to ensure Soviet survival by continuing the flow of Lend-Lease goods, the food and war materiel that had been going to Russia since the summer of 1941. Despite the menace of the German submarines, which took a terrible toll along the icy routes in the North Sea, the quantity of these supplies slowly increased. Finally, to relieve the pressure on the Soviet army, American and British forces had to launch a "second front" as soon as possible in the west.

758

SIEGE OF LENINGRAD
Their city surrounded by German troops, citizens of Leningrad dip water from a broken main. More than 600,000 died of starvation during the two-year siege.

The men who ultimately made these decisions were President Roosevelt and Prime Minister Winston Churchill, Britain's brilliant, calculating war leader. Their personal collaboration had begun at the Atlantic Conference of August 1941, which had declared to the world that the United States and Great Britain stood together against the Axis. From December 1941 to January 1943, through a series of private meetings, the two men grew closer. Although Russia's fate also hung on the decisions that Roosevelt and Churchill made, the Soviet Union remained a distant ally, declaring its needs and awaiting a response from the Western powers.

The initial American impulse was to open at least a token second front in western Europe during 1942. But no one had anticipated the complexities of global warfare. Although the United States pushed the German submarines away from its coast, the Nazis more than held their own during 1942 in the battle for the Atlantic sea lanes. Without guaranteed supplies, the

Allies would never breach the coast of France. And such crucial items as landing craft were still very scarce. Moreover, the Pacific war also demanded attention and resources, especially because the attack on Pearl Harbor gave it a special importance to the many Americans who favored a Pacific-first strategy.

The United States began to stabilize its position against the weaker but more remote foe in Asia. Because Congress had authorized a program of naval construction well before Pearl Harbor, the American fleet was able to return in strength to the Pacific less than a year after Japan's devastating attack. In May 1942, even as Japan was overrunning the Philippines, a successful American assault on Japanese shipping in the battle of the Coral Sea secured Australia. A month later, a Japanese naval force was repulsed at the battle of Midway, west of Hawaii. Then in November 1942 the American navy won a three-day encounter off the Solomon Islands near Australia, and the balance of sea power shifted back to the United States. Meanwhile,

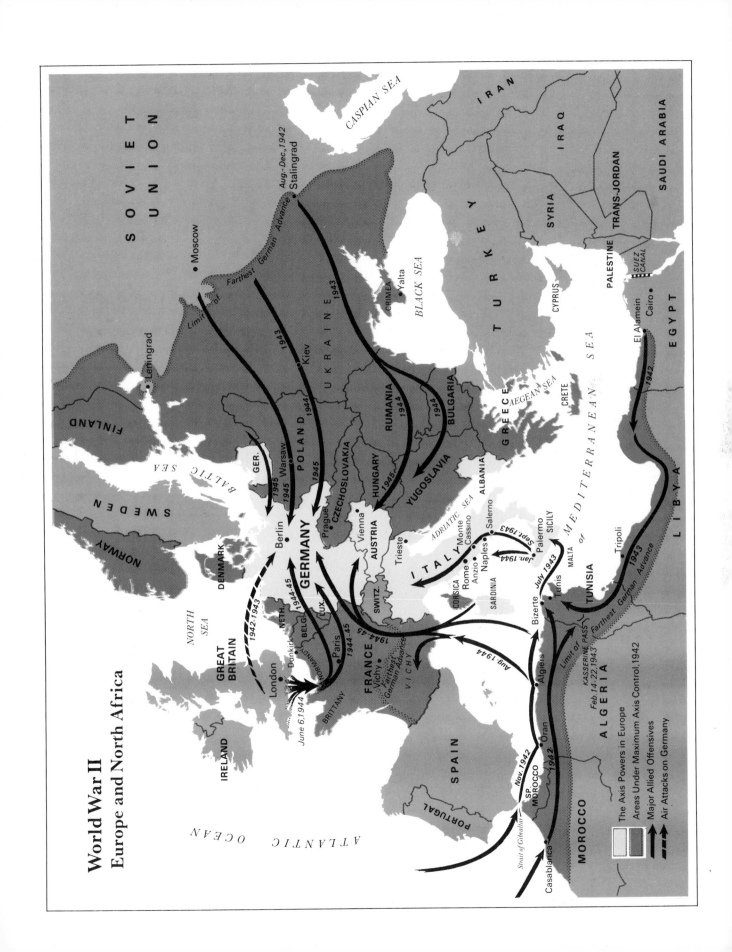

World War II
Europe and North Africa

SOVIET UNION

CASPIAN SEA

IRAN

IRAQ

SAUDI ARABIA

TRANS-JORDAN

SYRIA

PALESTINE

Aug.-Dec., 1942
Stalingrad

• Moscow

Farthest German Advance

Limit of

1943

TURKEY

SUEZ CANAL

• Leningrad

Kiev •

UKRAINE

1943

1944

CRIMEA
Yalta •

BLACK SEA

CYPRUS

EGYPT

El Alamein •
Cairo •

1942

FINLAND

1944

RUMANIA

1944

BULGARIA

GREECE

AEGEAN SEA

CRETE

SWEDEN

BALTIC SEA

Warsaw

POLAND

1945

1945

CZECHOSLOVAKIA

1945

HUNGARY

1945

YUGOSLAVIA

ALBANIA

ADRIATIC SEA

MEDITERRANEAN SEA

of

LIBYA

NORWAY

GER.

1945

1945

Berlin

GERMANY

1944-45

Prague •

Vienna •

AUSTRIA

Trieste •

Monte Cassino

Salerno

Sept. 1943

Palermo

SICILY

Tripoli •

1943

DENMARK

NORTH SEA

NETH.

BELG.

Lux.

Paris •

1944-45

Dunkirk •

London •

SWITZ.

ITALY

Rome •
Anzio •
Naples •

Jan. 1944

CORSICA

SARDINIA

MALTA

July 1943

Bizerte •

Tunis •

TUNISIA

Farthest German Advance

1943

GREAT BRITAIN

IRELAND

NORMANDY

June 6, 1944

BRITTANY

FRANCE

Vichy •

VICHY

Farthest German Advance

Aug. 1944

Limit of

KASSERINE PASS
Feb. 14-22, 1943

Algiers •

Oran •

ALGERIA

ATLANTIC OCEAN

SPAIN

PORTUGAL

Nov. 1942

1942

SP. MOROCCO

Strait of Gibraltar

Casablanca •

MOROCCO

The Axis Powers in Europe

Areas Under Maximum Axis Control, 1942

Major Allied Offensives

Air Attacks on Germany

1942-1943

LANDING OPERATIONS, SOUTH PACIFIC, 1944
American troops step ashore from an LST (landing ship tank) in the South Pacific, where U.S. forces have gained an advantage on a Japanese-held island.

with an eye to morale back home, American forces in August launched small, difficult counteroffensives at Guadalcanal in the Solomon Islands and on the far larger contested island of New Guinea.

Sobered by the complications of a global war, Roosevelt and his advisers, despite complaints from Moscow, abandoned plans for a quick attack on France and accepted Churchill's alternative of a North African campaign. In November 1942 Operation Torch under General Dwight D. Eisenhower invaded French Morocco and Algeria. As British General Bernard Montgomery pushed Rommel's *Afrika Korps* from the east, Eisenhower's troops swept westward. By May 1943 they had eliminated Axis power throughout North Africa.

During the North African campaign the tide of battle began to shift around the world. The Soviet Union had already won the pivotal engagement of the European war. Hitler, in an effort to crack Russia's resistance before another winter froze his army in place, gambled recklessly on an assault against Stalingrad. During the winter's war of 1942–43, a relentless Soviet counterattack not only saved Stalingrad but

actually cost Germany half a million troops. The following summer the Soviet army took the initiative against its weakened, overextended German enemy and began the drive westward toward Berlin. In the Southwest Pacific, American forces cut the first wedge through the enemy perimeter north of Australia, placed the Japanese on the defensive, and charted the winding trail of island conquests that led to Japan itself. In the summer of 1943, radar, long-range air patrols, and Ultra, Britain's ability to read coded German messages, finally tipped the balance against the German submarines in the battle of the Atlantic.

Victory in Europe. When the United States and Great Britain bypassed France for North Africa in 1942, Soviet Premier Josef Stalin was again promised a second front in Europe for the following year. But in 1943 Churchill once more persuaded Roosevelt to postpone an attack on France, which he feared would fail, and to strike instead at the weakest Axis power, Italy. That July, in the most dubious strategic decision of the war, an Allied force landed in Sicily; in September it crossed into Italy. Nothing in the campaign went well.

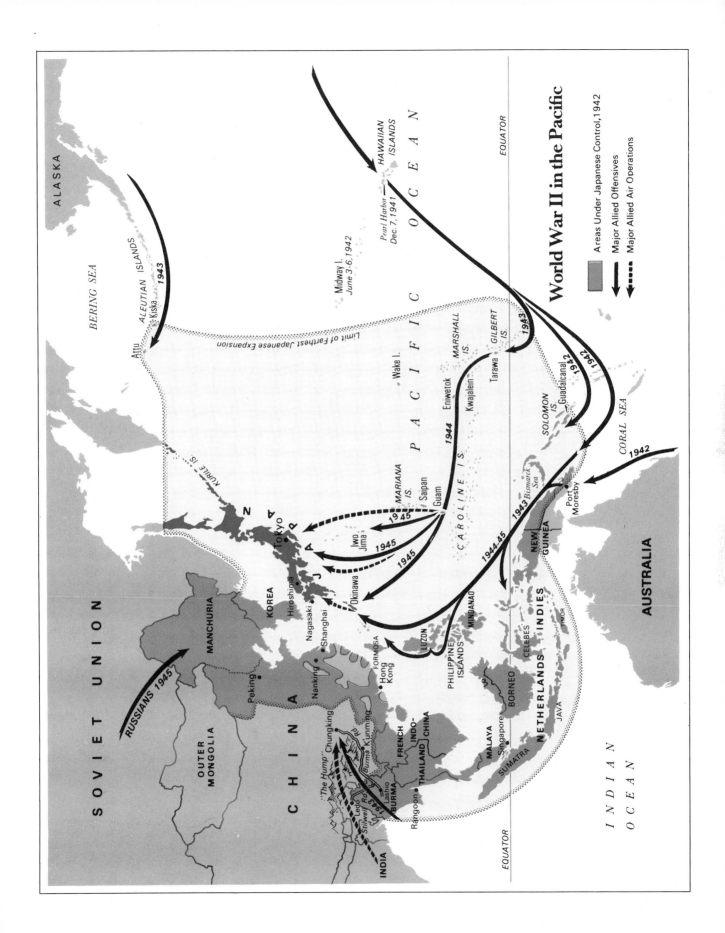

World War II in the Pacific

Areas Under Japanese Control, 1942

Major Allied Offensives

Major Allied Air Operations

The following account by *Life* correspondent Jack Belden graphically depicts the terrors and hazards of an amphibious assault during the Second World War. The largest and most successful of this kind of attack was the invasion of France on June 6, 1944.

A War Correspondent Lands in Salerno (1943)

*T*HE Germans knew we were coming and waited for us. All they had to do was study the map and see the obvious place for us to strike was south of Naples. Even correspondents who were not briefed before the operation and who possessed no special information guessed, on the basis of logic, that was where we would land. While we were steaming toward our objective the Swiss radio announced that an Allied invasion fleet was carrying the Fifth Army toward Naples. . . .

As late as 5:30 on the afternoon of Sept. 8 the naval commander on the forces I was with said that a bombardment was scheduled. Yet it never came off. Perhaps the Army, wishing to rely on suprise, didn't want the bombardment. If that is so, it was a repetition of tactics that already had been used in landings in Sicily. A repetition of tactics as a general rule is bad. It plays into enemy hands.

Perhaps the announcement of the Italian surrender made the authorities change their minds. Maybe neither of these reasons is correct. But whatever the reason we had little or no supporting fire on the American part of the beach. That announcement of the Italian surrender which we heard at 6:30 on our radios had an unfortunate effect on the troops. We all cheered the news and shouts from the whole fleet echoed over the Mediterranean. . . .

Everything seemed to be going too smoothly. While we were still under way our ship slung boats and even "ducks" over the side. As soon as the anchor was down the boats of the first assault wave were away and circling in the water. It was the smoothest debarkation I'd ever seen. . . .

"Why should we be afraid?" said a private. I couldn't answer him. I couldn't say it was wiser to be afraid. Lack of fear is the mark of well-trained and disciplined troops but it is also the mark of inexperience. These men were not scared and I didn't like it. . . .

Before us all was quiet and dark. We broke our circle and headed in a column toward shore. Above the roar of our motors we did not hear the approach of that first shell. But I saw the flame leap out of the boat next to me and simultaneously the crash shook our boat and it jerked once or twice and then went on. Abruptly I sat down in the bottom of the boat, not

as a precaution but because I was afraid. I heard a soldier say, "I saw a shell close like that in training once," and I was more afraid.

Though we were still a good distance from the beach, the German guns were already on us. As we learned later, the Germans were so sure of where we were going to land that they brought their defenses right onto the beach. Trees, brush and all obstacles were cut down so as to give them a clear field of fire. Nothing was left to chance. Machine guns fired only in certain zones, the zones interlocked. Almost on the water's edge, in some cases only 50 yards apart, machine guns were set up facing toward the sea. Fifty yards from the beach heavy machine guns threatened death to anyone coming out of the boats. In back of those were mortars. . . .

Shells were flashing in the water, flames were yellowing the sky and bullets slapped into our boat. They snapped over our heads, rattled against the boat sides like hail and beat at the ramp door seeming to say, "When you open the door, I'll get you, get you, get you." The coxswain shouted, "Get ready!" The boat shuddered and the ramp creaked open. A man leaped into the void and his legs flailed the sea which was bubbling and breaking in a white froth on the white sandy beach. I stepped down. My legs sank down to the knees and my feet touched the sandy soil of Italy. At last I was on the continent of Europe.

That great and significant affair was a thing of insignificance to me then. I was possessed by no thought of liberating a continent but only by the frenzied fancy that yellow tracers were flashing on the left and right, that flares were curving in golden parabolas onto the beach, that the boats were illuminated and gray and ugly, that they were disgorging dim and menacing figures and everything was unfriendly, miserable and wet.

Although Italy immediately surrendered, German troops filled the vacuum from the north, fortified the critical mountains and passes, and stalled the large Allied army. Stalin, whose soldiers continued to bear the primary burden of the ground war against Germany, was furious.

Not until June 6, 1944, did the United States and Britain finally establish a successful second front in France. By then Rome had fallen, and the Soviet army had reached Poland. The systematic bombing of Germany, after accomplishing relatively little in 1943, was now devastating its cities. The Allies commanded the air, and American supplies flowed across the Atlantic. While feints to the northern coast of France confused Germany's waiting army, Operation Overlord struck the beaches of Normandy on June 6 in the greatest amphibious assault in history. After six weeks of struggle, the Allies broke through Germany's coastal defenses, opening northern France to the Allied army. In August another force invaded southern France, and that same month Paris fell.

Hitler's last thrust came a week after Overlord, when the first rocket-launched bombs whined across the English Channel. In September the silent and more deadly V-2 rockets, replacing the V-1 "buzz bombs," hit London. They brought terror to England but no success for the Nazis. That same month British and American troops entered Germany. The Russian army pressed through Poland and the Balkans. Except for a desperate Nazi counterattack at the German-Belgian border—the "battle of the Bulge," in December 1944—Germany's army collapsed inside the Allied vise. By the end of April, Russian troops were fighting in the streets of Berlin. Hitler, ill and deranged, committed suicide in a hidden bunker in Berlin, and on May 7, 1945, German officers formally capitulated to the Allied command.

Russian lives and American productivity had been the basic contributions to victory in Europe. About 20 million Soviet citizens died in the conflict with Germany. By contrast, British losses were about 500,000, and American losses in both theaters of war about 300,000. The United States served as the arsenal of the Allied cause. By 1942 America's war production equaled the combined output of the Axis powers; by 1944, it doubled the enemy's total. When Germany could no longer slow the delivery of American goods, the Nazis were doomed to fall beneath the crushing weight of war materiel.

After Germany's surrender, the numbing facts about the Nazis' Jewish policy began to be fully disclosed. Systematically, the German government had applied the most effective techniques of modern organization to destroy 6 million European Jews. Although the Roosevelt administration had had substan-

U.S. Army photograph

THE INFANTRYMAN'S WAR
Behind every move on the generals' maps lay a terrible price in human suffering. This soldier, wounded by shrapnel, receives a transfusion of blood plasma as a Sicilian family looks on.

tial knowledge during the war of what was happening, it had refused to make any special effort to rescue the victims of the Holocaust and had even rejected plans to bomb the transportation lines into the death camps. Arguing that "rescue through victory" was the best policy for saving people from the Holocaust, the Roosevelt administration resisted suggestions for anything that might divert resources from the war effort and retard Nazi defeat. If the policy seemed wise at the time, in retrospect it has impressed people as callous insensitivity to a problem that could not wait.

Bloody Advances in the Pacific.
While American troops had fought through the Italian mud in 1943, the pace of the Pacific war had remained slow. That November, on the assumption that only an occupation of Tokyo itself could end the war, naval forces under Admiral Chester Nimitz, along with a combination of American, Australian, and New Zealand ground forces under General Douglas MacArthur, began a grim, two-pronged assault toward the Japanese mainland. Nimitz's com-

mand had to regain control over the myriad islands in the central Pacific. Bloody links lay in the chain ahead: Tarawa in the Gilbert Islands, Saipan in the Marianas, Iwo Jima, and then Okinawa at the tip of Japan's homeland. From the south, MacArthur's command had to hack its way through the jungles of New Guinea and converge with Nimitz's forces on the Philippines.

Early in 1944, as America's production expanded to serve both the European and Pacific wars, the drive to Japan gained momentum. By summer, the United States controlled the central Pacific. Then in October, with General MacArthur dramatically leading his troops to the site of a humiliating defeat early in the war, American forces invaded the Philippines. That same month, in the battle of Leyte Gulf, Japanese naval power was destroyed. Fierce Japanese resistance continued to keep casualties high. As late as March 1945, a month's fight for the tiny, desolate island of Iwo Jima left 20,000 Americans dead and wounded. But Japan now lay open to systematic bombing. Napalm raids burned its compact cities, one by one. In March 1945 a single attack on Tokyo killed more than 80,000 inhabitants. When Germany surrendered in May 1945, an utterly exposed Japan was already tottering.

The Atomic Bomb.
The climactic blow of the Asian war had been in preparation even before Pearl Harbor and had been originally aimed at Germany, not Japan. In 1939 refugee physicists from Europe, fearing the potential of Germany's military technology, began urging the American government to explore the possibility of producing an atomic bomb before the Nazis could develop it. Within a year the awesome project was under way. In utmost secrecy, groups of scientists at separate laboratories struggled against time to master the secrets of the atom. They learned to control a chain reaction of atomic fission so that it would generate enormous power that they then translated into a technically practical military device. In July 1945 the task was finally completed at a lonely center in Los Alamos, New Mexico, under the direction of physicist J. Robert Oppenheimer. By then, however, Germany had fallen. A new, inexperienced president, Harry S Truman, sat in the White House. An array of military and civilian advisers counseled the president to use the new weapon against Japan, explaining that it might eliminate the need for an invasion of the Japanese home islands, which was expected to produce heavy American casualties. On August 6 a single bomb demolished the city of Hiroshima, immediately killing about 80,000 people and maiming and poisoning thousands more. Three days later, just as the Soviet Union declared war on Japan, a second bomb razed Nagasaki. On August 14, Japan surrendered.

D-DAY
Taking cover behind barriers that had blocked their landing craft, these Allied soldiers fought for a piece of the Normandy beaches.

Robert Capa/Magnum Photos, Inc.

The Home Front

The Second World War ended the depression in the United States. Before the war was over, net farm income almost doubled, and corporate profits after taxes climbed 70 percent. From a total of more than 8 million unemployed in 1940, the curve dropped below a million in 1944. Moreover, an abundance of jobs and an industrial wage scale that rose 24 percent drew into the labor market an additional 7 million workers, half of whom were women. There had been no comparable economic boom in American history.

The Wartime Boom.
Economic organization for a worldwide conflict required an extraordinary expansion of government power. Washington suddenly teemed with hundreds of thousands of new arrivals who jammed themselves into cubbyhole offices with a bewildering array of alphabet labels. The main divisions of the government bureaucracy matched the major functions of the modern economy. The War Production Board, the Office of Price Administration, the War Manpower Commission, the Office of Defense Transportation, and the War Food Administration each had broad authority to manage its subdivision of the economy. Beginning in October 1942, the skillful South Carolina politician James Byrnes ruled these agencies through the Office of Economic Stabilization, and subsequently through the Office of War Mobilization.

Allocating scarce resources and controlling inflation were the problems that most bedeviled the wartime agencies. Because the United States was blessed with an abundance of natural resources, it had enough raw materials for most wartime programs.

When a shortage of rubber created a crisis, the rapid development of synthetic rubber soon resolved it. The shortage of skilled labor, however, defied solution. Not only did the armed services absorb over 15 million men and women, but civilians could not resist hopping from job to job in search of better wages. "Stabilization," or job-freeze, orders from Washington had little effect on labor turnover, and Roosevelt's proposal in 1944 to draft workers into an industrial army collapsed in the face of united opposition from employers and unions alike.

The demand for a larger body of laborers at home to provide materiel to troops at the front greatly expanded the role of women in the work force. During the war years some 6.5 million women took jobs; more than half of them had previously been unpaid housewives. By the spring of 1945, 57 percent of all employed persons in the United States were women, an unprecedented proportion of American laborers. Equally striking, the percentage of married working women jumped from 36 percent in 1940 to 50 percent in 1945.

Scarce labor and scarce goods drove up prices during the early months of the war. The Office of Price Administration (OPA), under the able but politically obtuse economist Leon Henderson, lacked the power to control inflation because Congress refused to hold down the rise of agricultural prices. Only late in 1942, when Byrnes took charge of the entire mobilization program, did a semblance of order begin to emerge. By mid-1943, a broad legal ceiling over prices, wages, and rents finally stopped the upward spiral. Although the cost of living increased about 33 percent during the war, relatively little of that increase occurred after the summer of 1943.

Library of Congress

ON THE HOME FRONT
Wartime labor shortages brought women into the work force in great numbers. By 1945 they made up 57 percent of all employed persons in the United States.

Finance posed another basic wartime problem. Although more than half the costs of war accumulated as a national debt, massive new funds still had to be raised. The answer came in the revolutionary Revenue Act of 1942, which established America's modern structure of taxation. The heart of the measure was a steeply graduated income tax that for the first time covered most middle-income and lower-income groups. As a result, the number of families paying income tax quadrupled, and by 1945 revenues from the tax were an astronomical twenty times above their level in 1940. To ease the pain yet increase the flow, the government withheld most of these taxes directly from workers' paychecks rather than demand them in a lump sum once a year.

Inside the intricate framework of wartime rules, extreme decentralization prevailed. The tax laws contained numerous loopholes for the wealthy. Thousands of local draft boards decided who should fill the quotas for military service. To get the planes and tanks and beef and wheat it needed, the government simply offered to pay a lot of money. It signed lucrative contracts with individual companies guaranteeing costs, profits, and large tax write-offs. Companies negotiated these contracts through the various bureaus of the wartime government, then fought with one another for the labor and raw materials all of them needed. After the government allowed farm prices to skyrocket for a year, it continued to subsidize many farmers at a level above the market price for their products. Even the unpopular OPA, which rationed such scarce commodities as gasoline, meat, shoes, and sugar among a nation of grumbling consumers, exercised little control over the widespread violation of its rules. The government's chief administrators intervened only when the many small decisions below them had created a hopeless mess.

In the wartime scramble for advantage, the strong reaped the greatest benefits. In 1940 the 100 leading companies manufactured 30 percent of the nation's output. By 1943 the 100 leaders produced 70 percent. The conservative coalition in Congress grew larger and bolder. As the unemployed came back to work, Congress in 1942 terminated the WPA. Calling the Farm Security Administration a "communist" center, its congressional opponents abolished the agency's social programs for the rural poor. Despite President Roosevelt's efforts, Congress lightened the tax burden on the rich in 1943.

The one child of the thirties to thrive during the war was the union movement. In 1941, two more citadels of the open shop—Ford and the corporations in "Little Steel"—surrendered. During the war itself union membership rose 40 percent. Even more important, many employers, in an effort to hold their workers and maintain production, actually bargained with the unions for the first time. Yet here also the conservatives had their say. Although the number of strikes remained quite low between 1941 and 1945, important ones in the coal and railroad industries during 1943 triggered an angry public reaction, and Congress responded with the Smith-Connally Act, which authorized the president to postpone a strike for thirty days and seize a plant that had been struck. Strikers could be fined and imprisoned.

Above all, the conservatives fought every executive agency that tried to make economic plans for the postwar years. Not one of these proposals survived the congressional budget cuts. As the war drew to a close, the only significant preparation for peace was the Servicemen's Readjustment Act of 1944, popularly known as the GI Bill, which provided unemployment compensation, medical care, mortgage funds, and educational subsidies for the returning veterans. An ailing Roosevelt did little to arrest the confusion. Investing most of his energies in world problems—"Dr. Win-the-War" had replaced "Dr. New Deal," he said—the president left the home front to his subordinates.

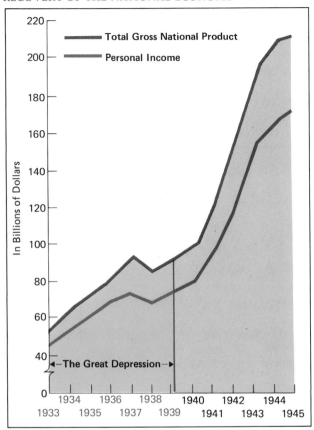

Except in military affairs, Roosevelt had lost almost all influence in Congress by late 1943. At the beginning of 1944, when, in the most radical speech of his career, he announced an economic bill of rights for the postwar era, it received an unfriendly response in Congress. Further, when the Democrats nominated him for a fourth term in 1944, he campaigned listlessly against Thomas E. Dewey, the smooth and capable but aloof Republican governor of New York. Although Roosevelt's percentage of the popular vote declined, he still won handily, 439 to 99 electoral votes. Perhaps the nasty Democratic comment that no one wanted "little Tom Dewey sitting on two Washington telephone books" at the peace conference captured the essence of Roosevelt's strength. At a grand juncture in world affairs, the president had an appropriately grand international prestige. But domestically, America had no strong leadership entering 1945.

Racial Crosscurrents. While the Roosevelt administration struggled to win the war and ensure postwar peace and prosperity, racial conflicts raised basic questions about traditional commitments to equality and free-

dom. Assertions that the Second World War was a crusade for democracy stumbled over the fact that white Americans subjected Japanese, Mexican, and black Americans to racial prejudice that deprived them of basic rights.

The most shocking example of arbitrary government power occurred on the West Coast immediately after the Japanese attack on Pearl Harbor. A large majority of whites along the West Coast had nursed a traditional hostility toward Asians. After the surprise attack on American territory, they readily believed rumors of a Japanese seditious "fifth column" in the United States that was planning extensive sabotage and communicating with enemy submarines off America's shores. The government, they cried, must destroy the danger from within. These popular, bipartisan emotions found a willing servant in Lieutenant General John DeWitt, who headed the army's Western Defense Command. Responding to DeWitt's request, Washington gave the general broad powers in February 1942 to solve the Japanese problem as he chose.

At the outset, DeWitt planned to use stronger measures against the 40,000 alien Japanese (immigrants who by law were denied the right to become American citizens) than against the 70,000 who were American citizens by birth. But that distinction quickly disappeared. Early in 1942 DeWitt ordered all Japanese Americans along the coasts of Washington, Oregon, and California and in southern Arizona to abandon their homes. From temporary stockades, they were transported to ten inland centers where the Army Relocation Authority guarded them for the duration. In *Korematsu* v. *United States* (1944), the Supreme Court upheld these policies on grounds of national security. Along with their liberty, Japanese Americans lost about $350 million in property and income.

Concentration camps for 110,000 Japanese Americans were an embarrassment to the Roosevelt administration, which officially described them as "relocation centers." After the initial wave of panic passed, government officials discussed ways of reversing their policy and releasing the prisoners. But public opinion was against this policy change. The administration was told that no communities would accept the Japanese Americans. As a compromise, the army during 1943 and 1944 issued individual leaves to 35,000 imprisoned Japanese Americans, most of whom served in the United States armed forces. Finally, in January 1945 the prison gates were opened to everyone.

Meanwhile, in response to the desperate wartime need for unskilled labor, the United States in 1942 negotiated an agreement with Mexico for the importation of *braceros*, or temporary workers. Los Angeles, booming with war contracts and bursting with new arrivals, was a favorite destination for both legal

PRISONERS
With pride as their only defense, these Japanese Americans await shipment to one of the wartime concentration camps.

and illegal immigrants from Mexico. City officials did nothing to ease the newcomers' transition. Ethnic tensions simmered in the overflowing metropolis until the local hostility toward Chicanos erupted in the "zoot suit"* riots, which in most cases meant the beating of young Mexican Americans.

Racial tensions between black and white Americans thrown together in northern cities were even sharper. During the depression, when the unemployed crowded the large cities, 400,000 blacks had left the South and gone north. Then during the early 1940s alone, another million responded to the wartime jobs that beckoned from Los Angeles to Boston. By 1950 approximately one-third of America's black population lived outside the South.

The small economic gains made by blacks under the New Deal had provoked black leaders to press for more. In 1941 A. Philip Randolph, the shrewd president of the Brotherhood of Sleeping Car Porters, intro-

---

*"Zoot suits" were baggy suits popular among poor and lower-middle-class youths in the 1940s.

duced a new tactic in the fight for black rights. As the economy was mobilizing for war, Randolph rallied blacks throughout the nation for a mass march on Washington that would publicize America's racial discrimination around the world and possibly disrupt the early stages of war production. Randolph's price for canceling the march was President Roosevelt's intervention in behalf of black workers. Despite his irritation at Randolph's threat, Roosevelt on June 25, 1941, issued a precedent-setting executive order that banned discriminatory hiring "because of race, creed, color, or national origin" both within the national government and throughout its expanding network of war-related contracts. The executive order also established the Fair Employment Practices Committee (FEPC) to oversee these rules.

But it was the need for labor, not the weak FEPC, that broadened economic opportunities for blacks during the war. Both in the war industries and in the armed services, Jim Crow rules weakened slightly under the pressure of an increasingly severe manpower shortage. However, racial tensions were mounting, especially over access to housing and public facilities in the swollen industrial areas of the large cities. During the summer of 1943, these emotions exploded from coast to coast in a series of violent racial encounters.

The worst of the riots occurred in Detroit, a primary center of war production, where 500,000 newcomers, including 60,000 blacks, had been squeezed in since 1940. On a hot Sunday in June 1943 a fight between teenage whites and blacks ignited two days of guerrilla warfare and widespread looting. Twenty-five blacks and nine whites were killed, hundreds wounded, and millions of dollars in property lost. By then, some Democrats were openly worrying about "the Negro vote." Yet every national election between 1936 and 1944 seemed to verify the political wisdom of Democratic policies. If blacks were really discontented, why did they vote as heavily Democratic as any other urban group? Wait until after the depression, the Roosevelt administration had told its black critics. Wait until after the war, it told them in the early 1940s.

Postwar International Planning for Peace

Even as the United States was fighting the war, President Roosevelt had been planning the peace. As in domestic affairs, the president was an inspired spokesman of hope, not only for Americans, but also for yearning peoples throughout the world. Even before Pearl Harbor, Roosevelt and Churchill had met to draw up the Atlantic Charter, which proclaimed their ideals for the postwar world. These ideals recalled the Wilsonian principles of political self-determination, free economic exchange, and international cooperation. Roosevelt's broad goal of the "Four Freedoms"—freedom from want and fear, freedom of speech and religion—became international bywords.

International Organizations. During the war the president emphasized his hope for postwar international cooperation between Britain, China, the Soviet Union, and the United States, and he envisioned all peace-loving nations joining in a new world league. To achieve these goals, the Roosevelt administration moved decisively to create new international organizations. At a conference in Bretton Woods, New Hampshire, in 1944, the United States took the initiative in developing a program for international monetary stabilization. The American dollar became the basis for most international monetary transactions. To facilitate global finance, the conference planned two new agencies—the World Bank, which would help to regularize transactions among the industrial powers, and the International Monetary Fund, which would issue loans to the poorest nations.

At the same time, the Roosevelt administration

led the movement for another attempt at worldwide collective security. Secretary of State Cordell Hull, a devoted Wilsonian, deserves the primary credit for negotiating the establishment of the United Nations (UN). Recalling Wilson's failure to win approval of the Versailles Treaty and the League of Nations, the secretary successfully wooed the Senate. He included prominent Republicans in the planning of a new league, and he persuaded isolationist senators like Arthur Vandenberg of Michigan to accept the need for participation in it. At every opportunity, Hull also pressed America's wartime allies for firm commitments to an international organization. When the secretary retired in 1944, the hardest work had been done. Despite Britain's fears for its empire and Russia's fears for its security, their representatives came to San Francisco to join delegates from forty-six other nations in founding a world organization. Overcoming final Soviet resistance, the delegates signed the charter of the United Nations in June 1945. In July the United States Senate overwhelmingly approved America's participation.

Soviet-American Relations: Alliance and Mistrust. Between the Bolshevik Revolution of 1917 and the German invasion of Russia in 1941, Soviet-American relations had been an almost unrelieved story of mutual hostility. Until 1933 the United States had not even recognized the Soviet Union. Americans had responded with disgust to the Nazi-Soviet Pact of 1939 and the Russian war against Finland that winter. Even after the United States and the Soviet Union had become wartime allies, their early exchanges were sometimes sharp, especially over delays in opening a second front in western Europe. To assure the Soviets that they had no intention of abandoning Russia part way through the war—and to prevent a possible separate Nazi-Soviet peace—FDR and Churchill in January 1943 announced their commitment to "unconditional surrender."

In November 1943, at the depths of Russia's wartime doubts, Roosevelt opened a dialogue with the Soviets when he, Stalin, and Churchill held their first joint meeting in Tehran, Iran. Their conversations ranged over the second front in Europe, Russia's entry into the Asian war, and punishment for Germany. Roosevelt responded to Stalin's proposals in encouraging tones. During a second meeting, at the Black Sea port of Yalta in February 1945, Roosevelt renewed his conciliatory efforts. At the very end of the European war, when Churchill argued for troop movements that would place the Western powers, not the Soviet Union, in Berlin and the Balkans, Roosevelt refused to play military chess with Stalin. It was not a case of a politically minded Churchill and a militarily minded

THE YALTA CONFERENCE
Flanked by Churchill on his right and Stalin on his left, an ill and weary Roosevelt prepared to negotiate the preliminaries for a postwar settlement.

Roosevelt; the president simply had different political objectives.

Roosevelt's goals were twofold. First and foremost, he wished to ensure that the United States would emerge from the war ready to shed its isolationist past. He hoped that wartime cooperation with the Allies would lead to postwar collective security arrangements that would make the Wilsonian vision of a world at peace a reality. To succeed, however, he believed that he must guarantee Soviet security through concessions to Stalin in Europe and Asia.

Yet at the same time, the president knew that he had only narrowed, not closed, the gap between the United States and the Soviet Union. Roosevelt's second postwar aim, therefore, was to maintain the modern American tradition of a tacit Anglo-American alliance. Although Roosevelt twitted Churchill about the British Empire, he used none of his wartime leverage to alter Britain's colonial policies. Churchill—but not Stalin—was informed about the atomic bomb as it was being developed. If Soviet-American relations deteriorated, American diplomats seemed to feel, the

United States could always rely on this Anglo-American basis for a broad structure of international cooperation.

Roosevelt spoke of "four policemen"—Great Britain, the Soviet Union, the United States, and China—maintaining the postwar peace. But he also expected each policeman to patrol his natural region of influence, a division that might draw the United States back to its old role as the great power of the Western Hemisphere. Even during the war, the presence of American troops abroad had seemed unnatural. Almost everyone expected the soldiers to come home and stay home after the war; Roosevelt himself voiced this assumption to Stalin at Tehran. For emotional as well as logistical reasons, therefore, Americans increasingly favored a powerful air force to provide a maximum of protection with a minimum of involvement. As the fighting came to an end, Chief of Staff General George C. Marshall was planning the nation's postwar defense in these terms. But no one had a clear picture of what the United States would be defending, or against whom.

The Truman Presidency, 1945-1949

On April 12, 1945, only a few weeks after his fourth inauguration, Franklin Roosevelt died. As millions mourned in public, they worried about the future under the new president, Harry S Truman. The new chief executive was an able Missouri judge who had entered the Senate in 1935 and built a reputation for hard work, party loyalty, and stubborn determination. During the war he had gained prominence by heading a Senate committee investigating government waste and corruption. At the 1944 convention Democratic leaders had selected the reliable, unobtrusive Truman to replace Vice-President Wallace, whose desire to expand the New Deal and usher in the "century of the common man" had alienated conservative Democrats. Yet no one—including Truman himself—had thought of the little man from Missouri as a possible president. Republican senator Robert Taft of Ohio once said, in rejecting the office, that the vice-president had nothing to do except "inquire about the president's health." Truman had not even done that. During his short time as vice-president, he had little contact with FDR, and he had gleaned no definite idea of what Roosevelt intended to do in his fourth term.

Perhaps Roosevelt himself had had no clear plan. Washington had become a bewildering place in which to try to shape any kind of policy. The last years of the New Deal and the war years had seen innumerable special interests fighting with one another in Washington for the government's favor. The stakes were high, the rules loose, and the results chaotic. By the end of the war the big economic associations of bankers, manufacturers, and farmers were shattered. Even the oligopolies were less integrated, for the latest wave of corporate consolidation was tending to produce purely financial combinations of distinct and often very different kinds of business firms.

A permanent professional bureaucracy, moreover, was taking shape in Washington to deal with each specialized subdivision of the economy. During the war the government bureaucracy had swelled to four times its 1939 size; and once created, the bureaucracy tended to perpetuate itself. A job in Washington now became what it had rarely been before—a career. Administrators grew accustomed to protecting their domains from outside intrusion and to developing intricate links with private groups and friendly congressmen. Any president who sought to regain control over the bureaucracy and to create a broad public policy faced an immense task.

The Transition to Peace. Without a blueprint of where FDR was headed, Truman had to devise his own plans for mastering the chaos in Washington and guiding the nation's transition from war to peace. Even the most experienced leader would have had difficulty guiding America's economy out of the war. Lost in a maze of complex problems, "quick and brittle" in his decisions, Truman simply foundered. Even before Japan surrendered in August 1945, he could not withstand the popular pressures for a rapid demobilization of the armed forces and a rapid dismantling of most wartime regulations. Industries now made their own decisions in their own behalf, and during the first postwar year corporate profits shot up 20 percent.

Labor discontent spread across the nation. By January 1946, 3 percent of the labor force, including auto, steel, electrical, and packinghouse workers, were simultaneously on strike. When a new round of strikes occurred that spring, a furious president went before Congress to threaten the railroad workers with an army draft even though the railroad brotherhoods had already canceled the strike. Of the wartime controls, only those governing prices remained, and a feud between the president and Congress needlessly allowed these to end all at once in June 1946, producing the highest rate of inflation in the nation's history. Farm prices rose almost 14 percent in a month and nearly 30 percent before the end of the year. As the saying went, "To err is Truman." "Had enough?" asked the Republican campaign slogan.

Apparently many Americans had, for the off-year elections of 1946 cost the Democrats eleven seats in the Senate and fifty-four in the House. When the Eightieth Congress convened in 1947, the Republicans were the majority party for the first time since Hoover's administration. With the cooperation of conservative Democrats, they could even override the president's veto. Yet the Eightieth Congress had little to offer as an alternative to Truman's erratic policies. Its primary contribution was the Taft-Hartley Act of 1947, a culmination of the congressional antagonism toward unions that had been growing for a decade. A complicated law, Taft-Hartley required financial reports from the unions, restricted their political activities, and prohibited a list of "unfair" labor practices. It also empowered the president to postpone a major strike for an eighty-day "cooling-off" period and allowed state governments to pass antiunion "right-to-work" laws. But despite these new rules and the howls they brought from the unions, labor-management relations proceeded much the same after Taft-Hartley as before.

The Beginnings of the Cold War. At the same time the Truman administration wrestled with domestic problems, it had to confront a crisis overseas. Within two years after Truman took office, the United States and the Soviet Union were engaged in a "Cold War" along a line approximating the location of their victorious armies in the summer of 1945. Although no experienced observer had expected a smooth transition from war to peace, relatively few people anticipated the bitter animosity that in fact developed. The United States and the Soviet Union both seemed to desire some accommodation, but the two nations found it impossible to compromise on a set of basic problems. The underlying causes of the rift were extremely complex, and for decades reasonable people would differ sharply over their meaning. The immediate source of conflict, however, was obvious to everyone. Now that the war had been won, what should be done about conquered Germany and Soviet-occupied eastern Europe?

At the Yalta Conference, in February 1945, Roosevelt, Churchill, and Stalin had taken a first step toward resolving this complex package of problems. Stalin stated the Soviet position in detail: for Germany, which had invaded Russia twice in thirty years, he demanded a harsh settlement. He insisted that Germany be stripped of the potential to make war and that it send massive reparations in machinery and labor to the Soviet Union. In eastern Europe, which had been Germany's avenue for invasion, Stalin wanted friendly governments from Poland in the north to the boundary of Greece in the south. Where Stalin was rigid and determined, Roosevelt, who was by then gravely ill, seemed vague and agreeable. The president apparently accepted Stalin's argument that these measures were essential to Russian security. It was Churchill, not Roosevelt, who futilely resisted $20 billion as an estimate for German reparations. Again it was Churchill, more than Roosevelt, who forced the insertion of the words "free and unfettered elections" into the Yalta agreement on the postwar Polish government. Neither Churchill nor Roosevelt challenged a general Soviet sphere of influence covering Hungary, Rumania, Bulgaria, and Yugoslavia.

All parties regarded the agreements at Yalta as no more than the outline for a later settlement. But instead of proceeding toward a full-scale peace treaty, the Soviet Union and the United States each began reshaping the Yalta decisions to suit its own ends. Stalin made it clear that his candidates would have to be elected in Poland. Truman not only attacked Russia's coercion of Poland, but also challenged the entire concept of a Soviet sphere in eastern Europe. Meanwhile, the United States reconsidered the plans for a harsh peace in Germany. As a temporary measure, Germany had been divided into American, British, French, and Russian zones of military occupation. By treating these zones as self-contained administrative units, the United States was able to shield the western industrial portions of Germany from most Soviet demands for reparations.

By summer, Soviet-American tensions were so high that any meeting between Stalin and Truman was in doubt. In July 1945, however, the two did confer at Potsdam, outside Berlin. Although they issued bland statements of unity and Stalin renewed a promise to declare war on Japan, it was an unhappy conference for both leaders. The crucial exchanges concerned Germany. Unable to find a common ground, the great powers accepted the separate ground that each one already held. The Soviet Union could set its own policy in the Eastern zone of Germany; the United States, Great Britain, and France would determine policy in their Western zones. The divisive issue of German reparations was cast vaguely into the future. After Potsdam, neither Truman nor Stalin sought another summit meeting.

The Iron Curtain Falls. There were many other sources of Soviet-American friction in 1945 and 1946. At the San Francisco conference to found the United Nations, the Russian delegates had come close to disrupting the proceedings. The Soviet Union continued to view the UN as a league of potential enemies and often obstructed its work. Moreover, to contest American and British influence in the Middle East, Russia kept its troops in Iran and withdrew them early in 1946 only after strong protests. On its part, the United States abruptly ended economic aid to the Soviet Union after Germany's defeat, despite Russia's desperate need for assistance. Bluntly, Truman made any future assistance dependent on a Soviet acceptance of American policies. In addition, the United States excluded the Soviet Union from the occupation government of Japan, as it already had from the occupation government of Italy.

Yet each of these problems by itself was either negotiable or tolerable. Only the issues of Germany and eastern Europe defied any accommodation. In what Soviet officials viewed as an assault on their vital interests, the Truman administration pursued a policy of reconciliation with Germany and demanded independent governments throughout eastern Europe. The German zones rapidly became permanent Eastern and Western spheres; the Soviet Union tightened its authority over Poland and the Balkans. "From Stettin in the Baltic to Trieste in the Adriatic," Churchill declared in a speech of March 1946 at Fulton, Missouri, "an iron curtain has descended across the Continent." More and more stories of mass killings, deportations, and labor camps filtered through that curtain. Although there were moments of hope for a year after the Potsdam Conference, the main trend in Soviet relations ran strongly toward suspicion and anger. By the end of 1946, even the occasional hopes disappeared.

American Rationale for Confronting the Soviets. What led the United States to confront the Soviet Union in Europe? The answer has four parts. The most elusive element, but perhaps the most important, was a powerful tradition of mutual distrust. There was a natural inclination in both the United States and the Soviet Union to regard the other nation as the "communist" or the "capitalist" enemy. During the war people had become accustomed to thinking of the world as composed of two diametrically opposed philosophies—fascism and democracy. Now, by substituting "communism" for "fascism," many Americans assumed a simple response to a bewildering snarl of global problems. At the founding of the UN, the influential Republican senator Arthur Vandenberg noted in his diary, "The basic trouble is that we are trying to unite two incompatible ideologies." Americans favored universalist or Wilsonian measures to inhibit postwar aggression, while the Soviets trusted only traditional power arrangements—alliances and spheres of influence. Moreover, because both Soviet and American leaders viewed their counterparts as inherently expansionist, feelings of distrust easily turned into fears of aggression. There was little distinction between Hitler and Stalin as mass murderers. But in 1945 Stalin, ruling a decimated land, showed little urge for expansion beyond eastern Europe. It was the United States that filled the great vacuums of power in the Pacific, the Middle East, and western Europe. Nevertheless, as power met power in the middle of Europe, each nation assumed the worst of the other.

The second reason why the United States confronted the Soviets concerned American expectations following a victory. The United States, never before in a position of world supremacy, assumed that it would control the terms of a postwar settlement. An "American century" was dawning, declared the prominent publisher Henry Luce. Policymakers could hardly resist acting as lords of the domain. After the war the United States made its own decisions on distributing American food abroad instead of relying on a neutral international relief agency (UNRRA), and Washington treated both the World Bank and the International Monetary Fund as instruments of American policy. Under the Baruch Plan of 1946, the United States offered to internationalize the control of atomic power only if America retained an indefinite monopoly and was assured that no other nation was developing its own atomic weapons. The Soviet Union hotly rejected the plan as no bargain at all. In this climate of national self-confidence, most Americans assumed that an able president could manage any international problem. Such a high level of popular expectations and low level of popular patience contributed to a hard line in foreign affairs in 1945 and 1946.

The third element in America's postwar policy was Truman's personal inclination toward a hard line. By temperament he was a fighter. In a characteristically Trumanesque way, the president wrote his secretary of state in January 1946, "I'm tired of babying the Soviets." Moreover, Truman took pride in his ability to reach a decision promptly, then hold to it firmly. After a meeting with J. Robert Oppenheimer over the moral implications of the atomic bomb, the president snapped: "Don't ever bring the damn fool in here again. He didn't set that bomb off. I did. This kind of snivelling makes me sick." With the unyielding, intensely suspicious Russians on one side and the pugnacious Truman on the other, the possibilities of a compromise were always slender.

Truman's advisers made the fourth contribution to America's postwar foreign policy. In his first months as president, Truman turned everywhere for advice on foreign affairs. The group of counselors whom he inherited from Roosevelt could not look at Truman without seeing the giant shadow of FDR behind him. Understandably the new president allowed them to drop away one by one. Harry Hopkins, Roosevelt's most intimate aide, and Henry Wallace, now secretary of commerce, were particularly unhappy about Truman's hard line with Stalin. By the fall of 1945, Hopkins lamented that "we are doing almost everything we can to break with Russia, which seems so unnecessary to me." After a long period of strain, Wallace finally cut ties with the Truman administration in a major speech of September 1946: "'Getting tough' never brought anything real and lasting—whether for schoolyard bullies or businessmen or world powers. The tougher we get, the tougher the Russians will get."

Truman found more support among his former political associates from Congress. One of these, James F. Byrnes, became secretary of state in July 1945. Following an impressive career in Congress, the Supreme Court, and as "assistant president" in charge of America's wartime mobilization, Byrnes took his new office with the attitude that he himself, not Truman, really should have been Roosevelt's successor. Although Byrnes was a firm anticommunist, he was also a bargainer, and he kept an element of flexibility in America's relations with the Soviet Union.

The State Department in the Cold War. Discreetly at hand stood a third group of advisers, whose base of operations was the State Department. As America's world affairs increasingly demanded a wider range of diplomatic services, the State Department emerged as a significant center of government power, with extensive connections in those business, military, and publishing circles that affected its work. The expanding department attracted an able and strong-minded set of leaders, including W. Averell Harriman, the son of a railroad magnate and ambassador to the Soviet Union; George F. Kennan, a career diplomat with special talents as a writer and planner; and Dean Acheson, a wellborn lawyer who had found his true calling in the State Department. Through such men as Harriman, Kennan, and Acheson, the department offered Truman something that his other advisers failed to provide: the outlines for a systematic world policy.

As the leaders in the State Department interpreted Soviet behavior, the Russians were following a long-term plan to destroy all capitalist societies. Communist ideology made them fanatics. Despite the needs of their war-ravaged nation, Soviet officials kept a large army mobilized after Germany's surrender. State Department leaders thought that if weakness in a neighboring country gave the Russians the opportunity, they would seize it. The Soviet army had already attempted such a probe in Iran. From its base in central Europe, the Soviet Union could strike the devastated, chaotic nations of western Europe at any time. To counter this broad threat, the United States, too, needed a long-term plan. American power had to meet Soviet power on a global scale. Otherwise, as Harriman warned, the Russians would pursue their goal of world domination by continuing to build "tiers [of satellites], layer on layer," until they crushed the forces of freedom. Only firmness, or a policy of "containment," as Kennan called it in 1947, could stop them. As the history of fascism proved, appeasement merely whetted a dictator's appetite.

To meet the Soviet challenge, government officials saw the need for both a unified defense establishment to coordinate the armed services and an intelligence organization to deal with worldwide Soviet subversion. Consequently, in 1947 Congress passed the National Security Act creating the Department of Defense, headed by a secretary and subordinate secretaries of the army, navy, and air force. It also set up the National Security Council (NSC) to advise the president on national security matters, and the Central Intelligence Agency (CIA), a successor to the wartime Office of Strategic Services (OSS), responsible for all spy activities.

The Truman Doctrine and the Marshall Plan.

With the United States hesitating at an important crossroads in its foreign policy, Truman was ready to follow the State Department's guidance. In January 1947 Byrnes was replaced as secretary of state by General George Marshall, a man of flawless integrity but limited imagination who, like Truman, relied heavily on the judgment of Assistant Secretary Dean Acheson. In February, one of Roosevelt's four policemen, Great

Britain, greatly weakened by its war effort, informed Washington that it was retiring from the force. American, not British, aid would have to save the conservative government in Greece, which was racked with civil war between communists and anticommunists. President Truman, addressing Congress in March on aid to both Greece and Turkey, dramatically announced the new "Truman Doctrine." "At the present moment in world history nearly every nation must choose between alternative ways of life," Truman declared. One way of life was freedom and democracy. Communism, Truman warned, was the alternative:

The second way of life is based upon the will of a minority forcibly imposed upon the majority. It relies upon terror and oppression, a controlled press and radio, fixed elections, and the suppression of personal freedoms. I believe that it must be the policy of the United States to support free people who are resisting attempted subjugation by armed minorities or by outside pressure.

Meanwhile, the State Department was preparing strategy for a general European defense "against totalitarian pressures." Through the Marshall Plan, which took shape in the summer of 1947, America eventually sent more than $12 billion in American aid to its European allies and enabled their shattered economies to achieve a minor miracle of recovery. The Marshall Plan brought the United States an extraordinary amount of goodwill in western Europe. Moreover, in July 1947 Washington made a formal commitment to rehabilitate West Germany as part of a "free Europe." Although the communist nations of Europe were officially invited to participate in the Marshall Plan, participation would require Russia to break its security system for eastern Europe. As American leaders expected, the Russians refused and demanded that their European allies refuse as well. Hungary in May, and then Rumania in December, fell totally under Soviet control. American trade with the Soviet Union, which had flourished in 1946, dwindled to a trickle.

Czechoslovakia Falls; Berlin Stands.

In Czechoslovakia—the very symbol of a liberated Europe—political turmoil precipitated by the Communist party in February 1948 allowed it to take power. Communications across the Iron Curtain virtually ceased. That spring, rumors raced through Washington that a real war was imminent. Instead, between April and June 1948, the Soviet Union cut the transportation lines to Berlin, which lay deep within the Russian sector of Germany. Berlin, like Germany as a whole, was administered through zones. Now the American, British, and French zones within Berlin were under siege. The United States re-

TRUMAN ON THE NATIONAL LTD.
Truman's 1948 whistlestop campaign, in which supporters
urged him to "give 'em hell," led to his startling upset of
Thomas Dewey.

Division of Political History, Smithsonian Institution

sive party, like earlier American parties of the same
name, depended on the reputation of one man, Henry
Wallace, who symbolized the New Deal liberalism at
home and accommodation with the Soviet Union
abroad. In Birmingham, Alabama, a new states' rights
Democratic party—the Dixiecrats—attracted southern leaders who feared an assault on southern race
relations. The Dixiecrats nominated Governor J.
Strom Thurmond of South Carolina and dreamed of
carrying the entire South. The Roosevelt coalition, it
seemed, was crumbling. Above all, Truman faced a
formidable Republican opponent in Governor Dewey
of New York, who had done better against the indomitable Roosevelt in 1944 than any of the three
Republican candidates who had preceded him. The
only argument among the experts was the margin of
Dewey's victory.

Truman made fools of the experts in 1948 because
he responded so shrewdly to the prevailing disorganization in political and economic affairs. In a nation of innumerable scattered interest groups, no one
knew how to provide effective leadership. Using a
carefully devised strategy, the president shifted the
blame for weak leadership to the Republican majority
in the Eightieth Congress, which he scorned as the
"Do-Nothing Congress." After the nominating conventions, he called Congress into special session and
challenged the Republicans to enact their program. Of
course little happened. The paralysis in public policy
appeared to be specifically a Republican malady.

To attract voters, Truman compiled a long list of
favors and promises. He reminded the unions that he
had vetoed the Taft-Hartley Act of 1947 and that Republican votes had overridden him. He reminded
business groups of tax benefits and government contracts. He promised subsidies for everything a farmer
could produce. He recommended enlarging the TVA,
increasing public housing, and broadening Social Security. He favored government aid to education. At the
national convention in 1948, with Mayor Hubert H.
Humphrey of Minneapolis leading the drive, the Democrats committed themselves to federal laws against
job discrimination, lynching, and poll taxes. Truman
not only endorsed this platform, but took the cause to
Harlem, where no presidential candidate had ever
campaigned. Even more striking, the president embarked in 1948 on the long, difficult course of desegregating the armed forces.

Dewey took the high road, blandly promising a
sound, sane administration. Voters judged him dull
and pompous; they thought he looked like "the little
man on the wedding cake" and agreed with the observation that he could "strut sitting down." Truman, the
bantam rooster from Missouri, fought an arduous
cross-country campaign, running for president like a

sponded with an impressively organized airlift that
brought essential supplies to the citizens in these isolated zones. In May 1949 the Russians finally abandoned the blockade. More than any other event, the
Berlin blockade seemed to verify the Truman administration's warnings about Soviet aggression. Although
some commentators saw Soviet actions in Czechoslovakia and Berlin as defensive reactions to the resurgence of German power, a substantial majority believed them to be a test of Western resolve to resist
Soviet expansion. Consequently, American opposition
to the Cold War collapsed, and anti-Soviet sentiments
spread in western Europe, where communists were
ejected from the governments of France and Italy.

The Election of 1948. Troubles at home and abroad made
Truman a poor bet for election in 1948, and most Democratic leaders prayed that he would not run for president. With little choice, less enthusiasm, and no hope,
the national convention dutifully nominated him. Immediately after, two additional parties formed to attract the votes of dissident Democrats. The Progres-

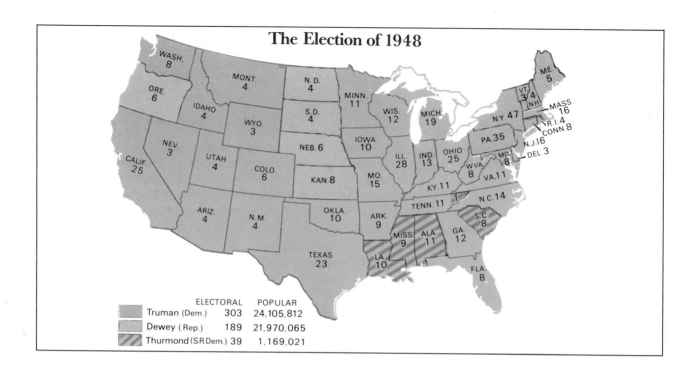

The Election of 1948

	ELECTORAL	POPULAR
Truman (Dem.)	303	24,105,812
Dewey (Rep.)	189	21,970,065
Thurmond (S.R.Dem.)	39	1,169,021

country politician. His remark to one audience summarized his message: "Vote your own interests." In 1948 Truman's provincial style was highly effective. Meanwhile the deepening Cold War with the Soviet Union eroded the Progressives' appeal and made Wallace appear to be the candidate of the Communist party. On election day, only a stubborn handful voted the Progressive ticket. Thurmond kept only the four southern states that he had controlled in July. Truman, with 303 electoral votes to Dewey's 189, scored the most stunning upset in modern politics and instantly joined America's folk heroes in the grand old tradition of the underdog triumphant.

Truman's Second Term, 1949–1953

Memories of FDR cast less of a shadow over Truman after he had been elected in his own right in 1948. The hallmarks of his second administration, he decided, would be the Fair Deal—as he called his program—at home and the containment of communism abroad. Although Congress passed some of his domestic programs, the president fell well short of achieving the reforms he proposed. One reason for his relative lack of success was the turmoil that erupted over exaggerated fears of a domestic communist threat; another reason was the limited war in Korea that frustrated Americans and undermined Truman's popularity. Although Truman has subsequently been seen as a near-great president, he was vilified in his own day. He left

office as one of the least popular chief executives in American history.

The Fair Deal. In 1946, amid the confusion of wartime demobilization and the jostling of interest groups, Truman had demanded that Congress make the maintenance of "full employment" a matter of urgent national priority. Public opinion had strongly backed the president, and thus Congress had responded with the Full Employment Act. But Congress had carefully avoided specifying *how* full employment was to be maintained. Nor had it undertaken any social reforms. The sprawling, government-oriented economy had been changing too rapidly, and neither the Democrats nor the Republicans had found a satisfactory technique for managing it.

Now, having been elected president in his own right, Truman announced a comprehensive domestic reform policy. It offered, he said, a "fair deal" for "every segment of our population and every individual." And Congress responded by passing the most progressive group of bills since 1938. It extended such New Deal measures as Social Security and the minimum wage, and it remedied substandard housing with the Housing Act of 1949.

But Congress also rejected much of Truman's program, turning aside all reform proposals that broke new ground. Federal aid to education, national health insurance, a Fair Employment Practices Commission (FEPC), a new system of crop subsidies, and the cre-

In modern America the meaning of art expanded and blurred. A profusion of photographs, illustrations, movies, buildings, landscapes, fashions, and handicrafts hopelessly muddied the traditional questions about the appropriate subjects of art, the necessary training for artists, and the proper cultivation of the viewers. Could advertising qualify as art? Were the creators of comic strips artists? Did mass production destroy artistic taste or generate new forms of democratic art? Yet the endless quarreling over these unanswerable questions could not hide the timeless qualities of the debate. Now as before, each aspiring artist tried to determine *what* people saw and *how* they saw it. Each of these many images promised its viewers a special insight into what was real rather than merely superficial or transient. And these competing visions of reality, in turn, reflected the main lines of tension in modern American culture.

Varieties of Reality

Reprinted from The Saturday Evening Post
© 1929 The Curtis Publishing Company

For Americans without personal knowledge of small-town life, Norman Rockwell's famous drawings defined it as simple, friendly, and unaffected. In this fashion, Rockwell's imaginary town became part of modern America's reality. In contrast to Rockwell's cozy, vibrant town, the untouched wilderness had no place for people. Beneath this beautiful vision ran an undercurrent of hopelessness about modern American society.

Images, like other modern goods, were mass distributed, and, however unwittingly, Americans consumed them along with the myriad products of their society. As Americans took sides in a cultural conflict, therefore, they received images that helped them to understand their choices. During the 1920s and 1930s, for example, an aversion to city life was visualized in small groups of country people: a warm family gathering, an easy intimacy among friends, a mutual support between generations. The images of urban-industrial progress, on the other hand, were oriented toward things rather than people. A long, dramatic view of a fac-

tory, skyscraper, or the center of a city communicated the expansive grandeur of American technology. Americans came to know these images so well that in the 1960s environmentalists needed only a slight shift in focus to make ironic statements about modern progress. A tip of the camera accentuated the smoke belching from the factory. A longer view of the city juxtaposed its skyline with urban blight. By the sixties, the country town was slipping from memory, and the visual alternative to the city leaped past civilization to the wilderness. The image of pure nature, however, was a study in contemporary American frus-

Erich Hartmann/Magnum Photos, Inc.

"Gotham News" by Willem de Kooning.

tration, for it also offered no human comfort. As soon as people entered the virgin wilderness, they defiled it.

Another group of artists sought reality in a complex relation between the emotions of the viewers and the essential components of what they saw. They probed the same subjects of nature and urban-industrial society, but they rephrased these issues in abstract images. The flowering of American abstraction came in the years after the Second World War when Willem de Kooning was expressing the dynamism of modern life in rugged blocks and explosive colors, and the controversial Jackson Pollock was extending visual horizons with his flowing lines and subtle uses of depth. Then in the 1960s, as many Americans rebelled against the clutter and complexity around them,

painters of the minimalist and op art schools responded to these new yearnings with simple geometric abstractions.

Abstract artists, like other modern experts, developed techniques of expression that required special training simply to understand, let alone to use. Among their strongest defenders were professional and business people whose own success depended on expertise. Every subdivision of knowledge, they assumed, had special rules for understanding. But modern abstractionists, unlike the pioneers of the Armory Show in 1913, reached a nationwide audience. For millions of skeptical Americans abstract art was an incomprehensible jumble of shapes and colors. In art as in other areas of knowledge, they demanded a commonsense reality that anyone could grasp.

"Number 3," 1950, by Jackson Pollock.
Private Collection

Willem de Kooning, a major contributor to America's renaissance in painting after the Second World War, gave new vitality to the European cubist tradition. More innovative than de Kooning, Jackson Pollock was particularly ingenious in adapting modern technology to his art, as the aluminum paint on the above canvas demonstrates. In the 1960s the trends moved away from Pollock's complexity toward a simple, almost photographic reality. The reputation of Edward Hopper, whose best paintings had been completed three decades earlier, rose impressively. Almost no signs of life intruded on Hopper's brilliant, haunting scenes, and the loneliness of his stark art touched widespread anxieties about the individual's survival during the sixties.

Collection, The Museum of Modern Art, New York. Given Anonymously

"House by the Railroad" by Edward Hopper.

Photo by Milton H. Greene

Sex and violence—sometimes singly, sometimes in combination—dominated the popular arts after the Second World War. Mass-marketed stereotypes of sex and beauty reached their peak with the era of Marilyn Monroe, who exercised an extraordinary influence over American dreams and behavior. The vision of history's most horrible weapon as an awesome fantasy of color and clouds greatly strengthened the modern connection between violence and beauty.

The popular arts satisfied these demands. Through constant repetition the popular arts drilled a few simple images of truth and beauty into the American consciousness. The most familiar of all was the smooth, sexy, welcoming woman. From the Hollywood vamp of the twenties to the Petty girl of the forties to the *Playboy* centerfold of the sixties, a composite mo[del of fe]male beauty shaped men's assumptio[ns about] women and women's assumptions abo[ut them]selves. The popular arts also celebrated th[e dignity] of certain occupations. Under the auspic[es of the] New Deal, for example, public murals [and bas-] relief sculptures glorified manual labor wi[th]

U.S. Department of Energy

of proud, muscular men and women in the fields and factories. During the Second World War these handsome titans became soldiers and sailors. In fact, the Second World War introduced an elaborate aesthetic of violence that made instruments of destruction into objects of beauty: first the gleaming fleets of battleships and bombers, then the eerie majesty of the atomic bomb's mushroom cloud. The beauty of violence remained after the war as an important theme of the popular arts. A particularly striking example appeared in the climactic scene of the movie *Bonnie and Clyde*, which transformed the mutilation of the heroine's body into an arresting, slow-motion dance of death.

Subway Graffiti. Was it art or vandalism? The answer lay in the cultural standards of the beholder.

In reaction against these mass-produced images, some Americans swung to the other extreme and praised the beauty of almost anything unique. The market for handicrafts and homemade art objects thrived during the 1960s and 1970s. What popular primitivism lacked in refinement it contributed in personal expression, and its proponents contrasted the reality of a rough-hewn people's art with the artificiality of a slick commercial art. The urge for self-expression also spread into "street art," a new public outlet for the emotions of assertive, often angry city dwellers. None of the older art forms had to give way for the newcomers. A contemporary people's art simply added to the artistic variety of modern America.

ation of TVA-style controls in the Columbia and Missouri river valleys—all went down to defeat. Not until the 1960s would other Democratic administrations finally see many of these measures enacted.

Despite this resistance to expanding the federal government's role in managing domestic affairs, nothing could relieve the government of the responsibility it had assumed under FDR for general economic maintenance. No one could fail to recognize the intimate connection between government policy and the nation's phenomenal economic growth during the war. The gross national product (GNP) had risen a breathtaking 67 percent. Government expenditures accounted for an equally astonishing 40 percent of the GNP. The term *the government* became an everyday expression to designate this huge center of money and power. Although national expenditures dropped with the end of the war, they still remained six or seven times greater than in the 1930s, and double the percentage of the GNP under the New Deal. The tax laws now bound almost all Americans into the government's financial network. By 1946 the national debt had also risen sevenfold above the level of 1939, and funding this giant debt automatically made the government a dominant force in the nation's credit system. Moreover, the Federal Reserve's board of governors in Washington exercised an important general control over the nation's monetary affairs.

The most promising means for managing the economy seemed to be through fiscal policy—the control of tax and interest rates. If the economy faltered, the government could ease credit, lower taxes, and increase its deficit. If an economic boom threatened inflation, the government could tighten credit, raise taxes, and shrink the deficit. Fiscal policy at least minimized government interference with private groups or individuals, distributing its hardships and benefits impartially.

Truman, however, was not qualified to shape the government's fiscal powers into an acceptable public policy. Like Roosevelt, he disliked budget deficits and periodically led stern attacks on government spending. His secretary of the treasury regarded the national debt as simply an unfortunate government expense. Fiscal policy would not be used effectively until the 1960s.

Black rights was another issue on which the federal government could not avoid acting. Although Truman did not lead a general campaign for black rights during his second term, he did end segregation in the armed forces and appoint the first black to the federal bench. More important, the NAACP, which in the 1940s had increased its membership from 50,000 to 450,000, joined with northern whites in an increasingly vigorous fight for equal rights. This alliance produced a string of FEPC laws in New York, New Jersey, Massachusetts, Connecticut, and other states, and an attack on racism through the courts. In *Smith* v. *Allwright* (1944), the Supreme Court had outlawed all-white primary elections in the South. Then in *Sweatt* v. *Painter* (1950), it broadened an earlier ruling against segregated professional schools. The NAACP, behind its chief counsel, Thurgood Marshall, quietly prepared a legal assault on all segregated facilities.

Anticommunism. The issue that most strained the American social fabric at midcentury was not black rights, but anticommunism. A new wave of antiradicalism began to build after 1935, when enemies of the New Deal accused New Dealers of adopting communist ideas, and patriotic groups attacked the public schools for teaching radical doctrines. The House Committee on Un-American Activities (HUAC), established in 1938, gave lurid publicity to the charge that communists dominated the new industrial unions. Congress captured the spirit of this vague antiradicalism in the Smith Act of 1940, which set criminal penalties for teaching or advocating violent revolution, or for belonging to an organization that did either. Despite America's wartime alliance with the Soviet Union, anticommunist rhetoric remained fairly common during the early 1940s, and immediately after the war HUAC and numerous state antisubversive committees moved into action against an ever-widening range of expected dangers. For the next decade, clouds of uncertainty enveloped thousands of Americans who had once advocated a reform and left a record, or who had made an enemy. As one historian noted, "A perverse kind of democracy was practiced: all accusations, no matter from whom, were taken equally seriously." Reputations, friendships, and careers popped like bubbles at the prick of the charge, "Communist!"

In 1947 the Truman administration declared international communism the enemy of the United States. Prominent Americans of both parties echoed the alarm. Throughout the nation—in government, in the labor unions, in the communications industries, in public and private education—a variety of oaths and reviews screened those who were suspected of communist sympathies. Using both the Smith Act and a new Internal Security Act of 1950, the Justice Department prosecuted some members of the Communist party and forced the rest to disband. After a dramatic series of public hearings, Alger Hiss, once a respected official in the State Department, was convicted of perjury in January 1950 for denying that he had passed government information to a Soviet agent. In June came the shock of the Korean War, followed by arrests that eventually led to the execution of Julius and Ethel

SENATOR JOSEPH McCARTHY UNDER A HALO OF LIGHTS AND HIS AIDE ROY COHN AT THE ARMY-McCARTHY HEARINGS IN 1954
To millions of Americans in the early fifties, these were fearless patriots who defended the nation against an insidious network of communists.

Wide World Photos, Inc.

Rosenberg as Soviet spies. America seemed to be a bulwark of anticommunism.

But within this apparent consensus lay two profoundly different kinds of anticommunism. One, which appeared in strength around 1947, sought to defend the United States against an international challenge: the Soviet Union, the league of communist countries it headed, and the espionage system it directed. Abroad, this anticommunism tried to contain the power of the Soviet Union. At home, it concentrated above all on communists in government, because the enemy's agent at a crucial spot in the government could seriously damage the nation's defense. Hence, the revelations about Alger Hiss greatly aggravated these worries.

The other anticommunism expressed the fears and frustrations of average Americans. To them, communism was a pervasive web of dangers that might appear in the guise of atheism, sexual freedoms, strange accents, civil rights, or whatever most threatened a particular group's sense of security. Although this anticommunism was also concerned with national defense and international conflict, it equated these issues with threats to traditional institutions and moral standards. The actual sources of danger might well be some of the leaders in national politics. Splintered, diffuse, and eruptive, this was the truly popular anticommunism.

These two anticommunisms, one emphasizing power and the other emphasizing sin, were distinctly different. From a national vantage point, the many state and local committees that in the name of anticommunism attacked textbooks and library catalogues and civil libertarians were part of an aimless witch hunt. What possible relevance could these matters have to an international contest with Soviet communism? As one lawyer summarized the work of the Broyles Commission in Illinois, it "almost completely skirted . . . the operations of the Communist party in Illinois," and it failed totally "to cover evidence of actual subversion within the state." But such committees in Illinois, California, New York, Maryland, and elsewhere were not looking for that kind of communism. As the Broyles Commission stated, "Liberalism" was its enemy, and the educational system, the commission's primary target, was an excellent place to begin the battle. Sophisticated "Eastern internationalists" in the State Department were an equally logical target.

McCarthyism. In February 1950, a month after the conviction of Alger Hiss, an undistinguished first-term Republican senator from Wisconsin, Joseph McCarthy, elbowed forward to make anticommunism his personal crusade. For more than four years, this canny politician frightened government officials with charges of communist infiltration in their departments, staged melodramatic investigations of suspected enemy agents, exercised a powerful influence over government appointments, and won a nationwide following. McCarthy was the first politician to make effective use of national television, both in interviews and in broadcasts of his investigations. According to a poll early in 1954, three out of five Americans with an opinion about McCarthy favored his activities.

McCarthy opened his campaign by claiming that he had a list of authentic communists who were still employed by the State Department. Some thought he said 205. The senator later settled on 57. During Truman's administration McCarthy continued a scattergun attack on the State Department and helped to make "communism" a noisy issue in the elections of 1952. After Eisenhower's inauguration, McCarthy broadened his anticommunist fire until finally he hit the army itself early in 1954. Few politicians cared to risk an encounter with the Wisconsin slugger, because McCarthy quickly acquired a reputation for defeating his political enemies at the polls. Eisenhower also refused to engage him, saying privately, "I will not get into the gutter with that guy."

The key to McCarthy's success was his ability to raise fears over communists in government and domestic subversion. McCarthy repeatedly claimed that the sole purpose of his investigations was the exposure of communist agents in high places, and after the Hiss conviction no one in Washington could lightly dismiss that possibility. As cool a head as Senator Taft endorsed McCarthy's freewheeling search for spies. When McCarthy failed to find any Soviet agents, however, he shifted his attack to the books that his suspects had written, the reforms that they had supported, and the people who had associated with them. McCarthy invariably identified communism as "godless" and usually discovered its American disciples among the well born, well educated, and well placed. Despite the special attention that McCarthy attracted, others used even more extreme language. In 1952 Senator William Jenner of Indiana declared, "I charge that this country today is in the hands of a secret inner coterie which is directed by agents of the Soviet Union." Democrats, including Truman, contributed to the harsh anticommunist climate—in part to head off charges by such rabid extremists as Jenner and McCarthy that they themselves were part of the "communist conspiracy."

Still, McCarthy was the central figure in this unreasoning anticommunist outburst. Violating the customary procedures of the Senate, McCarthy called into question the personal integrity of his critics and branded them "gutless." The State Department, instead of selecting officials for their knowledge and skills, had to listen when it was told to "get rid of the alien-minded radicals and moral perverts." Years of such confusion in the standards of government eventually became intolerable. When McCarthy attacked the upper echelons of the army in 1954, his growing opposition in Washington began to organize. The senator and his aides did not fare well in a televised series of "Army-McCarthy" hearings. In August 1954 the Senate created a select committee to review charges of senatorial misconduct against McCarthy, and that December, by a vote of 67 to 22, his colleagues condemned him for his abuse of the Senate's rules. Without authority in the Senate, McCarthy faded into obscurity and died a few years later of chronic alcoholism.

Containment. As much as anything, McCarthy had used the continuing struggle with international communism in the years 1949–52 to exert his influence. The contest with Soviet power had grown even more intense in this period. To meet the threat, the Truman administration had completed negotiations for the North Atlantic Treaty, a pact for mutual assistance among twelve nations that was signed in April 1949.* Although the wording of the treaty was general, almost everyone interpreted it as the guarantee of American military support in case of a Soviet attack in Europe. In January 1949 Dean Acheson, the primary architect of Truman's European program, became secretary of state and received proper credit for this sweeping commitment of American power. Meanwhile, the Federal Republic of Germany evolved from the Western zones of occupation and was set on its way to independence. To each of these steps, the Soviet Union responded with a countermeasure: the German Democratic Republic in the east, then the Warsaw Pact, which formed a league of Russia's European satellites.

With breathtaking speed, the United States had fundamentally changed its role as a peacetime world power. During the rise of fascism in the 1930s, the United States had withdrawn more and more tightly into the Western Hemisphere. Now through the Truman Doctrine, the United States made an open-ended offer of assistance to nations everywhere in the world. Instead of demanding payment of its war debts, as the United States had done after the First World War, the government devised the Marshall Plan to underwrite the economies of western Europe. In 1940 even the fall of continental Europe had not brought the United States into the Second World War; in 1948 danger to the single city of Berlin threatened to trigger a third world war. In 1927 Americans had shied away from a simple bilateral treaty with France renouncing war; in 1949 the North Atlantic Treaty placed eleven other nations under the shelter of American power. As the

*The eleven other nations were Belgium, Canada, Denmark, France, Great Britain, Iceland, Italy, Luxembourg, the Netherlands, Norway, and Portugal. Soon Greece, Turkey, and West Germany joined.

United States' first military alliance since the treaty of friendship with France in 1778, the agreement represented a decisive break with America's isolationist past.

Despite these profound changes, however, the United States still did not have a clear and detailed foreign policy. What areas of the world did the Truman Doctrine cover? Under Acheson's guidance, the Truman administration concentrated on Europe and left the rest of the world in limbo. How did the United States plan to defend the nations that fell under its protection? No one expected American troops to be stationed throughout the world. Some people, including the influential columnist Walter Lippmann, hoped that American economic aid would enable groups of nations to organize their own regional leagues of defense. In his inaugural address of 1949, President Truman encouraged this kind of vision. "Point Four" of that address raised the possibility of exporting more technological skills and fewer weapons to the world's needy nations.

Communist Gains.
Two critical events of 1949 underlined the importance of these unresolved problems. One occurred in Asia; the other, in the Soviet Union.

In Asia, Mao Tse-tung's communists swept through China, driving Chiang Kai-shek's tattered remnants to the island of Formosa (Taiwan). That civil war had been brewing during the years of the Chinese resistance to Japan. At times Chiang, America's East Asian ally in the Pacific war, seemed more concerned about his domestic enemy than his foreign foe. Even before the end of the Second World War, American officials had begun their futile attempts to mediate between Chiang's nationalists and Mao's communists. Special American missions, including a highly publicized one in 1945–46 under General Marshall, had warned Chiang about the corruption in his government, dangled the prospect of economic assistance before the two camps, and struggled to arrange a truce between their armies. Unwilling to force concessions from Chiang, yet unable to intervene effectively in his behalf, the United States had invested some military aid and much larger amounts of hope in his cause. By 1949 the Truman administration could take comfort only in the fact that nobody had guessed right on the matter of China. Stalin, like Truman, had bet that Chiang would win, and had provided Mao's forces with only limited aid. Publicly the Soviets hailed the communist victory in China, but behind the scenes relations between the two Marxist regimes were tense from the start.

As the world's preeminent power, many argued, America could have saved China from communism—and according to the Truman Doctrine, they said, we

should have. But we did not. With no basis in fact, these critics irrationally attributed the communization of China to American irresolution, possibly even to betrayal in high places. The air was filled with bitter complaints about a vast territory and a huge population "lost" to the enemy. Adding China to the Soviet sphere in Eastern Europe indeed produced an appalling total effect. Simple maps traced the recent losses, and simple arithmetic summarized the human costs. In 1949, when Congressman Richard Nixon of California totaled the peoples inside and outside the communist domain, he concluded that "in 1944 . . . the odds were 9 to 1 in our favor. Today . . . the odds are 5 to 3 against us."

Before the communist victory in China, Americans had been comforted by the belief that people elsewhere, whenever free to choose, would select a political system similar to American democracy. The struggle against communism had continued, but many Americans had taken consolation in reassurances such as that by the sturdy liberal senator Robert Wagner of New York, who had observed, "History is on our side." In the administration's most cogent justification for the Truman Doctrine, George Kennan of the State Department had outlined what would happen if the United States were to apply steady, patient pressure along the perimeter of the communist sphere: in time, the communist domain would erode from its own weakness, and gradually more and more people would select freedom. But the communist revolution in China struck at the heart of this faith. For another quarter-century, the United States refused to recognize the communist government of China and many Americans clung to the belief that the Chinese, given a choice, would still follow the old warlord Chiang.

The second critical event of 1949 was the detonation of an atomic bomb by the Soviet Union. Since 1945, the American monopoly of atomic weapons had enabled the United States to expand its international commitments without spreading its military forces abroad. The Truman Doctrine seemed to say that American aid alone would protect its allies: American possession of the bomb would deter a large-scale Soviet intervention. A few months before the Soviets' atomic test, Secretary Acheson told the Senate Foreign Relations Committee that the North Atlantic Treaty Organization (NATO) would require no more than token American soldiers in Europe. Truman gave this claim the ring of truth in 1949 by insisting on a reduced military budget. No American leader seriously contemplated using the bomb; just having the bomb was enough.

How thoroughly the United States had relied on its monopoly of atomic weapons became clear after

The Shifting Front in Korea

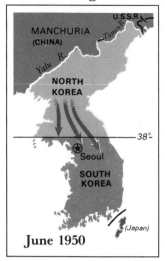

June 1950

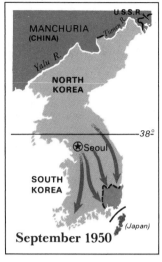

September 1950

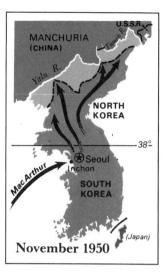

November 1950

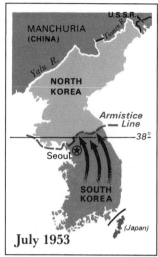

July 1953

that monopoly was broken. Suddenly the United States seemed terribly vulnerable. America's new security program for Europe no longer had teeth. In the scramble for alternatives, some government officials actually did suggest a preemptive atomic strike at the Soviet Union. Moreover, if Soviet society was inherently inferior, as Americans had been repeatedly told, how had it manufactured its own bomb so soon? Spies must have stolen American secrets. The Federal Bureau of Investigation proceeded to uncover the communists Julius and Ethel Rosenberg, who were charged with passing information about the bomb to the Soviet Union. They were found guilty and were executed. Judge Irving Kaufman, who sentenced the Rosenbergs to death in 1951, expressed the anger of a nation that had been stripped of its primary protection:

Your conduct in putting into the hands of the Russians the A-bomb . . . has already caused, in my opinion, the Communist aggression in Korea, with the resultant [American] casualties exceeding fifty thousand and who knows but that millions more of innocent people may pay the price of your treason. Indeed, by your betrayal you undoubtedly have altered the course of history.

The Korean War.

The Korean War, which began in June 1950, completed America's global policy of "containment" and marked a revolution in American–East Asian relations. Before 1945 the United States was friendly toward China, at war with Japan, and uninterested in Korea. By 1950 China was seen as an enemy, Japan as an ally, and Korea as a testing ground for the survival of freedom from communist aggression.

In 1945, during the Soviet Union's brief war against Japan, Russian troops had moved across Manchuria into the Korean peninsula before American troops could land from the sea. The two armies had hastily agreed to occupy northern and southern halves of the peninsula, divided at the thirty-eighth parallel, until their governments could settle the fate of this Japanese territory. As in many other cases after the war, delays, Soviet-American tensions, and then the Cold War had transformed a momentary convenience into a permanent solution. Under the auspices of the UN, which had assumed responsibility for a Korean settlement, the United States had backed one government in South Korea. The Soviet Union had sponsored a rival government in North Korea. Each Korean government had claimed the whole of the peninsula, and each was itching to fight for it. Because Korea had little significance in the complex contest between the Soviet Union and the United States, neither power had closely supervised its dependent government before 1950.

After the United States made clear that South Korea did not hold a significant priority in its defense plans for Asia, superior North Korean forces invaded South Korea. Although the Truman administration had not prepared for a crisis in Korea, it fought back, asserting that failure to meet aggression in Korea might lead to World War III. After sending the South Koreans light reinforcements from Japan, the United States took advantage of Russia's absence from the Security Council of the United Nations to place America's cause under the authority of the UN. On

U.S. ARMY ARTILLERYMEN IN KOREA, 1951
The Korean War, which settled into a stalemate in 1951, aroused widespread frustrations in the United States and undermined Truman's popularity.

June 27, the Security Council endorsed UN intervention. Officially, therefore, the United States did not fight a war in Korea; it cooperated in a UN police action.

By November American military power under General Douglas MacArthur had reversed the battle and driven the North Korean army past the thirty-eighth parallel back through its own territory to the Chinese border. The original purpose of the war had been protection of South Korea's territory. Now the goal seemed to be unification of the entire Korean peninsula. In response, large Chinese reinforcements surprised the American forces and pushed them once again below the thirty-eighth parallel. By early 1951 the war settled into a grudging, bloody struggle along the original boundary. Shortly after the inauguration of President Dwight Eisenhower in 1953, an armistice between the opposing armies more or less reestablished the division at the thirty-eighth parallel. A formal peace never came. Over a million Koreans and Chinese and about 23,000 Americans had died in the conflict.

Although this limited war aroused widespread resentment in the United States, the range of opposition was quite narrow. Critics filled the air with might-have-beens and should-have-beens that censured Truman and Acheson as shortsighted, fumbling leaders, but they almost never questioned the appropriateness of American military intervention. Nor did the administration's critics rally much support for a big war against either China or Russia. The center of such ambitions was the imperious General MacArthur, whose belligerent and insubordinate behavior after China's entry into the war forced Truman to recall him from Korea in April 1951 and relieve him of his command. As the hero of two wars and the successful director of America's occupation government in postwar Japan, MacArthur received an adoring welcome home after his recall. As the advocate of Asian conquest, however, MacArthur won no important endorsements. The Korean War was thoroughly unpopular, but the majority of Americans ratified the president's policy in fighting it.

The Election of 1952. Truman's second term had run into a buzzsaw of difficulties. Unable to master a Congress that was dominated by rural conservatives who held strategic committee chairmanships, the president had to be content with limited legislative gains. Second,

DWIGHT D. EISENHOWER
In Ike the Republicans finally found a winner. A war hero with such a smile was unbeatable in the fifties.

pressive talent for diplomacy as well as command. These qualities mattered very much at a tense, critical time in world affairs, and they contrasted with Taft's tendency to favor blunt, unilateral actions abroad. In a bitter contest, Eisenhower defeated Taft for the Republican nomination. Despite Taft's impressive strength among party regulars, the Republicans could not resist an immensely popular war hero.

The Democrats had more difficulty finding a candidate. A folksy campaign by the liberal Tennessee senator Estes Kefauver, replete with handshakes, barbecues, and coonskin caps, gave him an early lead in a crowded field, but Truman withheld his blessing. Instead, the Democrats finally drafted the witty but prudent governor of Illinois, Adlai E. Stevenson.

That fall, Eisenhower overwhelmed Stevenson, whom many ordinary voters rejected as an "egghead" intellectual. Emphasizing the administration's failings abroad in Korea, to which he promised personally to go to end the fighting, and at home, where corruption and communist subversion struck responsive chords in the electorate, "Ike" transformed his radiant smile, unaffected manner, and heroic reputation into a landslide victory. He captured over 55 percent of the popular vote, and thirty-nine states to Stevenson's nine. In Congress, however, the Republicans managed to win only a slim margin in the House and a tie in the Senate. The victory was more a personal triumph for Eisenhower than an expression of faith in the Republican party.

The American Spirit at Midcentury

With the outbreak of war in Europe in 1939, many Americans had sensed the coming of a new spirit of collective commitment to democratic values. After the attack on Pearl Harbor, the sense of a shared enterprise had spread throughout America. In ways that no government propaganda could have achieved, people linked all kinds of activities to a common cause: welding for the war effort, waking an hour early for the car pool, keeping tin cans for the scrap-metal drive, saving war stamps for a war bond. Factories were now pictured as vibrant centers of cooperation rather than as dreary mills of oppression. Intellectuals wrote confidently about "the public interest" as if everyone understood its meaning. For a brief period, the individual seemed to require no special reinforcements.

Then as soon as the war ended, the spirit of a common cause dissolved. The news told only of selfish strikers, business profiteers, and greedy farmers. The government seemed no more than an arena for squabbling interests. Where were the truly national goals? According to *The Best Years of Our Lives*, one of Hollywood's most acclaimed movies of the 1940s, the

the Korean War, producing thousands of military casualties and sharp domestic inflation, created frustrations that undermined Truman's popularity and ability to lead. Finally, in 1951–52, when evidence of corruption among Truman's associates and in the Justice Department sullied the administration's reputation, fewer than one in four Americans expressed approval of Truman's presidency.

Given the administration's unpopularity, Republicans looked toward the 1952 elections with high hopes for victories in both the presidential and the congressional contests. The two outstanding candidates for the Republican nomination were the brusque, efficient Robert Taft, son of a president and leader of his party in the Senate, and Dwight D. Eisenhower, hero of the Second World War and favorite of the party's moderates. Taft had established a long record of opposition to Washington bureaucracies and government interference with business. However, as a practicing politician, he had accepted the primary results of the New Deal and had acknowledged a government responsibility to protect the economy. Eisenhower, on the other hand, had established his record in the army, where he had demonstrated an im-

returning soldiers had to fight still another battle at home to preserve their dignity in an ungrateful society. In fact, what had the war meant? In its aftermath, total war raised questions about the threat of a technological barbarism that could no longer be attributed simply to the evils of fascism.

In these sobering postwar years, the question of the place of the individual in modern American society could be answered in four separate ways. Although each of the four was different, all dealt in some way with the clash between modern and traditional values, and all responded in some fashion to the problems and hopes of the vulnerable individual. Taken together these four answers outlined the central issues in modern American culture.

The Achieving Individual.

One answer was for the individual to learn the rules of the modern occupational system, abide by them, and succeed. The wartime economy had intensified the demand for greater numbers of specialists with higher levels of skill, and immediately after the war Americans turned to the schools to fill this demand. Bands of citizens campaigned to improve instruction in the basic skills. Funds flowed freely into the entire educational system. Between 1945 and 1950, expenditures in the public schools more than doubled; even more impressive, enrollment in higher education doubled. Just as the importance of the high school had dominated in the 1920s and 1930s, so the importance of higher education dominated the years after the Second World War. Now only colleges and graduate schools could satisfy a complex economy's need for specialized training. The greatest single impetus to college enrollment came from the GI Bill of 1944, which eventually subsidized the education of about 8 million former servicepeople. Along with the sheer numbers it funded, the GI Bill helped to democratize opportunities in higher education and hence in the upper ranks of business and the professions as well.

In *Death of a Salesman* (1949), the young playwright Arthur Miller created a brilliant morality tale about using these broadening opportunities. Immediately acclaimed as one of America's greatest plays, Miller's drama provided a painful lesson on how to fail in modern America. The play's hero, Willy Loman, lived by a weakened, vulgarized version of the traditional American dream of success. Having chosen the career of salesmanship, which in the 1920s had seemed the right avenue to wealth and importance, Willy found himself trapped in humiliating failures and endless debts. Hoping that his sons might still succeed, he taught them the only values he knew—a personal style, a winning appearance, and an eye for the main chance. But this only left them athletic, shal-

low, and morally stunted. In contrast, Willy's neighbor had simply relinquished his son to America's system of specialized occupations, enabling the young man to become a successful lawyer with a warm, easy relationship with his father. The young man's success explained Willy's failure and ultimate suicide. Modern America's avenue upward had been there all the while, but Willy's dream had hidden the only legitimate path to success.

The Humanistic Individual.

The second answer acknowledged that the individual would have to find an anchor of values outside science. Like the earlier critics of America's machine culture, a variety of intellectuals, educators, and publicists now warned that science and technology by themselves were amoral. Each person, they said, must find the fundamental principles in civilized life, and only the humanists—the philosophers and poets and theologians—could lead that search.

The quest for basic values was a nationwide preoccupation in the late forties. Some scholars explored the American past to discover its essentially American qualities, giving special attention to such brooding spirits as Thoreau, Melville, and the Puritans. Others examined the far richer resources of the Western tradition. Adults enrolled in well-attended classes on the "Great Books" of Western civilization. In colleges throughout the country, new and often required courses tried to distill wisdom not only from a long span of time, but also from a breadth of subjects such as an interdisciplinary examination of American culture or a humanistic understanding of science.

The fascination with fundamentals produced a strong reaction against the pragmatist's faith in an experimental, evolving truth. John Dewey, who more than any other intellectual leader was identified with a scientific method of ethics, became a particular target of attack in the late 1940s. Dewey's critics wanted certainties in place of his open-ended pursuit of truth. In foreign policy, for example, they sought to define a single unwavering "national interest" to guide America's international affairs. In civil liberties, they assigned to the freedoms of the First Amendment an absolute, timeless meaning that no judiciary, they asserted, should ever alter.

The critics of Dewey's scientific relativism accused its adherents of arrogance as well as fuzziness. The human mind, they claimed, was incapable of solving all of the world's problems through a scientific method. This line of opposition found its most effective spokesman in the theologian Reinhold Niebuhr, who believed that all actions reflected an inevitable human fallibility, and all choices involved moral risks. Nevertheless, individuals had a moral responsibility

HIROSHIMA, 1945
Was modern society on the brink of suicide? The awful power of the atomic bomb raised fundamental questions about the meaning of science, progress, and civilization.

to choose among alternatives and to act on their choices. The necessity of choosing from an inherently imperfect knowledge defined the human predicament. Niebuhr, supporting the containment of international communism, lectured Americans that "It is not easy . . . for an adolescent nation, with illusions of childlike innocency, to come to terms with the responsibilities and hazards of global politics." Yet meet them it must. Americans had to abandon their simple faith in man-made progress, face each situation as it arose, and, without arrogance, commit themselves to a course that might best fulfill their moral obligations.

The Heroic Individual. The third postwar answer was a defiant statement in behalf of the sovereign individual. Setting the individual at odds with modern society, it told him to overcome the dangers around him through his interior powers. In a few instances, this answer was addressed to the specialist. Ayn Rand's best-selling novel *The Fountainhead* (1943), for example, glorified the right of the creative professional to discard society's ordinary rules in order to realize his genius, and in the postwar years Rand cults mush-

roomed on college campuses. Usually, however, the hero had no special training and no resources except his hard inner core. During the forties a mass audience learned about this kind of hero through a host of movies, particularly those starring Humphrey Bogart, and through a flood of inexpensive paperbacks that suddenly deluged drugstores and newsstands.

Soon after the publication of his first book in 1947, Mickey Spillane became undisputed king of the new paperback market. In less than a decade, 30 million copies of his novels had been sold, a record that far surpassed any competitor's. His hero was a tough, resourceful private detective named Mike Hammer, who radiated an irresistible power. Although Spillane drew on a full tradition of fantasies about the all-conquering individual, he more than any of his predecessors gave them a contemporary urban setting pervaded by corrupt, ominous forces. It required an exceptional courage to break free from this threatening urban jungle. Those who succeeded, however, became true individuals and survived. The number of Spillane's imitators even more than the sale of his books indicated that his, of all the postwar answers, found the widest audience.

The Desperate Individual. The fourth postwar answer was the acceptance of despair that threatened to destroy the individual. In the late forties Americans were listening for the first time to those Europeans who had already peered inside a soulless society and found no individuals there. Suddenly relevant were Franz Kafka's nightmares of man as a nameless subject wandering through a fathomless system to a death he came to welcome, and the disturbing accounts of a devouring social organization in Aldous Huxley's *Brave New World* (1932), Arthur Koestler's *Darkness at Noon* (1941), and George Orwell's *1984* (1949). Because Orwell and Koestler were describing communist totalitarianism, Americans had a choice of reading their books as justifications for a free Western society. Instead, many Americans used them as a frame of reference for discussing the dangers in their own lives.

The Second World War, as it was viewed in retrospect, contributed significantly to this new spirit of despair. The best of the American war novels—Norman Mailer's *Naked and the Dead* (1948), Irwin Shaw's *Young Lions* (1948), and James Jones's *From Here to Eternity* (1951)—did not simply surround their characters with danger, as the war novels of the 1920s had done. Now individuals were sucked into the very center of destruction, and all characters were equally exposed to the stray bullet. No personal choice or inner strength affected these human specks that were being tossed by the fates.

Above all, the Holocaust and "The Bomb" posed the most profoundly disturbing problems of the postwar years. Had the Germans, in systematically destroying 6 million human beings, discovered an essential truth about the impersonal mobilization of power in modern society? And what of the American atomic bombs that had demolished the Japanese cities of Hiroshima and Nagasaki? Through the development and use of the bomb, scientific genius and human annihilation were juxtaposed so sharply, the concept of civilization was so directly challenged, and the terrors of nuclear death were so vividly imprinted on the minds of Americans, that even the most resolute Americans were unable to express its import.

The uniquely American way of expressing despair about the individual's lot appeared in a new image, "the Southern." In 1949 the southerner William Faulkner, with his finest writing already behind him, received the Nobel Prize for literature, and a favorite intellectual game of the late forties was unraveling the family histories in Faulkner's "Yoknapatawpha County," the fictional Mississippi setting for his greatest works. A year earlier, the young Tennessee Williams had been awarded a Pulitzer prize for *A Streetcar Named Desire*, which with another dramatic success in the 1940s established him as a leading playwright. These two, along with other gifted southern writers such as Carson McCullers and Flannery O'Connor, created a shockingly new American image.

Understanding the Southern depended on an appreciation of the Western, for intentionally or not, the Southern was a systematic attack on America's oldest myth of individual strength. In the Western, one man entered an open plain where he confronted a direct challenge, and by a clear moral choice he overcame it. He was the pure individual: a man alone, a man of simple, sovereign convictions, a man of action whose problem, once met, dissolved in a cleansing rite of violence. Not only had the movies, the radio, comics, and pulp fiction expanded the audience for this myth since the 1920s; such thoughtful writers as Hemingway had borrowed from it. The Western hero continued to stand tall in postwar America.

Like the Western, the Southern also used a regional stereotype to communicate a national message. Just as countless Americans associated the West with a new, formless land, many regarded the South as a decaying, backward region. This popular caricature helped southern writers reach a national audience. In contrast to the Western's openness, the world of the Southern was a suffocating prison—a town or household or room in which the inmates were held by invisible shackles they could never break. This world was filled with human vulnerability: children were caught in a whirl of adult terror, and adults locked in a desperate battle for sanity. These struggles, unlike the gun fights of the Western, showed women managing more effectively than men. Maleness and impotence were common companions in the Southern.

Where the Western hero acted, the characters in the Southern talked. They stabbed one another with words, searched in vain for the meaning of their lives through words, and covered their own anguish with words. Occasionally someone's hopelessness or passion would explode in violence, but violence only complicated the problems that no one would ever resolve. In *A Streetcar Named Desire*, Tennessee Williams let loose a caricature of the Western hero, the physical-sexual-nonverbal Stanley Kowalski, and he wrecked the fragile human defenses around him. Perhaps only a small minority listened carefully to the agonizing message of the Southern. Nevertheless, an exceptionally talented cluster of American writers were finally probing fundamental questions about the individual's chances for survival.

At midcentury one phase in the creation of modern culture was ending. An elaborate framework of modern values relating to occupational specialization, personal freedom, and mass manipulation lay across the top of American society. Beneath it a complex pattern of traditional values simultaneously resisted and assimilated these modern ways. The long overlapping frontier between the two spheres did not alter their basically antagonistic orientations. Hence, the range of answers to a problem common to both—the fate of the individual—revealed a wide diversity of standards, aspirations, and doubts. A distant viewer might well wonder if Arthur Miller's Achieving Man, Rein-hold Niebuhr's Moral Man, Mickey Spillane's Mike Hammer, and Tennessee Williams's Stanley Kowalski all belonged to the same human race. To maintain the uneasy coexistence among these conflicting beliefs required a good deal of mutual tolerance—or mutual indifference. Whether an increasingly nationalized American society would contain such leeway became a crucial question in the next quarter-century.

CHRONOLOGY

1941 Roosevelt bans racial discrimination in government and defense hiring.
FDR and Churchill meet in Atlantic Conference to prepare Anglo-American alliance.

1942 Japanese Americans moved to "relocation centers."
Revenue Act expands graduated income tax.
Government wage, price, and rent controls established.
Operation Torch, Allied invasion of North Africa.
American troops driven from Philippines.
U.S. inflicts first major defeat on Japan at battle of Midway.

1943 Allied invasion of Italy.

1944 Operation Overlord, Allied invasion of France.
Bretton Woods Conference on international monetary stabilization.
Roosevelt reelected president for an unprecedented fourth term.

1945 Yalta Conference.
Roosevelt dies; Harry S Truman becomes president.
UN charter signed by forty-seven nations.
Germany surrenders.
Potsdam Conference.

U.S. drops atomic bombs on Hiroshima and Nagasaki in Japan.
Japan surrenders.

1946 Republicans win control of Congress.

1947 Truman Doctrine calls for containment of communism.
Marshall Plan sends massive aid to Europe.
Department of Defense and Central Intelligence Agency established by National Security Act.
Taft-Hartley Act restricts actions of labor unions.

1948 Berlin blockaded by Soviets; U.S. organizes airlift.
Truman elected president.

1949 NATO established.
Soviet Union detonates atomic bomb.
Communist government controls China.

1950 Alger Hiss convicted of perjury in relation to espionage charges.
Senator Joseph McCarthy launches anti-communist crusade.
Korean War begins.

1951 Twenty-Second Amendment limits presidents to two terms.

1952 Dwight D. Eisenhower elected president.

1953 Rosenbergs executed as spies.
Armistice in Korea.

Gordon Wright, *The Ordeal of Total War, 1939–1945* (1968), gives an overview of the European theater in the Second World War. A. Russell Buchanan, *The United States in World War II* (2 vols., 1964), details America's military activities in both the European and the Pacific theaters; and Martha Byrd Hoyle, *A World in Flames* (1970), covers them more briefly. A famous naval historian, Samuel Eliot Morison, tells of the conflict at sea in *The Two-Ocean War* (1963). Morison's *Strategy and Compromise* (1958) and Kent Roberts Greenfield's *American Strategy in World War II: A Reconsideration* (1963) evaluate broad questions of military policy. Forrest C. Pogue, *George C. Marshall* (3 vols. to date, 1963–73), has followed the career of Roosevelt's chief of staff to 1945. Stephen E. Ambrose, *The Supreme Commander: The War Years of General Dwight D. Eisenhower* (1970), contains valuable insights. On foreign relations, Gaddis Smith's *Diplomacy during the Second World War, 1941–1945* (1965) is a convenient introduction. Herbert Feis, *Churchill, Roosevelt, and Stalin* (1957), and Robert Beitzell, *The Uneasy Alliance: America, Britain, and Russia, 1941–1943* (1972), examine the critical issues besetting the grand alliance.

Three fine books—Diane Shaver Clemens, *Yalta* (1970), Robert A. Divine, *Second Chance: The Triumph of Internationalism in America during World War II* (1967), and Michael Sherry, *Preparing for the Next War: American Plans for Postwar Defense, 1941–45* (1977)—chart paths into the postwar years. William Roger Louis, *Imperialism at Bay: The United States and the Decolonization of the British Empire* (1978), and Christopher Thorne, *Allies of a Kind: The United States, Britain, and the War Against Japan, 1941–1945* (1978), are also useful. For the development of the atomic bomb, see Richard G. Hewlett and Oscar E. Anderson, *The New World* (1962). Martin J. Sherwin, *A World Destroyed* (1975), Barton J. Bernstein (ed.), *The Atom Bomb* (1976), and Gregg Herken, *The Winning Weapon: The Atomic Bomb in the Cold War, 1945–1950* (1980), explore its international implications.

Specifically on the president's leadership, the concluding volume of James MacGregor Burns's biography, *Roosevelt: The Soldier of Freedom* (1970), and Robert Dallek, *Franklin D. Roosevelt and American Foreign Policy, 1932–1945* (1979), are basic. Robert Divine's *Roosevelt and World War II* (1969) is a keen and generally favorable appraisal. Valuable material on two of Roosevelt's advisers appears in Robert E. Sherwood, *Roosevelt and Hopkins* (rev. ed., 1950), and John Morton Blum, ed., *From the Morgenthau Diaries: Years of War, 1941–1945* (1967). Lloyd C. Gardner, *Architects of Illusion: Men and Ideas in American Foreign Policy, 1941–1949* (1970), is a perceptive essay on the men who won control of America's foreign policy; and Thomas G. Patterson, ed., *Cold War Critics: Alternatives to American Foreign Policy in the Truman Years* (1971), is a collection of essays on the men who lost. Additional information on the shapers of American policy appears in George Curry, "James F. Byrnes," in Vol. 14 of *American Secretaries of State and Their Diplomacy* (1965), Robert H. Ferrell, *George C. Marshall* (1966), which is Vol. 15 of the same series, Gaddis Smith, *Dean Acheson* (1972), which is Vol. 16, and Arnold A. Rogow, *James Forrestal* (1964), a study of the first secretary of defense. The writings of participants themselves include these particularly useful books: Harry S Truman, *Memoirs* (2 vols., 1955–56), Dean

Acheson, *Present at the Creation* (1969), Lucius Clay, *Decision in Germany* (1950), George F. Kennan, *Memoirs, 1925–1950* (1967), and Arthur H. Vandenberg, Jr., ed., *The Private Papers of Senator Vandenberg* (1952).

The history of the Cold War is a caldron of controversy. Two judicious guides are John Lewis Gaddis, *The United States and the Origins of the Cold War, 1941–1947* (1972), which tends to justify American policies, and Walter LaFeber, *America, Russia, and the Cold War, 1945–1980* (1980), which tends to criticize them. For a pungent taste of the battle, however, read on the one hand Herbert Feis, *From Trust to Terror: The Onset of the Cold War, 1945–1950* (1970), the last in his series of volumes explaining modern American diplomacy; and on the other hand Gabriel Kolko, *The Politics of War: The World and United States Foreign Policy, 1943–1945* (1968), and Joyce and Gabriel Kolko, *The Limits of Power: The World and United States Foreign Policy, 1945–1954* (1972), a thorough condemnation of Washington's policies. Louis J. Halle, *The Cold War as History* (1967), and Adam B. Ulam, *The Rivals: America and Russia Since World War II* (1971), are balanced accounts.

Several careful studies add substantially to our knowledge of the crucial issues dividing the United States and the Soviet Union: Lynn Etheridge Davis, *The Cold War Begins: Soviet-American Conflict over Eastern Europe* (1974), George C. Herring, Jr., *Aid to Russia, 1941–1946* (1973), Bruce Kuklick, *American Policy and the Division of Germany* (1972), and especially Thomas G. Paterson, *Soviet-American Confrontation* (1973). On problems that hardened the pattern of the Cold War, see Joseph I. Lieberman, *The Scorpion and the Tarantula: The Struggle to Control Atomic Weapons, 1945–1949* (1970), W. Phillips Davison, *The Berlin Blockade* (1958), Robert E. Osgood, *NATO* (1962), and Bruce R. Kuniholm, *The Origins of the Cold War in the Near East* (1980).

The origins and the course of America's postwar policy in East Asia are discussed in Akira Iriye's very perceptive *The Cold War in Asia* (1974), Kenneth E. Shewmaker's *Americans and Chinese Communists, 1927–1945* (1971), and Tang Tsou's *America's Failure in China, 1941–1950* (1963). For the background to the Korean War, see Leland M. Goodrich, *Korea: A Study of U.S. Policy in the United Nations* (1956), and Glenn D. Paige, *The Korean Decision* (1968). The policy struggles accompanying the war are discussed in John W. Spanier, *The Truman-MacArthur Controversy and the Korean War* (1959), and Trumbull Higgins, *Korea and the Fall of MacArthur* (1960). The indefatigable journalist I. F. Stone raises some intriguing questions in *Hidden History of the Korean War* (1952).

The domestic side of the Second World War has received much less attention from historians. Richard Polenberg, *War and Society: The United States, 1941–1945* (1972), provides a useful overview, and John Morton Blum, *V Was for Victory: Politics and American Culture During World War II* (1976), offers penetrating insights. Joel Seidman, *American Labor from Defense to Reconversion* (1953), deals primarily with government policy. William Henry Chafe, *The American Woman: Her Changing Social, Economic, and Political Roles, 1920–1970* (1972), includes a valuable discussion of women in the wartime economy. Roland A. Young, *Congressional Politics in the Second World War* (1956), reviews the legislative record. Davis R. B. Ross, *Preparing for Ulysses* (1969), explains the GI Bill, and Stephen K. Bailey, *Congress Makes a Law* (1957), analyzes the Full Employment Act.

A growing literature examines the place of racial minorities in modern America. Two surveys—John Hope Franklin, *From Slavery to Freedom* (3rd ed., 1969), and August Meier and Elliott M. Rudwick, *From Plantation to Ghetto* (rev. ed., 1970)—ably cover the years after 1920. Richard M. Dalfiume's *Desegregation of the United States Armed Forces* (1969), traces the most striking public gain for blacks during the Truman years. In *Black Bourgeoisie* (1957), E. Franklin Frazier offers a sharp analysis of relatively well-to-do blacks. Roger Daniels, *Concentration Camps, USA* (1971), is a brief study of the persecution of Japanese Americans during the Second World War; Jacobus ten Broek et al., *Prejudice, War and the Constitution* (1954), provides many of the details; and Michi Weglyn, *Years of Infamy* (1976), expresses the feelings of the prisoners.

For Truman's administration, see Cabell Phillips, *The Truman Presidency* (1966), a reasonable introduction, and Robert J. Donovan, *The Presidency of Harry S. Truman* (2 vols., 1977, 1982). Merle Miller, *Plain Speaking: An Oral Biography of Harry S Truman* (1974), helps to reveal the president's quality of mind. A considerably more sophisticated study, Alonzo L. Hamby's *Beyond the New Deal: Harry S Truman and American Liberalism* (1973), analyzes the place of the administration in a modern democratic tradition. A good place to begin exploring the election of 1948 is Samuel Lubell, *The Future of American Politics* (1952). Susan M. Hartmann, *Truman and the 80th Congress* (1971), covers important background in Washington. The meaning of Henry A. Wallace's third-party candidacy is evaluated in Norman D. Markowitz, *The Rise and Fall of the People's Century* (1973). V. O. Key, Jr., *Southern Politics in State and Nation* (1949), is a mine of information on its subject, and Robert A. Garson, *The Democratic Party and the Politics of Sectionalism,* *1941–1948* (1974), is a useful supplement. On particular areas of public policy, William C. Berman, *The Politics of Civil Rights in the Truman Administration* (1970), and Richard O. Davies, *Housing Reform During the Truman Administration* (1966), are both careful studies. Allen J. Matusow's *Farm Policies and Politics in the Truman Years* (1967) makes a thorough assessment in its field. More critical appraisals of the president appear in Barton J. Bernstein, ed., *Politics and Policies of the Truman Administration* (1970), especially the essays by Bernstein himself.

No domestic subject since the New Deal has attracted such scholarly attention as the anticommunist issue after the Second World War. Robert Griffith and Athan Theoharis, eds., *The Specter: Original Essays on the Cold War and the Origins of McCarthyism* (1974), Earl Latham, *The Communist Controversy in Washington* (1966), and Walter Gellhorn, ed., *The States and Subversion* (1952), suggest the wide range of topics and interests that were involved. Athan Theoharis, *Seeds of Repression* (1971), and Richard M. Freeland, *The Truman Doctrine and the Origins of McCarthyism* (1972), place a heavy responsibility for the rise of popular anticommunism on the Truman administration, and Alan D. Harper, *The Politics of Loyalty: The White House and the Communist Issue,* *1946–1952* (1969), significantly tempers that judgment. Robert Griffith, *The Politics of Fear* (1970), analyzes McCarthy's sources of power in the Senate. In *The Intellectuals and McCarthy* (1967), Michael Paul Rogin blames conservative academicians for inflating the record of McCarthy's popular appeal, and Mary Sperling McAuliffe, *Crisis on the Left: Cold War Politics and American Liberals,* *1947–1954* (1978), traces the capitulation of her subjects. On the most sensational espionage cases, see Walter and Miriam Schneir, *Invitation to an Inquest* (1965), and Ronald Radosh and Joyce Milton, *The Rosenberg File* (1983), which explore the Rosenberg case; and Allen Weinstein, *Perjury! The Hiss-Chambers Conflict* (1978).

31 Conformity and Conflict: The Modern Republic Under Eisenhower

The nationalistic upsurge that began in the 1930s and 1940s continued in somewhat different form in the 1950s. Rapid economic growth produced widespread affluence. Weary of the public concerns that had dominated their lives for twenty years, Americans now preferred private absorptions to public questions. Emphasizing similarities rather than differences, they insisted on conformity as the national style. "Togetherness" and "belongingness" became popular catch phrases. A best seller of the 1950s, William H. Whyte's *Organization Man*, depicted the eclipse of traditional individualism by an "organization ethic."

The Eisenhower presidency was a perfect reflection of this mood. An affable, benign, seemingly unpolitical figure, Dwight D. Eisenhower intended to take the country along "that straight road down the middle." His presidency, contemporary critics said, was a case study in "the bland leading the bland" and "mastery in the service of drift." Although recent historians have described Eisenhower as a more dynamic and thoughtful political leader, his presidency was largely an exercise in maintaining accepted standards and retarding change.

Yet the fifties saw upheavals at home and abroad. Within the United States, challenges to segregation, especially in the schools, pitted blacks against whites, federal authority against state and local control, and personal prejudice against the public good. In foreign affairs, the nation staunchly opposed communist advances in Asia, Europe, Latin America, and the Middle East. The Eisenhower administration struggled to contain and, if possible, to roll back communist power. The Cold War seemed to become a permanent fixture in American life.

Affluence and Unity

The 1950s, like the 1920s, were years of fulfillment. As the bitter strikes and angry rhetoric of the late forties subsided, so did most worries about a selfish, frag-

mented society. Despite two recessions during the decade, the GNP rose by 50 percent to half a trillion dollars, and the economy spread out a feast of goods and services. Echoing the claims of the 1920s, publicist Peter Drucker told Americans that their society had passed *"beyond Capitalism and Socialism."* Once again, millions believed that they not only had solved the major problems of the past, but had learned how to manage the problems of the future.

The Affluent Society. During the 1950s a combination of government expenditures, private investment, consumer borrowing, and a nearly 30 percent expansion of the population allowed the United States, which represented only 6 percent of the world's people, to produce and consume approximately 33 percent of the world's economic output. Although more than 20 percent of the nation's population continued to live in poverty during the 1950s, numerous Americans improved their standard of living and entered the middle class. By the early 1960s one Kentucky county, a center of long-standing economic distress, demonstrated the point: 59 percent of the families there owned automobiles, 42 percent had telephones, two-thirds had television sets, and nearly 90 percent owned washing machines.

Much of the secret of this economic upsurge can be found in the productivity of American agriculture and industry. Agricultural output began to increase substantially. During the quarter-century after the Second World War, the yield of wheat and cotton per acre doubled; the yield of corn tripled; food in America was abundant and cheap. While the number of farm laborers decreased by approximately 30 percent during the fifties, total farm production went up by a like amount. Relying on mechanical innovations that revolutionized the cultivation of crops, agribusiness made the nation's farms the most productive in the world. At the same time, American industry produced unprecedented amounts of goods by investing some $10 billion a year in new capital equipment, introducing more

efficient methods of automation, and relying heavily on electrical energy, the internal combustion engine, and the applied sciences, especially chemistry and electronics. Such light, relatively inexpensive materials as plastic and aluminum became widely used. Not only did these new materials expand the range of inexpensive goods; they created a mass market for cheap imitations of goods that had once been luxury items. Most American women could now afford to wear nylon stockings, whereas once only a few could afford silk ones. During the fifties America's largest corporations averaged $500 million a year in sales — ten times the volume of the 1920s.

The principal beneficiaries of this industrial boom were the country's consumers, who took full advantage of easy credit to borrow and buy at a dizzying pace. Between 1945 and 1957, consumer credit rose by a breathtaking 800 percent; and as credit swelled, revolving charge accounts, easy payment plans, and credit cards became increasingly popular. Devoting themselves to the good life, American consumers purchased not only household appliances that eased life's burdens, but also television sets, electric toothbrushes, sports equipment, and swimming pools—luxury goods that indulged their tastes and filled their leisure time.

In the fifties, entertainment became a major American industry. Expenditures on leisure activities jumped from 7 to 15 percent of the GNP during the decade. Working fewer hours at higher wages than ever before, Americans spent twice as much on vacations, travel, liquor, movies, and sports, taken together, as they did on rent. By 1960 the cost of satisfying American pleasures was approximately $85 billion a year.

The nationwide rush to the suburbs gave further evidence of an affluent, mobile society. During the depression and war years, the number of new dwellings had averaged about 300,000 a year. In the fifties, the annual average ran almost four times higher, and the demand for suburban housing seemed insatiable. By 1960 more than one in three Americans lived in suburbs—as many as lived in the cities. Instead of relying on the services of the inner city, as did the "bedroom towns" of the 1920s, the suburbs of the 1950s provided an increasingly self-contained life. Business firms, following the rush to the suburbs, sold their wares along miles of commercial avenues and inside countless shopping plazas, or malls, where suburban department stores displayed the national abundance. By the 1960s the typical American was no longer the farmer behind the plow, or the small-town dweller, or the busy urbanite, but the suburbanite with all the accouterments of the consumer culture, including house, car, commuter schedule, and golf clubs.

The Economics of Peace.

But a booming consumer sector did not entirely account for American prosperity. Military expenditures now dominated the national budget. The size of these expenditures alone, fluctuating at about 60 percent of the government's total costs, made them crucial to maintaining a healthy economy. Directly or indirectly, the military program financed the research behind America's most important technological innovations. Moreover, such giant corporations as General Electric, General Motors, and Douglas Aircraft subcontracted portions of their military work to smaller companies. If the government were to terminate a big defense contract, it might send shock waves through a large section of the economy and undo the government's efforts to sustain prosperity.

"Multinational" corporations also served to strengthen the connection between the domestic economy and world affairs. Before the Second World War, almost all the subdivisions that American corporations established abroad had remained small, dependent outposts of the parent companies. After the war, corporate expansion entered a new phase. American industrialists, from soft-drink makers to automobile and electronics manufacturers, gravitated to the capital-poor nations where production costs were low, governments encouraging, and ready markets inviting. Even more important than the sheer quantity of foreign subsidiaries was the fact that an increasing proportion of them duplicated the parent company's full corporate structure and dropped roots in the societies where they were planted. By the 1950s these corporate offshoots were thriving on every continent. Still tied to their parent companies in the United States, yet assimilated into the lives of foreign nations, they gave a new transnational cast to the American economy.

But multinational corporations were only the most striking part of a massive business expansion after the Second World War. In 1946 America's private investments abroad approximated their level in 1929. During the next decade foreign investments tripled. By the end of the 1960s, they stood almost ten times higher than in 1946. Much of this money was spent in search of minerals that the United States either lacked or used at a faster rate than it produced. Oil alone accounted for more than a third of these investments. Overall, American prosperity was becoming increasingly dependent upon foreign resources and markets and upon government policies in countries around the world.

The Other America.

For all the nation's wealth, there still remained an "invisible poor," poignantly described by the social critic Michael Harrington in his book *The Other America*. These black, Hispanic, poor white, and

THE OTHER AMERICA
These black children were part of the nearly 25 percent of Americans in the late 1940s who were, in Franklin Roosevelt's earlier observation, "ill-nourished, ill-clad, and ill-housed."

elderly Americans lived "on the outskirts of hope." One large component of this group was the some 2.5 million itinerant farm workers with an annual income of under $1,000. Other elements were the innumerable men and women working at menial labor and earning less than $1 an hour, and the countless unemployed Americans living on meager welfare doles. There were also as many as 8 million elderly persons who, with a mere $70-a-month Social Security payment, could not afford decent housing, proper nutrition, or adequate medical care. In all, between 20 and 25 percent of the population lived in misery and despair in urban ghettos, on tiny farms, or in rural shantytowns. In the midst of power and plenty, these Americans continued to suffer from powerlessness and want.

National Harmony. A national style of conformity emerged in the 1950s as Americans self-consciously strove for similarity and shunned difference. Consumerism contributed to this striving, and so did religion. Some Americans went so far as to burn "controversial books." Many more sought conformity by participating in a religious revival marked by an unthinking faith in shared assumptions; Congress captured the spirit of this revival by adding the words

under God to the Pledge of Allegiance and the phrase *In God We Trust* to all United States currency. These and many other instances of seeking conformity made the United States seem to one writer a "'Packaged Society,' for we are all items in a national supermarket— categorized, processed, labeled, priced, and readied for merchandising."

Affluence and consumerism drew Americans closer together, literally and figuratively. A postwar transportation revolution shrank the nation's great distances. Between 1946 and 1956, state governments tripled their investment in road construction, and the Federal Highway Act of 1956 committed the national government to subsidizing over 40,000 miles of super-highways that would connect America's major cities. In their high-powered postwar cars, Americans greatly expanded their range of travel. The airplane shrank distances even more dramatically. Between 1947 and 1957, as passenger service grew fourfold, the airlines became a normal, accepted means of travel.

The postwar advent of television greatly added to the sense of a shared culture and a common national experience. Fourteen thousand families had television sets in 1947; by 1960 the number had climbed to 46 million, meaning that TV was reaching into 90 percent

AMERICAN BANDSTAND
Responding to the national emphasis on traditional values in the fifties, most American teenagers were models of conformity.

Bruce Davidson/Magnum Photos, Inc.

of the country's homes. Filling 20 percent of the air time with commercials for cigarettes, deodorants, toothpaste, automobiles, beer, and other luxuries of the affluent society, TV broadcasters gave viewers a sense of sharing in the consumer culture and enhanced the feeling of national well-being.

Moreover, Americans appeared to unite just by acting as consumers. Common cars and clothes, common houses and vacations, common foods and recreations, gave the impression of a single national commitment to the same good life. In 1933 the Roosevelt administration had issued a 3¢ postage stamp to symbolize unity in a society of large economic blocs: a farmer, a businessman, a laborer, and a housewife, each in distinctive dress, marched shoulder to shoulder "in common determination." In the consumer society of the 1950s, a comparable image of unity would have shown an assortment of shoppers, in the same style of clothes, filling their carts with the same standardized products. Consumerism and the American way of life had become almost synonymous.

Another sign of the times was a widespread new faith in the unique powers of science and massed expertise. Following the awesome discoveries in atomic physics, the mass distribution of "wonder drug" antibiotics, and the conquest of polio, scientists had reached a new peak of prestige. An increasing number of Americans looked on the experts as the keepers of a vast national pool of skills that could be used in various combinations to suit particular problems. Scientifically coordinated teams, rather than just scientifically trained individuals, held the key to the future. It required a team of specialists to harness the atom, to operate on the human heart, to measure public opinion, or to run a giant corporation. Moreover, these teams now had a marvelous new technological aid, the computer. No lone genius could match the scientific range of computerized team research.

Voices of Discontent. Yet all was not togetherness and conformity during the fifties. Voices were raised in protest against the mindlessness of the consumer culture. One writer complained that "people no longer have any opinions; they have refrigerators. Instead of illusions we have television. Instead of tradition, the Volkswagen. The only way to catch the spirit of the times is to write a handbook on home appliances."

There was also considerable hand wringing over the fate of the individual. In the 1950s the more systematized American society became, the less significant, or even distinguishable, was any one person in its operations. Perhaps, as the most critical voices of the late forties had implied, there really were no individuals in a modern bureaucratic society.

What had become of the individuals? Such popular novels and movies as *On the Beach* and *Fail-Safe*, which portrayed life in a thermonuclear age, touched deep fears that the world would die in the ultimate holocaust. The audience for a dehumanizing science fiction expanded. The most intriguing new American writer of the 1950s, J. D. Salinger, and the most talented new American dramatist of the 1960s, Edward Albee, both emphasized the individual's agonizing, inescapable vulnerability in modern society. Many young writers accentuated the individual's isolation by using ordinary conversation as a way of hiding rather than communicating their characters' feelings. Only when the characters talked to themselves in lonely interior monologues did they honestly express their emotions. Such novelists as Saul Bellow and Joseph Heller relieved the individual's preposterous fate in modern society with a wild laughter.

As more and more jobs became mechanized and routinized, the individual laborer developed a new attitude toward work. During the 1950s employers noted that white-collar employees were inquiring more often about fringe benefits like vacations, company cars, and retirement plans than they were about the challenges of their jobs. By the 1960s many corporations were discovering a new problem of morale among those executives who ran the companies' daily affairs. Rising rates of absenteeism and declining rates of efficiency expressed the refusal of "middle managers" to devote themselves to jobs that were no longer rewarding. Indeed, white-collar efficiency had become a pervasive problem. On the average, white-collar employees worked only about 50 percent of the time they spent in the office. Somewhere outside of the job lay an elusive something called "fulfillment," and more and more Americans set out to find it.

It was a wide-ranging quest. Some cultivated their avocations instead of their vocations: more and more well-to-do Americans sought their primary satisfaction in boating or bridge, travel or tennis. Leisure became something much more basic in life than simply time to recuperate. Beginning with the modest "do-it-yourself" kits of the 1950s, handicrafts grew increasingly important in the lives of white-collar Americans concerned about the taste and quality of mass-produced goods. And a cult of the wilderness arose, which condemned the artificiality of modern society and advocated living close to nature. Part of this glorification of nature represented a reaction against the biological devastation that an indiscriminate use of insecticides was causing throughout America, eloquently publicized in Rachel Carson's chilling best seller, *Silent Spring* (1962).

The most general expression of the individual's modern quest was a nationwide fascination with personal power. Books coached Americans on games of "one-upmanship" in their everyday relations with friends and acquaintances. Commentators and historians praised the "strong" presidents. The preoccupation with personal power was a mass phenomenon, and it found a variety of popular outlets. The crunching game of football became America's leading sport. Its competitors adapted as best they could: through shortened fences and livelier balls in baseball, the "big game" in tennis, the "dunk" in basketball, and the "power play" in hockey. High-speed auto racing attracted more and more fans. By the 1960s everybody's car could be a personal vehicle of power: Cougar, Wildcat, Thunderbird, Stingray, Mustang. Promises of personal power suffused the advertising of everything from perfumes to breakfast foods. The theme of personal power saturated the movies and television, not only in the James Bond shows and their many "superspy" imitators, but just as thoroughly in children's cartoons. Yet no one knew how to restore a genuine sense of autonomy in a mass society dominated by huge, impersonal organizations.

"Modern Republicanism"

During his eight years as president, Dwight Eisenhower liked to describe his philosophy as "modern Republicanism," his followers as "progressive moderates," and his program as one of "dynamic conservatism." We will be "conservative when it comes to money, liberal when it comes to human beings," the new president declared. His administration would most of all try to find "things it can stop doing rather than new things for it to do." Much more in the Coolidge-Hoover than the Roosevelt-Truman tradition, Eisenhower prized individualism and visualized its operation through private groups—political, industrial, church, school, labor.

"It has been a group effort, freely undertaken, that has produced the things of which we are so proud," Eisenhower announced, and he expected his administration to serve this "American way of life." "Free enterprise," "private initiative," and the dangers of "regimentation" peppered his conversations. He regarded TVA as "creeping socialism." On election night, 1952, when Eisenhower finally broke loose from the happy mob of his supporters, his first telephone call was to Herbert Hoover.

The Washington Bureaucracy. But between Hoover's time and Eisenhower's, Washington had changed dramatically. During the New Deal and the Second World War, the federal bureaucracy had swollen to enormous proportions. By the early 1950s, physicists, chemists, biologists, engineers, hospital administrators, and a host of other scientific groups had become part of the Washington establishment, and government expenditures for scientific research and development skyrocketed from $74 million in 1940 to $7.3 billion in 1960. Other professionals, ranging from archivists and advertising specialists to experts in race relations and traffic management, found places in the government bureaucracy.

No one coordinated Washington's vast apparatus of government. On paper it looked as though the executive branch was the center of control. In 1950 Congress added to the executive's powers by giving the president the right to appoint his own chairman to the independent regulatory commissions. Now each new administration could have an immediate influence on the policies of the "Big Six": the Civil Aeronautics Board, the Federal Communications Commission, the Federal Power Commission, the Federal Trade Commission, the Interstate Commerce Commission, and the Securities and Exchange Commission. Then in 1953, the new Department of Health, Education, and Welfare (HEW) combined a great variety of services and programs under one executive chief.

Nevertheless, the larger the executive branch grew, the more its authority was scattered among innumerable offices and subdivisions. As powerful a politician as Eisenhower's principal domestic aide, Sherman Adams, could do no more than respond to the issues of government one at a time as they came to him. Fortunately for the president, the tests of good management required only a strong economy and a satisfied constituency of private interest groups. By these standards, the government functioned very well during the 1950s. Although Americans grumbled about incompetent bureaucrats, they generally approved the results of bureaucratic government.

Eisenhower's Conservatism.

President Eisenhower viewed himself less as a party leader or chief legislator than as a mediator. Believing that he should use his executive powers sparingly, he deferred to Congress and introduced few legislative proposals. Eisenhower's conception of the presidency, one political scientist has observed, represented "the greatest retreat in the national experience since the first battle of Bull Run."

The new president made clear at the start that his was to be a business administration dominated by a concern for "free enterprise." He gathered so many wealthy opponents of the New Deal into his cabinet that it was popularly described as "nine millionaires and a plumber"—and the "plumber," Secretary of Labor Martin Durkin, soon resigned. Because three of the president's appointees were General Motors executives, Adlai Stevenson could understandably quip that the New Dealers had "all left Washington to make way for the car dealers."

In its first months the new administration seemed bent on reducing federal controls over business and on generally reversing the flow of the past twenty years in domestic affairs. Secretary of Defense Charles E. Wilson, a former president of General Motors, declared that "what was good for our country was good for General Motors, and vice versa." Secretary of Commerce Sinclair Weeks fired the chief of the Bureau of Standards for reporting that a commercial battery additive, AD-2X, was useless; Secretary Weeks thought it should be allowed a "test of the marketplace." On other fronts, Secretary of Health, Education, and Welfare Oveta Culp Hobby opposed federal legislation providing free distribution of the Salk vaccine to prevent polio; it would, she said, be a major step toward "socialized medicine."

In cooperation with Secretary of the Treasury George Humphrey, the president set out to slash the national budget and minimize the government's influence in economic matters. Even during three recessions, when deficit spending seemed needed to revive the economy, the administration resisted an unbalanced budget and intervention in the private sector. Eisenhower opposed "going too far with trying to fool with our economy," and he objected to creating "huge federal bureaucracies of the PWA or WPA type."

These attitudes were given substantive expression in the Submerged Lands Act of 1953 and the Atomic Energy Act of 1954. The first bill shifted title to some $40 billion worth of disputed offshore oil lands from the federal government to seaboard states. The second act allowed the administration to oppose federal power projects, which it denounced as "creeping socialism," and to support government-financed atomic research by such private corporations as General Electric. Subsequently, when the Atomic Energy Commission requested a new steam-power plant for an AEC facility in Kentucky, the administration refused to let TVA build it. Instead, the contract went to a private utility syndicate, Dixon-Yates. But when cries of protest forced a disclosure of the contract, a conflict of interest was revealed. The administration had to cancel the agreement as "contrary to the public interest" and to accept a proposal from the city of Memphis to build a plant that could supply the steam power.

The Politics of Moderation.

The Eisenhower administration's opposition to government controls led it to dismantle the Reconstruction Finance Corporation, established by Hoover during the Great Depression. It also rejected significant federal support for education, public housing, and medical care for the aged—all of which Truman had proposed and for which the Democrats would keep pressing until the 1960s. Although New Deal programs generally remained intact, Eisenhower did what he could to cut back on many of them.

Yet the administration could not sustain its conservative intentions and make things work as it wished. Indeed, Eisenhower's attempts to revive the past quickly failed. Private groups welcomed favors, but almost none of them wanted responsibilities. Bipartisan leagues of businessmen, union leaders, and professionals demanded more, not less, money and assistance from Washington. For example, the farm associations were horrified when Eisenhower recommended phasing out their subsidies. Under pressure, the administration revealed that its devotion to free enterprise was more talk than action, and farm groups soon learned that in fact their subsidies would not disappear. To the contrary, in 1956 the administration introduced an additional form of federal support: the soil bank, a government program that paid farmers to remove land from cultivation. Scientifically advanced farmers who could grow more crops on less acreage found the soil bank a bonanza. By the close of Eisenhower's presidency, Republicans no longer repeated their earlier charges that the New Deal had

1956 CAMPAIGN PENNANT
Despite shortcomings as an effective leader, Eisenhower had a warmth and fairness that made him a most popular president.

made farmers dependent upon government handouts.

In other areas as well, the administration had to abandon its original intentions. The president's determination to balance the federal budget and resist interference in the economy foundered on the rock of recession. Eisenhower avoided deficits only three times during his eight years in office, and he ended his term with an annual budget nearly double what Truman's had been in 1950, before the Korean War. When Eisenhower responded to the recession of 1953–54 with a firm asssurance of no more New Deals and a willingness to wait for prosperity's return, he met a fearful nationwide outcry. Reluctantly but realistically, the president reconsidered. By March 1954 the Eisenhower administration had committed itself to protecting the economy with fiscal countermeasures; and, when the recession had passed, the president gave due credit to the "workings of the fiscal system."

A stamp of approval from impeccably conservative Republicans largely ended debate over the government's new approach to economic maintenance. By 1954 substantial majorities in Congress stood ready to support the economy by adjusting taxes and federal spending. The Treasury Department and the Federal Reserve both agreed that they should handle the national debt and regulate interest rates so that credit would expand in a weak economy and contract during inflation. In fact, the secretary of the trea-

sury now ranked with the secretaries of state and defense as a primary government leader. Many people accepted these fiscal techniques because they seemed so neutral. They did not inhibit the stream of favor seeking and favor dispensing that flowed through Washington's busy offices. Liberals could still plan to expand government services, and conservatives could still hope to preserve the government's detachment. For the Invisible Hand that had guided Hoover's cooperative commonwealth in the 1920s, the national government of the 1950s substituted the Barely Visible Hand of fiscal manipulation.

Eisenhower also found himself obliged to agree to other progressive measures that, on entering the White House, he had not intended to support. He approved the extension of Social Security benefits to 10 million more Americans; he backed the creation of the Department of Health, Education, and Welfare; and he agreed to an increase in the minimum wage. After the Soviet Union surprised the world by successfully launching the space satellite *Sputnik* in 1957, Eisenhower supported the National Defense Education Act, which financed student loans and the teaching of science, mathematics, and foreign languages. And at the end of his administration, he signed bills admitting Hawaii and Alaska to the Union.

In practice Eisenhower showed himself to be more a moderate than a staunchly conservative president. Consequently he entered the 1956 campaign for

JIM CROW, 1939
This "colored" entrance to a Deep South movie theater was one element in the rigidly enforced southern system of racial segregation practiced at midcentury.

reelection against Adlai Stevenson with the backing of the broad middle of the American electorate. Running on a platform of "Peace, Progress, and Prosperity," Eisenhower improved on his large popular majority of 1952, now receiving 58 percent of the vote and winning forty-one of the forty-eight states. Congress, however, was another matter. The Democrats retained the control they had won in 1954 over both the House and the Senate; and, for the first time since the election of 1848, a winning presidential candidate lost Congress to the opposing party.

Although Eisenhower maintained considerable popularity throughout his second term, many began to criticize him as a weak leader and to complain of a lost sense of national purpose. In 1958 a scandal broke involving Sherman Adams, and the Democrats increased their margins of control over both houses of Congress. In substantive terms, however, this Democratic dominance made little difference: the congressional session of 1959–60 produced almost no important legislation.

Civil Rights

The affluence and unity of the fifties could not mask underlying strains in American society over inequality and injustice suffered by the country's black citizens.

Throughout the nation—but particularly in the South, where a web of state and local statutes gave legal sanction to the practice—*de facto* segregation denied blacks admission to white schools and equal access to other public places. In restaurants, movie theaters, rest rooms, swimming pools, buses, and trains across the southern United States, blacks were compelled to use separate and almost always inferior facilities.

Opposition by blacks and northern white liberals to segregation had been mounting throughout the 1930s and 1940s, led principally by the NAACP. In 1944 the Swedish sociologist Gunnar Myrdal pricked the nation's conscience in *An American Dilemma*. The book described the country's antiblack prejudice as the one great contradiction to the "American creed," a nationally accepted set of beliefs in equality, opportunity, and justice for everybody. Few successful Americans could deny that segregation was inherently wrong. In their occupational world, distinctions based on skin color had no logical justification, and a rigid structure of Jim Crow drinking fountains and bus seats seemed absurd. In the postwar years, segregation had become an obvious affront to America's modern values. At home, it clashed with the ideal of an open society, in which citizens were free to acquire all the skills they could learn and buy all the goods they could earn. Abroad, it jeopardized America's chances

INTEGRATING LITTLE ROCK CENTRAL HIGH SCHOOL
President Eisenhower's unprecedented use of military power in 1957 did not change the basic pattern of segregation in the southern states.

of bringing people with brown or black or yellow skin into a worldwide anticommunist alliance. Prominent southern liberals, who had generally ignored the race problem before the late forties and early fifties, now gave increasing support to the critics of segregation. By the 1950s nationally minded Americans regarded Jim Crow as an anachronism that a modern society could no longer tolerate.

Legal Remedies.

One of the president's earliest appointments was a new chief justice of the United States Supreme Court. He chose the affable California Republican Earl Warren, who had been an extremely popular governor and the party's vice-presidential candidate in 1948. Warren, a "liberal Republican," was a skilled mediator with no record of interest in social experimentation. He had even participated in the drive to intern Japanese Americans during the Second World War. His appointment seemed to augur a safe, middle-of-the-road Court.

When Warren became chief justice in 1953, the most significant issue pending before the Supreme Court was racial segregation in the public schools. Precedents that challenged the Supreme Court's 1896 doctrine of "separate but equal" educational facilities had been accumulating for more than a decade, but the Court had not reversed itself on this defense of

segregation.* Few observers expected the moderate new chief justice to launch a fresh departure. But in a unanimous decision in *Brown* v. *Board of Education* (1954), the Court boldly declared separate educational facilities inherently unequal and unconstitutional. At a stroke the Court had undercut the entire structure of the Jim Crow laws.

Most Americans considered education an excellent place in which to begin racial desegregation. Because successful Americans based their own careers on specialized skills, they immediately recognized the serious consequences of an inferior education. Moreover, they believed that completely dismantling the caste system would require slow, careful adjustments over many years. If children in integrated schools grew up free of prejudice, these new generations, coming one after another, would eventually eliminate the last traces of racial hate. Time and the power of education lay on the side of progress. In this spirit of optimistic caution, the Supreme Court declared in the second *Brown* decision (1955) that school desegregation should proceed "with all deliberate speed."

During the next decade southern whites threw all manner of legal obstacles in the path of integration,

*For the 1896 *Plessy* v. *Ferguson* decision establishing the "separate but equal" doctrine, see chapter 25, p. 634.

MOBILIZING FOR CIVIL RIGHTS
Eloquence, courage, and ingenuity made Martin Luther King, Jr., an extraordinary public leader. In this 1966 photo he was speaking at the Antioch Baptist Church in Camden, Alabama.

rary. In 1958 and 1959 Faubus further defied the courts by closing Little Rock's high schools, and only another court order, in the fall of 1959, finally produced limited integration. In 1960, five years after the Supreme Court had ordered "all deliberate speed" in desegregating the nation's schools, only about 10 percent of southern school districts had complied.

The prospects were also bleak for southern blacks who wished to exercise the fundamental democratic right to vote. Arbitrary literacy tests and an atmosphere of intimidation kept most of them from the polls. In 1957 Congress took a small step to remove this obvious injustice. Passing the first civil rights law since 1875, Congress authorized federal court action to permit blacks to vote, and it established the Civil Rights Commission to monitor progress. In 1960 Congress went further, empowering the courts to appoint federal referees to protect voting rights, and making it a federal offense to threaten violent resistance to a court order. Despite these measures, however, three-fourths of eligible southern black voters were still unregistered in 1960.

Nonviolent Resistance. As the courts and Congress were promoting the cause of black rights in the fifties, blacks themselves mounted a highly effective campaign in their own behalf. Their movement quickly became identified with the intense, eloquent style of a young minister from Montgomery, Alabama—Martin Luther King, Jr. Not yet twenty-seven years old, he emerged in 1955 as the nationally publicized leader of a local boycott against Montgomery's segregated buses that began when Rosa Parks, a black woman, refused to give up her seat to a white man, as required by law. Through words and example, King provided blacks with a creative combination of the Christian love that their churches taught, the strategy of peaceful mass resistance that Mahatma Gandhi had formulated in India, and the self-discipline that relatively well-to-do blacks had long used to defend their rights in America's own caste system. While King was inspiring his fellow blacks with appeals for nonviolent direct action, he was also attracting wide support among whites who were committed to orderly behavior and peaceful change. Increasingly King was heralded as an American statesman.

In 1960 the Student Non-Violent Coordinating Committee (SNCC), throughout the cities of the South, applied King's tactics in a dramatic wave of "sit-ins" that desegregated numerous restaurants, then a variety of other public accommodations. The following year the Congress on Racial Equality (CORE), another organization of peaceful resistance, sponsored black and white "freedom riders" on a harrowing bus trip into the South that publicized the illegal segregation

ranging from the groundless constitutional doctrine of "state interposition" between the national government and citizens, to the substitution of private segregated schools for the public system. With increasing firmness the federal courts removed each impediment. But in 1957, almost three years after the Supreme Court's initial desegregation decision, there were no integrated classrooms in the Deep South. Finally, in the fall of 1957, a federal court ordered the schools in Little Rock, Arkansas, to begin integrating classes. When the city's Central High School accepted nine black students, Governor Orval Faubus called out the National Guard—ostensibly to prevent violence, but actually to halt integration. A federal judge compelled the withdrawal of the troops, but white mobs kept black students from reaching the school. A reluctant President Eisenhower, who had shown no sympathy for the Court's desegregation ruling and had denounced "extremists on both sides," felt compelled to call in federal troops to enforce the rule of law. Although this action allowed the black students to attend the high school, their attendance was only tempo-

"I HAVE A DREAM . . ."
During the 1963 march on Washington, a moving speech by Martin Luther King, Jr., further inspired participants to battle for landmark civil rights reforms that were enacted into law during the next two years.

in interstate travel. This pillar of Jim Crow also toppled. As in the case of Little Rock, the violent responses to these protests strengthened the bond between white liberals and black moderates. In 1963, when King led a movement against segregation in Birmingham, Alabama, national television vividly recorded the cattle prods, fire hoses, and snarling dogs that local police used to intimidate blacks. Murderers of civil rights activists that year in Birmingham and the next summer in Mississippi could not be prosecuted in the southern courts. King's Southern Christian Leadership Conference (SCLC) and SNCC seemed the embodiment of rationality in contrast to the revived Ku Klux Klan, the raucous rhetoric of local southern politicians, and the partiality of southern white courts.

White sympathy for King's inspired moderation continued to rise until, in the summer of 1963, a quarter-million Americans (including a significant minority of whites) dramatized the plight of the blacks by marching peacefully through Washington and gathering at the Lincoln Memorial. There they heard King's moving message of hope: "I have a dream that one day . . . the sons of former slaves and the sons of former slave-owners will be able to sit together at the table of brotherhood." He foresaw the day when "this nation will rise up and live out the true meaning of its creed: '. . . that all men are created equal.'" Only then would blacks have the redemption promised in a slave song: "Free at last, free at last, thank God Almighty I'm free at last."

The Eisenhower Foreign Policy: Cold War Orthodoxy

In foreign policy as in domestic affairs, the United States presented a new face of national unity and common purpose during the fifties. After the Korean War, no significant group of Americans challenged the basic outlines of the nation's containment policy. Both Republicans and Democrats defined international communism as a worldwide conspiracy directed from Moscow. The United States, they told the nation, must gird for a long, taxing struggle against the enemy. "Forces of good and evil are massed and armed and opposed as rarely before in history," President Eisenhower declared in January 1953. "Freedom is pitted against slavery, lightness against dark." To Secretary

JOHN FOSTER DULLES
Dulles, a steadfast opponent of communism, was the nation's dominant voice on foreign affairs in the fifties.

of State John Foster Dulles, the struggle between the United States and the Soviet Union was "an irreconcilable conflict." Dulles, the administration's dominant voice on foreign policy, was a staunch anticommunist with an evangelical commitment to rescuing peoples everywhere from "godless terrorism."

The Free World. At the start of its first term, the Eisenhower administration tried to answer the two most perplexing questions in America's international affairs. What was the scope of America's anticommunist policy, and what were the best means of implementing it? After several years of hesitation, the government interpreted the words in the Truman Doctrine literally: any nation willing to cooperate with America's worldwide anticommunist policy became a member of the "free world." Some of these nations, such as Great Britain and Canada, were old and trusted democratic friends. Others were recent enemies: West Germany was now preparing to enter NATO; and Japan, with which the United States, over vehement Soviet protests, in 1951 signed a formal peace, was incorporated along with Australia, New Zealand, and the Phil-

ippines in America's expanding scheme of defensive alliances. Some other members of the free world, such as Franco's Spain and South Korea, were authoritarian states. For Dulles, however, the dictatorial government of South Korea was part of "the great design of human freedom." Countries such as India that desired to remain neutral in the Cold War were denounced as indifferent to "human freedom."

Officially, every member of the free world was equally important in America's global policy. The government vowed never to repeat the Truman administration's mistake of announcing that South Korea lay outside the primary American line of defense, thus inviting North Korea's invasion. Viewing the communist camp as one interrelated whole and the free world as another, American policymakers interpreted a weakness in either bloc as the sign of greater changes to come. Free nations were likened to rows of dominoes, where the tipping of one into communism toppled the rest. From these concerns came the cardinal rule that would dominate the next two decades of American foreign policy: the free world must not relinquish a single additional piece of territory. No more Munichs; no more Chinas.

During the fifties, however, the Eisenhower administration went beyond this basic policy and urged the need for the "rollback" of communist power and the "liberation" of "captive" areas from communist control. Containment, a "negative, futile and immoral policy," was now to be replaced by the "contagious, liberating influences which are inherent in freedom." The administration coupled this pronouncement with a "New Look" in America's military program, described as "massive retaliation"—a primary reliance on nuclear weapons rather than conventional forces to meet a possible Soviet attack. Politically, the New Look appealed to the economy-minded, who were promised (in Secretary of Defense Charles Wilson's blunt phrase) "more bang for the buck." Militarily, however, the New Look represented only a slight change of emphasis from ground and naval forces to air and missile power.

The administration did not commit itself to military action to bring about "liberation" and did little to implement a "rollback" policy. Instead, it depended on a more elaborate version of the containment idea: it believed that the mere expression of hope for liberation would alter the mood of captive peoples and lead to the desired result. Yugoslavia's refusal to accept Soviet dictation after 1948, for example, kindled hopes for the liberation of all eastern Europe. But no liberation came.

The Middle East. The Eisenhower administration's central goals in the Middle East were to ensure the survival of the state of Israel, which had been formed in

1948, and to prevent the spread of communist power, especially in Iran. In 1951 the Iranian government, led by its intensely nationalistic prime minister, Dr. Muhammad Mossadegh, had nationalized the country's British-controlled oil industry. Fearful that Mossadegh might turn his country into a communist satellite, Eisenhower in 1953 approved a CIA plan to replace the prime minister with a more "reliable" ruler. In a cloak-and-dagger operation that the president later described as "more like a dime novel than an historical fact," the United States government secretly supported a successful coup against Mossadegh by the Iranian shah, Muhammad Reza Pahlevi. Unable to distinguish between Marxism-Leninism and militant nationalism in a country emerging from Western domination, the administration prided itself on having "saved Iran from communism."

A similar misinterpretation influenced the president's policies toward Egypt and Lebanon. In 1955, after President Gamal Abdel Nasser of Egypt arranged to buy arms from Moscow, the United States offered to help Nasser finance the building of the Aswan Dam, Egypt's highest economic priority at the time. But on reconsideration, the administration canceled the deal in 1956. "Do nations which play both sides get better treatment than nations which are stalwart and work with us?" Dulles asked.

The cancellation led to the Suez crisis in the fall of 1956. After Washington withdrew its offer of aid, Nasser nationalized the canal, on which Western countries depended for an uninterrupted flow of oil. Britain and France then joined Israel in an attack on Egypt. Eisenhower, who had not been informed of the attack in advance, feared that it would drive Egypt and other Arab states into the communist camp, and he pressed his allies into withdrawing from Egypt, which they did. At the same time, however, he worried that withdrawal would leave a vacuum for the Soviets to fill. As a preventive measure, he enunciated the Eisenhower Doctrine in January 1957: warning that Russia, under czars and Bolsheviks alike, had "long sought to dominate the Middle East," he asked Congress to approve economic and military assistance to Middle Eastern nations struggling to protect their independence. The president also requested permission to use American military power to defend those countries against "overt armed aggression from any nation controlled by International communism."

Eisenhower gave substance to his doctrine in the following year, when a coup toppled the pro-Western government in Iraq, and another pro-Western regime in Lebanon seemed vulnerable. Sending American forces into Lebanon in the summer of 1958, Eisenhower compared the situation to earlier ones in Greece, Czechoslovakia, China, and South Korea. The next year the United States fostered a Middle Eastern anti-Soviet alliance, CENTO. But not a single Arab state joined it.* Although critics of the president's policy complained that Arab nationalism, not Soviet communism, was the major problem, Congress followed his lead and supported the landing of troops in Lebanon. "America has either one voice or none," the Democratic Speaker of the House announced, "and that voice is the voice of the President—whether everybody agrees with him or not."

Brinkmanship in Asia. Although the Eisenhower administration warned of stronger action in response to the Asian crises it faced, the net result was much the same as in the Middle East. The United States government attempted no massive retaliation when a communist takeover loomed in northern Vietnam and when a Chinese communist offensive menaced the Chinese offshore islands of Quemoy and Matsu. Instead, the administration limited itself to actions that were calculated to narrow rather than broaden these conflicts.

In 1954, when French forces trying to maintain colonial rule in Vietnam faced a decisive defeat in a seven-year-old war against the Vietminh (the communist-dominated Vietnamese league for national independence), the American government confronted a difficult choice. Should it take military action? If so, should it strike with a tactical (that is, a small) nuclear bomb? Or should it avoid intervention and risk the loss of all Southeast Asia to communism? Although Eisenhower feared that a communist victory in Vietnam would set off a chain reaction that would topple one Southeast Asian country after another, he decided against intervention. It would, he believed, be a poor military gamble, and it might split America and its allies. Instead, the administration threw its support behind a pro-Western South Vietnamese government headed by Ngo Dinh Diem, a Catholic with strong American ties. At the same time, Dulles negotiated an alliance, the South East Asia Treaty Organization (SEATO), uniting France, Great Britain, the United States, Australia, New Zealand, Pakistan, the Philippines, and Thailand. But SEATO was more shadow than substance. Lacking automatic provisions for collective military resistance to aggression, the treaty created little more than a symbolic coalition of "free world" states. In backing the Diem government and engineering the treaty, the administration acted in a style more reminiscent of Truman's containment policy than of anything resembling "liberation" or massive retaliation.

The same was true of the Eisenhower administration's dealings with the two Chinas. Eisenhower had begun his term by reversing Truman's policy; no

*The members of CENTO were Great Britain, Iran, Pakistan, and Turkey.

"Don't Be Afraid—I Can Always Pull You Back"

Herbert Block, Herblock's Special for Today (Simon and Schuster, 1958)

"BRINKMANSHIP"

John Foster Dulles emphasized taking risks for freedom and peace by confronting the communist challenge all over the globe.

longer would the United States hold Chiang Kai-shek back from an offensive against the mainland and from answering communist artillery attacks on Nationalist-controlled offshore islands. But the president soon backed away from this policy, and Chiang was never "unleashed." In 1958, when another crisis erupted over the tiny offshore islands of Quemoy and Matsu, the administration made an about-face. Initially declaring themselves ready to meet any attack on the islands, Eisenhower and Dulles quickly moved to rein in Chiang and denied any intention of using "even tactical atomic weapons in a limited operation."

A confused American public took little comfort in Dulles's description of what journalists began to call "brinkmanship." "You have to take chances for peace," Dulles declared. ". . . Some say that we were brought to the verge of war. Of course we were brought to the verge of war. The ability to get to the verge of war without getting into the war is the necessary art. If you cannot master it, you inevitably get into wars. . . . If you are scared to go to the brink, you are lost." The administration's rhetoric and behavior in response to Asian problems demonstrated a combination of bluster and good sense. Further, all the talk of "liberation" and "massive retaliation" told more about the American mood in the fifties than about what the country intended to do abroad. Believing itself locked in an apocalyptic struggle against communism, the nation saw no room for dissent at home, and it called for an anticommunist crusade abroad. But when America confronted the reality that such action would risk a nuclear exchange, it reverted to the more judicious containment policy initiated in the Truman years.

Latin America. In Latin America, where geographical proximity allowed the United States to assert itself more forcefully, the Eisenhower administration gave freer expression to its anticommunist stance, particularly in the case of Guatemala. A democratically elected reform government under Jacobo Arbenz ruled the country in 1953. But because Arbenz had accepted some communists into his government and had expropriated idle lands owned by the American-controlled United Fruit Company, he came under attack from the Eisenhower administration as a tool of the worldwide Soviet communist conspiracy. Arbenz, Eisenhower believed, "was merely a puppet manipulated by communists."

Convinced that the Arbenz regime was a radical government that represented a threat to American security, President Eisenhower authorized the CIA to help oust Arbenz. Using the fact that Guatemala had accepted arms from Czechoslovakia, a Soviet satellite, and that the Guatemalan government had suspended civil liberties to prevent the CIA-planned coup, the Eisenhower administration in June 1954 aided an exiled Guatemalan army officer, who was operating from Honduras, to overturn the Arbenz government. Eisenhower and Dulles were convinced that the change of governments had "averted a Soviet beachhead in our hemisphere" and had little compunction about denying the American role in the coup. But, as columnist Harrison E. Salisbury subsequently wrote, the coup "was conceived by men who did not understand what was happening in Guatemala, who did not understand the nature of Latin America and its problems and who had no understanding of the consequences of the events they set in motion."

The Guatemalan coup, coupled with the administration's overt support of right-wing dictators in other Latin countries, aroused intense antagonism to the United States throughout the hemisphere. During a 1958 trip to eight Latin American countries, Vice-President Richard Nixon encountered a fierce outpouring of anti-Americanism, including an attack on his car in Caracas, Venezuela, that jeopardized his life. Instead of recognizing this hostility as a reaction to their indiscriminate support of anticommunist dictators, Eisenhower and Nixon believed that it confirmed the existence of an international communist conspiracy. The president described the hemisphere-wide anti-Americanism as part of "a pattern around the world—in Burma, in Jakarta, in South America, other places—that looks like there is some kind of concerted idea and plan. . . ." "The clear truth," Eisenhower said, is that "the threat of communism in Latin America is greater than ever before."

Nothing tended to confirm this belief more for the administration than events in Cuba. At the beginning of 1959, the victorious rebel leader, Fidel Castro, determined to end Cuban dependence on the United States, replaced Fulgencio Batista's right-wing military regime with a revolutionary government. Relying on American investments and markets for its economic survival, Cuba had essentially been an economic extension of the United States. American influence on the island had been so great, the United States representative to the country observed in 1960, that "the American ambassador was the second most influential man in Cuba; sometimes even more important than the president." Although Castro had initiated some overtures toward accommodation with the United States, his determined efforts in 1959 to break America's economic stranglehold made him seem another agent of the Soviet-communist drive for world power. When, in fact, Castro tied himself to Moscow in 1959–60 by increasing trade with the Soviet bloc fortyfold, the Eisenhower administration ordered the CIA to plot the overthrow of Castro's regime. This design was not acted upon until Eisenhower's successor, John F. Kennedy, took office in 1961.

The Limits of Orthodoxy. Despite Eisenhower's and Dulles's conviction that Soviet-American differences caused an irreconcilable conflict—one in which the United States must defeat the communist drive for world power—the realities of international affairs forced them into seeking an accommodation with the USSR. Above all, they found themselves compelled to respond to Soviet proposals for negotiations.

After Stalin died in March 1953, Russia's new leaders declared their desire for "peaceful coexistence" and their conviction that all unresolved questions between the two superpowers could be "settled peacefully by mutual agreement of the interested countries. . . ." Eager to head off the rearming of West Germany, the Soviets asked for direct talks between the Russian and American heads of state. Moreover, when Eisenhower called for Soviet demonstrations of good intentions as a prelude to meeting, Moscow responded by agreeing to a peace treaty with Austria making that nation a neutral buffer zone in the Cold War. The Soviet government also advanced a substantive proposal for arms limitations. The fact that the Soviets had followed America's lead in developing the H-bomb had convinced Eisenhower that "there is just no real alternative to peace" and that a summit meeting would have to be tried.

The two sides did meet in a summit conference at

Dwight D. Eisenhower Library

CLOSING THE MISSILE GAP
Soviet success in testing intercontinental ballistic missiles (ICBMs) touched off American efforts to close the so-called missile gap. Here, physicist Werner von Braun explains the Saturn missile to President Eisenhower.

Geneva, Switzerland, in July 1955; but they could not reach agreement on the two most important issues of the time, Germany and arms control. The United States proposed German unification "under conditions which will neither 'neutralize' nor 'demilitarize' united Germany, nor subtract it from NATO"; the Soviet Union rejected unification for Germany unless that nation was detached from "the military groupings of the Western powers." As to arms control, the Soviets wanted no part of an Eisenhower proposal called "open skies." An exchange of military plans and frequent aerial inspections by both sides to prevent surprise nuclear attacks, Eisenhower believed, "would undoubtedly benefit us more than the Russians," because the United States knew less about Soviet installations than vice-versa. Soviet Premier Nikita Khrushchev denounced "open skies" as "a very transparent espionage device," and the proposal came to nothing. But although the meeting in Switzerland produced no specific agreements, it did create what commentators called the "spirit of Geneva"—less fear and greater willingness to talk on both sides.

PRESIDENT EISENHOWER AND SOVIET PREMIER NIKITA KHRUSHCHEV, WASHINGTON, 1959
In foreign affairs Eisenhower, the military hero, commanded widespread American support as an effective defender of the national interest.

Still, tensions between the two superpowers remained high. In 1956, after Khrushchev denounced Stalin's crimes at the Twentieth Communist Party Congress and called for greater diversity in the communist bloc, the Poles and Hungarians rebelled against Moscow. A more independent-minded communist leader, Wladyslaw Gomulka, came to power in Warsaw and with considerable difficulty managed to placate his intensely anti-Russian people while staving off Soviet intervention. More rashly, a new Hungarian government declared its intention of withdrawing from the Warsaw Pact, the alliance of eastern European nations with Moscow. To prevent the collapse of their hold on Hungary—and perhaps on eastern Europe generally—the Soviets sent tanks and troops into that nation. Although the Eisenhower administration refused to intervene, it condemned this fresh demonstration of Soviet contempt for freedom and national sovereignty and reiterated the difficulty of reaching accommodation with the USSR.

A successful Soviet test of an intercontinental ballistic missile (ICBM) and the series of *Sputnik* launches beginning in 1957 dealt heavy blows to American self-confidence—and to conservative complacency about the nation's superiority in military power and space technology. Demands multiplied for upgrading American education. These concerns, coupled with the onset of a recession in 1958 and with Khrushchev's boasts about the rapidly growing Soviet economy "overtaking" its capitalist rival, led many Americans to worry about the prospect of being "buried" by the Soviet Union.

For Eisenhower, the need to avoid war with the Soviet Union remained so high a priority that he agreed to further face-to-face discussions with Khrushchev in 1959 and 1960. In September 1959 the folksy Soviet premier barnstormed across the United States on an official visit, and his candid private talk with Eisenhower about Soviet-American differences at the president's Maryland retreat created what Khrushchev called "the spirit of Camp David." One consequence of this improved mood was an agreement to hold a summit meeting in Paris in May 1960. But two weeks before the conference was to begin, an American U-2 spy plane was shot down 1,200 miles inside the Soviet Union. Acknowledging that he had approved the mission, Eisenhower said that he felt it better to drop the "false cloak of camaraderie" and confront the sharp differences between the two sides. The Russians denounced him; the conference was

KENNEDY FOR PRESIDENT
This broadside for Kennedy in the 1960 presidential campaign emphasizes the need for stronger leadership in the contest with communism. Making a campaign issue of the lost sense of purpose under Eisenhower, Kennedy also promised to get "the country moving again."

aborted; and Khrushchev declared that he would no longer deal with Eisenhower but instead would wait for his successor.

The Election of 1960. As long as the widely popular Eisenhower remained in the White House, for many Americans no one else seemed important as a national leader. Had Eisenhower been able to run for a third term, he probably would have won. But he was barred from running by the Twenty-Second Amendment, adopted in 1951; and Vice-President Nixon, who seemed the president's logical successor, became the Republican candidate. Sensing the need for a new figure to replace Adlai Stevenson, who had twice failed to win the White House, the Democrats chose the youthful-looking forty-three-year-old senator John F. Kennedy from Massachusetts. A well-organized and liberally financed primary campaign had given him a considerable edge over his competitors.

Both candidates came to the 1960 presidential campaign with handicaps. Nixon's history of red-baiting and his reputation of insincerity burdened him with a negative public impression that he felt compelled to refute. But his attempt during the campaign to appear as the experienced, judicious leader who had abandoned old habits and was ready for higher office partly backfired. Critics complained about the manipulation of his image and wondered "whether there is anything that might be called the 'real' Nixon, new or old."

Kennedy also had problems convincing the public that he was well suited for the White House. Numerous Protestant voters distrusted him as a Roman Catholic, and his political cautiousness during his senatorial career had caused many to doubt his capacity for independent judgment. During the campaign, however, he generally overcame these earlier impressions by forthrightly supporting the separation of church and state and by boldly appealing for a renewed sense of national purpose, for "getting the country moving again" after *Sputnik* and the 1958 recession. Moreover, his effective performance in four televised debates with Nixon added to the picture of a self-confident, dynamic candidate worthy of the highest office. Further aided by Lyndon B. Johnson of Texas, his vice-presidential running mate who helped balance the ticket, Kennedy won by the narrowest popular margin—two-tenths of one percent—of any winning candidate since James A. Garfield in 1880. Although the Democrats maintained control of Con-

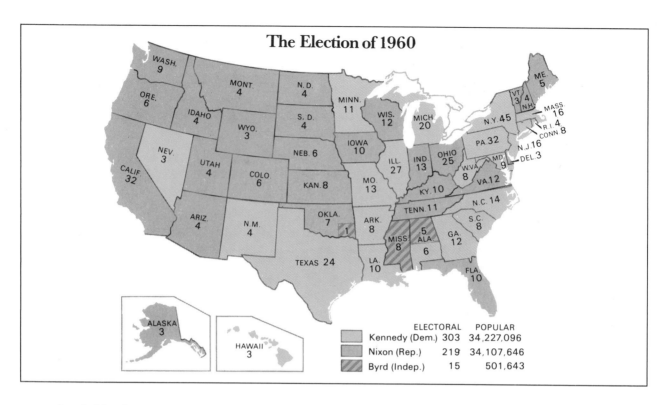

The Election of 1960

	ELECTORAL	POPULAR
Kennedy (Dem.)	303	34,227,096
Nixon (Rep.)	219	34,107,646
Byrd (Indep.)	15	501,643

gress, they held only a twenty-two seat margin in the House and a two-seat advantage in the Senate.

The Eisenhower Legacy

During Eisenhower's eight years in the White House, the meaning of the presidency had changed in two important respects. First, the office was separated from the normal patterns of electoral politics. Beginning with Eisenhower's triumph in 1952, the vote for president no longer followed the same curve as the nationwide vote for other Democratic and Republican candidates. Franklin Roosevelt's rising and falling majorities had roughly paralleled the majorities of the Democratic party. Even Harry Truman's surprising victory in 1948 had coincided with a similar Democratic revival. After 1952, however, the presidential vote set a course of its own. In 1954 the Democrats had recaptured both houses of Congress and continued to hold them, usually by substantial majorities. By contrast to this steady, partisan line, the presidential returns from election to election swung in big loops that expressed the public's specific choices between candidates.

As Americans detached their president from normal party politics, they were developing a new relation with him that had relatively little to do with the electoral process. Its crucial components were television and national opinion polls. The president spoke

directly to all the people through television; they responded directly to him through opinion polls.

A presidential election was merely the most formal and dramatic moment in a continuous dialogue. Between elections, a string of opinion polls charted results that were widely interpreted as substitute elections, measuring the success of the nation's leader. Any overwhelming endorsement of the president, such as Eisenhower's runaway victories in the 1952 and 1956 elections, became a sign of national strength. By the same token, a sharp drop in Truman's ratings during 1951 and 1952 signaled a severe national problem. Americans, in other words, made their month-by-month judgments of the president into a bedside graph of America's health.

The second significant change in the presidency involved the requirements for effective national leadership. The complex nature of the president's tasks forced him to act as a mobilizing leader for the whole nation and, at the same time, as a cautious manager of America's intricate foreign and domestic affairs. As early as the 1930s, Roosevelt had understood the need to be both inspiring and moderate. FDR, however, served during a bitterly partisan period when no one could hope to transcend parties and represent all the people. Moreover, his leadership was identified not with steady management, but with great emergencies: depression, then war. Truman was the last of the openly partisan presidents.

Eisenhower was the first to meet the modern demands on the president. The general's background allowed him to appear a man above the clamor of special interests. Each landmark in his military career—wartime commander of the Allied armies of Europe, chief of staff, and commander of NATO's forces—suggested the highest level of nonpartisanship. Even as president, Eisenhower liked to think of himself as a nonpartisan leader. He projected an instinctive fairness that promised to reunite the nation after the harsh years of Truman and McCarthy. Although his temper and tongue could match Truman's, Eisenhower was more restrained in public. Eisenhower never mastered the art of a formal television speech, but he was irresistibly attractive in casual shots. His incomparable smile, strong stride, and easy yet authoritative manner made him everybody's Ike. In a special sense, Eisenhower seemed able to speak to all Americans at home and speak for them abroad.

Eisenhower strengthened his position as national leader by delegating much of the controversial work of his administration. While his secretary of state used the militant language of the Cold War, the president spoke in a moderate, conciliatory tone. The world identified Dulles with "brinkmanship." It identified Eisenhower with "Atoms for Peace," a program to share America's scientific knowledge that the president first proposed in 1953 and then elaborated in 1955. In election years Eisenhower relied almost always on broad, bland pronouncements. Vice-President Richard Nixon was the administration's partisan voice, and every two years he flayed the Democrats with rawhide campaign rhetoric.

Much of this was by design. Although Eisenhower had a reputation as being above politics, he was, in fact, a more adept politician than his contemporaries understood. There is no better demonstration of Eisenhower's nonpartisan leadership than his last presidential address, warning the country against "the acquisition of unwarranted influence, whether sought or unsought, by the military-industrial complex."

Yet if Eisenhower re-created a sense of national unity and made important contributions to the office of the presidency, he also left a legacy of unsolved problems that have troubled his successors. In presiding over a consumer society devoted to indulging personal desires, he did little to address enduring public needs. America's "private opulence," Adlai Stevenson said, was matched by its "public squalor." Largely ignoring the suffering of poor Americans, urban blight, and unfilled promises of equal rights for all citizens, Eisenhower did little to advance the causes of economic and social justice and of civil rights. Likewise, although he refrained from direct challenges to the Soviets or from other actions in the developing world that might have involved the United States in combat, he clung to a Cold War orthodoxy that sustained, and at times intensified, Soviet-American differences and preparations for war.

CHRONOLOGY

1953 Department of Health, Education, and Welfare formed.

Submerged Lands Act.

1954 Atomic Energy Act subsidizes private development of nuclear energy.

Brown v. *Board of Education* outlaws segregation of schools.

1955 Formosa Resolution authorizes president to protect Taiwan.

South East Asia Treaty Organization (SEATO) formed.

Summit meeting at Geneva among leaders of the United States, Soviet Union, and Great Britain.

Merger of AFL and CIO, with George Meany as president.

1956 Federal Highway Act authorizes building of superhighways.

Suez crisis.

Hungarian uprising.

Eisenhower reelected president.

1957 Eisenhower Doctrine for the Middle East.

Federal troops enforce school desegregation in Little Rock, Arkansas.

First civil rights law since 1875.

Soviet Union launches *Sputnik*.

1958 National Defense Education Act.

American intervention in Lebanon.

1959 U.S. encourages formation of CENTO by Middle Eastern allies.

Castro comes to power in Cuba.

1960 U-2 incident.

John F. Kennedy elected president.

SUGGESTED READINGS

William E. Leuchtenburg, *A Troubled Feast: American Society Since 1945* (rev. ed., 1979), is a lively introduction to the postwar years. The confidence of the 1950s glows from *U.S.A., the Permanent Revolution* (1951) by the editors of *Fortune*, and from *The Big Change* (1952) by Frederick Lewis Allen. From a more critical perspective, the following help in assessing the political economy. E. L. Dale, *Conservatives in Power* (1960), and Harold G. Vatter, *The U.S. Economy in the 1950s* (1963), offer an overview. C. Wright Mills, *The Power Elite* (1956), explores what later came to be called the military-industrial complex. Grant McConnell, *Private Power and American Democracy* (1966), and Theodore J. Lowi, *The End of Liberalism* (1969), analyze the dangers to the public interest from pressure-group politics. John Kenneth Galbraith, *The New Industrial State* (1967), examines the influence of corporate managers in national economic policy, and Harry Braverman, *Labor and Monopoly Capital* (1974), surveys the influence of the corporate system on the working lives of its employees. John Kendrick's *Productivity Trends in the United States* (1961) and *United States Fiscal Policy, 1945–1959* (1961), and Herbert Stein's *The Fiscal Revolution in America* (1969), are useful specialized works. Michael Harrington, *The Other America* (1962), discusses poverty in the United States. The ferment in values after the Second World War has yet to find a historian. Something of the concern for the individual is communicated in two important sociological studies: David Riesman et al., *The Lonely Crowd: A Study of the Changing American Character* (1950), and C. Wright Mills, *White Collar: The American Middle Class* (1951). Also see William H. Whyte, *The Organization Man* (1956). Alexander Meiklejohn, *Free Speech and Its Relation to Self-Government* (1948), and Hans J. Morgenthau, *In Defense of the National Interest* (1951), illustrate the demand for fixed values. Also see Carl L. Becker, *Freedom and Responsibility in the American Way of Life* (1945). Robert M. Hutchins, *The Conflict in Education in a Democratic Society* (1953), and Arthur E. Bestor, Jr., *Educational Wastelands: The Retreat from Learning in Our Public Schools* (1953), discuss the place of fundamentals in education. The new tough-minded approach to social values is revealed in Arthur M. Schlesinger, Jr., *The Vital Center* (1949), Max Ascoli, *The Power of Freedom* (1949), and Reinhold Niebuhr, *The Irony of American History* (1952). For mass culture in the fifties, see Bernard Rosenberg and D. M. White, eds., *Mass Culture* (1957), and Eric Larrabee and Rolf Meyersohn, eds., *Mass Leisure* (1958).

The history of politics during the confident years focuses largely on the presidency. Herbert S. Parmet, *Eisenhower and the American Crusades* (1972), is a good general account of the Eisenhower presidency. Charles C. Alexander, *Holding the Line: The Eisenhower Era, 1952–1961* (1975), and Peter Lyon, *Eisenhower* (1974), cover the general's two terms. Marquis W. Childs, *Eisenhower: Captive Hero* (1958), gives valuable background. See also Sherman Adams, *Firsthand Report* (1961), the memoir by Eisenhower's primary domestic aide. Recent books on Eisenhower emphasizing his effective leadership include William Bragg Ewald, Jr., *Eisenhower the President: Crucial Days: 1951–1960* (1981), and Fred I. Greenstein, *The Hidden-Hand Presidency: Eisenhower as Leader* (1982). *The Life of Adlai E. Stevenson* (1976–77), a two-volume biography by John Bartlow Martin, sympathetically examines the hero of the liberals who twice lost to Eisenhower. Theodore H. White's *The Making of the President, 1960* (1961) includes shrewd observations on Nixon's losing campaign. In a deceptively entitled study, *The Revolt of the Moderates* (1956), Samuel Lubell explains moderate voting behavior that affected presidential politics.

Donald R. Matthews, *U.S. Senators and Their World* (1960), and William S. White, *Citadel: The Story of the U.S. Senate* (1957), contain interesting material on another center of political power. John D. Weaver, *Warren* (1967), and Leo Katcher, *Earl Warren* (1967), praise the controversial chief justice, and Milton R. Konvitz, *Expanding Liberties* (1966), evaluates some of the Warren Court's important decisions. How the national government has affected modern urban affairs is analyzed in Mark I. Gelfand, *A Nation of Cities* (1975). A crucial new political bloc is examined in Robert Gilpin and Christopher Wright, eds., *Scientists and National Policy-Making* (1964), and Don K. Price, *The Scientific Estate* (1965).

The hopes and concerns of the civil rights movement are revealed in Martin Luther King, Jr., *Why We Can't Wait* (1964); Stephen B. Oates, *Let the Trumpet Sound: The Life of Martin Luther King* (1982); Clayborne Carson, *In Struggle: SNCC and the Black Awakening of the 1960s* (1981); and two studies in public opinion by William Brink and Louis Harris—*The Negro Revolution in America* (1964) and *Black and White* (1967). Carl M. Brauer, *John F. Kennedy and the Second Reconstruction* (1977), analyzes a critical juncture in the movement. For background, see the first volume of Harvard Sitkoff's *A New Deal for Blacks: The Emergence of Civil Rights as a National Issue* (1978) and Charles F. Kellogg's *NAACP* (1967). For the beginnings of passive resistance, see William H. Chafe, *Civilities and Civil Rights* (1980). The sources of black militancy emerge from *The Autobiography of Malcolm X* (1965), Charles V. Hamilton and Stokely Carmichael, *Black Power* (1967), Eldridge Cleaver, *Soul on Ice* (1968), and James Forman, *The Making of Black Revolutionaries* (1972). Claude Brown's *Manchild in the Promised Land* (1965) is an eloquent statement on life and survival in the ghetto. On the travail of civil rights leaders, see David L. Lewis, *King: A Critical Biography* (1970), and August Meier and Elliott Rudwick, *CORE* (1973), the account of an organization transformed by the sweep of events. *Report of the National Advisory Commission on Civil Disorders* (1968) and Robert M. Fogelson, *Violence as Protest* (1971), reflect the complexity that came to surround the issue of black rights.

John W. Spanier, *American Foreign Policy Since World War II* (rev. ed., 1973), is a clear, largely favorable summary. For a more critical account focusing on domestic forces, see Robert Dallek, *The American Style of Foreign Policy: Cultural Politics and Foreign Affairs* (1983). A positive picture of Eisenhower's leadership is presented in Robert A. Divine, *Eisenhower and the Cold War* (1981). On the internationalization of American business, see Raymond Vernon, *Sovereignty at Bay: The Multinational Spread of U.S. Enterprise* (1971), and Mira Wilkins, *The Maturing of Multinational Enterprise: American Business Abroad from 1914 to 1970* (1974). In *The Politics of Oil*, Robert Engler examines some effects of internationalization. Paul Y. Hammond, *Organizing for Defense* (1961), discusses the place of the military in twentieth-century America. Maxwell D. Taylor, *The Uncertain Trumpet* (1960), is a prominent general's critical appraisal of the Eisenhower years that influenced the Kennedy administration; Richard A. Aliano, *American Defense Policy from Eisenhower to Kennedy* (1975), sides with Eisenhower. The sources and consequences of America's military foreign policy are explored in Richard J. Barnet, *Roots of War* (1972), and Alexander L. George and Richard Smoke, *Deterrence in American Foreign Policy* (1974).

Michael A. Guhin, *John Foster Dulles* (1972), praises one architect of American foreign policy for his flexibility, and Herman Finer, *Dulles over Suez* (1964), gives a detailed account of the international furor that the secretary of state raised in 1956 and 1957. For a critical appraisal of Dulles's leadership, see Townsend Hoopes, *The Devil and John Foster Dulles* (1973). A dangerous issue that spanned the Eisenhower and Kennedy administrations is examined in Jack M. Schick, *The Berlin Crisis, 1958–1962* (1971). Other books focusing on regional issues or American relations with specific countries are Barry Rubin, *Paved with Good Intentions: The American Experience and Iran* (1980); George McTurnan Kahin and John W. Lewis, *The United States in Vietnam* (rev. ed., 1969); and Stephen Schlesinger and Stephen Kinzer, *Bitter Fruit: The Untold Story of the American Coup in Guatemala* (1982).

32 The Modern Republic in Turmoil: The Sixties

The 1960s were tumultuous years for Americans. But the decade began with little indication of what was in store for the country. Although during his presidential campaign John F. Kennedy had summoned the nation to seek a "New Frontier," few commentators at the time had expected that his presidency would lead to important changes in American life. Having gained the White House by a narrow margin, the new president was confronted with a Congress dominated by conservative Democrats, and he had little room to maneuver. Moreover, many liberals doubted that Kennedy would be a strong leader. His cautiousness as a senator, especially in dealing with Joseph McCarthy, made them suspect that the theme of his book *Profiles in Courage* did not extend to the author, a man who had shown more profile than courage.

But before he was assassinated in November 1963, Kennedy had lifted the nation's spirits with his stirring rhetoric and dynamic style, and he was moving toward achieving major domestic reforms. These came to fruition under his successor, Lyndon Johnson, who provided the leadership for the greatest burst of innovative legislation since Franklin Roosevelt's New Deal. In an ironic turn of events, Johnson, a Southerner, presided over the boldest advances in civil rights since Reconstruction.

Stumbling actions abroad, however, eclipsed the forward movement at home. Problems in Latin America and a widening war in Vietnam cast a shadow over the Kennedy and Johnson presidencies by blighting America's reputation overseas and provoking turmoil in the United States. A counterculture of rebellious young Americans rejecting the accepted social norms, and a fierce opposition to the fighting in Vietnam, raised doubts about the country's domestic stability and its capacity to sustain traditional democratic customs. The role of the national government, the institution of the presidency, conventional habits of hard work and deference, and the national sense of cohe-siveness were all called into question by the crosscurrents of the 1960s. The nation's political leaders, who had been closely in touch with the mood of the country in the fifties, could not grasp what had gone wrong; and at the end of the sixties, it was still not clear that they would be able to surmount the crisis.

Kennedy's New Frontier

From his first day in office, Kennedy encouraged a fresh sense of hope in the nation. By the end of the Eisenhower years, many Americans had mourned a loss of national energy, symbolized by the sluggish economy and by embarrassment over the Soviets' *Sputnik* achievement and the U-2 episode. As the youngest elected president in American history, Kennedy at forty-three radiated vigor. His inaugural address was a summons to action and bold deeds.

Let the word go forth from this time and place, to friend and foe alike, that the torch has been passed to a new generation of Americans . . . unwilling to witness or permit the slow undoing of those human rights to which this Nation has always been committed.

Calling for "a struggle against the common enemies of man: tyranny, poverty, disease and war," he urged his "fellow Americans" to "ask not what your country can do for you—ask what you can do for your country." The "New Frontier," the name he had given to his program, described "not what I intend to offer the American people, but what I intend to ask of them."

By sponsoring a wide assortment of studies and reports, the new president imaginatively associated his office with broad national goals. Challenged by the Soviets in space, Kennedy promised to place a man on the moon before 1970, an objective that Americans of all kinds and ages would regard as a truly national enterprise. The organization of the Peace Corps in 1961, through which American volunteers took their

814

HUMANIZING THE WHITE HOUSE
Through his family as well as his presidential style, John Kennedy sent sparks of vitality and hope across the country. In 1962, five-year-old Caroline and two-year-old John, Jr., dance to their father's clapping.

skills to the world's poor nations, had a comparable appeal. Appropriate to his administration's image of youthful adventure, Kennedy appointed an extraordinary group of young men to high office, including his thirty-five-year-old brother, Robert, as attorney general.

The trim, handsome Kennedy made a striking appearance on television, as he had already demonstrated in his televised debates with Nixon during the 1960 campaign. As president, Kennedy continued to excel in both formal and informal uses of the medium. At home and abroad, he gained a reputation as a leader who was as comfortable with poetry as with power, and as one who was sensitive to the nuances of style. "In a single short speech at the University of Wisconsin in 1959," one commentator on the president's "style" notes, "Kennedy had quoted Goethe, Emerson, Swift, Faulkner, Tennyson, Woodrow Wilson, Lord Asquith, Artemus Ward, Finley Peter Dunne, and Queen Victoria. . . ." Kennedy's style became an object of international discussion, and "some even fancied that they saw in the White House circle the Arthurian idyll of Camelot." At times, his private affairs seemed to loom larger across the nation than his public actions. Through the eager cooperation of the news industry, the president and his stunningly attractive, photogenic family entered everybody's lives: Jack and his wife, Jackie; their children, Caroline and John Jr.; the president's brother, Bobby; and the rest of the vibrant Kennedy clan.

Limits of the New Frontier: The Domestic Record. What were the domestic consequences of Kennedy's presidency? The record is mixed. Kennedy's advocacy of the New Frontier and of the need to get the country moving again turned out to be more rhetoric than substance. Initially, the president spoke forcefully and persuasively about social programs that would ease the plight of the poor and the disadvantaged. But the administration's plans for Medicare, civil rights, tax reform, and federal aid to education and the cities through a department of urban affairs came to little. The conservative coalition of southern Democrats and Republicans that dominated Congress repeatedly blocked the passage of Kennedy's liberal reforms. Recognizing that he could have little impact on Congress, Kennedy thought it pointless to put "the office of the President on the line . . . and then be . . . defeated." To disgruntled liberals, Kennedy was continuing the same old "moderation" that they had seen under Eisenhower. Americans for Democratic Action, representing the most liberal wing of the Democratic party, concluded that Kennedy's actions "varied little from

LYNDON JOHNSON, ROBERT KENNEDY, AND JOHN KENNEDY
Three of America's most dynamic political leaders in the postwar era, these men served the nation in a time of extraordinary upheaval and change.

the formula developed when the Republican party controlled the White House. It is a formula of accommodation and compromise with the same coalition of Southerners and Republicans."

Yet despite a conservative Congress, and despite Kennedy's cautiousness, his administration ultimately managed to lead the legislature into passing some significant reforms—largely the consequence of the president's successful fight to break the conservative hold on the all-important House Rules Committee. The way was opened to the Trade Expansion Act of 1962, a law that, through the reduction of tariffs on goods exchanged between the United States and its major European trading partners, led to increased commerce and greater prosperity for both sides. The administration also had success in persuading Congress to raise the minimum wage, to approve a controversial day-care bill to aid working mothers, to expand Social Security benefits, and to increase public-works spending in impoverished areas like Appalachia.

Kennedy's greatest domestic achievements came in his management of the economy. To overcome a 7 percent unemployment rate inherited from the Eisenhower administration, he signed a number of con-

gressional bills that would promote economic expansion. These measures provided for investment tax credits, greater depreciation allowances, and increased government spending. He also fought to hold down price increases, issuing wage-price guidelines to which business and labor generally adhered; when U. S. Steel raised prices in April 1962 after its workers had agreed to a noninflationary contract, for example, Kennedy pressured the company into a turnabout. His economic policies produced an average annual GNP growth rate of 5.6 percent, a 1.3 percent inflation rate, and a reduction of unemployment from 7 percent to 5 percent. More important, he proposed a general tax reduction in 1963. A multibillion-dollar tax cut, he argued, would lead to greater consumer spending and business investment—and, in turn, to noninflationary economic expansion, more jobs, and greater prosperity for all. After its enactment in 1964, the tax cut produced just these results. "In economic management," wrote Arthur Schlesinger, Jr., the historian and Kennedy aide, "Kennedy was a most effective president." Where FDR and Truman had feared unbalanced budgets and deficit spending, Kennedy had acted boldly, initiating the first *deliberate* use of fiscal policy to spark and sustain an economic recovery. And the experiment worked: the economy boomed for the rest of the sixties, providing the foundation for the wide range of reform legislation enacted under his successor.

Further Limits: Civil Rights.

Kennedy's record on civil rights was also mixed. Despite the Democratic platform's strongest civil rights pledges in history, civil rights activists accused Kennedy of being "supercautious" about implementing them. During his first two years he refused to support major civil rights legislation, believing that doing so would alienate the conservative southern bloc in Congress—and hence would jeopardize the rest of his reform program and "divide the American people at a time when the international scene required maximum unity." But his strategy was misdirected. His efforts to win over southern Democrats failed: White House favors and flattery did not break southern legislators' resistance to Kennedy's larger reform plans. Internationally, moreover, his inaction cost him more than he gained, for his failure to move openly and vigorously to secure the civil rights of black Americans offended the leaders of the new, formerly colonial, nations then emerging around the globe.

Although the administration was held back by a conservative Congress, it had considerable leeway to support civil rights through executive action. But here the president was also very cautious. Kennedy had made campaign promises to end discrimination in public housing promptly, "with a stroke of the pen," but he took no such action until a flood of pens arrived in the White House mails in 1961–62; and even then, his executive order of November 1962 covered only future public housing. Under Robert Kennedy the Justice Department did make greater efforts in behalf of black rights than had the Eisenhower administration. Nevertheless, the Kennedy administration offered only "limited assistance" to southern blacks and to civil rights activists attacked by white racists. Only a major crisis over an attempt by a black student, James H. Meredith, to register at the University of Mississippi in 1962 persuaded the White House to make an all-out effort to defend a black man's rights. Martin Luther King, Jr., complained that while southern blacks had "marshaled extraordinary courage to employ nonviolent direct action, they had been left—by the most powerful federal government in the world—almost solely to their own resources."

Other administration actions hampered the civil rights cause. For example, Kennedy appointed a number of bitter-end segregationists as southern judges. He did this in the hope of appeasing Mississippi's Senator James Eastland, who as chairman of the Judiciary Committee had the power to clear other, more liberal nominees whom Kennedy had proposed. But in meeting Eastland's wishes, the White House made judicial appointments that perpetuated racism in the South under the cover of law. Further, the administration in 1963 agreed to FBI wiretaps on Martin Luther King, Jr. Intimidated by nonsensical charges that King was under communist control and that the civil rights movement was a communist conspiracy, the president and the attorney general thus allowed J. Edgar Hoover to violate King's constitutional rights and to attempt to destroy his reputation and public influence.

These facts, however, do not fully measure the history of civil rights in the Kennedy years. If the president initially held back from pushing civil rights legislation, he left little doubt that, unlike Eisenhower, he personally sympathized with the Supreme Court decisions in behalf of racial justice. If he moved slowly in issuing a directive against discrimination in federally assisted housing, it was in the hope of persuading Congress to establish a new department of urban affairs, which he wished to put under the direction of Robert C. Weaver, a black economist. If he appointed federal judges recommended by Senator Eastland, it was part of a strategy to win the approval of Eastland's Judiciary Committee for the appointment to the federal circuit court of Thurgood Marshall, the black general counsel of the NAACP, who had been active in securing the *Brown* decision. If his Justice Department did not use federal power at every turn to protect black rights, it went well beyond other administrations in the twentieth century—bringing lawsuits to defend voting rights, using federal marshals to protect "freedom riders" who challenged segregation on interstate buses and trains and in terminals, and pressing the Interstate Commerce Commission into compelling desegregation by interstate carriers in the south. If the Kennedys acceded to Hoover's wiretaps on King, they also told the civil rights leader that he was under surveillance and that they expected the allegations against him to be refuted.

Most important, by 1963 events—especially the acts of black civil disobedience reproduced on television screens—had driven the administration into a historic effort to end discrimination and segregation through federal legislation. In April, during a massive civil rights demonstration in Birmingham, Alabama, the strongest bastion of Deep South segregation, the city's police commissioner, Eugene "Bull" Connor, provoked international indignation when he ordered attacks on the marchers by police dogs, electric cattle prods, and water hoses under such high pressure that they tore the bark off trees. In June, after federalized National Guardsmen had forced the integration of the

University of Alabama, over the opposition of Alabama Governor George C. Wallace, President Kennedy threw the full force of his office behind the most comprehensive civil rights bill in history. Speaking to the nation on television, the president condemned the legacy of racial injustice and asked: "Who among us would . . . be content with the counsels of patience and delay? One hundred years of delay have passed since President Lincoln freed the slaves, yet their heirs, their grandsons, are not fully free. They are not yet freed from the bonds of injustice; they are not yet freed from social and economic oppression. And this nation, for all its hopes and all its boasts, will not be fully free until all its citizens are free." Asking Congress "to make a commitment it has not fully made in this century to the proposition that race has no place in American life or law," Kennedy described passage of the law as necessary "not merely for reasons of economic efficiency, world diplomacy and domestic tranquility—but above all, because it is right." Although Kennedy did not live to see the bill enacted, his action marked the first time in American history that a president had openly advocated the end of segregation.

The Kennedy Foreign Policy

By the time Kennedy had come to office in 1961, the idea of the Cold War as a worldwide contest between monolithic communist totalitarianism and American democracy had begun to erode. In the early fifties, after the Cold War had stabilized, few other nations gave anticommunism the same overriding importance that the United States assigned to it. With the delineation of clear spheres of control, diminished fears of Soviet aggression, and reviving prosperity, America's allies felt freer to follow their own inclinations in world affairs. France led the resistance. By refusing to join the European Defense Community (EDC) in 1954, France destroyed America's plans for a thoroughly integrated continental military force. After 1958 the government in Paris, under its imperious president, Charles de Gaulle, furnished a center for continuing European criticism of American policy. More subtly, Japan also maneuvered for greater independence from the United States. No sooner had the American occupation ended in 1951 than Japan sought full control over its own territory and policies. Here, as in western Europe, desire to trade with communist nations contributed to the tension, for the United States opposed almost all economic relations between the two international spheres.

Although the world's agrarian nations had a meager share in the prosperity of the 1950s, many of them, too, were marking their own separate paths. The elec-

tric names in Africa and Asia were those of fervent nationalists such as Nassar, Kwame Nkrumah of Ghana, Jawaharlal Nehru of India, and Sukarno of Indonesia. In a variety of ways, these leaders struggled to develop their nations without sacrificing their independence to either side in the Cold War. Extremely sensitive to pressures from the great powers, they retaliated in anger when the United States or the Soviet Union appeared to dangle economic aid as an incentive to enter their camps. Because the United States was allied with their former imperial masters in Europe, the recently emancipated colonies especially set themselves against American domination in the future. By the early 1960s, these new states were describing themselves as the Third World—nations equally independent of the two superpowers.

With Kennedy's inauguration, officials in Washington began exploring ways of responding to the diverse ambitions of many nations. The new president, who expected to build his reputation in foreign affairs, encouraged fresh ideas about America's policies. He promised to accept the new nations of Africa and Asia on their own terms and to negotiate with the established nations as equals. In 1961 Kennedy announced the "Alliance for Progress" with Latin America that would use economic aid from the United States to improve the quality of life in the Western Hemisphere. Insisting on steps toward greater economic and social justice as the only conditions for help, the administration hoped to "transform the American continent into a vast crucible of revolutionary ideas and efforts. . . ." The Peace Corps, which sent American volunteers to underdeveloped countries to help improve their educational systems and give their citizens needed technical skills, also placed individual human needs above international military policy.

Nevertheless, in the day-to-day conduct of foreign affairs, Kennedy, together with his primary adviser on foreign policy, McGeorge Bundy, and his secretary of state, Dean Rusk, gave priority to the containment of international communism. During the 1960 campaign Kennedy had claimed that Soviet technological advances had outstripped those of the United States, creating a "missile gap." Although no one ever found the gap, the new president launched the largest and fastest peacetime military buildup in American history. To make credible America's willingness to fight a nuclear war, the administration supported a fallout shelter program that was supposed to save 97 percent of the population from nuclear destruction. Through a flexible military power, Kennedy envisioned a new American mastery in the global battle against communism. In Latin America, United States policy aimed not to implement the Alliance for Progress, which came to little, but to isolate Castro's Cuba and to insu-

The following account by a Florida civil rights worker illustrates the idealism of young southern blacks and their dedication to ending legalized segregation a hundred years after the abolition of slavery.

A Black Student Fights for Equal Rights

I AM writing this in Leon County Jail. My sister Priscilla and I, five other A & M students and one high school student are serving 60-day sentences for our participation in the sit-ins. We could be out on appeal but we all strongly believe that Martin Luther King was right when he said: "We've got to fill the jails in order to win our equal rights." . . .

Students who saw the inside of the county jail before I did and were released on bond reported that conditions were miserable. They did not exaggerate. It is dank and cold. We are in what is called a "bull tank" with four cells. Each cell has four bunks, a commode and a small sink. Some of the cells have running water, but ours does not. Breakfast, if you can call it that, is served at 6:30. Another meal is served at 12:30 and in the evening, "sweet" bread and watery coffee. At first I found it difficult to eat this food. . . .

There is plenty of time to think in jail and I sometimes review in my mind the events which brought me here. It is almost six months since Priscilla and I were first introduced to CORE at a workshop in Miami. Upon our return we helped to establish a Tallahassee CORE group. . . .

Our first action in Tallahassee was on Feb. 13th. At 11 A.M. we sat down at the Woolworth lunch counter. When the waitress approached, Charles Steele, who was next to me, ordered a slice of cake for each of us. She said: "I'm sorry, I can't serve you" and moved on down the counter repeating this to the other participants. We all said we would wait, took out our books and started reading—or at least, we tried.

The regular customers continued to eat. When one man finished, the waitress said: "Thank you for staying and eating in all this indecency." The man replied: "What did you expect me to do? I paid for it."

One man stopped behind Bill Carpenter briefly and said: "I think you're doing a fine job: just sit right there." A young white hoodlum then came up behind Bill and tried to bait him into an argument. Unsuccessful, he boasted to his friends: "I bet if I disjoint him, he'll talk." When Bill didn't respond, he moved on. . . .

The second sit-in at Woolworth's occurred a week later. The waitress saw us sitting down and said: "Oh Lord, here they come again!" This time a few white persons were participating, secretly. . . .

At about 3:30 P.M. a squad of policemen led by a man in civilian clothes entered the store. Someone directed him to Priscilla, who had been chosen our spokesman for this sit-in. "As Mayor of Tallahassee, I am asking you to leave," said the man in civilian clothes.

"If we don't leave, would we be committing a crime?" Priscilla asked. The mayor simply repeated his original statement. Then he came over to me, pointed to the "closed" sign and asked: "Can you read?" I advised him to direct all his comments to our elected spokesman. He looked as though his official vanity was wounded but turned to Priscilla. We did too, reiterating our determination to stay. He ordered our arrest.

Two policemen "escorted" each of the eleven of us to the station. I use quotes because their handling of us was not exactly gentle nor were their remarks courteous. . . .

We were arraigned February 22 and charged with disturbing the peace by riotous conduct and unlawful assembly. We all pleaded "not guilty!" The trial was set for March 3. A week prior to that date the entire A & M student body met and decided to suspend classes on March 3 and attend the trial. The prospect of having 3000 students converge on the small courtroom was a factor, we believe, in causing a 2-week postponement. . . .

The 11 of us arrested on February 20 were tried on March 17. There was no second postponement. The trial started promptly at 9:30. Five additional charges had been made against us, but were subsequently dropped. During the trial, Judge Rudd tried to keep race out of the case. He said it was not a factor in our arrest. But we realize it was the sole factor. The mayor in his testimony used the word "nigger" freely. We were convicted and sentenced to 60 days in jail or a $300 fine. All 11 had agreed to go to jail but three paid fines upon advice of our attorneys.

So, here I am serving a 60-day sentence along with seven other CORE members. When I get out, I plan to carry on this struggle. I feel I shall be ready to go to jail again if necessary.

late other countries against similar revolutions. The United States aided Latin American nations in proportion to their commitment to anticommunism.

The Bay of Pigs.

The administration's focus on containing and defeating communism found direct expression in its dealings with Castro's Cuba. Plans made during Eisenhower's term to topple Castro's regime through either his assassination or an invasion of Cuban exiles were carried forward by the Kennedy government. Kennedy himself apparently was never informed of the assassination plot, despite the fact that the CIA continued to pursue the idea throughout his years in office. Indeed, on the same day in November 1963 that Kennedy was killed, the CIA was supplying weapons to a Cuban defector planning to murder Castro.

The invasion of Cuba by Cuban exiles in April 1961 was another matter. Kennedy had learned of the plan five months before its execution and had had ample opportunity to call it off. But he saw a compelling logic in its favor: an invasion might well bring down Castro and forestall the spread of anti-American revolutions in the hemisphere. If it failed, the invaders could still escape into the Escambray Mountains, where they could undermine Castro's power with guerrilla operations. As important, if the United States called off the invasion, the Cuban exiles would denounce Washington's loss of nerve, which the White House feared would encourage pro-Castro revolutions all over the Caribbean. Consequently, Kennedy allowed the CIA to complete preparations for a small army of the exiles to launch an attack. Ignoring the advice of Senator J. William Fulbright, chairman of the Foreign Relations Committee, who saw the operation as "wildly out of proportion to the threat," Kennedy approved what turned out to be a disastrous landing at the Bay of Pigs on the southern coast of the island. Attacking without sufficient air cover, the invaders were quickly defeated. The United States was widely denounced for its indifference to international law and for its hypocrisy in avowing a commitment to self-determination for nations everywhere. The defeat seriously injured the administration's prestige and self-confidence and emboldened the Soviet Union to commit acts of aggression that brought the two superpowers to the edge of war.

Soviet-American Relations: From Confrontation to Détente.

Even before Kennedy had come to office, the Soviets had signaled their intention to press vigorously for their interests against the young, inexperienced president-elect, whom they hoped to intimidate. At the beginning of January 1961, Khrushchev publicly predicted the ultimate triumph of socialism through national wars of liberation. In June, two months after the defeat at the Bay of Pigs had thrown his administration on the defensive, Kennedy met Khrushchev at Vienna. The Soviet premier bullied the president, forecasting the victory of communism over capitalism and insisting that the West sign a German peace treaty making West Berlin a "free city" or risk being ousted by Soviet arms. Viewing Khrushchev's threat as a first step toward the neutralization of all of western Europe, and as part of a larger design on Southeast Asia and the Western Hemisphere, Kennedy responded with a call-up of reserve forces and plans for a huge military buildup, including nuclear submarines, conventional army units for fighting limited wars, and special counterinsurgency forces to combat national wars of liberation. The Soviets answered by constructing the Berlin Wall in August 1961 to halt the migration of skilled East German workers to the West, as well as by resuming nuclear testing in the atmosphere, which produced radiation fallout. Detonating some fifty nuclear bombs during the next two months, the Soviets concluded the tests with the explosion of a fifty-seven-megaton weapon, the largest ever assembled. An attempt to intimidate the United States, the testing program only added to Soviet-American tensions by persuading Washington also to resume testing in April 1962.

The clash of wills culminated in the Cuban missile crisis, the most dangerous superpower confrontation in the Cold War era. In the fall of 1962 the Soviets began placing medium-range nuclear missiles in Cuba that could reach a large part of the United States. Khrushchev seems to have intended using the missiles to force Kennedy into accepting a German peace treaty and an arms-control agreement that would deter Communist China from building a nuclear arsenal. Apparently Khrushchev planned to appear before the United Nations, disclose the presence of the missiles, and offer to remove them in return for an agreement on Germany and on "atom-free" zones in central Europe and the Pacific. "If our two countries united their efforts . . ." Soviet Foreign Minister Andrei Gromyko had declared in 1961, "who would dare and who would be in a position to threaten peace?" In other words, the Chinese, with whom Moscow was coming into sharper and more open conflict, would be deterred from building weapons that could threaten the USSR.

Before Khrushchev could act, however, in October Kennedy revealed the existence of the Soviet missiles in Cuba. To prevent the Soviets from completing the installation of the weapons, the president announced a naval blockade of military shipments to the island. Although Kennedy recognized that the missiles would not have substantially altered the strategic balance between the two sides, he believed that it "would have

"CUBAN MISSILE SHOWDOWN"
The most dangerous confrontation between the two superpowers since 1945 occurred in October 1962 over the introduction of Soviet missiles into Cuba. The successful resolution of this crisis opened the way to the Test Ban Treaty in the following year.

politically changed the balance of power" and would have further thrown his administration on the defensive at home and abroad. Hence, he not only introduced the blockade, but also warned the Soviets that any use of the missiles would result in a full-scale attack on the Soviet Union. At the same time, however, he refused to launch a preemptive air strike against the missile sites that would have intensified the crisis. Instead, after days of excruciating tension when the world seemed on the verge of war, Kennedy and Khrushchev reached agreement. The Soviet leader promised to remove the missiles in return for a public pledge not to invade Cuba and a private one to dismantle American Jupiter missiles in Turkey.

The resolution of the Cuban missile crisis opened the way to a significant improvement in Soviet-American relations that came about principally through Kennedy's efforts. Recognizing more clearly than ever that "Mankind must put an end to war or war will put an end to mankind," the president used his diplomatic victory not to humiliate the Soviets, but to advance the cause of peace. He forbade members of his administration to gloat over America's tri-

umph and warned them against assuming that the Soviet pullback was a sign of weakness. Had Soviet national security been directly threatened in the confrontation, he said, they would have acted differently. Fortunately, this threat had not been present, and relations with the Soviet Union, he now concluded, "could be contained within the framework of mutual awareness of the impossibility of achieving any gains through war."

Kennedy eloquently expressed these views in a major address at American University in June 1963. In what Khrushchev called "the greatest speech by an American president since Roosevelt," Kennedy proposed a turn toward détente—a policy of lowering tensions between the Eastern and Western blocs. "What kind of peace do we seek?" he asked. "Not a *pax Americana* enforced on the world by American weapons of war. . . . Not merely peace for Americans but peace for all men and women—not merely peace in our time but peace for all time." He urged Americans and Russians alike to "re-examine our attitude toward the Cold War, remembering that we are not engaged in a debate. . . . We must deal with the world as it is." We are, he

The Kennedy Foreign Policy 823

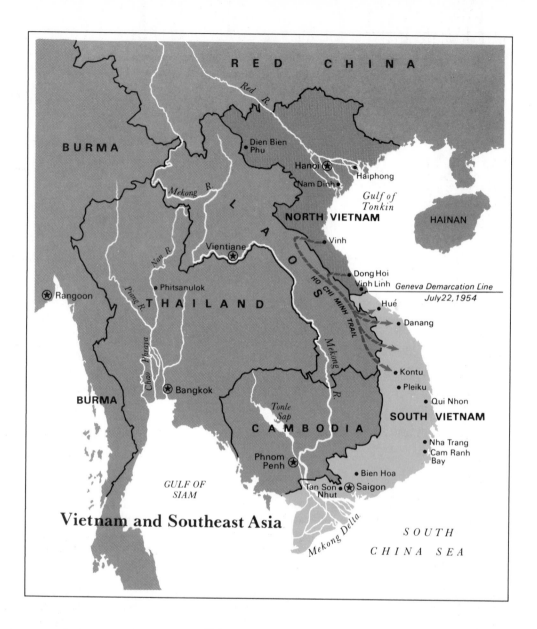

Vietnam and Southeast Asia

added, "caught in a vicious and dangerous cycle in which suspicion on one side breeds suspicion on the other, and new weapons beget counter weapons."

In the summer of 1963 Kennedy followed up his appeal for détente by successfully negotiating with the Soviet Union a ban on atmospheric and underwater nuclear explosions. Supported, according to one opinion poll, by 80 percent of the country, he overrode the objections of a minority who were predicting the loss of America's future security, and guided the treaty through the Senate. Had Kennedy lived to serve another term, perhaps he "might have taken the world a good deal farther along the road to disarmament and peace," as one historian has suggested.

Vietnam. Kennedy's historical reputation as a peacemaker is called into question by his actions in Vietnam. The difficulties he confronted in Southeast Asia were already well advanced when he entered the White House.* An international conference in Geneva in 1954 had created three independent states from the former French territory in Indochina: Laos, Cambodia, and Vietnam. Vietnam had temporarily been divided between a communist north and a noncommunist south, pending national elections and unification. But with American support, between 1954

*For the origins of the Vietnam problem under Eisenhower, see chapter 31, p. 805.

and 1956 the Diem government in southern Vietnam had rejected the Geneva plan for national elections and had established a permanent state. As Kennedy took office, the anticommunist governments in both South Vietnam and neighboring Laos were in jeopardy. Eisenhower told the new president that Laos was the key to all Southeast Asia and urged unilateral intervention, if necessary, to keep it out of communist hands.

Although Kennedy had doubts about Eisenhower's "domino" theory—the notion that the "loss" of any country in Southeast Asia would inevitably bring communist control throughout the area—he acted as if it were a sound idea. In his first State of the Union message, Kennedy warned that "the relentless pressures of the Chinese communists menace the security of the entire area—from the borders of India and South Vietnam to the jungles of Laos, struggling to protect its newly won independence." Kennedy believed the freedom and independence of the Laotian people to be at stake in the conflict, and he promised that "this Nation shall persevere in our pursuit of these objectives."

The United States was able to negotiate the neutralization of Laos with the Soviets, but South Vietnam was a less manageable problem. The Vietcong, South Vietnamese guerrillas backed by North Vietnam and China, refused to negotiate; and Kennedy and his advisers were provoked into seeing the Vietnamese struggle as part of a worldwide communist drive for power. The battle of "freedom versus tyranny," Kennedy told Congress in May 1961, was being fought in Vietnam. "We must decide whether to help these countries [in Southeast Asia] to the best of our ability or throw in the towel in the area and pull back our defenses to San Francisco and a 'Fortress America' concept," Vice-President Lyndon Johnson declared. Kennedy's military advisers also urged a strong American effort, including a force of possibly 10,000 men. ". . . As I knew from experience with my French friends," George Ball, Kennedy's under secretary of state, later said, "there was something about Vietnam that seduced the toughest military minds into fantasy."

Kennedy was convinced that the Vietnamese struggle was primarily a fight to halt the advance of communism in Asia, and he expected that by defeating the communists with a successful American-sponsored "democratic revolution" the United States would send the world a powerful signal of its progressive intentions. Thus he committed American men, materiel, and prestige to the defense of South Vietnam. To his satisfaction, moreover, the policy seemed to work. In 1962 Secretary of Defense Robert McNamara reported that "every quantitative measurement we have shows we're winning this war." Others in the American government echoed this belief, and by the beginning of 1963 Kennedy was telling the nation that "the spearpoint of aggression has been blunted in South Vietnam." At the same time, Secretary of State Dean Rusk saw Diem's regime making "steady movement toward a constitutional system resting upon popular consent."

These appraisals were far too optimistic. By the fall of 1963, the Saigon government had made little progress toward winning (in a phrase popular at the time) "the hearts and minds" of the South Vietnamese people. Unbiased reporters concluded that Diem was losing the war. When public demonstrations by South Vietnamese groups led by the Buddhist clergy made this point clear, the Kennedy administration acquiesced in a military coup against Diem, who was killed. The American government at once recognized the new regime and renewed its commitment to keep South Vietnam free. Having put 16,000 American military advisers in the country by November 1963, it seems likely that Kennedy, had he lived, would have expanded United States involvement to prevent defeat. But there is also evidence suggesting otherwise. Two months earlier he had said that it was up to the people of South Vietnam to win or lose the war, and he made plans to withdraw all American military advisers from the country in 1965. He had confided these hopes to at least two American senators, contending that he felt compelled to wait until after the 1964 election, when he could be less concerned about Republican assertions that he might be "losing" South Vietnam.

On November 22, 1963, questions about what Kennedy might do in a second term suddenly became unanswerable. Kennedy was struck down in Dallas, Texas, by Lee Harvey Oswald, a drifting malcontent who had lived for a while in the Soviet Union; and Oswald in turn was murdered in the Dallas city jail by the nightclub operator Jack Ruby. It was the most unexpected and devastating single event in the nation's history since Lincoln's assassination almost a century earlier—and owing to modern media, no event had ever been so thoroughly national and yet so intensely personal. During a long weekend of mourning, the nation immersed itself in every detail of the tragedy and its aftermath. Through television, Americans traced the president's motorcade through Dallas, saw Kennedy jarred by an explosion of shots, shared the vigil outside the hospital, witnessed Oswald's incredible murder, and then followed the somber state funeral through the gray streets of Washington. Almost two decades later, with important questions about the assassination still unanswered, millions could re-create those "six seconds in Dallas" as if their lives, too, had hung in the balance. In memory, Kennedy's popularity soared. But as time passed his record was subjected to scrutiny and controversy, and his place in history remains an open question.

Domestic Affairs Under Johnson

Lyndon Baines Johnson, Kennedy's vice-president, was sworn in as the new president on the airplane that carried Kennedy's body back to Washington. It was soon obvious that Johnson could not command the public affection that Kennedy had won. The tall, overbearing Texan, best known as a political wheeler-dealer, entered the White House with little fixed national support. Many doubted that he would be able to overcome his regional and personal limitations to become an effective national leader. But he quickly removed these doubts. Although a less polished figure who could not match Kennedy's high style, Johnson was a man of boundless drive, keen intelligence, and great compassion for the disadvantaged. Eleven years as a congressman and, beginning in 1949, twelve years as a senator, during which time he served as majority leader, had prepared Johnson particularly well to lead the nation.

Johnson's five years in the White House are among the most important in this century. Eclipsing every American president except Franklin Roosevelt in leading Congress to pass major domestic reform legislation, Johnson fought an "unconditional war on poverty" that he aimed to win through the creation of what he called the Great Society. Johnson described his program as leading "not only toward the rich society and the powerful society but upward to the Great Society," which "rests on abundance and liberty for all. It demands an end to poverty and racial injustice, to which we are totally committed in our time." Further, the Great Society was to be an America in which "men are more concerned with the quality of their goals than with the quantity of their goods."

The Election of 1964. From the moment he assumed the presidency, Johnson set about winning the office in his own right and going down in history as a great leader. With the election of 1964 less than a year away, he moved quickly to appeal to Democratic constituencies outside the South. His primary goal was the passage of the Kennedy civil rights bill, which had become a rallying point for liberal and moderate Americans across the land. On November 27, 1963, Johnson told Congress that "no memorial oration or eulogy could more eloquently honor President Kennedy's memory than the earliest possible passage of the civil rights bill. . . . We have talked long enough in this country about equal rights. . . . It is time now to write the next chap-

LBJ FOR THE USA
Johnson's 1964 presidential campaign emphasized his qualities as a national figure who spoke for all Americans. Running against Senator Barry Goldwater, who impressed most as a radical of the right, LBJ won a landslide victory.

ter, and to write it in the books of law." The following July, after defeating a fifty-seven-day southern filibuster in the Senate, Johnson signed the 1964 Civil Rights Act into law. It prohibited discrimination in places of public accommodation such as hotels and restaurants, required equal treatment for all in public facilities like parks and swimming pools, forbade the use of federal funds in specific hospitals, universities, and the like that practiced discrimination, and protected blacks against being barred from voting.

Johnson won a number of other victories that raised his standing with liberals and partly satisfied his drive for economic and social justice in the United States. Under his prodding, Congress greatly expanded federal aid to education and approved an urban mass transit subsidy, a food stamp program, and an $11.5 billion tax cut to fuel economic expansion and greater prosperity for all. He also persuaded Congress to pass the Economic Opportunity Act of 1964, which created the Office of Economic Opportunity

(OEO) to advance the "war on poverty" that he had declared in January 1964.

Having identified himself so strongly with the liberal side of the Democratic party, Johnson worried that the Republicans might seize the middle ground from him in the campaign of 1964 by nominating New York's moderate governor, Nelson Rockefeller. But the Republicans obliged Johnson by choosing Senator Barry Goldwater of Arizona, a militant conservative who candidly advocated the return to a pre–New Deal era in which social welfare and civil rights laws would be repealed and the United States would free itself from the burdens of the Cold War by decisively defeating the Soviet communist threat. By telling the Republican convention that "extremism in the defense of liberty is no vice," Goldwater identified himself all the more with the radical right, which was anathema to the majority of voters. When Goldwater bumper stickers declared "In your heart you know he's right," the Democrats, playing on fears of nuclear war, countered with "In your heart you know he might."

Despite his obvious advantages in running against so impolitic a candidate, Johnson worried that Goldwater would arouse patriotic support by attacking the administration's "no win" actions in Vietnam. Although Johnson announced that he would not escalate the war—"We are not about to send American boys nine or ten thousand miles away from home to do what Asian boys ought to be doing for themselves"—he ordered United States forces to bomb North Vietnam during the campaign, after North Vietnamese gunboats allegedly launched an unprovoked attack on American destroyers in the Gulf of Tonkin. In addition, he extracted from Congress the Tonkin Gulf Resolution, authorizing the president "to repel any armed attack against the forces of the United States and to prevent future aggression." While campaigning as a "peace" candidate, Johnson also made sure that Goldwater could not attack him as too weak a defender of American interests. Johnson's appeal was reminiscent of Wilson's in 1916 and of FDR's in 1940—and, like theirs, was doomed to disappoint many who voted for him.

Johnson's strategy could not have been more effective. He handed Goldwater the worst defeat ever suffered by a major party's presidential candidate up to that time. Winning 61.1 percent of the popular vote—43 million votes—as against Goldwater's 38.5 percent and 27 million, Johnson held the largest popular vote, the greatest margin of victory, and the highest percentage of the vote in history. With advantages of 295 to 140 in the House and 68 to 32 in the Senate, the Democrats were in a position largely to fulfill the president's program—to carry out the agenda of liberal social reform dating back to Truman's presidency.

The Great Society.

Under Lyndon Johnson's direction in 1965–66, the Eighty-Ninth Congress became, in the words of its Speaker, "the Congress of accomplished hopes . . . of realized dreams." In a whirlwind of activity that astonished even the most optimistic reformers, Congress passed a series of laws that made fundamental changes in American life. Medicare provided medical and hospital insurance for the elderly under Social Security, and Medicaid meant that the indigent could also receive health care. Cabinet-level departments were created to oversee new federal programs in transportation and in housing and urban development. A new immigration statute ended the system of national-origin quotas established in the 1920s. Education bills provided aid to elementary, secondary, and higher institutions of learning. A housing act created federal rent supplements for the poor, and the Model Cities program encouraged the redevelopment of decaying urban communities. Highway, traffic safety, and clean air and rivers acts were passed, and there was even a highway beautification law. To wage the war on poverty, Johnson pushed through the Appalachian Regional Development Program, a domestic peace corps called VISTA (Volunteers in Service to America), the Head Start program for disadvantaged preschool children, the Neighborhood Youth Corps to help unemployed teenagers, the Job Corps for school dropouts, the Upward Bound drive for sending more underprivileged young people to college, and the Community Action Program, promoting direct participation by poor people in easing their plight.

The combination of the 1964 tax cut and the wide-ranging attack on poverty produced dramatic results. The gross national product nearly doubled during the 1960s, and the economy added 10 million new jobs. Like the GNP, median family income nearly doubled, while the number of Americans living below the poverty line fell by approximately 50 percent, to 11 percent of the total population. Yet Johnson's program was never as "revolutionary" as some feared and others hoped it would be. The annual budget for the war on poverty never went much above $2 billion—less than one-quarter of 1 percent of the GNP. The program did little to redistribute income and nothing to guarantee jobs. "For a mere $11 billion," the economist Robert Lekachman complained, "we could raise every poor American above the poverty line." But the administration had no intention of making the war on poverty a "handout program" and instead relied on traditional American assumptions about ambition, education, opportunity, and success. Still, the Great Society went well beyond what had been done earlier: in announcing his program, Johnson committed his administration to a vigorous national management of

"WE SHALL OVERCOME" President Lyndon Johnson's enthusiasm for racial equality is apparent in this scene as he reaches out to black children and their parents.

matters that once were controlled by localities. Justifiable comments were heard that the Great Society gave the government more control than ever before over American economic and social life, and one critic wrote that the country had "moved . . . nearer to state collectivism at the federal level than in any previous period."

Civil Rights.

Johnson's efforts to advance black rights coincided with the climax of the black activist drive for equality. But the president's intervention in the civil rights cause produced ambiguous results.

Behind the civil rights movement lay a faith that the American creed would inevitably triumph over its antiblack contradictions. The Warren Court depended on the creed to give social authority to its legal rulings against segregation. Martin Luther King, Jr., depended on the creed as a national white conscience that his strategy of civil disobedience could stir. The Johnson administration depended on the creed to rally the people who were still resisting a national program to eliminate racial inequalities from American life. Because of their common faith in the creed, a disciplined black minority and a well-to-do white minority had been able to work together for black rights. As a climax to the biracial civil rights movement, whites had enthusiastically applauded in 1964 when King rose in Oslo to receive the Nobel Prize for Peace.

Early in 1965, civil rights activists under King's leadership attacked southern restraints on black voting. Throughout the South, but particularly in Alabama, black registration was far below what it could have been. To dramatize the issue, King led a series of demonstrations in Selma, Alabama, where blacks had been systematically excluded from the franchise. After several violent clashes provoked by local authorities, and the killing of a white Unitarian minister from Boston, Johnson asked Congress for a voting rights law that would "establish a simple, uniform standard which cannot be used, however ingenious the effort, to flout the Constitution." In a moving address praising the courage of black Americans fighting for freedom, as America's rebels had at Lexington in 1775, Johnson pledged to wipe out the prejudice that blighted the lives of all Americans. "It is all of us who must overcome the crippling legacy of bigotry and injustice, and we shall overcome."

After a widely publicized march from Selma to Montgomery in March 1965, which Johnson agreed to protect with federalized National Guardsmen, Congress passed a voting rights statute in the summer of 1965. Under the law, federal agents were authorized to register qualified voters in counties where 50 percent or more of voting-age citizens were unregistered. The law had immediate and substantial consequences: in the three years following passage, voter registration

CHICAGO STREET IN THE AFTERMATH OF THE DEATH OF MARTIN LUTHER KING, JR.
King's assassination in April 1968 triggered a fresh burst of rioting in America's urban ghettos. The mid-sixties saw repeated explosions of black anger over economic and social conditions perpetuating black inequality.

among southern blacks increased by almost 50 percent. Black registration in Mississippi alone quadrupled. Political participation by blacks increased not only in the South, but in other parts of the country as well. In every region of the nation black Americans made some political gains, winning election to high city, state, and federal offices.

Along with judicial rulings securing civil rights for blacks, the mid-1960s also saw a series of Supreme Court decisions that significantly extended the rights of social outcasts, such as persons accused of spreading obscenity or breaking the criminal law. The majority of Supreme Court justices, including Chief Justice Earl Warren, viewed these decisions as part of a broad pattern of "incorporating" the Bill of Rights into the everyday procedures of local courts and police forces. This was the same rationale that the Supreme Court used in broadening the civil rights of racial minorities.

Civil Disorder. The Johnson administration's belief that it was easing the plight of black Americans received a rude jolt in the summer of 1965. On August 11, five days after the Voting Rights Act became law, the black neighborhood of Watts in Los Angeles exploded in

some of the worst racial rioting in American history. Although disturbances had erupted in northern cities in the past, including several in the summer of 1964, none of them was quite like the Los Angeles upheaval. Unlike the black slum areas of New York, Chicago, Philadelphia, and other major cities, Watts was a comparatively well-off area with numerous private homes and little evidence of substandard dwellings and littered streets. But an adult unemployment rate of 30 percent, combined with a bitter antagonism on the part of Watts residents toward a largely white police force, created tensions that made the community an emotional tinderbox. Instead of easing these problems, the existing civil rights laws and modestly funded government programs had brought only frustrated hopes. The Johnson reforms had produced not optimism, but feelings of despair that there was no way out of the poverty with which most Watts residents lived. The consequence was a riot costing 34 lives and over $35 million in property damage. The injured numbered 856, with more than 3,000 people arrested. An investigating commission described the bitterness and despair that had generated the rioting and warned that if the existing racial breach were allowed to continue, it "could in time split our society irretrievably."

As the commission had foreseen, Watts was "only a curtain-raiser" for what occurred during the next three summers. Between 1966 and 1968 Cleveland, Chicago, Detroit, Newark (New Jersey), Jacksonville (Florida), and other cities experienced similar racial eruptions in which death, injury, and destruction were widespread: forty-three people died in Detroit, for example, where another 2,000 suffered injuries and thousands of fires gutted the inner city.

Martin Luther King, Jr., who had preached nonviolence, now seemed hopelessly out of step with black militants preaching black nationalism and "black power." Rejecting King's call for love and understanding, dynamic new leaders appeared who alarmed even sympathetic whites. Stokely Carmichael of SNCC and Malcolm X, at first a spokesman for the separatist-minded Black Muslims and later an advocate of a more purely (but still black-oriented) Islamic religion, urged their followers to separate themselves from their white oppressors. It was the whites' hatred and abuse, the militants said, that had forced blacks to fight back. Whites did not really believe in equality and justice for all: on the contrary, white values created a self-serving institutional structure that made blacks a colonial people inside American society. Only an exclusively black, racially proud movement could hope to break these institutional shackles.

In April 1968, in a tragic confirmation of this message of hate, a white escaped convict named James Earl Ray killed Martin Luther King, Jr., as he stood on the balcony of a Memphis motel. A fresh outburst of rioting shook the nation's ghettos, taking an additional thirty-nine lives and giving added meaning to the report that the National Advisory Commission on Civil Disorders had issued a month before: "Our nation is moving toward two societies, one black, one white—separate and unequal."

The commission was acutely aware of the entrenched poverty and despair of the ghettos, which the Great Society had barely begun to relieve. The rise of black separatism and the outbursts of ghetto rioting, which the commission attributed largely to the continuing effects of economic deprivation and white racism, frightened the progressive camp. Liberal whites and moderate blacks had united around the assumption that blacks desired—and should desire—peaceful integration into a hitherto white-dominated society. Thus warnings about a drift to "two societies" were not mere rhetoric: they arose from the fear that separatism, racial disorder, and the squalor that spawned them would, if not overcome, destroy the liberal dream of social justice and equality, thrusting the nation back into its segregated, violence-ridden past.

The Johnson Foreign Policy

As a rising tide of troubles beset the Johnson administration at home, it was confronted with distracting problems abroad. Johnson's background and experience made him far more comfortable with domestic than foreign affairs, and he was frustrated by his inability to control overseas events. Moreover, he had little patience with internal divisions over foreign policy. In his view, presidential direction of diplomacy was not a fit subject for domestic debate. "I am the only president you have," he was fond of saying; when the safety of the nation was at stake, he believed it unpatriotic for Americans to question the government's policy, especially in dealing with the "worldwide communist threat." Like those of so many others of his generation, his views on foreign affairs had been shaped by the experience of the thirties. Johnson deplored any hint of appeasement as certain to undermine national security. He believed that every challenge to American power must be met with a vigorous response. His dealings with Panama and the Dominican Republic, for example, evoked memories of Theodore Roosevelt's "big stick" diplomacy. And in Southeast Asia Johnson became mired in a Vietnam war he could neither win nor end.

The advances that LBJ achieved at home were soon tarnished and blocked by the violence he perpetrated abroad. Vietnam, one critic complained, is "poisoning and brutalizing our domestic life. . . . 'The Great Society' has become the sick society." The war split the country and blighted Johnson's presidency. By the time he left the White House, many Americans spoke of "the tragedy of LBJ"; but his was only part of the larger tragedy of a postwar liberalism that had failed in its drive to ensure social justice and halt communism in a single, simultaneous burst of progressive action.

Latin America. Policy toward Latin America, where Johnson was determined to have no more Cubas, demonstrates LBJ's difficulties in overseas affairs. When, in January 1964, President Roberto Chiari of Panama broke relations with the United States and demanded renegotiation of the 1903 Panama Canal Treaty, Johnson took a hard line, saying that he would not knuckle under to a "banana republic" no larger than the city of St. Louis. When the Organization of American States proposed formal negotiations, Johnson contemptuously refused. Subsequently, however, the president did agree to a "review" of outstanding issues between the United States and Panama, which led to a new treaty giving Panama a greater voice in the management of the canal and a larger financial return.

WAR IN VIETNAM
Who was the enemy in Vietnam? Perhaps this Vietnamese woman knew, but increasing numbers of Americans could not say.

Johnson's intervention in the Dominican Republic in the spring of 1965 had a less satisfactory outcome. In April a group of Dominican army officers who were committed to replacing an unpopular conservative regime with a more liberal one under Juan Bosch, a former head of government, revolted. Informed by the American embassy that American lives were in danger and that communists were playing a significant part in the uprising, Johnson immediately decided to send in the marines. The American troops, numbering over 20,000, quickly overcame the rebels, and the existing government was preserved. Juan Bosch justifiably complained that his had been "a democratic revolution smashed by the leading democracy of the world."

To justify his actions, Johnson grossly overstated the dangers. Almost none of what the president said was true, and the Dominican episode helped create what became known as the credibility gap. The invasion did little, if anything, to serve national security; and, by raising doubts about the administration's capacity to pursue a rational foreign policy, it intensified a growing concern over the wisdom of Johnson's course in Vietnam.

The Vietnam Disaster. Like Eisenhower and Kennedy, Johnson felt compelled to stave off a communist victory in Vietnam. He believed that such an outcome would pave the way to Chinese communist domination of all Southeast Asia and would encourage Moscow and Peking to take more aggressive steps that might provoke a nuclear war. The president also feared that failure in Vietnam would touch off a fierce domestic debate like the one of the early 1950s over the "loss" of China. Thus Johnson vowed that he was "not going to lose South Vietnam." But he always regarded Vietnam as a frustrating obstacle to the enactment of his reform program at home. In order to dampen domestic challenge to his military plans, as well as to avert congressional balking over the expensive Great Society programs, Johnson never asked for a tax increase to fight the war in Southeast Asia. Only in the 1970s would the inflationary consequences of this decision become fully apparent.

In February 1965, after the Vietcong killed 8 Americans and wounded another 108 in an attack on an American base at Pleiku, 240 miles northeast of South Vietnam's capital, Saigon, the president ordered retaliatory air strikes. Three weeks later he authorized the continuous bombing of North Vietnam in the hope of forcing the North to the conference table. At the same time, he sent the first American combat units into South Vietnam—to do the fighting that he had promised only Asian boys would do.

Once he had committed American forces, Johnson was drawn ever deeper into a quagmire. By the end of April 1965, American forces in South Vietnam numbered almost 50,000. By June their mission, which had been to protect air bases and support South Vietnamese units in grave danger, was broadened to allow them to engage in combat as local commanders saw fit. In July the administration committed itself to sending another 150,000 troops, who were to carry out an aggressive "search-and-destroy" strategy against the enemy. Although the American commander, General William Westmoreland, predicted that this would produce victory by 1967, an end to the fighting was nowhere in sight during that year. Worse yet, by then the number of American ground forces had risen to 400,000; as many as 543,000 were fighting in 1968. The cost in dead and wounded also grew alarmingly. By the end of 1968, more than 30,000 Americans had died and another 100,000 had been wounded. Repeated assertions from American political and military chiefs that they could see the light at the end of the tunnel evoked the cynical comment that "sometimes the light at the end of the tunnel is from an onrushing train."

Simultaneously the air war escalated in numbers and ferocity. In order to kill guerrillas in the South, disrupt supply lines from the North, and demoralize the North Vietnamese government and people, American planes assaulted "free fire zones" in South Vietnam and struck at North Vietnam's capital, Hanoi, and its main port, Haiphong. By 1968 the total tonnage of bombs dropped on Vietnam reached nearly 3 million tons—almost 50 percent more than had been dropped by U.S. air forces during the Second World War.

All this had astonishingly little effect in breaking the will of the Vietcong and North Vietnamese to fight. To be sure, tens of thousands of Vietnamese lost their lives and far more were wounded or driven from their homes. But according to numerous estimates at the end of 1967, the killing had "not discernibly weakened" the Saigon government's opponents. The Tet, or lunar New Year, offensive begun by the communists on January 30, 1968, underscored this. Attacking most of South Vietnam's provincial capitals, briefly capturing Hué, and assaulting the American embassy in Saigon, the communists demonstrated how far the United States remained from victory. Although American officials called the offensive "a complete failure" and discussed the possibility of sending another 206,000 troops to finish off the enemy, Johnson had to

concede that further escalation was out of the question. On March 31 he rejected the proposal for sending more troops, announced a reduction in the bombing of North Vietnam, proposed the start of peace talks, and revealed his decision not to run for reelection in 1968. The war had been lost not so much through military defeat as through the collapse of general public support for it at home.

Opposition to the War. Johnson withdrew from the presidential race because he believed he could not win. His record-breaking support in 1964 had disappeared in the debate over Vietnam. Far from being a nation of contented citizens thankful to their president for peace and prosperity, America in 1968 seethed with racial and political strife.

Early in 1965, when Johnson had begun to expand American commitments in Vietnam, he had hoped that the war would be over in twelve to eighteen months—that is, before serious domestic opposition to the fighting could emerge. To his distress, protests had begun at once. In March 1965 students and faculty held the nation's first teach-in at the University of Michigan, where they presented the case against the war. Others followed across the country. But instead of bringing about any change in administration policy, these protests only promoted a sense of betrayal among Johnson and his aides. Secretary of State Rusk, for example, criticized "the gullibility of educated men" and "their stubborn disregard of plain facts."

As the gap between opponents and supporters of the war widened, the minority opposition adopted more extreme tactics. Young men, many of them affluent university students, began to burn their draft cards and took up the chant, "Hell No, We Won't Go!" Demonstrations and marches turned into violent clashes with the police. Angry college students seized campus buildings, roughed up university officials, and forced the temporary shutdown of several institutions of higher learning. Privately calling dissenters "crazies" and publicly denouncing them as "nervous Nellies" ready to "turn on their own leaders, and on their country, and on our own fighting men," Johnson drove them into a greater sense of alienation. Frustrated opponents of the violence in Vietnam and of American racism, which many saw reflected in the disproportionate numbers of blacks serving and dying in the war, seized upon the administration's unbending attitude and began to advocate their own brand of self-righteous violence. Proclaiming violence to be "as American as cherry pie," and declaring that "to get rid of the gun it is necessary to take up the gun," radicals urged an all-out assault on the status quo, on an "Amerika" that had turned into the "Fourth Reich"—a nation much like Hitler's Germany.

Countercurrents

Americans in the Eisenhower era, filled with a sense of the nation's wholeness, had placed vast faith in scientific and technical expertise and in the powers of national governmental management. Many had come to believe that every problem had a national, managerial solution. Kennedy and Johnson acted upon this expectation by enlarging the scope of the federal government's responsibilities. Meanwhile, from its frustrating beginnings in the 1950s, the nation's space program became a dazzling success in the 1960s, and the astronauts—the decade's heroes—seemed to merge into a composite of the healthy, balanced American male. Americans of all ages were caught up in the ferment of the times, inspired by Kennedy's charisma, by the nobility of the civil rights cause, and by the visible signs of technological triumph.

But as the national government extended its power into new, formerly local and even private areas of concern, complex new problems arose. The nation grieved over Kennedy's assassination, not only as a personal loss, but also as the beginning of national disintegration. Uneasiness over the implications of scientific progress deepened; the computer, which in the fifties had promised impartial answers to the world's problems, began to seem a threat to personal autonomy. The "military-industrial complex," against which Eisenhower had warned in 1961, became a national obsession. And millions felt their hopes for social justice and progress betrayed as the Washington "experts" led the United States into a war it could not win.

These crosscurrents generated a sense of alienation throughout American society. Alienation was most obvious among those young people, white and black, who protested against the war, denounced American institutions, and adopted lifestyles that shocked their elders; Marxism, which gave the question of alienation a revolutionary twist, attracted some. And although most upper-middle-class Americans rejected the young rebels' methods, they shared some of their children's alienation. Discontent with their jobs and family life, for example, drove elders restlessly to search for "fulfillment"; and worry over the dangers that technological progress posed to the individual knew no age boundaries. Alienation also extended to millions of ordinary, or "middle," Americans who felt threatened by the rapid social change around them. The "generation gap" was separating them from their children; traditional institutions and ideals such as the family, sexual morality, the work ethic, and patriotism were under attack; and black activism and expansive federal power challenged the familiar world of white power and community mores.

Counterculture. Against this background of doubt and searching, bands of well-to-do white youths came into the streets as the hippies, flower children, dropouts, and rebels of the 1960s. Although a minority of their age group, they were so visible and so audible that they always seemed far more numerous than they were. They clustered in parks to smoke marijuana and sing. They crowded the sidewalks around college campuses. They became the most committed white partisans of black rights and the bulwark of a marching, chanting peace movement. Although some of these protestors were self-indulged dropouts, many were thoughtful, nonviolent young people with legitimate concerns about the state of American affairs. Beginning with the free speech movement at Berkeley in 1964 and culminating in the nationwide activities of Students for a Democratic Society (SDS), their protest groups rallied many more young people behind specific campaigns for student rights and social justice. By 1967 and 1968, student strikes were commonplace. So were colonies of young people, including swarms of teenage runaways, who experimented with communal life, drugs, and poverty. In the late 1960s the largest of these colonies occupied much of the Haight-Ashbury district of San Francisco.

In many ways these young dissenters were acting out just one more variation of the modern adolescent rebellion. All the standard elements of the past forty years were there. Increasingly, hard rock set a musical barrier between the generations. Trust no one over thirty, the rebels declared. Even their primary areas of rebellion—dress, language, drugs, and sex—were the familiar ones from the 1920s.

This noisy rebellion made a penetrating commentary on contemporary life. It focused on the most sensitive problems of the individual in modern society. In response to a dehumanizing bureaucracy, the young dissenters assaulted the nation's important institutions. Some pointedly rejected the products of these institutions—the government's laws, the party's candidates, the corporation's goods, the university's degrees—and many more young people cheered them on. Rather than postpone gratifications in the name of a career, the young dissenters wanted the good life now. In response to feelings of loneliness, they emphasized community and loyalty and love. Craftsmanship, nature, and a "whole earth" were sacred causes. A few rebels tried to build an entire life around these values in self-sufficient rural communes. Young radicals even reflected their society's preoccupation with power. The abuse of power, they claimed, lay at the root of America's social evils. "Power to the people" would bring a new era of justice.

As they probed their doubts about their parents' lives, the young rebels divided the older generations.

SISTERHOOD
The women's movement, the last great outpouring of the sixties, raised fundamental questions about sexual discrimination and human fulfillment.

A minority of their elders defended the right of their sons and daughters to a dissenting lifestyle. Often these adults found courage to act out their own feelings. Some marched for civil rights and peace. Others, acknowledging the need for a new intimacy in human relations, experimented with "encounter" and "sensitivity" groups and greater sexual freedom. A few joined the youthful dropouts. But a majority of adults opposed the new youth movement. By making public their private anxieties, the young rebels threatened the balance that older people were trying to maintain between adult responsibility and adult discontents. The more extreme the rebellion, the more widespread the opposition became. By 1970 the young radicals had lost almost all their adult sympathizers.

Women's Rights. The most lasting outgrowth of the rebellious sixties was a revived movement for women's rights. After a promising search for new directions in the 1920s, the women's movement had collapsed in the depression. Although during the forties women poured into the labor market to stay, and during the fifties expanded the range of their public activities, the question of basic rights remained dormant. Only in their private world away from work did women enjoy anything approximating the freedom of men. As dressing styles, leisure activities, and public behavior increasingly became "unisex," men continued to keep the best jobs. By the 1960s close to half of the women in America held paying jobs, partly because more than

one-third of the marriages in America ended in divorce. Most women received lower salaries or wages than men did for the same work, and an even larger proportion of women were blocked somewhere along the ladder of promotion in their occupations. Meanwhile, women's responsibilities at home scarcely changed. The widespread concerns about individual fulfillment, the anxieties about powerlessness, and the increasing doubts about the quality of American consumerism had particularly sharp application in the lives of women.

In 1963 Betty Friedan's *Feminine Mystique* broke the silence. By the end of the decade, a host of books and articles had appeared that analyzed the evils of sexism. The drive for black rights, in which women took a significant part, contributed a vocabulary to communicate women's feelings of oppression; antiwar activity, especially draft counseling, also helped sensitize and politicize college-age women. The civil rights movement inspired the acronym of a new pressure group, the National Organization for Women (NOW), which appeared in 1966. ("What do you want?" the civil rights marchers chanted. "FREEDOM!" "When do you want it?" "NOW!")

One portion of the swelling movement explored the myriad psychic and cultural ways in which women were bound into the role of "the second sex." Consciousness-raising activities that ranged from public bra burnings to private seminars sought to define women's special needs and give them outlets. A second

NOW's bill of rights lists women's grievances against American society and calls for an end to the economic and social injustices traditionally suffered by them.

The NOW Bill of Rights

WE demand:

I. That the United States Congress immediately pass the Equal Rights Amendment to the Constitution to provide that "Equality of rights under the law shall not be denied or abridged by the United States or by any State on account of sex," and that such then be immediately ratified by the several States.

II. That equal employment opportunity be guaranteed to all women, as well as men, by insisting that the Equal Employment Opportunity Commission enforce the prohibitions against sex discrimination in employment under Title VII of the Civil Rights Act of 1964 with the same vigor as it enforces the prohibitions against racial discrimination.

III. That women be protected by law to ensure their rights to return to their jobs within a reasonable time after childbirth without loss of seniority or other accrued benefits, and be paid maternity leave as a form of social security and/or employee benefit.

IV. Immediate revision of tax laws to permit the deduction of home and child care expenses for working parents.

V. That child care facilities be established by law on the same basis as parks, libraries, and public schools, adequate to the needs of children from the pre-school years through adolescence, as a community resource to be used by all citizens from all income levels.

VI. That the right of women to be educated to their full potential equally with men be secured by Federal and State Legislation, eliminating all discrimination and segregation by sex, written and unwritten, at all levels of education, including colleges, graduate and professional schools, loans and fellowships, and Federal and State training programs such as the Job Corps.

VII. The right of women in poverty to secure job training, housing, and family allowances on equal terms with men, but without prejudice to a parent's right to remain at home to care for his or her children; revision of welfare legislation and poverty programs which deny women dignity, privacy, and self-respect.

VIII. The right of women to control their own reproductive lives by removing from penal codes laws limiting access to contraceptive information and devices and laws governing abortion.

portion of the movement concentrated on women's economic plight, and this agenda met far less male resistance. Gender, like race or culture, was irrelevant to the skills standards that prevailed in most white-collar occupations. Here women's demands for an equal opportunity were an irrefutable claim. Both the federal courts and the national executive made commitments to enforce equal access to jobs, and equal pay for equal work. Although extensive discrimination against women remained, an important start had been made.

Counterattack. The counterculture and radical protests provoked a national backlash aimed at inhibiting federal intrusion on behalf of minorities, restoring conventional values, and reestablishing white, middle-class citizens at the center of American life. This eruption of middle America's anger reached full force in 1968, and as late as the 1980s its power was not yet spent.

The period of acute crisis over federal intrusiveness had begun in 1957, when Congress passed the first civil rights law since Reconstruction, federal troops enforced school desegregation in Little Rock, and the Warren Court stepped up its activism. By 1965 the barriers against national power appeared to be smashed: federal officials were registering Southern black voters, and federal funds for the war on poverty bypassed white middle Americans in favor of the people economically below them. Not only did the public welfare rolls swell enormously in the mid-1960s, but some agents of OEO even encouraged welfare recipients to demand more.

The first line of middle America's counterattack was against the blacks' drive for full equality. Contrary to the hopes of those in the civil rights movement, millions of whites understood the American creed not as a common system of national values, but as the justification for their particular set of values. Turning inward, they continued to be concerned only with their own families, cultural identities, and special local ways. Attempts to draw Americans into a uniform system of national rules arrived like an enemy invasion. In most cases they could not grasp the legal and bureaucratic procedures behind such rules, and many were "functionally illiterate" in the face of tax forms, insurance claims, credit contracts, and similar fine print.

Across America, skin color was a primary means of establishing protective barriers. White wage earners, who increasingly had to work with people of other colors, still refused to accept them into their daily lives. During the fifties these insular feelings had exploded in anger throughout the South, where the civil rights movement had begun. But temperatures were also rising in the North, where every city suffered from housing shortages and where local resources were increasingly strained, partly as a result of new migrations. Rural blacks and whites who had been replaced by mechanical cotton pickers, consolidated farms, and mechanized coal mining, poured into the city slums. So did Mexican Americans and Puerto Ricans, trying to escape their own grinding poverty. In the crowded, competitive northern cities, racial antagonisms turned into hate. When Martin Luther King, Jr., took his civil rights campaign north in 1964, the ferocity of the white reaction matched anything he had encountered in the South.

By itself, the civil rights movement would not have provoked a white revolt against federal authority. But the movement was accompanied by a broader drive for power. Many of the Warren Court's decisions interfered with the censorship of films, schoolbooks, and pornography by middle Americans. Its defense of the rights of accused alarmed these Americans, who feared street crime and thought that they could not walk in their neighborhoods if the police were hampered in the pursuit of suspects. The Court's outlawing of prayer and Bible reading in the public schools deeply offended the many Americans who continued to believe that religion belonged in the schools as well as the home. And the Court's use of the "one person, one vote" principle in redrawing state election districts undermined the customary way in which voters and politicians had sought to protect small towns against outside, urban intrusion. Thus the Supreme Court came to symbolize a wholesale assault on traditional American values. "Impeach Earl Warren" became a popular slogan of resistance.

American liberals had convinced themselves that their understanding of equality, opportunity, and justice was everybody's American creed. As they used this creed to make national policy, they assumed that no one would seriously question the new policy's impartiality. Bursts of opposition, they believed, were only temporary interruptions in the march toward nationwide acceptance. But this nationalizing process had the opposite effect. Instead of creating a nonpolitical consensus, it ignited fresh political conflicts. By 1965 not a great deal had actually changed. Only a small percentage of black children attended integrated classes. Many communities still found ways of keeping Christianity in and "alien" books out of their schools. Police procedures altered very little. Nevertheless, when conservative whites saw a solid phalanx in the national government arrayed against them, they prepared to fight for their traditional rights.

In northern and southern cities alike, advocates of traditional rights combated the racial integration of the schools, especially when integration meant busing

LOCAL AMERICA STRIKES BACK
The assault on traditional values and local rights triggered a nationwide response in the late sixties. In Cocoa Beach, Florida, marchers show their disdain for antiwar demonstrations.

black and white children. Numerous white Catholics in New Orleans, Philadelphia, and Boston actively resisted their church's policies of integration. Urban politicians attacked the local agencies of OEO and lobbied in Washington to disband it. In the towns as well as the cities, bumper stickers reading "Impeach Earl Warren" and "Support Your Local Police" signaled a growing opposition to judicial restraints and supervisory review boards. The Crime Control Act of 1968, which generally endorsed strong police action, was considered a significant victory in this cause. In many white communities Mayor Richard Daley of Chicago became an instant hero when he reportedly instructed the police to maim looters and kill arsonists during a ghetto riot.

The second line of conservative America's counterattack was directed at the youth rebellion. "Sideburns . . . shall not extend lower than the bottom of the ear opening and shall be of uniform width," the regulations of the Louisville Fire Department stated. "Beards, goatees or any other extraneous facial hair will not be permitted." Opinion polls showed consistently large majorities favoring severe punishment for drug users, including marijuana smokers. Although the Vietnam War was unpopular throughout the United States by 1968, waving a Vietcong flag or burning an American one, as television reported some radicals doing, evoked widespread anger. By traditional

values, affluent students had no right to insult their nation or squander its educational privileges. The New York police who cracked heads while breaking a campus strike at Columbia University in 1968, the townsmen who took a crowbar to the flower children, or the construction workers who roamed lower Manhattan beating up long-haired youths were expressing the feelings of innumerable fellow citizens. In May 1970, when four students at Kent State University were killed for no apparent reason by the National Guard, a nationwide poll tallied four out of five Americans on the side of the guardsmen.

What happened at Kent State typified what was happening throughout the country at the end of the decade. University administrators relied more and more on the local police to control student unrest. Law enforcement agencies killed, jailed, or scattered the leadership of a small, militant black power organization, the Black Panthers. After 1967, the peace marches in Washington were battling, antagonistic affairs, and the peace organizations, always a quarreling lot, became increasingly fragmented. Occasionally a happy episode broke the pattern. In the summer of 1969, "the nation of Woodstock," perhaps 400,000 young people, gathered at White Lake, New York, for a rock festival and a holiday frolic. But a few months later in Altamont, California, an attempt to repeat the joys of Woodstock dissolved in violence.

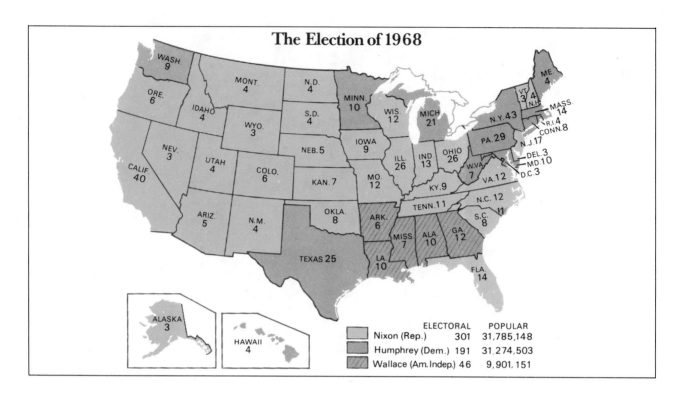

The Election of 1968

	ELECTORAL	POPULAR
Nixon (Rep.)	301	31,785,148
Humphrey (Dem.)	191	31,274,503
Wallace (Am. Indep.)	46	9,901,151

The Election of 1968. These crosscurrents dominated the presidential campaign of 1968. At the beginning of that year, the forces of protest and reform seemed on the verge of capturing the national government. The summer before, a quarter-million Americans had marched quietly through Washington in behalf of peace in Vietnam. Both their number and their discipline gave the movement a new respectability. The inheritor of this strength was a thoughtful, enigmatic Democratic senator from Minnesota, Eugene McCarthy, who in November 1967 opened his campaign for president on a peace platform. In January and February 1968, as the Tet offensive exposed the military failure of America's policy in Vietnam, McCarthy was touring New Hampshire in preparation for the first presidential primary. That March, the idealistic candidate no one had taken seriously received almost as many votes as President Johnson himself.

A few weeks after the New Hampshire primary, Johnson quit the race. A second peace candidate, Robert Kennedy, entered the lists. The boyish Bobby Kennedy, who had been attorney general in John Kennedy's administration and then senator from New York, attracted an even more zealous following than his older brother had. The favorite of the youth movement, however, was still McCarthy. His willingness to fight a lonely battle and his cool, moral style converted tens of thousands of college students, "Clean for Gene" with shaves and neckties, into his campaign workers.

McCarthy could not match Kennedy's broad appeal. In a decisive showdown in California, Kennedy won the primary and seemed assured of the Democratic nomination. But in the midst of a victory celebration in a Los Angeles hotel, Robert Kennedy was shot and killed by Sirhan B. Sirhan, a Jordanian immigrant ostensibly angered over Kennedy's support of Israel. The shock of a second Kennedy assassinated only two months after Martin Luther King's murder, and in the train of so much public violence, spread the numbing sense that society was consuming itself through paroxysms of hate. Eugene McCarthy, now the sole leader of the peace movement, unaccountably allowed his own presidential drive to lose momentum. That August in Chicago, while policemen were banging their way through a park full of young demonstrators outside convention headquarters, the Democrats nominated a very different Minnesota politician, the talkative, middle-of-the-road vice-president, Hubert Humphrey. Although Humphrey had a strong record on civil rights and other liberal causes, many Democrats felt that he had hopelessly compromised himself on Vietnam, and they greeted his nomination with anger and despair.

Liberal frustration was heightened when the Republicans nominated Richard M. Nixon. For the former vice-president, it was a remarkable political comeback from his defeats in the 1960 presidential campaign and the 1962 California gubernatorial election. Effectively taking advantage of widespread weariness with social divisions and national self-reproach, Nixon in 1968 declared himself the candidate of the "silent majority" who yearned for a restoration of public peace and unity. Yet the effectiveness of this appeal was undermined by Nixon's choice of a running mate, Governor Spiro Agnew of Maryland. Agnew, an abrasive man who offended many with his tasteless comments about various ethnic groups, aroused fears of a divisive Nixon presidency that would offer no relief from the troubles of the previous four years.

Agnew's actions were partly calculated to offset the appeal of Governor George C. Wallace of Alabama, who was running as an independent. Wallace claimed to be the advocate of "poor folks" against invading bureaucrats and of decent citizens against subversive youths, and he identified himself with patriotic virtues and conventional truths. Exploiting the white backlash against minorities and radicals, Wallace won 10 million votes. But he remained far behind Nixon and Humphrey, who almost evenly divided the remaining 86 percent of the popular vote.

The Nixon and Wallace campaigns increased Humphrey's attractiveness to moderates. Moreover, when Humphrey announced that he would stop the bombing of North Vietnam—and when Johnson did just that a few days before the election—Humphrey came within a hair of winning the presidency. But Johnson's failure in Vietnam was more than Humphrey could overcome. With only 43.4 percent of the popular vote and a margin of less than seven-tenths of one percent, Nixon gained the White House.

"Of all the extraordinary developments of 1968," one commentator observes, "perhaps least expected was the durability of characters and institutions in the face of defiant challenge." Events in the sixties had strained American political and social institutions to their limits, but the election of 1968 demonstrated that they were highly resilient and unlikely to break. Events in the next six years further testified to this fact.

United Press International, Inc.

PEACE AND FREEDOM

Shortly after this lively scene outside the 1968 Democratic convention, Chicago police attacked the demonstrators and the Democrats nominated Hubert Humphrey.

CHRONOLOGY

1961	Peace Corps organized.
	American-backed invasion of Cuba at Bay of Pigs fails.
	Berlin Wall erected.
1962	Cuban missile crisis.
1963	Kennedy proposes major tax reduction and civil rights bills.
	Test Ban Treaty between United States and Soviet Union.
	Kennedy assassinated; Lyndon B. Johnson becomes president.
1964	Johnson announces national war on poverty.
	Free speech movement at Berkeley.
	Major Civil Rights Act passed.
	Tonkin Gulf Resolution.
	Johnson elected president.
1965	Johnson sends American combat troops to Vietnam; bombing of North begins.
	American intervention in Dominican Republic.
	Johnson's Great Society programs enacted.
	Second major Civil Rights Act passed.
	Ghetto riots in Watts section of Los Angeles.
1966	National Organization for Women (NOW) founded.
1968	Martin Luther King, Jr., and Senator Robert Kennedy assassinated.
	Richard M. Nixon elected president.
1969	U.S. puts first man on the moon.
1970	Four students killed by the National Guard at Kent State University.

SUGGESTED READINGS

William E. Leuchtenburg, *A Troubled Feast: American Society Since 1945* (rev. ed., 1979), and Lawrence S. Wittner, *Cold War America: From Hiroshima to Watergate* (2nd ed., 1978), are contrasting surveys of the sixties. On John Kennedy and his administration, Theodore C. Sorensen, *Kennedy* (1965), and Arthur M. Schlesinger, Jr., *A Thousand Days* (1965), are appreciative assessments by insiders. Bruce Miroff, *Pragmatic Illusions: The Presidential Politics of John F. Kennedy* (1976), emphasizes Kennedy's limitations. In *The Promise and the Performance: The Leadership of John F. Kennedy* (1975), Lewis J. Paper tries to find a middle ground. Aida DiPace Donald, ed., *John F. Kennedy and the New Frontier* (1966), is a useful anthology. Herbert Parmet, *Jack: The Struggles of John F. Kennedy* (1980), is a recent critical account. Richard E. Neustadt, *Presidential Power* (1960), is an analysis of leadership that reputedly influenced Kennedy. Tom Wicker, *JFK and LBJ* (1968), finds Kennedy wanting as a political leader alongside of Johnson. Arthur Schlesinger, Jr., *Robert Kennedy and His Times* (1978), is the fullest account of John Kennedy's younger brother. Also see the articles on the twentieth anniversary of Kennedy's death in *The New Republic*, Nov. 21, 1983.

Initial accounts of Lyndon Johnson's personality and presidency can be found in Robert Novak and Rowland Evans, *Lyndon B. Johnson: The Exercise of Power* (1966); Eric Goldman, *The Tragedy of Lyndon Johnson* (1969); Doris Kearns, *Lyndon Johnson and the American Dream* (1976); and Ronnie Dugger, *The Politician: The Life and Times of Lyndon Johnson* (1982). For the most comprehensive account of LBJ's early life, see the first volume of what will eventually be a three-volume study, Robert A. Caro, *The Years of Lyndon Johnson: The Path to Power* (1982). For a useful but critical recounting of Johnson's Great Society, see Marvin E. Gettleman and David Mermelstein, *The Great Society Reader* (1967).

The references in the previous chapter are also useful on the civil rights movement in the sixties. In addition, August Meier and Elliott Rudwick, eds., *Black Protest in the Sixties* (1970), and Robert Conot, *Rivers of Blood, Years of Darkness* (1968), on the Watts riots, are both of value.

The violence of the sixties is analyzed in the *Report of the National Advisory Commission on Civil Disorders* (1968). The background to the violence of the decade is explored in Hugh Davis Graham and Ted Robert Gurr, *The History of Violence in America* (1969), and Richard Hofstadter and Michael Wallace, eds., *American Violence: A Documentary History* (1970), which also includes an important essay by Hofstadter. Nathan Glazer, *Remembering the Answers* (1970), explores the campus upheavals.

The literature of the youth rebellion, or counterculture, begins with Jack Kerouac's *On the Road* (1957) and more or less ends with Charles A. Reich's *The Greening of America* (1971). The world against which these youths rebelled is discussed in William H. Whyte, *The Organization Man* (1956), and Scott Donaldson, *The Suburban Myth* (1969). Theodore Roszak, *The Making of a Counter-Culture* (1969), and Richard Flacks, *Youth and Social Change* (1971), attempt to probe the rebellion's inner meaning. Philip E. Slater, *The Pursuit of Loneliness* (1970), contrasts the rebel culture with establishment culture. In *Young Radicals* (1968), Kenneth Keniston analyzes leaders in the rebellion. Kirkpatrick Sale, *SDS* (1973), is a sympathetic study of its most prominent campus organization. Four fine books add historical perspective: John P. Diggins, *The American Left in the Twentieth*

Century (1973), Rosabeth Moss Kantor, *Commitment and Community* (1972), James Weinstein, *Ambiguous Legacy: The Left in American Politics* (1975), and Lawrence S. Wittner, *Rebels against War: The American Peace Movement, 1941–1960* (1969). Tom Wolfe's *The Electric Kool-Aid Acid Test* (1968) and Joan Didion's *Slouching Towards Bethlehem* (1968) comment on the culture of Haight-Ashbury.

A fine general survey of women's history is Nancy Woloch, *Women and the American Experience* (1984). Three outstanding books—Betty Friedan, *The Feminine Mystique* (1963), Kate Millett, *Sexual Politics* (1970), and Robin Morgan (comp.), *Sisterhood Is Powerful* (1970)—suggest the range and force of the women's movement. Peter G. Filene's *Him/Her/Self: Sex Roles in Modern America* (1975) is also useful. The best historical account of American women in the half-century after 1920 is William H. Chafe, *The American Woman* (1970). Sara Evans, *Personal Politics: The Roots of American Women's Liberation in the Civil Rights Movement and the New Left* (1979), should also be consulted.

Sources on the resistance to national liberalism and young radicalism are scattered. Arthur B. Shostak's *Blue-Collar Life* (1969) summarizes an array of studies on white urban wage earners and their families. Bennett M. Berger, *Working-Class Suburb* (1960), Herbert J. Gans, *The Levittowners* (1967), and William Kornblum, *Blue-Collar Community* (1974), add substantially to this analysis. Robert A. Caro, *The Power Broker: Robert Moses and the Fall of New York* (1974), Herbert J. Gans, *The Urban Villagers* (1962), and Sam Bass Warner, Jr., *The Urban Wilderness* (1972), include perceptive accounts of how government policies have damaged inner-city life. In *Small Town in Mass Society* (1958), Arthur J. Vidich and Joseph Bensman describe the defenses of townspeople against external authority. In *All Our Kin* (1974), Carol Stack explains the creative adaptations among poor black families. Peter Binzen, *Whitetown, U.S.A.* (1970), discusses urban dwellers in rebellion against government authority, and Numan V. Bartley, *The Rise of Massive Resistance* (1969), and Neil R. McMillen, *The Citizens' Council* (1971), trace an earlier rebellion in the South. The new explicitness about ethnic identities is explored in Michael Novak's *The Rise of the Unmeltable Ethnics* (1972).

References in the previous chapter are again of use in consulting additional materials on American foreign relations in the sixties. Walter LaFeber, *America, Russia and the Cold War, 1945–1980* (4th ed., 1980), contains a fine survey of the decade. On Kennedy's foreign policy the following books are particularly useful. Richard J. Walton's *Cold War and Counterrevolution* (1972) takes a negative view of Kennedy's foreign policy. The decline of Kennedy's Alliance for Progress is traced in Jerome Levinson and Juan de Onís, *The Alliance That Lost Its Way* (1970). On the Cuban missile crisis, Graham T. Allison, *Essence of Decision* (1971), offers an intriguing set of alternative explanations, and Herbert S. Dinerstein, *The Making of a Missile Crisis: October 1962* (1976), tries to view the confrontation from Moscow's perspective. The best account of the Test Ban Treaty is in Glenn T. Seaborg, *Kennedy, Khrushchev, and the Test Ban* (1981). The Kennedy-Johnson policies in the Caribbean are discussed in Lester D. Langley, *The United States and the Caribbean, 1900–1970* (1980).

The Kennedy-Johnson policies in Vietnam are the subject of numerous books. George McTurnan Kahin and John W. Lewis, *The United States in Vietnam* (rev. ed., 1969), is a solid introduction to the war in Southeast Asia. Most writers on the war condemn the United States, and *The Indochina Story* (1970) by the Committee of Concerned Asian Scholars is a particularly striking example. Donald S. Zagoria, *Vietnam Triangle: Moscow, Peking, Hanoi* (1967), and Gunther Lewy, *America in Vietnam* (1978), are two of the relatively few defenses of American policy. Henry Brandon, *Anatomy of Error: The Inside Story of the Asian War on the Potomac, 1954–1969* (1969), and Arthur M. Schlesinger, Jr., *The Bitter Heritage: Vietnam and American Democracy, 1941–1966* (1967), seek a middle ground. David Halberstam's fascinating *The Best and the Brightest* (1972) dissects the policymaking in Washington, and Frances FitzGerald's excellent *Fire in the Lake* (1972) analyzes the consequences of this policy in Vietnam. J. William Fulbright, *The Arrogance of Power* (1967), expresses the opposition from Congress. A notorious massacre of civilians in Vietnam is exposed in Seymour M. Hersh, *My Lai 4* (1970). Two recent works are particularly worth attention: Arnold R. Isaacs, *Without Honor: Defeat in Vietnam and Cambodia* (1983), and Stanley Karnow, *Vietnam: A History* (1983).

33 An Elusive Stability: The Modern Republic Since 1969

Cycles of advance and retreat have been central features of twentieth-century American history. The return of "normalcy" in the twenties followed the intense battles for domestic and world reform in the progressive era and the First World War; the conventionality of the fifties succeeded the far-reaching alterations of the New Deal and the Second World War. The idealism and conflict of the sixties gave way to a new period of conservatism in the seventies and early eighties. In response to the big-government programs of the Great Society and the turmoil unleashed by the Vietnam War and the counterculture, the Nixon, Ford, Carter, and Reagan years saw a demand for less governmental power, the reassertion of old values, and a renewed emphasis on America's virtues.

The conservatism of the period from 1969 to 1984, however, was no guarantee against upheaval and change. Just as the twenties and the fifties had their unsettling social alterations and scandals, so the fifteen years after Lyndon Johnson left office had their share of disturbing events. Although Americans could savor their nation's scientific expertise in a series of extraordinary achievements in outer space—the moon landing in 1969 and the space shuttle launchings a decade later—the possibility and even the desirability of economic expansion and technological advance became nagging problems during the seventies and eighties. Unprecedented shortages of basic raw materials and soaring costs of oil and natural gas; "stagflation" (sluggish economic growth combined with persistent inflation); defeat in Vietnam; the Watergate scandal and a president's ejection from office; the two worst economic downturns since the Great Depression; and the largest government deficits in the nation's history—all these shook confidence in the foundations of American strength and made the years from Richard Nixon's presidency to Ronald Reagan's a time of elusive stability.

The Imperial Presidency: Nixon

Richard Nixon's five and a half years in the White House are a study in contradictions. Mistrustful and tending to see a "crisis" in every political squall, he nevertheless handled international affairs skillfully and shrewdly. A conservative Republican opponent of liberal social programs and relaxed moral standards, he dismantled some of Johnson's Great Society, resisted demands for further advances in civil rights, and appointed federal judges who would stem the tide of social permissiveness. Yet his administration also supported social reforms that pleased even his sharpest critics. An advocate of orthodox economic ideas, the president initially limited federal intrusion into the workings of the marketplace. But during his first term the country was wracked by a bad recession and rising prices, let loose by spending on the Vietnam War and Great Society programs—and Nixon tried to slow inflation and restore prosperity by using liberal devices. A staunch Cold Warrior with a record of unswerving hostility to communism, Nixon continued the war in Vietnam for another four years and carried it into Cambodia and Laos as well. But his administration eventually negotiated a "peace with honor" in Vietnam, and Nixon startled the world not only by pursuing a policy of détente with the Soviet Union, but also by opening the door to improved relations with the communist People's Republic of China, America's harshest enemy in the fifties and sixties. "Law and order" conservatives, Nixon and Vice-President Spiro Agnew ridiculed the "long-haired" radicals who rejected American conventions. Yet both men, greedy for money and indifferent to democratic traditions, violated fundamental canons of American law and politics, and both were driven from office in disgrace.

The Politics of Moderation. Nixon took office in 1969 under a cloud. He had been elected with a minority of the

popular vote, and he was a stiff, uninspiring speaker. Liberals bitterly disliked him, remembering his red-baiting as senator and vice-president, his alliance with Joseph McCarthy, and his transparent posturing to gain political ends. "He is the least 'authentic' man alive," one critic said. Countless intellectuals nursed a hatred for "Tricky Dick" Nixon unlike anything a new president had faced in the twentieth century.

Yet Nixon initially surprised his critics, showing himself politically more moderate than they had expected. This was partly the result of any modern president's inability—regardless of his intent—to reverse the historical growth of federal power. Moreover, determined to have eight years in the White House and to make his mark on history, especially in foreign affairs, the new president worked hard to establish his credibility with moderates. In his inaugural speech he called for a lowered political temperature in the United States and tried to position himself at the center of domestic affairs. "America has suffered from a fever of words," he said, "from inflated rhetoric that promises more than it can deliver; from angry rhetoric that fans discontents into hatreds. . . . We cannot learn from one another until we stop shouting at one another—until we speak quietly enough so that our words can be heard as well as our voices." Underscoring this appeal to the political center, Nixon appointed a number of moderate Republicans or independents to his cabinet. Daniel Patrick Moynihan, a Democratic adviser to the president on urban affairs, and Assistant Secretary of HEW James Farmer, a black leader, also helped give Nixon's program a centrist tone.

In addition, the administration backed a number of reform measures that surprised liberals and strengthened Nixon's hold on moderates. The president's Interior Department made conservation of natural resources its highest priority, while Nixon himself proposed establishing the Environmental Protection Agency (EPA) in 1970. Largely leaving Great Society programs intact, the White House also successfully promoted a 50 percent increase in Social Security benefits, a greater federal role in medical education through increased grants, and the lowering of the voting age to eighteen, which became part of the Constitution when the Twenty-Sixth Amendment was ratified in 1971.

Nixon proposed a fundamental change in the country's welfare system. Instead of maintaining the cumbersome bureaucracy and varied levels of state support that were central features of existing programs, the administration developed the Family Assistance Plan that would guarantee all welfare recipients a minimum income and encourage many adults receiving such help either to work or to register for job training. Although Congress rejected the program, Nixon's plan demonstrated a commitment to helping the poor and streamlining the bureaucracy that might have issued from a liberal Democratic administration. At the beginning of 1971 Nixon also called for a "New American Revolution." His program fell far short of what its name promised, but it did include a plan, which Congress enacted, for sharing revenue between the federal and state governments.

Nixon's close identification with America's successful space program also contributed to the image of a progressive, innovative administration. In July 1969 John F. Kennedy's pledge to put men on the moon by the end of the decade was fulfilled when American astronauts Neil A. Armstrong and Edwin E. Aldrin, Jr., stepped onto the lunar surface. Television cameras recorded Nixon talking to them by telephone and greeting them on the deck of the aircraft carrier that retrieved their spacecraft in the Pacific Ocean.

On civil rights as well, the Nixon White House managed to identify itself with significant gains. Making four appointments to the Supreme Court, including Chief Justice Warren Burger, Nixon received partial credit for some of the Court's surprisingly liberal decisions. These included ensuring women's constitutional right to abortion in *Roe* v. *Wade* (1973), and upholding the constitutionality of busing to achieve school desegregation in *Swann* v. *Charlotte-Mecklenburg Board of Education* (1971). The administration sued the state of Georgia for maintaining separate school systems for blacks and whites. When the number of students in all-black schools declined by almost 75 percent in the first two years of Nixon's term, the White House was able to take substantial credit for promoting minority rights. Under Nixon, the federal bureaucracy and courts promoted affirmative action programs to open educational and employment opportunities for women and minorities who had encountered past discrimination. And in 1972 Nixon raised no objections as Congress sent to the states for ratification the Equal Rights Amendment (ERA), providing that "Equality of rights under the law shall not be denied or abridged . . . on account of sex."

The president's economic policies also showed the administration as more flexible and moderate than opponents had thought it would be. Serious economic problems had confronted the new president, in large part a legacy of Johnson's refusal to raise taxes to finance the Great Society and the Vietnam War. With inflation accelerating, Nixon first tried standard conservative remedies: reduced federal spending and a slower growth of the money supply. But these policies only produced a sharp economic downturn without a corresponding drop in prices. During 1970–71 unemployment doubled to 6 percent, while inflation ran at about 5 percent, the worst since the Korean War. In addition, for the first time since 1893 the United States suffered a trade deficit, paying more for the goods it bought than it sold abroad. To meet these difficulties, Nixon sharply reversed course, embracing the doctrines of the British economist John Maynard Keynes that once had been the exclusive preserve of liberal Democrats and that Republicans had scorned. Declaring frankly that "I am now a Keynesian," Nixon adopted the strategy of deficit spending to stimulate economic growth, introduced wage and price controls to hold down inflation, and devalued the dollar to boost American exports. These departures from traditional free-market ideas produced a strong economic rebound and smaller price increases in the first half of 1972. Although the president's policies did not provide permanent relief from the unprecedented stagflation that persisted throughout his first term, they did promote temporary gains and strengthened impressions that Nixon was more a practical political leader than a doctrinaire conservative.

The Appeal to Conservatives.

Yet just as Nixon was struggling to win the favor of the political center, he was also trying to outflank George Wallace on the right by appealing to "middle Americans" fed up with street rioting and the counterculture's attacks on traditional values. Nixon aimed to create a Republican majority of middle Americans, chiefly white suburbanites. He selected an all-white, all-male Republican cabinet, including the outspoken conservative John Mitchell as attorney general; as his principal White House aides he chose a pair of hard, austere organization men, H. R. Haldeman and John Ehrlichman, who were strongly identified with middle America. Thus the new president left no doubt that his administration would reflect conservative views. And no administration figure expressed the conservative outlook more strongly than Spiro Agnew. Nixon had been the harshly partisan voice of the Eisenhower presidency; now Agnew served the same function. He heaped scorn on "an effete corps of impudent . . . intellectuals," accused the television networks of bias, and locked horns with such influential liberal newspapers as the *New York Times* and the *Washington Post*. The vice-president attacked peace demonstrators as "ideological eunuchs," deplored the "spirit of national masochism," and flayed upper-middle-class snobs whose permissiveness was producing a generation of immoral "potheads." He was praised for his efforts by such reactionaries as Senator Strom Thurmond of South Carolina, who compared him to John C. Calhoun, "the greatest vice-president in the history of America."

Several administration actions were calculated to appeal to the right. Despite some steps toward social reform, the White House clearly rejected starting new social programs, and it cut back on existing ones. Limiting the activities of such Great Society agencies as OEO and Model Cities, the administration in 1972 also began to withhold funds appropriated by Congress for social programs. At the same time, Nixon vetoed health, education, and welfare bills passed by the Democratic-controlled Congress, and he even failed to protest when Congress killed most of his own proposals for social advance.

The administration's occasional steps forward on civil rights were counterbalanced by undisguised efforts to accommodate southern segregationists—a political strategy aimed at ensuring Nixon's popularity in the South in the 1972 campaign. Nixon's Justice Department opposed an extension of the Voting Rights Act of 1965, asking instead for a law that would remove federal commitments to enforcement in the South. In addition, the administration won a delay in desegregating Mississippi's schools that remained in effect until October 1969, when the NAACP gained a favorable ruling on the issue from the Supreme Court. After the Court in 1971 ordered school busing to promote desegregation, the White House asked Congress for legislation restricting future busing. "For the first time since Woodrow Wilson," declared the NAACP, "we have a national administration that can be rightly characterized as anti-Negro." The accuracy of this charge was confirmed by Nixon's efforts in 1969 and 1970 to appoint to the Court two southern jurists with white supremacist views. Although the Senate rejected both as lacking sufficient distinction, Nixon publicly assured southerners that men with a similar outlook would one day sit on the high court.

Other minority groups also clashed with the administration. Numerous migrants from Latin America, many of whom had crossed into the United States illegally and could not speak English, struggled to overcome their poverty. Although these immigrants participated in the various affirmative action programs begun in the sixties, they were only beginning to use group pressure to win a larger share of jobs. Their most effective organization developed in California's "farm factories," where Mexican American labor supported a thriving commercial agriculture. Under the patient, persistent leadership of César Chavez, the United Farm Workers rallied national support through boycotts of non-union lettuce and grapes. By the seventies Chicano farm workers had built a solid union base in areas where exploitation had long been a way of life, but they and other Hispanics viewed the Nixon administration as hostile to them and insensitive to their needs.

The same was true of native Americans. In the 1950s, after the Republicans had declared an end to

STRENGTH IN UNION
Through persistence and publicity, the moderate César Chavez organized Chicano laborers in California's "farm factories."

the national supervision of native Americans and had placed their reservations under the laws of the individual states, various tribes had suffered grievous losses. The Klamath Nation in Oregon had promptly lost its rich lumber resources, and the demoralized Menominee Nation in Wisconsin had seen its small, tight economy disappear in a rush of panic sales. Not until the late sixties did a significant change occur. Adapting the protest tactics of the time, groups of native Americans, led by the Sioux Nations, occupied sites that symbolized the burial of their heritage beneath white civilization: Alcatraz Island, Mount Rushmore, Fort Sheridan, and Wounded Knee, South Dakota, where in 1973 they engaged in a bloody confrontation with law enforcement agents.* Overlapping these public and often violent protests, striking victories occurred in the courts. In a wave of separate actions that began in 1969 in the Alaskan hinterland and that extended from the Northwest fisheries to the Maine woods, some native Americans transformed their endlessly violated treaties from another century into a legal basis for claiming important economic rights through the processes of law. As a whole, however, native Americans in the seventies continued to suffer

* For the Wounded Knee massacre, see chapter 22, p. 557.

more severely from poverty and disease than any other cultural group in the United States, a situation largely unrecognized by the federal government.

The ambiguities of the administration's approach to civil rights, the social and political crosscurrents of the period, and the momentum of federal power were all illustrated by the fate of affirmative action programs in the Nixon years. Affirmative action was one of the most effective weapons that the national government developed in combating racial and sex discrimination. It was also one of the most controversial, for it involved setting goals (critics called them quotas) for admitting women and minorities to higher education institutions and labor unions, as well as for employing and promoting these victims of past discrimination in colleges and universities, local police and fire departments, and a host of white- and blue-collar jobs funded by federal contracts. Affirmative action programs were largely created by federal officials and judges, interpreting a section of the 1964 Civil Rights Act. Once set in motion, the policy won strong support from minority and women's organizations.

Affirmative action struck at the core of white male dominance in society and the economy, and it raised thorny problems of deciding who should bear the burden of reversing past discriminatory patterns. Especially because a sluggish economy made the 1970s

NIXON AND KISSINGER
Starting as Nixon's adviser, Henry Kissinger became America's most prominent diplomat in the seventies.

a period of intense competition for jobs and promotion, it evoked angry cries of "reverse discrimination." Along with busing, affirmative action thus proved to be one of the most divisive consequences of the federal government's advocacy of disadvantaged groups' rights. But unlike busing, which Nixon and many other politicians felt free to denounce, affirmative action did not become a major political issue until the Reagan presidency. Undeniably affirmative action speeded up the entry of minorities and women into upwardly mobile careers that modern social and economic change had set in motion. And if critics worried that affirmative action was making the law more, not less, gender- and color-conscious, supporters welcomed the widening of opportunities for pursuing a well-paying occupation or professional career.

Foreign Affairs: "An Enduring Structure of Peace."

Unlike most twentieth-century American presidents, Nixon came to the White House better prepared to deal with foreign relations than with domestic affairs. Through extensive reading and travel he had prepared himself for major undertakings abroad, and during his term he devoted himself principally to solving world problems. He found a congenial partner in Henry Kissinger, a Harvard professor who became first his national security adviser and then his secretary of state. A brilliant analyst of world problems, Kissinger became known as a realist who understood the nature of power and how to defend American interests.

Nixon and Kissinger assumed that they were facing a new era in international relations, one in which the Soviet-American power struggle could no longer be Washington's all-consuming concern. "The rigid bipolar world of the 1940s and 1950s," Nixon said in 1971, had given way "to the fluidity of a new era of multilateral diplomacy." The number of independent nations had increased from 51 in 1945 to 127 in 1970, and the communist bloc had fragmented into what Nixon called "competing centers of doctrine and power." Thus had arisen "an increasingly heterogeneous and complex world." To meet these changed circumstances, Nixon and Kissinger aimed to encourage local and regional initiatives by groups of nations and to foster individual nations' independence and self-sufficiency. Through the recognition and acceptance of international diversity, they hoped to bring about widespread cooperation among nations that would lead to "an enduring structure of peace." This grand design included plans for improving relations with Russia and China. But Nixon and Kissinger believed that their vision could not be realized until they settled the war in Vietnam.

The Slow Retreat from Vietnam. Ending the conflict was thus their first aim. But achieving "peace with honor" in Vietnam proved unexpectedly difficult. Instead of a speedy conclusion to the fighting, which Nixon had promised in his 1968 campaign, the struggle lasted four more years and the United States lost 27,000 more lives. The bloodshed was prolonged because the administration sought an unrealizable objective: before quitting the war, Nixon wished to be sure that South Vietnam would survive as an independent state, so that the United States would not face renewed domestic recriminations over another Asian "loss." But as a client state ruled by unstable governments lacking widespread popular support, South Vietnam could not defend itself without the benefit of continuing American military aid. This the Nixon administration could not give.

Washington tried to negotiate a settlement with the North Vietnamese in 1969. Hanoi refused to talk. Nixon thereupon announced a program of Vietnamization, whereby the United States would withdraw from the fighting as the South Vietnamese became capable of defending themselves. Although the administration reduced the number of American troops in Vietnam from half a million to 39,000 over the next three years, fierce fighting punctuated these withdrawals. In April 1970 American and South Vietnamese ground forces widened the war by striking at North Vietnamese units in Cambodia (Kampuchea). When the invasion provoked renewed campus demonstrations in the United States, which led to the death of six students in Ohio and Mississippi and the early closing of some colleges and universities, Nixon defended his action as necessary to the survival of free institutions everywhere. If "the world's most powerful nation acts like a pitiful helpless giant," he said, "the forces of totalitarianism and anarchy will threaten free nations . . . throughout the world."

The president's militancy, however, did not immediately bring Hanoi to the peace table, nor did it advance the cause of Saigon's independence. In March 1972, after further U.S. efforts at negotiation with Hanoi came to nothing, the North Vietnamese launched a large-scale invasion of the South. Nixon answered with massive B-52 attacks, the mining of Haiphong harbor, and a naval blockade of North Vietnam. This round of fighting at last produced an American–North Vietnamese agreement to halt the war. But Saigon refused to go along with the settlement, which called for an American withdrawal while leaving North Vietnamese forces in place in the South. To force both Vietnams into an agreement, Nixon used the carrot and the stick. Promising the South Vietnamese an additional billion dollars in military supplies, and warning that Saigon would have to

go it alone if it did not conform to Washington's demands, Nixon also committed himself to "swift and severe retaliatory action" if Hanoi broke the peace agreement. At the same time, he ordered twelve days of air attacks on the North in December 1972, during which the United States dropped more bombs than in the entire period from 1969 to 1971.

Unable to resist, both Vietnams agreed to a settlement in January 1973 that finally extricated the United States from its longest war. But "peace with honor" came at a high price. The war had cost over a million Vietnamese lives; 57,000 Americans were killed, and close to 300,000 were wounded. In the end, these losses were in vain, for in the spring of 1975 Saigon fell to communist arms. Although Nixon had promised the South Vietnamese that they could "count on us," he had failed to reckon with public and congressional determination to halt America's "endless support for an endless war."

Détente with China and the Soviet Union. While the Nixon administration wound down the war in Southeast Asia, it also tried to create a "structure of peace" through improved relations with Peking and Moscow. The hostility between the two communist superpowers, coupled with the desire in each nation to devote more energy to its internal affairs, made both receptive to achieving a better understanding with the United States. Preliminary conversations in 1971 between Peking and Washington indicated that both sides were ready for a major change in relations. To facilitate détente with China, Kissinger first met secretly with Premier Chou En-lai; then, in the summer of 1971, the president broke the news that he would visit China.

In February 1972 Nixon made good on his commitment to better relations with China by traveling to Peking. His objectives were to end twenty-two years of mutual hostility and to ally China to the United States in a drive to curb Moscow's "geopolitical ambitions." "What brings us together," Nixon told Chairman Mao Tse-tung, "is a recognition of a new situation in the world and a recognition on our part that what is important is not a nation's internal political philosophy. What is important is its policy toward the rest of the world and toward us." One of the most significant acts of his presidency was Nixon's abandonment of his doctrinaire anticommunism in order to reach an accommodation with the People's Republic of China. In the Shanghai communiqué at the close of the talks, the United States and the People's Republic announced their rejection of "foreign domination" over "any part of China or any independent country in this world." Obviously referring to the Soviet Union, they agreed to oppose the "efforts by any other country . . . to estab-

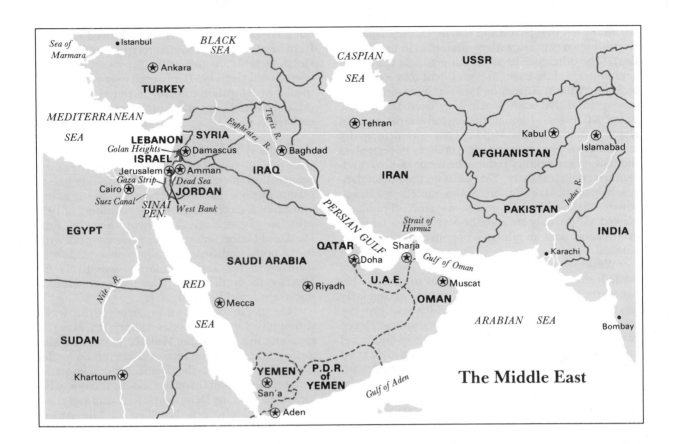

The Middle East

lish . . . hegemony." They also agreed to disagree about Taiwan: Nixon acknowledged that the island was a part of China but warned that the United States would not abandon it or allow it forcibly to be incorporated into the People's Republic.

In May 1972 Nixon and Kissinger followed their successful negotiations in Peking with a visit to Moscow. The Soviet leader, Leonid Brezhnev, who sought to limit the range of Russia's international involvements, willingly grasped a chance to lessen the tensions with his country's chief rival. Nixon and Kissinger shrewdly perceived that their acknowledgment of the Soviet Union as a unique state determined to follow its own destiny would produce meaningful agreements congenial to a new world order. "There must be room in this world for two great nations with different systems to live together and work together," Nixon declared in Moscow. As a consequence of this realism, as well as of Soviet eagerness to forestall a full-scale Sino-American rapprochement and to achieve greater economic well-being for its own people, Russia's leaders agreed to sign the Strategic Arms Limitation Treaty (SALT I) with the United States, to expand Russian-American trade, and to avoid international tensions that could play havoc with détente.

The Continuing Cold War: Asia, Latin America, and the Middle East. Yet these advances toward a new "structure of peace" did not mean the end of the Cold War. At the same time the Nixon administration was improving relations with China and Russia, it was also demonstrating its reflexive anticommunism in Asia, Latin America, and the Middle East. This helped perpetuate the East-West struggle. For example, Nixon saw the war between India and Pakistan in 1971 less as a regional conflict than as a battle between Soviet and Chinese client states in which the United States should side with Peking. Convinced that Pakistan was responsible for the crisis, which was essentially a local affair, administration critics complained that American policy was essentially a throwback to the same kind of Cold War orthodoxy that had sucked the nation into Vietnam. Similarly, the White House worked to topple Chile's socialist regime under Salvador Allende, whom it considered pro-Soviet and dangerous to United States interests in Latin America. Although numerous American officials believed that Allende's government presented no serious threat to the United States, the Nixon administration helped bring about the military coup of September 1973 that cost Allende his life.

Many felt that Nixon and Kissinger also displayed an overblown concern with communism in the Middle East. "The difference between our goal and the Soviet goal in the Middle East," the president told Secretary of State William Rogers in 1969, "is very simple but fundamental. *We* want peace. *They* want the Middle East." Kissinger, although not entirely agreeing with Nixon's view that the Middle East was principally an arena of Soviet-American conflict, nevertheless thought it "essential to reduce the scope of Soviet adventurist policies" there. This focus on the Soviet danger helped tie the United States closely to Israel, which Nixon—like all presidents since Truman—viewed as "the only state in the Middle East which is pro-freedom and an effective opponent to Soviet expansion."

Washington's close identification with Israel made it difficult for the United States to mediate between the Israelis and the Arab states, particularly Egypt, Jordan, and Syria, all of which had lost important territories to Israel in 1967. For almost eleven years after the Suez crisis of 1956, the Arabs and Israel had remained on the edge of war. Guerrilla attacks on Israel by Palestinians, who contended that the Jewish state had driven them from their homeland, kept the area in constant tension. In June 1967 these difficulties led to the Six Day War in which Israel seized the Sinai Peninsula from Egypt, the Golan Heights from Syria, and all territory on the west bank of the Jordan River from Jordan. Convinced that these Arab states would not risk further losses in another war with Israel, and that the Soviets, whom they credited with excessive influence, would hold the Arabs back from another conflict, the Nixon administration failed to anticipate the Egyptian-Syrian surprise attack on Israel on the Jewish holy day of Yom Kippur in October 1973. The administration played a major part in arranging a cease-fire and used the conflict to adopt a more even-handed approach to Arab-Israeli differences. Nevertheless, because the United States resupplied Israel with weapons during the fighting, the Arab states proclaimed an oil embargo against the West. Cutting oil production by 25 percent from the September 1973 output, Arab oil producers deprived the United States and its allies of needed supplies. Their action led to fuel shortages, long lines of automobiles at filling stations, and a doubling of gasoline prices in the United States during the fall of 1973.

Recognizing America's economic dependence on Arab oil and the unproductiveness of a narrow anti-communist view of Middle Eastern events, Nixon sent Kissinger to the area. The secretary of state shuttled between Israel, Egypt, and Syria trying to find diplomatic solutions to the region's conflicts. Between November 1973 and September 1975, Kissinger worked out a series of agreements that removed Israeli forces from newly captured Syrian territory and a part of the Golan Heights, reopened the Suez Canal (which had been closed since 1967), restored part of the Sinai Peninsula to Egyptian control, initiated indirect peace talks between Egypt and Israel, and ended the Arab oil embargo.

The Election of 1972. Nixon entered the 1972 campaign with a solid record of achievement overseas and an economy on the mend at home. Yet neither his accomplishments nor his popularity was so strong as to guarantee him a second term. At the beginning of 1972, his principal Democratic opponent, Senator Edmund Muskie of Maine, was running neck and neck with him in the polls, and George Wallace, who made a strong showing in the early primaries, was likely to cost Nixon votes on the right. Thus the president faced an uncertain reelection bid.

Circumstances, however, opened the way to a stunningly lopsided Nixon victory. In May 1972 a spectator in a crowd shot Wallace, paralyzing him and forcing him out of the race. Muskie ran an ineffectual campaign and lost the Democratic nomination to Senator George McGovern of South Dakota, who was identified with the Democratic left wing and the counterculture. McGovern horrified middle Americans with talk of giving welfare recipients a thousand dollars a year, cutting the defense budget, and crawling to Hanoi to beg for peace. Moreover, he stumbled badly when he had to replace his vice-presidential nominee, Senator Thomas Eagleton of Missouri, who revealed that he had been hospitalized three times for emotional disorders. Instead of being able to focus on Nixon's failings, McGovern had to appease conservative Democrats and defend his integrity and capacity for the presidency. Most voters gave him negative marks. Winning only 37.5 percent of the popular vote, and only 17 electoral votes (from Massachusetts and the District of Columbia), McGovern fared even worse than had Goldwater against Johnson in 1964. Nixon's 60.7 percent of the popular count and 520 electoral votes made him the third most successful victor in a presidential contest in American history. But the Democrats kept control of Congress, and Nixon became the only president to begin two terms with the opposition dominant in both houses.

Watergate. Nixon's second term found him immersed in a series of scandals revealing the worst constitutional abuses by high officials in the country's history, and it ended in the most serious crisis that the office of the presidency had ever faced.

Vice-President Agnew was the first administration figure to leave office in disgrace. Early in 1973 the

"He says he's from the phone company . . ."

PRESIDENT AND MRS. NIXON LEAVING THE WHITE HOUSE, AUGUST 1974
Provoking one of the worst political crises in American history, the Watergate scandal made Richard Nixon the only president ever to resign from office.

Justice Department reconstructed a long history of secret payments that engineering firms, in return for government contracts, had been making to Agnew throughout his rise in Maryland politics. Couriers had even sat outside the vice-president's office waiting to deliver the cash. After a frantic attempt to save his career, the vice-president suddenly resigned in October as part of a bargain with the Justice Department. Agnew received a light sentence for evading income tax but avoided the much more serious penalties for extortion and bribery. He was the first vice-president ever forced to resign because of wrongdoing. To replace him, Nixon appointed Congressman Gerald R. Ford of Michigan, an honest but undistinguished conservative Republican.*

The loss of the vice-president was stunning enough. Yet Agnew was only the prologue. As he fell, President Nixon himself was toppling. In June 1972 five men had been arrested for burglarizing Democratic headquarters at the Watergate Apartments in Washington, D.C. After a flurry of attention, the story had slipped from sight. Despite the clear connection between the burglars and the Republican Committee to Reelect the President (CREEP), McGovern had not

* The Twenty-Fifth Amendment, approved in 1967, had specified a procedure for filling a vice-presidential vacancy through appointment and congressional ratification.

been able to rouse much interest in the incident during the campaign. Then in the spring of 1973, as the *Washington Post* and Federal District Judge John J. Sirica pressed for more information about the break-in, one of the burglars decided to cooperate with the government investigators. As that culprit was confessing, John Dean, a close presidential adviser, acknowledged his own part in the incident. Behind these two, a long line of penitents began to form.

The stories they told spread in two directions. One traced a variety of activities through the executive's most powerful offices: the use of campaign contributions to win government favors, the illegal handling of those funds, devious techniques for making the president a millionaire, and assorted tactics of political sabotage to ensure Nixon's reelection. In order to discredit Defense Department consultant Daniel Ellsberg for having leaked to the press a confidential Pentagon study of American involvement in Vietnam, the White House had also sanctioned the burglary of Ellsberg's psychiatrist's office. Although all this provided a sordid view through the keyhole of national politics, it attracted far less attention than the second trail of evidence, which carried the burglary's planning and the subsequent suppression of evidence to Nixon's inner staff—Dean, Attorney General John Mitchell, and Haldeman and Ehrlichman. All these men had to resign and eventually served short prison terms. Would the trail lead to the president's desk?

For more than a year, Nixon fought to block the investigation. In public, the president repeatedly declared his innocence. In private, he plotted ways of obstructing a grand jury under the tenacious Judge Sirica and a Senate investigating committee under Sam Ervin of North Carolina, a staunch defender of the Constitution. Forced to accept a special Watergate prosecutor within the Justice Department, Nixon in October 1973 fired the first one, Archibald Cox of the Harvard Law School, because Cox was preparing to sue for evidence that the president would not relinquish. Cox's replacement, the conservative Houston lawyer Leon Jaworski, proved just as dogged and carried his demand for the evidence to the Supreme Court.

The evidence in question lay in a vault of tapes recording almost every conversation that had been held in President Nixon's private office. These tapes, which in a 1984 interview Nixon said he wished he had destroyed, eventually wrecked his defenses. Someone tried erasing portions of the tapes. The White House issued an edited transcript of parts of them. Finally, the president decided to withhold them altogether. But in July 1974 the Supreme Court unanimously awarded the tapes to Judge Sirica's grand jury and, through the grand jury, to the public. As the House of Representatives was preparing to vote articles of impeachment against the president, Nixon acknowledged much of what the tapes would verify about his intimate involvement in the Watergate affair. Admitting the facts but denying guilt, Nixon resigned on August 9, 1974.

This last and mightiest fall set the most astonishing of precedents. After receiving 97 percent of the electoral vote, the president—the indispensable leader—had been driven from office in midterm. Moreover, his replacement had been elected to no office higher than representative from the Fifth Congressional District of Michigan. Gerald Ford had a mandate for national leadership only from the two houses of Congress.

The Watergate scandal and its outcome greatly undermined the prestige of what historian Arthur Schlesinger called the "imperial presidency," and it meant a considerable resurgence of congressional power. Congress, however, was to prove generally ineffectual in exercising its revived authority to deal with the nation's increasingly serious economic problems.

The Custodial Presidency: Ford

The transition from Richard Nixon to Gerald Ford was remarkably smooth. Most Americans thought that a man, not the system, had failed. The news media interpreted Nixon's disgrace as a lesson proving that even the most exalted would suffer for the sin of pride.

The amiable, unaffected Ford, a study in contrast with the dour, withdrawn Nixon, eased the country's way through the first resignation by a chief executive. In his initial address, Ford promised to represent all the people; and he began his presidency with a cautious, congressional style of leadership, offering a little for this group, a little for that one. Telling the country that its "long national nightmare is over," he implicitly promised a period of healing in which the abuses of imperial presidents like Johnson and Nixon would be things of the past. "I am acutely aware that I have received the votes of none of you" he said on taking office. "I am a Ford, not a Lincoln," he said on another occasion. Well before Nixon's resignation, only about one in four Americans was supporting his presidency. At the start of Ford's term, three out of four citizens described themselves as behind the new president.

But much of this goodwill evaporated when, a month into his term, Ford pardoned Nixon unconditionally for all federal crimes he committed or may have committed as president. Ford's action angered many and rekindled feelings of alienation toward government officials. Under Nixon cynicism about Washington politics was widespread and intense, with four out of five Americans saying that, while he may have been lying, Nixon was no more corrupt than his predecessors. In 1974, 43 percent of the respondents in a national survey revealed that they had "hardly any" confidence in those running the executive branch of government. The nation's legislative branch fared even worse: in 1976 only 17 percent of Americans expressed respect for the United States Congress. The Republican party was particularly damaged by this mood of alienation. In 1974 the party claimed only 18 percent of the registered voters, and, in the congressional elections that year, the Democrats substantially increased their hold on both houses.

"YOUR MONEY OR YOUR WAY OF LIFE!"
In the seventies the Organization of Petroleum Exporting Countries helped spur inflation in industrial nations by sharply increasing oil prices. During the decade American leaders made only limited gains in meeting this challenge to the country's economic stability. In this 1975 cartoon by Draper Hill, the artist has captured the reluctance with which Americans, represented here by Henry Kissinger, faced the energy crisis.

Ford tried to achieve a record that would warrant his election in 1976. But he fell far short of his goal. By no standard can he be described as an outstanding president. He was an uninspiring speaker who exercised little control over Congress and made no major gains in foreign affairs. Most citizens thought Ford "a nice guy" but doubted his command of serious issues.

The Energy Crisis.   One reason for this negative perception of Ford's leadership was his inability to deal with a deepening economic crisis that only in part reflected the residual effects of President Johnson's deficits.

The Arab oil embargo of 1973 had dramatically revealed the West's growing dependence on Third World petroleum producers and its vulnerability to the monopolistic practices of the Organization of Petroleum Exporting Countries (OPEC), a cartel of these producers. In 1974 OPEC unilaterally announced a fourfold increase in international oil prices. Led by energy costs, inflation in the United States shot up to 11 percent, and other industrialized countries suffered similarly. It was one of the most momentous events of the postwar era, signaling the West's loss of control over the sources of cheap energy that for decades had sustained its economic growth and prosperity. Americans reacted with shock and disbelief. Much was said about the end of Western economic growth in the dawning new era of scarcity, and some talked wildly of seizing Middle Eastern oil fields. There were many scapegoats: Arab nabobs, greedy oil companies, obtuse politicians, even American manufacturers of gas-guzzling automobiles—but no heroes. Perceptive observers, however, realized that the answer would have to be found in conservation and the ultimate development of new energy sources. Meanwhile Western consumers would have to reconcile themselves to paying the sky-rocketing OPEC prices, financing new technologies, and enduring more stagflation.

Ford responded unimaginatively, offering no plan to meet what everyone soon called the energy crisis. Preoccupied with restraining price increases, Ford issued WIN (Whip Inflation Now) buttons, cut government spending, supported tight money (which drove up interest rates), and urged a tax increase to reduce federal deficits. All this merely depressed an already faltering economy. By the spring of 1975, unemployment reached 9 percent, a level at which it remained for the rest of the year. A precipitous drop in stock prices and in the GNP showed that the country was caught in the worst economic downturn since the Great Depression. Instead of adopting a flexible policy to revive the economy, as Nixon had in 1971, Ford stuck with conservative ideas about wringing inflation out of the economy by slowing it down. Thus he vetoed numerous bills aimed at reviving the economy and helping the disadvantaged, and he refused to provide loan guarantees to New York City, which, trapped between swelling social service costs and shrinking tax revenues, had reached the verge of bankruptcy. Although congressional overrides of Ford's vetos and a presidential turn to a less hard-line approach stimulated a recovery by the end of 1975, the president was saddled with a reputation as rigid and unimaginative in dealing with domestic affairs.

The Ford Foreign Policy.

Ford fared little better in foreign affairs, an area in which he had limited knowledge and experience. To give his administration credibility, Ford kept Kissinger on as secretary of state. "I became the focal point of a degree of support unprecedented for a nonelected official," Kissinger later wrote. "It was as if the public and Congress felt the national peril instinctively and created a surrogate center around which the national purpose could rally." Yet even Kissinger's prestige could not move Congress and the public to rescue a collapsing South Vietnam. Nor could he persuade Americans that the United States should intervene against communist insurgents in Angola in southern Africa. Moreover, a military reaction to Cambodia's seizure of an American cargo ship, the *Mayaguez*, turned into a fiasco when forty American troops were killed while trying to rescue thirty-eight crew members who had already been released. Ford's only significant success was to outline a SALT II agreement with Brezhnev at a summit meeting in Vladivostok in November 1974. But the proposed treaty impressed relatively few voters and exposed him to right-wing Republican attacks.

The Election of 1976.

An undistinguished record during his more than two years as president seemed to make Ford an easy mark in the 1976 campaign. But the Democrats, running their own undynamic candidate, almost lost the election. In a surprising turn of events, they nominated the one-term former Georgia governor, James Earl Carter, Jr. Because voters were soured on government officials and skeptical about "pol-

Cartoon by David Levine c. 1974, © by NYREV, Inc.

THE CUSTODIAL PRESIDENT
A Michigan congressman who was appointed to the vice-presidency by Nixon, Gerald Ford impressed many Americans as incapable of being an effective president. In this 1974 cartoon by David Levine, the oversized chair, representing the presidency, appears to be swallowing up the uncertain Ford.

iticians," Jimmy Carter could turn to good advantage his obscurity and strong identification as a "born-again" Christian. Emphasizing his detachment from the Washington bureaucracy, and pledging that he would "never tell a lie," Carter touched responsive chords in a public eager for a less imposing, more open federal government.

Although Carter had begun his campaign against Ford with a 30 percent lead in the polls, most of his advantage had dissolved by election day. His ineptitude as a candidate foreshadowed his inexpert performance as president. On the campaign trail he tried to be all things to all people, raising suspicions that he had no fixed opinion on any major public question. Until the candidates held a televised debate in October, in which the president confirmed the public perception of him as uninformed and inept, it seemed as though Ford would catch and pass Carter. But Ford's astonishing remark during the debate that "there is no Soviet domination of Eastern Europe" reinforced a widespread feeling that he was unqualified to be an elected president of the United States. With the smallest proportion (53 percent) of eligible voters going to the polls since 1948, Carter won 51 percent of the popular vote to Ford's 48 percent. The division in the electoral college, 297 to 241, was the smallest since 1916.

The Faltering Presidency: Carter

Like his predecessor, Carter became an unpopular president. After a year and a half in office, his standing with the public was even lower than Ford's had been eighteen months into his term. Carter was a highly intelligent man (he had a degree in nuclear engineering) and an exceptionally hard-working president. But he lacked what people—still remembering Kennedy—called charisma, the ability to inspire and excite the media and the public. He was not short of political insight; in fact, Carter clearly understood the country's longing for a respite from imperious leaders. And thus he adopted an informal style that he believed would strike a resonant chord. After his inauguration he strolled down Pennsylvania Avenue hand in hand with his wife, Rosalynn; he attended town meetings in small communities, spending the night in local homes; he even gave a fireside chat wearing a cardigan sweater. Yet these gestures did not endear him to the public, which saw his actions as too contrived. Most Americans viewed Carter as an unspontaneous, dull speaker with a fine technician's grasp of issues but a limited capacity to inspire hope that the nation could master its problems. He was a poor administrator who got bogged down in detail by trying to exercise too much control over single issues. His image as the untainted leader of a scandal-free administration was shattered when Bert Lance, his budget director and a close friend from Georgia, was forced out of office by revelations of financial misdeeds. And when the press began to complain that an overly protective White House staff was insulating Carter from criticism, unhappy memories of Nixon were revived.

Domestic Affairs: The Unmanageable Economy.
Public confidence in Carter eroded chiefly because he could not restore a sound economy: for all the criticism of the "imperial presidency," Americans still expected their presidents to continue the Rooseveltian tradition of national economic management. Carter, like Nixon and Ford, had to wrestle with almost intractable problems of recession and inflation. On entering office, his first concern was to stimulate the economy and reduce unemployment, then running at nearly 8 percent. Since inflation had eased to 5.5 percent in 1976, only half of what it had been in 1974, Carter believed that he could concentrate on getting the economy moving again. Because fuel costs were so central to the recent price surge, Carter hoped to check the inflationary spiral by initiating a national energy policy that would hold down oil and natural gas prices.

During his first year in office, therefore, he pushed a number of bills through Congress that were directed at promoting economic expansion, and he pressed for a major energy law. The first half of his program succeeded. In 1977 Congress approved tax cuts totaling $34 billion and enacted public works and public service measures amounting to $14 billion, including an unprecedented national youth employment law. Congress also raised the minimum wage by nearly 50 percent, increased farm price supports, and eased environmental regulations on industries struggling to make a profit. The economy responded to this stimulus: unemployment fell from 7.9 percent at the start of Carter's term to 5.8 percent in 1979.

But Carter's energy proposals largely failed. In April 1977 he asked Congress for a bill that would reduce energy consumption by increasing taxes on gasoline and fuel-inefficient automobiles. Industries were to be encouraged to use coal instead of oil; natural gas and utility companies were to be induced to switch to nuclear power. In March 1979, however, the nation's faith in nuclear power was badly shaken by a near-catastrophe at the Three Mile Island nuclear power plant outside Harrisburg, Pennsylvania. Although the mishap led to no disaster, it focused public attention on the dangers inherent in using nuclear energy, including the release of radioactive materials into the atmosphere. Well before this part of Carter's program came into question, the rest of his plans had been largely turned aside by a deadlock among competing interests. Although Congress agreed to create the Department of Energy in 1977, it stalled on the balance of Carter's proposal until 1978; then it passed an ineffectual law promising little actual conservation and no meaningful restraints on rising energy prices.

Without an effective conservation program and with higher government spending, the economy again began to overheat. During 1978 inflation soared to 9.6 percent and kept rising. Shifting his attention to this problem, the president reduced the second of three proposed tax cuts by 20 percent and vetoed congressional appropriations for defense and public works that he feared would add to inflationary pressures. He also established voluntary guidelines on wage and price increases and promised to hold down government expenditures. But the economy took another nose dive when the Federal Reserve raised interest rates to slow economic expansion and bolster the dollar, which had tumbled in relation to other currencies. By the end of 1980 unemployment had shot back up to 7.4 percent, while the prime interest rate stood at an astonishing 20 percent and the federal deficit approached record highs. Even worse, the cost of living increased by 13 percent during 1980, and there was

PRESIDENT CARTER AT THE SIGNING OF THE PANAMA CANAL TREATY, SEPTEMBER 1977
Although generally unsuccessful in meeting the country's domestic economic problems, Jimmy Carter scored some successes in foreign affairs, particularly in the Panama Canal and Egyptian-Israeli negotiations.

little hope that these energy-driven price increases could soon be halted.

A second round of international oil shortages began in 1979, when a revolution broke out in Iran, one of the world's leading petroleum producers. World oil prices increased by another 50 percent; in the United States, gasoline now cost more than $1 a gallon. To meet the crisis—as well as to answer growing criticism of his ineptness and erratic policy shifts—Carter proposed a new energy program in mid-July.

In announcing his new energy plan on national television, Carter had prefaced his speech with a dramatic announcement that the country faced a "crisis of confidence" threatening to immobilize the national will and jeopardize American security. But having thus heightened a growing sense of national crisis, Carter reinforced perceptions of his administration's inability to cope: his second plan was no more acceptable to Congress than his first had been, and many thought it unworkable. As he approached the election of 1980, renewed and worsened stagflation made Carter vulnerable to attack from all points on the political spectrum. Admitting the mediocrity of his per-

formance in dealing with major domestic problems, Carter told a journalist after he left office that he deserved no more than a grade of "C."

A Moral Foreign Policy: Victories and Defeats.
Carter justifiably felt that he had done better in international affairs, although here too his administration suffered some setbacks. Unlike Nixon and Kissinger, Carter announced no ambitious new design for world peace resting on the realistic manipulation of power. Instead, he mounted an idealistic campaign to discourage human rights abuses by right- and left-wing regimes alike, and he thoughtfully identified the major international problems that his administration should address. These included resolving differences with Panama over the canal, thus enabling the United States to conciliate Latin American sensitivities; reducing tension in the Middle East in order to avert another war and another energy crisis; further normalizing relations with China; and reaching an arms-control agreement with the Soviets that would reduce the chances of a nuclear war.

Negotiating the canal treaties with Panama and

securing their Senate ratification formed one of the great success stories of Carter's term. Skillfully directed by Secretary of State Cyrus Vance, the State Department concluded fourteen years of negotiations over America's future role in managing and defending the canal. Under the two treaties signed in 1977, Panama and the United States agreed to abolish American sovereignty over the Canal Zone. Control of the canal itself was to remain in United States hands until the year 2000, but the Panamanians would take over after that time, on condition that the United States maintain the right to use and defend the waterway. The treaties provoked an outcry in Congress and among many Americans as a blow to national security and prestige. But with the help of amendments strengthening American rights unilaterally to protect the canal, the agreement won Senate approval in the spring of 1978, although by only one vote more than the two-thirds needed for passage. When the Carter administration also adopted a hands-off attitude toward a victorious left-wing revolution against the reactionary and repressive Somoza government in Nicaragua, U.S. standing in Latin America rose to a level not attained since the Kennedy years.

In the Middle East as well, the Carter administration built on the Nixon-Kissinger initiatives of 1973–75 and achieved a signal triumph. To break the bloody stalemate in the region, the Egyptian and Israeli leaders, Anwar Sadat and Menachem Begin, agreed to convert the indirect discussions Kissinger had fostered into direct negotiations and visits to each other's countries. And when Egyptian-Israeli negotiations reached an impasse in 1978, Carter invited the two leaders to Washington for further talks. After two intense weeks of meetings at the presidential retreat in Maryland, Carter mediated the Camp David Accords. An outline for an Egyptian-Israeli peace treaty, and a framework for peace in the region, the accords proposed Egyptian recognition of Israel's right to exist in return for restoration of the entire Sinai Peninsula to Egyptian control, as well as autonomy for Palestinians living on the West Bank and in the Gaza Strip. After further negotiations, which took Carter to Cairo and Tel Aviv, Egypt and Israel signed a peace treaty in March 1979.

Although the two sides also agreed to begin discussing the future of the West Bank and Gaza—that is, the fate of the Palestinians—it was clear that these negotiations promised little significant gain and that the Egyptian-Israeli accord represented the principal advance toward peace that could be achieved. With Cairo detached from the rest of the Arab world, it was almost impossible for other Arab countries to wage another all-out war with Israel. A civil war in Lebanon, beginning in 1975, provided plenty of opportunity for further bloodletting between Israel and its Arab neighbors, but the peace treaty with Egypt placed limits on the extent of the fighting. Thus the Camp David agreements were a genuine step toward peace.

The Carter administration also extended the Nixon-Kissinger policy of seeking better Sino-American relations. In January 1979 the administration established normal diplomatic relations with Peking and ended its official recognition of the Nationalist government on Taiwan. Although Washington also canceled a mutual defense pact with Taiwan, it maintained trade relations with the island and continued to sell it defensive weapons. The change in relations with Taiwan evoked strong criticism from conservative Americans; but the promise that the United States government would not permit Taiwan to be politically attached to the mainland against its will, as well as the realization that in recognizing Peking the United States was gaining a powerful anti-Soviet ally, made Carter's action popular in the United States.

At the same time that he improved relations with China, Carter also continued work begun under Ford for a second SALT agreement with the Soviets. But when the president openly encouraged Soviet dissidents in their struggle for human rights and asked for changes in the preliminary SALT II treaty negotiated by Ford and Kissinger, Moscow resisted further advances toward détente. By June 1979, however, the Soviets agreed to a SALT II treaty, apparently hoping thereby to discourage the development and deployment of new American weapons. Limiting the number of long-range missiles, bombers, and nuclear warheads held by each side, the agreement promised to ease the arms race and open the way to further talks on reducing nuclear stockpiles.

The treaty, however, could not withstand a deterioration in Soviet-American relations brought on by aggressive Soviet actions. The start of the difficulties dated from 1975–76, when Soviet-backed guerrillas, directly assisted by Cuban troops, had seized control of Angola, a former Portuguese colony in southern Africa. In addition, Soviet violations of the international Helsinki agreements of 1975, in which all parties promised not to violate human rights, and the USSR's deployment of new SS-20 missiles aimed at western Europe, raised strong American doubts about the sincerity of the Russian commitment to détente. Finally, in the winter of 1979–80, after a Soviet invasion of Afghanistan to preserve a Marxist government under attack from Muslim rebels, American outrage doomed the SALT II agreements. Although Carter tried to save the treaty by delaying a Senate vote until the outcry over Afghanistan cooled, he took other actions that reflected changed American attitudes: the adminis-

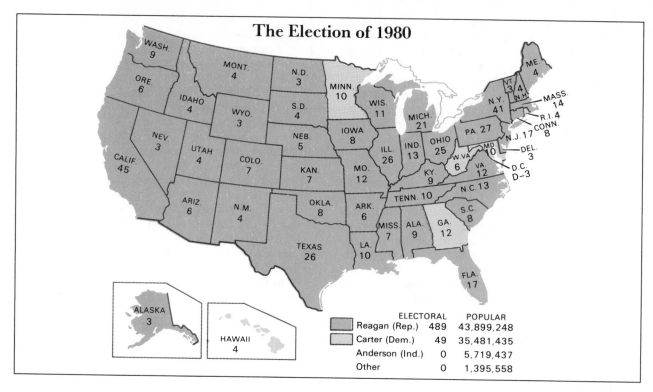

The Election of 1980

	ELECTORAL	POPULAR
Reagan (Rep.)	489	43,899,248
Carter (Dem.)	49	35,481,435
Anderson (Ind.)	0	5,719,437
Other	0	1,395,558

tration and its NATO allies agreed to install new intermediate-range Pershing-2 and cruise missiles to counter the Soviet SS-20s, and the United States halted grain and high-technology sales to the Soviets and boycotted the 1980 Olympic Games in Moscow.

This crisis in détente coincided with the worst foreign policy crisis of Carter's term, the seizure of American hostages in Tehran. Early in 1979 Ayatollah Ruhollah Khomeini, a revered and fanatical religious leader, drove the Shah out of Iran—a severe blow to American interests, for the United States had long supported the Shah despite his police-state methods and his disruptive modernization programs that alienated many Iranians. In November the American government allowed the exiled, dying monarch to come to the United States for medical treatment; in retaliation, Khomeini encouraged the seizure of the American embassy by radical students demanding the Shah's return for trial and certain execution. The students imprisoned fifty-three Americans, most of whom were entitled to diplomatic immunity under international law. After negotiations failed to effect their release, American forces attempted a rescue operation in April 1980. But the mission had to be curtailed when mishaps killed eight American troops and destroyed essential equipment. The resignation of Secretary of State Vance, who had opposed the mission, raised questions about the wisdom of the operation. Entering the 1980 presidential campaign, the admin-

istration carried the burden of a faltering détente policy and a humiliating inability to subdue the defiant Iranians.

The Election of 1980. The combination of stagflation and frustration over the hostage crisis undermined Carter's prospects. His chances of winning reelection depended chiefly on the effectiveness of the Republican campaign. To no one's surprise, the Republicans chose Ronald W. Reagan, a former movie actor and two-term governor of California. Reagan was sixty-nine years old, and a Republican victory would make him the oldest person ever elected to the White House. Further, he had a close association with right-wing groups that many feared would jeopardize social programs and peace. The Democrats seized upon these two issues and emphasized them throughout the campaign.

But Reagan quieted both concerns by running a vigorous campaign that appealed to a broad cross-section of the electorate. In his nomination speech he displayed the wit and charm that had endeared him to voters in California, emphasizing the themes that made him seem a pragmatic, steady man who could overcome the disarray that, according to opinion polls, seventy-five percent of Americans saw besetting their country. At the opening of his campaign, however, Reagan made a series of blunders. He supported an outdated concept of states' rights, called the Vietnam War "a noble cause," attributed fascism to the New Deal, aroused fears of a split with Peking, and endorsed the teaching in public schools of "creationism"—the biblical as opposed to the evolutionary explanation of the creation of the earth and the emergence of life. All this raised doubts about his commitment to moderation and his fitness for the presidency. Later, however, Reagan repaired the damage and put Carter on the defensive, using television to depict himself as a pleasant, reasonable leader who wanted peace as much as anyone else. He was particularly effective in a nationally televised debate with Carter a week before the election.

Reagan decisively defeated Carter, receiving 50.7 percent of the popular vote to Carter's 41 percent; most of the remaining votes went to John Anderson, a thoughtful liberal Republican congressman who had run as an independent. Reagan gained 489 electoral votes to the president's 49, which came from victories in only six states and the District of Columbia. But because only 55.1 percent of the electorate had gone to the polls, Reagan had actually captured the White House with a mere 28 percent of the eligible vote. Gaining 12 Senate seats, the Republicans won their largest majority in the upper house since 1928, 53 to 47. Although the Democrats retained control over the House of Representatives, 243 to 192, the Republicans reduced the Democratic margin by 33 seats, and the Republican–southern Democratic coalition that had frustrated Kennedy was reborn.

Reaganism

With Reagan's entrance into the White House in 1981—just as the Iranians were releasing the embassy hostages—conservatives had a fresh opportunity to direct national affairs and to test the validity of their ideas. To restore the nation's economic health and ensure its safety, Reagan proposed a conservative program of less government, lower taxes, balanced budgets, and peace through military strength. "In this present crisis," he said in his inaugural speech, "government is not the solution to our problem; government is the problem. . . . It is no coincidence that our present troubles parallel and are proportionate to the intervention and excessive growth of government. . . . It is time to reawaken this industrial giant, to get government back within its means and to lighten our punitive tax burden." At the same time, he intended to "rebuild" American military strength and close "a window of vulnerability" by modernizing the country's nuclear arsenal. The objective was to face down the Soviet Union, which, he said, "underlies all the unrest that is going on. If they weren't engaged in

this game of dominoes, there wouldn't be any hot spots in the world." Reagan launched his presidency intending to make dramatic changes in American policies at home and abroad.

Economic and Social Programs. To reduce the country's 13 percent inflation, 20 percent prime interest rate, $56 billion in projected federal deficits, and 7.4 percent unemployment rate, Reagan asked Congress to enact a series of measures described as supply-side economics: substantial cuts in domestic social programs and a 30 percent reduction in taxes over three years. The tax cut was supposed to produce a dramatic expansion of the economy that in turn would decrease unemployment and increase federal revenues; more could then be spent on defense, and the deficit would shrink. Ridiculed during the nomination campaign by his rival—and later his running mate—George Bush as "voodoo economics," the plan seemed unlikely to ease inflation and unemployment at the same time.

Yet the country and Congress were ready to try something new to break the stranglehold of stagflation. Consequently, in the spring and summer of 1981, Congress agreed to cut federal spending on domestic social programs by $41 billion, to reduce taxes across the board by 25 percent over three years, and to begin a $1.6 trillion expansion of defense spending. The president won most of what he had asked from Congress, and his initial triumph was labeled the Reagan Revolution by the news media. No president since FDR, a national magazine said, had "done so much of such magnitude so quickly to change the economic direction of the nation."

Three years into Reagan's term, the results of his program were uncertain. Between 1981 and 1983 the economy went into a sharp decline: unemployment climbed to 10.8 percent, the highest level since the Great Depression; capital spending, which was supposed to expand, dropped in each of the three years; and deficits soared higher than ever, reaching $195 billion in 1982–83. More Americans fell below the poverty level than at any time since Johnson launched his war on poverty in 1965. Under Reagan, the country's neediest citizens had to subsist with fewer government benefits. Reagan's cuts in domestic programs added up to fewer food stamps, public service jobs, student loans, legal services, child nutrition programs, and housing subsidies; they meant less Medicare, unemployment compensation, urban mass transit subsidy, and Aid to Families with Dependent Children, a major welfare program. The administration's critics complained about Reagan's "welfare for the rich"— tax cuts that gave only 8.5 percent of the reduction to the 31.7 million taxpayers annually earning $15,000 or less, whereas the 5.6 percent of Americans with annual

in five years—while inflation dropped to less than 4 percent. By the summer of 1984 unemployment had dropped even further, to 7.1 percent, and inflation was still under 5 percent.

This recovery, Reagan declared, proved that "our economic game plan is working." But many economists disagreed. They acknowledged that the administration had achieved an immediate improvement, but they were pessimistic about long-term economic prospects and were reluctant to credit "Reaganomics" with restoring a measure of economic health. With huge deficits of $200 billion being forecast for the next five years, they predicted that competition for loans between business and government would push up interest rates again, rekindle double-digit inflation, and stall the recovery. Economists also worried that business spending on new plants and equipment had shown no gain for three years. Since the supply-side policy aimed chiefly at expanding the economy's productive capacity, economists remained unconvinced that the Reagan program was working. The recovery, they believed, was essentially the result of government actions long advocated by liberal Keynesians: lower interest rates produced by easier monetary controls, and government deficits triggered by tax cuts and defense spending. Slackened international demand had also created an "oil glut" that undercut OPEC and stabilized energy prices. All this, critics thought, had given consumers the additional spending power to create a "demand-side" recovery through purchases of homes, automobiles, and other goods.

If the Reagan administration could claim some economic gains in its first three years, it was largely stymied on the social issues it had raised. Reagan advocated constitutional amendments against abortion and for public-school prayer; he opposed the ERA, affirmative action, and busing; and he proposed allowing segregated private schools to claim tax-exempt status. But except for the defeat of the ERA—which came in 1983, when the extended deadline for the amendment's ratification by the states expired—the administration achieved none of its conservative social goals. This failure came in part because the White House neglected to make the same strong effort on behalf of its social aims that it had made for its economic and defense programs. Reluctant to alienate minorities and women—groups that as a whole objected to the conservative agenda—Reagan gave only erratic backing to the social causes that he and the conservative "Moral Majority" believed essential to the restoration of a healthy nation.*

Indeed, to diminish the hostility of women and

PRESIDENT RONALD REAGAN
Although Reagan's policies as president have stirred considerable controversy, few question his effectiveness as a public speaker and politician. In the middle of 1984, after three-and-a-half years in office, Reagan was the most popular president since Eisenhower.

incomes of $50,000 or more kept 35 percent of the revenue lost by the federal government. In addition, liberal Democrats objected to a tax program that gave corporations a windfall by reducing their share of each federal tax dollar from 13 cents to 8 cents.

Yet for all these difficulties, the economy staged an impressive recovery. In the summer of 1982, abandoning supply-side doctrine about tight money and deficits, the White House effectively pressed the Federal Reserve into expanding the money supply and lowering interest rates. In response, the stock market rose to new highs in 1982–83. Meanwhile unemployment fell to 8.2 percent of the work force, and during 1983 the GNP grew at 3.3 percent—the quickest pace

---

* The Moral Majority is an especially clamorous evangelical Christian group, founded by the television preacher Jerry Falwell.

minorities, Reagan appointed the first woman to serve on the Supreme Court, Sandra Day O'Connor, and he gave token support to civil rights. After his administration came under attack for fostering a renewed atmosphere of racism in the country—the United States Civil Rights Commission, for example, criticized the White House for reducing the number of minorities and women in high government posts—the Justice Department filed a desegregation suit against Alabama's public higher education system. Reagan also proposed tougher antidiscrimination provisions in the fifteen-year-old Fair Housing Act.

The administration revealed its real intent in the Supreme Court cases it pressed on social issues, and here it won some significant victories. Between 1981 and 1984 the White House asked the Court to rule against busing to achieve desegregation, against women's right to an abortion, against the denial of tax exemptions to segregated private schools, and against the use of racial quotas in hiring. The Supreme Court had given conservatives some hope that the administration would win these cases. In *Bakke* v. *University of California* (1978), the Court had placed limits on racial quotas in admitting students to graduate programs. The Court had also held in 1978 that federal and state governments could refuse to provide public funds for abortions. But in responding to the cases brought by the Reagan administration, the Court was erratic. In 1981–83 it consistently refused to move in the direction that Reagan's Justice Department asked. In 1984, however, it sided with the administration by limiting liberal precedents on law-and-order issues, such as relaxing the rule on illegally obtained evidence, *U.S.* v. *Leon* (1984); on affirmative action, by giving priority to seniority over race in job layoffs, *Firefighters Local 1784* v. *Stotts* (1984); and on sex discrimination, by limiting cuts in federal aid to discriminatory school programs rather than to the whole school, *Grove City* v. *Bell* (1984).

As Reagan began his 1984 reelection campaign, he could point to lower inflation and an expanding economy, but he had no clear design for reducing unprecedented deficits that might halt the economic upturn, and he had some, but not many, gains to show for his efforts in behalf of the conservative social agenda. Least of all could he claim to have trimmed back the federal bureaucracy.

Anti-Sovietism. The distinguishing feature of Reagan's defense and foreign policies was anti-Sovietism. Like all presidents since 1945, Reagan had a legitimate concern about Soviet expansionism. But, more reminiscent of John Foster Dulles than of recent presidents, Reagan saw little room for reasonable compromise with Moscow and looked forward to the day when the West "will transcend communism." Soviet leaders, he said, were ready "to commit any crime, to lie, to cheat" to further their cause; the Soviet Union was an "evil empire" and the Soviet-American conflict a "struggle between right and wrong, good and evil." In September 1983, when a Soviet fighter plane shot down a South Korean passenger aircraft that had strayed into Soviet airspace, killing 269 civilians, Reagan declared that this action confirmed what he had been preaching about Soviet barbarism for more than thirty years.

Reagan's moralistic absorption with countering Soviet power and defeating "the communist threat," critics complained, made it difficult for him to deal realistically and constructively with foreign affairs. Supported by a minority of American defense specialists, Reagan insisted on the need for a buildup of the United States nuclear arsenal to overcome perceived Soviet advantages. The president pointed to the fact that the Soviet Union had eclipsed the United States in land-based ICBMs and that it had gained an advantage in Europe by targeting SS-20 missiles on NATO allies. But other knowledgeable Americans, including the Soviet policy expert George Kennan and the nuclear physicist Hans Bethe, disputed these conclusions. Emphasizing the "futility of any war fought with these weapons," Kennan asserted that the United States and the Soviet Union had achieved "levels of redundancy" in destructiveness "of such grotesque dimensions as to defy rational understanding." Although Bethe conceded that the Soviets held an advantage in land-based ICBMs, he argued that this did not give them overall superiority. He noted that, since the United States had "invulnerable nuclear-powered submarines" and bombers carrying cruise missiles—against which the Soviets had no effective defense—the United States still had the capacity to retaliate against any first strike and thus had no reason to feel inferior to Moscow in nuclear weapons. The greatest threat to American national security, Bethe said, did not arise from the United States' inferiority to Moscow in strategic weapons, but from "the grotesque size and continuing growth of both nuclear arsenals." But Reagan, who refused to concede this point, pressed forward with a buildup of weapons. In response, a "nuclear freeze" movement arose in the United States and western Europe, calling on the two superpowers mutually to cease producing and deploying more nuclear weapons.

The president offered a series of arms-control proposals on intermediate and long-range missiles, but the Soviet Union—as well as most American critics of the administration—dismissed them as ploys to appease the freeze movement in the West. And indeed, however eager Americans were for a strong defense, they also worried about the possibility of a nuclear

ANTINUCLEAR RALLY, NEW YORK CITY, 1982

Allan Tannenbaum / SYGMA

In the 1980s nuclear disarmament has become a critical issue for countless Americans and western Europeans.

war. In November 1983 a chilling television film depicting a nuclear exchange and its consequences, *The Day After*, attracted 100 million fascinated yet horrified viewers in the United States.

Nuclear arms talks between Moscow and Washington collapsed in late 1983. Supported by their electorates, several NATO governments (notably West Germany and Great Britain) had reiterated their support for the deployment of Pershing-2 missiles to counter the SS-20s; and as the weapons began arriving in Europe, the Soviets walked out of the arms talks. A new arms race appeared to be under way.

Foreign Policy: The Third World.
Reagan's foreign policies, most commentators also felt, did not offer realistic

solutions to other problem areas of the globe. Central America generally and El Salvador in particular were cases in point. At the start of Reagan's term, the administration described the situation in El Salvador as a "textbook case of indirect aggression by communist powers through Cuba"—an analysis that, as one Latin American expert pointed out, ignored local realities. In the administration's view, the Salvadoran insurrection had "no true domestic causes"; it stemmed not from indigenous poverty and political repression, but from "a virus imported from eastern Europe."

To combat this communist threat in El Salvador, the administration largely ignored the failings of the ruling junta, particularly its human rights violations, and urged a program of economic and military aid. It

THE U.S. IN GRENADA
In this photograph of October 27, 1983, an American soldier searches Grenadian houses for enemy troops.

asked Congress to fund arms shipments to El Salvador, to allow American military advisers to train Salvadoran government forces, and to permit the CIA's covert subversion of the Marxist government of Nicaragua. Reagan resorted to direct action on the tiny Caribbean island of Grenada in October 1983, when he dispatched American forces to stop a Marxist coup that allegedly threatened American lives. And in the spring of 1984 it was revealed that the administration was secretly helping Nicaraguan counterrevolutionaries mine their country's harbors. The outcry in Congress was so loud that the operations were halted.

Reagan's policy, critics said, was simplistic and counterproductive. In Central America, wrote the *New York Times* Mexico City bureau chief, "the administration has not found the right answers [because] it has not asked the right questions." Reagan seemed not to realize that political instability was indigenous, but instead blamed it on "external forces: . . . Moscow, Havana, Managua." Other critics, who acknowledged the real presence of a Marxist threat to United States interests in Central America, nevertheless felt that Reagan's military response to the problem was inappropriate. The critics pointed out that after three and a half years of the Reagan policy, Central American difficulties were as intractable as ever.

In the Middle East, Reagan initially focused on building a "strategic consensus"—that is, an anti-Soviet combination of Israel and moderate Arab

RONALD REAGAN IN CHINA
President Reagan's 1984 visit to the People's Republic of China served to reduce tensions between the administration and Peking.

states—to ensure the region's defense against communism. But this plan was strongly criticized as unrealistic. Moderate Arab leaders refused to believe that the Soviet threat to the area was a more urgent concern than the issue of autonomy for Palestinians living in refugee camps in Lebanon, Syria, and other Middle Eastern countries. Unwilling to accept this proposition, until September 1982 the White House made no major effort to address Arab-Israeli tensions over the Palestinian question and over Israel's continued occupation of the west bank of the Jordan River.

An Israeli invasion of Lebanon in June 1982, aimed at driving out Palestinian guerrillas who had repeatedly staged attacks on Israel, shocked the administration into adopting a more realistic Middle Eastern policy. Prodded by his new secretary of state, George Shultz, who had replaced Alexander Haig, Reagan advanced a comprehensive peace plan on September 1. Although neither Israel nor the moderate Arab states accepted Reagan's plan as a basis for nego-

tiations, the proposal at least focused on difficulties specific to the region rather than on some more general Soviet threat.

The difficulty of finding realistic answers to Middle Eastern problems was further underscored by the administration's inability to bring peace to Lebanon. Sending 1,500 American marines to Beirut in 1983 as part of a multinational peacekeeping force, the administration hoped to end civil strife between warring Lebanese and Palestinian factions. Divided between Yassir Arafat and other more radical leaders, the Palestine Liberation Organization (PLO), the political and military organization representing the Palestinian people, struggled within itself over an appropriate strategy for defeating Israel. The peacekeeping force also aimed to arrange the departure from Lebanon of Israeli forces and Syrian troops, who had been in northern Lebanon since 1976 trying to ensure Syria's strategic interests in a neighboring state. Instead, the peacekeepers became targets of violence.

Hundreds of American troops lost their lives before the rest were withdrawn in March 1984.

One of Reagan's few successes was to repair the damage that his own initial tilt toward Taiwan had done to Sino-American relations. Common concern about Soviet intentions, as well as growing commercial ties, gradually brought the administration and the mainland government together, and both sides acknowledged a more realistic understanding of their mutual interests. In 1984 Reagan made a successful visit to Peking, where he signed new agreements for the sale of nuclear power plants to the People's Republic and promised to reduce arms shipments to Taiwan. Success in this limited area, however, did not remove the serious doubts that many Americans had about Reagan's ability to supply effective answers to the varied and complex problems that the United States faced in its relations overseas.

Yet Reagan's meager foreign accomplishments were balanced by the dramatic improvement in the domestic economy during 1983 and by his extraordinary ability to maintain his popularity with the American public. "With Ronald Reagan, the blithe spirit entered the White House," the columnist Joseph Kraft observed. "He exudes charm, gentility, and good feeling. Even . . . massive inattention to the substance of policy has, with him, a positive side. He walks away from failure—changes policies in the middle of the debacle—in seeming innocence that anything much has happened." By his fourth year in the White House, Reagan seemed to be the most reassuring president since Eisenhower. And after more than two decades of tumultuous change and shattering disillusionment, it was above all reassurance that the nation craved.

A Cloudy Horizon

If the radicals of the sixties had trusted no one over thirty, an increasing number of Americans in the seventies and eighties wondered whether they could trust anyone at all. Worldwide terrorism—hijackings, bombings, assassinations—and violent domestic crimes were sensationalized in all the news media, conveying the persistent message that nobody was ever safe from random slaughter. The use of violence in countless TV shows said it again. In addition, the nation's official defenders of law and order, it seemed, were really specialists in deceit.

The Outrage of America. In 1971 the Pentagon Papers, leaked to the press by Daniel Ellsberg, exposed the government's secret maneuvers in Vietnam and its systematic lies about the Indochinese war. Each year brought more stories that discredited the agencies of law and order. President Johnson had approved a wiretap on Robert Kennedy, and President Nixon had authorized one on his own brother. The director of the FBI, J. Edgar Hoover, had waged a personal vendetta against Martin Luther King, Jr. The Bureau and military intelligence agencies had compiled mounds of dossiers on everybody from senators to singers, and the Internal Revenue Service had audited tax returns on the basis of citizens' political activities. Traditionally, Americans had enjoyed a bit of humbug now and then. But it was deadly serious business for them to learn that President Eisenhower had instructed subordinates to "confuse" the public on the matter of widespread contamination from the government's nuclear tests.

Some Americans slipped into a sense of helplessness. The computer only verified the intractability of the big problems: inflation and recession, crime and violence, domestic poverty and global hunger. A feeling of the individual being trapped in a vast web of uncontrollable forces characterized the important writings of Joyce Carol Oates, John Cheever, and Joan Didion. The most popular movies alternated between fantasies of terror like *The Exorcist* and *Jaws* and fantasies of escape like *Star Wars*, *Rocky*, and *E.T.*

Other Americans tried to reassert tough, fundamental values. "Permissive" child rearing fell into disrepute, and parents pledged their allegiance to maintaining clear authority and salutary discipline in the home. Hostility toward the rights of criminal suspects dominated the television dramas of the mid-seventies. With the Supreme Court's approval, infliction of the death penalty resumed in 1977, and by the mid-eighties hundreds of convicted criminals faced execution. The well-organized Right-to-Life movement fought abortion; a well-publicized campaign opposed homosexuality; and a spreading conservative mood helped stall the drive toward ratification of the Equal Rights Amendment, which in the early seventies had seemed assured.

Americans were most indignant about corporate abuses of consumers. In 1965 a zealous young lawyer named Ralph Nader had inspired a consumer movement with the publication of *Unsafe at Any Speed*, a detailed analysis of the dangers built into automobiles manufactured in Detroit. A shabby attempt by General Motors to discredit him only enlarged his fame. Nader's young volunteers—"Nader's Raiders"—rapidly produced a variety of additional exposés. By the 1970s innumerable journalists, scientists, and local committees were spreading the gospel of consumer standards, and new legal guidelines covered such areas as automobile safety, credit contracts, product labeling, and food adulteration. Despite its popular base, however, the consumer movement never had a disciplined, focused strength. For example, the latest American right that was proclaimed—the right to good health—generated a consistent, broad support

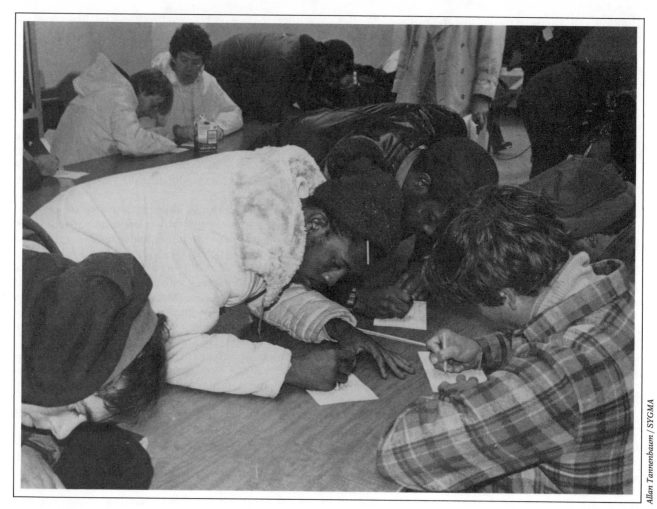

Allan Tannenbaum / SYGMA

JOB APPLICANTS, NEW YORK CITY, 1982
Unemployment remains one of the most vexing problems of the 1980s.

for a variety of national health plans that regularly appeared in Washington but that just as regularly died at the hands of lobbyists in Congress. Consumers were everybody in general and nobody in particular—and exceedingly hard to organize.

The most positive attempts to reclaim some measure of lost control were the many efforts to repair the urban-industrial society's damage to the physical environment. Images of an uncontaminated earth where man and nature were once again in harmony aroused a deeply embedded set of emotions during the sixties and seventies. In a crescendo of cries, more and more Americans demanded relief from the dangers of chemical sprays, industrial wastes, and automobile exhaust. "Organic" foods and "recyclable" products became increasingly popular. The national government responded to the public's demands by establishing a series of antipollution standards—beginning with the Clean Air Act of 1963—to protect the atmosphere and the waterways, and both state and local laws supplemented the ecology movement.

Some progress was made; yet here too the problems came to outweigh the prospects. As the economy faltered, the arguments that environmentalism cut into jobs, profits, and energy development sounded more and more persuasive. Bureaucratic confusion between Washington's Environmental Protection Agency (EPA) and the regulatory offices in local government hampered the enforcement of the new laws, and only widespread public outrage prevented the Reagan administration from virtually gutting them. Unfolding revelations about the extensive dumping and the gruesome toxicity of industrial wastes dimmed hopes of ever undoing the damage. The frightening crisis of Three Mile Island in 1979 dashed faith that government regulation could actually protect America from the worst environmental disasters, and in the early eighties the same fears focused on an inability to avert the ultimate threat to the human environment, a nuclear war. Graphic and pessimistic film versions of such catastrophes—*The China Syndrome* and *The Day After*—heightened these concerns.

The Republic in the Eighties. After six decades, the problems of America's modern state looked very similar to its earlier problems in broad outline, but they were very different in detail. The issue of a strong economy remained at the center of American life, and so did the obligation of public officials to oversee it. Governments at all levels had grown so luxuriantly that they took one-third of the nation's personal income in taxes and also accounted for one-third of the nation's personal income in salaries, wages, and other payments. The techniques of economic management, however, aroused fierce debate. Washington's standard fiscal formulas seemed inadequate, yet no substitute materialized to take their place. Most Americans, without easing their demands for prosperity and services, insisted on lower taxes and smaller bureaucracies. In hard times, the voters wanted more services for less money.

The revolt against taxes and rules was part of a general reaction against elite authority that included, but spread well beyond, government authority. Confidence in all major institutions—corporations, universities, medicine, law—dropped drastically during the seventies. Despite President Reagan's praise for traditional habits, the country remained irreverent toward its leaders. Interest in mysticism, astrology, and other supernatural forces thrived, and unorthodox routes to good health increasingly competed with traditional medicine. Fears spread that the United States was losing its technological edge to the Japanese and to other competitors, and that the educational system was in serious decay, as evidenced by declining college entrance examination scores. And the deeper the disenchantment with impersonal expertise, the stronger became the attraction of America's personal concerns. Innumerable Americans, for example, began to search for family and ethnic roots that could give life meaning apart from the hierarchical world of skills and careers.

The increasing skepticism about the system went hand in hand with a widespread caution about the future. In diverse ways, Americans were resisting long-term commitments. More and more pairs of people were substituting tentative living arrangements for marriages, and the practice spread from the young to older age groups. By the late seventies, courts were struggling to devise a new subdivision of the law that would cover these ad hoc partnerships. At the bicentennial, the birthrate reached its lowest level in American history. Such a large percentage of voters avoided party labels and declared themselves independents

Jean Guichard / SYGMA

U.S. MARINES IN LEBANON, NOVEMBER 1983

that each election became a surprise package of special whims. Commentators used such labels as "privatism" and "narcissism" to describe these trends. In the gradual development of modern culture, they were part of the continuing defense of the individual against a rationalized, routinized society. More and more Americans were trying to fashion lives that would maximize personal pleasure and personal growth by minimizing their formal ties in an imponderable society.

A growing aversion to constraints and commitments cast the nation's foreign policy in a haze of uncertainty. Clearly Americans now viewed world affairs with a greater impatience, with a lower tolerance for the ceaseless volatility of life around the globe. After the oil embargo of 1973–74, a number of writers and officials suggested a little gunboat diplomacy to seize the resources America wanted. In response to President Carter's moderate treaty gradually relinquishing the Canal Zone to Panama, a senator concluded that the United States had a right to keep the canal because "we stole it fair and square." Many Americans responded to the Iranian hostage crisis with demands to "nuke Iran," and Reagan's successful invasion of Grenada was widely applauded.

On the other hand, impatience generated a kind of indifference. As Third World revolutions unraveled America's network of global connections, a powerful urge welled up to stay clear of these eruptions. Fear of "another Vietnam" haunted the country, and the public dreaded the prospect of long-term military intervention in Lebanon and Central America.

The presidents of the seventies and eighties seemed to face almost insoluble problems. All of them were commanded to spin the gold of American prosperity from the straw of worldwide stagnation, to control global affairs despite America's waning international authority, and to elevate the national spirit through political institutions in which Americans had diminished faith. Yet the Reagan presidency suggested that traditional American optimism was not dead. The president's popularity rested less on substantive gains than on his ability to stir old feelings that America was a nation with a great past and a better future. Believing that history is on the Republic's side and that their ingenuity can meet any test, Americans have remained hopeful that the nation will find its way through the uncertain years ahead.

CHRONOLOGY

1970	Establishment of the Environmental Protection Agency (EPA).
1971	Twenty-sixth Amendment, giving eighteen-year-olds the right to vote. Wage and price controls introduced. Classified documents about the Vietnam War, the Pentagon Papers, leaked to the press.
1972	Nixon visits China and the Soviet Union. SALT I treaty signed. Watergate break-in. Nixon reelected president.
1973	American withdrawal from Vietnam. *Roe* v. *Wade* establishes women's constitutional right to abortion. Senate Watergate Committee begins hearings. Vice-President Agnew resigns; Gerald Ford appointed to succeed him.
1974	Worst economic recession since 1930s. Nixon resigns the presidency; Ford becomes president. Ford pardons Nixon.
1975	Government in South Vietnam falls. *Mayaguez* incident.
1976	James Earl ("Jimmy") Carter, Jr., elected president.
1977	Establishment of the Department of Energy.
1978	Panama Canal treaties ratified.

1979	United States formally recognizes China. SALT II treaty signed. Accident at Three Mile Island nuclear power plant. President Carter mediates an Egyptian-Israeli peace settlement. Iranian hostage crisis begins.
1979–80	Iranian revolution pushes up oil prices an additional 50 percent; U.S. experiences the worst stagflation yet.
1980	Boycott of Moscow Olympic Games in response to Soviet invasion of Afghanistan. Rescue mission in Iran fails. Ronald W. Reagan elected president.
1981	Reagan cuts domestic social programs and wins a 25 percent tax cut.
1982	Worst recession since the Great Depression, with 10.8 percent unemployment.
1983	Economic recovery combined with record deficit of $195 billion. American troops sent to Lebanon. Invasion of Grenada. Collapse of U.S.-Soviet arms talks.
1984	American forces withdrawn from Lebanon. Congress condemns covert administration help to rebels mining Nicaraguan harbors. Unemployment declines to 7.1 percent.

Three interesting books attempt general interpretations of contemporary U.S. politics: David Knoke, *Change and Continuity in American Politics* (1976); Everett Carll Ladd, Jr., and Charles D. Hadley, *Transformations of the American Party System* (rev. ed., 1978); and Kevin P. Phillips, *The Emerging Republican Majority* (1969). Accounts of Richard Nixon include a favorable one in Earl Mazo and Stephen Hess, *Nixon* (1968), and an unfavorable one in Garry Wills, *Nixon Agonistes* (1970). In *Kissinger* (1974), Marvin and Bernard Kalb raise Nixon's reputation in foreign affairs by deflating claims that Kissinger dominated the president. Tad Szulc, *The Illusion of Peace: Foreign Policy in the Nixon Years* (1978), is harsher still on Kissinger. Kissinger defends himself in his memoirs, *White House Years* (1979) and *Years of Upheaval* (1982). Seymour Hersh, *The Price of Power: Kissinger in the Nixon White House* (1983), raises disturbing questions about Kissinger's actions. Harland B. Moulton's *From Superiority to Parity: The United States and the Strategic Arms Race, 1961–1971* (1973) discusses some preliminary moves toward détente. On the Middle East, William B. Quandt, *Decade of Decision: American Policy Toward the Arab-Israeli Conflict, 1967–1976* (1977), and Robert W. Stookey, *America and the Arab States* (1975), are especially useful. Recent interest in the office of the chief executive has generated a variety of books, including George E. Reedy, *The Twilight of the Presidency* (1970); Arthur M. Schlesinger, Jr., *The Imperial Presidency* (1973), which is sharply critical of Nixon; and Otis L. Graham, Jr., *Toward a Planned Society: From Roosevelt to Nixon* (1976), which also faults Nixon for disrupting the evolution of national planning. The Watergate affair elicited its own special group of studies. Carl Bernstein and Bob Woodward, the reporters who helped to expose the affair, tell a fascinating tale of investigation and deception in *All the President's Men* (1974). Their sequel, *The Final Days* (1976), deals with Nixon during the year before his resignation. Among the many memoirs by participants, John Dean's *Blind Ambition* (1976) is particularly enlightening. Jonathan Schell, *The Time of Illusion* (1976), also illuminates the Watergate period. The conservative senator who led an early investigation into the mess is the subject of Dick Dabney's *A Good Man: The Life of Sam J. Ervin* (1976).

On minority groups, the essays in Michael V. Namorato, ed., *Have We Overcome?* (1979), assess the state of black rights, and Anthony Downs, *Opening Up the Suburbs* (1973), discusses race and social policy. Matt S. Meier and Feliciano Rivera, *The Chicanos: A History of Mexican Americans* (1972), is a general account of an increasingly important minority in American life. Also useful is Julian Samora, *Los Mojados: The Wetback Story* (1971). Wilcomb E. Washburn, *Red Man's Land, White Man's Law* (1971), details a record of mass injustice; D'Arcy McNickle, *Native American Tribalism* (1973), helps to explain the culture of recent protests; and Vine Deloria, Jr., *Behind the Trail of Broken Treaties* (1974), expresses the spirit of contemporary militancy. For a general survey and extensive bibliography, see Wilcomb Washburn's *The Indian in America* (1975).

Recent constitutional and political questions are addressed in Alexander M. Bickel, *The Supreme Court and the Idea of Progress* (1970), and in two books on Earl Warren: G. Edward White, *Earl Warren: A Public Life* (1982), and Bernard Schwartz, *Super Chief: Earl Warren and the Supreme Court* (1983). Martin P. Wattenberg, *The Decline of American Political Parties, 1952–1980* (1984), Walter Dean Burnham, *The Current Crisis in American Politics* (1983), and Theodore Sorenson, *A Different Kind of Presidency: A Proposal for Breaking the Political Deadlock* (1984), deal with problems in American political institutions.

The literature on the Ford-Carter-Reagan years is limited. On Ford, see his own account, *A Time To Heal: An Autobiography* (1979), and two books by journalists: J. F. ter Horst, *Gerald Ford and the Future of the Presidency* (1974), and Richard Reeves, *A Ford Not a Lincoln* (1975). The election of 1976 is covered in Elizabeth Drew, *American Journal: The Events of 1976* (1977), and Jules Witcover, *Marathon* (1977). Carter's term is recounted in his memoirs, *Keeping Faith* (1982), and in the memoirs of his two principal foreign policy advisers: Cyrus Vance, *Hard Choices: Critical Years in America's Foreign Policy* (1983), and Zbigniew Brzezinski, *Power and Principle: Memoirs of the National Security Advisor, 1977–1981* (1983). Carter, the man and the president, is also studied in James T. Wotten, *Dasher: The Roots and the Rising of Jimmy Carter* (1978); William Lee Miller, *Yankee From Georgia: The Emergence of Jimmy Carter* (1978); and Betty Glad, *Jimmy Carter: In Search of the Great White House* (1980). The 1980 election is the subject of Elizabeth Drew, *Portrait of an Election: The 1980 Presidential Campaign* (1981). On Reagan and the first years of his presidency, see Lou Cannon, *Reagan* (1982), and Laurence I. Barrett, *Gambling with History* (1983), both works by journalists. Initial accounts by historians are William E. Leuchtenburg, "Ronald Reagan," a chapter in *In the Shadow of FDR* (1983), and Robert Dallek, *Ronald Reagan: The Politics of Symbolism* (1984).

Appendix

PACIFIC OCEAN

C A

Tacoma• •Seattle
Olympia ⊛ Spokane•
Mt.Rainier WASHINGTON
14,410′ 1889
R.
Portland•
Columbia

Salem ⊛ Willamette R.
OREGON
1859

Helena ⊛ MONTANA
Butte• 1889
Yellowstone R.

NORTH DAKOTA
1889 ⊛ Bismarck

⊛ Boise IDAHO
1890

Snake R.

WYOMING
1890

Cheyenne ⊛

SOUTH DAKOTA
1889

Pierre
⊛

1867
NEBRASKA
Platte R.
Linco

Sacramento R. SIERRA
Reno• Carson ⊛ City

NEVADA
1864

Great Salt Lake
Salt Lake City ⊛
1896

UTAH

Denver ⊛

COLORADO
1876 +Pikes Pk. 14,110′

1861
K A N S
Wichi

Sacramento ⊛
San Francisco•

CALIFORNIA
1850

NEVADA
Mt. Whitney 14,495′

Los Angeles•

Colorado
Grand Canyon

R.

ARIZONA
1912

Santa Fe ⊛

NEW MEXICO
1912

Canadian R.
Oklaho
⊛
O K L A
190

San Diego•

Gila R. ⊛ Phoenix

•Tucson

•El Paso

M E X I C O

Ft.
Wo
Brazos
1845
T E X A S

Rio Grande

Pecos R.

San Antonio•

Aus
Colo

Nuec

SOVIET UNION
180°
ARCTIC OCEAN
Pt. Barrow
International Dateline (U.S.S.R.)
(United States)
ARCTIC CIRCLE
Attu
Nome• Yukon R.
BERING SEA
Fairbanks•
Mt.McKinley
20,300′
ALEUTIAN ISLANDS
Anchorage•
Kodiak I.
CANADA
Unimak
ALASKA
1959
Juneau ⊛
180°
PACIFIC OCEAN
0   600
Miles

KAUAI
NIIHAU
OAHU ⊛
Honolulu
MOLOKAI
PACIFIC
LANAI
KAHOOLAWE
MAUI
OCEAN
HAWAII
1959
•Hilo
HAWAII
0   150
Miles

Norman Clark Adams

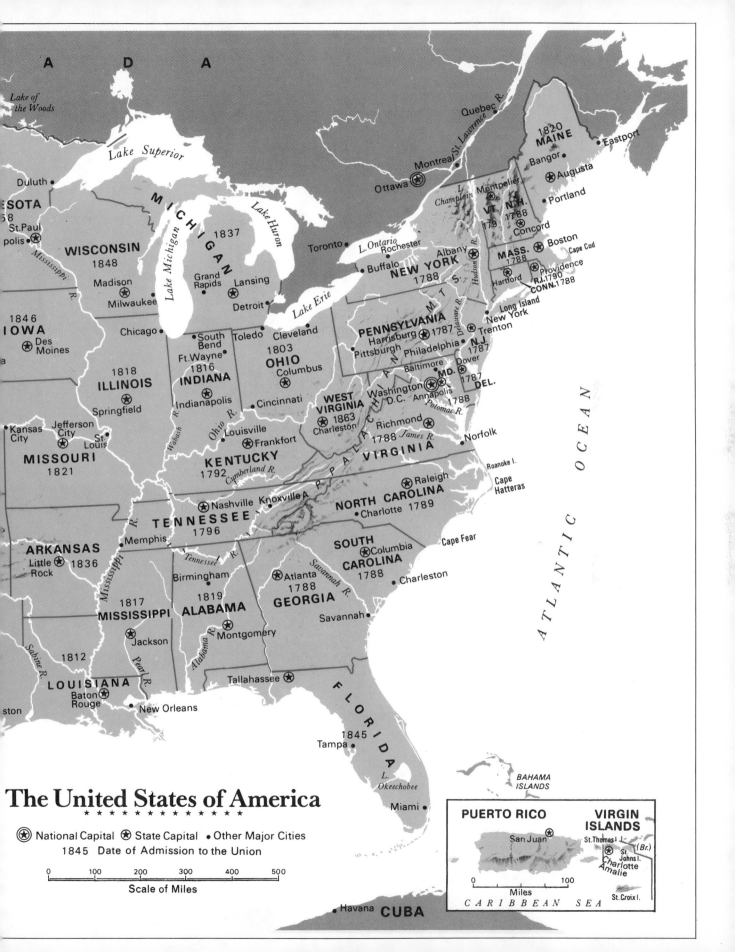

The United States of America
* * * * * * * * * * * * * *

⊛ National Capital ⊛ State Capital • Other Major Cities
1845 Date of Admission to the Union

0   100   200   300   400   500
Scale of Miles

CANADA

Lake of the Woods

Lake Superior

Duluth

SOTA
58
St.Paul
polis

MICHIGAN

WISCONSIN
1848

Madison

Milwaukee

1837

Grand Rapids

Lansing

Detroit

Lake Michigan

Lake Huron

Lake Erie

Quebec R.

Montreal   St. Lawrence

Ottawa

1820
MAINE

Bangor

Augusta

Eastport

Portland

L. Champlain   Montpelier

VT.   N.H.
179   1788

Concord

Toronto

L. Ontario   Rochester

Buffalo

NEW YORK
1788

Albany

Hudson R.

MASS.
1788   Boston

Cape Cod

Hartford   Providence
R.I.1790
CONN.1788

Long Island

New York

1846
IOWA

Des Moines

Mississippi R.

Chicago

South Bend
Ft.Wayne
1816
INDIANA

Indianapolis

Toledo

Cleveland

1803
OHIO

Columbus

PENNSYLVANIA
Harrisburg   1787
Pittsburgh

Philadelphia

N.J.
1787

Trenton

Dover

MD.
1787   DEL.

Delaware R.

1818
ILLINOIS

Springfield

Wabash R.

Cincinnati

Ohio R.

Louisville

WEST VIRGINIA
1863
Charleston

Washington
D.C.

Annapolis
1788

Baltimore

Potomac R.

Kansas City

Jefferson City

St. Louis

MISSOURI
1821

Frankfort

KENTUCKY
1792

Cumberland R.

Richmond

VIRGINIA
1788   James R.

Norfolk

Roanoke I.

Cape Hatteras

ATLANTIC OCEAN

Nashville

Knoxville

TENNESSEE
1796

Tennessee R.

Raleigh

NORTH CAROLINA

Charlotte   1789

Memphis

ARKANSAS
Little Rock   1836

Birmingham

1819

1817

MISSISSIPPI   ALABAMA

Jackson

Montgomery

Alabama R.

Pearl R.

Mississippi R.

Sabine R.

1812

LOUISIANA

Baton Rouge

New Orleans

ston

SOUTH CAROLINA
1788

Columbia

Charleston

Cape Fear

ATLANTIC

GEORGIA

Atlanta
1788

Savannah R.

Savannah

Tallahassee

FLORIDA

1845

Tampa

L. Okeechobee

Miami

BAHAMA ISLANDS

Havana   **CUBA**

Inset
PUERTO RICO

San Juan

VIRGIN ISLANDS

St. Thomas I.

St. Johns I.   (Br.)

Charlotte Amalie

St. Croix I.

0   100
Miles

CARIBBEAN SEA

Declaration of Independence

IN CONGRESS, JULY 4, 1776

THE UNANIMOUS DECLARATION OF THE THIRTEEN UNITED STATES OF AMERICA

When, in the course of human events, it becomes necessary for one people to dissolve the political bands which have connected them with another, and to assume, among the powers of the earth, the separate and equal station to which the laws of nature and of nature's God entitle them, a decent respect to the opinions of mankind requires that they should declare the causes which impel them to the separation.

We hold these truths to be self-evident: That all men are created equal; that they are endowed by their Creator with certain unalienable rights; that among these are life, liberty, and the pursuit of happiness; that, to secure these rights, governments are instituted among men, deriving their just powers from the consent of the governed; that whenever any form of government becomes destructive of these ends, it is the right of the people to alter or to abolish it, and to institute new government, laying its foundation on such principles, and organizing its powers in such form, as to them shall seem most likely to effect their safety and happiness. Prudence, indeed, will dictate that governments long established should not be changed for light and transient causes; and accordingly all experience hath shown that mankind are more disposed to suffer, while evils are sufferable, than to right themselves by abolishing the forms to which they are accustomed. But when a long train of abuses and usurpations, pursuing invariably the same object, evinces a design to reduce them under absolute despotism, it is their right, it is their duty, to throw off such government, and to provide new guards for their future security. Such has been the patient sufferance of these colonies; and such is now the necessity which constrains them to alter their former systems of government. The history of the present King of Great Britain is a history of repeated injuries and usurpations, all having in direct object the establishment of an absolute tyranny over these states. To prove this, let facts be submitted to a candid world.

He has refused his assent to laws, the most wholesome and necessary for the public good.

He has forbidden his governors to pass laws of immediate and pressing importance, unless suspended in their operation till his assent should be obtained; and, when so suspended, he has utterly neglected to attend to them.

He has refused to pass other laws for the accommodation of large districts of people, unless those people would relinquish the right of representation in the legislature, a right inestimable to them, and formidable to tyrants only.

He has called together legislative bodies at places unusual, uncomfortable, and distant from the depository of their public records, for the sole purpose of fatiguing them into compliance with his measures.

He has dissolved representative houses repeatedly, for opposing, with manly firmness, his invasions on the rights of the people.

He has refused for a long time, after such dissolutions, to cause others to be elected; whereby the legislative powers, incapable of annihilation, have returned to the people at large for their exercise; the state remaining, in the mean time, exposed to all the dangers of invasions from without and convulsions within.

He has endeavored to prevent the population of these states; for that purpose obstructing the laws for naturalization of foreigners; refusing to pass others to encourage their migration hither, and raising the conditions of new appropriations of lands.

He has obstructed the administration of justice, by refusing his assent to laws for establishing judiciary powers.

He has made judges dependent on his will alone, for the tenure of their offices, and the amount and payment of their salaries.

He has erected a multitude of new offices, and sent hither swarms of officers to harass our people and eat out their substance.

He has kept among us, in times of peace, standing armies, without the consent of our legislatures.

He has affected to render the military independent of, and superior to, the civil power.

He has combined with others to subject us to a jurisdiction foreign to our constitution, and unacknowledged by our laws, giving his assent to their acts of pretended legislation:

For quartering large bodies of armed troops among us;

For protecting them, by a mock trial, from punishment for any murders which they should commit on the inhabitants of these states;

For cutting off our trade with all parts of the world;

For imposing taxes on us without our consent;

For depriving us, in many cases, of the benefits of trial by jury;

For transporting us beyond seas, to be tried for pretended offenses;

For abolishing the free system of English laws in a neighboring province, establishing therein an arbitrary government, and enlarging its boundaries, so as to render it at once an example and fit instrument for introducing the same absolute rule into these colonies;

For taking away our charters, abolishing our most valuable laws, and altering fundamentally the forms of our governments;

For suspending our own legislatures, and declaring themselves invested with power to legislate for us in all cases whatsoever.

He has abdicated government here, by declaring us out of his protection and waging war against us.

He has plundered our seas, ravaged our coasts, burned our towns, and destroyed the lives of our people.

He is at this time transporting large armies of foreign mercenaries to complete the works of death, desolation, and tyranny already begun with circumstances of cruelty and perfidy scarcely paralleled in the most barbarous ages, and totally unworthy the head of a civilized nation.

He has constrained our fellow-citizens, taken captive on the high seas, to bear arms against their country, to become the executioners of their friends and brethren, or to fall themselves by their hands.

He has excited domestic insurrection among us, and has endeavored to bring on the inhabitants of our frontiers the merciless Indian savages, whose known rule of warfare is an undistinguished destruction of all ages, sexes, and conditions.

In every stage of these oppressions we have petitioned for redress in the most humble terms; our repeated petitions have been answered only by repeated injury. A prince, whose character is thus marked by every act which may define a tyrant, is unfit to be the ruler of a free people.

Nor have we been wanting in our attentions to our British brethren. We have warned them, from time to time, of attempts by their legislature to extend an unwarrantable jurisdiction over us. We have reminded them of the circumstances of our emigration and settlement here. We have appealed to their native justice and magnanimity; and we have conjured them, by the ties of our common kindred, to disavow these usurpations, which would inevitably interrupt our connections and correspondence. They, too, have been deaf to the voice of justice and of consanguinity. We must, therefore, acquiesce in the necessity which denounces our separation, and hold them, as we hold the rest of mankind, enemies in war, in peace friends.

We, therefore, the representatives of the United States of America, in General Congress assembled, appealing to the Supreme Judge of the world for the rectitude of our intentions, do, in the name and by the authority of the good people of these colonies, solemnly publish and declare, that these United Colonies are, and of right ought to be, FREE AND INDEPENDENT STATES; that they are absolved from all allegiance to the British crown, and that all political connection between them and the state of Great Britain is, and ought to be, totally dissolved; and that, as free and independent states, they have full power to levy war, conclude peace, contract alliances, establish commerce, and do all other acts and things which independent states may of right do. And for the support of this declaration, with a firm reliance on the protection of Divine Providence, we mutually pledge to each other our lives, our fortunes, and our sacred honor.

JOHN HANCOCK [*President*]
[*and fifty-five others*]

The Articles of Confederation and Perpetual Union

BETWEEN THE STATES OF NEW HAMPSHIRE, MASSACHUSETTS BAY, RHODE ISLAND AND PROVIDENCE PLANTATIONS, CONNECTICUT, NEW YORK, NEW JERSEY, PENNSYLVANIA, DELAWARE, MARYLAND, VIRGINIA, NORTH CAROLINA, SOUTH CAROLINA, GEORGIA.*

ARTICLE 1.

The stile of this confederacy shall be "The United States of America."

ARTICLE 2.

Each State retains its sovereignty, freedom and independence, and every power, jurisdiction, and right, which is not by this confederation expressly delegated to the United States, in Congress assembled.

ARTICLE 3.

The said states hereby severally enter into a firm league of friendship with each other for their common defence, the security of their liberties and their mutual and general welfare; binding themselves to assist each other against all force offered to, or attacks made upon them, or any of them, on account of religion, sovereignty, trade, or any other pretence whatever.

ARTICLE 4.

The better to secure and perpetuate mutual friendship and intercourse among the people of the different states in this union, the free inhabitants of each of these states, paupers, vagabonds, and fugitives from justice excepted, shall be entitled to all privileges and immunities of free citizens in the several states; and the people of each State shall have free ingress and regress to and from any other State, and shall enjoy therein all the privileges of trade and commerce, subject to the same duties, impositions, and restrictions, as the inhabitants thereof respectively; provided, that such restrictions shall not extend so far as to prevent the removal of property, imported into any State, to any other State of which the owner is an inhabitant; provided also, that no imposition, duties, or restriction, shall be laid by any State on the property of the United States, or either of them.

*This copy of the final draft of the Articles of Confederation is taken from the *Journals*, 9:907–925, November 15, 1777.

If any person guilty of, or charged with treason, felony, or other high misdemeanor in any State, shall flee from justice and be found in any of the United States, he shall, upon demand of the governor or executive power of the State from which he fled, be delivered up and removed to the State having jurisdiction of his offence.

Full faith and credit shall be given in each of these states to the records, acts, and judicial proceedings of the courts and magistrates of every other State.

ARTICLE 5.

For the more convenient management of the general interests of the United States, delegates shall be annually appointed, in such manner as the legislature of each State shall direct, to meet in Congress, on the 1st Monday in November in every year, with a power reserved to each State to recall its delegates, or any of them, at any time within the year, and to send others in their stead for the remainder of the year.

No State shall be represented in Congress by less than two, nor by more than seven members; and no person shall be capable of being a delegate for more than three years in any term of six years; nor shall any person, being a delegate, be capable of holding any office under the United States, for which he, or any other for his benefit, receives any salary, fees, or emolument of any kind.

Each State shall maintain its own delegates in a meeting of the states, and while they act as members of the committee of the states.

In determining questions in the United States, in Congress assembled, each State shall have one vote.

Freedom of speech and debate in Congress shall not be impeached or questioned in any court or place out of Congress: and the members of Congress shall be protected in their persons from arrests and imprisonments, during the time of their going to and from, and attendance on Congress, *except for treason*, felony, or breach of the peace.

ARTICLE 6.

No State, without the consent of the United States, in Congress assembled, shall send any embassy to, or receive any embassy from, or enter into any conference, agreement, alliance, or treaty with any king, prince, or state; nor shall any person, holding any office of profit or trust under the United States, or any of them, accept of any present, emolument, office or title, of any kind whatever, from any king, prince, or foreign state; nor shall the United States, in Congress assembled, or any of them, grant any title of nobility.

No two or more states shall enter into any treaty, confederation, or alliance, whatever, between them, without the consent of the United States, in Congress assembled, specifying accurately the purposes for which the same is to be entered into, and how long it shall continue.

No State shall lay any imposts or duties which may interfere with any stipulations in treaties entered into by the United States, in Congress assembled, with any king, prince, or state, in pursuance of any treaties already proposed by Congress to the courts of France and Spain.

No vessels of war shall be kept up in time of peace by any State, except such number only as shall be deemed necessary by the United States, in Congress assembled, for the defence of such State or its trade; nor shall any body of forces be kept up by any State, in time of peace, except such number only as, in the judgment of the United States, in Congress assembled, shall be deemed requisite to garrison the forts necessary for the defence of such State; but every State shall always keep up a well regulated and disciplined militia, sufficiently armed and accoutred, and shall provide, and constantly have ready for use, in public stores, a due number of field pieces and tents, and a proper quantity of arms, ammunition and camp equipage.

No State shall engage in any war without the consent of the United States, in Congress assembled, unless such State be actually invaded by enemies, or shall have received certain advice of a resolution being formed by some nation of Indians to invade· such State, and the danger is so imminent as not to admit of a delay till the United States, in Congress assembled, can be consulted; nor shall any State grant commissions to any ships or vessels of war, nor letters of marque or reprisal, except it be after a declaration of war by the United States, in Congress assembled, and then only against the kingdom or state, and the subjects thereof, against which war has been so declared, and under such regulations as shall be established by the United States, in Congress assembled, unless such State be infested by pirates, in which case vessels of war may be fitted out for that occasion, and kept so long as the danger shall continue, or until the United States, in Congress assembled, shall determine otherwise.

ARTICLE 7.

When land forces are raised by any State for the common defence, all officers of or under the rank of colonel, shall be appointed by the legislature of each State respectively, by whom such forces shall be raised, or in such manner as such State shall direct; and all vacancies shall be filled up by the State which first made the appointment.

ARTICLE 8.

All charges of war and all other expences, that shall be incurred for the common defence or general welfare, and allowed by the United States, in Congress assembled, shall be defrayed out of a common treasury, which shall be supplied by the several states, in proportion to the value of all land within each State, granted to or surveyed for any person, as such land and the buildings and improvements thereon shall be estimated according to such mode as the United States, in Congress assembled, shall, from time to time, direct and appoint.

The taxes for paying that proportion shall be laid and levied by the authority and direction of the legislatures of the several states, within the time agreed upon by the United States, in Congress assembled.

ARTICLE 9.

The United States, in Congress assembled, shall have the sole and exclusive right and power of determining on peace and war, except in the cases mentioned in the 6th article; of sending and receiving ambassadors; entering into treaties and alliances, provided that no treaty of commerce shall be made, whereby the legislative power of the respective states shall be restrained from imposing such imposts and duties on foreigners as their own people are subjected to, or from prohibiting the exportation or importation of any species of goods or commodities whatsoever; of establishing rules for deciding, in all cases, what captures on land or water shall be legal, and in what manner prizes, taken by land or naval forces in the service of the United States, shall be divided or appropriated; of granting letters of marque and reprisal in times of peace; appointing courts for the trial of piracies and felonies committed on the high seas, and establishing courts for receiving and determining, finally, appeals in all cases of captures; provided, that no member of Congress shall be appointed a judge of any of the said courts.

The United States, in Congress assembled, shall also be the last resort on appeal in all disputes and differences now subsisting, or that hereafter may arise between two or more states concerning boundary, jurisdiction or any other cause whatever; which authority shall always be exercised in the manner following: whenever the legislative or executive authority, or lawful agent of any State, in controversy with another, shall present a petition to Congress, stating the matter in question, and praying for a hearing, notice thereof shall be given, by order of Congress, to the legislative or executive authority of the other State in controversy, and a day assigned for the appearance of the parties by their lawful agents, who shall then be directed to appoint, by joint consent, commissioners or judges to constitute a court for hearing and determining the matter in question; but, if they cannot agree, Congress shall name three persons out of each of the United States, and from the list of such persons each party shall alternately strike out one, in the petitioners beginning, until the number shall be reduced to thirteen; and from that number not less than seven, nor more than nine names, as Congress shall direct, shall, in the presence of Congress, be drawn out by lot; and the persons whose names shall be so drawn, or any five of them, shall be commissioners or judges to hear and finally determine the controversy, so always as a major part of the judges who shall hear the cause shall agree in the determination; and if either party shall neglect to attend at the day appointed, without shewing reasons which Congress shall judge sufficient, or, being present, shall refuse to strike, the Congress shall proceed to nominate three persons out of each State, and the secretary of Congress shall strike in behalf of such party absent or refusing; and the judgment and sentence of the court to be appointed, in the manner before prescribed, shall be final and conclusive; and if any of the parties shall refuse to submit to the authority of such court, or to appear or defend their claim or cause, the court shall nevertheless proceed to pronounce sentence or judgment, which shall, in like manner, be final and decisive, the judgment or sentence and other proceedings being, in either case, transmitted to Congress, and lodged among the acts of Congress for the security of the parties concerned: provided, that every commissioner, before he sits in judgment, shall take an oath, to be administered by one of the judges of the supreme or superior court of the State where the cause shall be tried, "well and truly to hear and determine the matter in question, according to the best of his judgment, without favour, affection, or hope of reward": provided, also, that no State shall be deprived of territory for the benefit of the United States.

All controversies concerning the private right of soil, claimed under different grants of two or more states, whose jurisdictions, as they may respect such lands and the states which passed such grants, are adjusted, the said grants, or either of them, being at the same time claimed to have originated antecedent to such settlement of jurisdiction, shall, on the petition of either party to the Congress of the United States, be finally determined, as near as may be, in the same manner as is before prescribed for deciding disputes respecting territorial jurisdiction between different states.

The United States, in Congress assembled, shall also have the sole and exclusive right and power of regulating the alloy and value of coin struck by their own authority, or by that of the respective states; fixing the standard of weights and measures throughout the United States; regulating the trade and managing all affairs with the Indians not members of any of the states; provided that the legislative right of any State within its own limits be not infringed or violated; establishing and regulating post offices from one State to another throughout all the United States, and exacting such postage on the papers passing through the same as may be requisite to defray the expences of the said office; appointing all officers of the land forces in the service of the United States, excepting regimental officers; appointing all the officers of the naval forces, and commissioning all officers whatever in the service of the United States; making rules for the government and regulation of the said land and naval forces, and directing their operations.

The United States, in Congress assembled, shall have authority to appoint a committee to sit in the recess of Congress, to be denominated "a Committee of the States," and to consist of one delegate from each State, and to appoint such other committees and civil officers as may be necessary for managing the general affairs of the United States, under their direction; to appoint one of their number to preside; provided that no person be allowed to serve in the office of president more than one year in any term of three years; to ascertain the necessary sums of money to be raised for the service of the United States, and to appropriate and apply the same for defraying the public expences; to borrow money or emit bills on the credit of the United States, transmitting, every half year, to the respective states, an account of the sums of money so borrowed or emitted; to build and equip a navy; to agree upon the number of land forces, and to make requisitions from each State for its quota, in proportion to the number of white inhabitants in such State; which requisitions shall be binding; and, thereupon, the legislature of each State shall appoint the regimental officers, raise the men, and cloathe, arm, and equip them in a soldier-like manner, at the expence of the United States; and the officers and men so cloathed, armed, and equipped, shall march to the place appointed and within the time agreed on by the United States, in Congress assembled; but if the United States, in Congress assembled, shall, on consideration of circumstances, judge proper that any State should not raise men, or should raise a smaller number than its quota, and that any other State should raise a greater number of men than the quota thereof, such extra number shall be raised, officered, cloathed, armed, and equipped in the same manner as the quota of such State, unless the legislature of such State shall judge that such extra number cannot be safely spared out of the same, in which case they shall raise, officer, cloathe, arm, and equip as many of such extra number as they judge can be safely spared. And the officers and men so cloathed, armed, and equipped, shall march to the place appointed and within the time agreed on by the United States, in Congress assembled.

The United States, in Congress assembled, shall never engage in a war, nor grant letters of marque and reprisal in time of peace, nor enter into any treaties or alliances, nor coin money, nor regulate the value thereof, nor ascertain the sums and expences necessary for the defence and welfare of the United States, or any of them: nor emit bills, nor borrow money on the credit of the United States, nor appropriate money, nor agree upon the number of vessels of war to be built or purchased, or the number of land or sea forces to be raised, nor appoint a commander in chief of the army or navy, unless nine states assent to the same; nor shall a question on any other point, except for adjourning from day to day, be determined, unless by the votes of a majority of the United States, in Congress assembled.

The Congress of the United States shall have power to adjourn to any time within the year, and to any place within the United States, so that no period of adjournment be for a longer duration than the space of six months, and shall publish the journal of their proceedings monthly, except such parts thereof, relating to treaties, alliances or military operations, as, in their judgment, require secrecy; and the yeas and nays of the delegates of each State on any question shall be entered on the journal, when it is desired by any delegate; and the delegates of a State, or any of them, at his, or their request, shall be furnished with a transcript of the said journal, except such parts as are above excepted, to lay before the legislatures of the several states.

ARTICLE 10.

The committee of the states, or any nine of them, shall be authorized to execute, in the recess of Congress, such of the powers of Congress as the United States, in Congress assembled, by the consent of nine states, shall, from time to time, think expedient to vest them with; provided, that no power be delegated to the said committee, for the exercise of which, by the articles of confederation, the voice of nine states, in the Congress of the United States assembled, is requisite.

ARTICLE 11.

Canada acceding to this confederation, and joining in the measures of the United States, shall be admitted into and entitled to all the advantages of this union; but no other colony shall be admitted into the same, unless such admission be agreed to by nine states.

ARTICLE 12.

All bills of credit emitted, monies borrowed and debts contracted by, or under the authority of Congress before the assembling of the United States, in pursuance of the present confederation, shall be deemed and considered as a charge against the United States, for payment and satisfaction whereof the said United States and the public faith are hereby solemnly pledged.

ARTICLE 13.

Every State shall abide by the determinations of the United States, in Congress assembled, on all questions which, by this confederation, are submitted to them. And the articles of this confederation shall be inviolably observed by every State, and the union shall be perpetual; nor shall any alteration at any time hereafter be made in any of them, unless such alteration be agreed to in a Congress of the United States, and be afterwards confirmed by the legislatures of every State.

These articles shall be proposed to the legislatures of all the United States, to be considered, and if approved of by them, they are advised to authorize their delegates to ratify the same in the Congress of the United States; which being done, the same shall become conclusive.

Constitution of the United States of America

PREAMBLE

We the people of the United States, in order to form a more perfect union, establish justice, insure domestic tranquillity, provide for the common defense, promote the general welfare, and secure the blessings of liberty to ourselves and our posterity, do ordain and establish this CONSTITUTION for the United States of America.

ARTICLE I

Section 1. All legislative powers herein granted shall be vested in a Congress of the United States, which shall consist of a Senate and a House of Representatives.

Section 2. The House of Representatives shall be composed of members chosen every second year by the people of the several States, and the electors in each State shall have the qualifications requisite for electors of the most numerous branch of the State Legislature.

No person shall be a Representative who shall not have attained to the age of twenty-five years, and been seven years a citizen of the United States, and who shall not, when elected, be an inhabitant of that State in which he shall be chosen.

Representatives and direct taxes shall be apportioned among the several States which may be included within this Union, according to their respective numbers, *which shall be determined by adding to the whole number of free persons, including those bound to service for a term of years and excluding Indians not taxed, three-fifths of all other persons.* The actual enumeration shall be made within three years after the first meeting of the Congress of the United States, and within every subsequent term of ten years, in such manner as they shall by law direct. The number of Representatives shall not exceed one for every thirty thousand, but each State shall have at least one Representative; *and until such enumeration shall be made, the State of New Hampshire shall be entitled to choose three, Massachusetts eight, Rhode Island and Providence Plantations one, Connecticut five, New York six, New Jersey four, Pennsylvania eight, Delaware one, Maryland six, Virginia ten, North Carolina five, South Carolina five, and Georgia three.*

When vacancies happen in the representation from any State, the Executive authority thereof shall issue writs of election to fill such vacancies.

The House of Representatives shall choose their Speaker and other officers; and shall have the sole power of impeachment.

Section 3. The Senate of the United States shall be composed of two Senators from each State, *chosen by the legislature thereof,* for six years; and each Senator shall have one vote.

Immediately after they shall be assembled in consequence of the first election, they shall be divided as equally as may be into three classes. The seats of the Senators of the first class shall be vacated at the expiration of the second year, of the second class at the expiration of the fourth year, and of the third class at the expiration of the sixth year, so that one-third may be chosen every second year; *and if vacancies happen by resignation or otherwise, during the recess of the legislature of any State, the Executive thereof may make temporary appointments until the next meeting of the legislature, which shall then fill such vacancies.*

No person shall be a Senator who shall not have attained to the age of thirty years, and been nine years a citizen of the United States, and who shall not, when elected, be an inhabitant of that State for which he shall be chosen.

The Vice-President of the United States shall be President of the Senate, but shall have no vote, unless they be equally divided.

The Senate shall choose their other officers, and also a President *pro tempore,* in the absence of the

NOTE: Passages that are no longer in effect are printed in italic type.

Vice-President, or when he shall exercise the office of President of the United States.

The Senate shall have the sole power to try all impeachments. When sitting for that purpose, they shall be on oath or affirmation. When the President of the United States is tried, the Chief Justice shall preside: and no person shall be convicted without the concurrence of two-thirds of the members present.

Judgment in cases of impeachment shall not extend further than to removal from the office, and disqualification to hold and enjoy any office of honor, trust or profit under the United States; but the party convicted shall nevertheless be liable and subject to indictment, trial, judgment and punishment, according to law.

Section 4. The times, places and manner of holding elections for Senators and Representatives shall be prescribed in each State by the legislature thereof; but the Congress may at any time by law make or alter such regulations, except as to the places of choosing Senators.

The Congress shall assemble at least once in every year, and such meeting *shall be on the first Monday in December, unless they shall by law appoint a different day.*

Section 5. Each house shall be the judge of the elections, returns and qualifications of its own members, and a majority of each shall constitute a quorum to do business; but a smaller number may adjourn from day to day, and may be authorized to compel the attendance of absent members, in such manner, and under such penalties, as each house may provide.

Each house may determine the rules of its proceedings, punish its members for disorderly behavior, and with the concurrence of two-thirds, expel a member.

Each house shall keep a journal of its proceedings, and from time to time publish the same, excepting such parts as may in their judgment require secrecy; and the yeas and nays of the members of either house on any question shall, at the desire of one-fifth of those present, be entered on the journal.

Neither house, during the session of Congress, shall, without the consent of the other, adjourn for more than three days, nor to any other place than that in which the two houses shall be sitting.

Section 6. The Senators and Representatives shall receive a compensation for their services, to be ascertained by law and paid out of the treasury of the United States. They shall in all cases except treason, felony and breach of the peace, be privileged from arrest during their attendance at the session of their respective houses, and in going to and returning from the same; and for any speech or debate in either house, they shall not be questioned in any other place.

No Senator or Representative shall, during the time for which he was elected, be appointed to any civil office under the authority of the United States, which shall have been created, or the emoluments whereof shall have been increased, during such time; and no person holding any office under the United States shall be a member of either house during his continuance in office.

Section 7. All bills for raising revenue shall originate in the House of Representatives; but the Senate may propose or concur with amendments as on other bills.

Every bill which shall have passed the House of Representatives and the Senate, shall, before it become a law, be presented to the President of the United States; if he approve he shall sign it, but if not he shall return it with objections to that house in which it originated, who shall enter the objections at large on their journal, and proceed to reconsider it. If after such reconsideration two-thirds of that house shall agree to pass the bill, it shall be sent, together with the objections, to the other house, by which it shall likewise be reconsidered, and, if approved by two-thirds of that house, it shall become a law. But in all such cases the votes of both houses shall be determined by yeas and nays, and the names of the persons voting for and against the bill shall be entered on the journal of each house respectively. If any bill shall not be returned by the President within ten days (Sundays excepted) after it shall have been presented to him, the same shall be a law, in like manner as if he had signed it, unless the Congress by their adjournment prevent its return, in which case it shall not be a law.

Every order, resolution, or vote to which the concurrence of the Senate and House of Representatives may be necessary (except on a question of adjournment) shall be presented to the President of the United States; and before the same shall take effect, shall be approved by him, or being disapproved by him, shall be repassed by two-thirds of the Senate and House of Representatives, according to the rules and limitations prescribed in the case of a bill.

Section 8. The Congress shall have power

To lay and collect taxes, duties, imposts, and excises, to pay the debts and provide for the common defense and general welfare of the United States; but all duties, imposts and excises shall be uniform throughout the United States;

To borrow money on the credit of the United States;

To regulate commerce with foreign nations, and

among the several States, and with the Indian tribes;

To establish an uniform rule of naturalization, and uniform laws on the subject of bankruptcies throughout the United States;

To coin money, regulate the value thereof, and of foreign coin, and fix the standard of weights and measures;

To provide for the punishment of counterfeiting the securities and current coin of the United States;

To establish post offices and post roads;

To promote the progress of science and useful arts by securing for limited times to authors and inventors the exclusive right to their respective writings and discoveries;

To constitute tribunals inferior to the Supreme Court;

To define and punish piracies and felonies committed on the high seas and offenses against the law of nations;

To declare war, grant letters of marque and reprisal, and make rules concerning captures on land and water;

To raise and support armies, but no appropriation of money to that use shall be for a longer term than two years;

To provide and maintain a navy;

To make rules for the government and regulation of the land and naval forces;

To provide for calling forth the militia to execute the laws of the Union, suppress insurrections, and repel invasions;

To provide for organizing, arming, and disciplining the militia, and for governing such part of them as may be employed in the service of the United States, reserving to the States respectively the appointment of the officers, and the authority of training the militia according to the discipline prescribed by Congress;

To exercise exclusive legislation in all cases whatsoever, over such district (not exceeding ten miles square) as may, by cession of particular States, and the acceptance of Congress, become the seat of government of the United States, and to exercise like authority over all places purchased by the consent of the legislature of the State, in which the same shall be, for erection of forts, magazines, arsenals, dock-yards, and other needful buildings;—and

To make all laws which shall be necessary and proper for carrying into execution the foregoing powers, and all other powers vested by this Constitution in the government of the United States, or in any department or officer thereof.

Section 9. *The migration or importation of such persons as any of the States now existing shall think proper to admit shall not be prohibited by the Congress prior to the year 1808; but a tax or duty may be imposed on such importation, not exceeding $10 for each person.*

The privilege of the writ of habeas corpus shall not be suspended, unless when in cases of rebellion or invasion the public safety may require it.

No bill of attainder or ex post facto law shall be passed.

No capitation, or other direct, tax shall be laid, unless in proportion to the census or enumeration herein before directed to be taken.

No tax or duty shall be laid on articles exported from any State.

No preference shall be given by any regulation of commerce or revenue to the ports of one State over those of another; nor shall vessels bound to, or from, one State, be obliged to enter, clear, or pay duties in another.

No money shall be drawn from the treasury, but in consequence of appropriations made by law; and a regular statement and account of the receipts and expenditures of all public money shall be published from time to time.

No title of nobility shall be granted by the United States: and no person holding any office of profit or trust under them, shall, without the consent of the Congress, accept of any present, emolument, office, or title, of any kind whatever, from any king, prince, or foreign state.

Section 10. No State shall enter into any treaty, alliance, or confederation; grant letters of marque and reprisal; coin money; emit bills of credit; make anything but gold and silver coin a tender in payment of debts; pass any bill of attainder, ex post facto law, or law impairing the obligation of contracts, or grant any title of nobility.

No State shall, without the consent of Congress, lay any imposts or duties on imports or exports, except what may be absolutely necessary for executing its inspection laws: and the net produce of all duties and imposts, laid by any State on imports or exports, shall be for the use of the treasury of the United States; and all such laws shall be subject to the revision and control of the Congress.

No State shall, without the consent of Congress, lay any duty of tonnage, keep troops or ships of war in time of peace, enter into any agreement or compact with another State, or with a foreign power, or engage in war, unless actually invaded, or in such imminent danger as will not admit of delay.

ARTICLE II

Section 1. The executive power shall be vested in a President of the United States of America. He shall hold his office during the term of four years, and, together with the Vice-President, chosen for the same term, be elected as follows:

Each state shall appoint, in such manner as the legislature thereof may direct, a number of electors, equal to the whole number of Senators and Representatives to which the State may be entitled in the Congress; but no Senator or Representative, or person holding an office of trust or profit under the United States, shall be appointed an elector.

The electors shall meet in their respective States, and vote by ballot for two persons, of whom one at least shall not be an inhabitant of the same State with themselves. And they shall make a list of all the persons voted for, and of the number of votes for each; which list they shall sign and certify, and transmit sealed to the seat of government of the United States, directed to the President of the Senate. The President of the Senate shall, in the presence of the Senate and the House of Representatives, open all the certificates, and the votes shall then be counted. The person having the greatest number of votes shall be the President, if such number be a majority of the whole number of electors appointed; and if there be more than one who have such majority, and have an equal number of votes, then the House of Representatives shall immediately choose by ballot one of them for President; and if no person have a majority, then from the five highest on the list said house shall in like manner choose the President. But in choosing the President the votes shall be taken by States, the representation from each State having one vote; a quorum for this purpose shall consist of a member or members from two-thirds of the States, and a majority of all the States shall be necessary to a choice. In every case, after the choice of the President, the person having the greatest number of votes of the electors shall be the Vice-President. But if there should remain two or more who have equal votes, the Senate shall choose from them by ballot the Vice-President.

The Congress may determine the time of choosing the electors and the day on which they shall give their votes; which day shall be the same throughout the United States.

No person except a natural-born citizen, *or a citizen of the United States at the time of the adoption of this Constitution*, shall be eligible to the office of President; neither shall any person be eligible to that office who shall not have attained to the age of thirty-five years, and been fourteen years a resident within the United States.

In case of the removal of the President from office or of his death, resignation, or inability to discharge the powers and duties of the said office, the same shall devolve on the Vice-President, and the Congress may by law provide for the case of removal, death, resignation, or inability, both of the President and Vice-President, declaring what officer shall then act as President, and such officer shall act accordingly, until the disability be removed, or a President shall be elected.

The President shall, at stated times, receive for his services a compensation, which shall neither be increased nor diminished during the period for which he shall have been elected, and he shall not receive within that period any other emolument from the United States, or any of them.

Before he enter on the execution of his office, he shall take the following oath or affirmation:—"I do solemnly swear (or affirm) that I will faithfully execute the office of the President of the United States, and will to the best of my ability preserve, protect and defend the Constitution of the United States."

Section 2. The President shall be commander in chief of the army and navy of the United States, and of the militia of the several States, when called into the actual service of the United States; he may require the opinion, in writing, of the principal officer in each of the executive departments, upon any subject relating to the duties of their respective offices, and he shall have power to grant reprieves and pardons for offenses against the United States, except in cases of impeachment.

He shall have power, by and with the advice and consent of the Senate, to make treaties, provided two-thirds of the Senators present concur; and he shall nominate, and by and with the advice and consent of the Senate, shall appoint ambassadors, other public ministers and consuls, judges of the Supreme Court, and all other officers of the United States, whose appointments are not herein otherwise provided for, and which shall be established by law: but Congress may by law vest the appointment of such inferior officers, as they think proper, in the President alone, in the courts of law, or in the heads of departments.

The President shall have power to fill up all vacancies that may happen during the recess of the Senate, by granting commissions which shall expire at the end of their next session.

Section 3. He shall from time to time give to the Congress information of the state of the Union, and recommend to their consideration such measures as he shall judge necessary and expedient; he may, on extraordinary occasions, convene both houses, or either of them, and in case of disagreement between them, with respect to the time of adjournment, he may adjourn them to such time as he shall think proper; he shall receive ambassadors and other public ministers; he shall take care that the laws be faithfully executed, and shall commission all the officers of the United States.

Section 4. The President, Vice-President and all civil officers of the United States shall be removed from office on impeachment for, and on conviction of, treason, bribery, or other high crimes and misdemeanors.

ARTICLE III

Section 1. The judicial power of the United States shall be vested in one Supreme Court, and in such inferior courts as the Congress may from time to time ordain and establish. The judges, both of the Supreme and inferior courts, shall hold their offices during good behavior, and shall, at stated times, receive for their services a compensation which shall not be diminished during their continuance in office.

Section 2. The judicial power shall extend to all cases, in law and equity, arising under this Constitution, the laws of the United States, and treaties made, or which shall be made, under their authority;—to all cases affecting ambassadors, other public ministers and consuls;—to all cases of admiralty and maritime jurisdiction;—to controversies to which the United States shall be a party;—to controversies between two or more States;—*between a State and citizens of another State;*—between citizens of different States;—between citizens of the same State claiming lands under grants of different States, and between a State, or the citizens thereof, and foreign states, citizens or subjects.

In all cases affecting ambassadors, other public ministers and consuls, and those in which a State shall be party, the Supreme Court shall have original jurisdiction. In all the other cases before mentioned, the Supreme Court shall have appellate jurisdiction, both as to law and fact, with such exceptions, and under such regulations, as the Congress shall make.

The trial of all crimes, except in cases of impeachment, shall be by jury; and such trial shall be held in the State where said crimes shall have been committed; but when not committed within any State, the trial shall be at such place or places as the Congress may by law have directed.

Section 3. Treason against the United States shall consist only in levying war against them, or in adhering to their enemies, giving them aid and comfort. No person shall be convicted of treason unless on the testimony of two witnesses to the same overt act, or on confession in open court.

The Congress shall have power to declare the punishment of treason, but no attainder of treason shall work corruption of blood, or forfeiture except during the life of the person attainted.

ARTICLE IV

Section 1. Full faith and credit shall be given in each State to the public acts, records, and judicial proceedings of every other State. And the Congress may by general laws prescribe the manner in which such acts, records, and proceedings shall be proved, and the effect thereof.

Section 2. The citizens of each State shall be entitled to all privileges and immunities of citizens in the several States.

A person charged in any State with treason, felony, or other crime, who shall flee from justice, and be found in another State, shall on demand of the executive authority of the State from which he fled, be delivered up, to be removed to the State having jurisdiction of the crime.

No person held to service or labor in one State, under the laws thereof, escaping into another, shall, in consequence of any law or regulation therein, be discharged from such service or labor, but shall be delivered up on claim of the party to whom such service or labor may be due.

Section 3. New States may be admitted by the Congress into this Union; but no new State shall be formed or erected within the jurisdiction of any other State; nor any State be formed by the junction of two or more States, or parts of States, without the consent of the legislatures of the States concerned as well as of the Congress.

The Congress shall have power to dispose of and make all needful rules and regulations respecting the territory or other property belonging to the United States; and nothing in this Constitution shall be so construed as to prejudice any claims of the United States, or of any particular State.

Section 4. The United States shall guarantee to every State in this Union a republican form of government, and shall protect each of them against invasion; and on application of the legislature, or of the executive (when the legislature cannot be convened), against domestic violence.

ARTICLE V

The Congress, whenever two-thirds of both houses shall deem it necessary, shall propose amendments to this Constitution, or, on the application of the legislatures of two-thirds of the several States, shall call a convention for proposing amendments, which, in either case, shall be valid to all intents and purposes, as part of this Constitution, when ratified by the legislatures of three-fourths of the several States, or by conventions in three-fourths thereof, as the one or the other mode of ratification may be proposed by the Congress; provided *that no amendments which may be made prior to the year one thousand eight hundred and eight shall in any manner affect the first and fourth clauses in the ninth section of the first article;* and that no State, without its consent, shall be deprived of its equal suffrage in the Senate.

ARTICLE VI

All debts contracted and engagements entered into, before the adoption of this Constitution, shall be as valid against the United States under this Constitution, as under the Confederaton.

This Constitution, and the laws of the United States which shall be made in pursuance thereof; and all treaties made, or which shall be made, under the authority of the United States, shall be the supreme law of the land; and the judges in every State shall be bound thereby, anything in the Constitution or laws of any State to the contrary notwithstanding.

The Senators and Representatives before mentioned, and the members of the several State legislatures, and all executive and judicial officers, both of the United States and of the several States, shall be bound by oath or affirmation to support this Constitution; but no religious test shall ever be required as a qualification to any office or public trust under the United States.

ARTICLE VII

The ratification of the conventions of nine States shall be sufficient for the establishment of this Constitution between the States so ratifying the same.

Done in Convention by the unanimous consent of the States present, the seventeenth day of September in the year of our Lord one thousand seven hundred and eighty-seven and of the Independence of the United States of America the twelfth. In witness whereof we have hereunto subscribed our names.

[Signed by]
Gᵒ WASHINGTON
Presidt and Deputy from Virginia
[*and thirty-eight others*]

Amendments to the Constitution

ARTICLE I*

Congress shall make no law respecting an establishment of religion, or prohibiting the free exercise thereof; or abridging the freedom of speech, or of the press; or the right of the people peaceably to assemble, and to petition the government for a redress of grievances.

ARTICLE II

A well-regulated militia being necessary to the security of a free State, the right of the people to keep and bear arms shall not be infringed.

ARTICLE III

No soldier shall, in time of peace, be quartered in any house without the consent of the owner, nor in time of war, but in a manner to be prescribed by law.

*The first ten Amendments (Bill of Rights) were adopted in 1791.

ARTICLE IV

The right of the people to be secure in their persons, houses, papers, and effects, against unreasonable searches and seizures, shall not be violated, and no warrants shall issue but upon probable cause, supported by oath or affirmation, and particularly describing the place to be searched, and the persons or things to be seized.

ARTICLE V

No person shall be held to answer for a capital, or otherwise infamous crime, unless on a presentment or indictment of a grand jury, except in cases arising in the land or naval forces, or in the militia, when in actual service in time of war or public danger; nor shall any person be subject for the same offense to be twice put in jeopardy of life or limb; nor shall be compelled in any criminal case to be a witness against himself, nor be deprived of life, liberty, or property, without due process of law; nor shall private property be taken for public use without just compensation.

ARTICLE VI

In all criminal prosecutions, the accused shall enjoy the right to a speedy and public trial, by an impartial jury of the State and district wherein the crime shall have been committed, which district shall have been previously ascertained by law, and to be informed of the nature and cause of the accusation; to be confronted with the witnesses against him; to have compulsory process for obtaining witnesses in his favor, and to have the assistance of counsel for his defense.

ARTICLE VII

In suits at common law, where the value in controversy shall exceed twenty dollars, the right of trial by jury shall be preserved, and no fact tried by a jury shall be otherwise reexamined in any court of the United States, than according to the rules of the common law.

ARTICLE VIII

Excessive bail shall not be required, nor excessive fines imposed, nor cruel and unusual punishments inflicted.

ARTICLE IX

The enumeration in the Constitution, of certain rights, shall not be construed to deny or disparage others retained by the people.

ARTICLE X

The powers not delegated to the United States by the Constitution, nor prohibited by it to the States, are reserved to the States respectively, or to the people.

ARTICLE XI
[Adopted 1798]

The judicial power of the United States shall not be construed to extend to any suit in law or equity, commenced or prosecuted against one of the United States by citizens of another State, or by citizens or subjects of any foreign state.

ARTICLE XII
[Adopted 1804]

The electors shall meet in their respective States, and vote by ballot for President and Vice-President, one of whom, at least, shall not be an inhabitant of the same State with themselves; they shall name in their ballots the person voted for as President, and in distinct ballots the person voted for as Vice-President, and they shall make distinct lists of all persons voted for as President, and of all persons voted for as Vice-President, and of the number of votes for each, which lists they shall sign and certify, and transmit sealed to the seat of government of the United States, directed to the President of the Senate;—the President of the Senate shall, in the presence of the Senate and House of Representatives, open all the certificates and the votes shall then be counted;—the person having the greatest number of votes for President shall be the President, if such number be a majority of the whole number of electors appointed; and if no person have such majority, then from the persons having the highest numbers not exceeding three on the list of those voted for as President, the House of Representatives shall choose immediately, by ballot, the President. But in choosing the President, the votes shall be taken by States, the representation from each State having one vote; a quorum for this purpose shall consist of a member or members from two-thirds of the States, and a majority of all the States shall be necessary to a choice. And if the House of Representatives shall not choose a President whenever the right of choice shall devolve upon them, before *the fourth day of March* next following, then the Vice-President shall act as President, as in the case of the death or other constitutional disability of the President.

The person having the greatest number of votes as Vice-President shall be the Vice-President, if such a number be a majority of the whole number of electors appointed; and if no person have a majority, then from the two highest numbers on the list the Senate shall choose the Vice-President; a quorum for the purpose shall consist of two-thirds of the whole number of Senators, and a majority of the whole number shall be necessary to a choice. But no person constitutionally ineligible to the office of President shall be eligible to that of Vice-President of the United States.

ARTICLE XIII
[Adopted 1865]

Section 1.   Neither slavery nor involuntary servitude, except as a punishment for crime whereof the party shall have been duly convicted, shall exist within the United States, or any place subject to their jurisdiction.

Section 2.   Congress shall have power to enforce this article by appropriate legislation.

ARTICLE XIV
[Adopted 1868]

Section 1. All persons born or naturalized in the United States, and subject to the jurisdiction thereof, are citizens of the United States and of the State wherein they reside. No State shall make or enforce any law which shall abridge the privileges or immunities of citizens of the United States; nor shall any State deprive any person of life, liberty, or property, without due process of law; nor deny to any person within its jurisdiction the equal protection of the laws.

Section 2. Representatives shall be apportioned among the several States according to their respective numbers, counting the whole number of persons in each State, excluding Indians not taxed. But when the right to vote at any election for the choice of Electors for President and Vice-President of the United States, Representatives in Congress, the executive and judicial officers of a State, or the members of the legislature thereof, is denied to any of the male inhabitants of such State, being twenty-one years of age and citizens of the United States, or in any way abridged, except for participation in rebellion, or other crime, the basis of representation therein shall be reduced in the proportion which the number of such male citizens shall bear to the whole number of male citizens twenty-one years of age in such State.

Section 3. No person shall be a Senator or Representative in Congress, or Elector of President and Vice-President, or hold any office, civil or military, under the United States, or under any State, who, having previously taken an oath, as a member of Congress, or as an officer of the United States, or as a member of any State legislature, or as an executive or judicial officer of any State, to support the Constitution of the United States, shall have engaged in insurrection or rebellion against the same, or given aid or comfort to the enemies thereof. Congress may, by a vote of two-thirds of each house, remove such disability.   .

Section 4. The validity of the public debt of the United States, authorized by law, including debts incurred for payment of pensions and bounties for services in suppressing insurrection or rebellion, shall not be questioned. But neither the United States nor any State shall assume or pay any debt or obligation incurred in aid of insurrection or rebellion against the United States, or any claim for the loss of emancipation of any slave; but all such debts, obligations, and claims shall be held illegal and void.

Section 5. The Congress shall have the power to enforce, by appropriate legislation, the provisions of this article.

ARTICLE XV
[Adopted 1870]

Section 1. The right of citizens of the United States to vote shall not be denied or abridged by the United States or by any State on account of race, color, or previous condition of servitude.

Section 2. The Congress shall have power to enforce this article by appropriate legislation.

ARTICLE XVI
[Adopted 1913]

The Congress shall have power to lay and collect taxes on incomes, from whatever source derived, without apportionment among the several States, and without regard to any census or enumeration.

ARTICLE XVII
[Adopted 1913]

Section 1. The Senate of the United States shall be composed of two Senators from each State, elected by the people thereof, for six years; and each Senator shall have one vote. The electors in each State shall have the qualifications requisite for electors of [voters for] the most numerous branch of the State legislatures.

Section 2. When vacancies happen in the representation of any State in the Senate, the executive authority of such State shall issue writs of election to fill such vacancies: Provided, that the Legislature of any State may empower the executive thereof to make temporary appointments until the people fill the vacancies by election as the Legislature may direct.

Section 3. This amendment shall not be so construed as to affect the election or term of any Senator chosen before it becomes valid as part of the Constitution.

ARTICLE XVIII
[Adopted 1919; Repealed 1933]

Section 1. After one year from the ratification of this article the manufacture, sale, or transportation of intoxicating liquors within, the importation thereof into, or the exportation thereof from the United States and all territory subject to the jurisdiction thereof, for beverage purposes, is hereby prohibited.

Section 2. The Congress and the several States shall have concurrent power to enforce this article by appropriate legislation.

Section 3. *This article shall be inoperative unless it shall have been ratified as an amendment to the Constitution by the legislatures of the several States, as provided by the Constitution, within seven years from the date of the submission thereof to the States by the Congress.*

ARTICLE XIX
[*Adopted 1920*]

Section 1. The right of citizens of the United States to vote shall not be denied or abridged by the United States or by any State on account of sex.

Section 2. The Congress shall have the power to enforce this article by appropriate legislation.

ARTICLE XX
[*Adopted 1933*]

Section 1. The terms of the President and Vice-President shall end at noon on the 20th day of January, and the terms of Senators and Representatives at noon on the 3d day of January, of the years in which such terms would have ended if this article had not been ratified; and the terms of their successors shall then begin.

Section 2. The Congress shall assemble at least once in every year, and such meeting shall begin at noon on the 3d day of January, unless they shall by law appoint a different day.

Section 3. If, at the time fixed for the beginning of the term of the President, the President-elect shall have died, the Vice-President-elect shall become President. If a President shall not have been chosen before the time fixed for the beginning of his term, or if the President-elect shall have failed to qualify, then the Vice-President-elect shall act as President until a President shall have qualified; and the Congress may by law provide for the case wherein neither a President-elect nor a Vice-President-elect shall have qualified, declaring who shall then act as President, or the manner in which one who is to act shall be selected, and such persons shall act accordingly until a President or Vice-President shall have qualified.

Section 4. The Congress may by law provide for the case of the death of any of the persons from whom the House of Representatives may choose a President whenever the right of choice shall have devolved upon them, and for the case of the death of any of the persons from whom the Senate may choose a Vice-President whenever the right of choice shall have devolved upon them.

Section 5. Sections 1 and 2 shall take effect on the 15th day of October following the ratification of this article.

Section 6. This article shall be inoperative unless it shall have been ratified as an amendment to the Constitution by the Legislatures of three-fourths of the several States within seven years from the date of its submission.

ARTICLE XXI
[*Adopted 1933*]

Section 1. The eighteenth article of amendment to the Constitution of the United States is hereby repealed.

Section 2. The transportation or importation into any State, Territory, or Possession of the United States for delivery or use therein of intoxicating liquors, in violation of the laws thereof, is hereby prohibited.

Section 3. This article shall be inoperative unless it shall have been ratified as an amendment to the Constitution by conventions in the several States, as provided in the Constitution, within seven years from the date of submission thereof to the States by the Congress.

ARTICLE XXII
[*Adopted 1951*]

Section 1. No person shall be elected to the office of President more than twice, and no person who has held the office of President, or acted as President, for more than two years of a term to which some other person was elected President shall be elected to the office of President more than once. But this article shall not apply to any person holding the office of President when this article was proposed by the Congress, and shall not prevent any person who may be holding the office of President, or acting as President, during the term within which this article becomes operative from holding the office of President or acting as President during the remainder of such term.

Section 2. This article shall be inoperative unless it shall have been ratified as an amendment to the Constitution by the legislatures of three-fourths of the several States within seven years from the date of its submission to the States by the Congress.

ARTICLE XXIII
[*Adopted 1961*]

Section 1. The District constituting the seat of Government of the United States shall appoint in such manner as the Congress may direct:

A number of electors of President and Vice-President equal to the whole number of Senators and Representatives in Congress to which the District would be entitled if it were a State, but in no event more than the least populous State; they shall be in addition to those appointed by the States, but they shall be considered for the purposes of the election of President and Vice-President, to be electors appointed by a State; and they shall meet in the District and perform such duties as provided by the twelfth article of amendment.

Section 2. The Congress shall have the power to enforce this article by appropriate legislation.

ARTICLE XXIV
[Adopted 1964]

Section 1. The right of citizens of the United States to vote in any primary or other election for President or Vice-President, for electors for President or Vice-President, or for Senator or Representative in Congress, shall not be denied or abridged by the United States or any State by reason of failure to pay any poll tax or other tax.

Section 2. The Congress shall have the power to enforce this article by appropriate legislation.

ARTICLE XXV
[Adopted 1967]

Section 1. In case of the removal of the President from office or of his death or resignation, the Vice President shall become President.

Section 2. Whenever there is a vacancy in the office of the Vice President, the President shall nominate a Vice President who shall take office upon confirmation by a majority vote of both Houses of Congress.

Section 3. Whenever the President transmits to the President pro tempore of the Senate and the Speaker of the House of Representatives his written declaration that he is unable to discharge the powers and duties of his office, and until he transmits to them a written declaration to the contrary, such powers and duties shall be discharged by the Vice President as Acting President.

Section 4. Whenever the Vice President and a majority of either the principal officers of the executive departments or of such other body as Congress may by law provide, transmit to the President pro tempore of the Senate and the Speaker of the House of Representatives their written declaration that the President is unable to discharge the powers and duties of his office, the Vice President shall immediately assume the powers and duties of the office as Acting President.

Thereafter, when the President transmits to the President pro tempore of the Senate and the Speaker of the House of Representatives his written declaration that no inability exists, he shall resume the powers and duties of his office unless the Vice President and a majority of either the principal officers of the executive department[s] or of such other body as Congress may by law provide, transmit within four days to the President pro tempore of the Senate and the Speaker of the House of Representatives their written declaration that the President is unable to discharge the powers and duties of his office. Thereupon Congress shall decide the issue, assembling within forty-eight hours for that purpose if not in session. If the Congress, within twenty-one days after receipt of the latter written declaration, or, if Congress is not in session, within twenty-one days after Congress is required to assemble, determines by two-thirds vote of both Houses that the President is unable to discharge the powers and duties of his office, the Vice President shall continue to discharge the same as Acting President; otherwise, the President shall resume the powers and duties of his office.

ARTICLE XXVI
[Adopted 1971]

Section 1. The right of citizens of the United States, who are eighteen years of age or older, to vote shall not be denied or abridged by the United States or by any State on account of age.

Section 2. The Congress shall have power to enforce this article by appropriate legislation.

ARTICLE XXVII
[Sent to States, 1972]

Section 1. Equality of rights under the law shall not be denied or abridged by the United States or by any State on account of sex.

Section 2. The Congress shall have the power to enforce, by appropriate legislation, the provisions of this article.

Section 3. This amendment shall take effect two years after the date of ratification.

Presidential Elections*

ELECTION	CANDIDATES	PARTIES	POPULAR VOTE	ELECTORAL VOTE
1789	**George Washington**	No party designations		69
	John Adams			34
	Minor Candidates			35
1792	**George Washington**	No party designations		132
	John Adams			77
	George Clinton			50
	Minor Candidates			5
1796	**John Adams**	Federalist		71
	Thomas Jefferson	Democratic-Republican		68
	Thomas Pinckney	Federalist		59
	Aaron Burr	Democratic-Republican		30
	Minor Candidates			48
1800	**Thomas Jefferson**	Democratic-Republican		73
	Aaron Burr	Democratic-Republican		73
	John Adams	Federalist		65
	Charles C. Pinckney	Federalist		64
	John Jay	Federalist		1
1804	**Thomas Jefferson**	Democratic-Republican		162
	Charles C. Pinckney	Federalist		14
1808	**James Madison**	Democratic-Republican		122
	Charles C. Pinckney	Federalist		47
	George Clinton	Democratic-Republican		6
1812	**James Madison**	Democratic-Republican		128
	DeWitt Clinton	Federalist		89
1816	**James Monroe**	Democratic-Republican		183
	Rufus King	Federalist		34
1820	**James Monroe**	Democratic-Republican		231
	John Q. Adams	Independent Republican		1
1824	**John Q. Adams** (Min.)†	Democratic-Republican	108,740	84
	Andrew Jackson	Democratic-Republican	153,544	99
	William H. Crawford	Democratic-Republican	46,618	41
	Henry Clay	Democratic-Republican	47,136	37
1828	**Andrew Jackson**	Democratic	647,286	178
	John Q. Adams	National Republican	508,064	83

* Candidates receiving less than 1% of the popular vote are omitted. Before the Twelfth Amendment (1804) the Electoral College voted for two presidential candidates, and the runner-up became vice-president. Basic figures are taken primarily from *Historical Statistics of the United States, 1789–1945* (1949), pp. 288–90; *Historical Statistics of the United States, Colonial Times to 1957* (1960), pp. 682–83; and *Statistical Abstract of the United States, 1969* (1969), pp. 355–57.

† "Min." indicates minority president—one receiving less than 50% of all popular votes.

ELECTION	CANDIDATES	PARTIES	POPULAR VOTE	ELECTORAL VOTE
1832	**Andrew Jackson**	Democratic	687,502	219
	Henry Clay	National Republican	530,189	49
	William Wirt	Anti-Masonic	33,108	7
	John Floyd	National Republican		11
1836	**Martin Van Buren**	Democratic	762,678	170
	William H. Harrison	Whig		73
	Hugh L. White	Whig	736,656	26
	Daniel Webster	Whig		14
	W. P. Mangum	Whig		11
1840	**William H. Harrison**	Whig	1,275,016	234
	Martin Van Buren	Democratic	1,129,102	60
1844	**James K. Polk** (Min.)*	Democratic	1,337,243	170
	Henry Clay	Whig	1,299,062	105
	James G. Birney	Liberty	62,300	
1848	**Zachary Taylor** (Min.)*	Whig	1,360,099	163
	Lewis Cass	Democratic	1,220,544	127
	Martin Van Buren	Free Soil	291,263	
1852	**Franklin Pierce**	Democratic	1,601,274	254
	Winfield Scott	Whig	1,386,580	42
	John P. Hale	Free Soil	155,825	
1856	**James Buchanan** (Min.)*	Democratic	1,838,169	174
	John C. Frémont	Republican	1,341,264	114
	Millard Fillmore	American	874,534	8
1860	**Abraham Lincoln** (Min.)*	Republican	1,866,452	180
	Stephen A. Douglas	Democratic	1,375,157	12
	John C. Breckinridge	Democratic	847,953	72
	John Bell	Constitutional Union	590,631	39
1864	**Abraham Lincoln**	Union	2,213,665	212
	George B. McClellan	Democratic	1,802,237	21
1868	**Ulysses S. Grant**	Republican	3,012,833	214
	Horatio Seymour	Democratic	2,703,249	80
1872	**Ulysses S. Grant**	Republican	3,597,132	286
	Horace Greeley	Democratic and Liberal Republican	2,834,125	66
1876	**Rutherford B. Hayes** (Min.)*	Republican	4,036,298	185
	Samuel J. Tilden	Democratic	4,300,590	184
1880	**James A. Garfield** (Min.)*	Republican	4,454,416	214
	Winfield S. Hancock	Democratic	4,444,952	155
	James B. Weaver	Greenback-Labor	308,578	
1884	**Grover Cleveland** (Min.)*	Democratic	4,874,986	219
	James G. Blaine	Republican	4,851,981	182
	Benjamin F. Butler	Greenback-Labor	175,370	
	John P. St. John	Prohibition	150,369	
1888	**Benjamin Harrison** (Min.)*	Republican	5,439,853	233

* "Min." indicates minority president—one receiving less than 50% of all popular votes.

ELECTION	CANDIDATES	PARTIES	POPULAR VOTE	ELECTORAL VOTE
	Grover Cleveland	Democratic	5,540,309	168
	Clinton B. Fisk	Prohibition	249,506	
	Anson J. Streeter	Union Labor	146,935	
1892	**Grover Cleveland** **(Min.)***	Democratic	5,556,918	277
	Benjamin Harrison	Republican	5,176,108	145
	James B. Weaver	People's	1,041,028	22
	John Bidwell	Prohibition	264,133	
1896	**William McKinley**	Republican	7,104,779	271
	William J. Bryan	Democratic	6,502,925	176
1900	**William McKinley**	Republican	7,207,923	292
	William J. Bryan	Democratic; Populist	6,358,133	155
	John C. Woolley	Prohibition	208,914	
1904	**Theodore Roosevelt**	Republican	7,623,486	336
	Alton B. Parker	Democratic	5,077,911	140
	Eugene V. Debs	Socialist	402,283	
	Silas C. Swallow	Prohibition	258,536	
1908	**William H. Taft**	Republican	7,678,908	321
	William J. Bryan	Democratic	6,409,104	162
	Eugene V. Debs	Socialist	420,793	
	Eugene W. Chafin	Prohibition	253,840	
1912	**Woodrow Wilson** **(Min.)***	Democratic	6,293,454	435
	Theodore Roosevelt	Progressive	4,119,538	88
	William H. Taft	Republican	3,484,980	8
	Eugene V. Debs	Socialist	900,672	
	Eugene W. Chafin	Prohibition	206,275	
1916	**Woodrow Wilson** **(Min.)***	Democratic	9,129,606	277
	Charles E. Hughes	Republican	8,538,221	254
	A. L. Benson	Socialist	585,113	
	J. F. Hanly	Prohibition	220,506	
1920	**Warren G. Harding**	Republican	16,152,200	404
	James M. Cox	Democratic	9,147,353	127
	Eugene V. Debs	Socialist	919,799	
	P. P. Christensen	Farmer-Labor	265,411	
1924	**Calvin Coolidge**	Republican	15,725,016	382
	John W. Davis	Democratic	8,386,503	136
	Robert M. La Follette	Progressive	4,822,856	13
1928	**Herbert C. Hoover**	Republican	21,391,381	444
	Alfred E. Smith	Democratic	15,016,443	87
1932	**Franklin D. Roosevelt**	Democratic	22,821,857	472
	Herbert C. Hoover	Republican	15,761,841	59
	Norman Thomas	Socialist	881,951	
1936	**Franklin D. Roosevelt**	Democratic	27,751,597	523
	Alfred M. Landon	Republican	16,679,583	8
	William Lemke	Union, etc.	882,479	
1940	**Franklin D. Roosevelt**	Democratic	27,244,160	449
	Wendell L. Willkie	Republican	22,305,198	82

* "Min." indicates minority president—one receiving less than 50% of all popular votes.

ELECTION	CANDIDATES	PARTIES	POPULAR VOTE	ELECTORAL VOTE
1944	**Franklin D. Roosevelt**	Democratic	25,602,504	432
	Thomas E. Dewey	Republican	22,006,285	99
1948	**Harry S Truman (Min.)***	Democratic	24,105,812	303
	Thomas E. Dewey	Republican	21,970,065	189
	J. Strom Thurmond	States' Rights Democratic	1,169,063	39
	Henry A. Wallace	Progressive	1,157,172	
1952	**Dwight D. Eisenhower**	Republican	33,936,234	442
	Adlai E. Stevenson	Democratic	27,314,992	89
1956	**Dwight D. Eisenhower**	Republican	35,590,472	457
	Adlai E. Stevenson	Democratic	26,022,752	73
1960	**John F. Kennedy (Min.)***	Democratic	34,226,731	303
	Richard M. Nixon	Republican	34,108,157	219
1964	**Lyndon B. Johnson**	Democratic	43,129,484	486
	Barry M. Goldwater	Republican	27,178,188	52
1968	**Richard M. Nixon (Min.)***	Republican	31,785,480	301
	Hubert H. Humphrey, Jr.	Democratic	31,275,166	191
	George C. Wallace	American Independent	9,906,473	46
1972	**Richard M. Nixon**	Republican	45,767,218	520
	George S. McGovern	Democratic	28,357,668	17
1976	**Jimmy Carter**	Democratic	40,276,040	297
	Gerald R. Ford	Republican	38,532,630	241
1980	**Ronald W. Reagan**	Republican	43,899,248	489
	Jimmy Carter	Democratic	35,481,435	49
1984	**Ronald W. Reagan**	Republican		
	Walter F. Mondale	Democrat		

*"Min." indicates minority president—one receiving less than 50% of all popular votes.

Presidents and Vice-Presidents

TERM	PRESIDENT	VICE-PRESIDENT
1789–1793	George Washington	John Adams
1793–1797	George Washington	John Adams
1797–1801	John Adams	Thomas Jefferson
1801–1805	Thomas Jefferson	Aaron Burr
1805–1809	Thomas Jefferson	George Clinton
1809–1813	James Madison	George Clinton (d. 1812)
1813–1817	James Madison	Elbridge Gerry (d. 1814)
1817–1821	James Monroe	Daniel D. Tompkins
1821–1825	James Monroe	Daniel D. Tompkins
1825–1829	John Quincy Adams	John C. Calhoun
1829–1833	Andrew Jackson	John C. Calhoun (resigned 1832)
1833–1837	Andrew Jackson	Martin Van Buren
1837–1841	Martin Van Buren	Richard M. Johnson
1841–1845	William H. Harrison (d. 1841) John Tyler	John Tyler
1845–1849	James K. Polk	George M. Dallas
1849–1853	Zachary Taylor (d. 1850) Millard Fillmore	Millard Fillmore
1853–1857	Franklin Pierce	William R. D. King (d. 1853)
1857–1861	James Buchanan	John C. Breckinridge
1861–1865	Abraham Lincoln	Hannibal Hamlin
1865–1869	Abraham Lincoln (d. 1865) Andrew Johnson	Andrew Johnson
1869–1873	Ulysses S. Grant	Schuyler Colfax
1873–1877	Ulysses S. Grant	Henry Wilson (d. 1875)
1877–1881	Rutherford B. Hayes	William A. Wheeler
1881–1885	James A. Garfield (d. 1881) Chester A. Arthur	Chester A. Arthur
1885–1889	Grover Cleveland	Thomas A. Hendricks (d. 1885)
1889–1893	Benjamin Harrison	Levi P. Morton
1893–1897	Grover Cleveland	Adlai E. Stevenson
1897–1901	William McKinley	Garret A. Hobart (d. 1899)
1901–1905	William McKinley (d. 1901) Theodore Roosevelt	Theodore Roosevelt
1905–1909	Theodore Roosevelt	Charles W. Fairbanks
1909–1913	William H. Taft	James S. Sherman (d. 1912)
1913–1917	Woodrow Wilson	Thomas R. Marshall
1917–1921	Woodrow Wilson	Thomas R. Marshall

1921–1925	Warren G. Harding (d. 1923) Calvin Coolidge	Calvin Coolidge
1925–1929	Calvin Coolidge	Charles G. Dawes
1929–1933	Herbert C. Hoover	Charles Curtis
1933–1937	Franklin D. Roosevelt	John N. Garner
1937–1941	Franklin D. Roosevelt	John N. Garner
1941–1945	Franklin D. Roosevelt	Henry A. Wallace
1945–1949	Franklin D. Roosevelt (d. 1945) Harry S Truman	Harry S Truman
1949–1953	Harry S Truman	Alben W. Barkley
1953–1957	Dwight D. Eisenhower	Richard M. Nixon
1957–1961	Dwight D. Eisenhower	Richard M. Nixon
1961–1965	John F. Kennedy (d. 1963) Lyndon B. Johnson	Lyndon B. Johnson
1965–1969	Lyndon B. Johnson	Hubert H. Humphrey, Jr.
1969–1974	Richard M. Nixon (resigned 1974)	Spiro T. Agnew (resigned 1973); Gerald R. Ford
1974–1976	Gerald R. Ford	Nelson A. Rockefeller
1976–1980	Jimmy Carter	Walter F. Mondale
1980–1984	Ronald W. Reagan	George Bush
1984–	Ronald W. Reagan	George Bush

Growth of U.S. Population and Area

CENSUS	POPULATION	PERCENT OF INCREASE OVER PRECEDING CENSUS	LAND AREA, SQUARE MILES	POPULATION PER SQUARE MILE
1790	3,929,214		867,980	4.5
1800	5,308,483	35.1	867,980	6.1
1810	7,239,881	36.4	1,685,865	4.3
1820	9,638,453	33.1	1,753,588	5.5
1830	12,866,020	33.5	1,753,588	7.3
1840	17,069,453	32.7	1,753,588	9.7
1850	23,191,876	35.9	2,944,337	7.9
1860	31,443,321	35.6	2,973,965	10.6
1870	39,818,449	26.6	2,973,965	13.4
1880	50,155,783	26.0	2,973,965	16.9
1890	62,947,714	25.5	2,973,965	21.2
1900	75,994,575	20.7	2,974,159	25.6
1910	91,972,266	21.0	2,973,890	30.9
1920	105,710,620	14.9	2,973,776	35.5
1930	122,775,046	16.1	2,977,128	41.2
1940	131,669,275	7.2	2,977,128	44.2
1950	150,697,361	14.5	2,974,726*	50.7
†1960	178,464,236	18.4	2,974,726	59.9
1970	204,765,770	14.7	2,974,726	68.8
1980	226,504,825	10.6	2,974,726	76.1

* As remeasured in 1940.
† Not including Alaska (pop. 226,167) and Hawaii (632,772).